ART AND CULTURAL HERITAGE

Art and Cultural Heritage provides appropriately more than a comprehensive in-depth analysis of national and international laws respecting cultural heritage. It is a bubbling caldron of law mixed with ethics, philosophy, politics, and working principles about how cultural heritage law, policy, and practice should be sculpted from the past as the present becomes the future. Art and cultural heritage are two pillars on which a society builds its identity, its values, its sense of community, and its individuals. The authors explore these demanding concerns, untangle basic values, and look critically at the conflicts and contradictions in existing art and cultural heritage law and policy in their diverse sectors. The rich and provocative contributions collectively provide a reasoned discussion of the issues from a multiplicity of views to permit the reader to understand the theoretical and philosophical underpinnings of the cultural heritage debate. Given the range of topics discussed with scholarship and clarity, the book is a resource to assist government and business policy makers, cultural resource professionals, and others whose activities impact the cultural and natural environment as well as the casual reader seeking to gain an in-depth understanding of the critical issues facing the protection of our global heritage in the twenty-first century.

Barbara T. Hoffman is a prominent New York arts lawyer who has taught and practiced in virtually every area of this specialized field for more than twenty-five years. She is a former chair of the Association of the Bar of the City of New York's Committee on Art Law and the immediate past chair of the International Bar Association Committee on Art, Cultural Institutions and Heritage Law.

Art and Cultural Heritage

Law, Policy, and Practice

Edited by

Barbara T. Hoffman

CAMBRIDGE
UNIVERSITY PRESS

COVER ILLUSTRATION CREDITS

Reading clockwise from the upper left:
1. Magpie Geese and Water Lilies at the Waterhole, by Johnny Bulun Bulun. Mr. Bulun Bulun is a well-known artist from Arnhemland. *Magpie Geese and Water Lilies at the Waterhole* is a bark painting created in 1978 by Mr. Bulun Bulun that depicts one of the most important cultural sites for the Ganalbingu people. The painting was altered and copied by a textile company in 1996. © Johnny Bulun Bulun. Museum and Art Gallery of the Northern Territory Collection. Licensed by VISCOPY, Australia, 2005.
2. Māori hei-tiki, or greenstone neck pendant. Museum of New Zealand Te Papa Tongarewa.
3. Cyprus image 1 (face image, up close). One of the Kanakaria mosaics that was successfully claimed by Cyprus in the case of *Autocephalous Greek-Orthodox Church of Cyprus and The Republic of Cyprus v. Goldberg & Feldman Fine Arts, Inc.* Photo by Petros Petrides.
4. Cambodian head. This head was found at the Metropolitan Museum of Art in New York, USA, in March 1994. The museum directors checked with ICOM and immediately made contact with the Cambodian authorities who made an official request for the return of the head. The Metropolitan Museum agreed to return the object in compliance with *ICOM's Code of Ethics for Museums.* Restitution took place in Phnom Penh on March 17, 1997. © Mention obligatoire Ecole française d'Extreme-Orient (EFEO)
5. Mayavase image. Maya limestone panel of a ballplayer from Site Q, Late Classic, 600 to 800 A.D. The Museum of the American Indian, Smithsonian Institution. © Justin Kerr. The limestone panel is one of more than two dozen sculptures that have entered this country since 1960, alleged to have been sawn off monuments at a place known to archaeologists only as Site Q. The search for Site Q began in the 1970s and has been suggested to lie along the Usumacinta River, the border between Guatemala and Mexico.
6. Preah Khan, a temple within the Angkor Wat complex in Cambodia. In 1992, the UNESCO World Heritage Committee declared the whole city of Angkor a World Heritage Site. Photograph courtesy of World Mounuments Fund. © World Monuments Fund.

CAMBRIDGE UNIVERSITY PRESS
Cambridge, New York, Melbourne, Madrid, Cape Town, Singapore,
São Paulo, Delhi, Dubai, Tokyo

Cambridge University Press
32 Avenue of the Americas, New York, NY 10013-2473, USA

www.cambridge.org
Information on this title: www.cambridge.org/9780521122979

First published 2006
This digitally printed version 2009

A catalog record for this publication is available from the British Library

Library of Congress Cataloging in Publication data

Art and Cultural Heritage : law, policy, and practice / edited by Barbara T. Hoffman.
p. cm.
Includes bibliographical references and index.
ISBN-13: 978-0-521-85764-2 (hardback)
ISBN-10: 0-521-85764-3 (hardback)
1. Cultural property – Protection – Law and legislation. I. Hoffman, Barbara T. II. Title.
K3791.A97 2005
344′.09 – dc22 2005012017

ISBN 978-0-521-85764-2 Hardback
ISBN 978-0-521-12297-9 Paperback

Contents

Contributors

George H. Okello Abungu, Ph.D. is a Cambridge-trained archaeologist and former Director-General of the National Museums of Kenya, who is also founder Chairman of Africa 2009, ISCOTIA, and Programme for Museum Development in Africa, among others. Mr. Abungu was most recently a Guest Scholar (May 2005) at the Getty Conservation Institute LA, researching strategies for sustainable management and utilisation of intangible heritage in Africa. He is the Chairman of the Kenya Cultural Center and the CEO of Okello Abungu Heritage Consultants. Apart from his work in the conservation of African heritage, he is also widely published in the disciplines of archaeology, heritage management, museology, and the subject of culture and development.
abungu@jambomail.com

Ignacio Gómez Arriola received his Bachelor of Architecture from the University of Guadalajara, where he also completed master level courses in Conservation of Monuments. He gives courses and seminars on cultural heritage conservation and is in charge of the World Heritage nomination dossier for the Agave Landscape and the old tequila factories. From 1996–2001, he was involved in the restoration and re-installation of the Renaissance altarpiece of the Great Holy Cross in the Hospital for Indians, the diagnostic and restoration project for the Degollado Theater in Guadalajara, and various restorative and rehabilitative activities in the Hopsicio Cabanas in Guadalajara. From 1997–8, he completed preparatory studies for the World Heritage nomination of the Hospicio Cabanas and from 1998–2000, restored a historic building for the Museum of Popular Arts of Jalisco. Mr. Arriola has been involved with numerous restoration projects as advisor and director and has received many awards for his work, among them the Franciscao de la Maza Prize, awarded by INHA in the field of heritage research, for the work done on the Hospital of Indians of Santa Cruz el Grande and the Jalisco Award given by the Jalisco Architectural Soceity for research. At the present, he is the Experto Restoratio Architect for the Instituto Nacional de Antrolpolgia e Historia in Jalisco and a member of the Board of ICOMOS Mexicano and ICOMOS Coordinator for the Satte of Jalisco.

Sir Ian Barker, QC practices as an arbitrator and mediator, both internationally and in New Zealand. He retired as Senior Judge of the High Court of New Zealand in 1997. He is a member of several international arbitration panels and is a Domain Name Dispute Resolution panelist for the World Intellectual Property Organisation. He was Chancellor of the University of Auckland from 1991 to 1999. He is New Zealand representative on the International Chamber of Commerce Commission on Arbitration and a nominee of the New Zealand Government on the International Centre for Settlement of Investment Disputes Panel.

Brenda Barrett serves as the National Coordinator for Heritage Areas for the National Park Service in Washington D.C. She provides budget, legislative, and policy support for the twenty-three Congressionally designated areas and for proposed heritage initiatives across the nation. She was formerly the Director of the Bureau for Historic Preservation at the Pennsylvania Historical and Museum Commission, the state's

public history agency in Harrisburg. Ms. Barrett received her Bachelor of Arts degree in anthropology from the University of Colorado in 1971 and her Master of Science degree in archaeology from the University of Wisconsin in 1974. She is also a graduate of the Dickinson School of Law – Pennsylvania State University and is admitted to practice in the Commonwealth of Pennsylvania.
Brenda_Barrett@nps.gov

Robert Bassett practices natural resources and international law at the firm Holland & Hart, LLP, in Greenwood Village, Colorado. He has worked in the natural resources industry for more than 20 years, representing clients in the United States, Europe, Latin America, Africa, and Canada. His practice has included advising natural resources companies during the acquisition of companies and properties, and providing counseling and advice on laws related to public lands, transportation, processing, sales, corporate, and litigation matters. Formerly, he was an attorney for Cyprus Amax Minerals Company, and practiced law with private firms in Alaska and New Mexico. Mr Bassett is Co-Chair of the Mining Committee of the Section of Energy and Resources Law of the International Bar Association, a past Trustee of the Rocky Mountain Mineral Law Foundation, an adjunct professor of International Mining Law and Policy at the University of Denver College of Law, and a lecturer on mining agreements at the Centre for Energy, Petroleum, and Mineral Law and Policy at the University of Dundee, Scotland.
bbassett@hollandhart.com

Jack Batievsky. The late Jack Batievsky was a partner in the law firm of Rodrigo, Elias & Medrano in Lima, Peru. He graduated in 1969 from the Law School of the Pontificia Universidad Católica del Perú, and taught law there from 1973. He was a member of the Colegio Abogados de Lima, the International Bar Association (where he chaired the Latin American and Caribbean Steering Group from 2000–2002), the Inter-American Bar Association, the International Fiscal Association, the American Bar Association and the Association of International Petroleum Negotiators. An obituary of Mr Batievsky may be found in the December 2002 *International Bar News*.

Forrest Booth is a *cum laude* graduate of Amherst College and the Harvard Law School. He has practiced admiralty, maritime, and insurance law for more than twenty-five years. He is a senior member of the 480-lawyer firm Cozen O'Connor. Until 2000, he headed his own nineteen-lawyer firm, which he founded in 1990. Prior to that, he was a partner in a large San Francisco law firm, where he headed the admiralty and maritime group. Mr. Booth served as a Lieutenant in the United States Navy, on sea duty between 1968 and 1972. He has taken more than a dozen cases to trial, and has handled thirty-four appeals before the U.S. Ninth Circuit Court of Appeals, the California Courts of Appeal, the California Supreme Court, and the U.S. Supreme Court in *Saratoga v. Martinac*. Most of these appeals resulted in published decisions. Forrest is the past Chair of the Pacific Admiralty Seminar, and past Chair, International Insurance Law Committee, American Bar Association Section of International Law and Practice. He specializes in casualty, salvage, marine insurance, construction, personal injury, cargo, insurance bad faith defense, oil and gas energy, and pollution matters. His legal publications include: *'Bad Faith' – Legal Trends in Suits Against Insurers*, 4 U.S.F. Mar. L.J. 1 (1992); *Who Owns Sunken Treasure? The Supreme Court, The Abandoned Shipwreck Act and the BROTHER JONATHAN*, 11 U.S.F. Mar. L.J. 77 (1998); and *Port and Maritime Security*, 15 U.S.F. Mar. L.J. 1 (2002). Mr. Booth is a member of the California and District of Columbia bars, the Maritime Law Association of the United States, the International Bar Association, the Association of Average Adjusters (UK), the Defense Research Institute, and the Pacific Admiralty Seminar Steering Committee. He is a regular speaker at insurance, legal, and marine industry conferences.

Manus Brinkman is the former Secretary General of the International Council of Museums (ICOM). He holds a doctorate degree in international relations from the University of Amsterdam. Mr. Brinkman has served as the Director of the Dutch

Museums Association and has edited the Association's magazine, *Museumvisie*, since 1990. He has been an active member of the Network of European Museum Organisations (NEMO) since its establishment, and served as its Chairman from 1995–8. He has also been actively involved in various international activities, including the campaign against the illicit traffic in cultural property.

Neil Brodie obtained a doctorate in archaeology from Liverpool University. Since 1998, he has been Coordinator of the Illicit Antiquities Research Centre at the McDonald Institute for Archaeological Research, Cambridge. He has published widely on the subject of illicit antiquities and carries out orthodox archaeological fieldwork in Greece.

Guido Carducci is Chief of the International Standards Section of UNESCO's Division of Cultural Heritage. He is a graduate of The Hague Academy of International Law and holds doctoral degrees in French law and Italian law. Mr. Carducci's recent publications in the field of the legal protection of cultural heritage and property include, "La Restitution Internationale des Objets d'Art et des Biens Culturels Volés ou Illicitement Exportés. Droit Commun, Directive CEE, Conventions d'Unesco et d'Unidroit" (1997 *L.G.D.J.* Paris), "L'Obligation de Restitution des Biens Culturels et des Objets d'Art en Cas de Conflit Armé: Droit Coutumier et Droit Conventionnel avant et après la Convention de La Haye de 1954. L'Importance du Facteur Temporel dans les Apports entre les Traités et la Coutume" (*Revue Générale de Droit International Public,* 2000, n. 2), "New Developments in the Law of the Sea : the Unesco Convention on the Protection of Underwater Cultural Heritage" (*American Journal of International Law,* 2002, n. 2), "The Expanding Protection of the Underwater Cultural Heritage: the New UNESCO Convention versus Existing International Law" (*The Protection of the Underwater Cultural Heritage* (T. Scovazzi, ed, Giuffrè 2002), and "Cultural Property and Works of Art in Public and Private International Law" and "Norme di Applicazione Necessaria" (*Enciclopedia Giuridica Treccani [Italian Treccani Legal Encyclopaedia]* 2000).
gcarducci@noos.fr

Trevor A Carmichael, QC was born in Barbados and was called to the United Kingdom Bar as a member of the Middle Temple. He is a member of the Inter-American Bar Association and an associate member of the Canadian Bar Association. He is the Barbados Country Chairman of the International Bar Association's International Litigation Committee on Business Law and served as its Deputy Secretary General for three years. He was one of eight Organization of American States experts responsible for drafting a Convention on International Contracts and is a member of the Committee on Joint Ventures Model Contracts of the United Nations Conference on Trade and Development. He has published widely and is the Principal of Chancery Chambers, a Barbados law firm engaged primarily in international business law, environmental law, and the law relating to charities.
chancery@caribsurf.com

Sara Castillo Vargas is the Executive Director of Costa Rica's National Commission for the Betterment of Justice Administration. She is an active member of ICOMOS-Costa Rica and represents the organisation on ICOMOS's International Legal and Administrative Affairs Committee. She has a degree in preservation studies from the University of Florida. Ms. Castillo Vargas took part in the drafting of Costa Rica's current legislation on the protection of cultural property. For several years, she served as the legal advisor of ICOMOS-Costa Rica.

Oscar Centurion Frontanilla is the Advisor for Cultural Affairs at the Ministry of Foreign Affairs of Paraguay. Prior to February 2004, he was at the Embassy of Paraguay in Washington, D.C. as Advisor for Cultural Affairs. He is former Chairman and CEO of the Centre for the Conservation of Cultural Heritage and ICOM-Paraguay (1995–2001), former Chairman of Asuncion's Historic Districts Office (1993–4), and former General Director of the National Office for Protecting Cultural Heritage at the Ministry of Education and Culture (1991–1993).

Kérya Chau Sun attended "Lycée Descartes," the French high school of Cambodia, and received a masters degree in Modern Literature at the Sorbonne University in Paris and a Diploma of Superior Specialized Study in Tourism, Culture, and Development. In 1990, after 21 years of absence from Cambodia, she returned to the country for a humanitarian mission. Deeply hurt by the loss of the majority of her family's members under the Khmers Rouges regime and distressed by the deprived situation of the country, in 1995, she returned to participate in the country's reconstruction. Since her return, she has been participating in the creation of the Authority for the Protection of the Site and Management of the Region of Angkor (APSARA Authority). She currently holds the position of Director of Angkor Tourism Development Department and is also vice-president of the national committee of ICOMOS and general secretary of the national committee of ICOM. She teaches the marketing and economy of tourism in the Royal University of Phnom Penh.

Richard Crewdson is a retired solicitor of London, England, and founder and Chair of the International Bar Association Cultural Property Law Committee 1986–90.

Alissandra Cummins, B.A.(Hons.), M.A., F.M.A. is Director of the Barbados Museum and Historical Society. She holds a Bachelor of Arts Degree with Honours in the History of Art from the University of East Anglia at Norwich, and a Master of Arts in Museum Studies from Leicester University. A recognized authority on Caribbean museum development and art, she was elected a Fellow of the Museums Association (U.K). She serves as Chairperson of both the National Art Gallery Committee and the Barbados National Commission for UNESCO. She is also a member of the Prime Minister's Task Force on the Cultural Industries and was recently appointed to Barbados' Advisory Committee on Intellectual Property. She was instrumental in formation of the Museums Association of the Caribbean (MAC) and became its founder President in 1989. She currently represents Barbados on UNESCO's Intergovernmental Committee for Promoting the Return of Cultural Property to its Country of Origin or its Restitution in Case of Illicit Appropriation (ICPRCP), and has served as its Chairperson from 2003–5. Miss Cummins served between 1998–2004 as Chairperson of the Advisory Committee of the International Council of Museums, following which she was elected as its president in 2004.

James Cuno is President and Director of the Art Institute of Chicago, having previously served as Professor and Director of the Courtauld Institute of Art, University of London, and Professor and Director of the Harvard University Art Museums. A Fellow of the American Academy of Arts and Sciences, he has also served as a Trustee of the Museum of Fine Arts, Boston and the Association of Art Museum Directors. He was President of the latter in 2002. Mr. Cuno has published widely on a number of topics, from French graphic art of the eighteenth and nineteenth century to contemporary American art and U.S. cultural policy as pertains to the purpose and mission of art museums in a civil society. His most recent book, *Whose Muse? Art Museums and the Public Trust* was published by Princeton University Press in 2003. Mr. Cuno has lectured and written frequently on the topic of U.S. art museums and the legal and ethical questions surrounding the acquisition of antiquities.
jcuno@artic.edu

Brooks Daly is the Senior Legal Counsel at the Permanent Court of Arbitration (PCA) in The Hague, The Netherlands. Mr. Daly counsels lawyers and arbitrators participating in international arbitration under PCA auspices on a variety of matters relating to arbitral procedure and international dispute resolution. He speaks frequently on international arbitration topics and lectures at Leiden University in the International Business Law and Public International Law LL.M. Programs. Prior to joining the PCA,

Mr. Daly acted as Counsel at the International Chamber of Commerce (ICC) International Court of Arbitration in Paris, France. He is a member of the California

Bar and practiced with the firms of Latham & Watkins (Los Angeles) and Hale & Dorr (London) before joining the ICC. He holds a Doctor of Jurisprudence from the New York University School of Law, a Master of Arts from the New York University Institute of French Studies, and a Bachelor of Arts from the University of California at Santa Barbara. He has acted as an arbitrator under the ICC Rules of Arbitration.
bdaly@pca-cpa.org

Ildiko Pogany DeAngelis is Associate Professor and Director of the Graduate Program in Museum Studies at The George Washington University in Washington, D.C. Professor DeAngelis holds Bachelor of Arts and Master of Arts degrees in art history and she was awarded a Certificate in Museum Administration from the Smithsonian Institution in 1976. In 1980, she earned a Juris Doctor degree *magna cum laude* from American University's Washington College of Law. She practiced law for 18 years before joining the faculty at George Washington University. The first four years, she practiced as an associate with the law firm of Steptoe and Johnson in Washington D.C., and the remainder, as Assistant General Counsel at the Smithsonian Institution, where she specialized in the legal issues arising from the management of museum collections. Professor DeAngelis is now the director of the largest graduate program in Museum Studies in the United States, with more than 115 graduate students studying for Master of Arts degrees and Certificates in Museum Studies. She teaches courses on the legal and ethical challenges of managing museum collections, including a seminar on stolen and illegally exported cultural property. Professor DeAngelis is the author of "Civil Recovery for Stolen Art: Lessons for Museums" an article published in the American Law Institute/American Bar Association's *Legal Problems of Museum Administration* coursebook. She also authored *U.S. Museums and the Nonprofit Sector: A Framework for International Dialogue*, published by the American Association of Museums; and she is a contributing author to Marie C. Malaro's *Legal Primer on Managing Museum Collections* (rev. 1998 ed.), published by the Smithsonian Institution.
ildikod@gwu.edu

Norma Rojas Delgadillo is the Legal Director of Mexico's National Council on Culture and the Arts. Prior to this, she served as the Director of Legal Affairs at the National Institute of Arts and Literature. Ms Rojas has participated in many international meetings and conferences on the protection of cultural heritage and intellectual property. She holds a law degree from the University of Coahuila's School of Law.

Charles E. Di Leva is Chief Counsel of the Environmentaly and Socially Sustainable Development and International Law Practice Group of the World Bank Legal Department. Since 1992, he has worked in all geographic regions, specializing on issues pertaining to sustainable development, such as carbon and green finance, development and implementation of multilateral environmental agreements, and national laws. From 1999 until 2001, he was Director of the Environmental Law Center of IUCN – The World Conservation Union, in Bonn, Germany. Mr. Di Leva served as trial attorney for four years with the U.S. Department of Justice, Environment and Natural Resources Division and for five years with the State of Rhode Island as Legal Counsel with the Department of Environmental Management and as Environmental Advocate in the Attorney General's office. He served for one year as Senior Program Officer with the Environmental Law Unit for the United Nations Environment Program in Nairobi, Kenya. He was also in private environmental law practice for three years in Washington D.C. Mr. Di Leva is an adjunct professor at the George Washington University School of Law, teaching International Trade and Environment, and an adjunct at the American University Washington College of Law teaching Legal Aspects of Sustainable Development. He is active with the American Bar Association, is Chair of the International Environmental Law Committee of the D.C. Bar Association, and is a graduate of Vermont Law School.
cdileva@worldbank.org

Alan Ereira studied history at the Exhibitioner, Queens' College Cambridge, and law as a Hardwicke Scholar at Lincoln's Inn. He joined the BBC as a history producer: prizes include the Japan Prize for Radio and the Royal Television Society award for Best Documentary Series. He helped the Kogi Mamas make a feature-length TV film offering Younger Brother advice. He has run Sunstone Films for ten years and is the founder of the Tairona Heritage Trust. The Tairona Heritage Trust (Fondacion Herencia Tairona) is a UK registered charity (no. 1012018). It provides assistance to the indigenous people of the Sierra Nevada de Santa Marta in response to requests from Gonawindua Tairona, which represents the Mamas. Its primary activities have been to assist in the physical requirements of communication between them and the wider world, reacquiring traditional lands to establish a frontier meeting-point, helping with the construction of an indigenous centre in the city of Santa Marta, and assisting in the physical establishment of an administrative centre there.

Craig Forrest is a lecturer in law and Fellow of the Centre for Public, International and Comparative Law, at the TC Beirne School of Law, University of Queensland, Australia. He is a graduate of Rhodes University (B.Com 1988), the University of South Africa (LLB, 1994; LLM, 1999) and the University of Wolverhampton (Ph.D., 2000). He participated in the UNESCO Conferences to draft the Convention on the Protection of the Underwater Cultural Heritage as a member of the South African delegation.

Mr. Forrest has published in the area of cultural heritage and the Convention on the Underwater Cultural Heritage. Recent publications include: "Salvage Law and the wreck of the Titanic" (2000) 1 *Lloyd's Maritime and Commercial Law Quarterly*, 1, "A New International Regime For The Protection of Underwater Cultural Heritage" (2002) 51(3) *International and Comparative Law Quarterly*, 511; "Defining 'underwater cultural heritage'" (2002) 31(1) *International Journal of Nautical Archaeology*, 3; "An International Perspective on Sunken State Vessels as Underwater Cultural Heritage "(2003) 34(1) *Ocean Development and International Law*, 41; "Has the Application of Salvage Law to Underwater Cultural Heritage Become a Thing of the Past?" (2003) 34(2) *Journal of Maritime Law and Commerce*, 309; "Strengthening the International Regime for the Prevention of The Illicit Trade in Cultural Heritage" (2003) 4(2) *Melbourne Journal of International Law*, 592; "The illicit trade in Iraqi heritage: Considerations for the Australian art and antiquities market" (2004) 29(3) *Alternative Law Journal*, 121; and 'Australia's Protection of Foreign States' Cultural Heritage' (2004) 27(3) *University of New South Wales Law Journal*. In 2005, he was a Visiting Fellow at the Illicit Antiquities Research Centre, McDonald Institute, University of Cambridge. His current research concerns the international law obligations of occupying forces to protected cultural heritage.
cforrest@law.uq.edu.au

Francesco Francioni was born in Florence, Italy. He received Dottore in Giurisprudenza, University of Florence (1966), and LL. M., Harvard (1968). He is a member of the Italian Bar; Chair of International Law, University of Siena and Professor of International Law and Human Rights at the European University Institute, Florence since 2003. He was Provost of the University of Siena from 1994 to 2003; legal counsel for the Italian Government on matters concerning the protection of cultural heritage, and President of the World Heritage Committee 1997–1998; consultant for UNESCO on matters concerning the intentional destruction of cultural heritage, and the safeguarding of intangible cultural heritage. He is a member of the American Law Institute and visiting Professor, Texas Law School, Austin, since 1988.
francesco.francioni@iue.it

Laura (Soullière) Gates received her Bachelor of Fine Arts and Master of Arts from the University of Massachusetts (Amherst). She worked as an architectural historian in planning and cultural resource management activities for the National Park Service in parks and central offices throughout the west and southwest. After moving into park management, she served as superintendent at Arkansas Post National Memorial, and presently is superintendent at Cane River Creole National Historical Park and a commissioner of Cane River National Heritage Area. She has lectured and written extensively on park architecture and design, civic engagement, and federal partnerships. She is past board member and former vice president of the George Wright Society, which is dedicated to the protection, preservation, and management of cultural and natural parks and reserves through research and education. She is a life member of the George Wright Society, and a member of the National Trust for Historic Preservation.

Ramon Gil was the child of an Asario father and Kogi mother. He comes from a line of Asario Mamas, but grew up part-acculturated on the wild borderlands between indigenous and Colombian territory. He was articulate and rebellious when he was taken in hand by powerful Kogi Mamas and trained to be their translator and representative. He is now a respected and energetic senior community leader working in extremely dangerous conditions.

Ariel W. Gonzales practices law, specializing in Public International Law. He is a member of the Faculty of Law at the University of Buenos Aires, as well as a diplomat, currently working at the Legal Advisor's Office of the Argentine Ministry of Foreign Affairs, International Trade and Worship. Mr. Gonzales was a member of the Delegations of Argentina at the negotiations that led to the adoption of the 1999 Second Protocol to the 1954 Hague Convention of Protection of Cultural Property in the Event of Armed Conflict, the 2001 Convention on the Protection of Underwater Cultural Heritage, the 2003 Convention on the Safeguarding of Intangible Cultural Heritage, and the 2003 UNESCO Declaration on the Intentional Destruction of Cultural Property and is Rapporteur of the World Heritage Committee. He is the author of several publications on the legal aspects of the international protection of cultural property, and an invited speaker at several seminars and regional meetings on the same subject, under the auspices of UNESCO and/or the International Committee of the Red Cross. awc@mrecic.gov.ar

Pearl Gourdon holds a bachelors degree with honors in business law and a masters in Art Law, from the University Jean Moulin 3, Lyon, France.

John Gribble has been the Maritime Archaeologist at the South African Heritage Resources Agency since 1996, responsible for managing underwater heritage nationally. He is also Director of the National Survey of Underwater Heritage, the first underwater heritage survey in South Africa. Mr. Gribble is a graduate of the University of Cape Town (Bachelor of Arts, Honours Archaeology, 1987; Master of Arts Archaeology, 1990). Nationally, he was Chairperson of the South African Archaeological Society: Western Cape (1997–2000), a Council Member of the South African Archaeological Society (1996–2000), and Secretary of the Southern African Association of Archaeologists (2000–4). Internationally, John was an associate member of the ICOMOS International Committee for Underwater Cultural Heritage (2000–1) and has been a full member since 2002. He was a member of the National Delegation to the UNESCO Conference of Experts to draft the Convention on the Protection of the Underwater Cultural Heritage (1998–2001). His current research interests include maritime cultural resource management and the archaeology of South Africa's small traders and coasters. Mr. Gribble's most recent publication is "The Past, Present and Future of Maritime Archaeology in South Africa,' in Carol V Ruppe and Janet F Barstad (eds.), *International Handbook of Underwater Archaeology* (2002).

Arapata Hakiwai has worked for the National Museum of New Zealand (now Museum of New Zealand Te Papa Tongarewa) for over twelve years. He has worked in a number of roles including exhibitions concept developer and research curator for the exhibitions for the opening of new Museum of New Zealand Te Papa Tongarewa

(Te Papa) in February 1998. Mr. Hakiwai was also the co-curator with John Terrell of a project team in partnership with Te Waka Toi (now Toi Aotearoa – Creative New Zealand) and the Field Museum of Natural History in Chicago on the restoration and renovation of the carved Mäori meeting house Ruatepupuke in 1991–93.

Arapata Hakiwai has worked for Te Papa National Services as the Community Partnerships Manager Mäori responsible for working with museums, galleries, allied organisations and Mäori tribes on cultural heritage initiatives. Before this he was the Bicultural Operations Manager for Te Papa. Arapata Hakiwai has been the Director, Mätauranga Mäori, Te Papa since late 2003 and is responsible for the care, management and research of the Mäori and Moriori collections held in Te Papa's care. His area of responsibility also includes advancing the development of mätauranga Mäori or Mäori knowledge into Te Papa's exhibitions and research projects. Arapata is presently a board member for Museums Aotearoa, the museum membership organization in New Zealand.

Yani Herreman, is an architect, holds masters degrees in History of Art and in Museology, with honors, and, is now studying for a doctorate in History of Art with a thesis on Museum Architecture in Mexico. She has worked in several museums where she has occupied positions such as Head of Exhibition Design, Department of the Museum of Cultures, at the National Institute of Anthropology and History and Director of the Natural History Museum of Mexico City. She was also Mexico City's Government Director of Museums, Libraries and Cultural Centers and Deputy Director for Cultural Action in the Ministry of Finance's Department of Heritage and Cultural Action. At the National University of Mexico, she was General Coordinator of the Cultural Action Department at the Iztacala Campus until she was asked to coordinate a postgraduate course on "Museum Planning and Exhibition Design" at the Center of Postgraduate Studies and Research of the School of Architecture, where she now works. She also teaches "Urban Art" at a Postgraduate level in the Arts School of the National University and "Exhibitions" at the CenCryM (Center for Conservation, Restoration and Museography of the National Institute of Anthropology). As an active architect and designer, she has designed exhibitions and has actively worked on museum planning and programming in different countries and works as a consultant. She has written on several topics related to museums, exhibitions, and architecture such as Planning, Programming, Museums and Tourism, Museums and Urban Planning, Exhibitions and Urban Environments. Active in ICOM, she was the founding Chair of its Latinamerican Region, first woman Chair of the Architecture Committee and VicePresident of the Executive Council.
yaniherreman@prodigy.net.mx

Christopher Hodges, Ph.D. has an international reputation as a leading expert in European product regulatory and product liability law. Dr. Hodges is currently an Associate Fellow, Centre for Socio-Legal Studies, Oxford University. He was formerly a partner in the international law firm CMS Cameron McKenna, and is now a consultant to them. At Oxford, Dr. Hodges is leading a major research programme on European and Comparative Product Liability and Regulatory Law. He has extensive experience in the regulation of pharmaceuticals and consumer products and is particularly well-known in the medical device field, being Chair of the Legal Committees of the European and UK medical device manufacturers' trade associations, EUCOMED, EDMA, ABHI and BIVDA. He is editor of the textbooks *Product Liability: European Laws and Practice* (Sweet & Maxwell, London, 1993) and *Multi-Party Actions* (Oxford, 2001) and co-author with Abbott, Howard and Tyler, Mark of *Product Safety* (Sweet & Maxwell, 1996). He undertook the European Commission's 1995 study on the Product Liability Directive and has assisted the Australian and Japanese governments in their liability or regulatory laws. He is the only practising lawyer on the Academic Advisory Panel on consumer law of the UK Department of Trade and Industry.

Barbara T. Hoffman, Editor and Contributor, is a prominent lawyer in private practice in New York City representing for-profit and non-profit entities in both transactions and litigation. She is highly regarded in the United States and internationally for her expertise in art and cultural heritage law. For more than twenty-five years, she has practiced globally in virtually every area related to the subject, including counseling various clients on cultural heritage issues, art restitution and provenance research, contracts for public and private art commissions including large-scale urban projects, international art transactions, and the mediation of art, cultural, and intellectual property-related disputes. She also advises artists and their foundations, museums, authors, filmmakers, and companies with respect to licensing, copyright, and other intellectual property issues. She is licensed to practice law in the states of New York, Washington and the District of Columbia, and is admitted to practice before various federal and state courts including the United States Supreme Court. She has also served as an arbitrator for the American Film Marketing Association.

Ms. Hoffman was associate professor of law at Seattle University, School of Law for nine years, teaching art law, constitutional law, copyright, land use and property. She has also been adjunct professor at the School of Architecture, University of Washington. She is a past chair of the Association of the Bar of the City of New York Committee on Art Law and immediate past chair of the International Bar Association Committee on Art, Cultural Institutions and Heritage Law. She has served as counsel to the College Art Association and was the founder of the Washington Volunteer Lawyers for the Arts. She is a frequent invited lecturer on topics of art and cultural heritage law and intellectual property law and has authored numerous articles and publications in her field, including *Exploiting Images and Image Collections in the New Media* (Kluwer Law International, 1998).

Ms. Hoffman holds a bachelor's degree with honors from Brown University in French and art history and masters degrees with honors from the Johns Hopkins School of Advanced International Studies and the London School of Economics. She received her Juris Doctor from the Columbia University School of Law, Harlan Fiske Stone Scholar. She was also a Fellow at the Centre du Recherche d'Urbanisme, Paris, France.
artlaw@mindspring.com

Bo Hammer Jensen is a European Patent Attorney with a long experience in biotechnology patenting. He has a masters degree in chemistry and physics from the University of Copenhagen, where he worked at the Institute for Physical Oceanography in the first part of his professional career. Subsequently he was trained in intellectual property law at the University of Copenhagen while getting practical training in private practice. In 1985, he joined the company Novo Industry (now Novo Nordisk), where he stayed till the demerger of Novozymes, formerly the Enzyme business unit of Novo Nordisk company in 2000. During these years, he has occupied different positions in the patent department, but today he is Director and Senior Patent Counsel to Novozymes with special responsibilities for policy issues and participation in international organisational work. He is a member of a number of organisations, including Chartered Institute of Patent Agents and Licensing Executives Society (International), and he is a member of Intellectual/Industrial Property Rights committees in various industry organisations, and presently chairing the EuropaBio IPR Working Group.

Jane L. Lennon AM (Member of Order of Australia), MA, is an adjunct professor at the Cultural Heritage Centre for Asia and the Pacific, Deakin University, Melbourne, Australia. She was a founding member of Australia ICOMOS in 1976 and a past president and spent nearly a decade managing historic places for the Department of Conservation and Natural Resources. Since 1993, she has been a consultant on a wide range of heritage issues, a member of the International Organization for Conservation and Cultural Heritage Council (1999–2003), and a 2003 Getty Conservation Institute guest scholar, and was appointed to the new Australian Heritage Council in 2004.

Federico Lenzerini was born in Poggibonsi (Italy) on 7 October 1968. *Magna cum laude*, University of Siena, 15 October 1998. He holds a doctorate and received a JD, in international law; is lecturer of European Union law and research fellow in international law, University of Siena; member of the Italian delegation in international negotiations concerning the protection of cultural heritage carried out under the auspices of UNESCO. He took part, as consultant to UNESCO, in the drafting of a preliminary report on the destruction of the Buddhas of Bamiyan in view of the adoption of the Declaration on the Intentional Destruction of Cultural Heritage. He participated, as member of the Italian delegation, in the twenty-eighth Session of the UNESCO World Heritage Committee, held in Suzhou (China) in June and July 2004. In addition to international protection of cultural heritage, his main areas of concern are international human rights, asylum law, rights of indigenous peoples, international environmental law and international trade.
lenzerini@unisi.it

Geoffrey Lewis chaired the ICOM Ethics Committee from 1996–2004. A past-President of ICOM and the Museums Association (UK) he directed the museums of Sheffield and Liverpool (now National Museums Liverpool) before becoming Director of Museum Studies at the University of Leicester. He holds a research degree in archaeology and the Diploma and Fellowship of the Museums Association. An honorary Fellow of his national professional association, he is also an honorary member of ICOM. Now retired, he continues to write and advise on museum matters.
mail@GeoffreyLewis.co.uk

Francisco Javier Lopez Morales, holds a doctorate in urbanism from the University of Grenoble, France. He has been a member of the ICOMOS Executive Committee since 1991, and is an expert consultant of UNESCO's World Heritage Committee. He has authored many books, among them *Arquitectura Vernacula en Mexico* (Vernacular Architecture in Mexico), for which he won the Juan Pablo Prize in Mexico. He has judged many national and international architecture competitions, and organized and participated in numerous international preservation conferences. He is a member of the National System of Researchers (Sistema Nacional de Investigadores – CONACyT), and professor-researcher in the Master's Program in Architecture of the School of Engineering and Architecture of the National Polytechnic Institute of Mexico. He has also consulted with the Andalucian Institute of Historic Heritage, Spain. In 2001, Dr. Lopez became Director of World Heritage at the National Institute for Anthropology and History, in Mexico City. Most recently, he participated in the committee drafting UNESCO's Convention for the Protection of Intangible Heritage.

Derek Luxford is a partner at the Syndey law firm, Hickson, and chair of the Land Transport Subcommittee of the Maritime and Transport Law Committee.

Patricia Madrigal Cordero is an attorney specializing in International Law at the University of Costa Rica and a candidate for a doctoral degree in Environmental Law at the University of Alicante, Spain. She has broad experience in interdisciplinary and institutional activities related to Legislative, Political, and Institutional Assessment, and in executing grassroots projects. She has held positions as a consultant on different projects for multilateral organizations such as the World Bank, the Interamerican Development Bank, the World Union for Nature in the Environmental Legislation Program, and the Wildlife Program for Central America in the Central American and Costa Rican Judicial School. She has been the Regional Collaborator for the International Environmental Law Year Book and was a director for the Costa Rican Bar Association. She is the President and founding member of the National Environmental Law Association in Costa Rica (ACDA). She is currently a member of the Council on Managing the Independent Professional Services Cooperative for Social Solidarity, Coopesolidar R.L. She has broad experience teaching at the university level, both nationally and internationally, and has published diverse articles and books related to

Costa Rican and Central American environmental legislation and policy, community use of wildlife, and biodiversity conservation.

Alberto Martorell-Carreño was conferred a Bachelor in Jurisprudence degree and the professional title of Lawyer by the Santa Maria Catholic University of Arequipa (Peru, 1991). He holds a masters degree in Protected Natural Areas from the Autonomous University of Madrid, Complutense University of Madrid, University of Alcala and Europarc (Spain) joint program. Mr. Martorell is Vice-President for International Affairs of ICOMOS Peru and member of ICOMOS Spain. In 2003 he was elected Vice-President of the International Scientific Committee on Legal, Administrative, and Financial Affairs of ICOMOS. He is Deputy Secretary General of the Iberoamerican Sub-Committee on Cultural Cities. He is also member of the ICOMOS Committee on Cultural Routes. Martorell has authored numerous books and articles in his areas of expertise. He is a candidate in the Doctoral studies Program on Political Sciences of the Autonomous University of Madrid, Spain. Martorell has evaluated the state conservation of World Heritage Sites in Peru, Aargentina, and Spain.

Nancy I. M. Morgan, Ph.D. is the Executive Director for the Cane River National Heritage Area Commission in Natchitoches, Louisiana. Since 2001, she has worked at the direction of a nineteen-member federal commission to preserve and promote the natural, cultural, and historical resources of the Cane River region. Morgan's interest in cultural landscapes was first realized in anthropological fieldwork in the Kaqchikel Maya region of Guatemala. Morgan's doctoral dissertation focused on the relationship between the residents of the Kaqchikel community of Santa María de Jesús and the Volcán de Agua (known as Junajpu in Kaqchikel), the sacred volcano on which the community sits. Morgan holds a masters degree and doctorate in Anthropology from Tulane University in New Orleans, Louisiana, and a Bachelor of Arts degree in History and Sociology/Anthropology from Colgate University in Hamilton, New York. Morgan was a Fulbright Fellow to Guatemala in 1999, and a Watson Fellow to Mexico and Central America in 1993.

Adrian Parkhouse is a partner of Farrer & Co in London. He is a litigation lawyer and head of the firm's Disputes Team. He is also Chair of its Art & Heritage Group, which focuses the many areas of the firm's practice in the art and heritage arena. He acts for collectors, dealers, galleries, and museums. He is an officer of the International Bar Association's Art, Cultural Institutions and Heritage Law Committee.
acp@farrer.co.uk

Gary L. Paulson is Assistant General Counsel, Upstream, Western Hemisphere for BP America, Inc., and is officed in Houston, Texas. In that position, he works with legal teams who provide legal services and support for BP's oil and gas exploration activities in the continental United States, the Gulf of Mexico, Latin American, and the Caribbean. Mr. Paulson received his Bachelor of Arts degree (with honors) from Colorado Sate University in 1970 and his Juris Doctor degree from the University of Denver in 1973, where he was an editor on the *Law Review.* Prior to joining the corporate predecessor of BP America, Inc. in 1981, he was engaged in a litigation and commercial law practice in Denver, Colorado. In his twenty-three year career with BP, his responsibilities have included oversight of legal issues relating to many facets of domestic and international energy operations including the exploration, production, marketing and sale of oil and natural gas; the refining and marketing of crude oil, and the manufacture and sale of chemical products. Mr. Paulson is licensed to practice law in Texas and Colorado and is admitted to practice before various state and federal courts, including the United States Supreme Court.

Matthew Peek is a senior career officer in the Australian Foreign Service. He has had a number of overseas postings including Australian Ambassador to Chile (with nonresident accreditation to Peru and Bolivia) and Australian Ambassador to the Kingdom of Denmark (with nonresident accreditation to Norway and Iceland). At the time of the presentation of this paper he was Australia's Ambassador and Permanent Delegate to UNESCO. Positions he has held in the Foreign Ministry include Assistant Secretary, Strategic Policy and Intelligence; Assistant Secretary, Economic Organisations; and Assistant Secretary, Staffing and Organisation. He is a graduate in Politics and History from the Australian National University.

Zelda Pickup, LLB., MA is a partner at CMS Cameron McKenna, a major transnational law firm with its main office based in London. Zelda qualified as a solicitor in 1977 and was subsequently awarded a masters degree in Healthcare Ethics. Following time spent in private practice and an academic career, during which she was published widely on various ethical and legal issues, Zelda joined AstraZeneca where she gained extensive experience as senior in-house counsel in the pharmaceutical sector. Zelda joined CMS Cameron McKenna in 2002 and specialises in advising on commercial agreements, regulatory issues and product liability for the pharmaceutical industry.

Hester du Plessis is a Senior Research Fellow at the Faculty of Art, Design and Architecture, University of Johannesburg. Her faculty responsibility is to structure, co-ordinate, and supervise research within the field of product design – industrial design, jewelry design, ceramic design, fashion design and architecture. Her field of research lies in philosophy and political science with the focus on social epistemology (women in design and indigenous knowledge systems). She has been working in close collaboration with scientists at the National Institute of Science, Technology and Development Studies, CSIR, in New Delhi, India, for the past five years. The focus of the research in India is on artisans and their traditional technologies. This cross-cultural collaborative research uses methodologies based in the research field of Public Attitude and Understanding of Science.
hettdple@mail.twr.ac.za

Peter Raue, Ph.D. Born in Munich in 1941, Professor Raue, a partner in Hogan and Hartson LLP, is one of the most well-known Berlin attorneys, with an excellent reputation in Germany, as well as in the international marketplace, specifically for his practice which covers all aspects of intellectual property rights (copyrights, publishers' right of publication, arts and entertainment, and unfair competition law). Among his many high-profile clients are numerous publishers, artists, actors, theaters, museums, and cultural institutions of all kinds. Professor Raue advises the Federal Government and the Berlin Government with regard to legal aspects of cultural politics. He lectures on copyrights at the Freie Universität Berlin. Professor Raue is co-founder of the Association of Friends of the National Gallery and its chairman since 1977.

James K. Reap is a Public Service Associate on the faculty of the University of Georgia College of Environment and Design and a Fellow of the Dean Rusk Center – International, Comparative and Graduate Legal Studies. He has broad experience in local and state government in the United States. His areas of specialization include heritage conservation, land use and environmental law, and local government and regional planning. He has participated in projects and conducted research in Ghana, Mali, Kazakhstan, Georgia, Ukraine, Croatia, Israel, France, Spain, and Mexico. He serves as President of the Committee on Legal, Administrative and Financial Issues of the International Council on Monuments and Sites, a nongovernmental organization affiliated with UNESCO.
jreap@uga.edu

Susan Reye, Ph.D. is a Senior General Counsel with the Australian Government Solicitor, where she specialises in public international law and environment and heritage law. From 1996 to 2003, she was the senior legal adviser to the Australian Department of the Environment and Heritage. She has also worked as an international lawyer with the Organization for Economic Co-operation and Development, as well as in the Australian Attorney-General's Department and Department of Foreign Affairs and Trade. She has a bachelor of arts (French and German Honors) from the

University of Queensland, an LL.B (Honors) from the Australian National University, and a Doctorate in public international law from the UniversitИ PanthИon-Assas (Paris 2). She can be contacted at susan.reye@ags.gov.au, or Susan Reye, Office of General Counsel, Australian Government Solicitor, Locked Bag 7246 Canberra Mail Centre, ACT 2610 Australia.

Mechtild Rössler, Ph.D. has a master of arts (1984) in cultural geography from Freiburg University (Germany) and a doctorate (1988) from the Faculty for Earth Sciences, University of Hamburg. She joined the Research Centre of the "Cité des Sciences et de L'Industrie" (Paris, France) in 1989 on a Centre National du Recherche Scientific (CNRS) post and worked in 1990–1 as visiting professor at the University of California at Berkeley (USA; Department of Geography). In 1991, Dr. Rössler, joined UNESCO Headquarters in Paris, first the Division for Ecological Sciences, and since 1992, the UNESCO World Heritage Centre as a programme specialist and responsible officer for natural heritage and cultural landscapes. In July 2001 she became Chief of Europe and North America, in charge of half of all World Heritage sites and fifty States Parties. She has published seven books, more than sixty articles, and contributes to the editorial board of three international journals.
m.rossler@unesco.org

Tullio Scovazzi, Professor of International Law at the University of Milano-Bicocca, Milan, Italy, is a legal expert of the Italian government to some negotiations relating to the international law of the sea, the environment, and cultural matters. Professor Scovazzi is the author of numerous publications, including *The Protection of the Underwater Cultural Heritage – Before and After the 2001 UNESCO Convention* (Leiden, 2003) and *La Protezione del Patrimonio Culturale Sottomarino nel Mare Mediterraneo*, (Milano, 2004).
tullio.scovazzi@unimib.it

Folarin Shyllon is Professor of Law at the University of Ibadan, Nigeria, where he was the Dean of the Faculty of Law from 1984 to 1991. He was educated at King's College, London. His current teaching and research interests are in the fields of cultural property law and intellectual property law. He was a contributor to UNESCO's maiden issue of World Culture Report (1998) and contributed a chapter to Halina Niec's *Cultural Rights and Wrongs* (Paris: UNESCO, 1998), published to mark the fiftieth anniversary of the Universal Declaration of Human Rights of 1948. He is a member of the Nigerian Bar and a former President of the Nigerian Association of Law Teachers. He was sent to Barbados by UNESCO in 2000 to advise the government on its accession to international instruments on cultural property. As a result of this visit, the government of Barbados decided to accede to all UNESCO conventions on the protection of cultural property, as well as the UNIDROIT Convention.
fshyllon@yahoo.co.uk

Gerald R. Singer joined the American Museum of Natural History in June 1995 as its first General Counsel. He is responsible for legal affairs and revenue security. Prior to joining the American Museum of Natural History, Mr. Singer was a corporate/litigation partner with a Chicago law firm representing both for-profit and nonprofit entities. Mr. Singer holds a Juris Doctor degree from the University of Michigan and a bachelor of arts degree from the University of Illinois.

Vivienne Solís Rivera graduated in biology from the University of Costa Rica (1983) and has a master's degree in ecology from the University of Lawrence, Kansas, in the United States. She has coordinated different interdisciplinary teams during her work experience. She worked on the Regional Master's Program for Wildlife Management at the National University in Heredia, Costa Rica. She was the coordinator for the Environmental Education Program for Fauna Management and the Environmental Education Program for the State Distance University. In addition, she participated as

the Executive Assistant in the National Conservation Strategy for Sustainable Development that the Ministry of Natural Resources and Energy of Costa Rica coordinated. She was President of the Board of Directors for the Foundation for the Development of the Central Volcanic Mountain Range in Costa Rica during the 1990–2 period. For 10 years, she was the coordinator of the Wildlife Thematic Area of the Regional Office for Mesoamerica of the World Union for Nature. She has written and edited more than twenty publications and articles linked to the issue of biodiversity and sustainable community management of natural resources. She is currently the manager of a cooperative (Coope Sol i Dar, R.L) dedicated to developing an interdisciplinary approach and encouraging actions to reduce biodiversity loss and to promote a better quality of life in local communities.
vsolis@coopesolidar.org

Maui Solomon (Moriori, Kai Tahu and Pakeha) is a barrister with twenty years' legal experience specialising in commercial law, resource management, intellectual property and Treaty of Waitangi/Indigenous Peoples Rights issues. Mr. Soloman has been actively involved in Maori fisheries issues for the past fifteen years and is currently a Commissioner on the Treaty of Waitangi Fisheries Commission. He represents three of the six tribes in the Wai 262 claim concerning indigenous flora and fauna and cultural/ intellectual rights of Maori, which seeks, among other things, to develop a unique system for protection and use of Maori traditional knowledge. Mr. Solomon maintains an active interest in international indigenous peoples issues and regularly attends meetings of the Convention on Biological Diversity and the World Intellectual Property Organisation. He is currently Co-Director of the Global Coalition of the International Society of Ethnobiology, an organisation committed to building closer working relationships among indigenous peoples, researchers, and scientists in the area of ethnobotanical studies. Maui has also been a key advocate and spokesperson for his own Moriori people over the past twenty years and is currently leading negotiations with the Crown regarding settlement of their Treaty claim.

Alvaro Soto is the Director of Expedition America and an Anthropologist from Universidad de los Andes. He received his master of arts and PhD. from the University of California, and completed his post-doctoral studies in Environment and Internacional Relations at the Royal Society of Canada. He is President of Neotrypico, a center for the study of the neotropics. He is also a University professor and serves as Executive Secretary for the Commission on Developing Countries and Global Change and was in charge of the preparation and publication of the book titled *For Earth's Sake*, presented as the position paper to the Earth Summit in Brazil in 1992. He is Senior Fellow of the International Federation of Insitutes for Advanced Studies. Has been Chairman of the Department of Anthropology at the Universidad de los Andes, Director-General of the natural parks system of Colombia, and Director of the Colombian Institute of Anthropology. Mr. Soto has published several articles and books on environmental issues and on his exploration and discovery of the Lost City of the Tayronas in the Sierra Nevada de Santa Marta, Colombia. He has produced several documentaries such as "Secrets of the Choco," a film on the Pacific coast of Colombia and its future. He has worked extensively among the indigenous and black communities of Colombia, particularly those on the Pacific coast, Amazonia, the Caribbean coast, and the Sierra Nevada.
neotropsoto@hotmail.com

María Margarita Suárez Garcia served as an expert at the National Museum of Fine Art in 1968 and has been the Director of the Museum of Colonial Art in Havana since 1969. She is currently also the Deputy Director of Museology in the Department of Cultural Heritage of the Office of the Historian of the City of Havana. Ms Suárez holds a degree in Art History from the University of Havana's Faculty of Arts. She completed her post-graduate studies in the same faculty, as well as at the Ministry of Culture's National Centre for Conservation, Restoration and Museology. She has undertaken research into museum collections and Colonial Cuban furniture, and has contributed to the Thesaurus of Decorative Arts, published by the Ministry of Culture. In 1987, Ms. Suárez attended a training course on museum work in the former USSR. She has also attended courses on educational work in museums and the protection of historical heritage organised by the Spanish Agency for International Cooperation. Ms. Suárez has participated in various national and international gatherings related to the registration and documentation of museum collections and colonial art.

Maria Rosa Suárez-Inclán Ducassi is a lawyer specializing in law and International relations. She is also one of Spain's most highly regarded experts based on her long experience in the field of conservation and the law as it relates to the legal protection of historic heritage. She is President of both the Spanish National Committee and the International Scientific Committee on Cultural Routes of ICOMOS. Ms. Suárez-Inclán Ducassi is also a member of the Executive Committee of ICOMOS.

Robert Sullivan is a descendant of the Nga Puhi and Kai Tahu tribes of Aotearoa/New Zealand. He was a member of the first International Indigenous Librarians' Forum Organizing Committee, 1999–2000, and edited their Proceedings (Auckland: Te Ropu Whakahau, 2001). He created and maintained the first Maori Web directory organized by subject, Nga Matatiki Rorohiko, 1995–2001, at The University of Auckland Library. In 2001, this directory was transferred to form the basis for the Maori section of the National Library of New Zealand's Te Puna Web Directory (<http://www.auckland.ac.nz/lbr/trout/trout.htm>). He is also a board member of the New Zealand Electronic Poetry Centre (<http://www.nzepc.auckland.ac.nz>).

Elizabeth Torres is an architect specialising in the restoration of monuments and historic sites. She holds a masters degree in social sciences, with a focus on anthropology, as well as a diploma in the rights of indigenous and primitive peoples. Ms. Torres is the Director of the National Museum of Bolivian Ethnography and Folklore. She was previously the Director of the National Institute of Artistic Heritage and Visual Arts of Bolivia and the Founder and Executive Director of the Rehabilitation of Sucre's Historic Areas Programme. Ms. Torres is Professor of Architectural History and the History of Latin-American Urbanism at Nuestra Señora de la Paz University and a consultant of the project to rehabilitate the historic areas of Cochabamba, organised by the University of San Simon. She is a member of the National Association of Architects of Bolivia, ICOMOS, ICOM, and SIARB.

Fred J. Truslow is the founder and chairman of the Board of the Institute for Latin American Art Documentation, a U.S. foundation for documenting and protecting Latin American cultural patrimony. As a lawyer (District of Columbia and New York), he specialised in housing and urban development (1970–80) and in corporate law, leveraged mergers and acquisitions, and financial transactions (1980–90). From 1990 to 1999, he was active in a private investment firm. During the 1980s, he represented the government of Peru in the recovery of cultural patrimony. Mr. Truslow was educated at Harvard Law School (Juris Doctor 1964 and Yale College, Bachelor of Arts, 1961).

Alida Tua is the Vice President of ARPAI. She received a doctorate in philosophy from the University of Rome and a doctorate in psychology from the University of Padova. She is a member of the Board of the Società Europea di Cultura, headquartered in Venice, and the Associazione per la Ricerca Contro il Cancro in Rome.

Juan Carlos Uribe was the Associate Director of the Intellectual Property Department of Cavelier Abogados (1990–3) and the founder, Partner and Director of the Intellectual Property Department of Vernot Abogados (1993–5). He currently lectures on Intellectual Property Law at the University Politecnico Grancolombiano. Mr. Uribe studied at the School of Law, Colegio Mayor de Nuestra Señora del Rosario (JD, 1988), the University of Kent at Canterbury (LLM in International Commercial Law, 1989), and the University of Pennsylvania (LLM in Intellectual Property and Entertainment Industries, 1990). His publications include *The Protection of Trade Secrets and Confidential Information* (1989). He is a member of the Copyright Society, the American

Intellectual Property Law Association, the Colombian Copyright Centre, an officer of the Committee on Art, Cultural Institutions and Heritage Law of the International Bar Association, and the University of Pennsylvania Alumni Association.

Juan Antonio Valdés received his Ph.D. in Archaeology from the Sorbonne University in 1983. He has published six books on Mayan civilisation and has lectured at many universities in the United States, Europe, and Latin America. He has written more than 100 articles on the results of his work at many first-class archaeological sites, including Tikal, Uaxactun, Copán, Dos Pilas, Kaminaljuyu and others. Professor Valdés has taught at San Carlos University since 1986 and served as Guatemala's Director of Cultural Heritage from 1996 to 1998.

Jorge Velarde is a senior partner of Rodrigo, Elias & Medrano Abogados. He chairs the Regulatory Group and is a member of the Finance Group in the firm's Lima office. He specializes in transportation finance, infrastructure, insurance, and mergers and acquisitions. He has participated in important international transactions, mainly representing foreign clients in the acquisition of Peruvian corporations and in the privatization of state businesses in several industries. Mr. Velarde is a graduate of the Catholic University of Peru and a member of the Lima, American, and International Bar Associations.
jvelarde@estudiorodrigo.com

Maria del Perpertuo Socorro Villareal Escarrega is the Coordinator of Legal Affairs of Mexico's National Institute of Anthropology and History. Prior to this, she worked for the Federal Electoral Institute.

Alexandra S Wawryk, Ph.D. received First Class degrees in Economics and Law, and a Ph.D. in Law, from the University of Adelaide, Australia. She is a lecturer at the University of Adelaide in Environmental Law, Minerals and Energy Law, and Contract Law. She is a barrister and solicitor of the Supreme Court of South Australia, and is a member of the South Australian Law Society's Planning, Environment and Local Government Committee, and the Environmental Defenders Office (SA). Dr. Wawryk has published articles in a number of journals, including the *Journal of Energy and Natural Resources Law*, the *University of New South Wales Law Journal*, the *Melbourne University Law Review*, the *Australasian Journal of Natural Resources Law and Policy*, and the *Environmental and Planning Law Journal*. She is the associate editor for renewable energy for OGEL, a specialist on-line database for Oil, Gas and Energy Law.
alex.wawryk@adelaide.edu.au

Wend Wendland is a lawyer, with a Masters of Law degree in intellectual property law. He practised as an intellectual property, competition law, and media law attorney, and is now Head of the Traditional Creativity and Cultural Expressions Section, Global Intellectual Property Issues Division, of the World Intellectual Property Organization in Geneva, Switzerland.
wend.wendland@wipo.int

Johannes Christian Wichard, a national of Germany, holds a masters degree from Harvard Law School and a doctorate in law from Tübingen University, Germany. Before joining WIPO in 1998, he was responsible for trademark and unfair competition law in the German Federal Ministry of Justice, and, before that, taught German and international private law at the Universities of Tübingen and Berlin.

Doğan Yağiz is head of the Legal Department of GAMA holding A.S., a leading Turkish contractor dealing internationally in large-scale industrial and infrastructure projects. He has represented the European International Contractors at the International Bar Association San Francisco Conference in 2003, where the paper formulating his chapter in this book was first presented. He is experienced in construction and energy law.

Preface and Acknowledgments

The field of art and cultural heritage law has expanded greatly since John Henry Merryman and Albert E. Elsen first published in 1979 their ground-breaking treatise based on the first course in art law at Stanford University, entitled, "Law, Ethics and the Visual Arts." The field of art law and cultural heritage law at that time was a specialty the contours of which were amorphous and not adequately defined.

As a young practitioner in the field in the early seventies, my starting point was always some other area of the law; i.e., commercial law, copyright, or trusts and estates, to which I tried to bring a special focus as to how those particular areas mixed with the specific concerns of artists or the particular qualities of artworks and the idiosyncrasies in the art world. Stephen Weil's decision to create the ALI-ABA Museum and the Law course was most welcome to assist practitioners and museum counsel in sharing information as the law developed. Similarly, the law of international cultural heritage and cultural heritage policy at that time was underdeveloped, causing Professor Merryman to apologize for so often quoting and citing his own articles.

Since that time, international protection of cultural heritage has become a common topic in legal literature, conferences, and international fora, with several international conventions having been negotiated and ratified. In addition, a specialized body of law is developing as it relates to artworks and cultural resources. At every level, from international conventions to national and local legislation, works of art and cultural resources are being singled out for special treatment; however, the mixture of art and law is still not entirely soluble and basic principles of general law applied to art and cultural property disputes may lead to incongruous and disparate results. It is still an ongoing debate as to how much more the law must change to accommodate the specific needs required to protect the natural and cultural heritage. Despite the growth in the fields, no comprehensive book on international art and cultural heritage law currently exists.

The occasion of the annual meeting of the International Bar Association in 2001 in Cancun, Mexico, and a generous grant from the Ford Foundation of US$40,000 permitted the International Bar Association's (IBA) Committee on Art, Cultural Institutions and Heritage Law, the Latin American and Caribbean Steering Group, and the International Council of Museums (ICOM), to organize an interdisciplinary conference and invite distinguished speakers from the region to discuss the various political and legal national initiatives of countries in Latin American and the Caribbean for protecting cultural heritage in the context of international law.

Referred to as "source nations" in literature and international debates, the voices of these nations had not often been heard in the legal and academic conferences in the United States and Europe. There is a tendency in this field to focus on the United States, Europe, and the Mediterranean; Africa, Latin America, and the Caribbean Basin are parts of the world that tend to be overlooked.

The success of the e-book and the interest of various communities within and outside the IBA, coupled with the growing interest in this field led to the decision to substantially revise and expand the publication beyond Latin America and, more importantly, to address other topical areas in greater depth, albeit maintaining our original vision and goals. *Art and Cultural Heritage: Law, Policy, and Practice* is the result of this decision. In addition to our original co-sponsor, ICOM, we are also joined in this publication by the International Council on Monuments and Sites (ICOMOS). The members of both organizations have contributed significant chapters to this book and literally helped to make it possible. The outstanding contributions of these two non-governmental international organizations in the ongoing struggle to preserve, protect, and manage cultural heritage is evident throughout the discussions in this book.

Art and Cultural Heritage: Law, Policy, and Practice was written and revised with the intention of appealing to a broad, as well as a specialized, readership. I have selected critical topics in cultural heritage law whose links are not often explored and sought to provide a global and international context to issues which, if discussed at all, have a local perspective. If I have omitted specific chapters on artists' rights and other topics related to the individual artist as well as the collector and the auction house – important players and stakeholders in the development of cultural heritage policy – it is not because such topics are unimportant to art law but because there is a surfeit of articles and literature on these topics, at least in the United States.

The book is unique in its breadth and in the voice it gives to constituencies who do not usually converse. It has been my privilege to invite from around the world, authors who are outstanding and distinguished in their area of expertise – experts, practitioners, academics, and individuals from diverse disciplines and sectors, including law, politics, museums, archaeology, anthropology, architecture, art history, business, and traditional knowledge. Obviously, each of the parts of this book could be the subject of a separate volume. Even each chapter could be the subject of a separate book. We have provided practical information as well as policy questions for further discussion. Most contributors have also provided useful Web site links and extended bibliographies to permit those interested in acquiring a more in-depth understanding of the subjects and issues presented to do so.

A publication such as this, taking nearly four years from its initial conception, can only be accomplished with the guidance and assistance of numerous people. At the outset, this book would not be possible without the authors' contributions. To them, I express my deepest gratitude for their wise counsel, generosity and dedication in managing to fine time in their active professional lives to share their valuable knowledge and expertise. Similarly, this book could not have been possible without the support of the co-sponsoring organization, and their officers and staff to whom I am also most grateful: Manus Brinkman, former Secretary General of ICOM; John Zvereff, Secretary General of ICOM; Alissandra Cummins, President of ICOM; Gaia Jungeblodt, Director of ICOMOS; James K. Reap, President, ICOMOS International Committee on Legal, Administrative & Financial Issues; and Michael Petzet, President of ICOMOS. I should also like to acknowledge the Ford Foundation and the International Bar Foundation, Inc. for their financial support.

Thanks also to the International Bar Association: Mark Ellis, its Executive Director, Andrew Primrose, Past President of the IBA Section on General Practice, Tom Forbes, Chair of the IBA's Public and Professional Interest Division, Paul Crick, its director of publications, the officers of the Committee on Art, Cultural Institutions and Heritage Law who have contributed their support before and during the time of my leadership as chair, particularly Judith Hill of Farrer & Co., John Heurta, General Counsel of the Smithsonian Institution, Juan Carlos Uribe of Triana Uribe and Michelsen, John Rubinstein of Rubinstein Phillips, and the chairs of the IBA committees who cooperated with us in the development of various programs from which some of these chapters are derived, notably Clive Elliott of Shortland Chambers, co-chair of the Committee on Intellectual Property and Entertainment Law; Dr. Christian Breitzke of Lebuhn & Puchta LLP, chair, Maritime and Transport Law; Michael E. Schneider of Lalive Partners, and Ange Sandberg of Skanska International Civil Engineering, co-chairs of International Construction Law; Gabrielle Williamson of Heuking Kuehn Luer Woitek, chair of the Environment, Health and Safety Law

Commitee; Louis van Wyck of Spoors & Fischer, vice chair of the Products Liability and Advertising Commitee; Russell Raikes of Cohen Highly LLP, and David Paterson of David Paterson Law Corp., chairs of the Indigenous Peoples Committee; Claus von Wobser of Von Wobeser y Sierra S. C. and Dominique Beserk Brown of BMG Avocats, chairs of the Dispute Resolution Section; and last but certainly not least the always inspiring and quick-witted chairs of the Committee on International Sales, James Klotz of Davis & Company and Jonathan P. Wood of Clyde & Co. I also note the contribution of Jack Batievsky, whose early support in his capacity as chair of the Latin American and Carribbean Steering Committee was critical to the initial success of the conference and e-book. His untimely death in 2002 is a significant loss to all of us. Of course, we are most grateful for the confidence of John Berger, Senior Editor, Cambridge University Press.

Finally, my acknowledgment must be made to my assistant, Abigail Martin. Without Abigail's dedicated and superbly competent support in helping to put this manuscript together and her enthusiasm for the subject, this book might not have been realized.

Barbara T. Hoffman
March 2005, New York

The International Bar Association
The Global Voice of the Legal Profession

In its role as a dual membership organisation, comprising about 16,000 individual lawyers and more than 190 Bar Associations and Law Societies, the International Bar Association (IBA) influences the development of international law reform and helps shape the future of the legal profession. Its member organisations cover all continents and include the American Bar Association, the German Federal Bar, the Japan Federation of Bar Associations, the Law Society of Zimbabwe, and the Mexican Bar Association.

Grouped into two divisions – the Legal Practice Division and the Public and Professional Interest Division – the Association covers all practice areas and professional interests. It provides members with access to leading experts and up-to-date information in addition top-level professional development and network-building opportunities through high-quality publications and world-class conferences. The IBA's Human Rights Institute works across the Association, helping to promote, protect, and enforce human rights under a just rule of law, and to preserve the independence of the judiciary and the legal profession worldwide.

The IBA, through the committees that make up its divisions, has a long tradition of publishing, in cooperation with leading publishers, books that offer the practitioner an in-depth analysis of current legal issues with a uniquely global perspective. *Art and Cultural Heritage: Law, Policy, and Practice* admirably continues this tradition. Its genesis was in the IBA Annual Conference held in Cancun in 2001, from which grew the IBA's first e-book. The interest in this, from various committees and fora within the IBA and beyond, led directly to this current volume, which the IBA is proud and pleased to support.

With topics as diverse as illicit traffic in cultural property, developing conservation strategies for national heritage areas, protecting underwater cultural heritage, and the role of museums and their stewardship of cultural property, *Art and Cultural Heritage: Law, Policy, and Practice* will be of interest to practitioners working in many areas of law, as well as museum professionals and anyone involved in the management and protection of cultural resources; indeed it will be of great interest to anyone who cares about the world's natural and cultural resources. Lawyers can and do play an important role, working alongside conservation and cultural heritage professionals, in safeguarding the treasures of the world, especially in today's international society, where national borders are becoming increasingly open. *Art and Cultural Heritage: Law, Policy, and Practice* not only comments on current issues in this arena, it moves the debate forward by highlighting new problems and issues.

As Editor, Barbara Hoffman has undertaken a huge task in bringing together contributors from all continents and from organisations such as the World Bank, the United Nations Educational, Scientific and Cultural Organization (UNESCO) and the World Intellectual Property Organization (WIPO or OMPI). The IBA would particularly like to note the support of the International Council of Museums and the International Council on Monuments and Sites. It is the IBA's aim to encourage exchange of information throughout the global legal community in accord with its role as the global voice of the legal profession. With this book, Barbara Hoffman has more than achieved this aim and I congratulate her and thank her for the many hours of work she has put into making it a reality.

Francis Neate
President, International Bar Association March 2005

The International Bar Association

As Co-Chair of the "Human Rights Institute" and former President of the International Bar Association, I am very glad to present this inspiring and interesting book.

Some years ago, I had the privilege and good fortune to learn about the energetic and challenging efforts Barbara Hoffman was undertaking in connection with her work as Chair of the International Bar Association's "Committee on Art, Cultural, Institution and Heritage Law."

Today such efforts have produced this splendid book.

Let me take this opportunity to remind that human rights are central among the purposes of the United Nations, as proclaimed in its own Charter, which states that they are "for all without distinction."

Human rights are not a privilege but, instead, they are natural-born rights of a universal nature, as written into the Universal Declaration of Human Rights, the Preamble of which proclaims that they are a "common standard" for all peoples and for all nations.

They are further of an indivisible, interdependent, and interrelated nature. This is to mean that political, cultural, social, economic, and civil rights are to be construed as a system, in their entirety.

Human rights, however, do not impose one single cultural standard. They respect every single one. Instead, they provide the minimum protection required to preserve human dignity. They are not oriented nor are they representative of any particular culture to the exclusion of others, but allow a healthy cultural variation without compromising the "minimum standards" they do set.

In fact, they facilitate respect for and protection of cultural diversity because they are predicated in the belief that every human being has the right to culture, which includes the right to enjoy his or her own particular identity.

On the other hand, cultural rights are not, however, unlimited.

They are clearly limited, like most rights, at the point at which they may infringe or violate the human rights of others.

This is so because no right can be abused at the expense or destruction of another. Cultural rights, therefore, cannot justify in any manner the denial or violation of human rights and fundamental individual freedoms.

Cultural "relativism"; i.e., the assertion that values vary a great deal according to different cultural perspectives, cannot – under any circumstance – be used or claimed as an excuse to violate or deny human rights.

The aforementioned means that there are substantive limitations on cultural behaviors or practices, even when they seem to be based in well-entrenched traditions.

No culture – as a nonstatic mutable historical formation – could, for example, be used to justify torture or slavery, nor to protect discrimination based on sex, race, ethnicity, or religion.

Having said that, it is also clear that there is a lot of room for cultural variation without compromising the "minimum standards" of human rights, as they are established by international law.

Let me say, in closing, that in our own daily efforts we are definitely encouraged by the fact that the author and all the collaborators who have produced this excellent book, whom we congratulate, have undertaken the adventure of putting together this useful tool that we definitely welcome.

Emilio J. Cárdenas
Co-Chair of the Human Rights Institute of
The International Bar Association

The International Council of Museums

The International Council of Museums (ICOM) was created in 1946, almost sixty years ago, and over this period some remarkable improvements have taken place in the field of cultural heritage protection. Nevertheless, the battle is far from won and this second edition of *Art and Cultural Heritage: Law, Policy, and Practice* provides valuable insight into current practices and policies. It is therefore a source of great pride for ICOM to be co-sponsoring this publication, which succeeds in putting the whole issue of cultural heritage legislation into perspective and will undoubtedly make a significant contribution to raising awareness at all levels.

ICOM is a nongovernmental organization and a nonprofit association, primarily financed by membership fees and supported by various public and private organizations. Today, six decades since its foundation, the organization has become a unique, culturally diverse network of individuals and institutions that voluntarily contribute their expertise and resources to the preservation and protection of cultural and natural heritage. ICOM's more than 20,000 members – institutional as well as individual – in 148 countries; its 116 national committees, twenty nine international committees, fifteen international affiliated organizations, and six regional organizations attest to its inclusive cultural diversity, and are a tribute to the role it plays for the profession and for the world community.

After the reconstruction from the devastation of World War II, ICOM's role has been in constant evolution, adapting its structure and focus to the needs of the times. From originally orchestrating the profession's response to the recovery of the damage inflicted upon the world's cultural heritage by the ravages of war, the organization has concentrated on communicating this very heritage as a means to ensure and preserve core values of humanity.

Throughout, ICOM never lost sight of its memberships' needs: publications, courses, training session, capacity building workshops, seminars, and regular General Conferences have been and are organized all over the world to promote networking and the exchange of expertise among museum professionals.

The organization recognized that it was also being called upon to set the standards for museum governance and professional practices and, in 1986, it established a Code of Professional Ethics, of compulsory adherence by all of its members and institutions. Translated into many languages, the Code of Ethics has become a benchmark for all its members and, indeed, for any professional museum body.

The awareness of a pervasive globalizing process that threatens the identity of minority cultures – and with it, world cultural heritage as a whole – prompted ICOM to embrace initiatives to protect cultural diversity. One such initiative is now one of ICOM's major commitments: the ongoing battle against the illicit traffic of cultural property that erodes the identity of communities by depriving them of referential elements of their cultural heritage. Public awareness campaigns were launched with the simultaneous publications of illicit traffic-prevention tools, such as the *100 Missing Objects* series (four volumes to date), later complemented by the Red List publications (Chapter TWO; see bibliography) featuring culturally protected objects, which were complemented by the more recent addition of Object ID, the minimum standards for describing art objects developed by the J. Paul Getty Institute and now administered by ICOM. Governments, international agencies, museums, and art institutions were all enlisted in this truly arduous battle, where ICOM has scored significant victories. Manus Brinkman, former Secretary General of ICOM, has devoted an article to this subject in the present volume.

As illicit traffic has increasingly become the object of international and national legislation, new issues are coming to the fore, issues on which ICOM will have to take a stance: restitution and repatriation of cultural property, as well as, perhaps, a role in mediating corresponding out-of-court disputes. In addition, ICOM will be taking a proactive approach to the preparation of mechanisms responding to the needs of countries caught up in the devastation that accompanies natural as well as manmade disasters. Already established is our Museum Emergency Preparedness Programme, recently supported by the creation of the Disaster Relief Web site and Task Force tasked with communicating needs and identifying the ways in which ICOM can best help in the event of an emergency.

ICOM has also identified the need for the complementary and comprehensive protection and preservation of both intangible and tangible heritage, positioning museums as essential partners in the process of developing national regional strategies for the implementation of the International Convention for the Safeguarding of the Intangible Cultural Heritage. This action signals ICOM's preoccupation with such global measures and mirrors the organization's active engagement in the process of elaborating a strong, principled position with respect to international conventions for the protection of cultural heritage. Working to advance the notion of an inclusive and unified approach to the safeguarding, identification, and conservation of cultural heritage in all its aspects is a challenge thrown out to all heritage agencies. ICOM, as mandated by its General Assembly, is poised to respond by reshaping itself into a more flexible and capable organization equipped to address the challenge of change and diversity. This it must do by fostering a visionary spirit capable of stimulating the increased involvement of the broad range of membership in upholding and fostering its core values.

This book will give the reader a comprehensive view of the present international legislative environment, which will, to a considerable extent, determine the future priorities and role of our Organization. We look forward to meeting the challenge.

Alissandra Cummins
President, International Council of Museums
Director, Barbados Museum and Historical Society

John Zvereff
Secretary General, International Council of Museums

International Council on Monuments and Sites

ICOMOS, the International Council on Monuments and Sites, is a nongovernmental organization of professionals dedicated to the conservation of the world's cultural heritage. It provides a forum for professional dialogue and a vehicle for the collection, evaluation, and dissemination of information on theory and practice of conservation. Founded in 1965, following the adoption of the Charter for the Conservation and Restoration of Monuments and Sites in Venice, ICOMOS has 8,000 members in more than 120 countries. Headquartered in Paris, ICOMOS is officially recognised as an advisory body to UNESCO, actively contributing to the World Heritage Committee and taking part in the implementation of the World Heritage Convention of 1972.

The International Scientific Committee on Legal, Administrative and Financial Issues (ICLAFI) is one of twenty-five ICOMOS International Committees of professionals with common interests who are organized for dialogue and dissemination of information specific to their particular disciplines. ICLAFI was established at a meeting in Weimar, Germany, in April 1997. The committee meets, generally on an annual basis, to explore the comparative legal aspects of a particular theme. Its objective is to promote, consistent with the aims of ICOMOS, international cooperation in the identification, study, and solution of legal, administrative, and financial issues in connection with the protection, maintenance, and conservation of monuments and sites.

It was therefore with great pleasure that we welcomed the generous offer of our ICOMOS colleague, Ms. Barbara Hoffman, Chair of the International Bar Association (IBA) Committee on Art, Cultural Institutions and Heritage Law, to make available the Committee's online publication, "*Legal and Other Issues in Protecting Cultural Heritage: The Latin American and Caribbean Experience in Context*" through a link on the ICOMOS Web site. The IBA solicited additional papers from interested ICOMOS members to expand the publication beyond its primary focus on the illicit traffic and looting of archaeological sites in Latin America to include materials on the preservation of immovable cultural heritage. Because ICOMOS provides the broadest worldwide forum for issues regarding preservation of monuments and sites, it seemed appropriate to provide our members an opportunity to share their professional perspectives, and their papers are included in the current volume, which is theculmination of the IBA effort to increases international dialogue on heritage conservation issues.

ICOMOS members are eager to develop an ongoing collaborative effort with IBA to promote a dialogue on issues involving cultural heritage in all its aspects. This publication is a positive step in that process. Certain papers may represent personal opinions, perhaps even controversial ones, but we believe that the expression of conflicting opinions is a positive contribution to the global debate.

ICOMOS is pleased to have been invited to foster discussion and advance the legal protection of the cultural heritage in all regions of the world through participation in this forum.

James Reap
President of ICLAFI

Michael Petzet
President of ICOMOS

INTRODUCTION

Exploring and Establishing Links for a Balanced Art and Cultural Heritage Policy

Barbara T. Hoffman

The original laws, the fundamental principles, are in *Sé*. *Sé* has no beginning, it has always existed. It is spiritual existence, the spiritual principle of existence. *Sé* is not a person, not a thing. It is the sum of things. *Sé* is complex. *Sé* brought the material world into being, but it embraces far more than that. *Sé* organises everything so as to create harmony. When everything was dark, on a level which our view can not reach, the first spiritual Parents originated spirit and thought. They created everything in spirit, in the non material world. They were not people, not air, not anything, just idea. These "spiritual Parents" are the ideas which precede all others. That is why they are called "Parents." They are aspects of *Sé* – ideas in the realm of ideas. They translate into our way of speaking as axioms, like the axioms of geometry. They are the fundamental concepts from which everything else arises. The Axioms of *Sé* need to be understood before beginning to discuss ideas of right and wrong.[1]

Ramon Gil, of the Kogi, a pre-Columbian high civilization in the Sierra Nevada de Santa Marta, in the first chapter in Part I explains how, from the Law of *Sé*, the Kogi derive their political, cultural and ecological theory. For the Kogi, as for many other indigenous peoples, the spiritual is linked to the material aspects of culture – artistic and natural heritage is preserved because it is a living link to their ancestors and their history.

Western origins of the idea of art and cultural heritage preservation as a matter of public concern are traced to France in the year 1794, "when the revolutionary government asked one of its members, Henri Gregoire" (who is referred to as Abbé Gregoire), to construct a response to a proposal to destroy all traces of Latin inscription on monuments and other "tainted art." He responded by urging "a focus on the creator of the art rather than on the patron, to bring the individual to the forefront and to present works of art as examples of the free spirit – genius and talent realized – triumphant over political repression, error and superstition . . . Because the Pyramids of Egypt had been built by tyranny and for tyranny, ought these monuments of antiquity to be demolished?" His goal was not only to bind the new republic to the greatness of its past, but to repudiate the distorted simplifications of revolutionary rhetoric which, by equating the destruction of all "tainted" works with the promotion of equality and liberty, seemed to honor what Gregoire called "the axioms of ignorance."[2]

Gregoire identified the existence of a national patrimony, and called for its preservation by stating that "those who were willing to see these artefacts destroyed, or sold abroad as if the nation cared nothing for them . . . were imperilling the most important symbols of national identity, those things that spoke for what France should aspire to be."[3]

In the past 50 years, but particularly in the past several decades, it has become apparent that culture matters and that protecting it is the concern not only of a people, and of sovereign nations but of the international community.[4] That concern is sustained by the emergence of principles that increasingly place weight on the concept of "common interests" to balance and to redefine traditional notions of state sovereignty and private property rights with respect to the protection of cultural heritage.

When the then Taliban government of Afghanistan in 2001 announced that "in view of the fatwa [religious edict] . . . it has been decided to break down all statues/idols . . . [including the great stone Buddhas at Bamiyan] because these idols have been gods of the infidels,"[5] the world community was stunned. Despite desperate efforts on the part of many individuals and organizations, including the United Nations Educational, Scientific and Cultural Organization (UNESCO), the Taliban destroyed the Buddhas. World reaction showed a remarkable universal consensus that the destruction of the Buddhas was wrong, whether the condemnation was justified on the basis of a violation of international law, the principle of humanity or the dictates of the public conscience, or a complex mix of the three.

After the Gulf War of 1990, there was a huge increase in global trafficking in Near Eastern art. Not surprisingly, archaeologists, art historians, and museum curators in the United States warned of the impact of another war on Iraq's cultural heritage when an attack by the United States in early 2003 appeared imminent. In the United Kingdom, the All-Party Parliamentary Group on Archaeology wrote to Prime Minister Tony Blair in February 2003 and asked that consideration be given to Iraq's sites and museums and their

[1] Gil, R., *Gozsezhi, 18 September 1998*, p. 2; translated by Ereira, A. See Chapter 2 this volume.

[2] Sax, J. L., *Heritage Preservation as a Public Duty: The Abbe Gregoire and the Origins of an Idea.* 88 Mich.L.Rev. 1142, 1156 (1990).

[3] Id at 1146.

[4] International law is the universal body of law that applies to all states regardless of their specific cultures, belief systems, and political organizations. The sources of international law are treaty and custom. Where there is no treaty and no contending executive or legislative act or judicial decision, resort must be had to customs and usages of "civilized nations." A prevailing custom of international law is one that arises from "a general and consistent practice of states followed by them from a sense of legal obligation (opinion juris)." See Restatement (third) of Foreign Relations Law of the United States Section 102 (2) (1987).

[5] Taken from an edict issued by Mullah Mohammed Omar, 26 February 2001. The text of the edict is available at <http://www.afghan-politics.org> (*Associated Press* source).

status in terms of world heritage archaeological significance. As Lieutenant-Colonel Tim Collins told the Royal Irish Battle Group on the eve of the conflict, "Iraq is steeped in history. It is the site of the Garden Eden, the Great Flood, and the birth of Abraham. Tread lightly there."[6]

Reports of widespread looting of Iraq's museums and archaeological sites and the burning of the National Library which followed in the immediate aftermath of the United States' invasion in March 2003 confirmed that the warnings were well-founded and brought to the forefront the inadequacy of international law to protect cultural heritage in times of armed conflict. Although Iraq had been a party to the 1954 Convention for Protection Cultural Property In The Event Of Armed Conflict (The Hague Convention),[7] neither the United States nor the United Kingdom had become a party.[8] The international community was quick to react to protect Iraq's heritage. In May 2003, the United Nations Security Council passed Resolution 1483 urging member states to facilitate the safe return to Iraqi institutions of Iraqi cultural property allegedly removed from the Iraq National Museum, the National Library, and other locations in Iraq since the adoption of Resolution 661 in 1990. Several nations, including so-called "market-nations" involved in the global art and antiquities market have taken steps to implement the Resolution. On 28 May 2003, the Swiss Federal Council imposed a ban that covers importation, exportation, and transit, as well as selling, marketing, dealing in, acquiring, or otherwise transferring Iraqi cultural assets stolen in Iraq since 2 August 1990, removed against the will of the owner, or taken out of Iraq illegally. It includes cultural assets acquired through illegal excavations. Such assets are presumed to have been exported illegally if they can be proved to have been in the Republic of Iraq after 2 August 1990.[9]

In the United Kingdom, the Iraq (United Nations Sanctions) Order 2003[10] brought these restrictions into effect on 14 June 2003. The Order prohibits the import or export of illegally removed Iraqi cultural property and creates a criminal offence with a maximum penalty of seven years imprisonment for "any person who holds or controls any item of illegally removed Iraqi cultural property . . . unless he proves he did not know and had no reason to suppose that the item in question was illegally removed Iraqi material."[11]

Initially, the United States left existing sanctions in place for illegally removed Iraqi cultural property when it lifted sanctions for most other commercial goods. On 19 November 2004, the United States Senate passed the "Emergency Protection for Iraqi Cultural Antiquities Act of 2004,"[12] which allows the President to impose import restrictions on any cultural materials illegally removed from Iraq. The legislation tracks Resolution 1483. At the time Senator Charles Grassley introduced the bill, he stated,

> I believe it is very important that we in Congress remain mindful of the need to take steps to protect Iraq's cultural heritage. Our bill will ensure that going forward we continue to adhere to the full spirit of Resolution 1483 and avoid any break in the protections afforded to Iraqi antiquities. Our bill also provides an important signal of our commitment to preserving Iraq's resources for the benefit of the Iraqi people.

On 17 October 2003, UNESCO General Conference adopted the Declaration Concerning the Intentional Destruction of the Cultural Heritage.[13] The text emerged mainly in response to the destruction of the Bamiyan Buddhas, but its language is broad enough to cover the destruction by rampant looting of Iraqi cultural heritage.[14] The Preamble begins, "[r]ecalling the tragic destruction of the Buddhas of Bamiyan that affected the international community as a whole."[15] The text then continues with the recommendation that the Member States commit to fight against the intentional destruction of the

[6] House of Commons, Select Committee on Culture, Media and Sport (First Report), Sec. 71, 2 December 2003. The full text is available at <http://www.publications.parliament.uk/pa/cm200304/cmselect/cmcumeds/59/5905.htm>.

[7] Convention for Protection of Cultural Property in the Event of Armed Conflict, May 14, 1954, 249 U.N.T.S. 240 ("Hague Convention"); Second Protocol to Hague Convention (The Hague, 26 March 1999). The Hague Convention expanded protection for cultural property from "war" to all armed conflicts. The Hague Convention also designated an international symbol for nations in order to protect cultural property. Finally, the Hague Convention created an International Register of Cultural Property Under Special Protection. The Hague Convention was drawn up with World Wars I and II in mind, but since then there has been an increase in the internecine strife, often along ethnic or religious divides, and the time-honored obliteration of an enemy's identity by destruction of its cultural heritage has become a frequent war aim. This failure of the Convention to prevent the loss or destruction of cultural material during times of war led to the formulation of a Second Protocol in 1999. Among its many provisions, it establishes that the destruction or appropriation of cultural material is a war crime, and includes a chapter that deals specifically with civil wars. <http://www.unesco.org/culture/laws/hague/html_eng/page1.shtml>.

[8] The strength of the Hague Convention principles was evident during the Persian Gulf War in 1990 ("Operation Desert Storm"). During Operation Desert Storm, the coalition forces adhered to its principles as tenets of customary international law. Kuwait, France, Egypt, Saudi Arabia, and other coalition members, as well as Iraq, are parties to the Hague Convention.

[9] Ordinance on Economic Measures against the Republic of Iraq of 28 May 2003, SR 946.206, available at <www.kultur-schweiz.admin.ch/arkgt/kgt/e/e_kgt.htm>.

[10] The Iraq (United Nations Sanctions) Order 2003, Statutory Instrument 2003, No. 1519 (UK, The Stationery Office Limited [TSO] 2003), ©Crown Copyright 2003. The Order inverts the burden of proof that usually applies in criminal prosecutions. Normally, the object is "innocent until proven guilty." In the case of Iraqi cultural property, the object is presumed guilty unless proven otherwise.

[11] The Order inverts the burden of proof that usually applies in criminal prosecutions. Normally, the object is "innocent until proven guilty." In the case of Iraqi cultural property, the object is presumed guilty unless proven otherwise. The British Art Market Federation reported to the House of Commons in 2004, that legitimate trade in Mesopotamian antiquities had collapsed to virtually nothing in the aftermath of the Iraq war and the related establishment of the specific legislation aimed at preventing illicit trade in cultural property sourced in Iraq.

[12] "Emergency Protection for Iraqi Cultural Antiquities Act of 2004," The House of Representatives, H.R. 1047, Title III, Iraqi Cultural Antiquities, Sec. 3001.

[13] UNESCO Declaration Concerning the Intentional Destruction of Cultural Heritage, October 17, 2003. The full text of the Declaration is available at <http://unesdoc.unesco.org/images/0013/001331/133171e.pdf#page=68>.

[14] The U.S. Department of State, through its Bureau of Educational and Cultural Affairs, maintains a constantly updated Web site on Iraqi cultural heritage at <http://exchanges.state.gov/culprop/iraq.html>.

[15] *Ibid.* fn. 13.

common heritage in any form so that it may be transmitted to succeeding generations.[16]

What obligations, if any, do the Hague Convention and the First Protocol place on an occupying force to safeguard antiquities, museums, and sites in situations such as those that occurred in Iraq, both before and after the declaration of the end of military operations? Do the principles of the Hague Convention apply once a war has been declared at an end? With the end of hostilities following the end of operations, the greatest threat to Iraq's cultural heritage is not from the "collateral damage of war," but from the civil disorder and the ensuing looting and destruction of museums, monuments, and sites.[17]

Professors Francesco Francioni and Federico Lenzerini, in their chapter entitled "The Obligation To Prevent And Avoid Destruction Of Cultural Heritage: From Bamiyan To Iraq," trace the evolution of the protection of cultural property in times of war and consider whether and to what extent contemporary international law protects cultural heritage of great importance for humanity against deliberate destruction perpetrated by a state in whose territory such heritage is located. They further consider the duty to prevent and avoid devastation of cultural heritage on the part of occupying forces, particularly with respect to the Iraqis' cultural treasures.

Beyond the question of cultural vandalism, Iraq introduces the reader to two other significant concerns in the development of cultural heritage policy: the illicit traffic in cultural property and the restitution to its place of origin of illicitly removed cultural property.

The illicit traffic in antiquities from Iraq followed a predictable path from the art-rich, usually extraordinarily poor nations – so-called "source nations" – to wealthy collectors and museums in so-called "market-nations" like the United Kingdom, Switzerland, and the United States. Our various authors lead others to the fact that looting archaeological sites and stealing artworks from museums and ethnological objects from rural areas have become frequent events the world over.

Although the looting of archaeological sites is hardly a recent phenomenon, it has grown dramatically, to crisis dimensions. Several generations ago, professional looters provided a select clientele of private collectors and well-known art museums with a modest but steady stream of minor archaeological treasures. Today, thefts of art and antiquities are reported to join drugs, money laundering, and the illegal arms trade as one of the largest areas of international criminal activity, although Interpol's Web site states, "we do not possess any figures which would enable us to claim that trafficking in cultural property is the third or fourth most common form of trafficking in an amount of five billion dollars, although this is frequently mentioned at international conferences and in the media."[18]

The ramifications of such looting go far beyond the theft of the object in question. Neil Brodie, in chapter 3, "An Archaeologist's View of the Trade in Illicit Antiquities," observes that archaeological sites and monuments are a source of historical information, often the only source, and when they are destroyed in the search for saleable antiquities the information is destroyed, too. An object taken from its cultural and geographic context may be stripped of its meaning and its significance lost to human knowledge. Thus Brodie argues that removing a cultural object from its place of origin is an affront to the common heritage of mankind.[19]

The problem of looted "cultural goods" that were plundered in wartime through acts of violence, confiscation, or apparently legal transactions, unfortunately remains part of human history even at the beginning of the twenty-first century. Such plundering occurred throughout the ages, but became more acute during the nineteenth and twentieth centuries. During World War II, cultural goods were looted on a massive scale never before seen.

In the 1960s and 1970s, the plundering of African cultural heritage assumed gigantic proportions, with dealers in ethnographic art organizing full-size expeditions into remote parts of Africa. Professor Folarin Shyllon in his chapter describes how light aircraft would land as close as possible to the cities, later leaving packed full of antiquities and other *objets d'art.* They flew to Mali's capital, Bamako, the headquarters for most of the illicit dealing, or to Senegal or Cote d'Ivoire, from where objects were sent to Paris or sold to the local dealers who shipped them to the United States.[20]

By 1970, thefts were increasing both in museums and on site, particularly in Latin American countries, with their wealth of archaeological sites of pre-Columbia material. In the North, private collectors and sometimes official institutions such as museums, were increasingly offered works that were fraudulently imported or of unidentified origin and buying them. In response to the crisis, UNESCO adopted the Convention on the Means of Prohibiting and Preventing the Illicit Import, Export and Transfer of Ownership of Cultural Property ("1970 UNESCO").[21] The 1970 UNESCO was conceived

[16] In Section II, the Declaration defines the meaning of "intentional destruction" as "an act intended to destroy in whole or in part cultural heritage, thus compromising its integrity, in a manner which constitutes a violation of international law or an unjustifiable offence to the principles of humanity and dictates of public conscience, in the latter case in so far as such acts are not already governed by fundamental principles of international law."

[17] See Franconi and Lenzerini, "The Obligation to Prevent and Avoid Destruction of Cultural Heritage: From Bamiyan to Iraq," Part I, this volume. Lehman, Jennifer N. Note: The Continued Struggle with Cultural Property: The Hague Convention, the UNESCO Convention, and the UNIDROIT Convention, 14 Ariz. *J. International and Comp. Law* (Spring 1997) 527, 537.

[18] <www.interpol.com/Public/WorkOfArt/conference/meeting04/recommendations.> Interpol has held numerous interdisciplinary conferences on the illicit traffic in cultural property and works closely with ICOM and UNESCO.

[19] Brodie, Neil. "An Archaeologist's View of the Trade in Illicit Antiquities," this volume.

[20] See Shyllon, F. "The Nigerian and African Experience on Looting and Trafficking in Cultural Objects," Part II of this book.

[21] United Nations Educational, Scientific & Cultural Organization Convention on the Means of Prohibiting and Preventing the Illicit Import, Export and Transfer of Ownership of Cultural Property, Nov. 14, 1970, Art. 1, 823 U.N.T.S. 232, 234–6. <http:www.unesco.org/culture/laws/1970/html_eng/page1.shtml>. Dr. Lyndel Prott, former

as the lynchpin of an international legal framework for controlling traffic in illegally exported or stolen cultural property and is based primarily on an essentially public international law and administrative law model.

Among other things, the final version of the 1970 UNESCO requires signatories to take appropriate steps to "prevent museums and similar institutions within their territories from acquiring cultural property originating in another State Party which has been illegally exported after entry into force of this Convention, in the States concerned." The 1970 UNESCO also calls for an embargo on cultural property "stolen from a museum or a religious or secular public monument or similar institution in another State Party... provided that such property is documented as appertaining to the inventory of that institution." In addition, it allows a member state whose cultural property is in jeopardy to request other member states to "participate in a concerted international effort to determine and to carry out the necessary concrete measures, including the control of exports and imports and international commerce in the specific materials concerned." The 1970 UNESCO is not retroactive, and enters into force three months after a state's ratification. It is, thus, not available for colonial and World War II claims.

Principally, 1970 UNESCO works at the level of government administrations: governments are required to take action at the request of a State party to the convention to seize cultural property that has been stolen. They must also collaborate to prevent major crises in the protection of cultural heritage, such as those now occurring in Iraq and Afghanistan.[22]

For example, in 1985, at the request of the Peruvian government, Canadian customs officers and investigators seized a large group of pre-Columbian objects, including ceramic pottery dating from 1800 B.C. to 1400 A.D. Illicitly exported from Peru, the objects were imported in violation of the Canadian Cultural Property Export and Import Act, and were destined for the United States. After having returned a first group of artefacts in 1997, Canada returned the remaining fifty-nine objects to Peru in April 2000.[23]

Requests for the restitution of cultural property are not a new issue in international law. In the famous case of the so-called "Elgin[24] marbles," or "Parthenon marbles," Lord Byron was among the first to criticize the removal of the collection of marble figures and a frieze from the Parthenon by Lord Elgin, who offered them for sale to the British Parliament in 1816. The formal request by Greece in 1983 by Melina Mercouri, its then Minister of Culture, for the return of the marbles remains the best known and most discussed paradigm in academic and political fora. Indeed, the Greek delegation included in its statement to the UNESCO Intergovernmental Committee for the Return of Cultural Property to its Country of Origin that all countries have the right to recover the most significant part of their cultural heritage lost during periods of colonial or foreign occupation.

With the independence of African nations, requests for restitution[25] and return of cultural objects had moved center stage at international meetings. In 1973, the United Nations General Assembly passed the first of a series of resolutions on the subject of Resolution 3187 (XXVIII) entitled "Restitution of Works of Art to Countries Victims of Expropriation." Amadou M'Bow, Director General of UNESCO, in 1978, issued a "Plea for the Return of an Irreplaceable Cultural Heritage to Those Who Created It."[26]

> The peoples who were victims of this plunder, sometimes for hundreds of years, have not only been despoiled of irreplaceable masterpieces, but also robbed of a memory which would doubtless have headed them to greater self knowledge...

Wars, colonialism, missionary and archaeological expeditions, looting, fraudulent "purchase," and even legitimate trade in antiquities thus led to a situation in which many nations and victims of war find their national and cultural heritage in foreign museums and private collections.

Requests for return or repatriation of cultural property may be placed in the larger context of an independence/post colonial universe. For example, the Icelandic demand for the return of the Codex Regius of the Poetic Edda and the compendium Book of Flatey (Flatey jarbok). The latter is a magnificent collection of the Icelandic sagas; the "former" contains the oldest text of the Edda, the most precious source of knowledge of ancient Norse myth and epic. The two books were the most valuable of thousands taken to Copenhagen by an Icelandic scholar, Arni Magnusson, in the eighteenth century. They became a focal point of the movement for Icelandic independence from Denmark, and demands for their return in Iceland began to be heard as early as 1830, reaching a level of intense and impassioned public debate in Denmark during the 60s. The Danes viewed the manuscripts held in the public Royal Library as well as those held in the private Arnamagnean Collection as a part of Danish cultural heritage. It took more than a quarter of a century before the books, reverently carried through Reykjavic by Danish sailors, finally came home.

Chief, Legal Standards UNESCO, has stated that it must be understood that the 1970 Convention did not emerge suddenly within the context of UNESCO. It was the end product of a long line of efforts to stop the pillaging of archaeological sites and the theft of cultural property of extreme importance.

22 In 1988, of the market nations, Canada and the United States had passed legislation implementing the 1970 UNESCO Convention. As of May, 15 2005, 107 states had ratified UNESCO. See introduction to Parts II and III, this volume.

23 See UNESCO's "No to Illicit Traffic in Cultural Property: Recent Examples of Successful Return of Cultural Property."

24 The French have coined the term of "Elginisme." 2 Grand Larousse De La Langue Francaise, 1528 (1972) n.m. (du n. de Bruce conte d'Elgin (1766–1841), diplomate anglais, qui constetua par des moyens parfois douteux d'importantes collections d'objets d'art etrangers.)

25 Some scholars distinguish between restitution based on violations of the prohibition of theft and pillage imposed by binding law and repatriation, which dates back to the nineteenth century when cultural heritage ended up outside its place of origin because of change of boundaries or loss by an ethnic group. See, for example, W. W. Kowalski Claims for Works of Art and their Legal Nature in Resolution of Cultural Property Disputes, Hague Peace Papers, 2004.

26 See also Shyllon, F., in Part II, this book for a discussion on "The Nigerian and African Experience on Looting and Trafficking in Cultural Objects."

In accordance with a special law passed by the Danish parliament and confirmed by its Supreme Court 1 April 1971, the first manuscripts, the Codex Regius and the Book of Flatey arrived on 21 April 1971. A committee of Danish and Icelandic scholars was appointed to determine which manuscripts were to be included for return under the provisos of the laws, which Solomonically divided the treasures based on closest links to Iceland or Denmark, and in 1986, the manuscript collection was finally fully divided. The return of the manuscripts was fully completed in 1997. After the division of the Arnamagnæan Collection, around 1,400 manuscripts and fragments remain in Den Arnamgnæan Samling in Copenhagen. The two Arnamagnæan institutes worked with close cooperation under the guidance of a committee consisting of two representatives from each institution.[27]

Iceland's successful negotiations opened the door to former colonies worldwide to petition for redress against historical imbalances of power that permitted the removal of valuable goods. However, the unique and complex relationship between indigenous and Western cultures makes the status of claims for returns and repatriation difficult to assess. Obviously, there are cases of outright theft and looting, but other documented situations of trade, barter, or gift suggest that good title passed.

In November 2004, Italy decided to end a long-standing feud with Ethiopia by returning one of Ethiopia's most cherished relics, the Obelisk of Axum, taken by Italian troops for political reasons as a spoil of war in 1937.[28] Axum (a town 350 kilometers northeast of Gonder) was Ethiopia's oldest city, 1000 years B.C. the capital of the Queen of Sheba and later the capital of the Axumite Empire. More than that the Ethiopian Orthodox Church was founded there in the fourth century, thus Axum became the holiest city of the country. The stele dates back to the 4th centry and is 24 meters high. It is supposed to range among the most outstanding examples of African stonemason art of its time.

For the transport to Rome in 1937, the stele was cut into three parts and shipped from Asmara. Mussolini erected the stele in front of his Ministry of Africa which later became the United Nations Food and Agricultural Organization, close to the Circo Massimo. In 1947, Italy signed an agreement for its return to Ethiopia. But it took close to 60 years to return it, despite the Italian commitment to send it back to Ethiopia.

Mr. Massimo Baistrocchi, Chief of the Italian Foreign Ministry's Art Recovery Section, reports that the obelisk was dismantled by Italian experts in 2004 at a cost of € 6m($7.7m), but due to "technical difficulties" more than another year was necessary to transport to Axum the ornate 24-meter obelisk (the largest and heaviest object to ever be transported by air). First of all the 160-ton monument had to be broken into three pieces, then the Axum's airstrip had to be improved and upgraded, also with installation of a radar, to handle the Antonov-124 aircraft, one of only two airplanes in the world large enough to carry the stones, one stone at the time. (The obelisk could not be shipped because Asmara is now part of Eritrea.)

The monument is scheduled to be re-erected in September, 2005; but, some other difficulties are now emerging. Near the car park site where the Axum obelisk is to be reconstructed, archaeologists using imaging equipment have found a vast new complex of royal burial chambers, older than the obelisk itself.

The British Museum prides itself on "holding in trust for the nations of the world" one of the finest collections of art and antiquities. According to critics, however, the museum's role as a primary custodian of world heritage was attained at the expense of the people whose treasures were raided, with the result that museums in the country of origin are obliged to display photographs and replicas of the cultural objects. In the face of mounting pressure, the British Museum has begun seriously to consider Ethiopia's request for repatriation of tablets known as the Magdala Treasures, looted by Britain from Ethiopia in 1869. The ten wooden tablets are regarded by the Ethiopian Orthodox church as representing the original arc of the covenant which housed the Ten Commandments. Ethiopia has been lobbying for their return for more than 50 years. What is remarkable is that the tablets are locked in a basement room underneath the British Museum and are covered in purple velvet. No member is permitted to access the room because of the sacred nature of the tablets. As a sign of the seriousness with which the British Museum is taking the case for restitution, in 2004, Neil MacGregor, the director of the British Museum, visited Addis Ababa to hear arguments in favour of return.[29]

Separate and apart from the moral and legal issues involved in restitution or reparation claims, the return of sacred or ritual objects raises particular issues for cultural policy makers, in particular museum staff: What is the proper response to claims for return of ritual, ceremonial, or religious objects, which in many cases, if returned, may be exposed to the elements or, if protected, kept in sacred places, unavailable for public viewing, or may be destroyed or allowed to deteriorate in accordance with spiritual policy.[30] A spokesperson for

[27] Before the manuscripts were returned, they were restored, photographed, and stored on microfilm to ensure that good reproductions were still available in Denmark for research and study purposes.

[28] On May 17, 2005, Massimo Baistrocchi reported another return. A stolen Gold Mask of the King of Sican (Peru) was given back to Peru. It was recovered in an artist collection in Turin and the widow of the artists, who bought it in good faith more than 20 years ago, donated it to the Italian State. The mask was shown at an exhibition at the Quirinale Palace, Rome, at the request of Peru, President Ciampi returned the mask at the end of the exhibition. There was another ceremony in Lima in April 2005.

The British Library will give back to the Arhibishopry of Benevento an ancient Codex (Messale) stolen during the Second World War. The decision was taken by a specially constituted panel on restitution which recognized the claim and recommended its return. By law, the British Library cannot relinquish any of its treasures, specific legislation must be enacted by Parliament. Of course, this will take a long time, but the Manuscript will be sent back under a loan.

[29] See comment by McGregor, N. in "The Universal Museum," Part VIII of this volume, "Museums and Cultural Heritage."

[30] Issues dealing with the intangible aspects of the display and collection of objects in museum collections are discussed in Part VIII, "Museums

the British Museum indicated that it is considering a loan to the Ethiopian Orthodox Church in London, renewable every five years to "circumvent issues of title and setting a precedent for return, which has only happened over Nazi era items."[31] This solution, as opposed to their return to a church in Ethiopia, is being proposed in part because of fear as to their proper preservation and conservation. Several other items, including the Emperor Tewodros I's crown and an amulet removed from his body after the battle of Magdala have already been returned to Ethiopia. The British Library currently holds 350 manuscripts from Magdala, and other artefacts are held by Cambridge, Edinburgh, the Royal Collection, and private collections.

The development of fair and equitable means to resolve the difficult issues posed by these examples is a significant challenge for museums in the twenty-first century and the subject of much thoughtful and provocative discussion in Part VIII of this book.[32]

With the fall of the Berlin Wall and the opening of archives in Eastern Europe and Russia, the world became aware of the enormous quantities of art, manuscripts, and antiques looted during the Second World War.[33] Although national laws adopted after the war in Switzerland, Belgium, France, Germany, Greece, Italy, and the Netherlands in recognition of title difficulties caused by gaps in provenance created a presumption in favor of the original owners of property looted during this period in title disputes, most of these national laws have lapsed. Thus, many of the legal hurdles faced by the claimants in a number of high-profile cases in Europe and the United States involving artwork stolen during the Second World War are similar to those faced by source nations seeking to recover artefacts lost during the colonial period: adverse possession, laches, provenance,[34] statutes of limitation, and the bona fide purchaser defence. Several contributors discuss whether special rules of evidence and a change in the traditional burden of proof may be appropriate in the context of the resolution of disputes involving art and "cultural property."

Somewhat different but nevertheless related obstacles may arise when cultural heritage claims are made by indigenous groups within their country of origin. Ancient human remains of a man who hunted or journeyed through the Colombia Plateau at least 8,340 to 9,200 years ago, dubbed "the Kennewick man," were discovered at an Army Corps of Engineers work site on federal aboriginal land along the Columbia River near Kennewick, Washington, in the United States. Five Native American groups (hereafter, the "Tribal Claimants") demanded that the remains be turned over to them for immediate burial at a secret location "with as little publicity as possible," and "without further testing of any kind." The Tribal Claimants based their demand on the Native American Graves Protection and Repatriation Act[35] ("NAGPRA"), enacted in 1990.[36] Under NAGPRA, "Native American" means of, or relating to, a tribe, people, or culture that is indigenous to the United States. On 13 January 2000, the Department of the Interior announced its determination that the Kennewick remains are "Native American" as defined by NAGPRA. The decision was premised on only two facts: the age of the remains, and their discovery within the United States. The agency's opinion stated: "As defined in NAGPRA, 'Native American' refers to human remains and cultural items relating to tribes, peoples, or cultures that resided within the area now encompassed by the United States prior to the historically documented arrival of European explorers, irrespective of when a particular group may have begun to reside in this area, and irrespective of whether some or all of these groups

and Cultural Heritage." See also Rosoff, Nancy B., "Integrating Nature Views in Museum Procedures: Hope and Practices of the National Museum of the American Indian." *Museum Anthropology* 22 (1998) 33–42.

[31] The Independent/The New Zealand Herald, 20 October 2004.

[32] See the discussion in part VIII, "Museums and Cultural Heritage" in particular, the statement of nineteen museum directors in "The Declaration on the Importance and Value of Universal Museums" and the comments thereon. See also the article by Lewis, G., "The Universal Museum: a Special Case?"

[33] For example, one million items – almost eighty percent of the Hungarian art treasures – were lost during the Second World War and its aftermath, either to Germany or the Soviet Union. See generally, Part I of this book "International Legal Tools and Viewpoints," and especially Carducci, G., "The Growing Complexity of International Art Law: Conflict of Laws, Uniform Law, Mandatory Rules, UNSC Resolutions, and EU Regulations"; Part III, "International Movement of Art and Cultural Property: Perspectives of the Market Nations," Hoffman, B., "International Art Transactions and the Resolution of Art and Cultural Property Disputes: The United States Perspective," Parkhouse, A., "The Illicit Trade in Cultural Objects: Recent Developments in the United Kingdom," and Raue, P., "Summum ius suma iniura – Stolen Jewish Cultural Assets Under Legal Examination."

[34] The words "provenance" and "provenience" are often used interchangeably but in the context of museum and archeological studies, they have different meanings. "Provenance" in both the art world and the museum world refers to the "history of ownership." Provenience refers to the geographical or geological origin or source of an artifact.

[35] 25 U.S.C. §3001 *et seq.*

[36] Although some consider claims for repatriation under NAGPRA as issues of sovereignty; others view repatriation as cultural property rights or human rights legislation, in particular based on spiritual and religious beliefs. When NAGPRA was passed, nearly 200,000 Native American remains were held in museums in the United States. Many Native Americans believe that reburial of disinterred remains is essential for the spirit of the deceased to return to rest. A controversial subject that surfaced repeatedly throughout the enactment of NAGPRA was the issue of what disposition should be required for prehistoric remains that have no discernable affiliation with any present-day Native American tribe or organization. Native American groups argued that these remains should be made available to them for reburial. Anthropologists believed they should be retained as valuable resources for scientific studies. Congress delegated the task of resolving the issue through rulemaking to the Interior Department. See Robert W. Lennon (22 Harv. Evntl. L. Rev. 369, 1998). NAGPRA requires *inter alia* federal agencies and museums that receive federal funds to inventory and, if requested, to repatriate Native American cultural items to lineal descendants or culturally affiliated Native American tribes and Native Hawaiian organizations. Cultural items under NAGPRA include human remains, associated and unassociated funerary objects, sacred objects, and objects of cultural patrimony. "Cultural objects" on federal land become the property of the tribe with the closest affiliation. Although human remains and funereal objects must be returned as right, the material is more nuanced regarding material of less cultural sensitivity. For an excellent discussion of NAGPRA, see Isaac Moriwake, "Critical Excavations: Law, Narrative and the Debate on Native American and Hawaiian Cultural Property Reparation," 20 Hawaii L. Rev. 261 (1998).

were or were not culturally affiliated or biologically related to present-day Indian tribes."

In response to arguments that scientific study could provide new information about the early history of people in the Americas, the Confederated Tribes of the Umatilla asserted, "We already know our history. It is passed on to us through our elders and through our religious practices. From our oral histories, we know that our people have been part of this land since the beginning of time. We do not believe that our people migrated here from another continent, as the scientists do."

Dr. Robson Bonnischen and other noted scientists challenged Secretary of the Interior Bruce Babbitt's interpretations of "Native American" and "cultural affiliation" and claimed further that the use of oral history to determine cultural affiliation violated the Establishment Clause of the First Amendment of the United States Constitution.[37]

Ultimately, after eight years of litigation, the Ninth Circuit Court of Appeals agreed with the scientists.[38] In the final outcome, the court set aside the decision awarding the remains to the Tribal Claimants, enjoined transfer of the remains to the tribes, and required archaeologists be allowed to study the remains. With respect to NAGPRA, the court said,

"The term 'Native American' requires, at a minimum, a cultural relationship between remains or other cultural items and a present-day tribe, people, or culture indigenous to the United States . . . The evidence in the record would not support a finding that Kennewick Man is related to any particular identifiable group or culture, and the group or culture to which he belonged may have died out thousands of years ago. . . . Congress did not create a presumption that items of a particular age are 'Native American . . . ' No cognizable link exists between Kennewick Man and Modern Columbia Plateau Indians."

The court concluded that no reasonable person could conclude by a preponderance of the evidence on this record that Kennewick Man is "Native American" under NAGPRA. The court also rejected evidence of oral tradition in this case as just "not specific enough or reliable enough or relevant enough to show a significant relationship." As the district court observed, 8,340 to 9,200 years between the life of Kennewick Man and the present is too long a time to bridge merely with evidence of oral traditions.[39]

In response to the Court's interpretation of NAGPRA as requiring that tribes must show a direct relationship to these human remains before they claim authority over them, Rob Roy Smith, attorney for the tribes, stated "that's the exact opposite of what Congress wanted. It places on the tribes the burden to prove the remains are Native American."[40]

The *Bonnischen* case presents the reader with themes discussed by several of this book's contributors relevant to the understanding and development of responsible and coherent cultural heritage policies. First, the world view of Native Americans and other indigenous peoples differs significantly from that of western industrialized societies. Second, how do we determine that an object is a "cultural object," and should "cultural affiliation" trump a more scientific definition of inheritance? Or, to put it in other terms, is the proper inquiry not whether commercial or scientific interests should be permitted to outweigh cultural property claims of indigenous peoples, but by what criteria and by whom is the decision made.[41] Once "Kennewick Man" was determined to be "ordinary bones," without tribal affiliation, scientists were at liberty to conduct their examination.[42]

Related to the determination of property rights in cultural objects is the issue of the type of evidence relevant to the proof of such claims. Similar to the case of source nation and World

[37] *Bonnischen v. United States*, 217 F. Supp. 2d 1116 (D. Or. 2002) aff'd and remanded 367 F.3d 864 (9th Cir. 2004).

[38] *Id.* 367 F 3d864 (9th Cir. 2004).

[39] Although Dr. Bonnischen died on December 25, 2004 at the age of 64 on vacation in Oregon, the case is far from over. The Court has identified the issues remaining in the case as follows: (1) the Court must determine the scope of permissible studies of the remains under the Archaeological Resources Protection Act of 1979 ("ARPA"), 16 U.S.C. §§470aa to 470mm. NAGPRA is Native American Law. ARPA deals with the rights of scientists to study archaeological resources on federal and Native American lands. (2) The Court must consider the appropriate remedy, if any, concerning the Court's finding that the Army Corp of Engineers violated the National Historic Preservation Act of 1966 ("NHPA"), 16 U.S.C. §§470 to 470w-6, by reburying the discovery site, and (3) whether the Tribes have a continuing legal interest in both these matters so as to permit their status as Interveners. Colorado Republican Sen. Ben Nighthorse Campbell is attempting to broaden NAGPRA so that any ancient skeletons can be claimed by modern Native American Tribes.

[40] In fact, many scholars and lawyers believed NAGPRA had effectively created a presumption in favor of tribal possession of cultural patrimony. Although there is no case specifically on point, NAGPRA appears to circumvent state statutes of limitation by recognizing traditional Native American concepts of strict inalienability and providing a federal cause of action for collective claimants. Presumably also the equitable defenses of adverse possession and laches do not apply.

[41] Some commentators assert that NAGPRA allows Native communities to "define themselves and their lifeways, including their own legal system's definition of what is a sacred object, what is cultural patrimony, what property may be transferred by individuals, and what property can be alienated", Strickland, R., "Implementing the National Policy of Understanding, Preserving, and Safeguarding the Heritage of Indian Peoples and Native Hawaiians: Human Rights, Sacred Objects, and Cultural Patrimony, *Ariz. St. L. J.* 24 (1992), 175, 180. For a more skeptical view, see Raines, J. C. B., "One is Missing: Native American Graves Protection and Repatriation Act: An Overview and Analysis," 17 *Am. Indian L. Rev.* (1992), 639, 658–63 (arguing that NAGPRA's value standards invite courts to rule against, as well as for, the interests of Native groups).

[42] See also Singer, G., "Unfolding Intangible Cultural Property Rights in Tangible Collections: Developing Standards of Stewardship" and other chapters in Part VIII, "Museums and Cultural Heritage." See also Isaac Moriwake, note 34, *supra*, discussing a dispute between two Hawaiian groups ("uttui malama"), and the City of Providence, Museum of Natural History, for the repatriation under NAGPRA of various culturally important items to their community of origin. The museum argues that the ki'i la'au is a utilitarian or decorative object and fails to meet the NAGPRA definition of cultural property. Even if NAGPRA applies, they argue that Hawaiian law and custom at the time of transfer did not render the object inalienable *per se*. In February 1998, after two years of litigation, under orders from the Rhode Island federal judge to mediate, the parties arrived at a settlement. In principle, the parties agreed to the repatriation of the ki'i la'au to the Hawaiians. The Hawaiian groups agreed to make a donation to the Museum to fund an exhibit in the Museum's Pacific Collection, where more than forty other Hawaiian objects remain. The Hawaiians and the City of Providence agreed to each select three representatives to sit on a six-member joint committee overseeing the proposed exhibit. In a provision deemed absolutely critical by the Hawaiian representatives, the agreement states that the Hawaiians are in no way, shape, or form purchasing the ki'i la'au from the City.

War II claimants, indigenous peoples have faced evidentiary burdens because of the passage of time in establishing title and provenance. In contrast to the rigid rules of ownership and proof under the common law, the repatriation criteria in NAGPRA arguably work in favor of the interests of the original owners. Although the court in *Bonnischen* rejected evidence of oral tradition as unreliable, NAGPRA declares that cultural affiliation may be substantiated by a preponderance of the evidence based upon "geographical kinship, biological, archaeological, anthropological, linguistic, folkloric, oral, historical, or other relevant information or expert opinions." By considering "oral history" as potentially of equal weight to scientific history, NAGPRA opens the restitution process to radically different ways of understanding culture, history, and ownership.[43]

Finally, NAGPRA and *Bonnischen* introduce us to issues surrounding communal ownership rights.[44] Indigenous groups worldwide have had difficulty in asserting property claims because national legislation and the courts did not recognize collective rights in cultural property.[45]

This tension between private rights of ownership created by western intellectual property systems such as copyright and communal ownership held by artists and their communities is an issue that has received attention by various scholars, policy makers, and courts. Recognizing a link between the spiritual and the material causes us to focus on the relationship between an individual artist/author as a possessor of intellectual property rights and collective ownership rights. Different conceptions of "ownership" within copyright law, on the one hand, and customary laws and protocols, on the other, may intersect, particularly in those cases in which an indigenous artist is entitled to assert copyright to prevent infringement of his creation and is simultaneously subject to parallel customary rules and regulations. Although intellectual property rights confer private rights of ownership, in customary discourse, to "own" does not necessarily or only mean 'ownership' in the Western nonindigenous sense. It can convey a sense of stewardship or responsibility for the traditional culture, rather than the right to exclude others from certain uses of expressions of the traditional culture, which is more akin to the nature of many intellectual property rights systems.

The issue was directly addressed in the Australian case of *John Bulun Bulun v R and T Textiles.*[46] Mr. Bulun Bulun is a well-known artist from Arnhemland, Gonalbingu, and his work *Magpie Geese and Water lilies at the Waterhole* was altered and copied by a textile company. In 1996, Mr. Bulun Bulun commenced action against the textile company for copyright infringement.

The Ganalbingu people are the traditional indigenous owners of Ganalbingu country. They have the right to permit and control the production and reproduction of the artistic work under the law and custom of the Ganalbingu people. The art work *Magpie Geese and Water lilies at the Waterhole* depicts knowledge concerning Djulibinyamurr. Djulibinyamurr, along with another waterhole site, Ngalyindi, are the two most important cultural sites in Ganalbingu country for the Ganalbingu people. Mr. Bulun Bulun noted that, under Ganalbingu law, ownership of land has corresponding obligation to create artworks, designs, songs, and other aspects of ritual and ceremony that go with the land.

The pertinent aspect of the case related to a claim by the clan group to which Mr. Bulun Bulun belonged that it, in effect, controlled the copyright in the artwork, and that the clan members were the beneficiaries of the creation of the artwork by the artist acting on their behalf. Accordingly, they claimed to be entitled to assert a collective right with respect to the copyright in the work, over and above any issue as to authorship.

Justice Von Doussa said, "Whilst it is superficially attractive to postulate that the common law should recognize communal title, it would be contrary to established legal principle for the common law to do so." The court looked at the relevance of customary law and decided that evidence of customary

[43] See Robert H. McLauglin, "The American Archaeological Record: Authority to Dig, Power to Interpret." *International Journal of Cultural Property* 7, 2 (1998), 359.

[44] NAGPRA supports claims made by lineal descendents, federally recognized Indian tribes, and Native Hawaiian organizations. If a lineal descendant cannot be identified, federally recognized Indian tribes and Native Hawaiian organizations may claim the objects. Only Indian tribes and Native Hawaiian organizations can claim communally owned objects of cultural patrimony. In this way, the law recognizes not only the property rights of individuals for all but communally owned property, but also the unique government-to-government relationship that exists between the U.S. government and the various Indian tribes.

[45] *Mayagna (Sumo) Indigenous Community of Awas Tingni v. Nicaragua*, 79 Inter-Am. Ct. H.R. (ser. C) (August 31, 2001), available at <http://www.corteidh.or.cr./seriecing/serie_c_79_ing.doc> revolved around efforts by the Awas Tingni and other indigenous communities of Nicaragua's Atlantic Coast to demarcate their traditional lands and to prevent logging in their territories by a Korean company under a government-granted concession. The Awas Tingni filed a petition with the Inter-American Commission on Human Rights (Commission), charging Nicaragua with failure to take steps necessary to secure the land rights of the Mayagna (Sumo) indigenous community of Awas Tingni and of other Mayagna and Miskito indigenous communities in Nicaragua's Atlantic Coast region. Evidence presented before the court included the oral testimony of members of the Awas Tingni community. Jaime Castillo Felipe, member of the Mayagna ethnic group, and lifetime resident of Awas Tingni, testified regarding the Tribe's ownership of the disputed territories. In explaining why he believed that the Tribe owned the land, he stated that they "have lived in the territory for over 300 years and this can be proven because they have historical places and because their work takes place in that territory." Other tribal members testified similarly regarding the significance of the land to the religion and cultural survival of the Awas Tingni people and their conceptions of collective ownership of the land and all the resources it encompasses. The Court ruled that the State violated, among others, the right to property as contained in Article 21 of the American Convention on Human Rights to the detriment of the members of the Mayagna (Sumo) community of Awas Tingni, and required the State to adopt measures to create an effective mechanism for official recognition, demarcation and titling of the indigenous community's properties. In particular, the Court acknowledged the Awas Tingni's communal form of property in the land and recognized the importance of the protection of this right to ensure the Community's cultural survival.

[46] 41 IPR 513. (1998) This case is one of the cases studied by Ms. Terri Janke in her study "Minding Culture: Case Studies on Intellectual Property and Traditional Cultural Expressions," commissioned by WIPO, and available at <http://www.wipo.int/globalissues/studies/cultural/minding-culture/index.html>.

law may be used as a basis for the foundation of rights recognized within the Australian legal system. After finding that Mr. Bulun Bulun's customary law obligations gave rise to a fiduciary relationship between himself and the Ganalbingu people, Justice Von Doussa stated:

> The conclusion does not treat the law and custom of the Ganalbingu people as part of the Australian legal system. Rather, it treats the law and custom of the Ganalbingu people as part of the factual matrix which characterizes the relationship as one of mutual trust and confidence. It is that relationship which the Australian legal system recognizes as giving rise to the fiduciary relationship, and to the obligations that arise out of it.

If *Bulun* raises the issue of whether and to what extent customary law may define property rights and whether traditional intellectual property law can accommodate very different notions of ownership, so as to protect traditional knowledge and designs, a final example looks at genetic resources and the traditional knowledge debate.[47]

There are increasing legal challenges to the patenting of traditional knowledge (TK) and its products such as grains, species, and traditional medicines. Two conflicting forces at the heart of this have been the attempts of nonindigenous individuals and organizations to claim ownership of indigenous knowledge for commercial gain; the other for indigenous peoples to seek means to protect their traditional knowledge or develop it in partnership with others.[48] The Neem tree, dubbed as the "corner drug store of rural India," is an integral part of India's cultural heritage. Known in Sanskrit as *Sarva Roga Nivarini*, "the curer of all ailments," Neem has been used in India for the past 2,000 years as an insecticide, fungicide, contraceptive, and antibacterial agent. Its twigs have been used as a tooth brush for time immemorial. An Indian cannot take a patent out on the Neem in India because Indian patent law restricts patentability to only process patents and not product patents. W. R. Grace obtained a U.S. patent on a pesticide derived from the seeds of the "Neem" tree in 1991. The patent was granted for an extraction process that produces a stable form of pesticide that could be stored and marketed globally. The patent was challenged on the grounds of "prior art" and "obviousness."[49] The U.S. patent office, however, denied the challenge; the European Patent office revoked the patent in November 2000.[50] South Asians claim that patents on the Neem tree involve "biopiracy."[51] A South Asian wrote that "an apt comparison to Americans patenting the Neem tree in the United States would be South Asians patenting the apple pie in South Asia."[52]

We have provided these examples as an introduction to the topics and themes discussed in *Art and Cultural Heritage: Law, Policy, and Practice*. A preliminary and fundamental question guiding the enterprise is to what extent traditional notions of property can provide an adequate framework to resolve the conflicts and contradictions presented by these examples.

Nonlawyers are accustomed to speak of the thing, the object itself, as "property." Although the term "property" is one that is often abused and seldom defined or subject to careful analysis, it is generally used to denote subject matter of a physical nature – a house, a car, or a cow.

As lawyers, however, we learn in the first year of law school, at least in the United States, that property is a concept, separate and apart from the thing. Property consists, in fact, of the legal relations among people in regard to a thing.[53] It is in this context that we may ask, using a traditional Western property analysis, whether the Ganalbingu people have a right to sue to protect their intangible property rights and if so, what is the scope of these rights.

In a complex society, individuals and the relations between groups of individuals are complicated. It follows that property

[47] These issues are discussed in Part VII, "Who Owns Traditional Knowledge?" Maui Solomon in "Protecting Moriori/Maori Heritage in New Zealand" questions whether the intellectual property system based on private property rights is adequate to protect traditional knowledge in the public domain.

[48] Whereas the international focus has been on the patenting of traditional knowledge, that topic seems today less important than the new thrust for claiming such knowledge from the herbal sector, which is experiencing a global boom. See Pickup, Z. and Hodges, C., "Recent Developments in the Regulation of Traditional Herbal Medicines" in Part VII, "Who Owns Traditional Knowledge?"

[49] The Indian government has created a Traditional Knowledge Digital Library (TKDL) to record systematically, in digital form, knowledge of Ayurveda, a traditional Indian system of medicine. The TKDL is perhaps the most self-conscious of the efforts to make traditional knowledge inalienable from the public domain, seeking explicitly to build the bridge between the knowledge contained in an old Sanskrit Shloka and the computer screen of a patent examiner in Washington, DC.

[50] The bioprospecting and patenting of Neem tree has parallels in Australia, as illustrated by the commercial exploitation of smokebush (*Conospernum*), an Australian plant commonly found in Western Australia. Smokebush has been used traditionally by Aboriginal peoples for a variety of therapeutic purposes. After initial unsuccessful tests by the U.S. National Cancer Institute in the 1960s, it was found in late 1980s that a substance called *Conocurvone*, that was isolated from smokebush, could be useful for destroying the human immunodeficiency virus in low concentrations. To develop this substance, in the early 1990s, the Western Australia goverment granted a license to Amrad Pty Ltd, a multinational pharmaceutical company. It has been suggested that Amrad has provided $1.5 m to gain access rights to smokebush. Further, the government of Western Australia would receive royalties exceeding $100 million by 2002 if *Conocurvone* is successfully commercialized. Aborigines, who have traditionally used the smokebush for its therapeutic and healing properties, would receive nothing from the commercial exploitation of the plant. See Professor Kamal Puri, Law School of University of Queensland, Australia, author's file.

[51] It should be noted that United States patent law, unlike many patent systems, does not utilize an "absolute novelty" rule for obtaining a patent, see *35 U.S.C. 102(a)*, but specifically permits the patenting of inventions known or used in foreign countries, so long as the invention is not patented or disclosed in a printed publication in the United States or a foreign country, the aim being to encourage importation of technology into the United States Claims of "biopiracy" are sometimes based on a misunderstanding of this facet of U.S. patent law.

[52] <http://www.thimmakka.org>. The Indian government was more successful. In a celebrated case, the Centre for Scientific and Industrial Research filed a reexamination in seeking revocation of a 1994 patent issued to the University of Mississippi (Patent 5,401,504), which claimed the use of turmeric for promoting wound healing. The Indian government argued that turmeric is a well-known traditional medicine used in India, and written about by Indian researchers as early as the 1950s.

[53] Some lawyers tend to forget that property represents this complex group of jural relations between the owner of the physical subject and other individuals. The result is a commodification of concept of the thing to the exclusion of a consideration of the relationship the object may have to others.

law as the product of society designed to maintain control over the use, allocation, and transmission of resources will be, too. The Anglo-Saxon notion of property can be best expressed as follows: "To the world: keep off unless you have my permission, which I may grant or withhold."[54] In the western world, property means private property. In the common law sense, "ownership" of ordinary physical things is often perceived of as private and unqualified. When you own something, it means you have title, benefit, exclusive use, and control. As Joseph Sax has opined, that concept enables owners to exercise unbridled power over owned objects, whatever the loss to science, scholarship, or art.[55]

For example, the reader may recall the story of Sue, "Tyrannosaurus rex," the best articulated fossil skeleton ever found – the "Mona Lisa" of dinosaurs. Sue was found in South Dakota, United States, by Peter Larson of the Black Hills Institute of Geological Research on federal land. Larson had paid Maurice Williams $5,000 to excavate the fossil. Williams, a Native American, had put his land in trust with the federal government under the Indian Reorganization Act of 1934. In 1992, a federal court had to decide who owned "Sue." That determination hinged on whether "Sue" was personal property, like a cow or tractor, or whether it was embedded in the land and thus the property of the United States government as trustee for Williams.[56] Three years and several court cases later, the courts ultimately found that "Sue" was part of the land and could be sold – that the fossil was once a dinosaur that walked the surface of the earth was irrelevant. Native Americans, as any other private landowner, were free to benefit by a sale to the highest bidder. Fortunately, in this case, it was the Field Museum of Natural History in Chicago for $8.36 million.

Contrast this with China's approach to fossils. In light of the large number of fossils discovered recently in China, and probably the loss of a great many of them to the growing international commercial fossil market, China amended its Cultural Relics Protection Law in 2002 ("CRPL") to provide more specific protection for paleontological fossils by defining them as "cultural relics." Like the French,[57] the Chinese government has a long-standing practice of grading "cultural property," and fossils fall within the category of objects of limited circulation.[58]

Intellectual property may be thought of as the use or value of an idea such as inventions, designs, literary and artistic works, and symbols, names, images, and performances. Most forms of intellectual property protection such as copyright, trademark, and patent law, grant exclusive proprietary rights to authors and artists in their creations. In the classic schema of intellectual property, the granting of private rights provides incentive for creation and invention and thus promotes knowledge and culture.[59] Intellectual property – like all property – remains an amorphous bundle of rights.[60] However, there are acknowledged limits to the bundle of

[54] Under the common law, property ownership begins with "first possession" and continues through subsequent owners in a "chain of title." In the case of "lost" or "mislaid" personal property or "chattel," either the finder or the owner of the premises gains the "right to possession" against all but the "true owner." The finder or landowner gains full title, however, to property classified as "abandoned." See Part VI, "Who Owns the Titanic's Treasures? Protection of the Underwater Archeological/Cultural Heritage," for a discussion of this concept as applied to the underwater cultural heritage.

[55] Sax, J. L., *Playing Darts with a Rembrandt*, p. 181, University of Michigan Press, 2002. Dr. Guido Carducci discusses Professor Sax's theory in "The Growing Complexity of International Art Law: Conflict of Laws, Uniform Law, Mandatory Rules, UNSC Resolutions, and EU Regulations" in Part I.

[56] Most Indian lands are held in trust by the United States for tribes or individual Indians. The United States holds "naked legal title" and the Indian landowners hold beneficial title. Indians have compensable property rights to mineral and timber resources on their trust lands, absent contrary indications in statute or treaty. In the same manner, historic properties, particularly archaeological resources, are attached to the land and belong to the landowner. As a result, Indian landowners hold beneficial title to, and "own," archeological resources on their lands. Paleontological resources, however, are not considered archaeological resources. In fact, fossils stand in a significantly different position to archaeological objects. Fossils are not human remains. Second, *in situ* preservation does not have the same importance to a paleontologist. Study of the fossils and knowledge of their location are important, but not necessarily their preservation *in situ.*

[57] See Gourdon, P., "Excerpts from the Memoire '*Le Regime Juridique et Fiscal Francais des Importations et Exportations d'Oeuvres d'Art*'" in Part III, "International Movement of Art and Cultural Property: Perspectives of the 'Market Nations'."

[58] Basic Principles of Civil Law 90 (William C. Jones, ed., 1989). According to the Civil Law, this property is not freely traded: it cannot be exported privately, it cannot be sold privately to foreigners, and it cannot be sold at a profit; therefore, it does not have the same characteristics generally attributed to the English term "property," quoted in Ann Carlisle Schmidt, "The Confuciusornis Sanctus: An Examination of Chinese Cultura," Property Law and Policy 23 B.C. Int'l Comp L. Rev 185 (2000). See also Michael Dutia, "How Much is the Ming Vase in the Window," 5 *Asian-Pacific L. & Poly'y J.* 62 (2004) for a detailed discussion of the 2002 CRPL.

[59] Modern copyright law derives its most fundamental principles from the Romantic conception of the author, a construct that emerged in the mid-eighteenth century and became the cornerstone for Western copyright law, establishing its structure and defining the parameters of the entitlements it extends to copyrightable works. Professor Jane Ginsburg of Columbia has asked, "Who is an author in copyright law?" Few judicial, decisions address what authorship means, or who is an author. Fewer laws define authorship. After studying legislative, judicial, and secondary authorities in the United States, the United Kingdom, Canada, and Australia, as well as in the civil law countries of France, Belgium, and the Netherlands, Professor Ginsberg's inquiry reveals considerable variation, not only in the comparison of common law and civil law systems, but within each legal regime. It is easier to assert that authors are the initial beneficiaries of copyright/droit d'auteur than to determine what makes someone an author. Jance C. Ginsburg, "The Concept of Authorship in Comparative Copyright Law." 52 *DePaul L. Rev.* (2003), 1063.

[60] In the United States, §17U.S.C. 106 grants to authors six exclusive rights, including the exclusive rights (i) to reproduce the work, (ii) to prepare derivative works, (iii) to perform the work publicly, and (iv) to display and (v) distribute the work. Sec. 106A provides limited moral rights protection. The source of the U.S. Congress' power to enact copyright laws is article I, clause 8, of the Constitution. According to this provision, "Congress shall have Power . . . to promote the Progress of Science and useful Arts, by securing for limited Times to Authors . . . the exclusive Right to their respective Writings." For "Progress in Science and useful Arts" to occur, the courts have stated that others must be permitted to build upon and refer to the creations of prior thinkers. The copyright law, thus, strives to balance the intellectual property rights of authors, publishers, and copyright owners with society's need for the free exchange of ideas. Accordingly, in addition to statutory exceptions, three judicially created doctrines have been fashioned to limit the copyright monopoly and promote its purpose. First, copyright law does not protect ideas but only their creative expression; second, facts are not protected, regardless

rights with respect to the (res) or idea. First, these rights invariably focus on physical manifestations of the idea. In the words of one commentator, "[a] fundamental principle common to all genres of intellectual property is that they do not carry any exclusive right in mere abstract ideas. Rather, their exclusivity touches only the concrete, tangible, or physical embodiments of an abstraction." Second, and importantly, the rights, with exception of "droit d'auteur," are for a limited period of time.

Unlike other forms of "property," to which traditional rights are more easily assigned, the formulation of cultural rights in property is extraordinarily complex. Questions about cultural identity and the ownership of culture, repatriation, and restitution implicate broader issues of ethics, globalisation, state sovereignty, governance, and distribution. The context in which cultural heritage is generated and preserved is important to its meaning and the terminology not only varies depending on the cultural community from which the term and definition emanate but also depends on the purpose and strategic use for which the term and definition are developed. A definition of "cultural property" or cultural heritage is not politically neutral.

THE INTERNATIONAL LEGAL LANDSCAPE

The contextual framework for a coherent cultural heritage policy begins with an analysis of the international legal landscape. Definitions of "cultural property" in international conventions determine not only what is protected under the conventions, but how stakeholders, be they museums, collectors, salvors, indigenous groups, or multinational companies, are affected. Beginning with Part I, various chapters discuss both the boundaries and philosophical underpinnings established by the standards set forth in international conventions relevant to the preservation, management, and protection of the cultural heritage.[61] In this section, the purpose is to simply and succinctly introduce the reader to the various concepts and definitions of cultural property through the lens of these conventions.

The current significant international conventions that form the legal regime for the protection of moveable and unmoveable "cultural property" are the Hague Convention, the 1970 UNESCO Convention, and its companion, the UNIDROIT Convention on the International Return of Stolen or Illegally Exported Cultural Objects[62] ("UNIDROIT"). The latter two are the keystone of a network of national and international attempts to deal with the "illicit" international traffic in smuggled and/or stolen cultural objects during peacetime.

Born from the ashes of the Second World War, the goal of the Hague Convention is to protect all culturally significant property during times of armed conflict. The rationale for this protection is found in the Preamble, which states that "damage to cultural property belonging to any people whatsoever means damage to the cultural heritage of all mankind since each people makes its contribution to the culture of the world." The Hague Convention introduced the term "cultural property" for the first time in an international agreement and defined the term broadly enough to encompass a very wide range of at-risk property.

The Preamble to the 1970 UNESCO states: "Cultural property constitutes one of the basic elements of civilization and national culture, and that its true value can be appreciated in relation to the fullest possible information regarding its origin, history and traditional setting."[63] The Preamble notes further that existing international conventions, resolutions, and recommendations on cultural and natural property "demonstrate the importance for all the peoples of the world of safeguarding this unique and irreplaceable property, to whichever peoples it might belong." The 1970 UNESCO specifically defines cultural property:

> as property which, on religious or secular grounds, is specifically designated by each State as being of importance for archaeology, prehistory, history, literature, art or science.

This definition is followed by a lengthy qualifying list of specific subcategories.[64] The 1970 UNESCO leaves to State Parties the precise designation as to which objects fall within the category of specifically protected items. It has been observed that this both reflects and reinforces the nationalistic notion that cultural property inherently belongs to and is within the exclusive control of the country of origin.

Both as a result of the enormous upsurge in the illegal trafficking of works of art and antiquities and the difficulty of implementing the private law aspects of Article 7(b)(ii)[65] of the 1970 UNESCO, after years of negotiations, the International Institute for the Unification of Private Law in Rome 1995 opened for ratification UNIDROIT.

UNIDROIT, being a scheme under private law, does not require that a "cultural object be designated by a state before it is covered." The definition of cultural object for the restitution

of the labor expended by the original author in uncovering them; and third, the public may make "fair use" of the copyrighted works.

[61] See Dr. Guido Carducci, "International Art Law" in Part I, "International Legal Tools and Viewpoints."

[62] International Institute for the Unification of Private Law Convention on Stolen or Illegally Exported Cultural Objects, June 24, 1995, *I.L.M.* 34 (1995), 1322; <http://www.unidroit.org/english/conventions/c-cult.htm>. It is also intellectually consistent to include the Convention on the Protection of Underwater Cultural Heritage; however, because it was adopted in 2001, I discuss it where it falls chronologically.

[63] An examination of the applicable international conventions offers no consistent pattern of definition of cultural property. Definitions of cultural property often fail to distinguish between "patrimony" and "property." The two words are used interchangeably, sometimes together with cultural heritage. The term cultural heritage appears in Article 4 of 1970 UNESCO but is used only once and appears without definition or operative significance.

[64] See Guido Carducci, Part I.

[65] Article 7(b)(ii) is concerned with cases of theft and illegal export and makes provisions for the restitution of an object when the object has been illegally exported from the territory of a signatory, provided that the object was stolen from a museum or a religious or secular public monument or similar institution and so documented, even if it is in the hands of a good faith purchaser, on payment of just compensation.

of stolen objects tracks 1970 UNESCO. Accordingly, cultural objects stolen from private homes, from all kinds of religious buildings, from private collections that are not yet registered with the state, and from traditional communities, can all be claimed back, even though the state, has neither registered nor designated them.[66] With respect to the return of cultural objects removed . . . contrary to a state party's law regulating the export of cultural objects for the purpose of protecting its cultural heritage, there are eleven broad categories of works that can properly be included in an export control scheme and recovered abroad. Virtually "nothing of the mind that a civilization produces would not qualify for an export control list," said one commentator.[67] UNIDROIT is a "lawyers" convention – dealing with legal concepts of title, ownership, statutes of repose, burden of proof, due diligence, reasonable compensation, and jurisdiction. UNIDROIT confronts crucial ethical and policy issues in the definition of basic terms, such as "stolen," "illegal export," "cultural property," and "reasonable compensation."

Dr. Guido Carducci, in Chapter 7 "The Growing Complexity of International Art Law" discusses the international standards created by these conventions and their intersection with private international law. Whatever the relevant legal regime of public or private ownership under domestic legislation may be, the protection of cultural property is governed by the rules laid down in the aforesaid international agreements on the articulation of movables, i.e., works of art and objects of artistic, historic, and archaeological interest.

What, if any, are the links between the conventions? Dr. Guido Carducci, in discussing the differences among these three international conventions, states that "these instruments are undeniably various in their subject-matter . . . such diversity should discourage easy and inaccurate comparisons or generalizations among these instruments . . . however, these instruments do share a link . . . as far as concerns: raising public awareness on, and especially ensuring a legal 'specificity' to 'cultural' property, as distinguished from (if not opposed to) 'ordinary' goods subject to a legal regime which usually is applicable territorially (*lex situs*) and favors rapid circulation and transfer of ownership."

War and illicit traffic in cultural property are not the only threat to cultural heritage. The UNESCO Convention Concerning the Protection of the World Cultural and Natural Heritage (the World Heritage Convention)[68] was adopted by UNESCO on November 16, 1972, partially in response to the changing social and economic conditions that aggravate the destruction of the cultural and natural heritage. Whereas the 1970 UNESCO and UNIDROIT dealt with illegal excavations, plunder, and the illicit traffic in movables, the World Heritage Convention is concerned with the natural and built environment.

The Preamble of the World Heritage Convention states that "parts of the cultural or natural heritage are of outstanding interest and therefore need to be preserved as part of the world heritage of mankind as a whole . . . that, in the view of the magnitude and gravity of the new dangers threatening them, it is incumbent on the international community as a whole to participate in the protection of the cultural and natural heritage of outstanding universal value, by the granting of assistance which, although not taking the place of action by the State concerned, will serve as an efficient compliment thereto (Legal Advice dated 30 November 2001).[69]

If the linking of culture and nature embedded in the World Heritage Convention was inspired by the environmental movement, so, too, is the linking of cultural diversity with biodiversity in the Convention on Biological Diversity[70] (the "CBD"), adopted in 1992 under the auspices of the United Nations Conference on Environment and Development, Rio de Janiero. The CBD embodies the idea that states should have ownership of the natural biological resources in their territories, including their genetic resources, and imposes obligations with regard to conservation and biodiversity, recognizes the value of intellectual property rights to protect "traditional" or "indigenous" knowledge, and seeks to address the needs of developing countries by requiring technology transfer and equitable benefit sharing in the results of research and discovery. Although work on the implementation of the CBD is ongoing, concern related to genetic resources and traditional knowledge particularly with respect to their interplay with intellectual property regimes, is being considered in a variety of international fora, including the World Intellectual Property Organization ("WIPO")[71], the Food

[66] A potential difficulty of the UNIDROIT Convention may result from the effort to resolve in one document disputes that involve two different areas of law – the restitution of stolen cultural property, which is typically a question of private law, and the illegal export of such property, which involves public law. These two areas of law typically result in different types of conventions. Conventions dealing with public law typically provide only a general framework and leave it to the particular states to apply their national laws to implement the Convention. This is often done to avoid conflict between nations as to particular provisions, thereby encouraging countries to participate in the Convention. In the case of Conventions governing private law, however, the norm is to provide more specific provisions, in order to achieve uniformity in the application and outcome of the proceedings.

[67] Both the 1970 Convention and UNIDROIT are discussed in Parts I, II, and III.

[68] Convention Concerning the Protection of the World Cultural and Natural Heritage, November 23, 1972, 27 U.S.T. 37, 1037 U.N.T.S. 151, <http://whc.unesco.org/world_he.htm>.

[69] The Chapters in part IV, "Protecting the World's Heritage: The National Dimension in the International Context," discuss the World Heritage Convention, its implementation in the courts, and its protection of cultural landscapes.

[70] Convention on Biological Diversity, June 5, 1992, U.N.E.P. (1992) <http://www.biodiv.org/convention/default.shtml>. As of May, 2005 187 states have subscribed to the CBD, but the United States has not ratified the Convention.

[71] The World Intellectual Property Organization ("WIPO") and the United Nations Environment Program ("UNEP") began work in the area by joint study in 1998 concerning the role of intellectual property rights in the sharing of benefits arising from the use of biological resources and associated traditional knowledge. See also Wend B. Wendland, "Intellectual Property and the Protection of Traditional Knowledge and Cultural Expressions," Bo Hammer Jensen, "Who Owns Traditional Knowledge," Maui Solomon, "Protecting Moriori/Maori Heritage in New Zealand," and other contributions in Part VII, "Who Owns Traditional Knowledge?"

and Agricultural Organization ("FAO"), the World Health Organization ("WHO"), and the World Trade Organization ("WTO").[72]

The CBD proposes a trust model for the management of natural and cultural resources wherein rights in cultural resources may be assigned to a party other than the TK community from which they originated. This model foregrounds the question of who, in the absence of a clearly identifiable individual or corporate creator, will administer and make decisions regarding the rights in traditional knowledge on behalf of a traditional knowledge community that has been identified as a beneficiary. One commentator has observed that whether or not the CBD can be characterized as customary international law, it offers an intellectual grounding for the claim that each state is obliged to protect the property rights of foreign states and communities to their genetic resources.[73]

Management of submerged cultural resources, particularly historic shipwrecks, has become a significant issue during the past three decades. The protection of wrecks like the Titanic in international waters and the sovereign immunity of a flag state's military or national vessels within the territorial waters of other countries is poorly regulated. Consequently, the effort by UNESCO spearheaded an international effort to prohibit commercial exploitation of underwater cultural heritage and improve international, regional, and national efforts to preserve these resources *in situ.*

On 6 November 2001, after many years of negotiating, the UNESCO Convention on the Protection of the Underwater Cultural Heritage[74] ("CPUCH") was adopted in Paris by vote (eighty-seven states in favour, four against,[75] and fifteen abstentions), thereby "acknowledging the importance of underwater cultural heritage as an integral part of the cultural heritage of humanity . . . "

When the CPUCH enters into force after the ratification or accession by twenty states, it will adopt a definition to include as cultural property "all traces of human existence having a cultural, historical or archaeological character, which have been partially or totally under water, periodically or continuously for at least 100 years (Art. 1 Para. 1(a)). The flashpoint of the debate among the various actors – original owners, salvors, insurers, and their representatives – in international fora and in Part VI of this book is whether the traditional admiralty law doctrine of salvage and finds should apply to underwater cultural heritage.

The Convention for the Safeguarding of the Intangible Cultural Heritage[76] ("2003 Convention") completes the current primary international legal framework for considering the principles affecting the protection of cultural heritage and the development of policy related thereto.[77] The 2003 Convention defines the intangible cultural heritage, or "living cultural heritage," as the practices, representations, expressions, and the knowledge and skills, which communities, groups and, in some cases, individuals recognize as part of their cultural heritage. As Mounir Bouchenaki, UNESCO's Assistant Director General for Culture stated, "Some of mankind's most enduring cultural achievements sprang from memory, such as the *Iliad* and the Indian epics. Each time a language disappears, it takes a wealth of tradition and culture with it. Culture is not only monuments. It is not only the stones that are important, but what they represent."[78]

The sections of this book are, for the most part, organized thematically as attention has been addressed to the subject via these international conventions.

[72] A discussion of the relationships between the Agreement on Trade Related Aspects of Intellectual Product ("TRIPS") and CBD is beyond this book. Essentially, the CBD takes the view that if a product or process has existed in a culture for a long period of time, it is owned and hence protected under intellectual property law. By contrast, the view under TRIPS is that if it is not patented, it is not owned. If it is not owned, it represents knowledge that is part of a global commons available for exploitation by all who so wish. See Charles R. McManis, "Intellectual Property, Genetic Resources and Traditional Knowledge Protection: Thinking Globally, Acting Locally," 11 Cardozo J. Int'l Comp. L 547, (Summer, 2003) discussing the growing awareness of interdependence of biotechnology and biodiversity, particularly as expressed at the Fourth WTO Ministerial Conference held in Doha Qator, November 2001, in the Declaration Doha, which specifically directed the TRIPS Council to examine the relationship between the TRIPS Council and CBD. "Agreement on Trade-Related Aspects of Intellectual Property Rights," 15 April 1994, *33 I.L.M. (1994), 81* ("TRIPS Agreement") available at <http://www.wto.int>.

[73] Anupam Chander and Madhavi Sunder, "The Romance of the Public Domain" 92 *Calif L. Rev.* 1331 (Oct. 2004) See also Shubha Ghosh, "Traditional Knowledge, Patents and the New Mercantilism" 85 *J. Pat* (2003), 885. See also Part IX, "Caring and Sharing: Innovative Solutions and Partnerships for Natural and Cultural Heritage Conservation."

[74] Convention on the Protection of the Underwater Cultural Heritage, November 6, 2001, 41 *I.L.M.* 40. <http://www.unesco.org/culture/laws/underwater/html_eng/convention.shtml>.

[75] Namely, the Russian Federation, Norway, Turkey, and Venezuela. The observer delegate of the United States, who was not entitled to vote (the United States not being a member of UNESCO at that time), regretted that his delegation could not accept the Convention because of objections to several key provisions relating to jurisdiction, the reporting scheme, warships, and the relationship of the convention to United Nations Convention on the Law of the Sea (UNCLOS). The negative votes of Turkey and Venezuela were because of disagreement on the Convention provisions on peaceful settlement of disputes (Art. 25) and reservations (Art. 30).

[76] Convention for the Safeguarding of the Intangible Cultural Heritage, October 17, 2003; the full text of the Convention can be found online at <http://unesdoc.unesco.org/images/0013/001325/132540e.pdf>.

[77] United Nations Convention on the Law of the Sea (Montego Bay, 1982) Dec. 10 1982, 1833 U.N.T.S. 3. <http://www.un.org/Depts/los/convention_agreements/texts/unclos/unclos_e.pdf>. Although the UNCLOS regime has some articles (Art. 303, 149) on underwater cultural heritage, salvage law and other rules of admiralty are given an overarching status; if there is a conflict between the objective to protect underwater cultural heritage on the one hand and the application of salvage law on the other hand, the latter prevails. See Part VI, Tullio Scovazzi. The WIPO is currently discussing the issues concerning the protection of traditional knowledge and genetic resources. The legal outcome, if any, of these discussions is not certain. See Wendland, W. B., "Intellectual Property and the Protection of Traditional Knowledge and Cultural Expression."

[78] *Int'l Herald Tribune*, Friday, November 15, 2002; for further discussion, see Cummins, A., "The Role of the Museum in Developing Heritage Policy; Carmichael, T., QC, "Cultural Heritage Preservation: A National Trust Perspective," Wendland, W., "Intellectual Property and the Protection of Traditional Knowledge and Cultural Expression"; and Solomon, M., "Protecting Moriori/Maori Heritage in New Zealand" in this book.

ABOUT DEFINITIONS, BOUNDARIES, AND VIEWPOINTS

The reader will learn that the entire question of the definition of such terms as "art," "cultural heritage," "cultural property," "cultural patrimony," "physical cultural resources,"[79] "indigenous," "traditional knowledge," and "folklore" for legal and policy purposes is difficult, fluid, and highly charged with political and social subtext.[80] As with art, there is no one single definition of what constitutes "cultural property." The progression toward an increasingly complicated set of broader definitions is particularly visible in the international conventions and the scholarly literature. This movement from the concept of "cultural property" to "cultural heritage" in the conventions, and the principles on which it is based, as several authors note, have different cultural policy implications and objectives.

Professor John Henry Merryman has written that the public interest in art and cultural property, which distinguishes it from ordinary things, is based on its expressive value, politics, religion, and utility. These reasons why we care about art and cultural property, taken together, imply a set of fundamental, related yet sometimes conflicted considerations that seem central to the development of cultural property policy. "They can be considered under the three headings Preservation, Truth and Access."[81]

In 1986, in an article entitled "Two Ways of Thinking about Cultural Property," and numerous other books and lectures,[82] Merryman constructed the paradigm that has often dominated a highly polarized cultural property debate with respect to movable cultural property.

> One way of thinking about cultural property – i.e., objects of artistic, archaeological, ethnological, or historical interest – is as components of a common human culture, whatever their places of origin or present location, independent of property rights or national jurisdiction.
>
> Another way of thinking about cultural property is as part of a national cultural heritage. This gives nations a special interest, implies the attribution of national character to objects, independently of their location or ownership, and legitimizes national export controls and demands for the "repatriation" of cultural property. As a corollary of this way of thinking, the world divides itself into source nations and market nations.
>
> Thus, in discussing the Greek demand for return of the Elgin marbles from England, the case is easy if only the assumptions and terms of cultural nationalism apply: the marbles are Greek, belong in Greece and should be returned to Greece. But if cultural internationalism is introduced into the discussion, the question becomes much more complex and interesting. The same is true of almost any other prominent cultural property claim: e.g., should Mexico return the Mayan Codex, stolen by a Mexican lawyer from the Bibliotheque Nationale in Paris, to France? The differences between cultural nationalism and internationalism become particularly significant in cases of what might be called "destructive retention" or "covetous neglect."[83]

For Merryman, the Hague Convention embodies cultural internationalism and 1970 UNESCO represents "retentive cultural nationalism." Professor of archaeology Clemency Coggins has attributed the division that characterizes the debate to the purpose and meaning attributed to cultural property: the legal mind treats antiquities as a commodity that must be shared, *Solomonically* between "interests" – all of which are accorded equal validity of primary importance: the country of origin, the archaeologists, the market, collectors,

[79] See Di Leva, C., "The World Bank's Policy on Physical Cultural Resources," in Part V, "A Consideration of Cultural and Natural Heritage Guidelines Applicable to InfraStructure Projects, Mining Operations, and Their Financing."

[80] The inconsistency of definition in the various legal instruments is, in part, explained by the often last-minute drafting efforts to reach compromise rather than any deliberate political intent. It is also a function of language. I noticed in editing and translating various papers from the French, Spanish, or Italian difficulty in finding the appropriate English term. This impression was confirmed as fact. In a most interesting article, "Cultural property v cultural heritage: a 'battle of concepts' in international law?", 86, 856 *IRRC* (June 2004), Manleo Frigo points out that while cultural property, as used in 1970 UNESCO, can be considered a subset of the notion of cultural heritage, "the equivalent of the term cultural property (e.g., '*beni culturali*') certainly includes not only immovables but also intangibles and/or nonmaterial elements at least for civil law countries." On the other hand, "the English usage of the term cultural property concerned as an expression of and testimony to human creation now has broader and more significant application.... Rather than a mere shortcoming arising from different language versions conveying the same concept, this becomes a more substantive matter of different legal concepts. This is particularly true when considered that the term cultural property is commonly translated into terms such as 'biens culturels,' 'beni culturali,' 'bienes culturales,' 'Kuturgut,' and 'bens culturais,' which are not only the (apparent) equivalent of it in other languages, but may also have a slightly but significantly different legal meaning in the relevant domestic legal systems." This is also confirmed in the definition attributed to cultural property by Paul Bator. In a seminal article, "An Essay on the International Trade in Art," 34 *Stan. L. Rev* 275 (1982) 250, 350–1. Professor Bator defined cultural property as "all objects that are in fact prized and collected, whether they were originally designed to be useful and whether or not they possess scientific as well as aesthetic value."

[81] Merryman, J. H., "*The Public Interest in Cultural Property*," 11 *Calif. L. Rev.* (1989), 339.

[82] See Merryman, J. H., "Two Ways of Thinking About Cultural Property," 80 *A.J.I.L.* (1986), 831, 853. See also, Merryman, J. H., "Trading in Art: Cultural Nationalism vs. Internationalism," 18 *Stan. L.* (1984), 24; "Thinking about the Elgin Marbles," 83 *Mich. L. Rev.* (1985), 1881; "Who Owns the Elgin Marbles?" *ARTNEWS* (Sept. 1986), 100; "The Public Interest in Cultural Property" 11 *Calif. L. Rev.* 339 (1989).

[83] See Merryman, J. H., "Two Ways of Thinking about Cultural Property," fn. 51 *supra*, *id* at p. [ ]. See also, Cuno, J., "Beyond Bamiyan: Will the World Be Ready Next Time?" "If endangered works were moved to some other nation, they might be better preserved, studied and displayed and more widely viewed and enjoyed." It is difficult to disagree with the conclusion of James Cuno following the destruction in Afghanistan and Iraq. Given the choice between decontextualization and destruction, the decision is not difficult.

Merryman says, "[t]o the cultural nationalist, the destruction of national cultural property through inadequate care is regrettable, but might be preferable to its "loss" through export. The cultural internationalist would oppose the removal of monumental sculptures from Mayan sites where physical damage or the loss of artistic integrity or cultural information would probably result, whether the removal was illegal or was legally, but incompetently, done. The same cultural internationalist, however, might wish that Mexico would sell or trade or lend some of its reputedly large hoard of unused Chac-Mols, pots and other objects to foreign collectors and museums, and he might be impatient with the argument that museums in other nations not only should forgo building such collections but should actively assist Mexico in suppressing the "illicit" trade in those objects."

and art historians. The object-oriented view of the ancient world is opposed to the scientifically designed, problem-oriented anthropological archaeology now practiced around the world. These are the two basic cultures that define the interests that might be described as scientific versus humanistic, but they are closer to cultural versus aesthetic.[84]

Professor James Cuno is a self-described cultural internationalist. In his thoughtful chapter in this book, entitled "Beyond Bamiyan: Will the World be Ready Next Time?" Cuno discusses, in part, why an object removed from its context still has value: "Works of art have many meanings, some of them historical, others aesthetic and philosophical. How, for example, can one inquire into the question of beauty without examples of beauty?"

For many contributors, however, the focus is not on "property," but the protection of "culture" as the unique mix of shared traditions, beliefs, relationships, practices, values, and their physical manifestation that hold together a community and give it an identity: "The work of art is the expression of extraordinarily patterned human behavior: it can be no more."[85] Trevor Carmichael defines culture as "the way of life of a people." Although cultural heritage may be reflected in various national and subnational institutions, it also transcends such institutions and is reflected in the essence of how people conduct their lives."[86]

Not only a different way of looking at "property," cultural nationalism may also represent a north-south response to a state's depletion of its cultural resources and a search for a postcolonial national identity. Folarin Shyllon observes,

> If we also accept that most of the singular objects that African nations would choose to keep are in the West . . . then the retentive nationalists are not those African countries who seek to have access to their treasures, but the former colonizers who have granted independence but are refusing to let go what they now consider to be part of their patrimony.
>
> 'Retentive nationalism,' 'cultural nationalism' and 'cultural internationalism' are not neutral terms after all.[87]

The complexities of the interaction of various nations and cultures with each other and the difficulties of finding concepts that are meaningful to all of them in order to find legal relationships makes a coherent development of cultural heritage law and policies a difficult task. Various treaties and nonbinding declarations have expressed the right of indigenous peoples to participate in international lawmaking. This current interest in the culture of indigenous people and their increased participation in the international arena, for example, has coincided with efforts to reconsider the meaning of "indigenous," as well as the meaning of cultural heritage in relation to such people.[88] In 2000, UNESCO adopted a Universal Declaration on Cultural Diversity. "The difference of cultural diversity is an ethical imperative. It implies a commitment to human rights and fundamental freedoms . . . "[89]

For example, in his chapter in this book, "Finding Solutions for Lost Cities: Indigenous Populations and Biological and Cultural Diversity," Alvaro Soto says, "all cultures are indigenous in the sense that they all originated in natural habitats, with communities developing their own particular strategies in order to adapt to and survive in particular surroundings. . . . All 'culture,' both past and present, is thus the result of the interaction of a particular community with a particular environment. There are therefore many different cultures, because there are many different types of environment."

Western notions of "property," "ownership," and "restitution" may not even translate to other cultures, whose entire system of belief and values runs counter to such notions. Several contributors suggest that ownership is not a universal law but a particular construct of some cultures. Whilst Western legal systems may regard cultural property in terms of proprietary rights and as a distinct category apart from other aspects of society, indigenous groups see it as interconnected within the society. Differences in perception produce challenges for lawyers and policy makers who seek ways to protect indigenous heritage within preexisting national legal frameworks as well as for others who would develop a global cultural heritage policy to guide international relations amongst nation states. The ideology undergirding the Law of Sé contrasts dramatically with the paradigm proposed by John Henry Merryman.[90] It is evident that in the twenty-first century, the debate and discussion have moved beyond two ways of thinking about "cultural property." From the point of view of policy

84 See Clemency Coggins, "United States Cultural Property Legislation: Observations of a Combatant," *International Journal of Cultural Property* 7, 1 (1998), 52, 57.

85 Willey, G. R. and Phillips, P., *Method and Theory in American Archeology*, University of Chicago Press, Chicago, 1958, p 2.

86 See "Cultural Heritage Protection: A National Trust Perspective" in Part IX.

87 Shyllon, F., "The Nigerian and African Experience on Looting and Trafficking in Cultural Objects," in Part II.

88 See Torres, E., "Chronological Overview of Developments in Bolivian and Latin American Cultural Heritage Legislation with a Special Emphasis on the Protection of Indigenous Culture" for a chronology of cultural heritage protection which dramatically describes the evolution of one country's policy from the protection of monuments to a broad definition of the protection of biodiversity, traditional knowledge, and the intangible heritage of the indigenous people. In particular, reference is made to the 1994 Draft Declaration of the Rights of Indigenous Peoples, which declares that indigenous peoples have the right to traditional knowledge and health practices. See also Charles Di Leva, "The World Bank's Policy on Physical and Cultural Resources" and World Bank Draft Operational Policies (Draft OP 4.10, December 1, 2004). "The Bank recognizes that the identities and cultures of Indigenous Peoples are inextricably linked to the lands on which they live and the natural resources on which they depend. These distinct circumstances expose Indigenous Peoples to different types of risks and levels of impacts from development projects, including loss of identity, culture and customary livelihoods, as well as exposure to disease. Gender and inter-generational issues among Indigenous Peoples also are more complex. . . . Because of the varied and changing contexts in which Indigenous Peoples live and because there is no universally accepted definition of 'Indigenous Peoples,' this policy does not define the term."

89 Adopted by acclamation, the Declaration illustrates that many states deserve recognition for the legitimate rights of states to support and create a favorable environment for cultural diversity through the creation of cultural policies. Universal Declaration on Cultural Diversity, Gen. Conf. of UNESCO, 31st Sess., art. 4, 2 November 2000.

90 Merryman's three principles of cultural internationalism are primarily property concepts.

makers, this means not only considering the uniqueness of indigenous culture but also respecting it and understanding that indigenous knowledge and Western knowledge are two parallel systems of innovation.[91] Law reflects the changing social norms of society as it also reinforces the social norms of that society. "Cultural property" and "cultural heritage" reflect different legal and social meanings.

But what is the link between "cultural property," "cultural heritage," and a concept discussed throughout this book, "the common heritage of (hu)mankind"?

The reader is particularly asked to consider the implications for the development of cultural heritage politics and policies in the different views and meanings attributed by our contributors and the international legal community to the term, "common heritage of (hu)mankind" or a reconfigured version thereof.

The term was derived from Hugo Grotius,[92] a renowned international legal scholar, and brought into contemporary usage by the Ambassador of Malta, to the United Nations Arvid Pardo, in an address on 1 November 1967 in which he spoke of the deep seabed. Although the terms are often used interchangeably, the concept of common property in international law should not be confused with this international law concept of the common heritage of (hu)mankind. The concept of the "common heritage of (hu)mankind" first found expression in modern times in such international treaties as the Agreement Governing the Activities of States on the Moon and Other Celestial Bodies of 1979 and, most importantly, the United Nations Convention on the Law of the Sea of 1982.[93] The international concept of common property and the concept of international common heritage of (hu)mankind share the principle of nonsovereignty over the resource in question. They differ, however, in that the concept of the common heritage of (hu)mankind envisions a strong international authority to govern the resource. It also involves the sharing of the benefits of the property concerned by all states, even if they are unable to participate in the actual extraction.

Such regimes grew out of an explicit concern among developing nations in the postcolonial era that technological advantage would permit richer nations unilateral domination of the global common spaces. Instead of *res nullius*, where the resources belong to no one and can be claimed by the first possessor, the *res communes* requires that any use be for the benefit of humanity.

The concept of *res nullius* or common property in international law is similar to the concept of a commons or public good in traditional property law. A commons is an area or a resource whose organizing premise is that it is available in principle for the use of every person. Typical examples include air, rainwater, and public parks.

Garret Hardin famously invites us to picture a pasture open to all. "It is expected," Hardin writes, "that each herdsman will try to keep as many cattle as possible on the commons." On this logic, the men will overrun the commons with cattle, eventually destroying it. Therein is the tragedy.[94]

Advocates who define the "common heritage of (hu)mankind" as a global commons often argue that raw, naturally occurring materials and cultural objects are free to the party that collects them, or owned by the party who first develops them, with the same consequences for natural resources as for cultural resources: a depletion of such resources in the poor source nations, and an asymmetrical flow to the wealthy industrialized nations, multinationals, and wealthy collectors. In the cultural property/cultural heritage debate, this position at the extreme commodifies art and cultural heritage property as stateless "goods" of commerce to promote free-trade principles in art and cultural artefacts.[95] The polar opposite of this debate is governed by what has been characterized as "retentive nationalism," fueled by the notion of sovereignty.

The example of the commons in copyright and patent law is referred to as the "public domain." The concept of the public domain as the equivalent of the common heritage of "hu" mankind is discussed in Part VII. Generally, the term public domain[96] refers to those aspects of intellectual property that are not, for a variety of reasons, made proprietary through patent and copyright law. The polarized arguments in the area of traditional knowledge and biodiversity, thus, play out between the "commons," free for all, and the "anticommons" (i.e., "private property").

[91] Janke, T., *Our Culture: Our Future – Report on Australian Indigenous Cultural and Intellectual Property Rights*, Michael Frankel and Co., Sydney, 1999, p. 112.

[92] Hugo Grotuis, II De June Belli Ac Paces: Libri Tres.

[93] Scholars, drawing on these two treaties, have identified five elements of the international common heritage of mankind: (1) exemption of the common area, such as the moon or the deep seabed and its resources, from appropriation by national governments; (2) international management of the area of resource through an international authority; (3) the sharing of benefits derived from the use of the area and its resources; (4) use of the area or resource solely for peaceful purposes; and (5) an obligation to protect the area or resource for future generations. Kemel Baslar, "The Concept of the Common Heritage of Mankind In International Law" (1998).

[94] Hardin, G., "The Tragedy of the Commons," 62 *Science* (December 13, 1968) 1243, 1244 (arguing that "ruin is the destination toward which all men rush, each pursuing his own best interest").

[95] Professor Merryman's position is obviously more nuanced and complex. For example, his distinction between "cultural moveability" and "cultural immovability" recognizes a right of return to the country of origin and retention for ceremonial objects that have a link to cultures whose export would result in significant loss. See Merryman, J. H., "A Licit International Trade in Cultural Objects," *Int. Jour. Cult. Prop.* 4 (1995).

[96] As Professor Jane Ginsburg notes in a view shared by the editor (see Barbara Hoffman, "Law for Arts Sake in the Public Realm," 16 *Columbia VLA Journal of Law and the Art* 16, 39 [1992]), "Copyright cannot be understood merely as a grudgingly tolerated way station on the road to the public domain. Much of copyright law in the United States and abroad makes sense only if one recognizes the centrality of the author, the human creator of the work. Because copyright arises out of the act of creating a work, authors have moral claims (*droit d'auteur*) that neither corporate intermediaries nor consumer end-users can (straightfacedly) assert."

Several contributors to this book propose that common cultural heritage is not, in a legal sense, the common property of all; it is thus distinguished from *res nulles* or "the public domain." The term common heritage, as used in the Hague Convention and other conventions acknowledges, however, a common duty of all states to protect and preserve the treasures falling under this category in the interests of the world community as a whole. The phrase "cultural heritage of all mankind" was intended to focus on state responsibility and not to define the rights of ownership or appropriation.

Preservation, truth, and access are unobjectionable goals of a cultural policy framework; however, should these goals be shared with other goals and objectives? What if the strategy were not "retentive nationalism" but the empowerment of less developed nations, and their indigenous communities, to participate fully in the global economy while retaining their own individual identity? In such a case, the reader may conclude that the considerations thought to undergird a framework for human rights may well be relevant to how we rethink our model of cultural policy. Concepts deemed fundamental to human rights – equality, participation, accountability, respect for diversity, international cooperation and solidarity – may balance and inform concerns about preservation, truth, and access. Can we construct a cultural heritage paradigm based on values of "preservation," "truth," and a reconfigured concept of access, prior informed consent (PIC), and its concomitant right to cultural objection? Trevor Carmichael's comments in this connection merit consideration.

> Today, fusion rules in a world that constantly flirts with the meaning of globalisation. Fusion in cuisine and lifestyles has now moved to the realm of musicals, where only a short while ago Sir Andrew Lloyd Webber spoke of his new 'Bollywood-inspired' musical 'Bombay Dreams,' and its Indian composer A. R. Ralman noted that 'the future of shows in the West lies in Indian music.' However, genuine fusion cannot be true to itself and is without merit if the primary product is not safe and sustainable.[97]

If our traditional property models so reconfigured become systems of social relationships regarding that property, then title does not necessarily give rise to entitlement. Obligations may accompany ownership and responsibilities may arise out of rights. From this perspective, each stick in the bundle of rights that describes property ownership is defined directly or indirectly in terms of the relationship between the owner and others in relationship to that property, whether the model begins with the paradigm of private property or instead focuses on a reconfigured public domain.[98] Each of us may perceive and weigh these relationships, goals, and principles differently but they belong in the mix.

Our authors realize the need to move beyond rhetoric and labels to engage in a constructive dialogue. Bo Hammer Jensen states,

> The results of this rhetoric are becoming more and more visible as many companies are cutting down departments involved in bioprospecting or even closing these departments and shifting to rely completely on other technologies to identify product candidates. This diminishes the market. It would therefore be desirable if in future debates about rights to traditional knowledge and the exploitation of this knowledge, the holders of these rights and the governments representing them in various forums could consider industry as their partners and not as adversaries.[99]

Neil MacGregor wrote,[100] "Most recently, as an example of what the British Museum means by claiming to be 'a museum of the world and for the world' we have developed a unique and path-breaking collaborative programme with the National Museum of Kenya. Their Keeper of Ethnology, Kiprop Lagat, is spending a period of time here in London choosing objects from the British Museum collection for an exhibition of East African cultures to go on show in Nairobi, Kenya, in 2006. This is the first time, to my knowledge, that a major Western museum has made a loan of this sort to a partner in sub-Saharan Africa, and certainly the first time that any such exhibition has been curated by an African colleague."

Arapata Hakiwai, Director, Mätauranga Maori, Museum of New Zealand, discusses in his chapter, Maori Taonga – Maori Identity, how museums can work together using the example of a project which is a collaborative initiative between the Field Museum and the Maori tribes with the closest connection to a Maori meeting house. Mr. Hakiwai is acting as a consultant to the Field Museum in Chicago.

Art and Cultural Heritage: Law, Policy and Practice is appropriately not solely about the law – national and international – respecting cultural heritage. Rather, it is a bubbling cauldron of law mixed with ethics, philosophy, politics and working principles about how cultural heritage law, policy, and practice should be sculpted from the past as the present becomes the future. Art and cultural heritage are two pillars on which a society builds its identity, its values, its sense of community and the individual. The authors explore these demanding concerns, untangle basic values, and look critically at the conflicts and their contradictions in existing art and cultural heritage law and policy in their diverse sectors. The rich and provocative contributions collectively provide reasoned and impassioned discussion of the issues from multiplicity of views to permit the reader to understand the theoretical and philosophical underpinnings of the cultural heritage debate.

To paraphrase Wend B. Wendland's remarks in his chapter in the context of the WIPO traditional knowledge debate,

[97] Trevor Carmichael, "Cultural Heritage Preservation: A National Trust Perspective" in Part IX.

[98] This is not to exclude nonproperty-based approaches. Customary law, codes of ethics and conduct, and documentation initiatives may all play a role in the shaping of rights in cultural property in cultural heritage protection.

[99] See Bo Hammer Jensen in Part VII . Also see V. Rivera and C. Cordero, "Costa Rica's Biodiversity Law, Cultural, and Biological Diversity: Searching for an Integral Approach" in Part IX. See also Editor's Note, "Caring and Sharing."

[100] Editor's files.

profound policy questions pulsate through these complex discussions: Who, if anyone, can or should enjoy the exclusive right to commercially exploit "cultural property,"? How should such assertions of exclusivity be reconciled with a balanced policy approach that encourages cultural exchange, promotes cultural development, and serves other goals such as research and education?[101]

Increasingly, not only the legal links, but the policy and practical links among culture, nature, and biodiversity are becoming more obvious and make it intellectually sound to construct a paradigm on which an integrated cultural policy is based. The contributions in the various chapters of this book reflect the general consensus that has emerged regarding the need to preserve and protect humanity's cultural, biological, and natural resources. The contributions also reflect the often divergent, sincerely-held opinions that exist regarding the means and ultimate goals of such efforts. There is no single, top-down, one-size-fits-all solution that can adequately protect the whole world's cultural heritage in a way that advances tha national development priorities of all countries, reflects ancient and diverse customary laws, and accommodates different values and cultural systems.[102]

[101] See Wend B. Wendland, Chapter 43, this volume, p. 327.
[102] Wend B. Wendland id. 101.

> Enabling diversity . . . entails admitting ambiguity – treating our own disciplinary inheritances as the fragile human creations they are – and opening up their inevitable aporias and listening for the meanings of their silences.[103]

What is evident is that whatever model one may choose, it is linked in a critical network with the other.

The challenges and issues addressed in *Art and Cultural Heritage: Law, Policy and Practice* are not only philosophical and intellectual. The world's underwater cultural heritage is a fragile, nonrenewable resource; we are losing languages and the cultures they sustain and biodiversity at an astonishing rate; and the illicit traffic in antiquities intensifies. Juan Antonio Valdez[104] sounds the warning, "the rate of destruction is spreading like a cancer and nobody is really listening to the warning voices. This means that, within a few decades, most of Guatemala's archaeological sites will have been plundered or destroyed by tractors. . . . We are facing a future in which there will be no other past than that which is already known and has been excavated. . . . What are we going to do about it?"

[103] Rosemary Coombe, "The Cultural Life of Things: Anthropological Approaches to Law and Society in Conditions of Globalization," *Am. U. J. Int'l L. & Pol'y* (1995), 791, 833.
[104] See his chapter, "Management and Conservation of Guatemala's Cultural Heritage, A Challenge to Keep History Alive" in Part II.

PART ONE

International Legal Tools and Viewpoints

CHAPTER ONE

The Law of *Sé*: Linking the Spiritual and Material

Ramòn Gil

Translated by Alan Ereira

Editor's Note: The following text is an annotated translation by Alan Ereira of a speech by Ramòn Gil, a trained spokesman for the Gonavindua Tairona. Gonavindua Tairona, an indigenous group that inhabits the Sierra Nevada de Santa Marta, Colombia, is the political organisation founded by the Mamas (priests) of the three tribes in 1987 in order to represent their interests in the face of increasing Western pressures.

High on a remote Colombian mountain, the Sierra Nevada de Santa Marta, a pre-Columbian high civilization still continues to preserve and protect its traditional life, practices, and way of understanding. The indigenous people there are the Asarios, and the most traditional of all, the Kogi. They call themselves the Elder Brothers of humanity, and regard us, their Younger Brothers, as rapacious and dangerous children incapable of concentration and analysis, and lacking respect for anything beyond our own individual greed.

In January 1999, I was invited to attend a gathering of tribal elders from all over America, held in the Sierra and hosted by the Arhuacos. The object was to explore their common concerns and try to develop some form of co-operation. The agenda had been set by a group of Mamas, their spiritual leaders, organised in a body they call Gonawindua Tairona. They demanded that each indigenous group describe their "Law of Origin" and then explain how they derived from that their political and ecological theory.

The Kogi Mamas sat and watched silently throughout the conference, as group after group struggled to understand and produce what had been demanded. On the final day, Ramòn Gil, their spokesman, made a presentation that had been prepared months before by the Mamas. It was not, of course, a Socratic dialogue as presented by Plato. But it follows the same course, deriving a political theory from a philosophical system. And that system is rooted in the notion of ideal forms preceding material structures.

It begins simply enough.

The Advisory Mamas of Gonawindua Tairona gathered together with the other organisations and authorities of the whole Sierra for more than a week . . . Their task was to study in depth the way in which we have been organised since before the dawn of time, and thus to trace the tasks, activities, programs and projects required by our indigenous vision, to achieve true development in the Sierra Nevada.

Consulting the *zhátukwa* our advisors conclude that the core of everything is *Sé*.

The *zhátukwa* is an oracle. The Mamas sit on a hillside with a bowl of water, meditate on the issue on which they seek advice, and cast a stone bead into it. The bubbles that appear are a form of speech.

Sé is another way of referring to *aluna*, the living essence of the cosmos. It carries an additional meaning that is also associated with the penis – that meaning has to do with penetration and fertilising. But fundamentally it refers to the realm of ideas, spirit, imagination, which exists independently of matter. And Ramòn now explained what that means.

The original laws, the fundamental principles, are in *Sé*. *Sé* has no beginning, it has always existed. It is spiritual existence, the spiritual principle of existence. *Sé* is not a person, not a thing. It is the sum of things. *Sé* is complex. *Sé* brought the material world into being, but it embraces far more than that. *Sé* organises everything so as to create harmony.

When everything was dark, on a level which our view can not reach, the first spiritual Parents originated spirit and thought. They created everything in spirit, in the non material world. They were not people, not air, not anything, just idea.

These "spiritual Parents" are the ideas that precede all others. That is why they are called "Parents."

They are aspects of *Sé* – ideas in the realm of ideas. They translate into our way of speaking as axioms, like the axioms of geometry. They are the fundamental concepts from which everything else arises. The Axioms of *Sé* need to be understood before beginning to discuss ideas of right and wrong.

The Axioms of *Sé*

1. *The Concept of Order.* The first step in creation is the idea of separation between one concept and another. It is the idea of setting things out, the difference between order and chaos. It is not the actual setting out or ordering of things, it is not bringing order out of chaos. It is the concept of order, the idea of setting things out.
2. *The Concept of Matter.* The next step is the idea of matter itself – the notion that there can be a physical, material world. It is not matter itself, but the idea of matter.
3. *The Concept of Time.* For a material world to exist there must be a concept of the past, of time. It is a very difficult idea to understand, because matter itself exists only in the present. But it is not continually re-created; the world does not collapse into chaos as each instant passes, to be re-made anew. The present has an ancestry that gives it form and defines it. If there was no concept of ancestry, there could be no world.

4. *The Concept of Gender.* The idea of generative energy is fundamental to the Kogis' understanding of the world. The material world is alive, filled with living things, and those living things are born through a combination of masculine and feminine energy. The world is charged with sexual energy, which they see as the basic life-force. That is why Ramòn speaks of "spiritual parents": *Sé* includes the concepts "mother" and "father."

On the basis of these (to the Mamas) self-evident axioms, Ramòn and the Mamas argued, it is possible to understand the rules by which people should live.

The law of *Sé* is the spiritual world that establishes material being. The law of *Sé* legislates everything in harmony from the beginning to the end of things. That is why our first step must be to recover the law of *Sé*, to fulfil it, to pay tribute according to the law of *Sé*, to direct our thought toward *Sé*. *Sé* is spiritual existence.

This "spiritual world" is not a vague area of emotions, feelings, and magical niceness. It is an intellectual arena, the place of abstract thought. The Mamas firmly believe that abstract thought underpins the material world, and material existence is utterly dependent on cosmic intelligence.

Sé is, as it were, the mind inside nature. The notion of "natural law" is not at all special to the indigenous people of the Sierra – or to Plato. It is an idea that has been revived whenever people have tried to establish political life on the basis of rational argument rather than tradition. It was especially influential in Europe and America in the Enlightenment of the eighteenth century, and provided the intellectual foundations of the American and French revolutions. But natural law was understood in a relatively narrow way; eighteenth century philosophers were concerned with human nature rather than the natural world as a whole. So they deduced that human society should be governed in a way that suited human nature (which generally meant that human beings needed to have a say in how they were ruled), but saw no need for human beings to worry about how they behaved towards plants, animals, or the natural resources of the world.

The indigenous understanding of nature is, of course, all-embracing, and that mind inside nature is seen as being actively concerned with the welfare of all it has created. Human life therefore ought to be a dialogue with the unseen thoughts that shape the material world.

Here is the crucial difference between indigenous and Western philosophy. It is a very different approach from our own, and the difficulty we have in understanding that approach has played a great part in shaping attitudes to indigenous people. This is why it has been asserted that they have a "pre-rational" mode of thought, and why they have been seen as living in a culture of superstition and child-like anxiety about hidden terrors. Descriptions of storm gods and water gods, witchcraft and fertility rites, offerings and rituals, have all been made through the lens of Western assumptions about "nature" which make the beliefs of these people appear irrational and, if truth be told, pretty stupid.

The vast scale of cultural destruction, the decimation and extermination of indigenous peoples conducted purposefully or simply carelessly by Western invaders, has been conducted against that background. It has been difficult to take seriously people who apparently see the world in terms of vengeful gods and dangerous spirits, when we "know" that there are no such things.

I hope that it is already clear that there is nothing "pre-rational" about the Kogis' way of thinking about the world. But to understand the dialogue they believe must be conducted with *Sé*, it might help to look at a major oddity in Plato's thought – one that set us on a path away from them, and from the rest of human society.

* * *

When most people hear the word "Platonic" they do not think about the philosophy of forms, or the difference between essence and existence. They think of relationships between men and women in which there is affection but no sex.

Plato described ideal forms (i.e., forms that existed as ideas), and said that material things are particular incarnations of those forms. But he went beyond that, to describe love itself as rooted in the ideal, and actual relations between human beings as particular material manifestations of the idea of love. Plato's whole purpose is to teach his students to detach the idea of love from fertility, and see it as the source of virtue and immortality rather than of life and mortality.

The link between creation and fertility, sexual energy and birth, was therefore put on one side. Sexual life and the life of the mind were split apart by Plato, and that became the dominant attitude of Western thought.

This was made easier by the fact that sexuality has normally been surrounded by taboos – especially the sexuality of women. It was therefore not hard, especially in societies dominated by men, to teach that the life of the mind and the intellect should be separated from the sexual life, and that one was actually a threat to the other.

Sexual taboos, however, have a quite different meaning. In any culture that understands that creation has a nonmaterial basis, fertility and birth are recognised as the bridge-head that links the "spirit" dimension with the material world. That is, after all, obvious and logical.

The realm of ideas, of *Sé*, is inherently dangerous. The material world is understood to be ordered, organised, a stable balance of living and dying. The nonmaterial world is the source of infinite possibilities, and a disruption of the delicate relationship between what is and what might be could change the material world in unimaginable ways. All human cultures have understood Divinity, or whatever shaped the world, to be dangerous as well as benevolent. And the sexual bridge-head through which fertility enters the world has always been a place of extreme danger.

Women's menstruation, for example, which signals their fertility, has been recognised in most cultures as a time of danger for the community, and it has been common for menstruating women to be kept apart in some way. Sexual activity and birth are kept apart from the rest of social life because they have sacred power.

Male sexual emission has a similar dangerous connection. Many cultures insisted that men engaged in any kind of ritual should avoid sex altogether, because ritual involves the ordering of sacred forces, and the door that sex opens between this world and the "other" invites disorder, an eruption from the incoherent nonmaterial cosmos.

The sacred dangerousness of sexuality meant that it was always treated as "apart." That meant that it was easy to transfer onto fertility, sex, and procreation the idea that they are base, distinct from the higher pursuits of men, and dangerous to the pursuit of virtue. That led directly to the idea that these aspects of life should be suppressed – that human beings would be better if they were not sexual animals at all. In place of the sacrament of sexual intercourse, Christianity preferred the idea of a "virgin birth," saying that when Jesus was born, the Divine entered the world as a human baby without a sexual act. St. Paul famously said that "it is better to marry than to burn," and clearly meant that a good Christian would not have sexual relations at all. Platonic love, devoid of sexual passion, combined easily with the suppression of women and repression of lust to produce a vision of the world in which fertility was base and mechanical rather than magical and sacred.

In order to understand the Mamas' concept of a dialogue with *Sé*, and so the importance of offerings and mediation, we have to step outside that framework. If we do not do that, most of human society throughout history will remain incomprehensible to us. For tens of thousands of years people made offerings and sacrifices and visited altars and sacred places in the certain knowledge that they were doing something meaningful and useful, helpful to themselves, their families, and their land. The Mamas' reasons for maintaining their traditional offerings are not irrational or illogical. The reasons follow, with strict logic, from the axioms of their philosophy.

Generative energy, fertility, is axiomatic to the existence of the material world. So is death: both are fundamental. The material world is the realm of mortality; the nonmaterial world is outside time, the place of immortality, where birth and death are ideas like all other ideas. But the presence of fertility in the world means that the link between the supernatural and the natural is still unbroken. Life comes into the material world, and goes out of it. Doors are forever opening and closing between the material and nonmaterial worlds.

But these dimensions are not fully compatible with each other. The material world is different from the nonmaterial. The world of *Sé* is the place of infinite possibilities, the whirling energy of the chaos that preceded even the idea of order. The very fact of fertility opens the door to chaos and disorder, and yet it was *Sé* that thought this world into being.

The world therefore requires some intermediary to stand at the door and manage the interface between the material and nonmaterial. That is why the Mamas are there. That is why human societies, as far back as we can detect them, have had priests. They are not there as agents of human society, although that can be part of their function. They are there because without them, fertility itself would destroy the world. They stand at the doors of life and death, and try to hold the dangerous balance between the seen and the unseen, the material and the transcendent.

* * *

There are many different forms of existence; one is the material world that arose from *Sé* but there is much that exists only in spirit. The law of *Sé* is to act thoughtfully. That is why we must ask permission to use what we need.

To act thoughtfully is the first logical rule of right action, the most basic starting point of natural law, because the world itself is constructed on the basis of ideas, of thought. Acting thoughtfully, acting in the realm of thought, means that a human being is directly participating in the larger, nonmaterial cosmos. The Mamas therefore place a great emphasis on thinking through what is to be done before undertaking any task. This process is an imitation of the way in which the world was created; it was thought through, created in idea, and then the idea was made real.

We speak of the world being made by God (a term I have never heard the Mamas utter), and of God making man "in his own image." There is a pun here: "image" is related to "imagination," and man was imagined before being made flesh – an idea the Mamas share. But it also means, of course, that Man is somehow like God. For the Mamas, the likeness between the cosmic intelligence and humankind lies in the power of thought itself.

To ask permission to use what we need is the second logical rule of right action, and goes to the very heart of indigenous ethics. The safety of the world requires priestly mediation with the power that makes the world fertile, but there is no logical reason to believe that this gives human beings dominion over everything in the world.

The material world is understood as an organised structure of almost infinite complexity, conceived by a process of thought far beyond human comprehension, and constantly endangered by the very life-energy that sustains it. Deliberate human interference in the world – such as agriculture, the killing of animals, or construction work – will inevitably have consequences which cannot be readily anticipated. The only way in which these things can be done safely is by involving the unseen creative power, the nonmaterial intelligence that shaped the world, as a partner in what is to be done.

The ancient tradition of making offerings and sacrifices, which has been universal in all "pagan" societies, is therefore an entirely rational business. That is why it has been the normal behaviour of human beings for tens of thousands of years. Our society, which sees these actions as meaningless superstitions, is unique in human history. Our society, as the Mamas are anxious to point out, has also been causing more extensive damage to the world than any other. They naturally see these facts as being closely connected.

That is what they want to explain.

It is necessary to educate people in the law of *Sé*. This law was given to the Elder Brothers and that is why it is our responsibility to protect all that exists.

* * *

***Sé* is the spiritual world and from it arose all that exists. It had no corporal being – no body, no organs. The first spiritual Parents began to study the organisation of spiritual diversity so that what now exists could materialise. Each species was given a specific function and a tribute to pay.**

One of the great problems in understanding what the Mamas are saying is the whole business of translation. Ramòn and the other Sierra Indians who translate into Spanish have to draw on a Catholic vocabulary that carries its own baggage and easily becomes very misleading. The nonmaterial dimension is described as "the spiritual world"; it could just as accurately be called "the world of essence" or "the cosmic mind."

A further complication is that everything is described in a metaphorical language that we tend to understand in a very literal way. The phrase *the first spiritual Parents* is, of course, a metaphor for what I have called, using a different metaphor, the Axioms of *Sé*. The image of those Parents carefully studying *the organisation of spiritual diversity* is an extension of the metaphor: extending my own metaphor, I would say that from the original axioms, the cosmic mind thought through the elaboration of the living material world, enabling it to come into being.

Because the world is a single, interconnected whole, everything in it has its own predetermined place. Living things are, of course, continually involved in the process of fertility. Plants and animals cannot exercise any control over that dangerous business, but that is clearly not in itself a problem. It follows that each species must have been created with its own specific behaviour, appropriate to its place in the world and allowing it to live and reproduce without endangering everything else.

But this elementary logic, supported of course by observation of the actual life of the natural world, does not hold good when it comes to human beings. We do not seem to have specific behaviour patterns in the same way. We shape our own lives. That is why we need the work of priests, handling the interface between the material and the nonmaterial, consciously making offerings and engaging the cosmic mind in a partnership with human activities.

When the Mamas meditate they are communicating with *Sé*, that is how they answer to the original spiritual law.

***Sé* has ultimate power over the world. It can end everything and re-build the world again because *Sé* does not die, it is always in charge, demanding obedience. When the law is not carried out *Sé* can destroy this world and make another, because *Sé* contains much that has not yet materialised. That is why the Mamas make this demand today for confession and spiritual offering. In other words, the spiritual world must be sustained by working in spirit: otherwise nothing could exist.**

Confession is another of those words whose meaning is changed by translation into the language of the Catholic church. I have on occasion been summoned to "confession" by a Mama. He sat on a rock in silence, his assistant explaining what was to be done. I was given a fragment of cotton thread to hold, and told to think deeply about what had brought me to this place – the whole process of my life which resulted in my being here on this spot. I was then asked to explain out loud what was my driving motivation. The language did not matter: I might as well speak in English as anything else. Then I was instructed to rotate, breathe on the cotton, and place it under the Mama's rock. During the whole of this process the Mama would pay no visible attention. It was not being done for his benefit, but for mine. *Confession* is a process of concentration on the things that matter. It really means adopting a public stance of responsibility and awareness.

* * *

Some of the laws of right behaviour that follow from the logic of *Sé* were listed by Ramòn. Many of them sound obvious and familiar – a litany that could fit readily into the Ten Commandments:

not to covet
not to want to kill
not to steal
not to work with lies or falsehood in thought

But there were others which, although equally fundamental, are no part of our moral code:

not to plunder the earth without paying tribute
not to plunder the water without permission
not to build housing without making a spiritual payment
not to make a road without making a spiritual payment
not to eat or drink without making a spiritual payment
not to breathe the air without making a spiritual payment
not to accept the light without making a spiritual payment

What exactly is meant by "paying tribute" and "making a spiritual payment"?

* * *

The simple translation would be to speak of "prayer," "blessing," and "sacrifice," but it is a translation that obscures meaning. These are such archaic ideas in our culture that we have to dig very deep to uncover what they are about.

Prayer is a version of "spiritual payment," related to the seriousness, responsibility, and awareness of "confession." It involves a connection with a creative power that transcends and includes all time. They say that what existed before creation, before even the idea of creation, was "memory and possibility" – that is the cosmos in which the material world is embedded. Ramòn once described the moment of creation to me as follows:

In the beginning everything was a plain cloth. And Serankua (*active creative energy, the male child of the Mother*) picked up a thread, and separated the cloth from the cloth. There was a space between the cloth and the cloth. In that space everything appeared – the earth, the trees, the animals, the material world.

The cloth was memory and possibility, past and future. The space opened between them, between past and future, was the present. Making the present was making the material world; the two are synonymous. Of course all this was simply the creation of ideas – what was being created was the idea of the present, and so the idea of a material world. But totality now embraced the past, future, and present of the verb "to be" – an idea expressed in our own Bible in God's identification of himself to Moses as "hayah hayah," translated as "I am that I am" but meaning something more like "I have been becoming, I have been becoming."

* * *

Many things come from the law of *Sé*, many of our principles like that of *Sentura Gwiawimundua*. It is good to know what that means, syllable by syllable:

Sen signifies the original darkness, before the universe was born. It is a word that represents the origin of everything and that, to the Kogi, signifies not vacancy but the essences of everything. So it conveys the idea of spirit, of soul, of thought, of life, and therefore of movement. Because this original darkness, the essence of everything, is the realm of ideas and ideas are understood to be words, *sen* also represents the idea of language. And because it is the place of origin, it is also the place of law.

tu is a word used in the story of Creation for the first food of the Great Mother. The Mother, *aluna*, began by conceiving the material of her own sustenance. So *tu* represents first contact with the Mother and food of the spirit and the soul, but it also signifies the nature of this food. It was not material food: the Mother fed on thoughts. *Tu* means omniscience and the power of deep thought, study, analysis, foresight – and care.

ra is a word that conveys the very essence of life, the principle of living movement and conception in the double sense in which we use that word – to mean the fertilising of an egg and the creation of an idea.

Deconstructing a Kogi word does not lead to an English word, but to a story. The story told by *Sen-tu-ra* is of the beginning of things, of the conceiving of life in profound thought. It is a story set in the time before the material world had come into being, the story of its preparation.

And the next word, *Gwi-a-wi-mun-dua*? Now we enter the real world.

Gwi is what Ramòn calls "the spiritual earth of *Serankwa*." *Serankwa* is not the Mother but her male child, a metaphor for the active energy that works in the physical world. The Mother conceived the world, gave it shape; her son operates in it. *Gwi* is the conceptual space in which he works and in which the present exists. To us it means the laws of nature. To them, it represents the spiritual force that sustains everything. It is the consistency, strength, and clarity of nature.

a is the word for the start of an agricultural cycle, the sowing of seed, the time of fertilisation.

wi means pregnancy, the time of the foetus.

mun means quick, alive, hidden – and, by extension, belly-button. It is also a word for sweet.

dua is "all the variety of life, all living things, sperm." And, because it is all-inclusive, it also signifies the union of masculine and feminine, positive and negative, *yin* and *yang*.

So the story moves forward; after the preparation for life in the world of thought and spirit, we move on. The laws of nature have come into being, life is planted, the foetus grows, all living things emerge in their infinite variety.

Sentura Gwiawimundua means "The Roots of Being." And because of the way this language works, it does not just mean it. It explains it.

In Ramòn's words:

Life is built on the basis of *Sentura*, the variety of life was harmonised in the original law, before the dawn of time. There, in *Sentura*, everything evolved in the spiritual depths before the first light, before the invisible became visible. When we are in *Sentura* we learn how to fulfil the law of *Sé* in spirit, to take care of water, wood and stone by making spiritual payments. Then thought dawns, the material world arises.

***Sentura Gwiawimundua* is the law. It is knowledge of the law of *Sé* and its execution in spirit. The indigenous people of the Sierra were given the law and the task of paying tribute for all that exists, the trees, the water, the stone, the rain, the sky, the lakes. All the Mamas were given this obligation.**

***Sentura Gwiawimundua* is the principle and the creation of the original spiritual law, it is the thought that shapes our original law, the protection, the permanent construction for our strength. It is ultimately the cycle of life.**

***Sentura Gwiawimundua* is the first step in thought, in the building of strength in diversity to make a single spiritual road.**

The blending of philosophy and myth in Ramòn's speech then involved a metaphorical explanation of the centrality of the ancestral territory of his own people, the Sierra Nevada de Santa Marta. But the mountain itself is also consciously understood as a metaphor for all mountains, and for the whole world.

To Serankua was given the task of organising the material world, this world, according to the law of *Sé*. The first thing that had to be done was to organise *Gwi*, the rock, the structure, the support, the column to give it consistency and strength.

The world has been built on solid foundations, the thought-constitution that fixes natural law as universal through time and space. We are familiar with this idea as the basis of science and mathematics.

Then Serankua crossed a thread of thought to make the centre and he lifted it. The peak Gonawindua appeared. There was a peak above and a peak below and it began to work as the motor of the world.

The peak is the mountain-peak, but the word Gonawindua is a story-word that represents the quickening pre-dawn first stirrings of life, the origin and variety of living beings. With life came death, and so the living world is mirrored in an underworld that is also of course the death that accompanies life.

Then, at each of the cardinal points, at each end of the world, he placed the kadukwa, shukwákula, shendukwa who would sustain the material world. At each of the four corners he put a guardian so that the material world turns with a cycle that constantly revitalises life.

The idea of four corners, each with its own guardian, is pretty much universal – expressed in our own language with terms such as "rightness" and "four-square" – and carries the idea of a link between law and what is seen to be proper. Although all this foundation-building is described as the work of Serankua, a masculine active principle working within a framework established by the feminine principle ("the Mother"), Ramòn explained that these ideas precede gendering of the world, because they are the prior conditions for the appearance of living nature.

Serankwa is the main organiser, the principle of authority. Serankwa gave each of the beings of the natural world their functions, the rules and right principles for harmony and coexistence. But at this time there was no masculine and feminine, no fertility in the material world. Then Seynekun appeared, much later, to find Serankwa. Seynekun is fertility – the woman, the fertile mountain. That is when Serankwa was able to give shape to the spiritual Parents of everything and of all that exists. It is Seynekun who organises the earth. Seynekun *Sé* was given the seed to organise the earth and all that exists. In her, in Seynekun are the books shishi and punkusa – the books that contain the law, the behaviour and functions of each species and also the ways to make payments to each being's Parents, what offerings, what tributes.

In the conjunction of Serankwa and Seynekun, of masculine and feminine, of positive and negative, the spiritual world becomes this material world.

The conjunction of masculine and feminine is the explosive moment when the material world comes into being – it is the tense space between past and future, between memory and possibility, quivering on the edge of collapse. That is why it is the realm where law must function – human law is a mere extension of natural law, metaphorically represented by mythical figures.

That is where each of the Fathers are assigned functions and responsibilities, giving them the character of authorities. There are, among others:

- **Kalashé and Kalawia: the lords of the trees, of the forest**
- **Nimaku and Nimekun: the authorities of water, of fish**
- **Gonduwashwi: of the air**
- **Mamatungwi: of the sun**
- **Zareymun and Zairiwmun: of the sea**
- **Zanani and Zarekun; of wild and domestic animals**
- **Ulukukwi and Ulukun: of the snake**
- **Seaga: of tigers and lions**
- **Kakuzhikwi: of the ants**

To all them and many others was given the task of communicating the law of *Sé* to the Mamas, so that with the four guardians (there were originally four tribal peoples of the Sierra) they would organise this material world based on the spiritual law of *Sé*.

And so we come to the place of humans, and their ability and responsibility to interpret this natural or original law, and act on its basis. It is a heavy burden, because the very survival of life depends on it. Humans, living lives of the mind in the realm of idea as well as lives of the body in the material world, are the necessary guardians at the gates between these worlds. Law is not something for the benefit of humans and their society. Humans and their society exist in the service of Law, to sustain the world.

***Sé*, Serankwa, Seynekun are fundamental principles that only the Elder Brothers know how to fulfil and our task is to do so. Neither Serankwa nor Seynekun organise the material world, nor do they maintain it. It is our task to do that, that is why we exist and that is why we conserve the knowledge and practices of the Mamas. We are the original inhabitants of this Heart of the World, we have the duty of doing this work. Order and harmony is in the law of *Sé*; authority and organisation is in Serankwa; handling things, the business of daily life, the use of our land is in Seynekun; these three combined summarise our vision of development, our ordering of this place.**

Ramòn's speech was not simply intended as a lesson in the roots of indigenous political philosophy. The reason for speaking, indeed the reason for the whole conference, was that the society that carries this burden is being destroyed. Our culture, which does not possess this sense of responsibility and regards the logic behind it as meaningless superstition, is demolishing theirs. And because their "superstitious" view is based on a chain of rational logical thought – as Ramòn tried to explain – they can see nothing but catastrophe unless we wake up and take notice.

The first step of the indigenous people of the Sierra in confronting this terrible danger was to call a halt to the invasion of their territory. They marked out a frontier, the Black Line, and persuaded the Colombian authorities to give it official status.

When we speak of the law of *Sé*, of Serankwa and of Seynekun, we are speaking with ancestral knowledge of a territory that was left to us as our own from the beginning of the world. That is a reality plain to all, indigenous and non-indigenous. The Colombian State recognised this when it published a resolution demarcating the Black Line, after consulting our Mamas.

Times are not the same as 500 years ago, when the Younger Brother made contact with us and began to interfere in our territory and our destiny. Many things have changed. For example, we have already lost a large part of the sacred sites fundamental to carrying on the law of Seynekun – to the continuance of nature and culture. This is not some capricious indigenous complaint; it is a problem that involves the whole of humanity. Why do we say this? The Sierra Nevada is the Heart of the World, here are the origins of all that exists, in accordance with the law of *Sé*. Spiritually we continue revitalising life, we carry on the practice, so far as we can, of communicating with the spiritual Parents of each and every one of the beings that make up the life of the world. Tragically, many of the places necessary to continue our work have been lost, or we do not have access to them, or because of the Younger Brother's concept of development (more and more mistaken) they have decayed.

When our Mamas explain the fundamental principles of harmony and coexistence, that is to say, the law of *Sé*, of Serankwa and of Seynekun, they simply confront us with the obligations and rights that as we have, as indigenous people with knowledge of these principles, concerning the survival of all that exists. And the only way we can act is to follow these guiding principles.

At the moment, our territory is dismembered into 14 municipalities, three departments, three autonomous corporations, two reserves, two parks and numberless entities and NGO's. Each one has its projects and its own development perspective. They all impact on our territory, confusing the work of our Mamas to apply the basic principles. Our elders have always maintained that the best help, is, in fact, to support the task that they were given in the beginning: to fulfil the principles of Serankwa and of Seynekun, principles that we alone know how to fulfil. That is the command that we were given.

It has been shown, and is accepted by the State, that indigenous people are the best experts in the territory of the Sierra Nevada. We believe that at the current time this assertion is beyond dispute. That is why our response to any development plan is to press that indigenous culture and the indigenous environmental vision should be the fundamental axes on which the Sierra can be made the territory that we all want: a territory that is conserved and is producing life.

This means that one of our tasks is to press for indigenous autonomy, political pressure. In fact it is the main task, when seeking to transform the worn-out schemes that have been functioning in the Sierra up to now. In indigenous thought no part of the world, not even the smallest, can be detached from everything else, which is how the Younger Brother thinks of things. This must be the conductive axis of any deep transformation set in motion to save the Sierra. We also have much to say about urban development, and about the so-called "megaprojects," since each and every one of these plans affects, in their combined impact, the indigenous traditional territory that is the Sierra Nevada.

Let us make clear that we are not demanding that all things should be done just as we want them, but to develop mechanisms and strategies that allow our voice to be heard, listened to, and, as much as possible, taken into account in the Younger Brother's perspectives of the future.

CHAPTER TWO

The Obligation to Prevent and Avoid Destruction of Cultural Heritage: From Bamiyan to Iraq

Francesco Francioni and Federico Lenzerini

INTRODUCTION

Throughout history, destruction and loss of cultural heritage have constantly occurred as a consequence of fanatic iconoclasm or as "collateral" effects of armed conflicts. As early as 391 A.D., the Roman Emperor Theodosius ordered the demolition of the Temple of Serapis in Alexandria to obliterate the last refuge of non-Christians. In 1992, Indu extremists were intent on the destruction of the sixteenth century Babri Mosque.[1] In more recent times, the Balkan wars have offered us the desolate spectacle of the devastation of Bosnia's mosques, libraries, and the ancient city of Dubrovnik. Extensive looting and forced transfer of cultural objects have accompanied almost every war, including the recent Iraqi war.[2] Aerial bombardments during the Second World War and in the more than one hundred armed conflicts that have plagued humanity since 1945 have contributed to the destruction and disappearance of much cultural heritage of great importance for the countries of origin and for humanity as a whole.

The violent destruction of the great rock sculptures of the Buddhas of Bamiyan by military and paramilitary forces of the Taliban government of Afghanistan in March 2001 could be seen as an ordinary example in this history of cultural infamy. At closer scrutiny, however, the violent acts themselves and the perverse modalities of their execution present various features that are new in the pathology of state behaviour toward cultural heritage.

First, unlike traditional war damage to cultural heritage, which affects the enemy's property, the demolition of the Buddhas of Bamiyan concerns heritage that belonged to the Afghan Nation. They were located in its territory and belonged to its ancient pre-Islamic past.

Second, the purpose of the destruction was not linked in any way to a military objective, but was inspired by the sheer will to eradicate any cultural manifestation of religious or spiritual creativity that did not correspond to the Taliban view of religion and culture.

Third, the modalities of the execution differed considerably from similar destruction that took in the course of recent armed conflicts. For instance, during the Balkan war of the 1990s and during the Iraq – Iran war in the 1980s, extensive destruction of cultural property occurred as a result of wanton bombardment, as in the case of Dubrovnik, or under the impulse of ethnic hatred. In the case of the Afghan Buddhas, the demolition was carefully planned, painstakingly announced to the media all over the world, and cynically documented in all its phases of preparation, bombing, and ultimate destruction.

Fourth, to the knowledge of these writers, the episode in point is the first one of planned, deliberate destruction of cultural heritage of great importance as an act of defiance toward the United Nations (UN) and the international community. It is not a mystery that the Taliban's decision to destroy the Buddhas of Bamiyan came in the wake of the sanctions adopted in 1999 and 2000 against the Afghan government because of their continuing sheltering and training of terrorists and planning of terrorist acts.[3]

Fifth, the destruction of the Buddhas and of other significant collections of pre-Islamic Afghan art took place as an act of narcissistic self-assertion against the pressure of the Director General of UNESCO, Ambassador Matsuura; his special envoy to Kabul, ambassador LaFranche; and the UN Secretary General, Kofi Annan, who all pleaded with the Taliban to reconsider their disgraceful decision to proceed with the destruction of all the statues in the country.[4]

Because of these elements, it is understandable that UNESCO and the international community as a whole

[1] See Saikal A. and Thakur R., "Vandalism in Afghanistan and No One to Stop it," in *The International Herald Tribune*, 6 March 2001, available at <http://www.unu.edu/hq/ginfo/media/Thakur38.html>.

[2] See the rich documentation provided by Boylan P., *Review of the Convention for the Protection of Cultural Property in the Event of Armed Conflict*, UNESCO, Paris, 1993.

This chapter is derived from a larger study undertaken by the authors on request by UNESCO in view of the development of an international instrument capable of clarifying in which circumstances deliberate destruction of cultural heritage constitutes a violation of international law (such instrument was finally adopted by the UNESCO General Conference on 17 October 2003 as *Declaration Concerning the Intentional Destruction of Cultural Heritage*). An earlier version of this study was published under the title "The Destruction of the Buddhas of Bamiyan and International Law" in the *European Journal of International Law*, vol. 14, 2003, p. 619–52.

[3] See, in particular, UN Security Council Resolution 1267(1999) of 15 October 1999; Resolution 1333(2000), adopted on 19 December 2000 with only the abstention of Malaysia and China (which provides for the strong condemnation of "the continuing use of the areas of Afghanistan under the control of [...] Taliban [...] for the sheltering and training of terrorists and planning of terrorist acts"); see also Resolution 1363(2001) of 30 July 2001.

[4] See also the appeal issued by ICOMOS and ICOM on 1 March 2001, where it is stated that the act of destruction "[...] would be a total cultural catastrophe. It would remain written in the pages of history next to the most infamous acts of barbarity." For a chronology of international efforts to dissuade the Taliban from carrying out their destructive plan see the Report of the Bureau of the World Heritage Committee, 25th Session, 25–30 June 2001, doc. WHO-2001/CONF.205/10.

reacted to the destruction of the Buddhas with shock.[5] There was great concern for the moral degradation shown by the authors of such acts, and a certain anxiety regarding the role of international law in preventing and suppressing such form of cultural vandalism which, in the words of the UNESCO Director General, can constitute a "crime against culture." This chapter is especially concerned with the latter point. It particularly addresses the question whether and to what extent contemporary international law protects cultural heritage of great importance for humanity against deliberate destruction perpetrated by a State in whose territory such heritage is located.

THE DESTRUCTION OF THE BUDDHAS OF BAMIYAN IN CONTEXT

The Taliban ("The Seekers") was formed in 1994 by a group of graduates of Pakistani Islamic colleges on the border with Afghanistan. The members of the group were led by *Mullah* (village-level religious leader) Mohammed Omar, a man who is said to have lost one of his eyes fighting the Soviets during their occupation of Afghanistan.[6] The Taliban advocated an "Islamic Revolution" in Afghanistan, aimed at the re-establishment of the unity of the country in the framework of the Islamic law *Sharia*.[7] Immediately after their rise, the Taliban were supported by most of the civilian population, which was frustrated by the situation of civil war persisting in the country since the end of 1970s. In particular, Afghan peoples were seduced by the hope of stability and restoration of peace promised by the Taliban, who seemed to be successful in stamping out corruption and improving living conditions.[8] For this reason, from 1994, the Taliban advance to gain effective power over Afghanistan had progressively intensified. At the critical date of the destruction of Buddhas, the Islamic Emirate of Afghanistan, established by the Taliban, covered some ninety to ninety-five percent of the Afghan territory, including the capital, Kabul. The rest of the territory, concentrated in the far northeast of the country, was still under the power of the Islamic State of Afghanistan, headed by the National Islamic United Front for the Salvation of Afghanistan ("United Front" or "Northern Front") that was led by B. Rabbani.[9]

Although at the end of the 1990s, the Taliban movement had gained effective control of the greatest part of the Afghan territory, this control was perceived by the international community as not being sufficient to confer on the Islamic Emirate of Afghanistan the attributes of legitimacy. Only a very small group of states (*i.e.*, Pakistan, Saudi Arabia, and the United Arab Emirates) had recognized the Taliban militia as the legitimate government of Afghanistan. The Afghan UN seat was still retained by the delegation of the Islamic State of Afghanistan,[10] which also retained control of most of the country's embassies abroad. President Rabbani continued to be acknowledged by most members of the international community, including Iran and Russia, as the rightful leader of Afghanistan.

War operations had intensified since June 2000 with the Taliban and the United Front receiving support, respectively, from Pakistan on the one side, and Iran, Russia, and some other former Soviet Republics on the other.[11] Nongovernmental organizations (NGOs) have reported both warring factions as systematically violating international humanitarian law and basic rights of individuals by burning houses, raping women, torturing, and executing peoples suspected of supporting the opposite faction.[12] For this reason, on 23 January 2001, *Amnesty International* urged the United States to support the establishment of an international tribunal for Afghanistan to investigate massacres perpetrated by the warring factions.[13] Afghanistan was estimated to have been at war for more than twenty years as of 2001. One of the worst effects of the conflict is the contamination of the Afghan territory with landmines. The Mine Action Programme for Afghanistan coordinated by the United Nations estimated that a known state area of 715 square kilometres was contaminated by landmines. Of this area, 333 square kilometres are considered as having a vital role for the accomplishment of basic social and economic human activities.[14]

Moreover, according to Human Rights Watch, during the war period, Afghanistan has lost a third of its population, with some 1.5 million peoples estimated to have died and another

[5] See, from a general point of view, the condemnation expressed by the UN General Assembly, in its Resolution 55/254 of 11 June 2001, on the protection of religious sites, with regard to "all acts or threat of violence, destruction, damage or endangerment, directed against religious sites as such, that continue to occur in the world."

[6] See "Who is Mullah Mohammad Omar?" at <http://www.afghan-web.com/politics/omar.html>.

[7] See UNHCR, "Background Paper on Refugees and Asylum Seekers from Afghanistan," Geneva, June 1997, at <http://www.unhcr.ch/refworld/country/cdr/cdrafg.htm>, at 2.4.

[8] See "Analysis: Who are the Taleban?" BBC News, 20 December 2000, at <http://news.bbc.co.uk/hi/english/world_south_asia.newsid_144000/144382.stm>.

[9] See Human Rights Watch, "Fueling Afghanistan's War" HRW World Report 2001: Asia Overview, at <http://www.hrw.org/backgrounder/asia/afghanistan/afghbk.htm>.

[10] See, at last, the UN General Assembly First Report of the Credentials Committee of the General Assembly Fifty-fifth session, UN Doc. A/55/537, 1 November 2000, at 6–8. See also Identical letters dated 14 September 2001 from the Permanent Representative of Afghanistan to the United Nations addressed to the Secretary-General and the President of the Security Council, UN doc. A/56/365–S/2001/870 of 17 September 2001.

[11] See Human Rights Watch, *cit.*, note 9.

[12] See Human Rights Watch, *cit.*, note 9; Clark K., "UN accuses Taleban of massacre" BBC News, 20 January 2001, at <http://www.afghan-politics.org>; UN Economic and Social Council, "Question of the Violation of Human Rights and Fundamental Freedoms in Any Part of the World," Report on the Situation of human rights in Afghanistan submitted by Mr. Kamal Hossain, Special Rapporteur, UN Doc. E/CN.4/2001/43, 1 February 2001, at 3 ff. and 41–4.

[13] See "Amnesty International Seeks US Support for Afghanistan International Tribunal," at <http://www.afghan-politics.org>.

[14] See UN General Assembly, "Emergency international assistance for peace, normalcy and reconstruction of war-stricken Afghanistan," Report of the Secretary-General, UN Doc. A/55/348, 31 August 2000, at 46. For a comprehensive survey on the effects of landmines on Afghan people see UN General Assembly, "Situation of human rights in Afghanistan," Note by the Secretary-General, UN Doc. A/55/346, 30 August 2000, at 42–7.

5 million fled as refugees to foreign countries.[15] Despite the promises made by the Taliban, Afghanistan managed in 2001 to reach the world's lowest life expectancy and, together with Somalia, was one of the two hungriest countries in the world.[16]

The persistence of war operations had induced, in the late 1990s, a large monetization of economic and social relations, combined with hyperinflation and the destruction of most of the subsistence economy.[17] Such sudden change produced abject poverty and the transformation of the internal economy into a system where, until recently, a significant part of the national income was obtained by the production of and trade in opium.[18] It may be supposed that by banning production of opium nationwide, the Taliban regime had tried to mitigate its international isolation by meeting one of the main requirements most often reiterated by the community of states. Similarly, the Taliban tried to take steps with regard to the discriminatory policy on grounds of gender, by relaxing the strict ban on female education previously imposed and by reinstituting the celebration of International Women's Day on 8 March.[19] However, this kind of measure, although welcomed, was nearly insignificant in a general context in which the conditions of women in the territories subjected to Taliban domination were of institutionalized virtual slavery.

Gender discrimination, together with a generally dramatic disregard of basic human rights,[20] was one of the consequences of extreme religious intolerance that characterized the Taliban regime. Such intolerance included absolute lack of freedom of expression and a total ban of pictures.[21] It is in this context of obscurantism that a decree promulgated by Mullah Omar on 8 January 2001 applied death penalty to Afghans who converted from Islam to Judaism or Christianity.[22]

Religious extremism and intolerance were not extraneous to the Taliban's decision to promote international terrorism. They hosted and supported Saudi Arabian dissident Osama Bin Laden in his fight against "imperialism of Western countries," especially by making Afghan territory available for hosting his training camps for terrorists.[23] This support was at the origin of the UN Security Council's decision to impose wide economic sanctions against the Taliban[24] and the concomitant downgrading of diplomatic relations between Afghanistan and Saudi Arabia, which, following the Afghan refusal to extradite Bin Laden, recalled its *charge d'affairs* from Kabul.[25] The Taliban leaders' response was that they would not take action against Bin Laden, who was considered a guest in their countries, and that any attempt to "try to change our ideology with economic sanctions will never work, because for us our ideology is first. The sanctions do have an effect, but exactly the wrong effect. The people are suffering."[26]

Even before the adoption of sanctions by the Security Council, the situation in Afghanistan had been the object of discussion within UNESCO with regard to the increasing threats to the cultural heritage of the country. Already in December 1997, the World Heritage Committee, the governing body of the 1972 UNESCO Convention on the protection of world cultural and natural heritage,[27] at its Naples meeting (under the Chairmanship of Professor Francioni) had adopted a resolution expressing concern at the reports about threats by the Taliban regime with regard to the Buddhist statues of Bamiyan. The resolution, unanimously adopted on a proposal by Italy, after having stressed that "the cultural and natural heritage of Afghanistan, particularly the Buddhist statues in Bamiyan [...] for its inestimable value, [has to be considered] not only as part of the heritage of Afghanistan but as part of the heritage of humankind," reads as follows:

"The *World Heritage Committee* [...] 1. *Reaffirms* the sovereign rights and responsibilities, towards the International Community, of

[15] See Human Rights Watch, *cit.*, note 9; UNHCR, "Background Paper on Refugees and Asylum Seekers from Afghanistan," *supra*, note 7, at 1.2, according to which, in 1996, the refugee population from Afghanistan was the largest in the world, standing at 2,628,550, whereas the number of internally displaced in Afghanistan reached 1,200,000 as of 31 December 1996. See also UN General Assembly – Security Council, "The situation in Afghanistan and its implications for international peace and security," Report of the Secretary-General, UN Doc. A/55/393–S/2000/875, 18 September 2000, at 39–42; UN General Assembly, "Situation of human rights in Afghanistan," Note by the Secretary-General, UN Doc. A/55/346, 30 August 2000, at 33–7; UN Doc. E/CN.4/2001/43, at 36–9; Finkel D., "The Road of Last Resort," in Washington Post, 18 March 2001, p. A01; Suarez R., "Afghanistan's Agony," *Online NewsHour*, 29 March 2001, at <http://www.afghan-politics.org>.

[16] See Human Rights Watch, *cit.*, note 9. According to World Food Program officials, in 2001, 3.8 million Afghan were facing severe shortage or absolute lack of food (See Suarez, *cit.*, note 15; see also UN Doc. E/CN.4/2001/43, at 53, according to which, in the past two years, Afghanistan's grain production has fallen by more than fifty percent, and now satisfies less than half of the whole national grain requirement); it was estimated that in 2001 the internal food production deficit amounted to 2.3 million tonnes, more than double the figure for 1999 (see UN Doc. A/55/346, at 29). Even before the beginning of the civil war, Afghanistan was among the world's poorest countries, but it did not experience the grinding poverty typical of ex-colonial societies characterized by a foreign economic dependence that generally magnifies social and economic disparities. In fact, it was characterized by a rural society in which human relationships were based on a system of solidarity and mutual help among social groups, which, in principle, maintained a fair distribution of resources (see Rubin B. R., "The Political Economy of War and Peace in Afghanistan," Sweden, 21 June 1999, available at <http://www.afghan-politics.org>, p. 3 f.).

[17] See Rubin, *cit.*, note 16, p. 6.

[18] Afghanistan is estimated to produce seventy-five percent of the world's raw opium, with a harvest estimated at 2,800 tons in 1998 (see Suarez, *cit.*, note 15; Rubin, *cit.*, note 16, p. 10). For the first time, on 27 July 2000, the Taliban supreme leader Mohammed Omar issued a decree imposing a complete ban on opium poppy cultivation in the controlled territory of Afghanistan (see UN Doc. A/55/393–S/2000/875, at 45).

[19] See UN Doc. A/55/346, at 53–54; UN Doc. E/CN.4/2001/43, at 50.

[20] See, in general, UN Doc. A/55/346 and UN Doc. E/CN.4/2001/43.

[21] See UN Doc. E/CN.4/2001/43, at 48.

[22] *Id.*, at 56.

[23] See, *supra*, note 3 and corresponding text.

[24] See UN Security Council Resolution 1333, *cit. supra*, note 3, paras. 4–7; see also UN Press Release SC/6979.

[25] See British Immigration & Nationality Directorate, "Afghanistan Assessment," October 2000, <http://www.ind.homeoffice.gov.uk/default.asp?pageId=162>, at 5.4.34.

[26] These words have been pronounced by the Taliban leader Sayed Rahmatullah Hashimi; see Suarez, *cit.*, note 15.

[27] See *infra*, note 38.

Image 1. Afghan Buddha before the destruction by the Taliban [© 2001 CNN], downloaded from <http://www.institute-for-afghan-studies.org/images/buddha_b1.jpg> (last checked on August 1, 2003).

Image 2. Destruction of Afghan Buddha by the Taliban [© 2001 CNN], downloaded from <http://www.institute-for-afghan-studies.org/images/buddha_d1.jpg> (last checked on August 1, 2003).

each State for the protection of its own cultural and natural heritage; 2. *Calls upon* the International Community to provide all the possible assistance needed to protect and conserve the cultural and natural heritage of Afghanistan under threat; 3. *Invites* the authorities in Afghanistan to take appropriate measures in order to safeguard the cultural and natural heritage of the country; 4. *Further invites* the authorities in Afghanistan to co-operate with UNESCO and the World Heritage Committee with a view to ensuring effective protection of its cultural and natural heritage [. . .]."[28]

THE TALIBAN'S "CULTURAL TERRORISM"

Unfortunately, the concern expressed by the World Heritage Committee at the Naples meeting proved to be well-founded. In March 2001, the Taliban regime defiantly announced its decision to put into practice its new form of symbolic politics consisting of the deliberate destruction of cultural heritage representing religious and spiritual tradition different from Islam. Much to the shock of the international community, such decision culminated in the destruction of two ancient Buddha statues, which were carved in sandstone cliffs in the third and fifth centuries A.D. in Bamiyan, about ninety miles West of Kabul.[29] The statues, which stood fifty-three and thirty-six metres tall respectively, probably represented the most important Afghan cultural treasures. According to press agencies, the destruction of the two Buddhas began on

[28] See UNESCO, Report of the XXI Session of the World Heritage Committee, Naples, Italy, 1–6 December 1997, doc. WHC-97/CONF.208/17 of 27 February 1998, par. VII.58.

[29] See Hammond N., "Cultural Terrorism," in *The Wall Street Journal*, 5 March 2001, available at <http://hss.fullerton.edu/comparative/wsj_bamian.htm>.

Thursday 1 March 2001.[30] Images 1 and 2, which show one of the two statues before and during smashing operations, remain as historical witness of such outrageous acts against the heritage of humanity.

According to the Taliban themselves, the destruction of the two giant statues was perpetrated in pursuance of an edict issued by their supreme leader *Mullah* Mohammed Omar on 26 February 2001,[31] proclaiming that

"In view of the fatwa (religious edict) of prominent Afghan scholars and the verdict of the Afghan Supreme Court it has been decided to break down all statues/idols present in different parts of the country. This is because these idols have been gods of the infidels, and these are respected even now and perhaps maybe turned into gods again. The real God is only Allah, and all other false gods should be removed."[32]

After the issuance of the order, Mohammed Omar declared that it was to be done for "the implementation of Islamic order."[33] Nevertheless, according to a major expert of Islamic religion, Egyptian Fahmi Howeidy, the Taliban edict was contrary to Islam, given that "Islam respects other cultures even if they include rituals that are against Islamic law."[34] However, despite the difficulties met by Afghan troops in destroying the solid rock carved statues,[35] the Taliban Ambassador in Pakistan, Abdul Salam Saif, confirmed on 6 March 2001 that the destruction of all statues, including the two Buddhas, was being completed.[36]

In addition, according to the Online Center of Afghan Studies, there is clear evidence that the destruction of the two Buddhas was not an isolated incident, but was the peak of a systematic plan, pursued by the Taliban regime, for the complete eradication of the whole Afghan ancient cultural heritage.[37]

After the 11 September terrorist attacks on the United States and the Taliban's refusal to extradite Bin Laden and the suspected terrorists, virtually no country has continued to support the Taliban regime. The antiterror campaign launched by the United States, with the support of many other countries, has led to extensive aerial bombardment of the Taliban military and logistic infrastructure and to their final demise in December 2001. At the time of this writing, a coalition government composed of the various factions opposed to the Taliban has been formed under the presidency of H. Karzai. Although this is a welcome development, it does not absolve the past regime from crimes connected to complicity in mass terrorism and crimes against culture perpetrated by the deliberate destruction of pre-Islamic heritage in Afghanistan.

As has already been pointed out in section 1, the acts of systematic and deliberate destruction of cultural heritage perpetrated by the Taliban raise the question whether such acts are internationally wrongful acts notwithstanding the fact that they are aimed at objects located within the territory and the effective jurisdiction of the acting government. We shall try to address such questions in the following section.

THE DELIBERATE DESTRUCTION OF THE BUDDHA STATUES AS A VIOLATION OF INTERNATIONAL LAW

The evolution of the international protection of cultural heritage that has taken place in the last decades has built upon the idea that cultural heritage is an element of the general interest of the international community. By destroying Afghan cultural heritage, the Taliban regime breached, indeed, a number of international obligations, existing on the basis of both conventional and customary international law. First of all, such destruction gave rise to a breach of duties lying on Afghanistan for its membership to the 1972 World Heritage Convention.[38] According to the Preamble of this Convention,

"deterioration or disappearance of any item of [. . .] cultural [. . .] heritage constitutes an harmful impoverishment of the heritage of all the nations of the world."

It is important to point out that, although at the relevant time there were no Afghan properties inscribed on the World Heritage List,[39] article 12 of the Convention expressly states that

"[t]he fact that a property belonging to the cultural or natural heritage has not been included in either of the [World Heritage List or the list of World Heritage in Danger] shall in no way be construed to mean that it does not have an outstanding universal value for purposes other than those resulting from inclusion in these lists."

[30] See "Afghan Taliban Have Begun Smashing Statues," *Reuters* agency, Thursday, 1 March 2001, 5:08 A.M. EDT, available at <http://www.afghan-politics.org>.

[31] See "Taliban: Statues Must Be Destroyed," *Associated Press* agency, Monday, 26 February 2001, 6:14 P.M. ET, available at <http://www.afghan-politics.org>.

[32] The text of the edict is available at <http://www.afghan-politics.org> (*Associated Press* source).

[33] See "Kabul defends plan to break statues," *France Press* agency, 27 February 2001, available at <http://www.afghan-politics.org>.

[34] See "Taliban gathers explosive to destroy renowned Buddha statues," *Reuters* agency, Friday, 2 March 2001, 4:18 P.M., available at <http://www.afghan-politics.org>.

[35] See "Taliban gathers explosive to destroy renowned Buddha statues," *supra*, note 34.

[36] See "Taliban stop destruction of the Buddha-Statues," *Reuters* agency, Tuesday, 6 March 2001, 23:05, available at <http://www.afghan-politics.org> (on 6 March 2001, the destruction was suspended for celebrating an Islamic celebration).

[37] See the "Communiqué By the Online Center of Afghan Studies Regarding the Destruction of Afghan National and Archeological Treasures" of 28 February 2001, available at <http://www.afghan-politics.org>.

[38] For the text of the World Heritage Convention (1972 *UNESCO Convention Concerning the Protection of the World Cultural and Natural Heritage*) see the UNESCO Web site, at <http://www.unesco.org/whc/world_he.htm>. Afghanistan ratified the Convention on 20 March 1979 (see <http://www.unesco.org/whc/sp/afg.htm>).

[39] After the destruction of the Buddhas of Bamiyan, the World Heritage Committee inscribed in the List the Minaret and Archaeological Remains of Jam in 2002 (see <http://whc.unesco.org/pg.cfm?cid=31&id_site=211>) and the Cultural Landscape and Archaeological Remains of the Bamiyan Valley (just the one in which the two Buddhas were located) in 2003 (see <http://whc.unesco.org/pg.cfm?cid=31&id_site=208>).

This provision must be read in connection with article 4, which points out that

"the duty of ensuring the [...] protection, conservation, presentation and transmission to future generations of the cultural [...] heritage [...] situated on [the] territory [of each State Party to this Convention], belongs primarily to that State,"

The joint reading of these provisions makes it clear that membership in the World Heritage Convention binds States Parties to conserve and protect their own cultural properties even if they are not inscribed in the World Heritage List. As for the Bamiyan Buddhas, there is no doubt that they were to be considered as included in the concept of cultural heritage relevant to the Convention.[40] Regardless of whether they met the text of "outstanding universal value" set forth in article 1, the Buddhas were certainly "works of monumental sculpture" of generally recognized historical importance. There can be no doubt that the deliberate, wanton destruction of the great Buddhas is inconsistent with the letter and spirit of the 1972 Convention. The World Heritage Committee, in the already cited resolution adopted in 1997, had considered the statues of "inestimable value" and "not only part of the heritage of Afghanistan but as part of the heritage of humankind."[41] In a gesture laden with symbolic value this characterization was confirmed by the World Heritage Committee's decision, in July 2003, to inscribe the remains of the two giants Buddhas and the area of Bamiyan in the World Heritage List, as cultural heritage of outstanding universal value pursuant to the World Heritage Convention. The Committee justified such inscription by reference to the value of the Bamiyan valley as, *inter alia*, an exceptional testimony to the interchange of different cultures and to a cultural tradition that has disappeared, and the statues themselves, although actually destroyed, were to be considered an outstanding representation of Buddhist art.[42]

Because Afghanistan was, at the time of the destruction of the Buddhas of Bamiyan, actually perturbed by a civil war,[43] the present inquiry must turn now to the relevant norms on the protection of cultural heritage during armed conflicts.[44] Several conventional instruments, pertaining both to the protection of cultural heritage and *iure in bello* or humanitarian law, are applicable in this context.[45]

First, the protection of cultural properties was included in the conventions on the laws and customs of war concluded in The Hague between the end of the nineteenth and the beginning of the twentieth century. In particular, article 27 of the Regulations annexed to the Convention IV of 1907[46] provided that

"[i]n sieges and bombardments all necessary steps must be taken to spare, as far as possible, buildings dedicated to religion, art, science, or charitable purposes, historic monuments, hospitals, and places where the sick and wounded are collected, provided they are not being used at the time for military purposes."[47]

The Hague conventions on the laws and customs of war are applicable only to international armed conflicts,[48] and only in the case that *all* belligerent States are parties to the conventions themselves (so-called *si omnes* clause). However, the aforementioned provision demonstrates that, at the time of their adoption, the protection of cultural heritage already constituted a common concern of the international community.[49]

The aforementioned limitations, which greatly impaired the effectiveness of the Hague conventions, were excluded from the 1954 UNESCO Convention for the Protection of Cultural Property in the Event of Armed Conflicts.[50] In

40 See article 1 of the World Heritage Convention (*supra*, note 45). The fact that the Bamyan Buddhas are included in the concept of cultural heritage as protected by the Convention is also demonstrated by the inclusion in the World Heritage List of a similar site, that is the Chinese *Mt. Emei and Leshan Giant Buddha*, inscribed by the World Heritage Committee in 1996 (see UNESCO Doc. WHC-96/CONF. 201/21 of 10 March 1997).

41 See *supra*, note 28 and corresponding text.

42 See *supra*, note 39. The Committee inscribed the valley of Bamiyan on the basis of the following criteria: *Criterion (i):* The Buddha statues and the cave art in Bamiyan Valley are an outstanding representation of the Gandharan school in Buddhist art in the Central Asian region. *Criterion (ii)*: The artistic and architectural remains of Bamiyan Valley, and an important Buddhist centre on the Silk Road, are an exceptional testimony to the interchange of Indian, Hellenistic, Roman, Sasanian influences as the basis for the development of a particular artistic expression in the Gandharan school. To this can be added the Islamic influence in a later period. *Criterion (iii):* The Bamiyan Valley bears an exceptional testimony to a cultural tradition in the Central Asian region that has disappeared. *Criterion (iv):* The Bamiyan Valley is an outstanding example of a cultural landscape that illustrates a significant period in Buddhism. *Criterion (vi):* The Bamiyan Valley is the most monumental expression of the western Buddhism. It was an important centre of pilgrimage over many centuries. Because of their symbolic values, the monuments have suffered at different times during their existence, including the deliberate destruction in 2001, which shook the whole world.

43 See *supra*, section 2.

44 Generally on this issue see Nalhik S. E., "La protection internationale des biens culturels en cas de conflit armé," in *Recueil des Cours*, vol. 120, 1967/I, p. 65 ff.; Panzera A. F., *La tutela internazionale dei beni culturali in tempo di guerra*, Torino, 1993; Francioni F., "Patrimonio culturale, sovranità degli Stati e conflitti armati," in Feliciani G. (ed.), *Beni culturali di interesse religioso*, Bologna, 1995, p. 149 ff.; Gioia A., "La protezione dei beni culturali nei conflitti armati," in Francioni F., Del Vecchio A., and De Caterini P. (eds.), *Protezione internazionale del patrimonio culturale: interessi nazionali e difesa del patrimonio comune della cultura*, Milano, 200, p. 71 ff.

45 On the protection of cultural heritage by international humanitarian law see Nahlik S. E., "Protection des biens culturels," in AA. VV., *Les dimensions internationales du droit humanitaire*, Paris, 1986, p. 237 ff.

46 See *Convention (IV) respecting the Laws and Customs of War on Land and its annex: Regulations concerning the Laws and Customs of War on Land.* The Hague, 18 October 1907, available at <http://www.icrc.org/ihl.nsf>.

47 The same principle is also expressed by article 56 of the Regulation annexed to the Hague Convention IV (*supra*, note 46) and article 5 of the *Convention (IX) concerning Bombardment by Naval Forces in Time of War* (available at <http://www.icrc.org/ihl.nsf>).

48 See Ronzitti N., *Diritto internazionale dei conflitti armati*, Torino, 1998, p. 94 ff.

49 This circumstance was confirmed in 1935 by the so-called *Roerich Pact* (*Treaty on the Protection of Artistic and Scientific Institutions and Historic Monuments*, Washington, 15 April 1935, available at <http://www.icrc.org/ihl.nsf>), a regional treaty concluded between the United States and other American states, the Preamble of which states that "immovable monuments [...] form the cultural treasure of peoples."

50 The full text of the Convention and of its 1954 and 1999 Protocols is available in the UNESCO Web site, at <http://www.unesco.org/culture/laws>.

particular, according to article 19 of this Convention, states parties must apply the provisions that relate to respect for cultural property even in case of noninternational armed conflicts. The preamble of the Convention also affirms the relevance of the protection of cultural heritage as a global value pertaining to the international community as a whole, proclaiming that

"damage to cultural property belonging to any people whatsoever means damage to the cultural heritage of all mankind, since each people makes its contribution to the culture of the world,"

and that

"the preservation of the cultural heritage is of great importance for all peoples of the world and [...] it is important that this heritage should receive international protection."[51]

Unfortunately Afghanistan was not party to the Hague Convention at the relevant time, and its provisions are thus not applicable as conventional norms to the case of the destruction of cultural goods perpetrated by the Taliban.[52] The same conclusion can be reached with regard to the 1977 Protocol II to the Geneva Conventions of 12 August 1949 on humanitarian law,[53] article 16 of which, entitled "Protection of Cultural Objects and of Places of Worship," states that

"[w]ithout prejudice to the provisions of the Hague Convention for the Protection of Cultural Property in the Event of Armed Conflict of 14 May 1954, it is prohibited to commit any acts of hostility directed against historic monuments, works of art or places of worship which constitute the cultural or spiritual heritage of peoples, and to use them in support of the military effort."

Although, according to article I, this provision would be, in principle, applicable to the Afghan situation,[54] such an application is prevented by the fact that Afghanistan was not a party to the Protocol at the time of the destruction of the Buddhas.[55]

However, the absence of specific treaty obligations – except those deriving from the 1972 Convention – does not relieve the Taliban regime from international responsibility deriving from the destruction of the Buddhas of Bamiyan, under general norms of customary international law. Indeed, such responsibility may arise as a consequence of the breach of at least two customary norms that have been formed as a consequence of the international practice in the field of protection of cultural heritage.

In this sense, it is to be emphasized, at the general level, that the reconstruction of relevant customary international law is not simply an academic exercise; where such law is found to exist, it has practical implications. First of all, unlike treaty law, customary international law is *ex se* of binding character for all the countries of the world because it needs no formal acceptance by governments, whereas treaties must be ratified or acceded to by the state concerned in order to produce any binding effect for such a State. In practical terms, this means that the international community (*i.e.*, states and international organizations) may lawfully claim (and eventually enforce through the adoption of appropriate counter measures) respect for the relevant customary provisions *vis-à-vis* any government, irrespective of its formal acceptance of the relevant obligation. In addition, customary international law may generally be invoked before national courts as law applicable in the state concerned. For example, the U.S. Supreme Court has proclaimed since 1815 that courts are "bound by the law of nations, which is part of the law of the land,"[56] thus instructing national judges to routinely enforce customary international law. In a recent judgment, a District Court of New York applied such principle by stating that "Congress's failure to ratify [an international treaty is not sufficient to exempt the United States from the obligation to respect] the customary international law principles contained in and underlying [such a] treaty,"[57] thus confirming the assumption that, when a customary norm actually exists, states are bound to respect it irrespective of whether or not they have ratified the existing international conventions proclaiming the rule that corresponds to the content of the customary norm itself.

The first of the two customary norms banning the intentional destruction of cultural heritage is to be found in the principle according to which such heritage constitutes part of the general interest of the international community as a whole. This principle belongs to the general category of norms establishing *erga omnes* obligations, a category enunciated by the International Court of Justice in the well-known *Barcelona Traction* case.[58] In this case, the Court distinguished between norms that create bilateral obligations of reciprocal character, binding upon individual states *inter sé*, and norms that create international obligations *erga omnes*, or obligations owed to the generality of states in the public interest. This category comprises the norms concerning the prohibition of force, the protection of basic human rights, or the protection of the general environment against massive degradation. In our view, the prohibition of acts of willful and systematic destruction of cultural heritage of great importance for humanity also falls in the category of *erga omnes* obligations. There are several manifestations of international practice that confirm the existence of such obligation. As early as 1907, the Hague Conventions on land warfare and naval bombardment proclaimed the principle that historic

[51] Generally on the 1954 Convention, see Nalhik, *cit.*, note 44, p. 120 ff.; Panzera, *cit.*, note 44, p. 30 ff. and 72 ff.; Gioia, *cit.*, note 44, p. 76 ff.

[52] For the updated list of the parties to the 1954 Convention, see the UNESCO Web site, at <http://www.unesco.org/culture/laws>.

[53] See *Protocol Additional to the Geneva Conventions of 12 August 1949, and Relating to the Protection of Victims of Non-International Armed Conflicts (Protocol II)*, *UNTS*, vol. 1125, p. 609.

[54] See article I of the Protocol II, *cit. supra*, note 53.

[55] For the updated list of the parties to the Protocol II to the Geneva conventions on humanitarian law see the United Nations High Commissioner on Human Rights Web site, at <http://www.unhchr.ch>.

[56] See *The Neriede*, 13 U.S. 388, 423 (1815). See also *The Paquete Habana*, 175 U.S. 677, 700 (1900).

[57] See *Beharry v. Reno*, 183 F. Supp. 2d 584 (E.D.N.Y. 2002), p. 29.

[58] See *Barcelona Traction, Light and Power Co.* case, *ICJ Rep.*, 1970, 3, p. 33–4.

monuments and buildings dedicated to art and science ought to be spared by military violence.[59] The *Roerich* Pact of 1935 went further to proclaim the principle that museums, monuments, and scientific and cultural institutions are to be protected as part of "common heritage of all people."[60] UNESCO has systematically restated this principle since the early 1950s. One can cite, among the several pertinent UNESCO recommendations,[61] the 1956 Recommendation on International Principles Applicable to Archeological Excavations,[62] and the Preamble, as well as Article 4, of the 1954 Hague Convention on the Protection of Cultural Property in the Event of Armed Conflicts.[63] More specifically, the idea of an international public interest in safeguarding cultural heritage is expressed by the 1972 World Heritage Convention, the Preamble of which states that

"the existing international conventions, recommendations and resolutions concerning cultural and natural property demonstrate the importance, for all the peoples of the world, of safeguarding this unique and irreplaceable property, to whatever people it may belong [...] [P]arts of the cultural or natural heritage are of outstanding interest and therefore need to be preserved as part of the world heritage of mankind as a whole."

A duty to preserve, and *a fortiori* not to deliberately destroy cultural heritage is also contemplated by the 1972 UNESCO Recommendation concerning the Protection, at National Level, of The Cultural and Natural Heritage.[64] The Preamble of this Recommendation states that

"every country in whose territory there are components of the cultural [...] heritage has an obligation to safeguard this part of mankind's heritage and to ensure that it is handed down to future generations."

and that

"knowledge and protection of the cultural [...] heritage in the various countries of the world are conducive to mutual understanding among the peoples."

If one considers the very high rate of ratification to the World Heritage Convention,[65] as well as the authoritative character of UNESCO recommendations, which really represent the near totality of the nations of the world that participate in the General Conference, it is not possible to deny that a general *opinio juris* exists in the international community on the binding character of the principles prohibiting deliberate destruction of cultural heritage of significant importance for humanity. This conclusion is reinforced by the fact that protection of cultural heritage as a matter of public interest, and not only as part of private property rights, is recognized in most of the mature domestic legal systems of the world. No civilized state, in the sense of article 38(c) of the Statute of the International Court of Justice, recognizes the right of the private owner of an important work of art to destroy it as part of the exercise of a supposedly unlimited right of private property. Catalogues and inventories of national treasures are generally intended to limit such private rights in view of safeguarding the public interest to the conservation and transmission of the cultural patrimony to future generations.[66] In the case of the Buddhas of Bamiyan, the injury to the international public interest, which consisted in the conservation of the monuments and in the prevention of their destruction, was all the more apparent because: (a) the destruction was motivated by invidious and discriminatory intent; (b) it was systematic; and (c) it was carried out in blatant defiance of the appeals coming from UNESCO, the UN,[67] ICOMOS, and many individual states.

The second customary principle pertinent to the present inquiry relates to the prohibition of acts of violence against cultural heritage in the event of armed conflicts.[68] Such a principle may be based on a consistent and unambiguous practice, which is demonstrated by the developments of international law in this field subsequent to the Hague conventions on the laws and customs of war. Besides the 1954 Hague Convention cited earlier,[69] one must consider the provision of article 53 of the 1977 Protocol I to the Geneva Conventions of 12 August 1949, relating to international armed conflicts, which states that

"[w]ithout prejudice to the provisions of the Hague Convention for the Protection of Cultural Property in the Event of Armed Conflict

[59] See respectively articles 27 and 56 of the Regulations annexed to The Hague Convention IV and article 5 of the Convention (IX) concerning Bombardment by Naval Forces in Time of War, *supra*, note 46.

[60] See *supra*, note 49.

[61] For a detailed examination of the relevant part of these recommendations, see Francioni, *cit.*, note 44, p. 152 f.; id., "Principi e criteri ispiratori per la protezione internazionale del patrimonio culturale," in Francioni, Del Vecchio, and De Caterini (eds.), *cit.*, note 44, p. 14 f. (the author notes that the relevance of these recommendations, for the formation of a customary norm in the field, is given by their reiterate repetition and by the fact that they are adopted by the UNESCO General Conference, which represents almost all members of the international community).

[62] 1956 UNESCO *Recommendation on International Principles Applicable to Archeological Excavations*, available in the UNESCO Web site, at <http://www.unesco.org/culture/laws/archaeological/html_eng/page1.shtml> (see, in particular, the fourth sentence of the Preamble).

[63] See *supra*, note 50.

[64] 1972 UNESCO *Recommendation concerning the Protection, at National Level, of The Cultural and Natural Heritage*, available at the UNESCO Web site, at <http://www.unesco.org/culture/laws/national/html_eng/page1.shtml>.

[65] The 1972 World Heritage Convention has been ratified by 178 states (updated 1 May 2004); see <http://www.unesco.org/whc/nwhc/pages/doc/main.htm>.

[66] See Sax J. L., *Playing Darts with a Rembrandt: Public and Private Rights in Cultural Treasures*, Ann Arbor, 1999.

[67] See *supra*, note 5.

[68] See Nahlik, *cit.*, note 44, pp. 89 and 145; Frigo M., *La protezione dei beni culturali nel diritto internazionale*, Milano, 1986, p. 62 ff.; Francioni, *cit.*, note 61, p. 13 ff.; Carducci G., "L'obligation de restitution des biens culturels et des objectes d'art en cas de conflit armé: droit coutumier et droit coventionel avant et après la Convention de La Haye de 1954," *RGDIP*, 2000, p. 289 ff.

[69] The 1954 Convention for the Protection of Cultural Property in the Event of Armed Conflicts has been ratified by 103 States, the 1977 Protocol II to the 1949 Geneva Conventions on humanitarian law by 152, and the 1977 Protocol I (see *infra*, note 70), by 159; see <http://www.icrc.org/ihl.nsf> (last checked on 7 August 2002).

of 14 May 1954, and of other relevant international instruments, it is prohibited: (a) to commit any acts of hostility directed against the historic monuments, works of art or places of worship which constitute the cultural or spiritual heritage of peoples; (b) to use such objects in support of the military effort; (c) to make such objects the object of reprisals."[70]

In addition, the acts of "seizure of, destruction or wilful damage done to institutions dedicated to religion, charity and education, the arts and sciences, historic monuments and works of art and science" are included by article 3(d) of the Statute of the International Criminal Tribunal for the Former Yugoslavia (ICTY) among the violations of the law or customs of war.[71] A similar approach is followed by the Statute of the International Criminal Court, whose articles 8(b)(IX) and 8(c)(IV), concerning, respectively, international and non-international armed conflicts, qualify as war crime any intentional attack directed, *inter alia*, against buildings dedicated to religious, educational, artistic, or humanitarian purposes, or historical monuments.[72] Finally, article 20(e)(iv) of the 1996 International Law Commission *Draft Code of Crimes Against the Peace and Security of Mankind* includes among war crimes all acts of "seizure of, destruction of or willful damage done to institutions dedicated to religion, charity and education, the arts and sciences, historic monuments and works of art and science."[73]

The customary character of the prohibition of destruction of cultural heritage (more precisely "destruction or willful damage to institutions dedicated to religion") during armed conflicts has been expressly confirmed by the ICTY in a recent judgment, in which both defendants, Dario Kordic and Mario Cerkez, have been found guilty of such a crime against cultural property because of their deliberate, armed attacks on ancient mosques of Bosnia Herzegovina.[74] According to the Tribunal, the act in point,

"when perpetrated with the requisite discriminatory intent, amounts to an attack on the very religious identity of a people. As such, it manifests a nearly pure expression of the notion of 'crimes against humanity', for all of humanity is indeed injured by the destruction of a unique religious culture and its concomitant cultural objects [...] [thus] amount[ing] to an act of persecution."[75]

The Hague Tribunal thus holds that this kind of crime may amount to an act of persecution included in the concept of "crimes against humanity" provided for by article 5(h) of the Statute.[76] In doing so, the Tribunal confirmed what it had already stated in one of its earlier judgements.[77] The same conclusion had been previously reached by the Nuremberg International Military Tribunal[78] and the International Law Commission.[79]

In addition, with regard to the shelling of the old town of Dubrovnik performed by the Yugoslav Forces on 6 December 1991, the ICTY held that

"the crime of destruction or wilful damage done to institutions dedicated to religion, charity, education, and the arts and sciences, and to historic monuments and works of art and science [...] represents a violation of values especially protected by the international community,"[80]

adding that

"the shelling attack on the Old Town was an attack not only against the history and heritage of the region, but also against the cultural heritage of humankind[81] [...] since it is a serious violation of international humanitarian law to attack civilian buildings, it is a crime of even greater seriousness to direct an attack on an especially protected site, such as the Old Town."[82]

There is a strong argument to hold that the description of the crime against culture as persecution, given by the ICTY in *Prosecutor v. Dario Kordic and Mario Cerkez*,[83] should also fit the factual situation with the case of the destruction of the Afghan cultural heritage perpetrated by the Taliban. In such a case, the discriminatory intent of destroying all signs of religions different from Islamism was declared by the Taliban themselves.[84]

We are aware that two objections may be raised with regard to our characterization of the destruction of the Buddhas of Bamiyan as an internationally wrongful act. The first stems from the circumstance that the practice cited earlier, especially the case law of the ICTY, relates to *individual criminal liability* and not to state responsibility. This is true. However, the objection is not persuasive, because, quite apart from

[70] See *Protocol Additional to the Geneva Convention of 12 August 1949, and relating to the Protection of Victims of International Armed Conflicts (Protocol I), UNTS*, vol. 1125, p. 5.

[71] The text of the Statute is available at <http://www.un.org/icty/basic/statut/statute.htm>.

[72] For the text of the Statute see *ILM*, 1998, p. 999 ff.

[73] The text of the Draft Code is available at <http://www.un.org/law/ilc/texts/dcode.htm>.

[74] See *Prosecutor v. Dario Kordic and Mario Cerkez*, judgement of 26 February 2001 (Trial Chamber), available in the ICTY Web site, at <http://www.un.org/icty> (see also the judgement of the Appeals Chamber of 17 December 2004, available at <http://www.un.org/icty/kordic/appeal/judgement/cer-aj041217e.pdf>); see, in particular, par. 206, in which the Trial Chamber states that the act of destruction or wilful damage to institutions dedicated to religion "has [...] already been criminalised under customary international law."

[75] *Id.*, par. 207.

[76] See *supra*, note 71.

[77] See *Prosecutor v. Tihomir Blaskic*, judgement of 3 March 2000, par. 227, available in the ICTY Web site, <http://www.un.org/icty>.

[78] See *Nuremberg Judgement*, pp. 248 and 302, quoted by the ICTY in *Prosecutor v. Dario Kordic and Mario Cerkez, cit.*, note 74, par. 206, note 267.

[79] See *Report of the International Law Commission on the work of its 43rd session*, 29 April–19 June 1991, doc. A/46/10/Suppl.10, p. 268, according to which the "systematic destruction of monuments or buildings representative of a particular social, religious, cultural or other group" is included in the concept of persecution.

[80] See *Prosecutor v. Miodrag Jokic*, judgment of 18 March 2004, available at <http://www.un.org/icty>, par. 46 (emphasis added).

[81] *Id.*, par. 51 (emphasis added).

[82] *Id.*, par. 53. The Old Town of Dubrovnik is inscribed in the UNESCO World Heritage List since 1979 (see <http://whc.unesco.org/sites/95.htm>).

[83] See *supra*, text corresponding to note 75.

[84] See *supra*, text corresponding to note 32.

the position one takes on the controversial problem whether individual criminal liability is an aspect of state responsibility or is totally autonomous,[85] it is clear that, in the case of the destruction of the Buddhas, the individual acts and the state conduct are one and the same, and form the inseparable elements of a single criminal design. The second possible objection could be that the alleged applicability of the prohibition of intentional destruction of cultural heritage is limited to international wars, to situations of military occupation of foreign territory, and should not be applicable to noninternational armed conflicts. This objection also is unfounded. The universal value of cultural heritage seems to exclude such a conceptual discrimination. In the last decades, international practice has extended the application of all main principles of humanitarian law, originally provided for international armed conflicts, to civil wars, ethnic conflicts, and conflicts of a noninternational character. This is apparent in the text of the 1999 Second Protocol to the 1954 Hague Convention[86] as well as in the recent statutes of international criminal tribunals.[87] The customary character of international rules protecting cultural heritage in internal armed conflicts has also been expressly confirmed by the ICTY in the foremost *Tadic* case, specifically referring to "Article 19 of the Hague Convention for the Protection of Cultural Property in the Event of Armed Conflict of 14 May 1954."[88]

If customary prohibition of deliberate destruction of cultural heritage of great significance for humanity exists in the event of internal conflicts, it would, indeed, be nonsense to maintain that similar intentional acts of destruction are permitted in times of peace.[89]

To conclude, the willful and discriminatory destruction of the great Buddhas of Bamiyan perpetrated by the Taliban in March 2001 constitutes a breach of the customary international law forbidding wanton destruction of cultural heritage. Additionally, the destruction in point entailed a specific breach of the World Heritage Convention commitment to ensure protection of cultural heritage situated in the territory of parties.[90]

Because international norms applicable to cultural heritage consider the destruction of any nation's cultural property as a loss and an injury to the collective patrimony of humankind's civilization, the deliberate devastation of cultural heritage of great significance for humanity entails a violation of an international obligation having *erga omnes* character. In the Afghan case, the *erga omnes* character of such obligation was confirmed by the fact that, although there was no directly and materially injured third state, because the act of violence was committed in the territory and against a value pertaining to the transgressor state as such, there was unanimous protest by the international community, including foreign governments and international organizations, against the destruction of the Buddhas. The customary obligation in point has the scope of limiting the power that the territorial state has over assets located within the sphere of its sovereignty, and it exists toward the international community as a whole, and thus, *a fortiori*, toward all states.

Such principle has been confirmed by the text and the spirit of the *Declaration Concerning the Intentional Destruction of Cultural Heritage*, adopted by the UNESCO General Conference on 17 October 2003, precisely as a reaction to the destruction of the two giant Buddhas of Bamiyan.[91] The first sentence of the Preamble affirms that the destruction of the Buddhas "affected the international community as a whole."[92] The sixth sentence reiterates, "one of the fundamental principles of the Preamble of the 1954 Hague Convention for the Protection of Cultural Property in the Event of Armed Conflict," according to which "damage to cultural property belonging to any people whatsoever means damage to the cultural heritage of all mankind." Article I affirms the recognition by the international community of "the importance of the protection of cultural heritage," and its commitment "to fight against its intentional destruction" in view of ensuring its transmission to "the succeeding generations." To this end, Article III recommends States to take "all appropriate measures to prevent, avoid, stop and suppress acts of intentional destruction of cultural heritage, *wherever such heritage is located*";[93] such duty is to be complied both in peacetime[94] and in the event of armed

[85] For a thorough discussion of this problem, with different conclusions, see Dupuy P. M., "International Criminal Responsibility and the Individual and International Responsibility of the State," in Cassese A., Gaeta P., and Jones J. R. W. D., *The Rome Statute of the International Criminal Court: A Commentary*, Oxford, 2002, p. 1085 ff.; Maison R., "La Responsabilité individuelle pour crime d'État en droit international public," thesis at the University of Paris, 2 January 2000, *passim*.

[86] *Second Protocol to the Hague Convention of 1954 for the Protection of Cultural Property in the Event of Armed Conflict*, in *ILM*, 1999, p. 769, particularly article 22.1.

[87] See, for example, the statutes of the International Criminal Tribunal for the Former Yugoslavia (*supra*, note 71), the International Criminal Tribunal for Rwanda (available at <http://www.ictr.org>), and the International Criminal Court (*supra*, note 72). See also the case law of the ICTY, especially the definition of armed conflict given by the Tribunal in *Prosecutor v. Dusko Tadic* (Appeal Chamber, 2 October 1995), in 35 *ILM* 1996, p. 32, paragraphs 66–70.

[88] See *Prosecutor v. Dusko Tadic, cit.*, note 87, par. 98.

[89] See Lenzerini F., "The UNESCO Declaration Concerning the Intentional Destruction of Cultural Heritage: One Step Forward and Two Steps Back," in 13(2003) *Italian Yearbook of International Law*, 2005, p. 131 ff.

[90] See the Preamble, article 4 and article 12 of the World Heritage Convention, *supra*, note 38.

[91] The full text of the Declaration is available in the UNESCO Web site, at <http://www.unesco.org>; for a critical comment see Lenzerini, *cit.*, note 89, *passim*.

[92] The very first sentence of the Preamble reads as follows: "[r]ecalling the tragic destruction of the Buddhas of Bamiyan that affected the international community as a whole." As already noted, the first version of the present chapter was elaborated, on a request of UNESCO, as a report having the purpose of investigating the status of international law concerning the matter of the deliberate destruction of cultural heritage in view of defining, at a preliminary stage, the possible content of an international instrument condemning such a kind of act; the 2003 UNESCO Declaration is actually that instrument.

[93] Emphasis added.

[94] See Article IV.

conflict ("in conformity with customary international law"), including the cases of internal wars and occupation.[95] The Declaration also affirms the responsibility of every State that "intentionally destroys or intentionally fails to take appropriate measures to prohibit, prevent, stop, and punish any intentional destruction of cultural heritage of great importance for humanity,"[96] as well as individuals who perform or order to be committed acts of deliberate destruction of such heritage.[97]

The deliberate and systematic destruction of cultural properties of pre-Islamic Afghanistan and, more particularly, of the Bamiyan Buddhas, in so far as this heritage constituted a representation of both a religious belief and the cultural identity of a people, could finally be envisaged as a violation of certain human rights; namely, the right to the preservation of one's own culture and the right to practice and obtain respect of one's own religion.[98] The destruction of religious symbols certainly is inconsistent with the obligation to respect cultural diversity and with religious toleration. These arguments remain valid, for even if the Buddhas of Bamiyan were no longer actively functional to the practice of religious rights, they nevertheless embodied an important testimony of past religious traditions and of cultural exchange among the peoples of Asia.

THE DUTY TO "PREVENT" AND "AVOID" DEVASTATION OF CULTURAL HERITAGE: OCCUPYING FORCES AND IRAQI CULTURAL TREASURES

As pointed out in the previous section, Article III of the UNESCO Declaration Concerning the Intentional Destruction of Cultural Heritage affirms the duty of States to, *inter alia*, prevent and avoid acts of intentional destruction of cultural heritage, irrespective of where such heritage is located. Article V then adds that such a duty exists also in the case of military occupation.

In this respect, the case of the devastation of the Iraqi National Museum of Baghdad and the arson of the Iraqi National Library, perpetrated in April 2003 after the entry of the U.S. forces in the city, is worth mentioning.[99] Absolutely priceless cultural treasures were conserved in such institutions, such as irreplaceable artifacts of Sumerian, Akkadian, Babylonian, Assyrian, and Arab art, including the Uruk vase (dating from 3500 B.C.) and artifacts excavated from the ancient Sumerian city of Ur, as well as thousands of Islamic ancient manuscripts. Many of these treasures have probably been irremediably lost as a result of the devastation of the National Museum and National Library. Although, properly speaking, the case of the Iraqi National Museum was a case of looting and not exactly of intentional destruction as such, it had, nevertheless, the actual effect of a severe loss of cultural treasures which, given their outstanding value, should be preserved in the interest of humanity as a whole. One may argue that such loss is equivalent to destruction both in terms of similar ideological condemnation and in terms of intolerability of the effects produced. It is thus not illogical to maintain that the legal regime provided for the cases of destruction of cultural heritage also extends to failure to prevent looting or any other form of annihilation of such heritage. As for the arson of the National Library, there is no doubt that it is precisely included in the concept of destruction of cultural heritage dealt with by the UNESCO Declaration.

Having this in mind, the core legal problem related to the devastation of the Iraqi cultural heritage consists of ascertaining whether and to what extent the occupying military forces can be considered responsible for such devastation according to relevant international law, as illustrated in the previous paragraph. In this regard, the obligation of occupying forces to preserve the integrity of local heritage derives not only from international principles applicable to intentional destruction, but also from the law concerning the protection of cultural heritage in the event of armed conflict. In particular, article 4, par. 3, of the 1954 Hague Convention imposes upon states parties the obligation of prohibiting, preventing, and putting a stop "to any form of theft, pillage or misappropriation of, and any acts of vandalism directed against, cultural property."[100] Although the United States is not party to the Hague Convention,[101] the content of the provision just reproduced corresponds to an obligation existing under customary international law.[102] This is confirmed by the treatment that U.S. war manuals reserve to these obligations as part of customary law.[103] If this is correct, then the question arises

[95] See Article V.

[96] See Article VI. The provision specifies that such responsibility exists irrespective of the fact that the cultural heritage concerned "is inscribed on a list maintained by UNESCO or another international organization."

[97] See Article VII (containing the same specification included in Article VI; see the previous note).

[98] The freedom of religion, which includes the right to freely manifest one's own religion in worship, observance, practice, and teaching, is stated by the main international conventional instruments on human rights; see, *inter alia*, article 18(1) of the 1966 *International Covenant on Civil and Political Rights* (UNTS, vol. 999, p. 171 ff.), article 9(1) of the 1950 *European Convention on Human Rights* (*European Treaty Series*, No. 5), and article 12(1) of the 1969 *American Convention on Human Rights* (*O.A.S. Treaty Series* No. 36). See also article 18 of the *Universal Declaration of Human Rights* and the UN *Declaration on the Elimination of All Forms of Intolerance and of Discrimination Based on Religion and Belief* (General Assembly res. 36/55 of 25 November 1981, available at <http://www.unhchr.ch/html/menu/3/b/d_intole.htm>.

[99] On this case see Francioni F., "Guerra e patrimonio culturale," in *Il Giornale dell'Arte*, June 2003, p. 1; Phuong C., "The Protection of Iraqi Cultural Property," in 53 *ICLQ*, 2004, p. 985 ff.

[100] See *supra*, note 50.

[101] See <http://erc.unesco.org/cp/convention.asp?KO=13637&language=E> (updated 17 November 2004).

[102] See Phuong, *cit.*, note 100, p. 987.

[103] Incidentally, the U.S. Government not only has signed the 1954 Hague Convention, but has also expressed the intention to proceed to its ratification by transmitting its text to the Senate, where consent to ratification has been pending for a while.

whether the United States' conduct, at the relevant time, involved a breach of its duty to prevent the looting to Iraqi cultural heritage. On the other hand, one must ask whether inaction of U.S. forces in preventing the devastation of Iraqi cultural heritage could be excused, thus excluding responsibility, in consideration of the possibility that the fighting taking place in Iraq at the relevant time could be so severe to materially preclude the U.S. army from having the chance of ensuring protection of cultural institutions in Baghdad. In this context, one must consider that U.S. forces did not arrive at the National Museum until 16 April 2003, whereas its looting took place between 8 and 12 April.[104] Was this attributable to negligence or to the actual impossibility of reaching the museum in time for preventing its devastation? This is a problem of fact on which there is disagreement. According to some sources, the American soldiers arrived in the place where the museum is located after many journalists were already there;[105] others maintain that the museum was being used by the Iraqi forces as a military position.[106] Of course, if the first set of facts is true, the United States could be considered responsible for failing to prevent the devastation of Iraqi cultural institutions because they actually had the means and material chance of preventing the pillaging and destruction of cultural treasures by swifter action and failed to do so. If on the other the museum was used by the Iraqi army for military defense,[107] then it is difficult to hold the United States responsible for negligent conduct since Iraqi resistance rendered impossible a timely advance to prevent the devastation of Iraqi cultural heritage: an outright attack on the museum and other cultural institutions if in fact such institution supported belligerent activities would have only worsened the degree of such devastation.

CONCLUSION

Destruction and dispersion of cultural heritage in recent years have caused not only shock and condemnation within the international community, but also a progressive development of pertinent international law. Individual states; international organizations, such as the United Nations and UNESCO; religious authorities, including some of the most influential Islamic authorities; NGOs; and people all over the world have called for international mobilisation against such acts of barbarity and religious intolerance such as the bombing of the Buddhas of Bamiyan. Is this sufficient to render such acts contrary to contemporary international law? This chapter has tried to provide a preliminary assessment of this question in light of contemporary international practice: the conclusion reached is rather promising. As in the area of fundamental human rights, first, and in the area of environmental protection, later, states may no longer invoke their sovereignty and domestic jurisdiction in order to justify acts of deliberate destruction of cultural heritage of great importance for humanity as a whole. Our analysis has tried to demonstrate also that, when such destruction is associated with the intent to discriminate or annihilate another religion and its forms of cultural expression, then the act amounts also to an attack on the very identity of the targeted people and religion and thus on the dignity and fundamental rights of its members. As the ICTY recently confirmed, such discriminatory destruction "[. . .] manifests a nearly pure expression of the notion of 'crimes against humanity', for all of humanity is indeed injured."[108] It is therefore rather evident that deliberate destruction of cultural heritage is a matter of concern not only for the people who own that heritage, but for humanity as a whole, and its perpetration entails a violation of an *erga omnes* obligations that each state is bound to respect *vis-a-vis* any other country and the international community as a whole.

QUESTIONS FOR DISCUSSION

1. Why should international law prohibit a state from destroying cultural property that is disliked or disapproved (see the destruction of monuments memorializing oppressive dictators, racism, or slavery)?

2. What is the status of customary international law concerning the intentional destruction of cultural heritage?

3. Why is it important that intentional destruction of cultural heritage is prohibited by customary international law besides international conventions?

4. Which objections could be raised with regard to the characterization of the destruction of the Buddhas of Bamiyan as an internationally wrongful act?

5. In what sense may the state obligation of refraining from and preventing destruction of cultural heritage of universal value be considered as having *erga omnes* character?

6. Which conditions should be satisfied in order to consider the occupying military forces responsible of the devastation of Iraqi cultural heritage?

[104] See Phuong, *cit.*, note 100, p. 985.

[105] See Hassan G., "The Pillage of Iraq," 7 July 2004, at <http://www.countercurrents.org/iraq-hassan070704.htm>, and the sources cited therein; in particular, according to the Middle East correspondent Robert Fisk, who witnessed the pillage himself, "US troops [. . .] did nothing to prevent looters from destroying priceless treasures of Iraq's history in the Baghdad Museum and in the museum in the northern city of Mosul, or from looting three hospitals," showing concern only for "the Ministry of Interior, of course – with its vast wealth of intelligence information on Iraq – and the Ministry of oil."

[106] See Phuong, *cit.*, note 100, p. 987.

[107] See Francioni, *cit.*, note 100, who emphasizes the fact that this possibility is not so implausible, given the reiterated practice of the Iraqi government led by Saddam Hussein to systematically place military objectives in the proximity of protected places such as hospitals as well as religious and cultural institutions.

[108] See *supra*, text corresponding to note 75.

USEFUL WEB SITE LINKS

http://portal.unesco.org/en/ev.php-URL_ID=12024&URL_DO=DO_TOPIC&URL_SECTION=201.html
(UNESCO Legal Instruments: International Conventions, Recommendations and Declarations concerning the protection of cultural heritage)

http://whc.unesco.org
(World Heritage Committee's home page)

http://whc.unesco.org/pg.cfm?cid=31&id_site=208
(World Heritage List: Cultural Landscape and Archaeological Remains of the Bamiyan Valley's page)

http://www.icrc.org/ihl
(International Committee of the Red Cross Treaty Database on International Humanitarian Law: all relevant treaties in full text, including ratification lists and search engine)

http://www.un.org/icty
(Web site of the International Criminal Tribunal for the Former Yugoslavia, including full text of judgements concerning destruction of cultural heritage)

CHAPTER THREE

Beyond Bamiyan: Will the World Be Ready Next Time?

James Cuno

A month after the destruction of the Bamiyan Buddhas, and in the company of the Taliban ministers of information and culture and of finance, several men with sledgehammers destroyed much of what remained of the collections of the National Museum of Afghanistan in Kabul. For those of us that read of this destruction, it was just as sad as the destruction of the Buddhas themselves.

The Kabul museum was the primary repository of the aesthetic and cultural achievement of the people that lived and traveled on the crossroads of Asia for thousands of years. All that remains of this once-renowned museum are the ghostly accounts of its installations in guidebooks from the 1970s and its description by Harvard professor Benjamin Rowland in the Asia House Gallery exhibition catalogue of 1966, Ancient Art from Afghanistan: Treasures of the Kabul Museum. There Professor Rowland wrote that

> "the single greatest discovery of the French [Archaeological] Mission [in Afghanistan], the treasure of Begram, comprising an amazing collection of Graeco-Roman sculpture and artifacts, Indian ivories, and Chinese lacquers, is displayed in one of the most beautiful installations to be seen in any museum in the world."

Years of civil war, bombardment, looting, neglect, and, most recently, iconoclastic hysteria, have reduced that once proud museum to a nearly empty shell. And now, reportedly, above its front door, frayed and flapping in the wind, hangs a banner that reads: "A nation stays alive when its culture stays alive."

This chapter focuses on the role of the museum after Bamiyan; that is to say, on the museum as an internationalist, preservationist institution in an age of resurgent nationalism. First, however, let me draw your attention to the promiscuous use by governments and international organizations of the terms archaeological artifacts and cultural property. Sometimes they are used to mean the same thing, and sometimes they are used to mean two very different kinds of things. The slippage between the two is crucial and almost always ideological. This is particularly important when one considers national policies – starting with those of the United States – with regard to the international exchange of archaeological artifacts and cultural property.[1]

The U.S. Department of State is responsible for implementing the Convention on Cultural Property Implementation Act. This is the enabling legislation for the 1970 UNESCO Convention on the Means of Prohibiting and Preventing the Illicit Import, Export and Transfer of Ownership of Cultural Property. In accordance with the Act, the Department of State accepts requests from countries for import restrictions on archaeological or ethnological artifacts, the pillage of which places their national cultural heritage in jeopardy. The Cultural Property Advisory Committee, appointed by the president of the United States, reviews these requests and makes recommendations to the Department of State. Under the president's authority, the Department of State makes a decision with regard to the request and may enter into a cultural property agreement with the requesting country. The cultural property staff supports these functions and related activities and serves as a centre of expertise on global cultural heritage protection issues.

On 19 January, 2001, the United States and Italy entered into a bilateral agreement under this provision of the Convention on Cultural Property Implementation Act to restrict the import into the United States of archaeological material from Italy that dates from the pre-Classical, Classical, and Imperial Roman periods, approximately covering the period between the ninth century B.C. and the fourth century A.D. The import of an article subject to this agreement into the United States from Italy will require certification or other documentation demonstrating that the article was not exported in violation of the laws of Italy.

It is hard to accept that all these objects are worthy of such restriction because they are important archaeologically or as cultural property, unless, of course, one believes that every old object is by definition of archaeological value or that every old object is culturally important to the people who now reside within the political boundaries of the country in which it was found. This is more or less what the U.S.–Italian Memorandum of Understanding does: it subsumes archaeological artifacts under the category of cultural property and assumes that everything – or almost everything – found or likely to have been found in Italy (given that this is almost always a judgment call and not a matter of fact), whether it was produced or imported there, is cultural property and thus crucial to the national identity and self-esteem of the Italian people.

[1] Of critical importance here is the distinction between cultural patrimony and cultural property. Article 1 of the UNESCO Convention defines cultural property broadly as "products of archaeological excavation . . . ; elements of artistic or historical monuments or archaeological sites which have been dismembered; antiquities more than one hundred years old, such as inscriptions, coins and engraved seals . . . ; [and] property of artistic interest." Differences between cultural property and cultural patrimony are often confused in these respects. Common sense would hold that cultural patrimony is a subset of cultural property. For example, all old bells are cultural property but the Liberty Bell is cultural patrimony. Cultural patrimony, in other words, suggests a level of importance greater than that of cultural property. It is not something owned by a people, but something of them, a part of their defining collective identity.

For example, the Memorandum states that (1) "the value of cultural property, whether archaeological or ethnological in nature, is immeasurable . . . such items often constitute the very essence of a society and convey important information concerning a people's origin, history, and traditional setting"; (2) "these materials are of cultural significance because they derive from cultures that developed autonomously in the region of present day Italy . . . the pillage of these materials from their context has prevented the fullest possible understanding of Italian cultural history by systematically destroying the archaeological record"; and (3) "the cultural patrimony represented by these materials is a source of identity and esteem for the modern Italian nation."

In other words, as the Memorandum of Understanding would have it, the destruction of the archaeological record in modern-day Italy is problematic not because the world has lost vital information about humanity and about the way our ancestors lived and ornamented their lives thousands of years ago, but because without it, "the fullest possible understanding of Italian cultural history" is impossible, and because the lost materials are "a source of identity and esteem for the modern Italian nation." The Memorandum's line of reasoning runs counter to the intentions of the 1983 legislation. It favors the retention of cultural property (of which it considers archaeological artifacts but a part) by modern nation states for the benefit of local peoples over the international exchange of archaeological artifacts and cultural property for the benefit of the world's peoples.

The stated policy of the United States is internationalist with regard to its own cultural property. The United States believes that exposure to works of art from the world's many cultures promotes cultural understanding, and it has made few laws restricting the export of its cultural property, limiting such laws to the protection of historically, architecturally, or archaeologically significant objects on land that is owned, controlled, or acquired by the federal government.

Other nations, like Italy, are nationalist in their cultural policy, restricting the export of objects found on their soil, whether on private or public land, because they are by definition state property and not private property. The unlicensed export of such objects therefore constitutes theft under Italian law. To be fair, as stated in the U.S.–Italian memorandum of understanding, Italy claims to permit "the interchange of archaeological materials for cultural, exhibition, education and scientific purposes." In practice, however, Italy almost never grants export licenses and limits the length of time an object can be on loan outside of Italy – if it may be loaned at all – to 12 months. Still, on the face of it, a loan policy of any kind would appear to be reasonable, even generous. It allows a nation to retain possession of its archaeological and cultural heritage, while sharing that heritage with the rest of the world on a temporary basis. But can one really expect a nation to risk loaning important archaeological material or rare, fragile cultural property? By definition, important archaeological material and rare, fragile cultural property are almost always too important to loan. In other words, Italy's promises to be more generous with the loan of archaeologically significant or culturally important objects means very little. It already has what it wants: a bilateral agreement with the U.S. government that affirms its nationalist policies.

So, what does all this mean for museums, which, as mentioned earlier, are internationalist, preservationist institutions, in an age of resurgent nationalism? As a partial answer to this question, a recent book by Patrick Geary of Princeton University, entitled *The Myth of Nations: The Medieval Origins of Europe*, is to be recommended. In his book, Professor Geary explores the role played by the academic discipline of history in defining nations and substantiating their nationalist claims. At one point, he writes:

> "Modern history was born in the nineteenth century, conceived and developed as an instrument of European nationalism. As a tool of nationalist ideology, the history of Europe's nations was a great success, but it has turned our understanding of the past into a toxic waste dump, filled with the poison of ethnic nationalism, and the poison has seeped deep into popular consciousness. Clearing up this waste is the most daunting challenge facing historians today."

It could be argued that museums face a similar challenge.

Museums are manifestly internationalist institutions. They were conceived as museums, as repositories of the world's greatest artistic achievements and of information about these achievements and the world in general. They were not conceived as national galleries, as collections of a nation's greatest art or artistic legacy. They were meant to collect, preserve, exhibit, and research the world's greatest artifacts forever and for everybody. And this was not imperialist looting. As Neil MacGregor, Director of the British Museum, likes to say, the British Museum is not an imperialist institution but an enlightened one, founded not at the height of the British Empire but in the middle of the eighteenth century, and dedicated not to the possession of the world's greatest objects but to protecting, studying, and providing informed and unfettered public access to them.

What is most worrisome about the language of the U.S.–Italian Memorandum of Understanding, the UNESCO Convention, and much of current political debate on the collection of antiquities by museums is, as already mentioned, the promiscuous slippage between the concepts of archaeological knowledge and cultural property. If only current international agreements were intended to preserve archaeological knowledge. If only they were meant to make sure that we know where the world's archaeological objects were found and that its archaeological sites are preserved. But they are not. They are intended instead to preserve the integrity of one nation's cultural property at the expense of the world's interest in international exchange. The most chilling part of Professor Rowland's introduction to the Asia House Gallery's exhibition of ancient art from the Kabul museum is his statement that

"... the fragmented beauties of thousands of years of Afghan history are represented in the collection of the Kabul Museum, an institution unique in the world in being composed entirely of objects acquired, not by purchase, but by excavations in the native soil."

In accordance with Afghan policy, the Kabul museum's collections comprised objects excavated in Afghanistan and kept within its political borders. As previous policies had allowed half the finds to go to the Musée Guimet, objects found on Afghan soil were subsequently considered property of the state and nonexportable. This is the policy advocated by UNESCO not only in Afghanistan – where the results have been so tragic – but everywhere where there are excavations or archaeological materials. In 1956, for example, UNESCO policy stated that

"Finds should be used in the first place, for building up, in the museums of the country in which excavations are carried out, complete collections fully representative of that country's civilization, history, art and architecture."

It did, however, concede that

"With the main object of promoting archaeological studies through the distribution of original material, the conceding authority, after scientific publication, might consider allocating to the approved excavator a number of finds from his excavation, consisting of duplicates or, in a more general sense, of objects or groups of objects which can be released in view of their similarity to other objects from the same excavation."

This is the kind of policy that kept the excavated artifacts in the Kabul museum at risk. The result is the almost total loss of the collection.

Early in the twentieth century, it was common practice for local governments to share archaeological finds with excavating parties, whatever their country of origin. This practice, called partage, meant that the world's greatest museums – whether in Paris, Berlin, London, New York, Boston, or Philadelphia – were able to preserve finds from excavations undertaken elsewhere, not just for the benefit of local audiences but for the benefit of all. As an example, Harvard University is opening an exhibition later this spring entitled Treasures from the Royal Tombs of Ur, which comes from the University of Pennsylvania Museum of Archaeology and Anthropology. It was shown two years ago at the Morgan Library in New York and comprises objects excavated by the University of Pennsylvania and the British Museum 80 years ago in what is now Iraq. What would the fate of these objects have been had they stayed in Iraq? It is hard to say, but it is clear that for much of the last quarter century they would have been inaccessible to most of the world, which would therefore not have had the chance to learn from them and to better appreciate their beauty and sophistication and the extraordinary abilities of their ancient makers.

The fact that they are in Philadelphia and have been there for decades at the University of Pennsylvania, where they have been studied by countless students and scholars and enjoyed by even more children and interested adults, as well as the fact that they have been preserved and documented and, for the past two years, have toured the United States, means that many more people have had access to these objects – and still more will – than would have been the case if they had remained in Iraq (and it is far from clear whether they would even have survived there).

One thing is clear and has been proved time and time again, not just in Iraq but also, most dramatically, in Kabul: archaeological objects and excavation sites are not protected by retentionist, nationalist cultural policies. Instead, all too often, they are put at risk. In addition, as pointed out again in an article in *The Economist*, much of what we know about the past has been deduced from ancient objects preserved in the world's museums.

Our critics, however, do not share this view. They believe that we should not acquire antiquities unless it can be proved that they were excavated and exported legally. They believe further that a work of ancient art is meaningless without knowledge of the archaeological circumstances of its "find spot." I disagree. Acquiring works of art advances knowledge. It is by making works of art available for study that we learn about their manufacture, style, iconography, date of execution, and relation to other works of art of similar characteristics. We may even learn about their original and subsequent uses and history. To declare, as some scholars have, that one should not publish, study, or teach from works of art without known provenance, and that museums should not acquire them, is not in the service of advancing knowledge but in opposition to it.

This point was raised recently in a 1998 article on the longstanding debate among Mayan scholars over the value of studying and teaching from objects without provenance, as objects without archaeological evidence are called.[2] The debate is all the more significant because so little is known of the "Post-Classic Mayan" history, the period after the Mayans left their cities in the jungle lowlands of what is now Central America and moved to highlands in the south and the upper Yucatan Peninsula. During this time period, the Mayans no longer carved stone monuments but continued to practice their religion and write hieroglyphs. The Post-Classic period lasted until the seventeenth century, when the Spanish finally succeeded in stamping out the Mayan religion by burning books and conducting an extensive anti-literacy campaign. What little is known of the final eight hundred years of Mayan civilization is preserved primarily in the painted images and hieroglyphic texts on manuscripts and ceramic pots.

The debate focuses on what can be learned from an object if its archaeological context is unknown, and whether, in fact, it is ethical even to study an unprovenienced object. Clemency Coggins, a Mayanist who wrote an article thirty years ago that pointed to the presence of looted Mayan artifacts in American museums, stated, "there's an

[2] See John Dorfman, "Getting Their Hands Dirty? Archaeologists and the Looting Trade," 8 *Linguafranca* 28 (1998).

aesthetic-versus-cultural division here.... One takes the short-term view – connoisseur-ship – and can't appreciate the broader view that sees the objects in historical context."[3] Another scholar, John Henderson from Cornell University, has said that unprovenienced "pieces have no research value, only aesthetic value."[4] On the one hand, the debate concerns aesthetic versus historical values, as if aesthetics bears no historical imprint. On the other, the debate focuses on the ethics of studying unprovenienced objects. Although the points are, for the sake of argument, on different hands, the hands are clasped and the points, like fingers, intertwined.

To be sure, as works of art, objects have value as documents of their use by a certain culture, of that culture's interest in specific decorative motifs and iconography, and/or of that culture's ability to manufacture and work the materials of which the objects are made. But even if we cannot know the specific culture that produced the objects in question, we can examine the objects for their manufacture, form, style, iconography, and ornamentation, and place them in the larger context of all we know about such objects. A piece of Roman glass (identified by comparison to glass excavated from a Roman site) with a very peculiar decorative motif, or of a much larger size, color or shape, tells us a something about the range of Roman glass types we did not know before even if we do not know where that specific piece of glass came from. Similarly, an object with an inscription may tell us something very important about its culture even if we have no knowledge of the circumstances in which it might have been found.

Works of art have many meanings, some of them historical, others aesthetic and philosophical. How, for example, can one inquire into the question of beauty without examples of beauty? By definition, works of art manifest beauty. To great benefit, they can be studied on for this reason alone. But works of art need not be studied to have value in our culture. They can provide pleasure, inspiration, even spiritual or emotional renewal. And, in their great variety, identifiable as Korean, Mexican, Mali, Greek, English, or Native American, they can remind us that the world is a very large and great place of which we, and our culture, are an important part.

Museums are dedicated to preserving the past for the sake of the future. They are havens for objects that are already, and for whatever reason, alienated from their original context. Museums do not alienate objects. They keep and preserve them and hold them in public trust. In this regard, museums are the allies of archaeologists. As the aforementioned article in *The Economist* points out, archaeology is in an ethical quandary in this day and age. It is a central paradox of archaeology that discovery involves destruction and that investigation involves intrusion. Archaeologists are now having to consider whether they should dig or save sites for future excavators, because questions not asked now might be unanswerable after one has dug through the layers of archaeological evidence. As one archaeologist puts it,

> "most archaeologists have had the experience of trying to discover something new about a site that was completely excavated only to find that the question they wanted to ask had not occurred to the original archaeologists. The intellectual health of the field, he says, depends on being able to address new questions or readdress old ones."

The one place archaeologists can return to time and time again is the museum that houses the finds of an excavation. There, they can take a fresh look at old discoveries and ask new questions about old finds. However, there has to be some kind of guarantee that those objects will be there, protected and available for study. For this reason, archaeologists should work with museums to change existing international policy to permit the sharing of excavation finds and the preservation and documentation of all ancient objects otherwise acquired. The lesson from the experience of the Kabul museum is that nationalist cultural policy is a failure: it either exposes the world's treasures to undue risks or creates an illicit market for antiquities. In Afghanistan it did both.

CONCLUSION

In the wake of Bamiyan, we must attach greater value to the preservationist role of museums in the world and reverse policies that favor the nationalistic retention of archaeological artifacts and cultural property over their international exchange. If we do not, we run the risk of becoming accessories to the crime against humanity that is the destruction of our common archaeological and cultural heritage, despite our best liberal intentions, which value the rights of the local community over those of the global community.

BIBLIOGRAPHY

Cuno, James, "Museums and the Acquisition of Antiquities," 19 *Cardozo Arts & Entertainment Law Journal*, 1 (2001): 83–96, Benjamin Cardozo School of Law, New York.

Cuno, James, "US Art Museums and Cultural Property," 16 *Connecticut Journal of International Law*, 2 (Spring 2001): 189–96.

QUESTIONS FOR DISCUSSION

1. With regard to the collecting of antiquities, are the claims of archaeologists and museums necessarily at odds? How do the claims of archaeologists and those of nationalist cultural policies differ? How are they similar?

2. On what grounds does a country decide to limit the import or export of cultural properties? Are these grounds different than those by which they might choose to limit the import or export of antiquities?

3. What international pressures are at play in setting and implementing cultural policies that might restrict the international movement in antiquities? Are these the same as those

[3] See also Clemency Coggins, "Illicit Trafic of Pre-Colombian Antiquities," 29 *Art J.* 94 (1969). See generally, Clemency Coggins, "United States Cultural Property Legislation: Observations of a Combatant," 7 *Int'l J. Cult. Prop.* 52 (1998).

[4] Dorfman, *supra* note 2, at 31.

that might restrict the international movement in cultural property? What do we expect of our art museums?

4. Should museums acquire antiquities for their collections? If so, under what circumstances is such acquisition appropriate?

A Suggested Response to Question 4

Guiding the professional practice of museum acquisitions is the concept of "due diligence," as set forth in Article 4 (4) of the 1995 UNIDROIT Convention.

In determining whether the possessor exercised due diligence, regard shall be paid to all the circumstances of the acquisition, including the character of the parties, the prices paid, whether the possessor consulted any reasonable accessible register of stolen cultural objects, and any other relevant information and documentation that it could reasonably have obtained, and whether the possessor consulted accessible agencies or took any step that a reasonable person would have taken in the circumstances.

Inherent in the concept of "due diligence" is acceptance of the fact that at the time of acquisition all evidence may not be at hand regarding the legal standing of the work of art in question. A museum is free to make the acquisition without such evidence only after certain procedures have been followed. If, after making the acquisition, convincing evidence is brought forward to prove that the work of art was illegally exported from its country of origin, then one is obliged to return it to the proper authorities in that country. It may result in money spent inappropriately, but that is part of the cost of doing business as a museum. The same would be true, of course, if a museum unknowingly purchased a "fake" work or a work later reattributed from a greater to a lesser master.

Let me offer a couple of examples from my own experience of how and why museums should acquire works of antiquity.

Nine years ago, when I was director of museums at Harvard, the Sackler Museum acquired a group of vase fragments that had been acquired by a scholar of Greek vases, Robert Guy. On seeing them, my first thought was how beautiful they were and how important they could be for teaching. They comprised more than two hundred fragments representing Greek vase painting from the sixth to the late fifth century B.C. The fragments contained Attic, Chalcidian, Corinthian, Laconian, and Etruscan examples. I saw immediately that a student could hold them in her hands and pass them around the seminar table, learning from the fragments things she could not from a complete pot. She could feel their texture and weight, see the depth of their clay walls, hold them up to raking light and see the clearly inscribed lines of their underdrawings and the different reflecting qualities of the blacks that comprise their outlines and painted bodies. Present and future students could learn a great deal about the materials and methods of Greek vase painting and about the particular stylistic qualities of some of its best and most influential artists. The vase fragments were not, to my mind, so much display objects as they were teaching and research objects. That is what interested me most about them.

As we proceeded to acquire the fragments, we contacted Mr. Guy and asked how and when he had acquired them, and if he had written evidence to back up his claims. He said he had no such evidence and that he had acquired them over many years from friends and dealers. Some of my colleagues would have wanted us to stop at that point, believing that such objects are presumed "guilty until proven innocent," and that not having positive evidence that they had been legally and ethically acquired was the same as admitting that they had been illegally or unethically acquired. I disagreed. We had no reason to believe that the fragments were illegally or unethically acquired. Just because other people had illegally acquired other fragments at other times – fragments that had been looted from archaeological sites – did not mean that ours were of dubious acquisition. The fact that many of ours had been acquired since the adoption of the UNESCO Convention did not mean that they had been removed from Italy (if, in fact, that is where they originated) after that date. They could just as easily have been out of the ground and on the market for many years prior to 1971. Who was to know?

I did know that Robert Guy was a scholar of considerable renown, former curator of ancient art at Princeton University and at Oxford, that he had built the collection over time with an eye to its potential for teaching, that we would publish an announcement about the collection in full and that his name would forever be associated with the fragments. He knew that the press and his colleagues, who would come to know of it through our publication, would scrutinize the acquisition carefully. If he thought that they had been illegally exported and acquired, or that his association with the collection would be detrimental to his standing as a scholar, he could easily have instructed the dealer who sold them to us to sell them a few at a time to private collectors, where they would have attracted little or no attention. Instead, he wanted the collection to be made public and to be held by a teaching museum, where it could be studied and appreciated by students, scholars, and the general public for many years to come.

I also know that these were vase fragments, of which there are no doubt tens of thousands in Italian museums. There was no evidence that these had come from a looted archaeological site, let alone an important archaeological site (as opposed to, say, found in a farmer's field). Thus, I had no reason to suspect that our acquiring these fragments was jeopardizing Italy's cultural patrimony. The matter would have been different if the objects in question had been Khmer temple sculptures because one would have been instantly suspicious of their status. (In this sense, I am reminded of Professor Colin Renfrew's statement that for many years the British Museum has followed a stringent policy, "which is to avoid acquisition [whether by purchase or bequest] of unprovenienced antiquities, defined as those on the market subsequent to 1970. Exception is made for minor antiquities and, in certain circumstances, for those originating from within the British Isles, for which the British Museum is the repository of last resort.") On these terms, so far as we could tell – and "the price paid" portion of the due diligence guidelines I cited previously would support this – the vase fragments were "minor antiquities."

Subsequently, I agreed that we should acquire the fragments and thus directed the Department of Ancient Art at the Arthur M. Sackler Museum to research them further and to prepare them for publication and exhibition. In December 1997, they were exhibited at our Fogg Art Museum. A fully illustrated and descriptive catalogue of the fragments was published and distributed. To date and to my knowledge, with the exception of letters from officials of the Archaeological Institute of America, a mention in the President's Column in the AIA's popular journal, *Archaeology*, and in conversations with a faculty colleague, we have been criticized only in the local press. No foreign government or cultural authority has suggested that the fragments were looted or illegally exported, despite our sending the Director General of the Italian Ministrero per i Beni Culturali e Ambientali a copy of our publication and asking his assistance in identifying any problems with the acquisition. The collection has been used in teaching, just as its collector and we had intended.

This is the process a museum should undertake when acquiring antiquities. Within the limited period of time preceding acquisition, museums should research the objects thoroughly, inquiring with colleagues into any problems known or suspected with the objects, the collector, or the dealer in question, and notify the appropriate governmental authorities of the likely country of origin. If nothing discouraging turns up, one is free to acquire such objects. However, the museum is still obligated to research the works further in anticipation of their being published and exhibited.

II

Sometimes it is only through the postacquisition process that one determines problems. This happened to us in 1991. We were given three Hellenistic, so-called Entella bronze tablets (from the Sicilian city of that name referred to in the inscriptions). They were given to the museum by someone who said he had acquired them in Europe in the early 1960s and had brought them to this country by 1965. We knew nothing about them and had no reason to disbelieve the donor, so we accepted them and set about cataloguing them. This required extensive research, undertaken by a graduate student in Harvard's Department of Classics.

Over the next few months, we learned that the texts of the tablets had been published in an Italian journal in 1980, but that the whereabouts of the tablets themselves were then unknown (one could only conclude that the texts were preserved from rubbings taken from the tablets before our donor purchased them).

We also learned that there were suspicions that these tablets, along with others, had been unearthed in clandestine excavations. With this information – that scholars did not know where our tablets were and that some believed them to have been excavated and exported illegally – we wrote the Soprintendente ai Beni Culturali of Palermo to report that we possessed the tablets. We asked for any evidence they had that showed they were indeed exported illegally. While waiting for a reply, we submitted our findings for publication in the international journal "Harvard Studies in Classical Philology."

Finally, in February 1996, almost four years after we had reported our acquisition of the tablets, we received a reply that presented us with convincing evidence that the tablets were indeed illegally exported. We promptly turned the tablets over to the Museo Archeologico Regionale di Palermo. I emphasize that the return of the tablets was made possible by our having acquired and researched them in the manner commonly practiced by art museums. Had they not been acquired by a museum, their whereabouts might not have been known for a very long time, if ever, and the tablets might never have made their way back to Palermo, where they belong. In the course of acquiring the tablets, we were able to rectify a wrong that had been done years before we acquired them.[5]

[5] Cuno, James, "Symposium: IV. Cultural Property: The Hard Question of Repatriation, Museums and the Acquisition of Antiquities," 19 *Cardozo Arts & Ent LJ* 83 (2001).

CHAPTER FOUR

The Role of the Museum in Developing Heritage Policy

Alissandra Cummins

INTRODUCTION

The late Denis Williams, Director of the Walter Roth Museum of Anthropology in Guyana, once stated that "the destruction and removal of our cultural heritage will not cease until everyone views it as a personal affront."[1] This short statement explains the decades of indifference and disrespect towards cultural patrimony in the Caribbean region as a direct consequence, largely subconscious, of the history of conquest, colonisation and colonialism, that has overshadowed the social, economic, and political development of the region. The observations in this chapter focus on the situation in the Caribbean Commonwealth (or CARICOM) countries, which, although bearing some resemblance to other countries in the region, differ significantly from both the Hispanic countries, where the tradition of independence and pride in identity is much older and more deeply entrenched, and the French and Dutch-speaking islands, where the maintenance of patriarchal control from Europe has, rather ironically, had an advantage in the form of the transfer of legislation, systems, standards, and policies that local governments have been able to use to protect their cultural heritage. The historic experience of the English-speaking countries includes neither of the these features. It is only recently, during the postindependence era that change is occurring, albeit slowly.

These patterns of destruction and power have so structured the history of these countries that it has been difficult to arouse either pride or respect for their culture and heritage as a legitimate basis upon which to build new national and regional identities. This has been greatly exacerbated by the official versions of said history, which have generally been European in focus and remote from the sensibilities of the Caribbean people, and the manner of their introduction into the educational system. As a result, Caribbean governments have historically displayed an official, almost benign neglect for the acknowledged cultural heritage (primarily European (or even Amerindian) originated monuments, sites, buildings, and artifacts remote from the majority populations' cultural experience) since they achieved independence from the 1960s onwards, making it acceptable for them to excuse themselves from their responsibility as guardians of this heritage.

In practice, this neglect took the form of an absence of policy that did not greatly concern the local communities, for which the absence of a tangible heritage, venerated elsewhere as "true" evidence of a "real" heritage, meant that all creative impulses and endeavours were concentrated on the intangible expressions of culture: festivities, folk tales, music, performances (including oratorical skills), traditional cuisine, funerary rites, language, and religious beliefs. In other words, they focused on those things that were intrinsic and almost instinctive, which could not be taken away from them and that could therefore serve as a basis for a heritage and a tradition that all could claim with pride. The absence of support for the preservation of a tangible heritage created a void that the region's museums, national trusts, conservation groups, and historical societies, which are largely nongovernmental in nature, have tried to fill by means of activities directed at the preservation of a heritage, so actively avoided or ignored by everyone else. This, then, is the psychological backdrop for the region's engagement with its cultural heritage. In my view, the parallels with the treatment of the Holocaust, for example, are very obvious. The changing perspectives, equally identifiable in both the European and the American context, are relevant to this discussion.

Dr Williams' remarks also underline the legitimization of official negligence and indifference, which, no matter how benign or passive, is indicative of the postcolonial perspective of policy makers on the subject of cultural heritage. Ironically, the only exception to this today is that heritage sites and monuments, which have been given new legitimacy as part of the heritage tourism resources of several nations, have now secured the imprimatur of acceptability. In practice, there was no policy apart from what had existed prior to independence, largely in the form of legislation enacted during the colonial period to establish archives, museums, and national trusts. Within this context, these institutions have done their best to sustain the heritage of the CARICOM countries, for the most part without significant government support, either in terms of resources or policy. It is only during the last 20 years that this situation has begun to change. However, it should be clear that governments did not attach much importance to cultural heritage or, by extension, to the institutions that served to protect and interpret this heritage. This has had the effect of restricting the scope of heritage management and rendering these institutions largely ineffectual, except among small enclaves of the population.

Effective legislation for the protection of cultural property has been a relative rarity in some countries, leaving the region's cultural heritage, particularly trafficable objects, open to the depredations of modern-day pirates. More significantly, this vulnerability has led to the transfer of important

[1] "Illicit Traffic in Cultural Property – A Status Report for Guyana," unpublished report presented at the CARICOM/UNESCO Regional Workshop on Illicit Traffic in Cultural Property, Grenada, 1997.

collections, specimens, and artefacts to the galleries and storerooms of foreign universities and museums and into the hands of private collectors. Until 20 years ago, recognition of the fact that the degradation, disappearance, and deterioration of cultural property impoverishes and damages the cultural identity of all people, as well as the fact that the theft of cultural property can cause irreparable damage to a society, was the sole preoccupation of the region's museums and heritage institutions. Conversely, the view that every state should recognise that the protection of cultural heritage contributes to the development of states, regions, and individuals, and that museum collections and exhibitions (as a collective interpretation of a nation's history) can usefully bring the stark reality of the colonial past into contrast with the confidence of a self-determined future, has only just begun to receive recognition among Caribbean governments. The following observations serve to illustrate these considerations.

STATUS OF HERITAGE AND HERITAGE INSTITUTIONS: THE PROBLEM

The omission of heritage education until recently from regional curricula and a lack of educational material have hindered the study and appreciation of various aspects of heritage by the local population. This has had the effect of compounding the lack of awareness, appreciation, and even basic knowledge of what constitutes cultural property in several countries. Few export controls exist for cultural heritage but where they do, the ignorance of officials regarding what constitutes valuable cultural property and their inability to identify material that is culturally unique to the region renders this form of control ineffectual. In addition, antique dealers have been permitted to trade largely unrestrained by policy, code of practice, and legislation. Dealers are not generally required to be qualified, or indeed licensed, to conduct business in this field, nor are they obliged to document, declare, or provide an independent assessment of the value of their sales or exports, except perhaps for tax or insurance purposes. Caribbean dealers are not constrained by a code of ethics or by requirements concerning the provenance or authenticity of their stock, except when such constraints benefit the state in the form of the payment of modest customs duties for genuine antiques.

This environment has contributed to the vulnerability of the region's cultural heritage by allowing the trade in antiques and collectibles to develop freely in the countries of the region. This situation has been compounded by foreign dealers and collectors who have exploited the advantages of trading in this very open environment. Lack of constraint on the part of collectors, particularly those protected by diplomatic protocols, has meant that certain antiquities, whether local or foreign, have been moved in and out of these countries without restraint. Although most CARICOM countries are currently signatories of the 1972 World Heritage Convention, of which the value, importance, and prestige for the development of heritage tourism is well recognized, very few have signed the 1970 UNESCO Convention on the Means of Prohibiting and Preventing the Illicit Import, Export and Transfer of Ownership of Cultural Property (or its counterpart 1995 UNIDROIT Convention) and few have put in place the mechanisms and infrastructures necessary for their implementation.

The disappearance of archaeological artefacts and the lack of control over the excavation of known archaeological sites, as described in expert John Whiting's 1983 UNESCO report on the Caribbean demonstrate the vulnerability of the Caribbean heritage over a period of several decades and remain critical factors even today. In addition, the possibility created by new technologies for underwater exploration have proved an additional menace to Caribbean heritage. Indeed, no CARICOM country has yet signaled acceptance of the 2001 Convention for the Protection of the Underwater Heritage despite convincing evidence of need. In addition, the lack of trained specialists and heritage managers in the region has led to a reliance on foreign specialists to implement national research, excavation and interpretation programmes in many countries.[2] However, without a functioning national heritage management structure, the Caribbean has provided opportunity without responsibility for some, and has contributed to the development of a climate of exploitation and opportunism that would be unacceptable in developed countries. Limited access to proper heritage management training, minimal budgets, and the chronic need for technical equipment, capacity, and facilities continue to be the greatest deficiencies.

Decades after the excavation of archaeological artefacts, the issues of ownership, censorship, and the control of cultural property that has been removed from its country of origin during the course of research projects continue to form the core of the problem. Efforts to repatriate collections to the region have not been wholly successful. On the other hand, it might have been expected that, with regard to the ownership of artefacts by the country of origin, the sharing and communication of information regarding finds and the careful handling of the documentary evidence that accompanies the collections, the actions of the researchers would ultimately be guided by the professional and ethical standards that apply in their own countries. Unfortunately, this has not always been the case.

The protection of copyrights and intellectual property is also critical. However, although all CARICOM countries benefit from some form of copyright legislation, there is little understanding as to how this may be extended to the protection of their cultural heritage because it focuses largely on the products of current manufacturers and not on tradition bearers. The 2003 UNESCO Convention for the Safeguarding of the Intangible Cultural Heritage offers some scope for appropriate management of these resources at the national level, but has yet to attract any significant support from regional governments, despite their reliance on these resources to give evidence or confirmation of national or cultural identity.

[2] These issues have been examined in depth in Cummins (1993) and (1999).

While much of the region's cultural heritage, including museum collections, now lies beyond the scope of copyright legislation, the ways in which these assets may be protected from unregulated exploitation need to be clarified. By the same token, museums must become more aware of the economic potential of their resources and explore various ways to exploit these resources (particularly through the development of digital resources and e-commerce capabilities) that do not threaten the integrity of the resources, the collection, or, indeed, the museum's own ethical policies. Government policy has so far refrained from tackling this issue, and the international exploitation of these assets has therefore proceeded without hindrance (except for institutional policy, where this exists). Such exploitation has even been encouraged by local tourism entities that actively endorse unrestricted access for and exploitation by foreign media in order – or so they claim with extraordinary circular logic – to portray the unique qualities of the region. The recent national intellectual property audit conducted in Barbados with a view to the establishment of a national IP Plan was a welcome departure from this oversight.

Caribbean countries have recently taken note of globalisation and its impact on the environment. In fact, current global consumption patterns render the small islands of the Caribbean among the most threatened territories in the world. The Caribbean possesses a rich trove of cultural property, much of which is suitable for preservation, interpretation, and future development as heritage education resources and tourist attractions. However, the development of heritage resources for tourism subjects this cultural property to considerable risks: uncontrolled exploitation by so-called developers has often led to inappropriate wear and tear, erosion, and – eventually – destruction. The tourism industry has not yet recognised the value of the museum experience in meeting the expectations of the visiting public. The failure to actively engage heritage institutions in tourism development represents a significant omission in the strategic planning process that small island developing states can ill afford. The special vulnerability of these countries means that their survival is contingent on their ability to maximize and manage their assets.

REGIONAL INITIATIVES OF CARIBBEAN MUSEUMS

In 1992, the CARICOM countries launched the Caribbean Regional Museum Development Project with funding from the United Nations Development Program (UNDP) and assistance from UNESCO. In the framework of the project, many of the aforementioned issues were addressed in a survey on the conservation status of Caribbean museums and a model cultural heritage act, which provided Caribbean governments with an outline for the preparation of cultural legislation (Cummins 1993 and Mottley 1993). The survey, which was designed and implemented under the auspices of the Museums Association of the Caribbean (MAC), sought to establish clear lines of responsibility for the management of the historical, cultural, and natural environment, and recommended the following actions for the protection of cultural heritage, including:

- adopting the ICOM definition of museums and Code of Ethics;
- developing minimum standards and policies for the management, documentation, and conservation of collections by museums;
- developing and adopting regional policies on standards for museum personnel;
- developing regional museum training programmes;
- ratifying international conventions for the protection of cultural property; and
- developing charters for museums that still lack them.

The Standing Committee of Ministers of Education (SCME) of the CARICOM countries subsequently endorsed these recommendations and incorporated them into the Regional Cultural Policy Programme, which was adopted in 1996. The SCME later called for the examination of existing national cultural heritage legislation in light of the aforementioned model act, in order to determine appropriate mechanisms for the incorporation and harmonisation of such legislation, and encouraged regional governments to introduce national legislation and policies where they did not already exist. A decade has now elapsed during which little has occurred at the governmental level to give impetus to this highly important process.

ROLE OF MUSEUMS IN THE POLICY DEVELOPMENT PROCESS

The development and implementation of national legislation, the examination of heritage sites for sustainable tourist development, and continuous consultation with the MAC are all consistent with the aforementioned regional programme. There have also been attempts to involve Caribbean museums in multidisciplinary planning processes, primarily in the fields of education, community development, and social transformation. Clearly, the reinforcement of collaborative efforts involving both governmental and nongovernmental agencies is vital to the success of these initiatives. A process of re-education (both at the governmental and the community levels) is needed to replace the negative attitude that arises at the thought of historical preservation with one that recognises the benefits that the authenticity of cultural property can provide. During the past 15 years, the Barbados Museum and Historical Society has continuously consulted with, advised, lobbied, shared documentation with, and researched the development of heritage legislation for the Barbadian government. At the same time, it has communicated its goals to the people through public information programmes, publications, and the reinforcement of professional standards in the field. The Preservation of Antiquities Bill, which identifies the nongovernmental Barbados Museum as the agency to manage the cultural heritage legislation on government's behalf, recognizes a uniquely resourceful partnership that represents the culmination of several years of effort.

The role of heritage institutions in this area should be recognised and coordinated with the role of their counterparts in the legal, security, and customs professions. Initiatives ensuring enhanced dialogue and coordination between the sectors include specialised training and public information programmes. The fact that the Barbados Museum has advised a variety of government departments and agencies on heritage-related issues, as well as its participation in a number of planning initiatives in the fields of tourism development, curriculum development, identification and evaluation of resources in the Exclusive Economic Zone, museum and national gallery development, coastal conservation, and land use planning, has revealed inconsistencies and gaps in the national planning process. The development and coordination of public policy that recognises and respects the importance of heritage in all sectors have recently been accepted as essential elements of national development strategy.

However, because there is no reliable knowledge base regarding antiquities within the regional customs authorities and police forces, dealers and collectors are not seriously challenged or confronted about their activities, even in countries that are currently signatories of the 1970 UNESCO Convention. What this means is that most instances of traffic in antiquities in CARICOM countries are, if not exactly illicit, almost certainly immoral – and disadvantageous to the country of origin. The initiative to develop an International Code of Ethics for antique dealers is therefore welcome, but the adoption of such a code will need to be coupled with comprehensive training for the officials who will be charged with implementing and enforcing it, at least in the Caribbean context. The role of museums is to bring these issues to the attention of the government, which will need to prepare for these changes by investing heavily in institutional reinforcement and capacity building.

Such steps are vital if Caribbean countries are to collaborate effectively with international organisations such as ICOM and Interpol on the retrieval of stolen or looted cultural property. In addition, they are crucial if regional governments are to accede to international heritage preservation conventions and make active use of their provisions. However, a lot more work remains to be done. The harmonisation of legislation at the national and regional level and closer collaboration between national agencies are essential aspects of the successful establishment of programmes for the protection of cultural heritage. Caribbean museums must work together with governments to encourage reciprocal arrangements among countries regarding the illicit export and repatriation of cultural property, especially human remains and sacred objects. Despite UNESCO's activities, including a regional consultation to encourage accession to the Underwater Heritage Convention in Jamaica in 2002, little progress has been made with respect to the protection of cultural property and familiarization with the mechanisms required for the implementation of the provisions of the 1970 UNESCO Convention.

Rather more success has been achieved through a series of regional technical workshops organized to help CARICOM countries to interpret the provisions of the 1972 World Heritage Convention. Instituted largely through the action of the World Heritage Committee from 2001, this policy gave priority to examining nominations of properties submitted by a state party with no sites inscribed on the List, as part of its *Global Strategy for a Balanced and Representative World Heritage List*. The Global Strategy is being implemented according to regional plans of action. Thematic meetings and technical studies on wooden built heritage, cultural landscapes, and Slave Route sites for example are leading to the preparation of new tentative lists and will encourage nominations of new types of properties to the World Heritage List. Strategies for the harmonisation of tentative lists and proposals for serial/transboundary nominations will require the harmonisation of legislations to assist with the management and protection of such sites, and the regular interventions of the World Heritage secretariat in the region have had the salutary effect of arousing governmental support for this activity. The same cannot be said, however, of the case for protection against illicit traffic in cultural property, which does not yet enjoy a similar level of esteem and value amongst Caribbean nations for the reasons stated earlier.

Conservation programmes and strategies devised to provide access to skills and resources at the regional level have achieved only limited success and have not been developed in a sustainable and progressive manner. Based on the recognition that individual countries have often been confronted with prohibitive costs when trying to establish their own conservation programmes, conservation services for a wide range of objects require urgent attention at the regional level. Short basic training programmes catering to a wide range of needs and capacities cannot begin to address the problem, but, in many instances, they provide the only real opportunities for reform. The issue is being addressed in part by the growth and development of the masters degree programme for Heritage Studies (established in the early 1990s at the Mona campus of the University of the West Indies, UWI) at the Cave Hill Campus of the UWI in Barbados, which serves to develop skills, knowledge, and an avocation for the field. The Barbados Museum serves as both site and tutor for the implementation of the programme, and is urging the creation of a sister programme in heritage resource management. In addition, the Barbados Museum has formulated briefing papers advocating the development of a comprehensive national heritage conservation strategy to form part of the national development process. Members of the museum's staff currently serve on several national committees and commissions established to respond to museum creation, heritage preservation and tourism development needs. Thus, the institution plays a unique role of institutional memory, in encouraging cross-fertilization of strategies and interdisciplinary approaches to shape Barbados' response to the heritage protection challenge. The publication of a national strategy entitled "Pathway to a Heritage Strategy" served as a public education tool by which the Barbados government seeks to involve and communicate with the national community in support of the implementation of a national policy.

Museums can play a role by lobbying and advising governments on effective, ecologically sound, community-oriented approaches to tourism that will be taken into consideration in the national planning process. Given the position of tourism as the most important economic activity in the Caribbean region, the countries should be poised to capitalize on the demand for tourism in a secure and peaceful environment and should seek to combine this experience with the preservation of their rich cultural heritage. A recent initiative, introduced in 2001 by the prime minister of Barbados, is the Heritage Assets Incentive Scheme. The Barbados Museum was asked to identify the criteria of heritage assets necessary for the implementation of such a scheme.

Although their own resources may not be adequate to the task of heritage preservation, museums can function effectively as lobbyists, to inform and advise governments on relevant issues through the regional and international associations to which they belong, while continuing to educate the public and implement activities at the grassroots level. The effective distribution of available information has been a key problem in this area, but the ability of museums to define and articulate major concepts gives them the potential to provide effective input at the stakeholder level in heritage protection. Caribbean museums can help to build consensus on sustainability, based on a commitment to transparency and inclusiveness, and certain regional institutions can also provide technical knowledge and expertise. In effect, this stimulates a participatory approach to the management of cultural heritage, critically important for a small state.

The Prime Minister of Barbados, the Rt. Hon. Owen Arthur, has clearly demonstrated the vital connection between cultural heritage and national development in his recent decision to take personal responsibility for the cultural heritage portfolio, and identifying as priority for his government the development of the cultural industries, including initiatives for the protection and preservation of the cultural heritage. The consequences of ignoring the process of globalisation are immense and threaten the factors underpinning the development of national identity in the Caribbean, which has already struggled to survive an earlier globalisation process: the transatlantic slave trade. The adverse effects of globalisation, which could impact on the future development of Caribbean countries by depriving people of the knowledge of their past and disconnecting communities from the symbols of their cultural identity (or destroying them altogether), are immeasurable.

QUESTIONS FOR DISCUSSION

1. Does/should the unique circumstance of the size of a state i.e., small, affect the scope and purpose of its policy for cultural heritage management?

2. Is the potential of the museum to function as a critically important advisor/facilitator of governmental policy fully recognized and appreciated?

3. To what extent should British common law, as it affects cultural property and antiquities, be regarded or accepted as "policy" or a "benchmark" for (Caribbean) Commonwealth countries where specific legislation governing the protection of these does not currently exist?

4. How can national policy be better defined/refined to effectively ensure the coordinated preservation and protection of both tangible and intangible heritage, while providing an environment in which it can be exploited (developed) for the public good?

BIBLIOGRAPHY

Cummins, Alissandra. 1993. Conservation Survey on the Status of Caribbean Museums. CARICOM/UNDP/UNESCO.

Cummins, Alissandra. 1999. The Role of Museums and Heritage Institutions in the Promotion and Preservation of Cultural Patrimony. OAS.

Mottley, Donna Scott. 1993. Model Cultural Heritage Act. CARICOM/UNDP/UNESCO.

Whiting, John. 1983. Report on Museum-Based Heritage in the Caribbean. UNESCO.

CHAPTER FIVE

An Archaeologist's View of the Trade in Unprovenanced Antiquities

Neil Brodie

INTRODUCTION

Archaeological sites and monuments are important sources of historical information. That is an archaeologist's view of archaeology, though it is not the only one and there are other perspectives that need to be considered. Today, many archaeological sites have a cultural or religious significance, sometimes they stand in the way of (or are destroyed by) agricultural or industrial improvement, and some may constitute an economic resource, to be exploited by means of tourism or looting. People even build homes in them. Thus the attitudes towards sites of people that live in their localities range from reverence, through indifference, to outright hostility. Diametrically opposed opinions may exist in the same community, sometimes even within the same family, structured by the sometimes complex intersections of cultural, religious, and economic interests. National governments, too, often take an interest in archaeological heritage, which may or may not be in accord with that of local communities and archaeologists. Governments may view archaeological heritage, or parts thereof, as a tangible and often very visible reminder – whether true or not – of national history and purpose, a justification of the nation state. They are also well aware of its economic potential. Archaeology, however, has no favourites: it can also be subversive when it provides a pole around which dissident views might gather. Thus, governments take a close interest in archaeological remains, and most countries today have subjected their archaeological heritage to some kind of state definition and control.

In the past, perhaps, archaeologists have taken a rather proprietorial view of archaeological heritage, believing that their scientific methods and objective research strategies have privileged their claim and lifted it above politics. However, it follows from what was said earlier that archaeological practice, whether as excavation or as an intellectual process, is inherently political. Any physical or intellectual intervention carries social consequences, and archaeologists are increasingly aware of this. Yet, while recognising that it is no longer possible to talk of a fully impartial standpoint from which a unique and objective account of the past can be delivered, they continue to maintain that their methods do produce a body of reliable historical knowledge that has general utility and that can protect against some of the wilder flights of fancy that are sometimes presented as fact to the public.

A central archaeological concept is context; that is to say, where an artefact is found and what is found with it. The methodology of archaeological excavation developed during the ninteenth and twentieth centuries to recover and record context, which was then regarded as the set of relationships among artefacts and between artefacts and their surrounding structures. However, the ever-growing battery of scientific techniques that is now available allows the reconstruction of context to go much further. For example, the analysis of lipid residues adhering to the walls of ancient pots makes it possible to identify the foodstuffs or goods that they may have contained. The soils and sediments in which artefacts are found can also be analysed microscopically to reveal information about past climates and environments. So today, when sites are excavated, contexts are carefully recorded. Indeed, in the expectation that methods of contextual analysis will continue to improve, and given the fact that the archaeological record is a limited resource, there is growing recognition that, where possible, archaeological sites should be conserved intact for future generations.

Most antiquities offered for sale on the international market have no provenance, which is to say that they have no accompanying information about findspot or previous ownership history. Most of these unprovenanced antiquities have probably been removed destructively and illegally from archaeological sites and monuments, so that their contexts have been destroyed, too. As a result, historical information is lost, and the reliability of any subsequent historical reconstructions is unavoidably reduced. The trade in unprovenanced antiquities has exploded over the past 40 years as barriers to communication have fallen and technology has improved. Antiquities are torn from standing monuments, secretly dug out from archaeological sites, or stolen from museums. They are exported illegally and traded around the world. It is a trade that antagonises all parties outlined earlier with a stake in archaeological heritage. Local communities may find their sacred monuments or statues defaced or their ancestral relics removed. The laws of states are ignored or subverted through corruption. But for archaeologists, an irreplaceable source of historical information is lost forever.

STRUCTURE OF THE TRADE

Although archaeological sites and monuments anywhere in the world may be plundered, most of the loot ends up in the private and public collections of Europe, North America, and, increasingly, the Far East. However, antiquities collecting in these countries is not an underground activity, as might be expected given the source of the collectables. People do not gather furtively at night to view one another's latest acquisitions. On the contrary, antiquities collectors see themselves as patrons of culture and the arts – as public benefactors. They expect others to see them in that light also. Many unprovenanced antiquities eventually come to rest in famous museums, which are the cultural repositories of Western society, a society that prides itself for being law-abiding, well-educated, and democratic; in other words, for being decent. How can it be, then, that this society is prepared to accept into its very heart material that carries with it the guilt of lost knowledge and the taint of corruption and criminality? How can this happen?

There are several factors in the antiquities trade that combine to disconnect the cultured world of museums and collectors from its antithetical underworld of criminality and destruction. First, all artefacts that are recovered by means of clandestine excavations will not have been seen in modern times, whether in a publication or in a museum's vitrine, so that when they appear on the market they cannot be recognised and identified as stolen. Second, many antiquities were removed from their countries of origin decades or even centuries ago, at a time when it was not illegal to do so. Some of these antiquities are still in circulation today and are therefore legally on the market. In other words, they are licit. Finally, most antiquities (between sixty and ninety percent[1]) are sold without provenance, which means that legal and illegal material have become hopelessly mixed on the market. Because most antiquities have not been recorded in any publication or entered into any database, it is difficult to investigate the pedigree of a single antiquity and virtually impossible to prove that any one particular piece has been looted. When asked by a discriminating customer, the vendor will have at hand a comforting homily about the grand tours of the eighteenth century, when European gentlemen travelled abroad and brought back with them antiquities as souvenirs for decorating their country homes. It is nondisclosure of provenance that allows illegal antiquities to infiltrate the market, and nondisclosure is a policy actively defended by dealers on the grounds of commercial necessity (keeping a source secret) or client confidentiality. However, many archaeologists today take the pragmatic view that an artefact with no provenance is most probably looted.

Nondisclosure of provenance also blocks investigations into the nature of the trade, and makes it difficult for outsiders to penetrate the trade's inner workings. Occasionally, however, often fortuitously, the economic and logistical structures of the trade are exposed. One example is the large-scale plunder and subsequent trade of Apulian vases that occurred during the 1980s and 1990s. Apulian vases were of Greek inspiration and made during the fourth century B.C. in what is today the southern Italian district of Puglia. They are to be found in all major collections of ancient Greek art and at auction regularly command prices in the region of U.S.$10,000 to $30,000 each. They comprise an unusual corpus of material in that they have been extensively catalogued (so that any previously unknown piece that arrives on the market is of questionable origin), and their looting and trade have been investigated by academic research and journalistic exposé.

During the 1980s and early 1990s, large numbers of Apulian vases were arriving for sale at Sotheby's auction house in London.[2] Many of them were consigned for sale by a Geneva-based dealer, who was shown to be acting as a front for an Italian dealer, who allegedly bought the vases directly from tomb-robbers in Puglia.[3] The tombs (often dug out with the aid of mechanical diggers) contained many objects of interest, but only the more valuable pieces were passed onto the international market, and many archaeological assemblages were irrevocably broken up, and contexts destroyed.[4] The vases were probably smuggled out of Italy in refrigerated trucks (customs officers are reluctant to search these trucks thoroughly for fear that their legitimate cargoes might perish), in consignments of modern reproduction ceramics, or in personal luggage (after first having been broken).[5]

In 1997, the Italian dealer was arrested in Italy and the Swiss police seized the contents of his four warehouses in Geneva Freeport. The warehouses were reported to contain around 10,000 antiquities from all parts of Italy, worth in total something like U.S.$40 million.[6] Also in 1997, the role played by London Sotheby's in marketing the vases was exposed in a book and on television,[7] and the company stopped its London antiquities auctions soon after. Sotheby's auctioned 1550 Apulian vases between 1960–98 but only 378 were known before their sale. None had any indication of findspot or context of discovery.[8]

Even when information concerning the findspot of an antiquity is provided in a sales catalogue, it is often ambiguous, using geographical or cultural terms that make historical sense but are of little relevance today. One auction house was quite happy to sell Mayan material from Petén, an area of Guatemala, until the United States imposed emergency restrictions on the import of material deriving from there in 1991. Objects offered for auction were thereafter more likely to be labelled "lowlands," an area encompassing parts of Mexico and Belize as well as Guatemala,[9] which, perhaps

1 C. Chippindale and D. W. J. Gill, 'Material consequences of contemporary classical collecting,' *American Journal of Archaeology* 104 (2000).

2 R. Elia, 'Analysis of the looting, selling and collecting of Apulian red-figure vases: a quantitative approach,' in N. Brodie, J. Doole and C. Renfrew (eds.), *Trade in Illicit Antiquities: The Destruction of the Archaeological Heritage* (Cambridge, McDonald Institute for Archaeological Research 2001).

3 P. Watson, *Sotheby's: Inside Story* (London, Bloomsbury 1997).

4 D. Graepler, *Fundort: Unbekannt. Raubgrabungen Zerstören das Archäologische Erbe* (Munich, Walter Bierung 1993).

5 G. Pastore, 'The looting of archaeological sites in Italy.' In N. Brodie, J. Doole and C. Renfrew (eds.), *Trade in Illicit Antiquities: The Destruction of the Archaeological Heritage* (Cambridge, McDonald Institute for Archaeological Research 2001).

6 P. Watson, 'The sequestered warehouses,' *Culture Without Context* 2 (1998).

7 P. Watson, *supra* note 3.

8 R. Elia, *supra* note 2.

9 E. Gilgan, 'Looting and the market for Maya objects: a Belizean perspective.' In N. Brodie, J. Doole and C. Renfrew (eds.), *Trade in*

fortuitously, made it more difficult for the U.S. Customs Service to identify material coming from Petén.

SCALE OF THE ILLICIT TRADE AND ITS CONSEQUENCES

The monetary value of the illicit trade, or the damage it causes, have rarely been quantified, largely because it takes place in secret. Interpol estimates that in monetary terms, the illicit trade in cultural property ranks third after drugs and weapons. There have been a few surveys of damage on the ground. In 1983, a study showed that 58.6 percent of all Mayan sites in Belize had been damaged by looters.[10] Between 1989 and 1991, a regional survey in Mali discovered 834 archaeological sites, but forty-five percent of them had already been looted – seventeen percent, badly.[11] Another survey in one district in northern Pakistan showed that nearly half the Buddhist shrines, stupas, and monasteries had been badly damaged or destroyed by illegal excavations.[12] In Andalusia, Spain, fourteen percent of known archaeological sites have been damaged by illicit excavation.[13] It is estimated that somewhere in the region of 11,000 graves must have been robbed to produce the number of Greek early bronze age Cycladic figurines that are now in collections worldwide[14] and that several thousand tombs must have been emptied in southern Italy to produce the 13,600 Apulian red-figure vases that have been recorded.[15]

ROLE OF MUSEUMS

Some illegal material ends up in museums, although many museums have now adopted acquisition policies that are designed to stop this happening. As long ago as 1970, the Museum of the University of Pennsylvania announced that it would no longer acquire antiquities of unknown pedigree, and it was followed by several other major museums in the United States. Also in 1970, the International Council of Museums (ICOM)[16] issued an influential statement on the ethics of museum acquisitions, and it has since been at the forefront of the fight against illicit traffic, with publications such as the *One Hundred Missing Objects* series and the Red Lists of African, Latin American, and Iraqi artefacts. Article 2.4 of the most recent (2004) ICOM Code of Ethics states that:

> "Museums should not acquire objects where there is reasonable cause to believe their recovery involved the unauthorised, unscientific, or intentional destruction or damage of monuments, archaeological or geological sites, or species or natural habitats. In the same way, acquisition should not occur if there has been a failure to disclose the finds to the owner or occupier of the land, or to the proper legal or governmental authorities."[17]

This article clearly states that a museum should not acquire any object when there is reason to believe that its initial recovery involved damage to an archaeological site or monument. Given that most unprovenanced antiquities have been obtained this way, their acquisition contravenes the ICOM code, and should be avoided. It is important that museums and their representative organisations take a strong stand against the trade in illegal material because they set a moral tone that the public will follow. As noted earlier, museums are seen to embody ideals that lie at the core of Western society. People trust museums, and it is for this reason that their actions should be beyond reproach.

Nevertheless, some museums are still happy to acquire material without provenance, particularly new museums with grand designs. The Miho Museum, which opened in November 1997 just to the north-east of Kyoto, Japan, is one such museum (both literally and figuratively). It is thought to have spent more than US$200 million on its collection, which has been published in a well-illustrated colour catalogue. However, most of the pieces in the catalogue have no provenance whatsoever, the implication being that they arrived on the market only recently and through dubious channels. This clearly makes archaeologists uncomfortable, and they are likely to decry the loss of context, but there are dangers too for the museum that buys such pieces without provenance – the twin dangers of fakes and stolen pieces.

Within four years of its opening, the Miho Museum had suffered. One of its most eye-catching displays is a collection of what is probably Iranian silver. This silverware is rumoured to be part of what is known as the Western Cave Treasure, a hoard of gold and silver thought to have been discovered by a shepherd in a cave in Iran in the late 1980s.[18] The pieces bought by the Miho Museum were apparently authenticated by a Western academic whose identity has been withheld, but

Illicit Antiquities: The Destruction of the Archaeological Heritage, 82 (Cambridge, McDonald Institute for Archaeological Research 2001).

10 M. Gutchen, 'The destruction of archaeological resources in Belize, Central America,' *Journal of Field Archaeology* 10 (1983).

11 M. Brent, 'The rape of Mali,' In K. D. Vitelli (ed.), *Archaeological Ethics* (Walnut Creek, AltaMira 1996).

12 I. Ali and R. Coningham, 'Recording and preserving Gandhara's cultural heritage,' *Culture Without Context* 3 (1998).

13 S. Fernandez Cacho and L. G. Sanjuán. 'Site looting and illicit trade of archaeological objects in Andalusia, Spain.' *Culture Without Context* 7 (2000).

14 D. W. J. Gill and C. Chippindale 'Material and Intellectual Consequences of Esteem for Cycladic Figures,' *American Journal of Archaeology*, 624 (1993).

15 Elia, supra note 2, 151. Many more figures are available in N. Brodie, J. Doole and P. Watson, *Stealing History*, (Cambridge, McDonald Institute for Archaeological Research 2000); and N. Brodie, J. Doole and C. Renfrew (eds.), *Trade in Illicit Antiquities: The Destruction of the Archaeological Heritage* (Cambridge, McDonald Institute for Archaeological Research 2001).

16 ICOM is a non-governmental organisation that maintains formal relations with UNESCO. It is dedicated to the development and management of museums and operates globally for the preservation of cultural heritage through its 108 national committees. More information on the organisation can be found at <http://www.icom.org>.

17 ICOM Code of Ethics for Museums, (Paris, ICOM 2004).

18 D. Alberge and D. McGrory 'Art mole threatens to turn tables on Yard handlers,' *The Times* (January 29 2000); E. Bleibtrau, 'Een verguld zilveren beker van koning Assurbanipal.' In E. Bleibtrau and H. D. Schneider (eds.), *Ritueel en Schoonheid: Antieke meesterwerken uit het Miho Museum, Japan*, 21 (Milan, Skira Editore 1999).

already the authenticity of one piece has been questioned. It is a gilt silver beaker that carries two inscriptions, both ancient but of different dates and in different scripts. One of the inscriptions is associated with engraved decoration in neo-Assyrian style that covers the outer surface of the beaker in four registers. The U.S. archaeologist Oscar Muscarella[19] has pointed to inconsistencies in the iconography of the decoration and suggested that it might have been added after the beaker's discovery in order to increase its value. On the other hand, it is possible that 2,600 years ago an inscribed beaker changed hands as loot or as a gift and was subsequently engraved and inscribed a second time. Perhaps the truth will never be known, or perhaps scientific examination of the surface will decide. In any case, another deceit of an object without provenance has been exposed – many museum collections containing such material are almost certainly adulterated by fakes.

Then there are stolen pieces. In April 2001, the Miho Museum announced that it was returning (of its own volition) a stone Buddha to the People's Republic of China. The Buddha, which stands nearly forty-eight inches high, had been stolen in 1994 from a public garden in Shandong Province before being bought by the Miho Museum from a dealer in London.[20]

In the United States, art museums are probably the largest collectors of antiquities. In an art museum, an antiquity is displayed as an art object, and little or no information is provided about its history, function, or significance. The object is left to "speak for itself." Thus, the acquisition and display of an antiquity that has been divorced from its context of discovery presents no challenge to the art museums' philosophy of purpose and preferred mode of display. Most art museums in the United States that collect archaeological material were incorporated in the late nineteenth or twentieth centuries, and since then have actively enlarged their collections, so that as the twentieth century wore on, art museum demand for antiquities grew progressively more acute. Unfortunately, for the museums, over the same period, most countries of the world placed their archaeological heritage under some kind of state control, which in most cases severely limits or completely bans the export of antiquities. Thus, the flow onto the market of legitimate material slowed at a time when demand was increasing, and the resulting shortfall was made good by looted material offered without provenance. Any museum that chose to enlarge its permanent collection (rather than embark upon a more ethical and economically advantageous programme of international loans and exhibitions) was forced to acquire unprovenanced material. The damaging effect of this continuing policy of indiscriminate acquisition could be demonstrated in almost any country of the world, but Nepal offers a well-documented example.

Art insiders suggest that demand for Nepalese religious sculpture dates back to the 1964 Art of Nepal exhibition held at Asia House Society in New York.[21] The exhibition attracted the attention of U.S. private collectors and museums, and in the decades that followed, they acquired large quantities of bronze devotional images and, when the supply of bronzes began to dry up, stone sculpture.[22] Over the same period, it is reported that Nepal lost more than half of its religious sculpture, and by 1998 most bronze images had been removed.[23] This sad synergy between the museum and the market has now almost ended Nepalese ownership of Nepalese heritage, and the pattern is one that has been repeated for many other countries in Asia[24] and, no doubt, for most other countries of the world. It is exactly this type of destructive collecting that the ICOM Code of Ethics is designed to prevent. Unfortunately, experience shows that all too often the ICOM Code is ignored. Comparable codes formulated by U.S. museum organisations are demonstrably weaker.

For example, the American Association of Museum's (AAM)[25] statement on the ethics of acquisition is briefer than ICOM's, and far less specific:

> "Acquisition, disposal and loan activities are conducted in a manner that respects the protection and preservation of natural and cultural resources and discourages illicit trade in such materials."[26]

There are no direct recommendations in the AAM's statement, although in the introduction to its code the AAM does ask that museums comply with applicable international conventions, which would include the 1970 UNESCO Convention on the Means of Prohibiting and Preventing the Illicit Import, Export and Transfer of Ownership of Cultural Property, implemented in the United States in 1983 as the Convention on Cultural Property Implementation Act (CCPIA), and in the afterword it emphasises that individual museums should frame their own individual codes of ethics, which should be in conformance with the AAM code and expand on it through the elaboration of specific guidelines.

In 2004, the Association of Art Museum Directors (AAMD)[27] published its "Report of the AAMD Task Force on the Acquisition of Archaeological Materials and Ancient Art,"[28] which contains seven guidelines to assist museums in

[19] O. Muscarella. *The Lie Became Great: The Forgery of Ancient Near Eastern Cultures* (Groningen, Styx 2000).

[20] C. Sims. 'Japanese agree to return a stolen statue to China,' *New York Times* (April 18 2001).

[21] P. Pal, *American Collectors of Asian Art*, 7 (Bombay, Marg 1986).

[22] N. Brodie and J. Doole, 'The Asian art affair: US art museum collections of Asian art and archaeology.' In N. Brodie and C. Hills (eds.), *Material Engagements: Studies in Honour of Colin Renfrew*, 101. (Cambridge, McDonald Institute for Archaeological Research 2004).

[23] J. Schick, *The Gods are Leaving the Country* (Bangkok, White Orchid 1998).

[24] N. Brodie and J. Doole, supra note 21.

[25] The AAM represents the interests of US museums and other cultural institutions. It currently has 3100 institutional members. More information can be found at <http://www.aam-us.org/index.cfm>.

[26] AAM Code of Ethics for Museums (1993).

[27] The AAMD represents the interests of art museums in the United States, Canada and Mexico through its membership of up to 200 museum directors. More information can be found at <http://www.aamd.org/>.

[28] AAMD Report on Acquisition of Archaeological Materials and Ancient Art (2004).

the preparation or revision of acquisition policies as regards antiquities (AAMD 2004).

The AAMD guidelines, too, ask that art museums conform to the law, but contain nothing to discourage the acquisition of material when there is reasonable cause to believe that its original recovery involved the destruction or damage of an archaeological site or monument (as under the ICOM code). Indeed, on the face of it, the requirement in Guideline D that member museums should not acquire any archaeological material or work of ancient art "known to have been 'stolen from a museum, or a religious, or secular public monument or similar institution'" or "known to have been part of an official archaeological excavation and removed in contravention of the laws of the country of origin" seem carefully (or carelessly) worded to allow the acquisition of material from excavations that are not official – in other words, antiquities from looted sites.

For a museum, an antiquity without provenance is a potential time bomb. It may have been in circulation for decades, which would make it a legitimate acquisition. It may have been first obtained secretly through clandestine excavation, which would make it unidentifiable and therefore a safe, if unethical, acquisition. However, it may also have been stolen from a preexisting collection, which would make it traceable. At any moment, new evidence may come to light that exposes the true nature of a piece. Public embarrassment, and possibly financial loss, will follow when the museum is forced to return the piece to its country of origin. In the United States, at least, by law, museum trustees have a fiduciary responsibility towards the institutions they serve, and it has been argued that they are in breach of this responsibility if they do not ensure acquisitions policies and diligence procedures that guard against such eventualities.[29]

ROLE OF PRIVATE COLLECTOR

Museums are not the only acquirers of unprovenanced antiquities. At one time or another, most antiquities pass through private hands, either in collections or as interior decorations. Like museums, though, the largest private collections provide the market with some kind of social legitimacy and an aura of respectability, even though they are often composed largely of antiquities with no provenance – even more so than museum collections.

One such collection was that of Barbara and Lawrence Fleischman, which was acquired by the J. Paul Getty Museum in 1996 by a mixture of gift and purchase. A catalogue of the collection was published in 1994. The dust jacket claims that "most of the objects have never before been publicly shown," and closer study has shown this claim to be true. The catalogue contains entries for 183 objects of which only thirty percent had been previously published and the remaining seventy percent were unknown. Worse still, there was an indication of the findspot in the case of only three of the objects.[30]

Inevitably, questions have been asked regarding some of the Fleischman pieces.[31] For example, Item No. 126 in the catalogue is a fragment of a fresco from a first century B.C. Roman house. No information about its provenance is provided, but the entry does reveal that the piece "matches precisely the upper portion of a fresco section in the Shelby White and Leon Levy collection . . . and is from the same room . . ."[32] But where was the room, and in what state is it today? What was found in the room? From the style of the paintings, a Pompeian provenance is suggested, but otherwise these are questions that the catalogue is sadly unable to answer.

Six months before acquiring the Fleischman collection, the Getty Museum had announced a new acquisitions policy whereby it would no longer collect pieces without provenance. However, the Fleischman collection was deemed to have a provenance because it had been published (by the Getty Museum!) before the November 1995 cut-off date.[33] But the time bombs are ticking. By 1999, the Getty Museum had already returned one of the Fleischman pieces – a Roman head – to Italy, where it had been stolen from an excavation storeroom.[34]

Museums may set the moral tone, but it is fair to say that the largest private collectors set the financial pace. The "collectors" themselves do not constitute a community, however. They are not unified by a common set of intellectual, aesthetic, or ethical dispositions, nor by social or economic circumstances. Although most antiquities collectors profess to be collecting ancient "art," it is clear that this is not always their true motivation. Many collectors collect antiquities as an easy (and relatively inexpensive) means to acquire the appearance, though not perhaps the substance, of connoisseurship that allows entry into the gala world of museum receptions and gallery tours. Thus, antiquities provide a source of cultural capital. Other collectors see antiquities as an investment opportunity, or as the latest "must-have" in chic interior decoration. But not all private collectors can be disparaged as social climbers. Some do take a genuine scholarly interest in the material they collect, and deplore the damage that indiscriminate collecting causes to archaeological heritage. It is interesting to recall that, as long ago as 1913, Charles L. Freer, whose collection formed the foundation of the Smithsonian Institution's Freer Gallery of Art, recognised the problem and lobbied the U.S. Government to ban the import of Chinese antiquities of uncertain provenance.[35]

29 P. Gerstenblith, 'Acquisition and deacquisition of museum collections and the fiduciary obligations of museums to the public,' *Cardozo Journal of International and Comparative Law* 11 (2003).

30 C. Chippindale and D. W. J. Gill, supra note 1, 474.

31 C. Renfrew, *Loot, Legitimacy and Ownership*, 28 (London, Duckworth 2000).

32 M. True and K. Hamma (eds.), *A Passion for Antiquities: Ancient Art from the Collection of Barbara and Lawrence Fleischman*, 251 (Malibu, J. Paul Getty Museum 1994).

33 J. E. Kaufman, 'Getty decides publishing equals provenance,' *Art Newspaper* 61, 17 (1996).

34 D. Lee, 'Getty returns three stolen works,' *Art Newspaper* 90, 1, 3 (1999).

35 W. I. Cohen, *East Asian Art and American Culture*, 58 (New York, Columbia University Press 1992).

The fact that some collectors understand the value of archaeological context and the desirability of a legitimate and ethical trade has led to the notion of the "Good Collector".[36] The Good Collector is also committed to making his or her collection available as an educational resource, and to supporting initiatives that aim to benefit the archaeology and archaeological institutions of countries whose heritage is being badly depleted by the market.

LOOTING DURING WARTIME

Events since the 1992 Soviet withdrawal from Afghanistan and the 1991 Gulf War in Iraq have shown once more how vulnerable archaeological heritage is in times of war. Monuments and historic buildings can be accidentally damaged or destroyed, and some might be deliberately targeted for religious or political reasons. But although in 2001 the world was shocked by the demolition of the Bamiyan Buddhas for what were ostensibly ideological reasons, in both Afghanistan and Iraq, most destruction has been wrought by gangs (that are often armed) searching for antiquities that can be sold on the international market. Archaeological sites around Afghanistan have been wrecked, sometimes with the help of bulldozers.[37] The situation in Iraq is no better. Archaeological sites have been continually attacked since the end of the 1991 Gulf War, and as the security situation has deteriorated through 2004, archaeological sites in the south of the country are being plundered on an unprecedented scale.

The reasons for widespread looting during wartime are obvious. As livelihoods are lost and public order breaks down, archaeological sites and monuments are left unprotected and offer a ready source of income. Unfortunately, there is evidence to suggest that much of the money made from the sale of looted antiquities is siphoned off by powerful political figures or warlords.[38]

What is happening in Iraq and Afghanistan is hardly a surprise. In recent times, archaeological looting has been a regular accompaniment of war,[39] but then cultural "treasures" and fine art works were long considered legitimate spoil for victorious or conquering armies. The difference today is that the international community has outlawed expropriation, so that now it is an activity of criminal rather than military organisations (though it is not always clear where to draw the line). Legislative attempts to protect cultural heritage in wartime can be traced back to the 1863 Lieber Code of the U.S. Federal Army, and were given force by the first Hague Convention of 1899. Today, the international disposition towards looting in wartime is determined by the 1954 Hague Convention for the Protection of Cultural Property in the Event of Armed Conflict, and, for movable heritage in particular, its 1954 First Protocol and 1999 Second Protocol. The Convention and its Protocols oblige a military force not to destroy or expropriate items of cultural heritage, but also require that it offers protection to enemy cultural heritage when possible.[40] Neither the United States nor the United Kingdom have ratified the Hague Convention, though both have signed it. The United Kingdom announced its intention to ratify the Convention and both Protocols in 2004.

The vulnerability of archaeological heritage during wartime and its attractiveness to thieves was highlighted by the ransack of Iraq's National Museum in April 2003. Before war broke out, staff had done what they could to protect the museum's collections, moving some into safe storage and protecting the larger or more fragile pieces *in situ*. Eventually, however, staff were forced to abandon the museum on April 8 as fighting closed in. Gangs of thieves broke in on April 10 and were not chased off until April 12, when the staff returned. It was not until four days later, on April 16, that U.S. troops were dispatched to guard the museum.

In the immediate aftermath of the museum's looting, wild estimates began to circulate of how many artefacts might have been stolen. A figure of 170,000 missing objects was frequently mentioned, although this figure was nothing more than a guess, based on the size of the museum inventory. Nevertheless, it was frequently quoted by the media as a true assessment of loss. Once staff and military investigators gained access to the museum, more sober assessments of the damage began to circulate, which triggered a reaction to the early sensationalist reporting. At a press briefing on 20 May, for example, the U.S. Secretary of Defense Donald Rumsfeld, keen to downplay U.S. culpability, announced that the theft at the National Museum was probably an inside job and that only an estimated 38 objects were confirmed as missing.[41] The situation has now been clarified by the report of the official U.S. investigation into the theft, led by Colonel Matthew Bogdanos. On 10 September 2003, he revealed that at least 13,515 objects had been stolen, of which 3,500 had been recovered – more than 1,700 returned under an amnesty and 900 through raids within Iraq. A further 750 had been recovered abroad. This figure of 13,515 is a minimum,

[36] R. T. McIntosh, T. Togola and S. K. McIntosh, 'The Good Collector and the premise of mutual respect among nations,' *African Arts* 27 (1995); S. K. McIntosh, 'Proposition,' *Public Archaeology* 1 (2000).

[37] A. W. Feroozi and Z. Tarzi. 'The impact of war upon Afghanistan's Cultural Heritage,' available at <http://www.archaeological.org/webinfo.php?page=10242>, accessed December 14 2004; see also the web site of the Society for the Preservation of Afghanistan's Cultural Heritage at <http://spach.info/>, accessed December 10 2004.

[38] M. Garen, 'The war within the war,' *Archaeology*, 30 (July/August 2004); T. McGirk, 'A year of looting dangerously,' *Independent on Sunday* (March 24 1996).

[39] N. Brodie, 'Introduction.' In N. Brodie and K. W. Tubb (eds.), *Illicit Antiquities: The Theft of Culture and the Extinction of Archaeology*, 6–8 (London, Routledge 2002); N. Brodie, 'Spoils of war.' *Archaeology* (July/August 2003).

[40] P. J. Boylan, 'The concept of cultural protection in times of armed conflict: From the crusades to the new millennium,' in N. Brodie and K. W. Tubb (eds.), *Illicit Antiquities: The Theft of Culture and the Extinction of Archaeology*, (London, Routledge 2002); P. J. O'Keefe, The First Protocol to the Hague Convention fifty years on.' *Art, Antiquity and Law* 9 (2004).

[41] 'US Department of Defense DoD News Briefing – Secretary Rumsfeld and Gen. Myers.' (2003). On line at <http://www.defenselink.mil/transcripts/2003/tr20030520-secdef0207.html>. Accessed 14 August 2004.

however, and might rise as recovery work in the museum progresses.[42]

Whether or not the sack of the Baghdad Museum could have prevented by the U.S. military is still a matter for conjecture. In January 2003, archaeologists and museum representatives had visited the U.S. Department of Defense and provided the locations of 4,000 (later increased to 5,000) archaeological sites that should be protected from military action in the event of war, and emphasised the danger that looting would break out afterwards.[43] By March 2003, the National Museum was in second place behind the Central Bank on a Pentagon list of places to be secured by U.S. forces to forestall looting, although this obviously never happened. Clearly, in the event, conditions on the ground were difficult and dangerous. U.S. troops were engaged in heavy fighting with Iraqi militia who had taken up positions in the museum's grounds. Nevertheless, the feeling persists in some quarters that a high-level decision not to offer protection was politically expedient because the museum had no direct economic importance. To some, it smacks of a conspiracy designed to leave the museum unguarded for the purpose of allowing looters to fulfil "orders" placed by rich U.S. collectors.

The need to protect the museum might not have arisen had it not been for the thriving black market in Iraqi antiquities. Throughout the 1990s and into the 2000s, a lot of material from Iraq (and Afghanistan) – presumably plundered – was flowing through London. This trade was carried on despite the fact that, under the 1990 UN Security Council Resolution 661, the export of material from Iraq was illegal. For all intents and purposes, the Resolution was simply ignored. However, soon after the outbreak of the current Iraq conflict, in June 2003, the UK Government implemented UN Security Council Resolution 1483 by the Iraq (United Nations Sanctions) Order (SI 1519), which specifically targets cultural material. This instrument has proved controversial because it abrogates the usual requirement in criminal law to prove guilty intent. Instead, anyone caught holding an Iraqi cultural object without verifiable proof that it was exported before August 1990 is in breach of the law, and should turn the object over to the police. Nevertheless, the law is effective. By late 2003, material that is identifiably Iraqi in origin had virtually disappeared from open sale on the London market,[44] thus confirming that most Iraqi objects offered for sale before June 2003 without provenance had not been from old collections, but in all probability had been looted. If strong enforcement of UN sanctions had been adopted sooner, sometime during the 1990s, it is at least arguable that by 2003 the market for Iraqi antiquities would have been much reduced, and the looting not so severe.

ARCHAEOLOGICAL RESPONSE

Proponents of the antiquities trade often argue that it is the responsibility of countries to protect their own heritage and to police their own borders, thereby implying that any material that slips out onto the market is fair game. Archaeologists are generally sceptical of this argument, because most countries whose archaeology is under threat are usually poor and cannot afford to enforce their heritage laws when they are threatened by powerful outside interests. Even a rich country like the United Kingdom has problems. In contrast, archaeologists and museum professionals have, for the past 30 years or so, been calling for the market to be made more transparent by means of statutory or voluntary regulation, so that illicit material can be more readily recognised. They have also been developing more ethical standards of professional behaviour with regard to their own activities.

Some professionals – individuals rather than representative organisations – continue to sell their expertise on the market. Two of them have already been quoted: the specialist who authenticated the Miho Museum's beaker (a former university professor) and the expert who wrote the catalogue entries for the Roman fresco fragments (a museum curator). It is the participation or, some might say, the collusion of these individuals that ostensibly keeps the market free from fakes and stolen artefacts. They are the guarantors of market confidence. (Dealers are often sceptical of this "expert" knowledge, but acknowledge the reassurance that customers feel when they see a signed certificate decorated with an academic qualification.) Although such behaviour may have been accepted in the past, today it contravenes the codes of practice that professional bodies have developed in recognition of the potential for destructive synergism that exists between the market and the professions. Two such codes of practice are mentioned here, but they are representative of many others.

The Society for American Archaeology (SAA)[45] adopted eight Principles of Archaeological Ethics in April 1996. Principle No. 3, "Commercialisation," reads in part:

> "Whenever possible [archaeologists] should discourage, and should themselves avoid, activities that enhance the commercial value of archaeological objects, especially objects that are not curated in public institutions, or readily available for scientific study, public interpretation, and display."

Article 5.1 of the 2004 ICOM Code of Ethics for Museums includes the paragraph:

> "Where museums provide an identification service, they should not act in any way that could be regarded as benefiting from such activity, directly or indirectly. The identification and authentication

[42] M. Bogdanos, Iraq Museum Investigation: 22 Apr–8 Sep 03 (2003). On line at <http://www.defenselink.mil/news/Sep2003/d20030922fr.pdf>. Accessed October 14 2004.

[43] M. Gibson, 'From the prevention measures to the fact-finding mission.' *Museum International*, 219/220 (2003); A. Lawler, 'Mayhem in Mesopotamia.' *Science* 301 (2003).

[44] N. Brodie, 'The plunder of Iraq's archaeological heritage 1991–2004 and the London antiquities trade,' in N. Brodie, M. Kersel, C. Luke and K. W. Tubb (eds.), *Transforming Values: Archaeology and the Antiquities Trade* (Gainesville, University Press of Florida, in review).

[45] The SAA is an international association of more than 6,600 archaeologists and other heritage professionals dedicated to the research, interpretation, and protection of the archaeological heritage of the Americas. More information on the organisation can be found at <http://www.saa.org>.

of objects that are believed or suspected to have been illegally or illicitly acquired, transferred, imported or exported should not be made public until the appropriate authorities have been notified."

Codes of practice are all very well, but the trick is in the enforcement. In 1998, the British Academy adopted a resolution on the illicit trade in antiquities that states in Article 7(d):

"Written certificates of authenticity or valuation (appraisals) should not be given for objects of doubtful provenance, and opinions on the monetary value of such objects should only be given on official request from museums or competent legal, governmental, or other responsible public authorities. Where there is reason to believe an object has been stolen the competent authorities should be notified."

Nevertheless, one Fellow of the British Academy has for a long time put his name to statements of authenticity. In the absence of any mechanism for enforcement, the resolution can function only as a set of guidelines, not a binding code of practice.

However, the powerful effect that professional archaeologists and museum curators may exert on the market goes beyond direct authentication or valuation because the study and publication of material without provenance will, in itself, provide a provenance of sorts: an academic pedigree. Once material is accepted into the validated corpus, its academic significance might translate into monetary value and provide a spur for further looting.

One response of the archaeological community has been to stop the study and publication of material that has no verifiable provenance. However, archaeological opinion is divided on the effectiveness of this tactic, for a variety of reasons.[46] In the first place, scholarly research on nonlooted material may also increase the market value of looted material: as more becomes known about a particular body of material, it becomes more collectable (and also harder to fake). In contrast, it has been argued that publication in the academic literature has little effect on the market. After all, who reads the academic literature? Then there is what Wylie[47] calls the "salvage principle." This principle asserts that some objects are of importance in themselves, even out of context, and that their importance is such as to warrant their study, so that some information at least is saved for posterity. A case in point is the large number of inscribed clay tablets that have appeared on the market since the 1991 Gulf War, in all probability extracted from sites in Iraq. The sale of these tablets would appear to be illegal, and in violation of trade sanctions, although once again this would be difficult to prove in each individual case. These tablets could arguably derive from Syria or other Middle Eastern countries, but they contain information about ancient administrations and economies. They are perhaps not as useful as tablets recovered through controlled excavation, but they are valuable nevertheless. Should these tablets simply be ignored? A related problem faces professional conservators. Without expert treatment, these tablets might deteriorate and be lost forever, yet their conservation supports the black market and may even encourage further looting.[48]

While the practicalities and ethics of working with looted material continue to tax archaeologists, they also help to reorient archaeological concerns. For a long time, U.S. and European archaeologists working in foreign countries were able to excavate, study, and (eventually) publish with little thought for the future of the sites, the sensibilities of local communities, the governments within whose jurisdictions they worked, or even the public at home, whose tax money had in many cases funded their research. However, it is increasingly accepted that archaeological research must have a public as well as an academic aspect, that it is the responsibility of archaeologists to ensure that their methods and aims are more widely understood – the stereotype of the archaeologist as treasure hunter still persists – that results should be widely publicised and that, where appropriate, archaeological sites should be prepared for public presentation, so that they can be incorporated into educational curricula and tourist itineraries. When this happens, local communities are included in the archaeological process and the sites in question fall under their protection. Archaeologists should also be prepared to support infrastructure development in host countries by training programmes aimed at archaeological, museum, and other heritage-related personnel.

Unfortunately, this is still largely abstract rhetoric. In Mexico, for example, there is only one case of research headed by a foreign institution that has concluded with the restoration of the site in question.[49] Archaeological expeditions still conform to the research ethic: the production of hard data followed by evaluation and interpretation in the academic literature. This ethic is structured by the debilitating symbiosis of professional expectations and funding constraints. Generally speaking, funds for the conservation or presentation of sites or for training programmes are not available from 'traditional' sources (usually government agencies or private foundations). Instead, such funds are available from organisations outside the "research" sector, but it is difficult to identify and approach them because doing so requires a type of knowledge, more commercial than academic, that is not offered to archaeologists during their professional training.

This is not to say that Western archaeologists working abroad have consistently failed their host countries. There are a number of large international projects of the kind

[46] A. Wylie, 'Archaeology and the antiquities market: The use of "looted" data.' In M. J. Lynott and A. Wylie (eds.), *Ethics in American Archaeology: Challenges for the 1990s* (Washington DC, Society for American Archaeology 1995).

[47] Wylie, *ibid*, 18.

[48] K. W. Tubb, 'Focusing beyond the microscope: ethical considerations in conservation,' *Art, Antiquity and Law* 2 (1997).

[49] E. Nalda, 'Mexico's archaeological heritage: A convergence and confrontation of interests.' In N. Brodie and K. W. Tubb (eds.), *Illicit Antiquities: The Theft of Culture and the Extinction of Archaeology*, (London, Routledge 2002).

described earlier, such as Butrint in Albania.[50] Angkor Borei in Cambodia,[51] the Mirador Basin in Guatemala,[52] and others, but at the present time it is probably true to say that most initiatives of this kind are home-grown. Since 1993, for example, there has been a great effort in Mali to win over the general public through the establishment of cultural missions and museums throughout the country. As a result, looting has now been virtually halted around the town of Djenne, site of the medieval town of Jenné-jeno, where the looting of terracotta statuettes produced between 400 and 1,000 years ago took on critical proportions in the late 1980s.[53]

One of the better-known developments of this kind has been at the spectacular site of Sipán in northern Peru. The archaeological site itself is a small complex of three eroded mud-brick pyramids located one kilometre outside the town. In the spring of 1987, a rich tomb of the Moche culture (early first millennium A.D.) was discovered in one of the pyramids and emptied by looters. Since then, the archaeologist Walter Alva of the Museo Nacional Brüning de la Región, has carried out a prolonged campaign of excavation – sometimes at great personal risk when disgruntled looters tried to resume their activities – and conservation at the site and has taken great pains to present his findings to the general public. What has been revealed at Sipán to date is a series of Moche royal tombs (three so far), the first to be discovered intact and undisturbed by looters, and their study has provided some unexpected insights into the previously obscure world of the Moche.[54] The results of the research have been made widely available through a range of media, including museum exhibitions, scholarly publications, a CD-ROM, a Web site, a series of popular publications, and even a comic book. The material from the excavations is now exhibited in a new purpose-built museum at the nearby town of Chiclayo, where it can be viewed by local people and tourists alike.

In 1993, building on the success of Sipán, the Museo Nacional Brüning de la Región established a programme of protection for archaeological sites in its area. Today, it has 350 volunteer members who help to watch over archaeological sites, and who are supported by the local media. It is thought that this programme has contributed to the collapse of local smuggling networks and a significant reduction in instances of looting.[55]

Another successful initiative in Peru was implemented at the first millennium B.C. site of Kuntur Wasi in the northern Andes. In 1994, with the help of archaeologists from Tokyo University, local villagers opened a small museum and educational centre, to which a library was added in 1996. Archaeological investigations continue at the site, which also remains free from the unwanted attention of looters.[56]

Local efforts in Mali and Peru were helped by bilateral agreements signed with the United States within the framework of the 1970 UNESCO Convention on the Means of Prohibiting and Preventing the Illicit Import, Export and Transfer of Ownership of Cultural Property. The U.S. implementation of this Convention, the 1983 CCPIA, specifically emphasises the importance of local measures in the field of education and protection.[57]

TOURISM

The positive impact of initiatives in Peru and Mali has been attributable in part, to the economic benefits that accrue from the increased tourist potential of curated and well-presented archaeological finds. Tourism has, in the past, been regarded by archaeologists as something of a mixed blessing. Tourist revenues are good, insofar as that the local people and governments that benefit are more likely to commit resources to site protection and conservation, but tourists themselves can be bad, especially in large numbers, because their endless propensity to touch and feel or simply walk about constitutes a relentless attack on the actual fabric of sites and monuments and can be a major cause of physical deterioration.

In 1999, the International Council on Monuments and Sites (ICOMOS)[58] adopted a new International Charter on Cultural Tourism. In its introduction, it states:

> "Tourism should bring benefits to host communities and provide an important means and motivation for them to care for and maintain their heritage and cultural practices. The involvement and cooperation of local and/or indigenous community representatives, conservationists, tourism operators, property owners, policy makers, those preparing national development plans and site managers is necessary to achieve a sustainable tourist industry and enhance the protection of heritage resources for future generations."

It has been estimated that foreign tourists coming to see the site and the excavated finds at Sipán spend something like

[50] R. Hodges, 'Rejecting reflexivity? Making post-Stalinist archaeology in Albania.' In N. Brodie and C. Hills (eds.), *Material Engagements: Studies in Honour of Colin Renfrew* (Cambridge, McDonald Institute for Archaeological Research 2004).

[51] M. T. Stark and P. B. Griffin, 'Archaeological research and cultural heritage management in Cambodia's Mekong Delta: The search for the "Cradle of Khmer Civilisation." In Y. Rowan and U. Baram (eds.), *Marketing Heritage. Archaeology and the Consumption of the Past.* (Walnut Creek, AltaMira 2004)

[52] R. D. Hansen, 'Marvels of the Ancient Maya,' *Archaeology* (September/October 2001); see also <http://www.miradorbasin.com/>.

[53] S. K. McIntosh, 'Reducing incentives for illicit trade in antiquities: The US implementation of the 1970 UNESCO Convention.' In N. Brodie and K. W. Tubb (eds.), *Illicit Antiquities: The Theft of Culture and the Extinction of Archaeology*, (London, Routledge 2002); T. Togola, 'The rape of Mali's only resource.' In N. Brodie and K. W. Tubb (eds.), *Illicit Antiquities: The Theft of Culture and the Extinction of Archaeology*, (London, Routledge 2002).

[54] W. Alva, W. and C. B. Donnan, *Royal Tombs of Sipán* (Los Angeles, University of California, Los Angeles 1994).

[55] W. Alva, 'The destruction, looting and traffic of the archaeological heritage of Peru.' In N. Brodie, J. Doole and C. Renfrew (eds.), *Trade in Illicit Antiquities: The Destruction of the Archaeological Heritage*, 95 (Cambridge, McDonald Institute for Archaeological Research 2001).

[56] Y. Onuki, 'Kuntur Wasi: Temple, gold, museum . . . and an experiment in community development,' *Museum International* 51(4) (1999).

[57] McIntosh, *supra* note 48, 243.

[58] ICOMOS is an international non-governmental organisation that acts as UNESCO's principal advisor in matters concerning the conservation and protection of the world's historic monuments and sites. It has national committees in over 100 countries.

U.S.$14 million a year in the area, which provides a welcome boost to the local economy.[59] However, this effect is moderated somewhat by the fact that, although some shops and cafes have appeared in the area of the site itself, the major beneficiary of the increase in tourism appears to be the nearby town of Chiclayo, which is located about ten kilometres away and handles all tourist arrivals and stopovers.[60]

Some tour operators have acted independently to protect threatened archaeological sites. The so-called Nazca lines in southern Peru are ground drawings or "geoglyphs" that were carved into the surface of the desert during the first millennium A.D. The individual glyphs take the form of giant naturalistic or geometrical figures, up to four-hundred metres across, that are visible in their entirety only from the air. They are a big tourist attraction, and it is estimated that the number of foreign tourists visiting the town of Nazca itself has tripled since 1995 to 70,000 a year. However, the geoglyphs, which are found scattered over an area of about two-hundred sq km, are increasingly under threat from looting, infrastructure development, and even the weather. Tomb robbing, in particular, has become a major problem in recent years, eroding glyphs and leaving ugly scars across the landscape. The problem is now so acute that the future survival of the Nazca lines is in doubt. In response, the Peruvian airline *Aero Condor* has established a joint protection programme with the local police and will mount airborne patrols to track thieves.[61]

TRADE RESPONSE

Several associations have been established to represent the interests of the trade, and they state publicly that their members are required to adhere to certain standards of behaviour, which are sometimes formulated as codes of ethics or practice. The existence of these codes allows the trade to argue that it is self-regulating and that therefore statutory control is unnecessary, an argument with political resonance in the ostensively free-trade jurisdictions of North America and Europe, where most of the end trading goes on. Unfortunately, it is questionable to what extent the codes are respected or enforced. In February 2002, for example, Frederick Schultz, a top Manhattan antiquities dealer and former president of the National Association of Dealers in Ancient, Oriental and Primitive Art, was convicted after appeal for trading in antiquities he knew to be stolen from Egypt.[62] Schultz may have been an exception. Most dealers are not criminals, but then they have no need to be. For reasons set out earlier, it is conveniently difficult to acquire knowledge of the illegal origins of unprovenanced antiquities. But professional codes of practice profess to offer a stronger standard of protection than is strictly required by law, by requiring that members show some degree of diligence when investigating the history of a piece. In the United Kingdom, for example, there are two trade associations (Antiquities Dealers Association and International Association of Dealers in Ancient Art), each of which has a code of ethics containing an identical Article 2:

> "The members of . . . [ADA/IADAA] . . . undertake not to purchase or sell objects until they have established to the best of their ability that such objects were not stolen from excavations, architectural monuments, public institutions or private property."

Unfortunately, what might constitute necessary diligence is not defined, and there is evidence to suggest that this article is often ignored, or at least only weakly respected. For example, large numbers of cuneiform tablets and other objects, probably from Iraq, have been offered for sale over the past ten years or so with a certificate of authenticity and translation provided by an Emeritus Professor of Assyriology at a top British University. Presumably, if a cuneiform tablet needs authenticating and translating in this way, it is because it has not previously come to the attention of the scholarly community, and therefore is probably fresh on the market. The professor has said as much himself. When interviewed by the *New York Times* in April 2003,[63] he was quoted as saying that when he authenticates an object he does not necessarily know where it comes from, and he suspects that very often the dealers themselves don't know either. Nevertheless, the high probability that these objects have been removed destructively and illegally from Iraq has not prevented their enthusiastic sale and collection. In 1999, UNESCO adopted its International Code of Ethics for Dealers in Cultural Property.[64] To date, however, this code has attracted little trade attention.

Although many archaeologists (and, indeed, museum curators, conservators, lawyers, and law enforcement officers) see the fundamental problem of the antiquities trade to be indiscriminate demand, among many proponents of the trade there is a strong opinion that many of its problems are an outgrowth of overregulation. This type of argument can be traced back to Paul Bator,[65] at least, who suggested that attempts to stifle the antiquities market by means of strong trade controls are futile because the controls will inevitably be circumvented by criminal means. Then, not only are archaeological sites offered no protection, but society is forced to suffer the adverse consequences of criminalization. The alternative strategy is to release more antiquities on to the market. An increased supply of legitimate antiquities would ameliorate demand, thereby removing the incentive to despoil

[59] P. Watson, 'The lessons of Sipán: Archaeologists and huaqeros,' *Culture Without Context* 4, 16 (1999)

[60] *Ibid*, 18.

[61] A. Faiola, 'Ancient history imperiled in Peru,' *Washington Post*, A20 (May 20 2001).

[62] P. Gerstenblith, United States v. Schultz. *Culture Without Context* 10 (2002).

[63] M. Gottlieb and B. Meier, 'Of 2,000 treasures stolen in Gulf War of 1991, only 12 have been recovered,' *New York Times* (April 30 2003).

[64] Available at <http://portal.unesco.org/culture/>, accessed December 16 2004.

[65] P. M. Bator, *The International Trade in Art* (Chicago, University of Chicago Press 1981). Paul M. Bator served as a member of the US delegation to the UNESCO Special Committee that negotiated and drafted the Convention on the Means of Prohibiting and Preventing the Illicit Import, Export and Transfer of Ownership of Cultural Property.

archaeological sites, and discourage the involvement of criminals. The antiquities to be released would be duplicates, or redundant, and either already exist in museum storage or be provided through future excavation. Unfortunately, there are many objections to this solution: stockpiles of objects might not exist, duplicates would not appeal to collectors, excavations do not routinely recover saleable objects, the release of legitimate material would further commercialise the market and act to increase rather than assuage demand, and more besides.[66] These objections have never been confronted.

CONCLUSION

The problems caused by the trade in unprovenanced antiquities will only be solved when it becomes possible to discriminate between antiquities that are on the market legitimately and those that are not. Self-regulation on the part of the trade has demonstrably failed, and so the answer seems to lie with museums. Museums can act by (1) acquiring only material acceptable under article 3.2 of the ICOM Code of Ethics, and (2) making public their accession records to facilitate provenance research.[67] The challenge for archaeologists is to develop more socially inclusive research strategies, and to recognise their responsibilities to the public that both funds and validates their activities.

QUESTIONS FOR DISUSSION

1. What standard of provenance should be regarded as acceptable for a museum intending to acquire a cultural object?

2. Should the fiduciary responsibilities of museum trustees impact upon the acquisition policies of museums as regards unprovenanced cultural objects?

3. Should private collectors receive tax benefits for donating unprovenanced cultural objects to museums or other cultural institutions?

BIBLIOGRAPHY

AAM. 1993. Code of Ethics for Museums.

AAMD. June 10, 2004. Report on Acquisition of Archaeological Materials and Ancient Art at <http://www.aamd.org/papers/guideln.php>.

Alberge, D. and D. McGrory, 2000. "Art mole threatens to turn tables on Yard handlers." *The Times*, 29 January, 2000.

Ali, I. and R., Coningham. 1998. "Recording and preserving Gandhara's cultural heritage." *Culture Without Context* 3: 10–16.

Alva, W. 2001. 'The destruction, looting and traffic of the archaeological heritage of Peru.' In Brodie, Doole and Renfrew (2001) pp. 89–96.

[66] N. Brodie, 'Export deregulation and the illicit trade in archaeological material.' In J. R. Richman and M. P. Forsyth (eds.), *Legal Perspectives on Cultural Resources* (Walnut Creek: AltaMira 2004).

[67] C. C. Coggins, 'A proposal for museum acquisition policies in the future,' *International Journal of Cultural Property* 7 (1998).

Alva, W. and C. B. Donnan. 1994. *Royal Tombs of Sipán*. Los Angeles: University of California, Los Angeles.

Bleibtrau, E. 1999. 'Een verguld zilveren beker van koning Assurbanipal.' In Bleibtrau, E. and H. D. Schneider (eds.). *Ritueel en Schoonheid: Antieke meesterwerken uit het Miho Museum, Japan.* Milan: Skira Editore. pp. 21–31.

Bator, P. M. 1981. *The International Trade in Art*. Chicago: University of Chicago Press.

Bogdanos, M. 2003. Iraq Museum Investigation: 22 Apr–8 Sep 03. On line at <http://www.defenselink.mil/news/Sep2003/d20030922fr.pdf> (accessed 14 October 2004).

Boylan, P. J. 2002. 'The concept of cultural protection in times of armed conflict: from the crusades to the new millennium.' In Brodie and Tubb (2002) pp. 43–108.

Brent, M. 1996. 'The rape of Mali'. In Vitelli, K. D. (ed.). *Archaeological Ethics*. Walnut Creek: AltaMira.

Brodie, N. 2002. 'Introduction.' In Brodie and Tubb (2002) pp. 1–22.

Brodie, N. 2003. 'Spoils of war.' *Archaeology* July/August: 16–19.

Brodie, N. 2004. 'Export deregulation and the illicit trade in archaeological material.' In J. R. Richman and M. P. Forsyth (eds.). *Legal Perspectives on Cultural Resources*. Walnut Creek: AltaMira. pp. 85–99.

Brodie, N. In review. 'The plunder of Iraq's archaeological heritage 1991–2004 and the London antiquities trade.' In N. Brodie, M. Kersel, C. Luke and K. W. Tubb (eds.). *Transforming Values: Archaeology and the Antiquities Trade.*

Brodie, N. and J. Doole. 2004. 'The Asian art affair: US art museum collections of Asian art and archaeology.' In Brodie and Hills (2004) pp. 83–108.

Brodie, N. and C. Hills (eds.). 2004. *Material Engagements: Studies in Honour of Colin Renfrew*. Cambridge: McDonald Institute for Archaeological Research.

Brodie, N. and C. Luke. In review. 'Conclusion. The social and cultural contexts of collecting.' In N. Brodie, M. Kersel, C. Luke and K. W. Tubb (eds.). *Transforming Values: Archaeology and the Antiquities Trade.*

Brodie, N. and K. W. Tubb (eds.). 2002. *Illicit Antiquities: The Theft of Culture and the Extinction of Archaeology*. London: Routledge.

Brodie, N., J. Doole and C. Renfrew (eds.). 2001. *Trade in Illicit Antiquities: The Destruction of the Archaeological Heritage*. Cambridge: McDonald Institute for Archaeological Research.

Brodie, N., J. Doole and P. Watson. 2000. *Stealing History*. Cambridge: McDonald Institute for Archaeological Research.

Chippindale, C. and D. W. J. Gill. 2000. 'Material consequences of contemporary classical collecting.' *American Journal of Archaeology* 104: 463–511.

Coggins, C. C. 1998. 'A proposal for museum acquisition policies in the future.' *International Journal of Cultural Property* 7: 434–7.

Cohen, W. I. 1992. *East Asian Art and American Culture*. New York: Columbia University Press.

Elia, R. 2001. 'Analysis of the looting, selling and collecting of Apulian red-figure vases: a quantitative approach.' In Brodie, Doole and Renfrew (2001) pp. 145–54.

Faiola, A. 2001. 'Ancient history imperiled in Peru.' *Washington Post*, May 20, A20.

Fernandez Cacho, S. and L. G. Sanjuán. 2000. 'Site looting and illicit trade of archaeological objects in Andalusia, Spain.' *Culture Without Context* 7: 17–24.

Feroozi, A. W. and Z. Tarzi. 2004. 'The impact of war upon Afghanistan's Cultural Heritage.' Available at www.archaeological.org.

Garen, M. 2004. 'The war within the war.' *Archaeology*, July/August: 28–30.

Gerstenblith, P. 2002. United States v. Schultz. *Culture Without Context* 10: 27–31.

Gerstenblith, P. 2003. 'Acquisition and deacquisition of museum collections and the fiduciary obligations of museums to the public.' *Cardozo Journal of International and Comparative Law* 11: 409–65.

Gibson, M. 2003. 'From the prevention measures to the fact-finding mission.' *Museum International*, 219–20: 108–17

Gilgan, E. 2001. 'Looting and the market for Maya objects: a Belizean perspective.' In Brodie, Doole and Renfrew (2001) pp. 73–87.

Gill, D. W. J. and C. Chippindale. 1993. 'Material and Intellectual Consequences of Esteem for Cycladic Figures.' *American Journal of Archaeology* 1997 Convention: 601–59.

Gottlieb, M. and B. Meier. 2003. 'Of 2,000 treasures stolen in Gulf War of 1991, only 12 have been recovered.' *New York Times*, 30 April.

Graepler, D. 1993. *Fundort: Unbekannt. Raubgrabungen Zerstören das Archäologische Erbe.* Munich: Walter Bierung.

Gutchen, M. 1983. 'The destruction of archaeological resources in Belize, Central America.' *Journal of Field Archaeology* 10: 217–27.

Hansen, R. D. 2001. 'Marvels of the Ancient Maya.' *Archaeology* September/October: 51–8.

Hodges, R. 2004. 'Rejecting reflexivity? Making post-Stalinist archaeology in Albania.' In Brodie and Hills (2004) pp. 145–64.

ICOM 2004. ICOM Code of Ethics for Museums. Paris: ICOM.

Kaufman, J. E. 1996. 'Getty decides publishing equals provenance.' *Art Newspaper* 61: 17.

Lawler, A. 2003. 'Mayhem in Mesopotamia.' *Science* 301: 582–8.

Lee, D. 1999. 'Getty returns three stolen works.' *Art Newspaper* 90: 1, 3.

McGirk, T. 1996. 'A year of looting dangerously.' *Independent on Sunday*, 24 March.

McIntosh, R., T. Togola, and S. K. McIntosh 1995. 'The Good Collector and the premise of mutual respect among nations.' *African Arts* 27: 60–9.

McIntosh, S. K. 2000. 'Proposition.' *Public Archaeology* 1: 73–6.

McIntosh, S. K. 2002. "Reducing incentives for illicit trade in antiquities: The US implementation of the 1970 UNESCO Convention." In Brodie and Tubb (2002) pp. 241–9.

Muscarella, O. 2000. *The Lie Became Great: The Forgery of Ancient Near Eastern Cultures.* Groningen: Styx.

Nalda, E. 2002. 'Mexico's archaeological heritage: a convergence and confrontation of interests.' In Brodie and Tubb (2002) pp. 205–27.

O'Keefe, P. J. 2004. The First Protocol to the Hague Convention fifty years on.' *Art, Antiquity and Law* 9: 99–116.

Onuki, Y. 1999. 'Kuntur Wasi: temple, gold, museum... and an experiment in community development.' *Museum International* 51(4): 42–6.

Pal, P. 1986. *American Collectors of Asian Art.* Bombay: Marg.

Pastore, G. 2001. The looting of archaeological sites in Italy. In Brodie, Doole and Renfrew (2001) pp. 155–60.

Renfrew, C. 2000. *Loot, Legitimacy and Ownership.* London: Duckworth.

Schick, J. 1998. *The Gods are Leaving the Country.* Bangkok: White Orchid.

Sims, C. 2001. 'Japanese agree to return a stolen statue to China.' *New York Times*, April 18.

Stark, M. T. and P. B. Griffin. 2004. 'Archaeological research and cultural heritage management in Cambodia's Mekong Delta: the search for the "Cradle of Khmer Civilisation." In Y. Rowan and U. Baram (eds.). *Marketing Heritage. Archaeology and the Consumption of the Past.* Walnut Creek: AltaMira, 117–41.

Togola, T. 2002. 'The rape of Mali's only resource.' In Brodie and Tubb (2002) pp. 250–6.

True, M. and K. Hamma (eds.). 1994. *A Passion for Antiquities: Ancient Art from the Collection of Barbara and Lawrence Fleischman.* Malibu: J. Paul Getty Museum.

Tubb, K. W. 1997. 'Focusing beyond the microscope: ethical considerations in conservation.' *Art, Antiquity and Law* 2: 41–50.

US Department of Defense 2003. 'DoD News Briefing – Secretary Rumsfeld and Gen. Myers.' Online at <http://www.defenselink.mil/transcripts/2003/tr20030520-secdef0207.html>. Accessed 14 August 2004.

Watson, P. 1997. *Sotheby's: Inside Story.* London: Bloomsbury.

Watson, P. 1998. 'The sequestered warehouses.' *Culture Without Context* 2: 11–14.

Watson, P. 1999. 'The lessons of Sipán: archaeologists and huaqeros.' *Culture Without Context* 4: 15–20.

Wylie, A. 1995. 'Archaeology and the antiquities market: the use of "looted" data.' In M. J. Lynott and A. Wylie (eds.). *Ethics in American Archaeology: Challenges for the 1990s.* Washington DC: Society for American Archaeology. pp. 17–21.

CHAPTER SIX

Reflexions on the Causes of Illicit Traffic in Cultural Property and Some Potential Cures

Manus Brinkman

Over the past four decades, an increasingly acrimonious debate has developed over the role played by antiquities collecting in the destruction of world's archaeological heritage. Most collectors and dealers protest that the link made between collecting and looting is grossly overstated and that most of their purchases are from old collections.[1] Members of the archaeological community argue, in my view, persuasively, to the contrary. The causes of the illicit international traffic in cultural property are, in fact, very similar to those of drug trafficking. On the one hand, there is a demand from wealthy consumers, and, on the other, there is a huge supply in regions where poverty reigns. It is rather strange that the collection of cultural objects of unknown provenance by wealthy private individuals is still widely considered to be socially acceptable. Nobody has to collect illicit material.

Although reputable auction houses and dealers act within the parameters of the law, previously their trade associations did not support initiatives to actively restrict the free trade in cultural objects on the theory that the black market thrives from overly retentive trade in cultural objects: as the demand for antiquities grows, the supply is cut off.

Auction houses, however, create and stimulate demand for objects from source nations. The best known auction houses do not wait for trends but develop them aggressively. In the past decade, auction houses have turned to Asian art as the newest "trend" with a considerable number of major works of art said to have come out of Southeast Asia and China. In 1996, the strong demand for Southeast Asian paintings among an increasingly affluent Asian middle class became apparent when Christie's withdrew five Indonesian paintings from its Singapore sale after the National Museum in Jakarta saw them and identified them as stolen. "I think it is our duty to report if we know something . . . but we don't go out and look for lost paintings," Christie's then Singapore manager is reported as saying at the time of the return.[2] Because auction houses are bound only by the law of agency, it is easy for them to consider only an obligation to the auction house's individual consignor rather than a broader fiduciary duty to the international community. Singapore is a free port with few regulations.

Whether as a result of public pressure, self-interest, legal developments or conscience, auction houses have become more active in policing the illicit traffic in art. Sotheby's and others in the international art market established the Art Loss Register – one of the largest and best-known databases of stolen and missing art and cultural objects – to assist in provenance enquiries and help ensure that stolen or looted property is not circulated in the legitimate market. If an object is reported stolen in the archives of the Art Loss Register or Interpol, it will not appear in a Sotheby's or a Christie's catalogue.

In 1984, a Code of Practice for the Control of International Trading in Works of Art was signed by representatives of several British auctioneers and dealers, including Christie's and Sotheby's. They agreed "to the best of their ability not to import, export or transfer the ownership of objects" exported illegally from their country of origin.

In 1994, ten years after the British initiative, a newly formed association of antiquities dealers in Europe and the United States, The International Association of Dealers in Ancient Art, aims "to actively encourage the protection and preservation of ancient sites."

In 1991, UNESCO adopted an International Code of Ethics for Dealers in Cultural Property, which could be useful if adopted by dealers' associations. It can only be hoped that art dealers around the world will be informed of its principles and adhere to them.

Although private collectors play a major role in the stimulation of illicit traffic, the general public should also be held responsible. More and more tourists return home with artefacts that are protected in their countries of origin. Although the individual objects may not be valuable, the sheer volume of this form of illicit traffic is staggering.

The local inhabitant may also be a participant. Poor farmers may suddenly see an opportunity to earn some money by selling pottery from an archaeological site. Local officials are often also involved in this trade, either openly, for the purpose of "making their village or county rich," or clandestinely, as part of a network of illegal excavation and smuggling.

Take, for example, the case of Qixing, a town in the Hunan province of China. Most of China's cultural heritage is owned by the state, administered by different levels of local government and managed by each unit at the grass roots level.

[1] Although the focus here is on the role played by the collector in the illicit antiquities trade, the collector has a complex role in the preservation of cultural heritage. Collectors are by definition acquisitive people and collect for a variety of reasons. Those who own important works often describe themselves as "trustees" or "stewards." Private collectors are essential to museums and play a central role both in sustaining the art heritage of the past, as well as collecting it for the future. As Bernard de Mandeville put it succinctly two hundred years ago: "Private vices, public benefits," quoted in Joseph L. Sax, *Playing Darts with a Rembrandt*, p. 63 (Univ. of Michigan Press, 2003).

[2] Leong Weng Kam, "Indonesian Art Heads Home," *Singapore Strait Times*, Oct. 4, 1996.

The Cultural Heritage Department, the Finance Department, and the Police Department all have obligations. The authorities were informed that illegal excavations were taking place and promised to take action. In practice, nothing happened, because the authorities either failed to take appropriate action or blamed bureaucratic restrictions for preventing them from doing so.

As He Shuzhong, Founder and Director, Cultural Heritage Watch, Beijing, observed, authorities are generally reluctant to take action because action to protect the sites costs them money and because they may come into conflict with construction companies. Besides, taking action would make them responsible for preventing a very lucrative trade. Of the 70,000 officially designated archaeological sites in China, the central government has taken responsibility for 1,269 sites; approximately 7,000 sites are protected at the provincial level; and an astounding 60,000 sites are the responsibility of county and local governments. It is estimated that about 400,000 need protection. Even if a site is officially registered, there is often little visible protection in practice. Sometimes the people responsible for protecting several square kilometres of archaeological property possess no telephone or means of transport. In addition to ineffective law enforcement, Shuzhong identifies the following flaws in China's system for protection of its cultural heritage: (1) failure to codify cultural heritage legislation, (2) ambiguity over the scope of protection, (3) absence of a system of registration, (4) export licensing, (5) absence of control of the relics market.[3]

The situation in other parts of the world is similar. In Peru, for example, fifty percent of all known archaeological sites have been looted. In Belize, the figure is seventy-three percent, and in south-west Niger (Bura system), almost ninety percent.[4] As my predecessor, Elisabeth des Portes, noted, the extent of the situation can be judged by the example of Ecuador, which, in 1983, retrieved 9,236 archaeological objects that had been illicitly taken out of the country and were in the possession of a single Italian collector. Churches throughout Latin America are also systematically looted.[5]

The situation in Cambodia is also well known. Despite some progress, objects continue to be smuggled in trucks to Thailand. Craftsmen in Thailand frequently change the features of statues to prevent them from being recognised. Objects are then sold in Bangkok antique shops or sold on the international market. The Thai government recently intercepted truckloads of smuggled Khmer antiquities and sent them back to Cambodia.

European countries are not spared from robbery or looting. In Italy, as many as 100,000 Apulian graves have been destroyed.[6] Every year, moreover, tens of thousands of objects are stolen from museums, castles, country houses, private collections, and churches. In Italy, tens of thousands of objects have disappeared from churches in the last 20 years. This is why ICOM published a fourth volume in its One Hundred Missing Objects series, entitled One Hundred Missing Objects in Europe, that focuses exclusively on the theft of religious artefacts.

The solution to the illicit trade in cultural material is not a simple one. I have already discussed the importance of codes of ethics. In addition, core requirements include an effective international legal framework and well-crafted domestic legislation, education of the public, a clear definition of cultural property, an inventory, and adequate security. The last three are more fully discussed subsequently.

DEFINING A COUNTRY'S CULTURAL PROPERTY

Without a definition of cultural property, it is difficult for a country to recover lost or stolen objects; and defining cultural property is not an easy matter. A definition of cultural property may include artefacts that are expressive of a specific culture and are unusual or uniquely characteristic of that culture. Examples of such artefacts include rare collections of fauna and flora, archaeological finds, and antiquities. A definition based on these criteria would be so broad however, that it would only be effective if national governments made a list of protected cultural property. For African and Pacific countries, such a list might include native crafts and objects used for ritual purposes, whereas in Mediterranean countries it might cover antiquities and in Western European countries, fine art.

ESTABLISHING AN INVENTORY SYSTEM AND MAINTAINING COMPREHENSIVE DOCUMENTATION

The story of Nepal is very poignant. Jurgen Schick, a German national living in Nepal, devised a plan to produce a comprehensive set of documents on the art of the Kathmandu valley. However, he increasingly found himself standing in front of empty alcoves, disfigured temple walls, shrines plundered down to their last artefacts, and headless statues of deities. In the 1980s, Nepal's art treasures were systematically plundered by well-organised bands of thieves that stole the images of Nepal's deities on the orders of an international art theft network and smuggled them abroad to collections and museums in richer countries. In the past 40 years, more than half the works of art that Nepal created during 2,000 years of cultural history have been stolen and taken out of the country. According to Schick, "of the hundreds of temples in the Kathmandu valley, not a single one exists that does not bear

[3] Shuzhong, He. "The Mainland's Environment and the Protection of China's Cultural Heritage: A Chinese Cultural Heritage Lawyer's Perspective." 5 *Art Antiquity and Law* p. 19–35. (March 2000) See also <http://www.chinacov.com/EN/displaynews.asp?id=99> (last visited January 2005).

[4] *No To Illicit Traffic: Some Facts on Illicit Trafficking in Cultural Property* (information pack). 2000. Paris: UNESCO International Standards Unit.

[5] Elisabeth des Portes, Secretary General of ICOM in 1996.

[6] *One Hundred Missing Objects: Looting in Europe* (2002: 30–31)/ Information provided by the Carabinieri Unit for the Protection of Artistic Heritage.

the clear marks of theft." The fact that UNESCO placed the valley on its World Heritage List did not help. Schick managed to photograph many sites "before" and "after" the theft, and by doing so he has provided documentation that may be used to support demands for the repatriation of certain artefacts. As a rule, such artefacts cannot be repatriated after they have been discovered, because there is no proof that they originate from the alleged country of origin.

In all programmes relating to risk preparedness, registration should always be a high priority. If registries, inventories, and descriptions do not exist, it will be very difficult to establish later where an object came from and to whom it really belongs.

At the international level, however, it is important that these descriptions and lists are more or less standardised. Standardisation in the field of cultural property protection is a particularly difficult task, although there have been some initiatives. In 1995, ICOM's International Committee for Documentation (CIDOC) published the *International Guidelines for Museum Object Information.* In 1996, ICOM published a *Handbook of Standards for African Collections*, based on the CIDOC Guidelines. CIDOC and six African museums participated in the production of the Handbook, which can be consulted on ICOM's Web site. In addition, Interpol has developed standardised forms for documenting stolen objects to help police officers describe stolen artworks.

The Object Identification (Object ID) system, an international standard for recording basic data on movable cultural property, was developed by the J. Paul Getty Trust (today the Getty Foundation). ICOM has always supported the Object ID, not as a documentation system in itself, but as a tool in the fight against the illicit traffic in cultural property, which allows for immediate transmission of essential information to law enforcement agencies on identifiable characteristics of stolen objects. In 2004, the Getty Foundation transferred the worldwide license on Object ID to ICOM in recognition of its commitment to the international promotion of this invaluable documentation tool. Lists of stolen objects are still available, but the information contained in these lists tends to vary. Some countries, like France and Italy, maintain extensive databases on stolen objects, but they focus mainly on objects stolen from the countries themselves. Since 1969, Italy has had a special branch within its police force that is responsible for the recovery of stolen art. This special branch maintains an extensive database that can be consulted on its Web site.

The International Foundation for Art Research (IFAR) in New York publishes information on art that has been reported as stolen, and its database is now part of the Art Loss Register. Based in London, this is a private database that mainly serves insurance companies and private collectors. Although the register is a valuable resource, it is of limited use because it is still far from being comprehensive. For example, it does not contain details of antiquities that have been illegally excavated and smuggled without trace, nor does it contain the details of objects that, for one reason or another, have never been properly registered or documented in their country of origin.

The Illicit Antiquities Research Centre of the McDonald Institute for Archaeological Research also provides information on missing and stolen objects. The Institute has cooperated with ICOM-UK and the United Kingdom Museums Association to produce a research report on the illicit traffic in cultural objects.[7]

ICOM has produced four volumes in its One Hundred Missing Objects series. As a result of the series, various objects have been found and even returned to their countries of origin, although the series is meant to be a tool for raising awareness rather than a database of stolen objects.

For example, an eleventh-century stone statue of a four-headed Brahma, sold by Sotheby's in London on 21 October 1993 for £2,070 was proven to be looted from Angkor. A photo of the head was included on page 92 of the first edition of *Looting in Angkor* (DCA 3489). The object was formally identified by ICOM and the Ecole Francaise d' Extreme Orient (EFEO). After several years of discussions between the Cambodian authorities, Sotheby's, and the possessor of the object, it was returned in Phnom Penh on 4 December 1996.

The Metropolitan Museum in New York had, as part of its South and Southeast Asian display, an early tenth-century head of the Brahmanic god Shiva that had been removed from a sculpture held in an Angkor conservation storehouse. The object is referenced in *Looting in Angkor* (first edition, p. 80, DCA 5729). The Metropolitan informed ICOM it was in possession of the piece. After several years of correspondence between the Cambodian authorities and the Metropolitan, the latter returned the sculpture to Cambodia in March 1997.

On 2 June 1992, in a sale of Southeast Asian art held at Sotheby's in New York, ICOM found a torso of an eleventh-century feminine figure listed as stolen in *Looting in Angkor* (first edition, p. 46, DCA 7081) to have been sold to a Swiss gallery for US$63,250. The object was subsequently returned, alternately, to several of its previous owners. In August 1996, it was finally in the possession of a New York art gallery (Doris Wiener Gallery). In May of 1997, the gallery returned the statue to the Cambodian authorities.

PROTECTING MUSEUMS, EXCAVATION SITES, AND OTHER LOCATIONS CONTAINING CULTURAL PROPERTY

Although more attention is being paid to security issues in the current climate, they are still not very high on the agenda of many museums. Most of the time, security is more a question of risk management and general risk awareness rather than of identifying the appropriate technological resources. It is also a question of money. Protecting large archaeological sites requires a car and a telephone system at the very least, which, in many parts of the world, are not always available for

[7] <http://www.mcdonald.cam.ac.uk/IARC/cwoc/issue5/stealinghistory.htm>.

this purpose. However, money alone will not help. Awareness is also a key factor, and involving local people in the protection of their heritage may also have a significant impact. ICOM has an International Committee for Museum Security that offers advice and recommendations on the protection of museums, excavation sites, and other locations containing cultural property.

ICOM has organised training workshops for police and customs officers in Africa, the Middle East, and Southeast Asia to provide them with some basic knowledge about protected objects and the seriousness of the illicit traffic therein. ICOM also works closely together with Interpol, but until recently, the latter has had very limited resources for the retrieval of cultural property.

BIBLIOGRAPHY

Books

One Hundred Missing Objects: Looting in Europe. (ICOM, Paris 2000.)

One Hundred Missing Objects: Looting in Africa. (ICOM, Paris 1997.)

One Hundred Missing Objects: Looting in Angkor. (ICOM, Paris 1997.)

One Hundred Missing Objects: Looting in Latin America. (ICOM, Paris 1997.)

Rascher, Andrea F. G. 2000. Kulturguter-transfer und globalisierung. Zurich.

Red List: Stop the Looting of African Archaeological Objects. 2000. Paris: ICOM.

Renfrew, Colin. 2000. Loot, Legitimacy and Ownership. London.

Schick, Jurgen. 1998. The Gods Are Leaving the Country. Bangkok.

Wiederkehr Schuler, Elsbeth. 2000. Kulturgueterschutz-Freier Kunstmarkt. Zurich.

Journals and Periodicals

Culture without Context (newsletter of the McDonald Illicit Antiquities Research Centre, Cambridge).

ICOM News (newsletter of the International Council of Museums, Paris).

International Journal of Cultural Property (bi-annual journal published by Cambridge University Press for the International Cultural Property Society).

The Art Newspaper (monthly publication of Umberto Allemandi & Co. Publishing, London).

Web sites

International Council of Museums (ICOM), <http://icom.museum/>

The McDonald Institute for Archaeological Research, <http://www.mcdonald.cam.ac.uk/>

Museum Security Network, <http://www.museum-security.org/>

Cultural Heritage Watch, <http://www.heritagewatch.org/index.html>

Object Identification System (Object ID), <http://www.object-id.com/about.html>

International Foundation for Art Research (IFAR), and the Art Loss Register (ALR), <http://www.ifar.org/index.htm>

The Growing Complexity of International Art Law: Conflict of Laws, Uniform Law, Mandatory Rules, UNSC Resolutions and EU Regulations[1]

Guido Carducci

To the memory of Dr. Georges Droz, Former Secretary General of the Hague Conference of Private International Law, inter alia *for his contribution to the shift from Private International Law to International Uniform Law specifically designed for Cultural Property.*[2]

International transactions of "works of art" or "cultural property" raise a variety of private and/or public international law issues.[3] The occasionally related claims for restitution raise legal but also sensitive and complex moral issues.[4]

Before entering into the complex legal issues related to such international transactions, a preliminary and broader issue needs to be addressed.

[1] Prof. (MC Paris) Dr. Guido Carducci (ICC/CCI Arbitrator; Diploma, Hague Academy of International Law, awarded in 1991). The author is currently Chief, International Standards Section, (CLT/INS), United Nations Educational, Scientific, and Cultural Organization (UNESCO Headquarters, Paris). The article is written in the author's personal capacity and does not commit the Organization. (Any comment to this article may be addressed to: gcarducci@noos.fr.)

This article originates from a contribution the author had the honor to be invited to give at the last International Bar Association (IBA) Annual Meeting in Auckland, New Zealand (24–29 October 2004), on "Licit international transactions in works of art and antiquities." Some elements of a second contribution as commentator on "International arbitration and ADR in art and cultural heritage disputes" serve as a basis for this article.

[2] See G. Droz, *The International Protection of Cultural Property from the Standpoint of Private International Law,* in International Legal Protection of Cultural Property (Workshop in Delphi, 20–22 September 1983, 1984 p.114–116). Dr. Droz also contributed to designing thoughtful and balanced solutions during the UNIDROIT Diplomatic Conference in June (7–24) 1995. See also G. Droz, *La Convention d'Unidroit sur le retour international des biens culturels volés ou illicitement exportés (Rome, 24 juin 1995),* RCDIP, 1997, p. 239. For a brief summary of his contribution to private international law, see P. Lagarde, *Ad memoriam,* RCDIP no. 3, 2004.

[3] Usually studies on legal protection in international law of cultural property proceed from a public or private law perspective. In our view, in spite of their respective complexities, both perspectives and their interactions must be considered to provide an accurate analysis of such protection (G. Carducci, *Beni culturali in diritto internazionale pubblico e privato,* in Enciclopedia giuridica italiana G. Treccani, Rome 2000).

[4] As respect for, and protection of, the integrity of national cultural heritages vis-à-vis cultural objects illicitly removed from the country of origin.

1. ON CULTURAL AND LEGAL "SPECIFICITY" OF WORKS OF ART AND CULTURAL PROPERTY

Indeed, depending on the position national authorities take on this specificity, the legal regime and status of works of art and cultural property may differ substantially at various levels: domestic law (below:1.2), private international law (below: 5), international treaty law (below: 6) or *ad hoc* measures (below: 8 and 9).

1.1. Cultural and Legal Specificity

Are works of art and cultural property "specific" vis-à-vis, and as such distinct from, "ordinary" objects? The answer is rather clear in general terms, as are the protection and conservation needs, as well as the cultural and scientific values of such objects. However, it is necessary not to confuse and, on the contrary, maintain distinct "cultural" and "legal" specificity of such objects: even if the former is certain vis-à-vis a given object (or category of objects) the latter does *not automatically* follow. A legal specificity of such objects exists if the national authorities (government, law-maker, judiciary through case-law) deem it appropriate and consequently provide specific provisions which result in a legal regime for these objects which is (in part or in its entirety) different from the regime applicable to "ordinary" objects. Each legal system decides if, to what extent and under which forms and contents, legal specificity is added to the cultural specificity of a given object (or category of objects). Although the terminology of objects (or movable property) is used here, the same reasoning applies generally to immovable (cultural property).

The length of this article does not permit a full development of the various and rather well-known reasons underlying the specificity of works of art and cultural property. The article focuses more on the legal specificity of these objects.

1.2. The Example of the Legal Regime Applicable to Movable Property

Domestic regimes which favor circulation of movable property are fully justified vis-à-vis "ordinary" objects. In particular, for transactions (*a non domino*) made by a "seller" who is not the owner, civil law legal systems generally favor such circulation, while common law legal systems tend to rely on the "nemo dat"[5] (or "nemo plus"[6]) rule and therefore protect the original owner (see below: 5.2).

Leaving aside these different legal traditions, clear in comparative law, the realm of regimes enabling non-derivative acquisitions follow the logic favoring circulation of movable property. Such regimes are based either on "instantaneous"[7]

[5] *Nemo dat quod non habet.*

[6] *Nemo plus juris ad alium transferre potest quam ipse habet.*

[7] Actually, in spite of this eye-catching formulation, what is at stake under such provisions is the *instantaneous acquisitive effect* they grant to possession.

or prolonged possession (acquisitive prescription[8]). They favor circulation by providing acquisition of title with no requirement for proof of the validity of all the previous transfers of the object, differently from what may be required for derivative acquisitions.

However, such regimes do not necessarily appear appropriate for objects as specific as works of art and cultural property. This is confirmed by all those legal systems that prefer imprescriptibility (exclusion of adverse possession and acquisitive prescription) and therefore reject the idea of extending to such specific objects the applicability of the ordinary regime designed primarily for commodities and in a *favor commercii* philosophy.

More generally, depending on the country and legal system, such specific protection regimes may vary in content: from imprescriptibility to inalienability, including a state's preemptive right and the prohibition, or at least the control,[9] of export.[10]

The length of this chapter does not permit a comparative analysis of various relevant legislations. However, among other possible examples, one can note the Portuguese law no. 13/85 on Portuguese Cultural Heritage (6 July 1985), which extends protection measures to immovable. It entails several protective measures for cultural property, such as: limits to the owner's freedom to dispose of the object (duty to take care and maintain the object[11]; objects required to be catalogued[12]), state's preemptive right to purchase in case of planned sale,[13] exclusion of adverse possession and acquisitive prescription,[14] limits to, and in some cases prohibition of, export.[15] A more exceptional provision goes as far as declaring void and deprived of legal effect any transaction in Portugal on cultural property imported in violation of the exporting country's legislation on export or transfer of ownership. Even if this provision expressly operates under the condition of reciprocity vis-à-vis other concerned countries,[16] it represents a valuable testimony of openness towards foreign law and international solidarity against illicit trafficking of cultural property.

As will become clearer in the following developments of this article, in international art law, the expertise of a comparative lawyer is most valuable to appreciate the legal cultures and policy differences as well as to predict the consequences, inter alia on the transaction, of such a variety of domestic regimes on works of art or cultural property.

1.3. Legal Specificity, Private Ownership, Academic Proposals

Though necessarily briefly, these issues deserve to be raised here. As was said above, the variety of legal regimes that exists in comparative law reflects the fact that each legal system decides if, to what extent and under which forms and contents, legal specificity is added to the cultural specificity of a given object (or category of objects).

Professor Joseph Sax undertook a stimulating analysis of current American law vis-à-vis treasures. After having recalled how ordinary private property is well-rooted in American law and noting how this characteristic reduces, in various regards, the chance for archaeological and paleontological objects to benefit from a different and specific legal regime,[17] he concludes, among others, by expressing a call for the recognition of a species of qualified ownership.[18] Two brief observations seem necessary.

First of all, even where private property is well-rooted and acknowledged in broad terms (as subject-matter and/or legal effects), as in the majority of legal systems at present, by its legal and cultural significance this may delay and/or hinder, but does not *per se* and from a *legal* perspective prevent, two distinct developments. The first, elaborating on the "specificity" of works of art, and even more of "cultural" property or heritage. Then – the second – granting to such acknowledged specific category of property a concrete legal significance, which implies a (given degree of) *specificity of regime*, more protective and less commerce-oriented than ordinary regimes designed for commodities. This observation is also supported by the fact that such legal specificity has been granted also in legal systems where private ownership is not only rooted in their traditions but is protected as such, though in coexistence with the general interest, even at the constitutional law level, as for instance in Italian[19] or French law.[20]

[8] In spite of the traditional distinction between the "two" prescriptions, the "extinctive" (bar to a lawsuit or statute of limitations) and the "acquisitive" (of title) both undeniably based on legal consequences of time, under French law a unitary theory of the two prescriptions, based on possession, has been proposed (F. Zenati, S. Fournier, *Essai d'une théorie unitaire de la prescription*, RTDCiv. 1996, p. 339).

[9] Examples are numerous. To limit references to recent cases, in the French market a Verlaine's work (" Cellulairement ") was sold by Sotheby's. However, it will normally be excluded from export as it is being classified as national treasure. (Le Figaro, 7 January 2005).

[10] See G. Carducci, *La restitution internationale des biens culturels et des objets d'art. Droit commun, Directive CEE, Conventions de l'UNESCO et d'UNIDROIT*, LGDJ Paris 1997 (p. 1–446), Foreword by Prof. P. Lagarde (University Paris I), p. 43–88.

[11] Art. 15 and 27, 2.

[12] Art. 19 and 20.

[13] Art. 17.

[14] Art. 28

[15] Art. 33–35.

[16] Art. 31, 2 and 3. The provision reads in Portuguese:

2 – São nulas e de nenhum efeito as transações realizadas em território português sobre bens culturais móveis provenientes de países estrangeiros quando efectuadas com infracção das disposições da respectiva legislação interna reguladora da sua alienação ou exportação.

3 – O disposto no número anterior será aplicável, relativamente a outros países, em termos de reciprocidade.

[17] J. L. Sax, *Playing Darts with a Rembrandt. Public and Private Rights in Cultural Treasures*, Michigan Press, 1999, for instance, at p. 184 "The United States stands virtually alone in its reluctance to restrict landowners from treating archaeological and paleontological objects as ordinary private property."

[18] J. L. Sax, *Playing Darts with a Rembrandt*, cited, p. 197.

[19] Art. 42, 2–4, Italian constitution. On Art. 9 of the Italian Constitution and its provisions on cultural promotion, see M. S. Giannini, *Sull'articolo 9 Costituzione.*, in *Scritti in onore di A. Falzea*, Vol. III, 1, Giuffrè 1991 p. 433.

[20] On the case-law developed by the *Conseil constitutionnel* on private ownership, see Th. S. Renoux, M de Villiers, *Code constitutionnel*, Litec 2001 p. 144.

Secondly, Professor Sax's call for the recognition of a species of qualified ownership not only deserves serious consideration but, in its essence, reflects a general concern already shared by some scholar contributions on the regime of cultural property, at least, in continental Europe. Among these, of primary importance is the growing awareness that "cultural" property or heritage, as such, deserves specific legal protection regimes *regardless* of traditional (private law) considerations, such as ownership and the fact that its owner is a "private" individual or a "public" entity.[21] Such regimes vary in their contents, depending on the category of "cultural" property concerned, but share the same protection function, by providing rules, distinct where appropriate, from rules designed for "ordinary" objects or immovable property. The rationale behind this has, to various extents, been adopted by numerous law-makers (and/or judiciaries through case-law) which undeniably recognize and express the specificity of cultural property.

Several well-known international cases have brought attention to such protection legislations. The *United States v. F. Schultz* case has inter alia recalled that Egyptian law 117 considers property of the State all Egyptian antiquities (objects over a century old having archeological or historical importance).[22]

Another similar example, a decade before, demonstrated that under Guatemalan law, upon illegal export, cultural property becomes property of the Republic of Guatemala.[23]

Each legal system, generally through its authorities and sources, finds its balance of interests somewhere between the two ends of the spectrum, unlimited trade (and circulation) on one side, and absolute protection of art or cultural objects excluding, or at least limiting, trade (and circulation) on the other.

1.4. Variety of Contents, Forms, Scopes

A legal system which grants a legal "specificity" to works of art and cultural property may do so through a variety of contents, forms, and scopes.

1.4.1. Domestic Situations

The most visible and frequent specificity is the one expressed in domestic law in terms of *substantive rules*, i.e., those establishing the regime directly applicable to works of art and cultural property. Relevant in this respect are for instance provisions on imprescriptibility (exclusion of adverse possession and acquisitive prescription), inalienability, a state's preemptive right on purchase etc.

1.4.2. International Situations

For private international law issues, such as on contracts and property, states usually rely on their conflict of laws rules. In this case works of art and cultural property are subject to the same law that an ordinary object would be subject to under general private international law (see below: 5). Then the normative content of this law indicates, case by case, the regime applicable, more or less protective as it may be.

If states wish to depart from this state of affairs and ensure internationally a (certain degree of) legal specificity to such objects, they may do so, either jointly by elaborating and/or adhering to an international Convention (see below: 6), or individually, through amending their ordinary private international law mechanisms.

Two main technical possibilities can be illustrated, bearing in mind that they demand careful consideration in each legal system and are not very frequently used in comparative law.

i) A first possibility is elaborating a conflict of laws rule specific to works of art and cultural property. To this category belongs, for instance, the rule in favor of the *lex originis* adopted by the Institute of International Law at the 1991 Basle Resolution (see below: 5.4). In this case the forum does not predict the normative content of such law and the outcome of the dispute, but ensures that the law of the most culturally concerned state applies.
ii) A second possibility exists *outside* the dominant technique of multilateral conflict of laws rules, and consists in elaborating a *substantive unilateral rule* which would apply within its scope to any international (private law) case relating to such specific objects brought before this state's courts. However, the applicability of such a unilateral rule becomes obviously uncertain if a foreign court has jurisdiction on the case. Such rule would qualify as international mandatory rule and is considered below (10.2).

A completely different situation is at stake where a legal system qualifies a (category of) cultural property as *res extra commercium* and, as such, inalienable and imprescriptible (exclusion of adverse possession and acquisitive prescription). Differently from the way the two techniques considered above (i and ii) operate, this status of cultural property which is very protective under domestic law as long as the object is on the territory, is generally not recognized *per se* internationally if the object is imported in a different legal system. Usually, such specific status disappears unless the importing country qualifies, from *its own* perspective, the object as *res extra commercium*. This outcome is recurrent though, technically speaking, a form of recognition may be envisaged in private international law.[24]

[21] See in particular M. S. Giannini, *I beni culturali*, Riv. Trim. Dir. Pub. 1976 p. 3.
[22] United States of America v. F. Schultz, January 3, 2002, United States District Court, S.D. New York, 178 F.Supp.2d 445.
[23] United States of America v. Pre-Columbian Artifacts and the Republic of Guatemala, United States District Court, N.D. Illinois, E.D., October 14 1993, 845 F.Supp. 544.
[24] See G. Carducci, *La restitution internationale*, cited, p. 308–311.

2. OBJECTIVE

2.1. Favoring Licit Trade and Legal Predictability in International Transactions

Transactions concerning works of art and cultural property have increased in the last decades, for several reasons, including an increased strong, genuine interest of collectors, a broader public wishing to possess art in whatever form and of whatever significance,[25] and financial reasons moving investors towards potential speculative purchasing.

If the demand for works of art in the market may be presumed to be generally satisfied by objects of licit provenance, it is a fact that the stronger the demand becomes, the more cultural objects of illicit provenance enter the market. The phenomenon is widely recognized as being a growing reality and threat even by non-specialist and large-public-oriented journals or magazines. For instance, the cover page of Time Magazine, dated 3 November 2003, read "Tomb raiders" on Asia's looted treasures.[26] Other regions of the world could substantiate similar and not less alarming reports.

The focus of this chapter is therefore on international transactions, not on specific risks, particularly in a material sense, which may affect works of art and cultural property. Such risks are of differing natures: risks in material sense, such as destruction and damage to, and risks taken more in a legal sense, as looting, theft, illicit export or trafficking. It is clear that, depending on circumstances, more than one of these risks, and both "material" and "legal" risks, may in reality affect the same object.

The famous looting of the Baghdad Museum, as well as the deliberate destruction of the Buddhas of Bamiyan[27] that led the international community represented within UNESCO to adopt the UNESCO *Declaration concerning the Intentional Destruction of Cultural Heritage*,[28] recently reminded in a tragic magnified scale how at risk cultural property is. It is only exceptionally that we witness the opposite, a positive outcome concerning objects feared destroyed.[29]

In spite of its daily massive use, the term "transaction" offers various meanings. Although this is the case more in common law[30] than in civil law jurisdictions,[31] the term is taken here in its predominant use, as a business agreement. Depending on the parties' needs and the applicable law, its content may vary, such as a sales agreement, a loan or exchange agreement on works of art, very common for temporary exhibitions, or even insurance related contracts. A transaction concerning works of art raises several (legal/financial) risks which are generally higher than if ordinary commodities were at stake. This is easily reflected inter alia by issues such as authenticity and the buyer's cautious approach imposed by the *caveat emptor* principle in the acquisition of such specific "art" objects or "cultural" property. The complexity of legal issues and related risks increases even further as soon as the transaction presents a "foreign element" – recurrent in the flourishing international art market on *movable* objects – which characterizes it as a (private law) "international" case from the forum's perspective.

This chapter illustrates how the characterization of a transaction as international, when duly analyzed, raises a variety of factors resulting in a growing complexity of international art law. This chapter originates from a contribution the author had the honor to be invited to give at the International Bar Association (IBA) Annual Meeting in Auckland, New Zealand (2004). Among others, it is worth observing how, during an interesting debate on *international* transactions on works of art or cultural property,[32] several interventions focused on freedom of contract and the need for drafting proper contract clauses on risk allocation between seller and buyer. These terms ("freedom of contract") and exercises ("clauses drafting") are obviously important. However, if they are not properly spatially defined at law, such terms and exercises recall *domestic* rather than *international* transactions reasoning. Scarcely, if ever, were mentioned terms as "applicable law," "international conventions," "mandatory rules" (neither "domestic" nor "international"), or exceptionally and for some categories of objects at particular risk, United Nations or European Union international measures. Apparently overlooked is that, in an international transaction, freedom of contract as well as the legal effects of the contract (its binding effect on the parties and transfer of title on movables) depends on the coexistence and interactions of these terms and the normative rules they represent. Elaborating and drafting contract clauses merely on commercial inputs and regardless of such coexistence and normative interactions may reveal a costly and vain exercise as soon as the contract is brought to the attention of a judge (or an arbitrator[33]). Such an exercise may be, for instance, the agreement to sell and export important cultural property without ensuring its alienability, transferability and exportability under the relevant provisions.

[25] Cultural, artistic, historical (significance) etc.

[26] The title continues, "Thieves and smugglers are stripping away Asia's precious artifacts and selling them to dealers in Europe and the U.S. inside a global black market."

[27] From a legal perspective, see F. Francioni – F. Lenzerini, *The Destruction of the Buddhas of Bamiyan and International Law*, in *European Journal of International Law*, 2003, p. 619–651.

[28] See the text under: <http://portal.unesco.org/culture/en/ev.php-URL_ID=17125&URL_DO=DO_TOPIC&URL_SECTION=201.html>.

[29] Most recently, for instance, more than twenty thousands cultural objects feared destroyed have been found intact in Afghanistan (the last part of the recovery is reported in The Art Newspaper, December 2004).

[30] For instance, the Black's Law Dictionary provides not less than four different meanings.

[31] In French law, compare G. Cornu (sous la dir.), *Vocabulaire juridique*. Parallel remarks are possible in other civil law legal systems.

[32] As announced in the Programme: "Licit international transactions in works of art and antiquities."

[33] Bearing in mind however that the extent the positions of an arbitrator and a (state) judge differ depending on the rules applicable to the international arbitration and its outcome (award).

Furthermore, restitution of illicitly removed works of art and cultural property, far from solely raising moral issues and being a complex and technical field of law, is also a growing reality. It is worth to recall, among others indicators reflecting this state of affairs and its growing awareness in the international market, Christie's recent decision to follow Sotheby's in appointing a "director of restitution."[34]

2.2. From "Traditional" to "New" Complexity of International Art Law

This chapter aims at illustrating how much more complex the legal issues are in reality, as soon as the international character of the transaction is duly taken into account. Actually, two different levels of "complexity" of international art law are discussed.

2.2.1. Private International Law as Minimum and Traditional Complexity

The first level results from the ordinary operation of private international law: this rather sophisticated and technical branch of law may be seen as a synonym of complication by art professionals or even practicing lawyers not familiar with it (see below 4). Among others, it should be noted that not only conflict of law rules (and the numerous related issues[35]) and rules on jurisdiction, but even the definition of an "international" (as opposed to "domestic") contract, vary from jurisdiction to jurisdiction.

This remains true also, at the European level, under the rather sophisticated 1980 Rome Convention on the Law Applicable to Contractual Obligations: it applies to contractual obligations raising a conflict of law without providing a uniform definition of the "international" contract raising it.

2.2.2. Proper Use of Private International Law and Complexity Inherent to International Transactions

The usual reaction to an acknowledged international character of the transaction is for the practicing lawyer to attempt to reduce legal unpredictability and reassure the client through proper use of choice-of-law and/or forum-selection (or arbitration) clauses.[36]

However, international contract negotiations require certain specific insights and skills, and depend particularly on cultural factors.[37] The suggested use of such clauses may not meet the counterpart's acceptance. Furthermore, this outcome (absence of such clauses) becomes chronic for those parties that do not even suggest to discuss such clauses fearing it would be misinterpreted as an unacceptable questioning of the counterpart's present commitment and future good faith, or a too blunt proposal, having an indirect impact on the merits, where disagreement may turn into a deal-breaker of the whole transaction.

Even assuming that agreement on these clauses is reached, while extremely important they do not solve *per se* all relevant issues.

The principle of party autonomy, in spite of its remarkable diffusion in comparative law, may find different degrees of acceptance/conditions and/or obstacles, as international mandatory rules, depending on the forum (below: 10.2). If the forum has been chosen by the parties, an optimizing choice from a party autonomy perspective may be presumed. However, practice shows from time to time unfortunate forum selection clauses in this regard. Furthermore, some key issues for international transactions on movable property as title or ownership transfer generally do not even belong to the category of "contracts" and, as such, in most jurisdictions, do not benefit from party autonomy (below: 5.1). The parties then cannot rely on the predictability they generally expect under an express choice-of law clause.

Assuming that the parties have been well advised and have maximized the predictability of their transactions through proper use of choice-of-law and/or forum-selection (or arbitration) clauses, it is time to illustrate that in some circumstances and jurisdictions, the current normative complexity of international art law may "unexpectedly" interfere with the desired predictability. This article wishes to anticipate these possible outcomes and contribute to the increase of legal predictability.

2.2.3. "New" Complexity beyond Traditional Private International Law

The second level of complexity results from a more exceptional set of combinations of national and international rules which evolve outside and beyond traditional private international law (at least in its dichotomy *lex fori – lex causae*). With a view to increasing legal predictability, this article aims at drawing practitioners' attention to possible outcomes, unexpected under "ordinary" conflict of laws. These may result from the interactions among multiple – basically *five (at present) – different sources* of rules each of which operates under its *specific methodology, conditions* and *effects*. Such rules encompass conflict of laws rules, international uniform law, mandatory rules and, more exceptionally but concerning *per se* the international or the European community, United Nations Security Council Resolutions or *ad hoc* EU Regulations. As such, these normative interactions may be deemed a "complication" not only in general legal practice but even by private international lawyers.

Furthermore, such interactions also demand a sensibility for, and an expertise in, public international law on issues as law of treaties, implementation of international or European *ad hoc* rules at national level etc. Differently from what over-specialization (academic and/or professional) trends may

[34] The Art Newspapers, December 2004.

[35] Characterization, *Renvoi*, Public Policy, Status of Foreign Law, etc.

[36] If maximizing predictability is the priority "and/or" should be replaced by "and": both choice-of-law and forum-selection (or arbitration) clauses should be used.

[37] What Professor A. T. von Mehren (*Significance of Cultural and Legal Diversity for International Transactions*, in *Ius Privatum Gentium*, Festschrift für M. Rheinstein, Tübingen 1969, p. 249) authoritatively wrote nearly four decades ago still applies to quite a number of international negotiations.

generally recommend, a serious knowledge of *both* private and public international law is most desirable for lawyers dealing in international art trade. In a broader perspective the Institute of International Law recommends both private and public international law to be included in admission exams to practice of law and considers knowledge of international law as necessary to discharge a wide range of professional responsibilities.[38]

Although not all their consequences and ramifications may be analyzed here,[39] both levels of complexity, and especially the latter, result in, as summarized in the title, "growing complexity" of international art trade law, and are presented here. This approach differs from some traditional presentations essentially based on private international law where the work of art falls under the general category of chattels or movable personal property.

3. SOME CAVEATS

3.1. Intent

i) It is useful to clarify immediately that this chapter does *not* intend to present an alarming state of "double complexity" in international art law as *the* reality *everywhere* (in *any* jurisdiction) and vis-à-vis *any* work of art or cultural property.
ii) This complexity becomes a reality, to different extents, if and where states, individually or jointly, grant a high degree of importance to a given (category of) work(s) of art, and usually even more if they consider it (them) "cultural" property or heritage.
iii) Furthermore, such complexities are here illustrated for not yet experienced international art lawyers.

3.2. Subject-matter

In order to keep this chapter concise, the following public international law issues are not considered:

i) protection of cultural property during an armed conflict[40];
ii) the existence and the content of a customary international obligation to restitution of cultural property removed during such conflict[41];
iii) the impact that treaties – UNESCO treaties *inter alia* – may have on international customary law[42];
iv) the adjustments that the legal qualification of such an impact may be subject to vis-à-vis less recent treaties and customs. If applied to cultural property, this issue deserves consideration with regard, inter alia, to both *ad hoc* treaties, as peace treaties, and codification treaties, as 1899 Hague Convention II and 1907 Hague Convention IV (Articles 27 and 56 of the annexed Regulations)[43];
v) specific jurisdictional and immunity issues as those illustrated in the recent case Republic of Austria v. Altmann[44];
vi) specific period-related claims, as on Nazi-looted art, which may require, depending on the specificity of a given case, further legal developments.

3.3. Comprehension

i) The terms "work of art" and "cultural property" are hereafter used jointly, to facilitate the reading of the article. One should bear in mind however that, beyond the numerous *subjective* conceptions or definitions of "art" and "culture," their respective *legal* definition and significance (as applied to objects) depend on the legal (primarily domestic, sometimes international) regulation applicable, in *each case* (as characterized in fact and law). Generalizations in this field would be particularly unfortunate.
ii) In spite of some undeniable national differences that appear by comparing legal systems, generally national authorities (governments, law-makers, judiciary through case-law) consider "cultural" property or heritage as distinct from, and more characterized as a category than,

[38] Institute of International Law, Recommendation on "Teaching of Public and Private International Law," adopted at the Strasbourg Session (1997) (Art. 5 and the Preamble).

[39] For a thorough analysis of these consequences for movable cultural property (with the exception of consideration of the *ad hoc* international measures generated by the Iraqi conflict), see G. Carducci, *La restitution internationale*, cited. The term "droit commun" (in French) refers to private international law as applicable where no international convention (basically of a uniform law nature with regard to cultural property) applies (in a given jurisdiction).

[40] For the armed conflict perspective, see S. E. Nahlik, *La protection internationale des biens culturels en cas de conflit armé*, in *Recueil des cours de l'Académie de droit international (La Haye)* [Collection of Lectures of the International Law Academy (The Hague)], vol. 120, II, 1967, pp. 61–163. More generally, P. Verri, *Le destin des biens culturels dans les conflits armés*, in *Revue internationale de la Croix-Rouge*, no. 752, 1985, pp. 67–85 et no. 753, 1985, pp. 127–139.

[41] See G. Carducci, *L'obligation de restitution des biens culturels et des objets d'art en cas de conflit armé: droit coutumier et droit conventionnel avant et après la Convention de La Haye de 1954 (L'importance du facteur temporel dans les rapports entre les traités et la coutume)*, *Revue générale de droit international public*, 2000 p. 289.

[42] On the potential effects of treaties on the customary process, see R. R. Baxter, *Treaties and Custom*, *Collected Courses*, 1970, I, p. 25; K. Doehring, *Gewohnheitsrecht aus Verträgen*, Zeitschrift für ausländisches öffentliches Recht und Völkerrecht, 1976 p. 77 ; O. Schachter, *Entangled Treaty and Custom*, in Essays S. Rosenne, Kluwer 1989 p. 717 ; U. Scheuner, *Internationale Verträge als Elemente der Bildung von Völkerrechtlichem Gewohnheitsrecht*, F. S. für F. A. Mann, 1977, p. 409 s.; L. B. Sohn, *Unratified Treaties as a Source of Customary International Law*, Essays W. Riphagen, 1986, p. 231 s.; H. W. A. Thirlway, *International Customary Law and Codification*, Leiden 1972, p. 80; M. E. Villiger, *Customary International Law and Treaties*, 2 Ed. 1997.

[43] For the analysis of our proposal to distinguish two possible effects of treaties on customary rules depending on the time period and prevailing conception of the custom concerned, see G. Carducci, *L'obligation de restitution des biens culturels et des objets d'art en cas de conflit armé: droit coutumier et droit conventionnel avant et après la Convention de La Haye de 1954*, cited (at p. 292, 309–315). The proposal was briefly presented at the SFDI (*Société française pour le droit international*) Paris Workshop (*La Sorbonne*, Paris, 25–27 May 2000), *Le droit international et le temps*, Pedone 2001, p. 170.

[44] Republic of Austria *et al.* v. Maria V.Altmann, 541 U.S. 2004.

"works of art." This is often reflected in a more protective legal regime for such cultural objects (or immovable cultural heritage).

iii) In spite of the international character of their subject-matter (international private law situations), private international law solutions (both on conflict of laws and jurisdiction) belong primarily to domestic law and, as such, vary from jurisdiction to jurisdiction.[45] This is also true, at least to some extent, for *national* implementation of international law rules which are *not directly* effective in domestic law. Therefore, generalizations should be omitted and a case by case analysis of the legal treatment and outcome of each situation in a given jurisdiction should be used.

iv) This chapter covers primarily the private law aspects of international art trade. Public and criminal law rules are considered only to the extent they may have an impact on such aspects. For instance, even "public" law rules (as export controls) are considered to the extent that they are likely to have an impact on an international transaction and may, under some conditions, qualify as international mandatory rules (below: 10.2).

v) Though necessarily legal in nature and facing particularly complex issues because of its subject-matter, this article attempts to be informative and accessible also to art and cultural heritage professionals.

4. DEFINING "ILLICIT" TRADE IN, OR ACQUISITION OF, WORKS OF ART OR CULTURAL PROPERTY

4.1. Some Certainties

How does one define "illicit" trade in or acquisition of art? The reply may vary.

Archeologists have been described as generally assuming that an ancient object is "illicitly acquired unless there is convincing proof to the contrary."[46]

However, "licit" and "illicit" characterizations ought to be treated for what they are, i.e. *legal characterizations*.[47] As such they are relative and variable in time and space, depending on a given applicable (primarily domestic) legal framework and the way it evolves (relativity in time) and/or the extent it differs from others (relativity in space).

Indeed, such a variety can be found in comparative law where states regulate to various extents transactions in works of art and cultural objects (above: 1.3) and outlaw some related "illicit" conduct. If we consider international trade, states generally qualify illicit situations covering primarily theft, looting and illicit export of art objects or cultural property. At the international treaty-law level this is best demonstrated by the most recent multilateral treaty negotiated on restitution of cultural property: the 1995 UNIDROIT *Convention on Stolen or Illegally Exported Cultural Objects* establishes, with different conditions, a right to restitution of cultural property concerned by either form of illicit trade: theft or illicit export.[48] Differently from what is sometimes misleadingly presented as the "mere equivalence of theft and illicit export" under the UNIDROIT Convention, the latter rejects such an equivalence and distinguishes stolen and illegally exported cultural objects, submitting them to *different* regimes.[49]

Factually speaking, circumstances favoring "illicit" conduct vary from place to place and time to time. For instance, situations of poverty and lack of judicial and social control in some periods and countries, such as during or in the aftermath of armed conflicts, facilitate and increase illicit trade, among others, in works of art.

4.2. Some Academic Debate

In one of his stimulating articles on art and cultural property law, Professor John Merryman attempts to redefine "licit" and "illicit" international trade in cultural objects. He premises that "whether *international* trade in specific kinds of cultural objects is licit or illicit accordingly depends on *international* law, not on the source nation's characterization, and international law on the topic is at present fragmentary and amorphous." He suggests to consider "internationally licit" trade in "culturally moveable" objects, objects that bear no significant relation to the national culture, or redundant archaeological objects, whether or not their export was prohibited by the source nation. The eminent author qualifies his suggestion as "redefinition of a licit international trade" in cultural objects.[50]

However, two different elements are at stake here, the definition of categories of objects subject to trade and the legal characterization of conduct related to such objects. Both elements should be internationally regulated if setting an *autonomous* and purely *international* definition of licit/illicit trade is the target. However, Professor Merryman's suggestion addresses only the first element, not the second. Even if international treaty-law were one day to endorse the suggestion and define directly the categories of objects in which the international trade is *licit*, in spite of an illicit export,[51] as

45 With the notable exception of applicable international Conventions, as the 1980 Rome Convention (see below: 10.2.2).

46 Clemency Chase Coggins, *A Licit International Traffic in Ancient Art: Let There Be Light !*, IJCP 1995, p. 61, at 62.

47 This is obviously true also of "unlawful" or "illegal" characterizations, associated to criminal offences in some jurisdictions.

48 To simplify the text the terminological distinction between "restitution" and "return," retained also in the UNIDROIT Convention, is not used here.

49 See Chapters II and III, and in particular Art. 5, 3, which has no equivalent in Art. 3.

50 J. H. Merryman, *A Licit International Trade in Cultural Objects*, IJCP, 1995, p. 13–60, at 28 and 29.

51 J. H. Merryman (at p. 29) envisages in his suggestion of "internationally illicit" trade stolen objects (with no precision on such characterization) and culturally immovable objects, but not "illicit export." Such an illicit export (from a source nation's perspective) is dealt with under "internationally licit" trade and is deemed irrelevant, not an obstacle *per se* to such a licit trade.

soon as the opposite portion of the trade – "illicit" – is considered, then the legal characterizations of conduct relating to cultural property ("illicit export," "stealing" etc.), are no longer international but national,[52] and therefore variable in time and space.

4.3. On the Legal Effects of Domestic Characterizations

Without entering here into the debate between "cultural or retentive nationalism" and "cultural internationalism,"[53] to the extent that it may be assumed to be transferable to trade in cultural property, it is difficult to deny the fact that in the past and still at present international law refers to notions as "theft" or "illicit export," and therefore "stolen" or "illicitly exported" cultural property or heritage, but does not properly define them and, implicitly or explicitly, leaves their characterization to the relevant domestic legislation.

This realism is reflected in both international customary and treaty law related to cultural property. The former, to the extent that it is identified, is unlikely to provide autonomous (non-domestic) accurate and operational definitions. The latter, is even more explicit: at present the existing (multilateral) international treaty-law instruments as the 1970 UNESCO *Convention on the Means of Prohibiting and Preventing the Illicit Import, Export and Transfer of Ownership of Cultural Property*, the 1995 UNIDROIT *Convention on Stolen or Illegally Exported Cultural Objects*, as well as European instruments as the Council *Directive 93/7 of 15 March 1993 on the return of cultural objects unlawfully removed from the territory of a Member State*,[54] grant legal consequences to what states qualify, from their perspective, illicit conduct (theft and/or illicit export).

Where such multilateral instruments do not apply and within the (scarce) limits imposed by (public) international law the situation may be different. Prof. Merryman, quoting also Prof. Lalive, recalls that the importing country may ignore on its territory the "illicit" (export) characterization given by the country of origin.[55] Technically speaking this is certainly a possibility. However, some observations appear useful.

i) If this possibility is retained by the importing country, the forum (jurisdiction in the importing country) deprives the "illicit" conduct (export) from the legal characterization and effects that the *lex originis* would correlate to it. However, this attitude in the importing country poses a different issue, i.e. the (denied) consideration or application of, or just giving effect to, foreign law, which does *not* make *per se* the characterization of "licit/illicit" less a national law issue, or a purely international law issue.
ii) As observed above, existing European and international instruments reject this possibility and do not ignore States parties' characterizations within their scope of application. It remains to be seen if states, when drafting future international treaties, will go so far as defining *directly* and *autonomously* international illicit trade in art or cultural property, and by opposition determine its licit trade.
iii) It is worth recalling that at the academic level, the authoritative Basel Resolution (1991) of the Institute of International Law[56] adopted a different position for works of art: it considers that their export is governed by the relevant provisions of the country of origin.[57]

5. INTERNATIONAL ART LAW AND PRIVATE INTERNATIONAL LAW

In terms of legal outcomes, it is important to illustrate that, in spite of the illicit provenance of the object, the normal operation of private international law does not necessarily guarantee the restitution of the object. However, before entering into such outcomes, some preliminary remarks are necessary.

5.1. Preliminary Remarks

5.1.1. The Distinction Between Contract and Ownership Issues

Depending on the perspective used, international art law may cover several fields of law. With reference to private law issues, such as contracts or property, it covers private international law as applicable to movables, works of art or cultural property.[58] Leaving aside jurisdictional issues[59] and their obvious practical importance,[60] each forum possesses its conflict of laws rule to determine the applicable law.

A preliminary distinction is crucial in private international law for movable property. On one side, contractual issues are subject to the law applicable to the contract. On the other, ownership issues, such as the legal status of the object and the validity of its transfer are subject to *lex situs*. Both common

[52] If the hypothetical future international treaty-law provisions were to refer to illicit export – even if deemed irrelevant in its effects for the purposes of defining a licit trade – and/or to theft, the legal characterization of such terms would be basically left to domestic law. An international standardization of what amounts to "illicit export" and/or "theft" of cultural property appears a difficult task.

[53] In addition to J. H. Merryman's famous studies, see also, generally, L. V. Prott, *Cultural Heritage Law: The Perspective of the Source Nations*, Art Antiquity and Law, 2000, p. 333.

[54] See for instance Council Directive 93/7 of 15 March 1993 on the return of cultural objects unlawfully removed from the territory of a Member State, Art. 1 (2).

[55] J. H. Merryman, *A Licit International Trade in Cultural Objects*, cited, p. 28.

[56] Resolution "The International Sale of Works of Art from the Angle of the Protection the Cultural Heritage."(Below: 5.4).

[57] Art. 3, for works of art identified as belonging to the cultural heritage of a country.

[58] Generally, see also L. V. Prott, *Problems of Private International Law for the Protection of the Cultural Heritage*, Hague Academy Collected Courses, 1989, p. 219; 1993 K. Siehr, *International Art Trade and the Law*, Hague Academy Collected Courses, 1993, p. 9.

[59] Assuming that a national system of private international law covers both conflict of laws and jurisdiction (and recognition of foreign judgments).

[60] Varying mainly on the forum's distribution between "substance/procedure" issues.

law jurisdictions, as the United States[61] or United Kingdom,[62] and civil law jurisdictions, as France,[63] Italy[64] or Germany,[65] recognize this well-rooted distinction.

5.1.2. Crucial Importance of Party Autonomy and Contractual Issues

Although party autonomy does not solve all forms of legal complexity in international art transactions, its proper use remains recommended (above: 2.2.2). Choice-of-law clauses refer traditionally to the law applicable to the contract. This remains true nowadays in spite of the fact that comparative law has shown in the last two decades that party autonomy has partially penetrated other branches of conflict of laws as well.[66]

Although each private international law (primarily domestic, convention if applicable) system may vary in the issues it subjects to the law of contract,[67] selecting properly such law enables predictability on numerous crucial issues, inter alia:

i) if lack of authenticity of a work of art verified after the conclusion of the contract, qualifying as mistake by the buyer (generally) or misrepresentation by the seller, leads to rescission and/or damages or other remedy;
ii) identifying the mandatory rules (below: 10.1) to comply with;
iii) the concrete significance of distinctive terms as void, voidable and unenforceable contracts, inter alia in case of violation of such mandatory rules;
iv) the relationships and possible overlapping among expectation, reliance and restitution interests and remedies;
v) if breach of contract entails damages and/or specific performance;
vi) if rescission and/or termination operates retrospectively; etc.

[61] See Scoles, Hay, Borchers, Symeonides, *Conflict of Laws*, Third Edition, 2000, n. 19.12 p. 962.

[62] See Collins (Gen. Ed.) Dicey & Morris, *The Conflict of Laws*, 13 Ed. Vol. 2, 2000, p. 965 n. 24–005.

[63] See Batiffol, *Les conflits de lois en matière de contrats*, Paris, 1938, n. 477 p. 397, Batiffol & Lagarde, *Droit international privé*, II, Paris, 1985, n. 524 p. 193; Audit, *Droit international privé*, Paris, 1997 n. 750, p. 618; Mayer, *Droit international privé*, Paris, 1998, n. 654 p. 424.

[64] See Vitta, *Diritto internazionale privato*, Torino, 1975, III p. 46; Venturini, *Diritto internazionale privato. Diritti reali ed obbligazioni*, Padova, 1956, p. 29; Balladore Pallieri, *Diritto internazionale privato*, Milano, 1974, p. 248; Cassoni, *La compravendita nelle Convenzioni e nel diritto internazionale privato italiano*, in *Rivista di diritto internazionale privato e processuale*, 1982 p. 429 (459).

[65] See Kreuzer, *Münchener Kommentar zum BGB, Internationales Privatrecht*, n. 28 p. 2014, Stoll, *Staudinger Kommentar, Internationales Sachenrecht*, n. 113, p. 58, n. 226 p. 114, V. Bar, *Internationales Privatrecht*, II, Müchen 1991 n. 774 p. 561, Kegel, *Internationales Privatrecht*, 7 Ed., München, 1995, p. 571.

[66] Cf. Carlier, *Autonomie de la volonté et statut personnel*, Bruxelles 1992 ; Gannagé, *La pénétration de l'autonomie de la volonté dans le droit international privé de la famille*, RCDIP 1992, p. 425; P. Picone, *Autonomia della volontà e pluralità dei metodi di coordinamento tra ordinamenti*, in *La riforma italiana del diritto internazionale privato*, Cedam 1998, p. 515; Stoll, *Die Rechtswahl im Namens-, Ehe- und Erbrecht*, München 1991.

[67] Depending inter alia on the relationships of contract to other sources of obligations, as tort and others – if accepted under a given jurisdiction – as trusts and restitution. At European level, see Art. 10 of the 1980 Rome Convention on the Law Applicable to Contractual Obligations.

5.2. The Case of Theft

In this case the transfer is (*a non domino*) done by a "seller" not owner by definition.[68] However, depending on the content of the applicable law, title may be acquired by adverse possession or prescription. Examples are numerous. As shown in the famous British case *Winkworth v. Christie's Ltd*,[69] the law applicable did not lead to the return of stolen material. Works of art were stolen in England, then brought to and sold in Italy. The buyer later brought the objects to London and assigned them to Christie's to offer for sale. In spite of two non insignificant facts (objects were stolen in, and reimported to, England and English law if applicable would in principle protect the original owner), the judge applied the forum's rule of conflict on interests in moveable property, the *lex situs* at the time of the transaction. Italian law was then declared applicable and the original owner was divested of his title. The assignee had acquired title in spite of the fact that the "seller" was not the owner.

Movable works of art and cultural property not only have no natural situs, as any movable, but because of their speculative potential and sometimes also for laundering purposes, they are even likely to be rapidly internationally displaced. In view of this specificity, it should be noted, without entering here into all the ramifications of complex issues ("conflit mobile" and domestic variations on the theme), that once title is acquired, it is generally recognized abroad, in the subsequent importing country. This is generally true even if the new local law would require a longer term of possession, or different characteristics of the possession regardless of its term, to grant title.

In terms of substantive law, the logic which favors circulation of movable property – as in Italian law in the Winkworth v. Christie's Ltd case – is well known in civil law jurisdictions.[70]

The outcome is different where the applicable law does not pass title to the assignee. Among other examples, in the *Autocephalous Greek-Orthodox Church v. Goldberg* case, the law of Indiana was applied and it recognized the Republic of Cyprus' replevin action to recover wrongfully taken or unlawfully detained goods. Actually they were mosaics stolen in 1979 by vandals in the Kanakaria Church in Cyprus.[71]

5.3. The Case of Illicit Export

Illicit export: The variety of prices worldwide can tempt owners to export, certainly legally but in some cases even illegally, their works of art to sell them abroad at a higher price. In some cases a theft may precede illicit export. Then the author

[68] Unless the seller is not the thief but a person having already acquired title under the applicable law. In this case his/her transfer is a derivative one from the purchaser's point of view.

[69] Chancery Division [1977 w. No. 2296] W.L.R.

[70] For a comparative analysis see G. Carducci, *La restitution internationale*, cited, p. 397–408.

[71] *Autocephalous Greek-Orthodox Church v. Goldberg*, S.D. Ind. 1989, 3 August 1989, 717 F.Supp.1374; US Court of Appeals for the 7th Circuit, 917 F.2d 278, 24 October 1990.

of the export is the thief or, as the case may be, a receiver of stolen property, or even a "new" owner if the applicable law has granted the transfer of title (above: 5.2).

In a traditional private international law system based on the distinction between private and public law provisions, illicit export is considered, from the import country forum's point of view, simply a violation of foreign public law and as such it generally does not directly constitute *per se* a (private law) ground for restitution of the illicitly exported objects. The few cases where the foreign government obtained restitution are usually based on the government's title on the object, not on its illicit export *per se.*[72]

The qualifications of the foreign provision may vary depending on the forum's legal traditions or views. With regard to a valuable Maori carving illicitly exported from New Zealand, in the well-known case *Attorney General of New Zealand v. Ortiz*, it is worth noting that first Lord Denning (Court of Appeal) then the House of Lords, envisaged several qualifications of the New Zealand Historic Articles Act of 1962, as (foreign) revenue, penal and/or public law. Ultimately, the enforcement in England of such a foreign provision was excluded. The New Zealand Crown also could not benefit from a claim based on title as the forfeiture, under New Zealand law, of the illicitly exported Maori carving was deemed not to operate automatically.[73]

The case *Kingdom of Spain v. Christie's* shows yet another situation. Here the claimant alleged illicit export not to claim title[74] but simply to seek a declaration on given facts. The relevant facts were that the Goya oil painting "La Marquesa de Santa Cruz" had been illicitly exported from Spain and that the existing export permit had been forged.[75] Such situation does not pose particular legal difficulty and the claim is generally acceptable as long as it is deemed justified.[76]

5.4. Some Academic Debate and Suggestions Favoring the Lex Originis

If the current state of law in several jurisdictions has been briefly considered (above: 5.2 and 5.3), the academic debate also deserves some attention. For the sake of brevity and clarity we will consider such a debate in one of its most authoritative and accessible forms[77]: the Resolution on the "International Sale of Works of Art from the Angle of the Protection the Cultural Heritage" adopted by the Institute of International Law at its Basel's session (1991).

This Resolution considers in its Preamble that every country has the right and the duty to take measures to preserve its cultural heritage, that in a number of cases such measures entail restrictions on the free movement of works of art which are considered integral elements of the cultural heritage of the country, and that such measures, while being justified by the need to safeguard this heritage, should be reconciled as far as possible with the general interests of the international trade of works of art. These "considering" in the Preamble having set the broader picture, it is important to focus on the content of such "reconciliation" between the two protection and trade interests.

Such content is not disclosed as such in the Preamble, although in it the drafters of the Resolution consider, inter alia, "desirable that measures to protect the cultural heritage which are in force in the country of origin of the work of art be recognized in other countries, in particular in those in which such property is actually located."[78] Such "desirable recognition" is not irrelevant in the debate.

More explicit and most important as it does not merely stand in the Preamble, is the provision in Article 2: the transfer of ownership of works of art belonging to the cultural heritage of the country of origin shall be governed by the law of that country. The provision in article 3 follows the same logic: the provisions of the law of the country of origin governing the export of works of art shall apply. Under both articles, the forum ensures that the law of the most culturally concerned state applies to the object, although – and this outcome is normal for a conflict of law solution – it can not predict the normative content of the *lex originis* and therefore the outcome of the dispute.[79] The Resolution defines the country of origin as the one most closely linked to the object from the cultural point of view.[80]

These articles specifically designed for works of art and cultural property[81] clearly depart from current private international law solutions designed for ordinary chattels and movable property and which are *de facto* extended, at least in most jurisdictions, to movable works of art or cultural property. As briefly illustrated above (5.2 and 5.3), under such solutions the *lex generalis* has generally no particular status. However, the *lex originis* may exceptionally gain some international effects if its relevant provisions are deemed international mandatory rules (see below: 10.2).

Under ordinary conflict of laws, in terms of property law issues, the *lex situs* of the place of acquisition is relevant, not *per se* the *lex originis*. An exception would be the case where the *lex situs* at the time of acquisition and the *lex originis* happen

72 From a more general point of view, compare in the past J. Basedow, *Private Law Effects of Foreign Export Controls*, GYIL 1984, p. 109, at 117.

73 Attorney General of New Zealand v Ortiz and others, Court of Appeal, 21 May 1982 [1982] 3 All ER, p. 432; House of Lords, 21 April 1983, [1983] 2 All ER, p. 93.

74 Actually claimant did not even present a claim against defendants by way of injunctions or for damages.

75 *Kingdom of Spain v. Christie's*, [1986 S. No. 1308], W.L.R. 1986 p. 1120.

76 At least as long as the judge declares – as he did in this case – the claim was justified by a serious concern (preventing further circulation of a work of art with a forged export permit) and therefore did not strike it out as an abuse of process.

77 A systematic presentation of this and other academic suggestions, in this (effects abroad of the *lex originis*) and other regards, is in G. Carducci, *La restitution internationale, cited.*

78 Preambular paragraph (*Considering*) no. 6.

79 The *lex originis* is deemed the applicable law without considering its content at this stage (public policy test intervenes at a later stage).

80 Art1, b.

81 Although the title of the Basle Resolution refers to works of art, Art. 1 clarifies that such works are identified as belonging to the cultural heritage of a country (by registration, classification or by any relevant internationally accepted method of publicity).

to be the same legal system; this is an exceptional situation, although the case *Winkworth v. Christie's Ltd* reminded that re-importation into, and (re)sale and (re)acquisition of the object in, the country of origin are possible. On the contrary, under the Basel Resolution, the *lex originis* gains a special status: it represents the only law applicable to the transfer of ownership of works of art.

In terms of illicit export issues, differently from the general irrelevance of the *lex originis* under ordinary conflict of (private) laws, the Basel Resolution declares that the export of works of art is governed by the relevant provisions of the country of origin.[82]

It remains to be seen if private international law (domestic or international in case of a treaty) systems will in the future evolve towards the use of the *lex originis*. For the time being, the issue is certainly part of the academic debate.[83]

6. FROM PRIVATE INTERNATIONAL LAW TO INTERNATIONAL UNIFORM LAW

6.1. Preliminary Remarks

International uniform law has progressively gained in importance. It offers the remarkable advantage for states to negotiate specific solutions, tailored to the needs of their subject-matter, leaving aside the unpredictability of the normative content of a given law applicable under ordinary conflict of laws. As a counterpart, this technique exposes states to the difficult task of finding consensual solutions where divergences may exist in legal traditions and/or current policies.

A well-known example is provided by the 1980 United Nations *Vienna Convention on International Sale of Goods* (CISG). It offers a regime specific to such international sales, exempted from the shortcomings that may generate the application of those national laws whose regime is too rooted in domestic sales and not sufficiently flexible to adapt to the needs of international sales. However, the Convention is not completely uniform; negotiating in the rather legally and economically heterogeneous universal framework, its drafters were not in a position to completely avoid making reference to private international law, and therefore to national applicable laws, as concerns crucial issues, such as the applicability of the Convention,[84] the validity of the contract or the transfer of title.[85]

6.2. Uniform Law, Works of Art and Cultural Property

Private international law solutions, as briefly described (above: 5.2 and 5.3), do not necessarily ensure the return of cultural property stolen and/or illicitly exported. This outcome is rather principle in most jurisdictions vis-à-vis an illicit export, while in case of theft return is a possible outcome depending on the law applicable in a specific case.

6.2.1. International Instruments

6.2.1.1. *On the Limited Significance of the 1980 Vienna Convention.* The 1980 United Nations *Vienna Convention on International Sale of Goods* (CISG) offers a regime specifically designed to meet the needs related to the international sales of goods. However, it is of a very limited significance for international sales of works of art and cultural property. Briefly, it should be stressed that:

i) its scope (*ratione materiae*) excludes: a) sales of goods bought for personal, family or household use; and b) sales by auction.[86] In most cases only some sales of works of art and cultural property between museums or similar entities may still fall under the scope of application of the Convention;
ii) even in the cases where the Convention applies, its provisions do not rule on crucial issues as the validity of the sales contract and the transfer of ownership it is expected to generate, directly or indirectly.[87] Such issues remain regulated by relevant applicable laws under private international law as well as, more exceptionally, by other sources considered in this article;
iii) last but not least, the Vienna Convention permits the parties to exclude its application or derogate from, or vary, the effect of any of its provisions.[88]

6.2.1.2. *Specific UNESCO and UNIDROIT Instruments.* Reacting to the continuous increase of illicit traffic in works of art and cultural property, the international community initiated multilateral negotiations to adopt treaties specific to such objects. Obviously such treaty-law making exercises were not unprecedented in general terms. However, the new treaties did innovate substantially from private, and private international, law perspectives because they established a new uniform law regime specifically conceived for cultural property. As such, these regimes apply within their scopes (in particular vis-à-vis their States Parties and according to their definition of cultural property) regardless of the State Party's private international law rules.[89]

For instance, if such instrument obliges a possessor of stolen cultural property to return it, the obligation remains even if the law usually applicable in that (State Party) jurisdiction would generally grant title to the possessor. Differently from the Vienna Convention and its explicitly stated non binding nature (above: 6.2.1.1), a clause between seller and buyer would not exclude *per se* the applicability of these interstate uniform instruments.

As the only United Nations agency with a mandate for the protection of cultural heritage, since its inception the United

[82] Art. 3

[83] See G. Carducci, *La restitution internationale*, cited, p. 147–186. Most recently, Ch. Armbrüster, *La revendication de biens culturels du point de vue du droit international privé*, RCDIP 2004, p. 723.

[84] Art. 1, 1.

[85] Art. 4.

[86] Art. 2, a) and b).

[87] Art. 4.

[88] Art. 6 and subject to article 12.

[89] Such rules remain applicable outside the scope of these instruments or, if circumstances so require, to fill a gap in them.

Nations Educational, Scientific, and Cultural Organization (UNESCO) has elaborated several standard-setting instruments thereon. Leaving aside Recommendations and Declarations and focusing only on Conventions and Protocols, binding instruments for their respective States Parties, the following are most relevant.

First, the 1954 Protocol to the Hague *Convention for the Protection of Cultural Property in the Event of Armed Conflict*[90] represents the first multilateral treaty addressing specifically illicit export and restitution of movable cultural property in armed conflict and is currently in force among 89 States.[91] Second, the 1970 UNESCO *Convention on the Means of Prohibiting and Preventing the Illicit Import, Export and Transfer of Ownership of Cultural Property* represented a strong position against illicit traffic at the time of its adoption, and is currently in force among 106 States.[92] This Convention has been a "pioneer" instrument if compared to traditional private international law solutions for illicit traffic cases available in the late 1960's.[93] Twenty five years after its adoption, the 1970 Convention has been complemented primarily on the private law aspects of restitution (good faith acquisition, duty of care, indemnity etc.), by the UNIDROIT *Convention on Stolen or Illegally Exported Cultural Objects* adopted in 1995, currently in force among 23 States.[94]

Although none is explicitly retroactive,[95] all these instruments are operational according to their respective contents and scopes of application. While it does not affect, technically speaking, the non-retroactivity principle, the 1995 UNIDROIT Convention contains in its Preamble a paragraph which clearly reflects the sensitivity of the issue, at least for some countries, and the lengthy debates it generated during the negotiations.[96] Under different conditions specific to each treaty, all these texts set an obligation, the return of cultural property having illicit provenance. Such instruments differ inter alia in the mechanisms they establish (request presented through diplomatic channel or state courts and authorities, etc.).

Even the least recent instrument, the Protocol dating back to 1954 and celebrating its 50th Anniversary just last year, sets out clear provisions and obligations for its States Parties in armed conflict situations.[97] This set of rules clarifies at the multilateral treaty-law level the issue of restitution in armed conflict beyond some uncertainties that may exist in general customary international law, such as the period starting from which a general customary obligation of return should be deemed to exist, and its precise content.[98] Last but not least, the Protocol establishes another crucial principle: cultural property removed during armed conflict shall never be retained as war reparations.

The famous 1970 UNESCO Convention applies both to "ordinary" peacetime situations as well as to periods of military occupation[99] where poverty and difficult conditions are likely to increase looting and theft, among others, of cultural property. The most recent and sophisticated multilateral treaty on restitution is the 1995 UNIDROIT Convention. Whatever the views one may have on restitution, this Convention deserves consideration, inter alia, as it provides two *distinct* and detailed regimes, for stolen or illicitly exported objects, which are to be returned pursuant to certain conditions even if they were not stolen before being illicitly exported.[100] Such regimes reflect the balance of interests achieved during the Diplomatic Conference in June 1995.

6.2.2. European Specific Instruments

Outside the UNESCO or UNIDROIT instruments, but influenced by the *travaux préparatoires* of the latter, at the European level the Council Directive 93/7 of 15 March 1993 on the return of cultural objects unlawfully removed from the territory of a Member State, has established an important return scheme to counterbalance the establishment of the internal market and its impact on customs controls among Member

[90] See generally, J. Toman, *The Protection of Cultural Property in the Event of Armed Conflict. Commentary on the Convention for the Protection of Cultural Property in the Event of Armed Conflict and its Protocol, signed on 14 May 1954 in The Hague, and on other Instruments of International Law Concerning such Protection*, Dartmouth Publishing Company/UNESCO, 1996, p. 333–351; P. O'Keefe, *The First Protocol to the Hague Convention Fifty Years on*, Art Antiquity and Law, 2004 p. 99; On the relationships between the Protocol, States practice, *ad hoc* (peace) and codification treaties, and customary law developments, G. Carducci, *L'obligation de restitution des biens culturels et des objets d'art en cas de conflit armé: droit coutumier et droit conventionnel avant et après la Convention de La Haye de 1954*, cited.

[91] See the up-dated list under: <http://erc.unesco.org/cp/convention.asp?KO=15391&language=E>.

[92] See the up-dated list under: <http://erc.unesco.org/cp/convention.asp?KO=13039&language=E>.

[93] For the comparison, and current interactions, between uniform law instruments and general private international law, see G. Carducci, *La restitution internationale*, cited. For a commentary, see P. O'Keefe, *Commentary on the UNESCO 1970 Convention on illicit traffic*, IAL, 2000.

[94] On the 1995 Convention see G. Carducci, *La restitution internationale des biens culturels et des objets d'art, cited.*, L. V. Prott, *Commentary on the UNIDROIT Convention*, IAL, 1997, P. Lalive, *Une avancée du droit international: la Convention de Rome d'Unidroit sur les biens culturels volés ou illicitement exportés*, Uniform Law Review, 1996 p. 40. The text and up-dated list of States Parties is available at <http://www.unidroit.org/english/conventions/1995culturalproperty/main.htm>.

[95] Non-retroactivity of treaties to acts or facts which took place or situations which ceased to exist before their entry into force, unless "a different interpretation appears from the treaty or is otherwise established" is a fundamental principle (1969 Vienna Convention on the Law of Treaties, Art. 28).

[96] "AFFIRMING that the adoption of the provisions of this Convention for the future in no way confers any approval or legitimacy upon illegal transactions of whatever kind which may have taken place before the entry into force of the Convention."

[97] i) To prevent the exportation, from a territory occupied by them during an armed conflict; ii) to take into their custody (either automatically or at the request of the authorities of the State concerned) cultural property imported into their territories; and especially iii) to a) return, at the close of hostilities, to the competent authorities of the territory previously occupied, cultural property which is in their territories, if such property has been exported in contravention of the obligation to prevent the exportation from a territory occupied; and b) pay an indemnity to the holders in good faith of any cultural property which has to be returned.

[98] Some doctrinal statements and State practice (and *opinio iuris*) do not appear necessarily consistent. See G. Carducci, *L'obligation de restitution des biens culturels et des objets d'art en cas de conflit armé, cited.*

[99] Art. 11.

[100] Under the conditions set out in Art. 5.

States. Differently from the UNESCO or UNIDROIT Conventions, the Directive operates exclusively for cases of illicit export,[101] regardless of the preexistence of a theft, and solely for objects qualified as national treasures in the sense of former Article 36, currently 30, of the Rome Treaty.[102]

The European authorities may one day wish to consider revising this text in order to better counter the increasing illicit traffic which affects most frequently stolen cultural property not necessarily "illicitly" exported and qualified as national treasure. Although it does not currently seem to be on the agenda,[103] such revision would therefore probably imply extending the Directive, or an analogous mechanism, to theft, regardless of an "illicit" export (of the stolen object), and to cultural property not necessarily qualified as national treasure. In terms of European treaty-law, such a revision would imply departing to some extent from the restrictive textual base, limited to national treasures, in Article 30.[104]

7. UN-RATIFIED OR INAPPLICABLE INTERNATIONAL CONVENTIONS AND PUBLIC POLICY

Although international uniform law is generally designed to replace private international law, practice shows that often such a replacement is a reality only in part and the two systems coexist, as in the example provided above (1980 Vienna Convention; above: 6.1).

From a public international law perspective treaties are binding on their respective States Parties. Un-ratified treaties generally do not receive a great deal of attention, if not vis-à-vis potential crystallization of, or developments in, customary international law.[105]

From a private international law perspective, un-ratified treaties attract generally even less attention. Unless the treaty is one of private international law or one establishing a (private law) uniform regime, the momentum of multilateral codification vis-à-vis interstate practice is not even directly at stake in this perspective.

However, it would be erroneous to completely disregard un-ratified, or even ratified but just inapplicable, treaties in private international law, at least in the field of cultural property. The important Republic of Ecuador v. Danusso case provides an example. With regard to a collection of archaeological objects illicitly removed and exported from Ecuador and imported to Italy, the Turin Tribunal applied to ownership issues the *lex situs* rule, at the time of the acquisition, and considered legitimate and grounded the restitution claim filed by the Republic of Ecuador. If the reasoning was so far no more than ordinary and to be expected in those circumstances, the judge was innovative by making reference to the 1970 UNESCO Convention, although it was not applicable (*ratione temporis*) to the dispute.[106] The Convention served as a relevant threshold to measure the compatibility of foreign law (Ecuadorian law) to the forum's fundamental public policy.[107]

8. EMERGENCY SITUATIONS AND *AD HOC* UNITED NATIONS SECURITY COUNCIL RESOLUTIONS

The end of the cold war was a significant event not only for its numerous socio-political consequences, but also for the activity of the United Nations Security Council whose primary responsibility is the maintenance of international peace and security.[108] Indeed, since then not only has this activity radically increased,[109] but also enforcement actions under Article 41 of the United Nations Charter have become the ordinary tool for peace maintenance.[110] The variety of measures the Security Council may take results from two distinct sources, operating at different levels: first, Chapter VII and the powers it grants the Security Council,[111] secondly, Article 41 which allows a broad range of measures, through a non-exhaustive enumeration, with the exclusion of those involving the use of force.[112]

It is therefore clear that in exceptional situations, the international community may deem it appropriate to operate through the Security Council to adopt *ad hoc* international law rules to be applied, inter alia, to illicit trafficking and restitution of cultural property. This has been the case for the situations linked to armed conflicts.

Important in this regard have been the two wars in Iraq and some of the Resolutions they generated. For instance, Resolution 686 (1991) adopted on 2 March 1991, demanded that Iraq, inter alia (paragraph 2, d) "Immediately begin to return all Kuwait property seized by Iraq, the return to be completed in the shortest possible period."

However, more important and articulated is Resolution 1483 (2003) adopted by the Security Council on 22 May 2003. Among others, its Paragraph 7 so reads:

7. *Decides* that all Member States shall take appropriate steps to facilitate the safe return to Iraqi institutions of Iraqi cultural property and other items of archaeological, historical, cultural, rare scientific, and religious importance illegally removed from the Iraq National Museum, the National

[101] Art. 1, 1.
[102] Art. 1, 2.
[103] Amendments of substance, besides updating the amounts indicated in the Annex, seem to be currently excluded by the Commission in its Report to the Council, the European Parliament and the Economic and Social Committee, p. 16–17.
[104] The restrictive effect this textual basis had in the elaboration of the Directive is unquestioned, even self-explanatory in its Preamble.
[105] For instance, L. B. Sohn, *Unratified Treaties as a Source of Customary International Law*, Essays W. Riphagen, 1986, p. 231.
[106] *Tribunale di Torino*, 25 March 1982, RDIPP 1982, p. 625.
[107] Public policy in private international sense ("ordine pubblico internazionale").
[108] Art. 24, Par. 1, UN Charter.
[109] Cf. *United Nations: Law, Policies and Practice*, (Editor-in-chief R. Wolfrum), Vol. II, 1995, p. 1158.
[110] *The Charter of the United Nations. A Commentary*, (Ed. by B. Simma), Oxford University Press, 2002, p. 738.
[111] For instance, besides establishing positive or negative (refraining from) obligations, the Security Council may inter alia deem appropriate establishing a committee (as for States to report to on the implementation of a Resolution, as in the recent Resolution 1540, n. 4, Apr. 28, 2004).
[112] These latter measures are generally based on Art. 42.

Library, and other locations in Iraq since the adoption of resolution 661 (1990) of 6 August 1990, including by establishing a prohibition on trade in or transfer of such items and items with respect to which reasonable suspicion exists that they have been illegally removed, and *calls upon* the United Nations Educational, Scientific, and Cultural Organization, Interpol, and other international organizations, as appropriate, to assist in the implementation of this paragraph.

All United Nations Member States have the obligation to implement the measures decided upon by the Security Council.[113] Their applicability and effects depend on the specific content of the measures and their implementation at domestic level, and indirectly on the existing balance between monist or dualist approaches in the target state.

The above-mentioned Resolution 1483 (2003) has resulted, for instance, in the United Kingdom example, in steps taken at national level under *The Iraq (United Nations Sanctions) Order 2003* adopted on 12 June 2003 and which came into force on 14 June. For illegally removed Iraqi cultural property the Order prohibits both importation and exportation.[114] Among others, a self-explanatory, important provision qualifies "illegally removed" Iraqi cultural property[115] as property illegally removed from any location in Iraq since 6 August 1990, and declares immaterial whether the removal was illegal under the law of a part of the United Kingdom or of any other country or territory.

Depending on the scope of these *ad hoc* international rules and the resulting domestic implementations in the various target states, the legal complexity of international transactions concerning cultural objects may vary domestically and globally increase. For instance:

i) Private law sanctions (void, voidable, unenforceable contract; operating retrospectively or not etc.); for violations of the measures, if not (indirectly or directly) determined by the Resolution, may vary from country to country.
ii) If generally a target state implements the measure decided upon by the Security Council within the scope of validity of the Resolution – as for instance did the United Kingdom with regard to Resolution 1483,[116] other states may, on their own initiative and if not precluded to do so under international law, deem appropriate to prolong the measure – actually its domestic implementation – beyond the original scope of, and timeframe indicated in, the Resolution.

More generally, the Security Council may extend the timeframe of a previous Resolution.[117]

9. EMERGENCY SITUATIONS AND *AD HOC* EUROPEAN UNION REGULATIONS

Though operating at a regional and not universal level, the European Union has initiated important initiatives to reduce illicit trafficking of cultural property and works of art. Leaving aside regular activities, as the control operated through the Council Directive 93/7 of 15 March 1993 on the return of cultural objects unlawfully removed from the territory of a Member State and the Council Regulation 3911/92 of 9 December 1992 on the export of cultural goods (as amended), most relevant in terms of *ad hoc* measure is Council Regulation 1210/2003 of 7 July 2003 concerning certain specific restrictions on economic and financial relations with Iraq and repealing Regulation (EC) 2465/96. EU Regulations are directly effective in the legal systems of Member States.

Regulation 1210 prohibits import of (or introduction into the territory of the Community), export of (or removal from such territory) or dealing in, Iraqi cultural property as defined by the Regulation.[118] Regulation 1210 is obviously a self sufficient normative EU instrument, with a determined scope of application (*ratione temporis*,[119] *loci* and *personae*[120]).

However, its nature and scope reflect the fact that it represents a valuable, concrete example of the coexistence of, and interactions between, the two complementary *ad hoc* international (UN) and European (EU) instruments for the protection of the Iraqi cultural property. This explains why the prohibitions established by Regulation 1210 cease to apply if it is shown that the cultural items were either exported from Iraq prior to 6 August 1990, or are being returned to Iraqi institutions in accordance with the above-mentioned UNSC Resolution 1483.[121]

It is worth observing that 6 of August 1990 is the date of adoption of UNSC Resolution 661 (1990) and the time limit of removal of cultural property from Iraq before which both the UNSC Resolution 1483 (2003) and the (EU) Regulation 1210/2003 cease to apply to such property.

Both crucial tasks of defining, and ensuring the implementation of, sanctions applicable to infringements of the Regulation 1210 are left to EU Member States. The discretionary nature of these tasks at national level is however limited. On one side, sanctions provided for must be effective, proportionate and dissuasive. On the other, Member States shall be responsible for bringing proceedings, under their jurisdictions, against any person in cases of breach of the restrictive measure laid down in the Regulation.[122]

Important also is the scope of the prohibitions established. Regulation 1210 expressly clarifies that it applies notwithstanding any rights conferred or obligations imposed by any international agreement signed or any contract entered into or any license or permit granted before its entry into force.[123]

[113] Art. 48, UN Charter. [114] Art. 8.
[115] And any other item of archaeological, historical, cultural, rare scientific or religious importance.
[116] Which is also reflected by the provision (Art. 1, Par. 2) in The Iraq (United Nations Sanctions) Order 2003 linking the effects, in whole or in part, of the to those of the Resolution 1483.
[117] For instance Resolution 1579 (2004), 21 December 2004, renewed measures imposed by Resolution 1521 (2003).

[118] Art. 3, c) and Annex II. [119] Art. 18.
[120] Art. 16. [121] Art. 3, 2.
[122] Art. 15. Some anticipation is to be found in Preamble (13).
[123] Art. 14.

10. PRIVATE INTERNATIONAL LAW AND "MANDATORY RULES"

"Mandatory rules" represent another set of rules which is a growing potential source of international art law and that may have an impact on international transactions of art in their validity and effects, impact which is not necessarily expected under "ordinary" private international law. Depending on their nature and objectives under their respective legal systems, mandatory rules may vary in their target and scope and, as such, deserve a distinction.

10.1. "Ordinary" Mandatory Rules

10.1.1. Nature

We favour this terminology of "ordinary" to avoid misunderstanding. They are the rules that the parties may not contract out. It is a common phenomenon in many jurisdictions to observe that the "freedom of contract," i.e. the freedom to choose if, with whom and on what, to contract, is less and less an operational freedom and a philosophical dogma. In view of its crucial importance for economy and trade, such freedom is increasingly a policy tool for the national regulatory authorities.

Mandatory rules operating as limitations, under various forms and contents, to the freedom of contract are, for some time already, a reality both in common law jurisdictions, as the United Kingdom[124] and the United States,[125] and in civil law legal systems, as France,[126] Germany[127] and Italy.[128] Art objects, and usually even more so "cultural" property and heritage, are no exception to such regulatory trend. Furthermore, in many jurisdictions their significance attracts, or generates, a particular legal protection for which rules on contracts (sale, loan etc.) are generally mandatory. Depending on jurisdictions, non-compliance leads generally to unenforceability or to a void contract.

From a substantive law (public policy and law of obligations) perspective, the complexity of exploring what is an "illegal" contract must be evaluated case by case, under the relevant legal system, without relying solely on the recurrent and well-settled "causes" of illegality.[129] Evaluation of illegality, both in its causes and effects, increases in complexity vis-à-vis "international" contracts: not only the spectrum of potential mandatory rules varies depending on the applicable law, and sometimes even *beyond* it (see below 10.2), but even the characterization of rules as "mandatory," if not statutorily provided for, is generally (even) more complex vis-à-vis foreign law.[130]

10.1.2. Scope

For international (private law) situations, from a conflict of laws perspective mandatory rules are applicable from the forum's perspective simply to the extent that they belong to the proper law/*lex causae.*

More exceptionally, mandatory rules of other jurisdictions may be taken into account, not as ruling norms but basically as mere fact, whose legal effects are ruled by the applicable law. Such taking into account generally occurs when the foreign rules have an impact locally, inter alia on the performance of the contract.[131]

In a not recent but still interesting decision, the German *Bundesgerichthof* (BGH) accepted to appreciate under the (German) applicable law a violation of the Nigerian law on export of cultural property (masks and statues). The insurance contract relating to the transport of such cultural objects was declared void for violation of German mandatory rules (in the framework of the compatibility test to *gute Sitten*, §138 BGB).[132]

10.2. "International" Mandatory or "Overriding" Rules

10.2.1. Nature and Identification

These are not multilateral conflict rules, as those generally indicating the law applicable, inter alia to contracts or chattels, where depending on circumstances such law may be a foreign law or the *lex fori.* They are unilateral rules that determine, explicitly or implicitly,[133] their own spatial scope, regardless of the ordinary operation of the forum's conflict of laws rule. Such rules have been identified by scholars,[134] and in case-law, but are more rarely acknowledged as a category by law-makers.[135] If a statutory clarification fails, the context, nature and purposes of the provisions usually enable the judge to clarify and, where appropriate,[136] to declare them

[124] For instance, A. Grubb, *The Law of Contract*, Butterworths, London 1999, p. 31 ; Chitty, *On Contracts, General Principles*, Vol. I, 1994 London p. 65.

[125] Cf. E. Farnswort, *On Contracts*, 1990, Vol. II, p. 15–67; Id. *Contracts*, 2004, p. 20–23.

[126] Among others, F. Terré, Ph. Simler, Y. Lequette, *Droit civil. Les obligations*, 7th Ed. 1999, p. 37.

[127] K. Larenz, *Allgemeiner Teil des deutschen Bürgerlichen Rechts*, 7ème éd. München, 1989, p. 427 s., p. 560 s.; D. Medicus, *Allgemeiner Teil des BGB*, 6ème éd. Heidelberg 1994, p. 74 s.; W. Fikentscher, *Schuldrecht*, 8ème éd. Berlin 1992, p.77–85; Krame, *Vor §145 BGB*, Münchener Kommentar BGB, I (Allgemeiner Teil), 3ème éd. 1993, p. 1219 (1226 s.).

[128] G. B. Ferri, *Il negozio giuridico tra libertà e norma*, 4th Ed. 1992; C. M. Bianca, *Il contratto*, 1987 Giuffrè, p. 18 s.; R. Sacco, *Obbligazioni e contratti*, Vol. X, in *Trattato di diritto privato* (dir. P. Rescigno), UTET 1988, p. 247 s.

[129] One of the not so numerous first studies that had the credit of refraining from (excessively) relying on such causes, was M. P. Furmston, *The Analysis of Illegal Contracts*, The University of Toronto Law Journal, 1966 p. 267.

[130] It is assumed that: i) the judge has succeeded in learning the content of foreign law, only its interpretation remaining an issue; ii) the rule at stake is not statutorily characterized as mandatory; iii) its judicial interpretation may lead to such characterization.

[131] Zweigert K., *Nichterfüllung auf Grund ausländischer Leistungsverbote*, Rabels Z. 1942, p. 283.

[132] BGH, 22 June 1972, BGHZ 59 n. 14, 82.

[133] In the latter case, judicial interpretation of the nature and objective of the relevant rules is particularly important.

[134] Primarily in 1941, by W. Wengler, *Die Anknüpfung des zwingenden Schuldrechts im internationalen Privatrecht*, Zvergl R W 1941, 168.

[135] This used to be generally the case until some recent (national and mostly European) codifications of private international law.

[136] For a negative example, where the characterization of "overriding rule" has been denied, French *Cour de cassation*(*Chambre commerciale*), 28 Nov. 2000, RTDCom. 2001, p. 1067.

overriding rules and, as such, distinguish them from "ordinary" mandatory rules (provisions which can not be contracted out). It should however be clear that, in some cases, a single provision may be at the same time an ordinary mandatory and an overriding rule.

More generally, the identification of overriding rules is complicated by some elements, such as:

i) *Interpretation*: each legal system determines, explicitly or implicitly, the scope of its provisions. If this is generally not problematic for the judge vis-à-vis the provisions of the *lex fori*, as soon as the provision belongs to foreign law and its spatial scope is not statutorily expressed, ascertaining such scope raises all the known difficulties in interpreting foreign law.
ii) *Variety of terminologies*:
   a. The situation is rather clear in all those jurisdictions where the terminology is clearly distinct from "ordinary" mandatory rules, as in French (*Lois de police*[137] or *Lois d'application immediate*[138]), Italian (*Norme di applicazione necessaria*[139]) or German (*Eingriffsnormen*[140]). All these terminologies have the credit of being at the same time, distinct from "ordinary" mandatory rules, and refraining from going as far as "international" mandatory rules. Indeed, this latter terminology may be misleading to the extent that such rules are most often domestic, and only exceptionally European[141] or international rules.
   b. However, the situation is somehow more difficult in the English language where can be found, depending on the authority considered, both a distinctive terminology, as "overriding rules"[142] or "statutes,"[143] and mere "mandatory rules" as in the official version of the Rome Convention or some doctrinal presentations.[144]
iii) *Misleading terminologies*: such rules are sometimes defined as self-limiting rules. This terminology is accurate for its reference to a unilateral approach ("self"). However, it is somehow misleading because, if compared to the scope of application that ordinary conflict of law rules grant to private law provisions, generally these rules do not limit, but extend their scope of application.[145]

10.2.2. Scope

The specific category of norms which is "overriding rules," reflects the growing interest of States to ensure enforcement of some of their policies in, or having at least an effect on, international private law situations. Depending on the prevailing policy at stake, such interest may also address cultural property in view of its importance for the nation's heritage, and for instance ensure its inalienability or prevent its unauthorized export. In some cases, the state may also wish to ensure respect of a foreign country's cultural heritage, for instance against illicit looting. Overriding rules deserve consideration to prevent unexpected (mandatory) interferences on the contract, even if they are not very numerous in number and manifestations, with some exceptions as exchange controls, and as such risk to be ignored or disregarded in everyday legal practice.

If the law of the forum possesses overriding rules, the judge generally applies them directly instead of the usually applicable (foreign) law.[146] If they belong to the applicable law, they are generally automatically applied as part of it, unless they raise, in a specific case, a conflict with the forum's priority policies, be them expressed in terms of public policy or overriding rules.

The application of mandatory and overriding rules belonging to the proper law of contract or the forum's law are to some extent predictable since the parties are usually permitted and advised to choose both the applicable law and the court having jurisdiction on a possible dispute. However, international art dealers and lawyers may find more unpredictability with regard to overriding rules of a "third" country, which is neither the applicable law nor the forum's law.

Exceptionally and under some restrictive conditions, such rules may be taken into account and even applied in the framework of the European law of international contracts, the

137 P. Mayer, *Les lois de police*, Communication au Comité Français de d.i.p. du 23 novembre 1985 p. 105 ; Id. *Les lois de police étrangères*, Clunet 1981 p. 277 s.;

138 Ph. Francescakis, *Conflits de lois (principes généraux)*, Répertoire de droit international, Dalloz, n. 122 et s. p. 31; Id. *Quelques précisions sur les "lois d'application immédiate" et leurs rapports avec les règles de conflits de lois*, RCDIP. 1966 p. 2 et s.;

139 G. Carducci, *Norme di applicazione necessaria (diritto internazionale privato)*, Enciclopedia giuridica Treccani (1999); R. De Nova, *Self-limiting Rules and Party Autonomy*, F. S. W. Wengler, Vol. II Berlin 1973 p. 617; P. Picone, *Norme di diritto internazionale privato e norme materiali del foro*, 1971; G. Sperduti, *Norme d'applicazione necessaria e ordine pubblico*, Riv.dir.intern.priv.proc. 1976, p. 467.

140 F. A. Mann, *Sonderanknüpfung und zwingendes Recht im internationalen Privatrecht*, Festschrift Beitzke, Berlin 1979 p. 607; K. Siehr, *Ausländische Eingriffsnormen im inländischen Wirtschaftskollisionsrecht*, RabelsZ 1988 p. 41; K. Schurig, *Zwingendes Recht, "Eingriffsnormen" und neues IPR*, RabelsZ 1990 p. 217.; I. Schwander, *Lois d'application immédiate, Sonderanknüpfung, IPR-Sachnormen und andere Ausnahmen von der gewöhnlichen Anknüpfung im internationalen Privatrecht*, Zürich 1975; K. Siehr, *Normen mit eigener Bestimmung ihres räumlich-persönlichen Anwendungsbereichs im Kollisionsrecht der Bundesrepublik Deutschland*, Rabels Z 1982, p. 357.

141 As, already since 1957, Art. 81, 2 of the Rome treaty (former Art. 85, 2).

142 See Dicey and Morris (ed. L. Collins), *Conflict of Laws*, 13th Ed. 2000, Vol. II, p. 1243 (although in Rule 175, II the terminology of mandatory rules emerges again, though duly spatially qualified; i.e. as mandatory irrespective of the fact that foreign law is applicable).

143 J. H. C. Morris, *Statutes in the Conflict of Laws*, in F. S. K. Lipstein, 1980, p. 187, at p. 200.

144 See for the latter, Scoles, Hay, Borchers, Symeonides, *Conflict of Laws*, Third Edition, 2000, n. 18.4, p. 863 and 867 even with an explicit reference to Art. 7 (I) of the 1980 Rome Convention.

145 See G. Carducci, *Norme di applicazione necessaria*, cited.

146 See, for instance, Rome Convention, Art. 7, II. Opposite to this principle is an academic proposal made in the 60's (T. Treves) to consider that the overriding rule should apply not instead of, but at the same time as, the conflict of law rule and therefore the applicable law, under the condition of an identity of results. This proposal has been redeveloped thirty years later by A. Bonomi, *Le norme imperative nel diritto internazionale privato*, Schulthess Zürich 1998, p. 154. In our view, this proposal is not only far from reality in most jurisdictions but is also not desirable *per se*, for different reasons (see G. Carducci, *Norme di applicazione necessaria*, cited, Enciclopedia giuridica Treccani, 1999, p. 3).

1980 Rome Convention on the Law Applicable to Contractual Obligations[147] or in some national private international law systems, as is the case in Switzerland,[148] primarily if they present a link to the contract. The qualification as "private" or "public" law is not here directly relevant. For instance, under the Rome Convention national provisions on export control of cultural property are not excluded from qualifying as foreign overriding rules in their *private law effects* on the contract (for instance declared void in case of illicit export) for the simple fact that they are qualified as belonging to "public law" from the forum's perspective.[149]

10.2.3. European and American Methodological Divergences v. Comparable Results

It is well-known that continental European conflict of laws differ in several regards, primarily in terms of methodology, from the Anglo-American conflict of laws. Savigny's famous objective to ensure international uniformity of decisions, and therefore continuity in international (private law) relations regardless of the country of litigation, naturally opposes to *lex fori* favouritism as Currie's. It is worth observing that, paradoxically enough, such favouritism is generally *de jure* rejected but *de facto* used in several jurisdictions in the United States.[150] In most of Europe *lex fori* favouritism is certainly weaker, if not rejected at least in principle. However, differently from such favouritism which covers the applicable law as a whole, it is undeniable that international mandatory rules are unilateral provisions and reflect the historic resurgence and growing trend towards the acknowledgment of a forum's interest to apply *systematically* (at least) *some* of its (most important) substantive provisions in international private law cases.

In spite of several differences, it is important to observe that American conflict of laws may reach solutions not too distant from those made possible under the more explicit and analytical wording of Article 7, I of the Rome Convention, through Restatement (Second) on Conflict of Laws (§187).[151] Under the latter provision, a genuine interest of the law whose mandatory rules are at stake should prove to be stronger than the interest of the law normally applicable to the issue. In any event, both Article 7, I and §187 reject generalizations: their outcome depends on the specific (factual and legal) elements of each situation and their evaluation by the judge.

[147] Art. 7, 1. On this rather complex question with various ramifications vis-à-vis movable cultural property, see G. Carducci, *La restitution internationale des biens culturels et des objets d'art*, cited, p. 314–339.

[148] Swiss law (18 December 1987) on Private International Law (art. 19).

[149] See also P. Lagarde, *Le nouveau droit international privé des contrats après l'entrée en vigueur de la Convention de Rome du 19 juin 1980*, RCDIP 1991, p. 287 (at 322).

[150] See S. C. Symeonides, *The American Choice-of-Law Revolution in the Courts: Today and Tomorrow*, Hague Academy, Collected Courses, 2002, p. 9 at 382.

[151] For a comparison, see T. C. Hartley, *Mandatory Rules in International Contracts: the Common Law Approach*, Hague Academy, Collected Courses, 1997, p. 337, at 378–380.

Reservation to Art. 7, I, of the Rome Convention v. Comparable Results

Some European States, as Germany[152] or the United Kingdom,[153] have rejected the applicability of Article 7, I of the Rome Convention.[154] An art lawyer may be tempted to disregard all the related complexities and basically reinsure his/her client by merely focusing on the proper law of the contract.

However, it would not be an excessive precaution to verify if, in a given legal system, for instance German law, in spite of its rejection of the applicability of Article 7, I, and the debates it raised,[155] some pre-existing judicial conflict of laws techniques may lead, still at present and in some circumstances, to results similar to those expected under Article 7, I.[156]

* * *

CONCLUSIONS

(Potentially Contributing to Legal Predictability)

1) Besides the variety of opinions that may exist on the "cultural" specificity of some (categories of) objects, national authorities (governments and/or law-makers and/or the judiciary through case-law) decide upon the question whether and to what extent works of art and cultural property deserve a "legal" specificity and therefore a specific legal regime, that differ, completely or in part, from the regime designed for, ordinary property. Whether this specific regime exists and, if so, what its content and effects are, are issues to be evaluated on a case by case basis as to prevent unfortunate generalizations.
2) Such specific regimes are common in many legal systems. As such they apply directly to domestic situations on the territory, but also to (the private law aspects of) international situations if they are part of the applicable law from the forum's perspective.
3) Such specific regimes are generally elaborated and adopted by states (national authorities) acting individually on their domestic substantive provisions and/or (more exceptionally) conflict of laws rules; however, they are increasingly adopted also by states acting jointly, at regional or universal level, through setting regular standards (as international conventions) or *ad hoc* standards as the Iraqi situation as shown.
4) Legal predictability of international transactions can only be improved by duly acknowledging the potential complexity of international art trade in both degrees and various forms and contents described in this article. Obviously, in particular cases even more variables and factors

[152] Art. 34 EGBGB.

[153] Contracts (Applicable Law) Act 1990, Section 2 (2).

[154] Art. 22 (1, a).

[155] See for instance, K. Kreuzer, *Erklärung eines generellen Vorbehalts zu Art. 7 Abs. 1 des Übereinkommens vom 19.6. 1980 über das auf vertragliche Schuldverhältnisse anzuwendende Recht?*, IPRax 1984, p. 293.

[156] See for instance, D. Busse, *Die Berücksichtigung ausländischer "Eingriffsnormen" durch die deutsche Rechtsprechung*, ZVR 1996, p. 386.

of complexity may exist and their case by case accurate assessment is appropriate.

5) Proper use of private international law tools as choice of law and jurisdiction selection clauses is recommended, although it is realistic to say that a number of variables remains outside the scope and effects of such clauses in legally complex international art transactions. Vis-à-vis such variables, making assurances to interested parties merely on the basis of such clauses may be inappropriate.
6) In art and cultural property law an unlimited freedom of contract should not be assumed. Mandatory protection regimes are a reality in the numerous legal systems where the (legal) treatment and destiny of art and cultural property are not just the concern of the parties to the contract, whatever its content (sale, loan etc.).
7) The example of Christies' recent decision to follow Sotheby's in appointing a "director of restitution,"[157] reflects the growing reality of restitution (with its legal and moral complexity) and awareness by the international market of it.

[157] The Art Newspaper, December 2004.

PART TWO

Keeping Culture Alive

The Source Nation's Efforts to Manage, Protect, and Preserve Heritage Resources

CHAPTER EIGHT

Introduction to Parts II and III: Cultural Rights, Cultural Property, and International Trade

Barbara T. Hoffman

Monsieur Gerard Sousi, Directeur du diplome Droit et Fiscalité du Marché de l'Art, has remarked that in the twenty-first century, each stakeholder in the international art market is part of a global network of cultural and economic exchanges. "Mondialisation, globalization, internationalism, peu importe le terme, le marché de l'art ne connaît pas du frontière."[1] Globalization is not universally welcomed with the same warmth by each stakeholder. Each country will balance globalisation with other values, interests and goals it seeks to achieve on behalf of its citizens in the formulation of policies with respect to the protection of its cultural property.

Parts II and III discuss the international movement in works of art and cultural property or "cultural objects" and its interface with cultural heritage law and policy. Obviously, the legislative programs of countries in Latin America and the Caribbean and around the world, for the protection of artistic, archaeological, ethnological, and historical properties differ both with respect to the objects protected and the scope and method of protection. How do countries implement their goals? What policies do they use? What instruments do they employ? Is there a central authority or is control decentralized. How do different agencies within a central government relate to each other? Any one involved in the formulation of cultural heritage policy as well as those involved in the international art trade must become familiar with the legal, financial and administrative regime for protecting such heritage.

The authors in Part II are from what are commonly referred to as "source nations" because these nations are the sources of cultural objects for which there is a world market. When cultural objects leave source nations they go to market nations where the demand exceeds the supply for such objects. The international trade in cultural property is most often regulated through export controls. The theory is that in the absence of such controls, the source nation's export of cultural objects would far exceed its import of cultural objects.[2] In speaking in support of the Law of 31 August 1920, which imposed a tariff on the exportation of ancient objects that could be as high as 100% of the value, President Edouard Herriot opined that it was necessary to struggle against "le collectioneur qui a remplacé le pillage par droit de conquête par une autre forme de pillage qui ne paraît quère plus interessante: le pillage par le droit d'argent."

Part III looks at the international art trade and the protection of cultural heritage from the point of view of the "market nations," principally the United States, the United Kingdom, and Germany, with special reference to cases arising from World War II in the case of the latter.

Mention has previously been made of the debate between cultural internationalist policies and "national retention policies." One point of contention is export controls.[3] Not surprisingly, the reader will discover that many of the source nations in Latin America have broad export controls. The United Kingdom, Japan,[4] and Canada[5] have narrowly drawn export restrictions. A distinction is made between "cultural patrimony" or "national treasure" and other cultural objects, which may be freely traded.

In addition to export restrictions, many source nations have enacted, in various forms, "national ownership laws." These laws present important issues discussed by the authors of Parts II and III.

If there is a strong focus in Parts II and III on the illicit rather than the licit traffic of works of art, it is in part because of the magnitude of the problem particularly as regards antiquities,

[1] Gérard Sousi, "L'Oeil Hors-série," *Le marché de l'art*, 2003, p. 12. "Globalization, internationalism, whatever the term, the art market knows no boundaries." The editor is an occasional lecturer in this master's program Jean Moulin 3.

[2] France is considered both a market nation and a source nation, whilst Switzerland, Japan, Germany, the United States, and Canada are considered market nations.

[3] For the cultural internationalist, export controls do not necessarily protect cultural property. Professor Merryman posits the example of a great work of art from a private collection in France, where it was unavailable for public viewing, classified as a national treasure, and then exported illegally to the United States where it hangs today in a great museum, properly identified as the work of a great French artist. See also for a contary view, Dr. Guido Carducci in International Legal Tools and Viewpoints in this book.

[4] In Japan, registration is undertaken under the Law for the Protection of Cultural Properties. There are two categories under the law: one is "National Treasure" and the other is "Important Cultural Property." Once the items are registered under one of these categories, exporting them is strictly prohibited. Dealers will handle other non-registered items. In that case, the certificate of audit for export is necessary. The certificate requires a photo to accompany each item so that customs officers can identify it. The application for the certificate with a photo must be submitted to the Agency of Cultural Affairs. The Agency then verifies whether or not the item in question is registered as an Important Cultural Property or National Treasure, or neither. If it is not registered under either of the two categories, the item is available for export. In the case that an application comes under consideration and the Agency for Cultural Affairs has not been aware of the existence of the object, and that object happens to be extremely important, the Agency is allowed three months to decide if it should be registered as an Important Cultural Property. It also can decide to purchase the item so that the item cannot be exported. This is the current situation.

[5] The Canadian Cultural Property Export Control List provides a detailed description of the classes of objects. Export controls apply if the expert examiner determines that the object meets the criteria of "outstanding significance" or "national importance."

as discussed by many of the authors. In general, there are three variations on the international movement of stolen works of art. First, cases of illegal export involve the smuggling out of its country of origin, a privately owned work of art that is classified as a "national treasure." Second, many countries declare contents of tombs and other relics of earlier civilizations found or built on the earth to be the property of the state and, as such, the taking of these objects in violation of said laws is "theft." The final variation is simple theft, in which an object of art is owned by an individual in one country and eventually appears in a private collection in another country. As one leading art scholar points out, simple theft cases are the least complicated to resolve, whereas illegal export and archaeological theft cases usually present more complex ethical issues, and the applicable law is far less clear or simple.

Protection is provided to the bona fide purchaser of property in most legal systems, except if the property is stolen. This principle stems from a recognition of the intolerable disruptive effect that a contrary rule would have on a free market economy and a system of private property.

In part, the lack of harmony in national law on the transferability of title to stolen property, the bona fide purchaser defence, limitations on the time within which an action may be brought (statues of limitation or repose), and allocation of the burden of proof, facilitate the laundering of and illicit trade in stolen art and antiquities. Under the Anglo-American common law rule – generally known as the *nemo dat quod non habet* rule – no one can give what one does not have,[6] a thief could not convey good title. As a result, in common law jurisdictions, the original owner retains title to the property even after it has been stolen and even if there have been several subsequent purchases by individuals who were unaware they were buying stolen goods.[7]

The vast majority of civil law systems, including most of Western Europe, Japan, and Mexico, accord greater protection to the possessor in good faith[8] of stolen property. Generally, civil law jurisdictions favour a shorter statute of limitations period. To civil code jurisdictions that favour the bona fide purchaser (BFP) of stolen goods over the original owner, the security of commercial transactions of personal property is a sacrosanct principle. In the civil law system, the original owner bears the risk of loss by theft or sale to a BFP. In the common law, the BFP bears the risk that the seller might not have good title.

Much cultural property that is the subject of dispute has moved across national borders. A court is called upon to decide under choice of law analysis which law to apply and then apply it to determine title. *Winkworth v. Christie, Manson & Woods, Ltd.*, provides an example of this process. Japanese artworks were stolen from the residence of a collector domiciled in England and were subsequently sold in Italy to a good faith purchaser who brought them back to England and delivered them to an auction house for sale. The original owner brought an action in an English court to affirm his title and recover the artworks. The English court chose to apply the law of Italy – the place of the transaction (*lex situs*) – whose short period of repose gave superior title to the good-faith purchaser. This, despite the argument of the original owner that several strong connecting factors to England, including that the theft had occurred there, the owner was domiciled there, the owner did not know that the art had ever been removed from England, the art had been voluntarily returned to England, and that an English court was hearing the action, supported the application of English law.

Stolen art is generally smuggled out of art-source countries, such as Cambodia,[9] Greece, Italy, Mali, Turkey, and, recently, Eastern Europe, Afghanistan, and China, and is then taken to countries like the United Kingdom, France, Switzerland, Thailand, Hong Kong, Singapore, and Japan, where liberal laws protecting the good-faith purchaser permit the property transferred to such a jurisdiction to be purged of its tainted title.[10]

UNIDROIT sets up two regimes: one for "stolen objects" and one for return of "illegally exported objects." Article III provides that the possessor of a cultural object that has been stolen shall return it. UNIDROIT endorses the *nemo dat* rule and makes it easier for aggrieved countries to recover cultural objects in three ways.[11] First, objects taken from illegal excavations will count as "stolen" objects. Second, the burden of proof will be reversed, with buyers of ancient artefacts having to prove that they did everything to ascertain that an object was not stolen in order to receive compensation. The issue of compensation is one of the most quarrelsome issues because

[6] It is codified in the United States in the Uniform Commercial Code, which states: "A purchaser of goods acquires all title which his transferor had or had power to transfer . . ." U.C.C. @ 2-403(1)(2000). It is codified as applied to goods in England in the Sale of Goods Act, 1979, c. 54, @21(1)(Eng.).

[7] Courts and legislatures, however, have modified the common law by imposing a statute of repose or limitations to limit the time in which a plaintiff possesses the legal right to assert a valid claim for the return of stolen property in court.

[8] Art. 3 of the Swiss Civil Code states . . . (1) Good faith is presumed when it is a legal condition for the existence or the effect of a right. (2) No one can claim being in good faith if it is incompatible with the attention that he should have shown in the given circumstances. But see the Cultural Property Transfer Act (CPTA) discussed *infra*.

[9] The first stop for many objects from Cambodia is Thailand, then Singapore, Japan, Western Europe, or North America. Thailand is not a signatory to the UNESCO Convention. Both the Thais and the French have a strong passion for collecting Khmer art. French law provides that the BFP of stolen goods acquires title, even from a thief, after the expiration of a three-year limitation period that runs from the time of the theft.

During a visit by the author in 1994 to a World Monuments Fund project at Angkor Wat in Cambodia, John Sanday, project manger for the team that is helping to preserve the Preah Khan, said that five Nagas, each weighing over a ton, were stolen from the site in the summer of 1994. Since the early 1990s, 60 sculptures have been beheaded at Preah Khan and countless others have been stolen in their entirety or defaced at Banteay Srei. According to King Norodom Sihanouk of Cambodia, Angkor has lost ten times the number of its statues, statuettes, lintels, and Buddha heads since 1970 that it lost between the eighth century and 1970.

[10] See B. Hoffman, "How UNIDROIT Protects Cultural Property," *New York Journal* (March 3–10, 1995).

[11] The UNIDROIT Convention is discussed by Guido Carducci in Part I of this book.

it strikes at the heart of the conflict between common law and civil jurisdictions. Attempting to discover a balance between these two interests, Article 4 offsets restitution against compensation but only for "stolen" goods. The Convention states that it is the current possessor who must establish that he or she followed the due diligence standard set out in Article 4 of the UNIDROIT Convention. Third, Article 5 permits a foreign government to lodge claims with either an administrative body or courts, at the election of the forum state, to recover objects based on violation of its export laws if it can "establish" certain evidentiary criteria or "establish" that the object is of important cultural significance. The UNIDROIT Convention has not proposed any rule relating to the burden of proof in illegal export cases, leaving it to national states in the implementation legislation. UNIDROIT also addresses another criticism of 1970 UNESCO by establishing a period of prescription of "three years from the time when the claimant knew the location of the cultural object and the identity of its possessor, and in any case within a period of fifty years from the time of theft."

The principles embodied in UNIDROIT thus distinguish between title to the object (i.e., right to compensation) and the right to decide where the object is located (i.e., the state of origin need not have any title).

Adherence to UNIDROIT has been slow. UNESCO, however, has fared better. Although initially the only market nations to ratify were Canada and the United States (1983), Japan, France, and, most recently, the United Kingdom[12] and Switzerland, have also ratified.[13]

Switzerland is fourth behind the United States, the United Kingdom, and France as a hub in the international art trade with sometimes controversial connections to the illicit trade in art and antiquities. The terms of Swiss law, until 2005, considered cultural objects as ordinary commodities with a five-year statute of limitations from the time of purchase. In addition, good faith on the part of the purchaser was presumed. Apparently, there is no statute of limitations for a bad-faith purchaser. Switzerland is often a destination for laundering material smuggled out of Italy.

In June 2004, Switzerland adopted the Federal Act on the International Transfer of Cultural Property or the Cultural Property Transfer Act (CPTA), which has been effective from June 2005. It is interesting to note that the legislation uses both "cultural object" and "cultural heritage" and establishes the link between the two. Switzerland has adopted the approach of the United States to enforcement of UNESCO with bilateral treaties under Article 9, rather than the Canadian model at the other end of the spectrum.[14]

The CPTA provides that importation of cultural property is illegal only if it violates the terms of a bilateral treaty between Switzerland and one of the hundred countries parties to the 1970 UNESCO Convention. Cultural property illegally imported into Switzerland under a bilateral treaty will be returned to the country of export if it is of significant importance to the heritage of that country and the claim is brought within (1) thirty years from the date of the export and (2) one year from the date when the country of origin located the property and the possessor. Illegally imported cultural property may be seized. The possessor is entitled to compensation if the property has been purchased in good faith and may retain possession until compensation is paid. Illegal importation is a criminal offence.

Article 16 requires art dealers and auction houses operating in Switzerland to exercise due diligence in order to avoid dealing in cultural property that may have been stolen, illegally excavated, or illegally imported into Switzerland.

Furthermore, dealers and auction houses are required to:

i. verify sellers' identities and require them to sign a warranty that they have good transferable title to the property
ii. provide clients with information on export from and import into countries parties to the 1970 UNESCO Convention
iii. maintain a register of data regarding cultural property they sell, and
iv. keep all documentation and registers for a period of thirty years

Article 17 permits the inspection of storage houses and business rooms of people active in the art trade or auction business. The Act requires Swiss museums to verify that cultural property they acquire or exhibit has not been stolen or illegally excavated, and that it is not part of the heritage property of a foreign country and was illegally exported from that country.

The time limit for adverse possession in accordance with Article 728 and the time limit for the return under Article 934, Swiss Civil Code, have been increased from five to thirty years under Article 32, CPTA.

Thus, not only are items stolen in Switzerland or abroad subject to return, but also, cultural goods removed against the will of the owner or otherwise lost to the owner are subject to a thirty-year limitations period for Cultural Property. The same applies to clandestine excavations and palaeontological objects to where the state of origin, for example, Egypt, Italy, or Turkey considers itself the owner of the objects found in the ground. The absolute time limit of thirty years is

[12] See A. Parkhouse, "The Illicit Trade in Cultural Objects: Recent Developments in the United Kingdom," in Part III of this book, "International Movement of Art and Cultural Property: Market Nations."

[13] See G. Carducci, Part I *supra*.

[14] The Cultural Property Export and Import Act came into force on 6 September 1977 and is administered by the Movable Cultural Property Program and the Canadian Cultural Property Export Review Board. The Act regulates the import and export of cultural property and provides special tax incentives to encourage Canadians to donate or sell important objects to public institutions in Canada. It is illegal to import into Canada all cultural objects illegally exported out of a state that is also a cosignatory of the 1970 UNESCO Convention on the Means of Prohibiting and Preventing the Illicit Import, Export, and Transfer of Ownership of Cultural Property. The Cultural Property Export and Import Law provides a mechanism to recover and return such foreign cultural property.

supplemented by a relative time of one year: the person entitled to file action must do so within one year of determining where and with whom the object is located.

Professor John Henry Merryman, in an address entitled "Cultural Property, International Trade and Human Rights,"[15] poses the question of why a nation's law should prohibit the export of privately held works of art? Why should other nations be expected to recognize and enforce such laws? He then answers that the obvious response – that there is a public interest in cultural property, and the state, as guardian of the public interest, acts to protect it – raises a variety of troubling questions.

Professor Merryman then argues that "courts do not routinely enforce foreign claims based on such laws in the absence of a treaty or special legal provisions as a subset of the principle based on state sovereignty that normally states do not enforce the public laws of another state. The source nation seeking the return of a cultural object that is illegally exported is limited to diplomatic or executive channels."[16]

Dr. Carducci suggests in his chapter in this book that, to the contrary, evolving principles of international customary law[17] support a sovereign nation's right to have another nation return those objects that are an essential part of their cultural heritage and are illegally taken from it. The reader may consider the following three cases in support (admittedly all three cases deal with theft, not illegal export) of Dr. Carducci's proposition.

In the English case of *Bumper Development Corporation, et al. v. Commissioner of Police for the Metropolis,*[18] a number of Indian claimants, including a temple and its idols, were successful in recovering possession of a bronze sculpture, the "London Nataraj," a stone object of religious worship known as the "Swalingam," that was proven to have been stolen in India after 1976.[19] On June 10, 1982, Bumper purchased the sculpture in good faith from a dealer in London, although it was later conceded the provenance documentation was false. Under English common law, the claim of the plaintiff's was not time barred.

The novel question presented was whether a foreign legal person who would not be recognised as a legal person under English law can sue in the English courts. The particular difficulty arose out of English law's restriction of legal personality to corporations or the like; that is to say, the personified groups or series of individuals. The Court reasoned as follows:

> This insistence on an essentially animate content in a legal person leads to a formidable conceptual difficulty in recognising as a party entitled to sue in our courts something which on one view is little more than a pile of stones.... in the Court's judgement there was sufficient evidence to justify findings that under Hindu law, the temple was a juristic entity. We therefore hold that the temple is acceptable as a party to these proceedings and that it is as such entitled to sue for the recovery of the Nataraja.
>
> We are fortified in reaching this conclusion since it accords with what we consider to be the intent and purpose behind the principles of comity. Furthermore, it avoids the danger of there being any fetter of an artificial procedural nature imported from the *lex fori* which might otherwise stand between a right recognised by and enforceable under the *lex causae.*

In Arrêts du Tribunal Suisse 1 April 1997 134, 143–144, a work of art stolen from a French collector in France was located in Switzerland. The French owner asked that pursuant to the European Convention of Mutual Assistance, the painting be returned to France as the proceeds of a crime. The Swiss Federal Court, at the end of its opinion, stated:

> Lorsque, comme l'espèce, la demande porte sur la restitution d'un bien culturel, le juge de l'entraide doit veiller à prendre en compte l'intérêt public international, comme à la Suisse et à la France, lié à la protection de ces biens [citing UNESCO and UNIDROIT]. Ces normes, qui relèvant d'une commune inspiration, constituent autant d'expressions d'un ordre public international en vigueur ou en formation ... Ces normes, qui concrétisent l'impératif d'une lutte internationale efficace contre le trafic de biens culturels ...[20]

The case of *Autocephalous Greek-Orthodox Church of Cyprus et al. v Goldberg et al.*[21] raises several issues discussed elsewhere,[22]

[15] Cardozo, Arts and Entertainment Law Journal, 9 (2000).

[16] See J. H. Merryman, "The Retention of Cultural Property." 21 University of California Davis Law Review 477, 484 (1988). Italy has been exemplary in the use of diplomacy for the repatriation of its cultural patrimony. In this regard, we may note the efforts of Ambassador Mario Bondiolio Osio, Minister for the Restitution of Art Works, Ministry of Foreign Affairs, Rome, Italy and Former Minister of Culture Provisional Authority, Iraq.

[17] See G. Carducci, "op. cit. Introduction," in Part I, "International Legal Tools and Viewpoints"; and B. Hoffman, "International Art Transactions and the Resolution of Art and Cultural Property Disputes: The United States Perspective" in Part III.

[18] *Bumper Development Corporation v. Commissioner of Police of the Metropolis and others* {1991} 1 WLR 1362, CA (1991). See also *Bulun Bulun v R & T Textiles.* Many commentators speculate that the judgement shows that Aboriginal customary laws, interests, and obligations are relevant source to provide for rights that will be recognized and protected by the Australian legal system.

[19] In August or September 1976, an Indian, variously described as a "coolie" or "landless labourer," called Ramamoorthi who lived in a hut near the site of the ruined Hindu temple at Pathur in the State of Tamil Nadu was excavating sand or similar material when his spade struck a metal object. There was a suggestion that it might have been a year earlier, but this was not accepted by Ian Kennedy J, whose finding has not been questioned. The place where he was excavating was close to the hut in which he lived and was either immediately adjacent to or formed part of the site of the temple. The name of the temple was the Arul Thiru Viswanatha Swarmy Temple. The object that Ramamoorthi struck formed part of a series of bronze Hindu idols later identified as members of a "family" and was a major idol known as a Siva Nataraja. The overwhelming probability is that they formed part of the religious objects in the temple, which had been endowed in the late thirteenth century by a Hindu notable called Avui Thiru Viswanatha. It was later accepted by all parties that the temple had lain in ruins and unworshipped for a matter of centuries. Notwithstanding his lowly status, Ramamoorthi realized that he had discovered objects of value. As they say, the rest is history.

[20] Translation: When, as in this case, the request is for the return of a cultural object, the judge must be careful to take into account the interest of the international community, as well as that of Switzerland and France, tied to the protection of cultural property (citing UNESCO and UNIDROIT). These provisions are based on a common inspiration which constitutes a principle of the world community, which is in the process of developing. These provisions established the importance of a unified international struggle against the traffic in cultural property.

[21] 717 F. Supp. P. 1374 (Ind. 1989), 917 F. 2d p. 278 (7th Cir. 1990).

[22] See G. Carducci, *supra* note 16. Dr. Carducci cites *inter alia,* Hague 1954, 1970 UNESCO, UNIDROIT, Council Directive 93/7/EEC 15 March 1993, and scholarly commentary in support of his thesis.

but it also relates to the issue under consideration: the use of a source nation's laws to facilitate the return of its illegally removed "cultural patrimony."

Peg Goldberg, an art dealer, refused to return mosaics to the church and republic of Cyprus, and the church and the government brought an action to recover possession of the mosaics. The lower court awarded the mosaics to the church. On appeal, the court affirmed the right of the church to proceed. The proof included evidence that the church was a distinct juridicial entity under the law of Cyprus, and a citizen of Cyprus. In awarding the mosaics to the church, Chief Judge Bauer began his opinion with an excerpt from *The Siege of Corinth* by George Gordon (Lord Byron).

There is a temple in ruin stands,

Fashion'd by long forgotten hands;
Two or three columns, and many a stone, Marble and
Granite with grass o'ergrown!
Out upon Time! it will leave no more
Of the things to come than the things before!
Out upon Time! who for ever will leave
But enough of the past and future to grieve
O'er that which hath been, and o'er that which must be:
What we have seen, our sons shall see; Remnants of
Fragments of stone, rear'd by creatures of clay!

Chief Judge Bauer then continues,

Byron, writing here of the Turkish invasion of Corinth in 1715, could as well have been describing the many churches and monuments that today lie in ruins on Cyprus, a small, war-torn island in the eastern corner of the Mediterranean Sea. In this appeal, we consider the fate of several tangible victims of Cyprus' turbulent history: specifically, four Byzantine mosaics created over 1400 years ago. The district court awarded possession of these extremely valuable mosaics to plaintiff-appellee, the Cutocephalous Greek-Orthodox Church of Cyprus ("Church of Cyprus" or "Church").

As Byron's poem laments, war can reduce our grandest and most sacred temples to mere "fragments of stone." Those who plundered the churches and monuments of war-torn Cyprus, hoarded their relics away, and are now smuggling and selling them for large sums, are just such blackguards. The Republic of Cyprus, with diligent effort, has been able to locate several of these stolen antiquities; items of vast cultural, religious (and, as this case demonstrates, monetary) value. Among such finds are the pieces of the Kanakaria mosaic at issue in this case.

In affirming the order, he concludes,

Lest this result seem too harsh, we should note that those who wish to purchase art work on the international market, undoubtedly a ticklish business, are not without means by which to protect themselves. Especially when circumstances are as suspicious as those that faced Peg Goldberg, prospective purchasers would do best to do more than make a few last-minute phone calls. As testified to at trial, in a transaction like this, "All the red flags are up, all the red lights are on, all the sirens are blaring."

Judge Richard Cudahy, in his concurring opinion, provides even stronger support for a country of origin's right of return.

A second and unrelated, but important, aspect of this case involves the treatment of the cultural heritage of foreign nations under international and United States law. At the very least, we should not sanction illegal traffic in stolen cultural property that is clearly documented as belonging to a public or religious institution. This is particularly true where this sort of property is "important to the cultural heritage of a people because of its distinctive characteristics, comparative rarity, or its contribution to the knowledge of the origins, development, or history of that people." *19 U.S.C. @ 2601* (2)(C)(ii)(II).

Focusing on a relatively short segment of what might otherwise be considered its "history," the United States chooses in considerable measure to ignore the ancient cultural heritage of the land which it now occupies. But a short cultural memory is not an adequate justification for participating in the plunder of the cherished antiquities that play important roles in the histories of foreign lands. The UNESCO Convention and the Cultural Property Implementation Act constitute an effort to instill respect for the cultural property and heritage of all peoples. The mosaics before us are of great intrinsic beauty. They are the virtually unique remnants of an earlier artistic period and should be returned to their homeland and their rightful owner. This is the case not only because the mosaics belong there, but as a reminder that greed and callous disregard for the property, history and culture of others cannot be countenanced by the world community or by this court.

CHAPTER NINE

Management and Conservation of Guatemala's Cultural Heritage: A Challenge to Keep History Alive

Juan Antonio Valdés

INTRODUCTION

Despite disturbing news about increasing levels of looting in countries around the world, the UNESCO Convention on the Means of Prohibiting and Preventing the Illicit Import, Export and Transfer of Ownership of Cultural Property was only adopted in 1970. This slow awakening led some museums in the United States to issue a direct response to the phenomenon, such as the Pennsylvania Declaration, the Harvard Report, and the policy statements from the Field Museum of Natural History and the Brooklyn Museum. According to these documents, which were adopted between 1970 and 1972, the museums undertook not to acquire any archaeological or ethnological property that had been illegally exported from its country of origin (Meyer 1990).[1] A similar line was taken by other museums and by the U.S. administration itself when the United States finally signed the UNESCO Convention in 1983. This provided a short breathing space to countries with a rich archaeological and ethnological heritage, both tangible and intangible, such as Guatemala, Mexico, Ecuador, Peru, Italy, Greece, India, Cambodia, China, and Egypt. Most of these are in the developing world, and their national budgets are therefore well below the level that would allow them to tackle the problems arising from the destruction of and illicit trade in their cultural property.

On the other side of the Atlantic, European countries have not taken an official stance on the issue, nor have they signed an agreement with Guatemala to collaborate in the fight to restore objects illegally removed from the country because it might put European museums and private collectors in an embarrassing position. Proof of this can be seen in the legal claim issued by Guatemala in 2001 for the return of a jade mask that was looted from a royal tomb on the Río Azul archaeological site and now resides in the Barbier-Muller Collection in Barcelona. The Spanish government has not offered to cooperate in the return of the mask however, pointing out that it is being held in a private collection. In fact, there is not even any cooperation between the nations of the Old Continent. To illustrate this point, it is enough to recall the British government's repeated refusal to accede to the claims of the former Greek Minister of Culture, Melina Mercouri, who died without securing the return of the famous Caryatids and many other Greek sculptures on show in the British Museum.

Guatemala is one of the world's richest countries in terms of tradition and cultural heritage, but this wealth is being destroyed at a rate that is unprecedented in the country's history. Economic necessity, ignorance, and a lack of awareness concerning the real significance of cultural heritage, combined with a desire to make money quickly and easily, are the three main causes of this situation. As a result, the growing interest in objects from Guatemala, be they pre-Hispanic, Colonial, or from a later period, has increased their value at auctions held by art galleries in New York and Paris. This means that the problem is far from being solved. In fact, it has led to the formation of new gangs that continue to plunder archaeological sites in addition to stealing pre-Columbian artefacts from museums and religious objects from Catholic churches. In the southern coastal region, the problem is even worse, although it is seldom mentioned. Instead of simply being plundered, archaeological sites are torn up indiscriminately with tractors and heavy machinery in order to free up more land for cultivation. And the landowners know exactly what they are doing.

The rate of destruction is spreading like a cancer, and nobody is really listening to the warning voices. This means that, within a few decades, most of Guatemala's archaeological sites will have been plundered or destroyed by tractors. There is no doubt that, in the words of Karl Meyer

> we are facing a future in which there will be no other past than that which is already known and has been excavated. Or, what is equally sad, that which has been so ruinously mutilated that it only offers us a meagre fragment of a lost legacy.[2]

This statement applies equally to documents kept in archives and looted tombs. In both cases, the pages of history are being torn out, which means that history can never again be related or understood in a complete context.

Despite the fact that Guatemala is a country with a rich historical past, the relevant authorities have done little to protect its heritage. The main reasons for this are the meagre resources set aside by successive governments and the ignorance of the authorities with regard to the issue. Although institutions like the Institute for Anthropology and History and the National Institute of Indigenous Studies were created in the 1940s, successive governments have never provided the necessary support. The creation of the Ministry of Culture and Sport 15 years ago has provided the government with a certain amount breathing space. It was a sign that the authorities were showing more interest in cultural issues, although

[1] Meyer, Karl. 1990. El Saqueno del Pasado (Fondo de Cultura Económica).

[2] *Id.* at p. 16.

the Ministry's small budget has meant that it was unable to carry out major projects, which, when the chips are down, is what produces positive results.

It is fascinating to discuss Guatemala's cultural heritage, but it is a difficult and often delicate matter to suggest how to go about managing and conserving it. One is confronted not only by a wall, but also by a whole series of barriers and interests, in which the state bureaucracy, private collectors, and a lack of funds all play decisive roles.

What is to be done about this? Is it the sole responsibility of governments to take protective measures? What is the responsibility of ordinary citizens? What should it be done first? What measures need to be taken? These and other questions add to the many anxieties that torment the minds of people who see what is happening to Guatemala's heritage on a daily basis but usually passes unnoticed by the public. What has actually been done about the problem so far?

THE PROBLEM OF LOOTING IN GUATEMALA

Guatemala's pre-Hispanic heritage is under constant threat as a result of continuous looting from eighty-five percent of the country's 5,000 or so recognised archaeological sites, which contain the remains of the ancient Maya and Xinca civilisations. Collectors in Guatemala and abroad will go to any lengths to acquire beautiful polychrome artefacts, fine jade objects, and fragments of stelae (carved stone monuments) from any part of the country on the black market, for no other reason than the desire to possess them. In the last few decades, there has also been a constant theft of valuable images, gold ornaments, and gold and silver religious objects from Catholic churches.

Looting is a social phenomenon that reflects the economic state of the nation and the lack of public awareness with regard to the meaning of cultural heritage. In Guatemala, ninety percent of the looting is done by illiterate farmers from the region surrounding the site of the looting, at the instigation of an intermediary or an individual who is in charge of the looting. This person offers the farmers a way of earning a better living – more money for less effort – without informing them of the crime they are committing or the risks they are running. The intermediary pays the farmers a minimal sum and then earns three times that amount by selling the artifacts to an international trafficker or to a contact higher up the chain, who in turn sells the artefacts to collectors in Guatemala and abroad. These collectors are the ones who provide the original incentive for this ever-expanding network. The looting networks are becoming increasingly complex and are now involved with bands of drug traffickers based along the border with Mexico and Belize in the north of Guatemala. These people are armed with high-calibre weapons and threaten to kill archaeologists and their teams if they refuse to leave the site they wish to rob.

Soon after the discovery of the cultural riches of Petén Province in the north of Guatemala, looters focused their attention on sculpted stone monuments with hieroglyphs, such as stelae, altars, lintels, and staircases, simply because of the aesthetic and artistic values they represent for collectors. These artefacts were easily accessible in the abandoned buildings in the middle of the dense rainforest. Later, collectors began to acquire fine ceramic pieces painted with polychrome scenes and valuable jade artefacts deposited in tombs inside the buildings. To reach them, looters dug huge, uneven trenches in the buildings, destroying everything that got in their way. If they did not find the tombs, they would ransack the building until all that was left were a few walls, which later collapsed as a result of the damage inflicted and the deleterious effect of the rain. Cases of this kind have been extensively documented, especially along the border between Guatemala and Mexico, at Río Azul, Nakbé, El Mirador, Tintal, Naachtun, La Muralla, Wakna, and many other sites, and at Naranjo, Holmul, Dos Aguadas, Jobal, and other sites on the border with Belize.

Problems such as these led to the establishment in 1975, at Guatemala's Institute of Anthropology and History, of the Department of pre-Hispanic and Colonial Monuments, whose job it is to protect and guard archaeological and Colonial sites throughout the country. At present, some 5,000 sites are registered, but only forty-five are under permanent surveillance. A shortage of personnel and the Department's limited resources mean that protection is inadequate, especially considering the fact that there are archaeological artefacts scattered all over the country. Having said that, however, some artefacts are much more significant than others, and looters do not make any distinctions in their efforts to get hold of artefacts from which they can make money.

GOVERNMENT MEASURES FOR THE PROTECTION OF GUATEMALA'S CULTURAL HERITAGE

Soon after achieving independence in 1821, Guatemala began a modest campaign to conserve its heritage. The first national museum was founded in 1831. It was later transformed into the National Museum of Archaeology and Ethnology by a government measure of 14 July 1922. The foundation in 1946 of Guatemala's Institute of Anthropology and History was a major step forward. So, too, was the establishment in 1986 of the Cultural Heritage Directorate, which is responsible for the protection of the nation's cultural property, and the aforementioned Department of pre-Hispanic and Colonial Monuments. To formalize this range of measures, the Ministry of Culture and Sport was established in 1985, confirming the government's intervention at the national and international levels. The Ministry is now the body responsible for drafting legislation to present to the Guatemalan Congress for approval and implementation.

An endless number of laws have been passed by the aforementioned bodies. Even Guatemala's Constitution incorporates various statutes concerning the protection, preservation, restoration, and recovery of the nation's cultural property. The Constitution states that archaeological sites should receive special government attention in order to preserve their characteristics and safeguard their historical value. Likewise, it declares that monuments and archaeological objects are government assets and therefore the inalienable property of the state. Private collectors can never own these objects. They are what may be regarded as "trustees," on the understanding that at all times the sole legal owner is the state of Guatemala.

Full backing for this approach came in the form of the Law for the Protection of the Cultural Heritage of the Nation (1999), which was approved by Guatemala's Congress by means of Statute 26–97 and was later amended by means of Statute 81–98. Although the Law was the subject of some controversy, all the social and professional sectors concerned clearly realized the importance of its existence. Under the auspices of the Ministry of Culture and Sport, the interested parties were brought together to work on its drafting and ultimate approval. The importance of the Law lies not only in what it says, but also in the fact that it makes all Guatemalans aware of the richness of their culture and the need to protect their historical legacy. It lays the foundations for a better understanding by the people of Guatemala of an important part of their national identity.

Among the Law's most recent achievements are the creation of a special department within the State Prosecutor's Office to prosecute crimes against cultural property and the establishment of an interinstitutional commission for the protection of cultural property, which comprises some fifteen institutions, including the airport security authorities, Public Prosecutor's Office, Ministry of Culture, Guatemalan Institute of Tourism, and national and international police authorities.

INTERNATIONAL AGREEMENTS

In order to tackle the problem of looting, the authorities have to be able to count on the cooperation of local individuals and organizations, but they also need the support of the authorities in other countries, underpinned by legal mechanisms that regulate the return of cultural objects to their country of origin. Signing such international agreements seems to have an effect, because it is a way of reducing the incentive to loot. By cutting down the circulation of cultural property on the illegal market, demand will diminish, and areas of archaeological interest can thus be preserved for scientific investigation.

Agreements between Guatemala and the countries of Central America, Mexico, and the United States for the return of objects of Guatemalan origin found on these territories have proved effective. Under the terms of such agreements and with the support of Interpol, many objects have been returned to their country of origin. Of special interest is the Memorandum of Understanding signed by the governments of the United States and Guatemala on 29 September 1997. This Memorandum concerns the protection of archaeological objects and is based on an emergency agreement between the two nations that has been in force since 15 April 1991. What is new in the case of the Memorandum is Guatemala's contention that the area that is to be protected by the agreement should be extended to include objects not only from the Petén region but from the whole country, including artefacts produced by the pre-Columbian cultures of the highlands and the southern coast of Guatemala. Under this new arrangement, Guatemala no longer needs to be involved in slow and costly legal proceedings on U.S. territory when objects are seized by customs. All it takes is for a representative appointed by the Guatemalan government to certify that the object is of Guatemalan provenance, and the object can then be returned. This development has speeded up the return of thousands of objects.

The Memorandum of Understanding was drawn up while this author was Director of Cultural Heritage in Guatemala, with the support of the Ministry of Culture and Sport, which was eager to fight the illegal traffic in artefacts. However, the authorities in the United States rejected Guatemala's contention that protection should be extended to objects produced in Guatemala during the Colonial Period (1524–1821) and during the centuries following independence. It was pointed out that they were not of particular ethnographic interest because the paintings and sculptures of the famous Antigua School were executed by various artists, in some cases by Spaniards born in Guatemala rather than by Creoles. Although the matter was discussed, there was no way of persuading the U.S. authorities that these works should be included on the list of protected works.

Nevertheless, it is worth pointing out that, although it is not written into the Memorandum of Understanding, the importance of Guatemalan objects produced after the Spanish conquest is tacitly understood by some of the customs authorities that monitor compliance with the agreements in the United States. One example of this is the return to Guatemala of valuable nineteenth-century documents that were taken from the General Archive of Central America in Guatemala City.

On 18 August 2002, the Assistant Secretary of Educational and Cultural Affairs, Department of State, concluded that the cultural patrimony of Guatemala continues to be in jeopardy from pillage of irreplaceable materials representing its pre-Columbian heritage and made the necessary determinations to extend the import restrictions for a period not to exceed five years.[3] Negotiations are also under way for comprehensive agreements with Spain, Italy, and Colombia, but no progress has been made in this area so far.

WHO SHOULD MANAGE AND CONSERVE GUATEMALA'S HERITAGE?

In the past, this was exclusively the job of the state, which created specific institutions to protect cultural property. With the passage of time and as a result of insufficient economic

[3] The List of Designated Archaeological Material from Guatemala describing the materials covered by these import restrictions is set forth in T.D. 97–81. The list and accompanying image database may also be found at Web site address: <http://exchanges.state.gov/culprop>. The restrictions on the importation of these archaeological materials from Guatemala are to continue in effect for five years from 29 September 2002.

resources to fulfil the task, however, other institutions and private individuals have also pledged their support. The country is reaching the stage at which responsibility has to be shared between government institutions and private actors. The answer to the question of who should manage and conserve Guatemala's heritage is that all Guatemalans have a duty to support the protection of everything that forms part of their heritage.

However, because Guatemala is a multicultural country where ethnic groups are fragmented rather than integrated, the questions arise: Does anyone "own" cultural heritage? To whom does this heritage belong? Does it belong to the indigenous people descended from the Mayas or to the mestizos? Should more attention be paid to the Mayas when they ask that they alone be allowed to administer pre-Hispanic sites? What about the mestizos and ladinos? How much interest in or understanding of Guatemalan heritage do they have? Who will protect the pre-Hispanic heritage of eastern Guatemala when the Xincas have all but disappeared? Who should dictate cultural policy in Guatemala, and how? Many of these important questions are being ignored. Some of them can be answered; others still await a response.

With the signing of the 1996 peace accords between the government of Guatemala and the guerrillas, new ideas began to take hold in the region. Some have brought progress, but others have been exploited by people intent on making a profit.

Guatemala is a nation made up of many cultural groups and although some groups have been here much longer than others, all of them currently exist in a place on the planet that, for historical and political reasons, is called Guatemala. The ancient inhabitants of this land formed many alliances and carried out many conquests. The result was the mingling of blood between Olmecas and Mayas, Mayas and the people of the high plains of Mexico, Mayas from the centre of the country with the peoples of the south coast, and Mayas from the Guatemalan highlands with Mayas from the lowlands of Yucatan, Belize, and Petén. On the whole, people representing a wide range of colors and languages have lived in the lands of Mesoamerica (what is now known as part of Mexico and Central America). After the Spanish conquest, it was logical that the union of the two dominant cultures would produce the mestizo population, which over the centuries has become as strong and as solid as it is today. The conquistadors could not wipe out the rich indigenous culture. It survived by intelligently and subtly integrating itself into the new way of life. The cult of the dead, the oral tradition, and respect for ancestors are but some of the cultural elements inherited by new generations of Guatemalans as a result of this ethnic mix. Ladinos and mestizos are both products of this intermingling, although they often fail to recognize the value of their origins or treat one bloodline as more important than the other.

There is no doubt that centuries of oppression of the indigenous population have, with justification, polarized attitudes. Whether they like it or not, however, this does not alter the fact that all Guatemalans share a greater or lesser percentage of the same blood. That is why all Guatemalans have the same duty to protect, care for, and administer Guatemala's cultural and natural heritage, whether it be 300, 2,000, or more than 4,000 years old. This is an important point, because Mayan groups are currently claiming the exclusive right to manage and administer their sacred sites, including archaeological sites, lagoons, volcanoes, caves with river sources, and hot springs. With the greatest respect to Mayan priests and their religious beliefs, all Guatemalans have equal rights to protect archaeological sites for the reasons outlined previously. The differences probably stem from a question of perception. Mestizos perceive archaeological sites as part of their heritage whereas, for Mayan priests, they have spiritual value.

Guatemalans must work together to protect their heritage and to avoid breaking up into ethnic groups, because instead of forming a nation this would leave them even more divided. There must be changes in the institutions responsible for protecting the country's cultural and natural heritage, and these should be open to the creation of new structures and frameworks that would allow the involvement of groups traditionally relegated to the sidelines, such as the Mayas and the Garifuna. The idea that the Mayas should manage their sites, the Garifuna should manage theirs, and the mestizos should manage sites dating from after the conquest is not constructive, because it would lead to a tremendous conceptual division and the creation of little fiefdoms. If this were to happen, who would take care of the palaeontological remains that stand as silent witnesses in the middle of this ethnic discord? Perhaps prehistoric man – who lived 10,000 years ago – will also return to claim what is rightly his! The situation is clearly getting out of hand. The results of the reclamation phenomenon that has spread across the American continent since the celebration of the five hundreth anniversary of Columbus's arrival are varied, but they have included the total prohibition of archaeological investigations in certain places.

FACTORS AFFECTING HERITAGE

Under the administration of President Alvaro Arzú (1996–2000), tourism was treated as a major currency-earner in Guatemala, much as it has been in neighboring countries like Mexico, which has enjoyed considerable economic success as a result. Guatemala decided to focus on ecotourism and cultural tourism. Not surprisingly, the latter tends to appeal to more mature tourists with greater financial resources, who have the time and desire to devote several days to a single country, as opposed to younger tourists who frantically rush to visit 15 countries in a fortnight. There is no doubt that the best way to attract more visitors is through the word-of-mouth recommendations of the tourists themselves.

In an entertaining and extremely readable article by Juan Ignacio Macua (1997), "Tourism and Heritage: A Marriage of Convenience," the author shrewdly opens the reader's eyes to the advantages and disadvantages of tourism and its effect on heritage sites, museums, collections, and documents. It goes without saying that tourism brings economic benefits to the country, its advertising agencies and tour operators, and many other businesses that fall under the tourism umbrella. Even so, care must be taken with regard to the number of people that, in a few years from now, will throng the same sites, cities, and museums. Without forward planning, the crowds may do more harm than good, as the cultural property in question is liable to suffer both damage and wear and tear. Panajachel, Antigua, and Tikal are just some examples of the effects of increasing the number of visitors. The access routes, management priorities, and visitor capacity of each potential tourist site must be carefully studied before launching massive advertising campaigns that can affect heritage of all kinds: tangible and intangible, movable and immovable. One solution might be decentralization and the creation of new places of interest with controlled or restricted access. This would avoid a repetition of what happened at the famous Altamira caves in Spain, which had to be closed to visitors because of the damage caused to the cave paintings by carbon monoxide. The excessive number of people visiting Madrid's Museo del Prado, where it is impossible to stop to admire the paintings and sculptures without someone bumping into you, is another case in point.

Admitting visitors to archaeological sites is one way of keeping the sites alive and protecting them from constant looting. In addition, many of these sites, which are located in archaeological parks that embrace both nature and culture, are being invaded by indigenous groups that are reclaiming the land for cultivation. Although the problem of looting is not new, rising and falling levels of looting continue to reflect the economic state of the nation. Looting increases in times of crisis, only to decline when the situation stabilizes. In addition, however, it appears that catalogues and books on Mayan civilization that have been published in recent years have been used by collectors to place orders "from the catalogue" with minor figures in the hierarchy of the looters' organizations. Evidence of this can be seen at archaeological sites such as Aguateca and El Perú, where looters have only removed certain parts of the stelae, especially those in which the glyphs are better preserved or the features of the human figures are sharper and more clear-cut (Valdés 1995). The same has occurred with regard to Guatemalan colonial artefacts: after the publication of several beautifully illustrated books, images of archangels were stolen from a number of churches. Images of the archangel Michael and the archangel Gabriel are most likely to be removed from altars in towns and villages that bear their names. Neither the church authorities nor the government have been able to stop these thefts.

A recent phenomenon, which occurred between 1996 and 1999, was the occupation of archaeological parks by farmers reclaiming land for cultivation. Although the occupiers cited economic reasons for their actions, what is certain is that they destroyed trees that for centuries have enabled the land to breathe. The animals in the parks, many of which are threatened with extinction, flee or die during the disturbances. Archaeological sites like Dos Pilas, Machaquilá, and, more recently, the areas around Aguateca, Yaxhá, and many other ancient cities have been ransacked. It has even happened in the satellite sites of Tikal, Guatemala's most cherished archaeological site, where more resources have been invested than in any other site. The land in the area of Tikal is used for growing maize, a crop that requires increasingly large areas of land. Because the soil in Petén contains limestone, the yield is not high and before long the locals will start chopping down more trees to create more land for cultivation. Following lengthy discussions, an understanding was reached between the government and the farmers and specific arrangements were made in each case. The occupiers left the parks but remained in the vicinity, apparently continuing to cause minor damage.

LOW GOVERNMENT BUDGETS VERSUS SUPPORT FROM PRIVATE ACTORS

Another issue that must always be considered is the budget that is needed to administer and safeguard heritage sites and objects. It is widely recognized that the share of the state budget that is allocated for this task is negligible and is not enough to start developing recovery projects in remote areas where no roads have been built because they fall within the Maya Biosphere Reserve, Mesoamerica's greatest "lung" in the heart of the rainforest. Many administrations have given up too soon, though some have made substantial efforts to raise funds. Some of these campaigns have borne fruit, helping to preserve Guatemala's heritage. This has always been regarded as the sole responsibility of the government, and only in relatively recent years has the way been opened for private organizations and individuals to contribute.

Having accepted that protecting Guatemala's heritage is everyone's job, various private institutions and foundations have responded to the call for help by supporting museums. In each case, a special agreement has been signed. This being the first time the strategy has been tried, the results have not always been as good as might have been hoped, although the cooperation has proved productive in most cases. Among the most outstanding examples is the Granai and Townson Foundation's support of the National Museum of Archaeology and Ethnology and the Museum of Modern Art. Another success story is "Operation Quetzal" at the National Museum of Natural History, where a highly satisfactory campaign has concentrated on the education of children and young people.

This same openness on the part of the authorities has prompted some private collectors to ask Guatemala's Institute of Anthropology and History to officially register items in their collections. An example of this is provided by the Hotel Casa Santo Domingo in Antigua, Guatemala, which now runs two museums that are open to the public inside the hotel complex. There are similar cases in Panajachel, Cobán and Petén, where, following official registration of artefacts, small private museums have been opened to visitors. They have become both educational centers and tourist attractions, drawing school parties and visitors from Guatemala and abroad.

Another example of collaboration between the government and private actors will shortly come to fruition with the inauguration of the Miraflores museum. The museum is the result of intense archaeological investigation in the southern sector of the ancient city of Kaminaljuyu, carried out within strict scientific parameters by a team of twenty professionals from five countries who have analyzed and interpreted the remains (Valdés 1998). This privately funded project will give the public an insight into the daily lives of the early inhabitants of the valley. It will show their daily activities, their diet, agricultural systems and products, the technology used to irrigate fields under cultivation, trading relationships with neighboring settlements, and much more. The agreement signed with the Ministry of Culture and Sports put a positive seal on the initiative of showing the people of Guatemala the results of this research in a museum, thus contributing to education and culture.

CONCLUSIONS

Guatemala's cultural heritage is vast and immensely valuable. Cooperation among institutions and friendly governments has opened up a new stage in the struggle to safeguard the ancestral treasures of Mayan culture as well as artefacts produced in the centuries following the arrival of the Spanish conquistadors. The use of modern technology is proving to be an unprecedented resource, enabling organizations to communicate the theft or loss of registered objects swiftly and on a global scale using the Object ID checklist.

Of course, the prudent management of a suitable budget plays an important role. Without this, the situation will remain problematic. Often, seminars and conferences have been organized, future plans have been discussed and approved, and castles have been built in the air, but in the end it all comes back to the same problem: no money. This has led to the demoralization of those working in the cultural sector and, quite frankly, a loss of belief in the powers that be, who never keep their promises. In four years' time, there will be a new government, and the whole process will begin all over again: seminars, proposals, preparation of budgets, budgetary cuts, etc.

Another factor that makes it impossible to find quick and viable measures to protect cultural heritage is the excessive bureaucracy that has invaded the offices of the Ministry of Culture and Sport and the Cultural Heritage Directorate. In addition, staff training is inadequate and decision making is characterized by a lack of confidence. All this is the result of continuous changes in senior management. Over the last three years, there have been three different Directors and Deputy Directors of Cultural Heritage and five Directors of Guatemala's Institute of Tourism, which is unfortunate, because it means that projects were not continued and commitments were not met. This state of affairs has, on occasion, resulted in an obvious power vacuum, which slows down the staff's activities, delays action plans, hinders research, and ends in anarchy. It also means that people with a certain amount of power within the organization are able to impose their own rules, overriding the statutes and laws of the institution. Regrettably, this is happening right now, and, as a result, the institutions are losing their prestige and their credibility at an alarming rate.

It is not desirable to conclude on a negative note, but such is the reality. Whereas some institutions have come up with brilliant ideas and initiatives, others have shown a lack of vision with respect to the future. It is to be hoped, however, that the budding cooperation between the government and private actors will continue to develop, provided that the latter are genuinely concerned about Guatemala's cultural heritage, in order to continue the struggle to protect the cultural property and the identity of Guatemala's citizens.

BIBLIOGRAPHY

Ley para la Protección del Patrimonio Cultural de la Nación. Guatemala: Ministerio de Cultura y Deportes. Instituto de Antropología e Historia.

Macua de Aguirre, Juan Ignacio. 1997. "Turismo y Patrimonio: matrimonio de conveniencia." El Impacto del Turismo en el Patrimonio Cultural. Spain: Agencia Española de Cooperación Internacional, pp. 71–90.

Meyer, Karl. 1990. El Saqueo del Pasado: Historia del trafico internacional ilegal de obras de Arte. Mexico: Fondo de Cultura Económica.

Valdés, Juan Antonio. 1995. "Saqueo y depredación en Tamarindito y otros sitios arqueológicos de la región de Petexbatún." Proyecto Arqueológico Regional Petexbatún. Informe Preliminar No. 6. 1995. Guatemala: IDAEH, pp. 14–1 to 14–8.

——— 1997. "Turismo y Patrimonio: El caso de Tikal." 1997. El Impacto del Turismo en el Patrimonio Cultural. Spain: Agencia Española de Cooperación Internacional, pp. 243–51.

——— 1998. "Kaminaljuyú, Guatemala: Descubrimientos recientes sobre poder y manejo Hidráulico." Memorias del Tercer Congreso Internacional de Mayistas, 1995. Mexico: UNAM. Centro de Estudios Mayas, pp. 752–70.

CHAPTER TEN

The Protection of Cultural Patrimony in Peru

Jack Batievsky* and Jorge Velarde

Irrespective of the decision in this matter, the court has considerable sympathy for Peru with respect to the problems that it confronts as manifested by this litigation. It is evident that many priceless and beautiful Pre-Columbian artifacts excavated from historical monuments in that country have been and are being smuggled abroad and are sold to museums or other collectors of art. Such conduct is destructive of a major segment of the cultural heritage of Peru, and the plaintiff is entitled to the support of the courts of the United States in its determination to prevent further looting of its patrimony.

However, there is substantial evidence that the subject items [were purchased] in good faith over the years, and the plaintiff must overcome legal and factual burdens that are heavy indeed before the court can justly order the subject items to be removed from the defendant's possession and turned over to the plaintiff. The trial of this action has shown that the plaintiff simply cannot meet these burdens.[1]

PERUVIAN CULTURAL PROPERTY LEGISLATION

Peruvian legislation has historically recognised private ownership over cultural property. Under Spanish colonial rule, private ownership of movable and immovable cultural property was recognised.

Following its independence from Spain in 1821, and until 1929, Peru's cultural property legislation protected archaeological objects, regulated investigation and excavation activities, and prohibited their export, while maintaining the principles of private ownership and free domestic trade.

At the beginning of the twentieth century, Peruvian legislators tried to halt the plundering of the country's cultural patrimony. As a result, cultural property had to be registered and could not be exported without authorisation. With certain exceptions, newly discovered cultural objects became the property of the state.

[1] (*Government of Peru v. Benjamin Johnson and others.* United States District Court for the Central District of California – Case No. CV 88-6990-WPG – 29 June 1989, Decided – 29 June 1989, Filed.)

*The editor notes with sadness the passing of Jack Batievsky in November 2002.

Supreme Decree No. 2612, enacted on 19 August 1911, laid down that the title to objects yet to be discovered in excavations belonged to the state, but recognised private ownership of cultural objects excavated prior to the enactment of the Decree.

However, the 1852 Civil Code established that archaeological finds generally belonged to the discoverer, except when they had been discovered on private land, in which case they belonged equally to the discoverer and the owner of the land. Supreme Decree No. 2612, a norm of lesser hierarchy, therefore violated the Civil Code and, hence, was unconstitutional.

In 1929, Law No. 6634 established that cultural objects belonged to the state and that the state was entitled to expropriate the land on which such objects were located. Accordingly, all future discoveries of movable property would automatically take place on state-owned land and therefore belonged to the state. The Law implied the confiscation of cultural objects from their true owners and violated the constitutional right to private ownership. In practice, property can only be expropriated by the state subject to due process and prior payment of fair market value in compensation.

In accordance with the criteria established by Supreme Decree No. 2612, Law No. 6634 recognised private ownership of movable cultural property discovered prior to its enactment, but also established that all future discoveries were to be treated as state property. As an exception, private ownership was permitted to the discoverer of cultural objects similar to those already held in museums. This innovation meant that movable cultural property that consisted of unique objects or had been discovered on state-owned land belonged to the state, whereas objects that were not unique when they were discovered could be privately owned.

In addition, a special register was to be established to keep records of existing cultural objects. Privately owned cultural property had to be recorded in the register within one year of its discovery. Otherwise, said property would become the property of the state. From a legal standpoint, absent an expropriation process and fair market value compensation, this provision violated the aforementioned principle of private ownership guaranteed by the Civil Code and the Constitution.

However, the whole issue depended on the date of discovery, which was very difficult to prove. There is no doubt that the date of origin of a cultural object can be determined, but ascertaining the date of its excavation in order to establish whether the discovery was made before or after the enactment of Law No. 6634 is practically impossible. The state was relieved from the burden of proof and insisted that objects discovered prior to Law No. 6634 be registered. The intention was that objects that were then not registered within the aforementioned one-year term would become the property of the state.

The result was that the register was not introduced on schedule and, in fact, never functioned properly.

In 1958, an attempt to reintroduce the register was made by means of Law No. 12956. The presumption of state ownership in the case of unregistered objects was eliminated, but the register still failed to function properly, mainly because it lacked the resources that were required for registering the enormous amount of cultural property involved and because private owners lacked confidence in future arrangements even after registering their property.

In accordance with Law No. 6634, the 1936 Civil Code ruled that "archaeological monuments and historical objects that are subject to special legislation are the property of the state."

In 1971, Decree Law No. 19033 laid down that immovable monuments (real estate) and historical objects were inalienable and nonprescriptible. However, like all other legislative attempts to establish state ownership, the Law was deemed unconstitutional and had a short life.

In 1985, Congress approved Law No. 24047 which stated that all pre-Hispanic movable property, regardless of whether it belonged to a private owner or to the state, was presumed to be cultural property.

The Law also established that movable cultural objects could circulate (traded) freely within Peruvian territory, except when this caused them to be separated from a set or a registered collection. In such cases, the prior approval of the National Institute of Culture was required.

Cultural property could not be exported without prior authorisation granted by Supreme Resolution.

An inventory of movable cultural property was kept by the National Institute of Culture, where an individual entry was made for each artefact. Registration was not mandatory, as it was under earlier regimes. No reference was made with regard to the ownership over new discoveries.

Law No. 28296, recently enacted, has abrogated and replaced Law No. 24047.

CURRENT LEGISLATION

Legislative attempts to establish state ownership of cultural property proved to be impracticable because of the lack of material resources for the establishment of a register, as well as to their constitutional and legal violations. The modern legislative treatment of cultural property has proved to be more realistic by allowing private ownership of such property.

The 1993 Peruvian Constitution expressly acknowledged the right to private ownership of cultural property that is recognised as such or presumed to be part of the country's cultural heritage. Previous versions of the Constitution had established that archaeological property and monuments were protected by the state. Thus, prior to the enactment of the 1993 Constitution, the question of whether or not cultural property that qualified as national heritage could be privately owned had not been addressed specifically at the constitutional level.

Article 21 of the 1993 Constitution states that, regardless of whether it is privately or publicly owned, cultural property is protected by the state and that legislation guarantees private and public ownership of such property. Article 21 also encourages private participation in the conservation, restoration, exhibition, and diffusion of Peru's cultural heritage, as well as its restitution if it has been removed illegally from Peruvian territory.

In addition to the relevant provisions in the Constitution, the current rules on cultural property are laid down in Law No. 28296, which was published on 22 July 2004, whereas the current regulations on the exploration and excavation of cultural property were approved by Supreme Resolution No. 559-85-ED, which was published on 16 September 1985.

Also, the 1991 Criminal Code treats the unauthorised excavation, extraction, or export of cultural property as criminal offences.

Article III of Law No. 28296 lays down that all pre-Hispanic, colonial, and republican material or inmaterial property, regardless of whether it belongs to a private owner or to the state, is presumed to be cultural property. Ex officio or upon request, this presumption can be confirmed or, if evidence exists that the property lacks cultural value, dismissed by a formal statement from the National Institute of Culture. Because all pre-Hispanic, colonial, and republican artefacts are presumed to be items of cultural property, including copies of original archaeological objects, customs officials always request an authorisation or a certificate of noncultural value prior to their export.

Movable cultural objects can circulate (be traded) freely within the territory of Peru as long as the owner or possessor adopts all necessary measures to protect the integrity of said objects, as well as to previously communicate to the National Institute of Culture the moving or transfer and destination of the objects. Any transfer of cultural property must be registered with the National Institute of Culture.

Cultural property cannot be exported. However, under exceptional circumstances, it can be authorised by Supreme Resolution. Such authorisation may only be granted for the exhibition of cultural property for scientific, artistic, or cultural purposes, for the performance of studies or restoration work that is not available locally, or for the foreign stay of accredited Peruvian Heads of Ambassadorial Missions, Consuls, or Diplomats for as long as they remain abroad.

An inventory of movable and immovable cultural property is kept by the National Institute of Culture, where an individual entry is made for each artefact. According to Article 17 of Law No. 28296, registration is mandatory. In case a purchase does not meet all the requirements established in the Law, it will be presumed as an illicit purchase and the transaction will be void.

Unlike prior legislation, Law No. 28296 does make reference to the ownership over new discoveries. In fact, Article 5 of Law No. 28296 establishes that: (1) undiscovered movable or immovable cultural property belongs to the state; and, (2) known or discovered archaeological objects, not privately owned as of the enactment of the Law, keep their condition of state-owned property. The Law also states that such objects cannot be conveyed nor acquired by prescription. In accordance with this, Article 28 of the Regulations on Exploration and Excavation, which were approved by Supreme Resolution No. 559-85-ED, states that at the end of an excavation, every cultural object that has been discovered must be delivered to the National Institute of Culture for registration in the Inventory of Movable Archaeological Objects (now the National Registry for Property Part of the National Cultural Heritage). In addition, Article 28 states that the Institute will decide which state-owned museum will receive custody of the objects in question.

Article 226 of the Criminal Code classifies the plundering of archaeological sites, illegal excavations, and the removal of pre-Hispanic objects from such sites as criminal offences. These offences carry prison terms of three to six years. Article 228 of the Criminal Code provides that anyone who takes pre-Hispanic artefacts out of Peru or fails to return them in conformity with a prior export authorisation will face a prison term of three to eight years. Article 231 of the Criminal Code, finally, provides that all sanctions are accompanied by the forfeiture of the material, equipment, and vehicles used to commit the offence in question, as well as the cultural property thus obtained.

The period stipulated by the statute of limitations for criminal offences is equivalent to one-and-a-half times the maximum sanction. Therefore, with regard to cultural property offences, the statute expires after nine years in the case of Article 226 and after 12 years in the case of Article 228.

EXCAVATION AND EXTRACTION OF ARCHAEOLOGICAL PROPERTY

The National Institute of Culture is the governmental agency responsible for the preservation of the Peru's cultural heritage. It has been assigned the tasks of identifying, registering, investigating, and preserving said heritage and supervising the participation of the private sector in administration, investigation, protection, and promotion. In addition, the Institute registers, catalogues, investigates, restores, conserves, and protects the nation's movable and immovable cultural property.

No investigation, exploration, or excavation of archaeological or historical interest can be performed without prior authorisation by the National Institute of Culture, regardless of whether the site is located on private or state-owned property. Investigation and excavation permits are granted for a one-year term, subject to renewal. Excavations are also supervised by the Institute. Researchers can only request authorisation to excavate one site at a time. Investigation projects in archaeological zones (important archaeological areas that are subject to special treatment) will only be authorised if they are accompanied by a special agreement with the National Institute of Culture.

Archaeological investigations can only be carried out by members of national or foreign scientific institutions that are specialised in archaeology and by national or foreign scientists that hold academic degrees in archaeology and are listed in the National Register of Archaeologists at the National Institute of Culture. Applications to perform archaeological investigations must include a description of the project, a working plan, the curricula vitae of the participants and their registration numbers from the National Register of Archaeologists, as well as a formal presentation by the relevant embassy in the case of a foreign petitioner.

The description of the project must include specific information on its nature and purpose, including: exploration, excavation, and/or work site programmes; the location of the site and a geographic description of the area and property where the site is located; the various methods and procedures that are to be employed; the background of the participating technical team; a schedule describing the estimated duration of the work, excavation techniques, and dating, cataloguing, registration and restoration methods; the measures for the protection of the site; the material and financial resources of the project, including a detailed budget describing the total cost of the project, the amount and source of the funds, the material resources and types of technical assistance required; the system for the registration and analysis of the artefacts, indicating the place where the artefacts will be stored and registered; the estimated duration of the analysis and cataloguing of data regarding the artefacts that have been discovered; suggestions for the final destination of the collections and registers; and a publishing plan that addresses the dissemination of the results of the project and possesses the funding needed for the preparation and publication of a final report.

Immovable archaeological discoveries are to be immediately preserved and reported to the National Institute of Culture. Archaeological artefacts discovered during the course of the project belong to the state and are to be surrendered to the National Institute of Culture upon termination of the project for registration in the National Registry for Property part of the National Cultural Heritage. The Institute decides which museum will receive custody of the artefacts in question.

Every artefact discovered in accordance with the aforementioned regulations belongs to the state and will be placed in the custody of a state-owned museum. Because the state does not allow such objects to be transferred to private ownership, there actually is no way for a person to acquire private ownership of artefacts discovered in accordance with the current legal regime governing excavation.

RESTRICTIONS TO THE OWNERSHIP OF CULTURAL PROPERTY

Article 20 of Law No. 28296 states that the following are basic restrictions to the ownership of movable and immovable cultural property:

(a) Dismember or separate parts of movable or immovable cultural property.
(b) Alter, rebuild, modify, or totally or partially restore movable or immovable cultural property, without prior authorisation granted from the National Institute of Culture.

REGISTRATION OF CULTURAL PROPERTY

As mentioned earlier, according to the current legal framework, the registration of cultural property is mandatory. For such purpose, Law No. 28296 created the National Registry for Property Part of the National Cultural Heritage, in charge of the National Institute of Culture. In the case of state-owned cultural property, it shall be registered in the State-Owned Property Information System.

TRANSFER OF MOVABLE ARCHAEOLOGICAL PROPERTY

The owner of cultural property has the right to change its location within the Peruvian territory. This includes the right to sell or donate such property and to acquire it by purchase, gift, or inheritance, as long as such transfer is communicated to the competent authorities, but the state has a right of first refusal. In other words, privately owned cultural property can be traded within Peru like any other commodity subject to the restrictions aforementioned.

As a result, the sale and purchase of cultural property within Peru is subject to common legislation, and all issues related to its sale or purchase, such as authenticity, hidden defects, warranty of title, and right of possession, are governed by the general provisions of the Civil Code. However, the transfer of ownership or location of cultural property that is part of a set or a registered collection requires the prior approval of the National Institute of Culture. Likewise, the Criminal Code prohibits the transfer of ownership of cultural property to a convicted person while serving sentence for criminal offences against the national cultural heritage.

RIGHTS OF A BONA FIDE PURCHASER

In general, the Civil Code adopts the criteria of good faith. This means that good faith is always presumed to exist unless it is proved otherwise. Article 948 of the Civil Code states:

"He whom in good faith and as owner receives possession of a movable good from a third party, acquires title to the same even though the conveyor did not have the right to transfer said title. This rule does not apply to missing goods and goods acquired in violation of criminal laws."

Purchasers and beneficiaries of donations do not have to prove their good faith. Good faith is presumed, and it is therefore understood that whoever receives possession of movable property acts in good faith and hence acquires ownership. However, this presumption may disappear if it is proved that the purchaser or the beneficiary of the donation lacked good faith, or that the property in question happened to be lost or had been acquired in violation of criminal law.

Accordingly, the legal guarantee concerning the bona fide purchaser that appears in Article 948 of the Civil Code, namely, that acquiring possession implies acquiring ownership, does not apply to movable cultural property that was lost, stolen, or newly discovered or otherwise acquired in violation of criminal law. Should a criminal action be brought and the cultural property be identified as having been obtained, for example, by means of unauthorised excavation, the property in question must be forfeited by the discoverer or by the bona fide purchaser, provided that the latter has the right to claim the value of the forfeited property from the person from whom he or she purchased said property (Article 94 of the Criminal Code).

In addition to the aforementioned, Article 1542 of the Civil Code states that the movable property purchased in stores or locales that are open to the public are not recoverable, provided that the sale is supported by an invoice or policy issued by the seller. The affected party has the right to institute the applicable civil and criminal actions against the party who illegally sold him or her the property in question. This provision would not apply to newly discovered cultural artefacts, which belong to the State as a matter of law.

EXPORT OF CULTURAL PROPERTY

As a general rule, the export of cultural property is prohibited. However, temporary export authorisations may be granted for the exhibition of cultural property for scientific, artistic, or cultural purposes, for the performance of studies or restoration work that is not available locally, or for the foreign stay of accredited Peruvian Heads of Ambassadorial Missions, Consuls, or Diplomats for as long as they remain abroad. Temporary exports require the purchase of a comprehensive insurance policy covering the value of the cultural property, with the owner as beneficiary.

Temporary export licences may be granted for a period of up to one year and may be renewed once for a period of up to one more year.

An application for the temporary export of cultural property must be submitted to the National Institute of Culture and include information concerning the city, country, date, and location of the exhibition as well as the institution organising the event; a sponsorship letter from the Peruvian embassy in the country where the exhibition is to take place; a report on the physical and environmental safety of the exhibition site; a copy of the cultural property's registration and its photograph and full description; and the owner's written agreement, where applicable.

Export authorisations are granted by Supreme Resolution, on the proposal of the Ministry of Education.

BILATERAL AND MULTILATERAL TREATIES

The Peruvian Constitution provides that international treaties that are ratified by the state become part of the nation's legal framework.

Treaties on the protection of cultural heritage are approved and ratified by the President, who is obliged to notify Congress. If the treaty requires legislative action to enter into force, however, it must be approved by Congress and ratified by the President.

Peru is a state party to the following international treaties concerning the protection of cultural property.

Bilateral treaties

Agreement between Peru and Argentina for the Protection of Archaeological, Historical and Artistic Objects, executed on 14 May 1963 in Buenos Aires, Argentina, but not ratified by either country.

Agreement for Cultural Exchange between the Government of the Republic of Peru and the Government of the Popular Republic of Bulgaria, in force since 8 March 1978.

Agreement on Scientific Investigation and the Defence of Archaeological Heritage between Peru and Bolivia, in force since 20 February 1979.

Agreement with the United States for the Recovery and Return of Stolen Archaeological and Cultural Property, in force since 14 September 1981.

Agreement between the Republic of Peru and the Republic of Chile for Cultural Exchange, in force since 19 August 1982.

Cultural Exchange Agreement between the Republic of Peru and the Republic of Uruguay, in force since 24 July 1985.

Agreement between the Peruvian and Colombian Governments for the Protection, Conservation and Recovery of Stolen Archaeological and Cultural Objects, in force since 13 June 1995.

Agreement between the Republic of Peru and the Federated Republic of Brazil for the Recovery of Stolen or Illegally Exported Cultural Property, executed on 26 February 1996, not yet in force.

Agreement for the Protection and Restitution of Archaeological, Artistic and Historical Objects between the Governments of Peru and Mexico, in force since 13 June 1995.

Memorandum of Understanding between the Republic of Peru and the Republic of Austria to Prevent the Illegal Export of Cultural Property, in force since 29 March 1999.

Agreement between the Republic of Peru and the Republic of Bolivia for Recovery of Cultural Property and other Stolen, Illegally Imported or Exported Goods, ratified by Peru on 9 June 1999, not yet in force.

Memorandum of Understanding between the Republic of Peru and the Republic of Hungary for the Protection and Preservation of Archaeological, Historical and Cultural Property, ratified by Peru on 17 January 2000.

Agreement on the Protection and Recovery of Cultural Property between the Government of the Republic of Peru and the Government of the People's Republic of China, ratified by Peru on 2 June 2003, not yet in force.

Agreement on the Protection of Archaeological, Historical and Artistic Property between the Republic of Peru and the Republic of Paraguay, executed on 5 March 2001, ratified by Peru on 30 May 2001, not yet in force.

Agreement on the Protection, Preservation, Recovery and Restitution of Stolen, Exported or Illegally Transferred Cultural, Archaeological, Artistic and Historical Property between the Republic of Peru and the Republic of Uruguay, ratified by Peru on 11 February 2003, not yet in force.

Agreement on the Protection, Preservation, Recovery and Restitution of Exported or Illegally Transferred Cultural, Archaeological, Artistic and Historical Property between the Republic of Peru and the Republic of Turkey, ratified by Peru on 19 March 2003.

Agreement on the Protection, Preservation, Recovery and Restitution of Exported or Illegally Transferred Archaeological, Artistic, Historical and Cultural Property between the Republic of Peru and the Republic of Panama, in force since 3 April, 2003.

Agreement on the Protection, Preservation, Recovery and Restitution of Stolen, Exported or Illegally Transferred Archaeological, Artistic, Historical and Cultural Property between the Republic of Peru and the United Mexican State, in force since 17 July 2003.

Agreement on the Protection, Preservation, Recovery and Restitution of Stolen, Exported or Illegally Transferred Archaeological, Artistic, Historical and Cultural Property between the Republic of Peru and the Republic of Argentina, in force since 11 July 2004.

Multilateral treaties

Convention on the Protection of Transportable Cultural Property (as approved by the Seventh International American Conference of Montevideo, 26 December 1933).

Convention on the Means of Prohibiting and Preventing the Illicit Import, Export and Transfer of Ownership of Cultural Property, UNESCO General Conference (Sixteenth Meeting, Paris, 14 November 1970), in force since 24 January 1980.

Convention on the Protection of the Archaeological, Historical and Artistic Heritage of the American Nations (Convention of San Salvador), Organisation of American States (Washington, DC, 16 June 1976), in force since 22 January 1980.

Convention concerning the Protection of the World Cultural and Natural Heritage, UNESCO (Paris, 23 November 1972), in force since 22 January 1982.

Second Protocol to the Convention of The Hague (1954), concerning the Protection of Cultural Property in case of War, in force since 22 June 2004.

CHAPTER ELEVEN

Cultural Patrimony and Property Rights in Peru

Alberto Martorell-Carreño

REFLECTIONS ON THE ESSAY BY JACK BATIEVSKY, "THE PROTECTION OF CULTURAL PATRIMONY IN PERU"

To present the legal regime for property as the main issue when analysing the Peruvian cultural heritage legal system is not productive. It has long been a fruitless discussion that does not contribute to the goal of developing an effective protective system. For this and other reasons, Peruvians have not been able to improve the current legal system. Consequently, the situation of destruction, illegal traffic, and plundering continues. We must begin by asking ourselves what our goal is when proposing a legal system to protect cultural heritage. From this author's perspective, the answer is too clear, convincing, and simple: it is to establish the juridical instruments to guarantee "cultural goods" continuity in time, preservation, and the best social and physical context.

It may not be accurate to state that Peruvian legislation, from its very beginning, has established private ownership rights for "cultural property." For example, Supreme Decree 89 from 2 April 1882 contained two main provisions: First, it prohibited the exportation of archaeological goods without previous governmental authorization; and secondly, it expressly declared that *all the monuments coming from Peruvian ancient times are the property of the Nation, because of the glory represented by them.*

Admittedly, the quoted article does not establish a "public ownership regime" for all cultural heritage goods. Nevertheless, its aim is even more important: setting up the rights of the nation to control its cultural heritage. Cultural property "belongs" to the Nation as a matter of law, whether it is in a private or public ownership system. For some authors, the State, as representative of the nation, would exercise property rights over "cultural property." This author disagrees with this position. The earlier referenced Supreme Decree did not establish a general public ownership system. To prohibit private ownership *for all* Peruvian cultural property was not the aim of the drafters.

The Supreme Decree 89 makes evident that the key issue is not ownership of cultural property. Rather, it is establishing that the rights of the nation over its cultural heritage are superior to title. For this reason, the cultural heritage property system is not analogous to those applied to other chattel. Cultural heritage property rules are *sui generis* because claims made on behalf of the public for its conservation and knowledge are superior to private property rights.

It is useful in this respect to consider the evolution of the conservation theory from "treasure trove" to "scientific discovery." Formerly, "treasures" were considered more valuable when containing gold objects or precious stones. Currently, the theory holds that the real value of heritage goods is determined not by its material nature, but by complex values like historical significance, information sources, identity meaning, etc. As we currently understand cultural property, even the concept of "work of art" is not sufficient. Artistic value is just one aspect to consider. Archaeologists emphasize the importance of authentic contextual environment for archaeological researching. This relationship between cultural goods and their social context irrespective of title is an accepted norm.

The so-called Franceschini Commission[1] has been key in this conceptual evolution. It defined "cultural good" as "all material testimony of a civilization's values." Nevertheless because cultural goods are evidence of anthropological, historical, and other natural and social processes, they are not "common goods."

This author's view is that Supreme Decree 89 established that there is a public interest on cultural goods. Notwithstanding, private collectors have continued to assert ownerships rights over such goods as if they were ordinary chattels.

Law 6634 (1929) is also discussed by Jack Batievsky. Even though some professionals, including archaeologists, consider that it is ideal for conservation purposes, this author believes it was not at all. Although Law 6634 was better than Law 24047 and even Law 28296 in many respects, it also presented some nonacceptable criteria and gaps.

Law 6634 established a public ownership system for all cultural heritage goods "prior to viceroyalty period," both of movable and immovable nature, that were not under previous private ownership. It means that found in-the-ground pre-Hispanic sites and objects were declared property of the state. Private ownership of archaeological artefacts was only to be recognized if such items were registered in a special register that was to be created in the National Museum of Natural History.

The property regime set forth in this legislation was as follows:

- All undiscovered pre-Hispanic goods belong to the State.
- Private ownership was recognized for all pre-Hispanic movable cultural goods in private possession on condition

[1] Franceschini Commission was created in 1964 by Italian Parliament to review the legal and administrative cultural system in Italy. Even though it was of national scope, its theoretic proposals are considered of great importance, initiating the so-called "cultural goods theory."

that such goods were inscribed within a period of one year.
- All immovable pre-Hispanic goods belong to the State.
- Cultural goods corresponding to other Peruvian historical periods than pre-Hispanic could be under public or private ownership.

Following the above, the next exceptions were established:

- Private ownership rights over immovable pre-Hispanic goods comprising a unique property with new buildings attached to them were recognized. In these cases, the state had the preferential right to buy the property if the owner wished to demolish it.
- Private ownerships of land where archaeological goods were discovered could acquire property rights over them if there were "similar objects" in public museums.
- Persons in charge of archaeological excavations could acquire property rights over "duplicated" cultural goods discovered by them.

The first of the previously quoted exceptions is easy to understand in certain cases like those in Cusco, where most of colonial buildings were built over Inca's walls and buildings. We are not just talking of churches like Santa Domingo (constructed over the Koricancha or "Temple of the Sun"). It was also the situation of many of the Spanish founders' houses. In those cases, it is clear that, from the beginning, these buildings have been private, and it is necessary to recognize acquired rights over them. However, this possibility must be strictly limited to such kind of "historical private rights." If it is not clearly limited, this possibility could comprise "any new work made over archaeological remains," with the possibility that valuable cultural objects would be lost to the heritage. The Law 28296 in article 6.1 continues.

Similarly, the exceptions founded on the supposed existence of "similar objects or duplicates" are not acceptable. Cultural goods are always unique and unrepeatable. Each artifact has its own intrinsic value. It was not correct to distinguish among "original artifacts" of public property and "duplicates" capable of private appropriation.

This author disagrees with the contention that "The Law implied the confiscation of cultural objects from their true owners and violated the constitutional right to private ownership"; owners, and even simple possessors of pre-Hispanic artifacts were able to register them. This decision is theoretical, however, given that the register was never created, leading to the problems faced today.

The register would have meant a very clear division: undiscovered archaeological goods are public property. Private owners have one year to register their archaeological goods. Failure to register would result in a loss of title to such goods.

Law 28296 establishes a recording system which, in the view of this author, is harmful to the value of conservation. It creates public records under the auspices of the National Institute of Culture, National Library, and National Archive. Public authorities shall inscribe on them cultural goods declared as cultural heritage of the nation. Nevertheless, it does not establish the obligation of private individuals to register artifacts under his/her possession. Furthermore, it promotes a progressive and permanent registration system for new acquisitions made by private owners. Those who request registration are required to prove their rights over the artifacts in their possession. The law establishes a presumption of illegal origin of the good, and if the requester does not prove his/her title, property rights will be assumed by the State. It is not clear at all how these "private property rights" must be established. Private owners are just obliged to record goods when constituting a private museum.

Title IV of the Law regulates private collections and private museums. Their legislatures need to be clarified and the law must clarify that no new rights over cultural goods from the pre-Hispanic period will be recognized.

The Law establishes that collectors shall have a private register of artifacts. Nevertheless, that kind of private register is not enough. To guarantee public rights, it is necessary to have a public recording system. It is one of the main failures of Law 28296.

The Peruvian Constitutional texts recognize private property but it is exercised *in harmony with social interest. The law establishes limitations and types of property rights.*[2] Cultural heritage is related to national rights; special limitations, and ways of exercising property rights over them are established by special legal and regulatory norms.

Professional standards applied to archaeological research are also important in order to avoid and control the illegal traffic of cultural movable goods. Law 6634 was a serious step in that way.

The legal situation of Viceroy and Republican cultural goods is different. Private property rights over such goods must be recognized; however, because of the serious problem of looting of colonial churches, a recoding system should be established.

THE NEW LAW 28296

Law 24047 (1984) replaced Law 6634 and, in 2004, Law 28296 replaced Law 24047. Most Peruvian archaeologists, art historians, lawyers, and other specialists in cultural heritage protection had criticized Law 24047 as legally deficient. Similarly, Law 28296 is also criticized for the failure to take into account the earlier indications of these professionals.

One of the most controversial issues contained in Law 24047 was the concept of "cultural heritage." All goods coming from pre-Hispanic and Viceroyalty periods, being testimony of artistic, scientific, historic, or technician creativity, are presumed to belong to the "Cultural Heritage of the Nation" category.[3] Although such a presumption is not unacceptable from a legal point of view, Peru is a Member State of the "Convention of San Salvador" ("Convention on

[2] Art. 34. Peruvian Constitution of 1933 (repealed; the quote is just referential).

[3] Art. 1 and 2, Law 24047.

the Protection of the Archeological, Historical, and Artistic Heritage of the American Nations [Organization of American States, 1976]"), which defines such goods as part of the cultural heritage of the American nations.

Article 2 of the Convention, containing the definition of "cultural heritage," includes on it:

a. Monuments, objects, fragments of ruined buildings, and archeological materials belonging to American cultures existing prior to contact with European culture, as well as remains of human beings, fauna, and flora related to such cultures;
b. Monuments, buildings, objects of an artistic, utilitarian, and ethnological nature, whole or in fragments, from the colonial era and the nineteenth century;
c. Libraries and archives; incunabula and manuscripts; books and other publications, iconographies, maps and documents published before 1850;
d. All objects originating after 1850 that the States Parties have recorded as cultural property, provided that they have given notice of such registration to the other parties to the treaty;
e. All cultural property that any of the States Parties specifically declares to be included within the scope of this convention.

It is clear that there are private and public goods belonging to the Cultural Patrimony. Nevertheless, this does not mean that private institutions or individuals can appropriate any cultural object, especially archaeological objects.

On the other hand, private property rights in cultural heritage objects have been constitutionally recognized.

The Constitucion Politica 1993[4] states:

> Los yacimientos y restos arqueológicos, construcciones, monumentos, lugares, documentos bibliográficos y de archivo, objetos artísticos y testimonios de valor histórico, expresamente declarados bienes culturales, y provisionalmente los que se presumen como tales, son patrimonio cultural de la Nación, independientemente de su condición de propiedad privada o pública. Están protegidos por el Estado. La ley garantiza la propiedad de dicho patrimonio.[5]

In the first place, the previous article makes the mistake of presenting presumption as provisional, conditioned on an express declaration. Notwithstanding this, it is clear that the objects set forth are the "cultural patrimony of the Nation." Whether public or private, those objects are included within the regime that is established. Secondly, the great respect for property rights does not necessarily imply a system of unrestricted access to "los bienes de dicho patrimonio." We argue that certain objects (bienes) by their qualities must always keep their public nature (as is the case for all undiscovered archeological objects).

The Law 28296 defines a general and extensive concept of cultural heritage of the nation. As did the former Law 24047, it specifies that the condition of cultural heritage will be expressly declared. "Cultural goods" not declared are protected by the presumption of belonging to the cultural heritage of the nation. Notwithstanding, it does not establish clearly the criteria to enforce the presumption or to revoke it.

The Civil Code provisions relating to treasures discovery are inapplicable to cultural goods. Supreme Resolution 559-85-ED[6] and further Supreme Resolution 004-2000-ED (in force) contain the rules for Archaeological Explorations and Excavations. None of them justify to affirm that "any accidental discovery must be divided into equal parts among the property of the land and the finder."

It is clear that there is a public guardianship over all archaeological goods. That's why there is a public control over scientific archaeological researching, public management of knowledge resulting from researching works (respecting copyrights), and the destination of artifacts discovered. The regime is contained in Supreme Resolution 004-2000-ED. If there is an accidental discovery, this fact must be informed immediately to INC.

DESIGNING A MORE COHERENT SYSTEM

No effective measure has been taken to overcome such a sad reality. Law 28296 (2004) has not successfully resolved the Peruvian heritage problem. It is necessary to face up to illegal trafficking of cultural goods. It is also necessary to control collectors and to establish very clear rules for this activity.

With the aim of contributing to this work, the following proposals are offered for consideration and discussion:

(1) A new definition of "cultural heritage" with reference to the Convention of San Salvador should be drafted.
(2) Registration of archeological treasures:
- Re-establish a registering system similar to that contained in Law 6634 for archeological or pre-Hispanic artifacts. It should be in the charge of the National Institute of Culture and its Regional offices. All persons possessing cultural goods belonging to national heritage should record them as the only one way to consolidate property rights. When registering, persons should inform on all references available on the cultural and geographic origin, time of discovery, available studies, etc.
- The period of time for this registration must be reasonable.
- Once the registration period expires, unregistered archaeological goods will be public property. Private possessors will lose all rights over them. An exception may be made for owners having historical

[4] Constitución Política del Perú de 1993. Art. 21° (derogada, se cita sólo de manera referencial).

[5] "Archaeological sites and remains, constructions, monuments, places, bibliographic and archive documents, artistic artifacts and evidences of historical value, expressly declared as cultural goods, and provisionally those presumed to be cultural goods, are cultural heritage of the Nation regardless if they are in private or public property. They are under State protection. Law guarantees property rights over such kind of heritage."

[6] Repealed.

documentation made by public notary as evidence of their rights.

With respect to Colonial and Republican cultural goods:

- Establish a nonobligatory register for private items of Colonial or Republican origin. All those goods properly registered should be fully recognized as private property of the registered titular and those acquiring legally goods from them.
- Reinforce the registration system existing for all cultural heritage goods property of the State (including pre-Hispanic, Colonial, and Republican items).
- Cultural goods belonging to the Catholic Church should be duly registered in a special register carried out by this institution (under public rules of management) or incorporated as a chapter in the existing national register.
- Those owners of Colonial and Republican items not registered should fulfill the next special rules: (a) to ask for authorization to transfer property rights over them; (b) to prove the legal origin of those goods.

(3) All cultural property goods (pre-Hispanic, from the Viceroyalty and Republican periods) under public ownership, including public societies, should be declared nontransferable to private sector. Only transferences among public organizations should be accepted, taking into account the correct conservation of the properties.

(4) Absolute prohibition to definitive exportation of cultural goods must be maintained and even reinforced regardless of whether they are in public or private ownership.[7]

(5) This author feels glad that new Law 28296 has considered his proposal of establishing a juridical measure consisting in the "automatic reversion of property rights in favor of the State" of cultural goods involved in cases of illegal exportation or attempted illegal exportation. By this mean, owners of cultural goods attempting or succeeding in exporting them would lose all property rights in favor of the State.

BIBLIOGRAPHY

Alibrandi, Tomasso. (1988). *El diritto dei beni culturali: la protezione del patrimonio storico-artistico.* Roma, Caroci.

Feliciano, Héctor. (2004). *El museo desparecido. La conspiración nazi para robar las obras maestros del arte mundial.* Barcelona, Destino.

Fuentes Camacho, Víctor. (1993). *El tráfico ilícito internacional de bienes culturales.* Madrid, Beramar.

ICOM. *Lista Roja de Bienes Culturales Latinoamericanos en Peligro.* <http://icom.museum/redlist/LatinAmerica/spanish/intro.html>.

Martorell, Alberto. (1994). *Patrimonio Cultural: protegiendo las raíces de nuestra historia.* Lima, Biblioteca Nacional de Perú.

Martorell, Alberto. (1998). *Patrimonio Cultural: políticas contra el tráfico ilícito.* Lima, Fondo de Cultura Económica.

Prott, L y O'Keefe, P. J. Medidas legislativas y reglamentarias nacionales de lucha contra el tráfico ilícito de bienes culturales. París, UNESCO, 1983.

Renfrew, Colin. (2000). *Loot, Legitimacy and Ownership.* Londres, Duckworth.

Watson, P. (1999). *'The lessons of Sipán: archaeologists and huaqueros.'* Culture Without Context 4: 15–20.

[7] Criterion established by Law 24047 for authorizing temporary exportation of goods of the Cultural Heritage of the Nation is right. Temporary exportation is allowed strictly for scientific, artistic, and cultural reasons, including specialized restoration works. It requires previous approval of specialized public organisms (INC, National Library, or National Record). The period of time is one year, but in case of renovation it is limited to one additional year.

CHAPTER TWELVE

Putting the IFAR Cuzco Inventory to Work

Frederic J. Truslow

PREFACE

In 1983–4, the International Foundation for Art Research (IFAR) organised, staffed, and found funding for a photographic inventory of 2,252 Spanish colonial paintings in thirty-four churches and one museum in and around Cuzco, Peru. The project was undertaken at the request of the Archbishop of Cuzco and the Peruvian government at a time of increasing thefts from vulnerable churches, but since that time these entities have not made use of the inventory. Plans are now under way for it to take on its intended role as a means of identifying the contents of these churches, protecting against theft, aiding in recoveries and supporting research and education. This article explores the additional steps needed, after the photographs have been taken and the index cards filled in, to turn these data into a useful tool for art protection and academic research.

* * *

As the seat of Spanish colonial government and the Catholic Church in South America for 300 years, Peru possesses an extraordinary heritage of religious buildings, art works, and furnishings. Much of this heritage, particularly the contents of rural churches, is disappearing through theft, dissipating an irreplaceable cultural record and scattering an essential resource for religious worship, tourism, academic research, and local development.

Official statistics of the National Police of Peru show, for example, that 130 churches reported thefts during the period 1996–2000, including seventy-four churches in the Cuzco area. The police estimate, however, that losses were underreported and that they actually affected more that 200 churches in the country during that period.[1] Over approximately the same period, some 2,700 works, valued at more than US$8 million, were estimated to have been stolen.[2] In some regions, the rate of loss is even greater. The Archbishop of Huancayo, in the central mountain region, estimated in December of 2000 that more than half of the sixteenth, seventeenth, and early eighteenth century art in the churches within his jurisdiction had been stolen, and a local art historian estimated that of 1,500 works originally in the area, only 500 remain.[3]

Although the losses and occasional recoveries are recurrent front page news in Lima newspapers,[4] Peru does not have an effective system for the protection of its colonial heritage. The quantity of places and works to be protected is huge (thousands of colonial churches, many in remote locations, and an estimated one million religious paintings and many more millions of objects of all kinds produced in the Colonial period). Rural churches often do not have priests, and sometimes not even custodians, in residence. Public resources are scarce, and other priorities, including poverty and terrorism, more pressing. The heads of relevant government agencies change frequently. Government, church, and private organisations have often been unable or unwilling to work together. Law enforcement is lax and convictions for theft rare. Meanwhile, the market value of colonial art increases, and with it the boldness and sophistication of thieves.

A major handicap has been that Peruvian churches and museums generally lack organised and accessible photographic inventories. Photographs are, of course, an essential part of any protection regime because they make it possible to identify and prove prior ownership of a stolen work.

How can this gap be filled? Commentators and policy makers in Peru tend to picture a comprehensive national inventory, extol its obvious virtues, and then bewail the difficulties of funding and organising such an enormous effort. They may be approaching the problem from the wrong end. A better place to start is with the photographic collections or inventories, like the IFAR inventory, that already exist, thanks to many different independent organisations or individuals, and cover thousands of colonial art works in every part of the country.

These existing inventories are not comprehensive, and vary in focus, quality, and availability, but provide important raw material for the creation, in the future, of an accessible, well-organised database. They have three great virtues. First, many of them were created by experienced art historians

This article was commissioned by IFAR and was originally published (with illustrations) in *IFAR Journal*, vol. 4, no. 4 and vol. 5, no. 1, 2001/02. It is reproduced here with the permission of IFAR and cannot be reproduced elsewhere in electronic or printed format without the express permission of IFAR. ©2002, Frederic J. Truslow. The Institute for Latin American Art Documentation (ILAAD) is a nonprofit organisation based in the United States that promotes the protection, study, and understanding of endangered national patrimonies throughout Latin America. ILAAD can be contacted at Latinartdoc@aol.com.

[1] *El Comercio*, Lima, Peru, 25 December 2000, p. 1.
[2] *El Comercio*, 21 June 1999, p. a2.
[3] *El Comercio*, 26 December 2000, p. a8.
[4] As recently as February 2002, two paintings were stolen from a church in Tinta, near Cuzco, covered by the IFAR inventory. Fortunately, good police work produced a recovery. *La República*, Lima, Peru, 10 February 2002, Web page 1.

or connoisseurs, and reflect the knowledge and sophistication of their creators. Second, they are literally irreplaceable because many of the art works photographed have since been stolen or disappeared. And third, it is considerably less expensive to start a database from existing photographs than from scratch.

What has to be added to make these existing inventories useful? First, the inventories generally predate the computer and need to be digitalised, using one of the powerful software programs now available for organising images and data. This will allow the structuring, searching, accessing, and communication, at low cost, of an otherwise unwieldy quantity of material. It is most important to design and input the database under the guidance of expert art historians with real knowledge of the material being inventoried because the database will need an accurate and well-designed classification system supporting both academic research and easy searches for specific works.

Second, it is necessary that the inventories reach critical mass: there should be enough works accessible in the database so that it is worth consulting. This can be accomplished at the start either through consolidation of existing inventories or the sharing of data between networked inventories. Thereafter, the database needs to continue to grow. A system should be created for adding new information steadily, both from other existing inventories and from new photographic campaigns.

Third, there needs to exist an ongoing organisation or alliance of organisations devoted to assuring that the database will be used both for academic purposes of education and research, and also to provide information about lost or recovered works to police and other art protection organisations. Well-established fields of art have their academic and cultural champions, but the field of Latin American colonial art is just getting started. The creation of the database would, in itself, advance this process of institutionalisation, providing a methodology and an encouragement to the owners and custodians of Peru's heritage to create more inventories, and to better use the available information for art protection. But the process must be a voluntary and cooperative one; it can succeed only if owners of existing inventories are willing to make them available, and if government, church, academic, and cultural organisations are ready to work together.

THE IFAR CUZCO INVENTORY

The IFAR Cuzco inventory is an important part of this mother lode of already collected information. I was fortunate to be present at its creation by the Comité Central de Defensa del Patrimonio Artistico Religioso del Cuzco in Cuzco in the summer of 1982. The Committee, a blue ribbon group including the Archbishop of Cuzco, the local director of the National Institute of Culture (INC), the Mayor, and other dignitaries, had been formed to combat thefts from churches in the area. My law firm in Washington D.C. was, at the time, counsel to the Government of Peru for the recovery of its cultural patrimony.[5] Some of the cases we had handled involved colonial art recoveries, but it was exceptionally difficult to recover the stolen works without a pre-theft photograph as positive identification. By pure chance, I was in Cuzco, and attended a meeting of the Committee at which this problem was discussed. The Committee decided to undertake an emergency photographic inventory in the churches of the Department of Cuzco.

On returning to the United States, I called Bonnie Burnham, then Executive Director of IFAR. IFAR had already established a reputation as a leader in the field of art theft recovery. Thanks to Bonnie's enthusiasm, IFAR spearheaded funding for the project through the Samuel H. Kress Foundation, the Organization of American States (OAS), and some private donors. The inventory was carried out jointly by IFAR, the Archdiocese of Cuzco, and the INC, and total IFAR funding was approximately US$47,000. Many people, too many to name here, generously volunteered their time and support.

Field work began in August 1983, when a group of six international volunteers assembled by IFAR, including four art historians and two photographers, joined a Peruvian cataloguing team from the INC and the lay organisation of the Archdiocese, the Asociación Populorum Progressio. The local communities take very seriously the protection of their churches; the first visit by the team to a church outside Cuzco, the richly decorated Church of the Immaculada in Checacupe, set off a riot led by the local mayor in defence of the town's patrimony, which was only calmed through the intervention of the Archbishop. As word spread, however, that the visitors were defenders, not looters, work proceeded more smoothly, and by the end of the first campaign, 327 paintings had been photographed, twelve churches inventoried, and IFAR and the team were declared honorary citizens of Cuzco.

On the second visit, in December 1983, the IFAR and Peruvian team focused on the Sacred Valley of the Urubamba, the valley that leads to Machu Picchu, photographing 637 paintings in sixteen churches. A third campaign, in July 1984, covered many of the larger collections within the city proper, photographing 1,288 paintings in six churches plus the Archbishop's museum. The inventory focused almost exclusively on paintings, inventorying in all 2,252 paintings in thirty-five churches and one museum. It also included about fifty silver objects. A particular accomplishment of the project, as an "Emergency Inventory" aimed at documenting works vulnerable to theft, was to include in its coverage about 750 paintings in twenty-two of the smaller, less protected rural churches.

The emergency nature of the project caused the team to limit itself to photographing and basic identification of the largest possible number of works. Attention was paid to lighting and, where necessary, works were brought down from the

[5] For a description of Peru's art recovery efforts at that time, see Frederic J. Truslow, "Peru's Recovery of Cultural Patrimony" *New York University Journal of International Law and Politics* 15 (1983): 839.

walls to get good pictures. Only a limited amount of other cataloguing information was recorded, generally the subject matter of the work, its location in the church, and sometimes its condition or the extent and nature of damage. In almost all cases, the authors of the works, painted in the sixteenth to eighteenth centuries, were anonymous, and styles and periods were not generally identified. Almost all photographs were 35 mm black and white, with several hundred larger negatives in the first campaign, and about 100 colour slides in the third campaign.

On completion of the first and second campaigns, IFAR prepared four sets of the inventory on index cards with photographs attached. One set was retained by IFAR, and three were delivered in mid 1985 to the new Archbishop of Cuzco, who had been appointed during the inventory. The Archbishop was expected to distribute the copies of the inventory among the Archdiocese, the INC, and the parish priests, but this never happened. The Church apparently became concerned that the inventory might actually stimulate thefts, and there were disagreements between the Church and the INC as to their respective roles and the best methods to protect colonial religious patrimony. Records are lacking as to the distribution of the inventory from the third campaign.

Lack of concerted direction from Peru, together with a shortage of staff, the pressure of other business at IFAR, and Bonnie Burnham's move to the World Monuments Fund in late 1984 brought the project to a close after the third campaign. IFAR had considered funding additional photographic campaigns, but concluded that it would be advisable to organise and publish the material already gathered before further expanding the inventory. Additional funding could not be obtained from the OAS, one of the Emergency Inventory's principal initial supporters.

AFTERMATH

As a consequence of the breakdown in cooperation between the two principal Peruvian entities concerned with Peru's colonial heritage, and lack of continuity in external support, the Church and the INC never worked out, much less implemented, a system for protecting and recovering church art in Cuzco. Thus, the Emergency Inventory was never made available in Peru for art protection or study. The INC office in Cuzco did keep on with the inventory, and by 2000 had catalogued about 9,000 pieces in more than 100 churches and chapels. Because the INC did not receive its copy of the 1983–4 inventory, about 800 of the works subsequently photographed by it duplicated photographs already in the IFAR inventory. The Archbishop did not participate in the INC inventory after 1984. IFAR's set of photographs and index cards and the negatives were stored for many years at the World Monuments Fund, where they were available to researchers but not widely known.

After completion of the Emergency Inventory, in the late 1980s and early 1990s, Peru, including the area around Cuzco, was plagued by terrorism. The Shining Path terrorist insurgency exacerbated the existing disorder and poverty, reduced tourism, and contributed to thefts and losses of art works. Lack of resources of both the Church and the State, and lack of cooperation between them, impeded an effective defence. Although the terrorists were brought under control by 1993 and tourism has since revived, art theft is still a major problem. Stolen works are commonly smuggled from Cuzco over the nearby border to Bolivia, and feed a thriving antiquities trade in La Paz, Bolivia's capital.

The history of the Emergency Inventory is instructive. First, it shows that institutional cooperation, though necessary, cannot be assumed, even when the institutions involved – the Church and the INC – have a clear common interest in addressing a problem as acute and obvious as that of religious art theft. Second, it shows the utility of intervention by an outside player, IFAR, which resulted in the production, if not the institutionalization, of a valuable, specific cooperative tool, the Emergency Inventory. Third, it shows that a project-by-project approach is not enough, and suggests the need for an ongoing institution that can, over an extended period of time, focus attention and resources on a specific objective, the protection of Peruvian colonial art.

CURRENT SITUATION

In July 2000, an assistant and I visited Cuzco for a week to see how the churches had fared during the sixteen years since the Emergency Inventory was completed. We were told that all the paintings in one church had been lost. We visited ten other churches and checked their paintings against the Emergency Inventory. Of a total of 397 paintings originally photographed in this nonscientific sampling of eleven churches, sixty-five paintings could not be found, for a loss rate of about one in six. Still, there are some great successes; the churches of Checacupe and Pitumarca, south of Cuzco, are beautifully restored and have suffered very few losses, wonderful images are to be found in almost every church, and the collections of the Archbishop's Museum and many of the larger churches of the city are extraordinary. Parishioners in many communities sleep in turns in their churches, and guard them vigilantly.

Art theft produced a diplomatic scandal in late 2000, when the Bolivian police seized more than 200 colonial artworks from the apartment of the cultural attaché of the Peruvian embassy in La Paz. Seven of the seized works were documented in the IFAR inventory, and this evidence was instrumental in establishing their provenance.

PUTTING THE INVENTORIES TO WORK

The Cuzco inventory offers an opportunity to protect Peruvian colonial art in a much more extensive way. The unfinished business that it so clearly represented led me to explore cooperation with Francisco Stastny, Professor of Art Emeritus of the University of San Marcos, Lima, Peru. Professor Stastny is recognised as one of Peru's foremost art historians for the Colonial period, and has, through decades of teaching, research, and directing two Peruvian art museums, built an extensive personal collection of more than 20,000 photographs documenting colonial works throughout Peru. These include a photographic inventory of 1,650 works in sixteen churches of the Colca Valley of Southern Peru carried out in 1987 with support from the Ford Foundation, as well as works in Lima, Trujillo, Arequipa, the Mantaro Valley, and other locations.

As part of this effort, there has been formed the Institute for Latin American Art Documentation (ILAAD), a nonprofit organisation based in the United States, to promote the protection, study, and understanding of endangered national patrimonies throughout Latin America. I welcome the participation of others who share these objectives. ILAAD's initial focus is to organise and make accessible, under appropriate safeguards, already existing Peruvian colonial art inventories, and to use them to protect the colonial cultural heritage of Peru and neighbouring countries. It will work closely with other organisations, including government agencies, foundations, churches, universities, museums, and libraries, in addition to private collectors and dealers, to achieve its purposes, recognising that the combined efforts of many independent entities will be necessary.

As part of this effort, ILAAD has made a proposal to the University of San Marcos, the Western Hemisphere's oldest university, to establish an Art Documentation Centre in Lima to catalogue, study, and protect Peru's colonial art heritage. In addition, ILAAD is hopeful that the new Archbishop of Cuzco, Mons. Juan Antonio Ugarte, a strong supporter of protection and restoration of the region's churches, will reactivate the original program of the Emergency Inventory, and find ways to cooperate productively with the Peruvian government's National Institute of Culture (INC).

ILAAD greatly appreciates IFAR's cooperation in allowing the Cuzco Emergency Inventory to be included in this programme. We also acknowledge the help, among others, of the staffs of the Frick Art Reference Library, the Cornell Institute for Digital Collections, and the Peruvian University of Applied Sciences, all of whom have provided technical advice and encouragement.

BENEFITS OF A CRITICAL MASS DATABASE

If the Stastny and IFAR collections can be combined, they will document well over 10,000 works from all parts of Peru. Similarly, the IFAR and INC collections together have documented more than 10,000 works, usefully concentrated in the Cuzco region. If the funding can be obtained to organise some or all of this material into a computerised, cross-referenced, searchable database, it should be immediately useful in a number of ways:

- It will provide a robust system of classification and cataloguing and an organisational model useful in the creation of inventories by other researchers, churches, museums, and collectors.
- It will provide, for the first time, a significant computerised archive of colonial works for identification and checking, under appropriate controls, by law enforcement agencies, owners, art dealers, and auction houses, thereby strengthening the protection and promoting the recovery of stolen works.
- A version of the database, on compact disc or other electronic format, can be developed for subscription internationally by universities and researchers, providing students and scholars with access to many more works, styles, and subjects, geographically and chronologically, than previously available. This will strengthen Spanish Colonial Art as an academic field, facilitate teaching, and help in preparing survey texts.

The database can and will continue to grow. For example, there have been identified photographic inventories covering 10,000 additional works in Peruvian museum and university collections that are currently inaccessible but would be logical additions to the database. ILAAD will also try to include or cross-reference other existing photograph collections in the United States. In addition, new photographic expeditions can be organised to document other works. ILAAD's efforts can complement inventory building by other organisations in Peru. The INC, in particular, is carrying out a pilot project with IBM and the Archdiocese of Lima to catalogue works in two of the principal churches of Lima, as well as objects from pre-Columbian periods. The Church's Episcopal Conference is planning a nationwide inventory, and the Archbishopric of Cuzco is launching "Salvemos Iglesias," its program for church protection and restoration. ILAAD expects to communicate and coordinate with these programmes.

ART PROTECTION ACTIVITIES

An effective protection program for Spanish colonial art building on the database implies cooperative relationships among at least five complementary but rather different groups: the academic community, the Catholic Church, the tourist industry, the INC and other government institutions that protect the national cultural heritage, and local and international law enforcement agencies. Clearly, creation of such relationships will require many years of work, necessarily supported by one or more catalytic private nonprofit organizations. Currently, no private organisation devoted to the protection and recovery of Spanish colonial art works exists, nor do I know of (although I would appreciate hearing about) other organisations protecting other specific categories of endangered patrimony that might serve as models for such an organisation. The closest model may be the Art Loss Register (ALR), a commercial organisation to which IFAR licensed its theft records in 1991, and the U.S. operations of which were managed by IFAR until 1997. ALR maintains a database of missing or stolen artworks of all kinds, a "negative" register, as opposed to the "positive" ILAAD database.[6] ALR

[6] A positive database records all works known in a given category, whether or not they are stolen or not.

compares its database constantly with auction and exhibition catalogues, and provides information to Interpol and national police organisations. It seems advisable to include in the ALR register those works in the database known to be lost or stolen, and cooperate with police organisations, both inside and outside Peru, as much as ALR does.

Perhaps the principal role of the photographic database in a joint protection effort involving the groups aforementioned would be to answer inquiries, from reputable and identified parties needing to determine or confirm provenance of particular works, concerning whether such works have been documented. The administrator of the database should follow procedures similar to those established by IFAR and continued by ALR to assure confidentiality of sensitive information, privacy of inquiries, and an audit trail. It will be important to publicise the availability of this search function to encourage government and religious organisations, auction houses, dealers, insurance companies, and documented owners of works to benefit from use of the database. To assure that searches are accurate and that the information in the database, particularly the location and ownership of works, is not misused and does not become a catalogue for thieves, the database should be kept confidential and all searches should be conducted by the administrator itself or in conjunction with similar established organisations or police agencies. The database should become a well-known and useful tool for art protection, which will, in turn, encourage churches, museums, and collectors to register their works. Colonial art has not usually been insured in Peru and elsewhere in Latin America, but creation of the database may encourage greater use of insurance.

Given the obvious security concerns affecting colonial artworks, and to preserve the privacy of owners, the administrator of the database should not as a matter of policy publish or publicly disclose the sites or ownership of works in vulnerable locations. On the other hand, nonsensitive information in the database should be made broadly available for education and research, as well as for art protection, recognising that owners of inventories will not contribute information on collections to the database unless their rights and concerns are respected. This includes restrictions on publication or educational use imposed by owners of such information.

Beyond administering the database search function and supporting activities such as the Documentation Centre, a supportive organisation should look for ways to fill gaps in the present art protection system in Peru. These gaps are extensive. Usually the owners of lost works are Peruvian churches, which have other, more pressing priorities than protecting their art, and lack any funds for alarm systems or advanced locks, or, often, even a telephone. They often do not have an inventory or photographs of their artworks.[7] Even if an inventory exists, such as those in the ILAAD database, it often has not been provided to the church, or, if once provided, has been mislaid. If a work is stolen, the priest or sacristan may not have reported the theft to the police, or know how to pursue its recovery. Police response is usually not vigorous. Years may pass before a work turns up, by which time the priest or sacristan may have changed, and any recovery effort has ended. The Peruvian government is charged with the responsibility to pursue and recover lost works, but its resources and energies are also limited.

It is not realistic to think that a small private organisation such as ILAAD can do a great deal to solve most of these problems, given its limited abilities and resources. Still, any organisation that strengthens the response of civil society to the problem will be helpful, provided that it works together with other public and private bodies. ILAAD can seek support for specific manageable activities or projects, such as:

- advice to owners on how to recover lost works;
- distribution of inventories to parishes; or
- preparation jointly with the government of a list of "most wanted" stolen works.

Publication of works that have been stolen can help in their recovery. These activities could help stimulate more concern about art theft in society at large, especially if two other events happen at the same time:

- there are successful recoveries;
- other institutions such as the Church and the universities spur student and tourist interest.

The best chance for success will come from simultaneous interrelated efforts on a number of fronts.

When the IFAR inventory was launched in Cuzco nineteen years ago, the plan of action was limited to the taking of photographs and collecting of identifying data. Now the task is broader: to incorporate that information into a system for art protection, and, to the extent that system does not exist, to encourage its creation. We hope the assembling of a database supplementing the IFAR inventory with other existing inventories large enough to be useful can have a catalytic influence, encouraging communication and action that begin to close the gaps in Peru's present art defences. An inventory is only one part of a system of art protection, but its creation may help jump-start other needed elements of that system.

[7] An important declaration of a supportive Church policy on art inventory and protection came in 1999 with the publication by the Pontifical Commission for the Cultural Heritage of the Church of a Circular Letter entitled, *The Inventory and Catalogue of the Cultural Heritage of the Church: a Necessary and Urgent Task.* Vatican City, 8 December 1999.

CHAPTER THIRTEEN

Cultural Property Legislation in Mexico: Past, Present, and Future

Norma Rojas Delgadillo

INTRODUCTION

For nearly 30 years, cultural property legislation in Mexico has remained unchanged. As a result, the circumstances and problems now confronting Mexico's great cultural heritage have outgrown the legal measures that are in force.

The legislation needs to be reformed so it can continue to conserve and protect Mexico's cultural heritage. This does not mean that new legal institutions need to be invented to resolve the problems in this area. Over the years, Mexico has been one of the countries of Latin America that have a significant tradition of regulations relating to cultural property.

Before offering some suggestions of what might be included in such new legislation, the next section briefly outlines the evolution of cultural property legislation in Mexico.

FIRST ATTEMPTS AT REGULATION

In the eighteenth century, the concept of the legal protection of historical and artistic property became more concrete in Spain,[1] and hence in its American colonies,[2] as the result of two important events: the foundation of the Academy of San Fernando in 1738 and the introduction of a series of legal measures relating to the safekeeping of historical and artistic property.[3]

In the nineteenth century, the Novísima Recopilación (Spanish Legal Code) was the first piece of legislation to offer a generic definition of a "cultural monument," in reference to a document from 1803 bearing the seal of King Carlos IV. At that time, the basic factor on which the definition was based was age, and neither the cultural value nor the historical interest of the property was taken into consideration.[4] From a modern point of view, a definition of a monument that is based merely on its age is clearly insufficient.

Following independence, Mexico developed an autonomous legal tradition on the treatment of this type of property. The main feature of Mexico's nineteenth century legislation was the establishment of regulations designed to prevent the looting of national historical monuments.[5]

DEVELOPMENTS IN NATIONAL LEGISLATION AFTER THE REVOLUTION[6]

Law on the Conservation of Historical and Artistic Monuments and Areas of Natural Beauty

The first time[7] that Mexico systematically enacted legislation to protect cultural property was when it passed the Law on the Conservation of Historical and Artistic Monuments and Areas of Natural Beauty,[8] which was published in the Diario Oficial de la Federación (Official Gazette) on 6 April 1914. The main objective of the Law was to conserve Mexico's historical and artistic heritage.

The consequence of this objective was that the ownership of national property or property that was in the public domain was inalienable and imprescriptible.[9] In the case of private property, the relevant cultural objects could not be transferred, restored, or modified without the permission of the National Inspectorate of Artistic and Historical Monuments, which was part of the Ministry of Public Education.[10]

[1] I use the term concrete because the concept originally dates from the Renaissance in Europe and the forms of patronage common to the period.

[2] Barrero (1990: 32 ff.).

[3] There are some examples of such measures in the Leyes de las Indias (Laws of the Native Americans), but their purpose was to prevent sites from being looted without awarding the Crown a share of the loot. For a summary of these measures, see Leyes de las Indias, vol. II, cl. 1 and vol. III, cl. 63v–64v(1975).

[4] Barrero (1990: 36). In Mexico, the first reference to the concept of a monument is in a Foreign Ministry circular dated 28 November 1835, which contains the obligation to verify compliance with the prohibition on the removal of Mexican monuments and antiquities. It is worth noting that the circular distinguishes between monuments and antiquities and also refers to the nature of the property, its value, and its interest, thus creating a much wider definition than was employed in Spanish legislation at this time. See King, et al. (1980: 184 ff).

[5] Examples of this are the Law of 16 November 1827 and the Decree of 3 June 1896, which enabled the federal government to grant permission to private individuals to undertake archaeological explorations. With regard to the treatment of cultural property, the Decree of 11 May 1897 reaffirms that archaeological monuments are the property of the nation.

[6] For a succinct analysis of legislative evolution, see Macedonio (1996).

[7] Strictly speaking, this is not the first time the protection of cultural heritage is mentioned. In fact, there is an indirect reference to the protection of monuments in the Law of 16 November 1827 on the Payment of Customs Dues at Ports and at the Frontiers of the Republic of Mexico. In Section IV, entitled "Concerning Exportation," Article 41 is worded as follows: "It is prohibited under pain of confiscation to export gold and silver in paste, solid or dust form, Mexican monuments and antiquities and cochineal seed. This prohibition does not include solid gold and gold dust in small quantities, provided that they are exported, in the judgment and with the knowledge of the government, to enrich scholarly collections, for which permission may be given on payment of the relevant duty." See Lombardo (1988: 56).

[8] The full wording of the law appears in Gertz (1976: 65 ff).

[9] Article 24 of the Law.

[10] Article 25 of the Law.

Law on the Conservation of Historical or Artistic Monuments, Buildings, Churches and Objects

January 1916 saw the enactment of the Law on the Conservation of Historical or Artistic Monuments, Buildings, Churches and Objects. The principal objective of the Law was the conservation of "all monuments, buildings, churches and objects that because of their artistic or historical interest are important to the history of the nation."[11] The only conceivable advantage of this Law was that it allowed for the possibility of expropriating – in the public interest – certain categories of private property covered in its provisions.

The first piece of legislation to accord special treatment to cultural heritage was the Law on the Protection and Conservation of Monuments and Areas of Natural Beauty, which was published in the Diario Oficial de la Federación on 31 January 1930. Under the terms of the Law, monuments were defined as movable and immovable objects the protection and conservation of which was in the public interest because of their artistic, archaeological, or historical value. The Law considered the protection and conservation of both monuments and areas of natural beauty to be in the public interest.[12]

The institution empowered to administer the Law was the Ministry of Public Education. In cases in which monuments or areas of natural beauty were not legally under its protection, the Ministry was required to issue a declaration extending such protection. Thus, a distinction was created between what the Ministry regarded as monuments and areas of natural beauty by law, and what it regarded as monuments and areas of natural beauty by declaration. In an emergency, the Ministry was authorised to issue a notification with the same effect as a declaration.[13]

The aforementioned declarations were issued by decree when the monuments and areas in question were privately owned. However, this formality was unnecessary in the case of public property. The declarations took effect on the date on which they were issued to the relevant organisation or institution.[14]

Law on the Protection and Conservation of Archaeological Monuments, Typical Historic Towns and Areas of Natural Beauty

The Law on the Protection and Conservation of Monuments and Areas of Natural Beauty was superseded by the Law on the Protection and Conservation of Archaeological Monuments, Typical Historic Towns and Areas of Natural Beauty, which was published in the Diario Oficial de la Federación on 19 January 1934. In this Law, the definition of an archaeological monument applied to the remains of indigenous civilisations that predated the Spanish conquest. Historical monuments, meanwhile, were monuments postdating the Spanish conquest the conservation of which was in the public interest because of their links to the political or social history of the nation or because their exceptional artistic or architectural value made them outstanding examples of Mexican culture. The works of living artists were not classified in this manner.[15] In fact, there was as yet no separate provision for artistic monuments because they still fell under the definition of historical monuments.

It is also worth noting that archaeological monuments were legally entitled to protection, whereas historical monuments required a declaration to this effect from the Ministry of Public Education.[16]

In addition, according to the terms of the Law, privately owned sites and areas required a decree whereas, in the case of public property,[17] it was sufficient that a declaration be issued to the authority that had jurisdiction over the property. The result was that any work carried out in such areas required the permission of the Ministry of Public Education.[18]

Finally, the Law was the first to have its own by-law, which was published in the Diario Oficial de la Federación on 7 April of 1934. The most important provision of this by-law was the creation of the Monuments Commission as an advisory body to the Ministry of Public Education.[19] The Commission had the final word on the issue of declarations and the performance of work on monuments, typical historic towns, and areas of natural beauty.

Federal Law on the Cultural Heritage of the Nation

The piece of legislation that finally united cultural and natural heritage was the Federal Law on the Cultural Heritage of the Nation, which was published in the Diario Oficial de la Federación on 16 September 1970. This Law defined the cultural heritage of the nation as all property that, under the terms of the law, was deemed to be of cultural value from the point of view of art, tradition, science, or technology.[20]

Although previous definitions of cultural heritage had made no reference to natural assets, this Law also regarded ethnological and paleontological items, specimens of flora and fauna,[21] and areas of natural beauty[22] as cultural property.

The institutions that were selected to apply the Law were the National Institute of Anthropology and History and the

[11] The full wording of the Law appears in Gertz (1976: 73 ff).
[12] *Ibid.*, especially Articles 1 and 4.
[13] This was the precursor of the provisional declaration currently provided for by the 1972 Federal Law on Archaeological, Artistic and Historical Monuments and Sites.
[14] See Article 25 of the 1930 Law.

[15] Article 13 of the 1934 Law.
[16] Article 14 of the 1934 Law.
[17] Article 22 of the 1934 Law.
[18] Articles 20 and 22 of the 1934 Law.
[19] Article 26 of the Law and Articles 36, 37, and 38 of the Regulations.
[20] Article 2 of the 1970 Law.
[21] This reference to specimens currently appears in paragraph XI of Article 2 of the General Law on National Property, which classifies them as property that is in the public domain. Despite their legal status, there is no secondary legislation that adequately regulates enjoyment of these assets.
[22] Sections IV, V, and XI of Article 3 of the 1970 Law.

National Institute of Fine Arts. Both institutions were decentralised bodies attached to the Ministry of Public Education.

To facilitate its own application, the Law defined the grounds of public interest, on the basis of which privately owned cultural property could be appropriated by the state. These grounds included the preservation of areas of natural beauty and the suspension of work that was being carried out in such areas.[23]

Under the provisions of the Law, all examples of movable and immovable property produced by cultures that existed before the arrival of Spanish culture in Mexico were to be considered archaeological monuments. These provisions also included human remains and the remains of flora and fauna associated with pre-Hispanic cultures. The definition of archaeological monuments also included movable property produced by primitive cultures that were not indigenous to Mexico.[24]

The Law defined historical monuments as all examples of movable and immovable property created after the arrival of Spanish culture in Mexico that were linked to the country's social, political, economic, cultural, or religious history and which, with the passage of time, had acquired cultural value.

The Law also provided for the protection of artistic monuments, including paintings, engravings, drawings, sculptures, architecture, and other objects of permanent aesthetic value, in addition to literary and musical works and archives, the importance or value of which was of an artistic nature.[25]

Finally, the Law defined areas of natural beauty as areas or regions, the combined aesthetic characteristics of which created an extraordinary public attraction.[26] Even so, the Ministry of Public Education only had jurisdiction over areas within the Federal District, the Federal Territories and those areas defined as cultural property[27] that were under federal jurisdiction. In the case of areas of natural beauty that belonged to a state or a municipality, the Federation would only have authority to act if it concluded an agreement with the appropriate state legislature or if it received government approval for the creation of an organisation to protect, conserve, and restore the area in question.[28] The National Institute of Anthropology and History was the competent authority with regard to the conservation of areas of natural beauty.

CURRENT SITUATION

The separation of legislation on natural and cultural heritage implies major legislative modifications at the national and the international level. For the purposes of this chapter, the discussion will be confined to the legal aspects of this separation, but this should not diminish the importance of real-world issues that have affected the development of cultural law.

CONVENTIONS

The most important international conventions now in force are the 1970 UNESCO Convention on the Means of Prohibiting and Preventing the Illicit Import, Export and Transfer of Ownership of Cultural Property (UNESCO Convention) and the 1972 UNESCO Convention concerning the Protection of World Cultural and Natural Heritage (World Heritage Convention).

The UNESCO Convention was signed in Paris on 17 November 1970 and was published in the Diario Oficial de la Federación on 27 October 1971. For the purposes of the Convention, cultural property means property which, on religious or secular grounds, is specifically designated by each state as being of importance for archaeology, prehistory, history, literature, art, or science and which belongs to the following categories, including rare collections and specimens of flora, fauna, minerals, anatomy, and objects of paleontological interest.[29]

The World Heritage Convention, which was adopted in Paris on 23 November 1972 and published in the Diario Oficial de la Federación on 2 May 1984, establishes that each state party to the Convention shall endeavour to the best of its ability to take measures to ensure the protection, conservation, and presentation of cultural and natural heritage located on its territory.

CONSTITUTIONAL REFORMS

The constitutional reforms of 6 July 1971, 3 February 1983, and 10 August 1987 have helped to shape Mexico's national heritage legislation. In 1971, the powers of the General Health Council were extended to enable it to adopt measures to prevent and combat environmental pollution,[30] thereby confirming a very important concept. In 1983, the concept of the "environment" was incorporated into the Constitution for the first time, and the use of valuable resources was made secondary to the protection of these resources.[31] In 1987, finally, the government was authorised to put in place measures that were necessary to preserving and restoring the ecological balance,[32] and Congress was authorised to draw up laws to determine the responsibility of various government departments for environmental protection and the preservation and restoration of the ecological balance.[33] It is on the basis of these constitutional reforms that Mexico seeks to regulate national cultural and environmental

[23] Section V of Article 38 of the 1970 Law.
[24] Articles 50 and 51 of the 1970 Law.
[25] Article 64 of the 1970 Law.
[26] Article 70 of the 1970 Law.
[27] Article 73 of the 1970 Law.
[28] Article 77 of the 1970 Law.
[29] Article 1(a) of the UNESCO Convention.
[30] Clause 4, Section XVI of Article 73 of the Constitution.
[31] Paragraph 6 of Article 25 of the Constitution.
[32] Paragraph 3 of Article 27 of the Constitution.
[33] Section XXIX-G of Article 73 of the Constitution.

heritage issues separately, in the manner discussed subsequently.[34]

FEDERAL LAW ON ARCHAEOLOGICAL, ARTISTIC, AND HISTORICAL MONUMENTS AND SITES

In this context, the first piece of legislation (which does not regulate areas of natural beauty) is the Federal Law on Archaeological, Artistic and Historical Monuments and Sites, which was published in the Diario Oficial de la Federación on 6 May 1972 and is currently in force (the Law).

According to this Law, archaeological monuments consist of movable or immovable property produced by pre-Hispanic cultures on national territory, as well as the remains of flora and fauna related to these cultures. It is understandable that natural phenomena can be of cultural importance, provided they are related in some way to pre-Hispanic cultures.[35] This would be the case with regard to remains found during the excavation of such monuments.

Furthermore, artistic monuments consist of movable or immovable property of outstanding aesthetic value, which is defined as such because of its significance, its place within specific artistic movements, its innovative quality, the materials and techniques used, and so on. In the case of buildings, their significance within the urban context is also taken into consideration.

Historical monuments, finally, consist of "property linked to the history of the nation, following the establishment of Spanish culture," as defined by a declaration or by law. According to the Law, historical monuments include:

- buildings constructed between the sixteenth and nineteenth centuries, including Church buildings and their annexes; archbishoprics, bishoprics, and ecclesiastical houses; seminaries, convents, and all other buildings dedicated to the administration, propagation, teaching, or practice of a religious cult; and buildings intended for education and teaching, social or charitable activities, public service, decorative purposes, or use by the civil or military authorities;
- movable property produced between the sixteenth and nineteenth centuries that is located or was discovered within such buildings;
- documents and files that belong or belonged to the offices and archives of the federal government, states, municipalities, or ecclesiastical houses, and original manuscripts related to the history of Mexico; and
- books, pamphlets and other material printed in Mexico or abroad between the sixteenth and nineteenth centuries, which, because of their rarity or importance to Mexican history, should be conserved in the country. Scientific and technological collections may also be added to this category by means of an appropriate declaration.

One of the most important innovations of the Law is the concept of the archaeological, artistic, and historical monument site. An archaeological monument site is an area in which several immovable archaeological monuments are located or are presumed to be located. The problem with this provision is that it is sometimes difficult to determine whether or not archaeological remains are present. Indeed, on what basis could one assume that this type of property is located in a given area?

SOME LEGISLATIVE PROPOSALS

On the basis of the legal and practical issues that have been discussed in this chapter, it is fair to say that the 1972 Federal Law on Archaeological, Artistic and Historical Monuments and Sites should be amended to include the following:

- a new classification of cultural property based solely on historical criteria, but incorporating characteristics that qualify such property for monument status;
- a redistribution of powers that strengthens the position of the federal government with regard to historical or artistic cultural property of local interest without removing the property in question from federal ownership;
- clearer and more explicit protection of intangible heritage and other types of cultural property, such as paleontological remains, shipwrecks, and cave paintings;
- an appropriate system of heritage protection that respects individual civic rights and also creates incentives for the owners of this kind of property;
- the creation of the necessary legislation to bring about coordination among the federal, state, and municipal authorities on issues of heritage protection;
- the appropriate regulation of the exploitation of the nation's cultural heritage;
- the establishment of a system of community participation, and the eventual integration of such participation, in policies on the protection and conservation of cultural heritage;
- the coordination of cultural heritage protection with other important legislative issues, such as the environment, urban planning, and tourism;
- the regulation of commercial activities in monument sites; and
- the creation of protection mechanisms to meet the specific needs of individual monument sites, on the understanding that a declaration that such sites are subject to protection and conservation is insufficient and that there is also a need for ongoing action plans in order to carry out the intentions of the Law.

[34] In the most recent constitutional reforms relating to environmental issues, which were published in the Diario Oficial de la Federación on 28 June de 1999, Articles 4 and 28 establish the right of every individual to an environment suited to his or her development and well-being and incorporate the concept of sustainability into the responsibilities of the state for development of the nation, the strengthening of national sovereignty, and democratic governance.

[35] Article 28 of the 1972 Law.

Obviously, it will not be a simple task to implement all these proposals. The only way to guarantee adequate legal protection of Mexico's cultural heritage is through the participation of all the relevant sectors and institutions.

BIBLIOGRAPHY

Barrero Rodríguez, Concepción. 1990. *La ordenación jurídica del patrimonio histórico. Col. Monografías Civitas.* Madrid: Civitas.

Gertz Manero, Alejandro. 1976. "La defensa jurídica y social del patrimonio cultural. México Fondo de Cultura Económica." *Archivo del Fondo:* No. 74.

Leyes de las Indias. 1975. Madrid: Cultura Hispánica.

Litvak King, Jaime, et al., 1980. *Arqueología y Derecho en México. Serie Antropológica: No. 23.* México: UNAM.

Lombardo De Ruíz, Sonia. 1988. *Antecedentes de las Leyes sobre Monumentos.* México: Instituto Nacional de Antropología e Historia.

Macedonio Hernández, Carlos A. 1996. "La Defensa Jurídica del Patrimonio Cultural de la Nación." *Revista Facultad de Derecho de Yucatán 22: 41–44.*

CHAPTER FOURTEEN

The Protection of Cultural Heritage in Colombia

Juan Carlos Uribe

This chapter seeks only to provide a brief outline of the evolution of the various legal acts designed to safeguard the cultural patrimony of Colombia, which, despite its richness, remains largely unknown to the majority of Colombia's citizens as well as to foreigners. To this end, the most relevant acts will be discussed in chronological order, with an emphasis on their most important features and, to some extent, the context in which they were adopted.

LAW NO. 47 OF 1920

The first law to define what type of objects are regarded as being of historic interest and in what manner the rights of the owners of such objects are to be limited was adopted in 1920. Its definitions were rather limited, however, because the law only covered (i) documents or objects belonging to a public museum or library, or (ii) documents or objects or having historic or artistic significance, or some other kind of importance, for the Colombian state. In fact, the law did not even attempt to define what it meant by a document of historic or artistic significance.

In addition, the rights of owners were not limited in a particularly serious manner, given that the law only established that protected documents and objects were not to be exported without government approval and, if approval for export was denied, that the documents or objects in question would be acquired by the state.

Because no one was really sure what type of objects constituted Colombia's cultural heritage, the museums and libraries were ordered to draw up an inventory of all the goods, documents, and objects of special significance that were not to be removed from the places where they were exhibited under any circumstances.

To introduce some authority and knowledge into this endeavour, the Academia Nacional de Historia (National Academy of History) was appointed as the government's advisory body for the organisation of museums and public archives.

LAW NO. 14 OF 1936

Over time, the work of archaeologists and their discoveries increased awareness and appreciation of Colombia's pre-Hispanic cultures and their creations. As a result of these developments, Colombia incorporated the Treaty on the Protection of Movable Property, signed in Washington in 1935, into local legislation. The Treaty provides a clear and specific classification of the types of documents and objects that are regarded as being of anthropological, cultural and historical value. These documents and objects are divided into three main categories:

- From the pre-Columbian period, objects such as: (1) weapons; (2) pottery; (3) woven fabrics; (4) Jewellery; (5) amulets; and (6) objects taken from monuments dating from this period.
- From the Colonial period, objects such as: (1) weapons; (2) tools; (3) costumes; (4) medals and coins; (5) amulets; (6) drawings, paintings, and plans; (7) codices and rare books; (8) silver and gold objects; (9) porcelain; and (10) other objects having artistic of historical value.
- From the period of the emancipation and the Republic, the same objects as from the Colonial period.

The following items also belong in all three categories: (1) official and institutional libraries; (2) private libraries that are valuable as a whole; (3) national archives and collections of public and private manuscripts; and (4) zoological specimens that are beautiful, rare, or threatened with extinction.

All the items just mentioned may only be imported or exported if accompanied by an official government authorisation. If this is not the case, customs authorities shall seize such items and return them to the Colombian government.

LAW NO. 36 OF 1936

Colombia is a State Party to the Roerich Treaty of 1935 for the Protection of Monuments and Cultural Institutions in Times of War. It should be noted that, during the last forty years, most of the violent destruction of Colombia's cultural heritage has occurred not as a consequence of international warfare, given that Colombia has not been involved in international warfare during this period, but as a consequence of the attacks of guerrilla groups on the civilian population and government buildings.

DECREE NO. 1060 OF 1936

As the discovery of archaeological sites became increasingly frequent and more widely known, both nationally and internationally, the study of the pre-Columbian period also gained momentum. The government was worried about the possible consequences of uncontrolled archaeological expeditions, so it regulated the admission and operation of such expeditions in the following fashion:

- All archaeological and scientific expeditions that wish to operate in Colombia must request a license and indicate the nature of their interest.
- Approved expeditions must be accompanied by Colombian personnel appointed by the Colombian government.
- Approved expeditions are not authorised to take archaeological, artistic, historic, or natural objects out of the country without the prior approval of the government.

LAW NO. 163 OF 1959

This Law expanded the list of objects that are regarded as being of artistic or historical value, including, in particular, objects from tombs and palaeontological finds, special architectonic works, and antique sections in some cities. City sections constructed between the sixteenth and eighteenth centuries also qualify for special protection to prevent their demolition or deterioration, and their original design cannot be changed or adapted without the prior approval of the Council of National Monuments. City sections of this kind include Cartagena, Tunja, Mompox, Popayan, Guaduas, Pasto, Villa de Leyva, and Santafe de Antioquia.

The adoption of the Law also coincided with the following innovations:

Movable or immovable property belonging to individuals may be expropriated by the government, as long as the latter indemnifies those individuals.

The Colombian Institute of Anthropology was placed in charge of granting licenses for anthropological expeditions and excavations, regardless of whether they take place on public or private land.

If a palaeontological or archaeological find is made during a mining or construction project, the activity in question must be postponed immediately until a proper assessment is made of the importance of the find and measures have been established to protect it.

The Council of National Monuments was created and was authorised to impose penalties in cases of the illicit export of cultural property and to obtain the return of the property in question if the supervision of the customs authorities is evaded.

Private owners of cultural property are required to register such property with the Office on National Monuments, although no sanction is imposed if they fail to do so.

DECREE NO. 264 OF 1963

This Decree specifies the functions of the Council of National Monuments, particularly in relation to its power to interact with local authorities for the preservation of architectural works.

LAW NO. 45 OF 1983

This Law incorporated the 1972 UNESCO Convention concerning the Protection of the World Cultural and Natural Heritage into national legislation.

DECREE NO. 12 OF 1984

In the past, the issue of shipwrecks had always lacked specific regulations. However, with the discovery of the San José off the coast of Colombia, near the city of Cartagena, the issue suddenly became very complicated as a result of the various interests involved in the case. This Decree represents an initial attempt to regulate the issue. The main points of the Decree are as follow:

- A shipwreck is composed not only of the vessel itself but also of its endowments and the movable assets that were part of it, regardless of whether they are within the vessel or dispersed on the bottom of the sea and regardless of the nature, cause, or time of the shipwreck.
- Both Colombians and foreign nationals are entitled to apply for a permit or a concession to explore a shipwreck. If anything is found, a report must be submitted indicating the precise geographic coordinates of the wreckage, and the finder will be entitled to a five percent share of the value of the discovery. Payment will be carried out by the party that is awarded the task of recovering the wreckage.
- The party that recovers the wreckage does not have any rights or privileges over the property recovered from the wreckage.
- The Direccion Maritima y Portuaria (Maritime and Ports Directorate) is in charge of awarding the aforementioned permits and concessions.
- Law No. 63 of 1986.

This Law incorporated the 1970 UNESCO Convention on the Means of Prohibiting and Preventing the Illicit Import, Export and Transfer of Ownership of Cultural Property into national legislation.

DECREE NO. 1397 OF 1989

This Decree provides guidelines regarding the right of the customs authorities to seize and withhold objects that might fall into the category of cultural property. An important limitation on this right is that any action in this regard must be based on an order of the Director of the Customs Office, and only if there is sufficient evidence that the property in question might be exported.

RESOLUTION NO. 50 OF 1990

This Resolution, which was issued by the Council of National Monuments, regulates the procedures that private individuals must follow in order to register the cultural property in their possession. Such registration must take the form of a declaration before the Colombian Institute of Anthropology, which will bear the cost of determining whether the pieces are authentic. Said institute must also be notified of all sales of such property.

DECREE NO. 329 OF 1997

This Decree regulates the temporary export of cultural property, stating that such objects may only leave the country for the purpose of temporary exhibitions of a cultural nature and only with the prior approval of the Council of National Monuments.

LAW NO. 397 OF 1997

This Law seeks to create a unified body of cultural law and to coordinate the governmental agencies entrusted with its protection. It is also known for creating the Colombian Ministry of Culture. The main characteristics of the Law are as follows:

- The status of archaeological heritage is extended to movable and immovable property that is currently part of the tradition and heritage of Colombia's indigenous populations.
- The Catholic Church and all other organised religions are recognised as the owners of the artistic objects created or acquired by them. The management and use of these objects will be regulated by means of special agreements with the Colombian government.
- In the case of shipwrecks, the license for their exploration must be obtained from the Ministry of Culture and from the Maritime and Ports Directorate.
- When an object is designated a monument or cultural property, a special plan must be developed for its protection, including specific management guidelines.
- All exports of cultural property are now strictly forbidden, except for temporary exports for the purpose of public exhibitions or scientific studies. In either case, the period of export should last no longer than three years.
- A Registry of National Heritage is created.
- Law 397 establishes that the National Museum of Colombia, as a Special Administrative Unit of the Ministry of Culture, is responsible for the oversight of existing museums, ensuring their ability to educate their audiences and protect their collections, and stimulating their active involvement in national, regional, and local cultural life and identity. The National Museums Network of the Ministry of Culture has organized museology seminars in Bogotá, Medellin, and Pasto where all those involved with and interested in museums have been invited to participate. Among their objectives is enhancing the abilities of the regional museums to operate effectively within the limits of their human and financial resources.
- The Law leaves many issues to future regulation, such as the procedure for awarding permits and concessions to explore shipwrecks and the management of the National Heritage registry.
- As can be gathered from the development of its legislation, Colombia has indeed gained a greater awareness of the riches its culture and traditions encompass. The current task is to obtain the necessary funds from the government and the private sector to create a coherent cultural heritage policy.

On April 21, 2004, the Government of the Republic of Columbia submitted, pursuant to Article 9 of the 1970 UNESCO Convention and in agreement with the Convention on Cultural Property Implementation Act, a request for U.S. import restrictions on pre-Colombian archaeological material and colonial period ethnological artifacts. Excerpts of the request can be found in the Appendix to this article.

APPENDIX

Request for Cultural Property Protection from the Government of the Republic of Colombia

PREFACE

This request is submitted to the Government of the United States under Article 9 of the 1970 UNESCO Convention and in agreement with the Convention on Cultural Property Implementation Act, Section 303.

The following memorandum may be found on the internet at <http://exchanges.state.gov/culprop/co04sum.html>.
Revised: June 16, 2004

1. THE HERITAGE OF COLOMBIA

a. The Archaeological Record

The ancient cultures of this northwestern corner of South America were a myriad of self-contained, small-scale chiefdoms and incipient state polities that first appeared in c. 3000 B.C. The many distinct culture groups produced a diverse and sophisticated material culture, of which – with few exceptions – only artifacts of stone, metal, and ceramic have survived the aggressive climate. While these cultures exchanged goods widely, artistic styles of the region are distinctive, and increasingly easily associated with specific locations. Tombs constitute the primary resource in this region on which scholars rely.

b. Legacy of the Colonial Era

The rich cultural range of pre-conquest Colombia was overwhelmed by the imposition of European values, language, aesthetics, and religion, starting the moment the Spanish established their first missions in the first part of the sixteenth Century. Elements of the late Gothic, Mudéjar, and Baroque sensibilities are seen in important civic architecture; stern symbols of the rigid orthodoxy of the Catholic Counter-Reformation, afoot at the time of the Conquest, are seen in religious buildings, objects, and paintings. Interesting mixtures of Spanish and native iconography are seen in mission features and ornamental arts.

c. The Changing Attitude Toward History

Several forces combine to promote a new attitude about Colombia's physical heritage, including the development of scholarly archaeological research with an emphasis on context and culture – not simply on objects, the opening of new lines of research in environmental and cultural studies, the response to the need for inventories and local museums, a welcoming of both national and foreign researchers into all these areas, and the increased sophistication and tightening of legal constraints on the acquisition and trade of objects of cultural significance.

Colombia sees itself as a multiethnic and multicultural nation building constructing its memory from the rich histories that have begun to emerge from academic research. With the encouragement of the Ministry of Culture, the results of two decades of archaeological investigation are starting to illuminate Colombia's culturally diverse past, and to provide detail on the human, ritual, and political realities of antiquity. Beautiful but disconnected objects are transformed into a legible, interrelated material culture that is the foundation of national identity.

2. PILLAGE AND ITS EFFECTS

The plunder of indigenous tombs in Colombia started in the sixteenth century with Spaniards extracting the rich offerings from burial mounds in the Sinu region of the Caribbean plains. Thereafter, the conquest routes followed the sources of gold, salt, emeralds and cotton blankets – useful for their monetary value. The monetary value of pre-Columbian archaeological artifacts and Colonial-era objects continues to tempt citizens and foreigners, even though the laws have changed.

An historic lack of appreciation by the population of the value of archaeological heritage to the nation, and the lack of preparation of official bodies have allowed the loss and destruction of irreplaceable archaeological material. Similarly, losses through theft and illegal appropriation of furnishings and religious art from churches across the country – from lack of security, attention, or threats of consequences – have depleted the national legacy from the Colonial and subsequent periods.

In many areas of Colombia, looting is commonplace, and crosses all social strata. The Colombian Institute of Anthropology and History (ICANH) and the Ministry of Culture – the agencies charged with heritage stewardship – must be creative and focused to educate citizens and stem the loss of objects that tie the country to its history. The practice is difficult to eradicate, and while various sectors are working hard on a range of mitigation measures, the help of the United States and other nations is crucial.

3. ILLICIT TRAFFIC OF COLOMBIA'S MOVABLE HERITAGE – THE UNITED STATES AS AN IMPORTER

The United States is one of several countries where the market is brisk in Colombian archaeological and Colonial period material, as evidenced by the U.S.-based Internet auction sites. Religious and decorative art from the Spanish Colonial period is more homogeneous throughout the region, and thus less easily associated with findspots. However, it is certain that thefts of these materials from Colombian churches is common.

Web sites and established galleries consistently offer an extraordinary range of ceramics, gold work, and stone sculpture easily identified with specific Colombian culture areas. Following a massive tomb-looting episode at Malagana in 1992, for example, highly recognizable objects flooded immediately onto the market, and these can now be seen in exhibitions and in circulation in secondary or tertiary sales.

4. MEASURES TAKEN BY COLOMBIA TO PROTECT MOVABLE HERITAGE

a. Legal Measures, Security, and Enforcement

The National Constitution [1991] takes a strong and constructive position on the importance of the physical cultural heritage, the common ownership of all heritage by the government on behalf of the citizens, and the obligation of the government at all levels, as well as all citizens to protect and preserve it. Specifically addressing these principles are Articles 63, 72, 82, 95, 101, 332, and 333.

* * *

b. Public Education

* * *

c. Archaeology, Museology, and Conservation

* * *

The ongoing conservation of research and exhibition collections is the responsibility of ICANH and the 50+ museums in the country, in which security and environmental controls [i.e., preventive conservation] are of the highest priority. Conservation of monuments and sites is programmed by ICANH, and supported by its own revenues, entry fees from archaeological parks, the Ministry of Culture, UNESCO [in the case of World Heritage Sites], and – on a limited basis – The Foundation for National Archaeological Research [FIAN].

d. Professional Development

Certain standards have been established to ensure best practices in fields affecting the archaeological and colonial heritage. First, all archaeological research in Colombia is undertaken only with permits issued by ICANH to registered and qualified archaeologists, following the submission, peer review, and approval of research plans, project descriptions, logistical, and staffing details. The applicant is required to ensure that the archaeological interventions are adequately staffed and capable of evaluating the impact of the project, and protecting archaeological information. ICANH publishes a "Manual of Preventive Archaeology," which defines minimum criteria for authorizing archaeological interventions.

As part of The National Campaign Against Illicit Trafficking of Cultural Goods, the Heritage Division of the Ministry of Culture created and promotes a training program course entitled Toward valuing and protecting movable cultural heritage, available to customs agents, police, prosecutors, art merchants, gallery owners, educators, etc., to familiarize them with the heritage and improve their abilities to protect the cultural heritage.

* * *

CHAPTER FIFTEEN

Chronological Overview of Developments in Bolivian and Latin American Cultural Heritage Legislation with a Special Emphasis on the Protection of Indigenous Culture

Elizabeth Torres

NINETEENTH CENTURY

The earliest example of Bolivian legislation in the field of cultural heritage preservation was a Supreme Decree adopted on 11 December 1825 – the year of Bolivia's independence – during the administration of Simon Bolivar. Articles 6 and 8 of the Decree mention the use and adaptation of old buildings for educational purposes, such as science and arts schools.

EARLY TWENTIETH CENTURY

In 1906, during the administration of Israel Montes, a Legal Regime for the Tiahuanacu Ruins, Ruins on the Lake Titicaca Islands and Ruins from the Inca and Preceding Ages was enacted as a Law of the Republic. Article 1 of this Law classifies the ruins as state property, engages the government in their care, and mandates an annual budget allocation. Article 2 prohibits the export of works of art from the ruins. Article 3 entitles the government to delegate preservation and restoration activities to the corresponding geographical societies. In 1909, during the administration of Eliodoro Villazón, a Supreme Decree establishing an Excavation Regime for Tiahuanacu and the Lake Titicaca Islands was promulgated in accordance with the aforementioned Law.

On 8 May 1927, during the administration of Hernando Siles, the National Monument Act was enacted. It created an ad honorem committee and a National Gallery of Fine Arts, History and Archaeology, both under the umbrella of the Ministry of Education, that were charged with classifying and protecting artistic and historical assets.

In 1930, in accordance with another Supreme Decree, a number of temples and important civilian and administrative buildings in the towns of La Paz, Sucre, and Potosi were declared national monuments by means of specific resolutions.

MID-TWENTIETH CENTURY

In 1945, during the administration of Gualberto Villaroel, Supreme Decree No. 400 (Norms on Bibliographic and Documentary Heritage) was promulgated. These Norms established that it was important to conserve the country's existing books, documents, and publications and that it was necessary to preserve the country's bibliographic wealth and maintain it properly in places created for this purpose.

In the late 1940s, archaeological research began in Tiahuanacu, Bolivia's main archaeological site.

In 1958, the Archaeological Excavation Regulations were issued. These Regulations were to be enforced on a nationwide basis by the Ministry of Education's Department of Archaeology.

Article 199 of the 1961 edition of the Bolivian Constitution provides that:

> "Archaeological monuments and objects are property of the State. Colonial, archaeological and historical goods, as well as objects related to religious worship, are part of the nation's cultural treasure, are protected by the State and cannot be exported. The State shall protect buildings and sites that are declared as being of artistic and historical value."

The awareness raised during the administration of Victor Paz Estenssoro, resulted in Supreme Decree No. 05918 promulgated on 6 November 1961. This Decree stated that it was the state's obligation to protect the nation's artistic and cultural heritage and to watch over the proper conservation of artistic, historical, and archaeological patrimony from pre-Columbian, Colonial, and Republican times.

The Decree complemented existing legislation with twenty-five regulatory articles and is still considered the most complete set of legal norms for the defence of Bolivia's cultural heritage. It classifies the following expressions of the human spirit as monuments and works of art:

1. architecture, including cities, monumental compounds, churches, and convents;
2. painting, including murals, paintings, engravings, drawings, and illustrations;
3. sculpture, including sculptures, reliefs, and retables;
4. fine art, such as goldwork, silverwork, tabernacles, jewellery, and other objects made before 1900;
5. furniture and accessories made before 1900;
6. rugs, tapestry, clothing, and hats made before 1900;
7. porcelain, china, crystal, glass, marble, and alabaster objects; and
8. books, including manuscripts, incunabula, musical scores, and musical manuscripts.

In addition, the Decree classifies all remains of human activity of artistic and scientific importance that date back to the pre-Hispanic period as monuments or archaeological objects, including:

1. monuments, ruins of towns, temples, fortresses, agricultural terraces, etc.;
2. archaeological sites, including middens and cemeteries, funeral pyramids, shrines, caverns, tombs, etc.;

3. archaeological objects, including statues, stelae, obelisks, sculptures of any material, quality, or significance, and utensils made of stone, wood, bone, or shells;
4. functional and ceremonial pottery;
5. weavings, baskets, nets, tapestry, embroidery, and featherwork; and
6. goldwork, silverwork, bronzework, and other objects made with precious or semiprecious stones.

The Decree prohibits the export of the aforementioned objects, including export via diplomatic channels. It also states that illegal exports are subject to confiscation, fines, and other penalties established by the criminal code.

On 27 November 1961, Ministerial Resolution No 1642 (Norms for Cataloguing and Guarding the Nation's Artistic Treasures) was issued. This Resolution charged the Directorate of Fine Arts and National Monuments and the Directorate of Anthropology of the Ministry of Education with responsibility for enforcing the aforementioned Decree.

In September 1962, during the interim administration of Juan Lechin Oquendo, Supreme Decree No. 06231 (Norms for Paleontology Research) was promulgated.

Despite the existence of a National Committee on Sacred Arts, a new Committee on Sacred Architecture and Arts was created in 1964. The new Committee was responsible for watching over the conservation of artistic, architectural, pictorial, and sculptural treasures and ornaments of a religious nature, and for accessories used by the Catholic Church.

In a similar vein, Supreme Decree No. 07234 (Norms on Archaeological Excavations and the Prohibition on the Sale of Archaeological Objects) was promulgated in 1965, during the administration of the military junta of Barrientos and Ovando.

LATE TWENTIETH CENTURY

In 1966, at its fourteenth session in Paris, the General Conference of UNESCO adopted the Declaration of the Principles of International Cultural Cooperation, the main purpose of which is to build peace through the respect and preservation of all cultures, which form the common heritage of mankind.

In 1967, the Bolivian Constitution was amended to make the state responsible for cultural heritage conservation. Article 191 of the 1967 Constitution states:

> "Monuments and archaeological objects are property of the State. Artistic, archaeological and historical goods, as well as object related to religious worship, are part of the nation's cultural treasure, are protected by the State and cannot be exported. The State shall organise a registry of artistic, historical, religious and documentary goods, and shall guard and conserve it. The State shall protect buildings and objects declared as being of historical or artistic value."

In 1973, Ministerial Resolution No. 792 (Norms Concerning Scientific Research into Anthropological Matters) identified the Ministry of Education and Culture as the agency responsible for the preservation of Bolivia's anthropological heritage.

It was at this time that ICOMOS-Bolivia was established as a nongovernmental organisation. Today, the organisation gathers together most of the professionals involved in the heritage conservation historic structures and restoration. Its advice regarding conservation and restoration and the training courses it provides in this field are extremely important.

In November 1975, Education Ministry Resolution No. 708 introduced the Norms for the Defence of the National Artistic Heritage (I). These Norms classified the works of art of renowned artists who died after 1900 as part of the national artistic heritage. These works were to be duly catalogued and incorporated into the provisions found in Article 3 of Supreme Decree No. 05918 of 6 November 1961, for the defence of the national artistic heritage.

The second half of the decade was notable for the establishment of the National Fine Arts Institute within the Bolivian Institute of Culture. In February 1978, the Institute expanded to become the National Artistic Heritage and Visual Arts Institute, with responsibility for national conservation and restoration regulations. At the same time, the National Directorate of Anthropology was also established under the auspices of the Ministry of Education and Culture. The Directorate introduced a registry of performers of folk music and a national copyright registry, the predecessor of Bolivia's current Copyright Directorate.

In 1976, a joint Ministerial Resolution of the Ministry of Education and the Ministry of the Interior, Migration and Justice introduced the Norms for the Defence of the National Artistic Heritage (II). These Norms granted custody to the National Museum of Art of all paintings and objects belonging to Bolivia's artistic and historical heritage in the churches, chapels, oratories, parishes, and sanctuaries of the Department of La Paz.

In August 1976, the Ministry of Education issued Ministerial Resolution No. 699 (Norms Concerning the Prohibition on Sending Works of Art Abroad), which expressly prohibits institutions or individuals from sending sixteenth, seventeenth, eighteenth, and nineteenth century paintings, in addition to paintings by artists who died after 1900, that are considered part of Bolivia's cultural heritage, abroad for restoration. Such paintings must be restored in Bolivia by the Institute of Culture's conservation and restoration workshop.

In 1976, the members of the Organization of American States adopted the Convention on the Protection of the Archaeological, Historical and Artistic Heritage of the American Nations (Convention of San Salvador). The purpose of the Convention is to identify, register, protect, and safeguard the property making up the cultural heritage of the American nations in order (a) to prevent illegal export or import of cultural property and (b) to promote cooperation among the American states for mutual awareness and appreciation of their cultural property.

In this international context, one of the first declarations on indigenous rights – the Barbados Declaration II – was adopted in Barbados in 1977. Through this Declaration, indigenous people from around the world publicised their discontent regarding the various forms of domination they endure, including economic domination, cultural domination, and so forth.

In 1982, UNESCO and the World Intellectual Property Organization (WIPO) issued their Model Provisions for National Laws on the Protection of Expressions of Folklore Against Illicit Exploitation and Other Prejudicial Actions for application by the international community.

In 1986, ICOM-Bolivia was established. It became the coordinating body for Bolivian museums, organising national and international conferences and providing short orientation courses to museum staff, especially in state capitals.

On 23 May 1988, Supreme Decree No. 21951 extended state protection to ethnographic and folkloric materials and resources, as well as locally produced artisanry and textiles that are more than thirty years old. Such objects are considered an inalienable part of Bolivia's cultural heritage, they are protected by the state, and their export is prohibited.

In 1988, the Declaration of Belem was adopted at the International Society of Ethnobiology's First International Congress in Belem (Brazil). In this document, the signatories strongly supported the following measures:

1. A substantial proportion of development aid should be devoted to efforts aimed at ethnobiological inventory, conservation, and management programmes.
2. Mechanisms should be established by which indigenous specialists are recognised as proper authorities and are consulted in relation to all programmes affecting them, their resources, and their environments.
3. All other inalienable human rights should be recognised and guaranteed, including the right to a cultural and linguistic identity.
4. Procedures should be developed to compensate native peoples for the utilisation of their knowledge and their biological resources.
5. Educational programmes should be implemented to alert the global community to the value of ethnobiological knowledge for human welfare.
6. All medical programmes should include recognition of and respect for traditional healers and incorporate traditional health practices that enhance the health of these populations.
7. Ethnobiologists should make the results of their research available to the native peoples with whom they have worked, including the dissemination of these results in the native language.
8. Exchanges of information should be promoted among indigenous and peasant peoples regarding conservation, management, and sustained utilisation of resources.

In June 1989, at its seventy-sixth session in Geneva, the International Labour Organisation (ILO) adopted the Convention Concerning Indigenous and Tribal Peoples in Independent Countries (ILO Convention 169).

According to Article 1(1), the Convention applies to:

(a) tribal peoples in independent countries whose social, cultural and economic conditions distinguish them from other sections of the national community, and whose status is regulated wholly or partially by their own customs or traditions or by special laws or regulations;

(b) peoples in independent countries who are regarded as indigenous on account of their descent from the populations which inhabited the country, or a geographical region to which the country belongs, at the time of conquest or colonisation or the establishment of present State boundaries and who, irrespective of their legal status, retain some or all of their own social, economic, cultural and political institutions.

Other important provisions include Article 8(1), (2), and (3):

In applying national laws and regulations to the peoples concerned, due regard shall be had to their customs or customary laws. These peoples shall have the right to retain their own customs and institutions, where these are not incompatible with fundamental rights defined by the national legal system and with internationally recognised human rights. Procedures shall be established, whenever necessary, to resolve conflicts which may arise in the application of this principle.

ARTICLE 23(1):

Handicrafts, rural and community-based industries, and subsistence economy and traditional activities of the peoples concerned, such as hunting, fishing, trapping and gathering, shall be recognised as important factors in the maintenance of their cultures and in their economic self-reliance and development. Governments shall, with the participation of these peoples and whenever appropriate, ensure that these activities are strengthened and promoted.

Also in 1989, at its twenty-fifth session, the General Conference of UNESCO adopted the Recommendation on the Safeguarding of Traditional Culture and Folklore.

Insofar as folklore constitutes manifestations of intellectual creativity, whether it be individual or collective, it deserves to be protected in a manner inspired by the protection provided for intellectual productions.

END OF THE MILLENNIUM

Toward the end of the millennium, the international community started searching for norms that would regulate professional ethics. Consequently, in June 1990, the Society for Economic Botany issued its Guidelines of Professional Ethics. These guidelines state that economic botanists are a diverse group with greatly varying scientific backgrounds and professional affiliations and that their ethical problems are both diverse and complex.

In 1990, during the administration of Jaime Paz Samora, Supreme Decree No. 22546 was promulgated to assist the first effort to recover Bolivian cultural objects (Coroma textiles) at the international level. This effort was undertaken by the Q'ipi Foundation, under the leadership of Cristina Bubba. The Foundation received funds from international organisations and based its efforts to recover a significant quantity of textiles that were more than thirty years old, with high-quality dyed fibres, on Bolivian legislation (for example, Supreme Decree No. 21951) and the UNESCO Convention. Within this framework, the government promulgated an extraordinary decree authorising the return of the textiles to their original communities, thus waiving the National Museum of Ethnography and Folklore's obligation to act as custodian.

On 11 July 1991, under pressure from the Bolivian Confederation of Indigenous Peoples (CIDOB), the government ratified ILO Convention 169 and enacted Law No. 1257, pursuant to Article 59(12) of the Bolivian Constitution.

In May 1992, in preparation for the 1992 Rio Summit, the World Conference of Indigenous Peoples on Territory, Environment and Development was held. Indigenous peoples from the Americas, Asia, Africa, Australia, Europe, and the Pacific participated in the Conference. They unanimously expressed their collective gratitude to the indigenous peoples of Brazil in the Kari-Oca Declaration, in which they stated, "We, the Indigenous Peoples, maintain our inherent rights to self-determination. We have always had the right to decide our own forms of government, to use our own ways to raise and educate our children, to our own cultural identity without interference."

They also issued the Indigenous Peoples Earth Charter, which outlines the following in its Section on Culture Science and Intellectual Property,

"86. The destruction of the culture has always been considered an internal, domestic problem within national states. The United Nations must set up a tribunal to review the cultural destruction of Indigenous Peoples....

88. The human remains and artifacts of Indigenous Peoples must be returned to their original peoples.

89. Our sacred and ceremonial sites should be protected and considered as the patrimony of Indigenous Peoples and humanity. The establishment of a set of legal and operational instruments at both national and international levels would guarantee this....

102. As creators and carriers of civilizations which have given and continue to share knowledge, experience and values with humanity, we require that our right to intellectual and cultural properties by guaranteed and that the mechanism for each implementation be in favour of our peoples, and studied in depth and implemented.

103. We should list the suspect museums and institutions that have misused our cultural and intellectual properties.

104. The protection, norms and mechanisms of artistic and artisan creation of our peoples must be established and implemented in order to avoid plunder, plagiarism, undue exposure and use....

106. In many instances, our songs, dances and ceremonies have been viewed as the only aspects of our lives. In some instances we have been asked to change a ceremony or a song to suit the occasion. This is racism....

108. All kinds of folkloric discrimination must be stopped and forbidden.

109. The United Nations should promote research into Indigenous knowledge and develop a network of Indigenous sciences."

In 1992, the UN Conference on Environment and Development, informally known as the Earth Summit or Rio '92, adopted the Convention on Biological Diversity,[1] which recognises,

"the close and traditional dependence of many indigenous and local communities embodying traditional lifestyles on biological resources . . ."

In June 1993, the Nine Tribes of Mataatua convened the First International Conference on the Cultural and Intellectual Property Rights of Indigenous Peoples. One hundred and fifty representatives from 14 countries attended. Japan, Australia, the Cook Islands, Fiji, India, Panama, Peru, the Philippines, Surinam, the United States, and New Zealand adopted the Mataatua Declaration. Its preamble reaffirms the United Nation's aim to "Adopt or strengthen appropriate policies and/or legal instruments that will protect indigenous intellectual and cultural property and the right to preserve customary and administrative systems and practices."

For Bolivia, 1994 was a very important year. A number of far-reaching reforms, including reforms to the Constitution, were implemented. As a result, Article 1 of the Constitution now states as follows:

Bolivia, a free, independent, sovereign, multi-ethnic and multicultural State, established as a unitary republic, adopts representative democracy as its form of government, built on the pillars of unity and solidarity among all Bolivians.

Other changes included the amendment of Article 171:

"The State recognises, respects and protects by law the social, economic and cultural rights of the indigenous peoples living in the national territory, particularly with regard to their communal lands of origin, guaranteeing their sustainable use of natural resources, their identity, values, languages, traditions and institutions.

The State recognises the legal personality of the indigenous and farming communities and farmers associations and unions.

The natural authorities of the indigenous and farming communities may exercise their own administrative regulations and alternative mechanisms of conflict resolution, in accordance with their traditions and procedures, in as much as they are not contrary to this Constitution and the law. The law shall make these functions and jurisdictions of the State compatible."

In April 1994, Law No. 1551 on Popular Participation was enacted. The Law's objectives are to recognise, promote, and consolidate the process of popular participation by integrating the indigenous, peasant, and urban communities into the country's legal, political, and economic life. The Law also strives to improve the quality of life for Bolivian men and women through the fairer distribution and better administration of public resources. The Law strengthens the necessary political and economic mechanisms to perfect representative democracy, facilitating popular participation and guaranteeing equal representation of men and women.

[1] See Part VII of this book, Bo Hammer Jensen, "Who Owns Traditional Knowledge: A Personal and Industry View." See also The Convention on Biological Diversity: <http://www.biodiv.org/>.

In order to attain these objectives, the Law:

(a) recognises the legal personality of the urban and rural grassroots territorial organisations and relates to them as public institutions;
(b) defines the territorial jurisdiction of the municipal governments as the section of a province. It also increases resources, expands the jurisdiction of the municipal governments and transfers responsibility for education, health care, and sports facilities, in addition to roads and micro-irrigation infrastructure, to the municipal governments for administration, maintenance, and renovation;
(c) establishes the principle of equal distribution per capita of the tax resources allocated to the departments through their municipalities and universities, thereby seeking to correct the existing historical unbalance between urban and rural areas; and
(d) reorganises the functions and competences of public institutions so that they can act in accordance with the legal framework of rights and obligations introduced by this Law.

Also in 1994, the UN Draft Declaration on the Rights of Indigenous Peoples was adopted. Its preamble states,

"Affirming that indigenous peoples are equal in dignity and rights to all other peoples, while recognising the right of all peoples to be different, to consider themselves different, and to be respected as such;

Affirming also that all peoples contribute to the diversity and richness of civilisations and cultures, which constitute the common heritage of humankind."

Other important provisions are the following:

ARTICLE 7:

Indigenous peoples have the collective and individual right not to be subjected to ethnocide and cultural genocide, including prevention of and redress for:

(a) Any action which has the aim or effect of depriving them of their integrity as distinct peoples, or of their cultural values or ethnic identities; . . .
(b) Any form of assimilation or integration by other cultures or ways of life imposed on them by legislative, administrative or other measures.

ARTICLE 12:

Indigenous peoples have the right to practice and revitalise their cultural traditions and customs. This includes the right to maintain, protect and develop the past, present and future manifestations of their cultures, such as archaeological and historical sites, artefacts, designs, ceremonies, technologies and visual and performing arts and literature, as well as the right to the restitution of cultural, intellectual, religious and spiritual property taken without their free and informed consent or in violation of their laws, traditions and customs.

ARTICLE 29:

Indigenous peoples are entitled to the recognition of the full ownership, control and protection of their cultural and intellectual property.

They have the right to special measures to control, develop and protect their sciences, technologies and cultural manifestations, including human and other genetic resources, seeds, medicines, knowledge of the properties of fauna and flora, oral traditions, literatures, designs and visual and performing arts.

In September 1995, implementation started on the Sucre Historical Sites Rehabilitation Plan for the purpose of preserving Sucre's urban architectural heritage, which has been declared cultural heritage of mankind by UNESCO. The plan took the Potosi Historical Sites Rehabilitation Plan (PRAHP) as model and was co-financed by the municipal government of Sucre, the prefecture of the department of Chuquisaca, and the Spanish Agency for International Cooperation. The first stage of the plan was to catalogue the city's historic centre, to make a socio-urban analysis of Sucre and its surrounding areas and to work on specific projects in the field of architectural and urban preservation. The plan was found to be in accordance with the Regulations on the Preservation of Sucre's Historic Centre. It is currently being implemented, together with a housing project to improve the quality of life in the preservation area and a tourist component.

In the 1990s, PRAHP became the model for all urban architectural preservation plans in Bolivia. It acquired several financial supporters, including such institutions as the Spanish Agency for International Cooperation, the municipal government of Potosi, and the Potosi Development Corporation (responsibility later taken over by the Prefecture of the Department of Potosi).

In July 1996, the Commission of the Andean Community introduced a regional measure on access and sharing of benefits, effective in Bolivia, Columbia, Ecuador, Peru, and Venezuela. Decision 391 introduces "The Common System on Access to Genetic Resources," which regulates "access to the genetic resources of the Member Countries and their derivatives." The goals of Decision 391 are to create the conditions for fair and equitable sharing of the benefits accruing from the access to genetic resources, to establish a basis for the recognition and appreciation of genetic resources, their derivatives, and related intangible components, particularly where indigenous, Afro-American, and local communities are involved.[2]

According to the Andean Common Law, Decision No. 391 has to be implemented by the member states at the national level.[3] Until now, however, the Decision has barely been operationalized within the member states. Only Bolivia has passed implementing regulations, but these have not yet been put into effect. Columbia and Venezuela have opted not to

[2] *Mogollón-Rojas*, "The Preservation of Local Biodiversity Inheritance and Indigenous People's Knowledge Proprietorship in the Venezuelan and Andean Community Legislation," Journal of World Intellectual Property, Col. 5, No. 4, July 2002, p. 540.

[3] *Gandarillas*, "The Impact of International Genetic Resources Policy on Developing Countries." Abstract for the XXVI International Horticultural Congress and Exhibition. Toronto, Canada, 11–17 August 2002 Available at <http://www.ihc2002.org/ihc2002/multi_day_symposia_S221_resume.htm>.

produce implementing regulation, but to apply Decision 391 directly.[4]

The regime covers genetic resources provided by Member Countries where they originate, and the genetic resources of migratory species found for natural reasons in the territory of the Member Countries. Like the CBD, Article 1 of Decision 391 defines genetic resources as "any biological material containing genetic information of actual or potential value." The country of origin is denied as the country that possesses "the genetic resources in *in situ* conditions."[5]

The Andean Community's Common System sets out the details of a process to permit the access to genetic resources, requiring public notification, the participation of nationals in research, support for conservation and sustainable use, technology transfer, scientific reporting requirements, and the deposit of voucher specimens. It obliges applicants seeking access to obtain the prior informed consent of, and to share benefits with both the Competent National Authority and indigenous, Afro-American, and local communities.

Decision 391 states that any rights beyond its "Complementary Measures," including intellectual property rights, to genetic resources, derivatives, synthesized products, or related intangible components obtained or developed through noncompliance with the Common Access System, shall not be recognized by the Member States of the Community.

In the Andean Community Decision, provisions of the Trade Related Aspects of Intellectual Property Rights (TRIPS) Agreement have been subordinated to the CBD.[6]

On 3–9 August 1996, the representatives of the organisations of indigenous peoples that make up the original Abya Yala nations (America) came together in Copenhagen to discuss their reality, vision, and culture in order to share experiences, initiate a dialogue, and present proposals to the European Community. They also issued the Copenhagen Declaration.

In February 1997, the Proposed American Declaration on the Rights of Indigenous Peoples was issued. Article VII(1) and (2) states,

> Indigenous peoples have the right to their cultural integrity, and their historical and archaeological heritage, which are important both for their survival as well as for the identity of their members.
>
> Indigenous peoples are entitled to restitution in respect of the property of which they have been dispossessed, and where that is not possible, compensation on a basis not less favourable than the standard of international law.

With regard to archaeology in Bolivia, Ministerial Resolution No. 082/97 (Regulations on Excavations) was issued on 3 June 1997. Article 1 states that no individual person or institution may undertake prospecting, excavation, or archaeological restoration in Bolivia without formal authorisation provided by the National Directorate of Archaeology and Anthropology (DINAAR).

On 30 July 1997, Secretarial Resolution No. 054/97 (Basic Regulations for Anthropological Research) was issued. The Regulations were to be enforced by DINAAR. One of the Resolution's main provisions institutes the obligation for institutions that are in charge of a particular research project to enter into an agreement with the people or community where the research is to take place, thereby allowing the local people the opportunity to clearly express their expectations regarding said research.

On 22–24 September 1997, a regional seminar on the application of the UNESCO Recommendation on the Safeguarding of Traditional Culture and Folklore in Latin America and the Caribbean took place in Mexico, after which the following recommendations were issued to UNESCO and the member states:

- to form a Regional Centre on Latin American and Caribbean Traditional Culture and Folklore, with a central office and three regional offices;
- to hold a meeting of cultural authorities in the region to prioritise traditional culture and folklore within the framework of their cultural policies in Oruro (Bolivia) in 1998;
- to create training workshops for promoters of folklore and an annual prize for individual or collective creators of traditional culture;
- to declare regional Creole languages of African origin part of the intangible cultural heritage of humanity and Bolivia's Oruro carnival an intangible cultural heritage site;
- to highlight the significance of legislation for the more effective protection of traditional culture and folklore;
- UNESCO should urge member states to allocate sufficient budgetary resources to carry out projects related to traditional culture and folklore.

In March 1998, the federal government of Mexico drafted an Initiative for Constitutional Reform on Indian Rights and Culture and submitted it to the Mexican Congress for approval. This proposal recognises indigenous peoples' right to the preservation and free development of their culture and the right to be accorded the full respect they deserve. It supports indigenous education with direct community involvement because education is the most powerful and effective instrument to achieve true equality. It recognises the indigenous communities' right to select their own forms of social organisation, with full internal liberties, insofar as they respect other free and legitimate forms of internal organisation of a state governed by the rule of law. The proposal establishes conditions for recognising indigenous traditions and customs, and strengthens regulations and actions to ensure

[4] *Mogollón-Rojas* (fn. 1), 539; *Seiler & Dutfield*, Regulating Access and Sharing of Benefits: Basic Issues, Legal Instruments, Policy Proposals; Doc. UNEP/CBD/WG-ABS/1/INF/4, p. 63 (fn. 261), p. 74.

[5] CBD, Access to Genetic Resources – Note by the Executive Secretary, Third Conference of the Parties, Buenos Aires 1996, Do. UNEP/CBD/COP/3/20, 5 October 1996, para. 36.

[6] *Dutfield*, IUCN – The World Conservation Union. Background paper for the intersessional meeting on the operations on the convention. Montreal, Canada, 28–30 June 1999, p. 69.

effective access to the national authorities, with special attention to the respect of human rights and women's rights.

Also in 1998, in Stockholm, the Intergovernmental Conference on Cultural Policies for Development issued an Action Plan on Cultural Policies for Development, which recommended that states adopt the following five policy objectives:

1. to make cultural policy one of the key components of development strategy;
2. to promote creativity and participation in cultural life;
3. to reinforce policy and practice to safeguard and enhance tangible and intangible, moveable and immoveable cultural heritage and to promote cultural industries;
4. to promote cultural and linguistic diversity in and for information society; and
5. to make more human and financial resources available for cultural development.

In August 1998, the Mexican state of Quintana Roo enacted the Quintana Roo Law of Indigenous Rights, Culture and Organisation, which recognises, preserves, and defends indigenous peoples' rights to improved social welfare and economic benefit and to their culture. In Chapter II, the Law established that indigenous peoples, whatever their nationality, shall be entitled to the protection of their rights, customs, practices, traditions, and language on entering the state of Quintana Roo.

On 3–5 December 1998, the First National Workshop-Seminar on the Protection and Rights of Traditional Culture and Folklore was held in Bolivia. The basic text of the Workshop states that, until today, the concept of cultural heritage protection has been limited to tangibles. However, when one speaks of intangible cultural heritage protection, one refers to safeguarding traditional culture and folklore, as defined by UNESCO:

> the totality of tradition-based creations of a cultural community, expressed by a group or individuals and recognised as reflecting the expectations of a community in so far as they reflect its cultural and social identity; . . .

The main objective of the aforementioned meeting was to define Bolivia's position on the protection of traditional culture and folklore in order to convene a Meeting of Latin American and Caribbean Cultural Authorities on the Protection of Traditional Culture and Folklore in Oruro in 1999.

The Workshop prepared and published a document, entitled Legal Protection of Traditional Culture and Folklore in Bolivia, that analyses and compares legislation in the field of intangible heritage protection. In its Conclusions and Recommendations, this final document included some specific legal recommendations:

- adoption of the 1989 UNESCO Recommendation for Safeguarding Traditional Culture and Folklore's definition of traditional culture and folklore;
- expansion of the period in which authors' rights are protected from fifty to seventy years after the death of an author in Law No. 1322 on Authors' Rights;
- replacement of the percentages established by Article 62 of Law No. 1322 with fifty percent for the originating community, twenty-five percent for the compiler, and two percent for the state;
- inclusion of the UNESCO definition of traditional culture and folklore in Article 5 of Law No. 1322;
- amendment and expansion of penal sanctions in Law No. 1322;
- treatment of the transgression of authors' rights as crimes against the public order;
- observance of the intellectual property rights established in TRIPs Agreement;
- amendment of Supreme Decree No. 23907 of 7 December 1994 in all relevant areas; and
- establishment of regulations on the tourist, scientific, cultural, and other uses of works and expressions of traditional culture and folklore.

On 11 December 1998, Bolivia and Mexico signed a General Collaboration Agreement on Archaeological, Anthropological, Cultural Heritage Protection and Conservation Issues. This Agreement aims to foster the necessary exchange of technical, academic, and legal information between the governments for the detection and restitution of archaeological, historical, and cultural property illicitly exported from Bolivia and Mexico. Both governments commit to adopting the necessary measures, in accordance with their own national legislation and pursuant to international treaties to which they are party, to stop the import, export, and transfer of illicitly acquired property that is part of their cultural heritage, be it archaeological or historical property.

On 14 December 1998, Bolivia and Peru signed an Agreement for Recovery of Cultural Property and other Stolen, Illegally Imported, or Exported Goods in order to establish common regulations to recover stolen, illicitly exported, or transferred cultural property.

Also in December 1998, CIDOB, CPESC and CABI published a set of recommendations, entitled Towards National Regulations for the Protection of the Traditional Knowledge of Indigenous Peoples of the Lowlands in Bolivia. This document asserts, *inter alia*, that indigenous cultural heritage is not currently protected by law in Bolivia. Current intellectual property laws do not encompass the cultural rights of indigenous peoples, and current legislation does not respond to the specific needs of indigenous peoples.

The document's final recommendations with regard to national policy are:

- a legal mediating structure, the main task of which shall be to protect knowledge beyond the existing system through the establishment of a knowledge registry;
- a legal structure to provide further protection under existing national regulations and legislation by making the current system more flexible; and

- a national policy to oversee the improvement of the enforcement of international legislation and regulations to be implemented by the Bolivian government.

The document's recommendations for the protection of indigenous cultural heritage are:

- The establishment of a knowledge registry. The idea was discussed at the workshops organised by the project. Debate centred on three issues:
  a. What should be registered: (1) verbal expressions, (2) musical expressions and dances, (3) works of art, and (4) traditional medicine.
  b. The seat of the registry: CIDOB.
  c. Access to the registry: restricted, with open access under certain circumstances.
- Protection of cultural heritage through the existing intellectual property system. Specific objectives with regard to the national protection of cultural heritage include:
  - demanding that the Bolivian government implement policies, strategies and legislation,
  - creating a support fund for culture and communication,
  - creating an archive of traditional knowledge,
  - elaborating a body of laws to protect and revitalise cultures and their:
    a. material property (objects) and intangible heritage (knowledge, practices and innovations),
    b. collective intellectual property rights,
    c. territories and natural resources,
    d. human resources and economies,
    e. collective and individual rights, and
    f. a code of ethics.

The strategy for achieving these objectives involves:

- creating a ministry of cultures and social communication,
- implementing the policies proposed by the National Cultures and Communication Council,
- creating an international network of communication,
- supervising the protection of indigenous cultural heritage,
- undertaking studies to identify the nature and scope of indigenous peoples' rights in relation to their traditional knowledge,
- collecting data on traditional knowledge to identify practices and innovations, and
- stimulating national policies to protect and promote indigenous intellectual property rights.

Specific actions include:

- encouraging academic institutions and nongovernmental organisations working as research centres to develop their activities in accordance with truly ethical conduct,
- managing the incorporation of provisions that mandate respect for all indigenous intellectual property in international cooperation accords,
- identifying all sacred and ceremonial indigenous sites for their protection, forbidding unauthorised access,
- fostering informed buyers who can prove that objects have been purchased licitly, and
- encouraging the state to support the development of educational, research, and training centres that are under indigenous authority and which strengthen the capacity of indigenous peoples to document, protect, teach, and apply all aspects of indigenous cultural heritage.

With regard to international protection, the document recommends international follow-up on the following issues:

- WIPO should establish an annual roundtable to facilitate the sharing of opinions and information with regard to protection of knowledge, innovations and practices of indigenous peoples.
- UNESCO should draft an annual report on the status of the protection of indigenous heritage worldwide.
- UNESCO should organise a technical conference to identify the methodology to be used in compiling and assessing information for future UNESCO reports.
- The United Nations should assign a member of the Working Group on Indigenous Populations a permanent mandate to exchange data with all sectors of the UN system on indigenous heritage.
- The United Nations should study the possibility of drafting a convention establishing international jurisdiction over overseas indigenous heritage recovery before the end of the International Decade of the World's Indigenous Peoples.
- A permanent forum within the UN system should oversee all issues dealing with indigenous cultural heritage protection.

At the end of 1998, the Lower Chamber of Bolivia's Congress convened a workshop to analyse a Draft Law for the Promotion and Regularisation of Artisanry. As is the case with many Bolivian laws, the main problem with this document was its disregard for originating communities and indigenous peoples. In addition, it did not offer a concept of artisanry, nor did it specify its possible scope. However, the Draft Law does touch upon the economic welfare of artisans through tax-reduction incentives, considering it a clear economic and commercial issue.

On 4 March 1999, Bolivia ratified the UNIDROIT Convention on Stolen or Illegally Exported Cultural Objects, which was adopted in Rome on 24 June 1995.

On 18 May 1999, International Museum Day, ICOM-Bolivia officially issued its Code of Professional Ethics, which regulates the performance and conduct of professional museum staff.

On 25 May 1999, in Cartagena de Indias (Colombia), the Andean Council of Foreign Ministers adopted Decision No. 460 on the Protection and Recovery of Cultural Artefacts of the Andean Community's Archaeological, Historical, Palaeontological and Artistic Heritage. This Decision is intended to promote common policies and regulations for the identification, registration, protection, conservation, oversight, and restitution of objects that are part of the cultural heritage of the Andean community of nations, and to design and implement measures aimed at stopping the illegal import, export, and transfer of such objects between the member states and third parties. The signatories take upon themselves:

a. the elaboration of laws and regulations allowing the protection of cultural heritage and, especially, the repression of illicit cultural heritage trade;
b. the establishment and updating of a list of the most important public and private cultural objects, the export of which would qualify as considerable impoverishment of the countries' cultural heritage;
c. the implementation of educational programmes aimed at stimulating and developing respect for all countries' cultural heritage; and
d. the effective dissemination among the member states of the Andean community of information regarding each case of cultural object disappearance or theft.

In June 1999, a consultant's report on the Preliminary Draft Intellectual Property Code was submitted for review to Bolivia's Ministry of Justice and Human Rights. This document adopts and defines the protection of traditional culture, folklore and artisanry, in accordance with the aforementioned definition from the UNESCO Recommendation on the Safeguarding of Traditional Culture and Folklore, adopted in 1989. According to the Draft Intellectual Property Code, community rights are protected in accordance with the UNESCO Convention, the UNIDROIT Convention, and WIPO's Model Provisions For National Laws on the Protection of Expressions of Folklore against Illicit Exploitation and Other Prejudicial Actions. With regard to proposed legislation, expressions of folklore, as defined in the report and to the extent of their utilisation as literary and artistic works, shall be considered as belonging to the national heritage, without prejudice to the protection regulations that may be adopted by other state agencies or through international agreements. It is mandatory to mention the origin of such works and, if at all possible, a clear reference to their community of origin. Law No. 1322 is partially modified in this regard. Expressions of artisanry and artisan designs shall be protected by the general regulations, especially those dealing with fine arts and national heritage. Law No. 1322 is not modified in this regard.

On 26 July 1999, Bolivia and Brazil signed an Agreement on the Repatriation of Stolen or Illicitly Imported or Exported Cultural Heritage Property and Others. According to this Agreement, each country is bound to prohibit and prevent the entry – into their respective territories – of cultural property that belongs to the other country and does not bear an explicit export authorisation.

At the end of August 1999, the Bolivian government officially submitted its Request for US Import Restrictions to Protect Bolivian Cultural Heritage to the US government in accordance with the UNESCO Convention. Under this Convention, the illegal import and export of cultural property is prohibited. The request was submitted in Spanish and English and contained information on cultures in Bolivia and archaeological and ethnographic objects for which Bolivia seeks protection, legal steps, and strategic actions taken by the Bolivia to protect its cultural heritage, illegal trafficking of Bolivian cultural heritage and the benefits of import restrictions, in addition to a bibliography and 20 annexes. A bilateral Letter of Understanding between the United States and Bolivia was approved by the US Congress and was signed at the end of 2001 in Washington.

In May 2001, UNESCO issued a declaration classifying the Carnival of Oruro as intangible cultural heritage of mankind. In addition, the Bolivian government has recently been working on the adoption of a bilateral agreement with Ecuador. Finally, a new Law on Bolivian Cultural Heritage is under discussion.

In December 2001, the United States and Bolivia entered into a memorandum of understanding pursuant to UNESCO and the Cultural Property Implementation Act.[7]

The first Ministerial Meeting on Cultural Diversity was held in Cartagena, Colombia, in July of 2002. The Cartagena Declaration and Plan of Action,[8] adopted on 13 July 2002, demonstrated the significance of cultural diversity to all member states of the Americas. Countries as diverse as Canada, Brazil, Antigua and Barbuda, the United States, and Mexico, agreed that greater inter-American cooperation was needed in order to preserve and promote the cultural diversity of the Americas.

EDITOR'S NOTE

Decision 391 was intended as an instrument to regulate the access to genetic resources and to help guarantee the conservation, sustainable use, and equitable distribution of the benefits derived from those resources. Nevertheless, the implementation of Decision 391 has seemingly been problematic and had the effect of hindering foreign and even most domestic access to Andean genetic resources, rather than promoting it.

This has resulted in a reduction in both national and international projects promoting research, conservation, and

[7] The "Memorandum of Understanding Between the Government of the United States of America and the Government of the Republic of Bolivia Concerning the Imposition of Import Restrictions on Archaeological Material from the Precolumbian Cultures and Certain Ethnological Material from the Colonial and Republican Periods of Bolivia" may be found on the internet in both Spanish and English at <http://exchanges.state.gov/culprop/bl01agr.html>.

[8] See The Cartagena Decalaration and Plan of Action at <http://www.forumunesco.upv.es/eng/red_forum/unesco_resoluciones/doc/1998cartagena_eng.pdf>.

use of Andean plant genetic resources, which seems to be contrary to what the Member States originally intended. To address the problems arising from overrestrictive legislation, the Andean countries are now seeking ways to implement Decision 391, not least with a view to the ratification of the International Treaty on Plant Genetic Resources. The goal will be to develop a mechanism that facilitates regulated and international access and exchange of genetic resources instead of complicating any measures of bioprospecting.*

* See: *Hanneman M.*, "Genetic Resources." In Silke von Lewinski (ed.), *Indigenous Heritage and Intellectual Property: Genetic Resources, Traditional Knowledge and Folklore*, Kluwer Law International, 2004.

CHAPTER SIXTEEN

Illicit Traffic in Cultural Heritage in the Southern Cone: A Case Study Based on the Paraguayan Experience

Oscar Centurion Frontanilla

CONVENTIONS, AGREEMENTS, AND SPECIAL LAWS

The 1970 UNESCO Convention on the Means of Prohibiting and Preventing the Illicit Import, Export and Transfer of Ownership Cultural of Property provided a basis for the consideration of the illicit traffic in cultural property by several countries that until then had not given the issue due attention. In the Southern Cone region, Argentina and Brazil were the first countries to ratify the Convention in 1973. Bolivia subsequently ratified the Convention in 1976, Uruguay did so in 1977 and, Paraguay in 2004 (November, 11). Peru's Acceptance dated 1979. As of 17 January 2005, Chile did not appear on the list of 106 states parties to the Convention. "The Convention entered into force on 24 April 1972. It subsequently entered into force for each State three months after the date of deposit of that State's instrument, except in cases of notifications of succession, where the entry into force occurred on the date on which the State assumed responsibility for conducting its international relations" (<http://erc.unesco.org/cp/convention.asp?KO=13039&language=E>).

In Paraguay, the protection of cultural heritage did not receive special treatment until the 1980s. This contrasts with the attitude of its neighbors, Brazil, Argentina, and Bolivia, which began to adopt special laws and establish specialized offices at government level in the 1930s and 1940s.

Law No. 946 on the Protection of Cultural Heritage was adopted in 1982, although the agency charged with the application of the law, the General Directorship for Cultural Heritage, a department within the Ministry of Education and Culture, was not officially or effectively established until 1992. In 1986, the National Congress approved and ratified the 1972 UNESCO Convention concerning the Protection of the World Cultural and Natural Heritage by means of Law No. 1231. The 1992 Constitution specifically refers to the issue of cultural heritage in Article 81.

In 1989, Paraguay began its transition toward democracy. The authorities began to introduce structures for dealing with cultural matters, and, in the context of new public freedoms, society was able to organize itself into various nongovernmental associations, some of which were devoted to the protection of Paraguay's movable and immovable cultural heritage, including sites and monuments. These associations existed at the national level or were affiliated to international organizations related to UNESCO, such as the International Council of Museums (ICOM) and the International Council on Monuments and Sites (ICOMOS).

A significant advance in the area of cultural heritage protection was achieved in 1995, with the signing of the UNIDROIT Convention on Stolen or Illegally Exported Cultural Objects in Rome. Together with Peru and Bolivia, Paraguay became one of the first three countries in the region to sign the Convention. Paraguay was the first to ratify in 1997, followed by Peru in 1998 and Bolivia in 1999. In addition, Brazil acceded to the Convention in 1999, and Argentina did so in 2001. As of 15 May 2005, according to the Convention's Status Report, Chile and Uruguay were not among the states that had signed (22), ratified (11), or acceded (12) to the Convention (Ecuador acceded to the Convention in 1997; El Salvador, in 1999; Guatemala, in 2003 and Venezuela in April 2005. No other countries from the Americas – Central America, the Caribbean, and North America – appear in the Status Report).

"The Convention entered into force on 1.VII.1998 _among other countries_ between Ecuador and, Paraguay, on 1.IX.1998 for Peru, on 1.XI.1998, on 1.IX.1999 for Brazil, on 1.X.1999 for Bolivia, on 1.I.2000 for El Salvador, on 1.II.2002 for Argentina, and on 1.III.2004 for Guatemala" (<http://www.unidroit.org/english/implement/i-95.htm>).

In spite of this indifferent behavior of some countries in the Southern Cone and other regions, namely, the Andean region, Central America, and the Caribbean, there are some positive signs, and it is possible to speak of a process to combat the illicit traffic in cultural property, starting with a specialized workshop in Cuenca (Ecuador) and the 1995 UNIDROIT Convention. This process was and continues to be promoted and supported by several national committees of ICOM, the local offices of UNESCO, Interpol, and the World Customs Organization. The General Secretariat of ICOM has drafted cooperation agreements and established a working group with these entities.

The process is strongly supported by the national committees of ICOMSUR, a regional branch of ICOM for the country members of MERCOSUR: Argentina, Brazil, Paraguay, and Uruguay (and countries associated to MERCOSUR: Bolivia, Chile, and Peru) and by the national committees of the Andean region, Central America, and the Caribbean, which belong to the regional branch of ICOM for Latin America and the Caribbean (ICOMLAC).

With reference to other chief international instruments on cultural heritage protection and illicit trade:

- Brazil (in 1958) and Uruguay (in 1999) have ratified the Convention for the Protection of Cultural Property in the Event of Armed Conflict (The Hague, 1954). Argentina and Peru acceded to it in 1989 and Paraguay and Bolivia, in November 2004.

All the MERCOSUR country members and associates have signed the 1972 UNESCO's Convention concerning the Protection of the World Cultural and Natural Heritage (Deposit of Ratification: Bolivia, 1976; Peru, 1982; Paraguay, 1988; or Acceptance: Brazil, 1977; Argentina, 1978; Chile, 1980; Uruguay, 1989).

- Panama is the first and only country of the Americas to have signed (deposit of Ratification), in 2003, the 2001 UNESCO's Convention on the Protection of the Underwater Cultural Heritage (Paris, 2 November 2001).
- Peru (in 1979), Argentina (in 2002), and Bolivia and Chile (in 2003) have signed the Convention on the Protection of the Archeological, Historical, and Artistic Heritage of the American Nations (Convention of El Salvador/ Organization of American States).

CAMPAIGNS AND MEETINGS

Within the framework of ICOM's international campaigns of 1997 and 1998, the Paraguayan National Committee of ICOM, like other national committees in the region, organized various meetings on the subject of the illicit traffic in cultural property and made contact with the local offices of Interpol, customs authorities, and other relevant government agencies. These encounters were widely covered in the media, and several committed cultural institutions participated in them. Promotional materials, such as posters and videos, supplementing the important publications on the situation in Latin America, were also produced and sponsored by ICOM.[1]

As a result of these activities, certain works of art that appeared in the aforementioned publication were recovered, including two polychromatic sculptures from the eighteenth century belonging to the collection of the Franciscan Church and Museum of Caazapa. On the basis of this case, which drew attention to the issue and laid the foundations for firmer action in the future, the Paraguayan National Committee of ICOM was able to develop contacts and joint procedures with the local offices of Interpol and various other government agencies, such as customs authorities, port authorities, and the ministries of foreign relations and education and culture, as well as with lawyers' associations and (even) law classes at local universities.

In addition to the meeting that took place in Cuenca (Ecuador) in 1995, important specialized meetings were convened in various parts of the Americas in recent years, including La Paz (Bolivia) in 1998, Cuzco (Peru) in 1999, and Bogotá (Colombia) in 2000. Specialized panels were also developed within the framework of meetings held in San José (Costa Rica) (Summit of the Museums of the Americas) and Sucre (Bolivia) in 1998, in Asuncion (Paraguay) in 1999, and in Trujillo (Peru) and La Paz (Bolivia) in 2000, where situations and problems common to all the countries of the region – including tourism and the development of museums and sustainable communities – were analyzed. Among other things, these situations and problems concern shortcomings in laws and regulations for the protection of cultural property, as well as the poor conditions and security strategies of museums and other cultural institutions and of the system for the protection of cultural property in general.

In April 2002 (in Bogotá), another important workshop was jointly organized by the Colombian Ministry of Education and Culture and ICOM, where a group of 60 heritage and museum professionals from the Americas and Europe drew up a "Red List of Latin-American Objects at Risk" to help put a stop to the illicit trade in cultural property. This list contains 25 examples of specific pre-Columbian and Colonial heritage categories that are systematically looted throughout Latin America and are in great demand on the illegal antiquities market. All the categories of objects in the Red List are protected by legislation and banned from export, and may, under no circumstances, be imported or put on sale. The Red List is an appeal to museums, auction houses, art dealers, and collectors not to acquire these objects. The Red List is also designed to help customs officials, police officers, and art dealers to identify them (<http://icom.museum/redlist>). Pre-Columbian Ceramic Moche Vessels, Wood Ceremonial Beakers (Inca Keros), Sculptures Carved Oars, or Fabrics Paracas Textiles from Peru are specified in this Red List; also Colonial Polychrome Wood Religious Sculptures from the Guarani-Jesuit missions on the borders of Argentine, Brazil, Paraguay, and Uruguay (Ancient Jesuit Province of Paracuaria) or the Chiquitos and Moxos-Jesuit missions in Bolivia.

A significant advance in the MERCOSUR's region was achieved in March 2004, with the organization by the President of Argentina, through the Secretary of Culture (and the support of UNESCO) of a meeting/seminar on "Illicit Traffic of Cultural Property in the southern Cone," which was the first official event of this type in the region. All the MERCOSUR's country members and associated members participated. This meeting set up the basis for a common operation in the struggle against the illicit traffic in cultural property in the region and established the foundations for an eventual memorandum of understanding among these countries on this particular subject (to be formalized in the near future).

At the aforementioned meeting in Asuncion, particular attention was devoted to the museums and agencies that are in charge of promoting tourism and security since their activities relate to the effects of tourism on cultural property, be it furniture, other movables, or sites and monuments. As a result of the participation of the National Secretariat for Tourism in the organization of the event, it was possible to include prevention of illicit traffic in cultural property in the master plan to develop tourism. Another important achievement, made possible by the participation of the National Institute of

[1] See, for example, *One Hundred Missing Objects: Looting in Latin America.* Paris: ICOM, 1997.

Culture and ICOM-Peru, was the establishment of the principles for the conclusion of a bilateral agreement between Paraguay and Peru on the recovery and return of illegally exported cultural property, which was eventually concluded in March 2001. Likewise, as a result of the participation of the General Directorship for Cultural Heritage and ICOM-Bolivia, the foundations for a similar agreement between Paraguay and Bolivia was set up and projected to a final document signed in April, 2004.

CHANGE OF FOCUS

Triangular traffic is in the interest of certain countries, such as those of the Southern Cone, that do not produce drugs or weapons and lack cultural property that is highly sought on the international market. These countries can serve as channels for the triangular traffic of goods and products that are bought or stolen in other countries and subsequently redirected to countries where there is a market for such goods and products, such as the United States, Canada, and European countries.

The second issue affects most Latin American countries, which are confronted with an increase in illicit activities in frontier areas that are sometimes beyond their control. There are not many specialized studies on this topic, but there are numerous reports on the illicit traffic in stolen vehicles, for example, to mention just one of the more popular targets of these activities. The situation is similar or worse in other parts of the Americas, even in countries that have more sophisticated border control arrangements, such as the United States and Mexico. In fact, according to various publications and recent movies like "Traffic," "Bread and Roses," and "Sin dejar huella," substantial quantities of drugs and even human beings are smuggled into these countries.

Other commodities, such as cultural property, may be even easier to transport than stolen vehicles or truckloads of illegal drugs. Some might argue that this only happens in the movies, but it will become a reality if the situation does not change. In other words, the possibility and the danger will continue to exist until total, permanent control of frontier areas is achieved, regardless of whether or not there is legislation in this field.

CONCLUSIONS AND RECOMMENDATIONS

These speculations (or logical assumptions) concerning the traffic in cultural property are directly related to current concerns that go beyond legal and cultural aspects and oblige us to devote more attention to the problem and to find new ways to tackle it. Other factors may be related to the problem, and new perspectives are therefore required. Such perspectives suggest the formation of broad coalitions involving all sectors of society.

In an analysis of the preservation process with regard to historical urban preservation in Latin America and the Caribbean, Eduardo Rojas asserts that, among other things, this process "is more sustainable when all the social actors become involved in the process, which guarantees a wide social support for the preservation actions." At the same time, this also facilitates the implementation of "reform in the action methods."

Should we follow these recommendations, which focus on long-term results, or should we switch to strategies that focus on short and medium-term objectives? One measure that should definitely be adopted is the establishment of graphical databases and multilateral agreements covering not only the MERCOSUR region but all the regions of the Americas. Countries that have experience with regard to agreements and emergency measures concerning the import and export of cultural property, such as Bolivia, Peru, or the United States, could lead the way in the pursuit of these objectives.

We should also find ways to live with the problem while we are fighting it. This may be achieved by following the example of the medical and veterinary sciences, which operate on the premise that it is necessary to live as well as possible with an illness until the appropriate cure is discovered.

The (IBA) International Bar Association's Committee on Art, Cultural Institutions and Heritage Law Cultural Heritage Conference of 2001 (Cancun, Mexico) was particularly significant, because professionals that until then were working almost exclusively with museums, cultural institutions or agencies specialized in cultural matters are now cooperating with lawyers, jurists, and law makers.

The events of 11 September 2001 which immediately preceded the IBA conference provided a wake up call to the importance of joining forces and sharing responsibilities to combat not only the illicit traffic of cultural property but also other illegal activities which continue to be an active part of daily life in several regions of the Americas.

Largely because of deficiencies that are particularly nourished by inadequate resources, local law enforcement in the Americas has often been an unreliable force to guard the region's borders. The triangle traffic, previously referred to is a problem of weak infrastructure, lack of concerted regional cooperation, widespread poverty, and porous borders. The recent activities discussed in this chapter thus represent not only positive steps in the combating of illicit traffic in cultural property but may also serve to combat other global problems arising from similar causes, including global terrorism and drug trafficking.

NOTES

The author gratefully acknowledges the assistance and documentation provided by the Paraguayan Ministry of Foreign Affairs, the Centre for the Conservation of Cultural Property of Asunción, and the Embassy of Paraguay in Washington, DC. All the opinions contained are the author's and do not reflect the opinions of any of the aforementioned institutions.

CHAPTER SEVENTEEN

The Nigerian and African Experience on Looting and Trafficking in Cultural Objects

Folarin Shyllon

INTRODUCTION

It has been observed that collecting objects from foreign countries and cultures flourished during the Nineteenth Century, especially after European powers were more firmly in control in Africa and Asia. Colonialism coincided with the development of new academic disciplines such as anthropology and archaeology. The material evidence of the newly discovered cultures was studied, catalogued, and displayed in European museums to illustrate the greatness of the colonial empire. Sometimes they were exhibited along with the colonial subjects.

Even in late Twentieth Century, a museum in Spain went further in the "affaire du Negre emphaille." The episode concerned the body of an African which was taken from a desecrated grave in Bechuanaland (now Botswana) in 1830, stuffed, and put on exhibition at Musée Darder de Banyoles in Spain, in violation of the concept of "Rest in Peace" to be found in every culture. Show-cased during the Barcelona Olympics, it was deplored by the then Organisation of African Unity as an unacceptable violation of African dignity. The Secretary-General of the United Nations and the Director General of UNESCO were duly informed. The "stuffed Negro" was eventually withdrawn from display, but by that time postcards and small sculptured copies of the exhibit had gone on sale. In October 2000, a BBC World Service Radio current affairs programme reported the homecoming of the human remains to Botswana, where it was laid to "Rest in Peace."[1]

In this chapter, I propose to look at the Nigerian experience in particular and the experience in Sub-Saharan Africa in general as concerns looting and trafficking in cultural objects.

TWO INFAMOUS EXAMPLES OF THE LOOTING OF AFRICAN ART TREASURES: ETHIOPIA AND NIGERIA

An article in *The Economist* of 10 July 1999, captioned "Let's Have Our Treasure Back, Please," opened with following account of the plunder of Ethiopia's cultural treasures in 1868.

> It took 15 elephants and 200 mules to carry off the loot from Ethiopia's old capital, Magdala. The brutal sacking of the mountain-top city in 1868, Britain's revenge on Emperor Tewodros for taking the British consul and a few other Europeans hostage, razed the city to the ground.

The hostages were released unharmed but the battle turned into a massacre and treasure hunt. Tewodros committed suicide and British soldiers stripped his body naked for souvenirs. They carted off his library and the treasures from a Coptic Christian church nearby. For four pounds sterling, Richard Holmes, the British army's "archaeologist," acquired the crown of the Abun, the head of the Ethiopian church, and a solid gold chalice from a soldier who had looted them. The booty was collected and auctioned off near Magdala. Holmes bought 350 illuminated bibles and manuscripts for the British Museum. Other books went to the Royal Library at Windsor and libraries at Oxford and Cambridge. They are still there, though odd treasures have been returned – usually the less valuable ones – as gestures, whenever the British needed to court Ethiopia.[2]

The plunder of Benin by the British forces took place in 1897. In that year, a British expedition led by Consul James Phillips tried to reach Benin City in what is now Nigeria at a time when the King was performing the most important religious rite of the year. During this period, the King is not allowed contact with foreign elements, including persons. The expedition was advised accordingly, but Consul Phillips still tried to force his way through to the city. One of the King's aides, acting without the King's knowledge, caused seven out of nine members of the expedition to be killed. The British reaction was swift. The city was invaded and the palace, where some tens of thousands of works of art in wood, ivory, and bronze were kept, was looted and eventually burnt down. The King was banished. The thousands of art pieces were first removed to London as spoils of war, and subsequently were dispersed throughout the world.

Among the objects captured is an exquisitely crafted ivory pendant now at the British Museum. In 1977, Nigeria requested the loan of the ivory mask for a pan-African cultural festival centred in Lagos, which had chosen the mask as its emblem. The British Museum initially requested an insurance bond of two million pounds sterling for the mask, but then argued that it was too delicate to be moved from its carefully controlled environment. In the event, the mask was not lent, leading to controversy.[3]

[1] F. Shyllon, "The Recovery of Cultural Objects by African States through the UNESCO and UNIDROIT Conventions and the Role of Arbitration" *Uniform Law Review* (2000–2), p. 219, p. 223.

[2] *The Economist*, 10 July 1999, 53.

[3] F. Shyllon, "Cultural Heritage Legislation and Management in Nigeria" *International Journal of Cultural Property*, 5 (1996) 235.

A LACK OF LAWS

In 1938, seventeen magnificent bronze heads and one-half figures were found in Ife, south-west Nigeria during the digging of foundations for a house that was being built not far from the Afin (palace) of the Oni (King) of Ife. Photographs of some of the heads were published by E. H. Duckworth, the Inspector of Education in Nigeria, in the *Nigeria Magazine*, published in London in June 1938; and also by William Bascom in *The Illustrated London News* of 8 April 1939. In 1940, an editorial note in the *Nigeria Magazine* titled "The Bronze Heads of Ife" linked the finds to appeals that had been made in the journal for the provision of a museum in Nigeria, adding that "the case of the Ife bronze heads, several of which have unfortunately been allowed to leave the country, furnishes one of the strongest arguments in favour of museum facilities and the preservation within Nigeria of objects illustrating the indigenous culture of the country."

Two of the bronzes were moved to the United States, and a third found its way to London through Paris, and was purchased by the National Art Collection Fund, which presented it to the British Museum. Sir Kenneth Clark, the distinguished director of the National Gallery, London, had no doubt that the discoveries at Ife were not merely of cultural or ethnographic interest; "they are works of art of a very high order, and should be preserved as part of the world's artistic inheritance." In 1910, the need for a museum had been seriously discussed consequent upon the incursion of Leo Frobenius, the German explorer, into Ife. When Frobenius was prevented from exporting some Ife bronze heads, he asked whether the exportation of antiquities had been forbidden by law. An unequivocal answer could not be given. Following the dispersal of the Ife bronze heads, the Nigerian government hurriedly passed an Order in Council to control the export of antiquities. The 1938 order was replaced by another Order in Council in 1943, next by the Antiquities Act of 1953, and then, in 1979, by the National Commission for Museums and Monuments Act.[4]

ENFORCING THE LAW

In an advertisement in the *Daily Times* of 5 June 1962, the Antiquities Commission drew the laws of Nigeria relating to the export of antiquities to the attention of those interested in acquiring traditional works of art. It warned that no antiquity could be exported from the country without a permit issued by the Commission, adding that "the definition of an antiquity is so wide as to include almost all objects of traditional art." Any person attempting to export a valuable antiquity without a valid permit was liable "to detention at the Customs barrier, and to prosecution for an offence punishable by heavy fines and a prison sentence." Furthermore, the advertisement warned buyers of traditional art objects to make every effort to ensure that the objects they wished to buy had been acquired legally; one dealer had recently completed a two-and-a-half-year prison sentence in Lagos. Nonetheless, the *Daily Express* of 30 May 1964 raised the alarm that "the problem of the disappearance of valuable Nigerian carvings and objects of artistic value had become increasingly serious." It added that many of these objects were taken out by expatriates who, when leaving the country, "smuggle out antiquities in their baggage."

The same article further disclosed that at a recent meeting of the Antiquities Commission, various strategies had been mapped out to combat the disappearance of these objects. The meeting, which specifically discussed "the collection, sale and illegal exportation of Nigerian antiquities," and had been called in response to several notorious cases, such as those discussed subsequently, was attended by senior members of the Department of Antiquities, the Antiquities Commission, the universities, the Nigeria Police, the Customs Department, the Ministry of Justice, and other prominent figures concerned about the theft of antiquities. The meeting emphasised the concern felt with regard to the continued illegal export of Nigeria's cultural property; and subsequently an intensive programme to stamp out the illegal traffic.

The *Daily Times* of 20 December 1963 reported the trial of Aharon Boas, an Israeli who had been convicted for illegally exporting terracotta heads and carvings the previous day. Boas was found to have exported nine antiquities, which had been recovered from Canada, America, Paris, and Amsterdam. But he was only ordered to pay a fine of fifty pounds, or to go to jail for three months in default.

In 1964, the trial of Dr. Winfried Rathke, a German eye specialist formerly of the University teaching hospital at Ibadan, was reported in the *Daily Times* of 29 and 30 October 1964. He was charged with attempting to smuggle thirty works of art out of the country. Other works of art were also found in his baggage, but these were covered by a permit that had been issued by the Director of the Department of Antiquities. He was found guilty and fined twenty-five pounds or two months imprisonment in default.[5]

A LACK OF MUSEUMS

The absence of a national museum facilitated not only the exportation of antiquities but also the destruction or damage of those that were not lost. Duckworth reported in 1938 that, at Ife, valuable treasures had not the slightest protection and "bronze heads and terra-cottas have to be stored on the floor or on a windowsill. With constant handling, the delicate terracottas are naturally falling to pieces." He also mentioned that "a few years ago one of the shrines outside the town possessed a collection of about 40 terracotta heads. Now they have all been stolen or broken." Likewise, Kenneth Murray, the father of the Nigerian antiquities movement, in urging for the provision of a museum for the country, used Ife as an example. Ife, he said, had an unknown number of ancient works in bronze,

[4] F. Shyllon, "One Hundred Years of Looting of Nigerian Art Treasures 1897–1996" *Art Antiquity and Law*, 3 (1998) 253, 255–256.

[5] Ibid; 257–258.

terracotta, and stone. Some of them "rank in quality with the finest works of the Renaissance" yet "some are kept piled in a cracked glass case in the palace . . . but others are quietly removed from the country." However, it was not until 1952 that the Jos Museum, Nigeria's first museum was opened.

AN OPEN SEASON

In the 1960s and 1970s, the plundering of African cultural property assumed gigantic proportions. Michel Brent, who had devoted several years to covering the pillaging of terracotta statuettes from Mali, regretted that it was precisely "at the moment when the African peoples have begun to acquire their independence, during the 1960s and 1970s, and thus begun to hold their heads high, to hope for the future, that this clandestine traffic of antique objects developed and took on such huge proportions."[6] The relentless looting and illicit trafficking in the plastic arts of Africa continued to cause alarm in various concerned quarters.

In 1971, Ekpo Eyo, as Director of the then Antiquities Department of Nigeria, made the ominous forecast that "unless the theft of Nigerian collections was arrested nothing will be left of Nigerian antiquities in about ten years."[7] Twenty-five years later, Nigeria's Minister of Culture, while inaugurating an Inter-Ministerial Committee on the looting of Nigeria's cultural property on 23 July 1996, warned that "we are losing our cultural heritage at such an alarming rate that unless the trend is arrested soon we may have no cultural artefacts to bequeath to our progeny."[8] Also in 1996, Henry John Drewal urged that drastic steps be taken to curb the activities of those plundering Africa's past, otherwise Africa will soon have a "landscape barren of cultural heritage."[9]

INTERNATIONAL STANDARDS AND AFRICA'S SCEPTICISM

There seems to be a pervasive lack of confidence among African nations in the efficacy of such international standards as exists to combat illicit traffic in their cultural property. This perhaps stems from disappointments and lack of movement or progress on the restitution issue. Ekpo Eyo wrote with some bitterness about Nigeria's experience when the Benin Museum was about to open in 1968. Faced with the problem of finding exhibits that should be shown to reflect the position that Benin holds in the world of art history, a draft resolution was tabled at the General Assembly of ICOM, which met in France in 1968, appealing for donations of one or two pieces from those museums that have large stocks of Benin works "so that Benin might also be able to show its own works at least to its own people." The resolution was modified to make it read like a general appeal for restitution or return, and then adopted. The adopted resolution was circulated to the embassies and high commissions in Nigeria of countries known to have large Benin holdings, but "no reaction was received from any quarters and the Benin Museum stays 'empty.'" In the end, as Biobaku wrote in 1972, the government of Nigeria had to compete with other countries at auction rooms in Europe to buy back for fifty thousand pounds sterling all but one of the Benin bronzes then on display in the Benin gallery in the National Museum, Lagos.

Again, in 1980, the government of Nigeria "as a matter of national honour and interest" bought at Sotheby in London five Nigerian works of art at a total cost of eight hundred thousand pounds sterling. The items bought include an early Benin bronze head of an Oba, fourteenth century; a Benin bronze head of an Oba, nineteenth century; and a Benin plaque of a Warrior Chief with Retainers, circa 1600.[10]

The other reason for African cynicism is the negative outcome of efforts to recover through foreign courts various art treasures, which had been illicitly exported because of the complex issue of conflicts of laws or enforcement of foreign penal statutes. Success in the foreign courts for the recovery of cultural property is often achieved at the cost of massively expensive litigation.

PRE-UNIDROIT CONVENTION OPTIONS FOR RECOVERY OF CULTURAL PROPERTY

There were (and are) four options available to any country that sought the return of its cultural property prior to the adoption of the UNIDROIT Convention:

(a) *Litigation in Foreign Courts.* Any State is at liberty to seek redress in the courts of the country or domicile of a defendant who is alleged to have stolen or illegally removed its cultural property, whether or not the requesting State is a member of the 1970 UNESCO Convention on the Means of Prohibiting and Preventing the Illicit Import, Export and Transfer of Ownership of Cultural Property. This option is bedevilled by two intractable problems.[11] The first is that prosecution is often difficult with regard to stolen objects because of evidentiary problems. The second difficulty relates to unlawfully exported objects in breach of export control and the widespread rejection or reluctance by foreign courts of legislative extraterritoriality, well exemplified in *Attorney-General of New Zealand v. Ortiz.*[12] In any case, few African countries can afford the expense involved in foreign litigation.

[6] M. Brent, "A View Inside the Illicit Trade in African Antiquities." In P. R. Schmidt and J. M. McIntosh (eds.) *Plundering Africa's Past.* (Bloomington and Indianapolis: University of Indiana Press, 1996) 63–78, 76.

[7] Nigerian *Daily Times*, 23 September 1971, p. 3.

[8] "Address by the Honourable Minister of Culture . . . At the Occasion of the Inaugural Meeting of the Inter-Ministerial Committee on the Looting of Nigeria's Cultural Property" 23 July 1966, Mimeograph.

[9] H. J. Drewal, "Past as Prologues: Empowering Africa's Cultural Institutions." In Schmidt and McIntosh, *Plundering Africa's Past*, 110–124, 116.

[10] Shyllon, (note 3 above), 249.

[11] J. A. R. Nafziger, "The New International Legal Framework for the Return, Restitution or Forfeiture of Cultural Property" *New York University Journal of International Law and Politics*, 15 (1983) 789, 794.

[12] *Weekly Law Reports* 2 [1982] 10; *Weekly Law Reports* 3 [1982] 570; *Weekly Law Reports*, 2 [1983] 809.

(b) *UNESCO Convention.* If the requesting State and the holding State are Parties to the Convention, then the requesting State can have recourse to the provisions of its Articles 3 and 7, but the object must be inventoried. As we shall see, African States still have some ground to cover in the area of systematic inventories of their cultural property collections. Furthermore, even where both States are States Parties to the Convention, it is not always easy to succeed, as is demonstrated in *R. v. Heller*,[13] in which the Government of Canada prosecuted a New York dealer who had imported into Canada a Nok terracotta sculpture illegally exported from Nigeria. Both Nigeria and Canada are Parties to the Convention. The prosecution failed on the technical ground that the Canadian statute implementing the Convention only applied to objects illegally exported after the entry into force of the Canadian legislation. Expert witnesses had been flown in from Nigeria, but despite the spirited effort of the Canadian Government, Nigeria could not recover the unlawfully exported cultural property. And that was in spite of the fact that the judge in the case accepted that Heller and his codefendant, Zango, knew before the import into Canada that the object had been illegally exported from Nigeria. Accordingly, African States that do not have the resources in any case to prosecute claims in foreign courts have ignored this option.

(c) *UNESCO Intergovernmental Committee.* In 1964, the General Conference of UNESCO, at its thirteenth session held in Paris, adopted the Recommendation on the Means of Prohibiting and Preventing the Illicit Export, Import and Transfer of Ownership of Cultural Property.[14] Another recommendation on the same theme was adopted at the twentieth session of the General Conference in 1978: Recommendation for the Protection of Movable Cultural Property.[15] The purpose of both Recommendations is to protect the national cultural heritage of States by countering the illicit operations that threaten it. It was, however, reaction within UNESCO to the UN General Assembly Resolution 3187 of 1973 that led to the establishment of the Intergovernmental Committee for Promoting the Return of Cultural Property to its Countries of Origin or its Restitution in Case of Illicit Appropriation in 1978 the "Intergovernmental Committee."[16] The Intergovernmental Committee held its first session at the UNESCO headquarters in Paris in 1980, and since then has met thirty times. The body, composed of twenty-two UNESCO member States,[17] is primarily a negotiating forum aimed at facilitating bilateral negotiations and agreements for the return or restitution of cultural property, particularly that resulting from colonisation and military occupation to its countries of origin either when all the legal means have failed or when bilateral negotiations have proved unsuccessful.

Surprisingly, African countries whose agitation at the UN General Assembly led to the establishment of the Intergovernmental Committee have made little use of the Committee's good offices in the recovery of their expropriated cultural property. It is only at the recently concluded thirteenth session of the Intergovernmental Committee meeting held at UNESCO's headquarters in Paris in February 2005, that Tanzania lodged a request with the IGC. This is sequel to Tanzania's request for the return of a Mankonde mask in the Babier-Mueller Museum in Switzerland. After negotiations among Tanzania, Interpol, and ICOM, the museum agreed to return the Makonde mask to Tanzania upon certain conditions, including the museum retaining ownership while the mask remains on permanent loan to the National Museum of Tanzania. This condition was unacceptable to both the Board of the National Museum of Tanzania and the Attorney General of Tanzania.

One explanation might be the difficulty of completing its Standard Form concerning Requests for Return or Restitution. But UNESCO assistance is always available to member States in this regard. It has been suggested that the lack of initiative is not because of lack of interest. "It is far more likely to be lack of resources, or a certain scepticism as to the likely effect of such initiatives in relation to the amount of work required."[17] African countries can point to the fact that Greece's request for the return of the Parthenon marbles, which goes back to 1984, remains unrequited. But Greece offers African countries an object lesson in determination and persistence, for it has never failed to raise the return of the marbles at all subsequent meetings of the Committee in spite of the regular negative British response. Indeed, the fourth Committee session convened at Athens and Delphi and the seventh in Athens, in 1985 and 1991, respectively, at the invitation of the Greek government. This leads us to say that the African inaction is attributable to lack of stamina for the necessary follow-up, as Salah Stetie has suggested.[18]

(d) *Bilateral Agreement.* In the context of bilateral negotiations, some outstanding examples of restitution have taken place since decolonisation. This includes the return of objects by Belgium to the Democratic Republic of Congo, by the Netherlands to Indonesia and by Australia and New Zealand to Papua New Guinea. It is noteworthy that countries that have achieved important return programmes have done so with the entire goodwill of the former holding States.

In the area of illicit trafficking in cultural property, both UNESCO and ICOM have been of great assistance to

[13] *Alberta Law Reports* (2d), 27 (1983) 346.

[14] UNESCO, *Conventions and Recommendations of UNESCO Concerning the Protection of the Cultural Heritage* Paris, UNESCO, 1985, 139–146.

[15] Ibid; 209–223.

[16] For accounts of how the Committee came into existence, see L. V. Prott and P. J. O'Keefe, *Law and the Cultural Heritage: Volume III – Movement.* Butterworths, London, 1989, 818–819.

[17] Ibid, 860.

[18] Ibid; 860.

developing countries in recovering stolen cultural property. The first step is to notify the international community of these thefts in co-operation with INTERPOL. To cite a famous example: In May 1987, UNESCO reported the theft of nine objects from the Jos National Museum in Nigeria. One of these objects, a fifteenth century Benin bronze head, was subsequently identified at an auction in Switzerland and returned.

In 1983, the U.S. Congress passed the Convention on Cultural Property Implementation Act to give effect to the 1970 UNESCO. The Act enables the President of the United States to enter into bilateral co-operation treaties pursuant to the UNESCO Convention Article 9 to apply import restrictions on cultural property from nations signatory to 1970 UNESCO, that request such co-operation from the United States. Mali is the only African nation to have requested such assistance. This exceptional measure was taken in the wake of the rampant pillaging of archaeological sites in the Niger River Valley. This is perhaps because of the fact that the then president of Mali was both a trained archeologist and a former president of ICOM. That Mali is the only African State that has entered into the special bilateral agreement with the United States, is a matter of surprise, since it is most evidently not the only African country troubled by the scourge of plundering of cultural property. Perhaps, there is a perception that such a requested to the U.S. may pose a highly technical and formidable challenge. This is incorrect. A State Party to UNESCO requesting bilateral assistance pursuant to Article 9 for import controls, may lodge such request on behalf of its government with the U.S. embassy, Deputy Ambassador or Head of Public Affairs. The Cultural Heritage Centre of the Bureau of Education and Cultural affairs of the U.S. State Department is quite willing to provide technical assistance to governments in preparing requests. Queries for assistance in preparing requests may be emailed to culprop@state.gov. Affrican states need only muster the initiative often lacking in matters of cultural property rescue.

Apart from Mali, six other countries – Burkina Faso, Cameroon, Chad, Ghana, Niger, and Nigeria – feature in the Red List with Nigeria listed in four out of eight categories identified. Given the pivotal position of the United States as an art importing nation, the lack of initiative on the part of African countries like Nigeria to take advantage of the U.S. scheme may be seen either as an illustration of the failure of African museum professionals to take measures to protect their cultural heritage or the lack of influence of such professionals in governmental decisions respecting the protection of cultural property.

It is not surprising, therefore, that at the Amsterdam Conference in October 1992 to discuss ways and means of protecting Africa's cultural heritage, some "Western experts demand[ed] that Africa first put its house in order."[19] The evidence adduced so far shows that the African States have not diligently pursued the options available to them for the protection of their cultural heritage. It is understandable if they stay away from litigation, but there is absolutely no excuse for not aggressively utilising the other options.

ARBITRATION OPTION UNDER THE UNIDROIT CONVENTION

The UNIDROIT Convention provides another option to the four discussed in the previous section for recovery of cultural property. Article 8(2) of the UNIDROIT Convention offers the avenue of arbitration for the recovery of stolen or illegally exported cultural objects. It provides that "[t]he parties may agree to submit the dispute to any court or other competent authority or to arbitration."[20] Arbitration is a civilized method of settling disputes, introducing, as it does, ideas of charity and fairness. Because an arbitral tribunal does not represent a national forum, it appears at first sight to be in a more neutral position than a national court to pronounce itself on a State claim that, among other issues, involves assessing issues of sovereignty and national cultural policy and law.

The Court of Arbitration for Cultural Property

Because uniform application of the UNIDROIT Convention will be crucial to its eventual success, it would be a good thing to have a specialised body devoted to arbitration of cultural property disputes, such as are already in existence for matters involving investment disputes, maritime claims, and, more recently, intellectual property disputes.[21] In course of time, such an institutional arbitration tribunal will be able to provide specialist services and cater to the special interests involved in cultural property disputes. Quite often, such disputes involve conflicting yet legitimate interests. It is suggested that such an institutional tribunal should operate under the aegis of either UNIDROIT or UNESCO; more probably the former because it already has a pool of lawyers versed in the complex legal and ethical issues that arise in the context of cultural property disputes. In this connection, the provision of Article 20 of the UNIDROIT Convention, which reads that the President of UNIDROIT "may at regular intervals, or at the request of five Contracting States, convene a special committee in order to review the practical operation of this Convention," could be used to facilitate the evolution of a Court of Arbitration for Cultural Property, as already exists in the field of sports law through the establishment of the Court of Arbitration for Sport.[22]

[19] H. M. Leyten, "African Museum Directors Want Protection of their Cultural Heritage: Conference on Illicit Trade in Cultural Heritage, Amsterdam (22–24 October 1997)," *International Journal of Cultural Property*, 7 (1998) 261, 264.

[20] E. Sidorsky, "The 1995 UNIDROIT Convention on Stolen or Illegally Exported Cultural Objects: The Role of Arbitration" *International Journal of Cultural Property*, 5 (1996) 19. Part X of this book discussed the arbitration and mediation of art and cultural property disputes in detail.

[21] G. Francis, The WIPO Arbitration Center," *Managing Intellectual Property* 4 (1994). WIPO is the World Intellectual Property Organisation in Geneva.

[22] At the Geneva Symposium on Resolution Methods for Art-Related Disputes, Gabrielle Kaufman, explained how what is being sought for cultural property had been achieved in the field of sports law through

Indeed, the same ideas lay behind the work of the Intergovernmental Committee for Promoting the Return of Cultural Property. As the representative of the Director-General said at the Committee's third session, "UNESCO's mission was to seek all ways and means to enable Member States to engage in fruitful dialogue on the basis of mutual respect and dignity and in a spirit of international solidarity. From such dialogue developed fruitful ideas."

The majority of African nations are among the world's poorest countries. Mali, for example, is one of the world's five poorest countries, and perhaps Africa's second in archaeological riches (after Egypt).[23] The option of litigation is therefore not a practical proposition for most African countries. The option of arbitration under the UNIDROIT Convention is an avenue that African countries should seize upon. It is therefore necessary for every African country to ratify the Convention to enable it to take advantage of the arbitration option. Only Gabon, however, among African nations has acceded to the UNIDROIT Convention with effect, from 12 May 2004.

The negative atmosphere concerning restitution points to a tactical error by postcolonial Africa. In the flush of independence, perhaps attention should have been focused more on the present-day illicit traffic of her cultural property which perpetuates, and in some cases even exceeds, the outflow of the past.

IMPORT CONTROL OF ILLEGALLY EXPORTED OBJECTS AND THE COROLLARY OF THE RED LIST

In 1998, ICOM, together with experts from Africa, Europe, and North America, drew up an inventory of African cultural objects that are the most endangered. This is known as the Red List, an instrument designed to create and heighten awareness of the problem. It contains a list of categories of African archaeological objects particularly at risk from looting and theft. These objects are protected by national legislation, banned from export, and may, under no circumstances, be put on sale. As Bator highlighted, import controls are somewhat less dependent than export controls on foolproof enforcement by border interdiction. "An illegally imported artefact continues to be contraband even though it penetrated the border, and if it later surfaces in a museum or collection, it can still be seized and repatriated."[24] Once objective criteria are in place, they would meet Bator's objection to a "blank check control" which was in the original "Secretariat" draft of the UNESCO Convention on the Means of Prohibiting and Preventing the Illicit Import, Export and Transfer of Ownership of Cultural Property. ICOM's Red List, it is submitted, provides such an objective criteria. Import controls would not, overnight, stop the illicit traffic in cultural objects but would do much toward its reduction. If progress cannot be made on the return of cultural property plundered during the colonial period, it would be double jeopardy to continue to allow passing of ownership after three years' possession of stolen objects. The rights of nations to their historical and cultural legacy must not continue to be sacrificed to rights of *bona fide* purchasers. The condonation of unjust enrichment should not be tolerated any longer in the comity of nations.

the establishment of CAS. See Q. Byrne-Sutton, "Resolution Methods for Art-Related Disputes," 7 (1998) Art-Law Centre, Geneva (17 October 1997) *International Journal of Cultural Property* (1998), 249, 255.

[23] S. McFadden, "Africa Plundered – How Collectors are Stealing the Art of a Continent", *The Bulletin – The News Weekly of the Capital of Europe*, 14 March 1996, 24 at 30.

[24] P. Bator, "An Essay on the International Trade in Art" *Stanford Law Review* 34 (1982), 275, 327; F. Shyllon, "International Standards for Cultural Heritage: An African Perspective" *Art Antiquity and Law* 5 (2000), 159, 165.

THE COROLLARY OF CITES AND THE COROLLARY OF THE CLANDESTINE NARCOTICS TRADE

An interesting comparison can be made for Africa and other Third World countries between the implementation of the Convention on International Trade in Endangered Species (CITES) of 1973 and the war against the clandestine narcotics trade. Indeed, there are many similarities between the art trade and the hard drugs trade. The art trade and the art market can be described as operating along illicit and mostly ignored paths, in the same way as clandestine narcotics traffic operates. And often the trade in cultural property is regarded as the most important trade after the drugs trade. It can be argued that although the West takes measures to combat the illicit drug trade, it has resisted the globalisation of measures to combat the illicit trade in cultural objects. Can it, therefore, be said that because the industrialised countries are the beneficiaries of the traffic in cultural objects, they are indifferent to the plight of Third World countries? Yet, in the case of Africa, illicit traffic in cultural objects constitutes as great a menace to its well-being as illicit trade in drugs. Its destructive effect on society is greater than the consumption of hard drugs, because it revives Africa's past emotional background of historical plundering and the negative outcome of efforts to recover stolen art treasures through foreign justice courts. Should we, therefore, not attach the same stigma to the illicit trade in cultural heritage as the entire civilized world does to the illicit trade in narcotics by prohibiting importation into all nations of the civilized world decontextualized cultural heritage objects?[25]

CULTURAL HERITAGE WELL-BEING INDEX AND AFRICA

Although there are no statistics or verifiable figures on cultural heritage management in black Africa, the massive literature on the subject indicate in an overwhelming manner that cultural heritage is an endangered species. If we look at five indicators:

(a) expenditure on sites,
(b) expenditure on museums,

[25] Shyllon, (note 10 above) 166–167.

(c) holdings of "art treasures which best represent their culture" or "irreplaceable masterpieces,"
(d) access to one's cultural treasures, and
(e) ability to taker care of cultural heritage objects

Africa will rank low in cultural heritage well-being. Impressionistic indicators abound. On expenditure and care of sites, Mturi,[26] Karoma,[27] and Kusimba,[28] in their contributions to *Plundering Africa's Past*, edited by Schmidt and McIntosh, exposed the deterioration, neglect, and destruction of archaeological and historical sites in Tanzania and Kenya. With regard to expenditure on museums, Gella, the former Director-General of Nigeria's Commission for Museums and Monuments, admitted that resources available to his establishment had become "very meagre."[29] When we come to holdings that "best represent their culture" and are "irreplaceable masterpieces," Benin objects provide an excellent illustration. Nigeria now holds the fifth largest collection after Berlin, London, Oxford, and New York. As we have seen, in 1977, Nigeria asked for the loan of the Benin ivory mask in the British Museum, earlier classified as "of extraordinary aesthetic quality" for a pan-African cultural festival in Lagos. It was not lent. The companion piece is at the Metropolitan Museum of Art, where it is "one of the Museum's prized possessions." Africa is denied access not only to her "irreplaceable masterpieces," but also hundreds and thousands of objects of importance. Dele Jegede summed up the situation when he wrote in *Plundering Africa's Past* that today, it is much easier to study African art in the West than it is to do so in Africa.[30] Yet, as Thurstan Shaw observed, original works of art are better studied and understood in the milieu that gave them birth.[31] It has been a fatal impact. As to Africa's ability to adequately take care of her cultural property, Africa remains the classic illustration of Bator's dictum that many countries rich in antiquities are far too poor otherwise to take adequate care of all of them.[32]

At the Amsterdam Conference on the Protection of African Cultural Heritage, some Western experts demanded that Africa should first put her house in order. African countries must indeed do so. Let us note, however, that even the richest countries, with state-of-the-art security, are seeing major thefts from the public museums and private collections as well as unauthorised digging at protected sites, doing irreparable damage to their archaeological heritage. Shaw has suggested that perhaps a more likely way of ensuring that cultural property is returned from richer nations to poorer and kept in satisfactory conditions of conservation and security, is that the rich cultural foundations should address themselves to the problem.

It is Bator's view that "[t]he Elgin Marbles are part of England's national patrimony."[33] If we also accept that most of the singular objects that African nations would choose to keep are in the West, which is refusing to contemplate the issue of significant loans or restitution, as suggested by Thurstan Shaw, then the retentive nationalists are not those African countries who seek to have access to their emigrated treasures, but the former colonisers who have granted independence but are refusing to let go what they now consider to be part of their patrimony. More than half a century ago, Kenneth Murray, the father of the museum movement in Nigeria, highlighted the anomaly in this thinking when he remarked that "the needs, indeed for a collection of Nigerian art in Europe cannot be as vital as the need for one in Nigeria. In Europe it would chiefly have academic purpose, but in Nigeria it is wanted for the cultural life of the country itself."[34]

Shaw has suggested a way out. We are accustomed to the idea of a "British School in Rome," a "British Institute" in Amman or East Africa, a "Cyprus American Research Institute," and so on. So why not a branch of the British Museum in Kumasi (Ghana), Benin (Nigeria), and other places? In order to overcome the legal difficulties, the objects in such extensions of the British Museum could be "on permanent loan."[35] There would be a dramatic rise in Africa's cultural heritage well-being.

Behind the criticisms of "retentive cultural nationalism" of source nations is the view that cultural objects can be possessed by all. Merryman has argued that the language of the preamble of the Convention for the Protection of Cultural Property in the Event of Armed Conflict 1954 is "a charter of cultural internationalism", because it talks of "damage to cultural property belonging to any people whatsoever means damage to the cultural heritage of all mankind."[36] This surely refers to ownership, and not international possession. Ownership and possession are two distinct legal concepts. Ownership connotes the right to exclusive enjoyment of a thing, whereas possession relates to physical detention. We cannot agree that the Benin ivory mask, by being on show at the British Museum, is in the possession of the international community. Yes, it is part of the "cultural heritage of all mankind"; that is, it is owned by all mankind. But who should

26 A. A. Mturi, "Whose Cultural Heritage? Conflicts and Contradictions in the Conservation of Historic Structures, Towns and Rock Art in Tanzania." In Schmidt and McIntosh, *Plundering Africa's Past*, 170–190.

27 N. J. Karoma, "The Deterioration and Destruction of Archaeological and Historical Sites in Tanzania." In Schmidt and McIntosh, *Plundering Africa's Past*, 191–200.

28 C. M Kusimba, "Kenya's Destruction of the Swahili Cultural Heritage" in Schmidt and McIntosh, *Plundering Africa's Past*, 201–224.

29 Y. Gella, "The Protection of Artistic and Cultural Property" Mimeograph. Paper given at Workshop on United Nations Model Treaty for the Prevention of Crimes that infringe on the Cultural Heritage of People in the form of Movable Property. Held at Coumayeur Mont Blanc, Aosta Valley, Italy, 25–27 June 1992.

30 D. Jegede, "Nigerian Art as Endangered Species." In Schmidt and McIntosh, *Plundering Africa's Past*, 125–142; 139.

31 T. Shaw, "Whose Heritage?", *Museum*, 149 (1986) 46–48, 48.

32 Bator, (note 12 above), 298.

33 Bator, (note 12 above), 303.

34 K. C. Murray, "Art in Nigeria: Need for a Museum" *Journal of the Royal African Society* XLI (1942), 241.

35 Shaw, (note 18 above), 47–48.

36 J. H. Merryman, "The Retention of Cultural Property," *U. Cal Davis L.R.* 21 (1988) 477; J. H. Merryman, "Two Ways of Thinking About Cultural Property" *American Journal of International Law*, 80 (1986) 831–853, 835–836.

have possession of it? The people to whom it matters most or those who merely enjoy its extraordinary aesthetic quality? It is more than nationalism to want to possess what symbolizes your very essence. Greenfield has observed that although cultural treasures may generate universal inspiration and appreciation, they are not universally created, nor can there be international possession.[37]

[37] J. Greenfield, *The Return of Cultural Treasures.* (Cambridge: Cambridge University Press, 2nd ed, 1966), 309.

CHAPTER EIGHTEEN

The Protection of Cultural Heritage Items in New Zealand

Sir Ian Barker

INTRODUCTION

It may be helpful in the debate about the resolution of art and cultural heritage disputes to set out the position of one small country that has many items of cultural heritage and that might be considered a "source nation" for such items.

New Zealand's short history of settlement goes back no more than about 1200 years, when its first inhabitants are thought to have arrived. European settlement is only of some 200 years' duration. Consequently, New Zealand does not have paintings that have been in existence for centuries. New Zealand does have a wide variety of cultural treasures (or *taonga* in the Maori language), some of which are centuries old. New Zealand is aware of the need to protect its antiquities and artifacts, especially those of significance to the indigenous Maori people and to the nation's history of settlement.

New Zealand cultural items – particularly Maori cultural items – attract international interest and demand. They are susceptible to illegal export. Heritage items from early European settlement – items as diverse as traction engines and classic yachts – also attract international attention.

New Zealand is a likely transit state for objects illegally stolen and exported from Pacific states. The citizens of many Pacific states share a Polynesian heritage with New Zealand Maori. Papers presented to a New Zealand Parliamentary Committee by the New Zealand Department of Cultural Heritage record the suspicion that heritage items from Pacific states have entered New Zealand under false identification so as to disguise their heritage value or to hide the circumstances of their export. New Zealand might then be identified as the country of origin on the import certification of destination states, thus disguising the true country of origin, which could be a country vulnerable to illicit trade. Many Pacific states have a small population and limited financial resources. Their ability to police illegal dealings with artifacts is not great.

CURRENT NEW ZEALAND LEGISLATION

Legislation aimed at protecting New Zealand's cultural heritage has its current expression in the Antiquities Act 1975 ("the Act"), which defines "antiquities" and "artifacts" as follows:

Antiquity means –

(a) Any chattel of any kind whatsoever, not being a chattel to which any of paragraphs (b) to (h) of this definition applies, which –
  (i) Is of national, historical, scientific, or artistic importance; and
  (ii) Relates to the European discovery, settlement, or development of New Zealand; and
  (iii) Is, or appears to be, more than 60 years old:

(b) Any artifact:

(c) Any book, diary, letter, document, paper, record, or other written matter (whether in manuscript or printed form), photographic negative or print, film, printed reproduction of any picture, or sound recording –
  (i) Which relates to New Zealand and is of national, historical, scientific, artistic, or literary importance; and
  (ii) Which is more than 60 years old; and
  (iii) Of which, in the case of a book first printed and published in New Zealand, no copy is in the custody of the National Library of New Zealand:

(d) Any work of art which relates to New Zealand, is more than 60 years old, and is of national, historical, or artistic value or importance:

(e) Any type specimen of any animal, plant or mineral existing or formerly existing in New Zealand:

(f) Any meteoric or part of a meteorite recovered in New Zealand:

(g) Any bones, feathers, or other parts or the eggs of the moa or other species of animals, birds, reptiles, or amphibians native to New Zealand which are generally believed to be extinct:

(h) Any ship, boat, or aircraft, or any part of any ship, boat or aircraft, or any equipment, cargo, or article belonging to any ship, boat or aircraft in any case where that ship, boat or aircraft has been, or appears to have been, a wreck in New Zealand, or within the territorial waters of New Zealand, for more than 60 years and that ship, boat, aircraft, equipment, cargo, or article, as the case may be, is of national, historical, scientific, or artistic value or importance:

Artifact means any chattel, carving, object or thing which relates to the history, art, culture, traditions, or economy of the Maori or other pre-European inhabitants of New Zealand and which was or appears to have been manufactured or modified in New Zealand by any such inhabitant, or brought to New Zealand by an ancestor of any such inhabitant, or used by any such inhabitant, prior to 1902."

The Act forbids the export of antiquities from New Zealand, other than with an official permit, which will be granted only after consideration of numerous matters on a statutory checklist. The Chief Executive of the administering Government Department (the person who grants permits) must refuse permission unless satisfied that the removal of any antiquity would not be to the substantial detriment of historical or scientific study or research in New Zealand and would not be contrary to the public interest.

Antiquities exported or attempted to be exported in breach of the Act are forfeited to the Crown but may be returned at the discretion of the relevant Minister subject to conditions. Any artifact (as defined) found in New Zealand or in its territorial waters is declared to be *prima facie* the property of the Crown, provided than any artifact, removed from the grave of any person or persons whose identity is known, is to be referred to the Maori Land Court to determine the proper person to hold custody of the artifact.

An artifact may not be sold otherwise than to a registered collector or to a public museum. Dispositions by gift *inter vivos* or inheritance are permitted. Collectors are to be registered on statutory conditions that include a requirement that the collection be available for examination by an authorised person. Auctioneers and dealers trading in artifacts must be specially licensed with the condition that they sell antiquities only to licensed dealers, collectors, auctioneers, or nominated museums. The major four museums in New Zealand are currently listed. Antique dealers in New Zealand are licensed as second-hand dealers under special legislation.

The predecessor of the Act was subjected to the scrutiny of the British Courts in the *Ortiz* case in the early 1980s (*Attorney-General of New Zealand v Ortiz & others* [1982] 3 All ER 432 (HC & CA): [1983] 2 All ER 931 (HL)). A carved set of doors of great Maori cultural significance had been purchased for NZ$6,000 by a dealer from a New Zealand Maori who had found it in a swamp. This intricately carved set of doors of considerable antiquity had then been removed by the dealer from New Zealand without a permit, in defiance of the then in force Act. The dealer sold the artifact to a well known collector of Polynesian artifacts named George Oritz living in Switzerland for US$63,000. Oritz then sought to resell the doors by auction through Sotheby's in London. The attempt of the New Zealand government in the British courts to prevent the sale and to recover the artifact for New Zealand was successful at first instance but failed in the Court of Appeal and House of Lords. The dealer was held to have obtained a valid title from the original finder of the artifact. The forfeiture provisions of the Act, as then existing, did not extinguish that title until there had been an actual forfeiture by the enforcement authorities. The statute had incorporated the seizure provisions of the customs legislation.

The British courts were sympathetic to the attempt of the New Zealand government to retrieve this valuable piece of cultural heritage, but felt unable to do other than apply the law, based essentially on proprietary rights to chattels. Another ground for the decision lay in the reluctance of British courts to uphold what they saw as a penal statute of another country.

Various points of interest that arise from the law reports of the Ortiz case are:

(a) At the time of the first-instance hearing in 1981, the panels were said to have been worth £300,000.
(b) There appeared to have been no challenge to the title of the individual who found the panel in a swamp and who sold it in 1973 to the dealer for NZ$6,000 – a fraction of the estimated value of £300,000 (sterling).
(c) The concluding comments in the judgment of Lord Denning in the Court of Appeal at pp. 458 9:

> "Returning to our present case, I am of opinion that if any country should have legislation prohibiting the export of works of art and providing for the automatic forfeiture of them to the state should they be exported, then that falls into the category of 'public laws' which will not be enforced by the courts of the country to which it is exported or any other country: because it is an act done in the exercise of sovereign authority which will not be enforced outside its own territory.
>
> On this point, therefore, I differ from the judge; but I would express my gratitude to him for his most valuable contribution to this important topic. He held that our courts should enforce the foreign laws about works of art by ordering them to be delivered up to the foreign government. He hoped that if we did this the courts of other countries would reciprocate and enforce our laws which prohibit the export of works of art. I regard this as too sanguine. If our works of art are sold to a dealer and exported to the United States without permission, as many have been, I doubt very much whether the courts of the United States would order them to be returned to England at the suit of our government, on the ground of forfeiture.
>
> The retrieval of such works of art must be achieved by diplomatic means. Best of all, there should be an international convention on the matter where individual countries can agree and pass the necessary legislation. It is a matter of such importance that I hope steps can be taken to this end."

(d) The collection of earlier English cases by Lord Denning from 1611 to 1971 which dealt with attempts by sovereign governments to confiscate valuable items.

In *Don Alonso* v *Cornero* (1611), Hob. 212, a Spanish Subject committed crimes in Spain and fled to England carrying 3,000 pounds of tobacco. His very flight was under Spanish law, a cause for forfeiture of the goods to the King of Spain "on the High Seas." On arrival in England, he sold the tobacco for £800. The Spanish ambassador took proceedings in England to recover the tobacco from the English purchaser because it had been forfeited to the King. The Court refused to enforce the forfeiture which had come into effect "on the High Seas." The forfeiture was an act of sovereign authority outside Spain.

Likewise a prohibition against the export of certain family papers was the exercise of sovereign authority by the King of Italy and was not enforced by an English Court in *King of Italy* v *Marquis Cosimo de Medici Tornaquinci* (1918), 34 TLR 623.

In *Brokair* v *Seatrain (UK) Ltd* [1971] 2QB 476, the English Courts refused to give effect to a levy against goods issued by the United States government while they were in transit on the High Seas.

The situation was different in *Princess Paley Olga* v *Weisz* [1929] 1 KB 718 where the Princess' valuable collection at her palace in St Petersburg was confiscated by decree of the Soviet State. When Mr Weisz, who had purchased some of the articles from the Soviet Government, brought them to England, the English Courts rejected the

Princess' claim to them because their confiscation had been the exercise of sovereign authority within a State's own territory and not outside that territory as happened in *Ortiz* and the other cases noted.

The Act establishes domestic control of the export of objects of cultural heritage but does not provide New Zealand with a means by which to recover illegally exported objects. Consequently, New Zealand has decided to accede to both the 1970 UNESCO Convention and the 1995 UNIDROIT Convention. Amendments to the Act are in train with the aim of incorporating both Conventions into New Zealand domestic law. Other amendments are proposed, the better to deal with the problems demonstrated by the *Ortiz* case.

Had the UNIDROIT Convention been in force between New Zealand and the United Kingdom, the result of the *Ortiz* case could well have been different. New Zealand could have requested the return of the carved panel under Article 5, provided it were "of significant cultural heritage" (as it clearly was). If New Zealand could have shown that Mr. Ortiz should have known that they had been exported illegally (based on his contract of purchase), then New Zealand would not have had to pay him compensation under Article 6. According to an article by R. R. Cater, "The Taranaki Panels – Case Study in the Recovery of Cultural Heritage" (1982), 35 Museum 256, the contract signed by Mr Ortiz included a provision that he should not show the panels to any archeologist of New Zealand extraction for two years nor entrust a photograph of them to any third party. Article 6(2) requires that regard be had to the circumstances of the acquisition, including the absence of an export certificate. That absence, plus the unusual provisions in the Ortiz contract, would have made an Article 6(2) defence to the payment of compensation likely to succeed.

OTHER NEW ZEALAND CASES

The Warrior's Head. A New Zealand judge has granted letters of administration in respect of the estate of a deceased Maori warrior, thought to have died in about 1820. The grant was made to the President of the New Zealand Maori Council, a representative organisation of the Maori people. The President had possible tribal links to the deceased, given that the deceased's tribal affiliation was indicated by tattooing on the head. The purpose of this grant was for the limited purpose of according to the deceased remains a proper burial in accordance with Maori custom and to prevent further indignity. The head was imminently due to be auctioned in London. The Judge expressed abhorrence at the sale and purchase of human remains for gain or curiosity (see re *Tupuna Maori*, P580/88 High Court of New Zealand, Wellington, 19 May 1988, Greig J).

The Cook Instruction – **Department of Internal Affairs v The Poverty Bay Club Inc** ***[1989] DCR 481.*** In 1988, the Poverty Bay Club removed from New Zealand a 1776 letter written by Captain James Cook to Captain Charles Clerke, and sent it to Sotheby's, London, for auction. The club was convicted of removing an antiquity from New Zealand without reasonable excuse and without a certificate of permission. The letter was acquired by the City of London for the purpose of returning it to New Zealand as a gift to mark the sesquicentennial of Cook's landing in New Zealand. The New Zealand government had made a decision not to bid for it at auction. Its return could not have been secured by existing legislation. The letter is now in the Archives New Zealand collection.

The Fowler Traction Engine – **The New Zealand Customs Service v (name suppressed)** ***(Unreported, District Court, Christchurch, CRN 27130, 17 July 2003).*** A 1996 application to export a "unique example" of an 1884 Fowler Traction engine was declined under the Antiquities Act. In 2002, the engine was found to be for sale in the United Kingdom. The exporter was convicted under section 203(4) of the Customs and Excise Act 1996 of knowingly making an erroneous Customs entry and fined $900 plus $175 solicitor fees. The engine was passed in at auction for UK£22,000.

The cases show that the New Zealand government has gone to some considerable trouble and expense to stop illegal traffic in New Zealand artifacts. Financing the *Ortiz* case in the full range of the British courts cannot have been a cheap exercise. But there is a limit to what a small country (population four million) can do. Only a determination by nations likely to receive artifacts to support the various international initiatives such as UNIDROIT will diminish the illegal trade in such objects; which trade can deprive a people of its cultural patrimony.

CHAPTER NINETEEN

Angkor Sites, Cultural World Heritage

Kérya Chau Sun

INTRODUCTION

Angkor, capital of the Khmer Empire from the ninth to the fifteenth centuries is, first and foremost, a unique cultural heritage of the Khmer peoples and a symbol of Khmer identity. Yet Angkor designates not only a geographical region and its remarkable monumental and artistic artifacts. Most importantly, it represents a dynamic cultural complex extending beyond national boundaries, and profoundly penetrating all aspects of Khmer society.

With more than forty significant monuments, Angkor is an outstanding heritage site, and the crown jewel of Khmer civilization. It is also a living site, home to many thousands of local villagers; a religious site, a place of pilgrimage for Buddhists both from Cambodia and from the rest of the world; and a natural site, where rice paddies intermingle with forests. From this subtle equilibrium comes the magic of Angkor . . .

Following a twenty-year period of war and neglect, the international community responded with the sincerest expression of friendship and determination to the petition that HRH Prince Norodom Sihanouk tabled before the UNESCO Director General on July 1, 1991, asking whether the Angkor monuments could be included on the World Heritage List.

The sixteenth ordinary session of the World Heritage Committee was held in Santa Fe, New Mexico, United States of America, from December 7–14, 1992. It was attended by the following members of the Committee: Brazil, China (People's Republic of), Colombia, Cyprus, Egypt, France, Germany, Indonesia, Italy, Mexico, Oman, Pakistan, Peru, Philippines, Spain, Senegal, Syrian Arab Republic, Thailand, Tunisia, and the United States of America.

The following State Parties to the Convention who are not members of the Committee were represented by observers: Algeria, Australia, Bangladesh, Belize, Bulgaria, Canada, Czech & Slovak Federal Republic, Finland, Greece, Guinea, Holy See, Japan, Netherlands, Poland, Russia, and Switzerland.

Representatives of the International Centre for the Study of the Preservation and the Restoration of Cultural Property (ICCROM), the International Council of Monuments and Sites (ICOMOS), and the World Conservation Union (IUCN) attended in an advisory capacity.

In order to guarantee the protection of the site for a three-year period (1993 to 1995), the Committee decided that a special in-depth study would be made of the Angkor site and that reports would be presented periodically to the Bureau and the Committee on the status of the monuments and the protective perimeter; the first report was to be presented by the July 1993 session of the Bureau and followed by a report to the Committee during its seventeenth session in December 1993.

In order to deal with the urgent problems of conservation quickly and effectively, the Committee inscribed the site of Angkor on the List of World Heritage in Danger, and requested, on the recommendations of ICOMOS, that the authorities concerned take the necessary steps to meet the following conditions:

a) enact adequate protective legislation;
b) establish an adequately staffed national protection agency;
c) establish permanent boundaries based on the UNDP project;
d) define meaningful buffer zones;
e) establish monitoring and coordination of the international conservation effort.

The Cambodian authorities went straight to work in the wake of the Paris Agreements to fulfil the conditions set in order to have the site put on the list on December 14, 1992.

The Royal Government of Cambodia was given three years in which to create an authority empowered to take charge of the protection and conservation of the sites and ensure the management thereof. Once this condition was met, the World Heritage Committee gave permanent status to the classification of the Angkor temples, which include the sites of Angkor as well as the Roluos group and Banteay Srei temple. Many other monuments in Siem Reap province could not be listed because of their inaccessibility at the time and the impossibility of giving them adequate protection.

The first of the five conditions met was the formation of the International Coordinating Committee for the Safeguarding and Development of the Historic Site of Angkor (ICC), which held its first meeting in December 22, 1993 under the co-chairmanship of France and Japan, just three months after the Tokyo intergovernmental conference.

The second condition was met when the Royal Decree on Zoning in the Siem Reap/Angkor Region was enacted on May 28, 1994. Under this legislation, the Siem Reap/Angkor

The author greatly acknowledges the contributions of Etienne Clement, and Sébastien Cavalier for this chapter.

region was divided into five zones, each with a specific level of protection:

- Zone 1: Monumental sites
- Zone 2: Protected archaeological reserves (or buffer zone)
- Zone 3: Protected cultural landscapes
- Zone 4: Sites of archaeological, anthropological, or historical interest
- Zone 5: Socioeconomic and cultural development perimeter of the Siem Reap/Angkor region.

These zones were defined using the findings of the project for the "Zoning and Environmental Management Plan" (known as ZEMP), now recognized as a model and consulted by numerous countries. Using an original approach, this project has provided the basis for land management in the entire Siem Reap/Angkor region. The definition of permanent protective boundaries and a buffer zone around the monument zones ensures that not only the monuments themselves are protected, but also their immediate environment by removing the risk of wildcat urban development or urban sprawl.

On February 19, 1995, the Royal Government of Cambodia issued an important decision, thereby fulfilling the third condition, that being a decree to create a national public establishment to take charge of management of the site: the Authority for the Protection of the Site and Management of the Region of Angkor, better known as the APSARA Authority.

The fourth condition required by the World Heritage Committee at the time of inclusion on the list was met on January 25, 1996, with the enactment of the Law on the Protection of Cultural Heritage, drafted with support from UNESCO. The last implementation subdecree relating thereto came into effect on September 18, 2002.

The Angkor site was included permanently on the World Heritage List in 1995.

PROTECTION AND DEVELOPMENT OF CULTURAL HERITAGE

The ICC

The ICC has been meeting twice a year since 1993, overseeing the safeguarding and development operations on the site.

The two co-chairs of this committee are France and Japan, the leading donors with regard to rehabilitation of the Angkor site. UNESCO provides the services of standing secretariat, and Cambodia is represented by the APSARA Authority.

The ICC is the international mechanism for coordination of assistances to be extended by different countries and organisations. It ensures the consistency of the different projects, and defines, when necessary, technical and financial standards and calls the attention of the concerned parties when required. It is primarily the political body in which all of the countries and international organizations are represented at the diplomatic level. In January 1997, it created a technical wing within itself, the Ad Hoc group of experts, in order to draw on high caliber, objective expertise. Upon request by the co-chairs of the ICC, it fulfills the following functions:

1. study the scientific and technical aspects of project proposals submitted by the ICC,
2. investigate technical issues relating to the Angkor site and its monuments,
3. give advice on any matter within its purview that the co-chairs may, from time to time, submit to it.

It has proven to be an invaluable means to assist both the ICC and the Cambodian authorities to take decisions in difficult cases. Its advice has prompted both of these levels to move toward developing a master plan for monument safeguarding and has encouraged international operators to investigate complex technical situations on their restoration work sites. Despite the long debate that preceded its coming into being, the Ad Hoc group of experts has taken on increasing importance and has now become an indispensable link in the ICC decision-making process. It now enjoys undisputed legitimacy: Far from being an agency of control, it has become an agency of discussion, exchange, and consultancy.

The APSARA Authority (Authority for the Protection of the Site and Management of the Region of Angkor)

The APSARA Authority was created by Royal Decree in 1995 in order to protect and develop the historical site of Angkor, with emphasis on tourism in close relationship to culture.

This government institution experienced growing pains during its early years, resulting from an overall lack of means – human, technical, and financial.

At the time of its inception, the APSARA Authority did not enjoy the support of the levels that were then in charge of managing the Angkor site with regard to both monument restoration and conservation and tourism management and regulation of construction. At the time it was set up, it did not have appropriate financial and political support of the government. Actually, this government institution was built on regulations put in place by foreign experts, albeit of high caliber, but because of their not being rooted in the local culture, they did not factor in the management difficulties linked to the weaknesses in the fundamental principles of the legislation and financial resources of a country lacking its own source income and depending upon international aid for reconstruction. This instrument, too refined for Cambodia (and called a world first at the 1995 World Heritage Conference in Berlin), had to be redesigned to enable it to operate in the field, failing in which it would simply have ceased to exist.

Furthermore, a lack of communication on the part of the APSARA Authority and the provincial authorities made it appear to hold "absolute power," with no one to answer to but the central level, whereas its area of concern was actually provincial in scope.

This rather negative image did not prompt the provincial authorities concerned by the projects to lend their assistance to implement them.

However, it must be acknowledged that there has been significant improvement since 2001 in the efforts put forth by the Authority to work with and seek to work with the provincial authorities, especially with regard to the very sensitive issues involving the abandonment and acquisition of illegally occupied land for the development needs of tourist facility infrastructure.

The Royal Government of Cambodia has since issued many decisions to enable it to achieve its three objectives:

1. ensure the protection, conservation, and showcasing of national cultural property, particularly with respect to the Siem Reap/Angkor region;
2. design and lead the management and development of tourism in the five zones of Siem Reap province;
3. assume the role of "project owner" for structuring activities carried out in the Siem Reap/Angkor region and draw up specifications in its capacity as "owner" of the projects carried out by establishments under its direct supervision, in partnership with the provincial authorities and in cooperation with the institutions, organisations, foundations, and associations, both Khmer and foreign, that are pursuing aims and objectives along the lines of its vocation and that are operating in the region.

A new decree signed on January 22, 1999, gave the legal status to the APSARA Authority as a public administrative establishment with administrative and financial autonomy and created the position of President Executive Director. In May of the same year, a governmental decision gave the APSARA Authority entitlement to receipts from the sale of entrance tickets to the site, which enabled it for the first time to have its own budget.

The revamping of the APSARA Authority decided by the Royal Government in early June 2001 and the putting in place of a team of technical officers on the institution's directorate had the basic purpose of reconciling the desire for sustainable economic development on the one hand and conservation of the cultural and social heritage of the Cambodian people on the other.

The APSARA Authority now has eight departments:

1. Department of Police: *(i)* Tourist Police Unit, *(ii)* Special Unit of Heritage Police, *(iii)* Joint Intervention Unit for cracking down on the destruction of forests, management of the domain, and elimination of anarchical activities in the Siem Reap/Angkor region;
2. Department of Administration, Staff, Finance and Public Relations;
3. Department of Monuments and Archaeology 1;
4. Department of Monuments and Archaeology 2;
5. Department of Tourism Development of Angkor;
6. Department of Urban Planning and Development of Siem Reap/Angkor Region;
7. Department of Demography and Development;
8. Department of Water and Forestry.

Heritage Management: Safeguarding the Site, Monument Maintenance, and Environmental Protection

Over the ten-year period, the international community has maintained its firm commitment to the Cambodian authorities to provide funding assistance for monument restoration, preservation, and presentation programs. Eleven different countries took on fourteen of the principal monuments, making Angkor the most extensive archaeological work site in the world.

The teams involved were constantly guided by three key principles:

1. Treat each monument as an integral part of an overall monument site or complex;
2. Study each monument in its archaeological, historical, environmental, and cultural context, as well as in the perspective of showcasing it in the future;
3. Involve national professionals and technicians in the operations and see to the gradual transfer of knowledge and skills.
   - France and Japan are funding several major work sites, whereas Germany is tackling the deterioration of the *apsara* sculptures in the Angkor Wat temple.
   - Other countries, such as Holland through Hungary, Russia, Italy, Indonesia, China, and India, are contributing to temple maintenance and safeguarding.
   - Switzerland has recently been added to the list with its monument management and maintenance program for the temple of Banteay Srei.
   - India has signed a memorandum of understanding with the APSARA Authority to care for the temple of Ta Prohm.
   - On December 16, 2004 the U.S. Department of State and the World Monuments Fund (WMF) announced a $550,000 grant from the State Department to WMF for the conservation of the Phnom Bakheng temple complex; Phnom Bakheng is perhaps the least understood and explored of the major temple complexes in what is today known as the Historic City of Angkor.
   - The State Department grant to establish the Phnom Bakheng Conservation and Presentation Project represents the first time that the U.S. government has directly supported conservation work in Angkor.

The Department of Monuments and Archaeology, renamed in 2001, has the assignment of protecting, preserving, conserving, and showcasing the archaeological, cultural, and eco-historic park of Angkor, which has been classified as a World Heritage site.

It is made up of four units that care for research work, structuring, maintenance, and archaeological operations, as well as a multipurpose technical office.

The various branches of these units undertake studies, perform planning operations, and work out in the field through mobile teams, caring for matters relating to the forest and archaeology. The administrative branch for the prevention of illicit trafficking in heritage artifacts produces the files or records needed by the competent authorities.

In order to preserve the archaeological heritage and deal with the increasing number of visitors to Angkor Archaeological Park, the Monuments and Archaeology Department drew up a program to put in the following infrastructure:

Monument Conservation. The key objective of this program is the training of specialized teams with the following missions:

- actual monument maintenance and establishment of a schedule of routine or exceptional upkeep activities, and
- working with the other technical units of the APSARA Authority to draw up a "Preservation Master Plan" highlighting emergency interventions from the standpoint of routine upkeep as well as that of major repairs (risk map and emergency intervention map).

Perimeter Area Management. The key focus of this program is the training of specialized teams with responsibility for:

- defining the general principles for management of the site; in particular, the monument approach area layout work and perimeter areas, and
- drawing up a "Management Master Plan," in keeping with the preservation master plan (risk map that this unit is helping develop).

Archaeology Survey. This unit was set up in June 2001 to meet an urgent ongoing need relating to the development of tourist amenities in the park:

- performing preliminary archaeological analyses that sometimes involve relatively complex evaluations, and
- drawing up an archaeological risk map based on both the preservation and management master plans.

Cultural Heritage Sites: Managing Tourism Congestion and Impacts of Development

Tourism in Cambodia must, first and foremost, be cultural tourism. Enhancement of the level of services offered in connection with this prime asset would give visitors an incentive to stay longer. However, implementation of such a policy is most challenging. Indeed, how can we say no to mass tourism – seen as a fast-track revenue solution for a people whose income is among the lowest in the world and who have suffered from the trauma of war? How can they resist the temptation to make money quickly?

Already, back in the 1960s, when Cambodia's economy was such that it was reasonably self-sufficient, King Norodom Sihanouk felt that no special emphasis should be put on tourism, that the number of visitors to Angkor should be kept low, in order to preserve the Angkor site.

The policy of cultural tourism that Cambodia intends to implement must have specific goals in order to prevent it from turning into commercial tourism, which would give rise to helter-skelter, wildcat development in the region.

For Cambodia, preservation tourism is the byword. The key concepts: Nature has an intrinsic value that can never be replaced. Heritage must be seen as a legacy received and to be passed on. There must be joint and several liability for the management of natural and cultural heritage and solidarity among the generations – past, present, and future. The quality of the intake facilities will have considerable impact on the long-term appeal of a tourist site. Objectives can no longer be thought out in the short term, but foresight is needed for proper adaptation to needs in the mid-term and long term.

We would like to refer to cultural tourism as defined in the Brussels Charter, signed in 1976 at a convention of ICOMOS: *Article 1:* "Tourism is an irreversible social, human, economic and cultural fact."

We all know that tourism is not just the industry of today, it is also the industry for tomorrow, and this gives clear focus to the policy that Cambodia must adopt in order to ensure sustainable development.

Angkor – the symbol of Khmer civilization and a world heritage protected site – must not be given over to wildcat tourism development with no master plan. Tourism development at Angkor must go hand in hand with monument preservation and safeguarding. A close link must be drawn between tourism and culture.

Statistics confirm that there has been a steady increase in the number of visitor arrivals since Cambodia's political situation has stabilized. Given the visitor concentration, tourism management on the Angkor site has become a key focus in the protection of Cambodian's historical and cultural heritage. Although international tourism is growing on the site, the fact remains that the majority of visitors are domestic tourists. Domestic tourism has been mobilizing considerably more visitors than international tourism.

Mass tourism and sustainable tourism go together. Tourism and environment have long been considered as an antinomy, the development of one being at the expense of the other. But we now understand that they can be mutually supportive. They are obviously closely interconnected; the success of the first – the contribution it can make to the overall economy of societies – depends on the quality of the second.

Tourism is a necessary partner, but its vitality must be channelled. This means understanding clearly the ins and outs of the industry, as well as the complex nature of its relationship with culture.

A tourism policy must be framed that respects societies, cultures, and nature while contributing to development. Tourism development must be part of overall development. Can sustainable tourism development be achieved if there is no overall development strategy? Can heritage be accessed as a means of showcasing the past for the present, while preserving it for the future?

A proper balance must be struck between cultural heritage and environmental protected activities and the inevitable development of the tourist economy, in order to meet the need for social and economic development in a country now fully in a reconstruction phase. This places Cambodia in a position that is both a strength and a weakness.

Management of Tourist Flows

The development of international tourism must not cause us to overlook the majority share of domestic tourism. Indeed, in-country tourism is prompting a much greater flow of visitors than international tourism.

The problems brought on by uncontrolled tourism can be resolved only with the establishment of partnership arrangements between the APSARA Authority and tour organizers. Carefully managing tourist flows in order to prevent the more popular monuments from being overcrowded needs consultation with all tourism stakeholders and appropriate authorities for the reinforcement of the solutions advocated.

But, can the APSARA Authority implement sound management practices in dealing with tourist flows?

The growing numbers of visitors have started to cause serious problems on some Angkor sites:

- Banteay Srei temple: The results of the tourist count done by surveyors working for the Investigations Visitors Unit have led the APSARA Authority to take emergency measures, setting up a conservation unit for this temple. The next step will involve the management of flows of visitors through a collaborative effort with tour itinerary organizers in order to schedule such things as the timing of visits.
- Angkor Wat: Surveys show that there are very distinct differences between the times foreign tourists and local Cambodian tourists prefer to visit this temple. This finding confirms that priority must be given to the program to develop the approach area in front of the temple. Furthermore, management of the chaotic sites around it – commercial and other – is a necessity.
- Phnom Bakheng: Chaotic traffic conditions have become the rule, with visitors cramming the site at sunset. Traffic conditions will be improved once the Angkor Wat approach area is properly developed and subject to appropriate regulations.

Training

Human resource development is also a major priority area. Cooperation with the provincial authorities and partnership with the private sector will enable the APSARA Authority to achieve a meeting of minds among all stakeholders in the tourism sector. They can thus unitedly contribute to tourism development on the Angkor site because the success of one means the success of all.

- The program to train guides working in Angkor Archaeological Park in cooperation with the Ministry of Tourism will enable a better service offering. The use of a quality label by the APSARA Authority will be a token of its desire to offer a service worthy of the site and thus enhance the prestige of the monuments.
- The training of monument guards is also necessary to improve their interaction with visitors and guides alike. They will become guardians of their own culture by providing insightful surveillance of their monument heritage.
- Organization of an awareness-raising seminar for local communities will involve them in the preservation and maintenance of the site.
- Involvement of tourism professionals will encourage them to inform their clients regarding the fragility of the heritage and elicit their compliance with the rules when visiting.
- Involving the park communities in the tourism development process by creating tourism-related jobs in keeping with their skills will enable them to benefit first-in-line from the revenue generated by this economy and contribute to poverty reduction, the backbone of government policy.
- Train APSARA Authority's staff with a keen awareness of heritage.
- Cooperate with various centers in the provision of training in tourism trade opportunities.

PREVENTION OF TRAFFICKING IN KHMER CULTURAL PROPERTY

Nearly three decades of civil war and a particularly rich heritage, have made Cambodia a distinctive haunt for traffickers in artifacts. Thefts of statues, temple dismantling, illegal diggings, and vandalism became commonplace in a country where the conditions for an exponential increase in the trafficking of cultural property could hardly have been better.

Yet, the Cambodian authorities were very quick to put in place, with support from UNESCO, an exemplary policy to prevent trafficking in cultural property. UNESCO's role therein was in response to a request made by HRH Prince Norodom Sihanouk in March 1992 (Subdecree No. ANK 60 of October 1997, establishing the Special Police Corps for the Protection of Cultural Heritage and fulfilling the fifth condition of the World Heritage Committee).

The founding principles of this policy and the steps to be taken were set forth in 1992, during a national workshop on the prevention of trafficking in cultural property held in Phnom Penh.

This was followed by numerous measures taken with a dual objective: to contain the looting going on in Cambodia and dissuade potential buyers on the international market.

Efforts to Contain the Looting

In order to halt the looting of the national heritage, the Cambodian authorities worked with the support of the international community to:

- develop a policy for the legal protection of cultural property,

- take steps to ensure the physical protection of the temples,
- raise awareness among the decision-makers and people in general with regard to the importance of preserving the national cultural heritage.

The Law on the Protection of Cultural Heritage was enacted on January 25, 1996. It provided for the protection of cultural property by classifying each individual object rather than following the Anglo-Saxon approach of protecting families of artifacts based on typologies. A subdecree went into effect on September 18, 2002 that spelled out these provisions.

Since classifying any artifact, either movable or immovable, implies having a thorough knowledge of the object in question, an inventory policy was launched in 1994. It began with an inventory of artifacts at the Angkor Conservation Office and National Museum of Phnom Penh and is being expanded to include an inventory of Cambodia's archaeological sites. Led by the Ministry of Culture and Fine Arts, both of these projects have had input from experts working with the "Ecole Française d'Extrême-Orient" (EFEO) and funding assistance from France. They are being complemented by the creation of an office for the prevention of trafficking in cultural property within the Ministry of Culture, with support from France, that has the responsibility of compiling a database of artifacts liable to being stolen, thus paving the way for a database of stolen objects.

Legal protection is only an academic exercise if it is not accompanied with physical measures of protection. For this reason, a special heritage police force responsible for protecting the monuments in the Angkor zone was established in 1994 with support from France and UNESCO. At the same time, the storerooms at the Angkor Conservation Office were renovated with funding assistance from Japan. An Interpol office was also opened in Phnom Penh as a means to disseminate information about the theft of Khmer artifacts, and an office for the prevention of trafficking in cultural property is in the process of being set up with assistance from the French authorities.

Physical protection of the monuments is not dependent upon the deployment of police forces alone. A consistent human presence on the sites is often just as dissuasive. When there are scientific teams on the sites or visitor flows, this helps protect them by making acts of looting more difficult to accomplish and by bringing new sources of income to the local communities. The rapid growth of tourism at Angkor and the gradual return of security to the country are therefore very positive factors.

The period since 1992 has also been characterized by numerous training and awareness-raising campaigns with regard to the protection of Cambodian cultural heritage: poster competitions, traditional theater shows, training of monks, customs officials, news reporters, and police officers, etc. Recent initiatives to date have included another training seminar on the prevention of trafficking in cultural property organized by the Ministry of Interior in October 1999 and attended by several hundred officials, as well as conferences for the general public held on this theme in 2001.

Dissuading Potential Buyers on the International Market

Trafficking in cultural property has considerably increased. In an attempt to regulate the international art market, two international conventions were adopted during the last thirty years. 1970 UNESCO and UNIDROIT both have been ratified by Cambodia:

- September 26, 1972: 1970 UNESCO and July 11, 2002, UNIDROIT.
- Pursuant to Article 9 of 1970 UNESCO, the Royal Government of Cambodia; requested bilateral assistance from the United States, one of the major importers of Cambodian art, and the United States imposed, in December 1999, emergency measures to prevent the import of some categories of Cambodian archaelological objects. According to this decision, a certain number of Khmer artifacts cannot henceforth enter the United States without an export license delivered by the Cambodian authorities. The ban was extended in 2003.

Adherence to UNESCO has enabled Cambodia to successfully seek the return of a number of items identified as missing based on the inventory of artifacts at the Angkor Conservation Office. A number of them have been sold through Sotheby's; others were in the possession of antique dealers or private owners, and still others had made their way to museums such as the Metropolitan Museum of Art and the Honolulu Academy of Arts.

These cases illustrate the great value of international awareness-raising campaigns regarding the protection of Khmer cultural heritage, a key weapon in the fight to reduce the international demand for Khmer artifacts on the art market. Such campaigns have taken various forms:

- International media campaigns have been conducted regularly to educate leading art market operators and collectors with regard to the problem of Khmer art being looted. Broad coverage was given to the most significant instances of artifact looting and returns (theft of fifty-square-meter of bas-reliefs at Banteay Chmar in late 1998; discovery of very large scale looting operations at Preah Khan of Kompong Svay in February 2000; return of two artifacts by the Honolulu Academy of Arts in 2001, etc.).
- Photographs of stolen items have been widely disseminated through international databases (Interpol, Art Loss Register, etc.).
- In 1993, ICOM put out a publication entitled *One Hundred Missing Objects – Looting at Angkor*, that was reprinted in 1997. It was given a broad distribution among culture ministries, museums, art dealers, and customs departments, and this has enabled the retrieval of eight artifacts stolen from the Angkor Conservation Office.

In June 1999, the National Museum of Phnom Penh held an exhibition to display the artifacts returned to Cambodia in the framework of actions to prevent illicit trafficking in cultural property and to pay tribute to what was being accomplished in this regard.

Notwithstanding these encouraging results, the fight is far from over. True, the Angkor site now enjoys a permanent level of security, but looting is continuing elsewhere in the Kingdom in more remote areas or places where there is less visitor travel. This is affecting many monuments in the northern and western parts of the country.

The Heritage Corp Police

Context

The French cooperation began promoting the protection of the temples of the region of Angkor in 1993, in order to sustain the Cambodian authorities for the creation of a Heritage Corp Police, specifically in charge of the prevention and the repression of the illicit traffic of artifacts in the archaeological sites.

The Cambodian authorities detached 325 policemen especially in charge of the protection of temples. France provided the vehicles, motorcycles, radios, uniforms, training, and technical advice. The material for the motorized brigade, provided in 1993, has been renewed via the organization of training for the team and the equipment of cross-country bicycles for two brigades of 100 people each. The number of policemen has been increased to 527 people.

Results

At the present, more than fourty most important temples are under the protection of the Heritage Corp Police.

The French police participated in the actions by giving technical advice for spreading the cover zone, and warning of the depredations that are focused henceforth on the unprotected temples.

The Inventory of the Objects

Context

For struggle against the illicit traffic of Khmer artifacts, an inventory of the most fragile pieces on the 2,500 archaeological sites inventoried by the EFEO in the country.

An office of prevention of the illicit trading of cultural goods has been installed in the Ministry of Culture, composed of four people, of which two are prospectors.

Results

- The first prospecting started at the end of November 2002, based on the information gathered since 1995 by the EFEO, of the southern regions of Cambodia, and spread today over the whole country and, in particular, the remote zones of the province of Prey Veng or Oudor Meancheay. Presently, 1,400 sites have been visited. The work in process is permitted to specify location and the configuration of numerous archaeological sites and gather an exceptional collection of photographs of the archaeological Khmer heritage.

  This information, in the setting of a GIS (Geographical Information System), gives an unexpected picture of the occupation of the territory during the ancient times, and permits the national authorities to have a management tool for its heritage, programs of regional development, tourist development, or prevention of the illicit traffic of artifacts.
- On March 27, 2002, a circular was signed by Prime Minister Hun Sen, which aimed to stop the illicit archaeological excavations. The Royal Government drew up a long list of the depredation sites and called on the Ministries of Culture, Defence, and Interior, as well as APSARA Authority, to take emergency measures, in collaboration with the local authorities, for protecting these sites. The circular also calls on the possessors of the hidden or stolen cultural goods from illicit excavations, to return them to the local authorities or to the museums within a period of six months. After the deadline of this period of leniency, the pillagers would be pursued judicially, according to the Law of 1996. This circular shows the will of the Royal Government to stop the vandalism.
- Encouraged by the international community, the governments of Bangkok and Phnom Penh also agreed to fight jointly against the traffic of the Khmer artifacts, that had spoiled the relations of cooperation and friendship between the two neighboring kingdoms. After this new understanding, the two countries signed, in June 2000, a bilateral agreement for controlling the traffic and returning stolen cultural goods. This bilateral agreement is welcomed enthusiastically by public opinion and by the experts on the protection of the heritage, particulary in view of the fact that Thailand has ratified 1970 UNESCO and UNIDROIT.
- Conscious of the international dimension of the problem, the Cambodian administration has decided to promote it at regional and international levels; such as these discussed in this section.
- To show its will to maintain the pressure and come to the end of this curse and continue to benefit support and sympathy of the international community in this domain, Cambodia welcomed, in March 2001, the Intergovernmental Committee of UNESCO for promoting the return of cultural goods to their country of origin or their restitution, in case of illegal appropriation. Although Cambodia is not a member of the Committee, holding in the country a demonstration of such size was the opportunity to organize a big media national debate on the theme of the cultural goods traffic.

THE ACTIONS OF ICOM

The International Council of Museums (ICOM) took things in hand and through a crusade attempted to convince all its members to apply its ethical rules that prohibit the museums from acquiring objects stolen in national collections of other countries. Some first emergency measures have also been taken in the field: reinforcement of the security of the Conservation of Angkor, training of civil servants, and growing awareness of populations and international community through UNESCO.

UNESCO called on France, which already had a police cooperation in Cambodia, to take charge of the training of 520 Cambodian policemen who will be armed and motorized and will spread out around the eighty monuments of the Angkor site. They will finally assure the minimum necessary security. In spite of it, the Conservation of Angkor was victim of a commando operation, resulting in twenty missing pieces! If the national and international mobilization to assure the security of the monuments succeeded in containing the lootings at Angkor, the traffic continued, through parallel networks that will be discovered later. They succeeded in dismantling the whole temple ornamentation of Bêng Mealea, in the northeast of Angkor.

In 1997, in spite of Cambodia's turbulent political climate in July, the world fair on Khmer sculptures took place in Paris, Washington, Tokyo, and Osaka. At this occasion, ICOM had republished *Hundred Missing Objects – Angkor's Lootings*, which had been published the first time in 1993, then updated in 1996. This was distributed extensively to international auction houses, museums, and antiquarians. Cambodia recovered several pieces mentioned in the book.

The campaign led by ICOM bore fruit. Some museums reported that they acquired or received objects, probably stolen. The Metropolitan Museum of New York, after repeated demands of the Royal Government of Cambodia, the campaign of ICOM, and a forceful article in the American press, ended up restoring to Cambodia a piece stolen in the Conservation of Angkor, and even facilitated the restitution of another piece by a private collector in New York. Some galleries in the United States, France, and Great Britain, ended up restoring some pieces that became embarrassing.

Other spectacular restitutions have to be noted following the negotiations undertaken by the Government of Phnom Penh. The Academy of Arts of Honolulu returned to Cambodia two masterpieces that were, in 1970, in the Conservation of Angkor in Siem Reap and that were represented in the book *Hundred Missing Objects – Angkor's Lootings.*

The spectacular seizures took place in Thailand, at the border, on the roads to Bangkok, and in galleries in the Thai capital. At the harbor of Rotterdam, some cargos have been seized by the customs department of the Netherlands and pieces restored to the embassy of Cambodia. These successes won't prevent what will probably remain in the history of Cambodia the most shameless of the depredations: the dismantling, piece by piece, of a whole wall of the temple of Bantaey Chmar, in the northwest of the country. One hundred-twenty two pieces cut by fretsaw crossed the border between Cambodia and Thailand. These historic stones were sent to one the antiquarians of Bangkok, but fortunately, a part has been seized by the Thai authorities and, after negotiation, restored to Cambodia.

With the Angkor site secured, the looters moved toward other, more distant sites. As the *mine clearance* of these distant places, one can discover the extent of the damage: at Kbal Spean, on the road of the Koulens mountain, an unique whole of set stones sculpted in the banks of the river is extensively mutilated. It is vandalism and rough and systematic cutting.

The Cambodian authority attention now turns therefore to smaller temples, more distant from the big sites, and difficult to control. Some international institutions bring their help: UNESCO and the World Monument Fund at Bantaey Chmar, for example. In 2000, the site of Kbal Spean, well-known as "river of thousand lingas," is placed within the jurisdiction of the APSARA Authority, in charge of the management of the Angkor site. Protective measures and conservation are also taken by the Ministry of Culture and Fine Arts, with the support of UNESCO, at the site of Koh Ker, former capital of the Angkorian empire during the X century, as well as at Sambor Prey Kuk. Given the will of the authorities to preserve major sites of the monumental Khmer heritage, the Royal Government proposed, in 2001, to UNESCO, the registration of Banteay Chmar and the temple of Preah Vihear on the World Heritage List.

LEGAL FRAMEWORK LEGISLATION AND NATIONAL ACTION

Cambodia's participation in international conventions and in adopting and implementing legislation has been discussed in the previous section. This section discusses legislation at the national level.

- Cambodia, since 1996, with the support of UNESCO, adopted domestic laws, and in 2001 began their implementation. A subdecree adopted in 2003 strengthens the legal provisions of the Law on protection of cultural heritage and puts into effect the definition of cultural goods and adjusts the modes of trade, export, and import of cultural goods as well as authorizations for archaelogical excavations. It is therefore important to train the civil servants of the concerned responsible institutions.
- August 1993: (Supreme Council on National Culture).
- September 1993: ICC, co-chaired by France and Japan with UNESCO as standing secretary.
- December 1993: first ICC meeting held in Cambodia, participated in by more than twenty countries and organisations (technical committee).
- May 1994: Royal Decree No. 001/NS establishing Protected Cultural Zones in the Siem Reap/Angkor Region and guidelines for their management.
- February 1995: Royal Decree No. NS/RKT/0295/12 for the creation of the Authority for the Protection and Management of Angkor and the region of Siem Reap.
- October 1995: Subdecree creating the Hotel Zone No. 079/ANKR/PK.

- January 1996: Law on the Protection of Cultural Heritage No. NS/RKM/0196/26.
- October 1997: Subdecree No. 60 ANK-PK establishing the Special Police Corps for the Protection of Cultural Heritage on the Heritage Corps Police supervised by the Ministry of Interior and in close collaboration with the APSARA Authority and the authorities of Siem Reap to assure the security in the Angkor Park and to fight against the illicit traffic of the artifacts.
- January 1999: Royal Decree No. NS/RKT/0199/18 strengthening the statute of the APSARA Authority.
- October 1999: Subdecree extending the Hotel Zone No. 093/ANKR/PK.
- December 2001: Subdecree creating a Tourist Police Corps No. 025/ANK/PK.
- September 2002: Subdecree spelling out the provisions of the Law on the Protection of Cultural Heritage.

After setting in place all the comprehensive and modern set of legal tools at the national level for protecting and managing the Angkor site, Cambodia, already party to three key international conventions on heritage safeguarding (1954 Convention on the Cultural Property in the Event of Armed Conflict, 1970 Convention on the Prevention of Illicit Traffic in Cultural Property, and 1972 Convention on World Heritage), ratified the UNIDROIT Convention on July 11, 2002.

PART THREE

International Movement of Art and Cultural Property

The "Market Nations"

CHAPTER TWENTY

International Art Transactions and the Resolution of Art and Cultural Property Disputes: A United States Perspective

Barbara T. Hoffman

The United States is the major art importing country in the world. It should be no surprise, therefore, that United States policy on the international movement and trade in cultural property, to the extent that one can speak of such a policy, is based on the free international movement of art works and cultural property and on the noninterference with private ownership of that art and cultural property.[1] The U.S. Congress has enacted few laws with respect to the regulation of private ownership of such property or its movement, interstate or internationally. The United States is perhaps unique in that it has no export restrictions on works of art. There are, however, growing limits on the export of archaeological objects and Native American cultural objects (NAGPRA 25 U.S.C. §3002–3007, 2000).

Historically, U.S. policy has been in favour of free imports of art and cultural property. Excluding politically embargoed goods and endangered species[2], the United States has few laws restricting the import of artwork and cultural property into the country. The fact that an art work has been illegally exported does not, in and of itself, bar it from lawful importation into the United States: illegal export does not itself render the importer (or one who took from him) in any way actionable in a U.S. court.[3]

U.S. courts, for the most part, have nevertheless been sympathetic to the claims of foreign governments for the return of stolen antiquities, despite the hurdles in litigating art and cultural property claims. Foreign claimants have achieved success in a number of recent cases. In part, this is because, under the common law, as more fully discussed in the introduction to Parts II and III of this book, a thief cannot convey good title. The U.S. government has also aggressively and successfully brought forfeiture actions under the National Stolen Property Act, customs statutes, and directives.

Current disputes concerning the ownership of art works and cultural property are characterized by often-complex fact patterns, multiple parties, and a host of potential implicated jurisdictions. The basic U.S. legal and institutional structure for recovery of looted antiquities and stolen art is a function of federal law, state legislation, and state common law, including choice of law, which may involve application of foreign law. Litigation related to cross-border purchases of art and cultural property confronts a lawyer with complex jurisdictional choices.[4]

This chapter provides a succinct overview of the applicable laws in the United States for resolving claims to stolen artwork, particularly those involving cultural patrimony of foreign nations. A primary purpose is to show the public policy issues involved in art litigation. The first two sections focus on a discussion of the relevant federal statutes, principally, the Convention on Cultural Property Implementation Act of 1983, civil actions for forfeiture based on U.S. customs law and customs directives. The third section looks at the National Stolen Property Act as given effect by the *McClain* doctrine and its early progeny. The principal concern in section four is private actions to recover cultural property, particularly state common law actions for replevin. The last section's, focus is on some of the themes developed in the prior sections in the context of recent developments with respect to the recovery of art looted during the Second World War.[5]

No discussion of the U.S. perspective on licit and illicit international art trade is complete without an understanding of the political and economic forces that have informed and shaped the debate about the formulation of cultural property policy. For more than 30 years, since the beginning of discussions on the implementation of the 1970 UNESCO Convention, art dealers, the American Association of Museums (AAM), the Association of Art Museum Directors (AAMD), and auction houses have lined up against archaeologists, ICOM, and others to debate whether and to what extent modern-day governments should be entitled to claim artefacts, works of art, and antiquities that originated in ancient civilizations now found within their borders. Museums have argued that the enforcement of such laws would hurt U.S.

[1] For the purposes of this chapter, cultural property may be broadly defined as antiquities and the generic term "works of art." The interchangeable use of terms is without significance. Other aspects of U.S. policy are discussed in other chapters.

[2] See the Convention on International Treaty of Endangered Species, Endangered Species Act of 1973. 16 U.S.C. §§1531 *et seq.* There is an exception in the Endangered Species Act for "antiques," which are defined as articles that are at least 100 years old. *Migratory Bird Treaty Act* 96 U.S.C. §701 and others.

[3] *United States v McClain*, et al, 545 F. 2d. 988 (5th Cir. 1977) appealed after remand 593 F. 2d 658 (5th Cir., 1979).

[4] The choice of forum may often be outcome derivative; however, a successful judgement may pose difficulties in enforcement. The scope of such concerns are beyond this chapter.

[5] Whereas the approach of this chapter is to provide a practical overview of significant cases, the subject is complex, and the reader should be aware that the cases are factually complicated, subject to nuanced discussion and multiple interpretations. The *McClain* decision and other cases discussed herein have generated or are likely to generate volumes of pages in the law reviews with excellent scholarship on all sides of the issue. Such depth is beyond the scope of this chapter which, because of the limitations of length and context, endeavours to provide only a useful reference and guide for the readers to the U.S. law and policy in this area and the considerations that undergrid it.

museums' abilities to collect and assemble collections and the public's access to information. At the heart of what is often a charged and emotional debate implicating law, politics, economics, archaeology, and education, are three issues: (1) whether the United States should enforce foreign cultural patrimony laws and which U.S. legal principles should govern the application of such law; (2) whether the United States should enforce the export prohibitions of foreign states with respect to cultural property disputes; and (3) what (if any) the applicable statute of limitations applied to the recovery of such property should be. Recent developments have further fueled this debate. The United States Court of Appeals for the 2nd Circuit's affirmance on 25 June 2003 of the conviction of New York art dealer, Frederick Schultz, on one count of conspiring to deal in stolen property, sent shockwaves through the dealer and collecting community, and confirmed that the United States, consistent with prior precedent as established by the *McClain* doctrine, would enforce, under appropriate circumstances the cultural patrimony laws of foreign nations on the theory that the cultural objects so exported were stolen. Although members of the archaeological community and others hailed the decision, members of the American Council for Cultural Policy (ACCP), an outspoken collectors and dealers groups were quick to condemn the decision. Kate FitzGibbon, editor of the ACCP writing in the Orientations, a journal for collectors of Asian art, March 2005, observes

> The collateral damage of the Frederick Schultz case to the reputations of legitimate dealers and collectors pales in comparison to the legal repercussions of that decision, in which a foreign law nationalizing antiquities was treated as an ownership law under the National Stolen Property Act. This decision potentially places title to thousands of objects in US museums and private collections in question and renders the safe harbor for objects long held in the United States under the Cultural Property Implementation Act meaningless.

Quite apart from its questionable accuracy, the extreme characterization reflects the paranoia and polarizing tendency of the group.

Similarly, battle lines have been drawn between primarily the same camps, in testimony before the Cultural Property Advisory Committee in February and March, 2005 over whether or not to grant the request by the Government of the People's Republic of China for a bilateral agreement restructuring the importation of Chinese cultural property over ninety five years old into the United States pursuant to Article 9 of 1970 UNESCO. The debate is more fully discussed in the next section.

THE INTERNATIONAL MOVEMENT OF WORKS OF ART AND THE CONVENTION ON CULTURAL PROPERTY IMPLEMENTATION ACT 1983 (PUBLIC LAW 97-446, 19 U.S.C. 2601 *ET SEQ.*, AS AMENDED)

U.S. ratification of the Convention on Cultural Property Implementation Act (CPIA) enables the United States to participate in the 1970 UNESCO Convention. In 1983, after more than 11 years of debate, Congress enacted the CPIA, fulfilling the U.S. government's obligations to implement 1970 UNESCO. The Act reflects the debate's painstaking attempts to balance the competing goals of archaeologists, anthropologists, academics, art collectors and museums, and relevant government agencies. The Department of State, in urging the adoption of the CPIA, argued,

> Governments which have been victimized by the spoliation and theft of cultural objects have been disturbed at the outflow of these objects to foreign lands and the appearance in the United States of objects has often given rise to outcries and urgent requests for return by other countries. The United States considers that on grounds of principle, good relations, and concerns for the preservation of the cultural heritage of mankind, it should render assistance to these situations.[6]

The delay in the enactment of the CPIA apparently was caused, in part, by pressure from art dealers and others in the trade, who argued that if the United States undertook unilateral import controls, illegal cultural property would simply be sold to those art market countries lacking similar import controls. In fact, some opine that the CPIA was perhaps finally enacted only because it was perceived as a restraint of sorts on certain customs officers. These officials had deemed all archaeological materials that a foreign country had claimed were stolen to be subject to seizure under the National Stolen Property Act, 18 U.S.C. §2311 *et seq.* (1934). The CPIA, therefore, emphasized the need for concerted action and, in particular, seemed to prefer action resulting from bilateral treaties between the United States and the affected source countries.

Under the CPIA, the term cultural property includes articles described in 1(a)–(k) of the UNESCO Convention.[7] The CPIA, 19 U.S.C. §§260-2613, did not implement all of the UNESCO Convention, but rather only implemented Article 7(i) and Article 9, which called for concerted action among nations to prevent trade in specific items of cultural property in emergency situations. A central element of the compromise between the government and the arts community embodied in the CPIA is that the United States would not give source nations a "blank check" by automatically enforcing their cultural property laws. Rather, the final legislation embodies a policy of prohibiting the importation of cultural property and returning it to the source nation only if (1) it was previously identified and then stolen from an institution or public monument (19 U.S.C. §2607), or (2) pursuant to a request from a foreign country to the extent necessary to prevent pillage (19 U.S.C. §2602-06). A country, the cultural patrimony of which "is in jeopardy from the pillage of archaeological or ethnological" materials, must demonstrate, in its request for assistance, that it has taken measures

[6] U.S. Code Cong. & Adm. News 4100 (1982).

[7] The CPIA regulates the import of certain types of archaeological and ethnological interest. The phrase "object of archaeological interest" refers to objects at least 250 years old and of "cultural significance," and "object of ethnological interest" is something from a tribal or pre-industrial society that is important to the cultural heritage of a people.

to protect its cultural property and that the requested import restrictions will benefit "the international community in the interchange of cultural property among nations for scientific and educational purposes" (19 U.S.C. §2602(a1)). In addition, the President may not impose import restrictions unless other nations – whether or not signatories to 1970 UNESCO – having a significant import trade in such objects also impose such restrictions (19 U.S.C. §2602(c)). The CPIA therefore adopts a highly selective approach to import restrictions.

Also as part of the compromise, Senator Daniel Patrick Moynihan of New York argued for the creation of the Cultural Property Advisory Committee ("The CPAC") to act on behalf of the President. The CPAC is meant to be representative of U.S. interests in this matter, with representatives of the archaeological community, the art museum community, collectors, art dealers, and interested citizens.[8]

CPAC convenes to review State-Party requests that have been submitted to the federal government under Article 9 of the UNESCO Convention. Such requests seek U.S. cooperation in restricting the importation of archaeological or ethnological material the pillage of which places a nation's cultural heritage in jeopardy. CPAC is responsible for reviewing such requests and recommending action by the United States. The U.S. Department of State provides CPAC with technical and administrative support to carry out its advisory function.

Temporary emergency import restrictions may be imposed upon request from a 1970 UNESCO State Party, if any archaeological or ethnological material of any source nation is:

(1) a newly discovered type of material which is of importance for the understanding of the history of mankind and is in jeopardy from pillage, dismantling, dispersal, or fragmentation;
(2) identifiable as coming from any site recognized to be of high cultural significance if such site is in jeopardy from pillage, dismantling, dispersal, or fragmentation which is, or threatens to be, of crisis proportions; or
(3) a part of the remains of a particular culture or civilization, the record of which is in jeopardy from pillage, dismantling, dispersal, or fragmentation which is, or threatens to be, of crisis proportions; and application of the import restrictions set forth in section 2606 of this title on a temporary basis would, in whole or in part, reduce the incentive for such pillage, dismantling, dispersal, or fragmentation.

A history of various restrictions is included with this chapter as Appendix 1.[9]

The import restriction becomes effective on the date that a descriptive list of the objects is published in the *U.S. Federal Register.* Thereafter, restricted objects may not enter the United States without an export certificate issued by the country of origin or documentation that the object left the country of origin prior to the effective date of the restriction.

Currently, the CPAC is considering two requests under. Article 9: Colombia and China.

As noted above, the request by the Chinese government to establish import bans to the United States for a wide spectrum of Chinese art and artifacts has generated intense debate. The lynchpin of the request and reaction to it is primarily based on whether or not the loss of Chinese archaeological sites and material is principally or substantially attributable to the market for Chinese art and antiquities in the United States.

In this connection opponents of the request argue that the request is too broad, does not meet the statutory criteria for such restrictions under CPAC, and that China has not taken sufficient steps to safeguard its own heritage.

Written comments from Sotheby's submitted in February and March are illustrative:

> Therefore, the United States may not accede to China's request without finding that other countries with a significant import trade in the materials have implemented or will implement import restrictions that are comparable in scope and substance to those under consideration by the United States. As mentioned above, Japan, Singapore, Taiwan, Switzerland and European Union members Great Britain, France and Germany have significant import trade in Chinese archaeological materials. We are not aware of specific import restrictions imposed by these countries on Chinese archaeological materials, nor are we aware of any requests from China to any of these countries about imposing such restrictions. . . .
>
> Even if the multinational response requirement was satisfied, China's request is further fundamentally flawed by reason of its overly broad definition of archaeological material. First, the Act defines archaeological objects as more than 250 years old and the request exceeds the 250 year requirement. Second, although there are objects in the request that satisfy the age requirement, they do not satisfy the other aspects of the statutory definition of "archaeological" in that they were not discovered as a result of scientific excavation, clandestine or accidental digging, or exploration on land or under water. Likewise, certain objects in the request could be either archaeological or non-archaeological depending upon the history of the object. . . .
>
> The third factor used to determine if an object is archaeological is whether it is of "cultural significance." Obviously, this factor was added to the law in order to limit the application of the other two factors which are much broader in scope.

Dan Monroe, member of the AAMD, Director of the Peabody Museum, former Chair of American Association of Museums and former President US ICOM, made similar comments noting the

> "excessively broad range of objects included in the request" and "the profound dampening effect the request would have, if adopted, on cultural exchange for the purposes of scholarship exhibition, and education. . . . Most important, though, is the fact that this request – targeted only to the United States – will do nothing to remedy problems associated with inconsistent enforcement of archaeological protection laws in China or the daily harm done to archaeological resources due to uncontrolled development."

[8] It has, in the past several years, come under attack as being biased in favor of source nations and a more restricted art trade. There was great uproar over the bilateral agreement entered into with Canada and that agreement has not been subsequently removed.

[9] See the U.S. Federal Cultural Property Legislation and U.S. Federal Preservation Laws Web site at: <http://exchanges.state.gov/culprop/uslaws.html> for additional information. The Chinese request for assistance is found in "A Guide to Art and Cultural Heritage Resources."

Anita Defunis, Governmental Affairs, AAMD argued that China should develop a licit traffic before applying such broad restructions.

Proponents argue that China has made efforts to combat pillage; the U.S. market is enormous and the U.S. should lead the global effort to protect the world's shared cultural heritage.

Without desiring to enter the fray, it is worth noting that bilateral Memorandum of Understanding (MOU) have produced effective results in eleven prior situations. The advantage of the U.S. process is that MOU's can be carefully calibrated to balance the various interests of collectors, archaeologists, art historians, museum curators, and others to achieve the goal of preventing illicit traffic. While not a total panacea, the MOU enables consideration of how to define the cultural objects denied importation, the development of incentives, police enforcement and compliance.

For example, consider the agreement with Italy which will soon be reviewd by the CPAC. The agreement would seem to represent a model of cooperation and cultural exchange in taking into account various interests; however, some members of the art trade are critical of any agreement with a developed country and argue against the broad definition of cultural objects it embodies. Under the Agreement with Italy to limit imports, the items covered encompass archaeological material from approximately the ninth century BC to the fifth century AD, representing pre-Classical, Classical and Imperial Roman periods, and including sculpture, monuments, wall paintings, vessels and ornaments in stone, metal, ceramic and glass. The restricted materials include not only objects originally made in what is now Italy, but red and black figured Attic vases and other Attic and Corinthian pottery that were widely exported from Greece to ancient Italy and the entire Mediterranean region. The restrictions encompass some of the Italian antiquities most sought after by collectors, such as Etruscan and Roman bronzes and Apulian vases.

The Agreement looks to Italy itself to take appropriate actions. Acknowledging the Italian effort in recent years 'to devote more public funds to guard archaeological sites and museums and to develop Italian tax incentives for private support of legitimate excavations,' the Agreement refers to Italy's need to institute more severe penalties and prompt prosecution of looters, regulate the use of metal detectors (used by potential looters), provide additional training for the Carabinieri Special Unit for the Protection of Artist Patrimony and intensify the investigations by the Carabinieri on the looting of archaeological sites and the routes out of the country taken by the smugglers of these artifacts.

Italy also agrees to promote agreements for long-term loans of objects of archeological and artistic interest to United States institutions, to encourage US-Italian archaeological expeditions and, very significantly, to continue to examine new ways to facilitate the export of archaeological items legitimately sold within Italy. See Memorandum of Agreement with Italy 66 Fed. Reg. (2001).

A U.S. leadership role in promoting a balanced policy of concerted international effort to stem the illicit antiquities trade is appropriate. The all or nothing rhetorical approach currently characterizing the debate is not fruitful and overlooks the common values shared by these opposing factions.

Violations of §§2606 or 2607 of the CPIA result in seizure and forfeiture of the property. The property will be offered for return to the source nation owner. If not returned to the source nation owner, it may be returned to a claimant who establishes that he is a bona fide purchaser (BFP) for value of the property with valid title. If the property is not returned to a source nation owner or claimant, it will be disposed of in accordance with customs laws regarding forfeited articles. Cultural property that is either stolen or not declared to the U.S. Customs Service when imported is subject to seizure and forfeiture under *18 U.S.C. 545, 19 U.S.C. §1497, and 19 U.S.C. §1595*(a). The person involved in such theft or unlawful entry may be subject to civil and criminal penalties under *18 U.S.C. §545, 19 U.S.C. §2314, 19 U.S.C. §1497, and 19 U.S.C. §1595*(a).

The specificity required to impose these emergency actions may also severely limit their effectiveness. For example, in In re Search Warrant Executed Feb. 1, 1995, the CPIA governed, because it was initially believed that the defendant had imported archaeological material from the Sipan region of Peru, thus, it was protected material under *19 C.F.R. §12.10*(g)(b). Failure to establish that the archaeological material was from Sipan made the CPIA inapplicable.[10]

Unlike the bilateral or emergency restrictions, §2607 of the CPIA does not require a state party request – only that the object be documented as pertaining to an inventory. This was the case in *United States of America v an Original Manuscript* Dated November 19, 1778 bearing the signature of Juniper Serra.[11] At a Mexico City flea market, a coin and manuscript dealer, Duane Douglas, paid $300 to $400 cash for the manuscript. Without declaring it to customs authorities, the dealer brought the manuscript to the United States. The dealer then sold the manuscript to the claimant Dana Toft for $16,000 cash. Seeking to return the manuscript to Mexico, the United States filed a forfeiture action against Toft pursuant to the CPIA, 19 U.S.C. §2609. The U.S. government moved for summary judgment.[12] The court granted the motion and held that the government met its burden of establishing that there was probable cause to believe that the seized defendant-in-rem manuscript was the same one that had been reported stolen from the national archives of Mexico.

The Court's discussion of the innocent owner or BFP defense is of particular interest. Toft had to establish he was not willfully blind to illegal activity in order to maintain an

[10] *In re Search Warrant Executed Feb. 1, 1995, No. M. 18-65 (RJW), 1995 WL 406276*, at *1 (S.D.N.Y. Jul. 7, 1995).

[11] 1999 WL 97 894 (S.D.N.Y.) 96CIV 6221 (Feb. 19, 1999).

[12] Summary judgement is appropriate when there is no dispute on the material facts that would warrant a trial, thus, permitting a judgement on the papers.

innocent owner defence. In rejecting Toft's claim, the court found the following facts of significance:

Toft claims that his entry into the area of valuable documents was a "very recent venture," yet Toft did not question meeting in a hotel room and exchanging $16,000 cash for the Manuscript. Furthermore, Toft claims he was given "representations" of the Manuscript's authenticity and felt it was a "righteous deal" based upon Douglas's willingness to enter into a bill of sale, yet Toft does not state that he was provided with any documentation supporting these "representations." Toft also does not state that he inquired any further into how the Manuscript came to be in Douglas's possession other than to ask Douglas if he "owned the Manuscript and was able to sell it." I find that Douglas's actions, his lack of documentation of the history of the Manuscript and his failure to inquire into the provenance of the Manuscript is highly suspicious and Toft cannot claim to be an innocent owner under such circumstances. Therefore, I do not find that "given Toft's conduct" he has established by a preponderance of the evidence that he is an innocent owner and entitled to that affirmative defense and as a result he is not entitled to compensation.

Rena Neville, Sotheby's Worldwide Compliance Director, is critical of the court's conclusion that the buyer was not a good faith purchaser, although not necessarily approving of Toft's conduct. Her inside knowledge of the art world and the court's lack thereof explains why she might have come to that conclusion. She states,

Moreover, the fact that the dealer was a foreigner may explain the cash nature of the transaction. The Mexican dealer may not have wanted an out-of-country check, which would have taken time to clear and incurred bank fees. Additionally, he may have been motivated to accept cash in order to avoid potential Mexican tax liabilities. Indeed, the buyer may have assumed that the seller was trying to avoid Mexican tax law obligations or to keep currency outside of Mexico, given the sometimes volatile nature of their currency. Although such motives are not admirable, purchasers do not have a legal obligation to ensure that sellers pay whatever taxes a seller may owe in connection with a sale.

On the contrary, had the buyer had any suspicion that he had purchased stolen property, he is unlikely to have consigned it to a high-profile international auction house whose catalogues are circulated throughout the world. Another fact that at least raises the possibility that the buyer did not suspect he was purchasing "hot" property at a discount price was that the auction house's published low presale estimate for the manuscript was $20,000, only $4,000 more than the buyer had paid.[13]

U.S. CUSTOMS POWER TO SEIZE ILLEGALLY IMPORTED GOODS: CIVIL FORFEITURE STATUTES

Civil forfeitures are civil suits instituted by the U.S. government at the discretion of federal prosecutors pursuant to federal statutes. In every forfeiture case, the government is acting to seize property that is alleged to be the subject of criminal activity. Any person who has a legal interest in the property may file a claim to defend against forfeiture, and a claimant with a meritorious claim will prevail.

Forfeiture is an unusual type of proceeding because it is not an action against a person for a criminal wrong, nor an action against a person for a civil wrong. The U.S. government has to obtain a warrant from a federal magistrate that lays out a predicate offense justifying forfeiture, for example, that a false statement was made or that documents simply weren't submitted at the entry of the cultural property into the United States. It is an action against the object, for example, "*the United States of America v. Portrait of Wally.*" It is a device that is important for law enforcement in drug crimes and the like and is an extraordinarily useful weapon for prosecutors. As the previous discussion with respect to the *Serra* case indicates, this weapon now permits an art object to be seized because it is stolen. Under either the CPIA or, as will be discussed in the next section, under the National Stolen Property Act, the U.S. government institutes the action and the owner can appear as a claimant. The burden of proof, however, is not on the government to show beyond a reasonable doubt that a crime was committed or on the prior owner to prove, by a preponderance of the evidence that the art object is theirs and that there are no statute of limitations problems; the burden is, rather, on the current owner, to show that, in fact, the property was not stolen.

Claimants satisfy this burden by proving that the predicate crime never occurred, or that the property lacks a sufficient nexus to the predicate crime to warrant forfeiture under the applicable statute. In addition, claimants often assert the innocent owner defence, arguing that because they have a legitimate interest in the property and did not participate in the predicate offence, the property should not be forfeited to the U.S. government. In the absence of an express innocent owner limitation in the applicable forfeiture statute, however, U.S. courts have held that the innocence of an owner is not a valid defence against civil forfeiture.[14]

18 USC §545 (1999)

This federal forfeiture statute prohibits the importing of merchandise "contrary to law" and allows the government to forfeit merchandise that has been determined as imported

[13] Neville, an invited panelist at the Internation Bar Association, Amsterdam, is also critical of the U.S. government's use of civil forfeiture in cases like *Serra*. She asserts that the alleged foreign government has an advantage over the U.S. defendant because the foreign government need only provide the U.S. government with sufficient information to establish a *prima facie* case using a probable cause standard of proof. In *Serra*, the government of Mexico did not appear as a party and only submitted affidavits at the request of the U.S. attorney. The court indicated that a careful reading of the legislative history of section 2610 leaves no doubt that Congress did not intend to exclude the more lax evidentiary standards with respect to the burden of proof and the hearsay evidence but, rather, intended to distinguish section 1615 to clarify that in a CPIA forfeiture, the burden of proof lies upon the government, not the claimant. Neville claims that it would be fairer if there was a presumption on the part of customs to use civil interpleader, unless the U.S. government intended to pursue a separate criminal action or the possessor had knowledge that the property was stolen. The U.S. government's standard of proof has recently been raised pursuant to the Civil Asset Forfeiture Reform Act of 2000.

[14] See David Pimentel. 1999. "Forfeiture Procedures in Federal Court: An Overview." 183 Fed. Rules Decisions 1, quoted in Ian M. Goldrich. 1999. "Comment: Balancing the Need for Repatriation of Illegally Removed Cultural Property with the Interests of Bona Fide Purchasers Applying the UNIDROIT Convention to the Case of the Golden Phiale." *Fordham International Law Journal* 23: 118.

contrary to law. In order to warrant forfeiture, the government need only show "probable cause." In *Steinhardt*, which is discussed *infra*, *McClain*'s definition of stolen provided the predicate for the civil forfeiture action resulting in the antiquity's return to Italy.

18 USC §542

This federal forfeiture statute prohibits the import of merchandise by means of a false statement and allows for seizure of the object. The case law interpreting §542 has imposed a requirement that the false statement be material.[15]

19 USC §1595a

This forfeiture statute permits the seizure or forfeiture of objects known to be stolen at the time of import, in accordance with 18 USC §1523. There is no BFP defence.

The Pre-Columbian Monumental or Architectural Sculpture or Murals Law[16] of 1972

This law authorizes the customs to seize a monumental or architectural sculpture or mural made by a pre-Columbian Indian culture of Mexico, Central America, South America, or the Caribbean unless the importer can show it was legally exported or was outside the jurisdiction prior to 1979.

Forfeiture of unlawful imports:

(a) Seizure. Any pre-Columbian monumental or architectural sculpture or mural imported into the United States in violation of this title shall be seized and subject to forfeiture under the customs laws.
(b) Disposition of Articles. Any pre-Columbian monumental or architectural sculpture or mural which is forfeited to the United States shall – (1) first be offered for return to the country of origin and shall be returned if that country bears all expenses incurred incident to such return and complies with such other requirements relating to the return as the Secretary shall prescribe; or (2) if not returned to the country of origin, be disposed of in the manner prescribed by law for articles forfeited for violation of the customs laws.

Customs Directive 5230-15, Cust B. & Dec. (18 April 1991)

This Directive explicitly references the *McClain* decision and informs officials that, if they are unsure of the status of a nation's patrimony laws, they should notify the Office of Enforcement. The Directive is a basis for finding that a false statement with regard to country of origin constitutes a material misstatement in violation of 18 USC §545. Under these circumstances, for example, knowing that the Phiale was from Italy would be of critical importance. See the discussion of *Phiale* (or *Steinhardt*) *infra*.

Also included in the Directive are the Pre-Columbian Monumental and Architectural Sculpture and Murals Statute (19 USC §§2091–2095 (1999)), the CPIA (19 USC §§2601–2613 (1999)), the National Stolen Property Act (NSPA), and *McClain*.

***United States* v. *An Antique Platter of Gold, Known as a Gold Phiale Mesomphalos, c. 400 B.C.*[17]**

In *An Antique Platter of Gold*, the U.S. Customs service seized a gold phiale of Italian origin upon the request of the Italian government via a Letters Rogatory Request. The government sought the civil forfeiture of an antique golden platter of Sicilian origin, known as a phiale (the "Phiale"), pursuant to 18 USC §§545 and 981 and seized the Phiale from *the apartment of an American Collector*, Michael Steinhardt. The Phiale become the defendant in rem and Steinhardt filled a motion to dismiss. Steinhardt purchased the Phiale through a New York art dealer who had brokered the transaction to obtain the Phiale from a Swiss art dealer. The New York art dealer flew to Switzerland and returned with the Phiale. The dealer's custom broker listed Switzerland as the Phiale's country of origin. The Italian government requested assistance from the United States government in invesitagting the Phiale's exportation and based its claim on Article 44 of Italy: Law of June 1, 1939 declaring that an archaeological item is presumed to belong to the state unless its possessor can show private ownership prior to 1902.

The court held that the government had met its initial burden of establishing that there is probable cause to believe that the Phiale is subject to forfeiture and denied Steinhardt's motion to dismiss.

> Applying the materiality standard here, the Court finds that the statements in the Customs forms – misidentifying Switzerland as the country of origin – were materially false and in violation of Section 542.

The court also reasoned that,

> Customs procedures provide that the country of origin is a significant factor in determining whether Customs officials should admit an object, hold it for further information, or seize it as smuggled, improperly declared or undervalued. Since certain countries have stringent laws to protect their cultural and artistic heritage, identification of such a country raises a red flag.
>
> Truthful identification of Italy on the customs forms would have placed the Customs Service on notice that an object of antiquity, dated circa 450 B.C., was being exported from a country with strict antiquity-protection laws.... Based on these facts, the Court concludes that the Government has met its burden of establishing that there is probable cause to believe that the Phiale is subject to forfeiture as merchandise imported contrary to law.

As an alternative basis, the government argued that the Phiale was subject to forfeiture pursuant to 19 USC §1595a(c) as stolen property imported contrary to law and in violation of the NSPA.

Michael Steinhardt appealed. The AAM, the AAMD, and others filed a friend of the court brief in opposition to the decision and in support of Steinhardt. The Archaeological Institute of America (AIA) and others filed a brief on behalf

[15] See *United States v. An Antique Platter of Gold, Known as a Gold Phiale Mesomphalos, c. 400 B.C.* 184 F.3d 131 (2d Cir 1999) *infra*.

[16] 19 USCS §2091–2095 (2002).

[17] *United States* v. *An Antique Platter of Gold, Known as a Gold Phiale Mesomphalos, c. 400 B.C.*, 991 F. Supp. 222; 1997 US Dist LEXIS 18899.

of Italy and the U.S. government. The briefs of the *amici curiae* read more like a text book on cultural property law in the United States than legal briefs, albeit from opposing standpoints.

The Second Circuit Court of Appeals affirmed the forfeiture on the basis that the Phiale had been imported by means of a false customs declaration with respect to value and country of origin and that such false statements were "material" in violation of 18 U.S.C. 545[18] and there was no innocent owner defence.

CASES CONSTRUING THE NATIONAL STOLEN PROPERTY ACT OF 1948[19] (18 USC §§2314–2315)

The NSPA provides in pertinent part as follows,

> "Whoever transports, transmits or transfers in interstate or foreign commerce, any goods etc. of value of $5,000 or more, knowing the same to have been stolen, converted or taken by fraud [shall be guilty of a crime]."

The statute was originally enacted to provide the assistance of the federal government in enabling states to recover stolen motor vehicles. Prior to the enactment of the CPIA, the NSPA enabled the United States to seize and return cultural property to its rightful owners.[20] Illegal export is not a crime under the NSPA, and the act of illegal export from the country of origin alone does not give rise to such a claim.[21] In principle, the fact that an object has been illegally exported does not prevent its lawful importation,[22] in the absence of a statute or agreement to that effect in the importing nation.

United States v. *Hollinshead*[23]

Hollinshead involved the theft of pre-Columbian artefacts originally discovered in 1961 at the Machaquila archaeological site in Guatemala, principally the Machaquila Stele 2. Sometime between 1968 and 1971, the Stele 2 was cut into pieces and brought to Hollinshead's codefendant's fish packing plant in Belize (British Honduras).[24] There, in the presence of Hollinshead, his codefendant, and some Guatemalan officers who departed after receiving bribes, the pieces were boxed and shipped to Miami, Florida, as personal property. In an effort to sell the Stele 2, Hollinshead's codefendant showed it to several collectors and museums in Georgia, New York, North Carolina, and Wisconsin without success. Thereafter, the Stele 2 was shipped to Hollinshead in California, from where he offered it to the Brooklyn Museum in New York for US$300,000. The curator of the Brooklyn Museum contacted Ian Graham, the archaeologist who discovered the Machaquila site, asking his opinion on the authenticity of the Stele 2. Mr Graham then contacted the authorities, which, in turn, led to Hollinshead's arrest.

Hollinshead and the defendants were convicted of conspiracy to transport stolen property in interstate commerce and for causing the transportation of property in interstate commerce in the U.S. District Court for the Central District of California.[25]

The Ninth Circuit Court of Appeals stated that it was not required to prove the defendant knew the law of the place of the theft. "Appellant's knowledge of Guatemalan law is relevant only to the extent that it bears upon the issue of knowledge that the stele was stolen." Based on the evidence presented at trial, such as the fact that the defendants were present in Belize when the Guatemalan officers were bribed and the packages were shipped to the United States, the Ninth Circuit held that the convictions were valid and affirmed the district court's decision.

United States v. *McClain*[26]

The leading case construing the NSPA as it relates to claims of ownership of cultural property by foreign countries is *United States* v. *McClain*. In *McClain*, the defendants were convicted of conspiring to transport and receive pre-Columbian artefacts from Mexico through interstate commerce, in violation of the NSPA. The legal theory under which the case was tried was that the artefacts were stolen in the sense that Mexico, over time, declared itself the owner of all pre-Columbian artefacts found in or on its soil. Thus, anyone who dug up or found such an item and dealt in it without government permission was regarded as having unlawfully taken the item from its prior owner. In *McClain I*,[27] the court held that the term stolen, as used in the NSPA, was not a term of art but rather a term that was broad in scope and with a wide ranging meaning. The court held that it was proper to punish encroachments upon legitimate and clear Mexican ownership through the NSPA, even though the goods may never be physically possessed by agents of that nation. However, the court also stated that a

[18] *U.S.* v. *An Antique Platter of Gold* 184 F. 3d 131 (2d Cir. 1999).

[19] 18 USC §2314 (1999).

[20] *US* v. *McClain*, 545 F. 2d 998 (5th Cir.) [*McClain I*], rehearing denied, 551 F. 2d 52 (5th Cir. 1977) (per curiam); *US* v. *McClain*, 593 F. 2d 658 (5th Cir.) [*McClain* II], cert. denied, 444 US 918 (1979); *United States* v. *Hollinshead*, 495 F. 2d 1154 (9th Cir. 1974).

[21] See *Jeanneret* v. *Vichey*, 693 F. 2d 259, 267 (2d Cir. 1982) "The Second Circuit recognizes the 'fundamental general rule' that 'illegal export does not itself render the importer . . . in any way actionable in a US court.'"

[22] In the United States, this general rule as applied to works of art or antiquities was first altered by the Treaty of Cooperation between the United States of America and the United Mexican States Providing for the Recovery and Return of Stolen Archaeological, Historical and Cultural Properties of 17 July 1970, US-Mex., 22 UST 494, TIAS No. 7088, 1971, and subsequently by a statute, entitled Regulation and Importation of Pre-Colombian Monumental or Architectural Sculpture or Murals, Pub. L. No. 92–587, 86 Stat. 1297 (1972), codified as 19 USC §§2091–2095 (2001). See Coggins, Clemency C. "United States Cultural Property Legislation: Observations of a Combatant," *Journal of Cultural Property Law 7, Vol. 1* (1998: 52, 54–55, 63–64). The import of archaeological materials was further regulated by the Agreement between the United States and Peru for the Recovery of Return of Stolen Archaeological, Historical and Cultural Properties of 15 September 1981, US.-Peru, 33 UST 1607. See also 19 USC §§2091–2095.

[23] *United States* v. *Hollinshead*, 495 F. 2d 1154 (9th Cir. 1974).

[24] See *Hollinshead*, op. cit. n. 12, at 1155–1156.

[25] Hollinshead's conviction was made possible because archaeologist Ian Graham had drawn and photographed the Machaquila ruins before the Stele's removal, clearly showing it in place on a critical date (after the enactment of Guatemalan law vesting ownership).

[26] *US* v. *McClain*, 545 F. 2d 998 (5th Cir.) [*McClain I*], rehearing denied, 551 F. 2d 52 (5th Cir. 1977) (per curiam); *US* v. *McClain*, 593 F. 2d 658 (5th Cir.) [*McClain* II], cert. denied, 444 US 918 (1979).

[27] McClain involved two convictions and three appeals from 1974 to 1979.

national law prohibiting export of cultural property was not enough to qualify that property as stolen under NSPA.[28]

The defendants in *McClain* argued that their offence constituted "mere illegal exportation," which was not covered under the NSPA. The court distinguished export prohibitions from sovereign ownership laws and observed that, whereas export restrictions did not create ownership in the state, a state's declaration of ownership was an attribute of sovereignty and that, where there was such a declaration of national ownership, illegal exportation of cultural objects would be considered theft within the meaning of the NSPA.[29]

However, not any declaration of ownership would be sufficient: It had to be expressed "with sufficient clarity to survive translation into terms understandable and binding upon American citizens." Only Mexico's law of 1972 satisfied that standard. Therefore, the Fifth Circuit upheld only the conspiracy convictions that were based on a smuggling scheme after the enactment of the 1972 law. Furthermore, the Fifth Circuit's decision to affirm the conspiracy conviction was based on the defendants' knowing violation of Mexican law and U.S. law,

> In the absence of compelling evidence of prejudice, we would be loath to reverse a conviction such as this where the evidence of guilt and of intent to violate both foreign and domestic law is near overwhelming. We believe, nonetheless, that reversal of at least the substantive count is required here. . . .[30]

The Fifth Circuit was arguably influenced by the fact that the defendants' conduct violated not only Mexican law, but also the U.S.–Mexico Repatriation Treaty and the Pre-Columbian Monumental Sculptures Act (see *infra*).

In *McClain*, in their first appeal, the defendants broadly argued that a reference to any foreign law for the purpose of determining what is or is not stolen would "inject an unacceptable view of uncertainty into the NSPA." The court rejected the argument that application of the NSPA to foreign exportation rendered the statute void for vagueness. The Court reasoned that the statute's specific scienter requirements eliminated the possibility that a defendant would be convicted for an offence he could not have understood. In both *Hollinshead* and *McClain*, there was ample evidence that the defendants knew beyond a reasonable doubt that the objects involved were stolen.

Peru v. *Johnson*[31]

The *McClain* theory of stolen goods, that is, a claim based on the assertion that the artefacts were "stolen because a nation has an umbrella law vesting the ownership of all of a certain class of antiquities in the nation" was argued in *Peru* v. *Johnson*. However, *Peru* was a civil, not a criminal, proceeding. Peru alleged that it was the legal owner of artifacts that had been seized by the U.S. Customs Service. The government of Peru brought suit against an art dealer and collector to recover eighty-nine pre-Columbian objects seized from them and sought an order for their return. The action for the return of the antiquities that were alleged to have been stolen from Sipan in 1986 was for conversion, an intentional tort under states law. The court ruled in favour of the individuals, holding that Peru failed to establish that the artefacts in question were excavated in modern-day Peru. In the absence of direct evidence of Peruvian origin, the possibility that the artefacts come from Colombia, Ecuador, or Mexico precluded a finding that they came from Peru.

Not only was Peru unable to establish the "find site," but equally importantly, it was also unable to establish that it legally owned the artefacts at the time of their exportation, because the laws of Peru were not precise and had changed several times over the years.[32]

United States v. *Pre-Columbian Artifacts*[33]

The United States filed civil interpleader action to determine who was entitled to certain pre-Columbian artefacts seized from defendant individuals. The defendant, the Republic of Guatemala, alleged that the artefacts were exported from Guatemala in violation of Guatemalan law. The individuals claimed a lawful interest in the property. The individuals filed a motion to strike Guatemala's claim of possession or, alternatively, for judgment on the pleadings.

The issue of whether or not artefacts were stolen property in violation of the NSPA required that the court construe Guatemalan law. Guatemalan law provided that upon illegal export, the artifacts become the property of Guatemala. The court held that the determination of foreign law is a legal question. "There is no requirement that foreign law and its supporting material be pleaded . . . alleging in a pleading that property is stolen under foreign law is a sufficient pleading . . ."[34]

The court next addressed the issue that the mere violation of export restrictions did not make possession of the illegally exported property a violation of the NSPA. "For the property to be stolen, it must belong to someone else."[35]

> There is no allegation that the artifacts were stolen from any Guatemalan individual. The only allegation is that the artifacts belong to the Republic. Guatemalan law (as assumed for purposes of the present motion) provides that, upon illegal export, the artifacts became the property of the Republic. Therefore, the moment the artifacts left Guatemala they became the property of the Republic. Thus, while traveling in foreign commerce, the artifacts were stolen in that they belonged to the Republic, not the person who unlawfully possessed the artifacts.[36]

[28] The decision has been criticised by museums, dealers, and auction houses as blurring, if not eliminating, the distinction between ownership and export laws, calling such laws that vest ownership of undiscovered antiquities in the governments as ownership laws in disguise.

[29] See *McClain I*, op. cit. n. 14, at 997–1000.

[30] *McClain III*, 593 F. 2d, 658, at 678 (5th Cir. 1979).

[31] *Peru* v. *Johnson*, 720 F. Supp. 10 (C.D. Cal 1989), aff'd sub nom; *Peru* v. *Wendt*, 933 F. 2d 1013 (9th Cir. 1991).

[32] See Jack Batievsky and Jorge Velarde, "The Protection of Cultural Patrimony of Peru" in Part II of this book.

[33] *United States* v. *Pre-Columbian Artifacts*, 845 F. Supp. 544 (N. Dist. Ill. Lexis 14656, 1993).

[34] Ibid., at p. 545.

[35] Ibid., at p. 545, citing *McClain I*. But see Part II, Sir Ian Barker's discussion of *Ortiz*.

[36] Ibid., at p. 545, citing *McClain III*.

To prove the three prongs of McClain, a country must meet "heavy legal and factual burdens" which include using evidence of geographic origin, eyewitness testimony, defendant admissions, and other evidentiary proof. In addition, in a criminal prosecution, the prosecutor must establish *mens rea* or *scienter*.

United States of America v. *Frederick Schultz*[37]

Frederick Schultz, a prominent New York antiquities dealer, was accused under the NSPA of conspiring to receive and possess stolen property. The indictment charged that Schultz conspired to smuggle ancient artefacts out of Egypt, in violation of Egyptian Law 117, which provides that, as of 1983, all Egyptian antiquities – that is, objects over a century old and having archaeological or historical importance – are considered to be the public property of the state.

Schultz moved to dismiss the indictment on three grounds,

> "(i) Law 117, despite its assertion of state ownership, is really more in the nature of a licensing and export regulation, the violation of which does not constitute theft of property in the sense covered by §2315; (ii) that, assuming Law 117 really does work an expropriation of property by Egypt, the special kind of property thereby vested in that foreign state does not give rise to interests entitled to protection under United States law; and (iii) that even if such foreign interests might sometimes be entitled to such protection, Congress, in enacting the Cultural Property Implementation Act of 1983, 19 USCS §2601 et seq., chose to substitute a civil enforcement regime for criminal prosecution."

Amicus curiae briefs were filed by the AIA on behalf of the government, and by the National Association of Dealers in Ancient, Oriental and Primitive Art, the Art Dealers' Association, and Christie's, Inc. on behalf of Schultz. The prosecutor, supported by the AIA, argued that the purpose of the CPIA was to enhance protection for foreign antiquities and not foreclose criminal prosecution of those who deal in stolen objects. Schultz's attorney and the amici curiae argued that *McClain* should be overturned, and that enforcing foreign patrimony laws by means of the NSPA was precluded by the CPIA, undermined it, and was contrary to U.S. law and policy.

Schultz's brief also included an extensive discussion and criticism of Egyptian law, which Schultz claimed lacked the clarity required by *McClain* and other cases. Lawyers and legislators drafting cultural patrimony laws may find the criteria informative.

> Among the factors these courts have considered in analyzing a foreign law's purported declaration of ownership are: whether the law declared the state's ownership in clear and unambiguous language; whether the law explicitly or implicitly recognized the right to private ownership; whether the nation actually sought to exercise its ownership rights such that, in practice, the statute acted as an export restriction; whether private citizens who possessed objects could transfer them by gift, bequest or intestate succession; and whether a designated government department had to make a determination of the object's artistic, archaeological or historical value in deciding the government's ownership interest. Applying these factors here demonstrates that Egypt's law does not withstand scrutiny.

The court ruled against Schultz on each of his arguments, reviewing the complaint as it is required to do: on Schultz's motion to dismiss, in the light most favourable to the government. After a separate hearing, the Court decided that Schlutz failed to prove his assertions with respect to Egyptian law and that the law clearly vested ownership in the state. The court, however, left open a critical loophole for Schultz to escape conviction under the NSPA on a strict interpretation of the *McClain* case.

> To be sure, even if the Government proves the defendant knew he was importing antiquities that were smuggled out of Egypt – an act that may not be inherently violative of United States law and policy, there may still be a jury question as to whether he knew he was dealing in stolen goods, an essential element of a section 2315 violation. But the indictment alleges he possessed such knowledge, and the Government asserts that it will prove, *inter alia*, that the defendant knew that at least two of the items he conspired to import had been stolen from the Antiquities Police. This is more than sufficient for the purposes of the present motion.

The government's case rested on expert testimony, bank transfers, and correspondence between Mr. Tokeley-Parry and Mr. Schultz, much of it collected by Scotland Yard. The scheme to smuggle antiquities out of Egypt through England to the United States "consisted of a fabricated tale" that the objects belonged to Thomas Alcock, who collected Egyptian antiquities in the 1920s. To bolster his claim, "the two made up labels that were baked in an oven to give them the authentic glow of age."[38]

Schultz indicates that the United States takes the threat to and consequences of plundering unexcavated archaeological sites seriously. The effect of recent legal developments will be to place a greater burden of due diligence on the good faith purchaser. This greater burden on purchasers does not necessarily relieve foreign claimants of the difficult evidentiary burden to overcome, although a diligent inquiry into the *Schultz* artefacts might not have yielded results given the forged documents.[39]

United States of America v. *Portrait of Wally*[40]

"Portrait of Wally" by Egon Schiele was brought to the United States for an exhibit at the Museum of Modern Art (MoMA), on loan from the Leopold Museum-Privatstiftung in Austria (Leopold). The painting was taken from a Jewish owner's private collection in 1938 after Germany annexed Austria.

[37] *United States of America* v. *Frederick Schultz*, 178 F. Supp 2d 445, 2002 US Dist. Lexis 15.

[38] *New York Times*, 30 January 2002. See Ildiko D'Angelis, Part VIII, "How Much Provenance is Enough? Post-*Schultz* Guidelines for Art Museum Acquisition of Archaeological Materials and Ancient Art" for an extended discussion of *Schultz* and its implications for museums.

[39] Recent developments may encourage the art trade to look more favourably on the implementation of the UNIDROIT Convention, which provides compensation for the BFP, conditions for repatriation, and a statute of limitations that is more favourable to the BFP than that of New York.

[40] *United States of America* v. *Portrait of Wally*, 99 Civ. 9940 (MBM) (11 April 2002).

The U.S. government sought a forfeiture of "Wally" predicated on a violation of 18 USC §2314, alleging that it was imported into the United States and about to be exported in violation of the NSPA.

A lawsuit involving the seizure of the work was originally commenced in the courts of the state of New York. Pursuant to a grand jury investigation, the New York district attorney's office served a subpoena duces tecum on MoMA for production of "Portrait of Wally" and another Schiele painting on loan from the Leopold, based on the allegation that the painting had been stolen by the Nazis during the German annexation of Austria.

The museum moved to quash the subpoena on the grounds that it was invalid under a New York law that protected works of art of nonresident lenders from any kind of seizure while on exhibit in New York. The court of first instance granted MoMA's motion to quash the subpoena duces tecum. The appellate court reversed the decision. The Court of Appeals, New York's highest court, then reversed the appellate court's decision and granted the motion to quash. The Court of Appeals held that issuance of the subpoena was forbidden by section 12.03 of New York's Arts and Cultural Affairs law. The Court of Appeals further concluded that the subpoena interfered significantly with the lender's possessory interests in the painting by compelling their indefinite detention in New York and thus effectuated a seizure in violation of the statute. The Association of the Bar of the City of New York, through its Committee on Art Law, filed a friend of the Court brief in support of MoMA in both the appellate court and the Court of Appeals in support of the court of first instance.[41]

The day of the Court of Appeals decision, the United States magistrate judge issued a seizure warrant for the painting and the U.S. government started the aforementioned forfeiture action. The government claimed that "Portrait of Wally" was stolen and that, therefore, it was imported and would be exported in violation of the NSPA, 18 U.S.C. 2314 (1994). The government argued that Austrian law controlled the question of whether the painting is stolen within the meaning of the NSPA.[42]

The Complaint alleged that the Leopold transported Wally knowing it to have been stolen by Welz.

MoMA, the Leopold, and various purported heirs of the alleged rightful owner, a Mrs Bondi, joined the suit as claimants.[43] The Leopold and MoMA, in their motion to dismiss, analogised the case to *McClain III*, arguing that §2314, "cannot properly be applied to items deemed stolen only on the basis of unclear pronouncements by a foreign legislature."

After seven years, discovery is now complete. The Leopold Museum has moved for summary judgment dismissing the complaint on several grounds including the act of state, comity and political question doctrine, no criminal conversion, and laches.

MOMA has explained its position by indicating it is bound by its loan agreement to return the "Portrait of Wally" position backed by the AAM. MOMA's defense can not only be attributed to the need to defend foreign art works from seizure. Most museums organizing international exhibitions in New York or elsewhere rely on 22 U.S.C. §2459. Enacted in 1965, the law provides the following:

> Whenever any work of art or other object of cultural significance is imported into the United States from any foreign country, pursuant to an agreement entered into between the foreign owner . . . and one or more cultural or educational institutions within the US . . . no court of the United States, any State, may issue or enforce any judicial process or judgment. . . .

The Act facilitates American exhibitions of cultural objects borrowed from foreign countries by providing legal assurances that no party may use the courts in the United States to deprive the borrower of custody and control of the object.

Even if "Portrait of Wally" need not have a chilling effect on international loans, the outcome is certain to have policy implications.[44] Given the resources expanded one may query, whether, as a matter of policy, civil forfeiture laws should be used to resolve title disputes over who owns property that was looted, confiscated or otherwise unlawfully acquired during World War II. As Judge Mukasey observed, "This is not [an] ordinary case. . . . This case involves substantial issues of public policy relating to property stolen during World War II as part of a program implemented by the German government. . . . There are more interests potentially at stake [in this case] than those of the immediate parties to this lawsuit."[45]

COMMON LAW CIVIL ACTIONS OF REPLEVIN

Because art and antiquities are treated as personal property (personal) under the law, each state's Uniform Commercial Code governs their sale and title.[46] Civil replevin or conversion actions are a means to recover personal property. In the past several years, foreign governments have sought to recover cultural patrimony on the basis of foreign patrimony laws. The claimants allege objects discovered in and removed from their territory constitute stolen property.

41 The author was chair of the Committee of Art Law of the ABCNY.

42 The government advances this argument in an effort to preclude the defendant from relying on U.S. common law doctrine, which precludes an object from being categorized as stolen after it has been recovered by another, such as law enforcement. The doctrine did not exist under Austrian law.

43 From the initial seizure, the art community has been almost entirely uniform in opposing the seizure of Wally, unlike prior cases that have been hotly disputed.

44 The New York exemption from seizure statute has been reenacted. Most museums, both before *Portrait of Wally* and subsequently thereafter, seek protection under the Federal Indemnity from Seizure Law.

45 *United States of America* v. *Portrait of Wally*, No. 99 Civ. 9940, 2000 U.S. Dist. LEXIS 18713 (S.D.N.Y. Dec. 28, 2000) id. at pp. 4–5.

46 Under U.C.C. §§2–403 a purchaser of goods can only acquire the title of the transfer; thus, a thief cannot convey good title. U.C.C. §§2–312 provides that in all sales contracts there is an implied warranty of title – i.e., that the seller has the right to sell the goods and that the buyer shall have quiet possession. Thus, although the BFP has no right to the stolen property, he may have a claim against the seller.

The civil and common law systems conceptualise claims to recover personal property in different ways. Civil law systems generally regard such claims as proprietary in nature, whereas common law systems generally treat them as personal claims in tort (civil wrongs). The civil law focus is the plaintiff's title, whereas the common law emphasis is on the defendant's retention of the property, which constitutes an interference with the plaintiffs possessory rights.[47]

Replevin is a legal action whereby the owner or person claiming the possession of personal goods may recover such personal goods where they have been wrongfully taken or unlawfully detained. The gist of the action is the defendant's unlawful detention of the plaintiff's property. The issue litigated is the present right to the possession of the property in controversy, and the purpose of the action is to determine who shall have possession of the property sought to be replevied. To recover the item sought to be replevied (which is the primary remedy in a replevin action), the plaintiff must generally establish three elements: title or right to possession, the fact that the property is unlawfully detained, and the fact that the defendant wrongfully holds possession.[48]

When claims for return are brought pursuant to cultural property ownership laws, three (if not a myriad) of issues will eventually arise. These are (1) the identity of the object sought to be recovered, (2) the right to possession, i.e., the legal theory (patrimony laws),[49] and (3) statute of limitations and laches.

The following discussion of cases is meant to highlight the fact that civil claims for the recovery of stolen art often involve difficult questions of conflict of law, statutes of limitations, and, as discussed in the Introduction to Part II, differences in the rights of the BFP and the original owner. The facts of the cases also provide an insight into transactions in the international art world. Some involve the resolution of the rights of two "innocent" parties. Finally, the cases provide an understanding of the complex and often contradictory policy considerations that fuel decisions in the area of cultural property.

Conflict of Laws

A detailed discussion of conflict of laws analysis is beyond the scope of this chapter.[50] The reader, however, in considering the various cases discussed herein and in other chapters in Parts II and III, should reflect on whether the choice of "the governmental interest test," the "*lex situs*" test, or any other variant encountered is a neutral choice. In the United States, a federal court deciding a case based on what is called diversity jurisdiction must apply the substantive law (including state conflicts of law rules) of the state in which it sits. The choice of law is often outcome determinative.

For example, in *Kunstsammlung zu Weimer* v. *Elicofon*,[51] the issue was whether to apply New York law or German law. Germany brought a replevin action to recover paintings stolen from German zones of occupation during World War II, claiming a right to possession in the paintings under allied military law in force at the time. German law, if applicable, would have provided a BFP defence defeating Germany's title. New York's law did not provide a BFP defence. The court applied New York law based on the fact that the paintings had been subsequently sold to a BFP in New York and on the interest of New York in regulating commerce within its borders. Noting New York's interest in maintaining honest transactions in the art trade, the court stated (Id. at 846):

> The fact that the theft of the paintings did not occur in New York is of no relevance. In applying the New York rule that a purchaser cannot acquire good title from a thief, New York courts do not concern themselves with the question of where the theft took place, but simply of whether one took place. Similarly, the residence of the true owner is not significant for the New York policy is not to protect resident owners but to protect owners generally as a means to preserve the integrity of transactions and prevent the state from becoming a marketplace for stolen goods.

In the case of *Autocephalous Greek-Orthodox Church of Cyprus* v. *Goldberg & Feldman Fine Arts, Inc.*,[52] the court applied the choice of law for torts because the claim of replevin was analogous to that of conversion – a tort. Under Indiana law, the *lex loci* rule had been modified so that it applied only when the place of tort is also the place of most significant contact. The court established a two step test:

(1) the place of the wrong and the legal action,
(2) which jurisdiction had the most significant contacts.

Applying the test, the court stated:

> Switzerland, "the place of wrong" because it was at the Geneva airport that Goldberg took possession and control of the mosaics – bears little connection to Cyprus' cause of action.

The district court went on to find that other *indicia*, such as those who financed the transaction and effected the transfer, are all Indiana citizens, the agreement stipulates that Indiana law will apply, and the mosaics are stored in Indiana supported the application of Indiana law.

[47] See generally Blom, Joost, "Laying Claim to the Long Lost Art: The Hoge Raad of the Netherlands and the Question of Limitation Periods." *International Journal of Cultural Property 9, Vol. 1* (2000), pp. 138–150.

[48] Establishing title in the case of stolen art is not a simple thing. Based on the customs of the art world and case law, the original owner or his or her successor in interest must rely on various indices of ownership or title, such as bills of sale, catalogue raisonée, provenance, insurance records, Art Loss Register, IFAR, Interpol, and other lists such as the ICOM lists.

[49] U.S. courts have generally required foreign claimants seeking to recover property on the basis of a foreign patrimony law to satisfy a strict burden of proof to the effect that (1) the foreign patrimony law at issue clearly and unequivocally vests title to the property in the state and is not a mere regulating exercise of the police power; (2) the object in question left the country at the time the law was in effect; and (3) the find site was within the current national borders.

[50] See Guido Carducci, "The Growing Complexity of International Art Law: Conflict of Laws, Uniform Law, Mandatory Rules, UNSC Resolutions, and EU Regulations" in Part I of this book.

[51] 536 F. Supp. 829 (E.D.N.Y. 1981) aff'd 678 F.2d 1150 (2d. Cir 1982).

[52] *Autocephalous Greek-Orthodox Church of Cyprus and The Republic of Cyprus* v. *Goldberg & Feldman Fine Arts, Inc.*, 717 F. Supp. 1374 (S.D. Ind. 1985), aff'd, 917 F. 2d 278 (7th Cir. 1990).

Proof of Title

Republic of Croatia v. *The Trustee of the Marquess of Northampton*[53]

This action for replevin involved the rights to possession and ownership of the Sevso Treasure, a collection of fourteen antique Roman silver pieces crafted in the fourth or fifth century A.D., and believed to have been hidden in the seventh century until they were unearthed in the 1970s. The collection was delivered to the Swiss auctioneer and art dealer Sotheby's AG in 1989 by the defendant, the Trustee of the Marquess of Northampton Settlement, a trust organised under the laws of Guernsey, one of the United Kingdom's Channel Islands, for the purpose of its sale as a unit in Switzerland in the fall of 1990.

Although the Trustee believed that the collection was unearthed somewhere in Lebanon in the 1970s, Sotheby's undertook to inquire of the cultural attaché at the embassy in Switzerland of each of the twenty-nine countries whose territory fell within the borders of the Roman Empire in the fourth century A.D. whether the pieces were recorded as stolen property. Similar inquiries were addressed to UNESCO, Interpol, the International Stolen Art Register, Europa Nostra, and the International Council on Museums. Sotheby's also announced that, should any claim arise, the Treasure would not be sold until the claim was resolved. As part of the procedure for ensuring that any possible claims would be made prior to resale, the auctioneer also issued a news release to the international media, containing the aforementioned information, on 9 February 1990, one day before the opening of an eleven-day exhibition of the Treasure at Sotheby's New York, as part of Sotheby's marketing campaign designed to culminate in the fall 1990 sale.[54]

The plaintiff, the Republic of Lebanon, demanded the return of the Treasure in New York on 15 February 1990. Subsequently, the Federal Republic of Yugoslavia (replaced before trial by Croatia) moved to intervene, asserting its own claim to the Treasure on the alleged grounds that it had been unearthed in Yugoslavia in 1971, and Lebanon withdrew from the case with prejudice. By the time of the trial, only Croatia and Hungary sought return of the Treasure based on umbrella national ownership laws. However, neither country was able to prove ownership by satisfying the court's requirement in each case that the foreign government establish and prove a find site within its territory and also prove that its laws vested ownership in the state at the time of the removal of the antiquities.[55]

Because Croatia and Hungary were unable to surmount the difficult legal and evidentiary burdens imposed by the court, the burden never shifted to the purchaser to establish a valid defence.[56] The appellate court distinguished this case from *Guggenheim* (see *infra*), in which the possessors' claim to title was based on a good faith purchase. In this case, the issue was whether Croatia and Hungary had a possessory right at all, and thus it was their burden to prove the find site. The burden of disproving the theft never passed to the Trustee, who, in fact, had abandoned the good faith purchase (BFP) defense. The court had previously denied the defendants' motion to remove the action to Switzerland on the basis of forum *non conveniens*. The appellate court stated,

> The Supreme Court's denial of the cross motion for forum non conveniens dismissal was correct, since defendant Trust failed to meet its heavy burden of demonstrating plaintiff's choice of forum was an inappropriate one. New York, as the situs of the disputed Treasure, resulting from defendants' intentional transportation of the Treasure to this jurisdiction as an integral part of their campaign to market and to establish clear title, has a valid and compelling interest in resolving the conflicting claims of possession and ownership.
>
> We note that litigating this action in New York will better serve the ends of justice than deferring to the proposed Swiss forum. New York permits more liberal discovery, which may be essential given the mystery surrounding the discovery of the Treasure, and also conducts its proceedings in the English language, a language with which more of the relevant documents are written than the German language, in which Swiss judicial proceedings in the Court of Zurich are conducted.[57]

Statue of Limitations

Solomon R. Guggenheim Foundation v. *Lubell*: New York's Demand and Refusal Rule

In the United States, each state has its own statute of limitations that determines the time in which an action must be brought. The statute of limitations in New York on actions

[53] *Republic of Croatia* v. *The Trustee of the Marquess of Northampton* 1987, Settlement 203 AD 2d 167, 610 NYS 2d 263 (Dept. 1994).

[54] Because the auction house acts as the agent of the consignor in offering property for sale, the legal relationship is one of principal to agent. The scope of the agent's fiduciary duty to the consignor is often the subject of litigation and is beyond the scope of this chapter. The consignor, under the standard consignment agreement, represents and warrants *inter alia* that "you have the right to consign the property for sale; that it is now and through and including the sale, free of . . . all claims of government or governmental agencies." In cases in which title is questioned, the auction house usually brings an interpleader action for determination of which of the parties claiming the art or cultural property has superior right, title, and interest in the property. Many art dealers acquire art and antiquities at auction. They cannot receive better title than the consignor.

[55] The difficulty of proving a find site within the confines of a modern nation in these situations suggests the wisdom of developing a regional approach, particularly with respect to the implementation of the UNESCO Convention. In this respect, see the *International Journal of Cultural Property*, Vol. 1 (2000), at p. 169, where a paper by Elizabeth Gilgan discusses the state of cultural heritage in Belize and more particularly analyses the market for antiquities from Belize in the United States. Mayan artefacts are found in Mexico, Guatemala, Belize, Honduras, and El Salvador. After the treaties with El Salvador and Guatemala on import restrictions, Gilgan saw a change in the description of Mayan artefacts used in auction catalogues. "During the 1980s, the catalogs routinely referenced to the origin of these antiquities as the Peten region in Guatemala. After the United States treaties, the provenience was given as 'Lowlands.'"

[56] The court stated,

> "The factual issues to be resolved at trial were whether Croatia or Hungary could prove by a preponderance of the evidence that the Treasure was discovered within its borders and whether the Trustee purchased the Treasure in good faith. . . ."

Croatia and Hungary argued on appeal that the court erred in refusing to shift the burden of proof so as to require the Trustee to substantiate his claim of title once Croatia and Hungary established *prima facie* their rights to possession of the Treasure.

[57] New York is a frequent locus for international art disputes, in part because of its law threshold for minimum contacts to establish jurisdiction.

for recovery of personal property is "three years from the time the action accrued."[58] With respect to actions for recovery of stolen art, New York has developed a rule entitled the Demand and Refusal Rule. Initially articulated in the case of *Menzel* v. *List* in 1938, the most recent articulation is in the case of *Guggenheim* v. *Lubell*.[59] In New York, the three-year statute of limitations governing a cause of action for replevin against a good faith purchaser of stolen chattel does not begin to run until the true owner makes a demand for return of the chattel and the current possessor refuses to return it.

In *Guggenheim*, the New York Court of Appeals decided that the statute of limitations for replevin against a good faith purchaser accrued when the museum made its demand. The Court held that there was no duty of reasonable diligence on the museum for statute of limitations purposes.

The Court in resolving the claim in favor of the Guggenheim, placed the New York rule in context:

> The backdrop for this replevin action (see, CLPR art 71) is the New York City art market, where masterpieces command extraordinary prices at auction and illicit dealing in stolen merchandise is an industry all its own. The Solomon R. Guggenheim Foundation . . . believes that the gouache was stolen from its premises by a mailroom employee sometime in the late 1960s. Rachel Lubell and her husband, now deceased, bought the painting from a well-known Madison Avenue gallery in 1967 and have displayed it in their home for more than 20 years. Mrs. Lubell claims that before the Guggenheim's demand for its return in 1986, she had no reason to believe that the painting had been stolen. . . .
>
> Precisely when the museum first learned that the gouache had been stolen is a matter of dispute. . . . It is undisputed, however, that the Guggenheim did not inform other museums, galleries or artistic organizations of the theft, and additionally, did not notify the New York City Police, the FBI, Interpol or any other law enforcement authorities. The museum asserts that this was a tactical decision based upon its belief that to publicize the theft would succeed only in driving the gouache further underground and greatly diminishing the possibility that it would be recovered. In 1974, having concluded that all efforts to recover the gouache had been exhausted, the museum's Board of Trustees voted to "deaccession" the gouache, thereby removing it from the museum's records. . . .
>
> Further our decision today is in part influenced by our recognition that New York enjoys a worldwide reputation as a preeminent cultural center. To place the burden of locating stolen artwork on the true owner and to foreclose the rights of that owner to recover its property if the burden is not met would, we believe, encourage illicit trafficking in stolen art. Three years after the theft, any purchaser, good faith or not, would be able to hold onto stolen art work unless the true owner was able to establish that it had undertaken a reasonable search for the missing art. This shifting of the burden onto the wronged owner is inappropriate. . . .
>
> New York has already considered – and rejected – adoption of a discovery rule. In 1986, both houses of the New York State Legislature passed Assembly Bill 11462-A (Senate Bill 3274-B), which would have modified the demand and refusal rule and instituted a discovery rule in actions for recovery of art objects brought against certain not-for-profit institutions. . . .
>
> Governor Cuomo vetoed the measure, however, on advice of the United States Department of State, the United States Department of Justice and the United States Information Agency (see, 3 U.S. Agencies Urge Veto of Art-Claim Bill, NY Times, July 23, 1986, at C15, col 1). In his veto message, the Governor expressed his concern that the statute "[did] not provide a reasonable opportunity for individuals or foreign governments to receive notice of a museum's acquisition and take action to recover it before their rights are extinguished." The Governor also stated that he had been advised by the State Department that the bill, if it went into effect, would have caused New York to become "a haven for cultural property stolen abroad since such objects [would] be immune from recovery under the limited time periods established by the bill."

The Court then concluded that, it would be difficult if not impossible to craft a reasonable diligence standard that would take into account all of these variables and would not unduly burden the true owner.[60]

The Discovery or Due Diligence Rule

Most states in the United States have adopted rules which are less favourable to the recovery by the original owner. Under the discovery rule enunciated in the seminal case of *O'Keefe* v. *Snyder*,[61] the cause of action does not begin to accrue until the true owner "first knew, or reasonably should have known through the exercise of due diligence, of the cause of action, including the identity of the possessor." In *O'Keefe*, Georgia O'Keefe sued Snyder, the possessor of three of her paintings, in replevin. O'Keefe alleged that the paintings had been stolen in 1946. Thirty years later, she learned of their whereabouts and demanded their return from Snyder. The New Jersey Supreme Court rejected the lower court's application of the adverse possession doctrine, finding adverse possession unsuitable to art objects. The court instead adopted the discovery rule, consciously shifting the inquiry to the conduct of the true owner, stating that the "focus of the inquiry will no longer be whether the possessor has met the tests of adverse possession, but whether the owner has acted with due diligence in pursuing his or her personal property." O'Keefe indicated that determining what constitutes "due diligence" is a fact-specific analysis that will vary depending on the facts of each case, including the "nature and value of the property."

The O'Keefe approach was followed by the Seventh Circuit in *Autocephalous Greek Orthodox Church of Cyprus* v. *Goldberg and Feldman Fine Arts, Inc.*[62]

The plaintiffs, the Greek-Orthodox Church of Cyprus (the "Church") and the Republic of Cyprus, brought a replevin action in which they sought the right to possession of four Byzantine mosaics that were removed without the Church's authorisation. The Church claimed that as between itself and the defendants, a purchaser and fine arts company, which had purchased the mosaics in good faith and without information

[58] N.Y. Civ Prac L. & R §203(a), McKinney 2005.

[59] *Solomon R. Guggenheim Foundation* v. *Lubell*, 153 A.D.2d 143, 149, 550 N.Y.S.2d 618, 621–22 (1st Dep.'t 1990), aff'd, 77 N.Y.2d 311, 567 N.Y.S.2d 623, 569 N.E.2d 426 (1999).

[60] The court specifically rejected the ruling of the Second Circuit in the case of *DeWerth* v. *Baldenger*, which, to avoid unreasonable delay, the original owner of the work must have exercised due diligence.

[61] *O'Keefe* v. *Snyder* 416A. 2d 862 870 (NJ 1980).

[62] *Autocephalous Greek-Orthodox Church of Cyprus and The Republic of Cyprus* v. *Goldberg & Feldman Fine Arts, Inc.*, 717 F. Supp. 1374 (S.D. Ind. 1985), aff'd, 917 F. 2d 278 (7th Cir. 1990).

or notice that they had been stolen, the Church was entitled to title and possession.

The church did not, therefore, rely on a foreign patrimony claim. Rather, the mosaics were stolen in the traditional sense from the church and documented as stolen. The court found that the church's action to recover the mosaics was governed by Indiana's six-year statute of limitations. The court held that the church's cause of action was filed in a timely manner and did not accrue until late 1988. The discovery rule prevented the statute from applying before then because the church had exercised due diligence and was not on reasonable notice of the identity of the possessor until then. The Republic of Cyprus, immediately upon learning that the mosaics at issue were missing, engaged in an organized effort to notify organizations that might assist, such as International Foundation for Art Research (IFAR). UNESCO, and other museums. Applying Indiana law, the district court found that the Church had proven its case for replevin and was entitled to the mosaics.

The district court concluded that the Church also had superior title under Swiss law, and Goldberg could not claim valid title as a "good faith purchasers"[63] because she only made a cursory inquiry into the suspicious circumstances surrounding the sale of the mosaics. (Under Indiana law, such considerations are irrelevant because, except in very limited exceptions not applicable here, a subsequent purchaser – even a "good faith, bona fide purchaser for value" – who obtains an item from a thief only acquires the title held by the thief; that is, no title.) The appellate court concluded that Judge Noland's extensive (and quite interesting) discussion of Swiss law, as well as Goldberg's lengthy attack thereon, need not be reviewed. "Cyprus adequately established the elements of replevin under Indiana law, on which ground alone we affirm the district court's decision to award the possession of the mosaics to the Church of Cyprus."[64]

The Laches Defense

The doctrine of laches is an equitable one – it states that a person cannot sit upon his rights to another party's prejudice. New York courts have specifically held that the laches doctrine may be implicated by the original owners' lack of diligence. Although the New York Court of Appeals in *Guggenheim* and the United States Court of Appeals for the Second Circuit in *DeWerth* v. *Ballinger* have disagreed as to whether the original owner need to show reasonable diligence in the context of a statute of limitations defence, both courts have explicitly ruled that an original owner's reasonable diligence in locating the lost property is highly relevant to a laches defence. A claim may be barred by the defence of laches when a plaintiff unreasonably delays commencing an action and that delay operates to the prejudice of the defendant. As an equitable defence, courts in Illinois and California have not applied it to replevin, an action at law.

Greek Orthodox Patriarchate of Jerusalem v. *Christie's, Inc.*[65]

The plaintiff, the Greek Orthodox Patriarchate of Jerusalem, brought this action seeking the return of a tenth century manuscript containing a copy of certain writings of Archimedes. The history of the Palimpsest recounted in the federal district court's decision is fascinating, but beyond the scope of this chapter.

The case is of interest for its discussion and resolution of choice of law issues, the statute of limitations discussion, and a more fully developed discussion of the laches defence in a replevin action.

Applying the law of the forum state, the court stated that in New York, questions relating to the validity of a transfer of personal possession are governed by the law of the state where the property is located at the time of transfer (*lex situs*). In this case, because title passed in France, if at all, French law was deemed to apply.

Although it was not necessary to the decision awarding title to the plaintiffs, the Court applied the laches defense, stating that:

> In the context of claims of lost or stolen works of art or cultural artefacts. . . . the doctrine of laches . . . safeguards the interests if a good faith purchaser of lost or stolen art . . . by weighing in the balance of competing interests the owner's diligence in pursuing his claim. . . .

The question of whether the Patriarchate was sufficiently diligent in searching for the Palimpsest to defeat the defendant's laches defense is easily answered. The Patriarchate was not diligent at all.

[63] Swiss law provides that "no one can claim to be in good faith if such claim is incompatible with the attention that he should have shown under the circumstances." It is interesting to compare the approach of the French court on the issue of good faith in the *Schloss* case. The Schloss collection was one of the world-renowned Jewish collections specifically targeted by the Germans, often helped by the Vichy Government. The collection (333 paintings, including masterpieces by Franz Hals, Rembrandt, Rubens, etc.) had been the property of the Schloss family since the nineteenth century. At the end of the war, the Musée du Louvre returned all the paintings remaining in France, *viz.* 162, to the Schloss family. The 171 missing paintings were displayed in a photographic catalogue that was widely published.

In 1990, one of the heirs to the Schloss family discovered the painting by Frans Hais in an art and antiques show organized in Paris, displayed by the American Art Gallery Newhouse Galleries. It was one of the 171 missing paintings of his family's collection. Long criminal proceedings took place against the Director of the New York Gallery, Mr. Williams. In the decision rendered in 1998 by the French Cour de Cassation, the latter held in particular that:

> Mr. A. W. . . . a well-informed art professional and a specialist of the seventeenth century, could not pretend to have ignored the historical circumstances surrounding the S[chloss] collection and more particularly the painting which he acquired.

The Court thus clearly considered in such (professional) circumstances that there was a presumption of bad faith, that – in the case at hand – could not be reversed by the fact that "the painting had been auctioned several times already despite the fact that it had been stolen during the war." Cour de Cassation, Decision of 4 June 1998, for a commentary on this decision, see Leila Anglade, *The Portrait of Pastor Adrianus by Frans Hals: A Landmark Criminal Decision on Looted Art is Finally Handed Down by French Court*, ART ANTIQUITY AND LAW, Vol VIII, March 2003, pp. 77 (2003).

[64] Indiana's statute of limitations for replevin actions is six years and the court applied the discovery rule.

[65] *Greek Orthodox Patriarchate of Jerusalem* v. *Christie's, Inc.*, 1999 US Dist. LEXIS 13257.

The only excuse the Patriarchate raised for its utter lack of diligence is that, as an order of monks, it could not be expected to search for a painting. Yet if the Patriarchate was able to retain counsel with impressive speed to bring the action the night before the Christie's auction, it could have retained counsel to search for the Palimpsest, or at least make some inquiries, at some point during the previous seventy years.

Warin v. *Wildenstein & Co.*

In *Warin* v. *Wildenstein & Co*,[66] the plaintiffs Francis Warin and En Memoire D'Alphonse Kann brought this action to recover eight rare and valuable illuminated manuscripts from the defendants, Wildenstein & Co., Inc., Daniel Wildenstein, Alec Wildenstein, and Guy Wildenstein. Plaintiffs claimed that the Nazis stole these manuscripts from Alphonse Kann's home in occupied France in October 1940.[67] They alleged that the defendants, who acquired the manuscripts from the French government between 1949 and 1952 after they were recovered from the Nazis, are not entitled to retain ownership and possession. The defendants moved for summary judgment, pursuant to CPLR 3212, dismissing the complaint on the grounds that plaintiffs' claims are barred by the statute of limitations and the doctrine of laches. Defendants also moved to dismiss the complaint against Daniel Wildenstein and Alec Wildenstein, pursuant to CPLR 3211(a)(8), for lack of personal jurisdiction. In turn, plaintiffs have cross-moved to dismiss the affirmative defenses of statute of limitations, laches, and lack of personal jurisdiction.

The parties disputed whether the limitations period for plaintiffs' claims is governed by French or New York law. Defendants argued that French law applied.[68] Plaintiffs asserted that it is New York law that governs the question of whether this lawsuit is time-barred.

The appellate court affirmed the lower court's dismissal of the case, indicating that whether French law or New York law was applied, the defendants prevailed on the laches defence.[69] It is very rare that laches, usually a fact-specific defence, is decided on summary judgement and lawyers for original owners have expressed some concern.

A common factor uniting U.S. decisions that also distinguishes them from the traditional European approach is that the courts seek to ascertain the merits of each party's claims rather than apply a rigid formula to determine ownership between two innocent parties. This is, of course, as Peter Raue in his chapter points out, at the expense of certainty, one of the cardinal reasons for statutes of limitation.

HOLOCAUST-RELATED DISPUTES

The public awareness of the extent and significance of Nazi looting that has occurred in recent years caused a shift in the stance of U.S. Museums on the issue of restitution. AAM has adopted Guidelines concerning the unlawful Appropriation of Objects during the Nazi era (<http://www.aamus.org/museumresources/ethics/nazi_guidelines>).

Similarly, in 1997 the AAMD formed a Task Force to draft guidelines on art looted by the Nazis during World War II. The Guidelines, which were published in June 1998, formed the basis of the Washington Principles drafted by the Washington Conference on Holocaust-era Assets, the first international conference held in the US addressing Holocaust assets. Among the AAMD's recommendations was the development of a centralized database using newly available technologies. The Task Force is now in the process of ensuring that the AAMD Guidelines are consistent with the Commission's recommendations. (Compare AAMD Guidelines June 10, 2004 on the Acquisition of Archaeological Materials and Ancient Art.)

The past few years has shown increasing sympathy to the claims of holocaust victims and their heirs notwithstanding the lengthy battle over "Portrait of Wally."

MOMA's deputy General Counsel Stephen Clark recently prepared for the annual ALI-ABA Legal Problems of Museum Administration Program, March 31, 2005, from publicly available information a selected list of World War II restitution cases from 1998–2004. The list included twenty cases which had been settled by United States' museums without litigation embodying solutions from restitution, to purchase by the museum, shared ownership and included another twenty one or so involving restitution to European claimants by European museums.

66 740 N.Y.S. 2d 331, 2002 N.Y. App. Div. LEXIS 3835 (App. Div. 1st Dep't 2002).

67 The Wildenstein Gallery is the most important and the wealthiest art gallery in the world. Its net worth is estimated to be $5.5 billion. The Wildensteins "aryanized" their gallery during the war by giving it to a former employee known to have Nazi sympathies. The Wildenstein family spent the war in New York and, for a commission, helped the Nazis get some of the looted art.

The Nazis plundered manuscripts from the Alphonse Kann collection, meticulously documenting their loot. Their description of the hand-painted manuscript called "The Master of Dredman Prayer Book," scripted by an anonymous late fifteenth century Flemish artist, leaves no doubt as to its authenticity. The manuscript is the only piece made by this artist and is the only looted manuscript of its kind. The "Annunciation," another late fifteenth century Flemish work, and a Louis XII prayer book manuscript are described in the inventory and are among the possessions of the Wildenstein Gallery. The Kann family's suit for the manuscripts failed in France because the court unanimously rejected the claim. See H. Feliciano, "Nazi Stolen Arts," O. Pell., 20 Whittier Law Rev 67 (1998).

68 In France, the statute of limitations is three years for a good faith purchaser. Under French law, even a thief can acquire good title if he maintains "continuous, peaceful, open, and unequivocal possession over a thirty year period."

69 See also *Wertheimer* v. *Cirker's Hayes Storage Warehouse, Inc.*, No. 105575/00, 2001 WL 1657237 (S. Ct. N.Y. Co. Sept. 28, 2001), aff'd 300 A.D. 2d 117, 752 N.Y.S. 2d 295 (1st Dep't 2002). In that case, an heir of Pierre Wertheimer, whose Pissarro painting was converted after he fled the Nazi invasion of France in June 1940, sought to recover the painting after it turned up years later in a warehouse in New York. In concluding that the claim was barred by laches, the trial court stated with respect to plaintiff's unreasonable delay:

> The Wertheimer family literally did nothing to recover the Pissarro painting since the early 1950s. . . . The painting apparently surfaced for a lengthy period, when it was advertised for sale by the Schoneman Galleries in New York City. Wertheimer was made aware by his grandmother in the early 1970s that some of the family property had been looted during the war. Plaintiff and his family did not report the Pissarro painting missing to the Art Loss Registry, or contact galleries or museums regarding the painting.

The next section discusses several significant cases which have not settled.

Holocaust cases in the United States have involved original owners versus the foreign governments civil forfeiture actions involving museums and heirs, and original owners (heirs) against good faith purchasers.

Altmann v. *Austria*[70]

Portrait of Wally (Wally III), brought allegations that the Austrian National Gallery possessed looted art. In response, the Austrian Minister for Education and Culture "opened up the Ministry's archives to permit research into the provenance of the national collection," and the Austrian government set up a Commission to advise on the return of artworks.

Adele Block-Bauer died in 1925. Her husband, Maria Altmann's uncle Ferdinand Bloch died in exile in 1945, leaving all his possessions to his nieces and nephews. Altmann, who arrived in the United States as a refugee in 1942, is the remaining survivor and a resident and citizen of the U.S. and California. Under post-war restitution laws, Austrian families whose possessions were stolen by Nazis were able to retrieve their property or receive compensation from the government. In order to recover the bulk of their property, the Bloch-Bauer family surrendered its claim to six Gustav Klimt paintings. The Austrian government turned the paintings over to the state museum.

Despite discovering documents that called into question the Austrian Gallery's legal claims to the Klimts through Adele Bloch-Bauer's will, the Commission recommended against returning the paintings.[71] Altmann tried to sue in Austrian courts to recover the paintings but could not afford the court's filing fee, a percentage of presumed recovery ($U.S.135,000). Altmann changed strategy and filed a lawsuit in the Federal District Court in California.

Altmann's lawsuit asserted jurisdiction under §2 of the Foreign Sovereign Immunities Act of 1976 (FSIA or Act), 28 U.S. C. §1330(a), which authorizes federal civil suits against foreign states "as to any claim for relief in personam with respect to which the foreign state is not entitled to immunity" under another section of the FSIA or under "any applicable international agreement."

In 2004, the United States Supreme Court decided the case of *Republic of Austria et al.* v. *Maria Altmann.* In many ways, the decision is a technical one in which the U.S. Supreme Court had to decide whether the FSIA applies retroactively to art that was looted during the World War II / Nazi era. The FSIA took effect in 1977 and permits lawsuits in the United States against foreign governments under certain limited circumstances. The U.S. State Department filed a friend of the court brief on behalf of the Republic of Austria, fearing a multiplicity of lawsuits that would interfere with U.S. foreign policy. The Supreme Court permitted the suit to proceed against the Austrian government and the Austrian National Gallery, concluding that the FSIA adopted in 1976, applies retroactively to divest Austria of immunity from alleged acts of expropriation even if such acts occurred in the 1940s.

On May 18, 2005, the Republic of Austria and Maria Altmann agreed to end their litigation in U.S. District Court regarding the Klimt paintings, and to submit the dispute to binding arbitration in Austria.

The agreement will clear the way for a prompt and conclusive decision on the ownership of the paintings, most of which have been housed in the Austrian National Gallery for more than fifty years. The Austrian National Gallery, as well as Mrs. Altmann's four co-heirs, are also parties to the agreement.

Under the agreement, the Los Angeles litigation will be dismissed and not subject to re-filing by any party. The agreement calls for the creation of a panel of three Austrian arbitrators chosen by the parties. The parties have agreed that they will accept the decision of the arbitration panel as final and without any right of appeal.

The issues before the panel are those previously addressed by the Austrian Art Advisory Commission.

Benningson v. *Alsdorf*

Picasso painted "Femme en blanc" in 1922, and Robert and Carlota Landsberg purchased it in 1926 or 1927 and took it to their residence in Berlin. After Robert died in 1932, and hostility against Jews in Germany increased in 1933, Carlota fled to New York where she settled in 1940 or 1941. Before Carlota left Berlin, she sent the Picasso to Paris for safekeeping with Paris art dealer J.K. Thannhauser. The painting was taken from Thannhauser's Gallery by the Nazis in 1940 during the occupation of Paris. James and Marilyn Alsdorf bought "Femme en blanc" from art dealer Stephen Hahn in New York the same year.

The Alsdorfs kept the Picasso in their Chicago apartment until Marilyn sent the painting to the David Tunkl Fine Art Gallery in Los Angeles for possible sale in September 2001. Tunkl located a Parisian art dealer interested in the painting, and sent the Picasso to Switzerland, where it was held in the Freeport for inspection by the prospective purchaser. The Parisian art dealer contacted the Art Loss Register (ALR) to conduct a provenance search on the Picasso. The search revealed that the painting had been stolen from Thannhauser's collection during the war after being placed there by Carlota. The ALR then contacted Carlota's grandson and heir, Thomas Bennigson, a law student at Berkeley.

Initially, negotiations concerning the Picasso were handled by the ALR, however, Bennigson brought a replevin action in California state court against Alsdorf and the Tunkl art gallery.

Bennigson also immediately filed an *ex parte* application for a temporary restraining order (TRO) in an attempt to keep the Picasso in Los Angeles. The TRO was granted the

[70] *Republic of Austria et al.* v. *Maria* v. *Altmann* 124 S.Ct 2240 (2004).

[71] The Austrian Parliament approved a law in 1998 that allowed return of 500 looted works in Austrian museums. Obviously, the Klimts were not among these works; however, the act returned 200 works to the Rothschild family, which netted the family nearly $90 million in a subsequent auction at Christie's.

next day (after Alsdorf's attorney was notified). But Alsdorf had already shipped the painting from Tunkl's gallery back to Chicago. Alsdorf then filed a motion to dismiss for lack of personal Jurisdiction which both the trial court and appellate court granted. Bennigson appealed to the states's highest court. On August 9, 2005, the parties announced a settlement of Bennigson's $10 million claim. Alsdorf will pay $6.5 million after the California court enters a consent judgment that Alsdorf has incontestable title.[72]

Sarah-Rose Josepha Adler, et al. v. *Elizabeth Taylor*[73]

Rightful ownership to "Vue de l'Asile et de la Chapelle de Saint-Remy," ("the painting"), which Vincent Van Gogh painted while a patient of the asylum at Saint-Remy, was the issue presented in this case brought against Elizabeth Taylor. Plaintiffs are heirs and descendants of an art collector who owned the painting in early twentieth-century Germany and claim it was stolen from their heir because of Nazi persecution. Taylor bought the painting in 1963 at a Sotheby's auction for US$257,000. The Sotheby's auction incorrectly stated that the painting had passed to Paul Cassirer in 1928 (he had died in 1926). The Sotheby's auction also referred bidders to two catalogues *raisonné*, which listed the history of the painting. This history of ownership identified a German woman named Maqurette Mauthner as the owner of the painting in the 1920s and 1930's. It included other information inconsistent with the Sotheby's auction's representations. Plaintiffs alleged that Taylor ignored these warning signs and bought the painting without properly investigating its ownership history. The court granted Elizabeth Taylor's motion to dismiss based on California's statute of limitations. The court reasoned:

California limits causes of action to recover Holocaust-era artwork from individuals. California passed a law giving heirs the right to sue *galleries and museums* for the return of such artwork until 2010, free from any statute of limitations. However, this exception does not apply to suits against individuals. In "[a]n action for taking, detaining, or injuring any goods or chattels, including actions for the specific recovery of personal property," a plaintiff must sue within three years. A newer version of the California law includes an explicit "discovery rule," which states that the statute begins to run when the plaintiff was on notice of the property's whereabouts. However, the parties agree that the Court should apply the old law given that Taylor bought the painting in 1963.

The discovery rule provides that, in an appropriate case, a cause of action will not accrue until the injured party discovers, or by exercise of reasonable diligence and intelligence should have discovered, facts which form the basis of a cause of action.

Plaintiffs' own Complaint establishes several key facts: (1) the world knew of Mauthner's prior ownership of the painting for years; (2) Mauthner was aware that the painting was lost or stolen; and (3) Taylor's purchase and ownership of the painting was common knowledge and easily discoverable.

Leonard Malewicz et al. v. *City of Amsterdam*

Until recently, as noted in the discussion *supra* of Portrait of Wally, 22 U.S.C. §2459 has served as an effective and efficient means for protecting visiting exhibits from litigation; however, its vitality has been called into question by *Malewicz* v. *City of Amsterdam* (362 F. Supp. 298 (D.C. March 30 2005).

The lawsuit attempts to correct an alleged wrong committed by the City of Amsterdam when it expropriated eighty-four works of art created by Kazmir Malewicz.

In denying the City of Amsterdam's motion to dismiss for lack of jurisdiction, the Court concluded that it could not determine on the record whether the City of Amsterdam's contacts with the United States were "substantial" within the FSIA.

Whether or not the case will be upheld on appeal is a matter of conjecture. What is interesting for the purposes of this chapter is that the Court, as in *Altmann*, declined to follow the recommendations of the Executive Branch on cultural policy.

In *Malewicz*, the United States submitted a Statement of Interest, which to this author was persuasive, but not to the Court arguing that because of the grant of immunity the artworks could not be present in the United States for the purposes of the FSIA.

The Plaintiffs filed their complaint two days prior to the close of the exhibition. A predicate for the exercise of jurisdiction was the immunized works presence in the United States.

The Plaintiffs contend that the expropriation exception to the FSIA 28 U.S.C. §1605 (a)(3) provides a jurisdictional basis for their claims concerning 14 works that were imported into the United States under a grant of immunity from seizure under section 2459. The works at issue were imported into the United States in 2003 to be part of a temporary exhibition of artwork at the Guggenheim Museum in New York City and the Menil Collection in Houston.

The Department of State granted the application for immunity based on the determination that the objects were of cultural significance and that the temporary exhibition of the works in the United States was in the national interest.

[72] A related case was filed in California against the gallery that sold to Mrs. Alsdorf. In *Claude Cassirer et al.* v. *Stephen Hahn*, plaintiffs pled only that the Stephen Hahn Gallery sold two Nazi-looted paintings by world-renowned artists Camille Pissarro and Pablo Picasso in 1975 and 1976 without the consent of the legal owners and kept the profits. Plaintiff Bennigson alleges as to the acquisition of the Picasso only that Hahn purchased the painting from an art dealer in Paris. The court framed the issue as one of choice of law, and applied California law to deny Hahn's statute of limitations defense.

"Under the governmental interest analysis, in general, the forum state applies its own law unless a litigant demonstrates that applying the law of another state would further the interest of the other state. There are three steps: (1) The court determines whether the foreign law differs from that of the forum. (2) If there is a difference, the court examines each jurisdiction's interest in the application of its own law to determine whether a true conflict exists. When both jurisdictions have a legitimate interest in the application of its rule of decision, (3) the court analyzes the comparative impairment of the interested jurisdictions, and applies the law of the state whose interest would be impaired if its law were not applied." On July 25, 2005, Bennigson arrived at a settlement with Hahn that should Bennigson recover the Picasso by judgment or settlement with Mrs. Alsdorf, Hahn would be obligated to pay Bennigson an amount that approximates Hahn's proper on the original sale.

[73] *Sarah-Rose Josepha Adler, et al.* v. *Elizabeth Taylor* (CV 04-H472 February 2005).

Confronted with an apparent conflict between the two acts, the Court reasoned as follows:

> Because the Malewicz Heirs are not seeking judicial seizure of the artworks, the City's and the United States' reliance on *§2459* is misplaced. Immunity from seizure is not immunity from suit for a declaration of rights or for damages arising from an alleged conversion if the other terms for FSIA jurisdiction exist.

CONCLUSION

What is clear from this brief overview is that cultural property in the United States legal system is not treated as ordinary personal property. A developing jurisprudence involves law, ethics, and policy considerations often beyond the case at issue. The results of efforts to recover looted art and cultural property either through litigation or other means transcend the issue of the return of such property to the claimant and look toward identifying those values and principles to contribute to a fair and equitable cultural heritage policy. As courts confront new and difficult applications for traditional legal doctrines, the U.S. law of cultural property is fluid and in a state of flux. Tread carefully.

POLICY QUESTIONS[74]

(1) Should we consider proposals by some that new restrictions on international acquisition be considered, including enhanced rights of return, limited to the "high-end" objects (which are the objects most likely to give rise to actions for return), return for relaxation of foreign export restrictions from source countries on mid-level objects? This approach has not been actively considered internationally, but has been raised from time to time informally by some in the United States.

(2) Is it time to legally distinguish between protection of objects because of their intrinsic nature as "cultural," recognizing the importance to particular communities such as those of Native Americans, on the one hand, and the protection of other property rights and territorial interests of states on the other? Both approaches to "protection" of cultural property have their adherents, but each would tend to produce different results.

(3) Should any new discussions at the international level on rights of return be coupled with undertakings on public access, conservation, and limitations on rights of resale? Should this be considered for discussions between the North American Free Trade Agreement member states?

(4) Should the trade, museums, and other acquiring institutions, and government agencies recognize the rapidly improving software capacity for low-cost, high-resolution recordation of objects, and expanded access internationally to such systems, which could be employed to significantly reduce the ease with which illegally acquired objects can overtly be sold or transferred through recognized outlets? Considerable work is under way in various international bodies on electronic registries for other types of commercial interests, which could perhaps be modified to accommodate international art object registries, if there is sufficient interest in doing so.

(5) Should specialized arbitration panels be promoted for transborder return cases? Proposals have been made for establishment of such a system, which could be composed of panels with expertise on the art trade, and could operate under professional guidelines agreed to in advance.

(6) Should we seek separate standards for the particular problems of archaeological site protection, and develop a dual approach to rights of possession and return, differentiating known art objects from those from protected sites? The preservation *in situ* of archaeological, ethnological, and other items often presents very different issues with regard to proof of origin, ownership, etc., as well as a level of purported "loss" that itself has different parameters. Efforts to combine both types of objects under the same rules or standards may need to be reconsidered.

(7) Under what terms and conditions should the United States consider ratification of the UNIDROIT Convention? It would, of course, be important to note that U.S. ratification would need to be accompanied by implementing legislation, as it was under UNESCO, which would have to set out in detail a number of points not clarified by the Convention, including standards to determine who could present claims, what evidentiary standards would be applied, whether any modifications to current state laws could be involved, etc.

(8) *Guggenheim* modified the holding of *DeWerth*, which had held that the demand and refusal rule, as interpreted by New York, required the exact opposite of the Guggenheim Court – that the original owner must exercise due diligence in the pursuit of his or her art and prove demand to be timely. Should *Guggenheim* be overruled and should *DeWerth* become the law of New York?

[74] Editor's Note: These questions were originally propounded by participants, including Herbert Hirsch, Chair, Committee, Art Law ABCNY 1997–2000, at the Cultural Property Round Table of the Association of the Bar of the City of New York, 12 November 1996.

APPENDIX I

Chart of Current and Expired Import Restrictions Under the Convention on Cultural Property Implementation Act*

Country	'87 '88 '89 '90 '91 '92 '93 '94 '95 '96 '97 '98 '99 '00 '01 '02 '03 '04 '05 '06 '07 08 09 '10
Bolivia	**March 14, 1989:** Emergency Action on antique ceremonial textiles from the community of Coroma, Bolivia. **(expired Sept. 11, 1996)** **Dec. 7, 2001:** Bilateral Agreement on pre-Columbian archaeological & Colonial and Republican ethnological material.
Cambodia	**Dec. 2, 1999:** Emergency Action on Khmer stone archaeological material. **Sept. 22, 2003:** Bilateral Agreement on Khmer archaeological material.
Canada	**April 22, 1997:** Bilateral Agreement on archaeological and ethnological material. **(exp. 2002)**
Cyprus Archaeological	**July 19, 2002:** Bilateral Agreement on pre-Classical and Classical archaeological material.
Cyprus Ethnological	**April 12, 1999:** Emergency Action (extended August 29, 2003) on Byzantine ethnological material.
El Salvador	**Sept. 11, 1987:** Emergency Action Cara Sucia pre-Columbian archaeological material. **March 10, 1995:** Bilateral Agreement **(**extended March 8, 2000, **and** March 8, 2005**)** on pre-Columbian archaeological material (continues protection for Cara Sucia material).
Guatemala	**April 15, 1991:** Emergency Action on pre-Columbian archaeological material from Peten. **Oct. 3, 1997:** Bilateral Agreement (extended Sept. 29, 2002) on pre-Columbian archaeological material (continues protection for Peten material).
Honduras	**March 12, 2004:** Bilateral Agreement on pre-Columbian archaeological material.
Italy	**Jan. 23, 2001,** Bilateral Agreement on Pre-classical, Classical and Imperial Roman archaeological material.
Mali	**Sept. 23, 1993:** Emergency Action on archaeological material from Niger River Valley, Bandiagara Escarpment. **Sept. 23, 1997:** Bilateral Agreement (extended Sept. 19, 2002) on archaeological material from the Niger River Valley and Bandiagara Escarpment (continuous protection).
Nicaragua	**Oct. 26, 2000:** Bilateral Agreement on pre-Columbian archaeological material.
Peru	**May 7, 1990:** Emergency Action on pre-Columbian archaeological material from Sipan. **June 11, 1997:** Bilateral Agreement (extended June 6, 2002**)** on pre-Columbian archaeological material and Colonial ethnological material (continues protection for Sipan material).

* Each country name is linked to its fact sheet. Shaded areas indicate continuous protection for restricted materials. Each action (agreement or emergency) is linked to the Federal Register notice which gives a detailed list of the archaeological or ethnological materials subject to restriction. The initial date indicates when the restriction went into effect. (A chart organized by date of original action is also available.)

CHAPTER TWENTY-ONE

The Illicit Trade in Cultural Objects: Recent Developments in the United Kingdom

Adrian Parkhouse

Fairly recent experience shows that, taking a relatively random group of people representing those with an interest in countering illicit trade in cultural objects, such people coming from a reasonable spread of countries across the world, and posing to them the simple question, "In terms of countering such illicit trade, do you regard the United Kingdom as on the side of the angels or not?" produces a considerable majority in favour of "no."[1]

It is material to the measure of the resulting disappointment to the English lawyer working in this area of law, that this experience post-dates many of the developments this chapter outlines. Given the experiment's lack of sophistication, the influences on the majority's thinking are not known. The suspicion may be that high-profile disputes, particularly that over the Parthenon Marbles, weigh heavily. That this might be the case, notwithstanding the real progress made in this area in recent years, is regrettable and one object of this chapter is to suggest that in most respects the United Kingdom has gone a considerable way to correcting many of the deficiencies that may have justified similar earlier criticism.

ANALYSING THE ISSUES

In 2001, Professor Norman Palmer presented a paper to the annual International Bar Association conference describing the work of the UK Illicit Trade Advisory Panel[2] ("the Panel").

The Panel, of which Professor Palmer had been Chair, was appointed by the then Minister for the Arts in May 2000 and reported in December that year. Its brief was to recommend what action, if any, the UK should take to stem the illicit trade in cultural objects.[3]

The Panel was at pains to recognise "*the dynamic and honourable licit trade*" in cultural objects that existed in the United Kingdom and the increasing influence of formal ethical guidelines and professional sanctions. It was concerned to ensure that this market would not be impaired by its recommendations. However, it was satisfied that there existed sufficient illicit trade in the United Kingdom to justify measured intervention by means of public and criminal law. It was concerned also that the United Kingdom should not be seen as offering a safer haven than other jurisdictions for those engaged in illicit trading.

The Panel surveyed the relevant law as it existed (and largely continues to exist today) in the United Kingdom. In particular, the following points were noted:

The Criminal Law: The existing law of theft applies where a person dishonestly appropriates property belonging to another with the intention of permanently depriving that other person of it.[4] A separate offence is committed when a person "handles" (which includes storage or transportation of an object or participation as an agent in its sale or purchase or facilitation of its disposal) a stolen object, knowing or believing it to be stolen,[5] and this applies even when the goods are stolen abroad.[6]

The Civil (Private) Law: Between the original owner and the thief, or anyone associated with the theft, the common law is a reasonably helpful tool to the owner. A combination of the tort of conversion, which entitles the owner to sue for the return of the object (almost) regardless of the knowledge of the possessor; the principle of *nemo dat*, meaning that the thief cannot pass a better title to goods than he himself has; and the fact that there is no limitation period on the bringing of an action against the thief (or anyone associated with the theft) means that the legal hurdles to recovery are minor.

In reality (a point implicitly recognized by the Panel), although this is true, where an object has passed through several hands, the *nemo dat* principle becomes less meaningful and the possibility of a limitation defence arises for the possessor. In such cases, the burden of proof of good faith acquisition is on the possessor, but, if established, the consequence is not only a defence but also the passage of title.[7] It is possible that the increasing availability of databases as everyday tools of the trade will make it very difficult for any dealer to satisfy the burden of good faith acquisition.[8]

[1] The reference is to a show of hands during a session on Illicit Trade in Heritage Objects at the International Bar Association Annual Conference in 2003.

[2] "*The Illicit Trade in Cultural Objects: Recent Developments in the United Kingdom.*" Professor Norman Palmer, 2001.

[3] Further information regarding the Panel can be found on <http://www.culture.gov.uk/cultural_property/illicit_trade.htm>.

[4] Section 1 Theft Act 1968.

[5] Section 22 Theft Act 1968.

[6] Section 24 Theft Act 1968. See *R* v. *Tokeley-Parry* [1999] Crim. L. R. 578. This was the English end of the removal of Egyptian artifacts that subsequently led to the conviction in New York of Frederick Schultz: *United States v. Schultz* 333 F.2d 293 (2d Cir 2003). Whereas Schultz's conviction for conspiracy was a matter of some controversy in the United States, Tokeley-Parry's went almost unnoticed in England.

[7] Section 4 Limitation Act.

[8] *De Préval* v. *Adrian Alan Ltd.* [1997] unreported 24th January, Arden J.

Foreign Law: Many cases involve the English courts taking into account the law of another jurisdiction, for example, where the law of another jurisdiction is the proper law of the material transaction. Sometimes – especially where the civil law may recognise as lawful an acquisition that the English law would not, that may not be to the advantage of the original owner.[9] The Panel took some comfort from the fact that the English courts retain power not to recognise either transactions or foreign limitation periods[10] that offend public policy. However, instances where such discretion is exercised are very few.

The general tenor of this review was not unduly critical of the then existing regime (particularly when there was added in the obligations on the United Kingdom of EU Council Directive 1993/7/EEC of 15 March 1993 – enacted into UK law by the Return of Cultural Objects Regulations 1994). Nonetheless the Panel's review of the existing legal structure concluded:

> These doctrines do not offer a definitive system for the deterrence of the cross-border illicit trade in cultural objects. If anything, they accentuate the general inadequacy of the common law in this regard. Their existence may, however, help in shaping and evaluating reforms.

Interestingly, shortly before the Panel's Report appeared, the House of Commons Select Committee on Culture, Media and Sport ("the Select Committee") had published its own Report into the same problem, that of "Cultural Property: Return and Illicit Trade."[11] In reviewing the problem of illicit trade, the Select Committee had greater sympathy than is evident in the Panel's Report for the "victim countries." Even so, having heard evidence on the legal framework and the trade's response to the problem, the Select Committee was also reticent in criticising either. Nonetheless, it concluded:

> . . . these arguments should not be interpreted as justifications for inaction in the United Kingdom. In examining the case for liberalisation of the trade in classical antiquities and of the export laws of some European States, it is possible to lose sight of the worldwide impact of the illicit trade in cultural property. The "victim States" are not simply countries such as Greece, Italy, Egypt and Turkey, but increasingly include countries such as Thailand, Cambodia, Mali, Peru, Mexico, Guatemala, Cyprus and Afghanistan. It is important to bear in mind the view that many indigenous communities have a prior claim to their own cultural property whatever the wishes of western collectors. In many cases, local populations are the victims rather than the perpetrators of looting. The burden of the illicit trade bears most heavily on developing countries, who lose both records of their past and opportunities for tourist development.
>
> The United Kingdom's voice as an advocate for legislative and practical action in other countries is unlikely to be heard while the perception remains that the United Kingdom has done little to contribute to the worldwide effort to combat the illicit trade in cultural property.

Thus the argument for change was one of setting an example. In the eyes of neither the Panel nor the Select Committee were there gaping holes in the then current framework.

THE RECOMMENDED RESPONSE

The principal recommendations of the Panel were:

(a) that the United Kingdom accede to the 1970 United Nations Educational Scientific and Cultural Organization (UNESCO) Convention on the Means of Prohibiting the Illicit Import, Export and Transfer of Cultural Property;
(b) that the United Kingdom not accede to the 1995 International Institute for the Unification of Private Law (UNIDROIT) Convention on Stolen Exported Cultural Objects;
(c) that a new criminal offence be created to impose penal sanctions on those who deal or are in possession of cultural objects unlawfully removed from overseas countries in breach of local laws on theft, removal from monuments, wrecks or sites, or illegal excavation;
(d) that databases be established to provide retrievable information on overseas law related to and on removed cultural objects; and
(e) that the United Kingdoms export licensing process be used as a means to observe the movement of unlawfully removed cultural objects.

Two of these recommendations justify further comment.

The Conventions – Question

The question of whether to accede to either or both of the UNESCO or UNIDROIT conventions occupied a significant element of the Panel's attention – as it had that of the Select Committee, looking at the same issue. The Select Committee had recommended accession by the United Kingdom to UNIDROIT but not to UNESCO – the reverse of the subsequent recommendations of the Panel.

What were the reasons for this divergence of view?

Both the Panel and the Select Committee were attracted by certain elements of UNIDROIT – in particular its grant of direct rights of action to dispossessed owners and the relative clarity and certainty of its language. However, according to the Panel, the factors counting against it were:

(a) the inability of a contracting power to make any reservations (and the Panel recommended certain matters be reserved in acceding to UNESCO);
(b) the relatively low level of accession to the Convention – only twelve countries at the date of the Panel's report, among which only France was regarded as a major "market nation"; and
(c) (the factor which many suspect to have been most material) the length of some of the applicable limitation

[9] See for example *Winkworth* v. *Christie, Manson and Woods Ltd.* [1980] Ch. 496.

[10] Section 2, Foreign Limitation Periods Act 1984.

[11] See Seventh Report of the House of Commons Select Committee on Culture Media and Sport, *Cultural Property: Return and Illicit Trade* (18 July 2000). <http://www.publications.parliament.uk/pa/cm199900/cmselect/cmcumeds/371/37102.htm>.

periods when compared with UK domestic law and the absence of any penalty for claimants who might have acted earlier but did not.

Regarding UNESCO, the Select Committee formed the view that the obligations placed on acceding states would require too much work on the part of the United Kingdom to be practical (for example: the obligation to have the trade maintain registers recording the origin of each item of cultural property, names and addresses of the supplier, description and price of each item sold, and to inform the purchaser of the cultural property of the export prohibition to which such property may be subject[12]). This finding echoed the reasoning of successive UK governments.

In contrast, the Panel was attracted by the UNESCO Convention, for the following reasons:

(a) reservations were permitted;
(b) the open-textured language introduced a welcome degree of elasticity into the Convention when applied in the contracting state; and
(c) there was a high level of accession to the Convention.

The Panel noted the nature of the Select Committee's concern about the work required to comply with the UNESCO obligations, but took a different view. They took each obligation in turn and decided that the "elasticity" of language meant that the United Kingdom, in fact, complied already with the greater part of the Convention requirements in one form or another. In the case of the example of register-keeping that worried the Select Committee, the Panel content that the records kept by dealers for Value Added Tax (VAT) reasons were sufficient.

In relation to reservations, the Panel recommended the United Kingdom make three when acceding:

(1) that the EU Council Directive 1993/7/EEC on unlawfully removed cultural objects apply exclusively to issues within the EU;
(2) that the definition of cultural objects adopted by the United Kingdom should be that used in the Annex to the EU Council Directive 1993/7/EEC; and
(3) that, where relevant, the limitation periods contained in the United Kingdom's domestic law should continue to apply.

In this discussion, the last of these points featured large. The Select Committee had been prepared to recognise a justification for treating cultural objects as unique for the purposes of limitation periods. It was willing to see the introduction into the United Kingdom of the far more lengthy periods of limitation required by UNIDROIT. The Panel took the opposite view. Its analysis of the current law led it to the conclusion that there were adequate protections already, and it was not satisfied that unique treatment was justified. Of all matters, the UNIDROIT limitation periods was the primary reason the Panel found against it.

The Criminal Offence

In relation to the proposed new criminal offence, the new offence was to extend the illegal action overseas from theft to matters such as unlawful excavation and removal. The Select Committee had made a similar recommendation.

DEVELOPMENTS SINCE 2001

Accession to UNESCO 1970

In March 2001, the UK government announced its commitment to accede to the UNESCO Convention. In October 2002, the United Kingdom contracted to the UNESCO Convention on the basis recommended by the Panel, but had not enacted implementing legislation.

The then Arts Minister's public statement was to the effect that "this will send out a powerful signal to those who do so much damage to the world's cultural heritage that the UK takes its responsibilities very seriously and is determined to act effectively." Others have taken a more sceptical view, asking what change accession makes given the limited consequence of its provisions?

At a practical level, it is the case that members of the Department of Culture, Media and Sport are working on implementing the Convention's requirements – in particular in liaising with and assisting foreign states when missing items appear in the United Kingdom. Whether this is more effective than prior to accession is not easy yet to judge. However, some commentators agree with the Panel – that the most important consequence of accession is to close an apparent or potential hole among the market nations, into which the trade in illicit items might move.

The Criminal Offence

The Dealing in Cultural Objects (Offences) Act became law in October 2003 and came into effect in early 2004. It creates the new offence of "*dishonestly dealing in a cultural object that is tainted, knowing or believing that the object is tainted.*"[13]

Why a new offence.

Although the offence of handling stolen goods contrary to section 22 of the Theft Act 1968 extends to goods that have been stolen abroad, there are a number of significant instances not covered by the handling offence. The offence does not apply to cases in which an item has been illegally excavated or removed in circumstances not amounting to theft; for example, where the item has been illegally excavated or removed with the consent of the landowner or owner of the building, or where there is no legal owner of the item.

[12] UNESCO Article 10.

[13] Section 1.

Furthermore, there may be cases in which an item has been stolen but a prosecution for the offence of handling is not feasible; for example, where there has been a break in the chain of the transaction, or where a person receives a stolen item for his own benefit, rather than for the benefit of another person. In such cases a prosecution for the new offence may be possible.

> The new offence is intended specifically to combat traffic in unlawfully removed cultural objects and will assist in maintaining the integrity of buildings, structures and monuments (including wrecks) world-wide by reducing the commercial incentive to those involved in the looting of such sites. It will send a strong signal that the Government is determined to put a stop to such practices.[14]

Any person found guilty of the offence is liable on conviction in the Crown Court to imprisonment for up to seven years and/or an unlimited fine and, on conviction in the Magistrates Court, a maximum of six months imprisonment and/or a fine up to £5,000.

The primary terms used by the Act are defined very broadly:

Cultural object is an object of historical, architectural, or archaeological interest. It is no defence not to know that an object is a cultural object.

Tainted. After 30 December, 2003, a cultural object is tainted if:

- the cultural object has been excavated;
- it has been removed from a building or structure of historical, architectural, or archaeological interest where the object has at any time formed part of the building or structure; or
- it has been removed from a monument of such interest; and such excavation or removal constituted a criminal offence at the time of such excavation or removal.

It is immaterial whether the excavation or removal took place in the United Kingdom or elsewhere or whether the offence is committed under the law of any part of the United Kingdom or under the law of any other country or territory.

The expression *monument* is defined as follows:

- any work, cave, or excavation;
- any site comprising the remains of any building or structure or any work cave or excavation;
- any site comprising the remains of any vehicle, vessel, aircraft, or other moveable structure, or part of any such thing;
- removing part of a vessel or objects from a vessel in a restricted area (section 1(3) Protection of Wrecks Act 1973);
- works affecting a scheduled monument (section 2, Ancient Monuments and Archaeological Areas Act 1979 (AMAAA));
- destroying or damaging a protected monument (section 28 AMAAA);
- operations in an area of archaeological importance (section 35 AMAAA);
- removal of an object discovered with a metal detector in a protected place (section 42(3) AMAAA);
- removal of remains of military vessels or aircraft (section 2, Protection of Military Remains Act 1986);
- demolition or alteration of a listed building (section 9, Planning (Listed Buildings and Conservation Areas) Act 1990);
- removal of part of a wreck (section 246(3) Merchant Shipping Act 1995)

and the removal or excavation constitutes an offence under the law of the UK or any other country or territory.

Deals in means, acquires, buys, hires, borrows, or accepts; disposes of, sells, lets on hire, lends, or gives; imports or exports.

So, for example, illegal removal of an object from a listed building in the United Kingdom, or illegal removal from a monument in China could trigger the offence. However, offences wholly unrelated to the process of excavation or removal – such as a breach of foreign export laws, a breach of local VAT regulations or health and safety legislation, an assault on an archaeologist or damage to excavation equipment – would not taint the object. The tainting of the object is triggered by the excavation of the object or its removal from a building structure or monument. It is immaterial whether the building or structure is above or below the surface of the land or the site is above or below water.

In the case of cultural objects that have been excavated, it does not matter whether the object has been excavated from a known archaeological site or elsewhere. The object will be tainted if such excavation constituted an offence at the time it was done.

This means that the illegal detachment or amputation of structural, architectural, or ornamental elements of a building will be tainted, but not chairs and tables or works of art hung in a building. However, where a structural, architectural, or ornamental element of a building has become detached, for example through natural causes, and is lying on the ground, it will be tainted if its removal constituted an offence.

The definition of "monument" covers a range of sites of historical, architectural, or archaeological interest. A work, for example, may include surface traces or contours of structural remains, such as a prehistoric hill-fort, a burial cairn, field system, or deserted medieval village; an excavation may refer to any site under archaeological investigation, including areas containing such artifact-rich deposits as votive offerings, cemeteries and graves, production sites, battlefields, or encampments. It also covers moveable objects such as the remains of vehicles, vessels, or aircraft, whether above or below water. Thus, a wreck on the seabed would be included.

[14] Department for Culture, Media and Sport Cultural Property Unit. "Dealing in Tainted Cultural Objects – Guidance on the Dealing in Cultural Objects (Offences) Act 2003" <http://www.culture.gov.uk/cultural_property/illicit_trade.htm>.

There is no mechanism in the Act for objects to cease to be tainted, even if they have been returned to the owner or relevant state authorities (unlike the express provision in section 24(3) of the Theft Act 1968 for stolen goods which have been returned). However, subsequent dealing in an object that has been returned to a legitimate owner is unlikely to be dishonest.

The Dealing in Tainted Cultural Objects Guidance Report explains the probable meaning of dishonesty. To be convicted of the offence, a person needs to act "dishonestly."

The question of whether a defendant acted "dishonestly" would depend on the normal test for dishonesty in theft cases, namely, whether the person's actions were dishonest according to the ordinary standards of reasonable and honest people and, if so, whether that person realized that his actions were, according to those standards, dishonest. Thus an auction house that accepted an object for the sole purpose of giving a valuation, or a restorer for the purposes of effecting restoration, would not be acting dishonestly by returning the object even though they had come to believe that the object was tainted. Of course, if the auction house or restorer were subsequently to deal in the object by, e.g. putting it up for sale, or arranging for it to be put up for sale, then an offence might well be committed.

To be convicted of an offence, a person also needs to know or believe that an object is tainted. (However, it will not be necessary to prove that the person knew or believed that the object was a cultural object.) The burden of proving knowledge or belief that an object is tainted rests with the prosecution and such proof must be beyond all reasonable doubt. This means that a mere failure by the accused to carry out adequate checks on the provenance of an object will not constitute knowledge or belief. However, knowledge or belief can be inferred from the circumstances surrounding the transaction.

For this purpose evidence could be adduced with regard to the following matters:

- the identity, period, nature, condition and general history of the object;
- the identity of any previous possessor;
- the consideration (if any) given for it;
- the existence and content (or otherwise) of any document indicating any transaction relation to the object;
- the legality (or otherwise) of any relevant export of the object;
- the existence and content (or otherwise) of any relevant export documentation.

Once the proposed database of stolen and illegally removed cultural objects is established, a failure to consult that database, or any alternative due-diligence service, would be a further evidential factor in determining whether the accused knew or believed that an object was tainted. Also relevant would be the degree of expertise of the accused and the knowledge of the trade by the accused.

The new offence is likely to be of concern primarily to collectors, auctioneers, and dealers in antiquities and architectural salvage rather than fine art dealers. However, the offence is not targeted solely at those who handle cultural objects in the course of their work. It will cover any person who dishonestly deals in a tainted cultural object, including, for example, a tourist importing a cultural object acquired abroad that has been illegally excavated or removed.

The Act does not necessarily oblige dealers to take steps to ascertain provenance or to exercise due diligence to avoid committing the offence. Knowledge or belief and dishonesty must be proved by the prosecution. Rather, the Act is designed to target irresponsible trading. It will inject greater transparency into the process of acquiring and disposing of cultural objects within the art market so that clear chains of ownership can be established in the event of suspected unlawful removal or excavation. In effect, the Act does not impose further costs in terms of due diligence checks but, rather, formalises them and encourages those not complying with industry-approved standards of good practice to come on board. The Act is designed to protect small business from the illicit trade, which threatens their commercial position through unfair competition. Any increase in costs to legitimate business, therefore, is likely to be minimal.

The Act applies to England, Wales, and Northern Ireland. It does not apply to Scotland because the criminal law is a devolved matter. However, it is likely that the Scottish Parliament will be enacting parallel legislation in the near future.[15]

The Database

The Panel's recommendations for the creation of a national database remain under discussion. The interests of law enforcement and access to information are not entirely aligned, meaning that the police and the art trade need to resolve the balance between discretion and free access.

One obstacle to achieving this goal has been the obvious one of who should pay – the government or the private sector. Commercial databases of stolen cultural objects such as the Art Loss Register (ALR) and Trace already exist, but when interviewed by the Select Committee, representatives of the British Art Market Federation (BAMF) stated that a fully comprehensive commercial database just isn't a viable proposition. The problem is that small businesses cannot afford to use them. James Ede, speaking on behalf of the BAMF, provided the argument and the figures when he said that

The vast majority of the members of my trade association [International Association of Dealers in Ancient Art <http://www.iadaa.org/index.html>] deal in objects that are worth between £1 and £500. It costs £30 to do a check with the ALR.

We cannot require our members to check things on that basis. We require them to check anything over £2000.

So, in view of this financial disincentive, the BAMF would like the government to fund a database aimed at screening all objects, no matter what their value. But what are these objects and what form do they take?

In February 2004, the Department for Culture, Media and Sport Home Office published the government's response to "Cultural Objects: Developments since 2000" (HC 59)

15 For more information on tainted cultural objects, see the Cultural Property page on the Department for Culture, Media and Sport Web site, <http://www.culture.gov.uk/cultural_property/illicit_trade.htm>.

Session 2003–2004.[16] In connection to the slow progress and the unresolved issue of funding, the committee notes,

The British Art Market told us that its reaction to absence of progress on a national database was "to sum it up in a word – frustration."

The committee goes on to say,

We regard the lack of progress made on a national database of illegally removed cultural objects to be lamentable. This is especially true given the existence of analogous systems in the commercial sector and elsewhere, as well as precedents for public/private co-operation in other areas where law enforcement is working alongside legitimate commerce to suffocate illicit markets.

The Government accepts that progress has been slower than hoped but the issues that we have had to deal with have been more complex and difficult to overcome than anticipated. Whilst not a top Home Office priority, for reasons already stated in written and oral evidence to the committee, the Government is determined to reach a conclusion on this issue. And we have made significant progress in the last year.

OTHER DEVELOPMENTS

Nazi Era Claims

The Spoliation Advisory Panel ("SAP") was set up by the UK government in April 2000. Its primary term of reference is:

to consider claims from anyone (or from any one or more of their heirs), who lost possession of a cultural object ("the object") during the Nazi era, where such object is now in the possession of a UK national collection or in the possession of another UK museum or gallery established for the public benefit ("the institution"). The Panel shall advise the claimant and the institution on what would be appropriate action to take in response to such a claim. The Panel shall also be available to advise about any claim for an item in a private collection at the joint request of the claimant and the owner.[17]

The reasons why the SAP was required stem in part from the UK limitation periods, which place considerable difficulties in the way of claims from the Nazi era and in part from the trustee obligations placed on the trustees of most of the United Kingdom's national museums and collections to retain, as well as maintain, the collections.[18] Faced with even a legitimate claim, the trustees (it is argued) are unable to volunteer to return an object.

The SAP works within these constraints, but beyond them also, inasmuch as, in addition to considering the facts and matters that would be relevant to a legal claim, the SAP is expressly required to "give due weight to the moral strength of the claimant's case" and to "consider whether any moral obligation, rests on the institution taking into account in particular the circumstances of its acquisition of the object, and its knowledge at that juncture of the object's provenance."

At the end of its investigation, the SAP is to advise the government what solution might be achieved. In this it is encouraged to use a panoply of remedial measures not limited to either restitution or compensation.

The Select Committee supported the work of the SAP, regarding it as recognition of the necessity to apply special rules to claims originating from this era.

To date, the SAP has reported on two cases: the painting "A View of Hampton Court Palace" by Jan Griffier the Elder at the Tate Gallery (18 January 2001)[19]; and "Still Life," formerly attributed to Chardin, at the Burrell Collection in Glasgow.[20] In the former case, the SAP recommended payment of £125,000 to the claimant together with the display by the Tate next to the painting of an account of its history and provenance during and since the Nazi era, with special reference to the interest therein of the claimant. In the Glasgow case, it recommended the return of the painting to the claimant.

As of May 2003, the SAP had received five claims for consideration.

Human Remains

Repatriation requests from groups claiming to be descendants of people whose remains are kept in the collections of UK museums have given rise to long-running and highly charged disputes. Many would argue that it is beyond the scope of this chapter (concerned as it is with developments in the area of *illicitly* imported items). However, others would argue differently and certainly some of the same questions that arise in claims for the repatriation of art and other heritage items arise here. In addition, this area raises new questions of law and morality. In law, for example, there is the question (not fully answered in English law) whether anyone can claim to own a corpse.

The moral issues – the claims of aboriginal peoples to the remains of ancestors – were recognised by the Select Committee Report in 2000.[21] In response to its recommendation, the government appointed the Human Remains Working Party in May 2001. The Working Party's Report was published in November 2003.[22]

The Report covers a lot of ground and is impossible to summarise here. However, two recommendations deserve emphasis:

- That any constraints on any museums preventing the de-accession from any collection of human remains be removed (such constraints including, in particular, the statutory constraints on the national collections noted earlier in relation to Nazi era claims); and

[16] "Government Response to 'Cultural objects: developments since 2000' (HC 59) Report of the Culture, Media and Sport Select Committee Session 2003–2004," (UK, The Stationery Office Limited (TSO), 02/04).

[17] See Department of Culture Media, and Sport Web site, <http://www.culture.gov.uk/cultural_property/spoliation_ad_panel.htm>.

[18] See, for example, Section 3 and of the British Museum Act 1963.

[19] See Department for Culture, Media and Sport Web site note 14 *supra*.

[20] See <http://www.gnn.gov.uk/content/detail.asp?NewsAreaID=2&ReleaseID=136585>.

[21] See note 11 *supra* paragraphs 153–66, 199 (xiv)–(xvi).

[22] The Report can be accessed through the Department for Culture, Media and Sport Web site at: <http://www.culture.gov.uk/cultural_property/wg_human_remains/default.htm>.

- That the model provided by the SAP (discussed earlier) be adopted for the resolution of any claim for the repatriation of human remains.

The Working Party's conclusions were not unanimous, indicative of the passions raised. By way of response, the government has commenced a consultation process[23] on what steps might be taken to change the current state of affairs.

CONCLUSION

Nothing that occurred in the past five years to the United Kingdom's law has any direct consequence on cases such as the Parthenon Marbles, which may be the cause of the unfavourable publicity, not to mention the interminable debate in the law schools and academic journals.[24] Nor can it be said that the United Kingdom has pulled out every stop: It has eschewed UNIDROIT and declined to ratify the UNESCO Convention on the Protection of the Underwater Cultural Heritage.

However, from a base of domestic law that, in favouring the original owner, is at least comparable to most other common law jurisdictions, the United Kingdom has moved forward in recent years in plugging any gaps that might have attracted the professional handler of illicit goods and in examining means of resolving difficult disputes.

[23] July 2004 – see <http://www.culture.gov.uk/global/press_notices/archive_2004>.

[24] Some would argue that the proposals to relax the bar on de-accession for human remains may be the thin end of a wedge leading eventually to total relaxation and the absence of any legal bar on de-accession of any part of the national collections.

CHAPTER TWENTY-TWO

Summum ius suma iniuria: Stolen Jewish Cultural Assets under Legal Examination

Peter Raue

It remains phenomenal that rather than explain, one can merely state:

60 years after the end of the so-called "Thousand Year Reich" which lasted for 12 terrible years (approximately the same period of time since the fall of the Berlin wall, but nevertheless an eternity!) discourse regarding Germany's "Wiedergutmachung" (reparations) for the injustices committed by the Nazi Regime has not simply been reduced to the question of provenance, but is more virulent than ever. Time has not succeeded in healing the raw wounds. On the contrary, the temporal distance to the Nazi terror has actually established the very prerequisites for re-opening and re-examining the issue of the so-called "Wieder-gut-machung."

Debates on compensation for forced labor have contributed considerably to the topicality of this discourse, and particularly to the question of the restitution of stolen art. Many restitution claimants refer explicitly to this debate if they have raised their claims only recently. Consequently, one's "*own story*" has never been told in full, but instead has actually created new problems in recent years. Of course, it should not really come as a surprise that many claimants hesitated for decades before asserting their claims. Is it not phenomenal that Holocaust literature by survivors possibly experienced its most important developments during the past few years? Imre Kertesz, Louis Begley, Ruth Klüger, Jorge Semprun, just to name a few, only wrote and published their memoirs during the last ten years.

To realize and understand this does not spare us from posing a simple question and from striving for an infinitely complicated answer: The question put to the legal expert is: Who owns the works of art which, let me put this deliberately in an open and neutral phrase, "*changed ownership*" under the Nazi regime? This question is highly complex, alone for the fact that a change in ownership may have various causes and can, therefore, provide various answers:

- ordinary sale, as is usual throughout the entire art world;
- as a consequence of direct force (confiscation and robbery); or (and these are the most complicated cases):
  - as a consequence of indirect force:
    - as a sale in order to finance a plan of departure/escape from Germany;
    - as a sale resulting from the fear of being persecuted for owning so-called "*degenerate art*" (such procedure is by no means restricted to Jewish ownership; other groups, in particular the opponents to Nazism, disposed of their "degenerate art" at that time so as to reduce the risk of persecution resulting from such possession).

As different, on the one hand, as prerequisites and reasons for abandoning such property were in each individual case, so the acquisition process from the first owner (often via numerous interim acquirers) to the present-day owner, is just as differentiable:

- auction sales in Berlin by Jewish auction houses, which were permitted until 1939, before international audiences – several of which achieved top prices;
- acquisition of confiscated, so-called "degenerate art" by art dealers who hoped to prevent the destruction of art and sold such pieces abroad;
- auction sales at the famous Swiss art auctions, where art works were bought by international art dealers, sold, and resold repeatedly up to the present day.

One must also differentiate among the various relationships between seller and purchaser. Often artworks were acquired on the market at internationally standard prices (which, however, seem to be distantly low today). However, whether the former owner (seller, supplier) benefited from the sale, or whether the proceeds were pocketed by the Nazis, must be investigated in each individual case: of course, it is readily assumed that families never saw any of the proceeds of the sale of art works deemed to be of so-called "Jewish ownership."

In the face of such highly complex legal considerations, the legal expert who is to decide a case will abstain from giving any general answer on the current fate of restitution claims, but will have to decide whether or not he/she may at least find a just solution for individual cases. In light of this, at least one fact seems clear and undisputable to me: The characteristics, conditions, and constellations of each, and I mean literally each, restitution case known to us vary to such an extent that different answers are required legally (as well as morally), and that generalized proposals for solving such cases would inevitably produce misjudgments.

Before I try to explain why a legal expert will probably have to capitulate in his/her quest for a solution to individual cases, which often remain merely rudimentarily solved, I would like to present examples of some significant restitution claims, given that it seems unavoidable to me to take a look at the hard facts in order to illustrate the complexity of the matter. Because these cases are well known, I shall summarize and simplify accordingly.

EMIL NOLDE: BUCHSBAUMGARTEN

The Jewish lawyer, Dr. Ismar Littmann, was a passionate art collector, with Buchsbaumgarten (1909) by Emil Nolde (1867–1956) among his collection. Distraught by the Nazi terror, Dr. Littmann committed suicide in 1934. The following year, his widow gave the Nolde piece to Max Perl, a Jewish auction house in Berlin. The painting was auctioned in 1935 at an auction with international attendance and renown, and the painting was purchased by Dr. Heinrich Arnhold, a Jewish banker, resident in Dresden. The Wilhelm Lehmbruck Museum acquired the painting in 1956 for DM 3,600 from the Arnhold family, who had emigrated to the United States of America. The painting has undisputedly been in the possession of the museum, where it has been on display, lent out, and made publicly available ever since.

In 1999, the last living daughter of the Littmann couple contacted the museum and demanded restitution of the painting or the value of the work at the current market value, minus a twenty percent discount.

PETER PAUL RUBENS: PORTRAIT OF THE MARCHESA VERONICA SPINOLA DORIA AND THE PORTRAIT OF THE MARCHESA IMPERIALE AND DAUGHTER

In 1933, the couple, Jakob and Rosa Oppenheimer, fled to France, where Jakob Oppenheimer died in 1941. Rosa Oppenheimer was deported to Auschwitz, where she was murdered in 1943. When fleeing to France, the couple's spectacular art collection was left behind in Berlin. A substantial part of the collection was auctioned by the Jewish auction house, Paul Graupe, in Berlin in 1935, among it the *Portrait of the Marchesa Veronica Spinola Doria* and the *Portrait of the Marchesa Imperiale and Daughter.* These works were acquired by Konrad Bareiss, who paid an international top price for a Rubens work for one of them. In 1964, Karlsruhe bought The *Portrait of the Marchesa Veronica Spinola,* whereas Stuttgart purchased the *Portrait of the Marchesa Imperiale and Daughter* in 1965. The paintings have been on public display ever since. In the 1990s, the heirs of the Oppenheimer couple demanded the return of both paintings.

When studying the case, Anja Heuß discovered almost incidentally that the family had already arrived at an agreement with Konrad Bareiss as regards restitution. Consequently, the Oppenheimer family abandoned their claim. However, there is one problem: how should such a claim have been handled, had there not been a settlement?

WASSILY KANDINSKY: COMPOSITION NO. 10 (1910)

This case is publicly discussed under the rubric of "Lissitzky/Beyeler." In summary:

Sophie Küppers, who had married El Lissitzky in 1927, was one of a series of owners of the painting named above by Wassily Kandinsky (1866–1944). Today, we can safely refer to this work of art as an icon of the twentieth century. In 1926, Ms. Küppers lent this piece to the Provinzialmuseum in Hannover, which had clearly submitted it voluntarily to the "Degenerate Art" exhibition in Munich in 1937. The painting was never returned to the museum, but was sold by the Nazis to the art dealer and collector, Ferdinand Möller, at a price of $100.00 Möller, who (often in rather problematic cooperation with the Nazi regime) sold many works confiscated by the Nazis, particularly to Switzerland, kept the painting. In 1951, the young art dealer, Ernst Beyeler, saw this piece in Möller's gallery in Cologne and bought it at a price of CHF 18,000.00 to re-sell it to a Swiss collector at, for that time, the very high price of CHF 28,000.00 Only three years later, Beyeler rebought the painting for CHF 45,000.00 (an incredibly high price at that time for a 20th century painting!). It has been in Beyeler's possession ever since and today belongs to the Beyeler foundation. For almost 50 years, this painting has been on display around the world without anyone asserting any claims – until one day in the 1990s, when one of the heirs of Sophie Lissitzkaja-Küppers, as opposed to the community of heirs, commissioned an agent specialized in this field to assert restitution claims. Evidently, this clever and equally unscrupulous agent was motivated by the current value of the painting, which can safely be estimated at CHF 100 million.

The fact that this publicly discussed case repeatedly leads to discussion of the restitution of formerly Jewish property, even though it has nothing to do with the fate of "Jewish property" but rather with the loss of property as a result of the Nazi cultural dictatorship, has not a little to do with the agent's cynical and unfounded formulations, and, moreover, only proves how important it is to consider each individual case in detail.

The agent, Toussaint, must have had his reasons for relating the fate of this work of art to the question of Jewish property, even if this has little to do with actuality. However, we shall forfeit every reasonable answer, if we fail to distinguish between the fate of

- art works that had been in Jewish possession (i.e., in no way restricted to "degenerate art");
- art works, deemed "degenerate" and confiscated by the Nazis;
- stolen art (which need mean neither Jewish nor "degenerate" art), to mention only the most important cases.[1]

LOVIS CORINTH: *WALCHENSEE AM ABHANG DES JOCHBERGES*

Today, this painting by Corinth (1858–1925) is in the Niedersächsischen Landesmuseum in Hannover (of all places!). It was confiscated by the Nazis from this museum in 1937 to suffer the same fate as so many other art works condemned as "degenerate." It was auctioned in Lucerne, bought by an unknown collector, and was brought to Hannover in 1953, at a cost of DM 20,000. The Schwerin museum demanded the return of the painting shortly after the fall of the Berlin Wall with the argument that because a restitution claim could not

1 The legal dispute over this painting was amicably resolved between the creation and publication of this article – much to the chagrin of the agent, no doubt.

have been made during the German Democratic Republic, restitution must be demanded now. However, once Hannover announced its refusal to hand over the painting, Schwerin, to the best of my knowledge, did not pursue its claim. Nevertheless, it is still necessary to consider the dimensions underlying this particular restitution claim:

The Schwerin museum states that 10,000 pieces of its pre-WWII collection are missing, and had been either confiscated by the Nazis, stolen by the Soviet occupational forces or lost in some other way. Now the museum wants them back – all 10,000 works?

DITTMAYER COLLECTION

Let us broaden our knowledge of this subject by examining a variation on the theme with the example of the Dittmayer couple:

Hans and Stephanie Dittmayer were passionate collectors of the type of art, which was promptly condemned as "degenerate" by the Nazis: Edvard Munch (1863–1944), Nolde, Lyonel Feininger (1871–1956), Ernst Ludwig Kirchner (1880–1938), Max Beckmann (1884–1950), just to mention a few. Stephanie Dittmayer was Jewish, whilst her "Aryan" husband was an industrialist, who worked in Dresden. Stephanie Dittmayer managed to disappear just as she was about to be deported to Theresienstadt in 1945. In 1944, her husband was conscripted to forced labor in a camp by the Gestapo, but was spared by a medical certificate. The son, Wolfram Dittmayer, was imprisoned in the concentration camp Osterode from October 3, 1944 to April 4, 1945.

In order to protect their art collection and avoid its confiscation by the Gestapo, the Dittmayer couple packed their art works into crates to be transported to Prague. At least one crate containing valuable pieces evidently survived the war because its contents can be found in private and public collections in Germany and abroad. Immediately after the war, the Dittmayer couple tried to have their art works returned to them from the CSSR, to no avail. The Dittmayer heirs, however, persist in their objective of having the art works returned from their current owners. This is a case, which is somewhere in between the debate regarding the history and return of so-called "degenerate" art, on the one hand, and about stolen art on the other. At any rate, this case shirks a single scheme of solution.

The Dittmayer couple are particularly engaged in their claims against public institutions, such as the Nationalgalerie Berlin, the Von-der-Heydt-Museum Wuppertal, and the Wilhelm Lehmbruck Museum Duisberg.

STOLEN ART – THE GERSTENBERG COLLECTION

During the war, the highly significant Gerstenberg family collection was stored in museums in Berlin before being removed to St. Petersburg and Moscow by the Soviet occupational forces. This case has relevance for the broader issue of restitution or the return of art work lost as a result of the war. It is clear that so-called "real cases of stolen art" cannot be subject to the statute of limitations because the possibility of filing restitution claims was not available during the Union of Soviet Socialist Republic dictatorship, which was not bound by rights or law.

Consequently, the question regarding the fate of art works that were confiscated and transported abroad by occupational forces in Germany after the end of the war remains controversial. That the subject of German art stolen by Soviet forces is particularly significant requires little explanation. However, one point seems equally self-evident to me: To commit oneself to the restitution of stolen art, is, in my opinion, a matter of course, but to restrict oneself to handling only the restitution of exclusively "Jewish" property hardly provides conclusive solutions for the questions raised by the scope of the problems depicted here. The expert required to consider the example cases described here from a legal point of view and prognosticate the outcome of a legal dispute regarding the return of the works mentioned here, can safely assert only one thing:

one would have to commission an expert for each case and be prepared to accept a different answer from each legal expert to the question "What would be the outcome of such a trial?"

In spite of possible, but understandable, aversion to legal argumentation, please allow me at least to present the legal instrumentarium, which shall be used to solve these cases. Nowadays, every restitution case is subject to at least three objections: (1) The statute of limitations, which seems straightforward, and yet how variably it can be viewed! Whereas in Germany the statute of limitations even for stolen items is thirty years, and for ownership in good faith is only ten years (legally, it is somewhat more complicated, but *de facto* this is correct), Switzerland does not recognize the statute of limitations for *in rem* restitution at all. The case becomes even more complicated if the art work has crossed more than one border and changed owner more than once: *lex rei sitae* determines whether the (German/Swiss/French/Austrian) statute of limitations is applied, as the statute of limitations of the country of the art work's ownership, i.e., *res sitae* prevails. This is the reason why it is difficult for any lawyer to provide a definitive answer regarding the statute of limitations, once a piece of art has been sold across several borders.

With this background, courts have additional room for interpretation. In the famous legal dispute, *the City of Gotha and the Federal Republic of Germany versus Sotheby's*, the London High Court stated that a *mala fide* acquirer's objection that the claim would be statute-barred would contravene public policy, which almost corresponds to the notion of *ordre public*. However, restitution claims are usually not asserted against the *mala fide* acquirer, but against the third or fourth acquirer. And what is the meaning of "mala fide acquirer" anyway? Those who acquired a work at an auction in Berlin in 1935 or in Lucerne in 1939 should hardly have to tolerate being called "mala fide."

It is hardly surprising that the son of the acquirer of Nolde's Buchsbaumgarten, the American, Henry Arnold, strongly protested in writing only last year against the lodging of legal objections against the acquisition process that took place in 1935. He stated that his father had been *bona fide* in every respect, had wanted to save banned art, acquired the work legitimately, and resold it to Germany at a truly moderate price, almost as an obligation toward Germany.

Those who intend to assert their restitution claims in the United States will, depending on the respective state in which the claim is filed, face different jurisdiction with regard to the statute of limitations. Never mind the fact that any prediction regarding a court decision in America is as good as reading tea leaves, as we know from the forced labor trials.

However, with regard to the first, most frequent, and "handy" objection to restitution claims, I would like to add one thing: Often this objection is deemed "indecent." As those opposing this objection ask: "Is a restitution claim doomed to be rejected simply because ten, thirty, or more years have passed since first being made?" Is such an objection not merely a formal objection and, therefore, even made in bad faith?

I do not find such "scruples" regarding the objection of being statute-barred convincing because they misjudge the actual character of the statute of limitations: All regulations on the statute of limitations are based on awareness of the notion that clarification of the facts becomes more difficult with the passing of time, and that it is a function of each legal system to refuse and even prohibit a case from being re-opened after a certain amount of time. This is the reason why almost all constitutional states also apply the statute of limitations to capital crimes, even to murder. Is it then so very strange to oppose restitution claims with the objection of the statute of limitations? Is there any rationally understandable reason for accepting the statute of limitations for murder on the one hand, but claiming it inadmissible in cases concerning the infringement of ownership rights on the other? Is this question, of whether the statute of limitations can be asserted in a restitution claim not to be answered in a different manner? Restitution claims filed by persons who were prevented from making such claims (because the opposing party was located in the Communist sphere of control, or the claimant was located in Russia, Hungary, or the German Democratic Republic) will have to be treated differently with regard to asserting the statute of limitations than claims by individuals who sat back and simply watched a work of art go around the world for decades (the Beyeler case!) as property of the lending party without asserting a claim. An individual who simply did not know what had happened to a confiscated painting which had once belonged to him/her, will be more entitled to call an objection to his restitution claim on the grounds of the statute of limitations "indecent" and "formalistic" than someone who asserts his/her claim because some clever and cynical agent promised that this would be a no-risk source of capital. However, the soldier who looted an art work in the chaos of the end of the war, took it abroad, hid it for thirty years and now thinks that he may openly and frivolously enjoy this stolen property (see the case of the "Quedlinburg Cathedral treasure") should be refused to apply the statute of limitations in restitution claims.

In any event, one must consider the moral or ethical justification of the statute of limitations differentially.

(2) Besides the objection that a claim has become statute-barred, a restitution claim may be opposed by the *objection of forfeiture*. This is an objection that may be made, if the possible claimant was aware of the whereabouts and situation of an art work for years but failed to take action. More than five decades after the war, this instrument has its own means of defense.

The German legal system prefers to solve the difficulties of providing evidence for cases of this nature with fixed statutes of limitations. However, to other legal systems, such forfeiture is a crucial element for the court's judgment. For example, in the highly publicized DeWeerth case in the United States, the restitution claim concerning a Monet painting was rejected on the grounds that the claimant did not make enough effort in his endeavors to relocate the painting after it had been left behind in the flight from the Nazis.

(3) In Germany, the claimant finally has to consider the *objection of preclusion*; i.e., the objection that he/she failed to adhere to the legal timeframe for restitution and compensation claims. After the war, the Federal Republic of Germany established norms for the so-called indemnification of Nazi wrongs and fixed preclusive periods during which claims could be asserted. Any claim asserted in Germany against public institutions certainly raises the question (but provides no answer) as to how restitution claims should be considered in the context of such preclusive periods. Again, one must differentiate between whether the person entitled to restitution was impeded from asserting his/her claims, or whether such inaction was attributable to the entitled parties "acquiescing."

In addition to these three formal objections (statute of limitations, forfeiture, preclusion), the claimant always has to consider an objection which is highly complex legally; i.e., the opposing party's claim that he/she acquired the work *bona fide* and is the legitimate owner of the work. This is a strong argument if the acquisition was not made in Germany as a direct result of Nazi seizure. Answering the question of *bona fide* property acquisition is also extremely complex and variable. Here too, determining whether the case is dealing with such "bona fide acquisition" and whether the owner can claim to have satisfied all legal elements constituting an acquisition differs greatly from country to country. Therefore, the first and often most difficult question in legal disputes is: "Which law is to apply in determining whether an acquisition is *bona fide*?" The fact that the country in which a painting is found has no bearing on which law is applied in establishing *bona fide* acquisition adds to the confusion. It may well be that a Swiss court has to determine *bona fide* acquisition according to German law (the Beyeler-Kandinsky painting, for example).

In order to outline the issue at least in some approximation of its actual complexity, may I add that even in those instances in which a German legal expert can predict the success or failure of a restitution claim with some certainty, he/she must recognize and admit that the ruling of a German court has no bearing on procedures elsewhere. This was made quite plain once more in the dispute over the *Tote Stadt III* by Egon Schiele (1890–1918).

Fritz Grünbaum, the Viennese cabaret artist who was murdered in a concentration camp, was the owner of Schiele's *Tote Stadt III*. Although it is not entirely clear as to how, the painting landed in the forerunner to the Berne auction house, Kornfeld, and passed through the hands of several collectors before being acquired by the important Viennese collector, Rudolf Leopold. When the collection was exhibited in the Museum of Modern Art in 1997, two ladies from New York claimed that Grünbaum was the cousin of their deceased father, that they were rightful heirs, and that they could make legitimate restitution claims for this piece.

Initially, this led to the painting being seized in New York, and it was later returned only on the grounds that it had come to New York with "safe passage," and should, therefore, be returned to Austria with "safe passage." There is no indication that the court had even the slightest doubt as to the legitimacy of the restitution claim of these two ladies!

Just how sensitively – and how unpredictably – the world reacts to so-called "Jewish property" can be seen not least in the case of Christoph Müller (Tübingen). Müller submitted a work by Oskar Schlemmer (1888–1943), which had been undisputedly in his family's possession, to Christie's in London. Shortly before the day of the auction, the Schlemmer family came forward with the unproven and the unprovable claim that the painting had been confiscated in Essen by the National Socialists, and had then landed in the hands of the Müller family through various dubious channels. It was only once the Schlemmer family had agreed to the auctioning of the painting on condition that the sale money was kept by Christie's, that the painting could finally be sold. The money, inaccessible for Müller, has remained in a Christie's account ever since. The auction house is only prepared to pay the money to Müller once a court reaches a binding decision that the painting came into the Müller family's possession legitimately. Such a decision can take years in the German legal system, which means that Christie's will withhold the money for years, even though the Schlemmer family cannot provide the slightest proof for their claim. This is further evidence that any prediction of the outcome of a legal case in the Anglo-American system is highly unreliable. Such uncertainties are highly unsettling for the loan of large collections on the international market; a marginal note, but not an insignificant consideration.

Back to the German legal system. Even if a restitution claim is not rejected on the grounds of the statute of limitations, forfeiture, preclusion, or acquisition in good faith, courts will have a hard time dealing with such claims:

> Should the Rubens paintings in Stuttgart and Karlsruhe be restituted, with the consequence that the investments (i.e. the money paid for the paintings in the millions) is lost? For, a museum obligated to restitute a work of art can never recover the purchase. Or, to give a concrete example, no-one can request the purchase price back from the seller Bareiss, since there is no legal basis for such a demand. A court seeking justice and propriety will question the appropriateness of whether a work of art should be valued by its current worth, or whether it should be limited to the value of the piece at the time when it could have been restituted justifiably and far more promptly?

The law and its jurisdiction provide no predictable means of assistance. In the pursuit of a just decision, it is a hazardous act of despair to awaken and utilize the submerged, Sleeping-Beauty-like norm of the "treasure trove law" of section 983 of the German Civil Code. Herein, the conflict of whether found "treasure" is the property of the finder, or the owner of the property on which it was found, is solved with Salomonian wisdom: "If a treasure is discovered and subsequently taken into possession, then it belongs in one half to the discoverer, and in one half to the owner of the property which harbored the treasure."

Nevertheless, it remains doubtful as to whether this "50/50" rule truly constitutes a model answer to our question.

And so, the legal expert leaves the test bench from where he is to submit his recommendations. The result of my considerations is nothing other than that the law fails to provide answers of convincing content to the question of restitution claims. Perhaps the following applies to all the examples I have provided and, furthermore, to all the cases with which I am familiar.

From a legal point of view, not a single case can be solved satisfactorily and convincingly. Yet, and with the greatest caution, I venture to say that, aside from the problem of stolen art, restitution claims should consistently be rejected within European legal jurisdiction on the grounds of the statute of limitations, forfeiture, preclusion, or the rightful acquisition of the current owner.

With respect to the different jurisdictions within Europe and the significant obstacles resulting from such diversity of rules, in December 2003, the European Parliament passed a Resolution (A 5-408/2003) calling for the European Commission and its Member States to consider formulating protocols to support and help owners of artworks looted by the Nazi regime regain their property. In particular, the Resolution by the European Parliament calls on the European Commission to undertake a study on:

- establishing a common cataloguing system to gather data on looted cultural goods and the status of existing claims;
- developing common principles with regard to access to public or private archives containing information on property identification and referring to existing databases about title to disputed properties;
- identifying common principles on how ownership or title is established, standards of proofs, and rights to export or import recovered property;
- exploring possible dispute resolution mechanism to avoid lengthy judicial proceedings;
- creating a cross-border administrative authority to deal with title disputes on cultural goods.

Apparently, the Resolution's recommendations have not been followed by a specific course of action.

In this context, appropriate rules of modification have to be considered: The fact that the strict application of the existing law, which is the only right and obligation of the judge, given that, as is well known, Justice is blind, achieves the highest law and simultaneously, the greatest injustice, was already acknowledged by Cicero in the famous legal phrase "*summum ius summa iniuria.*"

A person interested in criminal law is most familiar with the notion that a decision based on the strict application of the law can be so unjust that justice can only be achieved by exercising clemency. This explains why clemency does not need to be removed from the legal system as monarchic debris, but constitutes an indispensable legal institution even, and particularly, in a democratic legal state. Therefore, "clemency" does not signify the incursion of arbitrariness into a constitutional state, but is actually the modification of the strict application of the law, shaped by the ideas of democracy and justice.

It is on the basis of this notion, which is recognized as indisputable at least in legal literature, that restitution claims must be handled today. Because no one can dare to predict the outcome of a legal dispute because it cannot be denied that European decisions are often simply brushed aside in the United States, and because every decision, whether in rejecting or awarding restitution claims, can be problematic and unsatisfactory, the only way to solve the question discussed here lies in the establishment of a special board or commission. Only such a board could at least try to seek "material justice," in the sense of clemency as already discussed.

This board or commission should consist of people who make recommendations on the basis of justice, and ideally, even reasonably, with binding effect for both parties – an ethics board for restitution claims!

I am not so foolish as to believe that even with such a commission, answers to restitution claims can be easily found. However, I am convinced that if a balance of interests is to be found at all, it is only by means of such a board that peace and satisfaction can be brought in an individual case. The decisions made by the "Stiftung Preussischer Kulturbesitz" [Prussian Cultural Heritage Foundation] prove that decisions based on this idea, even though not without dispute, have been made in the past. Legal proceedings dragging on for years will not help us come to terms with our "own history." It is my opinion that only by mediating between different, legitimate interests can we find hope for a solution, which differentiates and acknowledges the individuality of each case. In other words, a solution which is committed to justice, but which at least bears some hope of achieving satisfaction.

It is indisputable:

- that state and municipal museums should be subject to different criteria than the private individual,
- that whether a ruling commission is suitable for claims against individuals requires further consideration,
- that claims from and in the Communist sphere of control, in which the mere thought of restitution was out of the question until its collapse, must be assessed differently than claims for well-known art works held in the West,
- that these are guidelines, which such a commission must first develop itself.

Not surprisingly, this brings me to recommendation No. 8 of the so-called "Washington Declaration" of December 3, 1998: "If the pre-War owners of art that is found to have been confiscated by the Nazis and not subsequently restituted, or their heirs, can be identified, steps should be taken expeditiously to achieve a just and fair solution, recognizing this may vary according to the facts and circumstances surrounding a specific case."

My considerations lead me to the conclusion that the tasks stipulated in the "Washington Declaration" can only be fulfilled by an arbitration board under the wing of the federal government (and vested with decision-making power). The question of which particular institution should incorporate such a commission is of secondary significance. However, the highly reliable "*Kulturstiftung der Länder*" (Cultural Foundation of the Federal States) readily springs to mind as a suitable domicile for such a decision-making body.

In order to avoid wasting more valuable time, those responsible must act quickly and effectively, establishing the ruling board, and museums and local authorities must submit to such procedure. This is the only way that the debate about restitution claims for property lost or seized under the Nazi regime can finally be settled in our time.

CHAPTER TWENTY-THREE

European Union Legislation Pertaining to Cultural Goods

Barbara T. Hoffman

Free trade in all goods within the internal market is a guiding principle of the European Union (EU), guaranteed under Articles 28 and 29 (formerly 30–38) and Article 23 (formerly Article 5). It was recognized, however, that there was need to reconcile free movement with that of legitimately protecting Member States' cultural and artistic heritage.

Article 30 (formerly Article 36) states:

> The provisions of Articles 28 and 29 shall not preclude prohibitions or restrictions on imports, exports or goods in transit justified on grounds of public morality, public policy or public security... or the protection of national treasures possessing artistic, historic or archaeological value" or the protection of industrial or commercial property.

Such prohibitions or restrictions shall not, however, constitute a means of arbitrary discrimination or a disguised restriction on trade between member states.

In order to preserve the principle of free movement and, at the same time, protect the cultural heritage, a double safeguard has been adopted at the community level. It rests on two legislative acts, a regulation and a directive, and also a regulation of implementation.

1. Council Regulation (EEC) No. 3911/92,[1] which covers the exportation of cultural goods, provides for uniform export controls for the cultural goods specified in it and requires a license to be issued by the competent authorities. The license must be presented together with the export declaration at the customs office where the export formalities are to be completed. For its implementation, Commission Regulation No. 752/93[2] lays down the types of export licenses that may be used, and the formalities for exporting such goods.
2. Council Directive 93/7/EEC[3] sets up a mechanism for the return within the Community of cultural goods belonging to the national artistic, historical, or archaeological heritage that have unlawfully left the territory of a Member State. One of the aims of the Directive is to create conditions for close collaboration among the Member States, particularly in investigating objects that have been removed illegally.

The Directive complements this preventive instrument by providing mechanisms and a procedure for returning national treasures unlawfully removed from the territory of a Member State. It is important to stress that although the aim of the Regulation is to avoid national treasures being taken out of the EU territory without controls, the Directive deals with the arrangements for restoring such treasures to the Member State of origin when they have been unlawfully removed from it and provides that illegally removed cultural objects have to be returned to that Member State from which they were removed. The original Member States of the EU and the European Economic Area (Iceland, Norway, and Liechtenstein) have implemented the Directive and the new Member States will have to do so after May 2004.

CATEGORIES OF GOODS COVERED BY EU REGULATIONS

The cultural goods covered by EU legislation – and for which an export license is required under Regulation (EEC) No. 3911/92 – are listed in the joint Annex to the two acts. They are divided into fifteen categories, according to their nature (corresponding as an indicative way to tariff headings in the Combined Nomenclature). The decisive criterion for being considered cultural goods is age (more than 50, 75, or 100 years old, with exceptions for certain collections or for certain objects of particular interest). This criterion is also combined with minimum value (between 0 and EUR 150,000). The list of these goods is set out in Annex 1.[4]

[1] Regulation (EEC) No. 3911/92 of the Council, of 9 December 1992, on the export of cultural goods (OJ No. L 395 of 31.12.1992). Modified by Regulation (EU) No. 2469/96 of 16 December 1996 (OJ No. L 335 of 24.12.1996) and by Regulation No. 974/2001 of 14.5.2001 (OJ No. L 137 of 19.5.2001).

[2] (OJ No. L 77 du 31.3.1993). Modified by Regulation No. 1526/98 of 16.7.1998 (OJ No. L 201 of 17.7 1998).

[3] Directive 93/7/EEC of the Council, of 15 March 1993, on the return of cultural objects unlawfully removed from the territory of a Member State (OJ No. L 74 do 27.31993). Modified by Directive No. 96/100/EC of 17.2.1996 (OJ No. L 60 of 1.3.1996) and Directive No. 2001/38 of 5.6.2001 (OJ No. L 187 of 10.7.2001).

[4] Until 2003, the EU and the United Kingdom applied broadly the same value thresholds to decide whether an antique or a work of art required an export license. For example, a painting required an export license from the United Kingdom if it was worth £119,000 or more. The same painting required an export license from the EU if it was worth EUR 150,000 or more. When converted into pounds sterling at the exchange rate set out in EU Regulation 3911/92 on the export of cultural property, EURO 150,000 was equal to approximately £119,000.

Following changes to EU and UK thresholds, the export of a painting worth £100,000 to France or Germany does not require a UK export license. If the same painting is exported to Switzerland or the United States, an EU export license is required. Before the changes came into effect, an export license was unnecessary in this circumstance.

In *Commission* v. *Italy*, the Court of Justice of the EU has had the opportunity to determine the interaction of Article 30 of the Treaty with Articles 28–29. In response to Italy's claim that the export tax on works of art was a protective measure, the Court, without defining national treasure, disagreed, stating that the tax had "the sole effect of rendering more onerous the exportation" of works of art "without ensuring attainment of the aim intended by [Article 30], which is to protect the artistic, historical or archaeological heritage."[5]

On an EU-level, Article 30 and the term National Treasure have been accorded widely divergent interpretations, resulting in two conflicting trends:

- an *'extensive' interpretation*: by countries largely in the south of Europe which are net exporters of cultural objects (e.g., Italy, Spain, France);
- a *'restrictive' interpretation*: by importing countries (e.g., the United Kingdom, one of the principal hubs of the art market)

In France, l'Conseil d'Etat dans l'arrêt Genty du 7 October 1987[6] affirmed the administrative determination to deny an export permit to certain Chinese jars as compatible with Article 28–30, without considering it necessary to go to the European Court in Luxembourg. It considered that a medieval Chinese jar presented a national interest of art and history, echoing the reasoning of the Kahn government on the matter of Talleyrand – Perrgod according to which the national character of a work derives "*bien plus que de la nationalité de son auteur . . . l'interet que lui porte ou est censeé lui porter la Nation.*"[7]

Another example of this 'extensive' interpretation and the difficulties faced by the collector under French law is provided by the Jacques Walter's matter. Walter, whose family had already donated to French museums some 144 paintings, mostly by Cezanne, Renoir, Modigliani, Matisse, Miro, or Picasso, wanted to sell a Van Gogh painting, "Jardin à Auvers" (Garden in Auvers), in 1982 but the French Ministry of Culture refused to issue an export license. Instead, the painting was listed as "National Treasure," with the consequence that it could not leave the country if sold.

The Van Gogh was eventually auctioned at Fr 55 million (US$11 million), three times less than its normal international art market value, because of this export restriction. Jacques Walter successfully sued the French state for damages in March 1994. Facing a Fr 422 million (US$84 million) compensation, the French Treasury immediately appealed the decision. The Court of Appeals confirmed the ruling, however reducing the compensation to Fr 145 million (US$29 million). The French Treasury then appealed to the Supreme Court of Appeal, which also ruled against the state.

Similarly, without directly challenging the Italian definition of national treasure, an applicant challenged the right of preemption and its exercise under the Italian export control regulations before the European Court of Human Rights under Article 1 of the First Protocol to the European Convention for the Protection of Human Right and Fundamental Freedoms (the "First Protocol"); the First Protocol provides that

> Every natural or legal person is entitled to the peaceful enjoyment of his possessions. No one shall be deprived of his possessions except in the public interest and subject to the conditions provided for by law and by the general principles of international law.

The applicant, Ernst Beyeler, a Swiss national, is a well-known art gallery owner. The case concerned a Van Gogh painting called "Portrait of a Young Peasant" which Mr. Beyeler bought in 1977 for 600,000,000 lira, or nearly 310,000 euros (EUR), through an intermediary without, however, disclosing to the vendor that the painting was being purchased on his behalf. Consequently, the declaration of sale the vendor filed with the Italian Ministry of Cultural Heritage in accordance with the requirements of Law No. 1089 of 1939 did not mention Mr. Beyeler. In 1983, the Italian Ministry learned that Mr. Beyeler was the real purchaser of the painting. On 2 May 1988 Mr. Beyeler sold the painting for US$85 million to the Peggy Guggenheim Foundation, which intended to include it in its Venetian collection. On 24 November 1988, Italy exercised its right of pre-emption and purchased the painting at the 1977 sale price, arguing that Mr. Beyeler had omitted to inform the ministry of the fact that in 1977 the painting had been purchased on his behalf.

Mr. Beyeler's primary claim was for restitution of the painting. He also claimed compensation for the damage sustained as a result of the length of time for which he had been deprived of the painting and the consequent loss of use of the amount he would have received had it been possible to perform the contract signed with the American corporation, less the amount paid him by the ministry on pre-emption of the sale, plus interest. His total claim thus amounted to US$13,444,358.52 (or more than EUR 14,000,000).

In the alternative, he claimed full compensation by way of payment of the value of the painting at the time of the "expropriation." He claimed an amount equivalent to the sum just indicated (namely, EUR 14,000,000).

By a vote of sixteen to one, the Court in *Beyeler v. Italy*[8] decided there had been a violation of Article I of the First Protocol.

The Court considered that the nature of the violation found in its principal judgment did not allow for restitution of the property. It pointed out that it had not concluded that the pre-emption had been unlawful as such. However, although it had not called into question the right of preemption, the Court

[5] See Case 7/68, *Commission v. Italy* (1968), ERC562.

[6] See Conseil d'Etat, 7 octobre 1987, *Ministre de la Culture/Consorts Genty*, Dalloz 1988, jurisprudence p. 269.

[7] Gourdon, Pearl. "*Le Regime Juridique et Fiscal Francais des Importations et Exportations d'Oeuvres d'Art.*" *Memoire – Droit et Fiscalité du Marché de l'Art, Université Jean Moulin*, Lyon 3, 2003–2004. *Diplôme d'Université de 3ème Cycle.*

[8] *Beyeler v. Italy (33202/96) [2002] ECHR 462 (28 May 2002).*

had decided that the conditions in which it had been exercised (five years after the ministry had become aware of the irregularities of which the applicant was accused) occasioned loss for the applicant as a result of the uncertainty and precariousness that prevailed throughout that period.

Thus, the Court decided that Mr. Beyeler should be compensated for the loss sustained as a result of being paid the same price in 1988 as he had paid in 1977, without any adjustment and that Mr. Beyeler should be compensated for the ancillary costs he had incurred between 1984 and 1988 in determining his legal position with regard to the painting.[9]

In respect of the costs incurred before the domestic courts, the Court found that although the proceedings brought by the applicant had, admittedly, sought to dispute the right of pre-emption, they had also sought to challenge the terms on which it had been exercised, including the lack of any adjustment of the sum paid in 1988, which was the pivotal element of the Court's finding of a violation. The domestic remedies had therefore also been partly aimed at remedying the violation of Protocol No. 1 found by the Court, which justified an order for reimbursement of part of those costs.

Professor Manlio Frigo[10] argues that the expensive application of the concept of National Treasure by Spain, Italy, and Portugal, can in part be attributed to the problem of translating various concepts into different languages.

For whereas, according to the Italian (Spanish, Portuguese) text of Article 30 of the Treaty, the provisions of Article 28 and 29 shall not preclude prohibitions or restrictions on imports, exports or goods in transit justified on grounds – among others – of the protection of the "*patrimonio artistico, storico o arqueologico nazionale*" ("*patrimonio artistico, o arqueologico nacional,*" "*património nacional de valor artistico, histórico ou arqueológico*"), other authentic texts (notably the English and the French texts) refer to the protection of "national treasures of artistic, historic or archaeological value" and to "*trésors nationaux ayant une valeur artistique, historique ou archeologique.*"[11]

In other words, it is clear that "national heritage" and "national treasures" evoke two difference concepts. Consequently, the Italian, Spanish, Portuguese texts appear *prima facie* to give the national authorities a broader discretionary power in deciding on the categories of goods to be included in the national protective legislation, and more specifically on limitations to their movement, a power which seems much more restricted in other authentic language versions.

Biondi states that the correct interpretation of National Treasures should not refer to the generality of all art or cultural goods but to a specific category that forms an indissoluble link with the cultural heritage of a particular nation.[12]

. . . It unquestionably follows that, in the light of the object and purpose of the Treaty, an extension of the national prohibitions or restrictions to categories of objects that fall within the definition of "national heritage," but not within the more restrictive notion of "national treasures," would not be adequately justified.[13]

[9] id.

[10] Professor of European Union and international law, Università degli Studi di Milano. Frigo, Manlio. "Cultural property v. cultural heritage: A "battle of concepts" in international law?" IRRC June 2004, Vol. 86, No. 854.

[11] Emphasis added. The German text of Article 30 of the EU Treaty is slightly different, as it refers to "*Kulturgu(t) von künstlerischem oder archäologischem Wert.*"

[12] Biondi, A. "The Merchant, the Thief and the Citizen: the Circulation of Works of Art within the European Union." Common Market Law Review. Vol. 34, pp. 1173–1195 (1997).

[13] Frigo, Manlio. *supra.*

CHAPTER TWENTY-FOUR

Hypothetical on the Enforcement of Export Prohibitions and a Commentary on the Hypothetical

Richard Crewdson

THE HYPOTHETICAL*

In 1921, France enacted a statute making it a crime to export works of fine art without an export permit, which permit could be denied if a Council of Experts determines that the artwork is part of the French national patrimony. The Council has been very expansive in its view of French national patrimony. In 1967, Ms. A exported from France a Leonardo drawing that belonged to her without obtaining any permits, and she is now attempting to sell the drawing in New York. France commences replevin proceedings to recover the drawing.

In 1987, France amended its 1921 export law to provide that the export prohibition thereafter would be limited to works of art created by French citizens or created in France by French residents. In 1989, Ms. A drove to Switzerland with her Monet watercolor and boarded a plane for New York where she sold her Monet at auction to Mr. Z for $19 million. She takes up residence in New York. The French Government attempts but fails to secure Ms. A's extradition from the United States. The French Government then brings an action against Mr. Z to recover the Monet. What should the outcome be?

Assume that there are no statute of limitations issues.

THE COMMENTARY

In the circumstances described, an equitable solution to the problem of who should possess respectively the Leonardo drawing and the Monet watercolor will be hard, if not impossible, to achieve.

Of the four parties involved (France, the United States of America, Ms. A, and Mr. Z), the first has patrimonial claims that are not recognised or matched by the second, Ms. A has property rights that will be recognised by the United States of America, in which she has taken up residence; Mr. Z has acquired property, which is not the subject of an involuntary transfer, in good faith, at a proper value. His property rights will therefore also be protected under U.S. law. Although the French government could therefore enforce its penal code against Ms. A if she ever again set foot in France, it is unlikely to receive a sympathetic hearing from a New York court in its efforts to recover either of the works of art. Relief would only be obtainable if there were an appropriate Convention to which both States were party.

A closer examination of the various parties' positions will indicate the following:

1. France: Export control of cultural objects (including a total prohibition on export of objects in the public domain), based on a system of classification, and extended in 1913 to privately owned goods of great historic or artistic importance, has been in existence since 1887. Total control of export of cultural objects was introduced in 1920 but abandoned in the following year. It was reintroduced by the "Vichy" government in 1941, and this law remained unchanged until 1992. The 1913 and 1941 Laws would therefore have been in force at the time of the two illegal exports.[1] It is fair to presume that both the Leonardo and the Monet would have been "classified" under the French system for export control purposes, and that an export license would have had to be applied for, and that this would have been refused in each case.

   However, such classification would not in any way have affected rights of ownership, nor would illegal export have given rise to the right of forfeiture. It is hard to see, therefore, how a replevin action by the French government could be initiated with any hope of success, in the absence of any title to the Leonardo.
2. United States of America: French claims in the U.S. courts to recover the two works of art would be confronted by two basic principles; first, the general principle that the United States of America is not obligated to enforce the export controls of another state, and second, the general principle that a foreign law would not be enforced if it was contrary to the "strong or fundamental" policy of the court's own legal system.[2] The result would be that in a case such as this, where ownership is not in question, the proprietary rights of a person resident within the jurisdiction take priority over a claimant foreign state.

* Editor's Note: In 1996, when the editor was chair of the Association of the Bar of the City of New York Committee on Art Law, the Committee organized a closed round-table discussion the Cultural Property Round Table with the objective of making a practical contribution to legal practice and scholarship. In addition to invited committee members, the committee invited distinguished lawyers, legal scholars, selected experts, and government officials to participate as either observers or as litigants in a debate of three mock hypotheticals, or as commentators on the panel. The committee developed three hypotheticals: (1) on enforcement of cultural patrimony laws, (2) on statute of limitations, and (3) on enforcement of export prohibitions. The editor would like to acknowledge the assistance of the members of the Hypothetical and Issues Committee, Herbert Hirsch, Lawrence M. Kaye, Alex A. Montague, Rena Moulopoulos Neville, Richard A. Rothman, and Daniel Shapiro, in the preparation of the hypotheticals, the third of which is reproduced in this chapter.

[1] See Chapter 25 for a discussion on the reform of the French Legal Framework in this century.

[2] Restatement of the Law, Second, Conflict of Laws ss 89, 90 (American Law Institute, St. Paul, 1971).

No law would have been violated,[3] and the United States of America, which has no export control (other than for pre-Columbian objects), offers no parallel code or system to the French export control laws.

It is, of course, true that, in its partial adoption of the UNESCO 1970 Convention,[4] the United States of America will bilaterally assist those States that it specifically recognises as being in need of emergency protection under the Convention, and also that the United States of America appears to be willing to restrict the import of cultural objects stolen from museums, places of religion, and public institutions, even if taken from a State that is not on the emergency list. But in this case, there is no question of any theft, and France is not on an emergency list, nor, indeed, a party to the UNESCO Convention, so the normal rules will apply.

3. Ms. A: Somehow, Ms. A succeeded in concealing the illegal export of the Leonardo drawing for a period of 20 years. If it had been discovered during that time, the full weight of the French penal code would have fallen upon her. Assuming that she had no intention at that time of taking up residence in the United States of America, the sympathy naturally felt for a person who migrates from one country to another is forced to leave her valuable property behind because of the rigour of export control, will not benefit her. Frankly, she has smuggled an extremely valuable, perhaps unique, piece (supposing it were the last Leonardo in private ownership), out of France for personal gain. But as we have seen, U.S. law will not, in the absence of Convention-based relations, interfere with private rights of ownership so long as they are *bona fide*, even where foreign export laws have been brazenly flouted. The Leonardo drawing may, however, prove hard to sell because of its notoriety and the circumstances of its removal from France.

   As regards the Monet, having by this time taken up U.S. residence, Ms. A's position is stronger than before, and in the eyes of the public and the court, she will be seen to be exercising her right freely to dispose of her property as a resident.

4. Mr. Z: The auction house from whom Mr. Z acquired the Monet will, no doubt, have made some enquiries as to the provenance of the watercolor, and have satisfied themselves that it was, indeed, Ms. A's property before including it in a sale, and they would have taken legal advice as to the consequences in the United States of the illegal export from France. Without giving any warranties as to the inviolability of Mr. Z's purchase, they would probably have felt confident that the drawing would remain in his possession so long as he wished to retain it.

[3] *US* v. *McClain*, 545 F.2d 988 (1977) at p. 996.

[4] 1970 UNESCO *Convention on the Means of Prohibiting and Preventing the Illicit Import Export and Transfer of Ownership of Cultural Property*, as translated into U.S. law by the *Convention on Cultural Property Implementation Act 1983* (19 U.S.C. s. 2601).

In official circles outside the United States of America, and among the international museum community, this overall conclusion may be felt to be provocative and a source of major irritation. Works of art that have been removed from their country of origin, or where they have been kept for more than 50 years, should be recoverable if their removal was illegal. Punishment of the miscreant cannot compensate for the loss of the artwork. Laws relating to export controls should be recognised by foreign courts, however tightly drawn. In international art sales, the export license should, in effect, assume a greater importance than the work of art itself.

This is the view of the majority of "art-rich" States, and is unlikely to change. But the opposite point of view taken by the "art importers" that foreign export control laws should not be recognised *per se*, because they are as likely as not to be unreasonable, is just as valid.

> "At the heart of recent debates about the international traffic in art has been the demand of the art-exporting countries that the United States bar the import of all art objects whose export was not itself legally authorized.... Such a rule would be undesirable.... Prohibiting imports in this way is a 'blank check' rule.... We should not abdicate our responsibility to decide whether the exporting country's decision to prohibit export represents a fair and acceptable accommodation among competing values (including the values served by allowing export)"[5]

The problem is how to reconcile the two positions, and this is what the UNIDROIT Convention[6] has attempted to do. The difficulties that arose in trying to find a solution is demonstrated by the fact that over a period of five years, far more time was spent, at successive meetings of government experts, in argument on a fair system of mutual enforcement of export controls than on the greater need to restrict international art theft, which, for the most part, was treated as being noncontroversial, despite the major change it would bring to the legal systems based on the *Code Napoléon*.[7]

Because of a late change in the wording of Article 5(3) of the Convention, the attempt to bridge the gap proposed by the Study Group that produced the Preliminary Draft of the Convention may prove to have been frustrated. In the Preliminary Draft, certain criteria were established that were designed to guide a court in its decision as to whether to order the return of an illegally exported object. The State seeking return of the object had to establish that the removal of the object from the territory:

> "significantly impaired one or more of the following interests:
> (a) the physical preservation of the object or of its context;
> (b) the integrity of a complex object;

[5] P. M. Bator: "An Essay on the International Trade in Art" (1982) 34 Stanford Law Review 327, as quoted in P. J. O'Keefe and L. V. Prott "Law and the Cultural Heritage" Vol. 3, p. 588.

[6] 1995 UNIDROIT Convention on *The International Return of Stolen or Illegally Exported Cultural Objects.*

[7] Effectively, the civil law countries were required to introduce the "*Nemo dat*" principle when dealing with cases involving international art theft.

(c) the preservation of information of, for example, a scientific or historical character;
(d) the traditional or ritual use of the object by a tribal or indigenous community [or established] that the object is of **outstanding** cultural importance for the requesting State."

Unfortunately, the delicate balance this carefully selected language was designed to set up was then upset by pressure on the government experts' drafting committee to delete the word "outstanding" and substitute the much weaker expression "significant."

Assuming hypothetically that both France and the United States had ratified the UNIDROIT Convention and the French government had established its right under the Convention to bring a claim to the U.S. courts, if one applies these two alternative wordings to the facts of this case, what would be the result, and would it be one that would satisfy informed U.S. public opinion?

Under the original wording of Article 5(3), it would be very difficult to make a case for the return of the Monet watercolor. In that medium, it would be looked upon as a minor work; a very substantial proportion of the painter's artistic legacy is already in permanent collections in France, much of it in the public domain. It would be easier to prove *per contra* that drawings of this nature were of greater educational value outside France than if they were held there. The only way of rebutting that argument would be if some special case, for example under 5(3)(c), could be made, relating to the preservation of information of a historical character, or perhaps if works by Monet in this medium were conspicuous by their rarity. The general sweep-up clause would not be effective.

Under the original wording, different considerations might apply to the Leonardo. The fact that the great artist spent his last years in France at the court of Francois I might lend some special significance to the surviving drawings of this still in France (whether in public or private ownership). This and other factors might tip the scales toward the "outstanding importance" classification, and an order for the return might therefore be obtained.

The actual wording of the Convention as signed does, of course, make it much easier for a requesting State to recover illegally exported cultural objects, and one is tempted to ask whether the categories (a)–(d) in 5(3) still have any relevance because most claims would now be framed under the sweep-up formula "of significant cultural importance." Both the Leonardo and the Monet could be reclaimed under this description.

If this is likely to be the effect of the unfortunate change of wording, it gives a convenient argument to those who would resist the ratification of the Convention by the United States of America. It would, however, be possible for the United States of America and any other country worried by this "abdication of responsibility," to use Mr. Bator's phrase, to introduce a statutory definition of the word "significant" when drafting the act of ratification. In the United Kingdom, for example, it would be possible to equate by statutory definition the concept of "significant importance" with the so-called "Waverley criteria"[8] on which the British export control system is based. There would then be a matching set of criteria that would be well understood by the legal courts. Even if these were to stretch slightly the plain meaning of the word "significant," it would not amount to a reservation in terms of the Convention itself.[9]

It is no secret that neither the United States of America nor the United Kingdom is in any hurry to ratify the UNIDROIT Convention. In fact, the pressure to do so will only be felt when it is realized how necessary it is in order to recover artworks stolen in either country and removed to continental Europe. Although this is a daily occurrence in England, it is probably a rare event in the United States. If and when the ratification takes place in both countries, it is to be hoped that there may be some mutual use of judicial precedent, which will help to minimize the damage caused by the article 5(3) amendment and to illustrate what the Bator principle means in practice. It may be worth mentioning in this connection that the EU Directive,[10] to which the United Kingdom is bound as a member state, has already set certain restrictions in terms of value and category to what a member state can classify as a "National Treasure" for purposes of export control, and it is possible for the European Court to further refine the national lists if it considers that free trade is being unduly restricted.[11]

It is ironical that the United States, which could be one of the last countries to ratify the UNIDROIT Convention (and, in fact, may never do so), is nevertheless the forum for most litigation related to art and cultural property.

[8] These criteria, known as the "Waverley Criteria," were established in 1952 by the Waverley Committee. The three tests applied to determine whether the object is of sufficient national importance to delay or deny export are: (1) Is the object so closely connected with the nation's history and current life that its departure would mean a misfortune for the nation? (2) Is it of outstanding artistic and aesthetic importance? (3) Is it of outstanding significance for the study of some particular branch of history, art, or learning?

If the decision is made that the object does sufficiently meet the criteria, the export license is not refused outright but a delay period is given, generally of between two to six months, to allow an offer from the state, a domestic institution, or public body to come forward. The right of the Committee to deny an export license is not absolute and can only be upheld if a *bona fide* offer is forthcoming from a state or public collection within the specified delay period; otherwise the license must be granted.

When a license is refused, the owner must be guaranteed a public offer to purchase the work at a "fair market price" or price obtainable on the open international market. The "fair market price" is determined by relevant experts and the Committee but generally implies: (a) if auctioned, the bid price + buyer's premium + dealer's commission; (b) if private sale, contractual price + dealer's commission, if applicable; (c) if no transaction, valuation by independent valuer or expert advisor; and (d) the price does not include insurance, storage, or interest costs of carrying the object while the export license remains pending.

[9] Article 18 prohibits reservations "except those expressly authorized."

[10] Council Directive 93/7/EEC (15 March 1993) *on the return of cultural objects unlawfully removed from the territory of a Member State.*

[11] Under Article 30 (formerly 36) of the Treaty of Rome, restrictions relating to national treasures "shall not constitute either a means of arbitrary discrimination or a disguised restriction on trade between Member States."

CHAPTER TWENTY-FIVE

Excerpts from the Memoire "Le Regime Juridique et Fiscal Francais des Importations et Exportations d'Oeuvres d'Art"

Pearl Gourdon

This note provides an analysis of the reforms undertaken by France early this century. In the beginning of this century, legislators enacted certain reforms relevant to the art market and the protection of the cultural patrimony: Promulgated the same day as the law dealing with the sale of furniture at public auction, the law of 10 July 2000, pertaining to the protection of national treasures, made important changes to the regime for the export of works of art. The law of 4 January 2002, dealing with the museums of France, in addition to the law of 1 August 2003 on patronage (*le mécénat achèvent*), allowing a reduction of taxes to companies who buy works of art presented from export, completed the reform of the control of the export of works of art. These laws are codified in the code of patrimony (*le Code du patrimoine.*)[1]

Regulation of the importation and exportation of works of art is a highly controversial subject divided by two contradictory imperatives: one, the indispensable free market in works of art, and the other, the necessity of preserving the national patrimony. Legislators have the task of navigating these two contradictions in order to find a delicate balance between them that offers the possibility of allowing the free circulation of works of art and antiquities except in such situations where it is of importance to the interests of the state to forbid it.

[1] Ordonnance no 2004-178 du 20 février 2004 relative à la partie législative du Code du patrimoine, J. O no 46 du 24 février 2004, p. 37048. Articles L. 111-1 à L 111-7.

Gourdon, Pearl. "*Le Regime Juridique et Fiscal Francais des Importations et Exportations d'Oeuvres d'Art.*" *Memoire – Droit et Fiscalité du Marché de l'Art, Université Jean Moulin*, Lyon 3, 2003–2004. *Diplôme d'Université de 3ème Cyvle.* Translated from French by the editor.

The law of 10 July 2000 has maintained the distinctions of prior laws dividing cultural goods into three groups of varying importance. The first, "*les trésors nationaux*," are classified as cultural goods that belong to cultural collections and, since the law of 4 January 2002, to the collections of French museums. The goods, which are classified according to the law of 1913 on the historic monuments or the law of 1979 on the archives or cultural goods, present an important interest to national patrimony from the point of view of history, art, or archeology. All the cultural goods in this category cannot be exported. Second are the cultural goods that are not national treasures but which have historic, artistic, or archeological interest. When they enter into one of the categories defined by the Annex of the Decree of 29 January 1993 (modified by the decree of 26 September 2001), their temporary export or definitive export outside the union must be submitted in order to obtain a certificate of export. It is this category that can be classified as potential national treasures. Finally, the last category pertains to cultural goods that do not belong in any of the other categories and can freely circulate without export controls.

For the first time, however, the law of 2000 protects the collection as an entity under certain circumstances with a view to preventing its dispersal. These building blocks added to the control of the exportation of works of art seems to preserve the required balance between the free trade in works of art and the preservation of the cultural patrimony. Through various measures, which have made the export of works of art easier and with a procedure that now permits more than one expert opinion through the Commission of National Treasure and also a procedure to obtain a reasonable price relative to the international art market. It appears that the reforms instituted by the law of 10 July 2000 and the regulations of 26 September 2001 have succeeded.

The search for equilibrium between the conservation of the national patrimony and the interest of the art market, as well as the intervention of the state and the liberty of the sellers and acquirers of works of art, must also be put within the context of tax structure. In effect, if the tax system determines the competitiveness of the French operators in the international art market, it is also one of the important weights sustaining cultural politics.

The existence of a T.V.A. at importation, even at the reduced tariff of 5.5 percent, when joined with other taxes like the taxation of greater value (*plus values*), seems to be stunting the growth of the French art market. A legitimate question to ask is whether or not our tax system poses an obstacle to the dynamism of the French art market.

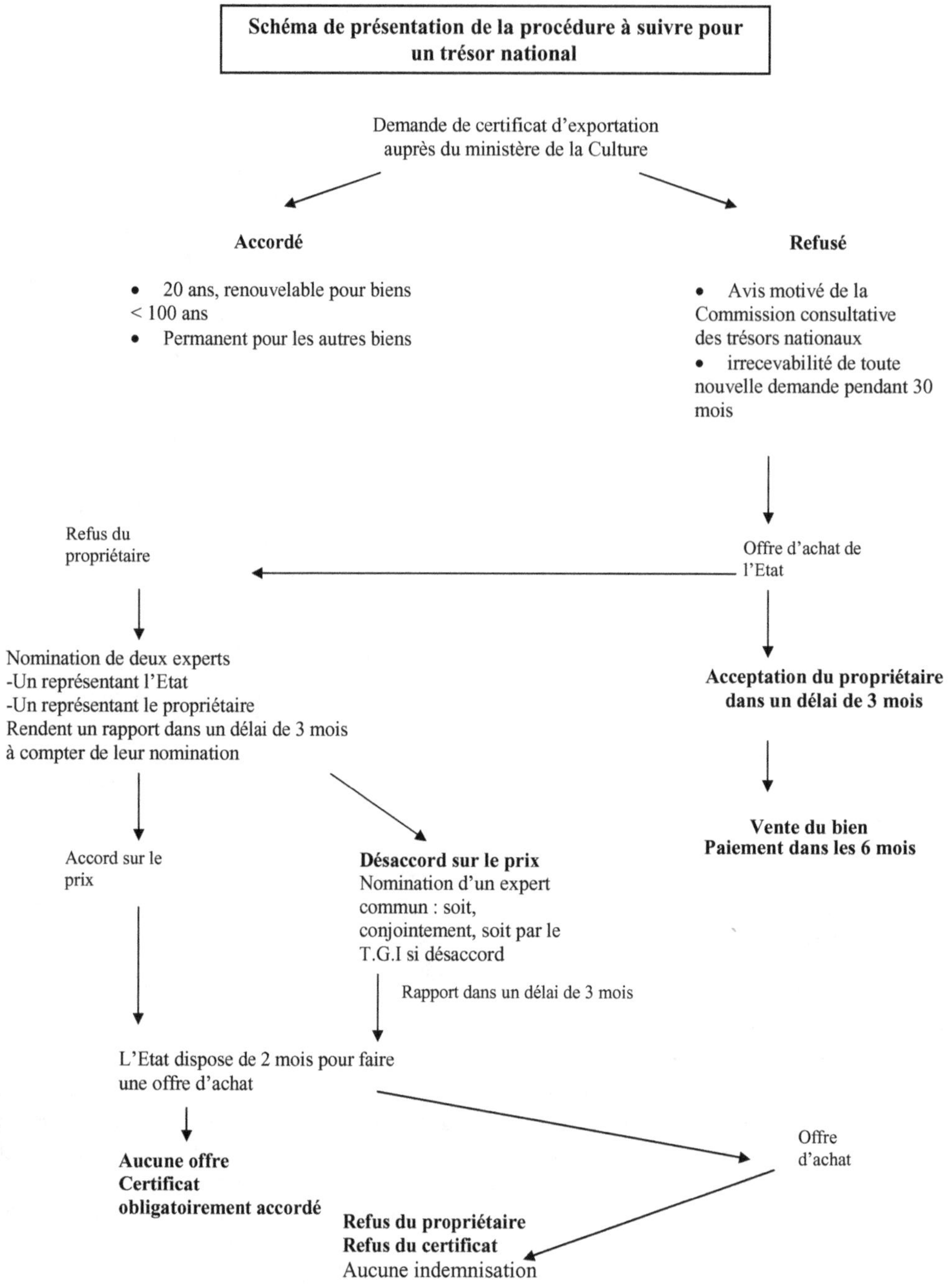

Image 1. Schéma de présentation de la procédure à suivre pour un trésor national.

PART FOUR

Protecting the World's Heritage

The National Dimension in the International Context

CHAPTER TWENTY-SIX

World Heritage – Linking Cultural and Biological Diversity

Mechtild Rössler

INTRODUCTION

The 1972 Convention Concerning the Protection of the World Cultural and Natural Heritage in short World Heritage Convention, is a unique international instrument that recognizes and protects both outstanding cultural and natural heritage. Although the World Heritage Convention's definition of heritage provided a pioneering approach for linking nature and culture, it took a long time for the recognition of the interaction between people and their environment; in particular, cultural landscapes.

NATURAL AND CULTURAL HERITAGE

The Convention defines *cultural heritage* as "monuments, groups of buildings, and sites," whereas *natural heritage* was described as "natural features consisting of physical and biological formations or groups of such formations, which are of outstanding universal value from the aesthetic or scientific point of view; geological and physiographical formations and precisely delineated areas that constitute the habitat of threatened species of animals and plants of outstanding universal value from the point of view of science or conservation; natural sites or precisely delineated natural areas of outstanding universal value from the point of view of science, conservation, or natural beauty." (UNESCO 1972)

"Mixed" sites, which would fall under both natural and cultural heritage, were covered as "combined works of nature and man." It is interesting to note that very few mixed sites, only 23, were inscribed in the 30 years of practice of the Convention, whereas 582 cultural and 149 natural properties from a total of 128 countries are now included on the World Heritage List. This result may also be because of the different approaches of the advisory bodies IUCN and ICOMOS in evaluating these properties. In the new Operational Guidelines (operational on 1 March 2004) the cultural and natural heritage criteria are merged and among the consequences may well be that heritage recognition and protection may be more integrated in the future.

The Convention became a key legal instrument in heritage conservation, both cultural and natural. It plays an important role in promoting the recognition of new heritage concepts, protection, and effective management in many regions of the world, as I will outline here in more detail.

LINKING NATURE AND CULTURE: CULTURAL LANDSCAPES

Interestingly enough, the interaction of people and their environment was covered until 1992 under the natural criteria for World Heritage and this definition was removed after the Caracas World Parks Congress (Titchen 1995). At the same time, in 1992, *cultural landscapes* were introduced into the Operational Guidelines, which provided a new and innovative approach toward linking culture and nature: The World Heritage Committee adopted three categories of cultural landscapes as qualifying for World Heritage status: (1) clearly defined landscapes designed and created intentionally by man; (2) organically evolved landscapes, which can be either relict landscapes or continuing landscapes; and (3) associative cultural landscapes.

In 1993, Tongariro National Park (New Zealand) became the first property to be inscribed on the World Heritage List under the revised cultural criteria and cultural landscapes categories. The Committee recognized that these mountains have cultural and religious significance for the Maori people and represent the spiritual links between this community and its natural environment. It was the first time that a natural World Heritage site received international recognition for its intangible cultural values. This decision illustrates the broadening of heritage definitions to include nonmaterial, intangible cultural heritage values. Among the diverse aspects of future heritage preservation is the acknowledgement of spiritual values associated with historical monuments, cultural landscapes, or natural features. This includes the necessity of documenting such traditions, including rituals, belief systems, and oral traditions, and the transmission to young people in order to preserve them in a living form underpinning people's cultural identity (Rossler, 2003).

The impact of the inclusion of cultural landscapes for the implementation of the World Heritage Convention was considerable in many ways:

- The category of the associative cultural landscape has been crucial in the recognition of intangible values and for the heritage of local communities and indigenous people.
- The importance of protecting biological diversity by maintaining cultural diversity within cultural landscapes was recognized.

This chapter was originally presented as a paper at the US/ICOMOS Symposium, "Learning from World Heritage," Nachitoches, LA, 2004.

- The inscription of sites as cultural landscapes on the World Heritage List had prime effects on the interpretation, presentation, and management of the properties.

Many cultural landscapes have been nominated and inscribed (35 by 2003 from all regions of the world) on the World Heritage List since the 1992 landmark decision. Often they are associative cultural landscapes, or sacred sites, which may be physical entities or mental images embedded in a people's spirituality, cultural tradition, and practice. The recent publications of the Ferrara meeting (UNESCO 2003b) and the study by Peter Fowler (2003) also show the importance of agricultural landscapes for the survival of humankind. Parallel, a project was developed by the Food and Agriculture Organization (FAO) on Globally Important Agricultural Heritage Systems, which focuses on outstanding agricultural systems and case studies, including World Heritage cultural landscapes, such as Cinque Terre (Italy).

The Cinque Terre (Italy): Many of the agricultural heritage landscapes of the world are threatened both by the failure of traditional ways to maintain production in a world of changing interests and needs, and the demands of mass tourism, whose impacts threaten the very qualities that attract tourists. The Cinque Terre, a World Heritage cultural landscape, exemplifies these dilemmas, but also offers hope that even in the most difficult situations, solutions may be at hand" (Stovel/De Marco, 2003). The unique and diverse cultural land- and seascape of wine-growing terraces and fishing villages was maintained over centuries. Since the 1970s, terraces have been abandoned and the impacts on this complex system, including collapses of dry stonewalls and landslides, have been severe. The World Heritage inscription gave a boost to the recognition of the people's pride in their heritage and territorial identity as well as to tourism and local produce. It brought direct economic benefits to the people and attracted international funding such as from the World Monuments Fund for terraces restoration and re-use. Subsequently, a *national park* was created that covers most (but not all) of the World Heritage cultural landscape.

NATURAL SACRED SITES AND PLACES TO PROTECT BIODIVERSITY

In the natural heritage field, local and indigenous knowledge, sacred places, and traditional skills were discovered as tools for the protection of both the natural environment and cultural diversity. UNESCO organized already in 1999, an international symposium on Natural Sacred Sites. The current UNESCO project, "Local and Indigenous Knowledge Systems in a Global Society" reflects this trend. More recently, a UNESCO-Man and the Biosphere workshop (Kunming, China, February 2003) led to the creation of an "International Network on Sacred Natural Sites for Biodiversity Conservation" in which scientists, conservation experts, and custodians of sacred natural sites collaborate to study and exchange information on the recognition and management of such sites for enhanced environmental conservation. These are only two examples of the implementation of this new approach. The Task Force on Cultural and Spiritual Values, IUCN World Commission on Protected Areas, is a crucial forum to discuss these concepts and this workshop can really bring us a step further in discussing the practical aspects of the many facets of traditional protection and the nonmaterial values of protected areas, including spiritual, cultural, and social values, cultural identity, artistic and aesthetic values, and the contribution of protected areas for peace (Rössler 2003).

The Quadisha Valley (Lebanon) is an interesting example of a site nominated as a natural property as the "Cedar Forest of Lebanon," but was not recommended by IUCN because of its small size and integrity issues. Subsequently it was presented as a cultural landscape and inscribed in 1998 as a monastic settlements landscape of the valley. The sacred cedars of Lebanon are already referred to in the Bible. The site has currently no protected area status and is located between two nature Reserves (Hosrsh Ehden and Tannourine Nature Reserves). A local association works toward better protection of the site and the World Heritage Committee in June 2003 requested better legal protection, management coordination, establishment of a nature reserve, and management plan.

CULTURAL SACRED SITES – CULTURAL DIVERSITY

"In sacred architecture, humans attempt to bring themselves closer to the divine by creating a special space to hold this powerful and precious contact." (Humphrey, Vitebsky, 2003, 8). Many World Heritage sites around the world are sacred places, ranging from Stonehenge to Borobudur, from Jerusalem to the shrines of Nara and the Kasubi Tombs in Uganda. However, we need to integrate the sacred and social dimensions into the interpretation and transmission to future generations of our World Heritage, and not only the outstanding architecture. This will contribute to a new understanding of the diverse interactions between people and their environment and culture's relationship with the divine.

TANGIBLE AND INTANGIBLE

The World Heritage Convention deals with tangible heritage, but embodies intangible values both for natural and cultural heritage. For natural heritage the concept of "natural beauty," which is reflected in one of the four natural criteria for the inclusion on the World Heritage List, is clearly illustrating intangible values: "*contain*[s] *superlative natural phenomena or areas of exceptional natural beauty and aesthetic importance....*" (UNESCO 1972). Similarly, the last criterion of the six cultural criteria is the intangible association (vi) "*with events or living traditions, ideas or with beliefs, with artistic and literary works of outstanding universal significance.*" However, the World Heritage Committee was struggling with the exclusive use of the intangible values and stated that it, "*considers that this criterion should justify inclusion on the list in exceptional circumstances and in conjunction with other criteria cultural or natural.*" Only in 2003 this approach changed, which will allow for a new drive for the recognition of intangible values of natural sites, for example. At the same time, UNESCO adopted a new Convention: the Convention for the Safeguarding of the Intangible Cultural Heritage, Paris, 17 October 2003.

The first cultural landscape from Africa, **Surkur Cultural Landscape (Nigeria)**, represents a case of traditional management and customary law. The Sukur Cultural Landscape encompasses the Hidi's stone henge palace (i.e., the dwelling place of the spirito-political paramountcy), dominating the villages below, the terraced fields and their sacred symbols with stone paved walkways linking the low land to the graduated plateaus. The landscape also features unique architectural elements, stone corrals for feeding domestic stock, grave yards, stone gates, and vernacular stone settlement clusters with homestead farms, all in the midst of rare species of flora and fauna. It is a remarkably intact physical expression of a society and its spiritual and material culture.

TRADITIONAL PROTECTION AND MANAGEMENT SYSTEMS: MANAGING CULTURAL AND BIOLOGICAL DIVERSITY

With the inclusion of cultural landscape categories in 1992, the World Heritage Committee recognized traditional management systems, customary law, and long-established customary techniques to protect the cultural and natural heritage. Through these protection systems, World Heritage sites contribute to sustainable local and regional development.

Cultural landscapes are particularly vulnerable to social, economic, and environmental changes. The maintenance of the fabric of societies, traditional knowledge, and indigenous practices is vital to their survival. In many cases, cultural landscapes and sacred natural sites are of vital importance to the protection of intangible values and heritage. World Heritage cultural landscapes and sacred properties can be models in effective landscape management, excellence in conservation practices, and innovation in legislative protection. They are places where we can learn about the relation between people, nature, and ecosystems and how this shapes culture and identity, and enriches cultural and, in some cases, biological diversity.

The Philippines Rice Terraces (Philippines) were included in the World Heritage List in 1995 and represent another agricultural landscape of unique scenic value of steep and small terraces. It represents a unique interaction between people and their natural environment. It was included on the World Heritage in-danger list despite efforts to safeguard the property by the Banaue Rice Terraces Task Force (BRTTF) and Ifugao Terraces Commission because the BRTTF lacks full Government support and needs more resources, greater independence, and an assurance of permanence. About twenty-five to thirty percent of the terraces are now abandoned, which has led to damage to some of the walls. This has arisen because parts of the irrigation system have been neglected, which, in turn, is because of people leaving the area. Most of the site is privately owned and traditionally managed.

CONCLUSIONS

The immense and forward-looking development in the interpretation of the World Heritage Convention represents only the beginning of a recognition of the complexity of nature–culture interactions and the wealth of intangible values in relation to protected areas, and in particular to sites of outstanding universal value. There will be many challenges in the identification, recognition, and protection of the intrinsic links between natural and cultural heritage, people and their environment and the tangible and the intangible values. An inclusive approach – both within UNESCO and with other institutions and organizations – is crucial for the designation and management of sites of outstanding universal value, for the benefit of the people living in and around these sites, the conservation community, and humanity as a whole.

World Heritage stewardship can promote diverse cultural and natural values relevant for protected areas globally. The variety of sites on the List demonstrates already that a great diversity of outstanding natural heritage sacred sites and cultural landscapes exists throughout the world. These combined works of nature and humankind express a long and intimate relationship between peoples and their natural environment. Powerful beliefs, traditions, and spiritual relationships of people with nature can contribute to global heritage conservation and, in particular, add a new dimension in linking culture and nature.

RECOMMENDATIONS

Some specific recommendations for the future following from my deliberations are:

(i) Encourage the development of specific guidelines and case studies of excellence on conservation practices and sustainable land use as cultural landscapes.

(ii) Support the effective management and legal/traditional protection mechanisms for cultural landscapes, particularly in Africa, the Pacific, the Arab States, the Andean sub-region, the Caribbean, central Asia and south-east Asia.

(iii) Enhance the identification of the interaction between people and the environment and encourage nominations of World Heritage cultural landscapes from under-represented regions and themes identified as gaps on the World Heritage List (e.g., agricultural landscapes, water and civilisation, sacred sites).

(iv) Raise awareness of the importance of nature–culture interaction through education and capacity-building programmes and through the UNESCO project on linking cultural and biological diversity.

(v) Encourage the re-interpretation of the existing World Heritage properties to enhance the understanding of the multifaceted and diverse human relations to nature and the universe in collaboration with both IUCN and ICOMOS.

(vi) Disseminate the results of the international workshop "Cultural Landscapes the Challenges of Conservation," Ferrara, Italy, November 2002, and the study by Peter Fowler (2003) to raise awareness within the professional community to raise standards in preparing tentative lists, nominations, and project development, and to improve evaluations and reactive monitoring.

The participants in the Ferrara workshop, which was held on the occasion of the thirtieth anniversary of the World Heritage Convention, concluded that "Cultural landscape management and conservation processes bring people together in caring for their collective identity and heritage, and provide a shared local vision within a global context. Local communities need therefore to be involved in every aspect of the identification, planning and management of the areas, as they are the most effective guardians of the landscape heritage. The outstanding landscapes are selected examples, which could offer stewardship, models in effective management and excellence in conservation practices."

QUESTIONS FOR FURTHER DISCUSSION

1. How do you see the future for an integrated global approach for natural and cultural heritage conservation?

2. How can European instruments co-exist with international instruments, such as the European Landscape Convention Florence 20 October 2000, (ETS no. 176) (2000) with the World Heritage Convention (1972)?

3. How would you describe the approach taken by the 1972 UNESCO Convention in comparison with other biodiversity-related Conventions and where do you see a potential for enhancing cooperation?

4. Are the new cultural heritage Conventions compatible with the 1972 Convention, such as the 2001 and 2003 UNESCO Conventions, as well as the planned Convention on Cultural Diversity?

5. Where do you see areas of cooperation between specialized UN agencies in cultural and natural heritage fields, such as United Nations Environmental Program, the Food Agricultural Organization, and UNESCO?

6. Are there international nongovernmental organizations that pursue an integrated approach for natural and cultural heritage conservation?

REFERENCES

Carmichael, D. L., J. Hubert, B. Reeves, A. Schanche (Eds.) 1998, *Sacred Sites, Sacred Places* (One World Archaeology, 23). Routledge London.

Beltran, J. (ed) 2000, *Indigenous and Traditional Peoples and Protected Areas. Principles, Guidelines and Case Studies.* World Commission on Protected Areas. Best Practice Protected Area Guidelines Series No. 4, IUCN Gland.

Beresford, M. and A. Philips, 2000, *Protected Landscapes: A Conservation Model for the 21st Century.* In: The George Wright Forum. Vol. 17, No. 1, (Landscape Stewardship: New Directions in Conservation of Nature and Culture), 15–26.

von Droste, B., H. Plachter and M. Rössler, (eds.) 1995, *Cultural Landscapes of Universal Value. Components of a Global Strategy.* Gustav Fischer, Jena.

von Droste, B., M. Rössler and S. Titchen (eds.) 1999, *Linking Nature and Culture.* Report of the Global Strategy Natural and Cultural Heritage Expert Meeting, 25 to 29 March 1998, Amsterdam, The Netherlands. UNESCO/Ministry for Foreign Affairs/Ministry for Education, Science, and Culture, The Hague.

Fowler, Peter: World Heritage Cultural Landscapes 1992–2003. World Heritage papers 6. UNESCO World Heritage Centre 2003.

Hamilton, L. S. 1993, *Ethics Religion and Biodiversity. Relations between conservation and cultural values.* Cambridge, The White Horse Press.

Humphrey, C. and P. Vitebsky 2003, *Sacred Architecture.* Singapore, Thorsons.

Lucas, B., 1992, *Protected Landscapes. A guide for policy-makers and planners.* IUCN – The World Conservation Union. London, Chapman and Hall.

Lee, Cathy and Thomas Schaaf (eds). The Importance of Sacred Natural Sites for Biodiversity Conservation. Proceedings of the International Workshop held in Kunming and Xishuangbanna Biosphere Reserve, China, February 2003, Paris: UNESCO, 2003.

Rössler, M. 1994, *Tongariro: first cultural landscape on the World Heritage List.* In: The World Heritage Newsletter, No. 4, March, p. 15.

Rössler, M. and G. Saouma-Forero (ed) 2000, *The World Heritage Convention and cultural landscapes in Africa.* Report of the Expert Meeting, Tiwi, Kenya, 9–14 March 1999. UNESCO/CRAterre, Paris.

Rössler, M. L. Towards linking the Tangible and the Intangible. In: *The Full Value of Pa* ed. by David Harmon and Allan Puttney, Rowe and Littlefieled, Oxford 2003, 197–210.

Thulstrup H. D. (ed), 1999, *World Natural Heritage and the local community. Case studies from Asia Pacific, Australia and New Zealand.* UNESCO World Heritage Centre, Paris.

Titchen, S. 1996, *Including Cultural Landscapes on the World Heritage List.* World Heritage Review, No. 2, 34–39.

Titchen, S. M. 1995, "*On the construction of outstanding universal value. UNESCO's World Heritage Convention (Convention concerning the Protection of the World Cultural and Natural Heritage, 1972) and the identification and assessment of cultural places for inclusion on the World Heritage List*", unpublished PhD dissertation, Australian National University, Canberra, Australia.

UNEP, 1999, *Cultural and Spiritual Values of Biodiversity. A complementary Contribution to the Global Biodiversity Assessment.* Intermediate Technology Publications. Nairobi Kenya.

UNESCO, 1972, *Convention concerning the protection of the world cultural and natural heritage adopted by the General Conference at its seventeenth session*, Paris, 16 November 1972.

UNESCO, 1998, *Natural sacred sites. Cultural diversity and biological diversity.* UNESCO/CNRS Conference, Paris, 22–25 September 1998 (abstract book).

UNESCO, 2001a, *Report of the Thematic Expert Meeting on Asia-Pacific Sacred Mountains* (Wakayama, Japan, 5 to 10 September 2001) WHC-2001/CONF.205/INF.9, 15 October 2001.

UNESCO, 2001b, UNESCO Universal Declaration on Cultural Diversity. 2 November 2001.

UNESCO, 2003a, *Convention for the Safeguarding of the Intangible Cultural Heritage*, Paris, 17 October 2003.

UNESCO, 2003b, Cultural Landscapes: the Challenges of Conservation. World Heritage 2002. Shared Legacy, Common Responsibility. Associated Workshops, 11–12 November 2002, Ferrara, Italy, World Heritage papers 7. UNESCO World Heritage Centre 2003.

REFERENCES TO IMPORTANT WEB SITES

<http://whc.unesco.org>

<http://www.unesco.org/mab/>

<http://portal.unesco.org/culture/>

<http://www.international.icomos.org/>

<http://www.iucn.org/>

<http://www.unep-wcmc.org/>

<http://www.iccrom.org/>

CHAPTER TWENTY-SEVEN

Judicial Interpretations of the World Heritage Convention in the Australian Courts

Matthew Peek and Susan Reye

Nation states have been around for a long time. As a means of organizing humanity, for better or worse, they are going to be around for an equally long time. Nation states exercise sovereignty over their territories. This is the key to their existence. They are jealous of their sovereignty.

From time to time, sovereign states join together to organize their relations and to achieve mutual objectives. They negotiate, sign, and ratify conventions. They do this essentially because they deem ratification to be in their national interest, however broadly they may choose to define this. The converse is also true: if a text is seen not to be in their interest, they will not ratify it; if the subsequent evolution of interpretation turns out not to be in their interest, they may choose to ignore provisions of the Convention or even withdraw from it. My point is that ideas for interpreting or implementing a Convention, interesting as many of them may be, must ultimately pass through the filter of how sovereign states, states as parties to the Convention, will respond. In other words, will these ideas work in practice?

This chapter provides an overview of the Australian judicial experience of the interpretation given to the World Heritage Convention over the last two decades. This may perhaps suggest some of the opportunities available, through law, for the protection of the world's natural and cultural heritage.

Australia was the first state party to enact specific national legislation to give effect to its Convention obligations. Initially this was done through the World Heritage Properties Conservation Act 1983, which has now been replaced by the world heritage provisions of the Environment Protection and Biodiversity Conservation Act 1999.

Australia is a federation, formed in 1901. Under the Australian constitution, the Commonwealth (or federal) parliament has no express power to legislate in relation to the environment or heritage, as such. But it does have power to legislate in relation to "external affairs." This includes power to give effect to international agreements to which Australia is a party. For this reason, the World Heritage Convention has provided an important basis for national legislative protection of the most valuable aspects of Australia's natural and cultural heritage.

Judicial interpretation of the Convention by the Australian courts has occurred in two broad contexts. First, the courts have had to decide the extent and nature of Australia's obligations under the Convention, so as to decide whether Commonwealth legislation that gives effect to those obligations is within constitutional power. Second, they have looked at the Convention in interpreting the legislation giving effect to the Convention's provisions.

The Australian courts' approach to interpretation will be familiar to many international lawyers. The judges apply the rules of interpretation set out in the Vienna Convention on the Law of Treaties, including consultation of the travaux préparatoires and subsequent agreements or practice of the parties, where appropriate.

Four key issues have been considered by Australian courts in relation to interpretation of the World Heritage Convention:

- the nature and extent of the obligations of state parties under the Convention, including the discretion allowed to each state party in determining the measures by which it will implement Convention obligations;
- the effects of inscribing a property on the World Heritage List and obligations on state parties in relation to non-listed world heritage;
- the meaning of "presentation" in Articles 4 and 5, and the relationship among the obligations of presentation, preservation, and conservation; and
- the meaning of "natural heritage" and how activities outside a property may affect this.

The first of these issues relates to the existence and nature of the legal obligations under the Convention.

In the Tasmanian Dam case, a landmark case, the state (provincial) government of Tasmania wished to construct a hydro-electric dam in an area recently entered on the World Heritage List. Tasmania challenged the constitutional validity of the World Heritage Properties Conservation Act under which the construction of the dam was prohibited. Tasmania argued that this Commonwealth (federal) Act was not a valid exercise of the Commonwealth's external affairs power, the power to give effect to treaties, because the World Heritage Convention did not impose binding legal obligations on states parties to protect a world heritage property. They argued that the Convention "imposed no real obligation and conferred no real benefit, and was no more than a statement of aspiration or political accord." However, by a majority of four to three, the High Court rejected this argument. Following a detailed textual interpretation of Articles 4 and 5, applying the usual rules of treaty interpretation, they concluded that although the Convention is not expressed with the precision that would be expected in a legal document under municipal law, this absence of precision does not imply any absence of international obligation.

Justice Deane said:

> Unless one is to take the view that over 70 nations have engaged in the solemn and cynical farce use of using words such as "obligation" and "duty" when neither was intended or undertaken, the provisions of the Convention impose real and identifiable obligations and provide for the availability of real benefits at least in respect of those properties which have, in accordance with the procedure established by the Convention, been indisputably made the subject of those obligations and identified as qualified for those benefits by being entered upon the nomination of the States in which they are situated, on the World Heritage List.

However, the High Court also recognized that the lack of precision in the language of the Convention has implications for the nature of the obligations imposed. In the Tasmanian Dam case, they pointed out that the Convention does not spell out either the specific steps to be taken for the protection, conservation, and presentation of the cultural and natural heritage situated on a state party's territory, nor the measure of the resources which are to be committed by the state party to that end.

The state party is thus left with discretion as to the manner of performance of the obligations under the Convention. This reflects general practice in relation to many treaties, and has been referred to by Sir Anthony Mason, former Chief Justice of the High Court, as "a certain margin of appreciation" left to the state in giving effect to convention provisions.

The nature of this margin of appreciation was considered in a subsequent case, *Richardson v. Forestry Commission*. In that case, the state of Tasmania challenged the constitutional validity of Commonwealth legislation that established an inquiry into whether a particular area was part of the natural or cultural heritage, and, related to this, an inquiry into the forestry industry and forestry resources in the area. The state claimed that an inquiry into the forestry industry was not related to giving effect to the World Heritage Convention. This argument was rejected by the Court. The High Court held that the Convention permits the state, in whose territory part of the world heritage is situated, to take into account economic and other factors in deciding how it will discharge the duty of identification imposed upon it by the Convention. Chief Justice Mason and Justice Brennan said:

> The terms of Art. 3, together with the second sentence of Art. 4 and the qualifications in the opening words of Art. 5 are entirely consistent with the acknowledgment of State sovereignty in Art. 6 and with the recognition that each State, in giving effect to the obligations imposed by the Convention, with respect to the heritage situated on its territory will naturally have to take account of competing considerations, economic and otherwise. Thus though each State has a duty to identify and delineate the heritage in its territory, the performance of this duty will depend in many respects on the judgment of that State.

Thus, in the opinion of the Court, because the Commonwealth government could take account of economic factors in deciding whether to nominate the area for listing, it could enact legislation for an inquiry into those matters.

In the Wet Tropics case, Queensland, another Australian state, argued that although the Wet Tropics Area had been included on the World Heritage List, it was not "cultural or natural heritage" within the meaning of the Convention, and so the Commonwealth had no power to protect it. The Court agreed that whether a property is part of the cultural or natural heritage depends on the qualities of the property, not on whether it has been listed.

However, the Court said:

> From the viewpoint of the international community, the submission by a State Party of a property for inclusion in the World Heritage List and inclusion of the property in the List by the Committee are the means by which the status of a property is ascertained and the duties attaching to that status are established. The State Party's submission of a property is some evidence of its status but the Committee's listing of a property is conclusive, for the benefits of listing are available only to properties having the status of being part of the cultural heritage or natural heritage.

Inclusion of the property in the List by the Committee, the Court said, is conclusive of its status in the eyes of the international community. It is therefore conclusive of Australia's international duty to protect and conserve it.

Of course, because the duties under Articles 4 and 5 to protect the cultural and natural heritage do not flow from listing, they are not limited to properties that have been entered in the World Heritage List. This is made clear in Article 12, and this has been recognized by the High Court. For example, in *Richardson v. Forestry Commission*, the Court considered legislation that gave interim protection to an area while an inquiry was held into its suitability to be nominated for world heritage listing. The Court held that the legislation gave effect to the Convention:

> The taking of action by a State to protect or conserve a particular property in its territory pending resolution of the status of that property as part of the heritage is to carry out and give effect to the Convention because the taking of the action is incidental to the State's duty to ensure protection of the heritage and to the attainment of the object of the Convention. The absence of such action by way of interim protection in the meantime would expose the property to the possibility of irreparable damage.

So far, this paper has focused on broad questions relating in general to the obligations under the Act. These questions have arisen mostly when the courts have considered whether legislation could properly be described as giving effect to the Convention. There have also been a limited number of cases in which the courts have looked at specific terms that are used in the Australian legislation and defined them by reference to the meaning in the Convention.

For example, the World Heritage Properties Conservation Act provided that, in determining whether or not to allow an activity that would otherwise be prohibited, the Minister "shall have regard only to the protection, conservation and presentation, within the meaning of the Convention, of the property." In *Friends of Hinchinbrook v. The Minister for the Environment*, a conservation group argued that the duty of "presentation" of natural heritage must be subordinate to the duties of protection and conservation. The full federal court rejected the argument. The Court looked at the context in which "presentation" is used in the Convention, and noted that it applies equally to cultural heritage and natural heritage. They considered that:

"The Convention is concerned that natural and cultural wonders should be seen and known, as well as protected and conserved."

They further considered that the Convention,

does not envisage that natural or cultural heritage is to be locked away from sight and made inaccessible to the public in all circumstances, or indeed in most circumstances. The Convention makes it clear that the values which it espouses are values which contemplate obligations on contracting States to render items of cultural or natural heritage accessible, but subject, of course, also to the obligations to protect and conserve. None of the objects of "presentation," "protection" or "conservation" is subordinate to the other. What is required in a particular case will be a balancing of the obligations of "protection" and "conservation," as well as "presentation," each given equal weight.

Another specific term to be examined is "natural heritage."

The Environment Protection and Biodiversity Conservation Act regulates actions that are likely to have a significant impact on the world heritage values of a world heritage property. The expression "world heritage values" is defined as meaning the "natural heritage" and the "cultural heritage" within the meaning of the Convention.

In *Booth v. Bosworth*, a conservation group claimed that the Act was being contravened by a lychee farmer who operated an electric grid to kill spectacled flying foxes that were feeding on the lychee fruit at harvest time. The farm was outside, but in the vicinity of, the Wet Tropics World Heritage Area, and the flying foxes that raided the lychee farm resided in the World Heritage Area.

To decide whether the electrocution of the flying foxes was likely to have a significant impact on the world heritage values – that is to say, the "natural heritage" of the Wet Tropics Area – the Federal Court had to consider the meaning of natural heritage under the Convention.

Applying the rules of treaty interpretation reflected in Article 31 of the Vienna Convention on the Law of Treaties, Justice Branson decided that in interpreting the definition of natural heritage in the Convention, it was appropriate to take account of the criteria for world heritage listing set out in the operational guidelines established by the Committee. She considered the documentation relating to the nomination of the particular property, the International Union for the Conservation of Nature report in relation to the listing, and especially the criteria under which the property was listed. The spectacled flying fox was not specifically mentioned in any of these documents (although a photograph of some spectacled flying foxes was among the attachments to the nomination document – a fact the judge considered significant enough to mention). On the basis of this material, and expert evidence relating to the spectacled flying fox, Justice Branson concluded that the spectacled flying fox contributed to the natural heritage of the Wet Tropics World Heritage Area, in relation to two of the criteria for which it was listed.

Justice Branson found that the probable impact of the operation of the grid, if allowed to continue on an annual basis during future lychee seasons, would be to halve the Australian population of spectacled flying foxes in less than five years, and render the species endangered. She said:

Is this impact on the population of Spectacled Flying Foxes to be equated in the context of the Act with a significant impact on the world heritage values of the Wet Tropics World Heritage Area? . . . I have concluded that in the circumstances of the present case it is. In this context, in my view, a dramatic decline in the population of a species, so as to render the species endangered, where that species forms a part (other than an inconsequential part) of the record of the Earth's evolutionary history or of the biological diversity of a most important and significant habitat for in-situ conservation of biological diversity is to be understood as having an impact that is important, notable or of consequence. I reject the submission of the respondents that before this conclusion can properly be reached it would have to be established that the Spectacled Flying Fox is itself, when compared with other species, a species of outstanding universal value.

Accordingly, she found that operation of the grid was likely to have a significant impact on the natural heritage, and therefore contravened the Act.

This case has shown the capacity of the Environment Protection and Biodiversity Conservation Act to control actions that are likely to have an indirect, but significant, impact on the world heritage values of a world heritage property regardless of how far from the property they may take place.

Of course, the Australian courts recognize that they do not have jurisdiction to make determinations that take effect as international law. In the Wet Tropics case, the High Court said:

The existence of . . . an international duty must be decided as a matter of fact, though this Court has no jurisdiction the exercise of which can affect the existence under international law of any purported obligation imposed on Australia.

. . . Although municipal courts do not administer international law, they take cognizance of international law in finding facts and they interpret municipal law, so far as its terms admit, consistently with international law. Regard may therefore be had to the terms of the Convention in deciding whether an international duty of protection and conservation exists, but the existence or otherwise of the duty is not necessarily concluded by the municipal court's construction of its terms or by its opinion as to the Convention's operation. The existence of an international duty depends upon the construction which the international community would attribute to the Convention and on the operation that the international community would accord to it in particular circumstances. The municipal court must ascertain that construction and operation as best it can in order to determine the validity of a law of the Commonwealth, conscious of the difference between the inquiry and the more familiar curial function of construing and applying a municipal law.

In summary, Australian courts have considered four main issues in relation to interpretation of the World Heritage Convention:

They have confirmed the nature and extent of obligations under the Convention, which imposes "real and identifiable obligations," and in recognition of other commitments on the part of states, have noted that each state party has discretion in determining the measures by which it will implement the obligations of the Convention:

- The effects of inscribing a property on the World Heritage List, confirming that the inclusion of the property in the List by the Committee is conclusive of its status in the eyes of the international community. It is therefore conclusive of Australia's international duty to protect and conserve it.
- Elaboration on the meaning of "presentation" in Articles 4 and 5, and importantly considering that none of the objects of "presentation," "protection," or "conservation" is subordinate to the other. What is required in a particular case will be a balancing of the obligations of "protection" and "conservation," as well as "presentation," each given equal weight.
- Consideration of the meaning under the Convention of "natural heritage" in relation to a specific world heritage property. The case also demonstrated the control of an action outside the boundaries of a world heritage property that has an indirect impact on the natural heritage within those boundaries.

The Australian experience in interpreting the World Heritage Convention has thus, from the point of view of this author, been a positive one. It underlines the importance Australia, its courts, its federal government, which turned to the courts for interpretation, and its civil society attach to honoring commitments made under the Convention.

QUESTIONS FOR DISCUSSION

1. What is the role of municipal courts in interpreting international agreements? Do difficulties arise from the different interpretative approaches for treaties compared with municipal legislation and private law instruments (e.g., contracts)? What effect can an interpretation by a municipal court have as a matter of international law?
2. What is the appropriate role of nongovernmental organizations in enforcing national legislation that implements a treaty, given that it is the state that is responsible for performing its obligations under international law?
3. What is the relationship between the duty of "presentation," on the one hand, and the duties of "preservation" and "conservation," on the other, under the World Heritage Convention?
4. Is Article 4 of the World Heritage Convention "aspirational," or does it impose obligations that can be identified with any precision? How does this relate to the "margin of appreciation" of a state in giving effect to its obligations under the Convention? To what extent can economic and social considerations be taken into account?
5. What is the effect of identification of world heritage by the territorial state, and of listing (or refusal to list) by the World Heritage Committee, in relation to the obligation of a state to protect world heritage within its territory? To what extent does a nomination document, or the World Heritage Committee's assessment of the property, determine the state's obligations in relation to the nominated property? Do these documents identify the "cultural heritage" or "national heritage" to be protected? If so, what is the situation relating to subsequent alterations or new discoveries in the property concerned?

USEFUL WEB SITE LINKS

<www.environment.gov.au>
Australian Government environment portal, linking to Web sites of state and federal (Commonwealth) authorities.

<www.deh.gov.au/>
Home page of the Australian (Commonwealth) Department of the Environment and Heritage, including material on world heritage areas and the Environment Protection and Biodiversity Conservation Act 1999.

<www.austlii.edu.au>
Database of Australian legislation and cases.

<www.law.gov.au>
Australian law online.

CHAPTER TWENTY-EIGHT

Paris Down Under – World Heritage Impacts in Australia

Jane L. Lennon

Australian heritage is dominated by landscapes representing wild nature and the product of Indigenous peoples. This landscape heritage is complex, woven by the interaction of people and their environment over time, including extensive shaping by Europeans. The development of Australia's landscape conservation has been influenced by changing perceptions of the relationship between nature and culture and has, for many years, placed a higher value on natural heritage. The development of heritage protection has been dramatically altered by the World Heritage Convention that ushered in many nominations of natural sites of global significance. This paper examines national characteristics, the shift in heritage protection to a values-based approach, the impact of tourism, and the rise of the cultural landscape concept as an integrating tool in producing a distinctively Australian contribution to heritage conservation.

Thirty years ago, Australia joined *The Convention Concerning the Protection of the World Cultural and Natural Heritage* and, ever since, World Heritage has had an impact on Australians – in their legislation, in their tourism, and in their concepts about nature and culture. Today the 16 World Heritage areas in Australia are household names, icons of popular heritage, and major tourist destinations, but only after bitter contests with a variety of communities and commercial interests. World Heritage in Australia has been a very political issue.

The Convention deals with heritage of outstanding universal value. UNESCO's Committee for the Protection of World Cultural and Natural Heritage referred to an "International Estate" but its use of the word heritage signalled a major shift in the understanding of this term applied to features of the built and natural environment rather than as a spiritual notion.

In 1973, a new Labor government led by Gough Whitlam, which had campaigned on a platform of environmental conservation, established a Committee of Enquiry into the National Estate. This committee recommended the creation of the Australian Heritage Commission, the primary role of which was to establish a Register of the National Estate of those "things we want to keep." Despite the name, places did not need to be of national significance to be listed. However, the name "National Estate" created confusion and controversy for the next 30 years. Historians saw this national heritage movement as part of a wider international trend in the 1960s and '70s, and the creation of the National Estate "might as readily be seen as an indirect creation of UNESCO as a symptom of Whitlam's new nationalism" (Davison, 1991:118).

NATIONAL CHARACTERISTICS

Australian landscapes are the product of 80 million years of evolution of the land and its flora and fauna since separation of the current land mass from Gondwana, and at least 60,000 years of Indigenous occupation and more than 200 years of European occupation (Lennon et al., 2001: 14–15). Australia, the only nation to occupy a whole continent, is biologically diverse and the undisputed world centre for marsupials and *Eucalyptus* vegetation. Australia has 7.6 million square kilometres of land, 70,000 kilometres of coastline, 16 million square kilometres of marine area, and 6 million square kilometres of Antarctica.

The first Australians, the Aboriginal and Torres Strait Islander peoples, modified the environment through the use of fire and hunting, changing the species composition of flora and fauna, and may have driven the Pleistocene mega-fauna to extinction as well (ASEC, 2001:7, 73). They also gave the landscape its creation stories and peopled it with heroic ancestors, and they created nonarchitectural but spectacular evidence of their culture in rock art, occupation sites, and sacred landscapes. They made the whole of Australia a cultural landscape, a fact not well recognized in heritage management practice in Australia.

The impact on the Indigenous landscape of the waves of European migration since the 1788 settlement of Sydney has been dramatic. Within a few generations, large tracts of the country were irreversibly modified by the introduction of sheep and cattle. Today, Australia's population of 20 million is highly urbanized, with sixty-two percent living in the five largest cities and eighty-five percent living within fifty kilometres of the coastline.

The Commonwealth of Australia was formed through the federation of the six separate British colonies in 1901. Under the constitution, the States and Territories are responsible for management of the environment, including national parks and heritage places, whereas the Commonwealth is responsible for other national matters like defence, quarantine, taxation, and matters associated with international treaties and conventions.

MANAGEMENT OF HERITAGE PLACES

In 1976, the Australian Heritage Commission was established to identify and conserve the National Estate, which was defined as:

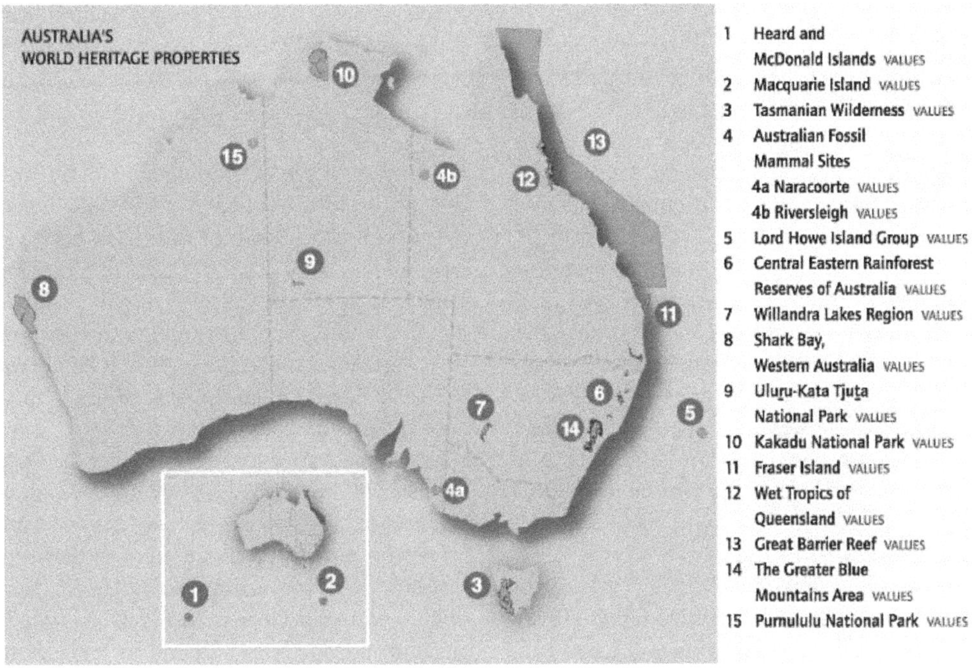

Figure 1.

. . . those places, being components of the natural environment of Australia, or the cultural environment of Australia that have aesthetic, historic, scientific or social significance or other special value for future generations as well as for the present community (section 4 (1), *Australian Heritage Commission Act, 1975*).

Soon after, Australia ICOMOS developed its Charter for the Conservation of Places of Cultural Significance, the Burra Charter, to assist in assessing the significance of cultural heritage values present at a place (<http://www.icomos.org/australia/charters>).

Creating the Register of the National Estate has kept Australians aware of heritage landscapes because of the many controversies about listing these places. In November 1976, the Federal government instructed that Fraser Island, the world's largest sand island, be entered in the Register and mining of mineral sands ceased after a decade of battling between the Queensland State government and the miners, notably US Dillingham Constructions. Some places such as Uluru-Kata Tjuta have iconic status, but listing others has been much contested. Where States had inadequate land-use protection, conservation advocates used the listing process to draw attention to threatened places, ranging from potential World Heritage sites to local landscapes with remnant natural vegetation.

In 1981, the Great Barrier Reef, the world's largest living organism; Kakadu with its rugged landscapes, expansive wetlands, and Aboriginal art; and Willandra Lakes, a series of former lakes and dunes containing the oldest documented human remains in Australia, were all entered on the World Heritage List. This reinforced the view that our big landscapes had international value. In 1982, the Tasmanian Wilderness, one quarter of the State of Tasmania, was World Heritage listed, despite complete opposition from the State government. A new Federal government had won the election on this issue of protection of wilderness using the external treaties power in the constitution and passed the World Heritage Properties Conservation Act in 1983, the only nation at that time to have legislation to protect World Heritage properties. World Heritage listing was truly used as a policy instrument to protect key Australian landscapes, especially in those States that did not use their land management powers appropriately for conservation.

In many ways, this set the scene for some of the key elements of World Heritage management in Australia – the emphasis on universal as opposed to local values, the emphasis on the natural as opposed to European heritage values, and the imposition of a centralist model of decision-making versus local involvement and consultation, a trend that is now being reversed. The problem of having no jurisdiction except through the external treaty power to prevent inappropriate land use is one of the reasons for the invention of the National List of Australian heritage places.

In 1996, the Australian Heritage Commission commenced community discussion about the best system for protecting Australia's heritage. It advocated moving to a systems model, which recognized that an integrated approach to heritage identification, conservation, and management was essential (AHC, 1996:14). It also recognized that more than 60 million hectares or eight percent of the Australian land mass was managed for nature conservation, with 4,100 protected areas (Worboys et al., 2001:75) and many of the 13,000 places entered in the Register of the National Estate now covered by State, Territory, and local government heritage legislation.

The area of protected land in Australia had risen by 2002 to over 10 percent or 77,462,000 hactares managed in 6,755 protected area reserves (<www.deh.gov.au/parks/nrs/capad/index.html>). In 2001 there were an estimated 163 million hactares of native forest in Australia. More than 12 percent of this forest was in nature conservation reserves (Bureau of Rural Sciences 2003, National Forest Inventory Database, Canberra).

Regional Forest Agreements (RFAs) were entered into between the Commonwealth and State governments to guarantee access to forest resources and to set up an adequate, comprehensive and representative reserve system for the biological diversity of Australian forests. As part of the process, places of heritage significance were identified and assessed. Five RFAs led to an increase of about 1.7 million hactares of forest area included in conservation reserves between 1997 and 2002.

In 2000, a new category of Indigenous Protected Areas was established and in March 2005 there were 19 Indigenous Protected Areas, totaling 13,240,016 hactares ranging from Ngaanyatjarra (Western Australia) covering 9,812,900 hactares to Chappell and Badger Islands (Tasmania) covering 1,270 hactares. These lands now account for 18 percent of Australia's protected areas (<http://www.deh.gov.au/indigenous/fact-sheets/ipa.html>). Traditional and ongoing Indigenous knowledge is increasingly accepted as a valid and necessary information input to biodiversity management, alongside scientific information. This new development also recognises the custodianship of Australia's biodiversity by Indigenous peoples.

The Council of Australian Governments reviewed the roles and responsibilities for heritage identification and environment protection, including the major gap between World Heritage and National Estate sites in their protection regimes. This resulted in the Commonwealth's new Environment Protection and Biodiversity Conservation Act 1999 (EPBC), which defines environment to include Australia's natural and cultural heritage. Actions "likely to have a significant impact on a matter of national environmental significance," require Ministerial approval. The matters of national environmental significance are: World Heritage properties, Ramsar wetlands of international importance, listed threatened species and communities; migratory species protected under international agreements, nuclear actions, and the Commonwealth marine environments (see <http://www.environment.gov.au/epbc>).

From 1 January 2004, amendments to the EPBC Act 1999 came into effect to create a new National Heritage List of natural, indigenous, and historic places with outstanding heritage value to our nation. Under the new system, National Heritage will join the other six matters of national environmental significance already protected by the EPBC Act. The primary purpose in managing National Heritage places is to identify, protect, conserve, present, and transmit to future generations the National Heritage values – the same purpose as for World Heritage values (<http://www.deh.gov.au/heritage/law/heritageact/distictively/index.html>).

VALUES-BASED MANAGEMENT

The impact of World Heritage in delineating a heritage values approach to the new system is obvious. For more than twenty years, the Commonwealth has been arguing about the types and levels of heritage values in places people wanted to protect as World Heritage – were the values of outstanding universal value, as required in the Convention?

In a statutory sense, the highest level of protection is given to World Heritage landscapes through this new Act, followed by national parks, protected areas, and heritage places, although these are mostly managed under State laws. Approximately 700 municipal governments look after identified places with local heritage values. The sixteen World Heritage properties are protected cooperatively between the Commonwealth and State governments, with the State agencies responsible for on-ground management. All properties now have plans of management and advisory committees with community and expert representation (<http://www.deh.gov.au/heritage/awh/worldheritage/index.html>).

Four of Australia's World Heritage Areas (Kakadu, Uluru, Willandra Lakes, and Tasmanian Wilderness) are inscribed as "mixed sites" for their Indigenous cultural World Heritage values, in addition to their natural values. These "mixed" site listings require the integrated management of both the cultural and natural values.

In Australia, this has meant the close involvement of the local Indigenous community, and the traditional owners have been essential partners in management decisions on the conservation of heritage values within the properties. This practice is now being extended to other protected areas.

Australians have traditionally perceived "nature" and Aboriginal culture as our heritage, which partly explains the absence of any World Heritage historic place in the representation of Australia's heritage of outstanding universal significance. The Royal Exhibition Buildings, Melbourne, has been nominated this year [added to World Heritage List in June 2004] and the nomination of the Sydney Opera House is still under development, as is a nomination of places exemplifying outstanding values in relation to convict history. The development of the National List should stimulate increased interest in establishing the historical contexts and assessing nationally significant places, and this in turn might convince the community and governments that there are Australian historic places of outstanding universal significance.

The history of the use of the World Heritage Convention to protect large expanses of the natural environment because of their pristine qualities has tended to mitigate against recognition of historic cultural values. Despite extended research into the range of cultural values in some natural areas like the Tasmanian Wilderness World Heritage Area, these values have not been officially recognized, yet they form the basis of popular tourist itineraries (Lennon, 2003). This is repeated in other World Heritage areas such as the Wet Tropics and Fraser Island.

The World Heritage Convention covers both natural and cultural heritage, but the prevailing view is that the natural environment of our continent is of outstanding universal value and wilderness is the most important category. Yet this denies the interaction of humans on the environment over long spans of time and reduces popular appreciation of cultural heritage to specific historic items. It also reflects ignorance of the importance of European settler heritage, which in turn is related to the history of World Heritage listing in Australia and the current feeling generated by the Greens party that a lot of cultural heritage is despoilation of natural heritage and best ignored or indeed "disappeared," such as mining relics or exotic plantings.

TOURISM

World Heritage Areas within Australia have become a drawcard for both domestic and international visitors. The Queensland coastal destinations serviced by two international airports attract many as a result of intense marketing. In fact, English is a minority language at many of these places. The Wet Tropics hosted an estimated one million visitors in 1999/2000.

Initially, the early World Heritage battles were predicated on the expectation of economic disaster for North Queensland and Tasmania by closing down mining and logging, but the opposite has occurred, with tourism as the new industry. The difference in people's attitude to World Heritage listing over the last twenty years is fascinating, from absolute horror at "UN intervention" and State delegations flying to Paris to try and persuade the World Heritage Committee not to list, to the present situation, in which everyone is clamouring for World Heritage status.

A total of 4.74 million international visitors arrived in Australia in 2003, compared with 4.93 in 2000. This significant fall is a result of the impact of terrorism, war, and Asia region health issues. The average visitor expenditure is approximately $4000 according to the Bureau of Tourism Research, and loss of visitors translates to an economic loss of around $1 billion for the 2001–3 period. This indicates the economic impact of World Heritage listing when combined with marketing and provision of infrastructure, and the impact is largely in regional communities.

CULTURAL LANDSCAPES

The 1992 amendments to the World Heritage criteria played a significant role in Australia in drawing attention to cultural values in the landscape. These amendments provided for the following cultural landscape categories: intentionally designed – as in gardens, relict – as in archaeological sites, organically evolving or continuing use with material evidence of its evolution, and associative landscapes with powerful religious, artistic, or cultural associations of the natural element rather than material cultural evidence. These categories have been applied by some managers at national park level and at local level as a means of protecting diverse heritage values in their landscapes.

The initial World Heritage listing of Uluru-Kata Tjuta ignored its associative cultural landscape values and management concentrated on getting Aboriginal people to help with wildlife conservation and education rather than encouraging them to maintain the traditional elements of Uluru as a story place. National publicity and new tourism promotion following its re-inscription in 1996 as a cultural landscape changed the popular view of Uluru as the "big rock in the Centre." The Park, covering about 1,325 square kilometres, contains some outstanding examples of rare desert flora and fauna as well as the major geological features of Uluru (a sandstone monolith some 9.4 kilometres in circumference rising about 314 metres above the plain and formerly known as Ayers Rock) and Kata Tjuta (some 36 rock domes rising about 500 metres above the plain and formerly known as the Olgas). It was already listed for these natural heritage values and is also an international biosphere reserve. But for the Anungu there was a time when ancestral beings in the form of humans, animals, and plants travelled widely across the land and performed remarkable feats of creation and destruction. The journeys of these beings are remembered and celebrated and the record of their activities exists today in the landscape. Anangu primary responsibility is to maintain these values by caring for the land in the Park using traditional methods.

Uluru is arguably the most distinctive current landscape symbol of Australia and conveys a powerful sense of the very long time during which the Australian continent has evolved. For all Australians Uluru is a symbol of the outback – the heart of the Red Centre – and over the last few decades it has become a popular icon in marketing our national identity.

State heritage agencies have also incorporated cultural landscapes into their categories of places in the 1990s using the World Heritage categories. Some local government authorities are using this concept as a means of protecting the diverse values in the landscapes and implementing zoning schemes to control development.

Whereas much practical conservation effort over the last decade has occurred as a whole-farm and water catchment levels through the federally funded National Heritage Trust, identifying and protecting remnant vegetation, there has been little effort at regional landscape protection and in managing delineated cultural landscapes, either on private property or in public land reserves. Since 1996, the Trust has invested $1.4 billion to help local communities support the sustainable management of Australia's natural resources through Landcare, Bushcare, Coastcare, and Rivercare programs (<http://www.nht.gov.au/overview.html>). Yet the historic components of the cultural landscape, such as historic roads and fences, place names, structures, and buildings, require identification as part of a whole landscape and funding for conservation treatments. The natural heritage view is so dominant that the cultural values in the landscape are ignored except for scenic ones.

Natural and cultural heritage values are given expression in various heritage-related disciplines, but our education and training has resulted in separating those values into natural, historic, and Indigenous categories in place-based frameworks separate from object-based or material cultures. The fundamental dichotomy of views expressed by the World Heritage Committee expert bodies – IUCN for natural heritage and ICOMOS for cultural heritage – flows down to the local landscape level and enshrines the actual separation of nature and culture despite the intention of the Convention to protect cultural landscapes as "the combined works of nature and of man." The separation of identification, assessment, and management of cultural and natural components in the landscape leads to conflict and unnecessary difficulties for managers. The World Heritage Committee has been trying since the mid-1990s to reform its operational guidelines and combine natural and cultural criteria.

CONCLUSION

Although environment is now defined in Australia to include natural and cultural heritage, new heritage legislation based on national values is a reflection of World Heritage methodology combining the works of nature and man and setting outstanding values as those to be protected. Some concepts from indigenous Australia may assist this integration of natural and cultural values in conservation practice. The Yolngu people use different words to describe "two way" exchange – *ganma* and *garma* (McConvell, 2000).

Both of these ideas are based on metaphors of place and space, and the first is also a water metaphor because water often represents knowledge in Yolngu philosophy. *Ganma* is defined as:

> "an area within the mangroves where the saltwater (non-Aboriginal knowledge) coming in from the sea meets the stream of fresh water (Yolngu knowledge). The water circulates silently underneath and there are lines of foam circulating across the surface." (Marika, 1999:112)

The metaphor here is that while the knowledge from different cultures gradually mix in the *ganma*, each system is preserved (as the sea and the fresh water remain distinct) and respected.

Garma is defined as:

> "an open ceremonial area that everyone can participate in and enjoy... Garma also means an open forum where people can share ideas and everyone can work hard to reach agreement." (Marika, 1999:114)

This sharing of the meanings and interpretation of different fields of heritage exhibited in Australian places is one of the key requirements for a more sustainable and holistic conservation practice. This principle of *ganma* occurring in *garma* could contribute a very special concept to the rest of the world and be particularly relevant to the reformed Operational Guidelines to the World Heritage Convention whereby the criteria are merged for determining outstanding universal values.

In contributing something distinctively Australian to the continuing evolution of World Heritage concepts for conservation, it is fitting to offer the words of a famous Australian writer:

> ...we need to keep in mind...the extent to which Aboriginal notions of inclusiveness, of re-imagining the world to take in all that is now in it, has worked to include us. (David Malouf, 1998:59)

QUESTIONS FOR DISCUSSION

1. Given that the environment is now legally defined in Australia to include cultural and natural heritage, what are the actual impediments to on-ground management of heritage values exhibited in a place?

2. How might one ensure that an integrated approach to management of identified heritage values occurs? Is monitoring an effective method of measuring this and if so, what indicators could be used?

3. What lessons can we learn from Australian Aboriginal methods of "caring for country"?

REFERENCES

Australian Heritage Commission, August 1996, *A National Future for Australia's Heritage*, Background Paper to the Discussion Paper.

Australian State of Environment Committee, 2001. *Australia State of the Environment, 2001*, CSIRO Publishing on behalf of the Department of Environment and Heritage, Canberra.

Davison, Graeme, A brief history of the heritage movement, in Graeme Davison and Chris McConville (eds), *A Heritage Handbook*. Allen and Unwin, Sydney, 1991, pp. 118–9.

Environment Australia, 1999. *Australia's World Heritage*, Department of Environment and Heritage, Canberra.

Lennon, Jane, Pearson, M., Marshall D., et al., 2001, *Natural and Cultural Heritage, Australia State of the Environment Report 2001* Theme Report, CSIRO Publishing on behalf of the Department of Environment and Heritage, Canberra (<http://www.ea.gov.au/soe/heritage>).

Lennon, Jane, 2003. Values as the Basis for Management of World Heritage Cultural Landscapes, in *Cultural Landscapes: the Challenges of Conservation*, World Heritage papers no.7, UNESCO World Heritage Centre, Paris, pp. 120–6.

Malouf David, 1998. A Spirit of Play, *The making of Australian consciousness*. ABC books, Sydney.

Marika, Raymattja, 1999, in McConvell, Patrick, 2000. Two-way research on indigenous languages in Australia: positioning resources in the *Garma*. Paper to Language Exploration Workshop, Philadelphia, <http://www.ldc.upenn.edu/>.

Worboys, Graeme, Michael Lockwood and Terry De Lacy, 2001. *Protected Area Management – Principles and Practice*, Oxford University Press, Melbourne.

PRACTICE TIPS

Australia ICOMOS produced an updated version of *The Illustrated Burra Charter: Good Practice for Heritage Places* by Meredith Walker and Peter Marquis-Kyle in 2004 that incorporates the major changes to the Burra Charter (the Australia ICOMOS Charter for Places of Cultural Significance) reflecting the evolution of heritage conservation practice in Australia (<www.icomos.org/australia>).

Tools provided by the Australian Heritage Commission such as the "how to do it" reference book, *Protecting Local Heritage Places, A guide for communities* (2000) will assist community groups interested in natural and cultural heritage identification and management. It was developed in consultation with professional heritage people and community-based organisations, provides ideas and options on how to identify and protect natural and cultural heritage places, outlines an integrated approach to the identification and management of natural and cultural heritage values, and provides lists of contact details for heritage agencies and useful references. It advocates ten steps to protect heritage places and provides guidance for each step in the process (<www.heritage.gov.au/protecting.html>).

Similarly, *Protecting Natural Heritage – Using the Australian Natural Heritage Charter* (2003) is a product of extensive community consultation, expands the principles of the Charter, and provides explanations and examples of process used in natural heritage conservation (<www.ea.gov.au/heritage/law/naturalheritage>), whereas *Ask First: A guide to respecting Indigenous heritage places and values,* (2002) offers practical assistance to those concerned with the protection and care of Indigenous heritage places (<www.heritage.gov.au/keyresources.html>).

Two major references for Australian practice are:

Kerr, J. S., 1996. *The Conservation Plan: A guide to the preparation of conservation plans for places of European cultural significance.* National Trust of Australia (NSW), Sydney.

Pearson, M. and Sullivan, S., 1995. *Looking After Heritage Places: The basics of heritage planning for managers, landowners and administrators.* Melbourne University Press, Melbourne.

CHAPTER TWENTY-NINE

The Cultural Landscape of the Agave and the Production of Tequila

Ignacio Gómez Arriola and
Francisco Javier Lopez Morales

Deste mesmo género de metl (...) sale mejor aquel vino que dije que beben algunos españoles, e yo lo he bebido (...) Éste cuecen en tierra, las pencas por sí y la cabeza por sí (...) y ansí lo llaman mexcalli; pero si las cabezas están cocidas de buen maestro y en algunas partes que son mejores que en otras, tiene tan buenas tajadas, que muchos españoles lo quieren tanto como diacitrón. Pues dirá alguno, si hay muchos destos metl; digo que toda la tierra está llena de ellos.

(from this genus of metl ... comes out better that wine which I have said some Spaniards drink and I have drunk it. ... this they cook underground; the leaf fronds by themselves, or the heads by themselves. ... and thus they call it mexcalli; but if the heads are cooked by a good master, and in those places that are better than others, it has good tajadas, which many Spaniards desire as much as dyacitron. If anyone asks if there exist many of these metl, I say that all the land is full of them.)

Fray Toribio de Benavente (Motolinía), 1541[1]

Our country is currently fostering the recognition of sites that imply a new manner of conceptualizing and valuing the fundamental legacy that Mexico has contributed to world culture. In 2002, the Mexican government presented UNESCO with its new Indicative List of sites to be proposed for inscription in the World Heritage List.

This Indicative List incorporates heritage categories not sufficiently represented or scarcely valued at the national and international levels, such as mixed natural–cultural sites, cultural landscapes, industrial heritage, the legacy of the twentieth century and cultural itineraries.

Among the sites selected are the Castle of Chapultepéc, the pre-Hispanic City of Mitla, the Church of Santa Prisca in Taxco, the Ahuehuete of Santa María del Tule, the House and Studio of Luis Barragán, the studio of Diego Rivera, the Aqueduct of Padre Tembleque, the campus of the Autonomous University of México, and, in the State of Jalisco, the historic town of San Sebastián del Oeste, *the Agave Landscape, and the ancient tequila industrial installations.*

[1] De Benavente, Toribio. *Relaciones de la Nueva España*. Ediciones de la Universidad Nacional Autónoma. México, 1956. P. 164.

The Proposal for the Tequila Region

According to our initial consideration, we found that in the mezcal plantations and the early tequila production sites, there are values that, in a global context, are unique, because they possess a cultural continuity that has its roots deep in the pre-Hispanic era.

This proposal represents the first time in our country that we explore the possibility of recognizing the cultural and heritage values of a broad region in their full complexity, and that do not necessarily refer to emblematic buildings or urban districts, but to the transformation of a landscape and the industrial heritage that stems from it.

Conceptual Aspects

Within this region, there have been unique cultural manifestations that involve the transformation of the natural landscape and the creation of architectural elements that, taken together, represent a set of values that can be recognized under the heritage category of cultural landscapes.

The World Heritage Convention establishes principles governing the protection of cultural and natural heritage places of universal value in member countries of UNESCO. The definition of cultural landscapes is based on Article 1 of the Convention, which under cultural heritage includes "the joint work of man and nature."

According to the definition provided by the World Heritage Committee, cultural landscapes are those resulting from the combined work of nature and humans, and which express a long and intimate relationship among people and their natural environment. The Committee recognized three categories of cultural landscapes:

a clearly defined landscape designed and created intentionally by man,
an organically evolved landscape,
an associative cultural landscape.

The Tequila region can be classified under the second category because it still maintains an active role in contemporary society that is intimately related to traditional lifeways, and where the evolutionary process is still ongoing.

From the time of their recognition in the early 1990s, 28 cultural landscapes have been inscribed in the World Heritage List. Salient among them are the medieval vineyards of Wachau in Austria and Hungary, the landscape of the Loire Valley in France, the tobacco plantations of the Valley of Viñales in Cuba, the royal gardens of Dessau – Worlitz in Germany, the Amalfi Coast in Italy, the wine producing region of the Alto Douro in Portugal, or the rice terraces of the Philippine Mountains.

Cultural Values Present in the Region of the Tequila Volcano

The region has maintained a cultural continuity that can be traced to the pre-Hispanic period. In it have evolved tangible and intangible manifestations that have shaped the landscape, the architecture, and the ancestral traditions.

As in all Meso-America, a culture of using the various species of "metl" or wild agave for a variety of uses had developed before the arrival of Spaniards in the region.

In western pre-Hispanic Mexico, two types of alcoholic beverage were derived from agave: One was *octli* or pulque, derived from the fermented juices of some varieties; and the other was the *mexcalli* or mezcal, produced from the fermentation of cooked agave hearts.

The culture of the builders of the concentric structures known as "guachimontones" and surrounding the Tequila Volcano maintained a type of regional commercial monopoly in the exploitation of *mexcalli*. With this goal, they modified their environment and the native flora over the centuries, adapting it for the cultivation of blue mezcal, or *mezcal azul*. This variety, the scientific name of which is *Agave Tequilana Weber Azul*, is found only in this region, and its origin has been pinpointed to the Canyon or Barranca of Río Grande de Santiago. For its exploitation, agave was subjected to a millenial process of domestication that eventually defined its particular characteristics. Insofar as we know, there is no evidence of this plant growing in the wild.

Its most important use was as a source of sugar for nourishment. It was produced by cooking (*tatemado*) the "pineapple" or center core of the plant. The *tatemado* took place in wells or circular ovens, similar to those later used in the colonial era.

The methods of cultivation were perfected through the centuries, giving rise to a pre-Hispanic agriculture-based culture that still exists in the region. The selection and planting of *hijuelos* (shoots), the *barbeo* (cutting), and the *jima* (harvest) are some of the elements extant from ancient traditions that continue in use.

After the contact between Spaniards and the indigenous people, a well-defined regional identity developed. Among its most salient elements is the production of *vino de mezcal* (mezcal wine), which is a process of *mestizaje* or syncretism of the pre-Hispanic tradition of fermenting and cooking the mezcal juice and European distillation technology, which results in an original new product the values of which were universally recognized early on.

Toward 1600, the distillation processes rooted in Arabic culture were introduced in the region for the production of the *Vino de Mezcal*, a name that was later replaced by the local toponymic: *Tequila*. The process is based more directly in the experience brought from the Antilles, where it was used for the production of rum from sugarcane.

Once the European approach to agricultural exploitation was adopted in the sixteenth century, along with the production of alcohol from a variety of sugar sources, humans systematically modified their agricultural surrounds and the native flora of the Tequila Valley to adapt them to the cultivation of this plant, which gave the region a unique character that has come to be defined by undulating lines of planting that respond to the irregular topography.

The Primitive Process of Producing *Vino de Mezcal*

The first step in the production of mezcal wine consisted of the *tatemado* of the mexcal pineapples or *piñas* in wells or conical ovens of stone, similar to those used in the pre-Hispanic period. To extract the *mosto*, or juice of the cooked mezcal, the *tahona* or Chilean mill was adopted. Its stone was moved with animal traction. The sweet *mosto* was fermented in underground stone vats for various days to produce the alcohol. Later, the vats were replaced by oak barrels or *pipones*. The final stage in the process of making vino mezcal was the distillation of the fermented *mosto* through evaporation in primitive copper or clay stills.

The First *Tabernas*

Toward the end of the seventeenth century, the first intensive plantations of blue mezcal and the Hacienda de Cuisillos were established. The hacienda was the first *Taberna*, or formal distillery for the production of *Vino Mezcal*.

Because of a vicerregal prohibition on the production of regional wines at that time, the early *tabernas* were located in isolated or out-or-the-way places, such as deep inside canyons, and in the Barranca of Río Grande de Santiago. In the early nineteenth century, the *taberna* was incorporated into the basic infrastructure of all haciendas throughout the region.

The Tequila Plantations or *Haciendas Tequileras*

Over the course of the nineteenth century, the rise of the port of San Blas as the viable center for exporting *vino mezcal* fostered a considerable increase in demand for the product, and brought about the growth of the haciendas in the region. The increase in production also drove the expansion of lands dedicated to cultivation throughout the region.

In response to the growing demand of the nineteenth century, the *tabernas* introduced new methods of fermentation, *tatemado*, and distillation. The increase in production caused the expansion of cultivation and the establishment of specialized industrial installations. The early well ovens in which the *tatemado* of the mezcal was fueled by wooden logs were replaced by masonry ovens that cooked with steam, thus establishing henceforth the difference of the *vino de mezcal de Tequila* from other similar ones.

The First Industrial Installations

The need for water in the production of vino mezcal brought about the establishment of the first industrial installations within the town of Tequila, on the banks of the Tequila River at the beginning of the nineteenth century. In these factories, now for the first time with an urban character, the traditonal production processes were maintained basically unchanged.

Over the course of the twentieth century, the industrial production of tequila became concentrated in the towns of Tequila, Amatitán, and Arenal, where modern production methods were gradually incorporated, including the mechanical grinding of cooked mezcal and the use of conveyor belts.

The Outstanding Universal Values Being Considered for the Nomination to the World Heritage List

To justify the nomination of the Agave Landscape and its inclusion in the Mexican Indicative List, the following World Heritage criteria for outstanding universal value have been identified as being applicable to this site:

Criterion II

Exhibit an important interchange of human values, over a span of time or within a cultural area of the world, of developments in architecture or technology, monumental arts, town-panning or landscape design.

The production of tequila is witness to the fruitful interchange of influences between two cultures in the early years of New Spain, which resulted in a process of *mestizaje* between the pre-Hispanic traditions of cooking and fermenting mezcal juices and European distillation techniques, giving rise to a product the values of which are now universally recognized.

Artistic trends from Europe were also introduced, producing over the long period of interchange of human values, a brief but significant architectural sampler of the evolution of architectural styles.

The Agave Landscape – the Paisaje Agavero – is the result of centuries of interchanges in human values through the convergence of pre-Hispanic and European technologies.

Criterion IV

Be an outstanding example of a type of building or architectural or technological ensemble or landscape which illustrates (a) significant stage(s) in human history.

The ancient *tabernas* or tequila distilleries and the cultural landscape of the blue agave cultivation constitute an outstanding example that, through their evolution over several centuries, illustrates a significant aspect in the process of human cultural development. The production of tequila has generated an identifiable variation of industrial installations that now constitutes a typology – originally defined in the eighteenth century, and continuing to evolve, with adaptations responding to new technologies, always respectful of the essence of the traditional processes.

A main gate, an office, the patios, the areas for cooking, grinding, fermentation, distillation, and aging are constant elements that recur in this industrial architectural typology, and that have responded to the architectural styles of the periods in which they were built.

Criterion V

Be an outstanding example of a traditional human settlement or land-use which is representative of a culture (or cultures), especially when it has become vulnerable under the impact of irreversible change.

The agave landscape and the ancient tequila industrial installations are the result of several centuries of refinement in the process of producing this beverage. Its recent demand in many regions of the world and the resulting process of economic globalization of which it is part could lead to vulnerability through a transforming process that would modify its essential characteristics.

Criterion VI

Be directly or tangibly associated with events or living traditions, with ideas, or with beliefs, or with artistic and literary works of outstanding universal significance.

The agave landscape and the ancient tequila industrial installations are associated with many cultural manifestations that define "what is Mexican" – "*lo mexicano*" – both inside Mexico and elsewhere.

The traditions that are linked to the elaboration and consumption of this alcoholic beverage have remote origins, and are kept alive, meaningful, and in constant expansion throughout the entire world. Literary works, movies, music, paintings, dance, and other broad cultural manifestations have been associated with tequila, its production, its rituals, and its traditional region.

Assurance of authenticity

The whole process of cultivation and production must meet traditional techniques and procedures by law. This is guaranteed by the *certificate of origin* required for this product and Official Mexican Standard NOM-006-SCFI-1994. The guarantee of authenticity, along with other legal instruments, will permit the endurance of the agave landscape and its installations.

Protected Area

The protected cultural heritage areas would include all archaeological remains, the architecture associated with the production of tequila, and the region of traditional agave landscapes.

Insofar as the agave landscape, the proposal is to protect and foster the traditional planting fields of blue mezcal. The majority of such fields are found in Arenal, Amatitán, Tequila y Magdalena, on the side of Tequila Volcano, and in the Canyon of Río Grande de Santiago.

As concerns archeology, all archaeological remains related to the production of tequila in the region of the volcano would be protected. A large number of pre-Hispanic sites from the *Teuchitlán traditon* are characterized by the *Guachimontones*, which are currenlty threatened by the indiscriminate planting of blue agave.

The protection of architectural elements and remains related to the cultivation of mezcal and the production of tequila in its original region would also be protected. This would involve approximately 200 haciendas and traditional industrial installations in nine municipalities.

The Work Ahead

The following work needs to be accomplished in order to complete the technical and legal sections of the nomination dossier:

(i) boundaries, inventory, and registry of archaeological sites and places with built heritage,
(ii) historic investigations,
(iii) assessments of condition and proposals for places with cultural and natural significance,
(iv) regulations for the protection of the archeological and built heritage in all municipalities involved,
(v) regional and urban development plans for all municipalities involved,
(vi) management plans for the conservation and enhancement of the agave landscape,
(vii) cooperative agreements among all concerned parties,
(viii) awareness campaigns within the local communities.

Governmental and Civil Society Participation

The aforementioned work, to be completed before the nomination can take place, will only be possible through the participation of public authorities, civil society stakeholders, and those interested in the conservation of this important heritage:

- **Federal agencies:** INAH, Tourism Secretariat, SARH, SEDESOL.
- **State agencies:** Executive, Secretaria de Cultura, SetuJal, SEDEUR, SEDER.
- **Municipal agencies:** City Halls of Tequila, Magdalena, Arenal, Amatitán, Teuchitlán, Tala, Ahualulco, A. Escobedo, and Etzatlán.
- **Industry organizations:** Agave plantation owners, Tequilera producers, industrial interests, etc.
- **Civil society:** ICOMOS, universities, research centers, local oraganizations, etc.
- **Local communities:** Those in the areas to be included in the nomination.

Window of Opportunity and Viability of This Nomination

The windows of opportunity for any nomination from Mexico are becoming increasingly more limited because of its overrepresentation under certain heritage categories. Only those categories that are less well represented in the World Heritage List will have a chance. Such is the case of Cultural Landscapes, proposed herein. This is an extraordinary example of adaptation and wise use of the natural environment.

CHAPTER THIRTY

National Heritage Areas: Developing a New Conservation Strategy

Brenda Barrett, Nancy I. M. Morgan, and Laura Soullière Gates

NATIONAL HERITAGE AREAS WITHIN A NATIONAL AND INTERNATIONAL CONTEXT

National heritage areas and national heritage corridors are large-scale living landscapes where community leaders and residents have come together around a common vision of their shared heritage. The process of developing a heritage area utilizes a strategy that encourages collaboration across political and programmatic boundaries on a plan for the conservation of valued assets in concert with compatible economic and community development. Overcoming obstacles to such partnerships is possible because, through extensive community involvement, the heritage area addresses the needs of the people who live in the landscape as well as the needs of their environment. The goals of most heritage areas are ambitious: to conserve both natural and cultural resources, to maintain community vitality, and to manage change while retaining an area's sense of identity.

Today, there are twenty-four congressionally designated national heritage areas and corridors in the United States.[1] Additionally, there are more than a dozen proposed for designation and almost that many for further study in the 108th Congress. The National Park Service (NPS) already has been directed to study four additional areas.[2] The heritage area concept and regional collaborative strategies extend beyond the federal government to the states as well. Louisiana, Maryland, New York, Pennsylvania, and Utah have heritage area programs, and there are hundreds of grassroots initiatives across the country.

The idea of working in partnership with residents and other partners to conserve significant living landscapes is not new. On the international level, there is increasing recognition that these landscapes have value and that their conservation can only occur in concert with local communities. Adrian Phillips, Senior Advisor on World Heritage to the International Union on the Conservation of Nature (IUCN), has written and spoken persuasively on the management of protected areas in cooperation with local people for multiple objectives.[3] In the United States, although the recent trend has been to bring parks and people more closely together, considering peopled landscapes as protected areas is something new. The barriers to recognizing and managing large and complex landscapes have seemed largely insurmountable without the use of regulatory power to direct or curb changes to resources.

With this perspective on the challenges of valuation and management of large living landscapes, the NPS's conservation role in these landscapes continues to evolve. The first national heritage initiative, Illinois and Michigan Canal National Heritage Corridor, was designated as recently as 1984. The ninety-seven-mile canal corridor connected Lake Michigan to the Illinois River and then the Mississippi via a long-used American Indian portage. Encompassing 1,067 units of local government, an active ship canal, and the remnants of the 1848 canal now managed by the State of Illinois as a park, the area displays both the scale and multijurisdictional nature of later heritage area proposals.[4] Most significantly, the area was to be managed not by the NPS in a traditional, hierarchical manner, but by a federal commission representing the interests and expertise of the local community.[5] This shift toward local control has become even more pronounced in recent years with the shift away from federal commissions, which are at least nominally Federal authorities, toward more flexible nonprofit organizations.[6] More recently, the agency's role has been limited to evaluating the

[1] The most recent heritage area, the Blue Ridge National Heritage Area in North Carolina, was designated as part of the Interior appropriations bill in December 2003 (P.L. 108-108).

[2] The National Park Service has been directed by Congress to undertake studies of the Buffalo Bayou in Houston, Texas, Low Country Gullah Culture in South Carolina and Georgia, Muscle Shoals in Alabama, and Niagara Falls in New York for possible heritage area designation.

Portions of this article have appeared in other contexts. The discussion of Cane River National Heritage Area builds on work done by Laura Gates and Nancy I. M. Morgan in an article titled "Report from the Field: The Whole is so Much Greater than the Sum of Its Parts" published in *The George Wright Forum*, Vol. 20 No. 2, June 2003, The George Wright Society, Hancock, Michigan. Parts of the discussion of measuring and evaluating national heritage areas were presented as a paper titled "National Heritage Areas: Developing a Model for Success" by Brenda Barrett and Suzanne Copping at the U.S. ICOMOS Annual Meeting, April 2004 in Natchitoches, Louisiana.

[3] Phillips, Adrian, 2003, "Turning Ideas on Their Head: The New Paradigm of Protected Areas," *The George Wright Forum* Vol. 20 No. 2. Adrian Phillips has made presentations on this theme at the International Heritage Development Conference in Pittsburgh, Pennsylvania, in June 2003 and at the Fifth World Parks Congress, "Benefits Beyond Boundaries" in Durban September, 2003.

[4] For more information on the Illinois and Michigan Canal National Corridor visit the following Web sites at <http://www.nps.gov/ilmi/home.htm> and <http://www.canalcor.org>.

[5] Members of the Illinois and Michigan Canal Corridor Commission include representatives of local government, the forest preserve district, five members with expertise in resource disciplines such as archaeology, conservation, history, historic preservation, and recreation, five with expertise in business and industry, and a representative of the National Park Service.

[6] At this time, six of the national heritage areas have federal commissions, and sixteen are managed by state agencies or nonprofit organizations.

feasibility and appropriateness of national designation,[7] providing assistance in the development of area management plans, and offering technical assistance on resource conservation and interpretation.

THE LEGISLATIVE FRAMEWORK FOR NATIONAL HERITAGE AREAS

National heritage areas, like units of the NPS, are designated on an individual basis by Congress. Each heritage area has its own legislative authorization that identifies the area's significant themes, sets boundaries, appoints a management entity, describes the management planning process, and prescribes the length of time and the amount of funding that the area can receive under the legislative authorization. The limits on funding assistance are not limits on the national designation. Once established, only congressional action can remove the national heritage area or corridor designation.

One of the challenges facing the national heritage areas is the lack of legislation establishing a programmatic framework. This is particularly problematic because there are no statutory criteria to evaluate proposals for national heritage area designation. The NPS has identified ten criteria that are useful in evaluating the feasibility of a proposed national heritage area and has promulgated them through testimony, before congressional committees, and through proposed legislation.[8] The core of this definition states that an area should contain:

> ... an assemblage of natural, historic, cultural, educational, scenic, or recreational resources that together are nationally significant to the heritage of the United States; represent distinctive aspects of the heritage of the United States worthy of recognition, conservation, interpretation, and continuing use; reflects traditions, customs, beliefs, and folk life that are a valuable part of the heritage of the United States; provides outstanding opportunities to conserve natural, historical, cultural, or scenic features; provides outstanding recreational or educational opportunities; and resources and traditional uses that have national importance.[9]

Along with a landscape that contains resources and stories of national importance, a proposed national heritage area must have the support of the people who live there. Because the hallmark of heritage areas is that they are locally supported and managed, the area must have the local capacity to work in partnership to develop a plan for preserving and enhancing the heritage of the region and to implement the plan.

The application of these proposed criteria to the evaluation of an area's significance and community readiness for designation is usually demonstrated by the preparation of a feasibility study. Although there is no legislative authority to require such a study before designation, increasingly the NPS and the relevant congressional committees are requesting this kind of documentation. In some cases the NPS is directed by Congress to undertake the preparation of a feasibility study on designating a proposed heritage area. In other cases, the areas, considering national designation, prepare their own study. This approach, having the region undertake its own feasibility study, has the benefit of building community appreciation of the heritage of a region and building confidence and capacity to manage it.

After designation, the authorizing legislation for every heritage area requires that the management entity prepare a management plan. The NPS provides advice and technical assistance, but does not take the lead. This planning process reaches out to the residents, businesses, related nonprofits, and government agencies to develop a vision for the future of the area. It is the next step in building public awareness and consensus on how the heritage of the region can be used to tell stories that resonate into the future. The plan should address resource protection, enhancement, interpretation, development, and funding. Identifying the financial resources to implement the plan is becoming more of a priority in the planning document.

When the plan is completed, it is forwarded through the NPS to the Secretary of Interior for review and approval. In most cases, the Governor of each state in which the national heritage area is located is consulted before the approval is finalized. The criteria for reviewing the plan are also dependent on the authorizing legislation for the designated area. Criteria range from none to assessing how the proposed plan sets priorities for resource conservation.[10]

The authorizing legislation also designates the management entity for each national heritage area. In many cases, this is an organization or governmental entity that is already in existence or has been created as part of the feasibility study. In other cases, the legislation proposes that a new entity be created and specifies the interests that will be represented on the board or commission and, in some cases, who will appoint them. For example, the recently established Blue Ridge National Heritage Area specifies that the management entity will be governed by a board of directors composed of five members who will be appointed by regional organizations within the heritage area, one member from the Eastern Band of the Cherokee and three members appointed by the

7 The specific criteria for designation may be found on the National Park Services Web site at <http://www.cr.nps.gov/heritageareas/>. The agency has identified four critical factors for a successful national heritage area: (1) completion of a suitability/feasibility study, (2) public involvement in the suitability and feasibility study, (3) demonstration of widespread public support among the area residents for the proposal, (4) commitment to the proposal from key constituents, which may include government, industry, and private nonprofit organizations, in addition to area residents.

8 The ten criteria for evaluating were first presented in testimony by National Park Service Deputy Director Denny Galvin in 1999 and, with some changes, have been incorporated into the NPS's legislative proposal presented to the Senate Committee on National Parks by Deputy Director Randy Jones in 30 March 2004.

9 See the National Park Service legislative proposal presented March 30, 2004.

10 For an example of priorities for the review management plans, see Ohio & Erie Canal National Heritage Area P.L. 104-333 Division II, Title VIII Section 808 (b).

Governor who reside in the area and have expertise in related fields.[11]

An effective and respected management entity is a critical element to the success of a national heritage area because it is that entity's responsibility to develop and oversee the implementation of the management plan. The structure of management entities varies and can even change over time. The earliest heritage corridors and areas were established with a federal commission as the responsible management body.[12] Although there is no legislative history on why federal commissions were selected, this strategy seems to have been a bridge between the interests of the National Park Service, a federal agency, and the local community represented by seats on the federal commission. The composition of these federal commissions is spelled out in the legislation and may include representatives from geographical regions in the heritage area, local governments, specified organizations, related disciplines, and state agencies. Appointments to the federal commissions are made by the Secretary of Interior.[13]

The federal commissions established to manage heritage areas are classified as operating commissions, with their powers enumerated in their authorizing legislation. These powers usually include the authority to receive appropriations, hire staff, develop a management plan, and take other appropriate actions. Federal commissions have the status of a federal entity, with all the attendant powers and obligations. Commission members serve without compensation beyond reimbursement for reasonable expenses.

Federal commissions have the benefit of the status as a federal entity and can serve as a neutral forum to bring together local, regional, and state interests. However, the effectiveness of commissions has been hampered by delays in appointing commission members and in filling subsequent vacancies. A 1992 NPS Advisory Board prepared *Report on Federal Commissions* noted this concern and recommended that the process be streamlined.

In the last decade, there has been a move away from federal commissions to designating governmental units or nonprofits as heritage area management entities. One approach has been to name a state agency to manage the heritage area. For example, the legislation for National Coal Heritage Area (1996) assigns administrative responsibility to the State of West Virginia. The South Carolina Heritage Corridor is to be administered by an entity selected by the Governor of the state.[14] State-managed areas have the benefit of having a permanently responsible entity, but can be made less effective during changes of administration. In addition, if the management is located in the state capitol, it may lose its connection to the heritage area community. Another variation on state management is the use of state-authorized authorities. The Augusta National Heritage Area is managed by the Augusta Canal Authority, a public body established under the law of the State of Georgia. The Lackawanna Valley National Heritage Area is also managed by an authority. Authorities have the advantage of more local accountability and oversight.[15]

Starting with the creation of the Quinebaug and Shetucket Rivers Valley National Heritage Corridor in 1994, the most common management structure for national heritage areas is the designation of a nonprofit corporation. Today, twelve of the twenty-four national heritage areas have adopted this approach. In most cases, a new nonprofit entity was created to manage heritage development in the region. The benefits of nonprofit management include the ability to move quickly in selecting and replacing board members and to respond to changes and opportunities on the ground. They can attract board members who understand that their fiduciary duty is to place the well-being of the organization's mission above the interests of its constituent groups and above local and state political interests.

The NPS does not play a direct role in the management of the national heritage areas. The agency does not hold a seat on heritage area boards unless directed to do so by the authorizing legislation. In almost all of the areas and corridors managed by federal commissions, the NPS, through its Director or designee, serves as an *ex officio* member. To avoid any conflicts of interest, NPS staff cannot sit on the board of nonprofit management entities that receive federal funding over which the agency has programmatic or financial oversight.

Another important element in the authorizing legislation is to establish the heritage area's boundaries. The overall legislation addresses the interpretive themes and purposes for which the national heritage area is being created. The boundaries of the area should reflect the location of heritage resources. Ideally, the boundary is developed in concert with the feasibility study and has had the benefit of widespread public review and comment. In some cases, the legislation refers to a map reference, as is done in establishing most units of

[11] The Blue Ridge National Heritage Area was authorized as part of the House Interior Appropriations Act of 2004 (P.L. 108-330).

[12] The Illinois and Michigan Canal National Heritage Corridor (1984), the (now) John H. Chafee Blackstone River Valley National Heritage Corridor (1986), the Delaware and Lehigh National Heritage Corridor (1988), the Southwestern Pennsylvania Heritage Preservation Commission (1988), and the Cane River National Heritage Area (1994) were the first five heritage areas or corridors and all were established with federal commissions as the designated management entity.

[13] Members on federal commissions must be appointed by the Secretary of the Interior. The authorizing legislation for the Cache La Poudre River Corridor (P.L. 104-323) designated as the management entity the Cache La Poudre Corridor Commission, to be established by the State of Colorado or its political subdivisions. The Secretary's role was limited to recognizing the commission. This was determined to be a violation of the appointments clause because state and local officials would be appointing members to a federal commission. To date, the proposed commission has not been seated.

[14] In practice, South Carolina's Office of Parks, Recreation and Tourism has managed the project out of the state office with state employees. Another project that is *de facto* managed by a state entity is the Hudson River Valley National Heritage Area. The management entities are the Hudson River Valley Greenway Communities Council and the Greenway Conservancy, both agencies established by the state of New York in its Hudson River Greenway Act of 1991.

[15] See Augusta Canal National Heritage Area P.L. 104-333 Division II, Title III and Lackawanna Valley National Heritage Act of 1999 P.L. 106-873.

the NPS.[16] In other areas, the boundary is identified more specifically as a political unit – often counties – or by other geographic features such as the border of a watershed.[17]

National heritage areas usually include multiple jurisdictions and may cross over state boundaries. The John H. Chafee Blackstone River Valley National Heritage Corridor boundaries include the Blackstone Valley in Massachusetts and Rhode Island, and the Quinebaug and Shetucket Rivers Valley National Heritage Corridor – originally in northeast Connecticut – now extends into the rivers' watershed in Massachusetts. One of the strengths of the heritage area strategy is to assemble communities with common stories and backgrounds to work together on preserving the past and planning for the future.

With the creation of a boundary comes the issue of what it means to be included within a national heritage area. What benefits accrue to related resources within the heritage area? What is the impact on owners of private property? The authorizing legislation, which is tailored to the needs and concerns of each heritage region, may address some of these issues. In developing the legislation for the Illinois and Michigan Canal National Heritage Corridor, the first of these areas, the business and industrial communities in the proposed corridor were concerned that the designation would effect adversely their operations within the corridor. Special guarantees were included to assuage these concerns, including assurances that the designation would not bring with it additional or increased environmental, occupational, or safety standards, or permitting requirements.[18]

Subsequent corridor initiatives seemed more concerned that the decisions of other federal agencies might adversely impact the corridor's resources, particularly water quality. The legislation authorizing the Delaware and Lehigh National Heritage Corridor states specifically that federal agencies whose actions might affect the flow of water of the canal or the natural resources in the corridor should consult with the corridor's commission and, if feasible, conform their actions to the corridor's management plan.[19]

All of this changed in 1995, when H.R. 1280 was introduced by Congressman Hefley (R-CO) to develop a programmatic approach to national heritage area designation.[20] Property rights organizations attacked the legislation as threatening to property owners, and the bill was not acted upon.[21] Subsequent legislative proposals to establish a heritage area program included an increasingly long list of private property right guarantees and protections, including, most recently, requirements that individual owners be notified and consent to the inclusion within national heritage area boundaries.[22] To date, all legislative efforts to reach consensus and to craft program legislation for national heritage areas have been unsuccessful in achieving passage of legislation for a national program. This is despite a recent General Accountability Office report, *National Park Service: A More Systematic Process for Establishing National Heritage Areas and Actions to Improve Their Accountability Are Needed*, that concluded that despite concerns about property rights, the agency was not able to find a single example of heritage areas directly affecting private property values or uses.[23]

The more recent concern for protecting private property rights is reflected in many of the provisions in individual designation bills post-1995. Most of these provisions clarify that designation shall not be construed to modify, enlarge, or diminish any authority of federal, state, and local governments to regulate the use of privately owned lands; and the designation shall not be construed to grant the powers of zoning, land use, or condemnation to the management entity of the heritage area. In addition, the management entities are specifically prohibited from using the federal funds received under the legislation to acquire real property or any interest in real property.[24] National heritage areas established post-2000 contain an even longer list of private property guarantees. The NPS legislative proposal has gathered together a broad array of protections in an attempt to meet concerns expressed by the property rights organizations, including statements that

[16] In establishing the Shenandoah Valley Battlefields (P.L. 104-333 Division I Title), Section 606 states that "The corridor shall consist of lands and interest therein as generally depicted on the map entitled 'Shenandoah Valley National Battlefields,' numbered SHVAA/80,000 and dated April 1994."

[17] In the legislation for the Tennessee Civil War Heritage Area (P.L. 104-333, Division II Title II), the issue of boundaries was not resolved and a provision was added that a compact would be prepared in the future that would address this issue by delineating at that time the boundaries of the proposed national heritage area.

[18] See Illinois and Michigan Canal National Heritage Corridor P.L. 98-398 Section 115.

[19] See Delaware and Lehigh National Heritage Corridor P.L. 100-692 Sec. 11.

[20] This was not the first attempt to pass legislation to set standards and criteria for a national heritage area program: Rep. Hinchey introduced H.R. 2416 "National Partnership System of Heritage Areas Act" (1993) at a hearing held in subcommittee; no further action was taken and if later was joined with H.R. 3707. Rep. Vento introduced H.R. 3707 "American Heritage Areas Partnership Program Act of 1993," which reported out of full committee to the House but was never brought up on the floor, Rep. Vento introduced H.R. 5044 "American Heritage Areas Act of 1994," an amended version which passed the House; no action taken in Senate, Rep. Hefley introduced H.R. 1280 "Technical Assistance Act of 1995"; hearing and mark-up held in subcommittee, voted favorable to the full committee, no action taken in full committee, Rep. Vento introduced H.R. 1301 "American Heritage Areas Act of 1995"; hearing held in subcommittee only, Rep. Hefley introduced H.R. 2532 "National Heritage Areas Policy Act of 1999"; hearing held in subcommittee only, Rep. Hefley introduced H.R. 2388 "National Heritage Areas Policy Act of 2001"; a hearing was held in the full committee, and Rep. Hefley introduced H.R. 1427 "The National heritage Areas Policy Act" (2003); no hearings have been held to date.

[21] Although H.R. 1280 to establish the "American Heritage Areas Partnership Program" was not enacted, Congress did establish nine individual national heritage area designations as part of Omnibus legislation (P.L. 104-333) in 1996.

[22] See H.R. 1427 (2003).

[23] *National Park Service: A More Systematic Process for Establishing National Heritage Areas and Actions to Improve Their Accountability* GAO-04-593T was presented as testimony before the Senate Committee on National Parks and Public Lands on March 26, 1994.

[24] The Shenandoah Valley Battlefields National Historic District is an exception to this prohibition. It is authorized to acquire land or interest in land by gift, devise, or with donated or appropriated funds from a willing seller. They may not hold land acquired by condemnation. (P.L. 104-333, Division I, Title IV, Section 606 (f) (2) (c).

the act does require property owners to participate in projects and programs or to permit public access; that the act does not change duly adopted land-use plans or affect water rights; that the act does not change hunting and fishing regulations; and, finally, does not create any additional landowner liability.[25]

Authorizing legislation for national heritage areas also establishes the length of time the Secretary of Interior can assist the areas and sets a limit on the amount of amount of money that the Department of Interior can appropriate under the terms of the legislation. The earliest heritage corridors all had these provisions, perhaps because of the experimental nature of the designation.[26] Starting with the Delaware and Lehigh National Heritage Corridor, appropriations authorized for national heritage areas required a 50% match for funds provided by the authorizing legislation.[27] At this time, the unofficial "formula" for funding is US$10 million over fifteen years with no more than US$1 million available for any fiscal year.[28] It is important to emphasize that the termination dates in legislation apply to funding under the terms of the legislation, not to the continued designation of the area as a national heritage area. Only Congress, by legislative action, can remove the national heritage area designation.

Questions about funding limitations and the length of time required to plan and implement programs over large geographic areas have led to continued tension between the NPS, congressional committees, and the national heritage areas about the success of the program. Also unresolved is the question of the long-term relationship between the heritage areas and other units of the National Park System.

The agency has continued to maintain a clear separation between units of the NPS[29] and national heritage areas. However, there is growing recognition that the heritage area strategy could provide significant value as a technique to develop a stewardship ethic in gateway communities and in landscapes around national parks. Cane River Creole National Historical Park and Cane River National Heritage Area in Natchitoches, Louisiana, were created within the same legislation in 1994 to preserve significant landscapes, sites, and structures – many associated with Creole culture – in both urban and rural settings. The park owns only sixty-three acres within its boundaries. The national heritage area includes 116,000 acres. Although this example is the most intentional adoption of unified strategies, many national parks have found heritage areas to be strong partners in interpretation, historic preservation, land conservation, and fund-raising.[30]

THE CANE RIVER MODEL: A CASE STUDY

The People and the Place

The Cane River region is in northwestern Louisiana, midway between Dallas and New Orleans, and its history is culturally complex. In 1714, the French became the first Europeans to establish a permanent settlement in the Lower Mississippi Valley at Natchitoches on the Cane River, the historic main channel of Red River. Their intentions were to revitalize trade with the American Indians and more fully exploit the agricultural and commercial potential of the region. Under the direction of Louis Juchereau de Saint Denis, the French gradually built up business interests in the area, much to the consternation of the Spanish, who, concerned about French incursions into the interior of the North American continent, established their mission post of Los Adaes just a few miles to the west shortly thereafter.

The transfer of the former French colony of Louisiana to Spain occurred in 1767, but despite Spanish rule, French Colonial culture flourished for several reasons. The Spanish regime caused little change in daily life around Natchitoches, and the Spanish retained the services of French Commandant Athanase de Mezières to maintain authority. Under his influence, the Spanish adopted the French manner of dealing with the tribes through trade rather than through missionary control. French remained the primary language.

By the late eighteenth century, commercial agriculture in the Cane River region replaced trade in animal skins and products as the primary economic base. French and Spanish land-grant farms produced indigo and tobacco, and farmers adopted the plantation system to work these large tracts of land with slave labor. Natchitoches, which had been a trade center prehistorically, remained an important crossroads of overland routes to the east, northeast, and southwest, and a water route to New Orleans and the Gulf of Mexico. The area was a cultural nexus of French, Spanish, American Indian, and African traditions, and out of this developed Creole culture – adaptations of French, Spanish, American Indian, and African peoples to the New World and to each other.

French and Spanish legal traditions allowed, at least nominally, for various sorts of manumission. In the Cane River region, the most famous instance was that of Marie-Thérèze

[25] See National Park Service legislative proposal March 30, 2004 and related legislation (S.2543) introduced by Senator Craig Thomas.

[26] The Illinois and Michigan Canal National Heritage Corridor (1984), the (now) John H. Chafee Blackstone River Valley National Heritage Corridor (1986), and the Delaware and Lehigh National Heritage Corridor (1988) were authorized by their original legislation for periods of five to ten years with the authority for extension of an equal period. All have been extended beyond their original authorization. The Illinois and Michigan Canal Commission expired as of August 2004.

[27] An exception to this rule is Cane River National Heritage Area (P.L. 103-449).

[28] This "formula" was first articulated in the eight national heritage areas created at the end of the 106th Congress in 1996. Since that time, this requirement has been included in all designation areas and it has been incorporated into proposed national heritage area designation bills in the 107th and 108th Congress.

[29] National Park Service, 1999, *The National Parks: Index 1999–2001*, US Government Printing Office, Washington, D.C. Popularly known as the *Index*, the booklet includes more than twenty classifications in the National Park System, including battlefields, historic sites, lakeshores, monuments, parkways, rivers and riverways, trails, and seashores. The national heritage areas are included in the *Index*, but are not considered part of the National Park System.

[30] Other examples include the Essex National Heritage Area in Massachusetts, which has a close relationship, including a shared visitor center, with Salem Maritime Historic Site and the Ohio and Erie National Heritage CanalWay, which expands the reach of Cuyahoga National Park north to Cleveland and south beyond Akron along the Ohio and Erie Canal.

Coin-Coin, who began life as a slave and by the end of her life owned about 5,000 acres of land and held ninety-nine slaves. Her twenty-five-year liaison with a soldier at the fort in Natchitoches resulted in ten children, whose freedom she acquired. Considered the matriarch of the Cane River *gens de couleur libre* (free people of color), she founded a family that at one point in the nineteenth century owned 19,000 acres of land, 16,000 of which remain in descendents' hands today.

During the nineteenth century, cotton became the principal crop for the agricultural lands, and plantation owners imported additional slaves from the southeastern United States. Although the 1803 Louisiana Purchase quickly brought about governmental changes, cultural changes lagged behind. French remained the primary language, and most people felt a cultural affinity to the French. The Red River Campaign during the Civil War and the violent decades that followed wreaked social and economic havoc along Cane River. Natural and human-caused changes on the Red River forced it to alter its course, and as a result Cane River became a virtual oxbow, cut off from lucrative river trade. In addition, the development of Shreveport as a successful river port rang a death knell for the economic progress of Natchitoches and the Cane River region. The area and its peoples were left in relative isolation. This lack of economic progress and in-depth interaction with the outside world resulted in the preservation of landscapes and buildings, but, more importantly, the conservation of cultures. Descendants of the early peoples of the Cane River area – French, Spanish, Africans, and American Indians – were from families who had interacted with each other for more than 200 years. Plantation owner, enslaved, free person of color, sharecropper, tenant farmer – all were related either through familial or geographic ties. Isolation had been an ally of preservation and cultural conservation.

Community Involvement and the Designation of a National Heritage Area

The community understood the rarity of the historical and cultural integrity extant in the Cane River region. Historic preservation was a long-standing value in the region, and groups had been active since the first half of the twentieth century. In 1964, a number of community members formed a nonprofit corporation with the express purpose of preserving historic properties. In the late 1980s, the group brought their congressman to the Cane River region to encourage his interest in the area's unusual resources and outstanding cultural significance. They discussed the possibilities for national park status, and he recommended they garner additional support in the region. When he lost his seat in the next election, community members began working closely with the staff of Senator J. Bennett Johnston to further this idea.[31]

In 1992, Congress directed the NPS to initiate a *Special Resource Study/Environmental Assessment* to "identify and evaluate alternatives for managing, preserving and interpreting historic structures, sites, and landscapes within the Cane River area of northwestern Louisiana, and how Creole culture developed in this area."[32] The special resource study, completed in 1993, identified Oakland Plantation and the outbuildings of Magnolia Plantation as nationally significant properties that met the National Park Service criteria for parklands. Although the study did not mention specifically the establishment of a "national heritage area," the seeds of the concept were there. The study recognized the community's commitment to historic preservation, and identified the cultural complexity of the area, past and present. The study even made suggestions on ways to manage the cultural landscape beyond traditional national park paradigms.

Laura Hudson, chief of staff for Senator Johnston, had worked extensively with the NPS on other park legislation. Hudson drafted the enabling legislation for Cane River Creole National Historical Park and Cane River National Heritage Area in consultation with Doug Faris, NPS Associate Regional Director for Planning and Compliance in the Southwest Region. They adapted existing national heritage area models to manage the conservation of cultural and historical resources in the Cane River region.

In 1994, Congress passed Public Law 103-449 (16 USC 410) enabling the creation of the national park and the national heritage area. The park included two former cotton plantations, both of which had been in the ownership of the same families since the time of Spanish land grants, and both of which contained nationally significant architectural and landscape resources. The heritage area included 45,000[33] acres of land that comprised the heart of Cane River's historic and scenic places – the national park, three state historic sites all tied to the historic roots of the area, and properties in the Natchitoches National Historic Landmark District that could be subject to cooperative agreements. Perhaps the most significant aspect of the heritage area was the continued use of the land in this small geographic area by the historic peoples who used it, combined with the highly visible, identifiable cultural landscape that gave this area an overwhelming sense of place.

The legislation for the park and the heritage area mandated the relationship between the two entities, inextricably linking them. Unlike most national heritage areas, in this instance two units of a national park anchored the cultural landscape that comprised Cane River National Heritage Area. The legislation specified the creation of a nineteen-member federal commission representing various community stakeholders. Among the purposes of this commission was to ensure a "culturally sensitive approach" be used in the development of both the park and the heritage area. This underscored the running dialogue between the two entities.

Implementation of the Heritage Area Model

Although the national park received funding immediately, the national heritage area received no funding for several

[31] Robert B. DeBlieux, personal communication, September 2, 2004.

[32] National Park Service, 1993, *Special Resource Study/Environmental Assessment: Cane River, Louisiana*, p. iii.

[33] The *Cane River National Heritage Area Management Plan* (2003) expanded the boundary to include 116,000 acres, per legislative authority.

years. Heritage area resources were in dire need of attention. The lack of financial backing for preservation of regional resources and development of programs created high levels of frustration in the community. The heritage area had no funding, no staff, and a volunteer commission. The community's hands were tied.

Cane River Creole National Historical Park began ethnographic, archeological, and historical studies in the heritage area soon after the legislation passed. The law specifically mandated that the park would coordinate a comprehensive research program on the cultural resource and genealogical topics, and this, along with a need to understand the cultural communities, provided the justification for studies completed for the park's general management plan. The research utilized extensive community involvement – often the team on a project included community members representing their own cultures. This project inclusion was a key factor in mobilizing some of the cultural groups in the heritage area.

The execution of a cooperative agreement between the park and the heritage area in 1998, and the subsequent transfer of funds provided a jump-start to the heritage area. The heritage area's funding has remained in the annual Department of the Interior appropriations bill since that time.

The second phase of development for the heritage area occurred between 1998 and 2002, after the execution of the cooperative agreement and the initial funds transfer. During this period, the heritage area commission was able to build on the groundwork laid by the National Park Service through Cane River Creole National Historical Park.

Two important tasks characterized the management of park and the heritage area during this phase. The first was to build an identity in a region where many long-standing public and nonprofit organizations had prospered for decades. The second was to expand partnership relationships with those existing organizations. The heritage area commission began developing a stronger identity through the creation of a map brochure, moving the concept of the heritage area from an idea to a tangible article that could be distributed widely to both visitors and residents for the first time. Also, the commission received a Save America's Treasures matching grant through the National Park Service to assist two local organizations in restoring two National Historic Landmark properties in the region. The park provided technical assistance on both projects. The Save America's Treasures grant allowed the commission and the park to cement community partnerships in the process of preserving nationally significant resources.

In addition, the heritage area commission established a competitive grants program in which individuals, organizations, and businesses could receive grants to carry out projects in the categories of historic preservation, research, and development. Through this program, a committee comprised of heritage area commissioners and community partners reviews grants annually, targeting projects that align with the heritage area's mission as outlined in the authorizing legislation. Begun in 1998, the grants program facilitates the process of moving federal seed money into the community to accomplish projects initiated by community members. Furthermore, the grants program builds partnerships among the commission, the park (which provides technical assistance to grantees), and grant recipients. In some instances, heritage area grants serve as a catalyst for extensive partnership building. The American Cemetery Preservation and Restoration Project provides an example in which a heritage area grant to a local nonprofit organization initiated a project that today involves city government, a landmark district development organization, Cane River Creole National Historical Park, and the NPS National Center for Preservation Technology and Training.

The Save America's Treasures award and the Cane River National Heritage Area grants program proved critical in raising awareness about the park's and the heritage area's existence and objectives, at the same time accomplishing projects central to the missions of both entities. This progress was complimented by staff development at both the park and the heritage area. With staff came the stability that is critical for long-term success in any organization.

At present, the park and the heritage area are entering a new phase of development, one characterized by a true joint effort. In 2004, both entities are in an operational phase, growing into the authorizing legislation that set their paths in 1994. The heritage area commission is orchestrating a shift from smaller, identity-building projects to larger projects that contribute to infrastructural development of the region. Several projects in the development concept planning stage and a comprehensive signage initiative mark the transition to this third phase. Similarly, new visitor facilities are coming online in the park, and attendance has increased significantly from early days. Funding for the park, the heritage area, and other local partners is relatively consistent at this juncture. These factors allow both park and heritage area to build a solid foundation for joint management now and in the future.

A strong framework built of three primary elements characterizes this third phase. Both the heritage area and the park have succeeded in developing effective programs. This proven track record provides a solid base for future projects, programming, and partnerships for both entities. Furthermore, by now all partners have built strong relationships in which the way everyone interacts is defined, yet flexible. Clear roles exist for the park, the heritage area commission, and their many partners; such definition makes partnerships more effective without putting limitations on future innovation. Finally, a foundation for continued communication built on openness, honesty, trust, and mutual respect exists among the park, the heritage area commission, and their partners. This foundation of trust and mutual respect is critical to the past success of the partnership region; maintaining it is essential to all future success.

THE CHALLENGE OF DEVELOPING A PROGRAM

With the increase in the number of national heritage areas and legislative proposals has come a renewed demand from Congress and the administration for a national policy to set standards and criteria for the establishment of new areas.[34] Even more challenging is the demand for clear measures to assess the benefit to both resources and communities of the program's federal investment and intervention. The growth of the NPS's programs and holdings has always been a dialogue between national goals and public demand.[35] The model of the great western parks carved out of public lands has been added to and amended for more than fifty years, with the addition of battlefields, memorial parkways, seashores, trails, and initiatives such as the National Underground Railroad Network to Freedom. Each of these designations and the complex new ideas that they represent have challenged the agency to think of new ways to conserve and interpret resources and brought them into closer contact with communities and the people who live there.[36] However, no idea has been as hard to conceptualize and reduce to standards, criteria, and measures of public benefit as that of national heritage areas.[37]

A generation ago, when the legislation passed for the first national heritage corridor, the NPS had no intention of creating a whole new category of designations. After several more were enacted and many more were proposed, both Congress and the agency developed several programmatic and statutory approaches. There were many countercurrents during this effort; some wished to harness the idea for broad landscape stewardship goals and others tried to rein in the idea as costly and unproven. Some resisted any standardization that might inhibit creativity and others, alarmed that the program threatened property rights, saw it as the first step toward federal land-use control. Although no agreement could be reached on an overall program approach, Congress and the administration were able to agree on a formula that set funding and time limits for the more recently designated areas on a case-by-case basis.[38]

Within the last two years, the idea of a national program has become more acceptable to all parties. In part, this is happening because there is a greater understanding of what makes these areas successful. Criteria have been developed, at least on paper, to ensure that community residents and leaders are fully consulted and committed before designation.[39] There is also general consensus that these areas, to justify the federal government's involvement, should contain nationally important resources and interpretive themes.

Still under discussion is how many national heritage areas should be created, what the long-term relationship should be between the NPS and the areas, and how to respond to proposals to extend funding support for areas that are reaching the end of their authorization. Finally, it is becoming more critical than ever to demonstrate what impact federal investment is having on heritage area goals of improving the conservation and interpretation of resources and the economic viability and sustainability of communities.[40]

USING DATA COLLECTION TO UNDERSTAND HERITAGE AREAS AND SHAPE FUTURE POLICY

Mounting pressures at the federal level to create criteria and guidance that guarantee the economic value and long-term "success" of heritage areas have led the NPS to utilize four concurrent data collection methods to attempt to quantify the physical, social, and economic characteristics of existing heritage areas and to create program accountability. Figure 30.1 demonstrates the categories of data that provide a basis for understanding and measuring the climate and impacts of heritage areas.

The first category (I) describes social, economic, and resource characteristics of the regions. Category two (II) describes additional overlapping designations, programs, and resources. The third category (III) counts heritage area-sponsored education and grants programs, partnerships, and impacts of heritage tourism. Category four (IV) reflects the aggregate economic leveraging impact of NPS appropriations. The fifth category (V) measures the regional economic impacts of heritage tourism.[41] Although some of the data being collected reflect the direct impacts of the presence of a heritage area, other categories are only informative of existing conditions. A major challenge lies in determining what programs and impacts can be attributed to heritage area activity.

Although data collection on national heritage areas is still in its early stages, preliminary findings provide some insights into both the characteristics of these areas and the outcomes of their efforts. For example, Category I information demonstrates that twenty percent of all National Historic Landmarks[42] are located within the boundaries of national

[34] Legislation has been introduced since 1993 to establish a programmatic approach to the creation of national heritage areas. However, Congress has not been able to agree on the terms of designation.

[35] Barrett, Brenda and Nora Mitchell, eds., 2003, "Stewardship of Heritage Areas," *The George Wright Forum* Vol. 20, No. 2. This issue of the *The George Wright Forum* examines the development of the national heritage area movement and its relationship to the National Park Service.

[36] National Park Service, 2003, *Branching Out: Approaches in National Park Stewardship*, Eastern National, Fort Washington, Pennsylvania. The booklet provides an excellent overview of the diversity of ways that the National Park Service designations and program have met the challenge of stewardship of the natural and cultural environment.

[37] Ibid, pp. 50–59.

[38] The formula that has been applied to most heritage areas created after 1996 is US$10 million dollars over fifteen years with no more than US$1 million dollars in any single year.

[39] For information on the national heritage area criteria, see footnote 7.

[40] The United States Senate, lead by Senator Thomas (R-WY), Chair of the Subcommittee on National Parks, has taken an active interest in the future of the national heritage area program. The Senate held an oversight hearing on the topic on March 13, 2002, requested assistance from the National Park Service Director Mainella in defining the purpose of the program and in developing "metrics for assessing progress" (March 21, 2003), and requested a review of the program by the General Accounting Office (May 1, 2003).

[41] The modified Money Generation Model (MGM2), developed by Michigan State University, considers the broader impacts that visitors to major visitor centers and attractions have on the surrounding region. The six areas are Silos and Smokestacks, Lackawanna Heritage Valley, Cane River National Heritage Area, Essex National Heritage Area, Augusta Canal National Heritage Area, and Ohio & Erie National Heritage Canal-Way.

[42] National Historic Landmarks are defined by the National Park Service as "... nationally significant historic places designated by the Secretary of Interior because they possess exceptional value or quality in illustrating or interpreting the heritage of the United States."

Data collection category	Purpose	Types of information	Sources	Reflected values and impacts
I. Baseline	describes social, economic and resource characteristics	population, age, race, income, unemployment, poverty, congressional representation, area, government, National Register and National Historic Landmarks listings, grants and tax credit projects	U.S. Census Bureau and National Park Service	social, historical, economic
II. Additional designations, programs and resources	indicates overlapping designations and resources, economic development and resource protection activities	federally managed parcels of land, designations and management by national conservation and preservation organizations (National Trust for Historic Preservation, National Scenic Byways, American Heritage Rivers)	websites and staff of Federal agencies and national organizations	historic, cultural, natural, recreational
III. Indicators	indicates impacts/ change more directly attributable to heritage area designation	visitation ,volunteerism, formal and informal partnerships, grants and enhancements to trails and historic properties, educational programs and participants	annual survey to designated areas	cultural, recreational, partnership
IV. Leveraging	assesses economic value and impact of Federal investment in local initiatives	National Park Service Heritage Partnerships Program Funding, Transportation Enhancements, Other Federal, state, local, private and non-profit	annual survey to designated areas	economic, partnership
V. Impacts of heritage tourism	measures the economic impacts of visitor spending on the surrounding region	Michigan State University modified Money Generation Model (MGM2)	visitor surveys collected at visitors' centers and major attractions in six heritage areas	economic, social

Figure 30.1. Categories of data collection.

heritage areas. This indicator supports the national importance of the resources and themes of these areas. Category III information demonstrates that in 2003, heritage areas were awarded 367 grants overall, which leveraged US$29,276,585. Sixty-seven of these grants were awarded for trails projects. Five hundred thirteen educational programs reached 740,775 students in 2003. These numbers indicate significant progress toward the national heritage areas' stated program goals of resource conservation and education. As this information is gathered on an annual basis, overall conservation and stewardship impacts can be tracked.

The goal of assisting regions with community and economic revitalization is reflected in both Categories III and IV. An estimated 31.6 million people visited heritage area attractions in 2003 (Category III), and a recently completed study on heritage tourism piloted by six of the national heritage areas demonstrates the economic impact of visitors on the heritage regions. Michigan State University based this modified study on the Money Generation Model long used by the NPS.[43] Preliminary findings have been so insightful that the remaining eighteen national heritage areas will be encouraged to participate in future studies. Measuring the impact of heritage tourism at a regional level helps national heritage areas gain local and Congressional support and offers the areas insight into how to better reach their constituents.

The data collection from Category III reflects some less tangible impacts of heritage areas on their regions. The national heritage areas reported that in 2003 they participated in more than 3,000 partnerships and generated 167,000 hours of volunteer service. Partnership commitment is also reflected in the amount of money that national heritage areas have leveraged with NPS funding: Partners committed more than eight times as much money from a diversified mixture of federal, state, local, and private funding sources.[44] Category IV information demonstrates to congressional appropriators, donors, potential partners, and investors the economic value of utilizing the heritage area strategy.

FURTHERING THE AGENDA – HYPOTHESIS OF CHANGE

Another area of inquiry involves looking at the characteristics of regions that adopt the heritage area strategy. Preliminary demographic and resource data suggest that certain factors set heritage areas apart from other landscapes. All of the heritage areas are or were "working landscapes" – their conservation and interpretation centers on a way of life that is becoming or has become obsolete. Particularly in the Northeast, heritage areas are regions that have experienced more out-migration than elsewhere in the country between 1995 and 2000.[45] Across the country, data from Category I show that heritage areas have a higher percentage of the population over 65 than the rest of the states in which they are located, and the average percentage of persons over 65 is higher than the national average, at 12.4 percent and

[43] For more information on the work of Michigan State University and the Money Generation Model, see <http://www.prr.msu.edu/mgm2/default.htm>, retrieved February 20, 2004.

[44] In 2002, the twenty-three national heritage areas were surveyed to determine the leveraging ratio of National Park Service Heritage Partnerships Funding to other federal, state, local, private, and nonprofit income. The leveraging percentages are available at <http://www.cr.nps.gov/heritageareas/research/>.

[45] The Northeast lost 1.2 million residents between 1995 and 2000. See <http://www.census.gov/population/cen2000/> for regional population statistics.

Heritage Area	Traditional economic base	Geographic landscape linkages	Type of change occurring	Mitigation techniques
Augusta, Blackstone, Cache La Poudre, D&L, Erie, Hudson, I&M, O&E, Wheeling, Yuma	transportation	canal or waterway	obsolete transportation corridors – regional loss of identity, depopulation	recreational trails and scenic byways (reconnecting transportation linkages), education
Blackstone, Lackawanna, MotorCities, National Coal, Path of Progress Rivers of Steel	industry	historic mills, factories plants and associated landscape formations	obsolete or severely declining industry – coal, steel, mining, textiles and manufacturing – depopulation	adaptive re-use, interpretation of industrial history, tourism (new uses for vacant structures)
Essex	maritime	water, colonial-era historic structures	development, loss of connection with history	tourism, interpretation and managed growth
Cane River, Hudson, Q&S, Silos and Smokestacks, South Carolina	agricultural	farmland and rural landscape	shift in use of land from agricultural to residential	conservation, tourism
Shenandoah, Tennessee	agriculture/ hybrid/ battlefield sites	battlefields and related historic sites, rural landscape	development, loss of connection with history	battlefield and site protection, interpretation

Figure 30.2. Heritage area change.

14.3 percent respectively.[46] Although these findings are not definitive, they do point to stress within a community as a factor in heritage area formation.

Whether the region is gaining or losing population, jobs, and young people, the desire to manage change brings together people of diverse cultures, interests, economic, and social backgrounds. Figure 30.2 illustrates one way of categorizing the national heritage areas in order to better understand and assess the complex shifts occurring and how heritage areas might address more effectively concerns about social, economic, and resource change. Drawing correlations between the characteristics of the landscape, the stresses occurring there, and the responses may shed light on why heritage areas form and how they can become successful in achieving their goals.

WHAT NEXT? IMPACTS AND FUTURE RESEARCH

Preliminary data collected on the heritage areas have been utilized to explain and justify the value of heritage area designation. The data are appearing in Congressional testimonies, NPS Special Resources Studies for proposed heritage areas, and the literature of the heritage areas.[47] The data collection is shaping draft program legislation and program direction. The information is also providing a more comprehensive picture of the national significance of the regions, which will improve technical assistance in the future. Also, the information highlights the federal, state, and local partners and programs within the regions that can provide future partnership opportunities. Finally, data collection is provoking a deeper questioning of the theoretical aspects of heritage development and creating dialogue that explores the larger social and value-based questions upon which the future of the movement will depend.

In addition to numbers collection and surveying, a series of workshops has brought professionals and academics together to discuss what is needed to further assess the present and future of the heritage movement. Outcomes of these workshops may include the development of a centralized database of legislation, management models, plans, and case studies, a publication series of best practices and guidelines, and an academic research forum to explore the impetus, practice, policy, and impacts of heritage development.[48]

Because of funding and time constraints, initial data collection has been focused on quantifiable things. This does not fully capture the impacts of heritage areas on the quality of life that the areas are attempting to conserve – intangible values that have made regions culturally or socially cohesive in the past. A model needs to be developed that accurately measures true heritage area "success." The model should consider both quantitative and qualitative data and draw stronger correlations between heritage area designation and management and its long-term impacts on the values that residents hold dear. Undoubtedly, research and data collection will evolve over time to encompass a broader range of resources and to

[46] U.S. Census Bureau statistics on age demographics are available by county for 1990 and 2000 at <http://www.census.gov>.

[47] Examples can be found in the National Park Service's Gullah/Guchee Draft Special Resource Study; congressional testimony on October 16, 2003 on H.R. 1862; and in the 2003 Annual Report on the National Heritage Areas, produced in partnership with the Alliance of National Heritage Areas and the National Park Service.

[48] Workshop reports and additional information are available at <http://www.cr.nps.gov/heritageareas/REP/research.htm>.

Figure 30.3. Buildings that were used first as slave quarters and later as housing for sharecroppers and tenant farmers at Magnolia Plantation, a National Historic Landmark that comprises one unit of Cane River Creole National Historical Park, which lies within Cane River National Heritage Area. Photo by Jack Boucher, National Park Service, HABS/HAER/HALS Division.

Figure 30.4. The Big House at Cherokee Plantation, an early nineteenth century French Creole house, is one of the privately owned historic properties that is an integral part of the cultural landscape in Cane River National Heritage Area. Photo by Jack Boucher, National Park Service, HABS/HAER/HALS Division.

Figure 30.5. Cane River winds through the entire length of the national heritage area. Photo by Jack Boucher, National Park Service, HABS/HAER/HALS Division.

Figure 30.6. A cotton gin that forms part of the working agricultural landscape of Cane River National Heritage Area. Photo by Jack Boucher, National Park Service, HABS/HAER/HALS Division.

identify the specific impacts that heritage areas are having on regions, people, and resources. Alternative conservation and international models, such as the Northern Forest Wealth Index and Quality of Life Reports completed in New Zealand and Canada,[49] will shape a new model for measuring the short and long-term successes of heritage area activities in communities undergoing change and stress.

HERITAGE AREAS AT THE CROSSROADS

Heritage areas tend to occur where the linkages between people and place, nature and culture, and the present and the past are traditionally connected, but currently are threatened or weak. Heritage areas focus on rebuilding these linkages through resource conservation, new partnerships, and economic development. At this critical juncture – as the future of heritage area policy is being determined – measuring, assessing, and understanding heritage areas will provide the federal government and the national heritage areas with information to improve the program and judge its ultimate success.

QUESTIONS FOR DISCUSSION

1. National heritage areas are long-term partnership strategies; how can the value of the partnership be measured over time?

2. What should the relationship be between national park units, protected areas, and the living landscape of national heritage areas?

3. What if the traditional communities and practices that defined the significance of a national heritage area change? What if the commitment of the communities in a national heritage area declines?

4. What level of governmental oversight is appropriate for designated national heritage areas?

5. How can partnerships between multiple governmental agencies be fostered to assist national heritage areas?

BIBLIOGRAPHY: HERITAGE AREAS

Alanen, Arnold R, and Robert Z. Melnick, eds. *Preserving Cultural Landscapes in America.* Baltimore: The John Hopkins University Press, 2000.

The essays provide an overview of the world of landscape classification and preservation from the perspectives of landscape architecture, geography, and anthropology. Good discussions on the dynamic nature of the field, nature versus culture, and the role of the National Park Service standards.

Archibald, Robert R. *A Place to Remember: Using History to Build Community.* Walnut Creek: Altamira Press, 1999.

The role history and place play in preserving workable communities and fostering civic involvement.

Barrett, Brenda. "Heritage Areas in the West." *Colorado Preservationist*, Vol. 17, No. 3, Autumn 2003.

Barrett, Brenda, "The National Register and Heritage Areas." *Cultural Resource Management*, 2002, No. 1.

Barrett, Brenda, and Augie Carlino, "What is in the Future for the Heritage Areas Movement?" *Forum Journal*, National Trust for Historic Preservation, Vol. 17, No. 4, Summer 2003.

Barrett, Brenda and Copping, Suzanne. "*National Heritage Areas: Developing a Model for Measuring Success.*" Paper presented at US/ICOMOS 2004 Annual Conference, Natchitoches, LA.

Barrett, Brenda and Nora Mitchell, eds., Stewardship of Heritage Areas. *George Wright Forum*, Vol. 20, No. 2, June 2003.

Billington, Robert. "Case Study of the Blackstone River Valley: Federal Investment Attracts Private Investment in Industrial Historic Sites." Unpublished.

[49] *The Northern Forest Wealth Index: Exploring a Deeper Meaning of Wealth.* Concord, NH: Northern Forest Center, 2000. *Quality of Life Report 2003.* Wellington, NZ: 2003. Available at <http://www.bigcities.govt.nz>, retrieved February 20, 2004. *Quality of Life in Canada: A Citizen's Report Card.* Canadian Policy Research Network: 2002. Available at <http://www.cprn.com/en/doc.cfm?doc=44>, retrieved February 20, 2004.

Bray, Paul. "The National Heritage Areas Phenomenon – Where it is Coming From." *Cultural Resource Management*, Vol. 17, No. 8, 1994.

Bray, Paul. "Rethinking Urban Parks." *Places*, Vol. 16, No. 2, Spring 2004.

Brown, Jessica, Nora Mitchell and Fausto Sarmiento. "Landscape Stewardship: New Directions in Conservation of Nature and Culture." *The George Wright Forum*. Vol. 17, No. 1, 2000, 12–70.

Brown, Jessica, Nora Mitchell and Jacqueline Tuxill. "Partnerships and Lived-in Landscapes: an Evolving US System of Parks and Protected Areas." *IUCN Protected Areas Program: Parks*, Vol. 13, No. 2 Category IV 2003.

Conservation Study Institute, IUCN-The World Conservation Union and QLF/Atlantic Center for the Environment. *International Concepts in Protected Landscapes: Exploring Their Value for Communities in the Northeast.* Woodstock, Vermont: Conservation Study Institute, 2000.

Cremin, Dennis H. "From Heartland to Nation: The National Heritage Area Movement at Twenty." *History News*, Spring 2004, 11–15.

Dorst, John D. *The Written Suburb: An American Site, an Ethnographic Dilemma.* Philadelphia: University of Pennsylvania Press, 1989.

Fowler, Peter J. *The Past in Contemporary Society: Then, Now.* London: Routledge. 1992.

Frenchman, Dennis. "*International Examples of the United States Heritage Areas Concept.*" Unpublished.

Handler, Richard and Eric Gable. *The New History in an Old Museum: Creating the Past at Colonial Williamsburg.* Durham, N.C.: Duke University Press, 1997.

Hart, Judy. "Planning for and Preserving Cultural Resources through National Heritage Areas." *Cultural Resource Management*. Vol. 23 No. 7, 2000, 29–33.

Hewison, Robert. *The Heritage Industry: Britain in a Climate of Decline.* London: Methuen, 1987.

Hirsch, Eric and Michael O'Hanlon, eds. *The Anthropology of Landscape: Perspectives on Place and Space.* Oxford: Clarendon Press, 1995.

Hirst, Paula S. "Heritage Areas and Heritage Corridors: the Next Step for Preservation." Thesis. Columbia University, 1998.

Hough, Michael. *Out of Place: Restoring Identity to the Regional Landscape.* New Haven: Yale University Press, 1990.
Looks at the conditions that create regional landscapes and those that work to degrade them. Offers some principles for regional design.

Hufford, Mary, ed. *Conserving Culture: A New Discourse on Heritage.* Urbana: University of Illinois, 1994.

Kirshenblatt-Gimblett, Barbara. *Destination Culture: Tourism, Museums and Heritage.* Berkeley: University of California Press, 1998.

Kunstler, James Howard. *The Geography of Nowhere: The Rise and Decline of America's Man-made Landscape.* New York: Touchstone, 1994.
Looks at the impact of car culture and car-based development on planning, communities, and residents.

Leuchtenburg, William E., ed. *American Place: Encounters with History.* New York: Oxford University Press, 2000.
A series of essays by historians on "historic places" and how they enrich the understanding of the past and the present.

Lowenthal, David. *The Past is a Foreign Country.* Cambridge: Cambridge University Press, 1985.

______. *The Heritage Crusade and the Spoils of History.* Cambridge: Cambridge University Press, 1988.

Meing, D. W., ed. *The Interpretation of Ordinary Landscapes: Geographical Essays.* New York: Oxford University Press, 1979.

Morse, Suzanne W. and Monica Gillespie. *Solutions for America, What's Already Out There: A Sourcebook of Ideas from Successful Community Programs.* Pew Partnership for Civic Change and the University of Richmond, 2002.
Highlights the work of Handmade in America, a community and economic revitalization project in North Carolina.

Nash, Dennison. *Anthropology of Tourism.* Oxford: Pergamon, 1996.

Peskin, Sarah. "America's Special Landscapes: The Heritage Area Phenomenon." Presented at Ferrara Paesaggio Conference, Ferrara, Italy, March, 2001.

Poria, Yaniv, Richard Butler, and David Airey. "The Core of Heritage Tourism." *Annals of Tourism Research.* Vol. 30, No. 1 (Jan. 2003): 238–254. [available on-line at <http://www.sciencedirect.com/science/journal/01607383>]

Regional Heritage Areas: Connecting People to Places and History. *National Trust Forum Journal*, Vol. 17, No. 4, Summer 2003.

Roe, Dilys, Nigel Leader-Williams, and Barry Dalal-Clayton. *Take Only Photographs, Leave Only Footprints: The Environmental Impacts of Wildlife Tourism.* London: International Institute for Environment and Development, 1997. [available on-line at <http://www.ecotourism.org/ conselefr.html>]

Rothman, Hal. *The Culture of Tourism, the Tourism of Culture: Selling the Past to the Present in the American Southwest.* Albuquerque, NM: University of New Mexico, 2003.

Smith, Valene L., ed. *Hosts and Guests: The Anthropology of Tourism*, 2nd ed. Philadelphia: University of Pennsylvania Press, 1989.

Turnbull, Alan J. "The Heritage Partnership Initiative: National Heritage Areas." *Cultural Resource Management* Vol.17, No.1, 1994.

Tuxill, Jacquelyn L. ed. *The Landscape of Conservation Stewardship: The Report of the Stewardship Initiative Feasibility Study.* Woodstock, Vermont: Marsh-Billings-Rockefeller National Historical Park, Conservation Study Institute, and The Woodstock Foundation, Inc., 2000.

Tuxill, Jacquelyn L. and Nora J. Mitchell, eds. *Collaboration and Conservation: Lessons Learned in Areas Managed through National Park Service Partnership.* Woodstock, Vermont: Conservation Study Institute, 2001.
Sets out a "to do" list for National Park Service partnership initiatives.

Tuxill, Jacquelyn L. and Nora J. Mitchell and Jessica Brown, eds. *Collaboration and Conservation: Lessons Learned from National*

Service Partnerships in Western U.S. Conservation and Stewarship Publication No. 6, Woodstock, Vermont: Conservation Study Institute, 2004.

West, Carroll Van. "Revisiting Our Civil War Legacies: Tennessee State Parks and the Tennessee Civil War National Heritage Area." *Tennessee Conservationist*. Vol. 69, No. 6 (Nov/Dec 2003): 28–31.

WEB SITES

<www.cr.nps.gov/heritageareas>

<www.nationalheritageareas.org>

For questions, please contact Nancy Morgan, Executive Director, Cane River National Heritage Area at 318.356.5555 or nmorgan@caneriverheritage.org.

CHAPTER THIRTY-ONE

The United States and the World Heritage Convention

James K. Reap

It would be fitting by 1972 for the nations of the world to agree to the principle that there are certain areas of such unique worldwide value that they should be treated as part of the heritage of all mankind and accorded special recognition as a World Heritage Trust. Such an arrangement would impose no limitations on the sovereignty of those nations which choose to participate, but would extend special international recognition to the areas which qualify and would make available technical and other assistance where appropriate to assist in their protection and management.

Statement of President Richard M. Nixon advocating the adoption of the World Heritage Convention, 1971

At best, world heritage . . . designations give the international community an open invitation to interfere in domestic land use decisions. More seriously, the underlying international land use agreements potentially have several significant adverse effects on the American system of government.

Statement of Congressman Don Young introducing the "American Land Sovereignty Protection Act", 1997.

It seems appropriate to examine the participation of the United States in the World Heritage Convention[1] almost thirty-five years after the Convention entered into force and to highlight several issues that have affected, and continue to affect, United States participation. Some of these issues, should other countries approach them in a similar way, also have the potential to affect the operation of the Convention from an international perspective.

What began with such idealism and enthusiasm appears to have become sidetracked by domestic political and parochial considerations. The United States had a major role in the creation of the Convention and became the first nation to ratify it in 1973 by a vote in the Senate of 95–0. The Convention entered into force on December 17, 1975 after ratification by the requisite number of States Parties. The United States has served as a member of the World Heritage Committee for much of that body's existence and in 1978 hosted the first Committee meeting that listed sites. Of the twelve sites listed at that time, two were in the United States: Mesa Verde and Yellowstone National Park. Since that time, implementing legislation and regulations have had the practical effect of limiting U.S. participation and legislation introduced in Congress in recent sessions to amend the implementing legislation could further cripple participation, should it pass.

After the U.S. Congress implemented the Convention by the 1980 Amendments to the National Historic Preservation Act (NHPA)[2]. These amendments gave the Secretary of the Interior the responsibility of directing and coordinating U.S. activities under the Convention in coordination with the Secretary of State, the Smithsonian Institution, and the Advisory Council on Historic Preservation.[3] Regulations setting forth policies and procedures used by the U.S. Department of the Interior to direct and coordinate participation were adopted in 1982 and continue in force. The regulations also address maintenance of the U.S. Indicative Inventory of Potential Future World Heritage Nominations[4] and the nomination of sites to the World Heritage List.[5] They established the Federal Interagency Panel on World Heritage to advise the Assistant Secretary for Fish and Wildlife and Parks, who is delegated responsibility to administer World Heritage activities by the U.S. government.

[1] The Convention Concerning the Protection of the World Cultural and Natural Heritage, popularly known as the World Heritage Convention, is truly universal in its scope. Promulgated at the General Conference of the United National Educational, Scientific, and Cultural Organization (UNESCO) 1972, it had been signed by 178 nations as of May 2004, making it perhaps the most widely accepted environmental and preservation agreement. At the end of 2004, 788 properties had been inscribed on the list – 611 cultural, 154 natural, and 23 mixed – located in the territories of 134 states parties.

[2] The National Historic Preservation Act of 1966, 16 U.S.C. *§470 et seq.*, is the key Federal statute in the area of historic preservation, establishing a partnership among Federal, state, and local governments following closely the approach set out in *With Heritage So Rich*, a report of a special committee under the auspices of the United States Conference of Mayors. The Federal approach involves the establishment of national standards, designation of properties worthy of preservation (National Register of Historic Places), protection of listed properties from federally licensed and funded projects (Section 106), appropriate management of federally owned properties, and the provision of incentives to state and local governments and private individuals. This law has served as a model for preservation laws in some other nations and represents a departure from the European model that traditionally focused on listing monuments to an approach focused on a broad range of heritage properties. It is at the local level in the United States where government has the "teeth" to protect heritage properties from damage or destruction by private owners. The regulation of land use through police power is one of the traditional powers of state government guaranteed through the Tenth Amendment of the U.S. Constitution. State governments have, in turn, authorized local governments to exercise this power by enacting historic preservation ordinances.

[3] Public Law 96-515, December 12, 1980, 94 Stat. 3000.

[4] The United States was the first nation to prepare such a list, and the current version is a slightly amended version of the document prepared in 1982. This list is intended to be an open-ended or revolving list. See James Charleton, "The United States and the World Heritage Convention," a paper presented at the annual symposium of US/ICOMOS in Indianapolis, Indiana in 2000, <www.icomos.org/usicomos/Symposium/SYMP00/charleton.htm>, accessed January 5, 2005.

[5] 36 CFR 73.

To date, twenty sites in the United States have been inscribed on the World Heritage List, two of which are sites jointly listed with Canada. Eight listings are cultural sites, however, no property has been added to the list since 1995.[6]

The relatively small number of U.S. inscriptions on the World Heritage List given the size of the country and its rich resources is attributable, in part, to the owner consent requirement included in the 1980 Amendments to the NHPA. The law prohibits any non-Federal property from being nominated unless the owner concurs in writing. The Interior Department has construed this language as requiring *written concurrence from 100 percent of property owners.* Additionally, each owner must pledge to protect the property. No other State Party to the Convention requires either government ownership or 100% private owner consent as a prior condition for nomination. This requirement is also more restrictive than other provisions of the NHPA pertaining to listing properties in the National Register of Historic Places or as a National Historic Landmark. A property may be listed under those programs unless there is a *notarized written objection* from the owner or owners of any single property or *a majority of the owners of such properties within a district.*[7]

Because of this restriction, it must be asked whether the United States has unreasonably limited its participation in the Convention. Of the properties listed, most are federally owned. No U.S. cities or historic districts have been listed, something quite common for other participating countries.[8]

A relevant case in point is that of Savannah, Georgia. In the late 1980s, there was increasing interest in listing the Savannah National Historic Landmark District on the World Heritage List. Through research and documentation, the district was placed on the Indicative List of Potential U.S. World Heritage Cultural Nominations. In 1992, the City of Savannah decided to move forward with the nomination process and a proposal was forwarded to the Federal Interagency Panel after two years of additional research. There was no question of significance or adequate protection, as required by the Convention. The district had been listed as a National Historic Landmark in 1966 and the area was protected against inappropriate development by a strong local historic district ordinance.[9] However, there was the issue of owner consent. Although local historic zoning had been the subject of a referendum that was approved by a three to one vote margin, discussions with the members of the Federal Interagency Panel made it clear that 100% written concurrence would be required. The likelihood of obtaining unanimous written consent from more than 1,000 property owners in Savannah, or any other American city, was inconceivable. The decision was therefore made to nominate the main components of the city plan, including the streets, 52 acres of tree-shaded squares, parks, and internationally acclaimed public monuments within a 2.2 square mile area. The Savannah city plan has been recognized as a unique artistic achievement in town planning and a masterpiece of creative genius on the part of the city's founder, General James Edward Oglethorpe. This creative solution to the owner-consent barrier proved to be unsuccessful, however. After reviewing the nomination, the ICOMOS World Heritage Coordinator informed the Mayor of Savannah he could not recommend inscription to the Bureau of the World Heritage Committee because the nomination was outside the operational guidelines for implementation of the Convention.[10] Since the rejection of the Savannah nomination, no further city or district nomination has been forthcoming from the United States.

A second, though less significant, problem with the U.S. nomination process concerns significance. The implementing statute simply states, "No property may be so nominated unless it has previously been determined to be of national significance."[11] Interior Department regulations for cultural properties recognize "national significance" as being limited to National Historic Landmarks (or areas of national significance established by the Congress or by presidential proclamation under the Antiquities Act of 1906). Further, the Department uses theme studies to identify and nominate as Landmarks properties associated with a specific area of American history, such as the fur trade, earliest Americans, women's history, Greek Revival architecture, etc. The nomination may face difficulties if no theme study exists, the theme study is incomplete or outdated, or the property does not fall into a particular theme category. Established Landmark themes and sub-themes must be cited in the World Heritage nomination form, and the nominator must refer to other theme studies (or historic contexts) already prepared that are relevant for a particular nomination.[12] At best, such a process may impose a lengthy delay and additional administrative hurdles in the nomination process.

Another contributing factor to the U.S. failure to nominate properties for World Heritage listing since the mid-1990s is undoubtedly the chilling effect caused by potentially damaging legislation introduced in Congress. The so-called "American Land Sovereignty Protection Act" (ALSPA) would have amended the NHPA to make World Heritage nominations significantly more difficult, requiring new administrative procedures and the approval of Congress before a site could be nominated to the World Heritage List or included on the List of World Heritage in Danger.[13]

[6] Of these sites, two were subsequently placed on the List of World Heritage in Danger: Everglades National Park and Yellowstone National Park. See <http://whc.unesco.org/nwhc/pages/doc/mainf3.htm>, accessed January 5, 2005.

[7] 16 U.S.C. 470(a)(6); 30 CFR 60.6.

[8] Examples include Islamic Cairo (Egypt); Historic Centers of Venice, Florence and Rome (Italy), Bath (UK), and Quebec (Canada); and the Medina of Fez (Morocco).

[9] City of Savannah Code of Ordinances, §8–3030.

[10] US/ICOMOS Newsletter, No. 4, 1995.

[11] 16 U.S.C. 470a-1(b).

[12] <http://www.cr.nps.gov/nr/publications/bulletins/nhl/nhlpt1.htm>, accessed 5 January 2005.

[13] Introduced in the 104th Congress as H. R. 3752 (no vote in the House); in the 105th Congress as H. R. 901(passed the House, no vote in the

Supporters of this bill expressed fear that environmental and cultural advocacy groups and federal agency managers would use World Heritage principles and processes in land management decisions without the knowledge of Congress or use designation to undermine local land use decisions without input from citizens and local governments. Federal regulatory actions, they assert, could have an adverse effect on the value of private property and a negative impact on local economies. However, under its current process, the Interior Department provides open public meetings and congressional notification when considering sites for nomination. The World Heritage Convention does not give UNESCO or the UN any authority over U.S. sites nor does it require changes in domestic law. The Convention does require that signatories protect their listed sites and settings, but that protection is provided under the laws of each State Party – in the case of the United States, the Constitution, along with federal, state, and local laws and procedures. The only way the Convention can affect land management decisions is by influencing public opinion or the decisions of the governing authority through the power of persuasion.[14] Even this is apparently a concern to those who fear limitations on unrestricted development of federal and private land.

These fears seem to have been fueled by a situation involving Yellowstone National Park. In 1995, the Interior Department notified the World Heritage Committee that the park was in danger and requested an on-site visit. After sending a special assessment team and further consultation with U.S. officials, the Committee placed Yellowstone on the List of World Heritage in Danger. Among the threats cited was a proposed gold mine just over a mile from the park. A number of U.S. environmental organizations were very vocal in their opposition to the mine. Much of the mining activity would have been on private land, but some Federal land outside the park would have been affected. President Clinton issued orders effectively creating a buffer zone on the Federal land prior to the listing. Mining and forest interests, along with others opposed to environmental legislation, asserted the World Heritage Convention had had a significant role in the Federal decisions affecting the mine and seized the issue as justification for introducing ALSPA.[15] Opponents of the bill contended that the problem with the mine had nothing to do with Yellowstone's World Heritage listing, but rather the fact that mining would adversely affect an important national park. Yellowstone was removed from the List of World Heritage in Danger in 2003.[16]

Proponents of ALSPA often tried to couple their concerns about the operation of the World Heritage Convention with the withdrawal of the United States from UNESCO in 1984. In fact, it was the policy of the Reagan Administration to retain U.S. participation in the Convention while withdrawing from UNESCO for other reasons.[17] In 1992, under former President Bush, Interior Secretary Manuel Lujan hosted the World Heritage Committee in Santa Fe, New Mexico. Perhaps this argument will have less weight now that the United States has rejoined UNESCO.[18]

Despite the assertion of its Congressional supporters that the ALSPA only ensured the involvement of the public and elected representatives in decision making and the protection of private property rights,[19] the publicity around the issue apparently tapped a deep vein of American xenophobia. Rumors spread on talk radio shows that the United Nations controls U.S. national parks or that the parks are being used as staging areas for UN troops.[20] So many inquiries were received about a foreign takeover of the Great Smokey Mountains National Park[21] that the Park Service had to include an article in the official visitors' guide under the title "Park Is Not Run by United Nations" assuring readers that the park "remains the property of the United States government." Politicians capitalized on these conspiracy theories.[22] In 1996, Rep. Don

Senate); in the 106th Congress as H. R. 883 (passed the House, no vote in the Senate), in the 107th Congress as H. R. 883 (assigned to committee). Companion bill was introduced in the Senate, the last being S.2575 introduced June 4, 2002, and assigned to committee but not sent to the floor for a vote. No similar bill was introduced in either chamber during the 108th Congress.

14 Machado, Matthew, "Land and Resource Management: X. Mounting Opposition to Bioshpere Reserves and World Heritage Sites in the United States Sparked by Claims of Interference with National Sovereignty," 1997 COLO. J. INT'L ENVTL L. Y. B. 120.

15 In spite of the fact that the mining company had settled its claims with the government and Congress had appropriated money for that purpose.

16 <http://whc.unesco.org//archive/decrec03.htm>, last accessed January 5, 2005.

17 Testimony of Brooks B. Yeager, Deputy Assistant Secretary for Policy and International Affairs, U.S. Department of the Interior, before the House Committee on Resources, March 19, 1999, citing letters from Reagan Administration officials in support of the Convention and a press release from then Interior Secretary Hodel indicating how proud the department was that the Statue of Liberty could be recognized as a World Heritage site.

18 Speech of President George Bush before the UN General Assembly, September 12, 2002. However, the reasons he cited for rejoining had nothing to do with environmental or cultural issues: "The United States is joining with the world to supply aid where it reaches people and lifts up lives, to extend trade and the prosperity it brings, and to bring medical care where it is desperately needed."

19 "And let's be clear, the goal of this measure is to abandon these programs, not simply to regulate them." Rep. Bruce Vento (D-Minn), statement before the House Committee on Resources, March 18, 1999.

20 In the case of Biosphere Reserves, a proposal for the Ozark Highlands Regional Biosphere was scuttled after conspiracy theorists claimed the designation was part of a plot by the UN to seize 55,000 square miles of the Ozarks using UN troops being trained in the Dakotas. One man reported seeing tanks in the woods and a woman asked if she could be shipped overseas and tried as an international criminal for picking wildflowers. "Black Helicopters Invade Ozarks," an editorial appearing in the *St. Louis Post Dispatch*, April 9, 1997.

21 This park has been designated an international "biosphere reserve," a program which is also a target of the ALSPA.

22 ALSPA opponent Rep. Jay Inslee (D-Wash.) suggested the bill be renamed the "American Land Paranoia Act," and Rep. Mark Udall (D-CO) claimed the bill "is primarily a means for supporters to take a shot at the UN and particularly UNESCO, and to demonstrate their solidarity with some who seem to view the UN as engaged in a vast multiwing conspiracy to overthrow our constitutional government." See "House Debated U.S. Participation in UNESCO Program and Implications for Americas Sovereignty; Senate Holds First Hearings," United Nations Association of the United States of America, June 1999,

Young (R-Alaska), the author of the ALSPA, sent a letter to congressional colleagues asking "Is Boutrous Boutrous-Ghali zoning land in your district?"[23] These fears and rumors even turned to personal attacks. Following his testimony against the ALSPA in 1997, US/ICOMOS Executive Director Gustavo Araoz received a threatening e-mail.[24]

The late Rep. Bruce F. Vento (D-Minnesota), speaking in 1999 in opposition to the bill, asserted, "The legislation sends a signal around the world that our nation, the United States of America, which forged the policy path to institute these various treaties and protocols, is undercutting the values and benefits of international recognition for important cultural or environmental sites."[25] The World Heritage Convention does not threaten the interests or sovereignty of the United States. The recognition brought through listing simply enhances the prestige of sites already protected by existing domestic law and brings economic benefits to local communities.[26]

In spite of attacks on U.S. participation in the World Heritage Convention from the property rights lobby, there is currently a renewal of interest in World Heritage listing from a number of quarters, particularly historic cities.[27] Those seeking to nominate additional sites have their work cut out for them. Although ALSPA was not enacted in previous sessions of Congress, the 109th Congress beginning in January 2005 is regarded as more conservative. However, supporters of congressional action may not feel the same urgency as during the Clinton Administration because the Bush Administration has given clear evidence of its sympathy for limiting the impact of environmental and land-use regulation. As the United States enters its fourth decade as a signatory of the World Heritage Convention, the question remains whether it will fulfill the vision it gave the world in 1972 and again step forward into a leadership position. In 1999, U.S. Rep. Bruce Vento pointedly put the question being asked by many advocates of cultural and natural resource conservation:

> When the United States is thrust into a role of dominant power and in the central role as a world leader in so many areas, why would we voluntarily abdicate perhaps the most important leadership position we occupy, that of a leader in an effort to make this life on this planet sustainable? (Statement of Congressman Bruce Vento concerning the "American Land Sovereignty Protection Act," 1999)

It would be unfortunate indeed if the very country whose inherently American national park ideal formed a philosophical underpinning for the Convention forsook leadership in the World Heritage Program.

QUESTIONS FOR DISCUSSION

1. How can the United States be a more effective participant in the World Heritage Convention?

2. What opportunities exist for better integrating the recognition and protection of cultural and natural properties in the United States?

3. What actions can be taken to nominate additional representative properties in the United States to the World Heritage List?

4. Is it reasonable for the United States to impose an owner consent requirement for World Heritage listing in the absence of any federal or state constitutional mandates for consent?

5. Should the desires of a local community – evidenced by action of its democratically elected governing body or by referendum – be overruled by one property owner in the nomination process, given that those communities have the constitutional power to designate and provide for the protection of historically significant properties?

USEFUL LINKS

<http://whc.unesco.org/>
The home page of the UNESCO World Heritage Center is the logical beginning point for investigation of the World Heritage Convention. The site contains internal links to the official text of the Convention, a list of States Parties, an overview, brief history, and benefits of ratification. There are also links to the List itself, along with the World Heritage in Danger List, information on key partners, and an overview of procedures and policy issues.

<http://www.nps.gov/oia/>
The U.S. National Park Service Office of International Affairs site contains information on the World Heritage Program in the United States, along with information on properties currently inscribed and the Tentative List of potential nominees.

<http://www.icomos.org>
The International Council on Monuments and Sites is the UNESCO partner that reviews cultural and mixed properties nominated to the World Heritage List.

<http://www.icomos.org/usicomos>
The United States Committee of ICOMOS site details the role of US/ICOMOS in World Heritage Program.

<http://www.iucn.org/>
The World Conservation Union is the UNESCO partner that reviews natural and mixed properties nominated to the World Heritage List.

<http://www.unausa.org/newindex.asp?place=http://www.unausa.org/policy/NewsActionAlerts/info/alspa3.asp>, accessed January 5, 2005.

23 Mann, Jim, "Dealing With Conspiracy Theories and Rumors Is No Walk in the Park," *Los Angeles Times*, September 2, 1966.

24 The text read: "America is "sovereign" soil that belongs to Americans; not the world! You will not confiscate our [*sic*] sacred soil without a battle . . . this is the bottom line! Your Treaty from hell will not succeed; for the Prince of Peace is Sovereign who will destroy you and your NEW WORLD ORDER! For God and Country, G. I. Jane P. S. Incidentally, with such a foreign-sounding name; where exactly is your native terrain; the Inferno, perhaps?"

25 *Supra*, Note 19.

26 During the period 1990–4, visitation to U.S. World Heritage parks increased 9.4 percent, as opposed to 4.2 percent for all national parks, and there is strong evidence that a significant part is derived from international tourism. Statement of Brooks B. Yeager. Note 17.

27 Newport, Rhode Island; Charleston, South Carolina; and Baltimore, Maryland are cases in point.

APPENDIX

Legal Resources for Protection of the Built Environment

INTERNATIONAL

The United Nations Educational Scientific and Cultural Organization (UNESCO) has an extensive Web site. Two areas have particular relevance for heritage law:

Legal instruments including conventions, recommendations, and declarations relating to culture may be found at: <http://portal.unesco.org/en/ev.php-URL_ID=13649&URL_DO=DO_TOPIC&URL_SECTION=-471.html>. The home page of the UNESCO World Heritage Centre is the logical beginning point for investigation of the World Heritage Convention: <http://whc.unesco.org/>.

The International Council on Monuments and Sites (ICOMOS) is an international nongovernmental organization of professionals, dedicated to the conservation of the world's historic monuments and sites: <http://www.vicomos.org/ICOMOS˙Main˙Page.html>

Other relevant ICOMOS pages include the ICOMOS Legal Committee: <http://www.icomos.org/iclafi/> and the ICOMOS Documentation Center: <http://www.international.icomos.org/centre_documentation/home_eng.htm>.

AUSTRALIA

Australian Department of Environment and Heritage, Heritage Laws and Notices: <http://www.deh.gov.au/about/legislation.html#legislation>.

CANADA

ICOMOS Canada includes links to information on Canadian heritage legislation, including the protection of heritage property, its development, and taxation of heritage and related development: <http://archive.canada.icomos.org/legis/04-.html.en>.

ENGLAND

English Heritage; follow the links to "Conserving Historic Places" and "Heritage Protection"; <http://www.english-heritage.org.uk/default.asp>.

SWEDEN, NORWAY, AND FINLAND

The national heritage administrations in the Nordic countries have Web pages in English relevant to preservation in their respective territories: Sweden, <www.raa.se>; Norway, <http://www.riksantikvaren.no/english>; and Finland, <http://www.nba.fi/en/>.

UNITED STATES

The Law Department of the National Trust for Historic Preservation is a key resource on preservation law and advocacy in the United States. Its Web site is: <http://www.nationaltrust.org/law/index.html>. The Legal Department has also produced a range of legal publications and the *Preservation Law Reporter*, a nationally recognized law journal.

The Advisory Council on Historic Preservation is an independent Federal agency that promotes the preservation, enhancement, and productive use of the United States' historic resources, and advises the President and Congress on national historic preservation policy. Its Web site contains information on the Federal historic preservation review process (Section 106) along with a synopsis and analysis of case law under Section 106: <www.achp.gov>.

Heritage Preservation Services, National Park Service, United States Department of the Interior Web site contains information on Federal programs for the protection of heritage properties. The home page of the site is: <http://www.cr.nps.gov/hps/>. A particularly useful page on the site provides links to laws, regulations, and standards pertaining to cultural resources: <http://www.cr.nps.gov/hps/laws/laws.htm>. Two online publications help explain the relationship between historic preservation and zoning and subdivisions regulations: Stephen A. Morris, *Subdivision Regulations and Historic Preservation*: <http://www2.cr.nps.gov/pad/partnership/Subdiv699.pdf> and *Zoning and Historic Preservation*: <http://www2.cr.nps.gov/pad/partnership/Zoning699.pdf>.

The National Conference of State Legislatures maintains a database on state historic preservation legislation: <http://www.ncsl.org/programs/arts/statehist.htm>. Caution: the database is current only through 1999.

The National Alliance of Preservation Commissions is the organization representing local government design review commissions in the United States. It is at the local level where the strongest protective legislation is enacted and administered. Their Web site is: <http://www.sed.uga.edu/pso/programs/napc/napc.htm>.

CHAPTER THIRTY-TWO

Cultural Heritage Legislation: The Historic Centre of Old Havana

María Margarita Suárez García

Since 1993, the historic centre of old Havana has undergone substantial changes as a result of the work carried out to restore and safeguard its social and cultural heritage. The organisation responsible for overseeing the work is the Office of the Historian of the City of Havana.

Covering an area of 2.1 square kilometres, the historic centre of Old Havana contains 3,744 buildings that greatly enhance the urban environment. Some 750 of these buildings have been declared heritage sites, which means that they are essential to the conservation of the authentic character of Cuban architecture and culture.

BACKGROUND

San Cristóbal de La Habana originally began as a settlement in the south-west of the island of Cuba in 1514, but the town was eventually established in 1519 on the northern coast of the island, close to the port of Carenas. The cabildo, or town council, a legal institution introduced by the Spaniards as an expression of justice, peace, and collective will, first met in the shade of a leafy ceiba tree. The first mass was also celebrated here, and both events were recorded in oils by the French painter Jean-Baptiste Vermay. The paintings are now displayed in a small neo-classical building that was built in the nineteenth century to commemorate these events.

Havana did not immediately grow into a major city because the surrounding countryside did not yield the hoped-for riches. Its development was rather the result of its magnificent coastal location. Its bay, which provided a fine natural harbor, and its strategic geographical position quickly made it an ideal port-of-call and rendezvous for Spanish galleons on their way to the mother country laden with treasures for the Crown. Later, the Spanish fleet would remain there for six months to defend its ships from constant attacks by privateers and pirates, hence the overwhelming need for the town to be fortified like no other in the West Indies.

Initially, three fortresses were built to defend Havana: La Real Fuerza, Los Tres Reyes del Morro, and San Salvador de la Punta, close to the sea wall. However, after the English captured the city, the defenses were shored up even further with the construction of new fortresses, watchtowers, and observation posts.

Havana differs from other eighteenth century colonial cities in Latin America in two basic respects: its system of large and small plazas that, combined with the irregular layout of the streets, create a unique cityscape, and its system of fortifications, without doubt the finest and most complex anywhere in Latin America. In the last century, the city has expanded, with the neighborhoods outside the city walls more heavily populated than those inside. Boulevards, parks, and large mansions were built to meet the needs of the Creole aristocracy.

During much of the nineteenth century, the city grew rapidly, especially on the eastern side, where new, exclusive districts sprang up, like Cerro and Vedado, and new architectural styles emerged. Later, residents moved away from the old town, and many of the fine old family houses were sold and put to other uses.

THE OFFICE OF THE HISTORIAN OF THE CITY OF HAVANA

Increased awareness of the importance of the historic centre and the need to conserve it is largely attributable to the existence of one institution, the Office of the Historian. Founded in 1938, the organisation can draw on many years of experience of protecting the old town.

The post of Historian of the City was created as long ago as 1925. The first Historian of the City was Dr. Emilio Roig de Leucheuring, appointed in recognition of the work he had already done to rescue and safeguard Cuba's cultural heritage, especially in Havana. Guided by the objectives outlined by Roig himself, namely, to foster the culture of Havana and encourage and assist in the promotion of that of Cuba and Latin America, and to act and plan in such a way as to involve the community, the Office of the Historian continues its work under the current Historian of the City, Dr. Eusebio Leal Spengler.

Until the twentieth century, there were no laws or regulations, nor any government support, for the protection of either movable or built heritage. Nevertheless, institutions and organisations made up of prominent intellectuals of the day, such as the National Council for Archaeology and Ethnology and the aforementioned Office of Historian of the City, fought tirelessly to protect the city's cultural and artistic heritage. Against this backdrop, the Commission for Monuments, Historic and Artistic Buildings and Sites of Havana was set up and the Historic, Architectural and Archaeological Monuments Bill was introduced in 1939.

After the triumph of the Cuban Revolution, the Department of Museums and Monuments of the National Council for Culture was created in 1959, and the real importance of the Office of the Historian for the safeguarding of Cuba's national, historical, and artistic heritage was fully recognised.

Later, in 1976, the Heritage Department of the Ministry of Culture was created. A programme of research and analysis was put in place to investigate and revitalise exceptional cultural properties in old Havana. The efforts to conserve and restore the built heritage, which began in the 1960s, were richly rewarded in 1978, when old Havana was added to the list of National Monuments.

In 1981, the Cuban government provided funds to the Office of the Historian to allow the process of restoring the historic centre to be speeded up. This move, as well as the quality of the cultural property in the old town, led UNESCO to declare it a World Heritage Site in 1982, occupying twenty-seventh place on the World Heritage List.

The major impact of the collapse of the Soviet Union and other socialist states in Europe at the beginning of the 1990s was soon felt in Cuba, where the national economy took a downturn. Until that time, the Cuban government had subsidised the restoration of the historic centre from the central budget, but now the need to prioritise the use of what little resources were available for more sensitive and vital sectors made it completely impossible to continue this support. However, this did not mean that the responsibility for saving the cultural heritage belonging to the Cuban people, as well as to humanity as a whole, would be ignored.

Following the grave situation in the first half of the 1990s, Cuba has experienced sustained recovery. As a result, even at the most difficult moments of the crisis, the Cuban government decided to give the Office of the Historian legal backing to enable the restoration and preservation of the historic centre to continue.

HERITAGE LEGISLATION AND THE HISTORIC CENTRE

The district that has come to be known as the historic centre of the city of Havana is made up of the whole of the municipality of old Havana, and parts of various adjacent municipalities such as Central Havana, Regla, and East Havana. It has enjoyed the status of a National Monument since 1978 and has been a National Heritage Site since 1979. It was designated a World Heritage Site in 1982, a Priority Conservation Zone in 1993, and a Zone of Special Significance to Tourism in 1995.

The area is protected by a special set of laws that is independent of the standard provisions of national and international law and that has been sanctioned and established by the state and by local legal provisions enacted especially for the city of Havana and the municipalities it embraces.

LAW NO. 1: PROTECTION OF CULTURAL PROPERTY LAW OF 4 AUGUST 1977

This Law lays down which assets should be considered part of the cultural heritage of the Cuban nation because of their special archaeological, prehistoric, historic, literary, educational, artistic, scientific, or general cultural relevance. In addition, it establishes appropriate measures for their protection.

The Law also provides for the creation of the Register of Cultural Assets of the Republic of Cuba, which is maintained by the Ministry of Culture. All assets covered by the Law may only be removed from Cuban territory with the express permission of the Ministry of Culture.

The principal legal implications of the status of cultural heritage of the Cuban nation are: the legal recognition of assets as being of public value and social interest, the establishment of a system of protection by legal, institutional, and technical means against such events as might endanger their survival, and the imposition of various levels of restriction as to the rights to their use and/or enjoyment.

LAW NO. 2: NATIONAL AND LOCAL MONUMENTS LAW OF 4 AUGUST 1977

This Law regards as a national monument any historic town centre, building, site, or object that, because of its exceptional nature, is worthy of conservation for its cultural, historical, or social significance, and has been designated as such by the National Monuments Commission.

Likewise, local monument status applies to any building, site, or object that combines the necessary conditions to be conserved for its cultural, historical, or social interest to a specific locality and has also been designated as such by the National Monuments Commission.

This Law thus gives the National Monuments Commission, which is attached to the Ministry of Culture, and the Provincial Monuments Commissions, which are attached to the cultural sections of the executive committees of the provincial assemblies, the authority to act under the technical and methodological supervision of the Ministry of Culture.

Designation as a national monument legally implies that the property in question is recognised as being of social interest and is subject to special regulations. These regulations primarily concern planning and building restrictions, the control and supervision of such monuments, and the exercise of ownership and other rights.

CONVENTION CONCERNING THE PROTECTION OF THE WORLD CULTURAL AND NATURAL HERITAGE

The principal objective of the Convention concerning the Protection of the World Cultural and Natural Heritage, which was adopted by the General Conference of UNESCO on 16 November 1972, is the establishment of an international system for the protection of the world's cultural and natural heritage against the traditional causes of decay, as well as those arising from changing social and economic conditions.

The World Heritage Convention was ratified by the Cuban government in March 1981 and came into force in Cuba on 24 June of the same year. It was not until 14 December 1982, however, that old Havana and its fortifications were granted their status as a World Heritage Site, introducing special regulations to protect the area.

The special status of old Havana, together with Cuba's concomitant accession to the World Heritage Convention, has a number of implications. First of all, the Cuban government is obliged to protect, conserve, and restore the area – single-handedly and using the maximum resources available – and to hand it on to future generations. In addition, it must undertake to pursue a general policy that enables old Havana to function as an integral part of community life. It must ensure that the protection of the area is taken into consideration in all urban planning, and it must conduct and encourage scientific, technical, and methodological studies and research to deal with any dangers threatening the area. Furthermore, the government is obliged to adopt suitable legal, scientific, technical, administrative, and financial measures to protect the area, to conserve, restore, and rehabilitate old Havana, and to do everything possible, for example, through educational programmes, to encourage those living there to respect and appreciate their environment.

LAW NO. 143: DECREE CONCERNING THE OFFICE OF THE HISTORIAN OF THE CITY OF HAVANA OF 30 OCTOBER 1993

This Decree designates the historic centre as a Priority Conservation Area, while Resolution No. 38 of 11 August 1997 of the Ministry of Finance legally implements a Special Taxation Regime for old Havana.

This Decree is significant in so far as it extends the authority of the Office of the Historian and confirms its status as a legally constituted cultural institution with a staff that is qualified to obtain the financial resources necessary for the restoration and conservation of the historic centre of Havana and an administrative arrangement through which it is able to supervise planning and manage the collection of taxes.

Another important aspect of this Decree is that it defines two areas of activity and competence of the Office of the Historian. The first is cultural and relates to the whole of the city of Havana. The second is cultural and administrative and relates to the historic centre.

AGREEMENT NO. 2951: A ZONE OF SPECIAL SIGNIFICANCE TO TOURISM

The Agreement of the Council of Ministers of the Republic of Cuba of 21 September 1995 grants the historic centre of Havana the status of a zone of special significance to tourism. It also extends the remit of the Office of the Historian, establishing a special administrative regime for housing and laying down rules covering the intervention of the Office in other administrative issues affecting the zone.

Other Means of Protecting Cultural Heritage

In addition to the laws, decrees, and regulations to protect cultural property in the historic centre, the Cultural Heritage Department of the Office of the Historian is engaged in a cultural project involving the 28 cultural institutions that form the Association of Museums and Specialist Institutions. The underlying premise of this activity is the importance of education as a major and determining factor in the protection of Cuba's heritage.

The basic objectives of this project are, *inter alia*, to contribute to the knowledge of Cuba's history and culture, to uncover and preserve material and spiritual expressions of Cuban nationhood in the cultural property that is in its care, to create materials and methods to teach and inform the population about tangible and intangible heritage, and to plan and carry out activities to help improve the emotional and cultural life of the community, particularly of its most vulnerable groups. With this in mind, a range of educational programmes that target different age groups and sections of the population has been created to encourage people to learn about and understand the significance of the movable and built heritage in the historic centre and to become actively involved in its preservation and protection.

One element of this project is an unique experimental programme known as "classrooms in the museum." The idea for this programme emerged when it became clear that the restoration work in the historic centre would affect the surrounding neighbourhoods, and that there was a need to improve the teaching environment of the primary schools and involve schoolchildren in the process of rehabilitating the historic centre. Their involvement is now a central aspect of the campaign to preserve the memory of old Havana and contribute to the educational, social, and cultural development of the children that live there with their families. This marks a break with traditional methods and also enriches the educational work of the museums and of the museologists, specialists, and teachers.

As a result of the fact that their lessons are conducted in classrooms inside the museum, the children have taken a greater interest in the museum itself. Discipline and concentration have improved and the lessons are more effective. The pupils acquire new knowledge as they become familiar with the museum collections, and their aesthetic awareness increases, enriching them spiritually and emotionally. Ensuring the future protection of Cuba's heritage by involving children in this novel experiment is just one aspect of the efforts of the Office of the Historian to conserve and safeguard Cuba's heritage.

PART FIVE

A Consideration of Cultural and Natural Heritage Guidelines Applicable to Infrastructure Projects, Mining Operations, and Their Financing

Illicit traffic in cultural property is not the only cause of the loss of national and international cultural heritage. Many aspects of economic development, urban sprawl, and exponential population growth also threaten our cultural legacy. In 1987, the World Bank issued a technical paper, entitled "The Management of Cultural Property in World Bank Assisted Projects: Archaeological, Historical, Religious and Natural Unique Sites" (World Bank Technical Paper No WTP 62, hereafter, "Bank Paper"). The Bank Paper analogizes the crisis of cultural property loss to that of decreasing biological diversity and identifies construction activities related to large public works, such as dams and reservoirs, large irrigation or other agricultural works, transportation corridors, and urban development as the agents most often responsible.

The World Bank and the International Finance Corporation (IFC) have developed a series of very specific standards and guidelines relating to cultural resource conservation, environmental protection, and related issues (for example, the relocation of people displaced by development projects). These policies include: the World Bank policy on Management of Cultural Property in Bank-financed Projects (September 1986), IFC General Environmental Guidelines (July 1998), the World Bank policy on Involuntary Resettlement (December 2001), and the World Bank Resettlement Sourcebook (2004).

According to its policy pertaining to cultural property, the World Bank will assist in the preservation of cultural property, and seek to avoid its elimination, and will not finance projects that will significantly damage nonreplicable cultural property, assisting only those projects that are sited or designed so as to prevent such damage.

Many of the actors involved in advising or representing private businesses, nongovernmental organisations, and local groups in private–public partnerships in the cultural heritage sector or in the development of travel and tourism projects in developing countries may already have had experience with the imposition of such preservation and sustainability standards. Nevertheless, the use of the lender – often the most powerful actor at the negotiating table – as a source of environmental and cultural heritage controls is not sufficiently exploited, if at all. The specific standards, guidelines, and checklists of the World Bank and the IFC can serve as a reference for public and private lending and funding communities and their attorneys in addressing cultural heritage issues in project finance agreements.

Lawyers serving clients in the fields of banking, business, cultural heritage and travel and tourism development, or representing nongovernmental organizations or other groups that have an interest in preservation and sustainability issues in relation to development projects, ought to be fully acquainted with the standards of the World Bank, the IFC, and other global financial institutions. Even if a cultural heritage project does not involve any of these institutions, the criteria they have established can still be adopted by a local bank or financing agency. As Joseph Harbaugh, Dean of the Nova Law School, has stated, "by including high standards of preservation and sustainability in the lending documents and deal instruments, the lender encourages project leaders to do what's 'right' and, at the same time, supports the successful completion of the project."

As several of the contributors in this book argue, preservation rather than the destruction of cultural property is more likely to generate economic benefits. Tourism, for example, represents a considerable percentage of income and foreign exchange in Latin America, the Caribbean, and Asia.

In the 1987 Technical Paper the World Bank identified positive trends in the incorporation of sustainability and cultural property policy in World Bank loan agreements.

"First, the incorporation of cultural material as a central aspect of a tourism project (as in Honduras – Tourism Development, or Jordan – Tourism) reflects the ability of the Bank and its borrowers to recognize and capitalize on the importance of cultural phenomena. This process promotes and ensures the survival of an historical monument by linking its future to the future of the country. These factors show the Bank's and the borrower's interest in, and willingness to promote, the cultural, historical, and artistic characteristics of the country. Success of such projects also helps to promote the view that cultural property is a potential source of income through tourism.

Second, in projects where a cultural survey was included as part of an environmental assessment, the effect of the project on potential cultural sites was determined early.

Third, although the archaeological components of Bank-financed projects have not always been carried out according to ideal archaeological standards (that is, complete, careful excavation, and preservation), they have at least been realistic. If the site was to be destroyed, time was allowed to survey and excavate. It is commendable that many of these projects also incorporated preservation, restoration, interpretation, and promotion of the archaeological artifacts and findings.

Fourth, the use of local (in-country) experts working with international specialists was effective. This practice allowed for the local people's involvement and expedited the overall project.

Finally, all the projects examined exhibited a sense of urgency; this recognition of the immediate loss of a non-renewable cultural resource reflected positively on project design.

Those in the lending sector as well as those charged with cultural heritage management may also consider the following excerpts from the World Bank's Technical Paper:

> Economic development should preserve and encourage the study of cultural property for five main reasons. First, the destruction of a site is irreversible. The stock of sites comprising a country's cultural heritage is unique and non-renewable; once destroyed or otherwise desecrated, the sites cannot be replaced.... The second reason is that a knowledge and understanding of a people's past can help present inhabitants to develop and sustain national identity and to appreciate the value of their own culture and heritage.... Third, each site has its own intrinsic value in the scientific study of the nature and development of the earth, its life, and civilization. Often only an experienced scientist will be able to recognize an important archaeological, historical, religious, or natural site.... The fourth reason is that development of cultural properties can have significant benefits for a nation's tourism industry. Surveys taken by the American Express Company have indicated that up to 50 percent of tourists make their destination decisions in large part because of their interest in visiting archaeological, historical, and natural attractions. The fifth, and possibly most relevant, reason to address cultural property concerns is that its preservation and study can be very useful in the successful design of present and future economic development projects.... For example, the thousand-year-old irrigation systems of Sri Lanka greatly aided in the design of the modern system and helped prevent errors. Knowledge of how the Mayan terraces, ancient raised fields, and irrigation works enabled that civilization to thrive in regions now considered marginal could greatly assist in devising sustainable agro-ecological development there. Similarly, the results of a UNESCO-backed study of 2,000-year-old techniques that enabled farms to flourish in Libya in Roman times may help (re)establish successful farms in parts of dryland North Africa.... The corollary is equally important. Archaeological studies can help us to understand why societies or civilizations changed, failed, or disappeared. Sedimentation of Mesopotamian irrigation works and the complete deforestation of Easter Island are cases in point.

And:

> Culturally significant areas and important archaeological sites are found all over the world. Clearly, it is not feasible to preserve every area or structure or to recover, document, and maintain detailed information on every archaeological find. The single-sheet 'Cultural Property Survey Form'... that describes the area's salient cultural aspects, however, is easily coded and stored. The need to systematically survey and record findings cannot be overemphasized. The procedural guidelines for the survey, salvage, excavation, or preservation of an archaeological site or culturally significant area are simple:
>
> (a) Never destroy before a professional survey is done;
> (b) Always survey, even if it is thought that nothing of cultural significance is present;
> (c) Treat every cultural site and artifact as a finite resource that can never be replaced;
> (d) Report all cultural discoveries to the responsible authorities;
> (e) Never dig an archaeological site or attempt to rehabilitate or preserve an important historical building or religious shrine without professional assistance.
>
> The guidelines and the suggestions outlined in this report, combined with an effort to work with the host country in the future of its cultural resources, should allow for the proper treatment and salvage of a significant number of the cultural sites encountered in future projects. Adherence to these principles and policies will ensure successful cooperation of the Bank, the borrower, archaeologists, and cultural experts to preserve at least a sample of the country's cultural patrimony.
>
> Not only will this cooperation promote preservation of important historical and religious structures, scenic or sacred natural areas, and valuable scientific information, it will also improve the economic development process, assist developing nations, and serve to enhance the quality of the Bank's and the borrower's investments.

Significant financial resources must be made available to preserve the cultural heritage of humanity. Innovative new forms of partnership for natural and cultural heritage by lenders and other actors are required to create the financial, institutional, and legal infrastructures adequate to this urgent task.

CHAPTER THIRTY-THREE

The World Bank's Policy on Physical Cultural Resources

Charles E. Di Leva

GLOBAL CONTEXT

There has been strong and renewed interest in the World Bank and the international community in preserving the world's physical cultural resources. With the end of the twentieth century, the international development community expanded its commitment to identify and protect the world's cultural properties. Of the 690 sites currently included on the World Heritage List, 370 sites were added between 1990 and 2000. Approximately fifty-five percent of these new sites are located in the countries of World Bank borrowers. In a recent publication, the World Bank identified the importance of incorporating physical cultural resources into its overall development strategy, stating:

> The increased recognition now being given to culture is part of the broad changes that have taken place in development thinking in the 1990s generally. Today, the World Bank is promoting a more encompassing development paradigm, as outlined in the Comprehensive Development Framework (CDF), which places the inducement of economic growth within its social context. This is why the Bank now recognizes, and advances the idea, that the cultural sector contributes to effective economic growth rather than just consuming budgetary resources. Furthermore, developmental assistance is not a narrow pursuit of economic growth alone but aims at broad social development. Culture and cultural heritage cannot be left out of development assistance programs. The Bank's deepening grasp of what makes nations prosper leads, among other initiatives, to including investments for culture in development lending.[1]

Unfortunately, successful management of physical cultural resources in many situations has been inhibited by inadequate resources from the global community. This unfortunate scarcity follows from the allocation of limited resources by governments, civil society, and international institutions to other commitments they appear to view with higher priority. For example, international institutions have channeled their resources with a focus on poverty reduction, health, and education as set forth in the Millennium Development Goals (MDGs).[2] In September 2000, the leaders of 189 member states of the United Nations (UN) unanimously adopted fundamental principles of developmental needs in the UN Millennium Declaration. Following the Millennium Declaration, the MDGs were developed by the UNs Secretariat along with the World Bank, the Organization for Economic Cooperation and Development, and the International Monetary Funds (IMF) to harmonize reporting on the development goals set forth in the declaration. The MDGs initiative aspires to reduce by half the number of people living in poverty and without access to basic needs such as water. More specifically, they establish precedent-setting specific targets to achieve a more sustainable world.

Moreover, the international community's recognition of the demand for critical infrastructure has required more funds for construction of roads and other facilities. It has become apparent that private-sector support for infrastructure services in the poorest countries has been flagging, falling from $128 billion in 1997, to $58 billion in 2002 (although this seems to have increased somewhat during fiscal year 2003).[3] As a result, the World Bank intends to increase its project lending for infrastructure. More than this, governments have directed funding to enhance national security and to finance the war on terrorism.

WORLD BANK CONTEXT

In the aftermath of the Second World War, along with the creation of Bretton-Woods organizations, there was a limited degree of focus on restoring the world's cultural property. Ironically, this prevailing sentiment did not find authoritative force in any particular policy instrument. It would be nearly three decades before the entry into force of the 1972 UNESCO Convention Concerning the Protection of the World Cultural and Natural Heritage (World Heritage Convention), which is the key international document defining and supporting cultural heritage. More than 160 of the World Bank's member states are parties to the convention, and the World Bank's lending operations are guided by the policy that such lending shall not contravene the borrower's treaty obligations or national laws.[4] At the national level, many member countries also have laws to protect physical cultural resources. Generally, these national laws prescribe specific conduct in the course of development activities, which include: (1) requiring

[1] World Bank, Middle East and North Africa Region, *Cultural Heritage and Development: A Framework for Action in the Middle East and North Africa*, p. 3 (World Bank 2001).

[2] The eight MDGs address extreme poverty, hunger, primary education, rights of women, child mortality, maternal health, combating pandemic disease, ensuring environmental sustainability, and developing a global partnership for development. The eighteen specific targets established to meet the MDGs include halving the number of people on abject poverty and hunger, reducing mortality in children under five by two-thirds, and halving and beginning to reverse the spread of acquired immunodeficiency syndrome and the incidence of malaria.

[3] The World Bank, *INFRASTRUCTURE SERVICES* (Sept. 2003).

[4] Borrowers of World Bank funds have to be members to the World Bank and IMF.

the performance of surveys that account for physical cultural properties, (2) demanding the stoppage of construction work upon the discovery of antiquities, and (3) encouraging mitigation in case of chance finds.

The World Bank is the first development bank to incorporate the international community's commitment of protecting physical cultural resources into its operations. Approximately 250 Bank funded projects have included at least a component of physical cultural resources. Equally important, the Bank has supported thirty-five stand-alone projects with funding between $300 and $400 million, including such examples as a five million dollar loan to Georgia and a $172,000 grant to Albania for ensuring the management and maintenance of physical cultural resources.

Beyond the international and domestic legal frameworks that preserve and manage physical cultural resources, the World Bank set out to develop its own internal policies. Initially, Operation Policy Note 11.03, "Managing Cultural Properties in Bank Financed Projects," was prepared, recommending certain measures devised to avoid harm to physical cultural properties in the undertaking of any World Bank-financed project. It was the adoption of the Environmental Assessment guidelines that first formalized a policy tool that supported physical cultural resources. In 1989, the World Bank developed a policy on Environmental Assessment, as well as an Environmental Assessment Sourcebook for the use of Bank staff and borrowers, incorporating considerations of PCRs through precautionary measures and proper management. Among other environmental and social concerns, the Environmental Assessment policy addressed issues of Indigenous Peoples, Natural Habitats, and Involuntary Resettlement. The new policy on Environmental Assessment implicitly encouraged review of potential impacts to physical cultural resources and development of mitigation plans to avoid and/or minimize damage to these values.

The Bank has continued to pursue a more definitive operational guideline to underscore the importance of protecting Physical Cultural Resources through the preparation of a draft operational policy that will soon be presented to the Bank's Board of Executive Directors for their consideration and approval. Concurrently, we can further point to the Bank's commitment to Physical Cultural Resources through its efforts with other multilateral development banks to harmonize approaches toward environmental and social safeguard policies, including cultural resources, as well as the collaboration between the World Bank and the International Finance Corporation in its promotion and support of the Equator Principles, which have been adopted by more than 25 commercial banks and include provision for the evaluation of physical cultural resources in the environmental assessment process.

Reflecting on the governing document for the World Bank's previous work with a cultural heritage component, Operation Policy Note (OPN) 11.03 "Managing Cultural Property in World Bank-Financed Projects" asserted and presented a general set of principles and guidelines in preserving physical cultural resources.[5] The over-arching objective of the policy was to "do no harm" with regard to cultural properties. This was stated by noting that projects should be planned in a manner to recognize and support important cultural sites. The note emphasized several other issues: (1) the World Bank should assist in the preservation and seek to avoid the elimination of the cultural properties; (2) if any significant damage of cultural sites were to be a product of the project activities, then the Bank should scale back its funding of the project; (3) Bank lending would provide training on the protection and management of Physical Cultural Resources; (4) if the World Bank is providing any financing, then the principle of preserving Physical Cultural Resources applies, despite the financing of the cultural component by another entity; and (5) Bank staff should support identification of all cultural property issues, although the borrower has the primary responsibility to protect Physical Cultural Resources that would be affected by project activities. Overarching the Note's recommendations is the commitment to the principle that the World Bank should "do no harm" in carrying out its development planning and financing of projects around the globe.

The move toward the development of a new policy for "physical cultural resources" was made more concrete in 1999. At that time, the World Bank's Board of Executive Directors identified a need for the Bank's Operation Evaluation Department (OED) to assess Bank work in the field to bring the lessons of experience with cultural heritage to bear on the revisions of OPN 11.03. Importantly, the OED study called attention to a perceived weakness of the OPN in its lack of a clear "do good" affirmative obligation with regard to preserving and managing cultural heritage. "The ambiguous approach to cultural heritage has led to high variability in Bank-financed work."[6]

OPN 11.03 and the World Bank's approach place the primary responsibility for management of cultural assets on the borrower. Borrowers, however, have often not recognized the economic and other values of Physical Cultural Resources to development. Moreover, institutional capacity in protecting and managing Physical Cultural Resources remains notably weak. There is a need to revive legal and institutional structures under which development projects proceed and it remains important for implementing agencies to involve members from the ministries of antiquities in the project planning and implementation process.

In the future, the World Bank will continue to expand its partnerships, which will foster Physical Cultural Resources commitments and establish synergies to expand on preservation initiatives. To a very important extent, this will include ensuring a demonstration to often-impoverished local communities of the link between poverty reduction and the effort

[5] OPN 11.03 was converted to Operational Policy 4.11 (August 1999) to fit with the new format of World Bank Operational Policies and Bank Procedures.

[6] World Bank, Operations Evaluation Department, *Cultural Properties in Policy and Practice: A Review of World Bank Experience*, p. vii. (World Bank 2001).

to preserve physical cultural resources. This is especially so given the difficulty in demonstrating any increase in overall overseas development assistance.

STRATEGY

Although it is clear that the World Bank and other members of the development community need to continue to ensure projects do not harm physical cultural resources, we also need to improve the institutional capacity of national, ministries and agencies, and train their staff in how better to preserve and manage these historic resources. More must be done to incorporate the principle and practice the management of cultural resources in regional, national, and local development strategies. There is an increase in demand from World Bank members throughout the world for support in this area. In the Bank's Middle East and North Africa Region, a framework for action demonstrates that those nations agree that cultural resources contribute to growth. For example, the Moroccan Country Assistance Strategy encourages investment in decaying urban historic enclaves. Interest in these issues also exists in the Africa Region, Europe and Central Asia Region, East Asia and Pacific Region. Most importantly, the President of the World Bank, James D. Wolfenson, has remained heavily involved on this issue.

NEW OPERATIONAL POLICY

The World Bank is drafting a new operational policy entitled "Physical Cultural Resources." The new draft policy will emphasize the important link for cultural resources as economic and social assets. The policy continues to apply to all components of a project whether or not it is receiving direct funding from the World Bank. The policy will address impacts and mitigation measures through the use of the Environmental Assessment process. The policy requires both an overall management plan and a plan for the management of chance finds. Importantly, the policy will also require assessment of the status of relevant national laws and their coverage of cultural resources.

It is expected that this new draft policy will be presented to the World Bank's Board of Directors early in 2005. The World Bank has made this draft policy publicly available and is appreciative of the members of the public who submitted comments on the draft. Those comments have all been considered in the process of finalizing the new World Bank policy on Physical Cultural Resources.

USEFUL LINKS

World Bank Operational Policy on Indigenous Peoples
http://wbln0018.worldbank.org/Institutional/Manuals/OpManual.nsf/0/0F7D6F3F04DD70398525672C007D08ED?OpenDocument

World Bank Operational Policy on Natural Habitats
http://lnweb18.worldbank.org/ESSD/sdvext.nsf/52ByDocName/NaturalHabitats

World Bank Operational Policy on Involuntary Resettlement
http://lnweb18.worldbank.org/ESSD/sdvext.nsf/52ByDocName/InvoluntaryResettlement

World Bank Operational Policy on Cultural Property
http://lnweb18.worldbank.org/ESSD/sdvext.nsf/52ByDocName/CulturalProperty

World Bank Operational Policy on Environmental Assessment
http://wbln0018.worldbank.org/Institutional/Manuals/OpManual.nsf/0/9367A2A9D9DAEED38525672C007D0972?OpenDocument

CONTRIBUTOR'S NOTE[7]

Founded in 1944, the World Bank Group is one of the world's largest sources of development assistance. The Bank, which provided US$19.5 billion in loans to its client countries in fiscal year 2002, is now working in more than 100 developing economies, bringing a mix of finance and ideas to improve living standards and eliminate the worst forms of poverty. For each of its clients, the Bank works with government agencies, nongovernmental organisations, and the private sector to formulate assistance strategies. Its country offices worldwide deliver the Bank's program in countries, liaise with government and civil society, and work to increase understanding of development issues. The World Bank is owned by 184 member countries whose views and interests are represented by a Board of Governors and a Washington-based Board of Directors. Member countries are shareholders who carry ultimate decision-making power in the World Bank.

The International Finance Corporation (IFC) promotes private sector investment, both foreign and domestic, in developing member countries. Its investment and advisory activities are designed to reduce poverty and improve people's lives in an environmentally and socially responsible manner. Its work includes activities in some of the riskiest sectors and countries. The IFC serves as an investor and an honest broker to balance each party's interest in a transaction, reassuring foreign investors, local partners, other creditors, and government authorities. The IFC advises businesses entering new markets and governments trying to provide a more hospitable business environment to create effective and stable financial markets or to privatise inefficient state enterprises. The IFC does continue to fund tourism projects. For example, see Project Report 10851, Abercrombie and Kent Hotels and Resorts: "This is a Category B project, according to IFC's Procedure for Environmental and Social Review of Projects because a limited number of specific environmental [and social] impacts may result which can be avoided or mitigated by adhering to generally recognised performance standards, guidelines or design criteria. The review of this project consisted of appraising technical and environmental[/social] information submitted by the project sponsor . . ." (27 April 2001). See the IFC's Environmental and Social Policies, available at http://www.ifc.org.

World Bank policy on Management of Cultural Property in Bank-financed Projects (September 1986). Other

[7] J. Harbaugh, "Committee Y Abstract," IBA Cancun, November 2001.

specific safeguard policies of the Bank apply to particular situations. Where the "natural unique" category of cultural property contains natural habitat, rare or endangered living species, or other sources of biological diversity (for example, the Galapagos Islands), the Bank's policy on Natural Habitats will also apply. Where the cultural property in question is a tribal sacred site, the Bank's policy on Management of Cultural Property in Bank-financed Projects and the policy on Indigenous Peoples are applicable. The preservation and handling of cultural property encountered in the Bank's work are important subsets of the broad environmental concerns addressed in the Bank's policy on Environmental Assessment. The Bank's safeguard policy, Management of Cultural Property in Bank-financed Projects, is soon to be reissued under the title Physical Cultural Resources. This policy will be implemented as an integral part of the Environmental Impact Assessment process.

CHAPTER THIRTY-FOUR

BTC Pipeline Project and the Preservation of Cultural Heritage

Gary Paulson

Large-scale construction and infrastructure projects may impact the communities in which they are constructed, in both positive and negative ways. Economic effects, both positive and negative, are often the subject of inquiry and discussion. Possible influence or impact on the environment in those communities – air, water and soil – is often the subject of study. Less focus has typically been placed on reviewing the cultural and natural heritage of regions in which these projects are undertaken. This chapter addresses one current oil industry pipeline project, its relation to the cultural heritage of the affected regions, and the relevance of the recent World Bank guidelines for such projects.

The World Bank intends to issue in summer, 2005, revised guidelines for the assessment of the impact of Bank-funded projects on cultural heritage. This Policy requires that applicants for such funding should develop a planning process that provides:

- for early consideration of cultural resources that might be impacted by the project (Section 4.11, Paragraph 5)
- for a preliminary investigation to identify likely major impacts on cultural resources (Section 4.11, Paragraph 7)
- for a plan to identify physical cultural resources likely to be affected by the project and an assessment of the project's potential impacts on those resources (Section 4.11, Paragraph 10)
- for a plan to mitigate anticipated adverse impacts on cultural resources, which should be created in consultation with project-affected groups (Section 4.11, Paragraph 11)
- for a management plan that should include measures for mitigating adverse impacts, a provision for the management of "chance finds" during the construction phase, and a monitoring system to track progress of these activities (Section 4.11, Paragraph 13)
- and also suggests that the borrower should consult in a timely manner with key groups (Section 4.11, Paragraph 14) and that the findings of the cultural resources investigation and assessment should be disclosed, except where borrower determines that disclosure might jeopardize the safety or integrity of the cultural resources involved (Section 4.11, Paragraph 16).

Although the project to be discussed herein was largely planned prior to the enactment of these World Bank guidelines, BP and other project sponsors, as will be seen, adopted a plan and process that meet, and often exceed, the requirements of the World Bank guidelines.

A consortium of state-owned and private companies, including BP, is currently constructing a large pipeline that will, when completed, move crude oil to market from newly discovered fields in the Caspian Sea. This pipeline will ultimately stretch to some 1,760 kilometers from Azerbaijan through Georgia to Turkey. The pipeline begins in the City of Baku, Azerbaijan on the Caspian Sea, passes east to a point near the town of Tbilisi, Georgia, and has its terminus in the port of Ceyhan, Turkey on the Mediterranean Sea – thus, the pipeline is often referred to as the BTC Pipeline.

Planning work on the pipeline began in 1995. Construction began in the year 2003 and proceeded at a fast pace. The BTC pipeline was inaugurated on May 25, 2005 in a ceremony presided over by President Ilham Aliyev of the Azerbaijan Republic, President Mikhail Saakashvilli of Georgia, President Ahmet Sezer of Turkey and President Nursaltan Nazarbayev of Kazakhstan at the Sangachal terminal, near Baku. The BTC partners have contributed more than $100 millon to community investment, environmental and cultural heritage protection programmes among 454 communities along the pipeline's route. At current oil prices the major oil and gas fields and pipelines will provide revenues to Azerbaijan, Georgia and Turkey of more than $150 billion between 2005 and 2024.

This is an enormous project and an enormous pipeline. It is a $2.9 billion investment intended to unlock a vast store of energy from the Caspian Sea by providing a new crude oil pipeline from Azerbaijan, through Georgia to Turkey for onward delivery to world markets. The pipeline diameter will be up to forty-six inches, almost large enough for a human to stand in its interior. Its capacity will be one million barrels per day, with the oil, at capacity, moving at the speed of approximately two meters per second.

The route of the pipeline proceeds from sea level in the Caspian and ascends to an altitude of approximately 2,800 meters and thence again to sea level on the Mediterranean. The terrain encountered varies greatly, from open plains to very mountainous sections. Through June 2004, approximately 85% of the pipeline had been substantially completed. The pace of the project is impressive. In June 2004 alone, more than 175 kilometers of pipeline right-of-way were opened, 170 kilometers of pipe joints were welded, and some 138 kilometers of pipeline were backfilled.

This pipeline will, when completed, constitute the first direct pipeline link between the land-locked Caspian Sea and the Mediterranean Sea. It will bring many positive economic advantages to the region. Currently, some 14,000 locally

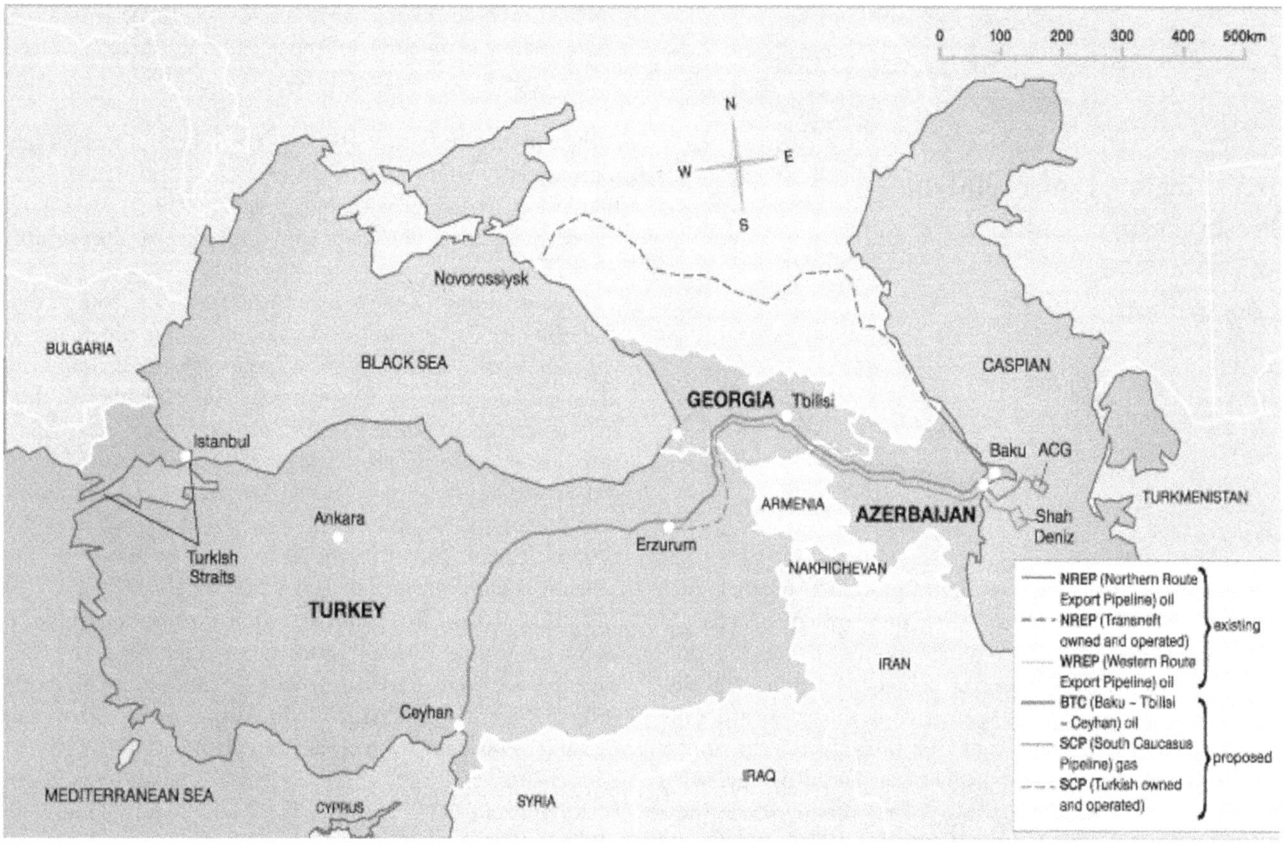

Figure 34.1. Project Area.

employed workers are engaged in work upon the pipeline. Substantial programs of social and environmental investment have been entered into that will ensure that peoples of the three host nations will share in the benefit of the pipeline. Completion of the pipeline will avoid increasing oil tanker traffic through the vulnerable Turkish straits and thus result in a substantial lessening of environmental risk.

As part-and-parcel of the BTC planning process, each of the three host governments (Azeri Republic, Georgia, and Turkey) required a comprehensive assessment of the environmental and social impacts associated with the construction and operation of the pipeline. Three separate but coordinated and complimentary Environmental and Social Impact Assessments (ESIAs) were completed to cover the length of the pipeline. Their preparation involved in-depth discussions with many different groups and organizations, including individual landowners, communities living near the pipeline route, governmental bodies, and nongovernmental organizations, a wide range of environmental specialists, archaeologists, and other academics.

The ESIAs run to many thousands of pages and cover a variety of topics. For the purpose of this chapter, we limit our discussion to a single topic, namely, the ways in which the pipeline consortium has dealt with the need to ensure protection of the substantial cultural heritage of these fascinating regions.

The route of the BTC (Figure 34.1) pipeline traverses many areas that are rich in cultural and archaeological heritage. It has been said that this region may be the longest continually inhabited land in the world. Architectural monuments and buried archaeological sites abound. Thus, the scale and scope of the project brings with it the potential for cultural heritage impact of the type contemplated in the World Bank guidelines.

Traces of prehistoric man may be found in many areas throughout the regions to be impacted by the construction of the BTC pipeline. The route of the pipeline traverses an area close to the Gobustan Reserve, located some 54 kilometers southwest of Baku. This area and its ancient rock carvings provide striking evidence of how early humans interacted with their environment, perhaps even as far back as 5,000–10,000 years ago. Although the archaeological and cultural wonders of Gobustan have been known for many years (in fact, petroglyphs of ancient boats there inspired the late Norwegian anthropologist Thor Heyerdahl to construct boats of balsa wood, papyrus, and marsh reeds for his famous transoceanic voyages). But for professional and amateur archaeologists alike, Azerbaijan, including much of the Gobustan Preserve, is still very much virgin territory where present day researchers have barely begun to scratch the archaeological surface. Opportunities abound to examine early human development, beginning with the Ice Age and the dawn of civilization up to the point at which humans began to settle down from Nomadic hunter–gatherer societies into an agriculture-based lifestyles requiring less frequent relocations.

The cultural heritage wealth in Georgia, alone, is exceptional. It is an archaeological treasure trove that enshrines *homo erectus* sites dating back some 1.5 million years. The oldest hominid remains found in Eurasia to date were discovered in Dmanisi, Georgia, approximately 40 kilometers from the BTC pipeline route. The region's archaeological sites and monuments are sometimes the only records that exist of the people and cultures that produced them.

The BTC owners and partners, together with the host governments, clearly identified preservation of this rich cultural and archaeological treasure as a high priority in the planning of the pipeline. As outlined hereinafter, the BTC pipeline project created a very substantial process to ensure the discovery, protection, and preservation of cultural and archaeological assets that might be impacted or threatened by pipeline construction. These protections were largely put in place prior to the enactment of the World Bank guidelines, but are fully in accord with the spirit and intent of the guidelines.

PRECONSTRUCTION PHASE

During the planning stages, the BTC consortium developed and is now implementing a multi-million-dollar Cultural Heritage Management Plan that ensured that valuable archaeological sites and architectural monuments along the pipeline right-of-way would be located, evaluated, preserved, and protected. BP teamed up with experts from the Centre for Archaeological Studies, the Georgia governmental agency responsible for archaeology and monuments; The Institute of Archaeology and Ethnography in Azerbaijan; and the Ministry of Culture in Turkey, to execute this Cultural Heritage Management Plan.

In the year 2000, a survey was conducted, in accordance with the ESIAs and the Cultural Heritage Management Plan, which was aimed at identifying heritage resources potentially affected by project activities. The procedure involved reviewing existing documentation on known sites and cultures, analyzing aerial photography for clues of heritage sites, and, ultimately, sending a team of people to walk the entire length of the pipeline route to document each identified site's potential interest. As a result, many hundreds of cultural heritage sites were identified along the pipeline route (206 architectural monuments and 56 archaeological sites in a single 250-kilometer section of the pipeline route in Georgia alone). Extreme care was taken in this preconstruction phase. During the preparation of the ESIA, every landowner (more than 35,000) in all communities (more than 500) within two kilometers of the route were contacted several times.

PLANNING AND CONSTRUCTION PHASE

All of the data reviewed and compiled during the preconstruction phase were carefully analyzed and mitigation measures which devised in each appropriate instance. Construction plans and processes included specific requirements to ensure that cultural resource expertise was available; that is, experts in archaeology and cultural heritage were included as part of the planning and construction teams to ensure that appropriate sensitivity was exercised at each step.

Also during the planning and construction, a provision was made for the management of "chance finds"; that is, archaeological and cultural treasures that were not identified during the preconstruction phase but were rather encountered as construction proceeded. This process included hiring cultural heritage mentors (as detailed hereafter) as well as training each member of the construction crews to be alert for evidence of items that might have cultural or archaeological significance and empowering each worker to shut down construction immediately if an item of interest was noted.

A monitoring system was set to carefully track progress against preconstruction and planning goals and objectives concerning the preservation of antiquities and heritage assets. The planning and construction process further provided for a system to appraise and record actions taken and information gathered.

In practice, mitigation processes worked well. The proposed pipeline route was significantly changed a number of times to avoid previously unknown cultural heritage sites. In one instance, the pipeline route was changed to bypass a Nadarbazeri Palace complex in the Tetritskaro region. In another instance, the route was changed to avoid substantial Bronze Age (3500–800 B.C.) remains, including settlements in Stone "Kurgan" burial sites near Salka in Georgia. Numerous other, smaller re-routes were undertaken as well.

In other areas, excavations were undertaken to assess the significance of finds in the right-of-way. In dozens of instances along the right-of-way, architectural monuments were identified and significant and mitigation measures were introduced to protect them.

In recognition of the fact that "late finds" were virtually inevitable, BP employed four cultural heritage monitors full-time on the project. Thus, as unexpected evidence of prior civilizations was discovered during construction, the cultural heritage monitors were available to ensure their evaluation and protection. The sole responsibility assigned to these monitors was to keep an eye out for archaeological sites. They were given the right to stop construction and recommend workarounds. As previously mentioned, all other personnel were also given training in the importance of the protection of these "late finds" and of their responsibility to keep a watchful eye out for them so that appropriate measures could be undertaken.

As the BTC project approaches completion, it is possible to assess the success of the efforts undertaken by the BTC consortium to protect cultural heritage of the regions through which the pipeline passes.

The artifact in Figure 34.2 was found at Eli Baba near Sulka in Georgia. It is believed it dates from the Mesolithic Period (12000–8000 B.C.). This is in an area where a major re-route of the pipeline was undertaken as a result of this discovery during the preconstruction phase. This represents a previously unknown necropolis that was identified and is now being excavated. To date, nearly one hundred graves have

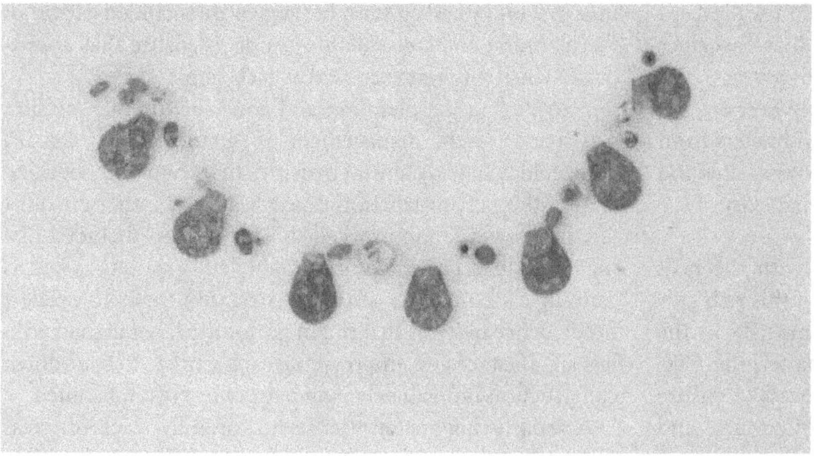

Figure 34.2. Artifact found at Eli Baba near Tsalka. It is believed to date from the Mesolithic Period (12000–8000 B.C.).

been found. It is thought that these beads were buried to accompany the deceased into the after-life. In this instance, thirty people from local villages are involved in the excavation work. All items recovered are transferred to the Georgian State Museum in Tbilisi for display.

Figure No. 34.3 represents a "late find" under the parlance of the World Bank guidelines. That is, it was discovered after the completion of the preconstruction investigation process. In this particular instance, the burial site was barely visible on the surface of the ground and simply looked like a nondescript pile of stones.

After having been discovered by the cultural heritage monitors, the site was protected and excavation of the site commenced.

To date, numerous intact plots and skeletal remains have been discovered, including the one depicted in Figure No. 34.3. At this same site, a possible Medieval Period trash pit was recently identified during the monitoring phase. Artifacts from that site include ceramics faunal remains and burnt floral materials. Also, stone tools from the middle Paleolithic Age were found near this area.

It can thus be persuasively argued that the efforts of the BTC consortium to identify, protect, and, where appropriate, recover cultural and archaeological artifacts have been a success. I believe it may also be said that our efforts will contribute to man's age-old quest to unlock the mysteries of our prehistoric ancestors. Failure to protect cultural heritage may inadvertently prevent the discovery of keys that might unlock those mysteries.

Figure 34.4 shows Ronny Gallagher and Abbas Islamov examining "cut marks" and water channels carved out of a stone surface on the Absheron Peninsula in Azerbaijan. Ronny Gallagher is BP's Environmental Manager in Baku. Abbas Islamov is BP's Safety Advisor in Azerbaijan. They are amateurs, intrigued by the mysteries of this ancient and fascinating region.

Figure 34.3. Skeletal remains found in a Middle Bronze Age burial site (kurgan) in Tetritskaro.

Figure 34.4. R. Gallagher and A. Islamov – Examining cup marks and water channels.

It is believed that cup marks, which vary in character a good deal, as depicted in Figures 34.5 and 34.6, were made by man during the Stone Age. But many questions remain – why are some cup marks larger than others? Why are some round and others, square? Why are some connected to channels but others are not? Why do some of them appear with the same design across vast territory? Why are some found on top of mountains and others in lowlands? Archaeologists surmise that some of these rock holes were used for cooking; others, possibly as sacrificial holes or site markers; and others were perhaps used to leave "messages" or items for following travelers. But most of them mystify us yet. Without making the effort to ensure that these clues to ancient civilizations are preserved, we may lose their meaning forever.

Ronny Gallagher and Abbas Islamov discovered other evidence of early man on the Absheron Peninsula. As Figure 34.7 shows, ancient peoples here cut strange parallel grooves in the rock. These amateur archaeologists, through research, discovered that similar grooves, known as "cart ruts," can be found throughout the Mediterranean along the sea coast of Malta, Greece, Italy, and Southern France. Some archaeologists

Figure 34.5. Cup marks – Absheron Peninsula in Azerbaijan.

Figure 34.6. Cup marks – Ancient doctor's office or wine press?

hypothesize that cart ruts may date back as far as the Neolithic age.

It is quite likely that these ruts pre-date the invention of the wheel. Other scholars have suggested that these cart ruts were lubricated with animal fat, which would have enabled sledges or heavy wooden sleds laden with heavy limestone blocks to have been dragged from the quarry to distant building sites.

Figure 34.7. "Cart" ruts on Aspheron Peninsula.

In this instance, we know that the cart ruts lead from what were clearly ancient quarries to the coast of the Caspian Sea. We also know that the water level of the Caspian would have been much lower during certain time periods. It is thus surmised that there are sunken buildings now located under the waters of the Caspian. Clues are needed to further the investigation. The efforts of Ronny Gallagher and Abbas Islamov again demonstrate the importance of preservation of antiquities and cultural heritage artifacts.

Preservation of historic sites and artifacts, such as those depicted, during the planning and construction of substantial infrastructure projects such as the BTC pipeline can help to ensure that our search for the answers to these ancient mysteries can continue. As Ronny Gallagher and Abbas Islamov have said: "Much has yet to be learned about the Stone Age, Neolithic and Bronze Age archaeology in these regions. Clearly, these untapped archeological riches need to be identified, protected and studied. With the right level of protection and the wealth of techniques now available to the modern archeologist, the history, ancient lifestyle and development of man in this region will become demystified."

It is argued, and rightly so, that these measures add cost and delay to projects and that a cost–benefit analysis is appropriate. But the World Bank guidelines represent a very helpful compilation of principles, processes, and procedures that can be considered by companies undertaking infrastructure projects in areas that hold the potential for discovery of artifacts and cultural heritage assets.

BP's CEO, John Browne, has famously said that BP will be a "force for good" as a world corporate citizen. It is my view that at BTC we are in some way fulfilling that promise.

CHAPTER THIRTY-FIVE

Tale of Zeugma and the Birecik Project

Doğan Yağiz

INTRODUCTION

Turkey is a country whose richnesses and endowments in terms of historical and natural features and cultural values can be found in very few other countries in the world. As it is a privilege to enjoy the benefits of these richnesses, it is necessary to fulfill the responsibilities deriving from the same fact.

It is common for economic and technological developments to bring with them some adverse affects on the cultural and social structures of nations and communities.

In a country like Turkey, where almost every place is an open air museum and where one can come across cultural properties in almost any spot, infrastructure, which serves as the basis of economic and social development, may unfortunately lead to the damage or destruction of such cultural properties. To prevent this, Turkey is cooperating with relevant organizations in the field of protecting cultural properties in a coordinated manner while maintaining its dedication to the process of full-fledged development. In this context, Turkish governments are increasingly incorporating the implications of public works and infrastructure development into its basic governmental duties and functions.

Although it is a pity that recent archeaological projects financed by domestic or foreign resources have not been sufficiently directed to rescue work, it is only natural that sites under threat are given priority in this regard. It must be recognized that financial support allocated for this purpose lags far behind what is actually required.

The story of Zeugma is a useful look into the issues associated with the protection of cultural property in the face of economic and technological development. This chapter discusses the development of an international hydroelectric power plant on the Euphrates River in the southeastern part of Turkey and its effects on a nearby archeological site called *Zeugma.*

ZEUGMA

The "Birecik Dam and HEPP Project" is known worldwide as the first large-scale international construction project implemented on Build-Operate-Transfer (BOT) basis. The project had attracted great enthusiasm around the globe when priceless mosaics and frescos from a Greco-Roman archeological site were coincidentally unearthed within the then unflooded reservoir area of the dam known as "Zeugma" or, in English, "the Bridge."

Anyone near a newsstand in May or June of 2000 probably met the mysterious eyes of a gypsy woman peering out from photos of a beautiful mosaic uncovered in the ancient city of Zeugma. Prior to this, most people had heard very little, if anything, about Zeugma. The media poured forth a plethora of stories, some true and some less accurate, about Zeugma and its threatened treasures, which were about to be lost forever to the rising waters of a new dam lake in southeast Turkey. Little did the gypsy woman know at the time of her photograph that her gaze would engage the world to embark upon one of the most ambitious archeological projects ever, aiming to rescue and preserve some of the most outstanding mosaics, frescoes, and other artifacts found between June and October of the year 2000.

But a good tale never comes easy and one must begin more than 2,300 years ago on the banks of the Euphrates river in an obscure area known as *Belkis-Zeugma.*

Zeugma is an amazingly well-preserved city, at one time hosting a Roman frontier city of grandeur equal to Pompei. In ancient times, for many people who inhabited the Mesopotamian region, it was an important crossing point of the river Euphrates. In modern times, the extent of Zeugma's rich remains were not clearly understood except by a handful of archeologists and researchers who were committed to finding Zeugma's past under the soil that covered it. With the completion of the Birecik Dam, this dormant area was thrust into the limelight in the summer of 2000 by a force greater than even the rising waters of the Euphrates River that were about to cover it.

THE BIRECIK PROJECT

The plans to build a dam down river from Zeugma, which would eventually cause part of the ancient city to be inundated, were not kept secret.

The Birecik Dam and HEPP is a significant energy and irrigation resource, which was established within the scope of the South East Anatolia Project ("GAP") and launched by the Turkish State in the early 1970s. The GAP, an ambitious effort for full-fledged and integrated socio-economic development based upon the principle of sustainable human development, envisioned achieving its goal by developing the land, water, and human resources in the South East Anatolian region, which constitutes about 10% of Turkey's population and geographical area.

The GAP had originally been designed as a package of thirteen projects, including the construction of energy plants and irrigation schemes over the Euphrates and Tigris rivers, which, when completed, will amount to twenty-two dams and nineteen hydraulic energy plants on these rivers. Today, in addition to dams, hydraulic plants, and irrigation systems, the GAP has evolved into a massive-scale economic development effort also covering investments in areas such as rural, urban, and agricultural infrastructure, transportation, industry, education, health, housing, and tourism.

When the GAP is completed, twenty-eight percent of the total water potential of Euphrates and Tigris rivers, which together flow more than fifty billion cubic meters of water annually, will be taken under control. It will also be possible to irrigate 1.7 million hectares of fertile land and to produce 27 billion kilowatts (kWh) of energy, representing twenty-two percent of the total hydraulic energy potential of the country.

In this context, the rationale for the Birecik Project was fourfold. The Government of Turkey (1) forecasted a continuing growth in its economy and in electricity demand, (2) desired the country's hydropower resources to be developed as environmentally acceptable energy sources, (3) wanted to accelerate development in the South East Anatolia region, and (4) wished to stimulate private sector involvement in electricity generation.

As a substantial step toward achieving the aforementioned goals, in December 1984, Law No. 3096 was passed, granting permission to private sector entities to produce, transmit, and trade electricity on the BOT basis. Under the terms of this law, the Turkish Ministry of Energy was authorized to grant permission to private sector entities to install and operate power generation facilities in Turkey. It is with the creation of this Law that the adventure of the Birecik Project and Zeugma began.

In 1986, the sponsors of the Project, consisting of Phillipp Holzmann from Germany; Alstom Group of Companies from France; Cegelec from Belgium; Strabag, Sulzer-Hydro, and Verbundplan from Austria; and, finally, GAMA from Turkey commenced negotiations with the Ministry of Energy to implement the Project on BOT basis. Being the first project of its kind not only in Turkey but in the world as well, the negotiation phase took almost ten difficult years and resulted in more than fifty executed contracts.

Among the most important of these contracts was the Implementation Contract signed between the Ministry of Energy and the Project Company formed by the sponsors, which established the principles of financing, constructing, operating, and transferring the Project. As defined under the Implementation Contract:

- The Project was to generate 2.5 billion Kwh energy per annum with six generating units of equal capacity.
- The total investment cost of the Project was approximately 2.3 billion Deutsche Marks, fifteen percent of which was to be funded by equity investments by the project sponsors and the balance by nonrecourse project financing from various lenders.
- Starting from the effective date, the investment period of the Project was agreed to be five and a half years, and thereafter the Project Company was granted an authorization to operate the facilities and sell electricity to an identified state-owned customer for a period of fifteen years at a predetermined unit price that would guarantee the repayment of the loans, the return of equity together with interest thereon, and all operating costs of the Project Company, including applicable taxes.
- Upon the expiration date of the operation period, the facilities, together with the shares of the sponsors at the Project Company, were required to be transferred to a governmental entity free of charge.
- Again, pursuant to the Implementation Contract: "Any archeological or historical findings" during the authorization period were accepted as an event of force majeure.

The force majeure clause was quite similar to those normally provided under classic construction contracts whereby, in order for an event to be accepted as an "event of force majeure," it had to first pass through specific tests such as "the event not being within the reasonable control of the party affected" or "the occurance of such event [which] could not have been prevented despite the exercise of reasonable diligence," etc. Then, as a second step, the event must have been listed as an event of force majeure under the contract. Finally the affected party must have notified the other party within a specified period of time of the occurance of the event and its effect upon the cost and time of performance.

If these prerequisites were duly fulfilled, the Project Company would be granted time and cost relief.

However, pursuant to another clause under the Implementation Contract, "if the effects of an event of force majeure had continued to materially and adversely affect the project for more than six months, the Project Company was accepted as being entitled to terminate the Contract and to serve a transfer notice to the Ministry of Energy." The effects of the Transfer Notice were threefold and were quite material for the Turkish State:

- First, upon receipt of a transfer notice, the Ministry (or its nominee) was obliged to purchase all the shares of the Sponsors in the Project Company at a predetermined price. The price, as such, did not only contain the nominal foreign currency value of the respective paid-in equities of the Sponsors but also included, *inter alia*, a specified compensation for loss of profit.
- Second, upon receipt of a transfer notice, all the loans provided by the lenders were required to be assumed by the Turkish State, and thus became sovereign liability. And
- Third, if the termination took place during the construction phase, the Turkish State would end up with an uncompleted facility and waste of substantial funds.

Another important project document was the Construction Contract entered into by and between the Project Company and the consortium formed by sponsor firms.

As far as the Construction Contract is concerned, suffice it to say that with respect to an event of force majeure, the parties thereto had followed the foot prints of the Implementation Contract and thus the summary presented in that regard applies *mutatis mutandis* to the Construction Contract as well.

Finally, both the Implementation and the Construction Contracts were screened by the lenders and were adopted to fully meet their requirements.

Financing of the loan portion of the total investment cost, representing approximately DM 1.8 billion, was arranged by the Project Company from several sources, on a nonrecourse basis.

Seventy-five percent of this amount was provided by export credit agencies, namely, HERMES from Germany, COFACE from France, DUCROIR from Belgium, and OeKb from Austria, and the balance as commercial loan by a syndication of commercial banks led by JP Morgan; all based on several agreements signed between the lenders and the Project Company.

Certain financing agreements that related to the rights and obligations of the Turkish State were also executed by the relevant instrumentalities thereof.

In this context, certain provisions of an umbrella document called the *Common Terms Agreement*, which, as the title implies, had set out common contractual terms to apply to all the financing agreements, should be considered.

In accordance with the Common Terms Agreement,

- if the Project was to be abandoned, terminated by either the Project Company or the contractor, or suspended for a continuous period in excess of 180 days, or
- if, in the opinion of the lenders, there existed a material adverse effect on the ability of the Company to implement the Project, insofar as the failure to comply had enabled a party to terminate the relevant Project Contract,

then, the lenders were declared entitled to treat such an event as an "event of default," and require the Ministry of Energy to terminate the Implementation Contract and take over the facilities and the shares of the sponsors in the Company.

Although the Common Terms Agreement did not make an express reference to the effects of archeological findings on the Project and thus impose any remedial measures with respect thereto, the umbrella language set forth earlier was deemed sufficient to provide a remedy.

THE PISTACHIO TREE

Based on this contractual framework, the construction of the Project started on April 1996, and progressed ahead of schedule until year 2000, when the impounding of the reservoir, commenced. The reservoir, when fully impounded, was to cover an area of fifty-six square kilometers and cause the rising of the water level of the Euphrates River from 352 meters up to a maximum of 385 meters above sea level. Based on the then available data, and especially the plans of Professor David Kennedy from the University of Western Australia, which had marked the borders of the town, this maximum water level as scheduled would have had no effect on Zeugma because the main city was believed to be established between 390–400 meters above sea level, and certainly above the flood basin of the Euphrates River, which, per the historical data, was not more than 370 meters.

When owners of pistachio trees within the reservoir area were asked to remove them, these assumptions were proven to be incorrect. Indeed, had the trees been left in the water uncut, they would have eventually decayed and jeopardized the safe operation of the power plant. By May 2000, only one of the local villagers complied with this instruction. This compliant individual not only cut the trunks of the trees, which was what had been asked of him, but decided to remove the roots from the ground as well. The surprise took place during the de-rooting of a pistachio tree at 369 meters' elevation.

The removal of the earth that covered the roots of this tree revealed an ancient Roman villa. The Project Company immediately notified the Ministry of Energy and the Ministry of Culture via the local museum.

Although this discovery was welcomed with enthusiasm by members of the archeology community, it was less warmly greeted by the Ministry of Energy and the Project Company. The initial surveys at the site revealed that there was much more than a Roman Villa resting under the ground. Indeed, the physical facilities were almost complete and the level of water in the reservoir was gradually increasing as the impounding continued, leaving very little time for rescue efforts before the impounding was completed and the operation of the power plant had commenced as scheduled.

This event, without any doubt, was an event of *force majeure* as provided under the Implementation Contract and the Construction Contract and had the potential of constituting an Event of Default under the Common Terms Agreement with the lenders. Rescue operations, if continued at the site, would be long term, with the inevitable result of the suspension of the impounding of the reservoir and the suspension of the operation of the Project. The Ministry of Energy was reluctant to undertake such activities because an extended suspension period would inevitably result in the termination of the Project contracts and the assumption of all the loans and payment of a compensation to the Project Sponsors, resulting in a cost of more than a billion dollars for the Turkish State.

On the other hand, the Turkish State did not want the treasures of Zeugma to disappear under the rising waters of the Birecik Lake, especially at a time when both the local and international media were bombarding the Turkish government with heavy critisisms for its actions concerning Zeugma.

The Turkish State was under a moral duty, and arguably a legal duty, to rescue and protect such remains pursuant to a number of international treaties it had ratified, including the UNESCO Treaty dated 1972, regarding the "Protection of World Cultural and Natural Heritage" and the Granada Treaty dated 1985, concerning the "Protection of European Architectural Heritage." Furthermore, in accordance with its local regulations, namely Law No. 2863, the Turkish State, represented by the Ministry of Culture, was obligated to ensure that such archeological sites were duly protected; however, the Ministry of Culture was also authorized to grant permission for construction activities within the protection zones, taking all relevant circumstances (such as public interest) into consideration. Violation of the provisions of this law did not only result in heavy fines, but also imprisonment for up to five years. The government was at an impasse as to how to best reconcile the competing interests.

THE MESSIAH

As is often the case, the impending loss of Zeugma focused world attention on its value. For years, only limited international funding had been channelled into archeological activities there. But, as we say, "every doomsday brings forth its Messiah." This was exactly what happened when, in the summer of 2000, after reading an article in the *New York Times*, David Packard of Packard Humanities Institute (PHI) became aware that a portion of Zeugma would soon be under water.

Through close Turkish friends, he was able to communicate his desire to mobilize a rescue effort at Zeugma. PHI made an offer of US$5 million toward excavation and research. Hence, the Messiah was found. This gracious offer triggered the commencement of a rescue initiative called the *Zeugma Archeological Project* (ZAP). ZAP represents one of the largest and most ambitious rescue operations of its type ever undertaken.

First, a memorandum of understanding was signed between PHI and Prime Ministry GAP Administration to make the offer official.

Then, the Ministry of Energy, Ministry of Culture, and other relevant Turkish governmental instrumentalies came to a mutual understanding to suspend the impounding of the reservoir for only four months.

The suspension per se had no effect on the Construction contractor because the construction activities were to progress independent from impounding. The Project Company was not affected either because the progress of construction activities was already ahead of schedule and the fifteen-year revenue generation period was to remain intact. Finally, from the perspective of the Ministry of Energy, the future of the Project would not be endangered because the 120-day suspension period fell sixty days short of the contractual termination threshold and, further, it had obtained the green light from the Ministry of Culture to continue with the Project.

THE RESCUE OPERATIONS

In June 2000, the rescue operations began under the leadership of GAP Administration, collaborating with PHI.

An international team coordinated by the Oxford Archeological Unit of England, and composed of specialists from the United States, Turkey, Britain, France, and Italy, cooperated to survey, excavate, record, and conserve the archeology of this unique site. The project was staffed by more than 150 archeologists and 250 workers helping to excavate and process the thousands of finds. The excavation works were accompanied by other teams, including the Zeugma Initiative, the University of La Rochelle from France, Centro di Conservazione Archeologica from Italy, and six Turkish Universities.

One of the unusual aspects of the ZAP project was the intense cooperation of the local residents who were dedicated to preserving the archeological treasures of Zeugma. It was estimated that the team of rescuers at Zeugma had accomplished in four months what normally would have taken up ten years. Obviously, the rising waters created a sense of urgency that is not the norm for excavation.

Taking all the restraints into consideration, the rescue team first conducted a walkover survey on the strip of land on the west bank of Euphrates, to establish how the area of the city could be divided into distrinct topographical zones.

This survey was then supported by a satellite imaging study, to identify the boundries of the site, and a ground penetrating radar survey, which is a nonintrusive survey providing three-dimensional profile of below-ground deposits and structures up to and beyond three meters.

As the result of the evaluation of the data obtained through such surveys, the site was divided into three areas, two of which (Areas A and B) required immediate excavation because the formation of the dam would have affected them. The remaining area, called *the Area C* comprised seventy percent of the city and would remain intact over the maximum elevation of the Birecik Lake. This evaluation phase led into the main phase of targeted excavation, including identification of trenches to be dug.

Overall, nineteen excavation areas were opened across the one-kilometer stretch of Areas (A) and (B). Among the many buildings found were houses, shops, and workshops, two series of buildings associated with different Christian ecclesiastical uses, and remains of temples. A cemetery site was discovered and extensive remains of the town's infrastructure, roads, and drains, as well as considerable evidence of the sophisticated system of water management. In total, the excavation has produced vast amounts of archeological records, including hundreds of drawings and thousands of written record sheets. Forty-five magnificent mosaics were recorded and conserved; of these twenty-two were complete.

Thousands of artifacts have been recovered. These range from simple objects associated with daily life, like the many cooking pots, to the richly decorated, high-status objects such as a small bronze figurine, golden rings, brooches, bracelets, etc., and certainly an unprecedented bronze Mars statue 155 centimeter tall, of exceptional importance, which was highlighted by the local and international media with great enthusiasm. Again, altogether, 90,000 pieces of bullae (seals) were recovered, making the local museum where they are kept now the possessor of the richest bullae collection in the world.

At the end of these efforts, it is alleged that eighty percent of the artifacts in Areas (A) and (B) have been rescued.

During these efforts, all such artifacts have been carefully excavated, removed, cleaned, recorded, transported, and preserved by using the latest technology available. For example, the mosaics uncovered have presented a challenge to archeologists and conservators alike. Prior to lifting, the mosaic floors were comprehensively recorded, including the full-scale tracing of figurative motifs on acetate film, accurately tied in by use of the Electronic Distance Meter. These tracings were later processed into auto-computer aided design to produce accurate records.

Among all, a very important part of the conservation work at Zeugma involved planning and supervising the long-term safe reburial of the excavated areas in order to limit the risks to archeological structures during and after flooding.

As part of these works, the wall paintings and the mosaics that were to be reburied were carefully prepared and protected from traumatic environmental change underwater. A lime whitewash had been applied to the surface, followed by a layer of a hydraulic lime mortar.

Reburial was the final step of conservation strategy for the site. At the end of the excavation work, all the trenches were backfilled following a carefully planned strategy in order to ensure mitigation of the environmental changes during inundation of wall paintings and mosaics and to prevent the collapse of the archeological structures unearthed.

CONCLUSION

- As of October 4, 2000, thirty percent of the Zeugma site was surrendered to the rising waters of the Birecik dam, to continue its new history underwater.
- After October 4, most of the members of the ZAP team left the site for their homes, somehow proud and somehow bitter.
- On October 2001, all the units of the Birecik Project entered into commercial operation with success, generating the energy contracted for, irrigating the surrounding land, and thus contributing to the economy of the region and Turkey.
- Today, while the archeological studies at Zeugma are continuing at the original slow pace, the sleeping beauty, left to rest under water for perhaps another 100 years, is waiting for a wake-up kiss from a future prince.

QUESTIONS FOR DISCUSSION

1. The World Bank Guidelines impose upon developing countries such standards which may not necessarily be applied in developed countries. That is, whereas the developed countries (not being dependent on external funding) will have flexibility in setting out their independant policies regarding funding of such infrastructure projects, the developing countries, being dependant on external funding for large-scale infrastructure projects, will be expected to comply with the said rules to obtain the required financing. In terms of fairness, and without querying the reasonableness of the World Bank Guidelines, shouldn't such restrictions apply (as an international policy matter) to all countries without distinction?

2. Is it likely that such Guidelines may be misused to limit and/or prevent the economical growth of developing countries?"

USEFUL LINKS

For additional information about Zeugma, the following Web sites are recommended:

http://www.arkeolojisanat.com.tr

http://www.gap.gov.tr

CHAPTER THIRTY-SIX

The Impact of Cultural Resources Laws on the United States Mining Industry

Robert A. Bassett

The mining industry provides the raw materials that form the foundation of our modern society; it is an industry that has an impact on us all. Many laws that preserve cultural resources, in turn, have an impact on the mining industry. This chapter presents an introduction to the mining industry, an overview of cultural resource preservation laws in the United States, and, finally, an example of how those laws can impact a mining project.

THE MINING INDUSTRY

Everything you see came out of the ground.
If it can't be grown, it has to be mined.

These truisms about the mining industry are meant to remind people of just how basic the industry really is. How often does one remember, for example, that the glass they use for drinking water is composed of various mineral materials, including silica sands and soda ash, and manufactured by machines made from iron, steel, aluminum, and other metals, which are fueled by electricity generated from gas, coal, or uranium?

Minerals must be taken out of the ground where they are located. The industry has limited ability to choose where its operations take place – operations must occur wherever the minerals are found. The land where the minerals are located is greatly impacted by the removal of minerals. Mining may appear to be a long-term endeavor, but, in fact, is an activity with a limited lifespan: When all the minerals have been removed from the ground, the mine must be closed, whether that occurs 5 years, 50 years, or 100 years after the mining began.

The modern mining industry is subject to extensive regulation in virtually every jurisdiction in the world. The countries where mining is most prevalent have both statutory and regulatory schemes governing the industry, particularly the United States, Canada, Australia, Chile, and Peru.[1] Mining laws govern the basic right to conduct mining activities (tenure laws), the operation of mines (including labor, safety, and tax laws), and the payment of royalties and other forms of rent to the government – the owner of the mineral in most jurisdictions.

The mining industry is also subject to general environmental laws, such as those aimed at protecting land, water, air, wildlife, or other ecosystems, and laws governing the disposal of unwanted mineral materials and hazardous wastes.[2] In addition to laws of general applicability that impact a mining project from start to finish, there is a unique set of laws that governs the end of a mining project. In most jurisdictions, a mining company must submit a plan to the government before beginning a particular project, describing its plans for the site once the mining is complete. Often, the company has to make a financial guaranty to ensure that the plan is followed. These "reclamation and bonding" laws require everything from replacing topsoil and re-establishing vegetation on the land[3] to backfilling the mined land[4] or returning the land to its approximate original contour.[5] No other industry must plan for its own demise in such a manner.

Recently, the mining industry has embraced the concept of sustainable development. As a result, in addition to planning for reclamation of the land, mining companies have accepted the broader social responsibility of studying the impact that their operations have on society in general.[6] Demonstrating this trend, recent studies have examined in detail how the mining industry is impacted by the related concepts of sustainable development[7] and public participation.[8] As part of this new responsibility that the mining industry has taken on, and as part of its obligation to mitigate environmental impacts, the mining industry is often faced with the task of preserving and protecting cultural resources.

The author thanks Kristin Kilpela Graham, Holland & Hart, LLP for her assistance on this chapter.

1 Many Web sites are excellent sources for locating these laws; see, for example, University of Denver, Natural Resources WebLinks, at <http://www.law.du.edu/naturalresources/default.htm>, Center for Energy, Petroleum, and Mineral Law Policy, Useful Links, at <http://www.dundee.ac.uk/cepmlp/main/html/links.htm>, and MRIC Online Services, at <http://www.mmaj.go.jp/mmaj_e/services.html>.

2 For a complete discussion of this type of law in the United States, see *5 American Law of Mining, Title XV (Environmental Laws) and Chapter 176 (Cultural Resources Protection)*, Rocky Mtn. Min. L. Fdn. 2003.

3 30 U.S.C. §1265(b)(19) (2000).

4 California Senate Bill 22 (2003).

5 30 U.S.C. §1265(b)(3).

6 See, for example, the Web site of Rio Tinto plc, <http://www.riotinto.com/community>.

7 "Breaking New Ground: Mining Minerals and Sustainable Development," published by the Mining Minerals and Sustainable Development Project of the International Institute for Environment and Development, available at <http://www.iied.org/mmsd/finalreport/index.html>.

8 Zillman, Lucas and Pring, eds., "Human Rights in Natural Resources Development," Oxford Press, 2002, sponsored by the Academic Advisory group of the Section on Energy and Natural Resources Law of the International Bar Association.

CULTURAL PRESERVATION LAWS AND THE MINING INDUSTRY – THE U.S. FRAMEWORK

In the United States, four federal laws concerning the preservation of cultural resources are of particular significance to the mining industry. In addition, most states have enacted laws regarding cultural resource preservation that can impact a project within a particular state. Most mining activity in the United States takes place in the western part of the country, including Alaska. Because nearly one-third of the land in the western United States is owned by the federal government, federal laws are of particular importance to the mining industry.

National Historic Preservation Act of 1966 (NHPA)[9]

The NHPA is the product of a series of earlier laws dating back to the beginning of the twentieth century. Most notable among these earlier laws is the Antiquities Act of 1906,[10] the first federal law that established a framework for preserving cultural heritage.

The NHPA has two basic parts, one substantive and one procedural. Substantively, the NHPA created the National Register of Historic Places.[11] This register is intended to catalogue districts, buildings, objects, and artifacts of historical significance that are at least fifty years old. Even historic mine buildings and workings can be cultural resources worthy of protection.[12] The National Register also covers "any property of traditional religious or cultural importance to Indian Tribes." Properties are nominated for inclusion on the list by local governments, Native American peoples, and the public at large. Once a site or object is placed on the National Register, it is given special protection under the NHPA.

Procedurally, the NHPA requires federal agencies to conduct a review of the potential impacts on "cultural resources" prior to any "undertaking." This review is a three-step process. First, the agency conducts studies to determine whether any protected properties will be impacted by the undertaking. As part of these studies, the agency consults with the relevant State Historic Preservation Officer, the Tribal Historic Preservation Officer (if Native American lands or properties are involved), and the general public. Second, the agency assesses the impact the undertaking will have on any properties identified in the review process. Third, the agency develops a plan to mitigate those impacts; the agency may enter into agreements with private entities, states, or Indian tribes to carry out the proposed mitigation measures.[13]

An early NHPA court case involving the mining industry called on the court to define "agency undertaking" for purposes of the statute. In the events leading up to *National Indian Youth Council* v. *Andrus*,[14] the Secretary of the Department of the Interior had approved the issuance of coal leases on approximately 40,000 acres of federal lands controlled by the Bureau of Land Management ("BLM"). The BLM had not, however, conducted a review under the NHPA prior to issuing the leases. The court held that the BLM was not required to conduct a NHPA review prior to issuing the leases because the mere act of issuing a lease, on paper, would not impact any cultural resources. Nonetheless, the court also held that a cultural resources review under the NHPA would be required prior to the BLM's approval of a mining plan on the lands because approval of such a plan, in the court's view, might allow activities that could have an impact on cultural resources.

Native American Graves Protection and Repatriation Act of 1990 (NAGPRA)[15]

The NAGPRA was enacted for the purpose of protecting human remains and funerary objects associated with burial sites of Native Americans. The NAGPRA also protects "objects of ceremonial, historic, or cultural importance" to Native Americans. Upon discovery of any remains or objects, the discoverer is required by the NAGPRA to immediately cease any activity at the site, and notify the appropriate federal agency and Indian tribe. An automatic thirty-day moratorium is placed on the activity, during which the site is studied, Indian tribes are consulted, and the discoverer is required to make a reasonable effort to protect the artifacts. The moratorium may be extended by the agency, as needed, to protect the artifacts. Ownership of any discovered Native American artifact automatically vests in the Indian tribe.

The NAGPRA has the potential to have a tremendous impact on any project located on federal lands. Mining companies that are aware of this potential impact understand the need to carefully conduct the studies required under the NHPA. That way, the company can identify in advance any Native American artifacts, rather than taking the risk of unexpected, chance finds that would halt the entire project.[16]

[9] 16 U.S.C. §§470–470x-6 (2000).

[10] 16 U.S.C. §461 (1976) (current version at 16 U.S.C. §432 (2000)).

[11] See 16 U.S.C. §470a (2000).

[12] W. Stern, "Potsherds and Petroglyphs: Effects of Cultural Resources Management on Public Lands Development," 41 Rocky Mt. Min. L. Inst. §14.01 (1995). The author is aware of one case where a mine was required to destroy an old "head-frame" by a State's mining authorities as part of reclaiming a mine site, but was also required by the same State's Historical Preservation Officer to preserve the head-frame as a historic structure.

[13] For purposes of this paper, the NHPA review process has been greatly oversimplified. The process is set forth primarily in sections 106 and 110 of the NHPA, *see* 16 U.S.C. §§470f–470h-2(a) (2000), and the implementing regulations. For a thorough treatment of the process, see Stern, *supra* note 13.

[14] 501 F. Supp. 649, 653 (1980).

[15] 25 U.S.C. §§3001–3013 (2000).

[16] In one project with which the author is familiar, several petroglyphs were discovered during the NHPA review that would be impacted by a coal mining project on federal lands. It took the mining company nearly a year and a half to locate an Indian Tribe that was willing to consult with BLM under the NHPA. Had this occurred as a "chance find" under the NAGPRA, the project would have been halted for this period simply because of the difficulty of finding a Native American group willing to review the artifacts.

National Environmental Policy Act of 1976 (NEPA)[17]

NEPA is an entirely procedural statute. Its key provision requires federal agencies to conduct an environmental analysis for any "major Federal action significantly affecting the quality of the human environment." What constitutes a "major federal action" under NEPA has been the subject of extensive litigation. The environmental studies required by NEPA for any such action are: (1) an environmental assessment ("EA") to identify the potential environmental impacts of the proposed action and (2) an environmental impact study ("EIS") if the EA reveals significant environmental impacts. In practice, mining activities on federal lands nearly always require the preparation of an extensive EIS.

In terms of cultural resources, the preparation of an EA or an EIS involves identifying any cultural resources within a project area and describing the impacts that the project may have on those cultural resources. Conducting either type of environmental analysis under NEPA has been held to be sufficient to satisfy the requirement of conducting a "review" under the NHPA. Thus, at least in most instances, compliance with NEPA equates to compliance with the NHPA.

Surface Mining Control and Reclamation Act of 1977 (SMCRA)[18]

SMCRA was the first U.S. environmental law that was passed specifically for the purpose of dealing with one particular industry – surface coal mining. SMCRA and its extensive implementing regulations govern all impacts of surface coal mining, as well as many of the surface impacts of underground coal mining. SMCRA specifically prohibits surface mining in locations listed on the National Register, and also forbids any mining that would impact historic lands or archeological sites. Furthermore, SMCRA prohibits mining activities that would impact "properties having religious or cultural significance to Native Americans," a definition that is nearly identical to that found in the NHPA.[19]

These four laws, along with other federal and state laws, create a statutory structure that protects cultural resources in the United States from inadvertent negative impacts by mining companies, particularly on federal lands (where much of the coal mining, and virtually all of the hardrock mining, take place).

NEPA's review process, which includes consideration of the NHPA, the NAGPRA, and SMCRA, is similar to the environmental assessments required in most developed countries with significant mining industries. The global reach of nongovernmental organizations focused on environmental, social, and cultural protection, and the desire of the mining industry itself to engage in "best practices," have led to the development of similar environmental review processes in virtually every country where major mining companies conduct activities.

The interplay of laws protecting cultural resources and permitting mining activity in the Unites States, however, sometimes produces extreme results, as demonstrated by the Glamis Imperial Project.

THE GLAMIS IMPERIAL PROJECT

Glamis Gold Ltd. is a Canadian gold mining company that owns a mining enterprise in the United States, Glamis Imperial Corporation.[20] In the late 1980s, Glamis discovered the gold deposit that became the subject of the Imperial Project. The deposit is located on federal lands in the desert of southeastern California. The site is in a historic gold mining district, only six miles from a mine that had been operated by Glamis for more than 20 years.

The BLM is the agency responsible for managing the federal lands upon which the Imperial Project is located. In 1987, the BLM prepared a "Resource Management Plan"[21] for the area. As part of that Plan, the BLM conducted a NHPA study to inventory any potential historic or Native American sites that might be subject to the NHPA's "preserve and protect" requirements. The BLM consulted with the local Indian tribe, the Quechan Tribe, as part of this planning process. The study identified no sites as being of cultural significance to Native Americans; the Plan specifically noted that there was "no evidence that the area is used today by contemporary Native Americans."

Glamis then performed additional mineral exploration on the Imperial Project site, and in 1991 it conducted a study of cultural resources at the site. This study, completed in 1990, also involved consultation with the Quechan Tribe. Like the 1987 BLM study, the 1990 study did not identify any Native American or other NHPA sites within the area.

In 1994, Glamis submitted a proposed mine operating plan to the BLM. By this time, Glamis had invested more than $15 million in the Imperial Project. In conjunction with submitting the plan, Glamis conducted a second study of cultural resources in 1995. Again, no Native American cultural site was identified.

In 1997, Glamis conducted a *third* study of the site that, like the prior BLM and Glamis studies, also entailed consultation with the Quechan Tribe. This time, however, the same tribal historian of the Quechan Tribe who had been consulted for the prior studies asserted that the Imperial Project area was considered "sacred" to the Quechan Tribe. This historian claimed that the site was part of the "Trail of Dreams," a 100-mile corridor stretching from San Francisco south

[17] 42 U.S.C. §§4321–4375 (2000). [18] 30 U.S.C. §§1201–1328 (2000).
[19] See 30 C. F. R. §762.5 (2003).

[20] For a complete history of the Imperial Project, see <http://www.nma.org/pdf/cong_test/glamis_testimony_092502.pdf>. For an opposing view, see <http://www.foe.org/cancun/glamis.pdf>.
[21] Resource Management Plans are developed under the Federal Land Policy and Management Act of 1976, see 43 U.S.C. §§1701–1785 (2000) and its implementing regulations.

through California into Mexico, which purportedly was used by early Native Americans as a route of transit. No physical evidence of this trail existed in its entire length, and no definition of the breadth or route of the trail was identified (even though the area described comprised a major part of southern California). Nevertheless, the local BLM office refused to grant approval of Glamis' proposed mining plan.

In the waning days of the Clinton Administration, Secretary of the Interior Bruce Babbitt issued the Department of Interior's "final decision" on the Glamis Imperial Project. This decision, issued January 17, 2001, concluded that the Department could exercise its discretion and deny a mining permit to Glamis. On November 23, 2001, the new Secretary of the Interior appointed by President Bush, Gail Norton, reversed Secretary Babbitt's decision, stating that the Department had no discretionary power to veto the mine proposal because Glamis had complied with all of the applicable mining and cultural resource protection laws. Secretary Norton's decision cleared the way for Glamis to begin mining at the Imperial Project.

Opponents of the project, however, sought support from the State of California. In December 2002, the California Mining Board adopted a regulation requiring all open pit mines to be completely backfilled. A Board report supporting this rule specifically cited the Glamis Imperial Project as an "emergency condition" justifying promulgation of the rule. The California State Legislature then passed Senate Bill 22, which was signed into law on April 7, 2003. Senate Bill 22, like the Board's regulation, requires backfilling of all open pit mines, especially those "on, or within one mile of, any Native American sacred site." California Governor Davis publicly stated that Senate Bill 22 "essentially stops the Glamis Gold Mine Proposal."

The story does not end there. On July 21, 2003 Glamis filed a "Notice of Intent" to make a claim against the U.S. government. This Notice was filed pursuant to Chapter 11, Article 1117 of the North American Free Trade Agreement (NAFTA). Glamis claims that the Department of Interior's actions, and those of the State of California, resulted in an expropriation of its property that is contrary to the provisions of NAFTA.[22] On December 9, 2003, Glamis filed a formal "Notice of Arbitration" under the UNCITRAL rules (as required by NAFTA) seeking not less than US$50 million in compensation for damages plus its costs and interest. The matter remains the subject of private arbitration at the time of this writing.

The Glamis Imperial Project is an example of cultural preservation laws run amok, of project opponents using those laws in an extreme fashion, and of a well-intentioned company doing all it could to plan in advance for compliance with those laws. It is hoped that the laws designed to preserve and protect cultural resources can be implemented in accordance with those purposes. It is further hoped that real mitigation can be performed whenever necessary, rather than having cultural resources laws become a platform for litigation against companies with a sincere desire to fulfill their duty to protect cultural resources.

DISCUSSION QUESTIONS

1. Who determines whether a specific site has cultural significance?

2. Who determines whether the cultural significance of a site outweighs a society's demand for production of minerals, especially minerals owned by the sovereign?

3. If a site is preserved for its cultural significance, how large a buffer zone around that site should also be preserved? What about view corridors to and from the sites?

4. When cultural artifacts can be safely removed from a site and preserved, is that a reasonable alternative, even though their significance will be segregated from the site itself?

5. If cultural preservation is determined to be a dominant use over the extraction of minerals, should a person who has the right to extract those minerals be compensated? By whom?

[22] Copies of the Notice of Intent, Notice of Arbitration and Agreement on Procedural Matters can be found at <http://www.naftaclaims.com/glamis.htm> (last visited January 6, 2005).

CHAPTER THIRTY-SEVEN

Minimising the Environmental and Cultural Impacts of Oil Operations in Emerging Economies: Transnational Oil Companies and Voluntary International Environmental Standards

Alexandra S. Wawryk

In the absence of adequate environmental laws and enforcement in emerging economies, there have been calls for oil companies to voluntarily adopt "best practices" in emerging economies. This article examines five environmental practices that can be seen as "best practices" through their endorsement in national and international oil industry association guidelines, and which will, when adequately implemented, reduce the negative environmental and cultural impacts of oil exploration and production.

INTRODUCTION

Emerging economies,[1] also known as developing countries, Third World countries, emerging market economies, emerging market systems, and emerging markets, hold the majority of the world's proved oil reserves, and account for the majority of the world's production of crude oil.[2] The exploitation of oil remains a priority for the governments of emerging economies because the revenue that comes from subsurface resource exploitation is a major source of foreign income for emerging economies, of which the majority are among the poorest countries in the world, and have large foreign debts. The oil industry is also a source of taxation revenue and employment, and offers the opportunity for the transfer of technology from developed to developing countries.

Oil and gas exploration and production have the potential to cause severe degradation to the physical environment and to the health, cultural, religious, and traditional economic activities of local and indigenous communities. The construction of access routes and roads, and the promise of employment in oil industry, may encourage the immigration of colonists into indigenous areas, leading to conflicts over land and access to natural resources, and the despoliation of sacred sites. Environmental impacts such as air and water pollution from the disposal of wastes, oil spills from pipelines, air and noise pollution caused by gas flaring, soil erosion from land-clearing activities, and the loss of biodiversity from forest clearing, can have devastating effects on human communities, particularly those who rely upon the natural environment to sustain a traditional lifestyle. In some cases, the impact of environmental degradation on the culture and traditional lifestyle of the community is so devastating that a breach of human rights occurs.[3]

The existence of national environmental laws that ensure that proper planning, pollution, prevention, mitigation, and monitoring techniques are employed by oil companies should minimise the risk of adverse consequences to health and culture caused by environmental degradation. However, environmental laws in emerging economies are often ineffective because they are substantively inadequate or because they are inadequately enforced. This has led to calls by academics, practising lawyers, and human rights and environmental activists for transnational oil companies to voluntarily improve their performance in countries with inadequate environmental laws.

Oil companies and industry groups have also recognised that international oil companies operating in emerging economies with inadequate environmental laws should adopt best practice. For example, members of the American Petroleum Institute are responsible for "obeying all laws and best practice" as part of the pledge to a program of continuous health, safety, and environmental improvements.[4] Principle 2 of the 1997 *Code of Environmental Conduct* of the Regional Association of Oil and Natural Gas Companies in Latin America and the Caribbean (ARPEL) states that "all plans, programs and actions that are developed by the oil industry must, at all stages, be guided by the best available environmental protection practices," whereas the 1997 *Environmental Policy* of the Australian Petroleum Production and Exploration Association (APPEA) states that APPEA encourages and supports member companies to "comply, at a minimum, with applicable laws, regulations, standards, and

[1] There is no single clear, fixed, and generally accepted definition of an emerging economy. For the purpose of this article, the term emerging economies refers to a group of countries that includes "countries in transition" from socialist to market economies, and "developing countries" that are, generally speaking, yet to undergo the industrialisation and development of high-technology societies of the Western developed countries. Development Assistance Committee, *Development Co-operation Report 1997* (OECD, Paris, 1998) p. A101; OECD, *External Debt Statistics* (OECD, France, 1997) at 4–5.

[2] As a general guide, at the end of 2003, the OECD countries held 7.5% of the world's proven reserves of oil and accounted for 27% of world production of oil: BP Amoco, *Statistical Review of World Energy 2004*, <http://www.bpamoco.com>.

B.Ec (Hons), LLB (Hons), PhD (Law) (Adelaide), Barrister and Solicitor of the Supreme Court of South Australia, Lecturer at the University of Adelaide.

[3] Inter-American Commission on Human Rights, *Report on the Situation of Human Rights in Ecuador*, OAS Doc OEA/Serv.L/V.II.96, doc 10, rev 1, 24 April 1997, Inter-American Commission on Human Rights, <http://www.cidh.oas.org/country.htm>.

[4] American Petroleum Institute (API), *API Environmental Stewardship Pledge for CAREFUL Operations*, <http://www.api.org>, accessed 5 July 2004.

guidelines for the protection of the environment and in their absence adopt the best practicable means to prevent or minimise adverse environmental impacts."[5]

But what is "best practice" in the international oil industry? What standards should be employed? No treaty has been negotiated with the specific aim of regulating the onshore activities of the oil and gas exploration and production industry operating within the borders of individual states. This stems historically from the view that the regulation of onshore resource exploitation falls within the domestic jurisdiction of states. In this context, the standards, guidelines, and best operating practices developed by oil industry association bodies, and nongovernmental and intergovernmental organizations (NGOs and IGOs) constitute the major efforts to achieve uniform standards and operating practices across the globe.

This chapter examines five environmental principles or practices that are emerging in the environmental codes of conduct, statements of environmental principles, and environmental guidelines that have been developed by oil industry organizations, NGOs, and IGOs, which can be identified as existing or emerging best practices. These practices should, when adequately implemented, help to minimise the negative environmental and cultural impacts of oil exploration and production.

The second part of this chapter identifies the types of standards that help protect the environment and describes the organizations that are the most influential in developing these standards and guidelines in the oil industry. The third part describes five major practices for protection of the environment that are emerging in the international oil industry and that will, when adequately implemented, reduce the negative impacts of oil and gas exploration and production on the physical and cultural environment. These practices are: environmental and social impact assessment (EIA and SIA), environmental management systems (EMS), environmental performance evaluation (EPE), environmental monitoring and auditing; and environmental reporting. The fourth part discusses the legal implications arising from the use of these standards and guidelines, whereas part five makes suggestions for future developments.

SOURCES OF INTERNATIONAL INDUSTRY AND GUIDELINES REGARDING OIL INDUSTRY EXPLORATION AND PRODUCTION PRACTICES

The development by major oil industry associations of internationally acceptable environmental standards and best operating practices, contained in industry guidelines, voluntary codes of conduct, and statements of environmental principles, is part of a broader and growing trend among industry in general.[6] These environmental codes and statements of environmental principles have arisen for a number of reasons. The genuine acknowledgment by industry of a duty to the environment is one reason for the growth of voluntary environmental guidelines and policies. Second, these codes are a response to shareholder, customer, interest group, and community pressure on companies to be transparent and accountable in environmental management, allowing industry to demonstrate environmental responsibility and enhancing public relations. Third, companies have adopted these cooperative and flexible approaches to environmental regulation in order to avoid prescriptive and costly command and control mechanisms.[7]

In the international oil exploration and production industry, the guidelines and standards of the International Association of Oil and Gas Producers (OGP; formerly the Oil Industry International Exploration and Production Forum) and the American Petroleum Institute (API) are particularly influential. The OGP represents oil and gas companies from around the world, and the API, through the history of the dominance of U.S. oil companies in the international oil industry, has a strong influence in the industry. The guidelines of various NGOs and IGOs are also influential, including the International Union for the Conservation of Nature (IUCN), the United Nations Environment Programme (UNEP), the International Standards Organisation (ISO), the World Bank, the International Chamber of Commerce (ICC), and the World Business Council for Sustainable Development.

The OGP has prepared several guidelines regarding onshore oil operations, on its own and in conjunction with IGOs and NGOs such as UNEP and IUCN, which represent "internationally acceptable operating practices" and "internationally acceptable goals and guidance on environmental protection during oil and gas exploration and production operations," including guidelines addressing: oil operations in tropical rainforests, exploration and production operations in mangrove areas, oil exploration in arctic and subarctic onshore regions, waste management, and decommissioning for onshore exploration and production sites.[8]

[5] Australian Petroleum Production and Exploration Association Limited (APPEA), *Environmental Policy*, June 1997, <http://www.appea.com.au/IndustryInformation/Environment/Policy/>, accessed 5 July 2004. Regional Association of Oil and Natural Gas Companies in Latin America and the Caribbean (ARPEL), *Code of Environmental Conduct*, May 1997, <http://portal.arpel.org/wps/portal>, accessed 15 July 2004.

[6] For example, the worldwide chemical industry has adopted the Responsible Care programme as a self-regulatory health, safety, and environmental management scheme, whereas examples of voluntary international environmental principles in the mining industry include the *Mining and Environment Guidelines*, adopted at the International Round-table on Mining and the Environment, Berlin, 25–28 June 1991, and the International Council on Mining and Metals' Sustainable Development Framework, *ICMM Sustainable Development Framework – Final Principles*, 29 May 2003, <http://www.icmm.com/icmm_principles.php>, accessed 5 July 2004.

[7] For example, the United Kingdom Offshore Operators' Association's (UKOOA) promotes "innovation rather than relying on compliance against prescriptive standards or technologies," and one of APPEA's key objectives is "self regulation through the formulation and acceptance of codes of practice in key areas of business activity": UKOOA, *Environmental Principles*, <http://www.ukooa.co.uk/issues/2000report/enviro00_vision.htm>, accessed 5 July 2004; APPEA, "Key Objectives," <http://www.appea.com.au/about/mission.asp> accessed 5 July 2004.

[8] Oil Industry International Exploration and Production Forum, *Oil and Gas Exploration and Production in Mangrove Areas: Guidelines*

The U.S. petroleum industry's commitment to protect the environment is embodied in the API's Environmental Stewardship Program, which is based on 11 principles contained in the *American Petroleum Institute Environmental and Safety Mission and Guiding Principles.*[9] These *Guiding Principles* became part of API's by-laws in 1990; therefore, acceptance of the principles is a condition of membership of the API. The API has also produced guidelines for environmental practices, including the 2001 publication, *Onshore Oil and Gas Production Practices for Protection of the Environment.*[10]

Other national and regional oil industry associations have also adopted environmental policies, codes, and guidelines for protection of the environment. These include APPEA's *Environmental Policy* (June 1997) and 1996 *Code of Environmental Practice* for companies operating in Australia, ARPEL's 1997 *Code of Environmental Conduct*, and the United Kingdom Offshore Operators' Association's *Environmental Principles.*[11]

The World Bank's *Pollution Prevention and Abatement Handbook* (1998) contains Guidelines for onshore oil and gas development, prepared by the Bank with assistance from intergovernmental organisations and the international oil and gas exploration and production industry. The Bank's Guidelines: set maximum levels for liquid effluents, air emissions, and noise levels, which are those "normally acceptable to the World Bank Group in making decisions regarding provisions of World Bank Group assistance"; describe industry practices, processes that can reduce, prevent, and control pollution, and treatment technologies; make recommendations for monitoring and reporting; and summarise the key production and control practices that will lead to compliance with emissions requirements.[12]

Environmental organisations that have produced guidelines for oil operations include the IUCN, in conjunction with the OGP or independently; for example *Oil Exploration in the Tropics: Guidelines for Environmental Protection*;[13] and Conservation International, which has also published recommendations regarding oil development in the tropics, in *Reinventing the Well: Approaches to Minimising the Environmental and Social Impact of Oil Development in the Tropics.*[14]

INTERNATIONAL ENVIRONMENTAL MANAGEMENT PRACTICES OF RELEVANCE TO THE OIL AND GAS INDUSTRY

The voluntary codes and guidelines of the international oil industry generally contain one or more of three broad types of standards or guidelines that assist in protecting the environment. The first of these are standards for equipment and products, such as construction requirements for underground storage tanks and pipelines. Poorly designed or constructed, or outdated equipment may pose a greater threat to the environment. Three major organisations that set standards in the international oil industry are the ISO, the API, and CEN, the European regional body corresponding to ISO.[15] Although product standards play a key role in preventing environmental pollution, they are not the focus of this article, and will not be discussed further.

The second type of standard addresses environmental practices, including the observance of environmental standards such as limits on emissions, and the implementation of recommended environmental practices such as waste disposal methods. Poor environmental practices, such as the unsafe disposal of toxic drilling wastes and gas flaring, generally pose a greater threat to the environment. A third type of standard assists the company to improve environmental performance by adopting environmental management procedures and systems. It is this type of environmental practice or procedure that is the focus of this article.

This section examines five emerging best practices for protection of the environment in the area of environmental management procedures and systems. These practices are: environmental and social impact assessment (EIA/SIA), environmental management systems (EMS), environmental performance evaluation (EPE), environmental monitoring and

for Environmental Protection (Gland, Switzerland: IUCN/E&P Forum, Report No. 2.54/184: 1993); *Oil and Gas Exploration in Arctic Offshore Regions – Guidelines for Environmental Protection*, Report No. 2.84/329, June 2002); *Oil and Gas Exploration in Arctic and Subarctic Onshore Regions: Guidelines for Environmental Protection* (Gland, Switzerland; Cambridge, UK: IUCN/E&P Forum, Report No. 2.55/185, 1993); *E&P Forum Oil Industry Operating Guideline for Tropical Rainforest*, Report No. 2.49/170, April 1991; *Exploration and Production Waste Management Guidelines*, Report No. 2.58/196, September 1993; *Decommissioning, Remediation and Reclamation Guidelines for Onshore Exploration and Production Sites*, Report No. 2.70/242, October 1996.

[9] See also the API's *Environmental Stewardship Program Pledge for CAREFUL Operations*; see note 4.

[10] American Petroleum Institute, *Onshore Oil and Gas Production Practices for Protection of the Environment* (Washington DC, API, 3rd ed, 2001).

[11] ARPEL, *Code of Environmental Conduct*, see note 5 APPEA, *APPEA Code of Environmental Practice* (1996 ed), <http://www.appea.com.au/Publications/docs/1996EnvCode.pdf>, accessed 5 July 2004; UKOOA, *Environmental Principles*, see note 7.

[12] World Bank, "Industry Sector Guidelines: Oil and Gas Development (Onshore)," *Pollution Prevention and Abatement Handbook 1998*, World Bank <http://www.worldbank.org/> at 361.

[13] International Union for the Conservation of Nature and Natural Resources, *Oil Exploration in the Tropics: Guidelines for Environmental Protection* (Gland, Switzerland: IUCN, 1991).

[14] Conservation International Policy Paper, Vol 2, 1997.

[15] The API has developed more than 550 technical standards. These "are so widely used both in the United States and around the world that they define standard industry practice". API, "Standards Safeguard the Environment and Human Health," 30 June 1999 (on file with author). ISO Technical Committee 67 is developing a series of technical standards for Materials, Equipment and Offshore Structures for Petroleum and Natural Gas Industries, based primarily on API standards. As of July 2004, there were 104 published ISO standards related to the Technical Committee and its Subcommittees: <http://www.iso.org/>. The OGP, which "strongly supports the internationalisation of key standards," promotes the publication, development, and use of ISO standards, and supports their use without modification wherever possible: *OGP Position Paper on Development and Use of International Standards* (Report No. 318, April 2001). The OGP's *Catalogue of International Standards Used in the Petroleum and Natural Gas Industries* (Report No 1.24/299, November 1999) lists nearly 800 international standards that are used in the international oil industry. Other organisations that produce technical standards adopted for international use include the International Electrotechnical Commission, the American Society of Mechanical Engineers, the American Society for Testing and Materials, and the National Association of Corrosion Engineers.

auditing; and environmental reporting. When successfully implemented by oil companies, these practices can significantly improve environmental performance and minimise the environmental destruction that occurs as a result of oil and gas exploration and production. These practices, and some of their main strengths and weaknesses, will now be discussed.[16]

Environmental and Social Impact Assessment

EIA is a procedure whereby the significant environmental impacts of a proposed development project are assessed prior to activity taking place.[17] EIA has the potential to be a powerful tool to ensure that the environmental and cultural impacts of proposed development activities are assessed, taken into account in decision-making, and mitigated. It is a process to which indigenous peoples should be able to contribute by providing knowledge and expertise about ecosystems and predicted environmental and cultural impacts of development.

Although the features of EIA vary between jurisdictions, there are a number of common elements. These are:

1. *Screening*: A mechanism to identify projects with potentially significant adverse environmental impacts in order to screen out proposals with minimal impacts.
2. *Scoping*: A process of determining the range of issues to be addressed in the EIA and identifying the significant issues relating to a proposed action.
3. *Alternatives*: The identification and measurement of the impacts of alternatives to a proposed development that may cause less environmental damage, including the option of no development.
4. *Baseline Environmental Study*: This provides a description of the existing environment of the proposed development site and its environs, including a cultural resources survey, prior to any activity taking place. The cultural resources of indigenous peoples include: places of traditional, cultural, spiritual, religious, and economic importance; cultural items including human remains, funerary items, sacred objects, and objects of cultural patrimony; cultural uses of the natural environment, such as subsistence use of plants and animals and ceremonial and religious use of plants, animals and minerals; and religious practices, particularly those related to specific sacred or spiritual sites.[18]
5. *Impact Prediction*: A procedure for ensuring that all potentially significant environmental impacts, including cultural and social impacts, are identified and taken into account.
6. *Mitigation Measures*: The identification and discussion of measures to mitigate predicted adverse environmental impacts.
7. *Environmental Impact Statement or EIA Report*: The document, usually prepared by the proponent of an activity, that describes a proposed development, discloses the predicted impacts on the environment, and sets out information on feasible alternatives and mitigation and protection measures.
8. *Public Participation and Review of EIS*: Public consultation and participation are an integral part of an effective EIA process, and may take place at all stages in the EIA process. As a minimum, EIA procedures in democratic countries allow for public review and comment on a draft EIS before a final EIS is prepared.[19]
9. *Decision*: After the final EIS has been prepared, the relevant decision-making body must make a decision regarding whether the proposed development should proceed, and if so, whether any conditions such as mitigation measures will be imposed. In most systems, the decision-making body is required to take into account, take due account of, or consider, the EIA when making a decision.
10. *Post-Project Analysis*: This includes ongoing surveillance and control over development activities and their effect on the environment through monitoring and auditing. Types of monitoring and auditing include: implementation monitoring, which involves checking that the project has been implemented in accordance with the approval, that mitigation measures correspond with those required, and that any conditions are met; impact monitoring, which involves measurement of the environmental impacts that have occurred, including cultural and social impacts; and impact auditing, which involves comparison between the predictions of the EIS and the results of the implementation and impact monitoring.[20]

Under most national EIA legislation, Social Impact Assessment (SIA), a method for assessing the impact of development strategies and projects on societies and cultures, is undertaken as part of the EIA process.[21] Social impacts are "the consequences to human populations of any public or private actions – that alter the way in which people live, work, play, relate to one another, organise to meet their needs, and generally cope as members of society." The term also includes

[16] The sections relating to environmental management systems, environmental performance evaluation, environmental monitoring and auditing; and environmental reporting, are shorter, updated versions of those appearing in Wawryk A, "Adoption of International Environmental Standards by Transnational Oil Companies: Reducing the Impact of Oil Operations in Emerging Economies" (2002) 20 JERL 402–34.

[17] There are numerous articles and books on EIA. See, for example, Gilpin A, *Environmental Impact Assessment (EIA): Cutting Edge for the Twenty-First Century* (Cambridge University Press, Cambridge UK, 1995); Glasson J, Therivale R, and Chadwick A, *Introduction to Environmental Impact Assessment: Principles and Procedures, Process, Practice and Prospects* (UCL Press Limited, London, 1994); Morris P and Therivel R (eds), *Methods of Environmental Impact Assessment* (London, UCL Press Limited, 1995); Wood C, *Environmental Impact Assessment: A Comparative Review* (Longman Group Limited, Essex UK, 1995).

[18] King T, "What Should be the 'Cultural Resources' Element of an EIA?" (2000) 20 *Environ Impact Assessment Rev* 5 at 15–16.

[19] Wood C, see note 17 at 227. [20] Ibid at 197–9.

[21] IUCN Inter-Commission Task Force on Indigenous Peoples, *Indigenous Peoples and Sustainability: Cases and Actions* (International Books, Utrecht, 1997) at 150.

cultural impacts involving "changes to the norms and beliefs that guide and rationalise their cognition of themselves and their society."[22]

For some developments, the social and cultural effects may be far more significant than the impacts of the project on the physical environment, and yet social impacts may be more difficult to assess, predict, and manage. Currently, methods for assessing the social and cultural impacts of oil projects are less advanced than methods for measuring effects of development activities on the physical environment such as the air, waters, and soils, although a number of organisations such as the Interorganisational Committee on Guidelines and Principles for Social Impact Assessment and the World Bank have produced guidelines for social impact assessment.[23] Challenges in the assessment and mitigation of social effects include: establishing clear benchmark criteria; identifying appropriate measures for impact assessment and mitigation; determining methods to address social impacts, which often require nonengineering solutions; and balancing the needs and desires of different stakeholders.[24]

Not only is EIA becoming "singularly important in both domestic and international environmental law," but the requirement for EIAs to be conducted as a prerequisite to the approval of major resource development projects is "one of the strongest trends in global mining."[25] EIA requirements are contained in treaties, national laws, and industry guidelines, and are imposed as conditions of lending and assistance by international financial organizations.

First, EIA requirements are contained in many instruments of international environmental law, including Principle 17 of the 1992 Rio Declaration on Environment and Development; Article 14(1)(a) of the 1992 UN Convention on Biological Diversity; and Article 4(f) of the 1992 UN Framework Convention on Climate Change, which were heavily influenced by UNEP's 1987 *Goals and Principles of Environmental Impact Assessment*, and a number of early regional treaties concerned with international watercourses and the assessment of transboundary environmental effects.[26] The most detailed procedures are contained in the 1991 Convention on Environmental Impact Assessment in a Transboundary Context, and the 1991 Protocol to the Antarctic Treaty on Environmental Protection.[27] The importance of EIA is also recognised in regional systems, most notably in Europe, where European Council Directive 85/337/EEC of 27 June 1985 obliged EC member states to have national EIA legislation in place by July 1988, and which has also formed the basis for EIA legislation by nonmember European States.[28]

Second, EIA is recommended in the publications of oil and gas industry bodies. The OGP recommends the use of EIA in the oil and gas industry in its publications *View of Environmental Impact Assessment* (1986) and *Principles for Impact Assessment: the Environmental and Social Dimension* (1997).[29] The latter document, which "highlights the importance of social and environmental assessment in all aspects of project planning to oil and gas companies and their contractors," recognises that EIA is an "integral part of projects management and engineering for all operations from seismic to decommissioning."[30] The OGP identifies consultation with stakeholders, including indigenous peoples, as a key aspect of environmental and social impact assessment.[31]

The OGP has recommended the use of EIA in a number of its guidelines.[32] These guidelines, which represent

[22] The Interorganisational Committee on "Guidelines and Principles for Social Impact Assessment" (1995) 15 *Environ Impact Assessment Rev* 11 at 11 (hereafter ICGPSIA, *Guidelines and Principles for SIA*).

[23] ICGPSIA, *Guidelines and Principles for SIA*; World Bank, *Social Assessment – Key Concepts*, <http://www.worldbank.org/>. See also the International Association for Impact Assessment, *International Principles for Social Impact Assessment* (Special Publication Series No. 2, May 2003) <http://www.iaia.org/Members/Publications/Guidelines_Principles/SP2.pdf>, accessed 5 July 2004; and the United Nations Environment Program, *UNEP Environmental Impact Assessment Training Resource Manual* (2nd ed, June 2002) Topic 13 – "Social Impact Assessment," 461–87.

[24] Oil Industry International Exploration and Production Forum, *Principles for Impact Assessment: the Environmental and Social Dimension*, Report No. 2.74/265, August 1997, (hereafter E&P Forum, *Principles for Impact Assessment*) at 3. See also Joyce S and MacFarlane M, *Social Impact Assessment in the Mining Industry: Current Situation and Future Directions* (International Institute for Environment and Development and the World Business Council for Sustainable Development, 2002), <http://www.iied.org/mmsd/mmsd_pdfs/social_impact_assessment.pdf – MMSD>, accessed 5 July 2004.

[25] Kiss A and Shelton D, *International Environmental Law* (Transnational Publishers Inc, Ardsey New York, 2nd ed, 2000) at 203; Pring G, Otto J and Naito K, "Trends in Environmental Law Affecting the Minerals Industry (Part I)" (1999) 17(1) *J Energy & Nat Resources L* 39 at 54.

[26] Rio Declaration on Environment and Development, adopted 14 June 1992, UNCED Doc A/CONF.151/5/Rev.1, (Vol I), Annex I, 13 June 1992, 31 *ILM* 874 (1992); Convention on Biological Diversity, adopted 5 June 1992, 31 *ILM* 818 (1992) (entered into force 29 December 1993); Framework Convention on Climate Change, adopted 9 May 1992, 31 *ILM* 848 (1992) (entered into force 21 March 1994); UNEP, *Goals and Principles of Environmental Impact Assessment*, UNEP Governing Council Res GC14/25, 17 June 1987; endorsed by the United Nations in UNGA Res 42/184 (1987).

[27] Convention on Environmental Impact Assessment in a Transboundary Context, (Espoo), adopted 25 February 1991, 30 *ILM* 800 (1991); the Antarctic Treaty (Washington), adopted 1 December 1959, 402 UNTS 71; 12 UST 794; UKTS 97 (1961), Cmnd 1535; TIAS 4786; 19 *ILM* 860 (1980) (entered into force 23 June 1961); Protocol to the Antarctic Treaty on Environmental Protection (Madrid), adopted 4 October 1991, 30 *ILM* 1455 (1991) (not yet in force).

[28] EEC Directive on the Assessment of the Effects of Certain Projects on the Environment, adopted 27 June 1985, 85/337/EEC, OJEC L 175 (5/7/85). For information on the Directive, see Kiss A and Shelton D, note 25 at 208–9.

[29] E&P Forum, *Principles for Impact Assessment*, see note 23. See also IPIECA/E&P Forum, *The Oil Industry: Operating in Sensitive Environments*, (Report No. 2.73/255, May 1997, revised version as of 5 July 2004, <http://www.ipieca.org/publications/biodiversity.html>) stating that "impact assessments are an integral part of project development and implementation"; APPEA's 1996 *Code of Environmental Practice* and ARPEL's *Guidelines for Environmental Impact Assessment (EIA) Process* (1992).

[30] E&P Forum, *Principles for Impact Assessment*, see note 24 at 1 and 3.

[31] *Ibid* at 4–7.

[32] E&P Forum, *Oil Industry Operating Guideline for Tropical Rainforest*, see note 8; *Oil and Gas Exploration and Production in Mangrove* Areas, see note 8; *Oil and Gas Exploration in Arctic Offshore Regions – Guidelines for Environmental Protection*, note 8; Oil *and Gas Exploration in Arctic and Subarctic Onshore Regions*, note 8; E&P Forum, *Exploration and Production Waste Management Guidelines*, note 8; *Decommissioning, Remediation and Reclamation Guidelines for Onshore Exploration and Production Sites*, note 8.

"internationally acceptable operating practices" and "internationally acceptable goals and guidance on environmental protection during oil and gas exploration and production operations," fully endorse the EIA process and provide recommendations and guidance to oil companies on the EIA process.[33] A key development in the EIA process as it applies to oil and gas companies is the expectation that companies will assess the impacts of oil and gas development not merely on the physical environment, but also on local and indigenous peoples. The OGP guidelines emphasise the importance of social and environmental impact assessment for assessing, predicting, avoiding, and mitigating the negative impacts of development on the physical and cultural environment of indigenous peoples, including impacts on cultural and religious practices, resource utilisation, and land use patterns.

The Arctic Onshore Exploration Guidelines contain comprehensive recommendations for identifying and minimising the negative effects of oil exploration and production operations on indigenous peoples, most of which are applicable to oil operations in general, not only operations in arctic and subarctic regions. The Guidelines state that the "customary rights and cultural heritage of indigenous peoples, including customary rights of access to land and other natural resources, and to exploit the 'products' of those resources, should be identified and respected throughout all phases of oil and gas operations."[34] The primary method by which the culture and environment of indigenous peoples are to be identified is by environmental impact assessment.

As part of EIA procedures, the Arctic Guidelines recommend the appropriate use of cultural resource surveys to: identify and document cultural resource sites; assess the likely impact of the proposed development on these sites; make recommendations for avoidance or mitigation of impacts; satisfy local and national regulation; and evaluate potential environmental factors of cultural importance. The Guidelines recognise that it is "likely that local residents will be the most important source of information" and suggest "full cooperation should be maintained at all stages." Survey results should be made known to the local community. "Appropriate consultation" throughout "all phases of oil and gas development" is seen as essential to ensuring "recognition and careful consideration of the culture and practices of indigenous peoples, including avoidance of sacred and archaeological sites."[35] The Guidelines recommend various measures to ensure that the predicted adverse effects resulting from their oil development activities are avoided, minimised, or mitigated.

Although the OGP has not produced any guidelines specific to social impact assessment, in 2002, the Association published, with the International Petroleum Industry Environmental Conservation Association, the joint report *Key Questions in Managing Social Issues in Oil & Gas Projects.*[36] The report contains ten lists of questions relating to a range of issues that may be encountered at all stages of an oil project, and which is intended to provide a tool in managing social planning. The lists of questions pertain to the following headings: legal and other agreements; safety and security; consultation and information disclosure; compensation; resettlement; cultural resources; employment and labour actions; local economic development, housing, and community impacts; national infrastructure and utilities; and health. Under each heading, the questions are grouped according to topics. For example, the topics under which the questions are grouped for cultural resources are: general background, project standards/commitments, potential lender/government standards/guidelines, sacred and religious properties, archaeological and historical sites/ palaeontological sites, archaeological sites, human remains, landscapes and other natural features, and underwater sites.[37]

As an example of the types of questions posed in the Report, those concerning human remains include the following: Are there human remains in the area? Is it possible to avoid them? Has a qualified professional positively identified them? Have the next of kin been identified and consulted? If not, when will this be completed? What are the regulatory requirements regarding the treatment of remains? If not recent remains, which groups, if any, may wish to claim the remains or have specific wishes about how they are to be treated? If the remains are to be removed, will specialists move them? Although there are some comments on key points in relation to each topic, it can be seen that these are not guidelines for protecting cultural resources. Rather, the questions are designed to raise awareness of issues that should be addressed in planning.

Third, many major multilateral and bilateral development institutions have adopted environmental policies and procedures. Of these, the most influential EIA requirements are those of the World Bank. The Bank's environmental and social impact assessment requirements are set out in the *Environmental Assessment Sourcebook*, and include Operational Policy 4.01 *Environmental Assessment*, Bank Procedure 4.01 *Environmental Assessment*, and Good Practice 4.01 *Environmental Assessment*, together with Annexes.[38] Oil and gas development projects are classified as projects that are "likely to have significant adverse environmental impacts that are sensitive, diverse, or unprecedented" and require an EIA.[39]

As with the guidelines of the OGP, the Bank's environment assessment requirements include special procedures for developments that affect indigenous peoples. These are

[33] *Oil and Gas Exploration and Production in Mangrove Areas*, *ibid* at 1; *Oil and Gas Exploration in Arctic and Subarctic Onshore Regions*, *ibid* at 1.
[34] *Oil and Gas Exploration in Arctic and Subarctic Onshore Regions*, ibid at 16.
[35] *Ibid* at 23.
[36] *Key Questions in Managing Social Issues in Oil & Gas Projects* (OGP/IPIECA, OGP Report No. 2.85/332, October 2002).
[37] *Ibid* pp. 30–3.
[38] *Environmental Assessment Sourcebook* (Washington DC, World Bank, 1991).
[39] World Bank, Good Practice 4.01 *Environmental Assessment*, "Annex B: Types of Projects and their Typical Classifications," January 1999.

Operational Directive 4.20, *Indigenous Peoples* (currently under revision), and Operational Policy 4.12, *Involuntary Resettlement* (revised April 2004). If a project raises issues covered by OD 4.20 or OP 4.12, it is considered "sensitive" for the purposes of categorisation of projects for environmental assessment. According to paragraph 13 of OD 4.20, where an investment project affects indigenous peoples, the borrower should prepare an indigenous peoples development plan that is consistent with the Bank's policy. The information to be contained in a plan includes: the legal framework regarding indigenous rights, baseline data, steps for recognising and protecting indigenous land tenure, strategies for local participation by indigenous peoples, technical identification of development or mitigation activities, assessing the capabilities and needs of government institutions assigned responsibility for indigenous peoples, an implementation schedule, provisions for monitoring and evaluation, and cost estimates and financing plans.

The World Bank's proposed support of an oil rehabilitation project in the Khanty Mansi Autonomous Okrug in Siberia demonstrates how EIA procedures operate with respect to indigenous peoples. The World Bank proposed to lend $500 million in the form of counter guarantees to commercial lenders backing a joint venture between Amoco Eurasia Petroleum Company and Yuganskneftegas to develop the North Priobskoye field situated in the Khanty Mansi Autonomous Okrug (KMAO) in Siberia.[40] As part of the loan package, the Bank required its EIA procedures, including the special procedures relating to indigenous people, to be met by Amoco Eurasia and Yuganskneftegas.

The draft EIA prepared by the proponents contained "rigorous safeguards designed to ensure that any environmental disruptions or damage would be kept to the lowest possible level," including multiple-well drilling pads and commingling of production from different geological strata; pipeline construction under the River Ob; detailed programs for waste management, well abandonment, and reclamation and replanting of disturbed lands; comprehensive emergency response procedures; and heath and safety systems. The proponents also engaged in negotiations for the creation of new environmentally protected areas in the KMAO.[41]

The Bank required the proponents to include a plan for the protection and support of indigenous peoples in the EIA, consistent with Operational Directive 4.20 on indigenous peoples, dealing with: impact assessment and monitoring, mitigation and compensation, local employment and training, and institutional strengthening. The proponents engaged in a consultation for more than three years with the affected local and indigenous peoples, which included meetings and community newsletters providing information on project progress and issues, signed a Protocol with one village (the Seliyarvo Protocol) regarding the protection of the village, and suggested "a number of micro projects to improve local conditions on a sustainable basis."[42] Unfortunately, it is not possible to measure the success in practice of the procedures because the project was cancelled because of a breakdown in negotiations between the Russian principals and Amoco Eurasia.[43]

The Bank, in conjunction with a number of oil companies and NGOs, has also set up an Internet site to harness knowledge on the social impacts of oil and gas operations. This site contains a virtual meeting place to share knowledge about the social and environmental impacts of oil and gas operations, and contains recommendations for best practice in impact mitigation, including a document that specifically addresses "emerging basic principles of best practice" for mitigation of the environmental and social impacts of oil and gas exploration and production activities on indigenous peoples. Prior environmental assessment is one of the key principles endorsed in the document.[44]

The adoption of the Equator Principles, initially by ten banks in June 2003, and currently by twenty-five financial institutions located in fourteen countries, demonstrates the influence of the World Bank Group's environmental policies and procedures.[45] Financial institutions that adopt the Principles will use common terminology to categorise projects for which they provide finance into high, medium, and low environmental and social risk, based on the categorisation process of the International Finance Corporation (part of the World Bank Group). Their customers must demonstrate in their environmental and social reviews and management plans the extent to which they have met the applicable World Bank and IFC sector-specific pollution abatement guidelines and IFC safeguard policies, and justify exceptions to them. Third, the loan documentation for high and medium risk projects will contain covenants for borrowers to comply with their environmental and social management plans. If those plans are not followed, financial institutions may declare the project loan to be in default.[46]

Finally, international business in general has supported the use of EIA, as demonstrated by the ICC's 1991 Business Charter for Sustainable Development. The Charter has been formally endorsed by hundreds of companies worldwide, including many major international oil and gas companies. The Charter comprises 16 principles for environmental management, which is stated to be a "vitally important aspect of

40 World Bank, *Russia – Petroleum Joint Venture*, Project Information Document No. RUPA8807, 30 September 1996, World Bank <http://www.worldbank.org/>, paras 10 and 13. For a critical report on the World Bank's role in the proposed development, see Schmidt E, *The World Bank and Russian Oil* (World Economy, Ecology and Development Association, Bonn, June 1996), <http://www.weedbonn.org/>.

41 World Bank, *Russia – Petroleum Joint Venture, ibid*, para 19.

42 Ibid para 20.

43 Personal communication with Mr. Charles McPherson, Task Manager, World Bank, 16 March 1999.

44 World Bank, "Environmental and Social Impact Mitigation Practices" (2001), <http://www.worldbank.org/ogsimpact/esimkrd.htm>, accessed 5 July 2004.

45 Equator Principles Web site <http://www.equator-principles.com/>, accessed 15 July 2004.

46 *Frequently Asked Questions About the Equator Principles*, <http://www.equator-principles.com/faq.shtml>, accessed 15 July 2004.

sustainable development."[47] According to Principle 5, entitled "prior assessment," companies should "assess environmental impacts before starting a new activity or project and before decommissioning a facility or leaving a site."

A thorough and well-conducted EIA provides a number of benefits, including the following: It provides a procedure for identification of likely adverse environmental impacts, including cultural impacts on indigenous peoples, *before* a decision to proceed with a development activity is made; it provides opportunities to the public and affected people, such as indigenous peoples, to present comments and recommendations to the decision-maker and participate in the development process; it precludes secrecy in official decision-making, and opens the process of development to scrutiny; it provides an opportunity to identify and take alternative development options; it presents an opportunity to identify and incorporate mitigation measures into a development activity; and conditions of approval may ensure monitoring of environmental (including cultural) impacts, annual reporting by the proponent, post-project analyses and independent environmental auditing.[48]

The OGP has identified a number of advantages of environmental and social assessment for oil and gas companies.[49] First, EIA can be beneficial to the project schedule and cost through the "significant financial savings" that can arise from the early identification and resolution of potential problems and conflicts, the avoidance of delays, and improved decision-making and project planning. Second, EIA allows companies to demonstrate a management capability for self-regulation, thus avoiding unnecessary regulation by governments. EIA assists companies to: demonstrate a scientific and technical credibility; "an integrated approach to social and environmental issues" that is "likely to lead to projects that are more acceptable and hence more likely to be supported, especially in sensitive areas," and a willingness to participate in local debate; address the information needs of stakeholders; and provide assurance to government and the public, thereby generating trust and confidence and enhancing the company image.[50]

Despite the potential benefits of EIA, in practice, where EIA is required by legislation, the procedure has suffered from a number of weaknesses. First, EIAs are usually produced by project proponents, who have the greatest stake in acceptance of the project, leading to the possibility of biased and inadequate environmental impacts statements.

Second, although EIAs should be conducted prior to the commencement of an activity, in practice environmental assessment is conducted only after economic and technical feasibility studies have been completed and investment decisions made, and the developer has already committed to a project in its proposed format. Furthermore, governments may give support to a project on economic grounds before an EIA is prepared, and pressure is then placed on the environmental agency not to delay the proposal by making "unreasonable" demands.[51]

Third, although public participation, including the participation of local and indigenous peoples, is an integral part of the EIA process, public participation may suffer from a number of deficiencies, such as difficulties in obtaining access to information. Fourth, while EIA systems generally require decision-makers to have regard to the EIS, the decision-maker is not obliged to base decisions on the EIS, so projects often are approved despite the results of the EIA. Contributing to most of these difficulties is the underlying attitude of many proponents and governments, who view EIA as a hurdle to development, rather than a useful tool for protection of the environment. Finally, EIA systems in general suffer from a lack of post-decision monitoring.[52]

In relation to the World Bank Group's environmental assessment procedures, the recent Extractive Industries Review (EIR) highlighted deficiencies in these procedures as applied to mining and energy projects.[53] Although it is beyond the scope of this chapter to examine the findings of, and responses to, the EIR, a report prepared for the EIR by the World Bank Group's own Operations Evaluation units identified a number of shortcomings in the environmental assessment procedures.[54] The most critical of these, in relation to the World Bank (the IBRD/IDA) are first, the incorrect categorisation of projects at the screening stage to a lower environmental category than should have been the case, with corresponding implications for the identification and implementation of applicable safeguards policies and the resources devoted to assessing and mitigating environmental impacts; second, inadequate supervision and monitoring, including a lack of employment of environmental and social specialists; and third, inadequate reporting.[55]

The EIA process has also been criticised with respect to its application in emerging economies. It is generally true that

[47] International Chamber of Commerce (ICC), *The Business Charter for Sustainable Development: Principles for Environmental Management*, accessed 5 July 2004, <http://www.iccwbo.org/home/environment_and_energy/sdcharter/charter/principles/principles.asp>.

[48] Gilpin A, note 17 at 3.

[49] OE&P Forum, *View of Environmental Impact Assessment*, Report No. 2.40/135, October 1986 at 3; E&P Forum, *Principles for Impact Assessment*, note 24 at 4.

[50] E&P Forum, *Principles for Impact Assessment, ibid.*

[51] Bates GM, *Environmental Law in Australia* (Butterworths, Sydney, 5th ed, 2002) at 325–8.

[52] *Ibid* at 328–33.

[53] For information and documents, see the EIR Web site, <http://www.eireview.org>.

[54] *Extractive Industries and Sustainable Development: An Evaluation of World Bank Group Experience*, Report No. 26373, 29 July 2003, <http://www.worldbank.org/oed/extractive_industries/>, accessed 15 July 2004. The Report is in four volumes. These are: Vol I: Overview; Vol II: World Bank Experience (Document of the Operations Evaluation Department, the World Bank, composed of the International Bank for Reconstruction and Development [IBRD] and the International Development Association [IDA]); Vol III: IFC Experience [Document of the Operations Evaluation Group, International Finance Corporation]; and Vol IV: MIGA's Experience (Document of the Operations Evaluation Unit, Multilateral Investment Guarantee Agency [MIGA]).

[55] *Extractive Industries and Sustainable Development: An Evaluation of World Bank Group Experience, ibid*, Vol I: Overview, pp. 6–7; Vol II: World Bank Experience, pp. 22–9.

EIA in many emerging economies is ineffective, for a number of reasons:[56]

- the coverage of EIA systems in emerging economies is inconsistent in relation to the types of projects covered and the impacts assessed;
- the consideration of alternatives in EIAs is often weak, and the alternative of "no-action" is often not a viable choice given the constraints of poverty;
- mitigation is often an afterthought, with insufficient opportunities to change previously designated plans;
- a lack of trained people and financial resources leads to the preparation of inadequate EIA reports;
- baseline socio-economic and environmental data are inaccurate, difficult to obtain, or nonexistent;
- EIA reports can also be extremely difficult to obtain by the public, often being classified as confidential, and with very limited numbers of copies available for public inspection, if at all. This is often exacerbated by lack of a culture of participation and low levels of literacy;
- EIA reports often have no influence on the decision that is taken; and
- monitoring of compliance with environmental controls and conditions, and of the EIA system itself, is ineffective or completely absent in developing countries.

In many emerging economies, poverty, the imperative of economic development, and the often-stated view that the country cannot afford to increase environment protection results in government approval of development projects that are not environmentally sustainable. The existence of widespread corruption, political pressures, and inadequate funding; the fact that the "organisations responsible for EIA are frequently new, lacking in status and political clout and working in a culture where an absence of information sharing considerably reduces their influence";[57] and the "bypassing" of that environment ministry by other, more powerful ministries, in particular the ministries concerned with resource exploitation, means that compliance with EIA legislation is inadequately monitored and enforced in the majority of emerging economies.

Environmental Management Systems

EMS are procedural rules or management processes that assist managers in preventing and detecting environmental violations. A number of organisations have produced standards and guidelines for EMS, including the ISO, an international federation of "standards bodies" from more than 100 countries, the European Union,[58] and oil and gas industry bodies. Most of the major international oil and gas companies have started to adopt detailed EMS.[59]

The ISO 14000 series standards are influential, international, voluntary standards that provide specific requirements and principles for environmental management. They give managers a structure for establishing, improving, and maintaining programmes for protection of the environment. The relevant standards are ISO 14001: Environment Management Systems – Specification with Guidance for Use; and ISO 14004: Environment Management Systems – General Guidelines on Principles, Systems and Supporting Techniques. ISO 14004 is a guidance document that explains environmental management concepts, defines key terms, and provides practical advice for the design and implementation of an EMS. ISO 140001 establishes a model EMS.[60] Various oil industry associations have set out requirements for EMS that are consistent with the ISO 14001 series, including the OGP,[61] the API,[62] and APPEA.[63]

The ISO 14001 series does not set environmental legal requirements; rather, it provides a management system to assist managers to comply with existing legal requirements, and to define management processes to be followed to control environmental impacts. A company can make a self-declaration of compliance with ISO 14001, or be audited and gain certification. A company with ISO 14001 certification can claim that it has a documented environmental management system that is fully implemented and consistently followed.[64]

[56] Wood C, note 17 at 302–8; Kerr T, "What's Good for General Motors is Not Always Good for Developing Nations: Standardizing Environmental Assessment of Foreign-Investment Projects in Developing Countries" (1995) 29(1) *Int Law* 153 at 160.

[57] Wood, *ibid* at 302.

[58] The European Union's Eco-Management and Audit Scheme (EMAS) is established by Regulation (EC) No 761/2001 of the European Parliament and of the Council of 19 March 2001 Allowing Voluntary Participation by Organisations in a Community Eco-Management and Audit Scheme (EMAS) (OJ L 114/1, 24/04/2001, pp. 1–29), plus the Corrigendum to Regulation (EC) No 761/2001 of the European Parliament and of the Council of 19 March 2001 allowing voluntary participation by organisation in a Community eco-management and audit scheme (EMAS) (OJ L 114/1, 24/04/2001, p. 10). This regulation replaces the former European Council Regulation 1836/93 of July 10, 1993, Concerning Voluntary Participation by Companies in the Industrial Sector in a Community Eco-Management and Audit Scheme OJ L 168/1.

[59] Wagner J, "Oil and Gas Operations and Environmental Law in Latin America" (1998) 16 *JERL* 153 at 179.

[60] Von Zharen W, *ISO 14000: Understanding the Environmental Standards* (Government Institutes Inc, Rockville, Maryland, 1996) at 51.

[61] Oil Industry International Exploration and Production Forum, *Guidelines for the Development and Application of Health, Safety and Environmental Management Systems*, E&P Forum, Report No. 6.36/210, July 1994. See also *Environmental Management in Oil and Gas Exploration and Production: An Overview of Issues and Management Approaches* (E&P Forum/UNEP, UNEP IE/PAC Technical Report 37, E&P Forum Report No 2.72/254, 1997).

[62] American Petroleum Institute, *Model Environmental, Health and Safety (EHS) Management System*, and *Guidance Document for Model Environmental, Health and Safety (EHS) Management System*, (API Documents 9100A and 9100B, October 1998).

[63] APPEA's *Code of Environmental Practice* provides guidance on the development and application of EMS consistent with the ISO 14000 Series Standards: *APPEA Code of Environmental Practice*, note 11.

[64] Ritchie I and Hayes W, *A Guide to the Implementation of the ISO 14000 Series on Environmental Management* (Prentice Hall Inc, Upper Saddle River, New Jersey, 1998) at 6.

A key benefit to the community of a "well-prepared and comprehensively implemented EMS" is that EMS have the potential to control and reduce environmental degradation by assisting companies to identify and manage their impacts on the environment.[65] Despite the benefits of the ISO 14000 Series standards, there are a number of limitations regarding these standards.[66] One of these is that the ISO 14000 Series does not set legal environmental standards. Certification indicates a corporation has a documented environmental policy, but makes no representation regarding the standard of environmental performance of the company. Thus, if environmental standards in developing countries are of a lower standard than in developed countries, EMS certification will not reveal that the environmental standards observed are not as stringent as those of developed countries. Public and government misconception that EMS set actual environmental standards can lead to misplaced confidence in the regime for environmental protection, providing a "shield" under which oil companies can operate using practices that are clearly below best practice.[67]

Environmental Performance Evaluation

EPE is a process by which a company measures its environmental performance against criteria set by management.[68] The most critical aspect of EPE is the choice of meaningful indicators to measure the environmental impact of activities. There are various sources of information for oil and gas companies to use in compiling indicators, including standards and guidelines produced by regulatory agencies, industry bodies such as the API, OGP and APPEA, and other organisations such as the World Bank.[69] The oil industry is engaged in collaborative efforts to develop indicators of environmental performance.[70]

The measurement of social and cultural performance by oil companies is also an emerging trend, although there are no common, standardised indicators in use, nor do the majority of companies yet report on their performance in these areas. Examples of indicators used by companies include: investment in educational and community programmes, taxes and social contributions paid, support for the Universal Declaration of Human Rights, the number of reported bribes, and the level of local content of projects in terms of jobs and procurement.[71]

The measurement of social and environmental performance has a number of benefits. Not only does it provide companies with benchmarks for improving their performance, but the publication of performance reports based on standardised, comparable criteria allows indigenous peoples, the general public, NGOs, shareholders, and the government to judge the performance of companies, both against their own performance in previous years, and against the performance of other companies. In the context of oil exploration and development, environmental and social performance reports will provide local communities and indigenous peoples with useful information on the past and current environmental and social policies and performance of oil companies that seek to operate on traditional lands, and will provide information to shareholders and the community that can be used to demand improved performance from oil companies.

Environmental Monitoring and Auditing

Monitoring

Environmental monitoring involves the ongoing, regular, and frequent inspection of equipment, management systems, operational activities, and their effect on the environment. Monitoring ensures compliance with environmental and social regulations and with any conditions imposed upon development on the basis of an EIA. It "provides a tool to evaluate and update mitigation strategies, if conditions change or original strategies prove not to be effective," allows anticipated impacts to be documented, and "can identify any unanticipated impacts" of development.[72]

Environmental monitoring is a key feature of EMS that is promoted by the ISO, EMAS, OGP, and the API. The OGP has stated that monitoring the environmental impacts of "all stages of a project is [the] key to responsible operations," whereas APPEA's Environmental Policy states that APPEA encourages and supports its members to "monitor environmental effects."[73]

Auditing

Environmental auditing is "the practice of comparing environmental regulatory and management requirements against the operational and management performance record of a facility by evaluating such records and systems against a set of predetermined standard."[74] In general, environmental audits may be performed in-house, by an independent third-party,

65 Wells D, "Corporate Environmental Management Systems" *1997 AMPLA Yrbk* 530 at 533.

66 Ritchie I and Hayes W, note 64 at 11. For a comprehensive, critical analysis of the ISO standards and the move to international standards in general, see Roht-Arriaza N, "Shifting the Point of Regulation: The International Organization for Standardization and Global Lawmaking on Trade and the Environment" (1995) 22 *Ecology LQ* 479.

67 For an example of this situation, see Kimerling J, "International Standards in Ecuador's Amazon Oil Fields: The Privitization of Environmental Law" (2001) 26 *Colum J Envtl L* 289.

68 Kuhre W, *ISO 14031: Environmental Performance Evaluation (EPE)* (Prentice Hall PTR, Upper Saddle River, New Jersey, 1998) at 3.

69 For examples of these indicators in the oil industry, see Kuhre W, *ibid* at 211–18; and API, *Environmental Performance Indicators: Methods for Measuring Pollution Prevention*, September 1994.

70 SustainAbility Ltd/UNEP, *The Oil Sector Report: A Review of Environmental Disclosure in the Oil Industry* (The Beacon Press, London, 1999) at 55.

71 *Ibid* at 44.

72 E&P Forum, *Principles for Impact Assessment*, note 24 at 11.

73 *The Oil Industry: Operating in Sensitive Environments*, note 28; APPEA *Environmental Policy*, note 6.

74 Prince W and Nelson D, "Developing an Environmental Model: Piecing Together the Growing Diversity of International Environmental

or by a combination of both. The use of an outside auditor may add credibility to the audit findings.[75] Over time, it is expected that increased international attention will be given to requirements for internal and independent third-party environmental auditing and public disclosure of audit results.[76] The OGP has affirmed the importance of environmental auditing for the oil and gas industry, stating that companies "should maintain procedures for audits to be carried out, as a normal part of business control."[77] To date, the ISO standards are considered to be the most influential effort toward standardising environmental auditing,[78] although these standards do not mandate third-party audits or external disclosure of audit reports, and are focused on audits of environmental management systems, rather than on compliance with legal regulations.[79]

In the context of oil exploration and production on indigenous peoples' lands, auditing has a crucial role to play not only in assessing the state of the environment on an ongoing basis, but as a means for determining the damage caused by oil companies in cases where indigenous peoples are claiming compensation for environmental destruction and demanding restitution of the land. For example, in 1992, Petroecuador contracted a Canadian consulting firm to conduct an independent environmental audit of Texaco's facilities in Ecuador. The audit, which was to be "a thorough study of the direct and indirect environmental and socio-economic impacts of Texaco's operations," and legally binding on Texaco, was seen by the indigenous peoples to offer a chance to hold Texaco accountable for the damage it had caused and provide an opportunity for restoration of the degraded environment and modernisation of outdated production methods.[80]

Standards and Agendas Affecting Mining Companies" (1996) 7 *Colo J Int'l Envt L & Pol'y* 247 at 292.

75 Third-party oversight may suffer from a major weakness: the vulnerability of independent monitors and auditors to "capture" by the firms they set out to audit. Where a corporation retains auditors from "for profit" auditing firms, there is a possibility the auditors will become aligned with the interests of the corporation they are monitoring, thereby undermining the independence, accuracy, and reliability of the audit results. On theories of regulation including regulatory capture, see Stigler G, "The Theory of Economic Regulation" (1971) 2 *Bell J of Economics & Management Science* 3–21, and more recently, Ayres I and Braithwaite J, *Responsive Regulation: Transcending the Deregulation Debate* (Oxford University Press, New York, 1992).

76 Wälde T, "Environmental Policies Towards Mining in Developing Countries" (1992) 10 *JERL* 327 at 348; Prince W and Nelson D, note 73 at 261–2.

77 E&P Forum, *Guidelines for the Development and Application of Health, Safety and Environmental Management Systems*, note 61 at 25.

78 The relevant standards are ISO 14010: 1996, *Guidelines for Environmental Auditing – General Principles;* ISO 14011: 1996, *Guidelines for Environmental Auditing – Audit Procedures – Auditing of EMS*; and ISO 14012: 1996 *Guidelines for Environmental Auditing – Qualification Criteria for Environmental Auditors.* Another influential audit scheme is the European Environmental Management and Audit Scheme (EMAS): see Regulation (EC) No 761/2001 of the European Parliament and of the Council of 19 March 2001 allowing voluntary participation by organisations in a community Eco-Management and Audit Scheme (EMAS), note 57.

79 Prince W and Nelson D, note 74 at 293.

80 Kimerling J, "The Environmental Audit of Texaco's Amazon Oil Fields: Environmental Justice or Business as Usual?" (1994) 17 *Harv Hum Rts J* 199 at 200. In the event, the terms of reference of the audit, its lack of independence, and the secrecy with which it was conducted, and its results, have been severely criticised.

Environmental and Social Reporting

As companies across all industry sectors are facing increasing pressure to disclose information regarding their environmental and social performance to governments and the public, a number of general mandatory disclosure requirements and voluntary reporting initiatives have arisen in recent years. To date, most environmental reporting initiatives are voluntary schemes led by industry organisations, IGOs, and NGOs, such as the Global Reporting Initiative, launched by the U.S.-based Coalition for Environmentally Responsible Economies, and the SustainAbility-UNEP "Engaging Stakeholders Programme."[81]

As regards environmental disclosure and reporting specifically in the international oil industry, in 1999, the UK-based group SustainAbility, in partnership with UNEP, produced *The Oil Sector Report: A Review of Environmental Disclosure in the Oil Industry*, which examined efforts at environmental and social disclosure for fifty leading oil companies. The Report found that among large international oil companies, environmental reporting is on the way to becoming standard practice, with most individual companies making some sort of environmental information publicly available.[82]

In addition, a number of oil industry associations publish environmental, health, and safety reports at an industry level. For example, the OGP has published aggregate exploration and production environmental performance data in an annual environment report since August 2000.[83] Other industry associations producing some type of aggregate industry performance data or reports include APPEA, the API, the Norwegian Oil Industry Association, the UK Offshore Operators Association Limited, and Canada's Petroleum Communication Foundation.

Despite the evidence that the oil industry "is taking the reporting agenda seriously," the *Oil Sector Report* found that the quality and content of corporate environmental reports varies considerably among companies. In particular, the overall quality and usefulness of the reports is undermined by lack of comparability from company to company; and a lack of clarity about the data reported in individual reports.[84]

Furthermore, social reporting, which is the process of accounting, preparing, and publishing information on social impacts and performance, including cultural impacts, lags well behind environmental reporting.[85] The *Oil Sector Report* found that "we are some way from seeing truly comparable social performance indicators," and that there is a "pressing need for greater coherence and convergence" in this area.[86] As yet, there is limited agreement on how to measure and

81 SustainAbility Ltd/UNEP, note 70, Appendix 2 at 64–5 lists a number of voluntary environmental reporting guidelines and initiatives.

82 *Ibid* at 10.

83 OGP, "Environmental Performance Indicators – Report for 1998," *Highlights*, August 2000, <http://www.ogp.org.uk/highlights/index.html>.

84 SustainAbility Ltd/UNEP, note 70 at 11–23.

85 *Ibid* at 41.

86 *Ibid* at 43 and 46.

monitor social performance, with the development of indicators being "extraordinarily difficult."[87] Nonetheless, some key clusters of indicators are emerging in the practice of oil companies. The *Oil Sector Report* identified eight categories for reporting, including the category "impacts on local communities," with potential aspects for indicator development in this category being: adherence to global operating standards, independent statements from groups most affected, use of community advisory committees, compensations and compensation policy for local environmental damage, impacts on community health and local economies, skills and technology transfer, and cultural sensitivity and management systems addressing indigenous issues.[88]

Following the publication of the *Oil Sector Report*, various members of the international oil industry have collaborated in a three-stage joint industry initiative – the Joint Corporate Reporting Task Force – to help improve the quality and usefulness of sustainability reporting. The results of the first stage, which assessed the current state of sustainability reporting and reporting trends, were published in February 2003.[89] A Web version of the *Compendium* will be established and regularly updated, allowing companies to revise their reporting practices and measure their performance against other companies and the industry. The second stage, guidance, will involve the development of common sustainability indicators, definitions, and data normalisation factors. The third phase, engagement, will provide means and resources to collect company performance data and provide an industrywide progress report.

As well as oil-industry specific measures, general research into the development of social impact indicators is being conducted by a number of bodies, such as the Institute of Social and Ethical Accountability.[90] A major development is the decision by the ISO in June 2004 to establish a new Technical Committee to develop a guidance document for social responsibility.[91] Also, the rise of "ethical" or "social" investing in the 1990s has contributed to the development of sustainability performance indicators and reports,[92] and various indexes have been developed to enable investors to compare the sustainability performance of companies. An example is the Goldman Sachs Energy Environmental and Social Index, developed for the United Nations Asset Management Working Group, and which relates specifically to oil and gas companies. It is based on an analysis of thirty environmental and social metrics in eight categories, including climate change, pollution, human rights, management diversity and incentives, investment in the future, work force, safety, and transparency and vision.[93] These general business developments serve as useful references to the oil industry's efforts to develop its own guidelines for sustainability.

LEGAL IMPLICATIONS OF STANDARDS

The continuing development and use of standards and guidelines regarding best practices for the protection of the environment, drafted by IGOs such as UNEP and the ISO, often in conjunction with oil and gas industry bodies, have legal implications beyond the formal status of these documents as nonbinding guidelines. In both the international and national sphere, these legally nonbinding guidelines have the potential to "harden" into binding law.[94]

First, in the international sphere, the norms, principles, or standards contained in the guidelines, declarations of principles and codes of practice of NGOs and IGOs, such as the nonbinding Rio Declaration on Environment and Development, can be seen as "soft law."[95] A norm is soft either when it is not part of a binding regime or when it is contained in a binding instrument but is not stated in obligatory terms. Soft

[87] *Ibid* at 43.

[88] *Ibid* at 43–7. The other seven categories are: business values and integrity, human rights, distribution equity, diversity, employee conditions, employee development, and social investment.

[89] IPIECA/API, *Compendium of Sustainability Reporting Practices and Trends for the Oil and Gas Industry*, February 2003, <http://www.ipieca.org>.

[90] SustainAbility Ltd/UNEP, note 70 at 46. The question of external verification of internal company sustainability reports has led to further concerns over the reliability, quality, and consistency of verification reports, which are usually conducted by accounting companies such as PriceWaterhouseCoopers. A number of guidelines for assurance providers have been developed, including the International Auditing and Assurance Standards Board of the International Federation of Accountants revised version of International Standard on Assurance Engagements (ISAE 3000), *Assurance Engagements other than Audits or Reviews of Historical Information* (December 2003).

[91] Greenbiz.com, "ISO to Go Ahead with Guidelines for Social Responsibility," <http://www.greenbiz.com/news/news_third.cfm?NewsID=26912>, accessed 6 July 2004. See also *Working Report on Social Responsibility*, prepared by the ISO Advisory Group on Social Responsibility, 30 April 2004, and *Recommendations to the ISO Technical Management Board*, ISO/TMB AG CSR N32, 30 April 2004, <http://www.iso.org>, accessed 6 July 2004.

[92] Ethical or social investing involves the purchase of securities in products in firms that meet positive criteria, such as environmental sensitivity, and avoiding investments in firms that meet negative criteria, such as weapons manufacturing: Zondorak V, "A New Face in Corporate Environmental Responsibility: The Valdez Principles" (1991) 18 *Bost Coll Env Aff L Rev* 457 (1991) at 481.

[93] *Global Energy: Introducing the Goldman Sachs Energy Environmental and Social Index*, Goldman Sachs Energy Environmental and Social Report, 24 February 2004.

[94] Armstrong K, "The Green Challenge – Managing Environmental Issues in Natural Resource Projects in Developing Countries" (1996) *42nd Rocky Mountain Mineral Law Institute* 3–1; Prince W and Nelson D, note 74; Pring G, Otto J, and Naito K, note 25; Pring G, Otto J, and Naito K, "Trends in Environmental Law Affecting the Minerals Industry (Part II)" (1999) 17(2) *J Energy & Nat Resources L* 151.

[95] For a discussion of soft law see Birnie P and Boyle A, *International Law and the Environment* (Clarendon Press, Oxford, 1992) at 26–30; Chinkin C, "The Challenge of Soft Law and Change in International Law" (1989) 38 *Intl and Comp LQ* 850; Dupuy P, "Soft Law and the International Law of the Environment" (1991) 12 *Mich J Int'l L* 420; Guruswamy L, et al., *International Environmental Law and World Order: A Problem-Oriented Coursebook* (West Publishing Co, St. Paul, Minnesota, 2nd ed, 1999) at 55–62; Hillgenberg H, "A Fresh Look at Soft Law" (1999) 19(3) *EJIL* 499; Kiss A and Shelton D, *International Environmental Law* (Transnational Publishers Inc, Ardsey New York, 2nd ed, 2000) at 46–52; Palmer G, "New Ways to Make International Environmental Law" (1992) *86 AJIL* 259; Szasz P, "International Norm-Making" in Brown Weiss E, *Environmental Change and International Law: New Challenges and Dimensions* (United Nations University Press, Tokyo, 1992) at 69–72.

law has emerged as a new and important source of international law, particularly in the fields of the environment and human rights, as the diversity of the international community and the complexity of the problems to be addressed have made it harder for states to obtain consensus on the creation of legally binding rules.

Over time, soft law may contribute to the formation of binding international law, either through the incorporation of initially nonbinding norms into a treaty, or, when these guidelines, codes, and principles are viewed as legally authoritative by a sufficient number of countries over a sufficient length of time, through the creation of customary law.[96] Thus, over time, measures for protections of the physical and cultural environment, including EIA, environmental management systems, monitoring and auditing, environmental performance evaluation, and environmental reporting, may become standard practices that the international community expects every government to require of oil and gas corporations by law in the future. Furthermore, the current leading international companies are preparing EIAs and implementing EMS, even when national laws do not require them, as "a hedge against future liability for failing to meet international standards."[97]

Nationally, industry statements of best practice may come to be binding through their application by national courts. If industry guidelines are generally endorsed and implemented by international oil companies, national courts can use the guidelines as evidence of industry best practice in litigation against the corporation. National courts can invoke the guidelines to interpret petroleum contracts negotiated with governments, such as service contracts and joint venture agreements, which require the use of best practice,[98] or to interpret legislative provisions that require the use of good international practice.

For example, in the Australian context, APPEA has stated that its voluntary Code of Environmental Practice "could reasonably be regarded as setting a benchmark for defining good oilfield practice on environmental matters," and, thus, implicitly invoked under Commonwealth and State offshore and onshore petroleum legislation such as the Petroleum (Submerged Lands) Act 1967 (Cth), which includes an obligation to conform to "good oilfield practice."[99] APPEA is so concerned with its own potential legal liability arising from reliance on the Code of Environmental Practice by its members, should the Code fail to satisfy legislative requirements, that APPEA has attached a disclaimer of liability to the Code. This disclaimer states in part that:

> The APPEA Guidelines are intended to provide general guidance as to those operating practices which are considered to represent good industry practices in the petroleum industry.
>
> **APPEA does not accept any responsibility or liability for any person's use of or reliance on the guidelines, or for any consequences of such use or reliance.**
>
> The Guidelines have not been reviewed or approved by Government bodies or regulators, and do not have legal force or effect. Therefore, compliance with the Guidelines will not necessarily mean compliance with legal obligations. Each person accessing the Guidelines must acquaint itself with its own legal obligations, and must, on a case-by-case basis, form its own judgement as to the conduct required in order to satisfy the individual circumstances.... It cannot be assumed that compliance with the Guidelines will in any way be sufficient.

Because best practice requirements are generally expressed in terms of the practices accepted *internationally*, an oil corporation is liable to a finding they did not follow best practice as set out in an international guideline, even if the corporation is not a member of an industry association issuing the guideline. Where a company is a member of the organisation that issued the guideline, there is an even greater potential for guidelines to be used as legal standards of industry best practice in legal proceedings because the company may be deemed to have "endorsed" the guidelines by virtue of its membership, even if the company was not actually aware of them.[100] The argument is even stronger in the case of oil companies that participated in the formulation of the industry standards.

As well as their use in interpreting petroleum contracts and legislation, national courts may invoke international guidelines in prosecutions for environmental offences. In particular, the ISO 14000 Series, or other industry standards for EMS based on the Series, may become the legal standard of due care in negligence cases concerning the environment. Alternatively, depending on the jurisdiction, the adoption and implementation of a comprehensive and effective EMS may provide the basis for a due diligence defence in cases of prosecution for environmental offences, reduce the risk of regulators implementing a prosecution, or, if a prosecution is mounted, mitigate the penalty imposed by the court.[101] For example, in *EPA* v. *Great Southern Energy*,[102] when imposing a penalty for pollution at the lower end of the range prescribed by legislation, the Land and Environment Court of New South Wales took into account the fact that the defendent had adopted an environmental policy using an EMS certified to ISO 14001 standards.

The implementation of an EMS may also be a penalty imposed on a corporation by judges for a breach of the law.

[96] Furthermore, IGOs and NGOs that have mechanisms for monitoring compliance with human rights and environmental norms may be able to shame governments and corporations into abiding by the norms: Szasz P, *ibid* at 71.

[97] Pring G, Otto J, and Naito K, (Part I), note 25 at 55.

[98] For example, clause 7.1.5 of Ecuador's Model for Service Contracts in Exploration and Exploitation of Hydrocarbons requires oil operators to "perform all of the services which are the object of this contract, according to the best techniques, equipment and generally accepted international practices for the hydrocarbon industry."

[99] *APPEA Code of Environmental Practice*, note 11.

[100] Armstrong K, note 94 at 3–41.

[101] Wells D, note 65 at 537; Trainor K, "Taking the Myth Out of Environmental Management Systems" *1997 AMPLA Yrbk* 555 at 557.

[102] [1999] NSWLEC 192. See also *EPA v. The Shell Company of Australia Ltd* [1999] NSWLEC 16.

This can be seen from the results of the prosecution of BP Exploration (Alaska) Inc (BPXA) in the United States in 1999 regarding the illegal disposal of hazardous waste on Alaska's North Slope. BPXA pleaded guilty in the U.S. District Court at Anchorage to failing to notify authorities immediately about a release of hazardous substances into the environment. As well as agreeing to pay the maximum criminal fine of US$5 million under the plea agreement, BP Amoco PLC must establish an EMS at all of its US facilities engaged in the exploration, drilling, or production of oil. This is the first system of its kind in the U.S. oil industry to result from a federal prosecution. BPXA must use best environmental practices to protect workers, the public, and the environment, with a court-appointed environmental monitor overseeing the implementation of BP Amoco's nationwide US$15 million EMS system during a five-year probation period.[103]

With increasing numbers of companies entering into negotiations and contracts with indigenous peoples, contracts for exploration and production on indigenous peoples' lands may include terms that demand exploitation that is consistent with international best practice for protection of the environment, including the cultural environment. Again, international guidelines can provide a useful source for identifying best practice, and provide a benchmark against which companies and human rights and environmental groups can monitor developments in guidelines to see whether practice corresponds with written endorsed codes and statements. Alternatively, the contract may contain a clause promising to operate in accordance with international guidelines.

International guidelines also raise the standard expected of oil companies in ways other than their application by the courts. For example, governments themselves may require implementation of good environmental practices as a condition for granting development approval, even where these practices are not required by legislation. The adoption and implementation of an EMS "is so important in today's operating environment that companies without a comprehensive EMS will find it increasingly difficult to gain approvals and ongoing cooperation from regulatory authorities."[104] Pressure for companies to adopt best practice also comes from banks, multilateral lending agencies, and insurance companies, the latter especially being concerned with avoiding the risks and costs of potential environmental litigation.[105]

Finally, the practices voluntarily adopted by one company may become a model for national oil and gas legislation, thereby raising the standard expected of other companies seeking to operate in that country in the future. For example, Texaco's procedures for the exploratory drilling of the onshore site Dao Ruang 1 in Thailand in 1993, conducted according to the company's *Worldwide Exploration and Production Environmental Practices*, were used by the Thai government as a model for drafting the Ministerial Regulations concerning Petroleum Environmental Management.[106]

Although the proliferation of national bodies with national standards may well raise the standards expected of oil companies in their operations overseas, there are a number of difficulties associated with the use of oil industry guidelines that may undermine their effectiveness in emerging economies (in addition to the various criticisms discussed above in relation to specific environmental practices).

The absence of the rule of law in many emerging economies, which undermines the effectiveness of national environmental laws, will impede the translation of nonbinding guidelines into binding national law in emerging economies. The potential use of guidelines depends on the existence of a strong and independent judiciary that is prepared to hold oil companies accountable for their actions and interpret phrases in petroleum contracts such as "good oilfield practice" to mean the strictest level of behaviour outlined in Guidelines and Codes rather than the lowest common denominator. In the absence of a tradition of judicial independence, and in the absence of a political system in which government action is restrained by the decisions of the judiciary, the likelihood that voluntary guidelines will harden into binding law is much reduced.

In particular, the ambiguity of the phrase best practice could provide considerable uncertainty when the phrase is used to interpret legislation, particularly in a country in which the rule of law is absent. On the one hand, phrases such as "internationally acceptable best practice" and "good oilfield practice" are used to allow the legal system to incorporate changes in technology in the oil industry. There is a trade-off between the need for flexibility, encapsulated in such phrases as "good oilfield practice," and the ambiguity inherent in these terms.

One source of ambiguity lies in determining which practices are or should be generally accepted as best practice. Some areas such as environmental reporting are still in a relatively early stage of development, and it is arguable that although environmental reporting is "cutting edge" and desirable practice, it is not yet a generally accepted practice in the industry. This is particularly so for the reporting of individual company performance rather than the reporting by an industry association of the aggregate performance of its members, and also for the measurement and reporting of cultural and social impacts as opposed to impacts on the physical environment. The actual practices of international oil companies, such as waste disposal methods, vary from company to company and, for one company, across jurisdictions, such as across

[103] "BP Amoco Admits Environmental Lapse," *Oil and Gas Journal*, 4 October 1999, 34–5.

[104] Wells D, note 65 at 534.

[105] Pitt H and Groskaufmanis K, "Minimizing Corporate Civil and Criminal Liability: A Second Look at Corporate Codes of Conduct" (1990) 78 *Georgetown LJ* 1559.

[106] *The Oil Industry: Operating in Sensitive Environments*, "Texaco Exploration in North East Bangkok" (IPIECA/E&P Forum, Report No. 2.73/255, London, May 1997). At the time of the report, the Thai government was intending to use Texaco's procedures for closure of the site as the case study for future reference for other concessionaire operations onshore in Thailand.

the different states of the United States, making it difficult to identify the best practices actually in use.

In this context, the five general practices for protection of the environment examined in this article are not the only emerging practices that are or will develop to be part of best practice. Companies should also use products that comply with API, ISO, and IEC standards; and should also incorporate best practice regarding specific aspects of oil operations, such as waste disposal, drilling, etc. Other principles include lifecycle assessment, green accounting, responsibility for restoration of the environment, and payment of compensation when harm has occurred. In these areas, the issue of restoring the cultural environment and measuring damages for compensation for destruction of the cultural environment, not merely the physical environment, will provide challenging developments in the legal arena.

Ambiguity also stems from the existence of many guidelines in the international oil industry, of varying detail and sophistication, so that there is no one international guideline that can be easily pointed to as representing internationally acceptable practice. For example, although I suggested that best practice or internationally acceptable practices for protection of the environment should include prior environmental assessment, including assessment of cultural impacts, the actual requirements for EIA differ among treaties, national laws, international and national oil industry guidelines, and institutions such as the World Bank, and there might be a number of standards that are suitable for adoption.

Furthermore, as time passes and guidelines become out of date, they must be revised and new guidelines prepared. There needs to be a mechanism whereby the standards and practices contained in the guidelines and documents of industry associations, NGOs, and IGOs are reviewed and updated. There is a danger that, in enforcement proceedings, a company may point to an outdated guideline as justification for its operations being best practice. However, expert evidence may be able to avoid this problem. Certainly it is not a problem that is specific to developing countries because issues of interpretation and evidence apply to both developed and developing countries where ambiguous phrases such as good practice or internationally acceptable practice are used.

A possible solution to the choice of guideline to be used as evidence of best practice is to require oil companies to refer to the most stringent guidelines of the industry association of which the oil company is a member. For example, a U.S. company operating in a Latin American country may be a member of the OGP, API, and ARPEL. The guideline that could be selected by the government (in enforcement proceedings) and/or by the relevant court may be the most stringent of these association guidelines. Alternatively, in proceedings before the court, the court could look at the operating practices of the same company in other jurisdictions and choose the most stringent practice as constituting best practice. The relevant court would need expert evidence to ascertain which is the best practice.

Although the need for interpretation of ambiguous phrases such as best practice is not particular to emerging economies because legislation in developed countries such as Australia also incorporates these phrases to capture flexibility and technological change, the absence of a strong and independent judiciary in many emerging economies, together with governments strongly committed to oil exploitation, often at the expense of the environment, mean that phrases such as best practice and internationally acceptable norms may be interpreted to require the lowest level of environmental protection rather than the most stringent practices.

In assessing whether or not international standards improve environmental performance, we see opposite forces at work. On the one hand, the absence of credible and effective voluntary monitoring mechanisms, inadequate enforcement of laws in emerging economies, and the short-term competitive disadvantage that may be faced by a company incurring costs to implement guidelines vis-à-vis competitors that do not incur these costs and/or flout environmental laws, means that relying on voluntary international guidelines drafted by industry to improve environmental performance may actually lead to a "race to the bottom," where the standards are adopted that are less stringent than those that would prevail under a well-enforced legislative regime. On the other hand, the adoption by transnational oil companies of international guidelines provides the leading companies with a competitive advantage in a number of areas, such as preference in gaining government contracts, expedited development approvals, and lower risks of litigation in the future. This leads to a "race to the top," with the leading companies imposing higher standards on their competitors in order to exploit this competitive advantage.[107]

The move toward privatisation of environmental law, where regulation is taken out of the public sphere and into the private sphere through the proliferation of voluntary codes and guidelines, raises issues of equity. For example, in the case of oil exploration and production on the traditional territories of indigenous peoples, those groups that live in an area that is under potential development by a transnational oil corporation applying international best practice will reap benefits that another group, subject to a development process by a corporation with lower standards, will not enjoy. The fairness of this dichotomy in the application of standards must be questioned.

SUGGESTIONS FOR THE FUTURE

An issue that deserves consideration in the future is the extent to which the oil industry associations should be responsible for rebuking member companies should they fail to observe the standards endorsed by the association. For example, Judith Kimberling has identified several areas in which Occidental falls short of best practice in its operations in

[107] Hepple B, "A Race to the Top? International Investment Guidelines and Corporate Codes of Conduct" (1999) 20 *Comp Labor Law & Pol'y J* 347.

the Ecuadorean Amazon.[108] Occidental is a member of the American Petroleum Institute, and the API's commitment to environmental stewardship is part of the association's bylaws. What is and should be the extent of the powers of the API to regulate the behaviour of its members? Should the API and other industry associations monitor their members' environmental (including cultural) performance? Should the API revoke Oxy's membership, and what effect if any, would this have on the company?

One solution to solving the problems of a multiplicity of standards, guidelines, and practices, and to establish standardised performance indicators and reporting formats in the international oil industry, is to develop a self-regulatory code of conduct for the international oil industry. Such a code could be based on the mechanics of the worldwide chemical industry's Responsible Care program, the most sophisticated self-regulatory environmental, health, and safety code in existence.[109]

Responsible Care is coordinated worldwide by the International Council of Chemical Associations (ICCA) through its members, the national chemical manufacturers associations. The core of Responsible Care (as adopted by the American Chemical Council in the United States) is a set of Guiding Principles and Codes of Management Practice. It is a condition of membership in the CMA that companies subscribe to the set of Guiding Principles, through the signature of the Chief Executive Officer, and incorporate the Codes of Management Practice into their operations. These Codes of Practice incorporate and go well beyond existing legal requirements. Each national association accepted as an ICCA member must report annually on its progress in the implementation of Responsible Care. National progress in implementing Responsible Care is measured internally through voluntary member self-evaluations and externally through a voluntary monitoring systems verification process, using independently verifiable performance measures for the six Codes of Practice.

An international oil industry code of conduct, which is drafted and implemented worldwide by an international industry association such as the OGP, and nationally through national or regional oil industry associations such as the API or ARPEL, could serve a useful role in providing uniformity to the body of principles and practices established in the international oil industry for the protection of the environment, culture, and human rights, while still allowing for innovative approaches to improving performance in these areas. An international industry code would also contain a number of limitations that would need to be addressed; for example, the free rider problem, the difficulty of developing a scheme that would involve all oil companies across the globe, including state-owned companies and geophysical contractors, and the establishment of effective sanctions for failure to comply with the code. In regard to this latter issue, governments may have a role to play in co-regulating an international oil industry association code. A global self-regulatory scheme would provide certainty with respect to the standards expected of oil companies as best practice and allow periodic review through the establishment of an appropriate review mechanism, and is an option that should be debated in the future.

[108] Kimerling J, note 67.

[109] For more information on Responsible Care, see Gunningham N, 'The Chemical Industry' in Gunningham – and Grabosky P, *Smart Regulation: Designing Environmental Policy* (Oxford University Press, New York, 1998), and the Chemical Manufacturers Association (US) Internet site, <http://www.americanchemistry.com/>.

QUESTIONS FOR DISCUSSION

1. Laws to protect environment and culture in emerging economies are often ineffective because they are substantively inadequate and/or inadequately enforced. This has led to calls for transnational oil companies to voluntarily improve their performance in countries with inadequate environmental laws. What are the benefits and risks to oil companies of voluntarily incorporating international best practices for protection of the environment, heritage, and culture in their operations in these countries?

2. The international chemical industry's Responsible Care code is one of the most sophisticated voluntary environmental, health, and safety codes in existence. There is no such industry code existing in the international oil industry. What are the strengths and weaknesses of adopting a voluntary industry code for protection of the environment?

3. What criteria or elements would be required to make a voluntary industry code successful? Is there a role for government in ensuring the success of a voluntary industry code? If so, what would that role be?

4. The environmental degradation caused by oil production may have such a devastating impact on the culture and traditional lifestyle of a local community that a breach of human rights occurs. Extractive industries have been linked to other abuses of human rights, such as breaches of human rights by the military or security forces that protect oil installations, and the nonobservance of labor rights. Some transnational oil companies have developed, or are in the process of developing, voluntary guidelines in relation to human rights. Is a voluntary approach to human rights appropriate? What are the arguments for and against incorporating principles relating to human rights in a voluntary industry code?

5. Assume you are a lawyer representing a group of indigenous peoples that has been approached by a mining or oil company interested in gaining access to land for operations. What terms or conditions would you suggest for negotiation in any agreement with the company, to ensure that the environment and culture heritage are duly protected?

BIBLIOGRAPHY AND SUGGESTED FURTHER READING

Armstrong K, "The Green Challenge – Managing Environmental Issues in Natural Resource Projects in Developing Countries" (1996) *42nd Rocky Mountain Mineral Law Institute* 3–1.

Ayres I and Braithwaite J, *Responsive Regulation: Transcending the Deregulation Debate* (New York, Oxford University Press, 1992).

Bell C, "International Environmental Standards and Industrial Codes of Conduct: Toward Sustainable Environmentalism" (2001) 47 *Rocky Mountain Mineral Law Institute* 25–1.

Deegan C, "Environmental Reporting for Australian Corporations: An Analysis of Contemporary Australian and Overseas Environmental Reporting Practices" (1996) 13 *EPLJ* 120.

Gilpin A, *Environmental Impact Assessment (EIA): Cutting Edge for the Twenty-First Century* (Cambridge UK, Cambridge University Press, 1995).

Glasson J, Therivale R and Chadwick A, *Introduction to Environmental Impact Assessment: Principles and Procedures, Process, Practice and Prospects* (London, UCL Press Limited, 1994).

Gunningham N and Grabosky P, *Smart Regulation: Designing Environmental Policy* (New York, Oxford University Press, 1998).

Gunningham N and Sinclair D, *Leaders and Laggards: Next Generation Environmental Regulation* (Sheffield UK, Greenleaf Publishing, 2002).

Hepple B, "A Race to the Top? International Investment Guidelines and Corporate Codes of Conduct" (1999) 20 *Comp Labor Law & Pol'y J* 347.

International Association of Oil and Gas Producers, *OGP Position Paper on Development and Use of International Standards* (Report No. 318, April 2001).

International Association of Oil and Gas Producers, *Catalogue of International Standards Used in the Petroleum and Natural Gas Industries* (Report No 1.24/299, November 1999).

IPIECA/E&P Forum, *The Oil Industry: Operating in Sensitive Environments*, (Report No. 2.73/255, May 1997, revised version as of 5 July 2004) <http://www.ipieca.org/publications/biodiversity.html>.

IPIECA/API, *Compendium of Sustainability Reporting Practices and Trends for the Oil and Gas Industry*, February 2003, <http://www.ipieca.org>.

International Standards Organisation, ISO Advisory Group on Social Responsibility, *Working Report on Social Responsibility*, 30 April 2004, and *Recommendations to the ISO Technical Management Board*, ISO/TMB AG CSR N32, 30 April 2004, <http://www.iso.org>, accessed 6 July 2004.

Joyce S and MacFarlane M, *Social Impact Assessment in the Mining Industry: Current Situation and Future Directions* (International Institute for Environment and Development and the World Business Council for Sustainable Development, 2002), <http://www.iied.org/mmsd/mmsd_pdfs/social_impact_assessment.pdf – MMSD>, accessed 5 July 2004.

Kerr T, "What's Good for General Motors is Not Always Good for Developing Nations: Standardizing Environmental Assessment of Foreign-Investment Projects in Developing Countries" (1995) 29(1) *Int Law* 153.

Kimerling J, "International Standards in Ecuador's Amazon Oil Fields: The Privitization of Environmental Law" (2001) 26 *Colum J Envtl L* 289.

King T, "What Should be the "Cultural Resources" Element of an EIA?" (2000) 20 *Environ Impact Assessment Rev* 5.

Kuhre W, *ISO 14031: Environmental Performance Evaluation (EPE)* (Prentice Hall PTR, Upper Saddle River, New Jersey, 1998).

Mays S, *Corporate Sustainability – An Investor Perspective* (Australian Department of Environment and Heritage, 2003), <http://www.deh.gov.au/industry/finance/publications/index.html>, accessed 5 July 2004.

Morris P and Therivel R (eds), *Methods of Environmental Impact Assessment* (UCL Press Limited, London, 1995).

Pitt H and Groskaufmanis K, "Minimizing Corporate Civil and Criminal Liability: A Second Look at Corporate Codes of Conduct" (1990) 78 *Georgetown LJ* 1559.

Prince W and Nelson D, "Developing an Environmental Model: Piecing Together the Growing Diversity of International Environmental Standards and Agendas Affecting Mining Companies" (1996) 7 *Colo J Int'l Envt L & Pol'y* 247.

Pring G, Otto J, and Naito K, "Trends in Environmental Law Affecting the Minerals Industry (Part I)" (1999) 17(1) *J Energy & Nat Resources L* 39.

Pring G, Otto J, and Naito K, "Trends in Environmental Law Affecting the Minerals Industry (Part II)" (1999) 17(2) *J Energy & Nat Resources L* 151.

Reinventing the Well: Approaches to Minimising the Environmental and Social Impact of Oil Development in the Tropics, Conservation International Policy Paper, Vol 2, 1997.

Ritchie I and Hayes W, *A Guide to the Implementation of the ISO 14000 Series on Environmental Management* (Prentice Hall Inc, Upper Saddle River, New Jersey, 1998).

Roht-Arriaza N, "Shifting the Point of Regulation: the International Organization for Standardization and Global Lawmaking on Trade and the Environment" (1995) 22 *Ecology LQ* 479.

Shoop M and Chiara P, "Sustainable Development and Mining: Oxymoron or Opportunity?" (2003) 49 *Rocky Mountain Mineral Law Institute* 11–1.

Stigler G, "The Theory of Economic Regulation" (1971) 2 *Bell J of Economics & Management Science* 3–21.

SustainAbility Ltd/UNEP, *The Oil Sector Report: A Review of Environmental Disclosure in the Oil Industry* (The Beacon Press, London, 1999).

Trainor K, "Taking the Myth Out of Environmental Management Systems" *1997 AMPLA Yrbk* 555.

United Nations Environment Program, *UNEP Environmental Impact Assessment Training Resource Manual* (2nd ed, June 2002) Topic 13 – "Social Impact Assessment."

United Nations Environment Program, Division of Technology, Industry and Economics, *Regulatory Approaches for the 21st Century*, Summary Report of the Workshop on 'How Government Regulations Interface with Voluntary Initiatives to Improve the Environmental Performance of the Mining Sector,' Toronto, Canada, 13–15 March 2002, <http://www.mineralresourcesforum.org>.

Von Zharen W, *ISO 14000: Understanding the Environmental Standards* (Government Institutes Inc, Rockville, Maryland, 1996).

Wagner J, "Oil and Gas Operations and Environmental Law in Latin America" (1998) 16 *JERL* 153.

Wälde T, "Environmental Policies Towards Mining in Developing Countries" (1992) 10 *JERL* 327.

Walker J and Howard S, *Finding the Way Forward: How Could Voluntary Action Move the Mining Industry Towards Sustainable Development?* (International Institute for Environment and Development and the World Business Council for Sustainable Development, London, 2002).

Wells D, "Corporate Environmental Management Systems" *1997 AMPLA Yrbk* 530.

Wood C, *Environmental Impact Assessment: A Comparative Review* (Longman Group Limited, Essex UK, 1995).

World Bank, *Environmental Assessment Sourcebook* (Washington DC, World Bank, 1991).

World Bank, "Environmental and Social Impact Mitigation Practices" (2001), <http://www.worldbank.org/ogsimpact/esimkrd.htm>, accessed 5 July 2004.

Extractive Industries and Sustainable Development: An Evaluation of World Bank Group Experience, Report No. 26373, 29 July

2003, <http://www.worldbank.org/oed/extractive_industries/>, accessed 15 July 2004.

World Business Council for Sustainable Development (WBCSD), *Meeting Changing Expectations: Corporate Social Responsibility* (1998), <http://www.wbcsd.ch/publications/csrpub.htm>.

Zondorak V, "A New Face in Corporate Environmental Responsibility: The Valdez Principles" (1991) 18 *Bost Coll Env Aff L Rev* 457.

Select Environmental Guidelines and Statements of Policy

American Petroleum Institute (API), *API Environmental Stewardship Pledge for CAREFUL Operations*, <http://www.api.org>, accessed 5 July 2004.

American Petroleum Institute, *American Petroleum Institute Environmental and Safety Mission and Guiding Principles*, <http://www.api.org>, accessed 5 July 2004.

American Petroleum Institute, *Onshore Oil and Gas Production Practices for Protection of the Environment* (Washington DC, API, 3rd ed, 2001).

Australian Petroleum Production and Exploration Association Limited (APPEA), *Environmental Policy*, June 1997, <http://www.appea.com.au/IndustryInformation/Environment/Policy/>, accessed 5 July 2004.

Australian Petroleum Production and Exploration Association Limited, *APPEA Code of Environmental Practice* (1996 ed), <http://www.appea.com.au/Publications/docs/1996EnvCode.pdf>, accessed 5 July 2004.

International Association for Impact Assessment, *International Principles for Social Impact Assessment* (Special Publication Series No. 2, May 2003) <http://www.iaia.org/Members/Publications/Guidelines_Principles/SP2.pdf>, accessed 5 July 2004.

International Association of Oil and Gas Producers (OGP), *Oil and Gas Exploration in Arctic Offshore Regions – Guidelines for Environmental Protection*, Report No. 2.84/329, June 2002).

International Chamber of Commerce (ICC), *The Business Charter for Sustainable Development: Principles for Environmental Management*, accessed 5 July 2004, <http://www.iccwbo.org/home/environment_and_energy/sdcharter/charter/principles/principles.asp>.

International Council on Mining and Metals' Sustainable Development Framework, *ICMM Sustainable Development Framework – Final Principles*, 29 May 2003, <http://www.icmm.com/icmm_principles.php>, accessed 5 July 2004.

International Union for the Conservation of Nature and Natural Resources, *Oil Exploration in the Tropics: Guidelines for Environmental Protection* (Gland, Switzerland: IUCN, 1991).

Interorganisational Committee on Guidelines and Principles for Social Impact Assessment, "Guidelines and Principles for Social Impact Assessment" (1995) 15 *Environ Impact Assessment Rev* 11.

Mining and Environment Guidelines, adopted at the International Round-table on Mining and the Environment, Berlin, 25–28 June 1991.

Oil Industry International Exploration and Production Forum (E&P Forum, now the OGP), *Principles for Impact Assessment: the Environmental and Social Dimension*, Report No. 2.74/265, August 1997.

Oil Industry International Exploration and Production Forum, *Decommissioning, Remediation and Reclamation Guidelines for Onshore Exploration and Production Sites*, Report No. 2.70/242, October 1996.

Oil Industry International Exploration and Production Forum, *Exploration and Production Waste Management Guidelines*, Report No. 2.58/196, September 1993.

Oil Industry International Exploration and Production Forum, *Oil and Gas Exploration in Arctic and Subarctic Onshore Regions: Guidelines for Environmental Protection* (Gland, Switzerland; Cambridge, UK: IUCN/E&P Forum, Report No. 2.55/185: 1993).

Oil Industry International Exploration and Production Forum, *Oil and Gas Exploration and Production in Mangrove Areas: Guidelines for Environmental Protection* (Gland, Switzerland: IUCN/E&P Forum, Report No. 2.54/184: 1993).

Oil Industry International Exploration and Production Forum, *Oil Industry Operating Guideline for Tropical Rainforest*, Report No. 2.49/170, April 1991.

Oil Industry International Exploration and Production Forum, *View of Environmental Impact Assessment*, Report No. 2.40/135, October 1986.

Regional Association of Oil and Natural Gas Companies in Latin America and the Caribbean (ARPEL), *Guidelines for the Elaboration of Terms of Reference for the Environmental Impact Assessment of Petroleum Industry Projects and Environmental Audits of Oil and Gas Industry Activities* (1998).

Regional Association of Oil and Natural Gas Companies in Latin America and the Caribbean, *Code of Environmental Conduct*, May 1997, http://portal.arpel.org/wps/portal.

Regional Association of Oil and Natural Gas Companies in Latin America and the Caribbean, *Guidelines for Environmental Impact Assessment (EIA) Process* (1992).

Regional Association of Oil and Natural Gas Companies in Latin America and the Caribbean, *Guidelines for Conducting Environmental Audits for Onshore Petroleum Operations* (1992).

The Equator Principles, <http://www.equator-principles.com/>, accessed 15 July 2004.

United Kingdom Offshore Operators' Association, *Environmental Principles*, <http://www.ukooa.co.uk/issues/2000report/enviro00_vision.htm>, accessed 5 July 2004.

United Nations Environment Program, *Goals and Principles of Environmental Impact Assessment*, UNEP Governing Council Res GC14/25, 17 June 1987; endorsed by the United Nations in UNGA Res 42/184 (1987).

World Bank, "Industry Sector Guidelines: Oil and Gas Development (Onshore)," *Pollution Prevention and Abatement Handbook* 1998, <http://www.worldbank.org/>.

INTERNET SITES

AccountAbility,
<http://www.accountability.org.uk/>

American Petroleum Institute (API),
<http://www.api.org>

Australian Petroleum Production and Exploration Association Limited (APPEA),
<http://www.appea.com.au/>

Chemical Manufacturers Association (US),
<http://www.americanchemistry.com/>

Dow Jones Sustainability Indexes,
<http://www.sustainability-indexes.com/>

European Commission Eco-Management and Audit Scheme,
<http://www.europa.eu.int/comm/environment/emas/>

FTSE The Index Company,
<http://www.ftse.com/index.jsp>

Global Reporting Initiative,
<http://www.globalreporting.org/index.asp>

International Association for Impact Assessment, <http://www.iaia.org/>
International Association of Oil and Gas Producers (OGP), <http://www.ogp.org.uk/>
International Chamber of Commerce (ICC), <http://www.iccwbo.org/>
International Council on Mining and Metals (ICMM), <http://www.icmm.com/>
International Petroleum Industry Environmental Conservation Association (IPIECA), <http://www.ipieca.org/>
International Standards Organisation (ISO), <http://www.iso.org/>
Regional Association of Oil and Natural Gas Companies in Latin America and the Caribbean (ARPEL), <http://portal.arpel.org/wps/portal>
The Social Investment Forum, <http://www.socialinvest.org/>
United Kingdom Offshore Operators' Association (UKOOA), <http://www.ukooa.co.uk/>
United Nations Environment Programme (UNEP), <http://www.unep.org/>
World Bank Extractive Industries Review, <http://www2.ifc.org/ogmc/>
World Bank Group <http://www.worldbank.org/>
World Business Council for Sustainable Development (WBCSD), <http://www.wbcsd.ch/templates/TemplateWBCSD5/layout.asp?MenuID=1>
World Conservation Union (IUCN), <http://www.iucn.org/>

PART SIX

Who Owns the Titantic's Treasures?

Protection of the Underwater Cultural Heritage

The chapters in Part VI explore the management, conservation, and protection of the underwater cultural heritage with reference to the international legal regime and its interface with the admiralty law, particularly the doctrine of salvage and finds. An often-polarized debate has pitted the archeological community against the commercial salvor community.

The terms of the debate are articulated in these excerpts from a letter written to the U.S. Commission on Ocean Policy on October 15, 2002, by Robert S. Neyland, Chair of the Advisory Council on Underwater Archaeology (ACUA), in connection with the United States Government's development of a policy on the oceans:

. . . In addition to shipwrecks, underwater cultural heritage includes physical evidence of past cultures preserved in submerged structures, buildings, aircrafts, artifacts, and human remains. Systematic archaeological investigation enables a "window" to this unknown past to be opened, and allows us to observe life as our forebears lived it. Scientific archeology's search for greater understanding of past history through the study of cultural material stands in direct contrast to the goals of treasure salvors, non-accredited "professional archaeologists," and other profit-minded entities who wish only to recover material from shipwrecks so that it may be sold or marketed for a profit. Despite frequent statements by the salvage community to the contrary, very little effort is made by these individuals to conduct proper scientific inquiry, conserve non-saleable artifacts, or adequately publish the results of their research . . .

. . . Most in the treasure salvor community contend that there are certain categories of artifacts (primarily coins, ingots and bars produced from previous metals) whose "economic resource value" outweighs their archaeological significance. Unfortunately, this is a shortsighted view of artifacts and their role in the overall interpretation of shipwrecks. The thousands of artifacts contained within an average shipwreck site have relationships not only to one another and the wreck fabric in which they are contained, but also to the larger culture that produced and placed them aboard the ship in the first place. To have any significant meaning, these relationships must be understood and recorded in great detail. In most instances, salvors are not willing to devote more resources than necessary to obtain the maximum return for their efforts. More often than not, this results in the complete loss of information and interpretation potential.

ACUA asserts that artifact assemblages and other cultural material recovered from shipwrecks and other submerged sites are the collective heritage of humanity. Consistence with this belief, ACUA does not support the sale of artifacts and objects or the dispersal of artifact collections. In addition to being inconsistent with accepted national and international professional museum standards and practice, the sale or dispersal of federally – owned artifacts is contrary to U.S. federal regulation, which states that an artifact collection "should not be subdivided and stored at more than a single repository unless such a subdivision is necessary to meet special storage, conservation, or research needs" [36 CFR 79.6(b)(2)].

Dispersal of artifact assemblages to different owners and facilities detracts from their value as cultural heritage and their collective ability to inform professionals and the public alike. Further, it limits the ability of researchers to locate, travel to, and study these materials. Perhaps worst of all, artifacts in dispersed collections end up being conserved (if at all) in markedly difference way, which frequently results in their deterioration and ultimate loss. None of the aforementioned scenarios are consistent with UNESCO's goal of "preserving underwater cultural heritage for the benefit of humankind." . . .

Can salvage law adapt to the demands of the new technology and through the guidance of the admiralty courts conform to the Convention? Or is any attempt to retrofit the admirality law doctrine as a vehicle for the preservation of the underwater cultural heritage the equivalent to buying new deck chairs for the Titanic?

The debate has intensified with the advances in sonar seabed scanning and imaging technologies and ocean robotics. New technologies allow archeologists to explore the human past in ocean depths beyond the fifty meter boundary set by scuba-diving. Since at least the discovery by Robert Ballard and his teams of the Titanic in the 1980s, it is clear the mysteries and answers about the human past are held in the deep oceans. Yet, can deep water archeology be done without exploitation of the ancient sites for private gain?

Just as technological developments over the past decade and a half have been fueled by archaeological and salvage expeditions, and salvage fueled by technology, so too, is the development of a jurisprudence of historic wrecks, deep ocean ancient sites, and the underwater cultural heritage enmeshed in a net of technological developments as increasingly sophisticated technology permits salvage operations beyond territorial waters.

Many archaeologists, lawyers, and scholars have argued that the law of salvage – motivated by economic gain – is fundamentally at odds with archeological values in preserving the underwater cultural heritage. It is the primary interpretation of Article 4 of the Convention. Can salvage law accommodate the values of archeology?

Courts have rarely questioned whether salvage law is appropriate at all for historic wrecks. To the consternation of many marine archaeologists, courts have uniformly found that shipwrecks and artifacts at the bottom of the ocean are as a matter of law in marine peril.

The authors of an article entitled, "Salvor in Possession: Friend or Foe to Marine Archaeology?" conclude that the legal framework is itself flawed by uncertainty and that the deliberations of the admirality courts are hampered by procedural deficiencies. The authors further conclude that in trying to assess the appropriateness of a salvor's conduct without reference to, and review by, the professionals, the courts have undertaken a difficult task with inadequate resources.

It is true that insufficient attention has been paid by the admirality courts to deep water archeological methodology. For example, in the 2002 U.S. federal apepellate court decision in *Bemis v. The RMS Lusitania*, a salvor was denied sole salvor status over the wreck of the Lusitania. "Bemis has expended significant resources; however, he has retrieved very few artifacts." The hull rests on the ocean floor off the coast of Ireland where it was sunk by a torpedo. The wreck is below 295 feet of water, making efforts to salvage the contents of the ship extremely difficult.

The appellate court affirmed the denial of a salvage award and restrained the salvor from taking artifacts from the wreck because of its scientific, historical, and archeological significance, concluding that the salvor did not use good archeological practice or due diligence. However, the court's emphasis on the recovery of the artifacts rather than their preservation *in situ* questions the flexibility of salvage doctrine to evolve so as to protect underwater cultural heritage. The law of salvage historically encouraged salvors to rescue ships and return the recovered goods to the stream of commerce.

Can the competing approaches to the management of the underwater cultural heritage find reconciliation in admiralty law? The answer depends on an admiralty court's receptiveness to evolving standards of international law and a willingness to redefine such old concepts as "marine peril," abandonment," "salvage," "clean hands," and "possession" to reflect the new technological realities.

If salvage law cannot accommodate the preservation of the underwater cultural heritage, can partnerships among states, salvors, and archeologists? The British government, on May 25, 2003, gave final approval to the recovery of a seventeenth-century shipwreck believed to contain history's richest sunken treasure. The British government believes the excavation site contains the wreckage of H. M. S. Sussex, which went down in a storm in 1694 with gold coins on board. Today, experts said, the cargo could fetch perhaps as much as $4 billion.

Odyssey Marine Exploration Inc. of Tampa, Fla., found what the British authorities believe to be the wreckage of the Sussex during four expeditions from 1998 to 2001. It is a disintegrating mound rich in cannons, anchors, and other artifacts. In September, 2003, the company signed an agreement with the British government to raise its remains from the bottom of the Mediterranean and split the proceeds.

Odyssey's plan, officials said, went through two drafts and five months of analysis and comment by the British government and its advisers. In the end, the parties agreed to two amendments relating to conservation of artifacts and remediation of the site after the excavation was completed.

The plan also features a new advisory body meant to oversee the recovery team and maintain high archaeological standards. The four-member body is named the Sussex Archaeological Executive. Odyssey and the British government will each appoint two members.

The agreement calls for archaeological integrity – a difficult feat a half-mile down. Even if that turns out to be feasible, many archaeologists abhor the sale of recovered artifacts, saying it inhibits scholarly analysis and public display. Responding to such criticism, the partnership agreement draws a distinction between classes of artifacts, saying cultural items like the ship's tools, cannons, and navigational gear have a greater archaeological value than its cargo of coins. These, it says, can be sold to help defray the millions of dollars in costs that Odyssey' will accrue from locating and recovering the remains of the Sussex.

EDITOR'S NOTE

The United States released its ocean policy, which contains virtually no mention of archeological cultural resources or the Convention on the Underwater Cultural Heritage. On September 20, 2004, the U.S. Commission on Ocean Policy fulfilled its mandate to deliver a comprehensive and coordinated national ocean policy to the President and Congress. The Commission's final report, "An Ocean Blueprint for the 21st Century," contains 212 recommendations addressing all aspects of ocean and coastal policy.

The Executive Order signed by President Bush establishes the Committee on Ocean Policy and states that, "It shall be the policy of the United States to: (a) coordinate the activities of executive departments and agencies regarding ocean-related matters in an integrated and effective manner to advance the environmental, economic, and security interests of present and future generations of Americans; and (b) facilitate, as appropriate, coordination and consultation regarding ocean-related matters among Federal, State, tribal, local governments, the private sector, foreign governments, and international organizations." Conspicuously omitted is any reference to the "cultural heritage," see <http://www.oceancommission.gov/>.

CHAPTER THIRTY-EIGHT

The 2001 UNESCO Convention on the Protection of the Underwater Cultural Heritage

Tullio Scovazzi

AN UNEXPECTED OBSTACLE

On 6 November 2001, the Convention on the Protection of the Underwater Cultural Heritage (CPUCH)[1] was signed in Paris with UNESCO. When entered into force,[2] it will apply to "all traces of human existence having a cultural, historical or archaeological character which have been partially or totally under water, periodically or continuously, for at least 100 years" (Art. 1, para. 1, a).

The CPUCH, which is the outcome of a longlasting negotiation, was adopted by vote (eighty-seven States in favour, four against,[3] and fifteen abstentions[4]). However, the lack of consensus at the moment of its adoption should not be considered as an irreparable flaw. Not only did the great majority of developing countries vote in favour, but also several among the industrialized countries and maritime powers were satisfied with the final outcome of the negotiations.[5]

To explain the merit of the CPUCH, a basic consideration must be made. Any attempts to deal with the cultural heritage at sea have inevitably to face an unexpected obstacle; that is, Art. 303 of the United Nations Convention on the Law of the Sea (UNCLOS; Montego Bay, 1982).[6] This provision is not only incomplete, but also counterproductive. It can be understood in a sense that undermines the very objective of protecting the underwater cultural heritage. Such a clearcut assumption about the deficiencies of Art. 303 requires some elaboration.

THE UNCLOS REGIME

The UNCLOS regime relating to the underwater cultural heritage is based on the following scheme.

Two General Obligations

Art. 303, para. 1, sets forth two very general obligations of protection and cooperation which apply to all archaeological and historical objects, wherever at sea they are found:

> States have the duty to protect objects of an archaeological and historical nature found at sea and shall co-operate for this purpose.

Because of its rather broad content, Art. 303, para. 1 does not say very much. Nevertheless, some legal consequences can be drawn from it. A State which knowingly destroyed or allowed the destruction of elements of the underwater cultural heritage would be responsible for a breach of the obligation to protect it.

A State which persistently refused any request by other States to establish some forms of cooperation aiming at the protection of the underwater cultural heritage could also be held responsible of an internationally wrongful act. An obligation to cooperate is not devoid of legal meaning. It implies a duty to act in good faith in pursuing a common objective and in taking into account the situation of the other interested States. As remarked by the International Court of Justice in the judgement of 20 February 1969 on the *North Sea Continental Shelf* cases,

> the parties are under an obligation to enter into negotiations with a view to arriving at an agreement, and not merely to go through a formal process of negotiation as a sort of a prior condition for the automatic application of a certain method of delimitation in the absence of agreement; they are under an obligation so to conduct themselves that the negotiations are meaningful, which will not be

[1] On this convention see O'Keefe, *Shipwrecked Heritage: A Commentary on the UNESCO Convention on Underwater Cultural Heritage*, Leicester, 2002; Garabello, *The Negotiating History of the Provisions of the Convention on the Protection of the Underwater Cultural Heritage*, in Garabello and Scovazzi (eds.), *The Protection of the Underwater Cultural Heritage – Before and After the 2001 UNESCO Convention*, Leiden, 2003, p. 89.

[2] The CPUCH will enter into force after the deposit of the twentieth instrument of ratification or accession (Art. 27). For the time being (December 2004), Panama, Bulgaria, and Croatia have ratified the CPUCH.

[3] Namely, the Russian Federation, Norway, Turkey, and Venezuela. The observer delegate of the United States, who was not entitled to vote (the United States not being a member of UNESCO at that time), regretted that his delegation could not accept the CPUCH because of objections to several key provisions relating to jurisdiction, the reporting scheme, warships, and the relationship of the convention to the United Nations Convention on the Law of the Sea. The negative vote of Turkey and Venezuela was attributable to disagreement on the CPUCH provisions regarding peaceful settlement of disputes (Art. 25) and reservations (Art. 30).

[4] Namely, Brazil, Czech Republic, Colombia, France, Germany, Greece, Iceland, Israel, Guinea-Bissau, Netherlands, Paraguay, Sweden, Switzerland, United Kingdom, and Uruguay. The abstentions were based on different, and sometimes opposite, reasons. For instance, the Greek delegate stated *inter alia* that "despite the fact that throughout the negotiations at UNESCO the majority of governmental experts were in favour of extending coastal rights over underwater cultural heritage on the continental shelf, the Draft Convention does not even mention the term 'coastal State.'" According to the French delegate, "la France est en désaccord avec le projet sur deux points précis: le statut des navires d'Etat et les droits de juridiction, dont nous considérons qu'ils sont incompatibles avec les dispositions de la Convention sur le droit de la mer."

[5] For example, Australia, Canada, China, Japan, New Zealand, and the Republic of Korea voted in favour. Among the member States of the European Community (at that time), Austria, Belgium, Denmark, Finland, Ireland, Italy, Luxembourg, Portugal, and Spain voted in favour, whereas France, Germany, Greece, the Netherlands, Sweden, and the United Kingdom abstained.

[6] Hereafter: the UNCLOS.

the case when either of them insists upon its own position without contemplating any modification of it.[7]

Cigarette Smugglers, Clandestine Immigrants, and Infectious Patients

Whereas underwater cultural heritage located within internal maritime waters, archipelagic waters, and territorial sea is subject to the jurisdiction of the coastal State,[8] Art. 303, para. 2, UNCLOS specifically relates to archaeological and historical objects located within the twenty-four-mile zone set forth by Art. 33 UNCLOS (the contiguous zone):

> In order to control traffic in such objects, the coastal State may, in applying article 33, presume that their removal from the sea-bed in the zone referred to in that article without its approval would result in an infringement within its territory or territorial sea of the laws and regulations referred to in that article (= customs, fiscal, immigration or sanitary laws and regulations).

Art. 303, para. 2, does give some rights to the coastal State. But the content of these rights is far from being clear because the wording of the provision gets entangled in mysterious complications. As provided for in Art. 33, in the contiguous zone, which is located between the external limit of the territorial sea (twelve nautical miles, in the case of most States) and twenty-four nautical miles, the coastal State may exercise control for customs, fiscal, immigration, or sanitary purposes. If literally understood, para. 2 suggests that the removal of archaeological and historical objects located in the contiguous zone can determine a violation of domestic provisions relating to matters which have little or nothing to do with the cultural heritage, such as smuggling, public health, and immigration. Under the UNCLOS logic, it is only as a consequence of the competences that it can already exercise in dealing with cigarette smugglers, clandestine immigrants, and infectious patients that the coastal State can exercise some other competences for the protection of the underwater cultural heritage located within twenty-four nautical miles from the shore. The wisdom of such a logic, which implies that underwater cultural heritage cannot be protected *per se*, is not fully convincing, to say the least.

Other problems arise from the wording of Art. 303, para. 2, if literally understood. The coastal State, which is empowered to prevent and sanction the "removal from the sea-bed" of objects of an archaeological and historical nature, is apparently defenceless if such objects, instead of being removed, are simply destroyed in the very place where they have been found.[9] Again, it is difficult to subscribe to the logic of such a conclusion.

All the textual complications of Art. 303, para. 2 are probably attributable to the obsession of the drafters of the UNCLOS to avoid any words that might give the impression of some kind of coastal State jurisdiction beyond the territorial sea (*horror jurisdictionis*, to say it in Latin). Rather than laying down a substantive regime to deal with a new concern, such as the protection of the underwater cultural heritage, the UNCLOS seems more interested in paying tribute to abstractions, like the attachment of some States to the almost theological dogma of freedom of the seas.

In any case, even if the spectre of cigarette smugglers, clandestine immigrants, and infectious patients does not seem the ideal way to transmit the message, from Art. 303, para. 2, the conclusion may be drawn that the coastal State can establish a twenty-four-mile so-called archaeological zone where it can apply its legislation for the aim of protecting the relevant objects.[10]

The Benefit of Mankind as a Whole

A specific provision of the UNCLOS (Art. 149) deals with the underwater cultural heritage found on the seabed and ocean floor beyond the limits of national jurisdiction (the so-called Area):

> All objects of an archaeological and historical nature found in the Area shall be preserved or disposed of for the benefit of mankind as a whole, particular regard being paid to the preferential rights of the State or country of origin, or the State of cultural origin, or the State of historical and archaeological origin.

Art. 149 appears rather vague in its content and devoid of details that could ensure its practical application. It, however, shows a preference for those uses of archaeological and historical objects that promote the "benefit of mankind as a whole." Private interests, such as the search for and use of the objects for trade and personal gain, are given little weight, if any.

Some categories of States which have a link with the objects (namely, the State of cultural origin, the State of historical and archaeological origin, the State or country of origin *tout court*[11]) are given preferential rights, although Art. 149 does

[7] I.C.J., *Reports*, 1969, para. 85 of the judgment. According to the arbitral award rendered on 16 November 1957 in the *Lake Lanoux* case (France v. Spain), the obligations to negotiate an agreement "take very diverse forms and have a scope which varies according to the manner in which they are defined and according to the procedures intended for their execution; but the reality of the obligations thus undertaken is incontestable and sanctions can be applied in the event, for example, of unjustified breaking off of the discussions, abnormal delays, disregard of the agreed procedures, systematic refusals to take into consideration adverse proposals of interests, and, more generally, in cases of violation of the rules of good faith" (*International Law Reports*, 1957, p. 128).

[8] The question of the regime of State vessels and aircraft will not be discussed here. According to certain States, such as the United States, the flag State retains title indefinitely to its sunken craft, wherever it is located, unless title has been expressly abandoned or transferred by it. Other States believe that there is no reason to envisage two different kinds of underwater cultural heritage. On the question, with special reference to the Spanish galleons, see Aznar Gomez, *La protección international del patrimonio subacuático con especial referencia al caso de España*, Valencia, 2004.

[9] Destroyed by a company holding a license for oil exploitation, for instance.

[10] In fact, a number of countries have already created such a zone.

[11] The imprecise wording of Art. 149 gives rise to some textual doubts. Should the State of historical origin be at the same time also the State of

not specify the content of these rights and the manner in which they should be harmonized with the concept of "benefit of mankind as a whole."

A Legal Vacuum

Although specific UNCLOS provisions apply to the space within twenty-four nautical miles, on the one hand, and to the Area, on the other, there is no clarification in the UNCLOS about the regime relating to the archaeological and historical objects found on the continental shelf or in the exclusive economic zone[12]; that is the space located between the twenty-four-mile limit of the archaeological zone and the Area. It is, however, clear that the rights of the coastal State on the continental shelf are limited to the exploration and exploitation of the relevant "natural resources," as explicitly stated in Art. 77, para. 1, of UNCLOS, and cannot be easily extended to manmade objects,[13] such as those belonging to the underwater cultural heritage.[14]

This legal vacuum greatly threatens the protection of cultural heritage because it brings into the picture the abstract idea of freedom of the seas.[15] It could easily lead to a "first come, first served" approach. Availing himself of the principle of freedom of the sea, any person on board any ship could explore the continental shelf adjacent to any coastal State, bring any archaeological and historical objects to the surface, become their owner under a domestic legislation (in most cases, the flag State legislation[16]), carry the objects into certain countries, and sell them on the private market. If this were the case, there would be no guarantee that the objects are disposed of for the public benefit rather than for private commercial gain or personal benefit. Nor could a State which has a direct cultural link with the objects prevent the continuous pillage of its historical heritage. The danger of freedom of fishing for underwater cultural heritage is far from being merely theoretical.[17]

During the negotiations for the UNCLOS, some countries were ready to extend, under certain conditions, the jurisdiction of the coastal State to the underwater cultural heritage found on the continental shelf. For instance, an informal proposal submitted in 1980 by Cape Verde, Greece, Italy, Malta, Portugal, Tunisia, and Yugoslavia provided as follows:

> The Coastal State may exercise jurisdiction, while respecting the rights of identifiable owners, over any objects of an archaeological and historical nature on or under its continental shelf for the purpose of research, recovery and protection. However, particular regard shall be paid to the preferential rights of the State or country of origin, or the State of cultural origin, or the State of historical and archaeological origin, in case of sale or any other disposal, resulting in the removal of such objects out of the Coastal State.[18]

The rejection of this kind of proposal, because of the already mentioned fear of creeping jurisdiction by coastal States (*horror jurisdictionis*),[19] led to the legal vacuum resulting from the present UNCLOS regime.

An Invitation to Looting

The danger of uncontrolled activities is aggravated by Art. 303, para. 3, UNCLOS, which subjects the general obligations of protection of archaeological and historical objects and international cooperation to a completely different set of rules:

> Nothing in this article affects the rights of identifiable owners, the law of salvage and other rules of admiralty, or laws and practices with respect to cultural exchanges.

In fact, salvage law and other rules of admiralty are given an overarching status by the UNCLOS. If there is a conflict between the objective to protect the underwater cultural heritage, on the one hand, and the provisions of salvage law

archaeological origin to get preferential rights? What is the meaning of the word "country" in the expression "State or country of origin"? Why is "country" not used in the cases of cultural, historical, and archaeological origin?

[12] The reference to the exclusive economic zone seems redundant (and will be hereinafter omitted) because the objects of archaeological or historical nature are more likely to lie on the seabed than to float in the waters of the exclusive economic zone. However, during the negotiations for the CPUCH, the highly hypothetical example was made of a bottle containing a message by the Italian national hero, Mr. Giuseppe Garibaldi, which is found floating in the exclusive economic zone of the United States or Uruguay, countries where Mr. Garibaldi had lived in certain periods of his life. Embarking on another effort of imagination, one could also think of an ancient little statue which has been eaten by a fish or cetacean swimming in the exclusive economic zone.

[13] As also stated by the International Law Commission in the commentary to the relevant provision of the draft Convention on the continental shelf: "It is clearly understood that the rights of the coastal State do not cover objects such as wrecked ships and their cargos (including bullion) lying on the seabed or covered by the sand and the subsoil" (U.N., *Yearbook of the International Law Commission*, 1956, vol. 2, p. 298).

[14] It seems too eccentric to assume (as assumed in a judgment rendered on 21 December 1983 by the United States District Court, District Maryland, in 577 *F. Suppl.* 597) that archaeological and historical objects found embedded in the sand or encrusted with sedentary living organisms can be likened to natural resources. But this approach is followed in the *Abandoned Shipwreck Act* adopted by the United States on 1987.

[15] Art. 59 UNCLOS ("Basis for the resolution of conflicts regarding the attribution of rights and jurisdiction"), the provision on the so-called residual rights in the exclusive economic zone, should also be taken into consideration. Under Art 59, "in cases where this Convention does not attribute rights or jurisdiction to the coastal State or to other States within the exclusive economic zone, and a conflict arises between the interests of the coastal State and any other State or States, the conflict should be resolved on the basis of equity and in the light of all the relevant circumstances, taking into account the respective importance of the interests involved to the parties as well as to the international community as a whole". In fact, the CPUCH regime could be seen as the application of UNCLOS Art. 59, as far as the underwater cultural heritage within the exclusive economic zone is concerned (see Migliorino, "*Submarine Antiquities and the Law of the Sea*," in *Marine Policy Reports*, 1982, p. 1).

[16] In this regard, the problems posed by flags of convenience must be taken into consideration.

[17] See, as regards the story of the expeditions made by Mr. Ballard in the Mediterranean and the various stories of Spanish galleons looted by treasure hunters, Scovazzi, *The Application of "Salvage Law and Other Rules of Admiralty to the Underwater Cultural Heritage,"* in Garabello and Scovazzi, *op. cit.*, pp. 20 and 38.

[18] Informal proposal by Cape Verde, Greece, Italy, Malta, Portugal, Tunisia, and Yugoslavia (U.N. doc. A/CONF.62/C.2/ Informal Meeting/43/Rev. 3 of 27 March 1980).

[19] Above, para. 2 B.

and other rules of admiralty, on the other, the latter prevail because they are not affected by any of the paragraphs of Art. 303.[20]

There is no clarification in the UNCLOS about what the expression, "the law of salvage and other rules of admiralty," means. In many countries, the notion of salvage (*sauvetage* in French) is only related to the attempts to save a ship or property carried by it from imminent marine peril on behalf of its owners. It has never been intended to apply to submerged archaeological sites or to ancient sunken ships which, far from being in peril, have been definitively lost.

On the contrary, in a minority of other countries of common law tradition, the concept of salvage law has been enlarged by some court decisions to cover activities that have very little to do with the traditional sphere of salvage. For example, the United States Court of Appeals for the 4th Circuit, in a decision rendered on 24 March 1999 (case *R.M.S. Titanic, Inc.* v. *Haver*), stated that the law of salvage and finds is a "venerable law of the sea." It was said to have arisen from the custom among "seafaring men" and to have "been preserved from ancient Rhodes (900 B.C.E.), Rome (Justinian's *Corpus Juris Civilis*) (533 C.E.), City of Trani (Italy) (1063), England (the Law of Oleron) (1189), the Hanse Towns or Hanseatic League (1597), and France (1681), all articulating similar principles."[21] Coming to the practical result of such a display of legal erudition, the law of finds seems to mean that "a person who discovers a shipwreck in navigable waters that has been long lost and abandoned and who reduces the property to actual or constructive possession becomes the property's owner." The application of the law of salvage, which appears to be something different from the law of finds, is also hardly satisfactory, in that it gives the salvor a lien (or right *in rem*) over the object. Yet the expression "the law of salvage and other rules of admiralty" simply means the application of a first-come-first-served or freedom-of-fishing approach that can only serve the interest of private commercial gain.

The fact remains that the body of "the law of salvage and other rules of admiralty" is today typical of a few common law systems, but remains a complete stranger to the legislation of other countries. Because of the lack of corresponding concepts, the very words "salvage" and "admiralty" cannot be properly translated into languages different from English. In the French official text of the UNCLOS, they are rendered with expressions (*droit de récupérer des épaves et... autres règles du droit maritime*) that have a broader and different meaning. No Italian lawyer (with the laudable exception of a few scholars) would today know what the "law of salvage and finds" is, despite the fact that the cities of Rome and Trani, which are said to have contributed to this body of "venerable law of the sea," are located somewhere in the Italian territory. Nor is it clear how a "venerable" body of rules – that is, believed to have developed in times when nobody cared about the underwater cultural heritage – could provide today any sensible tool for dealing with the protection of the heritage in question. All the lofty and almost theological expressions employed by the supporters of the law of salvage and the law of finds ("return to the mainstream of commerce," "admiralty's diligence ethic," "venerable law of the sea," etc.) are doubtful euphemisms. They dissimulate a first-come-first-served or freedom-of-fishing approach based on the destination of underwater cultural heritage for the exclusive purpose of private commercial gain.

This worsens the already sad picture of Art. 303 of the UNCLOS. Does this provision, while apparently protecting the underwater cultural heritage, strengthen a regime that results in the destination of much of this heritage for commercial purposes? Does Art. 303 give an overarching status to a body of rules that cannot provide any sensible tool for the protection of the heritage in question? The doubt is far from being trivial.[22]

Prospects for a Better Regime

It would be difficult to find elsewhere as many obscurities and contradictions as can be found in the UNCLOS regime of the underwater cultural heritage.[23] If the protection of the underwater cultural heritage is to be achieved "for the benefit of mankind as a whole" (as stated in Art. 149), why are salvage law and the other rules of admiralty, which only serve the purpose of private benefit and commercial gain, granted an overarching status (as stated in Art. 303, para. 3)? If the underwater cultural heritage is to be protected everywhere (as stated in Art. 303, para. 1), why is an evident gap

[20] Luckily enough, the drafters of the UNCLOS did not subject to salvage law and other rules of admiralty the heritage found in the Area, which falls under Art. 149.

[21] *International Legal Materials*, 1999, p. 807. For the details of the judicial "saga" of the *Titanic* see Scovazzi, *The Application* (quoted; see note 17), p. 60.

[22] "In recent decades treasure salvage has been added as an element of marine salvage under admiralty law. From an archaeological perspective, salvage law is a wholly inappropriate legal regime for treating underwater cultural heritage. Salvage law regards objects primarily as property with commercial value and rewards its recovery, regardless of its importance and value as cultural heritage. It encourages private-sector commercial recovery efforts, and is incapable of ensuring the adequate protection of underwater cultural heritage for the benefit of mankind as a whole." (The Archaeological Institute of America, "Comments on the UNESCO/ UN Division on Ocean Affairs and the Law of the Sea Draft Convention on the Protection of the Underwater Cultural Heritage," reproduced in Prott and Srong (eds.), *Background Materials on the Protection of the Underwater Cultural Heritage*, Paris, 1999, p. 176.) For other critical remarks about the results of the application of this body of law see Throckmorton, "The World's Worst Investment: The Economics of Treasure Hunting with Real Life Comparisons," paper published in 1990 and reprinted in Prott and Srong, *op. cit.*, p. 181. But see also the different views expressed by Hoffmann, "Sailing on Uncharted Waters: The U.S. Law of Historic Wrecks, Sunken Treasure and the Protection of Underwater Cultural Heritage," in Scovazzi (ed.), *La protezione del patrimonio culturale sottomarino nel Mare Mediterraneo*, Milano, 2004, p. 297.

[23] "The regimes for underwater archaeology resulting from the Convention are complicated and not complete." (Nordquist, Rosenne, and Sohn, *United Nations Convention on the Law of the Sea 1982 – A Commentary*, vol. V, Dordrecht, 1989, p. 161).

left open regarding the heritage located on the continental shelf?[24]

As a further surprise, it may be added that prospects of finding some remedy to the unsatisfactory regime of the UNCLOS could be drawn from para. 4 of Art. 303 itself. Under this paragraph, Art. 303 does not prejudice "other international agreements and rules of international law regarding the protection of objects of an archaeological and historical nature."[25] There is no reason why future agreements, such as the CPUCH, should not be covered by this provision. In other words, the UNCLOS itself seems to allow the drafting of more specific treaty regimes that can ensure a better protection of the underwater cultural heritage. The UNCLOS itself seems to encourage the filling of the gaps and the elimination of the contradictions that it has generated.

THE CPUCH AS A DEFENSIVE TOOL

The CPUCH may be seen as a reasonable defence against the results of the contradictory and counterproductive regime of the UNCLOS. The basic defensive tools are three; namely: the elimination of the undesirable effects of the law of salvage and finds, the exclusion of a first-come-first-served approach for the heritage found on the continental shelf, and the strengthening of regional cooperation.

The Rejection of the Law of Salvage and Finds

Although most countries participating in the negotiations for the CPUCH concurred in the rejection of the application of the law of salvage and finds to underwater cultural heritage, a minority of States were not prepared to accept an absolute ban. To achieve a reasonable compromise, Art. 4 (*Relationship to law of salvage and law of finds*) of the CPUCH provides as follows:

> Any activity relating to underwater cultural heritage to which this Convention applies shall not be subject to the law of salvage or law of finds, unless it:
>
> (a) is authorized by the competent authorities, and
> (b) is in full conformity with this Convention, and
> (c) ensures that any recovery of the underwater cultural heritage achieves its maximum protection.

This provision is to be understood in connection with Art. 2, para. 7, of the CPUCH ("underwater cultural heritage shall not be commercially exploited") and with the rules contained in the annex, which form an integral part of the CPUCH. In particular, under Rule 2 of the Annex,

> the commercial exploitation of underwater cultural heritage for trade or speculation or its irretrievable dispersal is fundamentally incompatible with the protection and proper management of underwater cultural heritage. Underwater cultural heritage shall not be traded, sold, bought or bartered as commercial goods.

The practical effect of the CPUCH regime is the prevention of all the undesirable effects of the application of the law of salvage and finds. Freedom of fishing for archaeological and historical objects is definitely banned. This seemed generally acceptable to all the States participating in the negotiation.

The Exclusion of a First-Come-First-Served Approach for the Heritage Found on the Continental Shelf

The majority of the countries participating in the negotiation were ready to extend the jurisdiction of the coastal State to the underwater cultural heritage found on the continental shelf or in the exclusive economic zone. However, a minority of States assumed that the extension of the jurisdiction of coastal States beyond the limit of the territorial sea would have altered the delicate balance embodied in the UNCLOS between the rights and obligations of the coastal State and those of other States. Such a difference of positions proved to be a thorny question.

During the negotiations, the chairman of Working Group 1 of the Group of Governmental Experts, trying to find a way out of the deadlock rather than merely recording the statements and re-statements of the opposing positions,[26] undertook to produce a tentative proposal.[27] It was based on a three-step procedure; namely, reporting of planned activities or discoveries; consultations on how to ensure the effective protection of the underwater cultural heritage; provisional protection measures. The coastal State was entitled to coordinate the consultations among the States that declared their interest,[28] unless it invited another State to act as coordinating State. Pending the outcome of the consultations, all States Parties had to comply with the provisional protection measures adopted by the coordinating State.

[24] The fact that the UNCLOS regime is far from being satisfactory seems implicitly acknowledged in the declaration made by the Netherlands on 28 June 1996 on ratification of the UNCLOS: "Jurisdiction over objects of an archaeological and historical nature found at sea is limited to articles 149 and 303 of the Convention. The Kingdom of the Netherlands does however consider that there may be a need to further develop, in international cooperation, the international law on the protection of the underwater cultural heritage."

[25] Under para. 3, Art. 303 does not affect salvage law and other rules of admiralty. Under para. 4, Art. 303 is without prejudice to other international agreements regarding the protection of objects of an archaeological and historical nature. If there is a conflict between salvage law and an international agreement covered by para. 4, which would prevail? To try to give an answer to the question, which is a consequence of the plethora of contradictions embedded in Art. 303, does not seem a sensible exercise.

[26] See *Final Report of the Third Meeting of Governmental Experts on the Draft Convention on the Protection of Underwater Cultural Heritage*, UNESCO doc. CLT-2000/CONF.201/CLD.7, para. 4 of Annex 1.

[27] UNESCO doc. WG1-NP3 of 6 July 2000 (reproduced also in the doc. quoted earlier; see note 26).

[28] To avoid the ghost of jurisdiction (*horror jurisdictionis*), the coastal State was not called coastal State, but was given a special responsibility under the following wording: "Taking into account its interest in avoiding unjustified interference with the exercise of sovereign rights and jurisdiction in its exclusive economic zone or on its continental shelf in accordance with international law, a State Party has a special responsibility for the coordination of activities directed at the underwater cultural heritage and for the protection of any discoveries made in its exclusive economic zone or on its continental shelf." (Art. D, para. 2, of the tentative proposals of the chairman of Working Group 1.)

During the same session, a "non-paper" was proposed by three unnamed delegations as a basis for discussion. Although different in several aspects from the proposal of the chairman of Working Group 1, the non-paper was also based on reporting and consultation.[29] It introduced two important elements; namely, that the States entitled to participate in the consultations were those that had a "verifiable link" with the underwater cultural heritage concerned, and that the coastal State[30] was entitled to impose requirements not in its own interest but on behalf of all States Parties as a whole.

Both proposals were inspired by a spirit of compromise and showed an effort to find reasonable solutions based on procedural mechanisms, without insisting on a mere extension of the jurisdiction of the coastal State. Both proposals led to the present Arts. 9 and 10 of the CPUCH, which were found acceptable by the majority of the States engaged in the negotiation. It is regrettable that, despite all the efforts to reach a reasonable compromise, a consensus could not be achieved.

It would be a difficult task to dwell upon all the nuances of provisions, such as Arts. 9 and 10, resulting from a stratification of proposals, counterproposals, last-minute changes, and "constructive ambiguities," which are not likely to lead to an easily readable text. The essence of the regime is the three-step procedure (reporting, consultations, urgent measures) it sets forth.[31]

Regarding *reporting*, the CPUCH bans secret activities or discoveries.[32] States Parties shall require their nationals or vessels flying their flag to report activities or discoveries to them. If the activity or discovery is located in the exclusive economic zone or on the continental shelf of another State Party, the CPUCH sets forth two alternative solutions:

> (i) States Parties shall require the national or the master of the vessel to report such discovery or activity to them and to that other State Party;
> (ii) alternatively, a State Party shall require the national or master of the vessel to report such discovery or activity to it and shall ensure the rapid and effective transmission of such report to all other States Parties. (Art. 9, para. 1, b)[33]

Although the wording leaves a certain margin of ambiguity, the State Party mentioned in sub-paragraph. (ii) is to be understood as the State to which the "national" belongs or the State of which the "vessel" flies the flag.[34] This interpretation is in conformity with the preparatory works of the CPUCH.[35]

Information is also notified to the Director-General of UNESCO, who shall promptly make it available to all States Parties (Art. 9, paras. 4 and 5).

Regarding *consultations*, the coastal State[36] shall consult all States Parties that have declared their interest in being consulted on how to ensure the effective protection of the underwater cultural heritage in question (Art. 10, para. 3, a, and Art. 9, para. 5). The CPUCH provides that any State Party may declare its interest in being consulted and that "such declaration shall be based on a verifiable link, especially a cultural, historical or archaeological link, to the underwater cultural heritage concerned."[37]

The coastal State[38] shall coordinate the consultations, unless it expressly declares that it does not wish to do so, in which case the States Parties that have declared an interest in being consulted shall appoint another coordinating State (Art. 10, para. 3, b). The coordinating State shall implement the measures of protection that have been agreed by the consulting States and may conduct any necessary preliminary research on the underwater cultural heritage (Art. 10, para. 5).

Regarding *urgent measures*, Art. 10, para. 4, CPUCH provides as follows:

> Without prejudice to the right of all States Parties to protect underwater cultural heritage by way of all practicable measures taken in accordance with international law to prevent immediate danger to the underwater cultural heritage, including looting, the Coordinating State may take all practicable measures, and/or issue any necessary authorizations in conformity with this Convention and, if necessary prior to consultations, to prevent any immediate danger to the underwater cultural heritage, whether arising from human activities or any other cause, including looting. In taking such measures assistance may be requested from other States Parties.

The right of the coordinating State to adopt urgent measures is the cornerstone of the CPUCH regime. It would have been illusory to subordinate this right to the conclusion of

29 UNESCO doc. WG.1/NP.1 of 5 July 2000 (reproduced also in the doc. quoted earlier; see note 26).

30 Again, the expression "coastal State" was not used in the "non-paper" either.

31 Under Arts. 11 and 12 CPUCH, a similar (although not identical) three-step procedure applies to the underwater cultural heritage found in the Area.

32 For obvious reasons, the principle of transparency of information is limited to the competent authorities of States Parties: "Information shared between States Parties, or between UNESCO and States Parties, regarding the discovery or location of underwater cultural heritage shall, to the extent compatible with their national legislation, be kept confidential and reserved to competent authorities of States Parties as long as the disclosure of such information might endanger or otherwise put at risk the preservation of such underwater cultural heritage." (Art. 19, para. 3.)

33 On depositing its instrument of ratification, acceptance, approval, or accession, a State Party shall declare the manner in which reports will be transmitted (Art. 9, para. 2).

34 The ambiguity lies in the fact that the "State Party" in question could also be understood as the coastal State.

35 A draft resolution submitted by the Russian Federation and the United Kingdom and endorsed by the United States tried to clarify the point by proposing the following wording: "When the discovery or activity is located in the exclusive economic zone or on the continental shelf of another State Party: (i) a State Party shall require its national or the master of a vessel flying its flag to report such discovery or activity to it and to that other State Party; (ii) alternatively, a State Party shall require its national or the master of a vessel flying its flag to report such discovery or activity to it and shall ensure the rapid and effective transmission of such reports to all other States Parties." (UNESCO doc. 31 C/COM.IV/DR.5 of 26 October 2001). The draft resolution was not adopted.

36 Here and everywhere else, the CPUCH avoids the words "coastal State" (because of the already mentioned *horror jurisdictionis*) and chooses other expressions, such as the "State Party in whose exclusive economic zone or on whose continental shelf" the activity or discovery is located.

37 The attempt to define what is a "verifiable link" was not made.

38 See note 36.

consultations that are normally expected to last for some time. It would also have been illusory to grant this right to the flag State, considering the risk of activities carried out by vessels flying the flag of non-Parties or a flag of convenience.[39] By definition, in a case of urgency, a determined State must be entitled to take immediate measures without losing time in procedural requirements.[40]

The CPUCH clearly sets forth that in coordinating consultations, taking measures, conducting preliminary research, and issuing authorizations, the coordinating State acts "on behalf of the States Parties as a whole and not in its own interest" (Art. 10, para. 6). Any such action shall not, in itself, constitute a basis for the assertion of any preferential or jurisdictional rights not provided for in international law, including the UNCLOS.

In any case, "a State Party in whose exclusive economic zone or on whose continental shelf underwater cultural heritage is located has the right to prohibit or authorize any activity directed at such heritage to prevent interference with its sovereign rights or jurisdiction as provided for by international law including the United Nations Convention on the Law of the Sea" (Art. 10, para. 2, CPUCH). This could mean that the coastal State can exercise broader rights if, for instance, a wreck is embedded in the sand or is encrusted with oysters, molluscs, or other sedentary living resources over which it already exercises sovereign rights under the UNCLOS provisions on the continental shelf.[41]

The Strengthening of Regional Cooperation

The CPUCH devotes one of its provisions (Art. 6) to bilateral, regional, or other multilateral agreements:

> 1. States Parties are encouraged to enter into bilateral, regional or other multilateral agreements or develop existing agreements, for the preservation of underwater cultural heritage. All such agreements shall be in full conformity with the provisions of this Convention and shall not dilute its universal character. States may, in such agreements, adopt rules and regulations which would ensure better protection of underwater cultural heritage than those adopted in this Convention.
> 2. The Parties to such bilateral, regional or other multilateral agreements may invite States with a verifiable link, especially a cultural, historical or archaeological link, to the underwater cultural heritage concerned to join such agreements.[42]

Art. 6 opens the way to a multiple-level protection of underwater cultural heritage. This corresponds to what has already happened in the field of the protection of the natural environment, where treaties having a world sphere of application are often followed by treaties concluded at regional and subregional levels. The key to coordination among treaties applicable at different levels is the criterium of the better protection, in the sense that the regional and subregional treaties are concluded to ensure better protection than the protection granted by those adopted at a more general level.

The possibility to conclude regional agreements should be carefully considered by the States bordering enclosed or semi-enclosed seas characterized by a particular kind of underwater cultural heritage, such as the Mediterranean, the Baltic, and the Caribbean. For instance, in a declaration adopted in Siracusa, Italy, on 10 March 2001,[43] the participants to an academic conference stressed that "the Mediterranean basin is characterized by the traces of ancient civilisations which flourished along its shores and, having developed the first seafaring techniques, established close relationships with each other" and that "the Mediterranean cultural heritage is unique in that it embodies the common historical and cultural roots of many civilizations." They consequently invited the Mediterranean countries to "study the possibility of adopting a regional convention that enhances cooperation in the investigation and protection of the Mediterranean submarine cultural heritage and sets forth the relevant rights and obligations."

CONCLUSIVE REMARKS

It is not likely that any sensible prospects for protecting the underwater cultural heritage may be drawn from the contradictory and counterproductive regime embodied in the UNCLOS, at least if it were literally read. The drafters of the UNCLOS could not forecast the subsequent progress in underwater technologies and the diffusion of treasure hunting activities in many seas of the world. They probably did not feel that the protection of the underwater cultural heritage was to be considered an urgent need.

For its innovative and pragmatic character, the CPUCH is a major step forward in the progressive development of international law. It has been criticized for the reason that, irrespective of Art. 3,[44] it departs from the regime embodied

[39] The present experience of the regulation of fisheries proves the dangers posed by vessels flying flags of convenience and engaging in so-called IUU (illegal, unreported, unregulated) fishing.

[40] On the contrary, the draft resolution submitted by the Russian Federation and the United Kingdom and endorsed by the United States (quoted earlier; see note 35) subordinated the right to adopt measures to prevent immediate danger to a specific condition: "... but in any event prompt assistance shall be requested from the State Party that is the flag State of the vessel engaged in such activities."

[41] The majority of countries participating in the negotiation rejected the assumption, put forward by the United States, that the only possibility for the coastal State to protect the underwater cultural heritage was based on its right to prevent interferences with its sovereign rights or jurisdiction as provided for by international law. This assumption is, in principle, unacceptable because it implies that oysters and other equally respectable living resources are more important than the cultural heritage. It is also dangerous because it can be interpreted in the sense that the salvor can retain the wreck after having given all the oysters to the coastal State!

[42] Under Art. 6, para. 3, the CPUCH "shall not alter the rights and obligations of States Parties regarding the protection of sunken vessels, arising from other bilateral, regional, or other multilateral agreements concluded before its adoption, and, in particular, those that are in conformity with the purposes of" the CPUCH.

[43] Text in Garabello and Scovazzi, *op. cit.*, p. 274.

[44] "Nothing in this Convention shall prejudice the rights, jurisdiction and duties of States under international law, including the United Nations Convention on the Law of the Sea. This Convention shall be interpreted and applied in the context of and in a manner consistent with international law, including the United Nations Convention on the Law of the Sea."

in the UNCLOS.[45] Perhaps it partially departs. But it must be stressed that the UNCLOS regime is so insufficient that it was impossible to protect the underwater cultural heritage without partially departing from it.

Variations from the UNCLOS regime are not a novelty. After the adoption of the UNCLOS, two multilateral treaties have been concluded that apparently "implement" the UNCLOS; namely, the 1994 Agreement Relating to the Implementation of Part XI of the UNCLOS and the 1995 Agreement for the Implementation of the Provisions of the UNCLOS Relating to the Conservation and Management of Straddling Fish Stocks and Highly Migratory Fish Stocks. In fact, because both agreements depart from the UNCLOS, the politically prudent label of an "implementing agreement" can be considered as a euphemism for the word "amendment," which would have been more correct from a substantive point of view. The reality is that, because it is, itself, a product of time, the UNCLOS cannot stop the passing of time. It is therefore subject to a process of evolution in the light of subsequent international practice.

The establishment of an effective protection regime for the underwater cultural heritage cannot be seen as an encroachment on the principle of the freedom of the sea. Nor is it the creation of other jurisdictional zones. It is difficult to see how rules and entitlements on the underwater cultural heritage found on the continental shelf could affect navigation in the superjacent waters. The concept of freedom of the sea is, today, to be understood not in an abstract way, but in the context of the present range of marine activities and in relation to other potentially conflicting uses and interests. Also, the idea that the coastal State can exercise rights on the oil found in its continental shelf corresponded, when it was initially proposed,[46] to an encroachment on the freedom of the high seas. Evident encroachments on the freedom of fishing on the high seas can easily be found in the aforementioned 1995 Straddling and Highly Migratory Fish Stocks Agreement, which introduces the innovative idea that States that persistently undermine the measures agreed upon by the others can be excluded from an activity taking place on the high seas. In this case, a new regime was considered a necessary tool to promote the conservation and sound management of living marine resources and, as such, was found reasonable by the great majority of States. Abstract principles and fears of creeping jurisdiction (*horror jurisdictionis*) were not sufficient to prevent the evolution of international law of the sea and the drafting of reasonable legal responses to emerging needs.

Similarly, effective solutions are today required with respect to the underwater cultural heritage. The protection of the underwater cultural heritage is endangered by an increasing number of unreported and unregulated activities that are the consequence of the improvement of underwater instruments and technologies. Should there remain a freedom-of-fishing type regime for objects of an archaeological and historical nature? Do they deserve less protection than fish? The CPUCH provides sensible answers to both questions.

Sadly enough, the message coming from the CPUCH has not yet been understood by many States. In particular, it is really disappointing to see that, by Resolution 59/24 adopted on 17 November 2004, the United Nations General Assembly:

> "urges all States to cooperate, directly or through competent international organizations, in taking measures to protect and preserve objects of an archaeological and historical nature found at sea, in conformity with article 303 of the Convention [= the UNCLOS]."

Not only is the CPUCH not even mentioned, but also, with regard to the two relevant UNCLOS provisions, Art. 149 is completely forgotten and Art. 303, the invitation to looting, is emphasized!

QUESTIONS FOR DISCUSSION

1. Is admiralty law a proper means to ensure the protection of the underwater cultural heritage?

2. How could States bordering enclosed or semi-enclosed sea join to ensure a better protection of their underwater cultural heritage?

3. Are the expressions "venerable law of the sea," "admiralty's diligence ethic," and "return to the mainstream of commerce" sufficiently impressive to qualify for a sort of legal theology that does not allow for any exceptions?

[45] See, for example, the intervention made on 28 November 2001 by the delegate of the Russian Federation, Mr. Tarabrin, at the United Nations General Assembly.

[46] See the Presidential Proclamation concerning the policy of the United States with respect to the natural resources of the subsoil and seabed of the continental shelf, adopted on 28 September 1945 (the so-called Truman Proclamation).

CHAPTER THIRTY-NINE

The Collision of Property Rights and Cultural Heritage; the Salvors' and Insurers' Viewpoints

Forrest Booth

INTRODUCTION

The draft UNESCO Convention on the Protection of the Underwater Cultural Heritage (the "Convention"), adopted on 2 November 2001, seeks to protect "underwater cultural heritage" in both the territorial waters of nations and the deep ocean. The Convention makes certain assumptions:

A. There is an underwater cultural heritage.[1]
B. Underwater cultural heritage can be protected by treaty or legislation.
C. International law has the right, by treaty, to supercede the maritime law of salvage and of finds.
D. All property on the ocean floor for more than 100 years is abandoned.
E. Preserving the underwater cultural heritage "for the enjoyment of all mankind" trumps individual property rights in underwater property.

As will be seen, each of these assumptions is subject to serious challenge, and several are flatly wrong. In addition, the Convention is flawed in that it violates Article 303 of the 1982 United Nations Convention on the Law of the Sea (UNCLOS).[2] Article 303, at paragraph 3, provides:

> Nothing in this article affects the rights of identifiable owners, the law of salvage and other rules of admiralty, or laws and practices with respect to cultural exchanges.

Admiralty and maritime law, including the law of salvage and the law of finds, is venerable, well-known, and established. The draft Convention blatantly tramples on property rights without achieving its desired goal, and improperly seeks to upset established international law as set forth, *inter alia*, in UNCLOS. The draft Convention should be rejected.

THE HISTORY OF TREASURE TROVE

Traditional maritime law emphasizes (and rewards) the recovery of property lost at sea or found on the ocean floor. For almost 3,000 years, the legal systems of the maritime nations of the world have uniformly recognized that those who voluntarily come to the assistance of fellow seamen in distress, and who recover property or perform salvage services on the high seas, are entitled to be rewarded for those services.[3] The earliest reference to such maritime law comes from ancient Rhodes, dating from 900 B.C. Codifications from Rome in 533 B.C., from England (the laws of Oleron) in 1189 A.D., from the Hanseatic League in 1597 A.D., and from France in 1681 A.D. are all noteworthy.[4] The law so codified constitutes a part of the continuing maritime law of nations – the *jus gentium*.[5] With certain limited exceptions, merchant seamen and others *not* employed by lifesaving organizations (such as the United Kingdom's Royal National Lifeboat Institution or the United States Coast Guard), are under no legal obligation to save life or property at sea. A salvor, as recognized in admiralty law, is one who *voluntarily* saves life or property at sea.[6] Salvors and treasure hunters act, not surprisingly, almost always out of a desire to earn money. They either seek a salvage award from the owner of the property (under the law of salvage), or they seek title to the property itself (under the law of finds), so they can either possess it or sell it. Much attention has been paid to Spanish galleons that sank in the Caribbean area while carrying riches from the New World back to Spain, such as the *Nuestra Snora de Atocha*.[7] Likewise, in North America, ships from the California Gold Rush in 1849, such as the *Central America*,[8] and from the Klondike Gold Rush in Alaska

[1] Obviously, the vast majority of artifacts and other material found underwater come from shipwrecks. Apologists for the Convention, in an attempt to direct attention away from this critical fact, have put forward the proposition that "underwater cultural heritage" and "historic wreck" are "roughly synonymous." James A. R. Nafziger, *The Evolving Role of Admiralty Courts in Litigation Related to Historic Wrecks*, 44 Harv.Int'l L.J. 251, 252 (2003). It is noteworthy that the apologists can find no support for this proposition, which is clearly indefensible. It has been asserted, with some credibility, that archeologists wish to prevent the salvaging of underwater wrecks, in order that they may recover or preserve historic shipwrecks themselves. Christopher R. Bryant, *The Archeological Duty of Care: The Legal, Professional, and Cultural Struggle Over Salvaging Historic Shipwrecks*, 65 Alb.L.Rev. 97, 99 (2001).

[2] United Nations Convention on the Law of the Sea, Dec. 10 1982, 1833 UNTS 3.

[3] *R.M.S. Titanic, Inc.* v. *Haver*, 171 F.3d 943, 960 (4th Cir. 1999).

[4] *Id.*

[5] *Id.* Even the opponents of marine salvage acknowledge that this is true. Nafziger, *supra*, n.1, at 260–261.

[6] *R.M.S. Titanic, Inc.* v. *Wrecked and Abandoned R.M.S. TITANIC, et al.*, 286 F.3d 194, 202 (4th Cir. 2002).

[7] *Treasure Salvors, Inc.* v. *Unidentified Wrecked and Abandoned Sailing Vessel*, 569 F.2d 330 (5th Cir. 1978) (hereinafter "*Treasure Salvors I*", and further proceedings *sub nom. Florida, Dept. of State* v. *Treasure Salvors, Inc.*, 621 F.2d 1340 (5th Cir. 1980) ("*Treasure Salvors II*"), *aff'd in part and rev'd in part*, 458 U.S. 670 (1982), 640 F.2d 560 (5th Cir. 1981) ("*Treasure Salvors III*"), and 556 F.Supp. 1319 (S. D. Fla. 1983) ("*Treasure Salvors IV*") (related case).

[8] *Columbus-America Discovery Group* v. *Atlantic Mut. Ins. Co.*, 974 F.2d 450 (4th Cir. 1992), *cert. denied*, 507 U.S. 1000 (1993), and further proceedings at 56 F.3d 556 (4th Cir. 1995) (hereafter the "*Central America*").

and Canada, such as the *Islander*,[9] conjure up images of vast amounts of gold coins, gold bars, jewels, and other riches. Some of these treasures have been recovered after truly Herculean efforts lasting decades,[10] often from extreme depths and in remote locations.

In the words of Virgil, cited by the U.S. Fourth Circuit Court of Appeals in the Central America,

"Quid non mortalia pectora cogis,
Auri sacra fames!"[11]

There are two separate and distinct legal doctrines that can apply when property is discovered and recovered from under the ocean; the law of salvage and the law of finds.

Salvage Law

Awards by courts to salvors, based on the law of salvage, are not based upon *quantum meruit*[12]; rather, they are a reward, an incentive to encourage others to take risks, in order to recover property that has been lost or is subject to a marine peril.[13] Salvage awards must be set high enough to encourage salvors to take the risks and expend the effort needed to recover property lost at sea.[14] It has always been the goal of civilized nations to encourage marine salvage, in order to recover or secure property that has been lost or is subject to threat of loss, as well as to protect the property rights of its owners. All maritime nations have adopted these principles as part of the *jus gentium*.[15]

Salvage law, as opposed to the law of finds, see discussion next section, gives the right of possession to the first salvor – i.e., he who first reduces the property to his possession.[16] Under the law of salvage, the salvor does not take title to the property.[17] Rather, the salvor receives an award, either from the owner or from the proceeds of the sale of the salved property (which amount is paid into the admiralty court).[18] The performance of salvage services gives rise to a common law maritime lien for the benefit of the salvor.[19] However, the salvage of a vessel or goods at sea, except in extraordinary circumstances, even when the goods have been abandoned, does not divest the original owner of title.[20] Salvage does not grant any direct ownership rights to the salvor.[21]

The Salvor's Award

Rescuing a vessel in peril that has lost propulsion or steering, and bringing such vessel safely into port or assisting it in recovering the ability to navigate, in a common law country, results in a salvage award to the assisting vessel.[22] Likewise, the raising of a sunken vessel, or part thereof, or its cargo, is deserving of a salvage award.[23] The greater the difficulty of the operation, the higher the award.[24] The factors that courts consider in making such an award are the labor expended, the skill required in rendering the service, the value of the salvor's equipment committed to the project, the danger to which that equipment was exposed, the risk incurred by the salvor, the value of the property salved, the degree of danger to which the property was exposed,[25] and the salvor's preservation of historical and/or archeological artifacts and data.[26] In setting such an award, the court is sitting as a court of equity.[27]

The Law of Finds

When no owner of property exists or can be determined, and no other interests such as liens or subrogation rights are proven to the satisfaction of the court, then a party who recovers property abandoned at sea traditionally is entitled to application of the law of finds. Under this doctrine, title to abandoned property vests in the person who reduces that property to his or her possession.[28] As the children's rhyme says, it is "finders, keepers."[29]

Either the property itself, or an award of the full value of the successful operation that was undertaken, goes to the person who is first able to seize possession of the valuable property.[30] However, unlike a salvor, a finder actually takes title to the property, good as against the world. The finder

[9] *Yukon Recovery, L.L.C.* v. *Certain Abandoned Property*, 205 F.3d 1189 (9th Cir. 2002), *cert. denied*, 531 U.S. 820, 121 S.Ct. 62 (2000) (hereafter the "*Islander*").

[10] The salvors searched for the wreck of the *Brother Jonathan* for more than nineteen years before finding and recovering its cargo of gold. *Deep Sea Research, Inc.* v. *BROTHER JONATHAN*, 102 F.3d 379, 382 (9th Cir. 1996), *aff'd in part, vacated in part sub nom. California and State Lands Comm.* v. *Deep Sea Research, Inc.*, 523 U.S. 491, 118 S.Ct. 1464, 140 L.Ed.2d 626 (1998) (hereafter the "*Brother Jonathan*").

[11] "To what cannot you compel the hearts of men, O cursed lust for gold!" *Aeneid*, III. 56, quoted in *Central America*, *supra*, n.8, 56 F.3d at 561 n.1.

[12] Implied contractual recovery of the reasonable value of services rendered. *T.G. Slater & Son, Inc.* v. *D. and P. Brennan, LLC*, 385 F.3d 836, 843 (4th Cir. 2004).

[13] *The BLACKWALL*, 77 U.S. (10 Wall) 1, 13, 19 L.Ed. 870, 875 (1869).

[14] The *CENTRAL AMERICA*, *supra*, n.8, 56 F.3d at 574.

[15] 3A M. J. Norris, *Benedict on Admiralty*, §14, 1–25 (7th ed. 1993).

[16] *Hener v. U.S.*, 525 F.Supp. 350, 354–5 (S.D.N.Y. 1981).

[17] *Wood* v. *Burg (The AKABA)*, 54 F. 197, 200 (4th Cir. 1893).

[18] *Treasure Salvors I*, *supra*, n.7, 569 F.2d at 337 n.11.

[19] *Treasure Salvors III*, *supra*, n.7, 640 F.2d at 567.

[20] *Id.*

[21] *Id.*; *The Akaba*, *supra*, n.17.

[22] *The Akaba*, *supra*, n.17, at 199.

[23] *Great Lakes Towing Co.* v. *St. Joseph-Chicago S.S. Co.*, 253 F. 635 (7th Cir. 1918).

[24] *Curry* v. *The BREWSTER* , 4 F.Cas. 82 (S. D. Fla. 1848) (No. 1852).

[25] *See generally*, *The BLACKWALL*, *supra*, n.13, at 13–14; the *CENTRAL AMERICA*, *supra*, n.8, 56 F.3d at 569 n.17. In the *CENTRAL AMERICA*, the court affirmed a finding that an award to the salvor of ninety percent of the value of the recovered property was appropriate because of the great depth of water, remote location, and extraordinary recovery efforts involved.

[26] Attention on the part of the court to matters of historical and/or archeological value is a recent addition to courts' considerations in this area. The *CENTRAL AMERICA*, *supra*, n.8, 56 F.3d at 573. This matter has recently been addressed by the U.S. Congress as well, as discussed in the section "The Abandoned Shipwreck Act of 1987" in this chapter.

[27] *THE BOSTON*, 3 F.Cas. 932, 937 (C.D.D. Mass. 1833) (No. 1673).

[28] *Treasure Salvors I*, *supra*, n.7, 569 F.2d at 337. *See also*, *Wiggins* v. *1100 Tons, More Or Less of Italian Marble*, 186 F.Supp. 452 (E. D. Va. 1960); *Nippon Shosen Kaisha, K.K.* v. *U.S.*, 238 F.Supp. 55 (N. D. Cal. 1964).

[29] *Int'l Aircraft Recovery, L.L.C.* v. *The Unidentified, Wrecked and Abandoned Aircraft*, 218 F.3d 1255, 1258 (11th Cir. 2000).

[30] *Treasure Salvors I*, *supra*, n.7, 569 F.2d at 337 n.11.

acquires title to lost or abandoned property by "occupancy." This is accomplished by taking possession of the property and exercising control and dominion over it.[31] Mere discovery of lost or abandoned property is not enough; the finder must take possession of it, and/or establish that he has full and unquestioned control over it.[32] In most cases, this will require bringing the property to the surface, transporting it to port, and landing it on shore. However, the law also affords its protection to the process of establishing the "occupancy" that cases such as *Treasure Salvors III* require.

Once the finder becomes actively engaged in reducing the property to his possession, with the necessary equipment and personnel to complete the task, he or she will be protected from interference by others.[33] If the finder abandons the project, however, or does not undertake to reduce the property to his or her possession after discovering its location in a timely manner, the finder will lose the protections of the court and his or her rights under the law of finds.[34]

Purpose of the Law of Finds

The law of finds supplements (but does not displace) the law of marine salvage. Finds provides a mechanism for determining the right of ownership of property when the owner is unknown, cannot be located, or for some reason fails to assert his or her rights before the court (i.e., abandons it). Most cases decided under the law of finds involve property that was lost long ago, which has remained under the sea and beyond the reach of its rightful owners for many years.[35]

Distinction has been made between the law of salvage and the law of finds since the Laws of Oleron.[36] Historically, the law of finds generally applied, not to manmade objects, but rather to unowned ocean resources, usually fish, whales, or other forms of aquatic life. He or she who found them and reduced them to possession was entitled to them as the owner, free and clear.[37]

Finder's Award

Unlike in the case of salvage, the court does not have to determine the appropriate award to be made to a finder; by definition, the finder takes title to the property or its proceeds, free and clear of all other claims, and in its entirety.[38]

THERE IS NO BASIS TO DIVEST VALID PROPERTY RIGHTS

All of what UNESCO, in the draft Convention, calls the underwater cultural heritage is manmade.[39] It is ships and the remains of ships, their cargoes, and other manmade objects and structures. The Convention only applies to such items when they are more than 100 years old.[40]

Assume that a venerable shipwreck lies on the ocean floor. That ship, as well as her cargo, had an owner (or owners) when she was loaded in port before her last voyage. She had an owner when she set sail from her final port of loading and embarkation. She and her cargo had an owner while she sailed on the high seas. Both the ship and her cargo had an owner when they encountered the storm, the iceberg, the rock or whatever else caused the ship to sink. Why, then, do the ship and her cargo not still have an owner when they lie on the ocean bottom? If they do have an owner, then what right does UNESCO, or any other governmental or intergovernmental agency, have to divest the owner of his rights in his property? Whether the owner is the original owner or an insurer that has paid for the loss of the goods and assumed subrogation rights, that owner's rights deserve the full protection of law, just as do all other property rights.

It is well-known that the major world insurance market for marine risks, Lloyds of London, began as a coffee house where shipowners gathered to discuss and do business, to buy and sell cargoes and to share risks.[41] For at least the last 200 years, most ships and their cargoes have been insured, at least to some degree because of the significant level of, and unique nature of, the risks entailed in maritime commerce.[42] When a loss has occurred and an insurer pays a claim, the insurer becomes subrogated to the rights of the owner in and to the damaged or lost property.[43] Indeed, hull insurance policies on ships and cargo insurance policies often specifically give rights of subrogation to underwriters, after they have paid a claim.[44] It is often said that a subrogated insurer "stands in the shoes of" his or her insured, having all of his or her rights, but also subject to all of his or her liabilities.

Obviously, one major purpose of subrogation is to keep insurance rates down. If insurers had to pay 100 percent of every loss, and could never recover any of the payments they made, the cost of insurance would be far higher. This point is well illustrated by the fact that insurance rates for commercial space satellite launches, although high, have been reduced

31 *Treasure Salvors III, supra*, n.7, 640 F.2d at 571.
32 *Id.*
33 *Treasure Salvors III, supra*, n.7, 640 F.2d at 572.
34 *Treasure Salvors III, supra*, n.7, 640 F.2d at 573.
35 The noted scholar Martin J. Norris believes the law of finds is properly limited exclusively to such wrecks and other property. 3A M. J. Norris, *Benedict on Admiralty* §158, 11–17 (7th ed. 1993).
36 *See generally, Hener* v. *U.S., supra*, n.16.
37 T. J. Shoenbaum, 2 Admiralty & Maritime Law, section 16–7 (2d ed. 1994).
38 *Klein* v. *Unidentified Wrecked and Abandoned Sailing Vessel*, 758 F.2d 1511, 1514 (11th Cir. 1985).
39 The Convention applies to "all traces of human existence having a cultural, historical or archaeological character which have been partially or totally under water . . ." Convention, Article 1, ¶1.(a)
40 Convention, Article 1, ¶1.(a).
41 *See generally, Edinburgh Assurance Co.* v. *R.L. Burns Corp.*, 479 F.Supp. 138 (C. D. Cal. 1979), *aff'd in part, rev'd in part and remanded*, 669 F.2d 1259 (9th Cir. 1982).
42 *See generally*, Leslie J. Buglass, *Marine Insurance and General Average in the United States*, 1–4, 50 (2d ed. 1981).
43 Buglass, *Marine Insurance and General Average in the United States, supra* n.42 at 417–422; Marine Insurance Act, 1906, Ch. 41, S. 79 [Eng.].
44 *See, e.g.*, Protection and Indemnity Form SP-23 (1/56).

in recent years, after a creative Lloyd's underwriter (Stephen R. Merrett) hired the U.S. National Aeronautics and Space Administration ("NASA") to use its space shuttle to recover two commercial satellites that had failed to achieve their desired orbits, and therefore were useless. Although Lloyds initially paid a loss of more than US$180 million for those satellites, their salvage value after recovery was about US$75 million, reducing the (net) claim by almost one half.[45]

UNDERWATER CULTURAL HERITAGE

It is presumptuous to argue that shipwrecks, lost cargoes, and other manmade items on the ocean floor are a common "cultural heritage." For one thing, they can almost never be seen or shared by anyone. Only the tiniest fraction of mankind are licensed scuba divers.[46] Scuba diving equipment is expensive, as is the training necessary to be certified as a competent diver. Furthermore, the depth limit of recreational diving using compressed air is approximately 180 feet (55 meters). Humans diving deeper than that must breathe exotic mixed gases (such as Nitrox, helium/oxygen or Trimix[47]), which (to do safely) requires considerable additional training and considerably more expensive equipment. This type of "technical" diving is very dangerous.[48] Alternatively, people must utilize a submarine, diving bell, or other submersible device, which are also very expensive; only a "handful of people" in the world can afford such an adventure.[49] Because the UNESCO Convention provides neither a regime for transporting large numbers of people underwater to see the supposed "cultural heritage," the funding to make that possible, nor resources to recover artifacts for public (museum) ownership/display, what the UNESCO Convention proposes is unrealistic, unworkable, and unfair.

If salvors recover property from the ocean floor, they can be paid for their efforts. This provides jobs and income for them, for the seamen and technicians they employ, and the shoreside facilities that support them and repair and maintain their vessels. The artifacts recovered can then be enjoyed by those who purchase them and, if they are purchased by museums or other public entities, can be put on display for many to enjoy. If they are of significant archeological or historical importance, they can be studied and tested by experts, professors, and scientists, and can thereby contribute to the sum of human knowledge. Lying on the ocean floor, out of reach and out of sight of essentially all of mankind, they can do none of those things.

The "Cultural Heritage" Is a Rapidly Wasting Resource

Much of what lies on the ocean floor is both fragile and rapidly decaying. A good example is the *R.M.S. Titanic*, which sank on 15 April, 1912.[50] The ship was not discovered until a joint American–French expedition located her in 1985.[51] The wooden decking has almost all wasted away. The hull is made of riveted ductile iron; it is steadily oxidizing (rusting) in the saltwater environment. Furthermore, rust-eating bacteria are feeding on the ship.[52] Up to 600 pounds of iron is being removed from the hull each day by microbial action.[53] Photographs of the ship show that some of the side shell plating has already rusted almost completely away. The remaining structure is substantially weakened, and it is clear that salvaging and raising even a portion of the hull would be essentially impossible. Masts and railings have fallen over, and decks have crumbled and caved in.[54] The mainmast has fallen over and been destroyed.[55] Furthermore, the wreck at a depth of more than 12,500 feet of water (3,788 meters), and is reachable by only four or five of the deepest-diving submersibles on earth. Anything that can be salved from the *Titanic* today should be because it will not survive (at least in any recognizable form) much longer in the deep ocean. The entire hull will collapse onto the seabed in the next twenty to thirty years.[56] Why should not the ship's bell, steering wheel, compass, and other recognizable artifacts, plus china and porcelain from the ship bearing the crest of the White Star Line, be recovered? They will never be seen *in situ*; to the extent they represent "cultural heritage," they may as well not exist at all, while they lie on the ocean floor. As with other such artifacts, they cannot be studied by scientists, professors, or technicians, cannot be probed, measured, or analyzed, and therefore cannot contribute in any way to the sum of human learning.

On July 26, 1956, the pride of the Italian line, the S.S. *Andrea Doria*, collided with the Swedish Lines *S.S. Stockholm*, approximately fifty miles southeast of Nantucket, Massachusetts. The *Andrea Doria* rolled on its side and sank approximately eleven hours later. It lies in about 240 feet of water (73 meters), and is occasionally visited by skilled sport divers who possess sophisticated mixed-gas diving equipment.[57] Recent photographs have shown that the hull of this ship, too, is rapidly deteriorating in the slightly warmer water and constant current to which it is exposed. Artifacts from the *Andrea Doria*, like those from the *Titanic*, will not be available for future generations to study, or view if they are not recovered soon. Although 240 feet (73 meters) is shallow by the standards of

[45] Elizabeth Tucker, *The Sky Wasn't the Limit*, Washington Post, 13th November, 1984, at D1.

[46] "Scuba" stands for self-contained underwater breathing apparatus. Scuba diving requires serious training and costly equipment, and therefore it is largely an elite, "first-world" sport. Yet even in the United States, only 0.68 percent of the population participated in the sport in 2003. <http://www.nsga.org/public/pages/index.cfm?pageid=159>.

[47] *See generally, Murley* v. *Deep Explorers, Inc.*, 281 F.Supp.2d 580, 582–583 (E.D.N.Y. 2003).

[48] *Id.*, at 581.

[49] <http://www.kbismarck.com/wreck.html>.

[50] At the age of 93, the TITANIC does not quite fall within the 100-year period of the Convention's applicability.

[51] *R.M.S. Titanic, Inc.* v. *Haver*, *supra*, n.3, at 951.

[52] <www.msnbc.msn.com/id/5139413/print/1/displaymode/1098/>.

[53] <http://query.nytimes.com/search/restricted/article?res=F70B13FF39550C7A8CDDA10894DB404482>.

[54] <www.msn.com>, *supra*, n.52.

[55] <Http://news.nationalgeographic.com/news/2004/06/0604_040604_titanic.html>.

[56] <www.nytimes.com>, *supra*, n.53.

[57] *Moyer* v. *The Wrecked and Abandoned Vessel ANDREA DORIA*, 836 F.Supp. 1099, 1102 (D.N.J. 1993).

most of the world's oceans, it is well beyond the capability of 99.9 percent of the world's population to reach. Mankind would be far better off if artifacts from that ship were recovered and sold for use, display, and/or study.

The U.S. Navy has recently completed a very expensive salvage operation to recover portions of the *U.S.S. Monitor*, one of the first two ironclad warships ever built.[58] The *Monitor* sank in the Atlantic Ocean, twenty miles off Cape Hatteras, North Carolina, in 234 feet of water (71 meters), on 31 December, 1862,[59] with the loss of sixteen lives. The primitive iron hull itself is so deteriorated that essentially nothing remains of it.[60] All the U.S. Navy was able to recover in August of 2002 were the engines, the round "pillbox" turret, and two eleven-inch Dahlgren guns. The U.S. Navy decided to recover what it could of the *Monitor* at this time because of the rapid rate of decay of the wreck. If they had not recovered the turret when they did, in a few years it would not be possible to recover it at all.[61] Therefore, valuable knowledge about the design, building, and history of the ship would have been lost forever.

The famous passenger liner *RMS Lusitania* was torpedoed by a U-Boat on 7 May 1915. It sank off the coast of Ireland, with the loss of 1,195 lives. Although it lies in 295 feet of water, a depth reachable by at least commercial divers, the ship lies on its side and the hull has collapsed to roughly half of its original width.[62] Much of the upperworks of the ship have collapsed into a heap of rubble on the seafloor, and the wreck has been further damaged by numerous fishing nets, and submarine depth charges during World War II.

In a few years, there will be very little left to see of any of these iron and steel vessels.

The fate of old wooden ships is even worse. The *Vasa*, pride of the Swedish Navy, was launched on 10 August 1628. It promptly rolled over and sank, with the loss of between thirty and fifty lives. Fortunately, mud soon covered the wreck, retarding (but not preventing) its deterioration. It was raised on 24 April 1961, from a depth of thirty meters. However, despite having been extensively treated and preserved by experts, sulfuric acid is continuing to destroy the ship.[63] If the *Vasa* had not been recovered when it was, much of what has been learned about fifteenth century shipbuilding in Scandinavia, by studying its remains, would today be unknown. *Vasa* is currently in a museum in Stockholm, open to the public for inspection and viewing.

The same is true of the British warship, the *Mary Rose*, which sank in 1545, during a battle with the French fleet. Although one of the best-preserved wooden vessels ever recovered when it was raised in 1982, the vessel is nevertheless substantially deteriorated.[64] Had the ship been left in the water, in a few more years, nothing would have remained. This is also true of wrecks of ancient Greek and Roman vessels located in the Mediterranean Sea, along with their cargoes; they will not last forever.

Deterioration is not the only reason why submerged property should be recovered whenever possible. Natural occurrences and disasters can eliminate the possibility to ever practically do so. Scuba and other sport divers, who can afford the extensive (and expensive) international travel involved, enjoy diving in the Pacific Ocean on many of the wrecks of warships and merchantmen left from World War II. One of the favorite locales of divers is near Rabaul in Papua New Guinea. There are fifty-eight shipwrecks from World War II at that one dive site alone. However, in 1994, a major volcanic eruption took place near Rabaul. Eight to ten feet of volcanic ash were deposited over the entire area; the ash in some places is twenty feet deep. Fifty of the fifty-eight wrecks have been covered by the ash and other material and are no longer visible or accessible to divers.

Recently, Indonesia suffered an earthquake measuring 9.0 on the Richter scale, which spawned at least one tsunami more than twenty feet high that traveled at several hundred miles per hour and caused hundreds of thousands of deaths in Sri Lanka, Bangladesh, India, and even thousands of miles away in Africa.[65] Coastal and estuarine areas in more than a dozen countries were decimated by the huge wave. One can only speculate how many shipwrecks and artifacts were either destroyed by this massive event, or buried too deep to recover.

Even if shipwrecks and other artifacts in the ocean are not destroyed by the marine environment itself, tsunamis, hurricanes, earthquakes, and other natural catastrophes from time to time cover and/or destroy them and prevent them from being seen and enjoyed by anyone.[66] For example, the wreck of the Spanish Armada ship *Girona*, which sank off the coast of Northern Ireland in 1588, has, over the years, yielded a rich bounty of artifacts. However, winter storms and heavy seas have pounded the site to the point that there is very little left of the *Girona*.[67] Storms and large waves frequently wash up pieces of centuries-old shipwrecks on the coast of Dorset, in southern England, as old shipwrecks steadily deteriorate.[68] Those pieces of wooden ships that remain underwater are consumed by certain species of worms and clams, which have evolved over time to be able to eat wood.[69]

These problems of deterioration, of course, are not confined to the marine environment. The damage to Greek

58 See <http://oceanexplorer.noaa.gov/explorations/02monitor/monitor.html>.

59 This wreck is exempt, as a government-owned vessel, but otherwise it would fall well within the Convention's 100-year period of applicability. *See supra*, n.40.

60 <http://query.nytimes.com/search/restricted/article?res=F20816F6345E0C718CDDAB0994DF494D81>.

61 *Id.*

62 <www.pbs.org/lostliners/lusitania.html>.

63 See <http://www.vasamuseet.se/aktuellt/eng/curing.html>.

64 See <http://www.maryrose.org/explore/ship1.htm>.

65 *Wall Street Journal*, 27 December 2004.

66 *Platoro, Ltd.* v. *The Unidentified Remains of a Vessel*, 518 F.Supp. 816, 821 (W.D. Tex. 1981), *aff'd in part, vacated in part*, 695 F.2d 893 (5th Cir. 1983) (finding that the annual threat of hurricanes destroys shipwrecks on the seabed).

67 *Belfast Telegraph*, 3 April 2004.

68 *Western Daily Press*, 23 February 2002.

69 *Washington Post*, 4 November 2004.

antiquities caused by air pollution is well known.[70] The former Nazi death camp at Auschwitz is also suffering substantial deterioration, and the Polish authorities who are determined to preserve it are currently debating the best method to do so. The barbed wire, the fence posts, and even the concrete used to keep the prisoners incarcerated is deteriorating so rapidly that, if not aggressively preserved, no trace will remain of the death camp in a few more years.[71]

To assert that manmade objects should be left on the ocean floor as the common cultural heritage of all mankind is both elitist and misinformed. If only archeologists have the right to conduct recovery operations, most shipwrecks will be lost forever because archeologists lack both the funding and the speed required to recover historic shipwrecks and their artifacts.[72] There are simply not the resources, either financial or technical, to mount publicly funded expeditions to recover even the most valuable historical artifacts from the seabed. Such expeditions, in the deep ocean, can cost more than US$30,000 per day to conduct.[73] Therefore, such artifacts will simply remain in the deep ocean, progressively decaying and wasting away, as are the *Titanic*, the *Lusitania*, and the *Andrea Doria*. Eventually, they will be lost or destroyed completely by this process or by some natural disaster. Ordinary people will never be able to see them, and even the most sophisticated sport divers are unable to reach them. However, if salvage (recovery) of such artifacts is allowed, the process of recovering them will pay for itself. The salvor will be remunerated either under the law of salvage or the law of finds, and the artifacts will then be made available for purchase. If they are of great historical, artistic, or archeological significance, museums can purchase them and place them on public display. However, even if they remain in private hands, they can be enjoyed by someone, which cannot be said of any artifacts on the ocean floor.

Abandonment

All nations of the world protect property rights to some extent.[74] To declare that property on the ocean floor is "cultural heritage," and to forbid it to be recovered, moved, or destroyed, is to divest the current owner of his or her rights in that property. Many courts have wrestled with the concept of whether or not such divestiture can be accomplished; if so, under what circumstances; and what constitutes "abandonment." Abandoned shipwrecks have been defined as those "to which the owner has relinquished ownership rights with no retention."[75] Logically, therefore, when an owner comes forward to state a claim of possession to undersea (or salved) property, abandonment cannot be implied.[76]

Most courts in the United States recognize that making a finding that property has been abandoned is a draconian step that should not be taken lightly. Therefore, courts require that a party show abandonment only by a clear and unmistakable affirmative act indicating an intent to repudiate ownership.[77] Some courts have noted that even when a vessel is abandoned, the original owner is not divested of title "except in extraordinary cases . . ."[78]

Of course, no divestiture is required if the true owner has consciously and voluntarily abandoned the property. Some courts therefore have disingenuously applied the legal fiction that, because the property has not been in the care, custody, or control of the owner for many years, it should be "deemed abandoned" by the passage of time.[79] However, one highly respected scholar has written that ownership (title) should *never* be divested *solely* by the passage of time.[80] In the view of this author, this is the better-reasoned, and only logical, position. ". . . [A] finding that title to such property has been lost requires strong proof, *such as the owner's express declaration abandoning title*."[81]

As noted earlier, expeditions to recover property from the deep ocean are enormously expensive. In addition, the technology to locate and recover such property, including deep-diving submersibles, remotely-operated vehicles, and scanning sideband sonar, has only recently been developed. Vessels such as the *Central America*, which lies 8,000 feet (2,424 meters) deep, or the *Titanic*, which lies 12,500 feet (3,788 meters) deep, could not have even been located until very recently, never mind recovered.[82] It would be unreasonable to conclude that an owner had abandoned such property simply because a great deal of time has passed since it was lost, especially when finding and recovering it during the intervening period would have been both physically and technologically impossible.

The Abandoned Shipwreck Act of 1987

The U.S. Congress passed the Abandoned Shipwreck Act of 1987[83] as an attempt to deal with ownership of certain very

70 See <learning.unl.ac.uk/humanIT/project/ parthenon/Centuries.htm>

71 Elizabeth Williamson and Bob Davis, "Burden of History; Auschwitz Repairs Force Tough Debate Over Preservation," *Wall Street Journal*, 14, August 2002, at A1.

72 *Bryant, supra*, n.1, at 115.

73 *Id.*, at 111.

74 See, e.g., the *English Human Rights Act of 1998*, Ch. 42, Sch. 1, Pt. II (Eng.), which provides, in pertinent part, that "[e]very natural or legal person is entitled to the peaceful enjoyment of his possessions. No one shall be deprived of his possessions except in the public interest and subject to the conditions provided for by law and by the general principles of international law." *See also, European Convention for the Protection of Human Rights and Fundamental Freedoms Rome, 4.XI.1950*, which provides that "[e]veryone has the right to respect for his private and family life, **his home** and his correspondence." *See also*, Article 17 of *European Union Charter of Fundamental Rights*, providing that "[e]veryone has the right to own, use, dispose of and bequeath his or her lawfully acquired possessions. No one may be deprived of his or her possessions, except in the public interest and in the cases and under the conditions provided for by law, subject to fair compensation being paid in good time for their loss. The use of property may be regulated by law in so far as is necessary for the general interest."

75 *Sea Hunt, Inc.* v. *The Unidentified Shipwrecked Vessel or Vessels*, 221 F.3d 634, 640 (4th Cir. 2000) (citing 43 U.S.C. §2101(b)).

76 *Id.*, at 641.

77 *Columbus-America Discovery Group, supra*, n.8, 974 F.2d at 461.

78 *Treasure Salvors III, supra*, n.7, 640 F.2d at 567.

79 *Treasure Salvors IV, supra*, n.7, 556 F.Supp. at 1327.

80 3A Martin J. Norris, *Benedict on Admiralty*, §157, 11–13 (7th ed. 1993).

81 *Adams* v. *Unione Mediterranea di Sicurta*, 220 F.3d 659, 671 (5th Cir. 2000) (emphasis in original) (citing *Hener* v. *United States*, 525 F.Supp. 350 (S.D.N.Y. 1981)).

82 *CENTRAL AMERICA*, supra, n.8, 947 F.2d at 457.

83 43 U.S.C. §§2101 *et seq.*, Public Law 100-298.

old shipwrecks. It applies only to wrecks found within the U.S. three-mile limit, which are embedded in submerged lands, or which lie on the seabed but are of historic value.[84] The Act takes title to such wrecks on behalf of the United States, and then immediately passes title to the state in whose waters the abandoned shipwreck is located.[85]

Although it has faced serious legal challenges, the Act has recently been held constitutional in a number of cases.[86]

Despite the Abandoned Shipwreck Act, several U.S. courts have recently upheld the rights of subrogated insurers to property on which they paid claims many years ago, overruling assertions that the property had been abandoned. In *Brother Jonathan*,[87] salvors, acting on behalf of subrogated insurers who had paid claims when the vessel sank in 1865 off Crescent City, California, were awarded the exclusive right to conduct salvage operations on that vessel and her cargo. Although the U.S. Supreme Court, in its decision, dealt with other aspects of the Abandoned Shipwreck Act, it declined to resolve whether or not the *Brother Jonathan* has been abandoned within the meaning of the Act,[88] but it refused to agree with the State of California that the doctrine of abandonment on account of the mere passage of time should apply.

Likewise, in the *Islander*,[89] the salvor, acting on behalf of subrogated insurers in the London Insurance Market, prevailed and was given the sole right to conduct salvage operations on the wreck of that vessel, which sank in 1901 off Juneau, Alaska. Another potential salvor had argued that the *Islander* had been abandoned, or should be deemed to be abandoned because of (1) the passage of time, and (2) the failure of a salvage operation in the 1930s to recover the vessel's valuable cargo of gold bars. The Court of Appeals refused to accept those arguments, noting that the technology needed to locate and recover such property had only recently been developed.

Research by this author has not disclosed the recovery of a single vessel, cargo, or historic artifact by any U.S. state, federal, or local agency, following passage of the Abandoned Shipwreck Act. Apparently all the Act has accomplished since 1987 is to effectively prevent all salvage operations within the three-mile limit of the United States' waters, leaving whatever property may be there to deteriorate unobserved in the corrosive saltwater environment.

[84] 43 U.S.C. §2105(a). [85] 43 U.S.C. §2105(c).

[86] *Zych* v. *Unidentified, Wrecked and Abandoned Vessel, Believed To Be The SB "SEABIRD"*, 746 F.Supp. 1334 (N.D. Ill. 1990), *rev'd and remanded*, 941 F.2d 525 (7th Cir. 1991), *on remand*, 811 F.Supp. 1300 (N.D. Ill. 1992), *aff'd*, 19 F.3d 1136 (7th Cir. 1994), *cert. denied*, 513 U.S. 961, 115 S.Ct. 420 (1994).

[87] *Deep Sea Research, Inc.* v. *BROTHER JONATHAN*, 102 F.3d 379, 382 (9th Cir. 1996), *aff'd in part, vacated in part sub nom. California and State Lands Comm.* v. *Deep Sea Research, Inc.*, 523 U.S. 491, 118 S.Ct. 1464, 140 L.Ed.2d 626 (1998) (hereinafter the "*BROTHER JONATHAN*").

[88] 102 F.3d at 388.

[89] *Yukon Recovery, L.L.C.* v. *Certain Abandoned Property, supra*, n.9.

CONCLUSION

No one would argue that the cultural heritage of mankind should not be preserved on land, in places where it can be enjoyed by many people, and studied and tested by experts with appropriate qualifications. The art in the Louvre in Paris, the Mayan ruins at Copan in Honduras, and the Parthenon in Athens come immediately to mind.[90] Visitors can simply walk up to and admire all of them. However, in the deep ocean, where visitation cannot occur except at prohibitive cost, it is difficult to support the draft Convention and its assumptions that nothing should ever be recovered or removed by private parties. There is much to be learned from artifacts that currently lie in the deep ocean, and they have beauty that many could enjoy and appreciate. A number of them also have great monetary value. However, unless they can be recovered by salvors, who, in turn, are compensated under either the law of salvage or the law of finds, those potential additions to our artistic heritage and mankind's store of knowledge will never occur. The benefits of the quest for knowledge will only be realized if the quest is undertaken.[91] Traditional maritime law concepts, including the law of salvage and the law of finds, have served us well for thousands of years, and they are now an accepted part of the *jus gentium*. UNCLOS correctly recognized that those generally accepted doctrines are important and should be honored. The draft Convention seeks to change and overturn them. It is in error, it abrogates generally accepted property rights, and it is contrary to prevailing (and morally correct) concepts of international law.

QUESTIONS FOR DISCUSSION

1. With artifacts that are iron/steel, wood, or other deteriorating materials, is it better to leave them in place on or in the seabed, or raise them and allow them to be preserved and displayed?

2. If the latter, who should be allowed to recover them, and on what terms? Who will own them after recovery? Who will pay for the recovery?

3. Does the passage of time alone divest the ownership rights of the heirs or successors to the original owners of such artifacts? Should it? If so, how long should it take?

[90] No one would argue, however, that such treasures are owned, collectively, by all mankind (i.e., are the cultural heritage of and belong to all peoples); the Louvre is free to sell or transfer one of its paintings or sculptures if it chooses to do so.

[91] *Bryant, supra*, n.1, at 145.

CHAPTER FORTY

Finders Keepers Losers Weepers – Myth or Reality? An Australian Perspective on Historic Shipwrecks

Derek Luxford

INTRODUCTION

Australia is the world's largest island and smallest continent. This may seem as something of an insult to the island state of Tasmania as well as the many smaller islands that lie off the Australian coast. However, the general aptness of the description should not be abandoned purely for the sake of geographic exactitude. As befits an island continent or a continent of islands (big and small), Australia has a massive coastline. The Australian coastline is littered with shipwrecks. There are some 6,000 to 7,000 shipwrecks along Australia's shores and in its internal waters, reflecting the history of Australia's discovery and development. This excludes the no doubt countless wrecks of small craft and boats used by the aboriginal inhabitants of Australia who first arrived in the country probably some 40,000 years before European discovery. Unfortunately, no remains survive of pre-European discovery aboriginal boats or the boats of pre-European Asian explorers.

In many ways, Australia was discovered almost by accident in the early seventeenth century. Dutch ships belonging to the VOC used the Roaring Forties to sail across the Indian Ocean from the Cape of Good Hope in South Africa to the Spice Islands (modern Indonesia). Unfortunately, sometimes, they overshot their mark and rather than turning north short of the Western Australian coast and heading up to Batavia, they went too far and were wrecked on the Western Australian coast. As we shall see later, it was the discovery in the twentieth century of some of the more famous of these wrecked Dutch ships that led the Australian Government to introduce relatively novel legislation to protect historic shipwrecks.[1] Until permanent European settlement was established in Sydney in January 1788, the only ships on the Australian coast other than visiting explorers (such as Tasman in 1642 and Dampier in 1688) were shipwrecks. Of the estimated 6,000 to 7,000 shipwrecks littering the Australian coast and inland waters, only some 1,800 wreck sites have been discovered. Most of those wreck sites have been discovered by accident, usually many decades after the ship was wrecked. Recreational diving rather than professional salvage has played a significant role in the discovery and subsequent exploration and recovery of relics and artefacts from those wrecks.

Although Australia lacks a *Titanic*, a *Central America*, or a *Geldermalsen*, it is not short of famous wrecks such as the *Batavia* (wrecked in 1629 off the Western Australian coast), the *Dunbar* (wrecked in 1857 off Sydney's South Head), and the more recent *Centaur* (an Australian hospital ship sunk by a Japanese submarine off the Queensland coast in 1943). Wrecks of Australian ships have usually not involved hoards of treasure such as bullion, which has often motivated professional salvors and wreck raisers in other parts of the world. That is not to say that the cargoes of vessels wrecked in Australia are not of very considerable historical and archaeological significance. Indeed, that is the very nature of a cargo of a sunken ship, whether it is treasure or something much more mundane such as commercial cargo and the belongings of the crew and passengers. In this respect, ships wrecked in Australian waters share something in common with the *Titanic* which really carried something for everybody interested in sunken ships.

The balance of this chapter is divided into three sections:

- a survey of the existing Australian law on historic shipwrecks and their treasures, looking at issues such as ownership, rights to possession, wreck notification, restrictions on wreck/treasure raising, and so forth;
- an analysis on how Australian law might change if Australia ratified the UNESCO Convention on the protection of the Underwater Cultural Heritage (UCH); and
- a brief analysis of whether there is any common ground or potential for common ground between the existing law and UCH.

THE CURRENT AUSTRALIAN LAW ON SHIPWRECKS AND THEIR TREASURES

Australia is a common law country. Much of its law is to be found in the judicial decision making of the courts, including the decisions of the courts interpreting legislation. Australia is a federal jurisdiction. This means that there is both federal (Commonwealth) and state legislation and federal and state courts. As a general proposition, federal courts determine questions involving federal legislation (such as the HSA) and the state courts determine issues arising out of state legislation. Sometimes there is a degree of overlap because many disputes that come before the courts (and this includes the area of historic shipwrecks) involve questions of both federal and state laws.

Each state has a Supreme Court from which an appeal lies to a Court of Appeal (sometimes called the Full Court) and

[1] Historic Shipwrecks Act 1976 (Cth) ('HSA').

at the very top of the legal hierarchy sits the High Court of Australia, the equivalent of the Supreme Court of the United States or the House of Lords in the United Kingdom. There is an equivalent appellate structure in the Federal Court system with the High Court again being the final Court in that system.

Issues of salvage and other aspects of maritime law, which can often be relevant to the issues discussed herein, can be heard either in the Federal Court or in the relevant State Supreme Court. Since the Australian Admiralty Act 1988 went into effect, the Federal Court has tended to acquire most maritime jurisdiction. Interestingly, and quite unlike the situation in the United States, for instance, there has been very little litigation in Australia involving competing claims to ownership/salvage/possession of historic shipwrecks and their cargoes and treasures. This may be partly because of the fact there have not been any finds of valuable treasures such as bullion in these shipwrecks, or it may, in part, be attributable to the fact that Australian legislation has given rise to a degree of certainty that the various players in the shipwreck "business" have not wished to challenge.

As a general proposition, Australia has been active in ratifying most international conventions affecting sea transport to and from Australia and around Australia's coasts, not only in relation to, for instance, the carriage of goods by sea (the original Hague Rules were adopted with few variations in the Australian Carriage of Goods by Sea Act 1924), but also in respect of, say, Limitation of Liability Conventions, marine pollution conventions, and the major conventions dealing with the safety of life at sea such as SOLAS and, more recently UNCLOS. Some of these maritime conventions have entered Australian domestic law as schedules to the Commonwealth Navigation Act 1912, which, to some extent, was an Australian version of the British Merchant Shipping legislation that Australia inherited when it was a British colony (or more correctly when its states were British colonies). Thus, SOLAS is Schedule 1 to the Navigation Act and Schedule 9 contains the International Convention on Salvage 1989.

Australia was a foundation signatory to UNCLOS when it came into force internationally in November 1994. Importantly, Australia has ratified the UNESCO Convention on the Means of Prohibiting the Illicit Import, Export and Transfer of Ownership of Cultural Property 1970 and the UNESCO Convention for the Protection of the World Cultural and Natural Heritage 1972 referred to in the preamble to UCH. The Australian Government is generally regarded as an enthusiastic supporter of UCH, having been one of the eighty-seven nations that voted to adopt UCH in November 2001. Interestingly, two countries with close maritime connections to Australia from the point of view of historic shipwrecks, namely the United Kingdom and the Netherlands, abstained from voting in favour of UCH in 2001. Indeed, vessels flying the flags of these two nations make up many of the larger and more famous shipwrecks around the Australian coast prior to the twentieth century.

THE COMMON LAW OF SALVAGE AND FINDS

As a common law country, Australia has inherited the maritime law of salvage and finds.[2] A crucial distinction between entitlements of salvors and finders is that a salvor is invariably entitled to a monetary reward for his services (usually on a no cure/no pay basis, but this is a matter of contract between the salvor and the other interested parties, including the shipowner or its successor in title), and the finder of an abandoned (and usually sunk) vessel is entitled to ownership of that vessel and its cargo on the basis that the abandoned vessel and cargo have become "derelict." A derelict is a vessel that has been abandoned at sea by those in charge of it without the intention of returning to it or attempting to recover it.[3]The relevant time of the intention is the time of leaving the vessel. A subsequent change of intention does not suffice to alter the fact that the vessel was derelict. It appears that the purpose of this policy involving derelicts is to prevent owners who have abandoned their vessels returning to them after the salvor has completed its successful salvage and then trying to reclaim ownership. Plainly, not all shipwrecks are abandoned or derelict. A vessel does not cease to belong to its owner merely because it has sunk and/or become a wreck, whether on the coast or at sea. It still belongs to its owner (or the successor in title) unless it is abandoned. The same principles apply to the cargo of wrecked vessels.

At common law, the finder of a derelict was allowed to keep possession *and* ownership of the derelict. This is to be contrasted with the position of a salvor, who does not become the owner of the vessel absent an agreement with the vessel's owners or successors in title. The salvor may have a lien on the salved vessel and cargo enforceable *in rem* (a dubious benefit in relation to a wreck but possibly very valuable in relation to salvaged cargo). In reality, in the case of constructive total loss of a vessel and cargo, the effective ownership may pass by the law of subrogation to the vessel's hull and machinery insurers and the cargo insurers. These issues have been litigated in the United States in the cases referred to by Forrest in his article, such as the *Central America*.[4] There has been a multitude of judicial decisions in the law of salvage in common law jurisdictions such as England and the United States, although there are relatively few such decisions in Australia.[5]

The distinction between salvor and finder (of a derelict), however important, should not be taken to mean that the two terms are mutually exclusive. The salvor can be a salvor of a derelict. In this case, he is also the finder and entitled under the law of finds to ownership of the find. Although the law of finds has been incorporated into Australian common law, it has not been very well developed and is nowhere near the state

[2] See Forrest Booth in this volume. [3] *Bradley v Newsom AC 16 (1919).*

[4] *Columbus-America Discovery Groups v Atlantic Mutual Insurance Co, 974 F.2d 450 (1992).*

[5] *The Oceanic Grandeur 127 CLR 312 (1972) (High Court)*; also reported in *2 LLR396 (1972).*

of development of that law in the United States. However, at this point, the law of finds in Australia departs from the law of finds in the United States by virtue of the provisions of specific Australian legislation. This is an appropriate point to turn to that legislation and to see how it has developed, not only in areas of finds of wrecks and their cargoes (whether derelict or otherwise) but where Australian legislation in relation to historic shipwrecks and their cargoes has to some extent moved away from the common law.

AUSTRALIAN SHIPWRECK LEGISLATION

An important distinction needs to be made between the law of finds as it applies to offshore wrecks versus onshore wrecks. The common law governs the former. Statute governs the latter. Since early colonial days, there has always been some legislative control over the control of wreckage on the shores in order to prevent pillage of wrecks. Initially, this legislation was in the form of adopted UK legislation, but with the passage of the Navigation Act 1912, specific Australian legislation was introduced. We now enter the realm of legislative definition and purpose.

Part VII of the Navigation Act entitles the Commonwealth Government to appoint an official called "the Receiver Of Wreck" (ROW). The ROW is charged with the responsibility over the wreck, which is defined in Section 294(1) as including: "jetsam flotsam, lagan and derelict found in or on the shores of the sea or any tidal water, and any article of goods of whatever kind which belong to or came from any ship wrecked, stranded, or in distress, or any portion of the hull, machinery or equipment on any such ship." The expression tidal water is defined as meaning that part of the sea or river within the ebb and flow and ordinary spring tides, but does not include a harbour. Jetsam is property jettisoned from the vessel; flotsam is property that has floated off the stricken vessel, and lagan is property cast overboard and which sinks (and is often marked for later recovery). A vessel that is merely in distress is not a wreck.[6]

As can be seen from the definition of Section 294(1), there needs to be a geographical nexus between the wreck and the shore. On this basis, once a vessel and its cargo are cast ashore, they come within these provisions about wreck. Because some salvages are carried out when the vessel has been cast ashore, it may be that the ordinary law on salvage does not apply to a vessel that has become a wreck. This is a grey area of law. There is also a constitutional argument as to whether the Navigation Act as a Commonwealth act applies above the low watermark, which is sometimes where the wreck or other property is cast up. These issues have yet to be determined by the Australian courts.

When any ship is wrecked, stranded, or in distress on or near Australian coast or tidal waters, the ROW must proceed there and take charge to preserve the ship and any lives in any wreck, provided that the ROW must not interfere with the master and crew in the management of the ship without a request from the master.[7] It is an offence to wilfully disobey the ROW's directions or to refuse to assist without reasonable course, to impede the ROW, or to take possession or make off with any wreck.[8]

A person finding or taking possession of a wreck is obliged to notify the ROW.[9] No person is to board a wreck without the authority of the master and under the Act, the master may repel by force any person acting in its contravention.[10] Once the ROW has taken possession of the wreck to which no one establishes a claim, the ROW may sell it to meet fees and expenses and must pay any remaining proceeds to the Commonwealth Treasury.[11]

An owner of any wreck in the possession of the ROW has one year in which to establish a claim, but is to pay all salvage, fees, and expenses before being entitled to retake possession of the wreck.[12] If there is a dispute as to title of any wreck, it can be determined by the courts.[13]

The Commonwealth has a power to require removal of a wreck by the owner under the Navigation Act 1912.[14] Interestingly, the cost to the owner of being required to remove a sunken vessel (a wreck) are not the costs that can be the subject of limitation.[15] Since that decision in 1988, the 1976 Limitation Convention has come into effect in Australia but because the Commonwealth Government has not legislated to bring wreck removal within the Limitation Convention, the decision probably stands as good law. Plainly, the effects of this decision will be of interest to marine insurers providing wreck removal expense and liability cover.

The provisions of the Navigation Act dealing with wreck removal do not deprive the owner of the vessel (or its successor in title) to title to the wreck, but they impose a one-year limitation period on its entitlement to establish its title as against the ROW. In practice, the ROW is not necessarily terribly keen to become the owner of a wreck because of the onerous obligations that dubious distinction can entail, particularly in the context of wreck removal and potential pollution damage. It is doubtful that the drafters of the relevant provisions of the Navigation Act dealing with wreck removal contemplated pollution concerns as being to the fore in this area of legislation.

Crucially, the wreck removal provisions of the Navigation Act do not apply to historic shipwrecks within the meaning of the Historic Shipwrecks Act 1976 or to an historic relic within the meaning of the HSA. In a sense, this appears logical because the wreck removal provisions of the Navigation Act are intended to apply to shipwrecks that have occurred

[6] *Australia United Steam Navigation Co v Lewis StRQd 217 (1937).*

[7] Section 296.

[8] Sections 297–303, 312.

[9] Sections 302 and 303.

[10] Section 313.

[11] Sections 306–310. The receiver has the same rights and remedies in recovery expenses as a salvor.

[12] Section 305.

[13] Section 311.

[14] Section 314A.

[15] *Barameda Enterprises v O'Connor 1 Qd R 359 1988.*

recently, where the vessel may still be in the process of foundering. Plainly, if the *Titanic* founded on or near the Australian coastline today, the provisions of Part VII of the Navigation Act would apply and the ROW would be in business to protect the wreck because the *Titanic* would have become a wreck within the definition of Section 294. However, if, hypothetically, the *Titanic* had sunk on or near the Australian coast and become a wreck in 1912 and salvors now wish to salvage it or raise it, the wreck would be protected by the provisions of the HSA. This is a good time to commence our survey of the HSA.

THE COMMONWEALTH HISTORIC SHIPWRECKS ACT

As mentioned, paragraph 2.14 Part VII of the Navigation Act, does not apply to historic shipwrecks or other historic relics. The terms historic shipwreck and historic relic are defined in Section 3 of the HSA. The HSA has its origins in the wrecks of four Dutch and one English ship in the seventeenth and eighteenth centuries; namely, the *Tryal* (wrecked in 1622), the *Batavia* (wrecked in 1629), the *Vergulde Draeck* (1656), the *Zuytdorp* (1712), and the *Zeewyk* (1727). All were wrecked on the Western Australian coast. The state of Western Australia passed the Museum Amendment Act 1964 specifically for the purpose of the recovery, preservation, and display of historic wrecks vested in the museum and, in particular, shipwrecks lost before 1900. The ownership of these vessels was vested in the Western Australian Museum. The four vessels just mentioned were listed in the schedule to that Act. In addition to the shipwreck sites themselves, the equipment, machinery, and other articles belonging to these ships (whether *in situ* or removed from the site) were protected. Other wrecks considered by the Director of the Museum to be of historic or scientific or archaeological, educational, or other national or local interests could be vested in the Museum. This Western Australian Act was modified subsequently and continues in force. In addition, in 1972, the Australian and Dutch Governments signed an agreement to vest the rights of the old Dutch shipwrecks in Australia, who, in turn, delegated authority to the Western Australian Museum. This is because the Dutch government was the successor entitled to the VOC the original owners of the vessels.

In 1976, a diver named Robinson contested the validity of the Western Australian legislation. He claimed he had first discovered the *Vergulde Draeck* in 1957 and rediscovered it in 1964 but that he had not been permitted to recover material because of the Western Australian legislation since then. His argument was that the relevant provisions of the Western Australian legislation were unconstitutional because they purported to have extraterritorial operation as far as the state of Western Australia was concerned. He also argued that its provisions were repugnant to either the Commonwealth Navigation Act 1912, the Commonwealth Seas and Submerged Lands Act 1973, or the English Merchant Shipping Act 1894. Eventually this case went to the Australian High Court.[16] The High Court split 3-3 but the Chief Justice's casting vote favoured Robinson. In the meantime, the Commonwealth government enacted the HSA, which was timely in having regard to the decision in *Robinson*. The enactment of the HSA required the Navigation Act to be amended in relation to the wreck provisions mentioned previously. Although the HSA initially applied only to the Commonwealth territories, subsequent proclamations made by each State government extended the operation of HSA to each state. The last state to proclaim the operation of HSA was Tasmania, in 1982.

The HSA protects shipwrecks and historic relics in *Australian territorial waters*. These waters are defined as the "territorial sea of Australia and waters of the sea (not being State waters) on the land side of the territorial sea of Australia." To give meaning to this definition, it is necessary to go to some other Commonwealth legislation. Basically, it is from the low watermark or from the end of jurisdiction of each state of Australia, out to a predetermined geographic coordinate that is approximately at the edge of the continental shelf. Interestingly, these provisions are parallel to the various definitions of territorial seas and other relevant types of waters contained in UNCLOS. Essentially, the territorial sea extends twelve nautical miles from the baseline.[17] The usual practice in administering the HSA is to protect a shipwreck and all the relics associated with that shipwreck, wherever located. Thus, if any relics have been removed from Australian waters and are now on land and located in a museum, they are protected.

There are two ways a shipwreck can become protected under the HSA. The main way is that if a ship is at least seventy-five years old from the date of the wrecking, then it and all articles associated with it are automatically protected. In relation to vessels that are less than seventy-five years old and their associated relics, it is by specific declaration.[18]

A shipwreck that has been declared as an historic shipwreck can be visited and dived on by anyone without a permit. However, without a permit, a person cannot interfere with, damage or destroy, dispose or remove an historic shipwreck or associated relics. There is an exception to this if a "protected zone" has been declared around the shipwreck. Such a zone can be declared for up to 200 hectares around the wreck, in which case the execution of any activity may be restricted unless a permit is obtained. The HSA provides for permits to be issued for people to enter a protected zone, to interfere (including excavation and recovery) with an historic shipwreck, and to dispose of an historic shipwreck and associated relics. There are significant penalties for breach of these requirements. In order to make the HSA effective in declaring a shipwreck and associated relics historic and to establish a protected zone, the Government must place an appropriate notice in the *Government Gazette* to make it public knowledge. This is the usual way in Australia in which regulations made pursuant to legislation are given public effect. Often one needs very good

[16] *Robinson v Western Australian Museum 138 CLR 283 (1977).*

[17] UNCLOS, Articles 2, 3, 4 and 8.

[18] *Section 4A of the HSA.*

eyesight to read the small print appearing in the *Government Gazette.*

The HSA sets up a public register for historic shipwrecks, historic relics, and protected zones. This register is being developed and currently mentions about 5,000 protected sites. The register is effectively operated by the Western Australian Museum, although it is supposed to be a joint venture among the various State governments. The HSA requires the discoverer of a new wreck to report it to the government.

Although the Commonwealth Government has the prime responsibility for administering the HSA, but in practice, it delegates that responsibility to each State government. The purpose of this system of administrative delegation is to provide for high levels of cooperation between the Australian and state agencies. To give effect to these objectives, the Commonwealth and State governments have joined forces to promote the historic shipwrecks program (HSP) to operate right across Australia. This dovetails with the administration of the preservation of historic shipwrecks and maritime relics in internal state waters (for instance harbours, rivers both coastal and inland) pursuant to the relevant legislation in each state. For instance, in New South Wales, the relevant legislation is the Heritage Act 1977.

Part 3C of the New South Wales Heritage Act governs the protection of historic shipwrecks. In most respects, the Heritage Act provisions mirror those of the HSA, although they are far less extensive. For instance, an historic shipwreck is defined as the remains of a ship (including any articles associated with a ship) that have been situated in state waters or otherwise within the limits of the state for 75 years, or that are the subject of an historic shipwreck protection order.[19]

In New South Wales, the Heritage Council administers the register of shipwrecks. The New South Wales Heritage Council employs several marine archaeologists specifically to look after the preservation of historic shipwrecks.

In order to avoid any constitutional clash, the New South Wales Heritage Act Part 3 C specifically does not apply to any State waters, which are waters to which the HSA applies.

There are approximately 1,800 shipwrecks in New South Wales and along the New South Wales coast. Hundreds of these are in rivers and harbours and may be protected under the New South Wales Heritage Act. Hence, if the *Titanic* had sailed up Sydney Harbour or the Parramatta River in 1912 before grounding and becoming a wreck, it would be subject to the provisions of the New South Wales Heritage Act. Similar provisions apply in all the other states. In New South Wales, the Maritime Archaeology Program, which began in 1988, forms part of the Commonwealth's HSP. Divers (both recreational and professional) are encouraged to report new shipwreck finds to the Heritage Council. Interestingly, there is a "wreck spotters" program run by the New South Wales Heritage Council in relation to historic shipwrecks. Also of some interest, at least one inland river non-shipwreck site has been declared as protected; namely, some ancient aboriginal fish traps on the inland Darling River in western New South Wales.

Under the HSA, it is an offence to do any of the following except in accordance with a permit:

- damage or destroy an historic shipwreck or a historic relic,
- interfere with an historic shipwreck or a historic relic,
- dispose of a historic shipwreck or a historic relic,
- remove a historic shipwreck or a historic relic from Australia (including State waters), or from Australian waters or from waters of the continental shelf of Australia.

There are significant fines for infringements against this prohibition of A$10,000 for an individual or A$50,000 for a body corporate.

It should be noted that the various prohibitions under the HSA do not mean that wreck recovering activities cannot take place. However, in practice, they restrict the commercial salvage and exploitation of historic shipwrecks in the way permitted in many other jurisdictions. Exceptions are made in relation to saving life or property. There is also a provision for rewards being paid to salvors or finders of historic shipwrecks. However, these rewards (up to A$50,000 in one case) are small compared with commercial salvage awards. In essence, such salvors are not allowed to recover and dispose of historic shipwrecks and relics on the open market in the way that has been done in the well-known cases of offshore salvage in other jurisdictions. The purpose of the Act has been to encourage marine archaeology and preservation of historic shipwrecks and relics either *in situ* or where they are available to the public at large such as in a museum. From time to time, amnesties have been granted to finders of wrecks, usually recreational divers, to encourage returning of artefacts to the authorities.

As a generalisation, Australian historic shipwrecks are given a wide berth because of their protection under the HSA (and corresponding State legislation) and probably just as much because they do not contain the "treasure" to make commercial exploitation viable on a large scale even if the authorities can be persuaded to grant an appropriate permit. In theory, there is no reason why the relevant government authorities could not grant a permit for commercial exploitation in the appropriate case. However, there are very strict public access guidelines published by the Commonwealth and State governments, including the use of artefacts. Essentially, their purpose is to make sure these things are available for public use and not for sale. Critics of the HSA and the HSP say that it worked very well for the first quarter of a century of its operation (after 1976), which was the process of discovering, mapping, and identifying historic shipwrecks. However, the critics see that the HSA is now centred too much on archaeological perspectives, on movable cultural heritage, and not enough on the sites themselves and that it is not the best way to effectively manage cultural heritage sites. The critics also say that the HSA should not be rewarding people with monetary rewards or samples of relics. The critics would like to see much better management plans for shipwreck sites developed before these disturbances are permitted. It has to be said that

[19] Section 47.

in Australia there does not seem to be any large-scale move to open up historic shipwrecks to commercial exploitation. This is perhaps ironic given that one of the world's most famous historic shipwreck salvors/raisers in the last two decades is Mike Hatcher, a native-born Englishman, although currently an Australian national, who has raised such famous treasure ships as the *Geldemalsen* (1985 off Malaysia in international waters) and the *Tek Seng* (1999 in Indonesia waters with the cooperation of the Indonesian Government).

Pursuant to the HSA and the relevant State legislation, there is little scope for the traditional role of the salvor or finder of wrecks/derelict in Australian territorial waters. Indeed, although Australia has ratified and adopted the 1989 Salvage Convention, it is questionable whether the rights given to the salvor under that Convention would be of any benefit in relation to the salvage of an historic shipwreck and its cargo. This is because the Convention does not apply to any salvage operation that involves property "that is maritime cultural property of prehistoric, archaeological or historic interests" and "is situated on the seabed."[20] This provision is a little unfortunate in its drafting in that it is doubtful that there would be any salvage from the sea that did not have some "cultural" aspect or is not of some "historic interest." This exclusion stems from the specific reservations contained in Article 30 of the Salvage Convention. This situation might be contrasted with UNCLOS, which recognises the duty to preserve objects of an "archaeological and historical nature."[21] This power of preservation may be limited to the jurisdiction of the territorial sea and is expressed to be subject to "the law of salvage and other rules of admiralty."[22]UNCLOS does not specifically refer to the traditional law of finds, although there is sufficient common law authority to place the law of maritime finds in the context of "admiralty" law in the broader perspective. Certainly, the old British vice admiralty courts recognise the law of finds in the maritime context. It is clear from Article 303(3) of UNCLOS dealing with the rights of "identifiable owners" that the laws of salvage and other rules of admiralty are not intended to be subordinated to the rights of states in carrying out their duty to protect objects of archaeological and historical nature found at sea and on the seabed.

Pursuant to UNCLOS, Australia, as a coastal state, is entitled to impose its laws not only on its internal waters but the waters of the territorial sea (up to twelve miles from the baseline), the waters of the contiguous zone (a further twelve miles), and in the EEZ, extending not more than 200 nautical miles from the baseline.[23] The rights exercised by Australia as the coastal state are subject to the "other rules of international law,"[24] and these include rights such as the protection of fishing stocks and resources. There is no specific provision in UNCLOS pertaining to the preservation of shipwrecks on the sea floor and the historic relics that go with it other than the general references in article 303 of UNCLOS. As mentioned earlier, Australian domestic law in the form of the HSA and the various state laws largely remove the law of salvage and finds from historic shipwrecks as defined in that legislation. There are similar provisions in the domestic legislation of other countries such as the United States and the United Kingdom.[25] However, this legislation does not extend beyond Australian territorial waters; that is to say it does not extend to the contiguous zone, the EEZ, or the high seas. If Australia adopted the UCH, then the UCH would apply to these areas to the extent that the Australian Government had jurisdiction in terms of regulating vessels flying its flag (including the vessels belonging to salvors) and its own nationals.

THE UCH IN OPERATION

The UCH proceeds on the assumptions set out very clearly in the introduction to Forrest Booth's chapter in this book. These assumptions are fundamentally at odds with the law of salvage and finds in the common law world in that precedence is given to the protection of underwater cultural heritage over legitimate property rights. UCH will supersede the maritime law of salvage and admiralty (including finds) and, in particular, all property on the ocean floor more than 100 years old will be treated as abandoned. The priority will be in preserving the underwater cultural heritage, apparently *in situ* although precisely for whose benefit is difficult to see unless one is very wealthy or possessed with the most up to date underwater technology. Usually, the two go hand-in-hand. There seems to be more than the touch of the academic daydreamer in UCH in these respects.

Put plainly, if the expressed purposes of UCH are given effect literally, let alone leniently, interpreted, then the sort of commercial salvage we have seen in relation to the great wreck explorations and treasure trove raisings will disappear. It will be in flagrant breach of UCH. The salvors will not be able to negotiate with the owners or successors in title to a shipwreck or its cargoes, whether they be the actual parties or their subrogated insurers. If the ship and/or cargo is abandoned (to become derelict) then under UCH there can be no law of finds. People cannot salvage the treasures of the *Titanic* or any other vessel more than 100 years old. They must leave it in place. This applies whether the vessel and its cargoes lie as shipwrecks within territorial or national waters (up to the extent of the EEZ) or under the high seas, in what is described as the "Area" in Article 1 of UCH. Interestingly, the inherent tension in the UCH between recognising some sort of right in underwater cultural heritage to remain *in situ* and the property rights of the owners or successors in title to the wrecks and treasures is, seemingly, avoided in relation to state-owned vessels. Article 2 of UCH provides that nothing in UCH shall be interpreted as modifying the rules of international law and state practice pertaining to sovereign immunities nor to

[20] *Section 316(3)(c) of the Navigation Act 1912.*
[21] Article 303(1) of UNCLOS.
[22] UNCLOS article 303(3).
[23] UNCLOS articles 55 to 75.
[24] UNCLOS article 2.

[25] The US Abandoned Shipwreck Act 43 USC and in the UK the Protection of Wrecks Act 1973 and the Protection of Military Remains Act 1986.

any state's rights in respect of its state vessels and aircraft consistent with state practice and international law, including UNCLOS. Article 3 of UCH provides that nothing in UCH "shall prejudice the rights, jurisdiction and duties of States under international law, including UNCLOS" and UCH must be interpreted and applied in the context of and consistently with international and UNCLOS.

In stark contrast to the apparently pre-eminent (or at the very least equal) prominence to be given to UNCLOS in international law is the poor neighbour relationship with the law of salvage and the law of finds. Article 4 of UCH provides that "any activity relating to underwater cultural heritage to which this Convention applies shall not be subject to the law of salvage or law of finds" unless it is authorised by the relevant authorities, is in conformity with UCH, and ensures that any recovery of underwater cultural heritage achieves maximum protection. In view of the purposes of UCH expressed in its preamble and in its Rules, in practice (if not in theory) this must mean that the preservation of underwater cultural heritage always comes out ahead of the rights of the parties under the law of salvage and finds. If a country adopts UCH, it must apply UCH in substance in its domestic legislation, applying not only to internal waters but also to a territorial sea, the contiguous zone, the EEZ, and to the extent that the state has jurisdiction over vessels and its nationals in the Area, to the Area as well. In other words, to the high seas in the broadest sense of the words.[26]

Indeed, Article 16 provides that State parties will take all practical measures to ensure that their nationals and vessels flying their flag do not engage in any activity directed at underwater cultural heritage in a manner not in conformity with UCH. State parties are even obliged to ensure that their warships operate as far as possible in conformity with UCH.[27]

Significantly, seizure and disposition of underwater cultural heritage recovered in an amount "not in conformity" with UCH is a breach of UCH and State parties are to take measures providing for that seizure and for appropriate sanctions. This article does not expressly prohibit any recovery of underwater cultural heritage (including treasures from vessels such as the *Titanic*) but in practical terms, it would make the commercial recovery and subsequent disposal of such treasures very difficult, having regard to the expressed purposes of UCH. Not impossible, but very difficult. On that basis, there appears to be a flagrant inconsistency with Article 303 of UNCLOS. This is not surprising, given that Article 4 of UCH throws out the law of salvage and finds. Plainly, this is a vicious circle to those wishing to pursue proprietary and possessory rights to historic shipwrecks and their treasures.

The effective (if not literal) prohibition of underwater property rights to historic shipwrecks and relics under UCH goes much further than the Australian HSA and State legislation. That legislation does not deny proprietary and other legal rights. In practice, it prevents the large-scale salvage and disposal of historic ships and treasures without a permit. A *Titanic* or *Geldermalsen* type of recovery permit might not be granted. However, this aspect has never been tested in the Australian courts. For the reasons mentioned earlier, it is unlikely to be so tested in the foreseeable future absent the discovery of a treasure ship.

Interestingly, if the *Titanic* had sunk in Australian waters (where the territorial seas or the extended seas under UNCLOS and UCH), UCH would not yet apply because the *Titanic* has not been a wreck for 100 years. However, it would be covered by HSA if it sank within twelve miles of the coast. Beyond that point, no current Australian legislation will apply. If Australia adopts UCH, then UCH will apply in all those waters to which it is applicable (including the Area as defined in Article 149 of UNCLOS). HSA's permit procedures might be seen as inconsistent with UCH's broader prohibitions. UNCLOS does not specifically deal with seabed wrecks and treasures, and arguably UNCLOS is not concerned with such matters at all in the Area because State rights in this particular part of the article seem to be confined to exploration and exploitation of natural resources.[28] It is arguable that in the Area there is something of a legal vacuum, as argued by Professor Tullao Scovazzi in his chapter in this volume. Professor Scovazzi gives some examples of what might be described as "first come first serve" or "finders keepers" marine archaeological finds, which he regards as inconsistent for the purposes of UCH. That may well be, but those finds proceeded on the basis that well-established property rights in the law of salvage and other areas take precedence over what are still ill-defined concepts of underwater cultural heritage. Of course, if UCH is ratified, those concepts will not be ill defined. They are defined in considerable detail in UCH and its Rules. Professor Scovazzi proceeds to paint what he describes as a "sad picture" of Article 303 of UNCLOS. Again, such a picture depends very much upon one's point of view. Professor Scovazzi criticises those who seek to support this system of law just because it is very old. However, simply because something is old and well-established does not mean it should be abandoned. Not even old wrecks are necessarily abandoned! If a law is a good law and has stood the test of time it should not necessarily be overthrown just for the sake of change or novelty. Such a concept can lead to anarchy and the very breakdown of any concept of law. However, this is to digress. I am sure that Professor Scovazzi does not intend to go that far. Plainly, UCH is intended to override the traditional law of salvage and other maritime/admiralty law in the areas of old shipwrecks and their relics. In countries such as Australia, that is not such a radical concept at all.

The HSA and other Australian legislation does not place an absolute bar on the commercial dealings with historic shipwrecks. Indeed, it is recognised that in appropriate cases they might well be removed to be put on display to the public in museums and so forth. As Forrest Booth coregently argues in his paper, who would have known anything about the

[26] Articles 7, 8, 9, 10, 11 and 12 of UCH.
[27] Article 13 of UCH.
[28] *Article 77(1) of UNCLOS.*

Mary Rose and the wonderful artefacts it preserved from 1545 had the vessel not been raised from the mud of the *Solent* in 1982 and placed in permanent exhibition in Portsmouth? Of what value was it to anybody lying in the mud of the Solent? The "rescue" of the wreck of the barge *James Craig* in the murky backwaters of Tasmania and its rebuilding in Sydney in recent years would not have occurred without commercial salvage technology. There are many cases that fall in between. Surely the answer must be to somehow work out a practical compromise between the two competing interests – namely, preservation of underwater cultural heritage (including historic shipwrecks and their cargoes and treasures) *in situ* and preserving them before they perish altogether. In this respect, the UCH strikes me as being chronologically short sighted. Old shipwrecks and their treasures will not last forever. However admirable the general principles set forward in the preamble to the UCH and many of the Rules to UCH, it strikes me that there is an element of lack of reality and even reasonableness in some of it. As a general proposition, it is doubtful as a matter of international law and commerce that the wholesale destruction of all forms of property rights to shipwrecks and their cargoes/treasures more than 100 years old is appropriate or desirable. In some circumstances it may be. The same comments might be made in relation to the wholesale prohibition of commercial exploitation of such shipwrecks and their cargoes/treasures. What constitutes commercial exploitation can vary from person to person. Piracy and unscrupulous theft for pure personal gain is at one end of the scale. However, one wonders whether there is not an element of unrealistic romanticism about the concept of some aspects of undersea cultural heritage. All shipwrecks result from either accident or war. They are unintended. Why should they be preserved *in situ* forever? Nobody would argue that buildings or land-side structures ought to be preserved in perpetuity if they are damaged as a consequence of natural disaster or war, and yet such land-side "wrecks" represent just as much a cultural heritage as their underwater brethren.

It is the position of this author, as a matter of fairness and practicality, that a compromise needs to be reached mid-way. Regulation, rather than outright prohibition, would appear to be the appropriate way to address the interests of all parties, including future generations. The dogma of UCH is unlikely of itself to lead to the preservation of any ancient shipwreck or its cargoes after an appropriate period of time. It cannot be merely coincidence that there are no shipwrecks left in Australia (with the possible exception of the *Mahogany Ship* in Victoria) from the pre-European age of discovery. Is not a museum or even some form of private collection (perhaps dispersed among vast numbers of people who purchased old porcelain from VOC ships) a fairer way of preserving the past than keeping it forever hidden under water until it rots away to nothing? That might be the outcome if UCH is enforced rigidly, as drafted. There is a great deal that is good, if not very good, in UCH. Regrettably, much of the benefit might be lost if its anti-property sentiments are taken literally.

To return to the title of the chapter, if there is nothing for finders to keepers, everybody will be a loser and weeper.

CHAPTER FORTY-ONE

The Shades of Harmony: Some Thoughts on the Different Contexts That Coastal States Face as Regards the 2001 Underwater Cultural Heritage Convention

Ariel W. Gonzáles

As it has been earlier argued,[1] the intense and complex negotiations that led to the adoption of the UNESCO Convention on the Protection of Underwater Cultural Heritage in November 2001[2] were unfortunately permeated by a misconception about the nature of such instrument. According to such misconception, the Convention has to do, exclusively, with the Law of the Sea: Its sole purpose is to specify the legal status of archaeological and historical objects found at sea. The stage was thus set for another round of confrontation between coastal and maritime States,[3] each side eager to advance its interests in the interpretation of an issue only generally regulated in the final clauses of the 1982 United Nations Convention on the Law of the Sea (UNCLOS).[4]

The delicate scheme of cooperation that was mainly set out by the governmental experts in the final stages of their debates restored to a great extent the dimension of the Convention as an instrument for the protection of the tangible cultural heritage – a missing block in the legal architecture that was developed for this purpose over the years under the auspices of UNESCO.[5] However, the misconception lingers on. A quick look to the voting records for the adoption of the Convention, both in technical and political instances (meetings of governmental experts and General Conference of UNESCO, respectively) reveals that the divisions on Law of the Sea issues could not be fully surmounted.[6] The persistent sensibilities regarding such issues may also underlie the difficulties that the Convention is currently encountering to receive its first ratifications.[7]

The recurrent anchoring of the Convention to the normative scheme codified by UNCLOS had a less evident, but more damaging, effect: The focus on the differences over the Law of the Sea aspects of the Convention led to overlooking the differences over the aspects that respond to the true nature of the Convention – that is, those reflecting its cultural dimension. This second set of differences, though, indicates subtle lines of fragmentation among coastal and maritime States. One such line of fragmentation suggests that a coastal State adjacent to the open seas – hereafter called "open-seas coastal State" (OSC) – tends to have a more cautious approach to the UCH Convention than a coastal State adjacent to a regional sea and which shares with other coastal States of the same condition an interest in such regional sea – hereafter referred to as a "regional sea coastal State" (RSC).[8]

The purpose of this chapter is to explore the source of these latter fissures in what was considered to be a monolithic block during the negotiations of the UCH Convention.[9] An attempt will be made to show that RSCs may be better prepared to implement aspects of the scheme of protection set out in the Convention that the OSCs perceive as difficulties or constraints. Three aspects will be highlighted in this regard: the extent of the principle of cooperation in the Convention, the linkage between the Convention and regional treaties on the same subject matter, and the role of the coastal State in the protection of the underwater cultural heritage in its jurisdictional waters. We will thus conclude that the

[1] González, *Negotiating the Convention on Underwater Cultural Heritage: Myths and reality*. In Camarda and Scovazzi (eds.), *The Protection of the Underwater Cultural Heritage – Legal Aspects*. Milano, 2002, pp. 105–11.

[2] Hereafter, "UCH Convention." Adopted by Resolution 31 C/24 (November 2001) of the General Conference of UNESCO.

[3] For the purposes of this presentation, the expressions "coastal States" and "maritime States" are used generally to refer to States whose primary concern is, respectively, the jurisdiction over maritime spaces and the advancement of the principle of freedom of the seas.

[4] Article 303 – Archaeological and historical objects found at sea.

[5] The 1954 Hague Convention on the protection of cultural property in the event of armed conflict, and its two Protocols; the 1970 Convention on the prevention of illicit import, export, and transfer of ownership of cultural property; and the 1972 Convention on the protection of World Heritage.

Legal Advisor's Office of the Argentine Ministry of Foreign Affairs. The opinions expressed in this paper – originally presented to the Mediterranean Congress on the Protection of Underwater Cultural Heritage (Siracusa; April 1–3, 2003) and updated (December 2004) – are exclusively the responsibility of its author.

[6] In fact, the interventions and explanations of vote at the referred instances show that the totality of the States that voted against the UCH Convention or abstained from such vote were concerned about a negative impact of the Convention on their rights and obligations as coastal or maritime States. For most of the statements on vote, see Camarda and Scovazzi (eds.), *supra*., footnote 1, pgs. 426–34.

[7] Pursuant to Article 27, the Convention needs a minimum of twenty ratifications – or similar expressions of obligation – for its entry into force.

[8] Once more, the voting records and statements on vote tend to be revealing – in particular, regarding coastal States in Europe, Latin America, and the Arab subregion. The European countries voting in favour of the Convention matched almost exactly the RSCs in such region – the exceptions being, possibly, Greece and Turkey, where issues unrelated to the cultural component of the Convention prevailed. The RSCs around the Caribbean Sea and the Persian Gulf also favoured strongly the Convention. Instead, almost all OSCs in Europe and Latin America abstained from the vote.

[9] Although they exceed the scope of this presentation, other lines of fragmentation concerning exclusively maritime States are also of interest. For instance, the Russian Federation, Japan, and the United Kingdom – three typical maritime States – voted against the Convention, in favour of it, and abstained, respectively!

RSCs could assume a "pioneering role" in the promotion and implementation of the Convention, with an overall benefit to the Convention that may largely exceed their own, partial interests.

IMPLEMENTING THE PRINCIPLE OF COOPERATION

From the very outset, the UCH Convention presents both its purpose and its philosophy. According to Article 2.1, the Convention *"aims to ensure and strengthen the protection of underwater cultural heritage."* This is a somewhat elegant way of expressing what most people expect from this instrument: that it prevents looting of underwater cultural heritage.

Such purpose is to be fulfilled not through a division of tasks among States Parties, in which they would have independent roles. On the contrary, the first principle of the Convention is that *"States Parties shall cooperate in the protection of underwater cultural heritage."*[10] It is only in the framework of such principle that *"States Parties shall, individually or jointly as appropriate, take all appropriate measures"* to protect such heritage.[11]

The privileged place of the principle of cooperation in the UCH Convention has two main advantages for all the States Parties. First, it is consistent with the nature of underwater cultural heritage, which is of the "interest of humanity."[12] Secondly, but no less important, it reinforces the understanding on the relationship between the Convention and UNCLOS: More specifically, the Convention confirms and puts into practice the cooperation required in UNCLOS for the protection of "objects of an archaeological and historical nature found at sea."[13]

A less amenable side of the principle of cooperation may regard its implementation. The UCH Convention would have been largely ineffective if it lacked some "teeth" to ensure that its purpose is fulfilled. It thus provides for very precise obligations for State Parties regarding activities that may affect the underwater cultural heritage. Such obligations – which are mainly set out in Articles 14 to 18 and in the Annex and, in a more indirect way, in Articles 4 and 5 – could be schematized as follows:

- the obligation to avoid an automatic assimilation of an element of underwater cultural heritage to a mere wreck – which would be subject to the law of salvage or the law of finds;
- the obligation to prevent the circulation of underwater cultural heritage illicitly exported and/or recovered, and to seize and put to a legal use such heritage;
- the obligation to not tolerate, in any way, activities directed at underwater cultural heritage that are not in conformity to the Convention;
- the obligation to share information and collaborate regarding the protection and management of underwater cultural heritage;
- the obligation of due diligence regarding activities under its jurisdiction that may incidentally affect underwater cultural heritage.

These obligations need also to be implemented in the context of the principle of cooperation. Such implementation, though, may be easier to achieve by RSCs than by OSCs. More specifically, when the list of corollaries to the principle of cooperation presented earlier is translated into practice, the following considerations arise:

- The legal systems of RSCs tend to belong to the same tradition, let it be "continental" or "common law." This facilitates a concerted position of such countries regarding the rule of exclusion of the law of salvage and law of finds, as well as to the exceptions to such rule. In contrast, an OSC will probably have to deal with a third country belonging to a different legal tradition and, thus, a different interpretation regarding the place of the referred laws in the scheme set out in the Convention.
- RSCs tend to suscribe cooperation agreements between their respective custom, fiscal or coast guard authorities, as well as to have harmonized regulations on the areas under the responsibility of such authorities. This normative network stimulates RCSs to collaborate against the circulation of underwater cultural heritage illicitly transferred of recovered. An OSC, instead, has to act alone, relying on its capabilities to sanction and persecute the authors of such illicit activities. For most OSCs – confronted with limited resources to police wide maritime areas – such capabilities are weak.[14]
- RSCs may look forward to the sharing of information on the protection and management of underwater cultural heritage. In fact, they understand that such heritage, whether it is protected *in situ* or recovered in conformity with the Convention, will stay in the region, close to them. Instead, an OSC could be more reluctant to

[10] Article 2.2. As the tenth paragraph of the Preamble to the Convention clearly indicates, the principle of cooperation is not just limited to States, but includes *"international organizations, scientific institutions, professional organizations, archaeologists, divers, other interested parties and the public at large."* With this understanding, and for the sake of simplicity, we will refer in this section just to "State Parties."

[11] Article 2.4. The subordination of this provision to the principle of cooperation is evidenced not only by its place at the end of the enunciation of principles, but – more importantly – by its own requirement that the measures to be adopted must be *"in conformity with the Convention."*

[12] Cfr. Article 2.3: *"States Parties shall preserve underwater cultural heritage for the benefit of humanity. . . ."* This idea is reinforced in the second paragraph of the Preamble to the Convention, in which it is recognized that the responsibility for the protection of such heritage *"rests with all States."*

[13] Article 303, paragraph 1.

[14] Canada could be considered an exception in this sense – which, in turn, helps to explain why, being an OSC, it has a favourable position on the UCH Convention. However, even when an OSC has strong capabilities of enforcement, in certain cases, a looter could circumvent its action by orienting its activities through another neighboring, more tolerating, OSC.

share information on the location of an underwater cultural heritage close to its coasts, which could lead to its recovery by a far away State with a verifiable link to such heritage.

- Finally, the various environmental and fisheries agreements that usually bind RSCs could make it easier for such States to mutually monitor the exercise of due diligence regarding activities that may incidentally affect underwater cultural heritage. An OSC, on the contrary, may have no similar incentives to refrain from such activities.

REGIONAL TREATIES AND THE UCH CONVENTION

As it may be seen from the previous section, RSCs seem better prepared to implement the principle of cooperation in the UCH Convention, mainly because of their usually intense normative interaction. This could explain, in turn, the interest and active participation of many of these countries during the negotiations that led to the adoption of the Convention, in the scheme that sets out the links between such instrument and other treaties on the same subject matter relating to the protection of underwater cultural heritage.

Such scheme is reflected in Article 6 of the Convention, which basically regulates two scenarios:

- *Ex post* – that is, after adopting the Convention[15] – States can enter into bilateral, regional, or other multilateral agreements on the protection of underwater cultural heritage that may be stricter but cannot be more flexible than the minimum standard of protection fixed in such instrument.[16] Furthermore, the referred agreements are not open to any third party, but only to *"States with a verifiable link, especially a cultural, historical or archaeological link to the underwater cultural heritage."*[17]
- *Ex ante*, it had to be admitted that the Convention could not alter the rights and obligations of States arising from agreements concluded before its adoption *"and, in particular, those that are in conformity with the purposes of the Convention."*[18]

RSCs may also be better positioned to respond to these two scenarios. In fact, such countries have gradually developed over the years a network of various instruments (arrangements, understandings, declarations, or agreements) related to the protection of underwater cultural heritage.[19] When this has not, in a straightforward manner, resulted in a regional agreement, it has established a sound basis for negotiating such an agreement with the background offered by the UCH Convention. Even where the referred development did not take place, the natural interaction resulting from the geographical proximity and shared cultural values of RSCs favours it. In any of these situations, then, Article 6 will not be perceived by RSCs as an obstacle for their ratification of the Convention.

Moreover, because RSCs will usually have similar views regarding the best way to protect underwater cultural heritage, a "State with a verifiable link" joining an agreement between such States will be perceived as an invitee, rather than a partner on an equal footing.[20] This may be an additional stimulus for such RSCs, who will be able to neutralize any particular divergent interest of the "outsider." For example, the parties may disagree on the need to preserve *in situ* a given underwater cultural heritage – the RSCs, mainly concerned with not affecting the cultural values of the area; the "State with a verifiable link" possibly more interested in display of the heritage in its national museum. In such a case, the concerted action of RSCs would reinforce the principle of considering such preservation as a first option for the protection of such heritage.[21]

In contrast, an OSC will have rarely entered into a bilateral agreement – and, even less, into a regional one – for the protection of the underwater cultural heritage in its adjacent waters: It will consider such protection to be of its primary – when not exclusive – responsibility. Most probably extraneous to the experience of RSCs as regards the gradual development of a body of practice and norms, the OSC will tend to react with suspicion to an offer to negotiate an agreement falling under Article 6.1 of the Convention. In particular, such an OSC will dislike the idea of accepting a bilateral commitment – usually, an agreement with a "State with a verifiable link" – that would reduce its degree of control over the referred underwater cultural heritage.[22]

[15] Strictly speaking, the link with other treaties would operate once the UHC enters into force. However, States that voted in favour of the adoption of the Convention at the UNESCO General Conference would find it difficult to enter into a regional or bilateral treaty not consistent with such instrument. This would represent, in fact, an act against the object and purpose of the Convention (Article 18 of the 1969 Vienna Convention on the Law of Treaties).

[16] Paragraph 1, which – in one of the strongest messages in the UHC Convention, asserts that these agreements *"shall be in full conformity with the provisions of the Convention and shall not dilute its universal character."*

[17] Paragraph 2.

[18] Paragraph 3. This last expression may be interpreted to convey the sense of frustation felt by many negotiators at not being able to overrule the principle of nonretroactivity of international treaties.

[19] The process that led to the adoption of the 2001 Siracusa Declaration on the Submarine Cultural Heritage of the Mediterranean Sea may be considered a model of such normative interaction. The English version of the Declaration can be found in Camarda and Scovazzi (eds.), *supra.*, footnote 1, pgs. 448–9.

[20] This, naturally, unless the State with a verifiable link is also a RSC in the same regional sea – in which case, there is an inherent convergence of interests and, thus, the problem would not arise.

[21] Article 2.5 of the UCH Convention and Rule 1 of its Annex.

[22] Not surprisingly, developing OSCs are particularly sensitive to this particular concern. It may have weighed heavily, for instance, in the decision of some South American States to abstain from the vote for the adoption of the UCH Convention. It is interesting to note, in this regard, that the quasi-totality of the bilateral agreements currently in force for the protection of a given underwater cultural heritage have only developed countries as Parties. And even then, such agreements pose quite sustantive limitations on the Party represented by a coastal State. For instance, the agreement between Australia and The Netherlands of 1972 regulates the creation of a Committee to deal with issues of disposition or ownership of underwater cultural heritage of Dutch origin, but located in the waters adjacent to the Australian coast.

THE COASTAL STATES AS "COORDINATORS"

The notions of responsibility and control over a given underwater cultural heritage bring us to what is perhaps the source of the biggest divide in the perceptions of RSCs and OSCs regarding the Convention: their role in the protection of such heritage in their jurisdictional waters.

This matter was possibly the most controversial during the negotiations, putting into question at a given moment the very adoption of the Convention. As it will be recalled, the negotiators finally managed to reach an almost complete consensus over a "normative package," which allowed cooperation to find its place within the rigid and highly politically sensitive categories of maritime spaces. In very broad terms, such normative package includes the following components:

- the exclusive right of a State Party to regulate and authorize activities directed at underwater cultural heritage located in its territorial waters but, at the same time, a moral commitment by such State Party to inform other State Parties and, when applicable, States with a verifiable link, about the discovery of identifiable State vessels and aircrafts that meet the definition of underwater cultural heritage[23];
- a mechanism of coordination for activities directed at underwater cultural heritage located in the Economic Exclusive Zone (EEZ) or on the continental shelf of a State Party to the Convention who is assigned in first instance the role of "Coordinating State." Such mechanism – which is at the heart of the scheme of cooperation and has the protection of underwater cultural heritage as its permanent objective – involves a detailed procedure of notifications and a network of interactions, which reunites the Coordinating State and the States with a verifiable link to the heritage concerned[24]; and
- a mechanism of consultation among interested State Parties for the protection of underwater cultural heritage in the Area.[25]

The fact that a given country is a RSC or an OSC does not alter in essence the way it perceives its role in the Convention regarding the protection of underwater cultural heritage in its territorial waters or in the Area. The same cannot be said for the mechanism of cooperation in the EEZ or on the continental shelf. Given the relatively circumscribed extension of its jurisdictional waters, a RSC may feel at ease in its function of "Coordinating State." It may even perceive such function as the codification of a practice already followed in its regional sea. Furthermore, the reasoning presented in the previous section regarding the reduced influence of a State with a verifiable link in a regional treaty can be extended to the mechanism of coordination.

Inversely, the logistical difficulties associated with the control of large maritime spaces may make the referred function of coordination nominal for an OSC. Such State may perceive as particularly frustrating a failure to exercise the rights that the UCH Convention assigns to it in terms of requiring reporting of activities directed at underwater cultural heritage[26] or of controlling whether the activity affects its sovereign rights or jurisdiction provided for in international law, including UNCLOS.[27] The OSC may prefer, therefore, to continue relying on the general obligation of cooperation currently stated in UNCLOS, rather than to be part of a mechanism that has an uncertain impact on its interests.

BY WAY OF CONCLUSION: A POSSIBLE PATH TOWARD THE ENTRY INTO FORCE OF THE UCH CONVENTION

As with most rational acts, the decision that leads a State to bind itself to an international treaty is the result of a cost–benefit analysis. This calculation is less based on facts than on perceptions: Instead of balancing its rights with its obligations under the treaty, the State will tend to assess how it can exercise such rights and fulfil such obligations in practice.

The UCH Convention is certainly no exception to such reasoning. At first glance, the Convention appears as a picture with clear-cut contrasts, notably, between coastal and maritime States, between States favouring *in situ* preservation of the underwater cultural heritage and those promoting its recovery, between States with an absolute or relative view of the protection of such heritage. A closer look, though, reveals that there are shades beneath the picture.

In the preceding sections, a group of these shades was outlined, namely those permeating coastal States. For some of these States, the ones referred to as RSCs, the UCH Convention reinforces their commitment to the regional sea to which they are adjacent: They simply add a "cultural heritage component" to the cooperation that already exists regarding such regional seas in various areas – for instance, defence, economics, environmental protection, and communication. Other States, the OSCs, perceive instead the Convention as a further complication of an already difficult task: how to preserve resources scattered in wide maritime spaces. Where the first see an opportunity and a source of inspiration, the latter fear a constraint or a risk.

The previous discussion does not necessarily conspire against the entry into force of the UCH Convention in a relatively short period, nor put into question its universality. Rather, it suggests a path for its ratification. In fact, it has been shown that the implementation of the different aspects of the Convention should be relatively easier for RSCs. Thus, the experience of these States as the first Parties of the Convention may represent a valuable evidence of the effectiveness of the

[23] Article 7.
[24] Articles 9 and 10.
[25] Articles 11 and 12. Generally speaking, the Area is the sea-bed beyond the continental shelf.
[26] Article 9.1(b)(i)
[27] Article 10.

mechanism it regulates.[28] This, in turn, may encourage OSCs to leave aside their concerns and also ratify or adhere to the Convention.[29]

[28] This rationale has certainly inspired the Siracuse Declaration on the Submarine Cultural Heritage of the Mediterranean Sea, adopted during the International Conference, "Means for the protection and touristic promotion of the marine cultural heritage in the Mediterranean." It is interesting to quote, in this regard, paragraph i.3 of such Declaration: "*The Mediterranean countries* [the typical RSCs in the European region] *have a* ***special responsibility*** *to ensure that* ***the submarine cultural heritage they share*** *is made known and preserved for the benefit of humankind*" (bold added by the author).

[29] In November 2004, the Colombian government, with the assistance of UNESCO, organized in Bogotá a Regional Seminar of Experts on Underwater Cultural Heritage. Among other interesting aspects, the Seminar showed the different realities faced by the Caribbean countries – the most likely RSCs in the Latin American region – vis-à-vis the OSCs embodied in many South American States. For instance, the latter tended to be more concerned than the former by the risks supposedly posed by the UCH Convention to their sovereign and/or jurisdictional rights in their maritime spaces. It was interesting also to note that the experts at Bogotá saw regional and subregional cooperation as one of the main means to augment the possibility of a relatively rapid entry into force of the Convention.

It is for RSCs, then, to open the way toward the entry into force of the UCH Convention.[30] These States have already shown preparation, practice, and commitment, the main attributes of the explorers of once uncharted seas. Now they need just to echo their boldness.

SUGGESTED READING FOR THIS ARTICLE

Camarda, Guido and Scovazzi, Tullio (eds.); *The Protection of the Underwater Cultural Heritage – Legal Aspects; Giuffré Editore; Milano*, 2002.

Garabello, Roberta and Scovazzi, Tullio (eds.); *The Protection of the Underwater Cultural Heritage – Before and after the 2001 UNESCO Convention;* Martinus Nijhoff Publishers; Leiden, 2003.

Scovazzi, Tullio (ed.); *La protezione del patrimonio culturale sottomarino nel Mare Mediterráneo;* Giuffré Editore; Milano, 2004.

[30] And it is revealing to note, in this regard, that the three countries that have ratified the UCH Convention to date – Panama, Bulgaria, and Croatia – can be described as RSCs.

CHAPTER FORTY-TWO

Underwater Cultural Heritage at Risk: The Case of the *Dodington* Coins

John Gribble and Craig Forrest

INTRODUCTION

Underwater cultural heritage is at risk: not only from the inevitable destruction of time and tide, but also from those for whom the lure of gold is more valuable than knowledge. Many States with a rich store of underwater cultural heritage have recognised the importance of this finite resource, not in monetary terms, but in archaeological terms – the knowledge that can be gleaned from an appropriately scientific excavation of a site. Unfortunately, giving effect to such a policy is fraught with difficulties. The nature of many underwater cultural heritage sites, lying often in treacherous waters beyond coastal state surveillance, makes enforcement of States' legislation perplexing. The low priority and consequent meagre budgets for most States' cultural heritage institutions exacerbate these difficulties. This is confounded by the lack of a truly international protective regime to prevent the illicit excavation and movement of cultural heritage between States.

These difficulties are exemplified in the case of the *Dodington* coins. Although this case has been instrumental in highlighting the inadequacies of the South African legislation, and provided insights necessary for law reform, it has also highlighted inadequacies in international law that cannot be remedied by individual States. Whereas a number of international and regional conventions exist that concern, in part, the complex issue of repatriation, neither the United Kingdom nor South Africa was a Party to any of these at the time the case arose. However, had these States been Party to these conventions, the inadequacies of the regimes provided for would not have aided South Africa in its attempts to have the coins repatriated.

This chapter is an updated version of Craig Forrest and John Gribble, "The Illicit Movement of Underwater Cultural Heritage: The Case of the *Dodington* Coins" (2002) 11(2) *International Journal of Cultural Property*, 267–93, by permission of Oxford University Press, and John Gribble, The Case of the Doddington Coins, presentation to the International Bar Association Annual meeting Johanesberg. 2002.

This chapter considers the difficulties and risks faced in protecting underwater cultural heritage in the form of the wreck of the vessel *Dodington*, and illustrates the positive results in historic shipwreck management and regulatory enforcement achieved in South Africa.

THE CASE OF THE *DODINGTON* COINS

On 1 October 1997, the then National Monuments Council (NMC)[1] of the Republic of South Africa received from London a copy of an article published in *The Times of London*[2] entitled "Clive of India's Gold Found in Pirate Wreck." The article was an advert for a forthcoming London auction at which 1,214 gold coins,[3] weighing a total of 620 ounces, were to be sold. What was important about these particular coins for the NMC was the claim made in the article that they were part of the 653 ounces of gold that Robert Clive – better known as Clive of India – took with him when he sailed from England for India via Africa, and which were part of the hoard lost when the East Indiaman *Dodington* was wrecked in Algoa Bay, South Africa, on 17 July 1755. The wreck and its contents lie within South African territorial waters, and are protected by South African heritage legislation.

For a variety of reasons, the NMC had historically not had a great deal of success prosecuting offences under the National Monuments Act,[4] even in South Africa. Reasons include the low priority and status cultural heritage offences carry within the justice system, and financial considerations such as the implications for the NMC's very limited budget of legal fees and costs. Perhaps the major constraint, however, was a lack of confidence on the part of the NMC itself in the legal strength and validity of sections of the Act, the result of which was that the NMC was unwilling to embark on costly legal proceedings with no guarantee of success.

In legal systems around the world, legislation is based within the framework of a country's legal system, is deemed to carry the force of law, and is legally binding upon it citizens. Laws, however, are open to various interpretations. It is not, therefore, until a piece of legislation and the principles and ideals enshrined in it have been tested in court, that it can claim to be worth more than the paper it is written on. Until that time, the legality and validity of that law, or section of a law, is questionable and its implementation is open to question and challenge. The National Monuments Act was a good example of exactly this dilemma. The result of the reticence to enforce contraventions of the Act was the development of a general perception of the NMC as a toothless dog, without the will to act, and this perception was abundantly clear in a

[1] Hereafter NMC. The National Monuments Council was renamed the South African Heritage Resources Agency (hereafter SAHRA) under the provisions of the National Resources Heritage Act, Act No. 25 of 1999.

[2] "Clive of India's Gold Found in Pirate Wreck," *The Times of London* Monday 29 September 1997.

[3] Although *The Times of London* article reported 1,400 gold coins, the total was, in fact, 1,214 coins weighing 620 ounces.

[4] Act No. 28 of 1969.

lack of respect for the Act, and for the NMC as the compliance agency. The need for the NMC to be seen actively enforcing the Act and not shying away from prosecuting offences was therefore of the utmost importance for improving the NMC's credibility, that of the Act, and that of heritage management in South Africa in general. The NMC needed to judge its decisions to prosecute offences against the Act not only according to likelihood of success, but had also to recognise the importance of demonstrating a will to fight and the legal importance of testing the Act in court.

THE LOSS OF THE *DODINGTON*

In late 1754, in an effort to force the French out of the Indian subcontinent once and for all, and to ensure the dominance of the British East India Company in the region, the Directors of the Company appointed Robert Clive – later to be known as Baron Plassey – to lead their forces in India.[5] A fleet of Company vessels, comprising the *Stretham, Dodington, Pelham, Edgecote*, and *Houghton*, was assembled, and sailed from the Downs near Dover on 22 April 1755.

The first half of the voyage was uneventful, with the *Dodington* proving herself a superior vessel by outstripping the rest of the fleet. After rounding Cape Agulhas, however, the master of the *Dodington*, James Sampson, committed a navigational error common at the time, which was to ultimately result in the loss of his vessel. The charts he was using were based on the original Portuguese Roteiro, or sailing instructions, compiled by Manuel de Mesquita Perestrelo in 1576,[6] and although remarkably accurate in other respects, showed the south-east coast of Africa cutting away too rapidly to the north. This meant that vessels sailing according to this chart were, in fact, closer to the coast than they realised, an error that put the *Dodington* directly on course to the low, rocky island named Chaos Island by Bartholemeu Dias in 1488, and today known as Bird Island, situated near Port Elizabeth in Algoa Bay.

Shortly after midnight on 17 July 1755, the *Dodington* struck a reef off Bird Island and, according to survivors' accounts, broke up within 20 minutes. Only 23 of the 270 people on board made it ashore. These survivors managed to salvage some items, including tools, food, and two chests of Company silver from the wreck before it disintegrated completely. They spent nearly seven months on the island building a small open boat they named *Happy Deliverance*, and eventually sailed to Mozambique, where they were rescued.[7]

When it was wrecked, the *Dodington* was carrying a cargo that included silver specie (35,000 ounces), copper ingots, military hardware and artillery pieces for Clive's campaign, and a variety of personal cargo. Historical records indicate that Clive was unable to get a passage on the *Dodington*, and had to settle for a berth on her sister ship, the *Stretham*. He nevertheless put his personal fortune of gold aboard the *Dodington*, as reflected in the "Manifest of private gold, silver and wrought plate Lycenced to be shipped on Board the *Doddington* (sic) for Fort. St. George," which is preserved in the Records of the East India Company, and reads: "For Robert Clive Esqr. Governor for Fort St. David, One Chest of Gold, Marked R.C. No. 1qt – 653 Oz, 6 pennyweight." Further evidence that this gold was indeed on board the *Dodington*, is to be found in a letter dated 5 October 1756, written by Clive to his father, in which he confirms that he lost £3000 when the vessel was wrecked.[8]

Although two chests of Company silver were recovered from the wreck by survivors and later returned to the Company through the unstinting honesty of the First Mate, Evan Jones, there is no evidence to suggest that the chest containing Clive's gold was ever recovered. In light of Jones' efforts with the Company silver, there is every reason to believe that had the gold been found, it too would have been returned to its owner.

DISCOVERY OF THE WRECK

The perception of the *Dodington* as a treasure ship ensured that she was never forgotten, but the location of the wreck itself was lost. It was only in 1977, after years of research, that the vessel was discovered off Bird Island by David Allen and Gerry van Niekerk. Based on archival research, and discounting later guesses as to the location of the wreck, it took Allen only ten minutes to find the wreck once he got into the water. The discovery of a number of bronze howitzers on the site, together with other artefacts, proved conclusively that the wreck was that of the *Dodington*.[9]

Allen and van Niekerk started excavating the wreck, and in 1982, following an amendment to the National Monuments Act, which made a permit from the NMC a requirement, applied for and were granted a permit to investigate the wreck. The Port Elizabeth Museum (now Bayworld) agreed to collaborate on the project and many of the historical artefacts recovered have been donated to the museum. The permit has been renewed a number of times, and after the death of Allen in 1987 was issued to van Niekerk, who held it thereafter.

SHIPWRECKS AND SOUTH AFRICAN LEGISLATION

In the nearly three decades since the wreck of the *Dodington* was found, there have also been sweeping changes in official attitudes to historical shipwrecks in South Africa, and a heritage resource that enjoyed no legal protection in 1977 is now covered by blanket legislative protection.

It is interesting to note here that it was, in fact, the discovery by Allen and van Niekerk of the *Dodington*, and an older Portuguese wreck, the *Santissimo Sacramento* (1647),[10] near Port Elizabeth in the same year, that was the catalyst

[5] G. Allen and D. Allen, *Clives's Lost Treasure* 9 (Robin Garton, London, 1978).

[6] E. Axelson (ed), *Dias and his Successors* (Saayman and Weber, Cape Town, 1988); R. Knox-Johnson, *The Cape of Good Hope: A Maritime History* (Hodder & Stoughton, London 1989).

[7] Allen, *supra* note 5, at 33–43.

[8] *Id.* at 10.

[9] *Id.* at 90–2.

[10] *Id.* at 70–3.

for the first legislation to protect historical shipwrecks. Their experience after locating the *Sacramento* of ruthless poaching and plundering of the site by other divers and salvors as soon as word of its discovery leaked out, led them to approach Mr. John Wiley, a Cape Town MP who had an interest in historical shipwrecks, with their concerns. Wiley took up the cause, and in an address to Parliament on 17 May 1977 called for legislation to protect historical shipwrecks.[11]

This resulted in an amendment to the National Monuments Act[12] that allowed the NMC to declare as a national monument any shipwreck in South African territorial waters more than 80 years old. Once declared, it was an offence to destroy or damage such a wreck. Where this legislation fell short, however, was in the fact that no legal protection was given to the contents of declared wrecks, which meant that artefacts could still be legally removed from sites. Furthermore, it was not until 1984 that the provisional declaration, for a period of five years and twenty-three wrecks – including the *Dodington* and the *Sacramento* – took place.[13]

The failure of this legislation to go far enough, and the fact that salvors were primarily interested in the contents of the wrecks, which were not protected, meant that artefacts and cargo continued to be removed from wrecks by salvors and divers at will. There was increasing concern on the part of both the NMC and coastal museums[14] that these individuals were profiting from the exploitation of a national heritage resource at the expense of the rest of the nation, and that because of their primarily commercial interest in the wrecks, their over-hasty methods were destroying valuable historical and archaeological sites and data.

As a result of pressure from the NMC and the South African Museums Association (SAMA),[15] a second amendment to the National Monuments Act[16] was passed, in the terms of which a permit was required from the NMC to "destroy, damage, alter or export from the Republic" any one of a list of artefacts known to have been in the country or its territorial waters for more than 100 years.[17] This piece of legislation attempted to control the movement of, and trade in, cultural property, but was largely ineffective because of a lack of personnel to implement and enforce it. Furthermore, because the legislation again did not make it an offence to remove material from a wreck or wreck site, the exploitation of sites did not diminish.

Continued lobbying by both SAMA and the South African Association of Archaeologists resulted in a third amendment to the National Monuments Act in 1986, which extended a blanket protection to all wrecks and wreck material over the age of 50 years, making it an offence to interfere with or disturb a wreck in any way, except under the terms of a permit issued by the NMC. This legislation provided the catalyst for the development by the NMC of a far stricter regime of wreck management through the permit system, and allowed real steps to be taken to conserve this heritage resource in South Africa. In addition it also supplied the impetus for the subsequent growth of a maritime archaeological capacity in South Africa.

In April 2000, the National Monuments Act, by then more than 30 years old, was replaced by the National Heritage Resources Act.[18] The Act, which established the South African Heritage Resources Agency (SAHRA) as the new national heritage compliance agency, also introduced greatly improved legal protection for underwater heritage and historical wrecks in South Africa.

As under the old Act, the new legislation also provides blanket protection for wrecks over a certain age – in this case sixty years. It is, however, in their definition within the Act that the real change in the status of wrecks becomes apparent. In terms of Section 2 (ii), wrecks form part of what is defined by the Act as "archaeological." This means that the legal ambiguity in the National Monuments Act with regard to whether or not wrecks were archaeological sites, and which was largely the result of their late inclusion within the ambit of that Act, is no longer there. Wrecks are archaeological sites and must be managed as such. Furthermore, all archaeological material is deemed to be the property of the State.[19] This is going to have profound implications for the general perception that wrecks are abandoned goods to be salvaged.

THE CASE FOR REPATRIATION

The historical association of the *Dodington* with Robert Clive, and the personal fortune he lost when the vessel was wrecked, meant that the announcement in the British press of the impending sale of coins reputed to be Clives' gold, set alarm bells ringing at the NMC. Although the announcement did not specifically refer to the coins as having come from the wreck of the *Dodington*, the claim was nevertheless that they were those lost by Clive.

According to *The Times* article, the claim made by the sellers was that the coins were recovered from the wreck of a small, heavily armed eighteenth-century privateer or pirate vessel which had stumbled upon off the South African east coast; this after an exhaustive search of the *Dodington* site itself failed to yield the gold. Although it is not entirely inconceivable that the wreck of a small wooden vessel could have been accidentally located on the vast expanse of seabed off the southeast African coast, the claim that the gold found was Clive's implies something along the lines of the following scenario: unseen by the *Dodington* survivors, Clive's gold was recovered from the wreck by pirates not long after the vessel was wrecked, was lost again when that vessel foundered, only to be found, quite by chance, by the same modern divers who had already visited the *Dodington*.

[11] Hansard, 1977, *Republic of South Africa House of Assembly Debates*, Vol. 68 (18 April–20 May), Column 7869–7872.

[12] Act No. 35 of 1979.

[13] J. Deacon, "Protection of historical shipwrecks through the National Monuments Act," in *Proceedings of the Third National Maritime Conference, Durban 1992*, (University of Stellenbosch, Stellenbosch 1993).

[14] G. Bell-Cross, Research Policy on Shipwrecks, 14 *South African Museums Association Bulletin* (1980).

[15] *Id.*

[16] Act No. 13 of 1981.

[17] Deacon, *supra* note 13.

[18] Act No. 25 of 1999.

[19] Section 3, Act No. 25 of 1999.

On top of that, the press report claimed that the wreck in question lay in international waters, thereby neatly and fortuitously placing it outside the legal jurisdiction of any adjacent coastal state. Because South Africa has chosen to include in its Maritime Zones Act[20] the provision in the United Nations Convention on the Law of the Sea[21] for a contiguous zone in which coastal states may choose to exercise jurisdiction over underwater cultural heritage, this would imply that the wreck in question would have to lie at least 24 nautical miles (44.4 kilometres) off the South African coast. At this distance from the South African east coast, average water depth is at least 200 metres, ruling out conventional diving, and requiring extremely sophisticated and expensive equipment and skills.

The suspicious nature of the entire claim was further fuelled by the fact that the identities of the divers involved in retrieving this material were kept secret, as was any other information regarding the identity and location of the alleged wreck of the privateer. This was ostensibly to "stop opportunists from profiting from the discovery,"[22] although *The Times* article seemed to contradict this statement by reporting that despite the wreck having been scoured by the divers, the only items of value found were the gold coins. Requests to the auctioneers for further information as to the identity of the seller/s and the location of the alleged second wreck were not successful. As a result of the NMC's enquiries, however, the auctioneers did withdraw the coins from the auction, and although immediately instructed by the seller/s to return the coins, decided to hold them until the matter of their origin, and any claims the Republic of South Africa may have had on them, were resolved.

The flimsy and suspicious nature of the claims made by the sellers as to the provenance of the coins, and their refusal to cooperate with the NMC, led the NMC to suspect that the alleged privateer was a fabrication designed to sidestep South Africa's heritage legislation and Customs and Excise regulations, and that the wreck of the *Dodington*, or possibly some other historical wreck in South African territorial waters, had been looted and the gold recovered illegally exported from the country. As the custodians of South Africa's cultural heritage, the NMC was bound to pursue the matter, and instructed its attorneys to take up the case.

THE FINANCIAL IMPLICATIONS OF LITIGATION

Increased interest in South African shipwrecks on the part of large, well-funded and well-equipped international salvage companies since the mid-1990s had been of concern to the NMC because of the limited capacity to effectively enforce the legislation and police the sites. This situation presented the possibility that salvors, international or local, could exploit South African wreck sites and leave the country with the material recovered, all without the NMC's knowledge. Although for these and other reasons the NMC had a policy of generally refusing permits to international concerns, interest by these companies and individuals had nevertheless set the stage for potential international litigation, and it was simply going to be a matter of time before the NMC would have to take up a case in a foreign court.

As in many other countries, heritage management in South Africa was, and still is, severely underfunded, and the compliance agency significantly understaffed. These financial and other resultant constraints were certainly one of the primary reasons for the NMC's seeming reticence in enforcing the Act and prosecuting offences. The cost, too, of launching legal proceedings – particularly in a foreign country – was a major issue, and had to be carefully considered given the NMC's meagre budget. In the case of the "*Dodington* coins," the NMC would not have been able to pursue the matter had the State, in the form of the then Department of Arts, Culture, Science and Technology not agreed to bear most of the legal costs.

During and since the case, there has been the opinion expressed in some quarters that the substantial legal bill this case generated was not justified, and that the money could have been better spent elsewhere in heritage conservation. However, it is important to view the issue of cost from alternative perspectives.

As mentioned earlier, the NMC's poor record in prosecuting and enforcing the Act had bred a culture of disrespect for the organisation and the Act, which the pursuit of this case would challenge. Having been alerted to the fact that the coins were for sale, and given the suspicious nature of information as to their provenance, the NMC was left with no moral or ethical alternative but to pursue the case. Furthermore, the opportunity that this case offered – no matter the outcome – to send a message to the country and to the world that the NMC would act to protect South Africa's cultural heritage, was of unquantifiable value, and therefore worth every cent in legal costs.

THE ISSUES

The attempt to repatriate the *Dodington* coins involved the central issues of the enforcement of South African export laws and questions of ownership.

The Application of the National Monuments Act in a Court of the United Kingdom

A fundamental principle of international law is the recognition of the equality of States and respect for the sovereignty of each State. From this concept derives the principle that no State will require another State to enforce its public laws. This would include not only penal and revenue laws, but also exportation laws, including those that prohibit the exportation of cultural heritage.

[20] Act No. 15 of 1994.
[21] U.N. Doc. A/Conf.62/122; (1982) 21 I.L.M. 1261.
[22] *The Times of London*, *supra* note 2.

The justifications for restrictions on the exportation of cultural heritage are diverse and controversial, and many commentators have criticised the strictness of the export limitation laws of many "source" States.[23] Although many of these criticisms may be well founded, the use of exportation limitation laws plays an important part in the protection of certain classes of cultural heritage, particularly archaeological material, and is an integral aspect of the protective system for archaeological sites that ordinarily would include the granting of excavation permits as well as export permits. It is within this framework of the protection of archaeological sites that the South African exportation limitation should be viewed.[24] As such, it is unfortunate that "market" States, such as the United Kingdom, have done little to aid source States in their fight to prevent the illicit excavation and exportation of cultural heritage.

The United Kingdom has long refused to enforce foreign public law. Although the determination of exactly what constitutes public law is uncertain, in cases of cultural property illegally exported from the source State, UK courts would appear to be opposed to repatriating them on these grounds. For example, in *The King of Italy and The Italian Government v. Marquis Cosimo de Merdici Tornaquinci and Christie, Manson and Woods*,[25] which concerned a petition for the granting of an injunction to prevent the sale of historic documents, Mr. Justice Peterson doubted whether the court would enforce the exportation laws of Italy in the case of exportation of historic documents that were not the property of the Italian State. Similarly, in *Attorney General of New Zealand v Oritz and Other*,[26] Staughton held that "an English court has no jurisdiction to entertain an action for the enforcement, either directly or indirectly, of a foreign penal, revenue or other public law."[27] The UK Government, in a response to a UNESCO inquiry concerning the 1970 UNESCO Conventionon on the Means of Prohibiting and Preventing the Illicit Import, Export and Transfer of Ownership of Cultural Property,[28] stated that "[i]t is not possible for HM Government to take measures against individuals or organisations unless the law of the United Kingdom is broken . . . There is no provision in the laws of the United Kingdom for proceedings to be taken against persons suspected of having infringed the export controls of other countries."[29] As such, the NMC recognised that the South African National Monuments Act could not be relied upon in a foreign court in a case for repatriation of the *Dodington* coins, and recourse would have to be had on grounds of ownership.

Ownership of the *Dodington* Coins

"All national legal systems prohibit and punish theft, and the courts of all nations are open to actions by foreign as well as domestic owners to recover their stolen property."[30] Thus, ownership laws of one State as they relate to whether or not the property is stolen will be recognised by another State subject to the possible rights of a purchaser in good faith and the operation of statutes of limitations or rules of prescription.

As was indicated earlier, a State will not enforce the public laws, including export laws, of another State in the absence of a bilateral or multilateral treaty.[31] The matter can be further confused when, as a result of the illegal export, the source State declares the cultural heritage to be confiscated and forfeited to the State.[32] Thus, questions of ownership become entangled with the application of public laws.

Difficulties may also arise where States apply laws that vest all cultural heritage found within the State to be State property, irrespective of whether the heritage is in a museum, in a private collection, or still undiscovered underground.[33] It is within this complex framework that attempts to repatriate the *Dodington* coins were made.

Perhaps one of the most contentious issues in the management of wrecks in South Africa relates to the ownership of wreck. The perception prevalent among divers and salvors is that wrecks and their contents are governed by the Roman Dutch legal concept of *res derelicta*, or abandoned goods, in terms of which the principle of finders keepers applies, ownership being vested in the *occupator*, or person who physically holds the material.[34] Although this is to some extent indeed the case with contemporary wreck and salvage, the NMC had always believed that by virtue of the fact that historical wrecks were archaeological sites (although this was not specifically

[23] The terms source and market States have been used in a very general sense to distinguish between those States recognised as having a net loss of archaeological material and those in which a thriving market for this material exists. It is, however, acknowledged that some States may exhibit both source and market trends.

[24] For example, the National Heritage Resources Act No. 25 of 1999 deals with the exportation of archaeological objects within the section concerning the protection of archaeological objects. Section 35(4) proves that: "No person may, without a permit issues by the responsible heritage resources authority – (a) destroy, damage, excavate, alter, deface or otherwise disturb any archaeological or palaeontological site or any meteorite; (b) destroy, damage, excavate, remove from it original position, collect or own any archaeological or palaeontological material or object or any meteorite; (c) trade in, sell for private gain, export or attempt to export from the Republic any category of archaeological or palaeontological material or any meteorite."

[25] 34 T.L.R 623 (Ch.Div 1918).

[26] [1984] 1 AC1, [1983] 2 All ER 93, [1983] 2 W.L.R 809.

[27] L. V. Prott and P. J. O'Keefe, *Law and the Cultural Heritage: Volume 3 Movement* 653 (Butterworths, London 1989).

[28] 10 I.L.M (1971) Hereafter "1970 UNESCO Convention." The Republic of South Africa accepted the Convention on 18 December 2003. The United Kingdom accepted the Convention on 1 August 2002 with implementing legislation adopted in October 2003. (See Part III, Parkhouse, Adrian. "The Illicit Trade in Cultural Objects: Recent Developments in the United Kingdom.") The Convention comes into effect for each state three months after the date of deposit of its instrument.

[29] UNESCO Doc. 20 C/84 p. 46, as quoted in Prott and O'Keefe, *supra* note 27, at 785.

[30] J. H. Merryman, A licit International Trade in Cultural Objects, 4(1) *International Journal of Cultural Property* 19 (1995).

[31] The 1970 UNESCO Convention was adopted to remedy this situation, but was only partly successful.

[32] See, for example, *Attorney-General of New Zealand v. Ortiz* [1982] 3 W.L.R. 570.

[33] See, for example, The Cultural Heritage Act No.3501 of July 2, 1979 of Ecuador.

[34] J. Hare, *Shipping Law and Admiralty Jurisdiction in South Africa* 171–190 (Juta & Co, 1999).

stated in the Act), and were protected by the National Monuments Act, this principle did not apply to them.[35] Although the question of ownership of this material was not explicitly addressed in the National Monuments Act, Section 12 (2)(c) did stipulate that all wreck recovered must be placed in the custody of a museum, which, in conjunction with the NMC, would decide on the disposal of the material. Although this implied ownership by the State, the issue was never satisfactorily addressed because it was never legally challenged. However, in the legal proceedings surrounding the *Dodington* coins, the NMC was obliged to resolve this lack of clarity on the question of the ownership of shipwreck material. On the basis of the Sea Shore Act,[36] which vests ownership of the sea, including the seabed and sea shore in the State President, and the Maritime Zones Act,[37] which defines the extent of South Africa's territorial waters, it could be argued that ownership of wreck material did vest with the State. As South Africa's statutory body for cultural heritage management, and an arm of the State, the NMC believed that if the *Dodington* coins came from South African territorial waters, the State, through the NMC, had a legal claim to their ownership. The legal opinion obtained on this issue was based on English Admiralty Law, and suggested that ownership of shipwreck material does indeed vest with the State, and more particularly with the State President as the representative of the nation. According to English Admiralty Law, the Crown is entitled to all unclaimed wreck found in its territorial waters as *droits* of Admiralty. As the legal successor to the British Crown, therefore, the South African State, in the person of the State President, was entitled to claim ownership of all unclaimed or abandoned wrecks within South African territorial waters. Furthermore, this would imply that the NMC, as the legislated State body for cultural heritage management, can assert ownership on behalf of the State President and the nation of all unclaimed or abandoned shipwrecks and their contents within South African territorial waters.[38]

More problematic was proving that the coins did indeed come from the archaeological site of the wreck of the *Dodington* within South African territorial waters, and if they did, when they had been removed. In this respect, the case of the *Dodington* is reminiscent of the facts in *Bumper Development Corp Ltd v. Commissioner of the Police of the Metropolis*.[39] In the *Bumper* case, the court had to rely on complex and expensive procedures to prove the identity of an illegally excavated idol of the Hindu God Shiva. This included proving similarities in metallurgical analysis, artistic style, soil samples, and termite runs found on the idol to those found on other artefacts from the illicitly excavated site that the idol in question was alleged to have come from. Similarly, in *R v. Heller*,[40] the Canadian court held that there was no evidence to prove that the cultural heritage, a Nok sculpture, had been exported after the imposition of export limitation by Nigeria.

The *Dodington* case further highlights how much more difficult it may be to prove that artefacts do indeed come from a specified underwater archaeological site than it would be if a terrestrial site was concerned. The very nature of seafaring means that the original vessel was capable of wide and easy movement, and once wrecked, of dispersing its contents over a wide area. The activities of contemporary salvors, rescuers, and abandoning crew could possibly result in further dispersal of artefacts. Thus, while artefacts may easily be associated with a particular wreck site, it may be more difficult to prove that the artefacts were found on that wreck site or within a limited circumference. These difficulties are exacerbated by the difficulties of surveillance and policing of protected underwater sites. Thus, although there was overwhelming evidence that the coins were from the *Dodington*, it was more difficult to prove that they were removed from the protected site of the wreck. Given that salvors are able to more easily remove artefacts from the territorial waters than from the land territory of a State, particularly because a site on the outer reaches of the territorial sea or contiguous zone may be well beyond the horizon, it is clear that protection of underwater cultural heritage based on ownership is extremely unreliable. As such, the NMC did not feel that it would be able to succeed in court, and a negotiated settlement was reached to return a percentage of the coins.

CONVENTIONAL INTERNATIONAL LAW AND REPATRIATION

The case of the *Dodington* coins clearly illustrates the problems associated with repatriation of cultural heritage illegally exported from the source State. Such problems are, however, not new and States have been grappling with possible solutions at an international level for a number of decades. Given the more recent advances in diving technology, this problem is perhaps newer in cases of underwater cultural heritage found at previously unreachable depths beyond the source State's horizon. It is unfortunate that international law was unable to render any assistance to the NMC in this case, not only because neither South Africa nor the United Kingdom was, at the time this case arose, a party to the existing international conventions, but also because these conventions are

[35] The Wreck and Salvage Act, Act No. 94 of 1996, applies to the salvage of all wrecks in South African Waters, including historic wrecks, with the proviso that the Wreck and Salvage Act would not derogate from the operation of the National Monuments Act, Act No. 28 of 1969, as amended. As to the difficulties in reconciling the provision of these Acts, compare Hare, *supra* note 34 and H. Staniland, "South Africa," in S. Dromgoole, *Legal Protection of the Underwater Cultural Heritage: National and International Perspectives* 139 (Kluwer Law International 1999).

[36] No. 21 of 1935. [37] No. 15 of 1994.

[38] It should be noted that since the *Dodington* coins case began, the National Heritage Resources Act No. 25 of 1999 was adopted, and declares all wrecks more than 60 years old in South Africa's territorial waters or contiguous zone to be the property of the State (sec.35(2)).

[39] [1991] 4 All ER 638 See also Peru V. Johnson 720 F. Spp. 810 (C.D. Cal. 1989) and Part III, Hoffman, Barbara. "International Art Transactions and The Resolution of Art and Cultural Property Disputes: The United States Perspective."

[40] (1983) 27 Alta. L.R. (2d) 346.

"at present fragmentary and amorphous"[41] and do not provide a sufficiently rigorous protective regime to provide for an occurrence such as that of the *Dodington* coins. Whereas South African legislation would regard the exportation of the coins without a permit as illegal, international law does not necessarily do so.

1970 UNESCO Convention on the Means of Prohibiting and Preventing the Illicit Import, Export and Transfer of Ownership of Cultural Property[42]

Arguably, the most important international convention to deal with the problem of the illicit movement of cultural heritage is the 1970 UNESCO Convention.[43] Nevertheless, it has, on the whole, proved ineffective in stemming the illicit excavation of archaeological material and its subsequent movement inter State.[44] These inefficiencies have been described by many commentators and will not be dealt with here.[45] However, the extent to which the Convention fails to deal with the particular problem of the *Dodington* coins will be considered.

The United Kingdom, as a market State, had long been opposed to interference with its prominent role as one of the world's leaders in the trade in art and antiquities and it is noteworthy that the United Kingdom did not even participate in the Meeting of Experts to discuss the Secretariat draft of the Convention in 1970.[46] This trade, however, has increasingly been under close scrutiny, and a report by the Government's Advisory Panel on Illict Trade in December 2000 revealed approximately thirty seizures of cultural goods by Customs and Excise every year. In 1999 alone, London Interpol Unit investigated 132 cases of illict traffic.[47] Although South Africa has been associated with market States in the past,[48] it is more likely that there is now a greater amount of African cultural heritage being exported than ever before, and thus South Africa can be regarded, as most African States are, as a source State.

At the time the *Dodington* case was being dealt with, neither the United Kingdom nor South Africa was a Party to the 1970 Convention. Both States are now Party to the Convention, and it is instructive to consider how the Convention might have applied had this occurred earlier and been applicable to the case of the *Dodington* coins because it clearly highlights the inadequacies of this international regime.

The definition of cultural property in the Convention is exhaustive and includes a number of overlapping categories, so that the *Dodington* coins would clearly fall within a number of these. For example, they could conceivably fall within Article 1(c), "products of archaeological excavations (including regular and clandestine) or of archaeological discoveries"; Article 1(d), "elements of artistic or historic monuments or archaeological sites which have been dismembered," or Article 1(e), "antiquities more than one hundred years old, such as inscriptions, coins and engraved seals." Falling within one of these categories would not, however, be sufficient because Article 1 requires that the cultural property be "specifically designated by each State as being of importance for archaeology, prehistory, literature, art, or science." The requirement of specific designation is susceptible to different interpretations and State practise has evidenced a range of responses, from a narrow interpretation in which the State specifically lists individual items, to a wider response by which a State designates all such items within their territory. As was indicated earlier, the site of the *Dodington* wreck was designated as a provisional national monument under the NMA in 1984, and as such, it is clear that for the purposes of Article 1 the coins would fall within the Convention's definition of cultural property. It is also clear that if the coins did indeed come from the site of the *Dodington* wreck, the coins would form part of the cultural heritage of South Africa pursuant to Article 4(b).[49]

Considerable differences of opinion exist as to whether the Convention requires State Parties to hold the importation of cultural heritage without an export permit as illicit.[50] Given that the United Kingdom has considered that its existing law is, on the whole, adequate to implement the Convention, it is clear that a narrow interpretation, similar to that of the United States, has been taken.[51] As such, Article 3, even if taken together with Article 6, would not require

[41] Merryman, *supra* note 30, at 28. [42] *Supra* note 28.

[43] For a detailed account of the 1970 UNESCO Convention, see P. J. O'Keefe, *Commentary on the UNESCO 1970 Convention on Illicit Traffic* (Institute of Art and Law, 2000).

[44] For a recent description of the traffic in illicitly excavated cultural heritage see N. Brodie, J. Doole and P. Watson, *Stealing History: The Illicit Trade in Cultural Material* (McDonald Institute for Archaeological Research, Cambridge 2000).

[45] See, for example, R. D. Abramson and S. B. Huttler, "The Legal Response to Illicit Movement of Cultural Heritage," 5 *Law and Policy in International Business* 932 (1973); A. G. Aldape, "The International Protection of Cultural Property," *Proceedings of the 71st Annual Meeting of the American Society of International Law* 196 (1977); W. P. Buranich, "The Art Collecting Countries and Their Export Restrictions on Cultural Property: Who Owns modern Art?" 19 *California Western International Law Journal* 153 (1988); J. F. Edwards, "Major Global Treaties for the Protection and Enjoyment of Art and Cultural Objects," 22 *University of Toledo Law Review* 919 (1991): J. B. Gordon, "The UNESCO Convention on the Illicit Movement of Art Treasures," 12 *Harvard International Law Journal* 537 (1971): R. H. M. Goy, "The International Protection of the Cultural and Natural Heritage," 4 *Netherlands Yearbook of International Law* 117 (1973): G. Reichelt, "International Protection of Cultural Property," I *Uniform Law Review Biannual* 43 (1985); R. Stahl, Retention and retrieval of art and antiquities through international and national means: the tug of war over cultural property, 5 *Brooklyn Journal of International Law* 103 (1979); J. Kifle, *International Legal Protection of Cultural Heritage* (Jurisfórlaget, 1994).

[46] Prott and O'Keefe, *supra* note 27, at 727.

[47] Dalya Albege, "Britain acts to prevent illict trade in art," *The Times*, 15 March, 2001.

[48] Prott and O'Keefe, *supra* note 27, at 576.

[49] Article 4 states that: "The States Parties to this Convention recognize that for the purposes of the Convention property which belongs to the following categories forms part of the cultural heritage of each State: . . . (b) cultural property found within the national territory." This would include the territorial sea.

[50] Compare Bator, *supra* note 24; Prott and O'Keefe, *supra* note 27; Edwards, *supra* note 44; and Abramson and Hutter, *supra* note 44.

[51] *The Ministerial Advisory Panel on Illicit Trade Report*, December 2000, 15.

illegally exported cultural heritage to be declared illict by the importing State.[52] Such a narrow interpretation would then only oblige an importing State Party "to prevent museums and similar institutions within their territory from acquiring cultural property originating in another State Party which has been illegally exported...."[53] Because the *Dodington* coins were not imported by a museum or other public institution, but by a private individual, the United Kingdom would not have been required to take cognisance of the fact that the coins were illegally exported from South Africa. Although Article 13(b) would require the United Kingdom to ensure that its competent authorities cooperated in facilitating the restitution of illicitly exported cultural heritage, it is likely that this article would be read down to relate only to that illicitly exported in Article 7.

Thus, the extent to which the Convention requires State Parties to give effect to the export laws of the source State are extremely narrow.

Although the Convention provides for the prohibition of the importation of cultural heritage, it is only in cases in which the cultural heritage has been "stolen from a museum or a religious or secular public monument or similar institution in another State Party to this Convention ... provided that such property is documented as appertaining to the inventory of that institution."[54] Although the site of the *Dodington* wreck is regarded as a National Monument, the coins could not possibly have been documented in an inventory and, thus, could not have been subject to this article. The uncertain status of the coins as having been stolen, based on South Africa's ownership of the coins, would also suggest that this provision is unsuited to the recovery of archaeological artefacts illicitly excavated and exported. This uncertainty would also leave Article 13(b) and (c) ineffective given that the restitution of illicitly exported cultural heritage would mean it has to be returned to the rightful owner, the only party able to institute actions for the recovery of stolen items.

Article 9, regarded by some as a core provision of the 1970 Convention, attempts to mobilise a concerted cooperative international effort to address situations in which a State's "cultural patrimony is in jeopardy from pillage of archaeological and ethnological material."[55] Although the utilisation of words such as pillage and jeopardy allow for a diversity of interpretations, it is clear that this article concerns situations in which the cultural heritage of a specific region or culture is in danger from repeated and widespread action, such as that which threatens terracotta statues of the Nok culture and figures of the Cycladic archipelago or of Mayan cultural heritage, especially Mayan stella. It is therefore unsuited to situations such as the *Dodington* coins, which represent a singular illict act against a unique cultural heritage.

Article 10 of the 1970 UNESCO Convention could have been of some assistance to NMC, had South Africa and United Kingdom been a Party to the Convention at the time. This article requires States Parties to oblige antique dealers to maintain a register recording the origin of each item of cultural property, names and addresses of the supplier, and description and price of each item sold. As such, the NMC would at least have been able to determine who the suppliers of the *Dodington* coins were.

Thus, although the *Dodington* coins fall within the definition of the cultural property subject to the protective regime of the 1970 UNESCO Convention, the ambiguity of articles such as Article 3, and the resulting narrow interpretations regarding the illicit import and export, are likely to render the Convention impotent in a case such as that of the *Dodington* coins and highlights a very real threat to underwater cultural heritage in any State's territorial waters or contiguous zone.[56]

The UNIDROIT[57] Convention on Stolen or Illegally Exported Cultural Objects[58]

Although the 1970 UNESCO Convention is important in laying the foundation for an international framework for the protection of cultural heritage, it lacks adequate enforcement mechanisms. In particular, the private law aspects of the Convention, principally contained in Article 7(b)(ii), that require a State Party to take appropriate measures to ensure the recovery and return of cultural property against just compensation to a purchaser in good faith and who has valid title to it, needed further clarification.[59] This resulted in the UNIDROIT Convention of 1995.[60] Although neither United Kingdom nor South Africa is a Party to the UNIDROIT Convention, it is instructive to consider the manner in which the provisions of the Convention could have aided South Africa in its quest for the repatriation of the *Dodington* coins.

The UNIDROIT Convention distinguishes between cultural heritage that has been stolen and that which has been illegally exported, although both could apply to any given case, such as that of the *Dodington* coins, subject to South Africa proving its claim of ownership.[61] The definition of the cultural heritage to be protected under the Convention closely

[52] O'Keefe, *supra* note 43, at 42. [53] Article 7(a).

[54] Article 7(b)(i).

[55] See O'Keefe, *supra* note 42, at 71; and Abramson and Hutter, *supra* note 44, at 962.

[56] Similar cases of historic wrecks being plundered and the artefacts being removed from the territory of the coastal State without the coastal State's knowledge or cooperation include that of the *Geldermalsen*, suspected of having been excavated in Indonesian territorial waters. G. Miller, "The Second Destruction of the *Geldermelsen*," in J. Barto Arnold III (ed.), 26(4) *Advances in Underwater Archaeology* 124 (1992).

[57] UNIDROIT is an independent intergovernmental organisation established in Rome in 1926 under the auspices of the League of Nations. Its primary purpose is to examine ways of harmonising and coordinating the private law of States.

[58] Signed on 24 June 1995.

[59] M. Schneider, The UNIDROIT Convention on Stolen or Illegally Exported Cultural Objects, Research Paper, UNIDROIT, Rome, 1995, See also Reichelt, *supra* note 44.

[60] For a general outline of the UNIDROIT Convention, see L. V. Prott, *Commentary on the UNIDROIT Convention* (Institute of Art and Law, 1997) and P. Jenkins, The UNIDROIT Convention on Stolen or Illegally Exported Cultural Objects, 1(2) *Art, Antiquity and Law* 163 (1996). See also the Introductions to Part II and III of this volume.

[61] Article 1.

follows that of the 1970 UNESCO Convention, repeating the exhaustive list of cultural heritage but not requiring it to have been designated by the State. Cultural heritage that is included in this list must be of importance for "archaeology, prehistory, history, literature, art or science."[62] Clearly, the *Dodington* coins are of importance to archaeology and history, and because they fall within the exhaustive list of the 1970 UNESCO Convention,[63] they fall within the terms of the UNIDROIT definition.[64]

Chapter III of the Convention concerns the return of illegally exported cultural heritage and provides that a contracting State "may request the court or other competent authority of another Contracting State to order the return of a cultural object illegally exported from the territory of the requesting State,"[65] which is precisely what the South African Government wished to request of the UK court. However, the court will only order the return if the requesting State can fulfil further criteria relating to the significance of the objects to the satisfaction of the court. These criteria, listed in Article 3, include establishing that the cultural heritage is of significant cultural importance for the requesting State, or that the removal of the cultural heritage would significantly impair the physical preservation of the object or its context, or the integrity of a complex object, or the preservation of information of, for example, a scientific or historical character.

It is clear that the removal of the *Dodington* coins certainly impaired the integrity of the wreck site, and therefore compromised the preservation of historical knowledge that could be gleaned from the site. Although the former cannot be reversed by the return of the *Dodington* coins, the non-return of the coins would certainly continue to prejudice the information that can be gleaned from the site and the artefacts derived from it. Because the coins are also clearly of significant cultural importance to South Africa, and provided that South Africa could furnish the necessary factual and/or legal information to back up its claim,[66] it would appear that a foreign court could conceivably return the coins under the terms of the UNDROIT Convention. Such a return would be subject to the application being made within three years from the time when the requesting State knew of the location of the cultural heritage and the identity of the possessor and within fifty years of the illegal export, and subject to the payment of compensation to *bona fide* possessor. The cost of returning the cultural heritage to the requesting State would also be born by that State. It would therefore appear that under the terms of the UNIDROIT Convention, South Africa could, had both parties in this case been State Parties to the Convention, been able to request the repatriation of the coins. However, it is evident that a considerable burden of proof will apply, as will the potentially costly burden of the exercise, particularly in cases in which there are *bona fide* possessors. This severely restricts the ability of developing States to take such actions, and given the difficulties in obtaining the finances to pursue this matter to date, it is unlikely that the NMC would have been able to make use of this avenue for the return of the coins had they been in the possession of a *bona fide* possessor.

A claim by South Africa for the restitution of the *Dodington* coins under Chapter II of the UNIDROIT Convention, relating to the restitution of stolen cultural heritage would, however, be less likely to succeed that that under Chapter III. Although Article 3(1) clearly requires that a possessor of cultural heritage that has been stolen shall return it, Article 3(2) requires that for the purposes of the Convention, "a cultural object which has been unlawfully excavated . . . shall be considered stolen, when consistent with the law of the State where the excavation took place." The combination of Articles 3(1) and 3(2) is potentially problematic in cases such as the *Dodington* coins. The court seized of the case will determine whether, in fact, the cultural heritage is stolen and therefore within the scope of the Convention, by reference to the rules of private international law. When undertaking this task in the case of illegally excavated cultural heritage, the court is bound to declare the goods as stolen only if that is consistent with the law of the State in which the illicit excavation took place. In the case of the *Dodington* coins, given the difficulties in proving ownership under the NMA, and the failure of the NMA to declare illegally excavated cultural heritage the property of the State, no such consistency would be immediately evident.

Although the UNIDROIT Convention offers some avenues for possible success in repatriation cases such as that of the *Dodington* coins, these are limited primarily by financial implications. More importantly, perhaps, is the reluctance of many States, particularly market States, to become a Party to the Convention. The United Kingdom, for example, declared the provision of the Convention unacceptable. Its objections, however, related primarily to what it considered to be an imprecise definition of cultural heritage and to the extended limitation periods.[67] There was, however, evidence that the United Kingdom supported much of Chapter III of the Convention, thus indicating perhaps some awareness of, and sympathy with, the problems faced by source States in controlling the export of cultural heritage.

The Commonwealth Scheme on the Protection of the Material Cultural Heritage

Although not a treaty, and therefore creating no binding obligations on States, the Commonwealth Scheme on the Protection of the Material Cultural Heritage could have provided a

[62] Article 2.
[63] See above.
[64] Article 2 and the Annex.
[65] Article 5(1).
[66] Article 5(4) requires that "any request made under paragraph 1 of this article shall contain or be accompanied by such information of a factual or legal nature as may assist the court or other competent authority of the State addressed in determining whether the requirements of paragraphs 1 to 3 have been met."

[67] Jenkins, *supra* note 60. The German Government also refused to sign the Convention on the grounds that the definition of cultural heritage was too broad. See P. Valentin, The UNIDROIT Convention on the International Return of Stolen or Illegally Exported Cultural Objects, 4(2) *Art, Antiquity and Law* 107 (1999).

framework within which the *Dodington* coins could have been returned because both South Africa and the United Kingdom are members of the Commonwealth.[68]

The *Dodington* coins fall clearly within the definition of the cultural heritage to be protected in that they are of national importance as a result of their archaeological significance.[69] However, a central problem in applying the scheme to the case of the *Dodington* coins is that both the export and import must take place after implementation of the scheme, and thus has no retrospective effect. Although the non-retrospectivity has its merits, it is problematic in that it is often difficult, if not impossible, to determine when the cultural heritage was illegally exported or when it was imported. This is certainly the case in the *Dodington* coins. A further disincentive to claim the return of cultural heritage illegally exported, much like that contained in the UNIDROIT Convention, relates to the cost of return that falls on the requesting State as well as the potential cost of paying compensation to a *bona fide* possessor.

It is unfortunate that the United Kingdom felt that it could not become a party to the scheme, citing difficulties "arising from its obligations as a member of the European Community and the placing of bureaucratic burdens on its large art trade."[70] It is, however, precisely the dangers posed by the large art trade that required the imposition of such a scheme, and the failure of the United Kingdom to become a party to the scheme had resulted in the *Dodington* coins appearing for auction as an object in this trade. The scheme thus proved to be of no value in the case of the *Dodington* coins.

The UNESCO Convention on the Protection of the Underwater Cultural Heritage

Negotiations through the agency of UNESCO to formulate and adopt a comprehensive Convention on the Protection of the Underwater Cultural Heritage were recently finalised, and a final draft of this Convention was approved at the General Conference of UNESCO in November 2001.[71] It is beyond the scope of this article to discuss the provisions of the new Convention,[72] but it is appropriate to consider those aspects of the treaty that may have an impact on the movement of illicitly excavated and exported underwater cultural heritage.

The Convention provides for a set of benchmark rules of good archaeological practise that States will agree to implement in areas under their jurisdiction and impose on nationals and vessels over which they exercise jurisdiction. Included in these rules is the requirement that before any activity directed at an underwater archaeological site is undertaken, an appropriate project design is drafted and authorised by the appropriate competent authorities.[73] In the case of the *Dodington* coins, this would be SAHRA because the site lies in South African territorial waters. Importantly, the rules also require that appropriate documentation of the excavation be undertaken, including "the provenance of underwater cultural heritage moved or removed in the course of the activities directed at underwater cultural heritage," and that a final report be submitted to the competent authority that includes an account of the objects recovered.[74] The project archive, which includes not only the documentation, but also the recovered artefacts themselves, is required to be kept intact as a collection and made available for professional study.[75] It would therefore be evident that the provisions of the Convention would not have been complied with had they been in force at the time of the excavation of the *Dodington* coins.

[68] The Scheme was agreed upon by the Commonwealth Law Ministers in November 1993 in Mauritius. For a detailed description of the scheme, see P. J. O'Keefe, Protection of the Material Cultural Heritage: The Commonwealth Scheme, 44 *International and Comparative Law Quarterly* 147 (1995).

[69] The scheme required that only cultural heritage that is of national importance as a result of (a) the close association of the item with the history or life of the country, (b) the aesthetic qualities of the item, (c) the value of the item in the study of the arts and science, (d) the rarity of the item, (e) the spiritual or emotional association of the item with the people of the country or any group or section thereof or (f) the archaeological significance of the item.

[70] O'Keefe, *supra* note 68, at 148.

[71] 41 ILM 37 (2002).

[72] For a more detailed discussion on the draft Convention see C. Forrest, "A New International Regime For The Protection of Underwater Cultural Heritage" (2002) 51(3) *International and Comparative Law Quarterly* 511–554; P. Fletcher-Tomenius and C. Forrest, The Protection of the Underwater Cultural Heritage and the Challenge to UNCLOS, 5(5) *Art, Antiquity and Law* 125 (2000); D. Bederman, The UNESCO Draft Convention on Underwater Cultural Heritage: A Critique and Counter-Proposal, 30(2) *Journal of Maritime Law and Commerce* 331 (1999); P. J. O'Keefe, Protection of the Underwater Cultural Heritage: Developments at UNESCO, 25(3) *International Journal of Nautical Archaeology* 169 (1996); P. J. O'Keefe, Second meeting of Governmental Experts to Consider the Draft Convention on the Protection of the Underwater Cultural Heritage, 8(2) *International Journal of Cultural Property* 568 (1999); P. J. O'Keefe and J. A. R. Nafziger, The Draft Convention on the Protection of Underwater Cultural Heritage, 25(4) *Ocean Development and International Law* 391 (1994).

[73] Rule 9 of the Rules in the Annex to the draft Convention states, "Prior to any activity directed at underwater cultural heritage, a project design for the activity shall be developed and submitted to the competent authority for authorization and appropriate peer review," whereas Rule 11 declares that "Activities directed at underwater cultural heritage shall be carried out in accordance with the project design approved by the competent authority." 41 ILA 37 (2002).

[74] Rule 28 of the Rules of the Annex states that "Documentation shall include, at a minimum, a comprehensive record of the site including the provenance of underwater cultural heritage moved or removed in the course of the activities directed at underwater cultural heritage, field notes, plans, drawings, sections, photographs and recording in other media" and Rule 32 states that "Reports shall include: (a) an account of the objectives; (b) an account of the methods and techniques employed; (c) an account of the results achieved; (d) basic graphic and photographic documentation on all phases of the activity; (e) recommendations concerning conservation and curation of any underwater cultural heritage removed as well as of the site; and (f) recommendations for future activities." 41 ILM 37 (2002).

[75] Rule 34 of the Rules in the Annex requires that "The project archive, including any underwater cultural heritage removed and a copy of all supporting documentation shall, as far as possible, be kept together and intact as a collection in a manner that is available for professional and public access (as well as the curation of the archive) as rapidly as possible and not later than 10 years from the completion of the project; in so far as may be compatible with conservation of underwater cultural heritage. 41" ILM 37 (2002).

The Convention addresses the question of the importation of illicitly recovered underwater cultural heritage in Article 13, which states: "A State party shall make it an offence to import into its territory underwater cultural heritage which has not been excavated in accordance with the Convention." The State is also under an obligation to impose sanctions for such importation as well as to seize the imported underwater cultural heritage.[76] Although the Convention does not deal with issues of ownership, nor does it explicitly require importing States to give effect to the exportation laws of another State, it will require the importing State to determine whether the competent authorities in the exporting State authorized the activities directed at the underwater cultural heritage and whether the Rules of the Annex were complied with. In the case of the *Dodington*, this would require the United Kingdom to determine whether Rules 9, 11, 28, and 32 were complied with. Although the importing State is required to seize the illicitly recovered underwater cultural heritage, the Convention does not specifically address the issue of its return.

The Convention may therefore offer some hope to States such as South Africa in the fight to recover underwater cultural heritage illicitly recovered and exported. Whereas South Africa supported the adoption of the provisions of the Convention at the UNESCO General Conference, the United Kingdom was not satisfied with the provisions included in the text and abstained from voting on the adoption of the Convention. Concerns expressed by the United Kingdom during negotiations and which the United Kingdom felt were not satisfactorily resolved in the final text related to the extent of coastal state jurisdiction, the inclusion of warships in the scope of the convention, and the failure to explicitly limit the scope of the convention only to UCH declared to be of archaeological or historical significance. The United Kingdom was also consistently opposed to any provision that would restrict the ability of private salvors to continue to recover and trade in underwater cultural heritage.

CONCLUSION

The Importance of the *Dodington* Case in South Africa

What the *Dodington* case has made clear is the fact – so obvious that it has tended to be overlooked – that historical wrecks are very different from other heritage sites and resources, and that they present different management and legal problems, which require different solutions. The assumption that the National Monuments Act was not only the appropriate piece of legislation for the prosecution of a wreck offence such as the case of the *Dodington* coins, but that it had international applicability has been clearly shown to be flawed. Fortunately, the avenue of Admiralty Law was open in this case. It is clear, however, that the new compliance agency, SAHRA, will have to reconsider its approach to international cases in the future, and further investigate the validity of national legislation abroad, as well as alternative approaches that exist for international cases of this nature.

The fact that wrecks are invariably found in internationally designated maritime zones has profound implications for their management and treatment under the law. Their relative inaccessibility and the fact that their exact locations are often not known means that their control and protection are fraught with difficulties not usually encountered with terrestrial heritage resources. Furthermore, disputes relating to wreck and other heritage resources will be heard in terms of different concepts of law in different courts that have different rules and procedures. This raises the question of the appropriateness of the inclusion of historical shipwrecks in a piece of general heritage legislation like the old National Monuments Act and the National Heritage Resources Act.

The scrutiny to which both of these pieces of legislation were subjected in the *Dodington* case has suggested that the provisions they contain relating to the protection of historical wrecks and artefacts are not clear, and that it is a flaw in both that the bulk of the legal provisions relating to wrecks are contained in the Regulations that accompany them, rather than in the legislation itself. In virtually all other countries with a rich shipwreck resource, separate legislation has been enacted for historical wrecks that acknowledges their unique legal status and management problems, and although the idea of a separate South African act for wrecks is not new, it has never been properly considered. The *Dodington* case has demonstrated some of the weaknesses of the present legislative protection of wrecks, and future cases are likely to show others. If the future protection and management of historical shipwrecks in South Africa are to do justice to the rich and internationally renowned resource in our waters, now is the time to consider the possibility of separate legislation for historical wrecks.

The case of the *Dodington* coins has thus served the important purpose of highlighting a number of fundamental problems, issues, and challenges relating to the management of historical shipwrecks in South Africa, and to South African heritage legislation. This case demonstrated the shortcomings of the heritage legislation, and suggested alternative legal avenues for shipwreck cases that have not been considered before. Its greatest importance, however, lies perhaps in the fact that through this case, the South African heritage compliance agency demonstrated to South Africa and the world that it not only has the will to enforce the legislation, but that its decision to do so will no longer be judged entirely according to whether or not SAHRA thinks the case will be successful. The pursuance of this case was important for the strong message it will convey to the ever-increasing numbers of foreign and local salvors wanting to work on South African wrecks that the heritage authority won't tolerate the plundering of our cultural heritage.

[76] Article 18.

QUESTIONS FOR DISCUSSION

The case of the *Dodington* coins highlights the difficulty that developing source States have in regard to repatriation of cultural heritage illicitly exported. Consider:

(a) how a developing source State might address the obligations in the 1970 UNESCO Convention in order to minimize the illicit excavation and exportation of cultural heritage without necessitating a large government budget;

(b) how the 1970 UNESCO Convention might be amended to overcome the difficulties experienced in the case of the *Dodington* coins; and

(c) the national policy difficulties that prevent some State from giving effect to other States' export laws, and how these might be overcome so as to allow for the establishment of an international regime in which all source States' export laws are effective.

BIBLIOGRAPHY

Allen, G. and Allen, D., *Clives's Lost Treasure* (1978) Robin Garton, London.

Garabello, R. and Scovazzi, T., *The Protection of Underwater Cultural heritage: Before and After the 2001 UNESCO Convention* (2003) Martinus Nijhoff Publishers.

Dromgoole, S., *Legal Protection of the Underwater Cultural heritage: National and International Perspectives* (1999) 139 Kluwer Law International.

Hare, J., *Shipping Law and Admiralty Jurisdiction in South Africa* (1999) Juta & Co.

O'Keefe, P. J., *Shipwrecked heritage: A Commentary on the UNESCO Convention on Underwater Cultural Heritage*, (2002) Institute of Art and Law.

O'Keefe, P. J., *Commentary on the UNESCO 1970 Convention on Illicit Traffic* (2000) Institute of Art and Law.

Forrest, C., A New International Regime for the Protection of Underwater Cultural Heritage (2002) 51(3) *International and Comparative Law Quarterly* 511–554.

Bederman, D., The UNESCO Draft Convention on Underwater Cultural Heritage: A Critique and Counter-Proposal, 30(2) *Journal of Maritime Law and Commerce* 331 (1999).

O'Keefe, P. J., Protection of the Underwater Cultural Heritage: Developments at UNESCO, 25(3) *International Journal of Nautical Archaeology* 169 (1996).

WEB SITES

South African Heritage Resource Agency,
<http://www.sahra.org.za>

United Nations Education, Science and Cultural Organization,
<http://www.unesco.org>

International Council on Monuments and Sites,
<http://www.icomos.org>

PART SEVEN

Who Owns Traditional Knowledge?

CHAPTER FORTY-THREE

Intellectual Property and the Protection of Traditional Knowledge and Cultural Expressions

Wend B. Wendland

INTRODUCTION

Indigenous art copied onto carpets, T-shirts, and greeting cards; traditional music fused with techno-house dance rhythms to produce best-selling "world music" albums; pharmaceutical drugs drawing upon traditional medicinal knowledge patented and commercialized; hand-woven carpets and handicrafts copied and sold as "authentic"; the process for making a traditional musical instrument patented; indigenous words and names trademarked and used commercially.

These are the kinds of examples that indigenous peoples and other traditional and cultural communities often refer to when arguing that traditional knowledge, creativity, and cultural expressions require greater intellectual property (IP) protection. But what exactly is the relationship between IP and the "protection" of traditional knowledge and cultural materials? Is IP part of the problem or is it part of the solution?

This chapter examines these and other questions further with reference to work taking place at the World Intellectual Property Organization (WIPO) concerning the protection of traditional knowledge and expressions of traditional cultures/folklore. The chapter also touches upon WIPO's related work concerning the IP aspects of access to and benefit-sharing in genetic resources.

WIPO is the United Nations (UN) agency responsible for the promotion and protection of creative intellectual activity and for the facilitation of the transfer of technology in order to accelerate economic, social, and cultural development.[1] IP protection is essentially implemented under national, and in some cases regional, laws. Internationally and regionally, existing agreements, conventions, and treaties help to establish the framework within which specific national laws operate.[2]

In particular, the chapter reports on ongoing deliberations within the WIPO Intergovernmental Committee on Intellectual Property and Genetic Resources, Traditional Knowledge and Folklore (the WIPO Committee). This committee, which met for the first time in April 2001 and has met seven times since then, brings together at each session some 250 representatives of States, indigenous peoples and other traditional communities, diverse nongovernmental organizations, and intergovernmental organizations.[3] Complementary practical and capacity-building initiatives of WIPO also are briefly described, and recent draft "instruments" addressing the protection of traditional knowledge and cultural expressions are introduced.[4]

To be clear, discussions within the WIPO Committee address, among other things, the possible recognition of enforceable IP-type rights in communally developed "traditional" knowledge systems and artistic expressions that are currently regarded by IP law as "public domain." Measures to control the gaining and exercise of conventional IP rights over creations and innovations derived from or based upon traditional knowledge and traditional cultural expressions or expressions of folklore[5] are also under discussion.

Profound policy questions pulsate through these complex discussions. To whom, if anyone, do or should traditional knowledge and expressions of intangible creativity belong as private property (including collective or communal property)? Who, if anyone, can or should enjoy the exclusive right to commercially exploit intangible traditional know-how and creativity? Should there be legal remedies against demeaning, derogatory, or offensive use of or derivations from expressions of traditional cultures? How should such assertions of exclusivity be reconciled with a balanced policy approach that encourages cultural exchange, promotes cultural development, and serves other legitimate goals such

[1] See <http://www.wipo.int/>

Head, Traditional Creativity and Cultural Expressions Section, Global Intellectual Property Issues Division, World Intellectual Property Organization (WIPO) in Geneva, Switzerland. The views expressed in this article are not necessarily those of WIPO or any of its Member States.

[2] Relevant international instruments would include many of the treaties administered by WIPO, such as the Paris Convention for the Protection of Industrial Property, 1883, as last revised in 1967; the Berne Convention for the Protection of Literary and Artistic Works, 1886, as last revised in 1971; the Madrid Agreement for the Repression of False and Deceptive Indications of Source on Goods, 1891; the International Convention for the Protection of Performers, the Producers of Phonograms and Broadcasting Organizations (the "Rome Convention"), 1961; the Lisbon Agreement for the Protection of Appellations of Origin and their International Registration, 1958, as last amended in 1979; the WIPO Copyright Treaty, 1996; and, the WIPO Performances and Phonograms Treaty, 1996.

[3] The Committee's working documents and reports are all available, in English, French, and Spanish, at <http://www.wipo.int/tk/en/igc/documents/index.html.> See also suggested Bibliography.

[4] Available as Annexes I to documents WIPO/GRTKF/IC/7/3 and WIPO/GRTKF/IC/7/5 at <http://www.wipo.int/meetings/en/details.jsp?meeting_id=6183>

[5] Expressions of folklore has been the term most commonly used in international intellectual property discussions and it still appears in many national laws. However, the word folklore has a pejorative meaning in some countries, communities, and cultures. On the other hand, many argue for the retention of the term expressions of folklore. The WIPO Secretariat often uses the term traditional cultural expressions as an interchangeable synonym for expressions of folklore.

as research and education? How should intellectual property mechanisms function to support and complement law and policy initiatives in other related fields, such as the safeguarding of cultural heritage and regulation of access to and use of genetic resources?

Above all perhaps, a sharpened focus on the "public domain" notion marks discussions on IP-related issues concerning genetic resources, traditional knowledge, and cultural expressions at WIPO and in other forums. Whereas biological and cultural heritage were previously considered common property (as part of the "universal heritage of humanity," as referred to, for example, in some cultural instruments and declarations[6]), there are growing calls for a re-evaluation of this public domain status, particularly by indigenous and local communities.

The legal, cultural, and political significance of this work is profound and potentially far-reaching. It is said by some to symbolize deep-running conflicts of values, notoriously difficult to settle. Technical IP questions are closely interwoven with broader agendas of economic, social, and political justice. Not unexpectedly, the debate among the various interests represented in the WIPO Committee is complex.

The remainder of this chapter covers the following issues:

(1) What are "traditional knowledge" and "traditional cultural expressions"?
(2) The meaning of "intellectual property protection";
(3) The IP-related needs and expectations of indigenous and traditional and other cultural communities;
(4) National and regional experiences;
(5) Cultural and legal policy challenges;
(6) WIPO's work so far: Latest developments;
(7) Concluding remarks.

WHAT ARE TRADITIONAL KNOWLEDGE AND TRADITIONAL CULTURAL EXPRESSIONS?

Introduction

Traditional knowledge and cultural expressions, often the product of intergenerational and fluid social and communal creative processes, reflect and identify a community's history, cultural and social identity, and values.

Although lying at the heart of a community's identity, traditional cultures are also "living" – they are constantly recreated as traditional artists and practitioners bring fresh perspectives to their work. Tradition is not only about imitation and reproduction; it is also about innovation and creation within the traditional framework. Over time, individual performers, composers, craftsmen, and other creators call communal motifs and styles to mind and rearrange and recontextualise them in new ways. Therefore, traditional creativity is marked by a dynamic interplay between collective and individual creativity.

In general, it may be said that traditional cultural expressions (1) are handed down from one generation to another, either orally or by imitation, (2) reflect a community's cultural and social identity, (3) consist of characteristic elements of a community's heritage, (4) are made by "authors unknown" and/or by communities and/or by individuals communally recognized as having the right, responsibility, or permission to do so, (5) are not made for commercial purposes but as vehicles for religious and cultural expression, and (6) are constantly evolving, developing, and being recreated within the community.

In this dynamic and creative context, it is often difficult, from an IP perspective, to know what constitutes independent creation. Under current copyright law, a contemporary adaptation or arrangement of old and pre-existing traditional materials can often be sufficiently original to qualify as a protected copyright work.

This is a key point, and it lies at the heart of extensive policy debate: Is the protection already available for contemporary tradition-based creations adequate, or is some form of IP protection for the underlying and pre-existing materials necessary? See further discussion under "Cultural and Legal Policy Challenges."

Relationship Between Traditional Knowledge and Traditional Cultural Expressions

There is an established approach in WIPO's work of considering the legal protection of traditional knowledge as such and expressions of such knowledge and of traditional cultures (traditional cultural expressions or expressions of folklore) in a parallel manner, there but distinctly. This is because the protection of knowledge as such and expressions thereof raise some distinct legal and cultural policy issues, involve different stakeholders and interests, and are each subject to different forms of exploitation and thus require specific solutions. Furthermore, there is already considerable national experience with the protection of traditional cultural expressions and expressions of folklore.

However, it is fully recognized that from an indigenous perspective, traditional cultural expressions and knowledge are often perceived as integral parts of an holistic cultural identity, subject to the same body of customary law and practices. WIPO's work on traditional knowledge and traditional cultural expressions is thus intimately complementary and coordinated. Furthermore, WIPO's work concerns specific means of legal protection against misuse of traditional materials by third parties beyond the traditional and customary context, and does not seek to impose definitions or categories on the customary laws, protocols, and practices of indigenous peoples and traditional and other communities. This approach is accordingly compatible with and respectful of the traditional context in which traditional cultural expressions and knowledge may be viewed as part of an inseparable whole.

[6] UNESCO's Convention Concerning the Protection of the World Cultural and Natural Heritage (1972), Recommendation on the Safeguarding of Traditional Culture and Folklore (1989), and Universal Declaration on Cultural Diversity (2001).

Working Descriptions

Purely as a working description, and drawn directly from existing laws and experiences, discussions within WIPO are currently using the following as a first draft basis for further consideration:

"The term 'traditional knowledge' refers to the content or substance of knowledge that is the result of intellectual activity and insight in a traditional context, and includes the know-how, skills, innovations, practices and learning that form part of traditional knowledge systems, and knowledge that is embodied in the traditional lifestyle of a community or people, or is contained in codified knowledge systems passed between generations. It is not limited to any specific technical field, and may include agricultural, environmental and medicinal knowledge, and knowledge associated with genetic resources."[7]

Similarly, the terms traditional cultural expressions or expressions of folklore are understood at present to refer broadly to:

"Productions consisting of characteristic elements of the traditional cultural heritage developed and maintained by a community, or by individuals reflecting the traditional artistic expectations of such a community. Such productions may include, for example, the following forms of expressions, or combinations thereof:

(i) verbal expressions, such as folk tales, folk poetry and riddles; aspects of language such as words, signs, names, symbols and other indications;
(ii) musical expressions, such as folk songs and instrumental music;
(iii) expressions by action, such as folk dances, plays and artistic forms or rituals; whether or not reduced to a material form; and
(iv) tangible expressions, such as:
  (a) productions of folk art, in particular, drawings, designs, paintings, carvings, sculptures, pottery, terracotta, mosaic, woodwork, metalware, jewelry, basket weaving, handicrafts, needlework, textiles, carpets, costumes;
  (b) musical instruments;
  (c) architectural forms."[8]

However, discussions within WIPO have stressed that the specific choice of terms to denote the protected subject matter, and the precise scope of protected subject matter, should be determined at the national and regional levels.

THE MEANING OF INTELLECTUAL PROPERTY PROTECTION

Intellectual property refers to creations of the mind such as inventions, designs, literary and artistic works, and symbols, names, images, and performances. Most forms of IP establish enforceable property rights in creations in order to grant control over their exploitation, particularly commercial exploitation, and to provide incentives for further creativity. Copyright, for example, protects the products of creativity, in the form of original literary and artistic works, against unwanted use and exploitation. The goals of copyright protection are to stimulate further creativity, to encourage public dissemination of works, and to enable creators to have the final say, subject to certain limitations and exceptions, over the use of their works. It can also provide protection against demeaning or degrading use of a work (referred to as moral rights).

Not all aspects of IP protection are focused directly on promoting innovation and creativity, particularly the law of distinctive marks, indications, and signs (laws governing trademarks, geographical indications, and national symbols) as well as the related area of the repression of unfair competition. These aim at the protection of established reputation, distinctiveness, and goodwill.

Nor do all forms of IP protection necessarily take the form of exclusive property rights. Equitable remuneration and compensatory liability schemes, compulsory licenses, moral rights, and unfair competition principles all provide protection of an IP nature without use of exclusive property rights.

Indeed, as argued by many of the indigenous peoples and others participating in WIPO's work, exclusive private property rights in traditional cultural expressions and knowledge, even if held by communities, may run counter to the characteristics of traditional forms and processes of creativity and may induce unforeseen side-effects, such as competition within and between communities.

Therefore, exclusive property rights, and IP-type mechanisms in general, should complement and be carefully balanced and coordinated with other nonproprietary and non-IP measures to reflect the characteristics of traditional forms and processes of creativity, the stakeholder interests involved, customary uses and practices, associated with such forms and processes, and community social structures, practices, and patterns.[9]

National legislative experiences are instructive. Among the many countries that have already enacted specific protection for traditional cultural expressions, for example, few provide for genuine exclusive property rights in traditional cultural expressions: Most aim, rather, at the regulation of their exploitation[10] (see subsequent discussions under "National and Regional Experiences").

Thus, IP-type exclusive property rights are not the only way to provide protection for traditional cultural expressions and knowledge. With this in mind, the WIPO Committee is actively examining possible *sui generis* adaptations to existing IP rights as well as entirely new *sui generis* IP-type laws, designed to respond to the particular characteristics of traditional cultural expressions and knowledge and the needs of their holders and custodians.[11] Comprehensive protection may require a range of proprietary and nonproprietary, including non-IP, tools (discussed subsequently).

[7] WIPO/GRTKF/IC/7/5.

[8] WIPO/GRTKF/IC/7/3.

[9] For example, statements by New Zealand (WIPO/GRTKF/IC/ 6/14, para. 41) and the Saami Council (WIPO/GRTKF/IC/ 6/14, para. 57).

[10] See WIPO/GRTKF/IC/ 3/10 and Lucas-Schloetter, "Folklore" in von Lewinski, S. (ed.), *Indigenous Heritage and Intellectual Property*, 2004 (Kluwer), page 291.

[11] See in particular WIPO documents WIPO/GRTKF/IC/4/INF 2 to 5 Add., WIPO/GRTKF/IC/5/3, WIPO/GRTKF/IC/5/8, WIPO/GRTKF/IC/5/INF 3, WIPO/GRTKF/IC/5/INF 4, WIPO/GRTKF/IC/6/3, WIPO/GRTKF/IC/6/4.

Relationship between IP "Protection" and "Safeguarding" of Cultural Heritage

Intellectual property protection, as described, is distinct from the notion of safeguarding in the way in which that term is often used in the cultural heritage context to refer to the identification, documentation, transmission, preservation, protection, revitalization, and promotion of cultural heritage in order to ensure its maintenance or viability.[12]

Clarity on what is meant by protection is key, because WIPO's work has shown that the needs and expectations of the holders and practitioners of traditional cultural expressions can, in some cases, be addressed more appropriately by measures for protection in the preservation and safeguarding sense rather than in the IP sense.

Take, as an example, a legend that was recorded centuries ago on a piece of cloth. "IP protection" of the legend would take the form of an IP-type right, preventing others from using the legend in a manner considered inappropriate by a community, such as reproducing the legend on a T-shirt. However, if only a few people know the legend and the language that should be used to recite the legend, protection may take the form of measures that would assist people to pass on their knowledge of the legend and the language to the next generation. If the cloth begins to decay, protection may take the form of measures to ensure that the cloth is preserved for future generations. In other instances, protection could take the form of promoting the legend outside the community in order that others may learn about it and gain a greater understanding and respect for the culture of the originating community.

There is an important relationship between IP protection and preservation/safeguarding in the sense used in the cultural heritage context, a relationship that requires balance and coordination, including that attained through continued cooperation between WIPO and UNESCO.

For example, the very process of preservation (such as the recording or documentation and publication of traditional cultural materials) can trigger concerns about lack of IP protection and can run the risk of unintentionally placing the materials in the public domain from the perspective of the IP system.

In this regard, WIPO is developing IP-related information and advice for folklorists, anthropologists and other fieldworkers, museums, archives, and other cultural heritage institutions, regarding the management of the IP rights that may vest in their collections. Although the activities of folklorists, collectors, fieldworkers, museums, archives, and other institutions are extremely important for the preservation of cultural heritage, indigenous peoples and local communities sometimes argue that their IP-related rights and interests are not always safeguarded when their cultural materials are first recorded and documented by folklorists and other fieldworkers or when they are subsequently displayed and made available to the public by museums, archives, and other collections.

The strategic management of the IP rights in field recordings and other forms of documentation of traditional cultural materials could be used, in a very practical way, to advance the rights and interests of the original providers and custodians of the materials.

THE INTELLECTUAL PROPERTY–RELATED NEEDS AND EXPECTATIONS OF INDIGENOUS AND TRADITIONAL AND OTHER CULTURAL COMMUNITIES

WIPO's work has, particularly since 1997, been informed by extensive consultations undertaken with representatives of indigenous, local, and other cultural communities.[13] Representatives of such communities remain closely involved in the work of the WIPO Committee. The effective participation of the peoples and communities whose knowledge and cultural expressions are the subject of discussion is obviously crucial.

In general terms, indigenous and other communities argue for the right to control access to and disclosure and use of their traditional knowledge and traditional cultural expressions. More specifically, and in respect of artistic expressions in particular, they call for:

(1) protection against unauthorized reproduction, adaptation, distribution, performance, and other such acts, in addition to prevention of insulting, derogatory, and/or culturally and spiritually offensive uses;
(2) protection against imitation of "style";
(3) prevention of false and misleading claims to authenticity and origin/failure to acknowledge source; and,
(4) protection against the registration of traditional signs and symbols as trademarks.

It is clear from the aforementioned examples that the notion of protection is used in at least two senses, one denoting "positive" protection (aimed at gaining IP rights over traditional cultural expressions in order to commercialize them and/or prevent others from doing so) and the other a form of "defensive" protection (aimed at preventing the gaining of IP rights over traditional cultural expressions and derivations therefrom).

In some cases at least, it would seem that defensive protection *against* IP can be more important to communities than positive protection by IP, especially in respect of sacred and spiritual cultural expressions. New Zealand, the United States, and the Andean Community have already put in place specific *sui generis* measures to combat the unauthorized

[12] See also "Glossary: Intangible Cultural Heritage," Netherlands Commission for UNESCO, 2002.

[13] In 1998 and 1999, WIPO undertook a series of fact-finding missions to 28 countries, interviewing some 3,000 holders and custodians of traditional knowledge and cultural expressions. The results of these missions have been published as "Intellectual Property Needs and Expectations of Traditional Knowledge Holders," which is available from the WIPO Secretariat or at <http://www.wipo.int/tk/en/tk/ffm/report/index.html>. Subsequently, roundtables, further fact-finding missions, and workshops involving community representatives have been and continue to be organized.

registration of indigenous and traditional signs and symbols as trademarks. In New Zealand, for example, it is no longer possible to register a trademark if its use or registration is considered likely to offend a significant section of the community, including the indigenous people of that country, Maori.[14]

In attempting to meet these needs, non-IP options are useful, too. So, in addition to existing IP systems, adapted IP rights (*sui generis* aspects of IP systems) and new, standalone *sui generis* systems, nonproprietary approaches that have been used include unfair competition; equitable remuneration schemes; trade practices and marketing laws; contracts and licenses; registers, inventories, and databases; customary and indigenous laws and protocols; cultural heritage preservation laws and programs; and handicrafts promotion and development programs.

For example, the Indian Arts and Crafts Act, 1990 of the United States protects Native American artisans by assuring the authenticity of Indian artifacts under the authority of an Indian Arts and Crafts Board. The Act, a truth-in-marketing law, prevents the marketing of products as Indian-made when the products are not made by Indians as they are defined by the Act.

These are not mutually exclusive options, and each may, working together, have a role to play in a comprehensive approach to protection. Which modalities and approaches are adopted will also depend upon the nature of the materials to be protected and the policy objectives that protection aims to advance.

There is no single, top-down, one-size-fits-all solution that can adequately protect all the world's traditional knowledge systems and artistic expressions in a way that advances the national developmental priorities of all countries, reflects ancient and diverse customary laws and protocols, accommodates different legal and cultural environments, and meets the various and locally rooted interests and needs of the world's cultural communities.[15] It is, after all, the precious *diversity* of distinct communities and cultures that is at stake. Forms of traditional creative expression and customary means of regulating their use, transmission, protection, and preservation are diverse. Concerns have been expressed that attempts to codify and institutionalize protection of cultural identity are undesirable and that a minimalist approach is preferable. An indigenous organization has put it best: "Any attempt to devise uniform guidelines for the recognition and protection of indigenous peoples' knowledge runs the risk of collapsing this rich jurisprudential diversity into a single 'model' that will not fit the values, conceptions or laws of any indigenous society."[16]

Provisions for the protection of traditional knowledge and cultural expressions adopted at the international level would also have to accommodate legislative and jurisprudential diversity within current national and regional approaches.[17] This is a relatively common approach in the IP field. Several IP conventions establish certain general principles and give scope for wide variation within the laws of the signatories.[18] Even where international obligations create minimum substantive standards for national laws, it is accepted that the choice of legal mechanisms is a matter of national discretion.

Thus, an approach of "flexibility for national policy and legislative development" underpins the work of the WIPO Committee.

In the shorter term at least, at the international level, some broadly agreed common objectives and principles might be the most appropriate and workable outcome. A wish for flexibility at the national and community levels will also need to be balanced with the desire on the part of many stakeholders for a form of international enforcement. In addition, IP-related outcomes must complement and take account of instruments and developments in other policy areas, necessitating close cooperation between WIPO and other relevant international forums. The challenges ahead are many.

NATIONAL AND REGIONAL EXPERIENCES

Certain States already provide specific legal protection for traditional knowledge subject matter, especially traditional cultural expressions or expressions of folklore, through one or more of several options (such as provisions based upon the *sui generis* Model Provisions for National Laws on the Protection of Expressions of Folklore Against Illicit Exploitation and Other Prejudicial Actions, 1982 or entirely new *sui generis* statutory systems); others do not, either because they do not believe it is appropriate or necessary to do so (for example, because they believe existing IP systems are adequate), or because they are still considering which approaches and systems are the most desirable.[19]

The debate about the protection of traditional knowledge and cultural expressions often centers on whether adequate and appropriate protection is best provided through either the conventional IP system or through an alternative *sui generis* system. Yet the documented practical experiences of many Member States reflect that existing IP rights and *sui generis* measures are not mutually exclusive but are complementary options.[20] A comprehensive approach is likely to consider

[14] New Zealand Trade Marks Act, 2002.

[15] Venezuela (WIPO/GRTKF/IC/6/14, para. 72), African Group (WIPO/GRTKF/IC/6/14, para. 73), Canada (WIPO/GRTKF/IC/6/14, para. 79), Syria (WIPO/GRTKF/IC/6/14, para. 80), New Zealand (WIPO/GRTKF/IC/6/14, para. 88), Kaska Dena Council (WIPO/GRTKF/IC/6/14, para. 59).

[16] Four Directions Council, "Forests, Indigenous Peoples and Biodiversity," Submission to the Secretariat for the CBD, 1996.

[17] See Final Report on National Experiences with the Legal Protection of Expressions of Folklore (WIPO/GRTKF/IC/ 3/10); Lucas-Schloetter, "Folklore" in von Lewinski, S. (ed.), *Indigenous Heritage and Intellectual Property*, 2004 (Kluwer); Kuruk, P., "Protecting Folklore Under Modern Intellectual Property Regimes: A Reappraisal of the Tensions Between Individual and Communal Rights in Africa and the United States," 48 American University Law Review 769 (1999).

[18] Such as the TRIPS Agreement, Article 1.1; Rome Convention, Article 7; the Satellites Convention, Article 2; the Lisbon Convention, Article 8; the Washington Treaty, Article 4; and the Phonograms Convention, Article 3.

[19] WIPO/GRTKF/IC/3/10.

[20] GRULAC (WIPO/GRTKF/IC/1/5), European Community (WIPO/GRTKF/IC/1/13, paras. 20 and 165), Canada (WIPO/GRTKF/IC/1/13,

each of these options, and apply them judiciously to achieve the objectives of protection, accepting the practical reality that the boundaries between these options are not rigid. Effective protection may therefore be found in a combined and comprehensive approach, with a menu of differentiated and multiple levels and forms of protection. The options selected by various countries have depended to a large degree on the policy objectives and national goals being served.

Use of Existing IP Mechanisms

Certain States believe that some, if not many, of the needs and concerns of indigenous peoples and traditional and other cultural communities and their members may be met by solutions existing already within current IP systems, including through appropriate extensions or adaptations of those systems.[21] For example:

(a) Copyright and industrial designs laws protect contemporary adaptations and interpretations of pre-existing materials, even if made within a traditional context.
(b) Copyright law may protect unpublished works of which the author is unknown.
(c) The *droite de suite* (the resale right) in copyright allows authors of work of arts to benefit economically from successive sales of their works.
(d) Performances of traditional cultural expressions are protected under the WIPO Performances and Phonograms Treaty (WPPT) 1996.
(e) Traditional signs, symbols, and other marks can be registered as trademarks.
(f) Traditional geographical names and appellations of origin can be registered as geographical indications.
(g) The distinctiveness and reputation associated with traditional goods and services can be protected against "passing off" under unfair competition laws and/or the use of certification and collective trade marks.
(h) Secret traditional cultural expressions may be protected as "confidential information" or under doctrines such as "breach of confidence."

In many of these cases, international protection is available by virtue of relevant treaties, such as the Berne Convention for the Protection of Literary and Artistic Works, 1971; the Agreement on Trade-Related Aspects of Intellectual Property Rights, 1994 (the TRIPS Agreement); and the WPPT, 1996. Collective and certification trademarks, geographical indications, and unfair competition law are particularly attractive options, not only because they already enjoy wide international recognition, but they also, not having been conceived with individuals in mind, can benefit and be used by collectivities such as indigenous communities. Experience with existing mechanisms and standards is also a useful guide.

In this vein, the Group of Latin American and Caribbean States (GRULAC) has, for example, stated within the WIPO Committee that "the resources offered by intellectual property have not been sufficiently exploited by the holders of traditional cultural knowledge or by the small and medium-sized businesses created by them."[22] Tradition-based creativity should also be encouraged and current IP protection for traditional cultural expressions and derivative works should be made use of as far as possible by communities and their members. For example, the African Group has noted that the protection of traditional cultural expressions and knowledge should aim to, among other things, "protect and reward innovations and creative works derived from traditional knowledge and expressions of folklore."[23]

A few States have provided information on actual and practical examples in which current IP standards have been used:

(1) Australia has identified four cases taht, in its view, demonstrate the ability of the Australian intellectual property regime to protect traditional knowledge: *Foster v Mountford (1976) 29 FLR 233,*[24] *Milpurrurru v Indofurn Pty Ltd (1995) 30 IPR 209,*[25] *Bulun Bulun & Milpurrurru v R & T Textiles Pty Ltd (1998) 41 IPR 513,*[26] and *Bulun*

paras. 46 and 166), Norway (WIPO/GRTKF/IC/1/13, para. 33), USA (WIPO/GRTKF/IC/1/13, para. 49), Poland (WIPO/GRTKF/IC/1/13, para. 156), the Asian Group (WIPO/GRTKF/IC/2/10 and WIPO/GRTKF/IC/2/16, para. 170), Ethiopia (WIPO/GRTKF/IC/1/13, para. 50), Asian Group (WIPO/GRTKF/IC/2/16 para. 170), Thailand (WIPO/GRTKF/IC/2/16, para. 172). African Group (WIPO/GRTKF/IC/4/15, para. 62), Brazil (WIPO/GRTKF/IC/4/15, para. 63), Venezuela (WIPO/GRTKF/IC/4/15, para. 65), Colombia (WIPO/GRTKF/IC/4/15, para. 67), Russian Federation (WIPO/GRTKF/IC/4/15, para. 68), Iran (Islamic Republic of) (WIPO/GRTKF/IC/4/15, para. 69), Indonesia (WIPO/GRTKF/IC/4/15, para. 74), Morocco (WIPO/GRTKF/IC/4/15, para. 76), Egypt (WIPO/GRTKF/IC/4/15, para. 80), Andean Community (WIPO/GRTKF/IC/4/15, para. 82), Peru (WIPO/GRTKF/IC/6/14, para. 77), India (WIPO/GRTKF/IC/6/14, para. 81), and New Zealand WIPO/GRTKF/IC/6/14, para. 88).

21 European Community (WIPO/GRTKF/IC/1/13, paras. 20 and 165), Canada (WIPO/GRTKF/IC/1/13, paras. 46 and 166), Norway (WIPO/GRTKF/IC/1/13, para. 33), United States (WIPO/GRTKF/IC/1/13, para. 49), Poland (WIPO/GRTKF/IC/1/13, para. 156), the Asian Group (WIPO/GRTKF/IC/2/10 and WIPO/GRTKF/IC/2/16, para. 170).

22 WIPO/GRTKF/IC/1/5, Annex II, page 2.

23 WIPO/GRTKF/IC/6/12. See also European Community (WIPO/GRTKF/IC/3/11.).

24 In this case, the Court used common law doctrine of confidential information to prevent the publication of a book containing culturally sensitive information.

25 This case involved the importation into Australia of carpets manufactured in Viet Nam, which reproduced (without permission) either all or parts of well-known works, based on creation stories, created by indigenous artists. The artists successfully claimed infringement of copyright as well as unfair trade practices because the labels attached to the carpets claimed that the carpets had been designed by Aboriginal artists and that royalties were paid to the artists on every carpet sold. In awarding damages to the plaintiffs, the judgment recognized the concepts of "cultural harm" and "aggregated damages."

26 This case arose out of the importation and sale in Australia of printed clothing fabric that infringed the copyright of the Aboriginal artist, Mr. John Bulun Bulun. A parallel issue was whether the community of the Ganalbingu people, to which Mr. Bulun Bulun and his co-applicant, Mr. Milpurrurru, belong, had equitable ownership of the copyright. The court said that, given that relief had been granted to Mr. Bulun Bulun through a permanent injunction, there was no need to address the issue of community's ownership. The assertion by the Ganalbingu of rights in equity depended upon there being a trust impressed upon expressions of ritual knowledge, such as the art work in question. The court considered there to be no evidence of an express or implied trust created in respect of Mr. Bulun Bulun's art. Nonetheless, in a *dictum*, the court recognized that

Bulun v Flash Screenprinters (discussed in (1989) EIPR Vol 2, pp. 346–55).[27] From these cases, Australia has suggested, protection under the Australian Copyright Act can be as valuable to Aboriginal and Torres Strait Islander artists as it is to other artists.

(2) Australia, Canada, New Zealand, and Portugal have given examples of the use of trademarks, particularly certification marks, to protect traditional knowledge and expressions of folklore. In Australia, certification marks have been registered by the National Indigenous Arts Advocacy Association. In Canada, trademarks, including certification marks, are used by Aboriginal people to identify a wide range of goods and services, ranging from traditional art and artwork to food products, clothing, tourist services, and enterprises run by First Nations. Many Aboriginal businesses and organizations have registered trademarks relating to traditional symbols and names. In Portugal, the Association of Carpet Producers of Arraiolos has registered a collective trademark in respect of its products. And, in New Zealand, the Maori Arts Board of Creative New Zealand is making use of trademark protection through the development of the "Maori Made Mark." It is a trademark of authenticity and quality, which indicates to consumers that the creator of goods is of Maori descent and produces work of a particular quality. It is a response to concerns raised by Maori regarding the protection of cultural and intellectual property rights, the misuse and abuse of Maori concepts, styles, and imagery, and the lack of commercial benefits accruing back to Maori.

(3) In Canada, copyright protection under the Copyright Act has been widely used by Aboriginal artists, composers, and writers of tradition-based creations such as wood carvings of Pacific coast artists, including masks and totem poles, the silver jewelry of Haida artists, songs and sound recordings of Aboriginal artists, and Inuit sculptures. Within the context of the WIPO Committee, Canada provided the following practical case study:

> "One practical example of how existing intellectual property laws can safeguard expressions of folklore involves the Snuneymuxw First Nation of Canada, which in 1999 used the Trademarks Act to protect ten petroglyph (ancient rock painting) images. Because the petroglyphs have special religious significance to the members of the First Nation, the unauthorized reproduction and commodification of the images was considered to be contrary to the cultural interests of the community, and the petroglyph images were registered in order to stop the sale of commercial items, such as T-shirts, jewelry and postcards, which bore those images. Members of the Snuneymuxw First Nation subsequently indicated that local merchants and commercial artisans had indeed stopped using the petroglyph images, and that the use of trade-mark protection, accompanied by an education campaign to make others aware of the significance of the petroglyphs to the Snuneymuxw First Nation, had been very successful";

(4) In Kazakhstan, the external appearance of national outer clothes, head dresses, carpets, decorations of saddles, national dwellings and their structural elements, in addition to women's apparel accessories, like bracelets, national children's cots-crib-cradles and table wares, are protected as industrial designs. The designations containing elements of Kazakh ornament are registered and protected as trademarks.

Some States have also put in place specific measures to supplement existing rights in order to meet a specific need. For example:

(a) In New Zealand, the Trade Marks Law now allows the Commissioner of Trade Marks to refuse to register a trademark where its use or registration would be likely to offend a significant section of the community, including Maori.

(b) In the United States, under Section 2(a) of the Trademark Act, 1946, as amended, a proposed trademark may be refused registration or cancelled (at any time) if the mark consists of or comprises matter that may disparage or falsely suggest a connection with persons, living or dead, institutions, beliefs, or national symbols, or bring them into contempt, or disrepute. The U.S. Patent and Trademark Office (USPTO) may refuse to register a proposed mark that falsely suggests a connection with an indigenous tribe or beliefs held by that tribe. The Trademark Law Treaty Implementation Act, 1998 required the USPTO to complete a study on the protection of the official insignia of federally and state-recognized Native American tribes. As a direct result of this study,[28] on August 31, 2001, the USPTO established a Database of Official Insignia of Native American Tribes, which may be searched and thus prevent the registration of a mark confusingly similar to an official insignia. "Insignia" refers to "the flag or coat of arms or other emblem or device of any federally or State recognized Native American tribe" and does not include words.[29]

Sui generis approaches

At the same time, many Committee participants have argued that current IP systems are not entirely adequate or appropriate, and that they should be modified or *sui generis* systems

the artist, as an indigenous person, had a fiduciary duty to his community. Therefore, there were two instances in which equitable relief in favor of a tribal community might be granted in a court's discretion, where copyright is infringed in a work embodying ritual knowledge: first, if the copyright owner fails or refuses to take appropriate action to enforce the copyright; and, second, if the copyright owner cannot be identified or found.

[27] Mr. Bulun Bulun brought a copyright infringement action in relation to the unauthorized reproduction of his artistic works on t-shirts by the defendant. The government of Australia informed that this was a clear-cut case of copyright infringement and that the case was settled out of court.

[28] Available at <http://www.uspto.gov/web/offices/com/sol/notices/insgstdy.pdf> (*30Nov99 entry*).

[29] Available at <http://www.uspto.gov/web/offices/com/sol/notices/insgstdy.pdf> (*30Nov99 entry*, pp. 24–26).

should be established.[30] Even if the protection already available under current laws is acknowledged, it has been argued that the focus of the Committee's work should be on those elements and forms of creativity not currently protected by IP laws.[31]

The main *sui generis* models, laws, or approaches concerning traditional cultural expressions, in particular, may be said to be:[32]

(1) the Tunis Model Law on Copyright for Developing Countries, 1976 ("the Tunis Model Law");
(2) the WIPO-UNESCO Model Provisions for National Laws on the Protection of Expressions of Folklore Against Illicit Exploitation and Other Prejudicial Actions, 1982 ("the Model Provisions");
(3) the Bangui Agreement on the Creation of an African Intellectual Property Organization (OAPI), as revised in 1999 ("the Bangui Agreement");
(4) the Special Intellectual Property Regime Governing the Collective Rights of Indigenous Peoples for the Protection and Defence of their Cultural Identity and their Traditional Knowledge of Panama, 2000 and the related Executive Decree of 2001 ("the Panama Law");
(5) the Pacific Regional Framework for the Protection of Traditional Knowledge and Expressions of Culture, 2002 ("the Pacific Regional Framework");
(6) the Indigenous Peoples Rights Act of 1997 of the Philippines ("the Philippines Law"); and
(7) the Indian Arts and Crafts Act, 1990 of the United States ("the U.S. Arts and Crafts Act").[33]

To expand upon one example only, the Panama Law creates the Department of Collective Rights and Expressions of Folklore within the relevant IP office. Panama's *sui generis* regime covers indigenous peoples' creations, such as inventions, designs and innovations, cultural historical elements, music, art, and traditional artistic expressions. The Department of Collective Rights and Expressions of Folklore has started a program for the archiving of expressions of folklore, and the functions and powers of this new authority are set out in some detail. The possibility to register collective exclusive rights is also provided for. The Kuna Yala territory has expressed interest in the registration of the handicraft known as the *mola* but no expression of folklore has been registered to date. The authority to attribute rights is vested upon the Congress(es) or the Traditional Indigenous Authority(ies). Some elements of knowledge may be co-owned by various communities, in which case benefits will be jointly shared. The Law also provides for exceptions to rights conferred as well as measures of enforcement. Collective indigenous rights may also be a basis for opposing unauthorized third party claims to IP, such as copyright, trademarks, and geographical indications.

As noted earlier, an exclusive rights approach to traditional cultural expressions may not necessarily be appropriate in all cases, and existing laws show the range of possible approaches. They evidence a wide range of underlying legal doctrines, which are, in sum:

(a) *exclusive property rights*, giving the right to authorize or prevent others from undertaking certain acts in relation to traditional cultural expressions.[34] An exclusive rights approach would be one way of giving effect to a principle of "free, prior and informed consent." Exclusive rights are provided for in the Tunis Model Law, 1976; the Model Provisions, 1982; the Panama Law, 2000; the Pacific Regional Framework, 2002; and the Philippines Law, 1997;
(b) entitlements under a scheme for *equitable remuneration/compensatory liability*, providing for some form of equitable return to the rightsholders for use of their traditional cultural expressions, without creating an exclusive right in them. This approach has been used in some systems for protection of traditional cultural expressions, often through a *domaine public payant* system;[35]
(c) a *moral rights* approach, normally providing the rights: of attribution of ownership; not to have ownership falsely attributed; not to have the protected materials subjected to derogatory treatment; and, in some jurisdictions, the right to publish or disclose (the right to decide if, when, and how the protected materials ought to be made accessible to the public).[36] "The integrity right that protects the reputation of creators may address the anxiety over the inappropriate use of expressions of folklore by preventing distortion, alteration, or misrepresentation of creators' works. This may provide redress against culturally inappropriate treatment of expressions of folklore . . . The

[30] Ethiopia (WIPO/GRTKF/IC/1/13, para. 50), Asian Group (WIPO/GRTKF/IC/2/16 para. 170), Thailand (WIPO/GRTKF/IC/2/16, para. 172). African Group (WIPO/GRTKF/IC/4/15, para. 62), Brazil (WIPO/GRTKF/IC/4/15, para. 63), Venezuela (WIPO/GRTKF/IC/4/15, para. 65), Colombia (WIPO/GRTKF/IC/4/15, para. 67), Russian Federation (WIPO/GRTKF/IC/4/15, para. 68), Iran (Islamic Republic of) (WIPO/GRTKF/IC/4/15, para. 69), Indonesia (WIPO/GRTKF/IC/4/15, para. 74), Morocco (WIPO/GRTKF/IC/4/15, para. 76), Egypt (WIPO/GRTKF/IC/4/15, para. 80), and Andean Community (WIPO/GRTKF/IC/4/15, para. 82).

[31] As the Delegation of Nigeria aptly put it at the sixth session, ". . . the concerns of many developing countries as far as folklore was concerned was to protect those elements of creativity for which authorship had become unidentifiable with a single individual either because of the affluxion of time or because of the communal nature in which the materials had evolved" (WIPO/GRTKF/IC/6/14, para. 43).

[32] These are analyzed and compared in WIPO publication, "Consolidated Analysis of the Legal Protection of Traditional Cultural Expressions" (Pub. No. 785 E) and in document WIPO/GRTKF/IC/5/INF/3.

[33] Also relevant are materials such as the Principles and Guidelines for the Protection of the Heritage of Indigenous People, prepared by Dr. Erica Irene-Daes for the UN's Working Group on Indigenous Populations, the recently adopted UNESCO International Convention for the Safeguarding of the Intangible Cultural Heritage and the Draft UNESCO Convention on the Diversity of Cultural Contents and Artistic Expressions.

[34] GRULAC (WIPO/GRTKF/IC/1/5, Annex I, p. 2 and Annex II, p. 5), Zambia (WIPO/GRTKF/IC/1/13, para. 38).

[35] GRULAC (WIPO/GRTKF/IC/1/5, Annex I, p. 2 and Annex II, p. 5), Bangui Agreement of OAPI, see WIPO/GRTKF/IC/5/INF 3.

[36] See Lucas-Schloetter, "Folklore" in von Lewinski, S. (ed.), *Indigenous Heritage and Intellectual Property*, 2004 (Kluwer), p. 298.

publication right is the creator's right to decide when, where, and in what form a work will be published. It may be effective in providing creators of folklore with a degree of control over the publication or disclosure of sacred works and thus reduce the possibility of inappropriate use. Furthermore, it could potentially be coupled with a breach of confidence action if the sacred information was communicated in confidence."[37] Protection of moral rights is found in the Model Provisions, 1982 and the Pacific Regional Model, 2002 (and, in relation to performances of TCEs/expressions of folklore, in the WPPT, 1996);

(d) an *unfair competition* approach, providing a right to prevent various acts that constitute unfair competition broadly speaking, such as misleading and deceptive trade practices, unjust enrichment, passing off, and taking of undue commercial advantage.[38] This approach underlies the U.S. Arts and Crafts Act, and is found in the Model Provisions, 1982;

(e) a *penal sanctions* approach, in which certain acts and omissions are treated as criminal offences. The Model Provisions, 1982 and the Pacific Regional Model, 2002 provides for certain criminal offences.[39]

Another key consideration has been the need to consider the customary law and practices of traditional communities. These can form the initial legal basis for the entitlement to exercise or withhold consent to using traditional knowledge. Customary law has also been recognized as an important mechanism for establishing appropriate procedures for consulting upon and affirming free, prior, and informed consent.

These various options are not necessarily mutually exclusive, and could be combined, in conformity with the guiding principle of flexibility and comprehensiveness. One option may, for example, be more relevant or suited for a particular form of traditional cultural expressions than another.

LEGAL AND CULTURAL POLICY CHALLENGES

The relationship between traditional cultural expressions and knowledge and IP raises complex and challenging issues. The challenges of multiculturalism and cultural diversity, particularly in societies with both indigenous and immigrant communities, require cultural policies to maintain a balance between the protection and preservation of cultural expressions – traditional or otherwise – and the free exchange of cultural experiences. A further challenge is to balance the need to preserve traditional cultures with the desire to stimulate tradition-based creativity as a contribution to sustainable economic development.

Addressing these challenges provokes some deeper policy questions. What is the relationship between IP protection and the promotion of cultural diversity? Which IP policies best serve a creative and multicultural public domain? When is borrowing from a traditional culture legitimate inspiration and when it is inappropriate adaptation or copying?

As noted earlier, a key legal and cultural policy question is: Is the protection that is already available for contemporary adaptations, interpretations, and performances of traditional cultural materials adequate, or should IP-type rights be established over the pre-existing, underlying, and communally developed materials regarded as public domain by the IP system?

Responses to this question are varied. Several States and other stakeholders suggest that the public domain character of folklore does not hamper its development – to the contrary, it encourages members of a community to keep alive pre-existing cultural heritage by providing individuals of the community with copyright protection when they use various expressions of pre-existing cultural heritage in their present-day creations or works. Such "forward-looking" incentives for tradition-based creativity can contribute toward the economic development of communities while also promoting and preserving their identities, it is argued.

On the other hand, indigenous and traditional peoples' representatives have strenuously argued at sessions of the WIPO Committee that the public domain is not a concept recognized by them and/or that because traditional knowledge and expressions of folklore have never been protected under IP, they could not be said to have entered the public domain. Should all historic materials be denied protection merely because they are not recent enough? Almost everything created has cultural and historic antecedents, hence systems should be established to yield benefits to cultural communities for all creations and innovations that draw upon tradition, it is pointed out.

Experts also point out that traditional cultural expressions do also not "reside" in particular countries or other geographical areas, but are rather carried, performed, and modified by people as they migrate within and across ethnic groups. And they have imprecise origins, often complicating efforts to determine or verify authenticity.[40] In practice, traditional cultures are not always created within firmly bounded and identifiable communities that can be treated as legal persons

[37] Palethorpe and Verhulst, Report on the International Protection of Expressions of Folklore Under Intellectual Property Law, 2000, p. 31.

[38] GRULAC (WIPO/GRTKF/IC/1/5, Annex I, p. 2).

[39] Sections 26 to 29.

[40] Stavenhagen, "Cultural Rights: a social science perspective," in UNESCO, *Cultural Rights and Wrongs*, 1998, pp. 2–7; Personal communications with, among others, Professor Dorothy Noyes, Associate Professor of Folklore, Ohio State University; Valdimar Hafstein, Researcher, Reykjavik Academy, Iceland and Adjunct Lecturer in Ethnology and Folklore, University of Iceland; see also: Valdimar Tr. Hafstein, 2004, "The Politics of Origins: Collective Creation Revisited" *Journal of American Folklore* 117 (465): 300–15, J. Sanford Rikoon, 2004 "On the Politics of the Politics of Origins: Social (In)Justice and the International Agenda on Intellectual Property, Traditional Knowledge, and Folklore." *Journal of American Folklore* 117 (465): 325–36 and Brown, M., *Who Owns Native Culture*, Harvard University Press, 2003. Proceedings of "Folklore, Aesthetic Ecologies and Public Domain," University of Pennsylvania, April 2 and 3, 2004, and 8th Congress of Societe Internationale d'Ethnologie et de Folklore/3rd Congress Association d'Anthropologie Mediterraneenne, Marseille, April 28, 2004.

or unified actors. Thus, traditional cultural expressions are not necessarily always the product of limited communities and the expression of local identities. Nor are they often truly unique, but rather the products of cross-cultural exchange and influence resulting from migration, pilgrimage, and sharing. In this context, the practical application of notions such as authenticity, community, origin, source, distinctiveness, and characteristic may require special attention.

WIPO'S WORK SO FAR: LATEST DEVELOPMENTS

The debate about protection – of an IP nature – of traditional knowledge and cultural expressions is a complex one. There is much at stake: strong aspirations; political, social, and legal issues, some of which are beyond the scope of IP; deep-rooted concerns about the appropriation of cultural heritage; apprehension about the loss of cultural identity; and fears that established balances in existing IP systems may be disturbed. The meanings of fundamental concepts are hotly contested – traditional, authentic, authorship, original, and public domain, to name a few. The sweep of technical, legal, and administrative challenges is broad.

Nevertheless, there has been significant progress on these issues within the work of the WIPO Committee. This work is based upon extensive consultations with indigenous peoples and traditional communities in twenty-eight countries, and involves direct participation by more than 100 NGOs, many of which represent the interests of indigenous peoples and traditional communities.

The Member States of WIPO have recently called for accelerated progress in this area, stressed the "international dimension" of these questions, and emphasized that no outcome of WIPO's work in this area is excluded, including the possible development of an international instrument or instruments.

Access to and Benefit-Sharing in Genetic Resources

With regard to the IP aspects of access to and benefit-sharing in genetic resources, discussions within WIPO and in other policy areas have focused largely on examining methods consistent with IP treaties for requiring the disclosure within patent applications of, among other things, genetic resources used in the development of the claimed inventions and the country of origin of those genetic resources; associated traditional knowledge used in the development of the claimed inventions and the source of that associated traditional knowledge; and evidence of prior informed consent. This work has, in large part, been undertaken at the request of the Convention on Biological Diversity (CBD), and is intended to support the objectives of the CBD.

A disclosure of origin requirement in patent applications is regarded by many States and others as an instrument to ensure the traceability of genetic resources and associated traditional knowledge, and to support compliance with a principle of "free, prior, and informed consent" (FPIC) and fair and equitable benefit sharing, in furtherance *inter alia* of the objectives of the CBD. FPIC is already a common feature of laws governing access to genetic resources and associated traditional knowledge, and its application has been further elaborated in the Bonn Guidelines established under the CBD. WIPO cooperates closely with the Secretariat of the CBD in relation to these questions.

There are diverse approaches toward establishing a disclosure requirement in patent applications for inventions based upon, derived from, or otherwise linked to genetic resources and associated traditional knowledge (see, for example, the WIPO Technical Study on Patent Disclosure Requirements related to Genetic Resources and Traditional Knowledge,[41] prepared by WIPO at the request of the Conference of the Parties [COP] to the CBD and submitted to the COP in 2004). A number of processes, within WIPO and elsewhere, are underway in which these complex and sensitive questions are being discussed by Member States, indigenous peoples, and traditional communities and other stakeholders.[42]

WIPO's program on genetic resources also responds to a widely felt need for more information about current practices concerning the IP aspects of agreements on access to genetic resources and the sharing of consequential benefits. In order to provide a practical IP contribution in this area, WIPO, in cooperation with the Secretariat of the CBD, is, *inter alia*, in the process of carrying out an examination of IP clauses in existing contractual agreements on access to genetic resources and associated benefit-sharing, with the specific aim of establishing a public, electronic database about this kind of contract.[43]

Traditional Knowledge and Cultural Expressions

In November 2004, Member States of WIPO examined specific draft proposals for recognizing, among other things, collective interests in traditional know-how and expressions of traditional cultures which are innovative or creative and characteristic of a distinct cultural identity.[44] These proposals are available on WIPO's Web site and will be subject to further revision in the light of comments and ongoing discussions among Member States and other stakeholders.

A key feature of these proposals is that they draw directly upon the full range of materials that have served as the basis of the Committee's work so far, such as the previous working

[41] WIPO Publication No. 786 E.

[42] Within WIPO, this issue has been mainly considered by the Intergovernmental Committee on Genetic Resources, Traditional Knowledge and Folklore (IGC), the Standing Committee on the Law of Patents, and the Working Group on PCT Reform. In early June 2005, a special one-day ad hoc meeting will be convened by WIPO to discuss a further invitation received from the Conference of the Parties of the CBD to examine issues concerning the interrelation of access to genetic resources and disclosure requirements in intellectual property rights applications. Proposals in this regard are currently available at <http://www.wipo.int/tk/en/genetic/proposals/index.html>

[43] See current database at <http://www.wipo.int/tk/en/databases/contracts/index.html>.

[44] See, in particular, WIPO documents WIPO/GRTKF/IC/7/3 and WIPO/GRTKF/IC/7/5.

documents prepared for the Committee[45]; interventions and submissions made by Member States, communities, and other stakeholders during Committee sessions but also at national and regional, consultations[46]; reports[47]; national, regional, and international laws and instruments[48]; studies[49]; responses to questionnaires[50]; and comments on the earlier working documents made at previous sessions of the Committee.[51]

For example, with regard to traditional cultural expressions, the draft proposals seek to:

(a) recognize and encourage the use of customary laws and systems and traditional governance and decision-making systems as far as possible;
(b) provide adequate guidance while being broad and flexible, leaving sufficient space for policy and legislative development at the national and community levels, with a view to establishment of options and mechanisms tailored to meeting specific national and community aspirations and circumstances;
(c) establish measures for legal protection that would apply only to uses of cultural expressions taking place beyond and outside of the customary and traditional context;
(d) respect and give effect to the right of communities to control access to their cultural expressions, especially those of particular cultural or spiritual value or significance, such as sacred or secret expressions, and expressions particularly vulnerable to exploitation. The suggested forms of protection are voluntary and communities would always be entitled to rely exclusively or in addition upon their own customary and traditional forms of protection against unwanted access, which might be the most effective in practice;
(e) address both economic and cultural aspects of the protection of traditional cultural expressions;
(f) complement and work together with laws and measures for the preservation and safeguarding of cultural heritage. In some cases, existing cultural heritage measures, institutions, and programs could be made use of in support of these principles, thus avoiding a duplication of effort and resources;
(g) recognize that private property rights in traditional cultural materials may run counter to the characteristics and nature of traditional cultures and the values of the communities that maintain, develop, and use them, and, therefore, that private property rights should complement and be carefully balanced with nonproprietary and non-IP measures, in addition to "positive" and "defensive" forms of protection;
(h) place particular emphasis on preventing the exploitation and insulting, derogatory, and offensive treatment of traditional cultural expressions of particular cultural significance;
(i) strike an appropriate balance between the rights and interests of communities, users, and the broader public. This includes taking international human rights standards into account, striking balances between, for example, the protection of traditional cultural expressions, on the one hand, and artistic and intellectual freedom, the preservation of cultural heritage, the customary use and transmission of traditional cultural expressions, promotion of cultural diversity, the stimulation of individual creativity, and access to and use of traditional cultural expressions and freedom of expression, on the other;
(j) address directly, in a practical and focused manner, the kinds of appropriations of traditional cultural expressions that previous consultations and discussions have identified as the most common and egregious;
(k) directly complement and be coordinated with parallel provisions for the protection of traditional knowledge;
(l) be closely guided by the nature, specific characteristics, and forms of traditional cultures, expression, and creativity.

The proposals set out suggested "Policy objectives" and "general guiding principles," in addition to specific provisions dealing with the main substantive issues that any approach, system, or instrument for the protection of traditional cultural expressions would need to deal with. These

45 Such as documents WIPO/GRTKF/IC/3/10, WIPO/GRTKF/IC/5/3, and WIPO/GRTKF/IC/6/3.

46 See, for example, document WIPO/GRTKF/IC/6/12. See WIPO/GRTKF/IC/4/4, WIPO/GRTKF/IC/5/4, and WIPO/GRTKF/IC/6/7, for example, for lists of these meetings and consultations.

47 Such as the report of the fact-finding missions conducted by WIPO in 1998 and 1999.

48 Such as the *sui generis* approaches in: Tunis Model Law on Copyright for Developing Countries, 1976 ("the Tunis Model Law"); the WIPO-UNESCO Model Provisions for National Laws on the Protection of Expressions of Folklore Against Illicit Exploitation and Other Prejudicial Actions, 1982 ("the Model Provisions"); OAPI, as revised in 1999 ("the Bangui Agreement"); the Special Intellectual Property Regime Governing the Collective Rights of Indigenous Peoples for the Protection and Defence of their Cultural Identity and their Traditional Knowledge of Panama, 2000, and the related Executive Decree of 2001 ("the Panama Law"); the Pacific Regional Framework for the Protection of Traditional Knowledge and Expressions of Culture, 2002 ("the Pacific Regional model"); the Indigenous Peoples Rights Act of 1997 of the Philippines ("the Philippines Law"); and the Indian Arts and Crafts Act, 1990 of the United States of America (the "USA Arts and Crafts Act"). These are summarized and analyzed in WIPO/GRTKF/IC/5/INF/3 and WIPO/GRTKF/IC/5/INF 4. Also consulted were the UNESCO International Convention on the Safeguarding of the Intangible Cultural Heritage, 2003; the draft UNESCO Convention for the Promotion and Protection of the Diversity of Cultural Contents and Artistic Expression; and the Principles and Guidelines for the Protection of the Heritage of Indigenous People, prepared by Dr. Erica Irene-Daes for the UN's Working Group on Indigenous Populations. In addition, several other national laws have been examined that are too numerous to mention. These are mainly the laws of African and other States that have enacted protection for TCEs/folklore based upon either the Tunis Model Law, 1976 or the Model Provisions, 1982. Particular attention has been paid, as examples only, to the copyright laws of Nigeria and Tunisia, both presented at the panel on Traditional cultural expressions held at the Committee's fourth session. The Peruvian Law of 2002 Introducing a Protection Regime for the Collective Knowledge of Indigenous Peoples Derived from Biological Resources ("the Peru Law, 2002") has also been analyzed.

49 Such as "Minding Culture" by Terri Janke and "National Experiences of India, Indonesia and the Philippines" by Valsala Kutty.

50 Such as WIPO/GRTKF/IC/3/10.

51 See, in particular, the reports of previous Committee sessions.

are: scope of subject matter; criteria for protection; beneficiaries; management of rights; scope of protection (such as utilizations requiring authorization); exceptions and limitations; term of protection; formalities; sanctions, remedies, and enforcement procedures; application in time; relationship with IP protection; and international and regional protection.

The suggested specific principles draw extensively upon existing IP and non-IP principles, doctrines, and legal mechanisms, and national and regional experiences, both practical and legislative. They recognize and take into account that some traditional cultural expressions and derivatives thereof are already protected by current IP laws, although addressing in particular, as many stakeholders have requested, the protection of subject matter that is not currently protected. The suggested principles, although extending protection for materials not currently protected by IP, are firmly rooted in IP law, policy, and practice, and seek to strike the required balances in a manner that is complementary to existing IP approaches.

More specifically, the draft provisions:

(a) regarding *scope of subject matter*, propose using as a starting point the description of expressions of folklore in the 1982 WIPO-UNESCO Model Provisions;
(b) regarding *criteria for protection*, propose that protection should extend to traditional cultural expressions that are creative (that is, the result of human intellectual activity but not necessarily original or novel) and characteristic of the traditional cultural heritage and identity of a community;
(c) concerning *beneficiaries*, establish that protection of traditional cultural expressions should be for the benefit of the indigenous peoples and traditional and other cultural communities who maintain, use, and develop them and of which they are characteristic;
(d) regarding the *management of rights*, authorizations to use traditional cultural expressions should be provided wherever possible by the relevant communities. An office, agency, or other authority, whether existing or specially created, could fulfill various tasks associated with the effective implementation of measures for the protection of traditional cultural expressions in the interests of and for the benefit of the relevant communities. An office of this kind, which might be governmental, quasi governmental or nongovernmental, might also receive applications for authorizations to use traditional cultural expressions and enforce rights on behalf of communities if they are not able to, in full consultation with the communities. Any benefits collected by such an office should be provided directly to the community concerned. Such an office would also be responsible for resolving competing claims by communities, according to customary laws and decision-making processes as far as possible;
(e) regarding *scope of protection*, recognize that varying and multiple levels and forms of protection may be appropriate for different kinds of traditional cultural expressions and depending also on the objectives intended to be served. For example, cultural expressions of particular cultural or spiritual value or significance (such as sacred expressions), or secret expressions may be the subject of strong forms of protection, in the form of exclusive rights or a principle of prior and informed consent, for example (to the extent that a community's control of access has been breached). Performances of traditional cultural expressions could also be the subject of strong protection, drawing directly from existing international law such as the WIPO Performances and Phonograms Treaty, 1996. On the other hand, for other traditional cultural expressions, especially those already, in practice, publicly available or accessible, the focus could rather be on regulation of their use, drawing upon principles relating to moral rights, equitable remuneration schemes, compensatory liability, and unfair competition;
(f) regarding *exceptions*, safeguard customary uses of traditional cultural expressions as determined by customary laws, extend only to uses of expressions outside the traditional or customary context whether or not for commercial gain, and otherwise render uses of traditional cultural expressions subject to the same kind of limitations applicable to literary and artistic works, trademarks, designs, and other forms of IP as relevant, save to the extent that such limitations might be offensive and culturally inappropriate in this particular context;
(g) concerning *term of protection*, protect traditional cultural expressions for as long as they continue to be maintained and used by, and are characteristic of, the relevant community. Regional and national implementation measures could specify circumstances in which a cultural expression will no longer be deemed to be characteristic of a community;
(h) in relation to *application in time*, provide that, although respecting as far as possible rights previously lawfully acquired and ongoing good faith uses of traditional cultural expressions, prior and ongoing uses of traditional cultural expressions should be regularized as far as possible within a certain period of measures for the protection coming into force;
(i) concerning *existing IP protection*, reinforce the notion that special protection for traditional cultural expressions should not replace, and is complementary to, any conventional IP protection applicable to the cultural expressions and derivatives thereof;
(j) concerning *formalities* and *sanctions, remedies, and enforcement*, establish measures that are practicable and effective, rather than systems of imaginative requirements unworkable in reality. No formalities for protection are suggested, although, in the interests of promoting certainty and transparency, the possibility of a notification system, for declaratory purposes, is identified, especially for cultural expressions of particular significance (which, it is suggested above, could be the subject of strong forms

of protection). Such notification should not involve the documentation, recordal, or public disclosure of the cultural expressions;

(k) regarding *regional and international protection*, provide for legal mechanisms and practical measures to recognize and enforce the rights of foreign rights holders in national systems. Existing or new regional organizations could be tasked with resolving competing claims to traditional cultural expressions by communities within distinct countries, using customary laws, local information sources, and alternative dispute resolution (ADR) as far as possible (see earlier discussion on ADR).

The WIPO Committee examined these proposals at its session in November 2004, and the proposals were left open for an initial round of comments until February 25, 2005. They will continue to be revised in the light of comments received on them and to be considered at future sessions of the Committee.

Policy development in the WIPO Committee is matched by complementary capacity-building assistance provided to States, regional organizations, communities, and other stakeholders. For instance, the provision of IP advice on the development of measures and laws (WIPO, for example, provided IP advice to South Pacific Island countries in drafting a *sui generis* law for the protection of traditional knowledge and cultural expressions); the organization of national and regional workshops for community representatives and Government officials; the undertaking of a practical study on customary laws; and the preparation of a "toolkit" for managing the IP aspects of documenting traditional knowledge and of 'practical guide' for the protection of TCEs.

CONCLUDING REMARKS

Aside from the specific proposals developed within the Committee, there has been other unmistakable progress of a more subtle nature: The needs and concerns of indigenous peoples and other cultural communities are now at the center of IP policy-making; the work of the WIPO Committee continues to be a process of reviewing the core principles and assumptions of IP; through the collection and analysis of actual experiences with IP and traditional cultural expressions and knowledge, extensive practical and empirical information is now available, helping to ensure that solutions eventually arrived at are workable, real-world, and actually useful to communities.

And, there have already been concrete and practical developments, such as: existing documentation of already disclosed traditional knowledge is now being included within the scope of prior art for patent examination purposes, helping to avoid cases in which patents are wrongfully granted over traditional knowledge-based inventions; geographical indications have been registered in respect of handicrafts in Portugal, Mexico, and the Russian Federation; Maori in New Zealand have recently registered a certification trademark to assure the authenticity and quality of Maori arts and crafts; Australia has recently tabled a draft amendment to the Copyright Act for the creation of communal moral rights in indigenous cultural materials;[52] and countries and regional organizations continue to experiment with new laws and approaches, such as Panama, Peru, and the Pacific Island countries, to name only a few.

The next sessions of the Committee in 2005 and beyond will, no doubt, advance understanding of the range of possible outcomes in this area, in which legal and policy evolution is still fast-evolving.

SELECTED BIBLIOGRAPHY[54]

Janke, T., Minding Culture – Case Studies on Intellectual Property and Traditional Cultural Expressions, prepared for WIPO

Kutty, P. V., National Experiences with the Protection of Expressions of Folklore/Traditional Cultural Expressions: India, Indonesia and the Philippines", prepared for WIPO

WIPO, "Intellectual Property Needs and Expectations of Traditional Knowledge Holders: WIPO Report on Fact-finding Missions (1998–1999)", WIPO Publication 768E/F/S

Group of Countries of Latin America and the Caribbean "Traditional Knowledge and the Need to Give it Adequate Intellectual Property Protection" (WIPO/GRTKF/IC/1/5)

European Community and its Member States "Expressions of Folklore" (WIPO/GRTKF/IC/3/11)

China "Current Status on the Protection and Legislation of National Folklore in China" (WIPO/GRTKF/IC/3/14)

WIPO Secretariat "Final Report on National Experiences with the Legal Protection of Expressions of Folklore" (WIPO/GRTKF/IC/3/10)

WIPO Secretariat "Presentations on National and Regional Experiences with Specific Legislation for the legal Protection of Traditional Cultural Expressions (WIPO/GRTKF/IC/4/INF 2 to 5Add)

WIPO Publication "Consolidated Analysis of the Legal Protection of Traditional Cultural Expressions/Expressions of Folklore"

WIPO Publication "Technical Study on Patent Disclosure Requirements Related to Genetic Resources and Traditional Knowledge"

WIPO-UNEP Study on the Role of Intellectual Property Rights in the Sharing of Benefits Arising from the Use of Biological Resources and Associated Traditional Knowledge"

WIPO Secretariat "Comparative Summary of *Sui Generis* Legislation for the Protection of Traditional Cultural Expressions" (WIPO/GRTKF/IC/5/INF 3)

WIPO Secretariat, "Traditional Cultural Expressions/Expressions of Folklore: Legal and Policy Options" (WIPO/GRTKF/IC/6/3)

WIPO Secretariat, "Traditional Cultural Expressions/Expressions of Folklore: Overview of Policy Objectives and Core Principles" (WIPO/GRTKF/IC/7/3)

WIPO Secretariat, "Traditional Knowledge: Overview of Policy Objectives and Core Principles" (WIPO/GRTKF/IC/7/5)

[52] For more information, see documents WIPO/GRTKF/IC/5/3 and 6/3.

[52] This list comprises materials prepared by or for WIPO. It does not seek to represent all relevant materials on these topics. There is a considerable amount of other valuable literature on these subjects, some of which is cited in these footnotes.

CHAPTER FORTY-FOUR

Who Owns Traditional Knowledge? A Personal and Industry View[1]

Bo Hammer Jensen[2]

WHAT IS KNOWLEDGE?

Working with the registration of inventions and obtaining intellectual property rights to protect these from unauthorised commercial exploitation inevitably brings you to sometimes more philosophical discussions regarding what constitutes knowledge.

- Many terms are in use for describing "knowledge," such as know-how, innovations, information, practices, skills, and learning.
- The Oxford English Reference Dictionary[3] defines knowledge as:
  (1) "awareness or familiarity gained by experience (of a person, fact, or thing)"; "a person's range of information"; or "specific information: facts or intelligence about something";
  (2) "a theoretical or practical understanding of a subject, language, etc."; "the sum of what is known"; or "learning, scholarship";
  (3) "true, justified belief"; or "certain understanding, as opposed to opinion."

  Similarly, it defines "know-how" as:

  (1) "practical knowledge; technique, expertise" or
  (2) "natural skill or invention."

  Innovation is defined as:

  (1) "the act of bringing in new methods, ideas, etc.," or
  (2) "the act of making changes."

  Information is defined as:

  (1) "something told" or "knowledge"; "items of knowledge" or "news";
  (2) [legal] "a charge or complaint lodged with a court or magistrate";
  (3) "the act of informing or telling; or an instance of this";
  (4) "that which is inherent in or can be conveyed by a particular arrangement or sequence of things" or [in information theory] "a mathematical quantity expressing the probability of occurrence of a particular sequence of symbols etc. as against a number of alternatives."

In my view, "knowledge" is that which is created through the generation and accumulation of experiences. In that sense, knowledge is empirical. Theories are speculative in nature – what if – whereas knowledge gives the impression, "I know" or "I have tested and found." Therefore, knowledge may not have any scientific, theoretical background or explanation.

Knowledge will primarily be created or obtained through our need for food, shelter, and other "necessities" and secondarily to satisfy human curiosity. The generation of knowledge happens – like everything else we do – in a cultural context in relation to the society in which the creator lives.

WHAT IS TRADITIONAL KNOWLEDGE?

In a recent document relating to the protection of traditional knowledge (TK),[4] it is "defined" as: "the content or substance of traditional know-how, innovations, information, practices, skills and learning rather than to the form of its expression."

If this is compared with the definition(s) for knowledge given earlier, it is seen that the only real difference is the word "traditional."

The debate about TK has, to a large extent, been fuelled by the text of Article 8(j) of the Convention on Biological Diversity (CBD), in which it is provided that:

Each Contracting Party shall, as far as possible and as appropriate:

(j) Subject to its national legislation, respect, preserve and maintain knowledge, innovations and practices of *indigenous and local communities embodying traditional lifestyles* relevant for the conservation and sustainable use of biological diversity and promote their wider application with the approval and involvement of the holders of such knowledge, innovations and practices and encourage the equitable sharing of the benefits arising from the utilization of such knowledge, innovations and practices;

The only difference between "knowledge" and "traditional knowledge" lies in the context in which the knowledge has been created and is being used (to the extent that it is still in use). TK could thus be defined as knowledge that has been created by "indigenous and local communities" and "embodies traditional lifestyles." However, for many purposes, such a definition may be considered too narrow because knowledge

[1] The views expressed in this presentation are personal.
[2] Director, Senior Patent Counsel, EPA, Novozymes A/S, Denmark.
[3] The *Oxford English Reference Dictionary*, Oxford University Press, 1996.
[4] WIPO/GRTKF/IC/7/5, at page 11.

that by many is considered "traditional" may not necessarily have been created by indigenous or local communities, and it may not embody traditional lifestyles (it may have been modified to suit modern times).[5]

Personally, I have always had a problem with the concept of "indigenous peoples or communities" in the international context. The concept is generally understood as defining people that are minorities, which have been (and often still are) discriminated against by immigrants who have taken over the land, etc. that was once the homelands of these peoples. Such a situation exists in some countries, but in most countries, indigenous peoples are the majority, and the minorities are immigrants or other groups defined by other criteria, such as religion, sexual inclination, and so on.

A completely different way to define TK would be to look at the societal context in which the knowledge is created. Thereby, the focus would be on the process leading to the knowledge, and not whether the result embodies a traditional lifestyle. TK could then be defined as knowledge created in a communal context in communities maintaining and developing traditional lifestyles. In this manner, knowledge created in societies, such as the Amish or Quaker societies in the United States, would also be covered.

IS IT POSSIBLE TO OWN KNOWLEDGE?

To own something means that it is your [private] property. It is in your possession and you have full control over it. If someone steals something you own, you may still claim ownership thereof and have it returned to you. Also, you may lose something you own, or it may be destroyed. After that, you do not own it anymore.

This is all very well for objects like chairs, houses, and ships. But is the concept of ownership still valid when we speak about knowledge?

In my view, it is not. The only situation in which someone can claim to own knowledge is during the period between the time, when the knowledge is created (if created by one person) and the time when this knowledge is shared with someone. From that crucial moment of dissemination and on, the knowledge is no longer the property of the person who created it.[6] If the knowledge is created by a group of people, it will never be the private property of any individual, but it may be considered as the property of the group, if the group agrees to keep the knowledge among them and not disseminate it to anyone outside the group. Therefore, it is my belief that the only knowledge that can be owned is "secret" knowledge or "know how," and the ownership is extremely volatile.

The discussions concerning the ownership of TK are, to a large extent, propelled by a misconception of the so-called intellectual (or industrial) property rights (IPR) and the perceived wrongs done when people or companies in industrialised countries apply for patent protection for inventions allegedly based on – if not simply consisting of – TK.

One of these misconceptions is that a patent provides ownership to the subject matter covered by the patent.

Knowledge disclosed in a patent application can never be considered as being owned by the owner of the patent. Even before the application has been published, the knowledge has lost the character of being the property of the creator because the application (in which the knowledge is disclosed) has been deposited with a governmental authority and read by people working there (although under a confidentiality restriction). In that process, the knowledge becomes no longer exclusively controlled by the creator.

It has been said many times, but apparently it cannot be said too often:

A patent provides the patent owner with the power to stop someone from exploiting the invention commercially. This power even exists only in countries in which a patent has been granted. For everyone, the knowledge embodied in the application is disseminated for their private use everywhere, and for commercial exploitation in all those countries in which no patent has been applied for or granted.

Also, because a valid patent can only cover inventions that are novel, a patent owner cannot stop anyone from doing what they were doing prior to the filing of the application resulting in the patent.

This principle may be expressed in another manner, namely – if not for the invention, then no one would be able to exploit it anyway.

Some economists believe that patenting may diminish "the common goods," but because a valid patent cannot cover anything that already is a part of the accumulated common knowledge, patenting cannot diminish the existing common goods. It may be that the increased use of patents in the business community reduces the volume of the future common goods, but this is based on the assumption that the innovation would happen and the knowledge thereof be disseminated anyway. The problem is whether or not this assumption is a sound one.

There is not a clear-cut answer to this because innovation has many incentives, of which the granting of an intellectual property right is only one. It is impossible to tell which innovation would happen in the absence of an intellectual property right.

Also, for most inventions, patent protection is only applied for in a very limited number of countries; normally between five and twenty, which leaves the invention open for commercial exploitation in more than 100 World Trade Organization (WTO) countries. For very obvious reasons, the patentee tries to cover as much of the potential market as possible by the selection of countries.

Even if the assumption were to be true, the situation is only of a temporary nature because the patent eventually expires, and the embodied knowledge is then made freely available for any exploitation to everybody, everywhere. Thereby, the volume of commonly available knowledge increases.

[5] See WIPO/GRTKF/IC/7/5 at page 12.

[6] This is also clear from the way in which we speak about knowledge; knowledge is shared or disseminated, not told or anything else.

Because of the conceived problem with people in the industrialised countries acquiring IPR covering TK, especially from developing countries, there now is a demand for the creation of an international system for the protection of TK.

Although generally supporting the creation of such a protective scheme, many in the industry have certain reservations and concerns, which I share and discuss in this article.

THE "TRADITIONAL" INTELLECTUAL PROPERTY "PHILOSOPHY"

The intellectual property rights we have today have been developed over a period of about 400 to 500 years, replacing former "monopoly" rights that were granted to certain people or groups of people. Normally, the old monopolies were granted either through apprenticeship or pure nepotism.

The "classical" disciplines are patents, copyrights, and trademarks. In more recent times, over the past 40 or so years, a number of rights normally designated as industrial rights have been created. These are plant breeder's rights, design rights, integrated circuit rights, database rights, and geographical indications. The reason to call these industrial rights is that they all have a strong element of real property rights in them (strongly attached to a specific product). Whereas a discussion of the development of these rights over time is beyond the scope of this chapter, it is worth noting the rationale behind them. Why have societies maintained such monopoly rights?

The Societal Aspect

Intellectual property rights are incentives to innovation and creativity. By granting for example, a patent to an innovator, the innovator is provided a time window in which he can stop competitors from exploiting his innovation, and thereby not only recoup his investments (time and money), but also gain a nice profit. The innovators and entrepreneurs in society are thereby encouraged to innovate instead of simply imitate.

Innovation and creativity are generally considered to benefit society, in that they create new products that may enrich our lives, create jobs through which people can maintain their standard of living, and improve our existing technologies, replacing less efficient processes, etc.

The Moral or Ethical Aspect

IPRs put creators/innovators in a position in which they can control the economic exploitation of their creation and be rewarded for their efforts, and this is only right. This principle finds support in Article 27(2) of the Universal Declaration on Human Rights.[7]

However, society has decided that the power to control the economic exploitation of the creation/innovation should only be available for a limited time period, after which it is being put into the hands of the general public, free to exploit for anyone.

The rules for obtaining IPRs are different, but generally the creator/innovator must apply for the right in order that it may be registered and administered. There is one exception to this, namely, the copyright that in most countries is generated simultaneously with the creation of the copyrighted work.

Like property, IPRs can be transferred between people, and they are thereby considered tradable goods. However, for copyrights there is, in most countries, one element of the rights that is not transferable, the moral right.

The moral right is a right that remains with creators, empowering them with the power to prohibit any exploitation that they (or society) consider abusive with respect to the creation.

In the context of the present discussion, it should be noted that for copyrights, there are two notable exceptions to general internationally shared norms; namely, the absence of the requirement for registration and the moral right. In some countries, copyrights have to be registered, and in some countries, the moral rights of the creator are not recognised.

PROTECTION OF TRADITIONAL KNOWLEDGE

As stated earlier, a more or less general demand for protecting TK has, in recent years, been expressed primarily by developing countries. The demand originated in various civil societies and indigenous peoples' organisations, but it is, today, supported by most governments in developing countries, and also by governments in many industrialised countries.

The discussion is mainly focused on two aspects, namely, a moral aspect and an economical aspect. The two aspects are very often intermixed in the discussions.

In 1998 to 1999, the UN organisation dealing with IPR, WIPO, in response to these demands initiated work on traditional knowledge consulting a wide range of stakeholders such as indigenous and local communities, nongovernmental organizations, governmental representatives, academics, researchers, and private sector representatives to determine the intellectual property needs and expectations of holders of TK. These so-called "fact finding missions" resulted in the publication of a number of reports.[8]

Based on this work, the WIPO General Assembly in 2000 agreed to establish an intergovernmental body to discuss intellectual property issues related to TK, genetic resources, and traditional cultural expressions (folklore). The Intergovernmental Committee on Intellectual Property and Genetic Resources, Traditional Knowledge and Folklore (the IGC) met five times in Geneva under the year 2000 mandate before reporting to the WIPO General Assembly in September 2003. The General Assembly prolonged the mandate for a period of two years, and also made certain revisions to the

[7] Article 27.

1. Everyone has the right freely to participate in the cultural life of the community, to enjoy the arts, and to share in scientific advancement and its benefits.
2. Everyone has the right to the protection of the moral and material interests resulting from any scientific, literary, or artistic production of which he or she is the author.

[8] <http://www.wipo.int/tk/en/tk/ffm/report/index.html>.

mandate.[9] The IGC ideally should therefore hopefully develop an instrument or instruments for international protection of TK during 2005. The seventh session of the IGC took place November 1 to 5, 2004, and the eighth session is scheduled for June 6 to 10, 2005.

It may be noted that this is not the first time that WIPO deals with TK. In the 1980s, WIPO drafted a model law on the protection of folklore in cooperation with UNESCO.[10] This was mainly fueled by the developments in audio-visual recording and the commercial exploitation in industrialised countries of recordings of expressions of folklore in developing countries. The first attempts to provide protection under copyrights for folklore dates back to the late sixties.

The present discussion is based primarily on documents prepared for the seventh session of the IGC, especially document WIPO/GRTKF/IC/7/5.

Before proceeding, it may also be appropriate to mention that the issue of TK is being dealt with in a plethora of intergovernmental organisations. For information, I only mention a few that may be considered the more important ones: UN Permanent Forum on Indigenous Issues, CBD, Food and Agricultural Organization, UNESCO, United Nations Development Program, United Nations Conference on Trade and Development, and the Office of the UN High Commissioner for Human Rights (all within the UN system). Outside the UN system, most noteworthy for this discussion is the TRIPs Council under the WTO. A comprehensive list of organisations involved in these discussions can be found as the participants listings in the reports of the IGC sessions.

Of special interest, it may be noted that the UN Permanent Forum on Indigenous Issues, in paragraph 20 of its "Millennium Development Goals and Indigenous Peoples," in 2000, provided "Forum recommends that the United Nations system should fully explore the protection, use and promotion of indigenous (including traditional) knowledge and ensure synergies across the relevant bodies currently investigating the issues and furthermore should invite the Forum to participate."

In stark contrast to the rationale behind the normal system of IPR, the creation of international agreed rights to protect TK is, for many of those involved in the debate, *not* to provide an incentive to promote the further creation of TK and disseminate this to the world – no – it is being thought of as an instrument to *avoid* the exploitation and use of TK.[11] Such a starting point is, in my view, negative and unacceptable.

It is also squarely against the spirit and wording of the CBD, according to which the member states shall

"*respect, preserve and maintain* knowledge, innovations and practices of indigenous and local communities embodying traditional lifestyles relevant for the conservation and sustainable use of biological diversity and *promote their wider application.*"

The CBD says nothing about protecting TK against exploitation – it talks about "preservation," which is protection against deterioration, but emphasises that the wider application thereof shall be

"with the *approval and involvement of the holders* of such knowledge, innovations and practices."

Furthermore, the member states shall

"*encourage* the equitable sharing of the benefits arising from the utilization of such knowledge."

Article 8(j) of the CBD is therefore a much better starting point for discussing the creation of a system for the protection of TK. The system should support the creation and maintenance (preservation) of TK by providing an incentive to do this. It should also be an incentive to disseminate knowledge of TK in order to create respect among other people for the achievements of its creators. Such developments must also happen with the approval and participation of those holding and creating the knowledge.

In the last decade or so, during the debates, especially within UN bodies dealing with human rights, concerning the protection and the rights of minority groups, such as indigenous peoples and others, the creation of special rights for these groups has also been an overarching issue, making the discussion of the protection of TK an even more sensitive issue. In these debates, it is my view that the consequences of creating special rights enjoyable only by special groups defined by ancestry or other special criteria must be evaluated very carefully because such rights may lead to the development of parallel societies within a society. The creation of rights may create imbalances within the society, and later lead to conflicts (it is good to fight discrimination, but not good to fight it by introducing privileges for those who formerly were discriminated against).

As indicated earlier, WIPO has made intensive investigations into the matter of protection of TK.

WIPO Work

In a general response to the call for the protection of TK, WIPO has noted that "a general requirement for protection and broad international standards may in practice be implemented by a wide range of distinct national legal mechanisms, ranging over diverse forms of IP right, adapted IP rights, the general law of unfair competition and various general legal mechanisms beyond the scope of IP law proper (such as the law of delict or torts, criminal law, access and benefit-sharing laws, customary laws, contract law, environmental law and indigenous rights law)."[12]

The main issue is not which law is used to establish the required protection, but whether the objectives set out will

[9] <http://www.wipo.int/documents/en/document/govbody/wo_gb_ga/doc/wo_ga_30_8.doc>.

[10] <http://www.wipo.int/tk/en/documents/pdf/1982-folklore-model-provisions.pdf>.

[11] N. S. Gopalakrishnan, EIPR, 2005, 1, 11–18, at page 15: "it is essential to find out the best possible way of protecting this knowledge to prevent exploitation."

[12] WIPO/GRTKF/IC/7/5 at paragraph 26.

be met. Therefore, it is most important that agreement [as far as possible] is established in respect of the objectives.

The Secretariat has, in document WIPO/GRTKF/IC/7/5, presented to the IGC for its discussion a comprehensive set of:

- *policy objectives*, which would set common general directions for protection and provide a consistent policy framework;
- *general guiding principles*, which would ensure consistency, balance, and effectiveness of substantive principles; and
- *substantive principles*, which would define the legal essence of protection, centered on the suppression of misappropriation of TK.

The objectives have been divided into several groups, namely:

(i) Objectives related directly to TK and TK holders:
  - to create an appropriate system for access to TK;
  - to ensure fair and equitable benefit-sharing for TK;
  - to promote respect, preservation, wider application, and development of TK;
  - to provide mechanisms for the enforcement of rights of TK holders;
  - to improve the quality of TK-based products and remove low-quality traditional medicine from the market;

(ii) Objectives related to biodiversity and genetic resource policy:
  - to promote the conservation and sustainable use of biological resources and associated TK;
  - to promote the legal safeguarding and transfer of genetic resources associated with TK;

(iii) Objectives related to indigenous peoples rights:
  - to promote development of indigenous peoples and local communities;
  - to recognize, respect, and promote the rights of indigenous peoples and local communities;

(iv) Objectives related to sustainable development and capacity building:
  - to enhance scientific capacity at the national and local levels;
  - to promote the transfer of technologies that make use of TK and associated genetic resources;

(v) Objectives related to innovation promotion:
  - to promote and recognize innovation based on TK;
  - to promote the development of Native arts and crafts;

And WIPO has indicated the possible means to be used as:

- Distinct IPR, including:
  - existing IP rights,
  - modified or adapted IP rights, and
  - stand-alone *sui generis* IP systems;
- Unfair competition law;
- Laws governing access to genetic resources and sharing of benefits;
- Trade practices and marketing laws;
- Use of contracts and licenses;
- Registers, inventories, and databases;
- Customary and indigenous laws and protocols;
- Cultural heritage preservation laws and programs;
- General law of civil liability and other remedies, such as rights of publicity, unjust enrichment, confidential information, and blasphemy; and, finally:
  - Criminal law.

Concerns Voiced in the Committee

During the work of the IGC, many concerns have been raised by various participating delegate and observers, some of which are listed subsequently:

- TK may have difficulties meeting requirements of the classical IPR disciplines, such as novelty or originality, and the innovation step or non-obviousness (this may be attributable at least in part to the fact that TK often dates back prior to the time periods associated with conventional IP systems, or are developed in a more diffuse, cumulative, and collective manner, making invention or authorship difficult to establish at a fixed time);
- the requirements in many IP laws for protected subject matter to be fixed in material form may be problematic (given that TK is often preserved and transmitted by oral, narrative, and other nonmaterial forms);
- the frequently informal nature of TK and the customary laws and protocols that define ownership (or other relationships such as custody and guardianship) which form the basis of claims of affinity and community responsibility are not in accordance with established IPR practices;
- the concern that protection systems should correspond to a positive duty to preserve and maintain TK, and not merely provide the means to prevent or exclude others from making unauthorized use (the characteristic function of IPR);
- the perceived tension between individualistic notions of IP rights (the single author or inventor), versus the tendency for TK to be originated, held, and managed in a collective environment (often making it difficult to identify the specific author, inventor, or analogous creator that IP law is viewed as requiring); and
- limitations on the term of protection in IP systems (which call for better recognition of TK, often highlighting the inappropriate nature of relatively brief terms of protection in conventional IP systems, as the need for protection is seen as enduring beyond individual life-spans for TK subject matter).

On the basis of this, WIPO has now set the course for the IGC to discuss the creation of a proposal for a system for the protection of TK that ideally should live up to the ambitious goals indicated subsequently.

Core Principles in the Proposal

- responsiveness to the needs, aspirations, and expectations of TK holders;

- understandable, effective, appropriate, and accessible protection;
- flexibility and comprehensiveness;
- equity and benefit-sharing;
- consistency with and supportiveness of existing IP systems;
- recognition of rights;
- complementarity of defensive and positive protection;
- coordination with laws governing genetic resources;
- concord with other international and regional instruments and processes;
- respect for customary use and transmission of TK; and
- recognition of the specific characteristics of TK.

It is difficult not to agree on all these points, but one could add some further points. For example, I would include easy identification of the rights by third parties. Another would be effective and economically feasible enforcement.

Experience has shown that some inventions are being created independently, several times, by different inventors (individuals or groups) at different points in time, and in order to respect somebody's rights, it is essential that it is easy to identify the rights and the proprietors thereof in order to obtain permission to exploit the invention, if this is desired.

Experience has also shown that in many instances it is difficult for economically weak parties to enforce their rights against economically strong offenders. In the present situation, in which most – if not all – holders of TK are economically weak, it is important that mechanisms be in place to secure them in this respect. On the other hand, the system should also prevent "gold diggers" among holders of TK from initiating frivolous cases with the aim of settling the case for a "reasonable compensation" (less than the legal costs for the "rich" party).

On the basis of these "Core Principles," WIPO then lists its proposed "Substantive Principles":

- prevent the misappropriation of TK;
- define acts of misappropriation such as acquisition and appropriation of TK by unfair means;
- provide examples of misappropriation, such as acquisition of TK by theft, bribery, coercion, breach or inducement to breach of contract, confidence, fiduciary duties, acquisition of TK without prior informed consent if such consent is required, and so on;
- protect TK against other acts of unfair competition;
- ensure maximum flexibility for national authorities to implement the principles in a legal form appropriate to their own legal systems, national priorities, and stakeholder needs;
- apply the principle of prior informed consent to TK;
- ensure equitable benefit-sharing from industrial and commercial uses made with gainful intent, if the TK conveys a technology-based advantage in industry and commerce to the user.

Again, it is difficult not to agree on all these principles.

THE WIPO PROPOSAL FOR PROTECTION AGAINST MISAPPROPRIATION

The WIPO paper emphasises the importance of providing protection against misappropriation, given that this quite obviously is a major concern for many parties involved.

WIPO recognises a widespread desire to prevent misappropriation and proposes to provide a foundational principle to clarify and structure the shared elements of the distinct concerns about misuse and misappropriation of TK that have been highlighted in the discussion both within and outside the Committee discussions. In particular, three broad aspects of misappropriation have been expressed in the debates:

- third parties acquiring illegitimate IP rights over TK;
- acquisition of TK without prior informed consent, where such consent is required; and
- commercial free-riding, or the inequitable use of TK for commercial gain without benefit-sharing.

A main feature to obtain this is suggested to be the general principles used against unfair competition that are also expressed in Article 10 *bis* of the Paris Convention. This has, in the past, been used to establish *sui generis* protection for new technologies (integrated circuits and databases) and new concepts (geographical indications). As a side remark, it can be argued that the protection of geographical indications is a system for the protection of a certain class of TK, where the protection takes the form of granting a monopoly to the use of the protected indication.

The substantive principles developed should, according to WIPO, frame a form of protection that provides: defensive protection; appropriate application of prior informed consent; equitable benefit-sharing for industrial and commercial uses of TK undertaken with gainful intent; and a sensitivity towards customary laws and understandings of TK holders.

These substantive principles would give effect to the objectives of protection, in line with the general guiding principles. They could help define a shared international understanding of protection characterized as follows:

- protection is balanced and proportionate, given the broader public interests and the specific interests of TK holder communities, recognizing fair use or fair dealing and the public domain, while seeking to repress truly inequitable conduct;
- misappropriation of TK is repressed as an act of unfair competition;
- benefits arising from commercial or industrial uses of TK are shared equitably;
- the principle of prior informed consent is applied to TK subject matter in harmony with existing national and international law;
- national authorities retain full flexibility to give effect to the principles compatible with their own legal systems, national policies, and stakeholder needs;

- TK holders retain full involvement and control in TK protection procedures;
- legitimate IP rights are not prejudiced;
- all existing TK laws described to the Committee are consistent with the shared international perspective;
- defensive and positive protections of TK are integrated and complementary;
- national authorities may choose to recognized or grant distinct, *sui generis* private property rights for TK, for either individual or communal owners, according to their own legal systems and national policies and stakeholder needs.

In my view, the introduction of this type of protection would be fine, but there is the drawback that the unfair competition rules, in their normal application, only protect against slavish imitation and, as I have understood the debate, this will not suffice for many purposes, given that protests are often raised against patents covering inventions developed from TK. Also, the initiation of action against unfair competition-based rights depends on the ability of the rightful holders of any such rights to identify violations, and to prove to the courts that they are the rightful owners. This may, in many instances, be very difficult for holders of TK.

Based on the discussions, WIPO has now proposed an outline for a system for the protection of TK against misappropriation. The core and substantial principles thereof are indicated in the Annex to this chapter. In the following I briefly touch upon the substantive principles as seen from industry as I perceive the concerns among industry people dealing with IPR.

The principles in B.1 (see Annex) are generally the same principles that we believe apply to the protection of know-how and proprietary information or knowledge. Holders of TK should enjoy similar rights. The first time a problem may arise is with B.3, wherein it is stated that the principles concern protection against misappropriation and "misuse" beyond its traditional context, but the term "misuse" is not defined anywhere, introducing uncertainty about the meaning thereof.

The principle defined in B.6:3 causes some concern because it assumes that one is always aware of making use of TK. This is not always the situation. It is possible, for example, for a pharmaceutical company in a screening programme related to a specific disease to identify an active component from a plant extract without having any knowledge of the plant having been used for medicinal uses for the same disease. The company will then not be aware of the possible conflict unless a system is established that makes it possible for the company to identify this. In such a situation, it is also difficult to determine whether or not there should actually be any acknowledgement, because the TK was not used and therefore did not make any contribution to the invention and development of a product.

In this context, it should also be mentioned that a large volume of TK has been made available to the public through the publications of ethnobotanists, ethnographers, and many others, and it is difficult to determine what "every reasonable endeavour to identify the source and origin of the knowledge" means.

As an example, the Danish "*People and Flora – Danish Ethnobotany (1978)*" demonstrates that practically each and every plant existing in Denmark, whether in the wild or cultivated, has been used at some point in time against quite a number of disorders or for other "medical" purpose. One source for the four-volume treatise is, "The Herbal Garden" by Henrik Smid, relating to medicinal use, first published in 1546 and with a subsequent reprint as late as 1923, indicating a continued use over a period of 400 years. Ethnobotanists, of course, also disclose many traditional uses of plants and plant materials other than medicinal uses.

This is very relevant in light of the fact that B.11 proposes that there should not be any formalities, such as registration of the rights identifying the knowledge and the right holders. It may therefore be difficult, if not impossible, for any third party to determine whether a piece of TK available in the public domain may be covered by a claim by any number of holders of TK somewhere in the world.

Industry Views and Concerns

In the industry, we are used to working with IPRs both in respect to obtaining and enforcing these rights and in relation to respecting the rights of other parties, especially the rights of competitors. We are also used to working with the laws and rules relating to unfair competition. Finally, we are accustomed to acquiring the right to exploit technologies necessary for doing business from third parties, if this is necessary and possible.

Most of these rights and the identities of the right holders are identifiable (registered), and they are generally limited in both time and geographical distribution.

One of the main tasks, and perhaps the most important one, is to produce so-called freedom of operation opinions, the purpose of which is to identify potential obstacles from IPRs belonging to other entities that may prohibit the putting on the market of a potential product. This is very important in the field of biotechnology, where development costs for new products are very high, especially in the pharmaceutical industries, but also in all other fields of biotechnology.

By their nature, such opinions are always subject to being faulty because some rights may never have been identified for various reasons, but they are always produced using all means available in order to obtain a high degree of certainty. Industry is therefore very concerned about the creation of a new type of rights that may not be registered, and therefore very difficult to identify.

It also causes concerns that these rights may be retroactive in the sense that they will cover knowledge that has been considered as being publicly available, maybe even for centuries, but now may belong to someone, the identity of whom may be very difficult to determine. Furthermore, even if one right holder has been identified, it may be that more right holders exist in various countries.

Further issues that cause concerns in industry circles are the scope of protection, the duration, and the lack of exhaustion regulations.

Scope of Protection

In the WIPO proposal, B.3 refers to the scope of subject matter, but no discussion is provided on the very important issue of "scope of protection" in the sense that, most often, TK is not simply copied without any modification, but provides the basis for further investigations that eventually leads to a novel product (that may be eligible for patent protection in itself). To what extent would the rights granted to holders of TK cover such "downstream" developments?

If it is correct that the protection afforded by the proposal covers only the copying of the TK, I do not see any problem for the industry, but I am afraid that some circles will not agree with this conclusion.

In respect of this, WIPO leaves open the possibilities for the creation of national or regional rights providing a broader scope that could "dominate" later rights, such as patents for inventions derived through the use of TK. Such national or regional rights may cause concerns in industry. This is the case with the laws introduced in, for example, the Philippines, Peru, and so on. However, discussion of these national laws is outside the scope of this chapter.

Duration

WIPO proposes the introduction of inalienable and perennial rights, for instance in relation to an entitlement to take action against derogatory or damaging activities, and to prevent illegitimate third-party IPRs. This sort of eternal right should only cover direct imitation, as stated earlier. As indicated earlier, WIPO further leaves open the possibility of introducing national or regional rights that may provide a broader scope of protection, and in respect of such rights, WIPO believes that a limited term must be applied.

Industry welcomes this, because one of the important concerns from industry, is "eternal" rights. Such rights may very easily become counterproductive in the sense that the right holder prohibits any exploitation whatsoever of something that could be of importance.

As I read the proposal, rights or entitlements would lapse when the original right holders cease to identify with the TK, meaning that the TK is no longer being used in its original cultural context. I believe that any rights should lapse if the TK no longer enjoys protection in its country of origin.

Exhaustion

In relation to most rights, the rights are exhausted if a product is brought on the market by the right holder. It is difficult to see from the WIPO proposal what remaining rights may be exercised by holders of TK. A short example may illustrate this.

The holders of some TK grant a company access to the TK and permission to develop a product. The product is successful; it may even be protected by patent rights, and appropriate compensations are provided to the right holders. Upon expiry of the patent, a number of competitors market generic products and the competition becomes fierce and prices drop.

Does the proposal provide that the competitors must also obtain permission from the right holders? They did not use the TK to develop their products!

What about the compensations (benefit-sharing) obligations of the original producer? Should they continue, thereby putting the original developer in a difficult situation with respect to still making profits?

Industry Requirements

Discussed earlier are some of the concerns I see with respect to the creation of systems for the protection of TK. Many other concerns could also be raised.

The most important requirements that industry would like to see fulfilled in such systems are:

- Transparency
- Flexibility
- Registered rights
- Easily identifiable ownership
- Easily identifiable and competent authorities
- Traditional knowledge in the public domain should not be "privatised" through exclusive rights that will prohibit exploitation in a "decent" manner.

Industry is a Partner

One very important point has been missing from the debate – namely that industry should be considered as a partner in this process. Very often, the rhetoric used implies that industry is more or less crooked, committing massive acts of "biopiracy." These allegations are founded on a handful of cases, most of which involve academic institutions or very small entities.

In reality, industry is essential in attaining the objectives of Article 8(j) of the CBD, namely to promote the sustainable use of TK to the benefit of all parties involved.

The results of this rhetoric are becoming more and more visible as many companies are cutting down departments involved in bioprospecting or even closing these departments and relying completely on other technologies to identify product candidates. This diminishes the market.

It is therefore important that the holders of rights to TK realise that if they have a desire to see their knowledge developed, it should be made attractive for industry to do this. On the other hand, as I noted earlier, for some people the objective is not as provided in Article 8(j), to promote, but rather to prohibit exploitation under any circumstances and, for that purpose, the less attractive, the better.

It would therefore be desirable if, in future debates about rights to TK and the exploitation of this knowledge, the holders of these rights and the governments representing them in various fora could consider industry as their partners and not as adversaries. The concerns we raise are real and deserve to be dealt with seriously. Similarly, industry should respect the concerns raised by the holders of TK, and deal with these in a serious manner. We are all in the same boat; let's pull together in order to make our journey successful.

Annex: Core Principles and Substantive Principles as Provided in WIPO/GRTKF/IC/7/5

CORE PRINCIPLES

General Guiding Principles

A.1: Principle of Responsiveness to the Needs and Expectations of TK Holders

Protection should reflect the aspirations and expectations of TK holders and, in particular, should: recognize and apply indigenous and customary practices, protocols, and laws as far as possible; address cultural and economic aspects of development; address insulting, derogatory, and offensive acts; enable full and effective participation by TK holders; and recognize the inseparable quality of TK and cultural expressions for many communities.

A.2: Principle of Recognition of Rights

The rights of TK holders to the effective protection of their knowledge against misuse and misappropriation should be recognized.

A.3: Principle of Effectiveness and Accessibility of Protection

Measures for protecting TK should be effective in achieving the objectives of protection, and should be understandable, affordable, accessible, and not burdensome for their intended beneficiaries, taking account of the cultural, social, and economic context of TK holders. National authorities should make available appropriate enforcement procedures that permit effective action against misappropriation of TK and violation of the principle of prior informed consent.

A.4: Principle of Flexibility and Comprehensiveness

1. Protection should respect the diversity of TK held by different peoples and communities in different sectors, should acknowledge differences in national circumstances and the legal context and heritage of national jurisdictions, and should allow sufficient flexibility for national authorities to determine the appropriate means of implementing these principles within existing and specific legislative mechanisms, adapting protection as necessary to take account of specific sectoral policy objectives.
2. Protection may combine proprietary and nonproprietary measures, and use existing IP rights (including measures to improve the application and practical accessibility of such rights), *sui generis* extensions or adaptations of IP rights, and specific *sui generis* laws. Protection should include defensive measures to curtail illegitimate acquisition of IP rights over TK or associated genetic resources, and positive measures establishing legal entitlements for TK holders.

A.5: Principle of Equity and Benefit-Sharing

1. Protection should reflect the need for an equitable balance between the rights and interests of those who develop, preserve, and sustain TK, and those who use and benefit from TK; the need to reconcile diverse policy concerns; and the need for specific protection measures to be proportionate to the objectives of protection and the maintenance of an equitable balance of interests.
2. Holders of TK should be entitled to fair and equitable sharing of benefits arising from the use of their TK. Where TK is associated with genetic resources, the distribution of benefits should be consistent with measures, established in accordance with the Convention on Biological Diversity, providing for sharing of benefits arising from the utilization of the genetic resources.

A.6: Principle of Consistency with Existing Legal Systems

1. The authority to determine access to genetic resources, whether or not associated with TK, rests with the national governments and is subject to national legislation. The protection of TK associated with genetic resources shall be consistent with the applicable law, if any, governing access to those resources and the sharing of benefits arising from their use. Nothing in these Principles shall be interpreted to limit the sovereign rights of States over their natural resources and the authority of governments to determine access to genetic resources, whether or not those resources are associated with protected TK.
2. TK protection should be consistent with, and supportive of, existing IP systems and should enhance the applicability of relevant intellectual property systems to TK subject matter in the interests of holders of TK and consistent with the broader public interest. Nothing in these Principles shall be interpreted to derogate from existing obligations that national authorities have to each under the Paris Convention and other international IP agreements.

A.7: Principle of Respect for and Cooperation with Other International and Regional Instruments and Processes

1. TK shall be protected in a way that is consistent with the objectives of other relevant international and regional instruments and processes, and without prejudice to

specific rights and obligations already established under binding legal instruments.

2. Nothing in these Principles shall be interpreted to affect the interpretation of other instruments or the work of other processes that address the role of TK in related policy areas, including the role of TK in the conservation of biological diversity, the combating of drought and desertification, or the implementation of farmers' rights as recognized by relevant international instruments and subject to national legislation.

A.8: Principle of Respect for Customary Use and Transmission of Traditional Knowledge

Customary use, practices, and norms shall be respected and given due account in the protection of TK, as far as possible and as appropriate and subject to national law and policy. Protection beyond the traditional context should not conflict with customary access to, and use and transmission of, TK, and should respect and bolster this customary framework.

A.9: Principle of Recognition of the Specific Characteristics of Traditional Knowledge

Protection of TK should respond to the traditional context, the collective or communal context, and intergenerational character of its development, preservation, and transmission, its relationship to a community's cultural and social identity and integrity, beliefs, spirituality, and values, and the constantly evolving character within the community.

Substantive Principles

B.1: Protection Against Misappropriation

1. TK shall be protected against misappropriation.

General Nature of Misappropriation

2. Any acquisition or appropriation of TK by unfair or illicit means constitutes an act of misappropriation. Misappropriation may also include deriving commercial benefit from the acquisition or appropriation of TK when the person using that knowledge knows, or is grossly negligent in failing to know, that it was acquired or appropriated by unfair means; and other commercial activities contrary to honest practices that gain inequitable benefit from TK.

Acts of Misappropriation

3. In particular, legal means should be available to suppress:
   (i) acquisition of TK by theft, bribery, coercion, fraud, trespass, breach or inducement of breach of contract, breach or inducement of breach of confidence or confidentiality, breach of fiduciary obligations or other relations of trust, deception, misrepresentation, the provision of misleading information when obtaining prior informed consent for access to TK, or other unfair or dishonest means;
   (ii) acquisition of TK or exercising control over it in violation of legal measures that require prior informed consent as a condition of access to the knowledge, and use of TK that violates terms that were mutually agreed as a condition of prior informed consent concerning access to that knowledge;
   (iii) false claims or assertions of ownership or control over TK, including acquiring, claiming, or asserting IPRs over traditional knowledge-related subject matter by a person who knew that the intellectual property rights were not validly held in the light of that TK and any conditions relating to its access; and
   (iv) commercial or industrial use of TK without just and appropriate compensation to the recognized holders of the knowledge, when such use has gainful intent and confers a technological or commercial advantage on its user, and when compensation would be consistent with fairness and equity in relation to the holders of the knowledge in view of the circumstances in which the user acquired the knowledge.

General Protection Against Unfair Competition

4. TK holders shall also be effectively protected against other acts of unfair competition, including acts specified in Article 10 *bis* of the Paris Convention. This includes false or misleading representations that a product or service is produced or provided with the involvement or endorsement of TK holders, or that the commercial exploitation of products or services benefits holders of TK.

Recognition of the Customary Context

5. The application, interpretation, and enforcement of protection against misappropriation of TK, including determination of equitable sharing and distribution of benefits, should be guided, as far as possible and appropriate, by respect for the customary practices, norms, laws, and understandings of the holder of the knowledge, including the spiritual, sacred, or ceremonial characteristics of the traditional origin of the knowledge.

B.2: Legal Form of Protection

1. Protection may be implemented through a special law on TK; the laws on IP, including unfair competition law and the law of unjust enrichment; the law of torts, liability, or civil obligations; criminal law; laws concerning the interests of indigenous peoples; regimes governing access and benefit-sharing; or any other law or combination of any of those laws.
2. The form of protection need not be through exclusive property rights, although such rights may be made available, as appropriate, for the holders of TK, including through existing or adapted intellectual property rights systems, in accordance with the needs and choices of the holders of the knowledge, national laws and policies, and international obligations.

B.3: General Scope of Subject Matter

1. These principles concern protection of TK against misappropriation and misuse beyond its traditional context, and should not be interpreted as limiting or seeking to define the diverse and holistic conceptions of knowledge within the traditional context.
2. For the purpose of these principles only, the term traditional knowledge refers to the content or substance of knowledge that is the result of intellectual activity and insight in a traditional context, and includes the know-how, skills, innovations, practices, and learning that form part of TK systems, and knowledge that is embodied in the traditional lifestyle of a community or people, or is contained in codified knowledge systems passed between generations. It is not limited to any specific technical field, and may include agricultural, environmental, and medicinal knowledge, and knowledge associated with genetic resources.

B.4: Eligibility for Protection

Protection should be extended at least to that TK that is:

(i) generated, preserved, and transmitted in a traditional and intergenerational context;
(ii) distinctively associated with a traditional or indigenous community or people which preserves and transmits it between generations; and
(iii) integral to the cultural identity of an indigenous or traditional community or people recognized as holding the knowledge through a form of custodianship, guardianship, collective ownership, or cultural responsibility, such as a sense of obligation to preserve, use, and transmit the knowledge appropriately, or a sense that to permit misappropriation or demeaning usage would be harmful or offensive; this relationship may be expressed formally or informally by customary or traditional practices, protocols, or laws.

B.5: Beneficiaries of Protection

Protection of TK should be for the principal benefit of the holders of knowledge in accordance with the relationship described under "eligibility for protection." Protection should, in particular, benefit the indigenous and traditional communities and peoples that develop, maintain, and identify culturally with TK and seek to pass it on between generations, as well as recognized individuals within these communities and peoples. Entitlement to the benefits of protection should, as far as possible and appropriate, take account of the customary protocols, understandings, laws, and practices of these communities and peoples. Benefits from protection should be appropriate to the cultural and social context, and the needs and aspirations, of the beneficiaries of protection.

B.6: Equitable Compensation and Recognition of Knowledge Holders

1. Commercial or industrial use of TK should be subject to just and appropriate compensation for the benefit of the traditional holder of the knowledge, when such use has gainful intent and confers a technological or commercial advantage, and when compensation would be consistent with fairness and equity in relation to holders of the knowledge in view of the circumstances in which the user acquired the knowledge. Liability for compensation should, in particular, arise where the knowledge was accessed or acquired in a manner that creates a reasonable expectation that benefits from such use should be shared equitably, and where the user is aware of the distinctive association of the knowledge with a certain community or people. Compensation should be in a form that responds to the express needs of the TK holders and is culturally appropriate.
2. Use of TK for noncommercial purposes need not incur an obligation for compensation, but suitable benefit-sharing from such uses should be encouraged, including access to research outcomes and involvement of the source community in research and educational activities.
3. Those using TK beyond its traditional context should make every reasonable endeavor to identify the source and origin of the knowledge, to acknowledge its holders as the source of the TK, and to use and refer to the knowledge in a manner that respects and acknowledges the cultural values of its holders.

B.7: Principle of Prior Informed Consent

1. The principle of prior informed consent should govern any direct access or acquisition of TK from its traditional holders, subject to these principles and relevant national laws.
2. Legal systems or mechanisms for obtaining prior informed consent should ensure legal certainty and clarity; should not create burdens for traditional holders and legitimate users of TK; should ensure that restrictions on access to TK are transparent and based on legal grounds; and should provide for mutually agreed terms for the equitable sharing of benefits arising from the use of that knowledge.
3. The holder of TK shall be entitled to grant prior informed consent for access to TK, or to approve the grant of such consent by an appropriate national authority, as provided by applicable national legislation.

B.8: Exceptions and Limitations

1. The application and implementation of protection of TK should not adversely affect:
   (i) the continued availability of TK for the customary practice, exchange, use, and transmission of TK by its holders;
   (ii) the use of traditional medicine for household purposes, use in government hospitals, or for other public health purposes; and
   (iii) other fair use or fair dealing with TK, including use of TK in good faith that commenced prior to the introduction of protection.

2. In particular, national authorities may exclude from the principle of prior informed consent the fair use of TK that is already readily available to the general public, provided that users of that TK provide equitable compensation for industrial and commercial uses of that TK.

B.9: Duration of Protection

Protection of TK against misappropriation should last as long as the TK fulfils eligibility for protection, in particular as long as it is maintained by TK holders, remains distinctively associated with them, and remains integral to their collective identity. Possible additional protection against other acts and more specific forms of protection, which may be made available by relevant national or regional laws or measures, shall specify the duration of protection under those laws or measures.

B.10: Application in Time

Protection of TK newly introduced in accordance with these principles should be applied to new acts of acquisition, appropriation, and use of TK. Recent acquisition or uses of TK should be regularized as far as possible within a certain period of that protection coming into force, subject to equitable treatment of rights acquired by third parties in good faith. Long-standing prior use in good faith may be permitted to continue, but the user should be encouraged to acknowledge the source of the TK concerned and to share benefits with the original holders of the knowledge.

B.11: Formalities

1. Eligibility for protection of TK against acts of misappropriation and other acts of unfair competition should not require any formalities.
2. In the interests of transparency, certainty, and the conservation of TK, relevant national authorities may maintain registers or other records of TK, where appropriate and subject to relevant policies, laws, and procedures, and the needs and aspirations of TK holders. Such registers may be associated with specific forms of protection, and should not compromise the status of hitherto undisclosed TK or the interests of TK holders in relation to undisclosed elements of their knowledge.

B.12: Consistency with the General Legal Framework

1. In case of TK that relates to components of biological diversity, access to, and use of, that TK shall be consistent with national laws regulating access to those components of biological diversity. Permission to access TK does not imply permission to use associated genetic resources and *vice versa.*
2. TK protection should be consistent with existing IP systems and supportive of the applicability of relevant international IP standards to the benefit of holders of TK.
3. Nothing in these Principles shall be interpreted to derogate from existing obligations that national authorities have to each under the Paris Convention and other international IP agreements.

B.13: Administration and Enforcement of Protection

1. An appropriate national or regional authority, or authorities, should be competent for:
   (i) distributing information about TK protection and conducting public awareness and advertising campaigns to inform TK holders and other stakeholders about the availability, scope, use, and enforcement of TK protection;
   (ii) determining whether an act pertaining to TK constitutes an act of misappropriation of, or another act of unfair competition in relation to, that knowledge;
   (iii) determining whether prior informed consent for access to and use of TK has been granted;
   (iv) determining equitable compensation; determining whether a user of TK is liable to pay equitable compensation; and, if the user is liable, as appropriate, facilitating and administering the payment and use of equitable compensation;
   (v) determining whether a right in TK has been acquired, maintained, or infringed, and determining remedies;
   (vi) assisting, where possible and appropriate, holders of TK to acquire, use, exercise, and enforce their rights over their TK.
2. Measures and procedures developed by national and regional authorities to give effect to protection in accordance with these Principles should be fair and equitable, should be accessible, appropriate, and not burdensome for holders of TK, and should provide safeguards for legitimate third-party interests and the interests of the general public.

B.14: International and Regional Protection

Legal and administrative mechanisms should be established to provide effective protection in national systems for the TK of foreign rightsholders. Measures should be established to facilitate, as far as possible, the acquisition, management, and enforcement of such protection for the benefit of TK holders in foreign countries.

CHAPTER FORTY-FIVE

Protecting Maori Heritage in New Zealand

Maui Solomon

INTRODUCTION

Increasingly, Maori traditional knowledge (TK) or matauranga Maori in all its various forms is being seen as a way of adding value to commercial products and services, ranging from Sony PlayStation games, to designer clothes, sports shoes, computer games, children's toys, pharmaceutical, food, and cosmetic products, sports, beverages, jewelry, telecommunication, airlines, rugby, motor vehicles, and even international singers, actors, and boxers sporting Maori-inspired images and designs on their bodies. And this is just a sample of what currently exists out there in the market place!

TK is also regarded as a valuable source of information by "bio-prospectors" searching for plants with bio-active compounds with potential for commercial exploitation, particularly in the so-called underdeveloped countries of the world.

So what is it about Maori knowledge and TK in general that makes it so appealing to western consumers? And what exactly is TK anyway, and what makes it so special that it should be afforded any different form of protection than any other knowledge? Who are the rightful proprietors of that knowledge and should access to its use be constrained or controlled in some way – and if so, by whom? Is the existing intellectual property rights (IPR) regime adequate for recognizing and protecting that knowledge? What are the issues and problems around access and use of TK? What is currently being done to address these issues both locally and internationally? These are some of the questions that I endeavour to address in this paper.

WHAT IS TRADITIONAL KNOWLEDGE?

A kaumatua of Ngati Kahungunu defined matauranga Maori or TK in these terms:

"Matauranga Maori in a traditional context means the knowledge, comprehension or understanding of everything visible or invisible that exists across the universe (i.e.: Aorangi sometimes referred to as Rangi and Papa). This meaning is related to the modern context as Maori research, science and technology principles and practices."

Tribal Elders giving evidence to the Waitangi Tribunal hearing the Wai 262 claim to indigenous flora and fauna and cultural and intellectual property rights ("the Wai 262 claim) explained that matauranga Maori has as its basis the notion of whakapapa or genealogical interconnectedness, leading to the following characteristics:

the inter-relatedness of all things;
the basis of knowledge being in the natural environment;
the inseparability of the spiritual (tapu) and life force (mauri) from every aspect of knowledge.

Seen in these terms, knowledge is not just an intellectual pursuit or outcome, it encompasses the physical and metaphysical, the tangible and the intangible. For Maori, the TK of a thing cannot be separated from its culture or context. The same or similar values and attributes of TK are held by Indigenous and traditional peoples the world over. The values associated with the knowledge cannot be separated from the knowledge itself.

This wide definition is consistent with the findings of Mrs. Erica Irene Daes, Special Rapporteur of the Sub-Commission on Prevention of Discrimination and Protection of Minorities, and Chairperson of the Working Group of Indigenous Populations, that it is more appropriate to refer to the collective cultural heritage of each Indigenous people rather than to make distinctions between Indigenous peoples' "cultural property" and "intellectual property." According to Daes, any attempt "to try to subdivide the heritage of Indigenous peoples into separate legal categories such as 'cultural,' 'artistic' or 'intellectual' or into separate elements such as songs, stories, science or sacred sites," would be artificial. She believes "all elements of heritage should be managed and protected as a single, interrelated whole."

Typically, the attributes of TK are collective by nature in that the knowledge belongs to the corpus of the tribe rather than exclusively to individuals. However, there are cases in which certain individuals within the tribe are the designated custodians of the knowledge, but this is usually held for the benefit of the group. The knowledge is also intergenerational in that it is passed from one generation to the next. It is the way in which tribes define who they are and their relationship to one another and to the world around them. For this reason, the IPRs as a system of private and exclusive property rights with limited duration as to time is not seen as the most appropriate means of recognising or protecting this wider concept of TK or what may better be termed "total heritage protection." However, in the absence of new legal frameworks, *sui generis* systems of protection and policies for protecting TK (which are currently the subject of discussion and debate by the Inter-Governmental Committee of The World Intellectual Property Organization [WIPO]), Indigenous peoples are examining ways in which the current system may be utilized as a means of affording some form of protection. Some of these means are discussed later in this chapter.

Thus, in the context of IPRs and commercialisation of TK, which focuses almost exclusively on financial incentives, problems are often encountered when that knowledge is used without the prior informed consent of the knowledge holders, is used in a culturally offensive manner, or is used in some other exploitative way inconsistent with the cultural mores of the knowledge holders.

CONTEMPORARY MANIFESTATIONS OF TRADITIONAL KNOWLEDGE

Indigenous and traditional peoples and their cultures do not exist in a vacuum. That is to say, their culture continues to evolve. So it is not just the past that is in need of protection but also the manifestations and expressions of that knowledge base for the present and future. For example, contemporary Maori artworks are rapidly growing in popularity worldwide. Many of these artworks are inspired by traditional designs from the tribe or culture of the artist concerned. An interesting issue is the extent of any obligations that these Maori artists have to acknowledge the provenance of their designs. Although this will depend largely on the individual concerned, most Maori artists (be they musicians, writers, performers, painters, or potters) I know take very seriously their obligations to their own and other tribes' knowledge and imagery. They would not consciously or deliberately use a design in a way that was offensive to their own or another tribe. One Maori artist whose paintings have a distinctive style bases her work on designs from her own hapu (sub-tribe) and marae (traditional meeting house), but does so with the support and approval of the hapu and marae concerned. Some years ago, this artist had to defend her works, which had been used by a large New Zealand corporate without her knowledge or consent. Eventually the matter was settled out of court because it was a clear case of copyright infringement.

A collateral issue would have been the right of the tribal collective to sue for misuse of their designs had the artist not done so. This issue has come up in the context of Aboriginal artists seeking to protect their designs (based on tribal collective knowledge) from being misappropriated. The courts in the Bulun Bulun case made observed that the artist has a fiduciary relationship to act in the best interests of his or her own tribe, however, the copyright laws as they stand today would not permit the community to sue independently if the artists did not do so. In Bulun, community was joined as a co-plaintiff.

WHO OWNS TRADITIONAL KNOWLEDGE?

"Everyone now speaks of their culture... in the context of national or international threats to its existence. This does not mean a simple and nostalgic desire for teepees and tomahawks or some fetishized repositories of a pristine identity.... What the self-consciousness of 'culture' does signify is the demand of the peoples for their own space within the world cultural order."

Nicholas and Bannister comment on the issue of cultural ownership that:

"A strong association between cultural knowledge and cultural identity is reflected not only in society's material culture... but in the intellectual aspects of cultural traditions. Language, for example, is a very important contributor to Indigenous cultural identity. Given the strength of this association, it is clear why control of knowledge is at the heart of the issue – not simply for economic reasons but because control is integral to the definition or restoration of cultural identity for present and future Indigenous societies."

For many, if not most, Indigenous peoples, control over their own destiny and reclamation of their identities as distinct and unique peoples is at the heart of their efforts to claim ownership and control over their own cultural knowledge and heritage. The globalization of world markets, the omnipotence of transnational companies, and the increasing trend towards homogeneity within western and developed countries in particular, are increasing the threats to the existence of many of these Indigenous cultures. Add to that the horrors that many of these cultures have endured over many centuries, the increasing instances of cultural rip-offs, 'bio-piracy,' and misappropriation of TK and it is little wonder that Indigenous peoples today are crying out "*enough*!" This is our culture; we "own" it; and we will decide how it is used, by whom it is used, and for what purposes it is used.

In the case of my own Moriori tribe, the Indigenous peoples of Rekohu or Chatham Islands (800 kilometres east of New Zealand), reclaiming our identity as a people has been fundamental to our cultural renaissance over the past 20 years. When my grandfather, Tame Horomona Rehe (also known as Tommy Solomon), the last known Moriori of full blood, died in 1933, the "race" was declared to be extinct. For decades prior to that, Moriori had been the subject of great fascination among historians, anthropologists, and enthnologists alike. Most had believed that Moriori, who had outlawed warfare and killing and had lived in peace for 500 years prior to the arrival of Europeans and Maori from New Zealand in the early 1800s, were racially inferior to Maori and a degenerate race of people. Anthropologists collected bones and skulls in an attempt to prove the Darwinian theory that only the fit survive: As Michael King records in "Moriori: A People Rediscoverd":

"Nobody in New Zealand – and few elsewhere in the world – has been subjected to group slander as intense and as damaging as that heaped upon the Moriori. They were regarded by many Victorians as the lowest in God's hierarchy of created beings; and by non-Christians as negative proof of the Darwinian precept that only the fit survived. After 1835 Maori colonists despised them, enslaved them for a generation and referred to them contemptuously, in the borrowed currency of racism, as "black fellas."

Generations of Moriori descendants had grown up trying to hide their identity for fear of persecution and ridicule and others, like my own family, knew precious little about our culture and were taught at school that we either never existed or we were just a "Pakeha" created myth.

Today, as a result of massive efforts that Moriori ourselves have made over the past twenty years, we are reclaiming our identity and our land and fishery resources in and around the Chatham Islands, and are currently in the process of negotiating a settlement of our Treaty claim with the Crown. On

21 January 2005, we officially opened our marae and cultural centre to the world, an occasion expected to double the size of the population of the Chathams (currently 700 people) and which included as invited guests the Prime Minister, Governor General, and Chief Justice of New Zealand and representatives and dignitaries from all the major tribal groupings throughout New Zealand.

The point of sharing this with you is to reinforce that no matter how dire the circumstances of a people or culture may be or become, there is a strong and indomitable human need to know who we are and where we have come from. The most rewarding aspect of the Moriori renaissance is the hope and joy that it has given to so many of our people who knew little or nothing of their Moriori heritage.

And what has this to do with owning TK? Without the control over our lands, our resources, and our stories, Moriori culture and identity were almost destroyed. To add insult to injury, historians distorted the truth about who the Moriori were and this became accepted orthodoxy within the educational system of New Zealand for 150 years. But we have struggled back from the brink of oblivion. And now that we are on the cusp of a new dawning for our people, we are acutely aware of the need to determine our own future. To do this, we must exercise a degree of control and, indeed, "ownership" over the means and the tools by which that will be accomplished. This includes our own hokopapa (genealogies) songs, legends, designs, histories, sites of significance, fisheries, lands, customs (many of which are now being "refurbished"), artifacts, human remains, and indeed all of our cultural and intellectual property. Already, there are examples of Moriori cultural images being used to sell clothing, cushions, jewellery, and other products and this is being done without consultation or permission of Moriori. But Moriori are determined that we will survive and prosper into the next millennium with our cultural values and knowledge base intact. That does not mean denying anyone else their culture or knowledge because fundamental to the Moriori ethos was the belief that different peoples could co-exist together in peace and share the resources the land has to offer.

Nor do Moriori have a problem with non-Moriori using our cultural images and designs, provided they ask us first and appropriate conditions are agreed upon. There are some images that are simply not appropriate for use on certain products such as food or clothing. Unless one knows the culture and stories of these images, one can easily cause offence without knowing it. It has been my experience that many unauthorised users of cultural designs are often oblivious of the offence they cause. To this extent, educational material and voluntary codes of conduct or guidelines would be very helpful to raise awareness of these issues among the wider general public.

OWNERSHIP VERSUS GUARDIANSHIP

In the context of many Indigenous cultures, the notion of ownership can be problematic. As one respected elder once told me, the only land that could truly be said to be "owned" in a traditional sense was the soil beneath the fingernails of a chief when he died. Many Indigenous cultures are uncomfortable with the idea of ownership because traditionally they have always acted as guardians and custodians of the land and knowledge for future generations. However, in today's modern, materialistic world, concepts of property and ownership are all pervasive. The more one owns, the better off one is said to be. Indigenous peoples, and certainly, Maori are no exception in this regard, are required to articulate their concerns and claims in the language and way of understanding of the majority culture. For generations, Maori have talked about and applied their responsibilities of kaitiakitanga (loosely akin to customary guardianship), but very little political or legal traction is gained and the point is often ignored or lost.

But as soon as legal claims to ownership over resources are made through the courts, suddenly everyone starts paying attention. It is the reality of the modern world we live in. The furore over the current foreshore and seabed debate illustrates the point. For many years, Maori endeavored to engage the government in constructive dialogue over the nature and extent of their rights and interests in the marine environment. For years, they were ignored. As a last resort, Maori sought redress through the courts to uphold their claims to customary "ownership" and having succeeded in convincing the highest court in the land that they have a right to be heard, the government introduced a bill to parliament that will effectively deny Maori their rights to legal redress. The issue did not start out as a dispute over ownership but has evolved into an issue that has now divided the nation.

Similarly, claims in relation to cultural and IP rights protection by Maori are being made in the context of having to fight fire with fire. If the knowledge and culture are being exploited and misappropriated by unscrupulous or uninformed companies and individuals, then Maori and other Indigenous peoples will be forced to assert their prior rights over their own culture and heritage and, if necessary, do so in the name of protecting and claiming ownership over their cultural and IP rights. As one commentator has astutely observed in a world in which it is hard for Indigenous peoples to make their voice heard:

> . . . intellectual property rights is a forceful sound bite. Precisely because it rolls so much up into a bundle, precisely because it has rhetorical inflationary potential, and precisely because it invokes property, it is a political slogan of power. Power is not always so easy to come by.

WHAT IS BEING DONE TO PROTECT TRADITIONAL KNOWLEDGE?

There are a range of tools, mechanisms, and processes that have been developed in recent years to protect TK and biological resources of indigenous peoples. These initiatives have been largely uncoordinated and ad hoc. They include:

- International Conventions (International Labour Organization [ILO] 169, CBD), WIPO, (International

Inter-Governmental Committee IGC) process, and the Draft Declaration on the Rights of Indigenous Peoples (DDRIP);

- Regional initiatives such as the Draft Model Law being proposed for the South Pacific relating to TK and genetic resources;
- National laws in some countries like the Philippines and Peru;
- Local initiatives by Indigenous communities, including advocacy, use of media, and awareness raising;
- Contractual arrangements between Indigenous communities, researchers and other users of TK, including know-how and licensing agreements;
- Voluntary codes of conduct and research protocols such as the Code of Ethics of the International Society of Ethnobiologists;
- Increasing use of IP tools by Indigenous peoples for claiming rights and defensive protection of TK such as copyright, trademark, and patents.

PROS AND CONS OF IPR AS A TOOL FOR "PROTECTING" TRADITIONAL KNOWLEDGE

As previously noted, the IP rights system in its current form is not adequate to protect TK in its widest context, particularly with regard to the relationship between indigenous peoples and biological resources. As noted by Darrell Posey:

"Intellectual Property Rights are inadequate and inappropriate for protection of traditional ecological knowledge and community of resources because they:

- Recognise individual, not collective rights;
- Require a specific act of invention;
- Simplify ownership regimes;
- Stimulate commercialisation [which may not always be negative];
- Recognise only market values;
- Are subject to economic powers and manipulation;
- Are difficult to monitor and enforce;
- Are expensive, complicated and time consuming."

To this list could be added the limited duration of IP rights, which do not accord with the intergenerational nature of Indigenous peoples' world view.

That is not to say that aspects of the IP rights system are not useful for the protection of aspects of TK and expressions of that knowledge. At best, the IP system can only offer piecemeal protection without addressing the underlying and fundamental issues that underpin Indigenous peoples' claims for self-determination and better protection of basic human rights. However, because of, in part, a lack of alternative mechanisms, Indigenous peoples are increasing their use of IP for protecting their rights. Examples of such use in New Zealand include:

Trademark protection – The Maori Made Mark, "Toi Iho," licences Maori artists to use the Mark to authenticate their works and provide consumers with quality assurance that the products are made by genuine Maori artists and to distinguish them from the many "copy-cat" products in the market place. Some key features of the process to establish the Mark are worthy of note as an example of how some of the expectations of Indigenous peoples can be accommodated within the current system:

The process followed a series of extensive hui (meetings) with Maori artists from around the country, who were involved in the key decision making around the words and designs used in the Mark.

The Mark was seen as an interim step to provide a level of protection to Maori artists under the current IP system until new and more responsive mechanisms to accommodate Maori aspirations for protecting their knowledge can be developed (such as the "Tikanga Maori Protection Framework" advocated by some of the Wai 262 claimants – see Appendix Two in this chapter).

Although the Mark is owned by a quasi-government agency (Te Waka Toi), there is an agreement with Maori that the proprietorial rights to the Mark will be transferred and assigned to an autonomous Maori body in due course.

Copyright protection – A Maori artist filed proceedings in the High Court claiming breach of copyright of her painting, which had been sold to one party and used by a third party without her knowledge or consent. The matter was eventually settled out of court. Had it proceeded to hearing, it would have been the first case of its kind to come before the New Zealand courts.

Contractual Agreements – A Maori tribe has entered into an agreement with a Crown Research Institute and a University to research "rongoa Maori" or Maori knowledge of certain plants and their medicinal qualities. The agreement provides that the TK remains in the ownership of the tribe and benefit-sharing arrangements have been negotiated, ensuring that the tribe receives at least thirty percent of any returns from any commercialisation of the knowledge. The agreement stipulates that any IPR arising from the project will be owned exclusively by the tribe. A Maori scientist is leading the project and is a critical factor in its success to date.

Patents – A Maori tribe from the North Island is working with the Cancer Genetics Research team at the University of Otago, to find a cure for a form of gastric cancer that has been prevalent in the family for generations. The project involves some 12,000 Maori who have agreed to provide genealogical and medical information to the research team in an endeavour to help identify and isolate the mutant gene causing the cancer. One aspect of the agreement is that any IPR arising from the project will be jointly owned and any financial benefits that arise will go towards further research.

OTHER INITIATIVES

Advocacy and Education – An increasing number of Maori individuals and organisations who are offended by the misappropriation of their TK by 'outsiders' are taking direct action in the form of writing to the companies concerned to express their objection and, in some cases, offering to work with the companies concerned, first, to help educate them and offer suggestions and alternatives to ensure that they understand why Maori are offended and, second, to explore ways in which the parties may work jointly together to develop a relationship beneficial to both (e.g., Lego, Sony Playstation, Microsoft, TechoMarine, Ford Motor Company, etc). In most of these cases, initial contact is made by writing to the company concerned. Invariably, the response comes back (if any) that they were not aware that any offence had been caused and that Maori should be grateful that their culture is being promoted internationally! In the case of Lego using Maori names on 'bionicle' toys, the media played a large part in raising the profile of the issue to a worldwide audience. Lego's response was to send a company representative to New Zealand from Denmark to meet with the Wai 262 claimants who had raised the concerns. The representative agreed not to make any second-generation toys using Maori names and expressed an interest in working with Maori to develop a voluntary code of conduct for toy manufacturing companies who were interested in using TK in developing products. Unfortunately, to date, no other company has expressed such an interest, so the initiative is on hold.

In all of these cases, the companies concerned were not applying for IP rights.

Personal experience to date leads me to the view that an education and awareness campaign about the use and misuse of TK by companies is needed.

Legislation – In the form of amendments to the Trade Marks Act 2002 providing for new grounds to reject an application if it is "offensive to a significant section of the community, including Maori." It also establishes a Maori Advisory Group to assist in determining whether any application is in breach of this provision. Amendments are also proposed to the Patents Act along similar lines.

THE CONVENTION ON BIOLOGICAL DIVERSITY, ARTICLE 8J AND RELATED PROVISIONS

The CBD and the IGC of the WIPO are two of the more prominent international initiatives exploring ways in which cultural and IP rights can be protected.

The maintenance of cultural diversity is now regarded by the world at large as necessary to the maintenance of biological diversity because Article 8j of the CBD talks about respecting, preserving, and maintaining TK as it relates to sustainable use of biological diversity and that this must be done with the approval and involvement of the holders of such knowledge. But it is subject to the caveat that such protections are "subject to national legislation." In other words, each Contracting Party (national government) is only obliged to respect and maintain such knowledge as far as possible and as appropriate to their own country's circumstances.

The establishment of the Ad Hoc Open-Ended Inter-Sessional Working Group on Article 8(j) and Related Provisions has enabled Indigenous peoples greater input into the work of the CBD process. But, although the work of that group is to be commended, there is still a feeling that ultimately the destiny of TK holders is in the hands of those who are Parties, as opposed to those (such as Indigenous and traditional peoples), who are merely Observers at the COP.

WORLD INTELLECTUAL PROPERTY ORGANISATION

Similarly, the WIPO, IGC process only permits Indigenous peoples observer status and their ability to have effective input is impeded by the lack of participation in these processes (attributable mainly to the high costs associated with attending conferences in Geneva) and the very limited amount of time allocated to Indigenous representatives to make their interventions. Nevertheless, there are governments in this forum, including the New Zealand government, who are supportive and sympathetic of initiatives to protect TK from misappropriation and advocate for the greater participation of Indigenous peoples.

One of the important initiatives being considered by the IGC is the elaboration of an international regime for protection of TK, genetic resources, and traditional cultural expressions. The Indigenous Peoples caucus representing the eleven indigenous organisations present at the Sixth Meeting of the IGC in March 2004 gave conditional support for an international regime and called for it to adopt the following fundamental principles:

> Indigenous peoples are recognized as custodians and owners of their knowledge, traditional cultural expressions and natural resources and have the exclusive right to control and manage their knowledge, expressions and resources. States must affirm that the land and territorial rights of Indigenous peoples are fundamental to the retention of Indigenous knowledge and cultural practices pursuant to the implementation of relevant international obligations.
>
> An international regime must expressly affirm the right of Indigenous peoples to restrict and/or exclude access to their knowledge, traditional cultural expressions and natural resources.
>
> An international regime must ensure that the right to prior informed consent of Indigenous peoples is guaranteed and protected, as a fundamental principle in the exercise of self-determination and sovereignty of Indigenous peoples.
>
> The right of prior informed consent must be maintained throughout any access and benefit sharing arrangements where there is potential change of permitted use or third party involvement.
>
> An international regime must enable the effective implementation, application and enforcement of Indigenous customary laws and cultural practices. In circumstances where there is a conflict, Indigenous customary laws and cultural practices shall prevail over domestic law or an international regime.

A full copy of the Indigenous intervention is attached as an Appendix to this chapter.

The seventh meeting of the IGC took place in Geneva (1–5 November 2004) and considered what the next steps will be in the process of elaborating an international regime.

ILO CONVENTION 169

The ILO Convention 169 is the only legally binding international instrument specifically intended to protect Indigenous and tribal peoples in its commitment to community ownership and local control of lands and resources. However, to date, only eleven countries have signed up to it.

DRAFT DECLARATION ON THE RIGHTS OF INDIGENOUS PEOPLES

For Indigenous peoples, DDRIP is the most important statement of basic requirements for adequate rights and protection. Some of the provisions include:

Right to restitution and redress for cultural, intellectual, religious, or spiritual property that is taken or used without authorisation;
Right to free and informed consent (prior informed consent);
Right to special measures to control, develop, and protect their sciences, technologies, and cultural manifestations, including human and other genetic resources, seed, medicines, knowledge of the properties of flora and fauna, oral traditions, literature, designs, and visual performing arts.

For more than twenty years, the DDRIP has been developed, guided by hundreds of Indigenous representatives in consultation with the UN Working Group on Indigenous Populations of the Geneva Human Rights Centre. However, the future of the Draft Declaration is by no means certain with recent attempts by member states to seriously water down the protections afforded to the Indigenous peoples under the declaration.

DECLARATIONS OF INDIGENOUS PEOPLES' ORGANISATIONS

In addition to international instruments, there are a plethora of Indigenous peoples' declarations that have been developed over the past 25 years calling for recognition and protection of rights. Included among these is the "Mataatua Declaration on the Cultural and Intellectual Property Rights of Indigenous Peoples" that was convened in Whakatane, Aotearoa/New Zealand by the nine tribes of Mataatua in June 1993 and currently has more than 150 organisations signed up to it.

C. Mohi, "Matauranga Maori – A National Resource," a paper prepared for the Ministry of Research Science and Technology, 1993, pages 1–3, quoted from David Williams' report on "Matauranga Maori and Taonga," Waitangi Tribunal Publication 2001, page 15. (Recorded as document #K6 on the Wai 262 Record of Inquiry).

L. Watson, "Test Tube and the Kete: Science and Matauranga Maori in the Wai 262 claim," paper to the Science, Culture and Fear Conference, 22 November 2002, Te Papa Tongarewa, Wellington.

Study on the Protection of the Cultural and Intellectual Property of indigenous Peoples, E/CN.4/SUB.2/1993/28, 28 July1993.

Quoted from Terri Janke, "Our Culture: Our Future" A Report on Australian Indigenous Cultural and Intellectual Property Rights, page 2. In her report, Janke adopts the following definition of "Indigenous Cultural and Intellectual Property":

> "Indigenous Cultural and Intellectual Property" refers to Indigenous peoples' rights to their heritage. Heritage comprises all objects, sites and knowledge, the nature or use of which has been transmitted or continues to be transmitted from generation to generation, and which is regarded as pertaining to a particular Indigenous group or its territory.

Heritage includes:

Literary, performing, and artistic works (including songs, music, dances, stories, ceremonies, symbols, languages, and designs);
scientific, agricultural, technical, and ecological knowledge (including cultigens, medicines, and phenotypes of flora and fauna);
all items of moveable cultural property;
human remains and tissues;
immovable cultural property (including sacred sites and historically significant sites and burial grounds);
documentation of Indigenous peoples' heritage in archives, film, photographs, videotape, or audiotape and all forms of media;
the heritage of an Indigenous people is a living one and includes objects, knowledge and literary and artistic works which may be created in the future based on that heritage.

Sahlins, M. 1999. 'What is anthropological enlightenment? Some lessons of the twentieth century'. *Annual Reviews in Anthropology* 29: i–xxiii.

Nicholas, G. P., and K. P. Bannister. 2004. "Copyrighting the Past? Emerging Intellectual Property Rights Issues in Archaeology," in *Current Anthropology*, Volume 45, Number 3, June 2004, page 339.

King, M. 1989. *Moriori: A People Rediscovered*, Penguin Books (NZ) Limited.

Strathern, M. 2004. Department of Anthropology, University of Cambridge, in a commentary on a paper by Michael F. Brown, "Can Culture be Copyrighted" *Current Anthropology*, Vol 39, No. 2 (April., 1998), pp 193–222 at page 216.

Posey, D. A. Chapter one, 'Introduction: Culture and Nature-The Inextricable Link' in "Cultural and Spiritual Values of Biodiversity." 1999, page 12. A Complimentary Contribution to the Global Biodiversity Assessment. 1999. Edited by Darrell Addison Posey.

A copy of all these declarations are included as Appendix 1 to the UNEP Publication "Cultural and Spiritual Values of Biodiversity." 1999. A Complimentary Contribution to the Global Biodiversity Assessment. 1999. Edited by Darrell Addison Posey.

THE WAI 262 CLAIM

The most significant attempt to date by Maori to protect their cultural and intellectual property rights has been in the form of a claim by a number of tribes to the Waitangi Tribunal. The Statement of Claim, which was filed in 1991 and amended in 1997, states as follows:

THE CLAIM

The claim relates to te tino rangatiratanga of Ngati Kuri, Te Rarawa and Ngati Wai in respect of indigenous flora and fauna me o ratou taonga katoa (and all their treasures) within their respective tribal rohe, including but not limited to te reo, matauranga, knowledge systems, laws, customs and values, whakairo, waahi tapu, biodiversity, natural resources, genetics and genetic derivatives, Maori symbols, images, designs, and their use and development and associated indigenous, cultural and customary heritage rights (including intellectual property and property rights) in relation to such taonga. 'Taonga' in this claim refers to all elements of the claimants' estates, material and non-material, tangible and intangible.

The claim has been described in various ways since it was filed with the Tribunal in 1991. It was the 262nd claim to be registered, hence the abridged version "Wai 262." It was initially described as a claim to indigenous flora and fauna. It has been called the "claim to intellectual and cultural property" or the "matauranga Maori claim." The statements of claim of some claimants refer to it as a claim to "indigenous flora and fauna me o ratou taonga katoa," a reference back to the second article of the Treaty of Waitangi. Perhaps it was best encapsulated by Professor Mason Durie, who, in giving evidence on behalf of the claimants in 2002, described the claim as "te ao Maori claim" – the claim about the Maori world.

Essentially, the claim is about ensuring that appropriate recognition, protection, and provision is made for Maori rights in relation to indigenous flora and fauna, their special relationship with that indigenous flora and fauna, and all knowledge and intellectual property rights that flow from that relationship. The claimants assert that these are rights that were guaranteed and protected under Article 2 of both the English and Maori versions of Te Tiriti o Waitangi/Treaty of Waitangi.

The Wai 262 claim seeks the protection of matauranga Maori from inappropriate use and its control by Maori. Included in the protection of knowledge is the knowledge system itself, and its internal mechanism for transmission, dissemination, tuition, and development. The evidence presented to the Tribunal has asserted that such systems existed at the time of the Treaty, but have been seriously eroded and disrespected to the point where the systems and the knowledge itself are at risk. This has been a consistent theme as the Tribunal has travelled from hapu to hapu to hear the testimony of elders.

In more recent times, there has been a growing recognition of the importance of matauranga Maori and its relationship and relevance to western science. As noted by Dr. Murray Parsons:

"If science is the study of the world around us using a hypothetico-deductive process (the scientific method) then this is not exclusive to western or European-derived cultural traditions but is also found in the cultures of all indigenous peoples. All indigenous peoples have science according to their needs and cultural understandings of their surroundings, the environment. The same thought processes that allowed Polynesians to voyage between the islands of the Pacific and to settle them, also has sent people into space. The term Maori Science has been used to emphasise Maori people too used the scientific method and that it is not the prerogative of western countries only."

Rongoa Maori or Maori Traditional Knowledge of Plants and Medicines

The Wai 262 claim also seeks to preserve and revive the practices of rongoa Maori or traditional Maori knowledge of native plants and their healing powers and the preparation of medicinal remedies based on those plants. Maori traditionally had an extensive knowledge of plants and their medicinal uses. The term rongoa Maori refers to traditional Maori medicine, to the practice of traditional Maori medicine, and the body of knowledge behind that practice. Tohunga or traditional healers had special knowledge of herbal plants and their uses. Many, if not most, of the practitioners of rongoa were elderly women. As one elderly expert on rongoa Maori explained in her evidence to the Waitangi Tribunal hearing the Wai 262 claim in 1997, "I know the plants and they know me." She knew what time of the year and what time of the day to collect plants from the ngahere or forest. She could not just collect from any forest but it had to be the forest with which she had a close physical and spiritual relationship. She described her power to heal as a gift from the Creator and that she was just a conduit between the gods and the plants in order to aid the healing process. She never demanded payment for her services because to do so would diminish the healing powers of the remedies she offered.

Robert McGowan, who is himself a practitioner of rongoa Maori, records that:

One of the most consistent themes that came through in my working with kaumatua and traditional healers, is that the foundation of rongoa Maori is taha wairua "spirituality"; not wai rakau "herbal medicine." The place of karakia (prayer) and tikanga (rules and protocols) – the appropriate rituals and traditions – is essential . . . There is an inclination in scientific research to reduce knowledge to terms that one can understand and then claim that that understanding is, in fact, an accurate description of the reality being investigated.

. . . What is needed is an understanding of the context in which that knowledge found its origins, an appreciation of the values and customs that govern its usage, and an acknowledgement of the priorities that experience has provided. Far from being subjective and therefore unscientific knowledge, such factors provide and enshrine a depth of knowledge that is both valid and important.

Figure 45.1. All Blacks.

Genetic Engineering Issues

The Wai 262 claimants have been concerned about issues of genetic engineering since prior to the lodgement of their claim in 1991. In particular, the likely prejudicial effects the release of genetically modified organisms (GMOs) into the environment will have on whakapapa of humans, plants, and animals and on the mauri and tapu of those organisms and the claimants responsibilities as kaitiaki. The claimants believe that there needs to be a great deal more research carried out under tightly controlled conditions to determine with more accuracy the long-term and cumulative impacts that the wholesale release of GMOs will have on the natural environment.

Commercial Interest in Maori Culture

This past decade has witnessed a marked growth in international interest in cultural heritage tourism and the use of Maori imagery, symbols, and designs to promote commercial products in a consumer hungry market increasingly seeking to gain an edge over their competitors. Tourists are attracted to the cultures of the Indigenous peoples, and their artwork, music, and designs are becoming highly prized commodities, and powerful marketing and branding tools. The use of Maori symbolism by Telecom, Air NZ, and Adidas in promoting the All Blacks, are some examples. More recently a plethora of internationally renowned companies including, Lego (use of Maori names on Bionicle toys), Sony (PlayStation game, "Mark of Kri," using Maori names and designs), TechnoMarine (watches and models with Maori names and imagery), Microsoft (use of Maori names and imagery in a computer game called "Asheron's Call"), a Danish restaurant (using Maori moko to promote food) and Ford Motor Company (Maori-inspired moko on a Hot Rod Pick-Up Truck), have jumped on the band wagon of using Maori designs and imagery to promote their products. The same phenomenon is being witnessed in other countries and states with Indigenous peoples, particularly Australia, North America, Hawaii, and Latin America.

* * *

Businesses in New Zealand are beginning to appreciate the added value and marketing opportunities that a distinctive Maori identity, Maori place names, and traditions give to

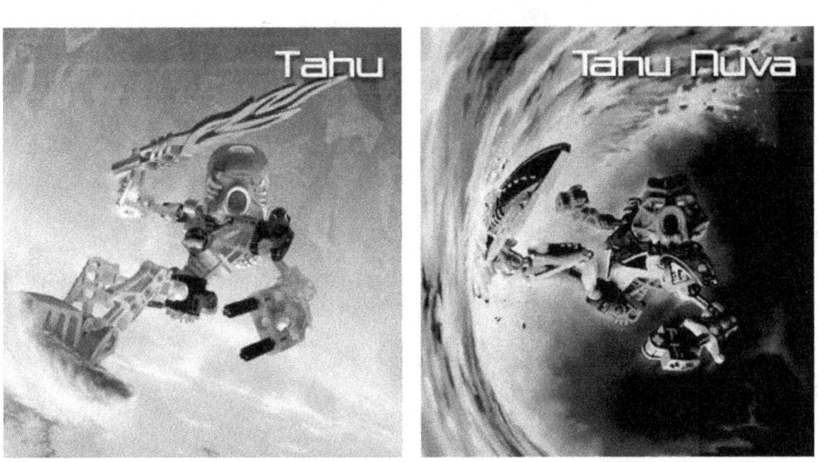

Figure 45.2. Lego.

100% PURE NEW ZEALAND
When we touch noses, or hongi, we're sharing the breath of life. With gentle presses, we offer peace, friendship and hospitality. It's a traditional welcome that is 100% pure New Zealand. www.purenz.com
New Zealand

Figure 45.3. Branding.

New Zealand businesses operating in the international market. As Brian Richards, marketing strategist for the Maori Made Mark, observed back in 1994:

> In worldwide research on New Zealand, 'sheep' and 'green' are the only two icons that stand out . . . we can actually add value using our indigenous products. It will come from our Maori people, our artists, our playwrights and designers. . . . Maori custom and culture is absolutely wonderful. There is potential for developing Maori icons to our culture. . . . I would love to see New Zealand borrow from Maori elements and use them in a modern context, because they help to position us worldwide. . . . By drawing on Maori culture and referencing, we could produce the most stunning textiles and fabric. Nobody yet has exploited Maori graphics and upholstery and curtaining fabrics etc. . . .

Some may argue that it is a positive thing for Maori culture to be promoted to an international audience in this way. Certainly, Maori are not against the use and development of their culture and intellectual property rights but insist that they have control over how their taonga (including in this context language, designs, symbols, and TK) are used, for what purposes they are used, and by whom they are used. It is offensive to many Maori (and certainly the Wai 262 claimants) that names such as "tohunga" are used on plastic toys and moko are used to promote food products, watches, and Hot Rod trucks. In the case of Ford Motor Company it purposefully associates the 'warrior' qualities of the wearer of traditional Maori moko with its Hot Rod truck, which is described on its Web site in the following manner:

> The leather-wrapped tonneau cover features a traditional Maori tribe tattoo that is die cut into the leather with black cow hair in the cut-out portions. The Maori are the Polynesian people of New Zealand. In moko, a type of Maori tattooing, shallow colored grooves in complex curvilinear designs were produced on the face by striking a miniature bone adze into the skin. Tattooed designs are thought by various peoples to provide magical protection against sickness or misfortune, or they serve to identify the wearer's rank, status or membership in a group.
>
> In Maori culture, an elegantly tattooed face was a great source of pride to a warrior, for it made him fierce in battle. . . . The F-150 has a great history and has consistently been the leader among full-size pick-ups – it is certainly fierce in battle.

In a letter written to TechnoMarine, Mr. Kingi Gilbert, a young Maori entrepreneur and an international advocate for better protection and respect for Maori cultural and intellectual property rights, had this to say about the unauthorised use of moko:

> There is a large body of [Maori] fighting against popular culture to have our designs respected. The widespread use of Maori images in pop culture is watering down the core values of Maori moko, it is making it less unique, and more commercial, but mostly, it loses its "ihi" or natural identifying force. It is seen as a commodity and not an identifying force, which a portion of it traditionally was.

Did you know that the moko was carved into the skin by bone chisel over a period of years? That it showed rank, achievements and history of the wearer? How do you think we feel today when we see those designs as "an identifying form" on people who know nothing about it? We don't receive any benefit from that at all, only hurt and pain. It doesn't respect our ancestors. It's like asking you to conduct a large press interview, but wear a Swatch branded hat and Mickey Mouse watch from Disneyland. Would you seriously allow yourself to be represented that way?

Another recent example of misappropriation of TK involves a German company registering a trademark over a Maori name. Moana Maniaopoto, a top New Zealand performing artist and musician who has written and produced a number of albums under her own name in New Zealand and has been a regular feature on the European touring circuit in recent years, was threatened in 2002 by the company with a court injunction and damages of 100,000 deutsche marks, for daring to use her own name, "Moana," on a CD of the same name. The company, Media XS, registered and based in Germany, had obtained a trademark for the name "Moana" with respect to a wide range of products and services throughout Europe, which included musical products. They argued that Moana could not use her own name on her CD because it was in violation of their registered trademark rights. Eventually, the matter was settled out of court by her German agents, agreeing to change the name on the CD to "Moana Maniapoto and The Tribe."

* * *

This case provides an example of the inadequacies of the current system of IPR to protect Maori TK in the public domain and how Maori names can be claimed and registered by others. Patent attorneys will argue that any knowledge in

Figure 45.4. Trademarking of Maori Names – "Moana."

the public domain is fair game for trademarking or other commercial use. The Wai 262 claimants and many other Maori have argued that it is not their fault that their knowledge has ended up in the public domain and has often got there through it being misappropriated in the first place. Just because it may be publicly available does not give people the right to misuse that knowledge for their own commercial gain without the consent of the custodians or proprietors of that knowledge.

As commercial interest in Indigenous culture, artwork, and knowledge continues to grow, tribes need to retain control over, regulate, and protect their cultural heritage rights if they are not to be debased in the pursuit of commercial gain. If companies want to use Maori images and designs then they should only do so with the consent and participation of those who are the knowledge holders. This would include acknowledgement of the knowledge holders and, where appropriate, the establishment of joint venture arrangements and the payment of royalties.

One of the difficulties for both Maori and private interests is the lack of any formal process for identifying where to go and to whom to speak in the rare instances in which commercial operators make efforts to obtain approval to use of traditional material. This is one of the key areas that the Wai 262 claim seeks to remedy by developing a framework and process within which these issues can be handled with efficiency and sensitivity. One proposal is to develop a framework of protection known as a "Tikanga Framework of Protection." This is set out in Appendix Two.

Unfortunately, the claim has been held up in the Waitangi Tribunal for the past two years because of administrative and resource difficulties. The claimants are understandably anxious to complete the hearing and obtain a report from the Tribunal so that appropriate recommendations may be made to ensure that the real work on developing a *sui generis* framework for protecting TK can begin.

Ka mutu (The End).

APPENDIX ONE

Sixth Meeting of the WIPO IGC on Intellectual Property and Genetic Resources, Traditional Knowledge and Folklore, Geneva, 15–19, March 2004.

Indigenous Peoples' Comments on Documents 6/6 and 6/12 Regarding a Prospective International Regime:

Mr. Chairman, this is a succinct statement representing a common ground among a group of Indigenous Peoples, particularly the following:

Aboriginal and Torres Strait Islander Commission, Australia (ATSIC), Foundation for Aboriginal and Islander Research Action (FAIRA), Assembly of First Nations, Call of the Earth, Canadian Indigenous Biodiversity Network, Coordinating Body of Indigenous Organizations of the Amazon Basin (COICA), Indigenous Peoples Caucus of the Creators Rights Alliance, Hoketehi Moriori Trust, Rekohu, Aotearoa (New Zealand), International Indian Treaty Council, the Kaska Dena Council and the Saami Council.

We are pleased to thank the Secretariat for its preparation of document 6/6 and the African Group on its thoughtful preparation of document 6/12, which we received on the first day of this meeting.

Mr. Chairman, we are supportive of the development of an international regime on the precondition that the following fundamental principles are included therein:

Indigenous peoples are recognized as custodians and owners of their knowledge, traditional cultural expressions and natural resources and have the exclusive right to control and manage their knowledge, expressions and resources.

States must affirm that the land and territorial rights of Indigenous Peoples are fundamental to the retention of Indigenous Knowledge and cultural practices pursuant to the implementation of relevant international obligations.

An international regime must expressly affirm the right of Indigenous peoples to restrict and/or exclude access to their knowledge, traditional cultural expressions and natural resources.

An international regime must ensure that the right to prior informed consent of Indigenous peoples is guaranteed and protected, as a fundamental principle in the exercise of self-determination and sovereignty of Indigenous peoples.

The right of prior informed consent must be maintained throughout any access and benefit sharing arrangements where there is potential change of permitted use or third party involvement.

An international regime must enable the effective implementation, application and enforcement of Indigenous customary laws and cultural practices.

In circumstances where there is a conflict, Indigenous customary laws and cultural practices shall prevail over domestic law or an international regime.

Mr. Chairman, we have studied document 6/12 with great interest. Even though we received it only on Monday, we have developed preliminary comments which we will provide to the Secretariat in written form. We emphasize that these amendments and additions are based upon a preliminary analysis. For clarity, we respectfully reserve our rights to revisit this framework document, if it becomes evolutionary in nature. Thank you, Mr. Chairman.

APPENDIX TWO

A Tikanga Maori Framework of Protection

A Tikanga Maori Framework of Protection would have some or all of the following features:

the system be developed by Maori;

the system be based in tikanga Maori, reflecting Maori cultural values and ethos;

inherent in this system will be the acknowledgement, protection and promotion of rights and obligations to manage, utilise and protect resources in accordance with Maori cultural values and preferences;

flexibility will be very important. Whatever structure or structures are chosen will need to be flexible enough to take account of issues that affect Maori in a national sense as well as at the regional and local marae level. The structure must also accommodate the rights of individuals such as Maori artists, carvers, musicians and designers.

how such a framework is mandated by Maori will be a vital and challenging ingredient. In New Zealand today there are many national bodies that represent Maori, including Maori Congress (an Iwi or tribal based organisation), New Zealand Maori Council (a statutory body), Maori Women's' Welfare League, The Confederation of United Tribes (based on the 1835 Declaration of Independence), and others. There are also various Iwi organizations and bodies, Land Trusts, Maori Incorporations and Marae trustees, to name a few. Indeed, one of the most challenging issues confronting Maoridom is the issue of mandate. Who speaks for the people? These issues will take some time to work through.

in terms of the resourcing of the framework, the claimants would seek an allocation of funds from the Crown (as part of their remedies package), to undertake nationwide consultation with tribes and urban Maori to discuss the formation of a structure. Funding would also be needed to implement and administer the new body on an ongoing basis.

Finally, there are considerations of enforceability. In order to enforce compliance with this new regime, some form of legal recognition and protection will be necessary within the current New Zealand legal system. But there may also be non-legal codes of ethics, and protocols containing rights and obligations, designed to educate and persuade voluntary compliance with the TMFP.

The TMFP might be responsible for:

- *acting as a referral body to Iwi (tribes), hapu (sub-tribes) or whanau (families) or individuals*
  Once it is determined at which level of Maori decision-making the relevant issue is most appropriately advanced. Where it was obvious that certain issues affected particular tribes, the issue would be immediately referred to that tribe to deal with. So, for example, if someone wanted to research the Pupu Harakeke (flax snail), they would have to deal with the Ngati Kuri people of the Far North. If it was a matter which affected Maori at a national level, then a national body could deal with and undertake research at that level;
- *acting as a support agency for Maori tribes and organisations in the undertaking of their own research*
- *liaising with mainstream government departments*;
- *consultative body with Maoridom*
  This would be a key component of the TMFP. Hui and consultation with Maori would need to take place on a regular basis;
- *assisting Maori in the formulation of policies to assist them in their role as kaitiaki of their various taonga (treasured things)*
  Policies might deal with issues of respect for cultural values, access, use and, where appropriate (and sanctioned by the tribe), commercial exploitation. Such policies themselves would have to be flexible to take account of the different tikanga and relationship that each tribe or hapu has with the taonga within their own rohe (tribal territories);
- *acting as a principal point of contact for those wishing to access and exploit traditional Maori knowledge of native flora and fauna for commercial gain*
- *education about Maori cultural values and their application within a modem day context*
  This might include the general public, government agencies, and the corporate sector.

CHAPTER FORTY-SIX

Culture, Science, and Indigenous Technology

Hester du Plessis

There is an urgent need for new forms of communication and cooperation, for instance, in the cultural industries, joint research and monitoring of cultural change and cultural development, integration of economy and culture. Faced with the questions of the relationship between culture, S&T development, commercialisation of culture, cultural industries and various alternative forms of culture, all countries are looking for new modes of communication. That is why the entire potential of South African – educational, technological, scientific – should become involved in cultural cooperation.

(Zegeye. 1998/1999:219)

INTRODUCTION

Discourse on research and research-related issues are currently taking place among developing countries within the academic, educational, social, political, and cultural arenas. Academic concepts and definitions of culture, identity, discourse, colonialism, and even politics and power structures are being redefined and adapted to comply with the new requirements of the technological era and its relevant issues and interests. Academic disciplines are, at the same time, being re-evaluated.

There is academic concern among researchers about this revision and the re-interpretation of these concepts and cultural concepts. The concern is that these concepts are being revised to comply exclusively with the new technological era's relevant issues and interests. The concepts and structures that form part of the indigenous knowledge of societies are not always included in these debates and are being neglected. This results in academics in developing countries beginning to query the basic research structures that are currently operating within various academic disciplines.

THE ARTS AND SCIENCE

Debates on issues like the differences and similarities between the arts and crafts have now shifted their focus to the differences and compatibilities between the arts and the sciences. Academics are striving to minimise the barriers between these various fields of study and are moving towards multidisciplinary and comparative investigation. In this way, the role of knowledge within developing countries is currently acknowledged as contributing towards valuable intellectual information and this input assist in the breaking down of academic barriers.

Leopold Senghor, an African intellectual, writes about Africa being partner to this new ambition and approach to do research in a more active, integrated, and creative manner. He discusses the characteristics of knowing (of knowledge) as not just a mere contemplative gaze, but also as a practical activity:

> To know an object, it no longer suffices to see it, to dissect it, to weight it, even if one has the most perfect precision instruments. One must also touch it, penetrate it from the inside – so to speak – and finger it.[1]

This understanding of knowledge is of special relevance when doing research on the knowledge of humanity and the human sciences. This plea is supported by a number of other African scholars.

> To know a human fact, psychological or social, no longer means to investigate it with the aid of statistics and graphs, but to live it: like the white man who, to understand the situation of Negro Americans, blackened his skin with a chemical product and worked as a Negro shoeshine boy. This is what phenomenological or existential thought reveals, as it follows the path of Marxism and exceeds it while integrating it. In this school of thought, the real coincides with thought, the content of a statement coincides with the form in which it is expressed, philosophy blends with science, as art merges with existence, with life.[2]

Understanding knowledge through this route has implications of a metaphysical kind. The fact that one cannot separate the knower from the known entails that one cannot make a distinction between two kinds of reality; one purely mental, the other merely material. For Senghor, it is the discovery of this dialectic method of acquiring knowledge about the self and the world that has shown up the true inadequacies of European scientific-technological culture. It is exactly this way of thinking that forms a bridge between European cultures and the cultures of developing countries. A paradigm shift in the way we conceptualise could provide the necessary intellectual tools for expressing the insights of traditional African thinking in a systematic way:

> This knowledge by confrontation and intuition is Negro-African knowledge. From our ancestors we have inherited our own method of knowledge. Why should we change it when Europeans now tell us it is the very method of the twentieth century – and the most fruitful method?[3]

Secrecy and control of knowledge, as is the norm in Africa, combined with the lack of interest in the personal pursuit of

[1] Senghor. 1965:72. [2] *Ibid.* 71.
[3] *Ibid.* 73.

knowledge or intellectual exploration, leads to the observation that:

The pursuit of science – the cultivation of rational or theoretical knowledge of the natural world – seems to presuppose an intense desire, at least initially, for knowledge for its own sake, not for the sake of some immediate practical results. It appears that our cultures had very little, if any, conception of knowledge for its own sake. They had a conception of knowledge that was practically oriented. Such an epistemic conception seems to have had a parallel in African conception of art. For it has been said by several scholars that art was conceived in the African traditional setting in functional (or teleological) terms, that the African aesthetic sense did not find the concept of "art for art's sake" hospitable. Even though I think that the purely aesthetic element of art was not lost sight of, this element does not appear to have been stressed in African art appreciation. This practical or functional conception of art, which dwarfed a conception of art for art's sake, must have infected the African conception of knowledge, resulting in a lack of interest in the acquisition of knowledge, including scientific knowledge, for its own sake.[4]

The conclusion can be made that the pursuit of knowledge in Africa inherited a past and a cultural attitude that consist of the following characteristics:

- The cultures did not have a commitment to the advancement of the scientific knowledge of the natural world.
- They made no attempt to investigate the scientific theories underpinning the technologies they developed.
- The disposition to pursue sustained inquiries into many areas of their life and thought does not seem to have been fostered by African cultures.
- Successive generations of cultural participants could not augment the compendium of knowledge they had inherited from their forefathers, but felt satisfied with it, making it into a hallowed or mummified basis of their own thought and action.

Some researchers lament the lack and absence of a scientific attitude towards life in general and research in specific:

In our contemporary world, where sustainable development, a great aspect of which is concerned with the enhancement of the material well-being of people, depends on the intelligent and efficient exploitation of the resources of nature – an exploration that can be effected only through science and its progeny, technology – the need to acquire the cultivation of the appropriate scientific attitudes is an imperative.[5]

In the light of this acknowledged lack of researched background knowledge, it becomes obvious that careful planning needs to be done by researchers in the future. Researchers need accurate understanding and documentation of the history of indigenous technology to help plan social and economic research and development programmes:

They need an urgent revival of research in the humanities (cultures) along with research on ancient technologies. Like science, technology – which is the application of 'knowledge' or discovery to practical use – is also a feature or product of culture. Technology is an enterprise that can be said to be common to all human cultures; it can certainly be regarded as among the earliest creations of any human society.[6]

It is not possible for researchers to ignore these issues. The recognition and acknowledgement of the inclusion of indigenous knowledge systems from the developing countries within current research structures is both necessary and expected.

THE SOUTH AFRICAN PERSPECTIVE

South Africa became a democratic country in 1994 and has since attempted to come to terms with and reposition globally in a rapidly changing world economy. This presents a unique set of challenges and restructuring of a national economy previously subjected to boycotts and sanctions. Sanctions made many new technologies either unavailable or very expensive. Coupled with this is the lack of recognition of indigenous technologies as part of the cultural and technological heritage of the South African society.

The consequence of this isolation goes beyond the industrial base, affecting tertiary education. Newly developed technologies and processes were, in many cases, not imported into South Africa and no education and training activities were developed around these innovations. As a result, the current lack of adequate education and training in new technologies and processes continues to render many industries uncompetitive on a global level.

The lack of technological development in South Africa adversely affects the internal economy. Technology is one of the most critical factors in production. Technological capability is, at the same time, important for most business strategies, including large and small enterprises. The upgrading of technology through research and innovation is a continuous process and is essential for the success of the local economy. The transfer of technology between countries, institutions, and industry is, at the same time, a prerequisite for development. Technology uses tools, techniques, and knowledge and deals primarily with how cultures use the environment to produce artefacts to fulfil their needs.

Technological ideas, processes, and skills moving from the developed to developing countries (as well as among developing countries themselves) imply technology transfer. The need to study the indigenous technologies and the necessary technology transfer and innovation that this brings about is currently considered to be important in research circles and forms part of the research, development, and training responsibilities of local educational institutes in South Africa.

Although industrial-level manufacturing is a main focus of government's industrialisation strategy, so too is the indigenous arts and crafts sector. In this sector, artefacts are produced within specific historical and cultural contexts and are for sale to both local and international tourists, in addition

[4] Eze. 1997:31.

[5] *Ibid*: 31.

[6] *Ibid*: 35.

to being exported. This sector has been targeted for aggressive development not only because it is seen to accompany the increase in tourism, but also because it is a seen as a sector that could play a critical role in poverty relief. It is the area identified as being in need of technological transfer and innovation and to upgrade the local manufacturing process. This is also the area where the impact of intellectual property rights takes place.

The phenomena of world markets brought about a combination of mass production coupled with mass marketing – this led to a homogenisation of products and designs (artefacts). The current consumer reaction against this is to rediscover and re-appreciate national and cultural diversity in product designs and production methods. This attitude towards design can be seen in context of a worldwide recession and the intensified competition between companies, global industries, and small businesses:

> A common feature of competition in all these markets is that the cost of translating technology into commercial products is as great as, or greater than, the cost of developing the technology itself; design, which is used to make products out of inventions, is thus one key determinant of costs and profitability.[7]

Designers are now offered a chance to rediscover indigenous styles and to return to craft as inspiration. This creates more scope for human involvement in design and manufacturing.

Because of South Africa's past political dispensation, development practitioners and academics paid little attention to indigenous knowledge systems and indigenous technologies (IKS&T). Very little attention was given to the potential or development of these technologies and designs in context of the socio-economic and cultural development of the country. At best, most of these practices were documented as examples of artefacts produced for daily use by artisans in the rural areas and considered as being curiosities within tribal context.

However, since the 1980s, increasing numbers of researchers became interested in the study of indigenous systems. Valuable new insights were added to the level of knowledge about indigenous knowledge systems and its development. A number of publications were produced. In most of the academic publications, concern is voiced about the lack of research on these knowledge systems and additional concern was voiced on the specific nature of research methodologies applied to research on IKS&T. The dominating influence of western methodologies used for research in developing countries is identified as being one of the problematic areas in this regard. Some of the theories and opinions that could impact on research are now taken into account:

- the alienation of the scientist from his/her culture/society;
- the role of the "other" in western society that attempts to define the *own* as an opposing factor;
- the role of power structures within a society that form and define its cultural practice;
- the problematic role of technology in the context of culture.
- the role of politics in determining concepts of culture;
- the concept of "cultural distance" between groups and/or within a discipline (Snow. 1998:4);
- the intellectual and scientific divide in culture;
- the role of intellectual property rights.

The common factor in these discussions is the quest of researchers to attempt and/or to renew efforts to look at society in an inclusive and representative way in combination with the acknowledgement of the idea of global cultural diversity. This includes all social and cultural aspects that infringe on daily life, identity, and the civil rights of the individual:

> To take more heed of the voices of marginalized people and minority groupings could contribute to a more empowering and creative approach to the empowerment of people.[8]

In the attempt to re-evaluate society, the responsibility of the researcher is the recognition of the complexities of societies, their unique rituals and customs, and the adoption of a culturally sensitive approach in order to develop appropriate research methodologies.

It is therefore important to recognise the importance of concentrating on the role and application of IKS as a part of this re-evaluation of the current South African society. The realisation that craft-based knowledge systems may have ecological and economic sustainability in the modern world has led to a re-evaluation of their contribution to society.

IKS&T IN THE DEVELOPING WORLD

In the developing world, IKS&T is now recognised as an important component of the science and technology wealth of former colonised countries. Increasingly, researchers realise that none of these colonised countries was spared colonial manipulation of science and technology. In an effort to decolonise research and research methodology on IKS, the motivation for the implementation of an organised structure within which such research can take place needs to be formalised.

Incorporating indigenous crafts into this reformulation of a unique South African identity will, by necessity, involve the sciences and indigenous technologies. The knowledge-base and indigenous technologies from which crafts people produce their artefacts have been transmitted through generations using ancient technologies and oral traditions. The advent of modern western S&T has, as mentioned before, left these crafts people isolated because of their marginal role in the global-market economy.

The concept of "knowledge" is considered to be the product of individual creativity. Historically, within research circles, this concept is based on western scientific thought and western systems of knowledge creation. The indigenous research

[7] Thackara. 1988:20.

[8] De Beer. 1997:56.

source by which information is gathered is viewed as being merely the gathering of *raw material* and not as knowledge in its own right. A need exists for the documentation, and in some cases the redocumentation, of these knowledge bases. Such a documentation process forms part of the debate around the reformulation of the basic concept of what research and research methodologies entail.

Support for this approach is inherent in a project that South African researchers have initiated with the National Institute of Science, Technology and Development Studies, Council for Scientific and Industrial Research, CSIR, in New Delhi, India.

THE RESEARCH PROJECT BETWEEN INDIA AND SOUTH AFRICA

Indigenous Knowledge Systems and Technologies among artisans in India and South Africa – a collaborative cross-cultural endeavour.

This project developed an appropriate research methodology to assist with the assessment of the indigenous artisan's socio-economic circumstances, attitude towards his/her craft and his/her understanding of the technology used during the manufacturing process of this craft.

- The project links the artisan's traditional "knowledge" under different research disciplines, public attitude towards and understanding of science, and IKS&T.
- It assists in the process of breaking down barriers between the two cultures; i.e., the humanities and the sciences.
- It promotes the concept of active field surveys as a valuable part of gaining insight into indigenous practises.
- It acknowledges the fact that the inability to understand culture inhibits the pace of acceptance of S&T in a society.
- This cultural gap between the socio-economical conditions of the West and the developing world is recognised as a problematic aspect that impacts greatly on IKS&T.

INTELLECTUAL PROPERTY RIGHTS AND THEIR ROLE IN DEVELOPING COUNTRIES

> Design is the most exiting area in relation to technological development. We are not strong on industrial design in South Africa and are often derivative or unoriginal by not drawing on our own experiences. Other countries have successfully developed programs that have transformed traditional (culturally specific) industries into mainstream products and markets. Technological innovation is a natural spin-off of the design process and there is every opportunity to begin to concentrate on South African design in order to maximise this potential.[9]

One of the foreseeable impacts that craft-based research will have is on aspects of innovation, production, and the accompanying processing of knowledge. Indigenous technologies are by nature influenced and changed by modern technologies and it is between the two worlds of technologies – IKS&T and modern technology – that innovation takes place. Indigenous technologies are, however, practised on the basis of traditional knowledge as transferred through centuries of artefact production. It is therefore critical that the role of intellectual property rights is understood and clarified, as it is an important aspect to take into account during the innovation and development process. It is also imperative, when doing international cross-cultural and comparative research, to look at the attitude and position of the partner country towards intellectual property rights. India has some very definite opinions expressed by its intellectuals within international debates concerning intellectual property rights.

Intellectual property rights concerns the area of "artefacts resulting from intangible intellectual endeavours, activities and creativity."[10] Although not tangible, this activity still possesses economical value. An argument can be formulated on the premise that this monetary value is of importance to the West and its multinationals. The argument around intellectual property rights – of knowledge having some monetary value – is a recent law concept formulated during the nineteenth century.

One of the subdivisions of intellectual property rights the so-called personality theory, mentions the fact that an idea is linked to the process of intellectual growth of the person and his or her personality. The results of such an intellectual endeavour is, however, also capable of an existence outside that of its creator. "This separate existence creates a lawful link and partnership between the idea and the creator."[11] When art is transformed into "physical form" it is classified as "artistic works." Pottery falls within this definition because the resultant artefacts (pottery) were, originally, defined as being: "art handwork/handwork of a technical nature" and later changed to "handworks." This description now includes artefacts that are not paintings, sculptures, drawings, gravures, photos, or building works as described by the copyright law, 25 of 1992.[12]

Technological innovation can take place in both the informal, rural community and/or the more formal academic sphere. Because indigenous technologies are predominantly based on marginalized and fragile rural practices and are being threatened by the process of globalisation, societies need to take informed protective action. India takes on a specific attitude towards intellectual property rights as expressed by their Director-General of the CSIR, Dr. R. A. Mashelkar:

> We need a particular focus on community knowledge and community innovation. To encourage communities, it is necessary to scout support, spawn and increase the grassroots innovation. Linking innovation, enterprise and investment is particularly important. New models and new thinking on IP will have to be envisioned to accomplish this.[13]

Current debates argue that a paradigm shift is needed for research to exist in opposition to intellectual property rights; intellectual property rights being representative of the economic property rights of the products of creativity. Knowledge and creativity are being so narrowly defined that

[9] DACST. November 1998. Report by the Cultural Strategy group.

[10] Klopper. 2002:1.
[11] *Ibid*: 4.
[12] *Ibid*: 15.
[13] Mashelkar in Hoppers. 2002:188.

the innovation of non-western knowledge systems has been ignored. The thrust of the western-based intellectual property rights regimes is therefore diametrically opposed to indigenous knowledge systems. Ignorance of IKS&T, among other things, often retards innovation and exploits people from developing worlds.

Most of the usual arguments for intellectual property do not hold up under scrutiny from this angle. In particular, in developing countries, the concept of the "marketplace of ideas" provides no justification for "ownership of ideas." To look at India's attitude towards intellectual property rights is therefore interesting. A host of craft activities are conducted in India on a daily basis. "The local communities active in craft production do not have the knowledge or the means to safeguard their property in a system that has its origin in very different cultural values and attitudes."[14] Mashelkar argues, quite correctly, that the existing intellectual property rights systems are "orientated on the concept of private ownership and individual innovation. They are at odds with indigenous cultures, which emphasise collective creative creation and ownership of knowledge. There is the concern that intellectual property rights systems encourage the appropriation of traditional knowledge for commercial use, without the fair sharing of benefits with the holders of this knowledge."[15]

Mashelkar identifies three different systems concerned with intellectual property rights:

1. industrial property systems for inanimate objects,
2. systems that deal with animate objects,
3. informal innovation systems.

He pleads for innovation in the westernised IPS systems. Because economics play a central role within these systems, intellectual property rights aspects of traditional knowledge are becoming a highly emotional issue in developing countries where poverty is the norm.

The solution to this problem is, according to Mashelkar, the creation of a Traditional Knowledge Digital Library. This library is housed at the National Institute of Science, Communication and Information Resources, CSIR, India.

> It could integrate widely scattered and distributed references on the traditional knowledge systems of the developing world in retrievable form. It could act as a bridge between the traditional and modern knowledge systems. Availability of this knowledge in a retrievable form, in many languages, will give major impetus to modern research in the developing world, as the developing world can then become involved in innovative research, adding further value to traditional knowledge.[16]

South Africa, in this case, is situated in a unique position. "South Africa shares many features with more advanced economies and it has a well-developed infrastructure, an advanced banking and financial system and a manufacturing sector that can produce varied and sophisticated products."[17] The wealth of the country is predominantly in the hands of the white minority in the country. South Africa posses a good industrial framework as the result of the colonial and apartheid infrastructures developed by the predominantly unskilled labour of the indigenous peoples. The truth is, however, "that a high percentage of the indigenous population exist outside this framework and falls more under the definition of developing countries that: tend to have economies in which agriculture is the dominant activity, and to have low per capita income, nutritional standards, literacy and productivity. Health, water and social service provisions and transport and communication facilities tend to be poor by comparison with the industrial countries of the 'developed' world. Developing countries also tend to have rather high birth and death rates, short life expectancy, and a marked incidence of ill-health, malnutrition and disease."[18]

Because this description is apt for South Africa, the country can thus be described as having "a dual social and economic structure with a minority of the population living according to the pattern of a 'First World' economy and the majority living according to the pattern of a 'Third World' standards or in socially and economically marginalized 'Fourth World' conditions."[19]

In the postmodern paradigm, indigenous communities are increasingly turning to their own cultures and using tradition as a critique of the new economic instrument of hegemony. "Traditional practises are being championed within this newly found arena of confidence and pride on indigenous people's systems of knowledge" (Sardar. 1998:161). The result of this is a new awareness of the value (monetary and intellectual) of these knowledge systems and related indigenous artefacts. "Indeed, in the decade ahead, it will not be so easy for western consumer industries simply to take indigenous knowledge from passive and compliant natives."[20]

A comment often heard in scientific circles is that all traditional knowledge and biodiversity should be patented. It is not possible, however, for traditional knowledge practitioners, or for a country's biodiversity, to be patented by its indigenous practitioners because, to indigenous societies, it is ancient knowledge. Western researchers argue differently: The reasons that the cumulative innovation of societies over thousands of years can be claimed as an "innovation" of western-trained scientists are two:

- the colonial legacy of the idea that science is unique to the West, and indigenous knowledge systems cannot be treated as scientific;
- countries like the United States, where most pirated indigenous innovations are filed for patenting, does not always acknowledge and/or recognise the existing indigenous knowledge of developing countries.

Thus, although patent regimes offer no protection to indigenous communities for their common innovation and their common resources, they used to allow the appropriation of their biodiversity and knowledge by scientists and commercial interests of other cultures, including members of the modern

[14] *Ibid*: 189.
[15] *Ibid*: 190.
[16] *Ibid*: 193.
[17] New Agenda. 2001:102.
[18] Bulmer. 998:3.
[19] New Agenda. 2001:103.
[20] Sardar. 1998:161.

scientific culture in their own societies. It is, however, necessary to voice some concern about the tendency to romanticise the traditional knowledge systems. Some of the traditional practises are embedded in myths; some are even quite dangerous to health. One example in South Africa was the use of cow dung to seal the navel of a new born baby – a use that caused numerous deaths attributable to tetanus.

What about the personal incentive to create? What about the lack of possibilities of wealth and fame that do not prevent creative individuals from nevertheless producing works of ingenious innovation? Most creative innovators in developing countries are motivated first by their need to survive, and secondly, their own intrinsic interest towards improving their lifestyle and/or production. It could be argued that monetary rewards actually reduce the quality of work. If the goal is different and more creative, then to pay creators on piecework basis such as through royalties could be counterproductive.

In a society without intellectual property protection, creativity is likely to thrive. Most of the problems that are envisaged to occur if there is no intellectual property – such as the exploitation of a small publisher who renounces copyright – are attributable to economic arrangements that maintain inequality. The soundest foundation for a society without intellectual property is greater economic and political equality. This means not just equality of opportunity, but also equality of outcomes. This does not imply uniformity. It means creative freedom and diversity and a situation in which people can get what they need but are not able to gain inordinate power or wealth by exploiting the work of others. India is not the only dissident voice against the mostly westernised intellectual property rights ideas. Even designers in the United Kingdom formulated opinions about the monetary value given to knowledge.

> . . . there is something basically wrong with the whole concept of patents and copyrights. If I design a toy that provides therapeutic exercise for handicapped children, then I think it is unjust to delay the release of the design by a year and a half, going through a patent application. I feel that ideas are plentiful and cheap, and it is wrong to make money from the needs of others. I have been very lucky in persuading many of my students to accept this view.[21]

For Papanek, the alternative to intellectual property is straightforward: intellectual products should not be owned. That means not owned by individuals, corporations, governments, or the community as common property. Ideas are available to be used by anyone who wants to. The alternative to intellectual property ownership is that intellectual products (artefacts and tools) cannot be owned. Strategies that can be deployed against intellectual property in developing countries may include civil disobedience, promotion of non-owned information, and fostering of a more cooperative society.[22] Intellectual property is one more way for rich countries to extract wealth from poor countries. Given the enormous exploitation of poor peoples built into the world trade system, it would also only seem fair for ideas produced in rich countries to be provided, at no cost or other restrictions, to poor countries.

[21] Papanek. 1985:xi.

[22] Martin. 1994:36.

CONCLUSION

Scientists do research and then publish their results. A large proportion of scientific knowledge is public knowledge. It can be argued that the most dynamic parts of science are those with the least secrecy. Open ideas can be examined, challenged, modified, and improved. Few scientists complain that they do not own the knowledge they produce. Indeed, they are much more likely to complain when corporations or governments try to control dissemination of ideas. Most scientists receive a salary from a government, corporation or university. Their livelihoods do not depend on royalties from published work.

Researchers at universities have academic freedom and tremendous research opportunities. The main reasons for doing research are for the intrinsic satisfaction of investigation and discovery and for recognition by their peers. To turn scientific knowledge into intellectual property would dampen the enthusiasm of many scientists for their work. However, as governments reduce their funding of universities, scientists and university administrations increasingly turn to patents and intellectual property rights as sources of income. Scientific knowledge is often, in this way, used for harmful purposes. It is difficult to imagine, though, how turning it into property could make it better. Vigorous intellectual activity is quite possible without intellectual property rights claims and, in fact, may be vigorous precisely because of the information not being owned.

QUESTIONS FOR DISCUSSION

1. There is a danger of romanticising IKS. What impact will such a perspective have on policy and academic endeavours?

2. The art and craft knowledge transmitted through IKS originated in ancient times. Will the encapsulation of these knowledge systems within intellectual property rights impoverish society and stop the continuous flow of information?

3. Most traditional technologies are embedded in sound science principles. Will the insertion of intellectual property rights within in these practises create conflict between individual right and public interest?

REFERENCES

Bulmer, M. & Warwick, D. 1998. *Social Research in Developing Countries.* Surveys and censuses in the third world. London: UCL Press.

Chambers. R. 1983. *Rural Development.* Essex: Addison Wesley Longman Limited.

Dacst. 1998. Department of Arts Culture, Science and Technology, South Africa. Report by the Cultural Strategy group.

De Beer, F. & Swanepoel, H. 1997. *Introduction to Development Studies.* Oxford: Oxford University Press.

Eze. E. C. 1997. *Postcolonial African Philosophy*. Oxford: Blackwell.

Hettinger. E. "Justifying intellectual property," in: *Philosophy and Public Affairs*, Winter 1989. Vol. 18, No. 1. See also David Vaver, "Intellectual property today: of myths and paradoxes," in: *Canadian Bar Review*, March 1990, Vol. 69, No. 1.

Hountondji, P. 1997. *Endogenous Knowledge*. Research Trails. Senegal: CODESRIA.

Klopper. H & Van Der Spuy. P. 2002. *Intellektuele goederereg*. Gezina: Printburo.

Martin, B. 1994. "Plagiarism: a misplaced emphasis," *Journal of Information Ethics*, Vol. 3, No. 2.

Mashelkar. R. "The role of Intellectual Property in building capacity for innovation for development" in HOPPERS C. 2002. *Indigenous Knowledge and the Integration of Knowledge Systems*. Claremont: New Africa Books (Pty) Ltd.

New Agenda. 2001. SA journal of social and economic policy. Issue 4. Cape Town: Institute for African Alternatives.

Papanek, V. 1985. *Design for the Real World: Human Ecology and Social Change*. London: Thames and Hudson.

Raza. G. & Du Plessis. H. 2002. *Science, Crafts and Knowledge*. Pretoria: Protea Book House.

Sardar, Z. 1998. *Postmodernism and the other*. London: Pluto Press.

Senghor. L. S. 1965. *On African Socialism*. Stanford: Pall Mall.

Smith, L. 1999. *Decolonising Methodologies*. London: Zed Books Ltd.

Snow, C. P. 1998. *The Two Cultures*. Cambridge: Cambridge University Press.

Thackara. J. 1988. *Design after Modernism*. Gloucester: Thames and Hudson.

CHAPTER FORTY-SEVEN

Recent Developments in the Regulation of Traditional Herbal Medicines

Zelda Pickup and Christopher Hodges

The use of traditional herbal medicine is widespread in many parts of the world, particularly in developing countries and even in Western society, where, for many years, it held only a minority appeal as an alternative to pharmaceutical medicine and now, more and more people are turning towards it. The total market for traditional medicinal products is growing and is now estimated to be around US$60 billion (£41 billion) worldwide.[1]

Reports of potentially life-threatening and fatal adverse events, together with concerns over quality, have led to calls for the strengthening and expanding of the regulatory regime that governs traditional herbal medicinal products, particularly in Europe. A tension exists between those who claim that as a result of increased regulation age-old remedies and the freedom to use them will be lost, and those who claim greater regulation is necessary to protect human health.

* * *

The popularity of herbal medicines continues to grow in the western world, notwithstanding a significant, continuing demand for pharmaceutical medicines. On both sides of the Atlantic, the annual rate of sales growth of popular herbs such as ginseng, St. John's Wort, garlic, aloe vera, and evening primrose oil are said to be greater than hundred percent.[2] In certain countries, herbal remedies are more popular than prescription alternatives; for example, Germany, where doctors themselves prescribed twice the value in prescriptions of St. John's Wort for depression (DM 61 million) as they did for Prozac (DM 30 million) in 1994.[3]

In the United Kingdom, it is difficult to gauge the extent of use of herbal medicines accurately because many herbal products may be designated as foods rather than medicines. However, a report prepared for the medicine industry in 1999 on over-the-counter (OTC) sales showed that around £50 million had been spent on herbal medicines.[4] This report also suggested that sales of OTC, complementary, and alternative medicines were increasing. A House of Lords report on complementary medicine estimated that market to be worth around £240 million in the United Kingdom per annum.[5] Business in traditional Chinese medicines [TCM] is booming both in China and in the West. A third of the global demand comes from European Union (EU) countries, turning TCM into a £18 billion industry in 2001.[6] All the indications suggest that the use of herbal medicines is likely to continue to grow.

This increasingly widespread use of herbal remedies has given rise to concerns about their safety, quality, and efficacy because at present such remedies are regulated in most countries in a piecemeal and inconsistent manner.

In the United Kingdom, for example, it has been estimated that about eighty percent of herbal remedies on the market are unlicensed by virtue of a clause exempting them from the provisions of the Medicines Act.[7] When the original medicines law was enacted, the herbal medicines market was small and no one imagined that so many products would eventually fall within the exemption. Except in countries such as Germany, France, and Australia, where special licensing procedures for herbal products have existed for some time, most regulatory regimes have allowed companies to choose between designating their product a food or a medicine. Under food regulations there are restrictions as to what may be claimed for the product and if manufacturers make what can be construed as medicinal claims (i.e., usually a claim for treatment, prevention, or cure for a specific disease or condition), herbal products can become subject to the much stricter medicines regulatory regimes. As a result, in the United Kingdom, herbal products have been frequently marketed with no explanation as to what they purport to do or indeed without any information relating to any risks such as contraindications or precautions in use.

In the United States, most herbal products are marketed as dietary supplements under the 1994 Dietary Supplement Health and Education Act.[8] Under the Act, the Food and Drug Administration (FDA) bears the burden of proof to show that a dietary supplement presents a significant or unreasonable risk to prevent it from being marketed, whereas for medicines, manufacturers bear the burden of proof of demonstrating that the medicine is safe and effective before it can be marketed. Therefore, herbal products may enter the marketplace without any formal safety review because there are no provisions

[1] World Health Organisation. Launch of Global Strategy on Traditional Medicine. May 2002.

[2] "Making Sense of Medicines," Jacky Law, *Scrip Magazine* May 1999.

[3] *Ibid.*

[4] Medicines Control Agency (now the Medicines and Healthcare products Regulatory Agency). Partial Regulatory Impact Report 27 March 2002.

[5] House of Lords Science and Technology Report on Complementary and Alternative Medicine, Nov 2000. See "Herbal Regulation, A Step Closer," Michael Baker, *PAGB Bulletin*, May 2002.

[6] "*The Times*" Oliver August, June 24th 2002.

[7] "Making Sense of Herbal Medicines," Jacky Law, *Scrip Magazine*. May 1999, referring to S.12(2) Medicines Act 1968.

[8] US Food and Drug Administration. Centre for Food Safety and Applied Nutrition.

for the FDA to approve supplements for safety or effectiveness before they reach the consumer, provided that the products' claims comply with labelling requirements and do not include unsubstantiated claims or claims that the product can prevent, treat, or cure disease.

The need for a thorough overhaul of the regulatory system covering such products to ensure consistent quality, safety, and efficacy was underlined during the 1990s, when irreversible and sometimes fatal side effects were reported with the use of herbs of the *aristolochia* species.

More than 100 cases of irreversible nephropathy have been reported in Belgium, since 1993, in young women attending a slimming clinic. The nephrotoxicity of the treatment has been traced to the inadvertent use of *aristolochia fanchi* in herbal formulations as a substitute for *stephania tetrandra.* One third of the Belgian patients are reported to have received a renal transplant. A number of the transplanted patients have also been found to have transitional cell carcinoma in the renal pelvis, ureter, and bladder. In thirty-nine patients who agreed to undergo prophylactic surgery, there were eighteen cases of urothelial carcinoma, seventeen cases of carcinoma of the ureter, renal pelvis, or both, and one papillary bladder tumour. Nineteen of the remaining patients had mild to moderate urothelial dysplaysia and two had normal urothelium. Since 1995, a total of seven cases of nethropathy have been reported in France in patients who took a preparation containing *aristolochia fanchi* instead of *stephania tetrandra* and in 1999, two cases of irreversible renal failure were reported in the United Kingdom in women taking unlicensed Chinese remedies for eczema. Both patients required renal transplants. Similar reports have been received from Spain, China, and Japan.[9]

Aristolochia is a toxic herbal ingredient used in TCM. A number of medicinal plants, which in themselves are considered harmless when correctly administered, are at high risk of being substituted by, or confused with, *aristolochia.* Following the cases of serious illness attributable to *aristolochia* in unlicensed medicines in Britain, a sampling and analysis exercise was carried out by the Medicines Control Agency (MCA).[10] This showed that a significant proportion of herbal remedies believed to be at risk of containing aristolochic acids did, in fact, do so. A number of plants may be confused with the *aristolochia* species because they have similar, common (or pin yin) names because in TCM certain herbs with similar medicinal properties are regarded as being interchangeable.

TCM herbal ingredients are often traded using pin yin names. These are not specific botanical names but are descriptions of the colour, shape, taste, or odour of the herbal ingredients or they may describe the actions or uses. It is common practice in this herbal tradition to substitute one herbal ingredient with another reputedly having similar medicinal properties, even though it may be botanically unrelated. Another issue is that unrelated pin yin names can be phonetically very similar. The risk of confusion between similar pin yin names is likely to be responsible for at least some of the cases in which *aristolochia fangji* (pin yin name: guang fangji) has been mistakenly used in place of *stephania tetrandra* (pin yin name: han fangji). The pin yin name, Mu Tong, is applied to a range of alternative herbal ingredients. Most of these are harmless, however, one possible ingredient is a species of *aristolochia,* thus, there could be a risk that *aristolochia* may from time to time enter the supply chain in products presented as containing Mu Tong.[11]

In October 2000, the European Medicines Evaluation Agency (now the European Medicines Agency) issued a position paper on herbal medicinal products, which considered the risks associated with the use of herbal remedies containing *aristolochia* species.[12] The MCA (now the Medicines and Healthcare products Regulatory Agency [MHRA]), having brought into force a temporary ban on herbal medicines containing *aristolochia* species and any others for which *aristolochia* may be inadvertently substituted, has now made this permanent, given that safety concerns have not been allayed by the temporary measure.[13] Recently, similar safety concerns have arisen over the use of *kava-kava.* About thirty cases of liver problems in Germany were reported in late November 2001. In the United Kingdom, the Committee on Safety of Medicines advised that, on the evidence available, the risk of hepatotoxicity (serious liver problems) appeared to outweigh the potential benefits of Kava-kava use. In 2002, a law was passed in the United Kingdom prohibiting the sale, supply, and importation of unlicensed medicines containing kava-kava, except for external use only.[14] Many other herbal ingredients are also prohibited or restricted in medicines.[15] There are also safety issues under discussion concerning several different herbal medicinal products.

Other problems encountered with herbal products are contamination and incorrect labelling. The addition of pharmaceutical drugs to TCMs and heavy metal contamination of Asian herbal products is not uncommon. A study of 2,609 samples of TCMs from eight hospitals in Taiwan found that twenty-four percent contained pharmaceutical products, the most common of which were caffeine, paracetamol, indomethacin, hydrochlorthiazide, and prednisolone. Outside Asia, benzodiazapines and nonsteroidal

[9] EMEA Working Party on Herbal Medicinal Products. "Position paper on the risks associated with the use of herbal products containing aristolochia species" 31 October 2000.

[10] Medicines Control Agency Consultation Document MLX 258 on "Further proposals to protect the public from unlicensed medicines containing herbal ingredients at risk of confusion with Aristolochia species" 17 Jan 2000.

[11] Medicines Control Agency Consultation Document MLX 254 "Proposals to protect the public from unlicensed medicines containing the herbal ingredient *Aristolochia*" 27 July 1999.

[12] See footnote 8 *supra.*

[13] The Medicines (*Aristolochia* and Mu Tong, etc.) (Prohibition) Order 2001 S1 1841.

[14] The Medicines for Human Use Kava-kava (Prohibition) Order 2002 S1 3170.

[15] See for example, the MHRA List of Herbal Ingredients, which are prohibited or restricted in medicines.

anti-inflammatory drugs have been identified in TCMs.[16] The MHRA has found toxic levels of arsenic or mercury in some TCMs and potent prescriptions-only medicines have been found in herbal medicines in the United Kingdom, including prescription-only steroids in "herbal" skin creams.[17] There are many examples of similar findings across Europe and the United States.

It appears that the great majority of quality-related problems are associated with unregulated herbal products. As can be seen from the previous discussion, these problems include deliberate or accidental inclusion of prohibited or restricted ingredients, substitution of ingredients, contamination with toxic substances, and differences between the labelled and actual contents.

The MHRA notes that these problems are further compounded by demand outstripping supply of good-quality ingredients, confusing nomenclature over plant species, cultural differences of view over toxicity, and traditional practices such as substituting one ingredient for another having a reportedly similar action.[18]

The lack of systematic and mandatory product safety information on unlicensed herbal remedies can compound public health risks. The use of St. John's Wort has become increasingly popular for the self-treatment of mild depression but it can have a variety of effects on the central nervous system and can reduce the effectiveness of some major prescription medicines, including, among others, oral contraceptives, antidepressants, anticonvulsants, and treatments for human immunodeficiency virus infection.

Herbs may mimic, magnify, or oppose the effects of conventional medicines if taken concurrently. For example, patients with clotting disorders, those taking anticoagulants or those awaiting surgery should avoid use of danshen, dongquay, papaya, and garlic because they increase international normalised ratio (blood clotting) rates. Devil's claw has been reported to cause purpura when combined with warfarin and ginkgo biloba should be avoided by people taking aspirin because of the risk of spontaneous hyphema. The combination of ginko biloba and warfarin can give rise to intracerebral haemorrhage and the combination of ginko with paracetemol and ergotamine/caffeine can cause subdural haematoma. Concurrent use of ginko and thiazide diuretics may give rise to hypertension.[19]

These safety and quality concerns have coincided with and reinforced a worldwide movement towards greater regulation of the herbal medicine industry. The World Health Organisation (WHO) has taken a great interest in this area because herbal medicines are vitally important to third world countries, where expensive prescription medicines can be afforded by few and herbal medicines are used in the traditional forms of treatment and healing. It has announced a global strategy on traditional medicines aimed at bringing complementary or alternative medicines into the mainstream of health services around the world.[20]

A working group of the WHO has already prepared guidelines for the use of herbal medicines in Western Pacific countries to respond to the widespread use in this part of the world, and the need for mechanisms to ensure these products are safe and effective yet remain broadly accessible. The working group report sets out a framework for developing national policies designed to control the safety, efficacy, and quality of herbal medicines, manufacturing practices, product registration, and labelling marketing trade.[21]

An Expert Committee of the WHO on the Specifications for Pharmaceutical Preparations has adopted guidelines for the assessment of herbal medicines. These guidelines define the criteria for the evaluation of the safety, efficacy, and quality of herbal medicines and are intended to assist national regulatory authorities, scientific organisations, and manufacturers in undertaking assessments of documentation, submissions, or regulatory dossiers on such products.[22]

In addition, the WHO has produced good manufacturing practice (GMP) guidelines for the manufacture of herbal medicinal products to address the manufacture of the products from material of plant origin that may be subject to contamination and deterioration and may vary in composition and properties.[23] It has also produced research guidelines for conducting specific research on the safety and efficacy of herbal medicines.[24] The guidelines are intended to facilitate the work of research scientists and clinicians while also furnishing some reference points for the governmental, industrial, and non-profit-making sectors.

The FDA in the United States is also proposing to issue regulations on GMPs, focusing on practices that ensure the identity, purity, quality, strength, and composition of dietary supplements (including herbal products).[25]

Against this background, the development of a Directive in the EU on traditional herbal medicines has taken several years. The purpose behind a Directive was to establish within the European Community a harmonised legislative framework for authorising the marketing of traditional herbal medicinal products involving a simplified registration procedure. The

[16] Dr. Adriane Fugh-Berman "Documented herb-induced interactions." *The Lancet* 2000, 355.134. Reported in the Pharmaceutical Journal Vol. 264.

[17] Medicines Control Agency Partial Regulatory Impact Assessment 27 March 2002.

[18] Safety of Herbal Medicinal Products. MHRA July 2002.

[19] Dr. Adriane Fugh-Berman, "Documented herb-induced interactions." *The Lancet* 2000, 355.134. Reported in the Pharmaceutical Journal Vol. 264.

[20] World Health Organisation announcement. 16 May 2002. <www.who.int>

[21] World Health Organisation "Guidelines for the Appropriate Use of Herbal Medicines."

[22] World Health Organisation "Guidelines for the Assessment of Herbal Medicines" 1991 as amended.

[23] World Health Organisation "Good Manufacturing Practices: Supplementary Guidelines for the Manufacture of Herbal Medicinal Products."

[24] World Health Organisation "Research Guidelines for Evaluating the Safety and Efficacy of Herbal Medicines."

[25] FDA. Centre for Food Safety and Applied Nutrition. Proposals issued on 13 March 2003.

Herbal Medicine Products Directive (the 'Directive') entered into force on 30 April 2004.[26]

In the recitals to the Directive, it is explained that a significant number of medicinal products, despite their long tradition, do not fulfil the requirements of a well-established medicinal use with recognised efficacy and an acceptable level of safety and are not eligible for a marketing authorisation. To maintain these products on the market, Member States have enacted different procedures and provisions, which may hinder trade in traditional medicinal products within the Community and lead to discrimination and distortion of competition. They may also have an impact on the protection of public health because the necessary guarantees of quality, safety, and efficacy are not always provided. Therefore, it was considered desirable to provide a special, simplified registration procedure for certain traditional medicinal products. This should be used only where there is a lack of sufficient scientific literature demonstrating a well-established medicinal use with recognised efficacy and an acceptable level of safety.

The Directive therefore provides for a special registration procedure allowing the registration and hence the marketing of certain traditional, herbal medicinal products without requiring the production of full supporting documentation on safety and efficacy. However, the same requirements apply (as for other medicinal products) to the manufacturing of these products and to their quality.

It is important to note that the scope of the proposed legislation is limited to traditional herbal medicinal products.[27] Herbal medicinal products, which can currently be authorised under Directive 2001/83/EC either on the basis of the results of new tests and trials on safety and efficacy or on the basis of referenced published scientific literature, are not eligible for simplified registration. The new provisions do not apply either to homeopathic medicinal products.

There are several conditions that have to be fulfilled to be eligible for registration under the new provisions.[28] The product must be an herbal medicinal product, the possible indications and ways of administration must be limited, and the product must be for administration at a specified strength. Finally, a specified period of traditional use must have elapsed and the information on the traditional use of the medicinal product must be sufficient to demonstrate its safety and efficacy.

In principle, the applicants for a registration under the new provisions have to provide the same particulars and documents as for any other application for authorisation of a medicinal product, including the results of physico-chemical, biological, or microbiological tests.[29] Thus, the usual provisions relating to establishing the quality of the medicinal product apply. However, instead of providing the results of tests and trials on safety and efficacy of the product, the applicant has to present bibliographical or expert evidence on the traditional medicinal use of the product as well as a bibliographic review of safety data, together with an expert report.

Well-established medicinal use, as defined for other medicinal products, requires at least ten years to have elapsed from the first systematic and documented use.[30] Bearing in mind that a traditional medicinal use under the new provisions does not require such systematic and documented use, a period of thirty years is considered appropriate to satisfy the requirements. In principle, only medicinal use within the Community is relevant because it is very difficult to verify whether information on use outside the Community provides a reliable basis to conclude on the safety and efficacy of the product. However, if the product has been in medicinal use within the Community for at least fifteen years, it will be acceptable that the evidence of thirty years of medicinal use may fully or partly relate to such use outside the Member States.

Because the regulatory status of herbal medicinal products varies greatly among the Member States and cannot immediately be harmonised in its entirety, the mutual recognition procedure for the registration of medicinal products cannot be applied to registrations of traditional herbal medicinal products. However, the new provisions oblige Member States to take account of authorisations or registrations granted to the product in other Member States when deciding whether to accept or reject an application.[31]

An application is to be refused under certain conditions.[32] It is to be refused if the evaluation shows that the qualitative or quantitative composition of the product is not as declared in the application, if the therapeutic indications do not comply with specific restrictions, if the product could be harmful in the normal conditions of use, if the data on the traditional use are insufficient, or if the pharmaceutical quality is not satisfactorily demonstrated.

It is intended to establish a list of herbal substances that fulfil the conditions of eligibility for the registration procedure (the European positive list). For each substance, the list will indicate the therapeutic indication, the specified strength and posology, the route of administration, and any other relevant safety information. If an application for traditional use registration refers to a herbal substance contained in that list, the applicant, instead of supplying the relevant documents, may refer instead to the details on the list. Nevertheless, the normal requirements regarding the quality of the product continue to apply.[33]

Where appropriate, existing medicines legislation will apply to the new registration procedure, including the control of manufacturers and importers bringing products from third countries into the EU, the obligation of the marketing

[26] Directive 2004/24/EC of the European Parliament and of the Council amending as regards traditional herbal medicinal products Directive 2001/83/EC on the Community Code relating to medicinal products for human use.

[27] Article 16a *Ibid.*

[28] *Ibid.*

[29] Chapter 1 Title III Directive 2001/83/EC. Directive 2001/83/EC has been amended by Directive 2004/27/EC which is to be implemented in Member States by October 30th 2005.

[30] Art 10(1)(a)(ii) Directive 2001/83/EC.

[31] Article 16d. Directive 2004/24/EC.

[32] Article 16e. *Ibid.*

[33] Article 16f. *Ibid.*

authorisation holder to take into account scientific and technical progress, the general provisions on manufacture and importation, the provisions on classification of medicinal products, and, importantly, the provisions on pharmacovigilance.[34]

In principle also, the general provisions on labelling and package leaflets, as well as on advertising, will apply. However, the European Commission believes it is necessary to give full information to the public, especially patients, about the individual characteristics of traditional herbal medicinal products registered under the Directive. The Directive contains, therefore, the obligation to include in the labelling, the package leaflet, and in any advertising, the information that the product is a traditional herbal medicinal product for use in specified indications exclusively based upon long-standing use and that the user should consult a doctor or a qualified health care practitioner if symptoms persist or if adverse events not mentioned in the package leaflet occur.[35]

A new committee on Herbal Medicinal Products is set up within the European Medicines Agency.[36] The committee's tasks relate to scientific issues with regard to herbal medicinal products and herbal substances. One of the major tasks of the new committee is to establish EU herbal monographs containing relevant information for herbal medicinal products such as the definition, the constituents, clinical particulars, pharmacological properties, and bibliographic references. As mentioned earlier, such monographs are relevant for the assessment of an application for a marketing authorisation based on well-established medicinal use, as well as for an application for registration under the new provisions. Whenever such monographs have been adopted, they must be used as a basis for any application for registration under the new provisions, with the intention of continuously harmonising the regulatory position of herbal medicinal products in Europe.

When considering the likely effect of the Directive on the Community,[37] the European Commission expects that it will make the most difference to small and medium-sized enterprises which, for the moment, do not market these products as medicines and will need to invest in the equipment and personnel necessary to achieve a licence for the manufacturing of medicines and to carry out the necessary quality assurance work to comply adequately with standards relating to the quality and safety of these products. At present, only some of these smaller enterprises have such facilities. This initial outlay is considered to be offset by the advantage that conditions for the marketing of these herbal medicinal products will be identical in all Member States and therefore will allow easier access to non-national markets.

However, it is clear that once the provisions of the Directive have been implemented in the Member States (by 30 October 2005, except where transition periods apply), a proportion of herbal products that cannot demonstrate efficacy (as a licensed medicine or by traditional use) or be legitimately covered under food, cosmetics, or general consumer product law, will not have a regulatory home and some existing products may be lost from the market. This possibility is a result of replacing a largely uncontrolled regime. It is considered likely by the MHRA that a substantial proportion of any products at risk in this way would be able to come within one of the relevant statutory regimes if there was some adjustment in the products' ingredients, strength, or claims. There is provision in the Directive for a seven-year transitional period for unlicensed herbal medicines legally on the market on 30 April 2004 to allow companies time to adjust to and comply with new arrangements.[38]

One concern raised has been whether the definition of traditional use is drawn too tightly so that some herbal remedies that have a traditional basis will be unable to meet the requirement. However, it has been proposed that the Directive should permit reference not only to information on specific manufactured herbal remedies but also to authoritative literature about the various herbal traditions practised by herbalists in the EU. The view of the MHRA is that the Directive will permit use of this kind of evidence.[39] The main non-western herbal traditions (TCM and Ayurveda) have been present in European Member States for more than the minimum fifteen-year period of EU usage specified in the proposals and appropriate evidence of traditional use should be available.

It has also been questioned whether the quality standards to be applied are inappropriate and too onerous for traditional herbal remedies. However, the existing quality requirements and European guidelines that apply to licensed herbal medicines are met successfully by large numbers of companies, including many that are at the smaller end of the spectrum. Licensed herbal and traditional herbal medicines will typically have very similar product characteristics and so it is argued that it should be equally feasible for companies to meet these requirements.[40] Quality guidelines are intended to be applied in a way that is appropriate to the product under consideration and there is flexibility to accept legitimate arguments from companies for which it is not feasible to provide data in a particular circumstance. It is expected that the guidelines would reflect the fact that the quality of data relating to efficacy will be of lesser importance.

The impact of the new provisions may be particularly significant to some TCM businesses because of the current variability and unreliability of quality standards in parts of the sector.[41] However, the direct impact of the Directive will be modified for this part of the sector because a significant proportion of TCM activity relates not to finished OTC remedies but to individual remedies made up following one to one consultations between practitioners and patients. These remedies will not be affected by the Directive and will continue to

[34] Article 16g. *Ibid.* [35] Article 16g(2) and (3). *Ibid.*
[36] Article 16h. *Ibid.*
[37] Impact Assessment Form on Proposed Directive.

[38] Article 2(2) Directive 2004/24/EC.
[39] MHRA Partial Regulatory Impact Assessment. 27 March 2002.
[40] *Ibid.* [41] *Ibid.*

be covered principally by other national regulations, such as the herbalist exemption to the Medicines Act in the United Kingdom.[42]

* * *

The Herbal Medicinal Products Working Party has been constituted and has held several meetings, discussing, among other matters, preparations for the implementation of the Directive as well as safety matters relating to St. John's Wort, Kava-kava, and other herbal products. Thus, in the EU traditional herbal medicines will now become subject to an expanded medicines regulatory regime, which will seek to ensure their quality, safety, and, to a lesser degree, efficacy. Given the safety and quality concerns that have arisen, it is difficult to argue that this is unnecessary interference in a traditionally unregulated area.

It is likely also that as a result of the WHO global strategy on traditional medicines, which urges countries to regulate and monitor the safety of herbal medicines and alternative therapies, to license and promote best practice among practitioners, together with the increasing interest of the U.S. FDA in this area, that there will be increasing regulatory activity and intervention in the field of traditional medicines.

[42] [It is worth noting that a separate review of this exemption in the UK (Section 12(1) Medicines Act 1968) is in progress and is also likely to lead to a requirement for higher standards. See Consultation Letter MHRA 2 March 2004].

PART EIGHT

Museums and Cultural Heritage

CHAPTER FORTY-EIGHT

The "Universal Museum": A Case of Special Pleading?

Geoffrey Lewis

The Declaration by nineteen of the world's leading museum directors on "the importance and value of universal museums" deserves our detailed attention. The statement argues that "the universal admiration for ancient civilisations would not be so deeply established today were it not for the influence exercised by the artefacts of these cultures, widely available to an international public in major museums." The concept of a universal museum and the attendant responsibilities implied by this are outside the scope of this chapter; for a view on this see O'Neill (2004).

The real purpose of this declaration is to establish for "universal museums" a higher degree of immunity from claims for repatriation from their collections. To this end, the declaration states, "calls to repatriate objects that have belonged to museum collections for many years . . . should acknowledge that museums serve not just the citizens of one nation but the people of every nation" (full text available in ICOM, 2004a) This then is a statement of self-interest, made by a group representing some of the world's richest museums. The presumption that a museum with universally defined objectives may be considered exempt from such demands is specious.

The key debate today among the world community of museums is not about the desirability of "universal museums" but concerns the ability of a people to present their cultural heritage in their own territory. This is reflected both at political and professional levels through UNESCO legislation and, for example, the International Council of Museums (ICOM) *Code of Ethics for Museums*, respectively. This group of museum directors also imply in their statement that they speak for the "international museum community." This also has seriously to be questioned.

The concept of universality is embodied in the origin of public museums. They were formed from private, often noble, and even royal collections, and were often the result of partnership between benefactor and state. Many of these collections were highly eclectic both in their subject coverage and geographical origin, a tradition that can be traced back to the European Renaissance but which took on new meaning as the spirit of the Enlightenment emerged. They were by then no longer collections of curiosities but well-ordered, classified assemblages from many parts of the world. Such was the case of the Tradescants' collection, which formed the basis of the Ashmolean Museum at Oxford, the first public museum, opened in 1683; sources for the animal collection alone included Arabia, Brazil, Cape Verde, Greenland, India, Ireland, Virginia, West Africa, and the West Indies (MacGregor, A 1983).

The encyclopaedic approach of this period, which contributed so much to the development of the arts and science at this time, undoubtedly influenced the formation of those two archetypal universal museums, the British Museum and the Louvre. The founding legislation of the former in 1753 states the encyclopaedic rubric "all arts and sciences have a connexion with each other. . . ." and then goes on to indicate its public function: "not only for the inspection and entertainment of the learned and the curious, but for the general use and benefit of the public" (Miller, 1973). Similar sentiments are expressed in the inscription above the entrance portico of the Altes Museum, Berlin, opened in 1830: It was for the study of all antiquities and liberal arts. These, and certain other public museums of the late eighteenth and early nineteenth century, are, themselves, documents of these important developments and cogent historical arguments can be invoked for the preservation of these assemblages of their time.

Much the same could be argued for other eighteenth and early nineteenth century museums; their collections testify not only to that encyclopaedic spirit but also the age of world exploration of which they are a part. They reflect the part played by the nation concerned, or the circumstances that trade, industry, or location contributed to the character they exhibit today. Not all of these are national museums, nor would they feature in a list of world class museums, but their role and character are as significant.

The universality of collections has not, however, been the only model for the development of museums. Museums of national identity were appearing alongside their "universal" counterparts by the beginning of the nineteenth century. Developing national consciousness led to the establishment of national museums in Budapest in 1802 and Prague in 1818. The following year, the Danish government founded the National Museum of Antiquities in Copenhagen. With this came subject as well as geographical specialisation, soon to be reflected within nations by regional and local museums (Lewis, 1992 & 2005).

There has been, therefore, a built-in tension for museums in their collecting for at least two hundred years. The national museum collects from a region, whereas a regional museum will house highly significant material from a locality. There is no satisfactory solution to this sort of dilemma although different approaches have been adopted by different nations. The legal and political structures of a particular country allow

Shorter versions of this chapter have appeared previously in *ICOM News* and *Museum International* (see references).

such matters to be determined but cultural identity is not always defined by national boundaries. The Lapp-speaking Sàmi, a clearly defined people culturally, inhabit the northern areas of Norway, Sweden, and Russia.

The co-incidence of national and cultural boundaries cannot be a foregone conclusion. The transitory nature of political boundaries, too, has been a feature of the European mainland over the last two centuries, not least recently in central and southern Europe. Here, and on other continents, changing boundaries and new nationhood have generated a heightened awareness of the significance of museum collections in establishing national and cultural identity. This is particularly poignant in Africa and among the first peoples of the Americas and Australasia. There can be no surprise that Nigerian commentators on the declaration on universal museums see it as retrogressive and far removed from "jump-starting the process of cultural repatriation and inter-museum cooperation" (Eluyemi et al, 2004). But they do identify with the view of George Abungu (2004) in Kenya that repatriation does not imply "emptying the vaults of the big museums" but involves the return of objects vital to understanding a nation's history and establishing its cultural identity as a people.

The debate that has followed the Declaration shows no sign of conciliation. Three directors of museums who, in different ways, could claim the universality of their collections, addressed the subject in a forum organised by ICOM; summaries of their papers have been published (Abungu, 2004; Gryseels, 2004; Schuster, 2004b). Five of the museum directors who claim "universal" status for their museums addressed a conference on the Enlightenment idea but none of their reported presentations recognised the real issues involved (de Montebello, 2004; Loyette, 2004; MacGregor, N 2004a; Piotrovski, 2004; Schuster, 2004). The goodwill of all parts of the "international museum community" is paramount if progress is to be made.

The legal framework to bring meaningful collections of a nation's dispersed cultural property together will normally transcend national laws. There is therefore a resulting dependency on such international legislation as there is, assuming that this has been adopted by the nations concerned and in a form that retains the spirit of the original legislation. Rarely is the transfer of cultural property included in treaties establishing or re-establishing nationhood. Perhaps the best known example is the Congress of Vienna in 1815, which resulted in the restitution of the collections appropriated from across Europe during the Napoleonic Wars. The last forty years have seen UNESCO legislation providing a basis for safeguarding cultural property both in the event of armed conflict and from illicit import, export, or transfer between nations. Implicit in this legislation is the principle that the cultural property of a nation provides an important means of expressing its cultural identity in its own territory. The doctrine of universal collections and universal museums does not fit comfortably in this.

The historical reality of the universality of culture, the universal museum, and the contributions made to cultural identity and understanding do not feature in the international legislation. This reflects a very different world order from that pertaining 200 years ago. These historical realities cannot be dismissed but international law is not retroactive, and in today's world order, the notion that the nation has priority to its cultural heritage is paramount. It seems therefore that the way forward is more likely to be achieved through partnerships between museums. A prerequisite of this is a clear understanding of the roles and needs of all concerned.

In this, ICOM provides clear guidance for all museums in the *Code of Ethics for Museums* approved at its General Assembly in Seoul in October 2004[1] (ICOM 2004b). This document states the principles on which excellence in the museum profession may be achieved and offers guidelines for desirable professional practice. It has much to say that is relevant in the present area of debate. This *Code* has the affirmation of the organisation's 20,000 members which, in itself, gives it strength and professional standing.

The *Code* requires that collecting is in accordance with a clear, published policy determined by the museum's mission and objectives.[2] This policy may be defined in agreement with neighbouring museums or, in some instances, through national legislation or other mechanisms. There is no case for indiscriminate collecting by museums today. It would be highly inappropriate for two public institutions in the same country to compete for the purchase of the same item of that nation's heritage and there are increasing cases of museums making joint purchases. Examples of joint acquisition include Joan Miró's *Head of a Catalan Peasant* by the Tate Gallery and the Scottish National Gallery of Modern Art or John Glover's painting, *Mount Wellington and Hobart Town from Kangaroo Point,* acquired by the National Gallery of Australia with the Tasmanian Museum and Art Gallery. Such partnerships have also extended beyond national boundaries in the case of joint acquisition of a work by American artist Bill Viola by the Pompidou Centre, the Tate Modern, and the Whitney Museum. This entails sharing ownership and alternating presentation of the work in the three museums. As the Director of the Tate Gallery said in this context, "we have to be both less possessive and more imaginative in sharing items which are already in the public domain" (Serota, 2003).

ICOM has had a clear statement on the ethics of acquisition since 1970 (ICOM, 1970), as have a number of museums, among them the University of Pennsylvania Museum (1970), the British Museum (1972), and the Berlin State Museums (1976). ICOM's *Code of Ethics for Museums* requires museums to ensure that they have valid title for any acquisition[3] and that the item has not been illegally exported from its country of origin[4] or resulted from unauthorised or unscientific fieldwork.[5] It should be noted that the term valid title has specific meaning in the Code. It excludes title that might be granted on stolen material after a set period of time under certain civil (Roman) legal systems if the acquisition is considered to have

[1] See Appendix XX.
[2] ICOM Code 2.1.
[3] ICOM Code 2.2.
[4] ICOM Code 2.3.
[5] ICOM Code 2.4.

been made in good faith. Common law systems favour the original owner, although, under certain circumstances, such claims may also be time [barred?].[6]

In exercising due diligence in this regard, it is reasonable for the full history of an item, from discovery or production, to be established.[7] This is not, of course, only a safeguard against illegal transactions but a key element in maintaining and furthering knowledge. Museums collect and preserve much of the primary evidence associated with different academic disciplines; objects without information are of limited value.[8] A recent international conference of archaeologists has recommended that all objects offered on the market should carry a "pedigree" providing verified support of their provenance and ownership (Heilmeyer et al 2003).

The eclectic collections of former years have a different significance today. They were made at a time when there were few museums and many national boundaries bear no relationship to those of today. Requests for the repatriation of cultural property are therefore inevitable. ICOM promotes a positive approach to this. Its *Code of Ethics for Museums* encourages the development of partnerships with museums where a significant part of the cultural heritage has been lost.[9] It advocates the initiation of dialogues that might lead to the return of cultural property and encourages prompt and responsible steps where specific requests are made.[10] It particularly encourages this activity at a professional rather than a political level. But each such claim has to be viewed and determined between the parties concerned with regard to all the circumstances.

The current debate is largely about ownership of collections. This is not the most propitious premise on which to argue a case when the circumstances are often buried in history and the doctrine of retroactivity mitigates against a legal solution. Some museums have responded positively on moral grounds as well as where the matter may be considered the solution to a lawful dispute.

Much more can be achieved by partnership between museums, not least through display, loans, and exchanges. This does not necessarily involve the preparation of major exhibitions but rather ensuring the availability of appropriate material at suitable locations. This would be undertaken to professional standards, as defined for example, in the *ICOM Code of Ethics for Museums*. The objectives should be to ensure both the public availability and the safety of the material. There are constraints where immunity from seizure cannot be assured. It was this that prevented the State Hermitage Museum, St. Petersburg, from lending Titian's *St. Sebastian* to London two years ago (Hope, 2003). On the other hand, the invoking of an order seeking to prevent the return to London of the Dja Dja Wurrung bark etchings lent for an exhibition in the Museum Victoria in Melbourne (*Melbourne Herald Sun*, 2004) will not encourage the wider international museum community in making further such loans.

[6] See Part III.
[7] ICOM Code 2.3.
[8] ICOM Code 3.1.
[9] ICOM Code 6.1.
[10] ICOM Code 6.2.

Successful partnership is based on mutual confidence and respect. There is a need for greater transparency by museums. It would be encouraging, for example, to see each of the signatories of the declaration on universal museums indicating clearly their acquisition policies, including their stance on the scourge of the contemporary cultural world – illicit trafficking.

Successful partnership among the international museum community needs to be addressed in the context of both the world order and the role and function of museums in the twenty-first century. The declaration on universal museums draws our attention, unwittingly, to some of the challenges facing the world's museums that are not currently being met. Museums should, in the words of the *ICOM Code of Ethics for Museums*, "work in close collaboration with the communities from which their collections originate as well as those they serve."[11] This could be a profitable partnership with museums in countries currently unable to present the primary evidence of their cultural heritage to their people.

APPENDIX I

DECLARATION ON THE IMPORTANCE AND VALUE OF UNIVERSAL MUSEUMS

The international museum community shares the conviction that illegal traffic in archaeological, artistic, and ethnic objects must be firmly discouraged. We should, however, recognize that objects acquired in earlier times must be viewed in the light of different sensitivities and values, reflective of that earlier era. The objects and monumental works that were installed decades and even centuries ago in museums throughout Europe and America were acquired under conditions that are not comparable with current ones.

Over time, objects so acquired – whether by purchase, gift, or partage – have become part of the museums that have cared for them, and by extension part of the heritage of the nations which house them. Today we are especially sensitive to the subject of a work's original context, but we should not lose sight of the fact that museums too provide a valid and valuable context for objects that were long ago displaced from their original source.

The universal admiration for ancient civilizations would not be so deeply established today were it not for the influence exercised by the artifacts of these cultures, widely available to an international public in major museums. Indeed, the sculpture of classical Greece, to take but one example, is an excellent illustration of this point and of the importance of public collecting. The centuries-long history of appreciation of Greek art began in antiquity, was renewed in Renaissance Italy, and subsequently spread through the rest of Europe and to the Americas. Its accession into the collections of public museums throughout the world marked the significance of Greek sculpture for mankind as a whole and its enduring value for the contemporary world. Moreover, the distinctly Greek aesthetic of these works appears all the more strongly as the result of their being seen and studied in direct proximity to products of other great civilizations.

Calls to repatriate objects that have belonged to museum collections for many years have become an important issue for museums. Although each case has to be judged individually, we should acknowledge that museums serve not just the citizens of one nation

[11] ICOM Code section 2.

but the people of every nation. Museums are agents in the development of culture, whose mission is to foster knowledge by a continuous process of reinterpretation. Each object contributes to that process. To narrow the focus of museums whose collections are diverse and multifaceted would therefore be a disservice to all visitors.

Signed by the Directors of:

The Art Institute of Chicago
Bavarian State Museum, Munich (Alte Pinakothek, Neue Pinakothek)
State Museums, Berlin
Cleveland Museum of Art
J. Paul Getty Museum, Los Angeles
Solomon R. Guggenheim Museum, New York
Los Angeles County Museum of Art
Louvre Museum, Paris
The Metropolitan Museum of Art, New York
The Museum of Fine Arts, Boston
The Museum of Modern Art, New York
Opificio delle Pietre Dure, Florence
Philadelphia Museum of Art
Prado Museum, Madrid
Rijksmuseum, Amsterdam
State Hermitage Museum, St. Petersburg
Thyssen-Bornemisza Museum, Madrid
Whitney Museum of American Art, New York
The British Museum

APPENDIX 2 COMMENTARY

THE WHOLE WORLD IN OUR HANDS[12]

Neil MacGregor[13]

For many, the icon of the British Museum is the Rosetta Stone, that administrative by-product of the Greek imperial adventure in Africa. But I want to begin with an object from the other end of the continent. It is a chair, pieced together from fragments of weapons decommissioned in Mozambique after the amnesty that ended the civil war in 1992, by the artist Kester as part of the project Transforming Arms into Plough Shares. It's almost the first thing the visitor now sees when entering the Africa Gallery at the museum and it is, I think, for any viewer, a disconcerting and thought-provoking object. When we look at the arms-chair, we realise we are looking at guns made in Britain, Europe, the US. It's a potent emblem, I think, of the complexities linking Africa to the rest of the world. On the one hand, the artist wanted his sculpture to be in the British Museum, and Mozambique at the end of the civil war chose to join the Commonwealth. Yet the chair speaks of a long relationship of commercial, political and military exploitation. It is also, I believe, an object that achieves one of the fundamental purposes for which the British Museum was set up by Parliament in 1753, and for which it still exists today: to allow visitors to address through objects, both ancient and more recent, questions of contemporary politics and international relations.

On a nearby plinth is another sculpture, Big Masquerade, by Sokari Douglas Camp, a Nigerian woman who for the last 20 years has lived in London. More than life-size, made of large chunks of metal styled as though fabric, it represents a masquerade of the sort that members of her family in Nigeria take part in. It is a view of Africa made by an African, but one that could have been given this physical form only outside Nigeria. Douglas Camp is very clear that she couldn't, as a woman, have had a career as a metal sculptor in Nigeria.

On display nearby are the Benin bronzes, some of the greatest achievements of sculpture from any period. The brass plaques were made to be fixed to the palace of the Oba, the king of Benin, one above the other, a display of technological virtuosity and sheer wealth guaranteed to daunt any visitor. At the end of the 19th century, the plaques were removed and put in storage while the palace was rebuilt. A British legation, travelling to Benin at a sacred season of the year when such visits were forbidden, was killed, though not on the orders of the Oba himself. In retaliation, the British mounted a punitive expedition against Benin. Civil order collapsed (Baghdad comes to mind), the plaques and other objects were seized and sold, ultimately winding up in the museums of London, Berlin, Paris and New York. There they caused a sensation. It was a revelation to western artists and scholars, and above all to the public, that metal work of this refinement had been made in 16th-century Africa. Out of the terrible circumstances of the 1897 dispersal, a new, more securely grounded view of Africa and of African culture could be formed.

What do these objects, singly and in combination, offer the viewer? It seems to me that the throne of weapons, the masquerade figure, the Benin bronzes, allow a range of different approaches – personal, political, sacred, military, historical, cultural and international. I don't know where else a visitor can apprehend Africa in so many contexts. A collection that embraces the whole world allows you to consider the whole world. That is what an institution such as the British Museum is for.

In 1753, Parliament decided to buy the collection and library of the scholar- physician Hans Sloane and set up the British Museum as the first national museum in the world. It was an act of intellectual idealism, and political radicalism. It is hard to know how far the MPs and grandees who presided over its birth had thought through the consequences of creating a public space for intellectual inquiry and the dissent that necessarily follows it. But the ideals articulated by the museum's founders were without doubt part of the Enlightenment conviction that knowledge and understanding were indispensable ingredients of civil society, and the best remedies against the forces of intolerance and bigotry that led to conflict, oppression and civil war.

It was one of the first institutions to be called British, and it's worth asking the question: "British, as opposed to what?" The first answer is surely that it was the British, not the Royal Museum. Unlike those princely royal collections across Europe, where the subjects were from time to time graciously admitted at the will of the sovereign (as was still the case with the royal pictures here in Britain), the new museum in London was to be the collection of all citizens, where they could come free of charge and as of right. This was an extraordinary notion in 1753. It laid the foundation of a quite new concept of the citizen's right to information and understanding, comparable to the founding of the BBC and the Open University, or the modern right of access to the internet.

Linda Colley, writing about the 18th-century construction of "Britishness", has focussed on two key elements: that it was anti-Catholic and, on the whole, anti-French. Only eight years before, in 1745, Britain had looked over the edge of the abyss at civil war, the Jacobite rebellion and the alarming possibility of a return to an authoritarian state on something like the French model. The foundation of the British Museum was part of the reaction to that defining moment.

The Catholic model of authority, as seen from London, was one where intellectual inquiry was limited, controlled, and often prohibited. On the political plane, France provided the clear demonstration

[12] *The Guardian*, Saturday 24 July 2004, at <http://books.guardian.co.uk/review/story/0,,1267250,00.html>. Reprinted with the permission of the author.

[13] Neil MacGregor is the director of the British Museum.

that in an absolutist society, even one only idiosyncratically Catholic, true intellectual liberty was denied. The British Museum is often contrasted with Diderot's Encyclopaedia. Where the conceptual French characteristically wrote a book, the empirical British collected things and put up a building. But the key difference is surely that Diderot was put in prison and the Encyclopaedia banned, whereas the British Museum was created by Parliament specifically to promote intellectual inquiry, and to encourage the discovery of new kinds of truth.

In 1753, London was a city prone to bouts of violent religious intolerance. In that year Parliament voted to give civil rights to the Jewish population only to withdraw them a few months later in the face of public protest. In 1780, the Gordon riots would show how explosively strong anti-Catholic feeling could be. Study of the different societies and religions of the world would, it was hoped, generate tolerance and understanding. Like Gulliver returning from his travels, the scholar and visitor to the British Museum would see that there are many good ways of organising the world.

The original collection contained books, rocks, plants, animals, and scientific instruments – all the world, physical, natural and human, under one roof. Artefacts from classical antiquity and ancient Egypt were complemented by objects from societies Europeans had hardly heard of. The new museum soon received objects and specimens collected by members of Captain Cook's expeditions from the islands of the Pacific, from the north-west coast of North America, and from Australia. These objects raised all kinds of questions about the origins and practices of communities dizzyingly remote from European understanding, and impossible to square with the received theories of world history.

To ensure that the collection would be held for the benefit of citizens, and not the purposes of the crown, Parliament hit upon a solution of extraordinary ingenuity and brilliance. They borrowed from private family law the notion of the trust. The decision that the museum would be run not as a department of state, but by trustees had – and still has – crucial implications. Trustee ownership confers duties rather than rights. Trustees must derive no benefit for themselves, but hold the collection exclusively for the advantage of the beneficiaries. The collection cannot be sold off. The museum was set firmly outside the commercial realm, a position epitomised by the principle of free admission. Even more astonishingly, it was in large measure removed from the political realm. Trustees are not allowed by law merely to follow government orders: they have to act as they judge best in the interest of beneficiaries, including, crucially, future and unborn beneficiaries.

Who are the beneficiaries for whom the trustees hold the collection? Startlingly, they are not just the citizens of Britain. The British Museum was from the beginning a trust where the objects would be held "for the use of learned and studious men [in 1753 they were mostly men], both native and foreign." In his will, Sloane had declared his desire that his collection should be preserved "for the improvement, knowledge and information of all persons." The rest of the world has rights to use and study the collection on the same footing as British citizens.

The original focus of the museum's curiosity was inevitably the ancient world and the cultures of Greece, Rome and the Bible that dominated 18th-century thinking about the world. The collections would enable these cultures to be addressed through things, not just words. The study and classification of objects began to reveal a history different from the familiar narrative of the texts known and studied for centuries. And soon other texts, long unreadable, complicated the story yet further.

The supreme example of this transformational new understanding is of course the Rosetta Stone. Once it was possible to read history from the perspective of ancient Egypt, it became clear that the account presented in the Hebrew Old Testament had to be robustly questioned. The literal truth, the absolute authority, of scriptural tradition could not easily resist the kinds of advances in historical knowledge unlocked by the Rosetta Stone. The deciphering of ancient scripts changed for ever the way Europeans were able to imagine the story of humanity, destroying centuries of received authority about the past with repercussions as important for our understanding of time and history as the geological studies of the same period.

And it was not just Egypt. In 1872, George Smith, an assistant in the museum, deciphered a neo-Assyrian seventh-century BC tablet from Nineveh. He found that it told the story of Utnapishtim, who had been warned by the gods that there would be a great flood that would destroy the world. He built a boat and loaded it with everything he could find. He survived the flood for six days while mankind was destroyed. At the end of the flood he sent a dove and a swallow out and they came back because they could not find dry land. Then he sent a raven, which did not return, and he knew the floods had subsided.

On reading the tablet, Smith "jumped up and rushed about the room in a great state of excitement, and, to the astonishment of those present, began to undress himself." Quite apart from being an understandable cause of extreme excitement, this was proof positive that the Biblical story of Noah was not unique. A different man in a different place was told by a different god, or, even more alarmingly several gods, to take his precautions. None of this proves or disproves any historical fact, nor indeed any religious creed. But this kind of comparative religious study changes the status of all claims to exclusive truth of whatever kind.

An essential part of such liberating understanding is the recognition that within the same museum object, different histories, meanings, and functions may freely cohabit. Here again, the fact that we are the British Museum, and not a French one, is significant. Implicit within French museum theory is the notion that sacred objects entering museum collections must be entirely divorced from their religious context and function and take their place exclusively within a secular human history. Is it necessary to make these kinds of separations?

When members of the London Maori community came to bless the installation in the museum of Maori objects, some of them given by their ancestors to Captain Cook, speeches, songs and prayers acknowledged different kinds of relationships – spiritual and academic – with the objects on display. It was an affirmation of an important principle: secular inquiry need not preclude the rights of the sacred.

Accommodations like this are perhaps harder when an object is tied to a particular notion of national identity, or comes to be appropriated to a particular political end. Such was the fate of the famous Cyrus Cylinder. Found in Babylon, this celebrates the conquest of Babylon by Cyrus, king of Persia, in 539 BC. It is, in other words, the record of the morning after the night of Belshazzar's feast. The writing was on the wall, Babylon fell, the Persians arrived, and Cyrus inscribed this clay cylinder to be used as the foundation document of a temple. In it he proclaims that he has returned statues of gods to their temples, and allowed deported peoples to return to their homelands. It is the archaeological evidence supporting the Old Testament narrative that Cyrus allowed the Jews to return from the waters of Babylon to rebuild Jerusalem.

When the last Shah of Iran decided to celebrate the 2,500th anniversary of the foundation of the Persian monarchy, he asserted that the Cyrus Cylinder was the world's first charter of human rights, whose birthplace was therefore to be located in Iran – an assertion that must have startled many who had tried to assert their human rights under his regime. The Cylinder became a mantra of his newly constructed national identity.

Comparison by scholars in the British Museum with other similar texts, however, showed that rulers in ancient Iraq had been making comparable declarations upon succeeding to the throne for two millennia before Cyrus. The Cylinder may indeed be a document of human rights and it is clearly linked with the history of Iran, but it is in no real sense an Iranian document: it is part of a much larger history of the ancient Near East, of Mesopotamian kingship, and of the Jewish diaspora. It is one of the museum's tasks to resist the narrowing of the object's meaning and its appropriation to one political agenda.

Which brings us to the Elgin Marbles. After the fall of the Colonels in 1974, strengthening democracy and joining the EU were naturally the prime aims of the new Greek government. Then for the first time the location of the Parthenon sculptures became not merely a matter of cultural debate, but an instrument of national politics. Ever since, the return of the Parthenon sculptures in the British Museum (about half of what survives from antiquity is already in Athens) has been a matter of Greek government policy. Melina Mercouri, Greek minister of culture, argued that the Parthenon and its sculptures embodied the values of democracy and indeed the very spirit of Greece as a modern, democratic, European nation, and were therefore the exclusive cultural patrimony of the Greek people. Well, up to a point. The problem is that they embody many other things besides. Their key purpose, as ornaments in a temple, was clearly as adjuncts to a religious cult. Athens may have been in some sense a democracy but it was also a slave-owning society and an imperial maritime power. Both the building and its sculptures were the subject of intense political controversy at the time of their creation, since they were funded from the proceeds of tribute extracted from fellow Greek city states in the name of defence against the Persian enemy.

What becomes evident in Bloomsbury is that the sculptures are, like the Cyrus Cylinder, part of a story that is not only national. Indeed it is not only European. In artistic terms the sculptures are clearly part of a process that embraces Egypt and Mesopotamia, Turkey, India, Rome and the whole of Europe. Over the centuries, the Parthenon itself has, like its sculptures, come to mean many other and contradictory things. The building has been a church and a mosque and is now a ruin, – a document of the Christian, Ottoman and Venetian history of Greece as well as the Classical. Its present expurgated state is a testament to the classical education and aspirations of the German kings who shaped modern Greece in the mid 19th century. And the sculptures, since coming to London, have become part of another European and world story.

The British Museum was founded with a civic purpose, to allow the citizen, through reasoned inquiry and comparison, to resist the certainties that endanger free society and are still among the greatest threats to our liberty. We see, for example, brutally oversimplified notions of identity manufactured and imposed upon cultures and communities throughout the Middle East, to sustain entrenched conflicts. It is no less an issue for our own country, where many English view the European continent in general, and Germany in particular, through a distorting myth of inherited enmity, while Scots can look upon the English through the fictional history of opposition and oppression served up by Braveheart. We need not dwell on the mythical Britain, racially pure, of BNP fantasy.

The cultural historian, Edward Said, in May 2003, after the invasion of Iraq and just a few months before his death, wrote a new preface to his book *Orientalism*: "The terrible reductive conflicts that herd people under falsely unifying rubrics like America, the West, or Islam, and invent collective identities for large numbers of individuals who are actually quite diverse, must be opposed . . ."

He goes on to say how we can oppose them. "We still have at our disposal the rational interpretative skills that are the legacy of humanist education. Rather than the manufactured clash of civilisations, we need to concentrate on the slow working together of cultures that overlap, borrow from each other and live together, but for that kind of wider perception, we need time and a patient and sceptical inquiry, supported by faith in communities of interpretation, that are difficult to sustain in a world demanding instant action and reaction." The British Museum, any world museum, seems to me to be indeed one of Said's "communities of interpretation."

A collection like that held in trust for the world by the British Museum is surely a powerful weapon in a conflict that may yet be mortal, unless we find means to free minds as well as bodies from oppression. World museums of this kind offer us a chance to forge the arguments that can hope to defeat the simplifying brutalities which disfigure politics all round the world. The British Museum must now reaffirm its worldwide civic purpose. That must be the goal that shapes our future plans. Where else can the world see so clearly that it is one?

THE TREASURES OF THE WORLD CULTURE IN THE PUBLIC MUSEUM[14]

Edited Remarks by
Peter-Klaus Schuster[15]

* * *

The collections in Berlin were acquired through the art market or private commerce. No deal was in fact possible without a contract of sale or permission to export. This does not mean that nothing was sold or exported. But it does mean that all objects came legally into the collections.

The Directors of the State Museums in West Berlin adopted a Declaration in 1976 which condemned illegal excavations, the concealment of origin and the illegal trade of archaeological objects. It argued for cultural exchange through loans between museums which would respect the requirements of preserving and restoring the works. As a consequence, long-term loan agreements have been introduced between Germany and both Italy and Greece. In 2002, we also prepared a Declaration to the effect that we, as Universal Museums, will not loan out for exhibition any objects of dubious legal background. Our international congress on Illegal Archaeology, planned long before the Declaration on Museums, again denounced unauthorized excavation and illegal art-dealing, and proposed solutions.

In connection with the demand for the restitution of art works in the possession of our museums, we distinguish four categories of case. Firstly, there are historical art works, which were as a rule purchased legally. Secondly, there is way booty seized on behalf of the State as reparation or as war trophy. This is the case between Germany and Russia. Thirdly, there are cultural possessions acquired as a consequence of persecution – art looted by the Nazis. And lastly, there are stolen goods from illegal excavations and plundering.

The cases in our second category are governed by the Geneva Convention. National and international property law applies to these cases, as it does to the cases of the third category, art looted by the Nazis. As for the last category, stolen goods from illegal excavations, this is now under discussion in the light of the UNESCO and UNIDROIT Conventions. That leaves us with the first category, legally acquired historical art works which are now ???demanded back by the legal successors of the sellers.

To date, we have restituted large numbers of art works. Furthermore, we have also returned objects of which the Berlin Museums

[14] The full text may be read at *ICOM News* <http://icom.museum/universal.html>.

[15] Mr. Schuster is the General Director of the State Museums of Berlin.

are indisputably the legal owner to their place of origin on the basis of permanent loan agreements in cooperation with our colleagues in the partner countries.

These are just some of the arguments and the realities which lie behind the Declaration on the Importance and Value of Universal Museums, and which prompted us to draft and publish this Declaration.

REFERENCES

Abungu, George (2004) 'The Declaration: A Contested Issue', *ICOM News* 57(1), p. 5.

de Montebello, Philippe (2004) 'Metropolitan Museum of Art, New York' *The British Museum Magazine*, 48, pp. 18–19.

Eluyemi, Omotoso & Akanbiemu, M O (2004), *Universal Museums: An anomalous declaration – a rejoiner*, Museums Association of Nigeria and National Commission for Museums and Monuments (May 2004, unpublished).

Gryseels, Guido (2004) 'Assuming our Responsibilities in the Present' *ICOM News*, 57(1), p. 8.

Heilmeyer, Wolf-Dieter & Eule, J Cordelia (2004), *Illegale Archäologie?* pp. 236–238, Staatliche Museen zu Berlin (for an English translation of the Berlin Resolution, 2003 see <http://www.unesco.org/culture/legalprotection/theft/images/berlin2003.pdf>.

Hope, Charles *et al* (2003) Titian, Exhibition Catalogue, National Gallery, London. See also Daily Telegraph, London 5 July 2004, p. 8.

ICOM (1970), 'Ethics of acquisition'/'Éthique des acquisitions', *ICOM News* 23(2), pp. 10–13 & 49–51, Paris.

ICOM (2004a) Universal Museums, *ICOM News* 57(1), Paris.

ICOM (2004b) *Code of Ethics for Museums*, available at <http://icom.museum> .

Lewis, Geoffrey (1992) 'Museums and their precursors: a brief world survey' in Thompson, J. *et al* (eds), *Manual of Curatorship: A Guide to Museum Practice.* Butterworth and Museums Association, London.

Lewis, Geoffrey (2004a) 'The Universal Museum: A Special Case?' *ICOM News*, 57(1), p. 3.

Lewis, Geoffrey (2004b) 'A Debated Museum Concept: partnership in universality', *Museum International* 224, 40–45. UNESCO/Blackwell, Oxford.

Lewis, Geoffrey (2005) 'Museums' in *Encyclopaedia Britannica*, 24, pp. 480–492 or *Britannica On Line.*

Loyette, Henri. (2004) 'The Louvre', *The British Museum Magazine* 48, pp. 20–21.

MacGregor, Arthur (ed) (1983), Tradescant's Rarities, p. 17. Clarendon Press, Oxford.

MacGregor, Neil (2004a) 'British Museum, London', *The British Museum Magazine* 48, pp. 20–21.

MacGregor, Neil (2004b), 'The British Museum', *ICOM News*, 57(1), p. 7.

Melbourne Herald Sun (2004) 'Fight for rare aboriginal artefacts', 10 November 2004, Melbourne.

Miller, Edward (1973) *That Noble Cabinet.* Andre Deutsch, London,

O'Neill, Mark (2004) 'Enlightenment Museums: universal or merely global?', *Museum and Society* 2(3), pp. 190–202.

Piotrovski, Mikhail (2004) 'State Hermitage Museum', St Petersburg', *The British Museum Magazine* 48, p. 19.

Schuster, Peter-Klaus (2004a) 'The Berlin State Museum' *The British Museum Magazine* 48, pp. 18–19.

Schuster, Peter-Klaus (2004b) 'The Treasures of World Culture in the Public Museum' *ICOM News*, 57(1), p. 4.

Serota, Nicholas (2003) *Why Save Art for the Nation?* Lecture given at the Art Fund Centenary Conference, and available at <www.tate.org.uk/home/news/whysaveart_11-11-03.htm>

CHAPTER FORTY-NINE

Africa and Its Museums: Changing of Pathways?

George H. Okello Abungu

INTRODUCTION

The concept of museums as it is today, including institutions in Africa, stems from western origins and practice. Museums have always been points of collections, and their origins lie within the human interest for the rare and unique. Although they started as individuals' hobbies, later they grew to become houses of collective memory, identity, and pride. Countries, particularly in Europe, opened museums that reflected the trends of that time. Gradually, they became places to exhibit and enjoy the unique and rare heritage of humanity, the wonders of the other worlds that were collected through adventures from the unknown lands and cultures. As museums developed into institutions of research, documentation, and exhibition to cater to the growing needs of a population thirsty for new ideas, they also became powerful symbols of representation of "us" as opposed to the "others." Museums became important symbols of a nation's achievements, attaining the status of "temples of heritage" with "don't touch" labels being a common part of their language.

Today, however, the role of the museums, particularly in Africa and the developing world, is being questioned; can the developing nations continue to sustain museums as "temples" and places of pride, without museums directly contributing to the well-being of the communities they are supposed to serve? Is the concept of a museum a universal one that implies similar functions and universal similar expectations? Judging from what is taking place in Africa in relation to the role of museums, the answer is no. This chapter discusses the changing roles of museums internationally, with special emphasis on Africa.

THE MUSEUM

Museums today are a world phenomenon, and are found in all parts of the world. Although museums started as individual hobbies with collectors of unique items doing it for personal satisfaction, today they are respected institutions carrying out diverse functions that range from research, collection development, documentation, and inventory, to exhibition and education. Museums are about people and are made by people for people. They have traditionally been places of identity and pride, temples of the best collections, put on display to facilitate human reflection and education.

Although some traditional museums have addressed socio-economic issues, most have been reflections of human pride and past achievements, rather than current issues and future projections. Today, museums must constantly remain up-to-date with the current social issues affecting the people they are founded to serve. This has become increasingly important since the majority of museums are funded through public coffers, as well as the public demand that museums and their professionals provide service and be accountable to the public.

ICOM's definition of the museum as a "non-profit making, permanent institution in the service of society and of its development, and open to the public which acquires, conserves, researches, communicates and exhibits, for purpose of study, education and enjoyment, material evidence of people and their environment" is broad and provides a wide range of opportunities for museums to involve themselves in the service of society. The statement that captures the museum's social role is "in the service of society and of its development," confirming the role of museum management towards the well-being of the people and their heritage as a dynamic element in society.

The museum today is the embodiment of the cultures of a people, particularly in societies that are devoid of "their own" culture; the museum becomes the temple of heritage; the representation of the identity or identities of a nation and its achievements. Museums have also become forums for dialogue and critical thinking, and in some cases museums provide spiritual spaces where a community can rally around shared heritage, problems, catastrophe, or happiness. Many museums today are moving away from the confines of their grand walls as houses of wonder, collections of the very rare, and fortification of the untouched, to open friendly spaces of memory, shared experience, and representation of identities.

It is clear that there are different types of museum, as defined by their activities and audiences. For example, museums dedicated to feathers or stamps may not share much with museums of natural history, and a numismatic museum is not easily comparable to a museum of art. Public expectation from a natural history museum may not be the same as from a numismatic museum or museum of stamps. They may, however, be connected by the same principles of serving the public and sharing common ethical standards.

Museums all over the world, particularly in Europe and North America, do not only depict "us" or "ours," but also "others." Equally important is the fact that some of the most popular exhibits in some of the largest museums worldwide come from "others." The exhibits are interpreted by "us" either as great achievements of humanity and unique or as a sign of a difference from "us."

In many cases, the objects are interpreted by "us" to demonstrate the difference between "us" and the "others." The interpretations were for many years the monopoly of curators and not of the makers or users or owners of the different heritage. Today, this monopoly of interpretation and representation is being challenged as museums play a major role in human relations. They do not only preserve world cultures, but are also guardians of their interpretation and hence of our understanding of the world. Therefore, museums shape how we understand our being. The traditional presentation and interpretation of material culture and other cultural symbols provide a challenge for museum curators as the diverse but globalized community asks for a stake in the production of its own history.

It must also be appreciated that the material culture of a people is a manifestation of their way of life and how they understand and treat their environment. Material culture bears messages that help us to understand why people behave in a certain way. In Africa, for example, much of material culture (objects) also holds symbolic meanings, and the objects are passed from generation to generation. Material culture is used in creating a coherent society through acceptance of the pieces as unifying factors. These pieces are grounded in the local cultural context and occupy special or defined spaces. They are often symbols of unity in a diversified society, some having spiritual connotations. Because many of these are currently found in museums, the museums in turn become the guardians of spiritual and symbolic heritage.

The new and emerging role of museums raises questions such as how can institutions bring this symbolic context closer to reality? More importantly, how can museums, particularly in Africa, make their objects have a positive impact on the lives of their people?

Unfortunately, many objects of cultural heritage continue to find their way onto the international markets of illicit trade, where they are taken from their context, abused, and subsequently lose their meaning. These same objects find their way into large and prestigious museums as major exhibits with elaborate and glossy catalogues aiming to legitimize their appropriation. The issue of holding heritage on behalf of those with inadequate security and inappropriate facilities is still a common excuse for the powerful to hold on to the others' heritage, irrespective of its provenance and how it was acquired.

Museums all over the world are at a crossroads, and in order for museums to gain respect, they must first clean up their acts, be transparent, and further the interest of the societies that they claim to represent. The privileged position of museums as the pride of the nation is beginning to be challenged by an inquisitive public. This is the case for African museums, the roles of which are becoming more diversified and inclusive. In doing this, museums compete for resources with many other bodies offering entertainment and education, and even institutions addressing human needs such as health and economics. The management of museums and the choice of their activities, particularly those that have an impact on society, are issues worth addressing in a holistic way.

MUSEUMS IN EUROPE AND NORTH AMERICA

Faced with the rising expectations from the public, dwindling budgets, and alternative sources of entertainment, the question "what museums for the twenty-first century?" is now a common one. In June of 2001 in Stockholm, Sweden, a gathering of more than 260 museum personnel from more than 40 countries grappled with issues like the role of museums, ethics, and relevance within society. Today, as people stop taking museums for granted, they are beginning to demand the removal of the monumental walls that surround the museum to create spaces with a human face, a forum for dialogue, and a neutral ground where many voices of various opinions have a chance of being heard. It is the opportune time for museums to move away from the traditional orientation and become dynamic, flexible, and proactive institutions recognizing change and diversity.

There are great opportunities for museums to play a central role in the national agenda, particularly in Europe and America. This is attributable both to good economic performance and to the lottery and other funds available for culture and the preservation of heritage, as well as the public's demand for leisure, entertainment, and education. Today, in Europe and America, there is growing desire for more free time from the work place. The free market and unrestricted use of science and technology are providing this opportunity. People are increasingly consumers of leisure but are also thirsty for fruitful educational activities.

What is not clear, however, is whether museums are prepared for this kind of challenge, addressing issues that affect humanity, offering products that bring repeat visits, and developing mechanisms for inclusion of changing cultures, all the while retaining their ethical stance.

AFRICA AT THE CROSSROADS

By contrast, museums in the developing world and particularly in Africa compete with other institutions such as schools, hospitals, and public works for the very scarce resources provided by the governments. Museums are not a priority and must strive to generate their own resources. If they are to attract central funding, they must play an even more important social role. This requires a broad mission, a proactive stance, and flexibility.

Museums in Africa in their present form are recent creations of the colonial era. Although material culture has always formed part of African life, it was never organized in the Western sense of display, as is the case in museums. It formed part of daily life, whether for ceremonial, ritual, functional, spiritual–religious, or political use. However, even objects in daily use have symbolic meaning and, when used for ritual or ceremonial purposes, attract varying degrees of reverence. Objects have a life and spirit of their own.

With colonialism, Europeans exposed to the outside world what they saw as the hidden "treasures" of Africa, the regalia symbolizing the "primitive" peoples of the continent. Over the years, the growing settler community in Africa wanted places of entertainment, which were provided, among others, by the display and consumption of African cultural and natural heritage.

Colonialism brought all kinds of people to the African continent; the missionaries, administrators, white settlers, collectors, marketers, and even vagabonds. All these groups were, in one way or the other, intrigued by the African cultural heritage, and to a certain degree became involved in its collection. Many of the collections that came to be housed in museums in and out of Africa were from missionary collectors, administrators, or rich white families who had previously indulged in the collection of African paraphernalia. With time, and as the collections grew, governments then established official museums in Africa.

In eastern and southern Africa, the fossil-rich Rift Valley offered opportunities for archaeologists and paleontologists to investigate the theory of human evolution. Africa, presented as the possible cradle of the human species, attracted the attention of scholars as early as the 1920s and 1930s. The early findings were placed in local museums because these specialists were associated with the museum institutions that they also often controlled. The collections strengthened the position of the museum as a centre for education and research, catering to a white elite.

Therefore, museums in Africa, especially the well-developed museums, were of little significance and benefit to the local people, as they strove to be centers of excellence for the outside world. Many museums in Africa had therefore become irrelevant institutions by the turn of the last century. Visitor statistics in many were low because people only visited them during school outings. The museums in Africa had to re-elevate their role in the new society. The question, "What museums for Africa?" first asked in November 1991 through an ICOM-organized brainstorming session of archaeologists and museologists, became a common cry across the continent. Africans began to reflect on museums that could address their needs and interests, and interpret their history as they saw it. It also became a question of empowering people to own their history and heritage. As public facilities, museums should have an influence on public life and development, increasing knowledge and making it accessible to the surrounding community.

It took many professionals and bodies to start these discussions; among them were the West Africa Museum Programme (WAMP), the West African Archaeological Association, ICOM, the South African Development Community Association of Museums, International Council of African Museums (AFRICOM), and various museum professionals in Africa.

In Africa, however, there is a long history of museums being divorced from the local communities, a period during which the museum was not managed for the well-being of the people. The former president of Mali, Alpha Oumar Konaré, when he was President of ICOM, remarked: "Who still doubts that Africa's museums never really left the cities, and even in those cities have remained things belonging to foreigners? Who doubts that museums in Africa have harbored illicit objects, or have often served to legitimise dubious traffic? Who doubts that the image of Africa transmitted abroad does not correspond to the reality of African life or to the views of African people? Who doubts that many museums continue to exist only because they are financed from abroad?" (Konaré O. 1995). This was Konaré writing and reflecting on the problems faced by African museums: the lack of vision, independence, transformation, and community participation. His prescription was "to eliminate the Western model for museums in Africa so that new methods for the preservation and promotion of Africa's cultural heritage can be allowed to flourish." It was necessary to cultivate willpower, to break away from dependence and to embrace dialogue. It was necessary for museums to include all members of society in their activities, to speak various national languages and to be open to science and technology.

Today, African museums must take the continent's needs into account and play a dual role as custodians of national heritage and forums for cultural development and exchange. The museums founded in the past decade not only respect new national identities, but also use the past through exhibitions and public programmes to instill a sense of identity and pride in the spectator. These museums are not shy to engage in issues that are traditionally seen to be outside the purview of the museums. They engage in issues of human rights, poverty alleviation, environmental degradation, cross cultural and gender matters, conflict resolution, street children, and protecting indigenous knowledge systems. These new developments reflect the desire for museums to take a central role in the political, economic, and social discourses of the various African countries, to present diversified activities, and to play proactive and significant national roles. They convey powerful messages of memory, responsibility, collective identity, and common destiny.

MUSEUMS IN THE SERVICE OF COMMUNITIES

The role of museums, therefore, ranges from educational facilities, platforms for dialogue, space of memory and common identity, to areas of resistance against oppression or a venue for economically and environmentally sustainable activities for local communities. Museums, to a certain extent, are removing the veil of the innocent nonaligned public institution to become a forum for dialogue. More and more museums on the continent of Africa are becoming a voice for the voiceless, and reconciler for different opinions. Although the museum cannot be everything to everybody, it can be something for everybody. That is the emerging scenario in Africa.

Many from the West would ask why and how can museums be involved in such "new" and "complex" issues. The answer is simple; the museum as a forum for different voices has the capacity to be inclusive. It may be the only space capable

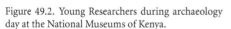

Figure 49.1. Two Young Researchers Club members in the National Museums of Kenya Osteology Lab.

of expressing the thoughts of any group who feels out of place; for example, the homeless and street children, the immigrants and refugees, the marginalized and the discriminated, all those who feel excluded and ignorant and who suffer in silence. In a continent plagued with economic, social, and political turbulence, the museum as the custodian of collective memory cannot have the pleasure of taking cover under research and education that is devoid from the existing reality. Examples of proactive museums in Africa abound today.

The National Museums of Botswana, through its desert Zebra Outreach Programme, has popularized museum activities at the rural level, taking the museum to the people while, at the same time, carrying out research on tangible as well as intangible heritage, like oral traditions. Because of its effectiveness, this programme receives substantial funding from the government, despite its high operating costs. It is a true reflection of the flexibility of the museum and its physical presence among the people in their own space.

Through the Museum Interactive Programme, the Education Department of the National Museums of Kenya (NMK) is involved in popularising science for young people by using museum specimens in interactive learning. In recognition of science as a means of national development, the programme has set up a club called the Young Researcher, for children between the ages of 8 and 13, to come every month to work behind the scenes with NMK researchers, in museum departments and laboratories (Figs. 49.1 and 49.2). The club is an important educational tool as well as a constructive recreational activity.

Through similar programmes, the NMK identified other weaknesses pertaining to education services within the country, especially in primary schools, where students were perceived only as listeners, and teachers as the owners and givers of knowledge. Through countrywide workshops, the NMK addressed this issue, developing the skills of primary school teachers in the promotion of analytical teaching.

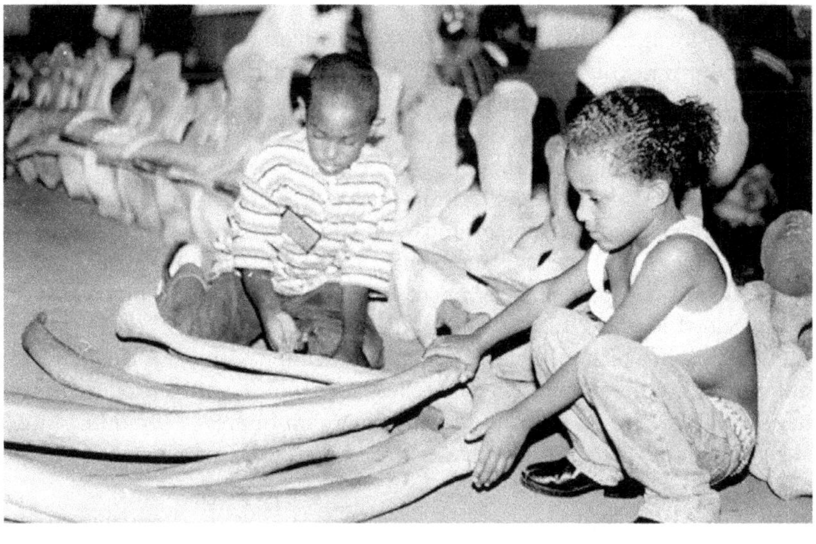

Figure 49.2. Young Researchers during archaeology day at the National Museums of Kenya.

Analytical teaching provides students with a capacity to take an active role in the exercise of learning.

Interactive learning exercises arose out of the need to bring museum objects to life and to endow them with meaning, for the benefit of communities, who are the stakeholders. Here, the museum was not only popularizing science and technology, but also encouraging the education of those people who will be responsible for running the country and deciding the destiny of the society. As Alpha Oumar Konaré once noted, "it must be clear that we are conserving objects not for their own sake, but for mankind in relation to man and society. If we pay more attention to the objects than to man or society, we shall conserve nothing. An object cannot be conserved outside the human and the social context" (Konaré O. 1995). The days when knowledge of museum specimens and collections, and the interpretation of material culture, were the preserve of a few "initiated" curators are fast disappearing.

MUSEUMS AS COMMUNITY SPACES

Museums in Africa are becoming platforms for expressing living communities' feelings and expectations; with the disappearance of many of their cultural and spiritual spaces, communities are beginning to regard museums as alternative spaces for cultural activities and community performances. Museums are becoming living spaces and forums for dialogue and free expression that also offer opportunities for recreating the "better past." In relation to the this, the Village Museum in Dar–es-Salaam, Tanzania, acts as a venue for the different Tanzanian ethnic groups to recreate their rich traditions in a town, but within rural setting. The various ethnic celebration days, during which people from a specific group go through their traditional practices, including food preparation and consumption, traditional folk singing, dance, and storytelling, are growing in popularity. The demand overstretches the available resources. The museum in this case provides opportunities for people to enjoy the rich traditions that have ensured the survival of the group, and for the young to learn from the old. It additionally enables each individual to identify his or her role within the community.

In Cape Town, South Africa, where thirty years ago a whole community was evicted from their homes in District Six, a museum was set up on that site, which helped to retain the spirit and cohesiveness of the community. The museum ensured, through community mobilisation, that no new construction should take place in the area, which was appropriated by the apartheid government. Today, the common memory of people of District Six is represented in the museum. After 30 years, the present government of South Africa has now decided to give back the land to the original owners. This is a case in which a simple community museum has not only helped in presenting a people's collective memory, but has played a successful role of resistance against an oppressive regime and has subsequently negotiated the return of the land by the new democratic government to its original owners. It is, therefore, the guardian and custodian of a people's memory, land, and dignity. It is a true testimony to the power of culture, that of memory, of the intangible heritage of a people. Nothing could sum up this power better than the quotation of Don Mattera in 1987 and found on the District Six Museum Web site, when he said, "Gone Buried Covered by the dust of defeat – or so the conquerors believed. But there is nothing that can be hidden from the mind. Nothing that memory cannot reach or touch or call back."

There are other African museums that have, through unfortunate events, demonstrated the power of heritage and museums as an institution of collective memory. When the king's Palace Museum in Antananarivo, Madagascar, caught fire, the entire town rallied together to extinguish the fire; subsequently, the whole of Madagascar was in mourning. Today, despite that little has been done to restore the museum, it is probably the only element that brings the people of the island together – including the 200 or so political parties. It became a symbol of the nation, a common identity for an otherwise diverse nation.

In Senegal and Mali, two museums have been set up to deal specifically with the issue of women. In both, the role of women as custodians of heritage, guardians of homes, mothers of the children, providers of food, and performers of other domestic chores is, for the first time, vividly put on public view through exhibitions. Women's roles in most African societies have not been given the attention of the public, unlike the roles of men, who are regarded as the "protectors" of the family. These museums are therefore trying to address gender issues that will not only bring the recognition of women's roles into a male-dominated society, but also to the forefront of the issue of gender equality, the sharing of responsibility, and the acknowledgement of the role of women as the backbone of the society. In this sense, the museum becomes the voice of the oppressed and the underprivileged.

AFRICAN MUSEUMS AS CUSTODIANS OF THE CONTINENT'S HERITAGE

In most African countries, museums are the custodians of the country's heritage. This role as custodians of both cultural and natural heritage has improved the status and made museums relevant to people's needs. Although some countries in Africa have two institutions in charge of cultural heritage – namely, museums for movable heritage and departments of antiquity for immovable heritage – many countries such as Kenya, Uganda, Nigeria, Ghana, Zimbabwe, and Botswana entrust this role to their national museums. The latter are empowered through relevant legislation to be custodians of heritage that includes antiquities and monuments. In Kenya, the old towns of Lamu and Mombasa have been registered as protected historical heritage, under the guardianship of the National Museums of Kenya. Furthermore, some museums have established training centres together with their local

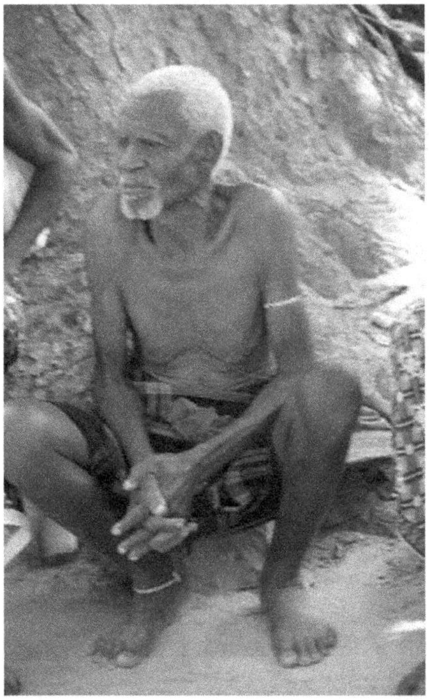

Figure 49.3. An attentive Kaya Elder.

communities, in order to train members of the community to carry out restoration, preservation, and renovation work. This is the case for the Swahili Cultural Centre in Mombasa and Lamu and the Great Zimbabwe Conservation Centre. The same applies to other cultural landscapes such as sacred places, where museums, in consultation and partnerships with the local communities (Fig. 49.3), have managed to conserve many of such heritage.

A number of museums also contain large collections of botanical and zoological specimens. For example, The NMK in Nairobi has the largest collection of plant specimens on the continent in its Herbarium; the same applies to the entomological collection. It also has the largest centre for Biodiversity in Eastern and Central Africa. Most of the museum's research facilities are directly related to human survival, existence, and the preservation of the environment. The department of entomology at NMK for years has contributed directly to pest control, and advised farmers on which insects are good and which are harmful to crops. It has also worked closely with the International Centre of Insect Physiology and Ecology for pest control in the region, given that it is the only institution engaged in the collection and maintenance of a permanent study collection.

The marine resources section of the Centre for Biodiversity, especially Ichthyology, has, over the years, worked with other institutions in improving fish stocks in the lakes of East Africa. It also helped operate the Aquarium of the NMK, which is both an educational and an entertainment facility.

Many African museums have so far appreciated the role of indigenous plants, especially food and medicinal plants. They have not only been able to exhibit indigenous food plants and medicines, but they have also been engaged in experimentation with the values attached to foods and the cultural significance of different plants. The issues of food security and poverty reduction have been part of museums' main activities. These are not only areas of interest but are practical human experiences that may enable museums to get better funding, given that museums are directly serving the people. The relevance of museums and hence the sustainable support they can now attract depend principally on their contribution to national development through tackling issues that affect their different communities.

Africa's position is unique because for a long time it has been a continent of conflict and wars. Most of the leaders have not lived up to the expectations that independence brought with it, and many countries are more divided than ever before. There has been, in many instances, a lack understanding about diversity as a resource. This has created a need for alternative forums for discussion that some museums have provided in order to fill the gap as facilitators of peace and co-existence. This, in turn, provides tremendous status opportunity and funding prospects for research and implementation of the museum's findings.

A number of museums in Africa (such as the NMK) have been involved for a long time not only in peace research, but also in peace exhibition, or similar projects. The traditional knowledge is there and, as Alpha Oumar Konaré, once said, "we must also be open to traditional knowledge, the knowledge of the people, of notables, men of culture." This knowledge should be protected, promoted, and used for the benefit of humanity; this includes the rich, intangible heritage of Africa (Fig. 49.4).

Africa is a continent of contrast, rich in tangible and intangible, movable and immovable, and cultural and natural heritage. The cradle of humankind, it boasts the Great Rift Valley, snow-peaked mountains on the equator, and prime beaches; the biodiversity of Africa is unrivalled and so is its contribution to the understanding of the origins of life. Africa itself is culture and many museums in the continent are today the custodians of this rich heritage. The museums have a special role therefore in the promotion of tourism as major attractions.

CREATION OF PARTNERSHIPS THROUGH NETWORKING

One area that museums can and, in some cases, have already started to exploit is the creation of partnerships and networks with other museums within and beyond the continent. An important example of partnerships in Sub-Saharan Africa is the twinning of African museums with European museums, most notably through ICOM's Swedish–African Museum Programme, sponsored by the Swedish International Development Cooperation Agency. This unique arrangement has

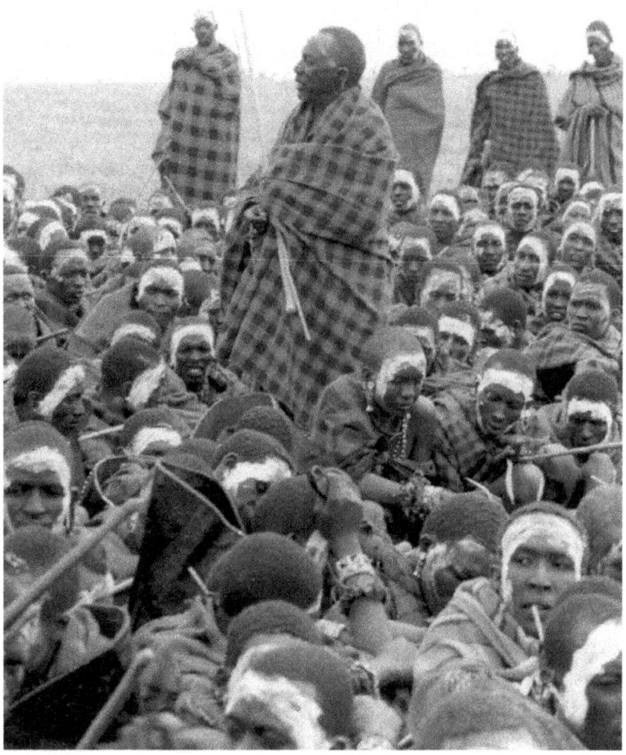

Figure 49.4. Maasai Elders with Morans discussing peace

seen museums in Africa and those in Sweden develop joint programmes to create equal partnerships that have produced rich cross-cultural exchanges as well as support for African museum programmes. Many of these programmes have identified local needs and created partnerships among people of different worlds, such as women's groups on the African continent and those from Sweden.

The umbrella body for African Museums, AFRICOM, has grown to meet the challenges of museums and museum professionals in the entire continent. Within the time AFRICOM has been in existence, it has developed a book of standards to assist African museums document their collections using a standard set of norms, thus making it easier for them to exchange information. In any museum or cultural institution, the whole proccess of inventory and documentation is paramount. Thus, the book of standards is a major contribution and a good example to be emulated internationally. Developed since 1995, it may have its weaknesses, however, its existence alone is a recognition for need for standards in the museum world.

AFRICOM has also cooperated with WAMP and produced a Directory of African museum professionals helping create a network of museums and museum professionals. By staging a successful General Assembly and conference, AFRICOM proved that the myth that Africans cannot run a successful continental organization is over. If anything, there are more successful heritage organizations found on the continent than before and some, such as Africa 2009, have become models for other continents. All these add confidence among the African museums that their approach is relevant to their situation. It is hoped that AFRICOM and other sister organizations will further help popularize the museums' social role all over the continent.

CONCLUSION

The roles of museums are changing from the all powerful "temples of state" to more inclusive, people-oriented institutions; ones that do not just present human and nature, but evoke dialogue with the very people represented. African museums are playing their rightful role by engaging in discussions pertaining to relevance to their communities. It is clear that African museums, apart from playing a crucial role in regards to exhibitions, education, and research, are also evolving into community facilities, creating forums and spaces where different voices can be heard. They are regionalizing and even globalizing their operations through partnerships, and enhancing the role of culture through understanding and appreciation of diversity. The museums have shown that culture can be a resource that can meet peoples' economic needs as well. African museums are well placed to play this unique role because they are also custodians of living heritage. In this sense, other museums have a lot to learn from developing countries, where the past and the present are still so tightly intertwined.

REFERENCES

Abungu, George H. O. 1993b "Museums, archaeology and the public in Kenya." In Ardouin, C. and Arinze (eds). *Museum and Archaeology in West Africa*. James Currey, London (1995).

Abungu, George H. O. 1994c "Museums, Archaeology and Conservation: the politics of cultural resource management in Kenya." Paper presented at WAC3, New Delhi December 1994.

Abungu George H. O. 1996b Heritage, community and the state in the 1990s: Experiences from Africa. Paper presented at the conference on The Production of History in a Changing South Africa. University of Western Cape, South Africa. 10–12 July 1996.

Abungu, George H. O. 2000 "Introduction to the visits of selected Kaya forests." In Rossler, M. and G. Saouma-Ferero. *The World Heritage Convention and Cultural Landscapes in Africa. UNESCO.*

Abungu, George H. O. 2001a "The Destruction of Archaeological Heritage: Examples from Kenya and Somalia." In Brodie N., Doole J., and Renfrew C. (eds). *Trade in Illicit Antiquities: the Destruction of the World Archaeological Heritage*, pp. 37–46. McDonald Institute for Archaeology, University of Cambridge, UK.

Abungu George H. O. 2001b "Museums: Arenas for dialogue or confrontation?". In "Managing Change: museums facing economic and social challenges." *ICOM News*, Vol. 54, no. 43.

Abungu George H. O. 2002 "Opening up new frontiers: Museums of the 21st century." In P. Agren (ed). Museum 2000: Contribution or Challenge? Folth and Hassler, Varnamo, 2002.

Ardouin, C. and Arinze, E. 1995 *Museums and the Community in West Africa.* James Curry, London.
Ardouin, C. and Arinze, E. 2000 *Museums and History in West Africa.* James Curry, Oxford.
Konaré, A. O. 1995, "The Creation and Survival of Local Museums." In Ardouin, C. and Arinze, E. *Museums and the Community in West Africa.* James Curry, London

ACKNOWLEDGMENTS

Okello Abungu Heritage Consultants, Nairobi – Kenya
International Council of Museums (ICOM), Paris – France
The Getty Conservation Institute, Los Angeles – USA
Teresa Duff, Getty Conservation Institute, Los Angeles – USA

CHAPTER FIFTY

The National Institute of Anthropology and History

María del Perpetuo Socorro Villareal Escarrega

Since it was first established sixty-six years ago, the National Institute of Anthropology and History has faced a wide range of challenges while trying to protect and conserve Mexico's archaeological and historical heritage. At the same time, it has been engaged in intense activity in the realm of Mexican culture. Today, the National Institute of Anthropology and History is represented throughout the country and its successes and achievements are widely recognised.

HISTORICAL DEVELOPMENT OF INSTITUTIONS RESPONSIBLE FOR PROTECTING CULTURAL HERITAGE

Since the pre-Hispanic period, there have been institutions whose functions included the protection and conservation of cultural heritage. The inhabitants of the territory now known as Mexico kept their heritage alive through the oral transmission of knowledge, stories, events, the teachings of their elders and priests, myths, legends, songs, and poetry. At the same time, communities that had devised hieroglyphic scripts recorded events by making inscriptions in stone or wood, or by painting figures and symbols on paper – made of amate or other plant fibres – or tanned leather, even producing genuine books and maps. These books were known as *amoxtli* and their authors as *amoxtlacuilos*. Their works, which are referred to today as manuscripts, were kept in special libraries.

Much evidence of the pre-Hispanic culture was lost during the Spanish conquest and colonisation. Great works of architecture, some containing evidence of mathematical knowledge and an understanding of the workings of the calendar, were deliberately destroyed or abandoned. Some manuscripts were burnt. However, hidden in the countryside, the mountains, and the rainforests were other cities, temples, palaces, tombs, and dwellings that survived the destruction, as did their contents. The relics of these pre-Hispanic communities now constitute Mexico's archaeological heritage.

Having evangelised the indigenous population, the conquistadors, in particular the religious ones, set about studying native languages and compiling primers and dictionaries. They also gathered information about the customs, beliefs, and history of the indigenous peoples. Meanwhile, some educated natives began to recover the contents of ancient pre-Hispanic books, which were eventually translated into Spanish. The rescued manuscripts and manuscripts represent an important source of information on Mexico's indigenous cultures and are now part of the country's cultural heritage.

With colonisation well under way, Spain established the Consejo de Indias (Council of the Americas). This move was to have important consequences. Through the Council, Spain claimed that the ruins of the pre-Hispanic sanctuaries, altars, and tombs, and the objects found inside them, were the property of the Spanish Crown. Spain also appointed a Cronista Mayor (Grand Historiographer) to write, as accurately and as truthfully as possible, the history of each Spanish province in the Americas.

After Mexico gained independence in 1821, the Antiquities Board was set up to protect and study the past. In 1825, President Lucas Alaman approved the establishment of the National Museum. This was a major step towards the establishment of other institutions to protect and preserve the nation's cultural heritage. For the first time, there was a set of rules governing the activities of a museum and the protection of the treasures housed there. With the arrival of Emperor Maximilian, the National Museum was renamed the Public Museum of History and divided into three sections: natural history, archaeology, and history. Following the restoration of democratic rule, the liberal government of President Juárez continued to support the museum, which reverted to its former name.

On 8 October 1885, during the regime of General Porfirio Díaz, a General Inspectorate of Monuments was created to manage ancient monuments and explore the areas surrounding them. In 1887, under the guidance of this Inspectorate, the National Museum took the major step of making public the contents of its archives, including the most important documents and studies relating to the ancient history of Mexico. The Inspectorate also promoted the dispatch of more scientific expeditions to study monuments around the country and the build up of archaeological and ethnographic collections. Also around this time, archaeology, ethnography, and history were recognised as academic disciplines, and professorships were created in these fields.

In 1905, in a climate that seemed to favour institutions involved in the protection of cultural heritage, the great Mexican educational reformer Don Justo Sierra established the Ministry of Public Education and Fine Arts. In 1909, with museum collections expanding, a decision was made to establish a separate museum of natural history. As a result of the restructuring, the National Museum was renamed the National Museum of Archaeology, History and Ethnography.

Departments of history, physical anthropology, ethnography, and retrospective indigenous industrial art were established within the Museum, along with a library and a number of workshops.

The Revolution of 1910 was a significant moment for Mexican institutions because it gave rise to new attitudes and fresh concerns that affected every aspect of national life. This period saw the establishment within the framework of the National Museum of inspectorates to supervise archaeological and historical monuments.

The current Ministry of Public Education was founded in 1921. In order to harmonise its activities with the objectives of the new Ministry, the Department of Archaeological and Ethnographic Studies – which until then had been part of the Ministry of Agriculture and Public Works – was moved to the Ministry of Public Education, and its archaeology and monuments sections were restructured. Later, in accordance with the Law on the Protection and Conservation of Sites of Natural Beauty of 30 January 1930, the archaeology and monuments sections were amalgamated to form the Department of Artistic, Archaeological and Historical Monuments within the Ministry of Public Education. The new Department was responsible for listing and protecting monuments and sites of natural beauty belonging to the nation or subject to federal government jurisdiction, in addition to monuments situated in the Federal District and the Federal Territories. It also received the legal backing of the 1933 Monuments Law, which defined it as a division of the Ministry of Public Education acting in matters related to cultural property and comprising a Department of Monuments of the Colonial Era and the Republic and a Department of Pre-Hispanic Monuments.

By 1938, the Mexican President, General Lázaro Cárdenas, was looking for better results from the federal government's endeavours to conserve national monuments and study indigenous groups. He presented Congress with a bill that sought to turn the Ministry of Public Education's Department of Artistic, Archaeological and Historical Monuments into an institute. The adoption of the bill led to the creation, on 3 February 1939, of the National Institute of Anthropology and History. This was a major step towards the organisation of anthropological studies in a unified and scientific way. The Institute was a legal entity in its own right, although it operated the Ministry of Public Education. Its remit was to explore archaeological sites and to protect, conserve, and restore Mexico's archaeological, historical, and artistic monuments.

The law that currently regulates the protection of Mexico's archaeological, artistic, and historical heritage came into force on 28 April 1972. It recognised the Institute's national dimension and reinforced its legal status as the body responsible for protecting Mexico's cultural heritage. With absolute clarity, the law identified built and movable archaeological property as belonging to the state and established legal and administrative provisions for the control, study, and protection of the nation's archaeological, historical, and artistic heritage.

LEGAL DEFINITION OF THE MAIN OBJECTIVES AND FUNCTIONS OF THE INSTITUTE

The legal framework governing the Institute lays down the Institution's general objectives and responsibilities, establishes the Institution's internal organisational structure on the basis of areas of activity and regional representation, and envisages the possibility of allowing members of the national and international academic community and the general public to participate in its activities. The law explicitly lays down the Institute's main objectives, which may be summarised as follows: scientific research into anthropology and history principally related to the domestic population; the conservation and restoration of Mexico's archaeological, historical, and prehistorical heritage; the protection, conservation, restoration, and recovery of cultural property; and the dissemination of information about the Institute's activities.

The law also outlines the functions assigned to the Institute to enable it to achieve its objectives. Accordingly, the Institute:

- issues permits for and supervises the work carried out by state and municipal authorities to restore and conserve archaeological and historical monuments;
- can conduct its own scientific research related to the archaeology and history of Mexico;
- can conduct explorations and excavations for scientific and conservation purposes at archaeological, historical, and paleontological sites and monuments in Mexico;
- can carry out the tasks of identification, investigation, recovery, reclamation, protection, restoration, rehabilitation, surveillance, and safekeeping of archaeological monuments and sites and the movable property associated with them; and
- is required to teach the subjects of anthropology, history, conservation, restoration, and museography at the technical, professional, and postgraduate level, to provide extension courses and to confer the corresponding degrees and diplomas through the National School of Anthropology and History and the National School of Conservation and Restoration.
- The Institute's functions fall into the following categories:
  1. research and conservation of cultural heritage
  2. professional training
  3. dissemination of knowledge and information on cultural property

In order to accomplish its various tasks, the Institute carries out various activities, including:

- encouraging and assisting the design of integrated programmes of protection, conservation, rehabilitation, and information for Mexico's principal historic centres at the federal, state, and municipal levels of government;

- promoting community involvement in conservation and in the dissemination of knowledge and information about cultural property;
- initiating, implementing, and monitoring projects for the management of archaeological sites, historical monuments, and museums in collaboration with government departments at the federal, states, and municipal levels;
- advising state and municipal authorities on the development of specific policies for the preservation of cultural property;
- encouraging various forms of public support, including councils, committees, sponsorships, volunteers, and societies of friends; and
- creating flexible and transparent plans for carrying out specific projects with community involvement.

The Institute works in consultation with various scientific bodies, notably the Archaeological Council and the Historical Monuments Council, the task of which is to study and propose projects involving the investigation, supervision, and restoration of cultural property.

PUBLIC SERVICES PROVIDED BY THE INSTITUTE

The work of the Institute, which is to preserve the cultural heritage of the Mexican people and disseminate knowledge and information about that heritage, is based on two guiding principles. The first is that cultural heritage should be accessible to everyone; the second, that it is the duty of the nation to protect this heritage.

These principles create the right conditions for more intense academic study and research, encourage the broader dissemination of information, and enlarge the field of activity and knowledge. At present, some 800 people are engaged in research relating to cultural heritage in the areas of history, social anthropology, physical anthropology, archaeology, linguistics, ethnohistory, ethnology, conservation, and restoration.

The aforementioned academic study and research are directly linked to the training of specialists at the National School of Anthropology and History and the National School of Conservation, Restoration and Museology, which are both part of the Institute. In addition, based on the desire to provide qualified people with specialised local knowledge that enables them to meet the specific needs of the regions, two more schools have been established: the National School of Anthropology and History at Chihuahua and the Western School of Conservation and Restoration at Guadalajara.

The Institute is responsible for setting technical standards for and implementing legal provisions regarding more than 110,500 historical monuments built between the sixteenth and nineteenth centuries, approximately 31,000 registered archaeological sites throughout the country (many more are believed to exist), and 173 archaeological areas that are open to the public.

In addition, the Institute is in charge of 110 museums across Mexico, which are divided into categories based on the nature of the museums and their collections. Accordingly, there are five national museums, twenty-one regional museums, fourty-three local museums, thirty-six on-site museums, and two metropolitan museums, in addition to three community centres. The Institute also advises more than 200 community museums. To give an indication of the cultural riches housed in the Institute's network of museums, suffice it to say that there are some 600,000 archaeological items and several hundred thousand pieces of movable cultural property dating from different periods of history.

In addition, the Institute is responsible for vast and valuable stores of documents, including those kept in the National Library of Anthropology and History, which holds Mexico's largest collection of historical and anthropological publications, as well as a collection of manuscripts so precious that they have World Heritage Status.

The National System of Photographic Collections, which consists of seventen archives containing more than 1.5 million items, preserves the pictorial memories of the Mexican people. It also boasts one of Latin America's most important sound archives devoted to recording and preserving the country's oral and musical traditions.

The dissemination of information and knowledge is carried out through a comprehensive programme of scientific and educational publications, as well as through the production of sound and video recordings, academic events, permanent contact with the mass media, and, of course, the aforementioned network of museums.

Overall, the work of the Institute has a considerable social impact, in that it collaborates with different levels of government and with the community to devise and implement conservation strategies, to raise public awareness of Mexico's cultural heritage and collective memory, and to formulate urban development programmes. Many of these activities are organised in collaboration with the federal, state, and municipal authorities and with groups and associations formed by members of the general public. For this purpose, the Institute has concluded a series of agreements with public and private organisations that enable it to work with them to protect, conserve, reclaim, and raise public awareness of Mexico's cultural heritage.

It is important to point out that anthropological research into the cultures that existed on the territory of what is now referred to as Mexico and the study of Mexican history since the introduction of Spanish culture are just as important to the Institute as the excavation, investigation, and rehabilitation of archaeological sites, the restoration of movable and immovable cultural property, and the conservation and protection of these priceless sources of learning.

Mexico is blessed with enormous cultural wealth. In many parts of the country, extraordinary manifestations of human creativity can be found. These treasures have had a profound impact on the country, but also beyond its frontiers, which is why Mexico is constantly searching for new ways to protect them.

During the course of a period now exceeding six decades, the National Institute of Anthropology and History has left its mark on Mexican society. Its accumulated experience has enabled it to create new and improved mechanisms to protect, conserve, restore, and disseminate information about Mexico's vast cultural heritage. The Institute is obliged to carry on creating effective conservation strategies, in order to guarantee that future generations will continue to enjoy the legacy that has been entrusted to it.

CHAPTER FIFTY-ONE

How Much Provenance Is Enough? Post-*Schultz* Guidelines for Art Museum Acquisition of Archeological Materials and Ancient Art

Ildiko P. DeAngelis

INTRODUCTION

It has been more than thirty years since major museums in the United States[1] voluntarily established (on a prospective basis) internal ethical guidelines restricting collecting practices in keeping with the goals of the then newly adopted UNESCO Convention on the Means of Prohibiting and Preventing Illicit Import, Export and Transfer of Ownership of Cultural Property of 1970 ("UNESCO Convention").[2] These voluntary ethical guidelines bar these museums to this day from acquiring objects when positive law does not forbid the acquisition.[3] Recent events in Afghanistan and Iraq have focused the world's attention on the increasingly widespread problem of looting of the world's cultural heritage. These events have created a new level of urgency for museum involvement in protection efforts. In addition, developments in the law have also called to museums to reexamine their existing acquisition practices.

Although many museums have had detailed acquisition guidelines for more than thirty years, others, most notably many private art collecting institutions, have not.[4] Indeed, in the United States, museum acquisition policies and practices continue to differ greatly. The nature of the museum doing the collecting will determine the quantity and type of information considered essential about the history of archeological materials and objects of antiquity being considered for acquisition.[5] The differing values important to the underlying academic discipline drive the collecting goals and policies, including the level of documentation. Art-connoisseurship-based museums place primary importance on an object's aesthetic value and, consequently, collecting practices will not preclude acquiring an object of aesthetic merit merely because the work may lack information about its "find spot" or what archeologists call "provenience."[6] By contrast, museums with an archeology focus place the greatest value in the

[1] See most notably the Harvard University Statement on Acquisitions (January 1972) and Smithsonian Institution Policy on Museum Acquisitions (May 1973) reproduced in Malaro, Marie C. *A Legal Primer on Managing Museum Collections* (Washington DC: Smithsonian Press, 2nd ed., 1998) Figures IV.1 and IV.2. The first museum to announce an acquisition policy of this nature was the University of Pennsylvania Museum on April 1, 1970. Others included the California State University at Long Beach; The Field Museum; Southern Illinois University; Washington State Museum in Seattle; Peabody Museum in Salem, Massachusetts; Arizona State Museum in Tucson; and the Utah Museum of Natural History. See Bator, Paul M. *The International Trade in Art* (Chicago: University of Chicago Press; Midway reprint, 1988) Note 144. No study has been done on the current status of implementation for these policies. See note 43 in this chapter regarding implementation. Notably absent from this original list are major private art museums.

[2] The UNESCO Convention's Article 7(a) urged member nations to control by domestic law the acquisition policies of museums within their borders. However, the history of the negotiation and ratification of the Convention shows that Article 7(a) would be interpreted by the United States to apply only to institutions whose acquisition policy is subject to national control under existing domestic law (for example, museums controlled by government agencies, such as the Department of Interior museums and museums of the Armed Forces) (Bator, 104). When the Convention was awaiting passage by an act of Congress for implementation in the United States, museums established voluntary ethical policies in keeping with 7(a). The U.S. law implementing the UNESCO Convention took more than a decade to pass. The Convention on Cultural Property Implementation Act was passed December 1982 as Title II, Pub. L. 97-446, 19 U.S.C. Secs. 2601–2613 ("CPIA") and expectedly did not include any provision dealing with the acquisition policies of museums but the legislative history cited voluntary compliance by the museum profession (Malaro, 91).

[3] UNESCO Convention's Section 5(a) urged adoption of "ethical principles" set forth in the convention by those concerned (curators, collectors, antique dealers). O'Keefe, Patrick J. "Museum Acquisition Policies and the UNESCO Convention" *Museum International* (January 1998) Vol. 50, No. 1, pp 20, 21. Thus, the UNESCO Convention provided moral backing for restrictions such as refusing to collect all illegally exported cultural property even if the government itself did not pursue this objective in the implementing legislation.

[4] See Herscher, Ellen. "Tarnished Reputations" *Archaeology* (Sept./Oct. 1998) pp 66–78. The Association of Art Museum Directors (AAMD) in June 2004 adopted its first comprehensive guidelines for its membership, consisting of 175 directors of art museums for collecting ancient art and archeological materials, discussed in detail subsequently (<http://www.aamd.org/papers/documents/June10FinalTaskForceReport_001.pd>, accessed January 5, 2005). One commentator notes that museums may have found it difficult to give up highly regarded objects on a point of principle (O'Keefe, 23).

[5] This chapter is limited to discussion of archeological materials and ancient art, which are subsets of the broader "cultural property" designation of objects that embody culture. Merryman, John H. *The Public Interest in Cultural Property*, 77 Calif. L. Rev 339 (1989). For purposes of this discussion, a broad definition of these terms will suffice. Archeological materials typically have an underground find spot, chiefly are the product of excavation, and represent a source of important information about ancient cultures based, in part, on the context of where the materials were found or excavated. "Art" is a subset of cultural property that has been determined to have aesthetic value and generally is collected for that purpose. For differences in acquisition policies, compare the AAMD Guidelines for art museum directors discussed later with the policies established for museums with archeology-based collections, such as the Smithsonian Institution's Acquisition Policy of 1972.

[6] The term provenance is used in art circles to refer to the history of the life of the work. See (<http://www.aamd.org/papers/faq.php>, accessed January 26, 2005). The art community also maintains that important information about a culture that created an object may be gleaned from the object's style and appearance even if its provenience is unknown. See, Cuno, J. "Building Collections and Housing Them: Acquisition, Renzo Piano, and a Master Plan for the Art Museums" *Annual Report of the Harvard University Art Museums* (1997–8).

information that an object of antiquity represents. Key information is determined from the context where the object was found and relationships with other things found around it and recorded in the excavation process using scientific principles and practices. As one commentator noted, "archeology is used to recover history, not just objects."[7] Undocumented objects – objects that carry little or no information of where they originated and how and when they were found and excavated – have little value for an archeological collection.[8] Removal of such objects from their "find spot" without documentation is condemned as an irretrievable loss of cultural heritage.[9]

Further division of views within the museum community on collecting practices may be based on differing loyalties. Art museums depend on donations from collectors who, in turn, depend on a free art market.[10] Museum archeologists may have ties to countries of origin ("source countries") needed for permission to excavate – the very same countries (typically developing nations) that seek to restrict illicit trade of their antiquities through stricter controls on the art market.[11] Given these differing values and loyalties, it is not surprising that the museum community does not speak with one voice on the scope, quality, and quantity of background information required for objects considered for acquisition. Nor do representatives share similar views on the ever-increasing legal restrictions burdening the international art market.

At the same time, all U.S. museums look to the same laws to ensure that clean, legal title is received for objects added to collections. Their collecting practices, at minimum, must conform to the law. As demonstrated by a recent case, *U.S. v. Schultz*,[12] discussed subsequently, the level of inquiry required about an object's past is increasing as U.S. law is being enforced more and more rigorously in response to international pressures to protect the world's cultural heritage. In addition, in order to promote additional values, the museum profession often sets higher ethical standards than required by positive law. However, the principle of protecting threatened international cultural heritage often competes with the missions of museums: to collect, preserve, and interpret the cultural objects for public benefit. Depending on the type of museum (aesthetic-based or science-based), the following issues may be resolved quite differently depending on how the museum's ability to meet its mission may be affected:

- acquiring objects that are undocumented – that lack some or all information on their history of ownership ("provenance") and/or history of excavation ("provenience") even after reasonable inquiry is made;
- acquiring objects that may have been subject to violation of foreign export laws (laws prohibiting export of cultural property from a source country) – such laws would not prevent legal importation into the United States and possession of such objects cannot be disturbed under U.S. law solely based on illegal export from another country.[13]

This chapter first examines the *U.S. v. Schultz* case that involved a criminal prosecution of a New York antiquities dealer accused of violating the U.S. National Stolen Property Act ("NSPA")[14] for conspiring to receive an undocumented Egyptian antiquity allegedly "stolen" from Egypt. The theft at issue was not based on standard notions of ownership, but rather on a 1983 Egyptian law that declares state ownership of all cultural property, including all undocumented and unexcavated cultural objects – a so-called "patrimony law."[15] For museums, previous practices thought to be legal under U.S. law (and perhaps restricted only by ethical rules adopted by segments of the museum community) have to be considered legally suspect.

Secondly, this paper examines the repercussions of the *Schultz* case on art museum collecting practices through the lens of a hypothetical art museum acquisition. Specifically, the ethical guidelines recently published (issued post-*Schultz*) by the Association of Art Museum Directors, "Report of the AAMD Task Force on the Acquisition of Archeological Materials and Ancient Art" ("2004 AAMD Guidelines") are applied to the case study and compared with existing policies of other museum professional groups and to internal policies of selected U.S. museums.[16]

[7] (Herscher, 66).

[8] Coggins, Clemency. "Archeology and the Art Market" *Science*, (January 21, 1972), Vol. 175, No. 4019, pp 263–8.

[9] "Accommodating these two fundamental values – the appreciation of beauty and the search for knowledge is the central challenge...." (Bator, 19).

[10] See AAMD, "Art Museums, Private Collectors, and the Public Benefit" (<http://www.aamd.org/pdfs/Private%20Collectors.pdf>, accessed January 7, 2005).

[11] See Vincent, Steven. "The War on Collecting" *Art & Auction* (February 15, 1999), at 39.

[12] *United States v. Schultz*, 178 F. Supp 2nd 445 (S.D.N.Y. 2002) *aff'd* 333 F3d 393 (2nd Cir. 2003).

[13] For cogent discussions of the illegal export problem, see Bator, 11, 52–4, and Merryman, John H. "The Nation and the Object," 3 *Int'l J. of Cult. Prop.* 64 (1994).

[14] The NSPA (18 U.S.C. Sec. 2315) makes it a crime to receive, possess, sell, and dispose of any goods valued at $5,000 or more that have crossed state or national boundaries after being stolen, knowing that the goods were stolen.

[15] Egyptian Law 117 (1983). The appeals court in *Schultz* concluded that "[w]e see no reason that property stolen from a foreign sovereign should be treated any differently from property stolen from a foreign museum or private home" for purposes of federal criminal theft law. 333 F3rd at 47. Critics observe that Egypt's "found in the ground" ownership statute "is utterly different from the U.S. definition of ownership." Hawkins, Ashton. "'*US v. Schultz*:' US Cultural Policy in Confusion" *The Art Newspaper* (January 9, 2003). (<http://62.253.251.9/access/artnewspaper.html>) (Record Number 17370).

[16] The AAMD Guidelines were issued June 10, 2004 and posted online at (<http://www.aamd.org/papers/documents/June10FinalTaskForceReport_001.pdf>, accessed January 5, 2005). One commentator argues that by failing to establish acquisition guidelines that respect the history of an object and its scientific value, museums are breaching their fiduciary obligations of due care. Gerstenblith, Patty. *Symposium: Traditional Knowledge, Intellectual Property, and Indigenous Culture: 'Acquisition and Deacquisition of Museum Collections and the Fiduciary Obligations of Museums to the Public*, 11 Cardozo J. Int'l & Comp. L. 409, 453.

U.S. v. Schultz

Frederick Schultz, a New York dealer and owner and president of the Frederick Schultz Ancient Art Gallery, arranged to purchase smuggled antiquities from a British restorer by the name of Jonathan Tokeley-Parry. Tokeley-Parry reportedly smuggled more than 3,000 antiquities out of Egypt during the early 1990s. His method was to make the objects look like cheap reproductions by covering them in plastic and then applying gold leaf and black paint. After an object cleared British customs, he restored and sold them on the international art market with Mr. Schultz's help. Ultimately, Tokeley-Parry was caught by New Scotland Yard, convicted in 1997, and served three years in jail. It was Tokeley-Parry who led investigators to Schultz by identifying him as his co-conspirator.

The facts uncovered by investigators unveiled a scheme worked out by the Schultz/Tokeley-Parry team to create fake documentation for the objects as originating from an old collection, called the Thomas Alcock Collection, dating from the 1920s. Labels for the collection were dipped in tea to give them an aged appearance. Thomas Alcock was one of Tokeley-Parry's deceased relatives. That relationship allowed Tokeley-Parry to present himself as Alcock's heir for purposes of selling the collection. Correspondence between Schultz and Tokeley-Parry indicated clearly that the co-conspirators were intentionally giving objects a fake provenance that placed them outside of Egypt and in Great Britain before applicable domestic and foreign laws were enacted.

Schultz was indicted in New York under the NSPA for one count of conspiring to receive stolen property. As noted previously, the stolen property was Egyptian antiquities illegally removed from Egypt after the 1983 law that vests ownership of all undiscovered antiquities in the national government.[17]

Schultz argued that he did not know he was engaging in theft under American law – in other words he did not know that the Egyptian law vested ownership in the Egyptian government would be recognized by U.S. courts. However, the court of appeals noted that the only requirement in the NSPA is knowledge that the goods were stolen. Because the jury found that Schultz knew all of the relevant facts, he could not escape liability by contending he did not know the law, given that ignorance of the law is no excuse. The court noted that Schultz's actions were not innocent, but fraudulent, and he was keenly aware of the illegality of his actions by forging documents, communicating in code, and even discussing the possibility of prison with his co-conspirator. In addition, at trial, the jury was instructed on "conscious avoidance," namely that one cannot purposefully remain ignorant in order to escape the consequences of the law. Although the jury instructions "could have been more precise," the appeals court found no reversible error. If Schultz was aware of the high probability that the objects were the property of the Egyptian government and did not, in fact, believe otherwise, then he can be found to have "known" that the objects were stolen. Five witnesses testified on their own personal knowledge of the Egyptian law to support the likelihood that Mr. Schulz had been aware as well. The witnesses included several museum curators who had been offered some of the smuggled antiquities by Mr. Schultz and someone who had worked previously with Mr. Schultz. The court held that such testimony was relevant, noting "as any acknowledged expert in the field of Egyptian antiquities, with many years of experience, it would have been natural for Schultz to know about the [Egyptian] law." Prior to this case, dealers, collectors, and museums may have ignored foreign patrimony laws relying on the 1989 *Peru v. Johnson* case in which a court held that Peruvian patrimony laws were unclear and akin to export controls, not statutes vesting ownership, and would not be given credence by U.S. courts. After the *Schultz* case, ignoring or dismissing patrimony laws may be reckless.[18]

[17] The theory behind this indictment was not new. In the late 1970s, in *United States v. McClain*, 545 F.2d 988 (5th Cir,. 1977); 593 F.2d 658 (5th Cir. 1979), several dealers were prosecuted under NSPA for dealing in Mexican antiquities subject to a 1972 Mexican law that vested ownership of undiscovered antiquities in the Mexican government. The *McClain* case was important for setting precedent that foreign patrimony laws may establish ownership of undocumented antiquities in the national government for purposes of U.S. federal law of theft. However, in a subsequent case, the weakness of the *McClain* doctrine became evident. In *Peru v. Johnson*, 720 F. Supp. 810 (C.D. Cal. 1989), *aff'd sub nom., Peru v. Wendt*, 933 F.2d 1013 (9th Cir. 1991), involving Peruvian patrimony laws, the court held that the national laws of Peru declaring public ownership of all undocumented cultural objects were not sufficiently clear as to provide notice to U.S. citizens required under the due process clause. This was a civil case seeking recovery of seized objects in which Peru carried the burden of proof of rightful ownership. The court noted that Peru's laws were akin to export controls, not statutes vesting ownership. Evidence that these laws were not consistently enforced in Peru as ownership laws further supported the court's conclusion that U.S. courts should not give them credence. In addition, there was no credible evidence as to whether the objects at issue were removed before or after Peru's laws went into effect. A further fatal flaw in the case was that the artifacts could not be traced as originating in the modern borders of Peru. Based on expert testimony, the court found that similar objects could be found in the neighboring countries of Bolivia and Ecuador and possibly other nations that were not a part of the suit. For more than twenty-five years, there were no further prosecutions under the *McClain* doctrine and its status and usefulness remained uncertain, especially after *Peru v. Johnson*, until *Schultz*. Expectedly, Mr. Schultz's counsel argued that the Egyptian law was not a true ownership law and that the indictment did not accord with U.S. law because the items were not "stolen" within the meaning of NSPA. The court held the opposite, finding the 1983 Egyptian law sufficiently clear and consistently enforced in Egypt as such.

[18] Schultz also argued that the enactment of the Convention on Cultural Property Implementation Act (CPIA) that implemented the UNESCO Convention in the United States shows that Congress did not intend the NSPA to apply to objects such as the ones at issue. On appeal, the Second Circuit rejected this argument and affirmed Schulz's conviction, holding that CPIA provides a mechanism by which the United States may recognize export controls of other nations, and does prevent criminal prosecution for theft of objects stolen from foreign nations. Because the CPIA is only a civil Customs statute, other types of theft would go unpunished if U.S. law enforcement were limited to the narrow category of cultural objects stolen from museums and cultural sites specified in the CPIA. Congress's intention to do so would have had to be expressed clearly, which the court found was not the case. 333 F.3d 393, 408. The Archeological Institute of America, the American Anthropological Association, the Society of American Archeology, the Society of Historical Archaeology, and the U.S. Committee for the International Council on Monuments and Sites filed amicus briefs arguing that applying the NSPA this way would go a long way in protecting archeological sites worldwide.

After the *Schultz* case, there is little doubt that a violation of federal criminal law for theft, including seizure of the object in the United States, is probable for objects covered by legitimate foreign patrimony laws. Moreover, ignorance of foreign laws by experts, such as museum curators, whether real or feigned, will not be excused. Information about where and when the object originated and knowledge of the scope, effective dates, and enforcement history of applicable foreign patrimony laws are no longer optional but necessary to avoid violating federal criminal law. Commentators note that following *Schultz*, U.S. courts will be left to determine the applicability of potentially more than 100 different foreign patrimony statutes, many dating back to the early twentieth century. It is argued that short of a court case, museums may not know whether a country's law is valid or not.[19] In addition, the current law leaves museum professionals, and others who participate in the international art market, in a difficult position because they could not prove that they did not know the law without being accused of consciously avoiding learning it.[20]

Given also the favorable U.S. civil law of recovery for stolen objects, title to undocumented antiquities can be subject to challenge by countries of origin in civil cases basing ownership on patrimony laws. The burden on a country of origin seeking restitution in a civil case or the burden on prosecutors in a criminal case is to prove that the illegal export of a state-owned object occurred after the ownership-vesting statute was enacted. The ability to trace the undocumented object to the source country after the effective date of the patrimony law is the remaining requirement.

It may be anticipated that as a result of the *Schultz* case, countries of origin without patrimony laws in place will now have ample incentive to quickly pass and enforce such laws. In addition, source countries should be increasing their efforts to document antiquities within their borders so that every undocumented object removed after the enactment of the patrimony law may be identified by default to have been looted from an unexcavated site. An undocumented object found abroad would be suspect unless there was evidence that the object was in a foreign jurisdiction prior to the effective date of the patrimony law at issue. Certainly, developments of technology and object identification through standardized data collection will make these documentation efforts easier and more effective in the future. Moreover, the problem that the objects must be traced to have originated within the modern-day borders of a source country for civil restitution may be resolved successfully if bordering countries were to agree to cooperate on such recovery efforts and seek return of objects as joint plaintiffs.[21]

From the perspective of proponents of greater restrictions, the *Schultz* case is a victory for the preservation of the full cultural record of the past. New legal consequences reduce the incentive to acquire and thus to loot or smuggle.[22] For those opposed, the *Schultz* case represents a victory for cultural nationalism by aiding source countries to embargo all cultural objects within their borders.[23] Clearly, *Schultz* (like McClain twenty-five years before it) is an example of a case with egregious facts that called for criminal sanctions. However, the impact of the case is far greater than as a renewed weapon to punish the smuggling activities of the most disreputable dealers. The safe harbors for museums and for all those who collect have been significantly narrowed.

Case Study: Post-*Schultz* Law, Policy, and Practice

Discussions regarding legal standards and ethical guidelines applicable to museum collecting are best examined in context. The following case study is examined to shed light on museum polices and practices in the post-*Schultz* era, specifically the Guidelines on Acquisition of Archeological Material and Ancient Art ("AAMD Guidelines") issued in June 2004 by the Association of Art Museum Directors:

Case Study: Arcadian Antiquities and Museum A

> Museum of Art ("Museum A") is offered a large art collection from the Estate of Collector Bill, who was known to the museum as a connoisseur and collector of Arcadian antiquities. Bill led a long and successful life, having made his fortune in real estate. However, all of his free time and energy were spent buying Arcadian art objects from dealers, at auction, and during his travels all over the world for the last 65 years of his life until he died in 2004 (1939–2004). He constantly upgraded his collection, selling things he purchased earlier and replacing them with objects of better quality. At the end of his life, his collection numbered in the hundreds. A selection of the most prominent pieces was featured in an exhibition of Arcadian antiquities and published in a dedicated catalog in 1973 by a New York museum.
>
> The paper documentation accompanying the collection is spotty at best. There are some invoices from dealers simply describing an object as "jade" or "pot." It is often impossible to establish which object belongs with which invoice. Some of the invoices are from foreign dealers in Switzerland and England. Others are from Hong Kong and some from New York dealers. However, the majority of the collection has no paper documentation. There is no evidence of any wrongdoing by Bill and title to his objects was never challenged in court during his lifetime, even after the 1973 public

19 Hawkins, *The Art Newspaper Archives* Record Number 17370.

20 "Culpable Ignorance? Museums Worry About Jury Instructions in Antiquities Conviction Case" *The Art Newspaper* (January 9, 2002) <http://62.253.251.9/access/artnewspaper.html>, accessed January 7, 2005) (Record Number 14994).

21 See *Peru v. Johnson*, 720 F. Supp. 810 (C.D. Cal. 1989), *aff'd sub nom.*, *Peru v. Wendt*, 933 F.2d 1013 (9th Cir. 1991) discussed earlier, in note 18.

22 Gerstenblith, Patty "An Internationally Respectful Application of National Law" *The Art Newspaper* (January 7, 2004); (<http://62.253.251.9/access/artnewspaper.html>, accessed January 6, 2005) (Record Number 19073). Schultz case is considered a "major setback for the beleaguered US antiquities market." Elia, Ricardo J. "A Move in the Right Direction" *The Art Newspaper* (January 9, 2003). <http://62.253.251.9/access/artnewspaper.html>, accessed January 6, 2005) (Record Number 17370).

23 Hawkins, *The Art Newspaper Archives* Record Number 17370.

exhibition. Through art historical research, the objects may be roughly dated and attributed to certain areas of the country of Arcadia, and a few objects to a specific archeological site. However, it appears that none can be traced directly to any contemporary looting activity, although Arcadia was subject to looting of archeological sites and graves for hundreds of years. Some pieces in the collection are truly unique, whereas others are good examples of so-called export ware that was created originally for foreign markets and are found all over the world.

The museum could benefit greatly from Bill's collection. The pieces would "round out" the museum's holdings in areas not adequately represented and are clearly within its collecting goals as directed by its mission. The museum has just hired a full-time conservator to do much-needed restoration of objects in the collection prior to the opening of a grand exhibit commemorating this major acquisition. The exhibition would require considerable scholarly examination of the collection and a catalog of the entire collection is planned.

If Museum A refuses the collection, it would fall into the residuary clause of Bill's Last Will and Testament, which directs liquidation of the entire collection at auction and distribution of the proceeds to Collector Bill's children. A New York auction house has already approached the family, ready to place the entire collection on auction, estimating that the collection would bring well over $50 million.

What should Museum A do? Assuming that Museum A follows basic legal principles and the 2004 AAMD Guidelines, the following steps may be taken.

Inquiry on the Reach of Foreign Law

Keeping the teaching of the *Schultz* case in mind, the first important step is for Museum A to examine the law of Arcadia. As the 2004 AAMD Guidelines state:

> Since the status of the work under foreign law may bear on its legal status under U.S. law, member museums must be familiar with relevant U.S. and foreign laws before making an acquisition. (Section C. (1))

This provision implements the lesson of the *Schultz* case that ignorance of a foreign law vesting ownership in the foreign government will not be excused for experts in the field. In this way, the AAMD Guidelines are recommending measures consistent with current law. The problem Museum A faces is finding, translating, and then interpreting the laws of Arcadia.[24] Researching foreign laws may difficult, although Internet Web sites now offer some English translations of foreign laws relating to cultural property protection.[25] The problem still remains whether the law at issue is sufficiently clear as an ownership law and enforced as such within Arcadia to prompt a court in the United States to recognize it under U.S. law. Museums may be required to seek legal counsel on these points. Prudence may dictate that when in doubt, Museum A should assume that a patrimony law will be effective and continue the inquiry about the objects based on that assumption.

> Upon conducting further research, Museum A discovers that Arcadia passed a law in 1950 prohibiting export of cultural property more than 50 years old without a permit. In fact, since the law was passed, no permits have been issued. Arcadia also passed a patrimony law in 1980 that vests ownership in the state of all cultural property within its borders, including any buried and yet undiscovered artifact. The crime of looting is subject to the death penalty and several death sentences imposed on looters have been reported in the press. Prior to 1950, there were no specific laws preventing the removal of cultural property from Arcadia. The United States has no (and never has had) temporary import restriction pursuant to the 1983 Cultural Property Implementation Act for Arcadian artifacts because Arcadia has never sought such protection.

Examine Documentation and Separate Objects into Categories

The second important consideration is that not all of Bill's objects present the same legal and ethical issues. The level of documentation for each object will determine the issues that need to be addressed. Therefore, Museum A is well advised to separate the collection into categories by levels of documentation available. In addition, the documentation must be carefully evaluated for authenticity, especially post-*Schultz*.[26] The remainder of this discussion will assume that the documentation Bill's estate provides is authentic. For Bill's collection, the following categories of objects may be advisable based, in part, on effective dates of applicable laws matched with the available documentation.

- Objects with no documentation prior to Bill's ownership
- Objects (described as significant) documented through the 1973 exhibition catalog
- Objects that may be identified as being in Bill's collection only after 1980 *and* no documentation exists that the objects had been removed from Arcadia prior to 1980 (effective date of Arcadia's patrimony law)

[24] It should be noted that if an object was known to have been located in a foreign country other than Arcadia, the laws of that country and the potential legal consequences should be investigated in a similar fashion. For purposes of this discussion, it will be assumed that only Arcadia's laws apply.

[25] For example, (<http://www.lootedart.com>) (accessed January 5, 2005), a site maintained by the Central Registry in London, contains foreign laws associated with looting that occurred in Europe during World War II, listed by country. No similar specialized legal resource site exists for patrimony laws of source countries related to antiquities. However, on the UNESCO Web site, the resource book published in 1988, *Handbook on national regulations concerning the export of cultural property* by Prott, Lyndel V and O'Keefe, Patrick J, is posted at (<http://unesdoc.unesco.org/images/0011/001191/119126eo.pdf>, accessed January 7, 2005). Creation of a comprehensive Web site of legal resources for anyone collecting antiquities and archeological materials of a foreign origin is long overdue.

[26] It has been noted that much documentation is manufactured and needs to be examined critically. Kaufman, J. "The Getty Sticks with Antiquities," *The Art Newspaper* (July–August 1996) pp 1, 17 (<http://62.253.251.9/access/artnewspaper.html>, accessed January 7, 2005) (Record Number 2386).

- Objects that may be traced to specific known excavation sites in Arcadia
- Objects that may be identified as being in Bill's collection after 1950 *and* no documentation exists that the objects had been removed from Arcadia prior to 1950 (the effective date of Arcadia's export law)
- Any remaining objects that may be identified as being in Bill's collection prior to 1950

Legal and ethical issues presented by each category follow:

Objects with No Documentation. As a general matter, any object acquired will come with some past history. Antiquities sold on E-Bay or off the back of a truck come without documentation. Even then, the history surrounding the acquisition provides information that should raise suspicion. Most museums stay away from suspect transactions. Although no study has been made on this point, it is likely that undocumented objects (objects with little or no provenance or provenience) are offered typically through bequests from private collectors, whose collecting standards often are unknown. These objects may have been purchased over a long period of time – throughout a testator's lifetime. Sufficient documentation on a place and time of purchase, and accompanying export and import permits, are extremely rare because such paperwork was not deemed important by the art trade.[27] Authenticity was the key inquiry, not documentation of legal title. What should a museum do in the absence of such information? Is an undocumented object presumed "guilty" until proven innocent or is it innocent until proven guilty? Should museums acquire only antiquities with a written, documented provenance?[28] For chain of title records, how far back is too far – when can we ignore misdeeds of the past?[29] Where is the line between benefiting the public through an undocumented acquisition versus fueling an illicit art market? Is there a benefit from an object "going public"? These are among the issues that need to be addressed in establishing an acquisition policy.

The "undocumented" portion of Bill's collection lacks any evidence of ownership history prior to Bill's. This category is likely to be the largest in terms of numbers and, indeed, most typical in terms of documentation for private collections accumulated during the last century. The dates Bill acquired these objects are undetermined. The objects are not traceable to any specific Arcadian excavation site, but stylistically, the objects are identifiable as ancient Arcadian. Research indicates that the modern day borders of Arcadia generally overlap ancient sites. Should the museum simply refuse to accept any object from the Estate of Bill that is not documented as being free from any potential legal problems (such as evidence showing that the object was removed from Arcadia before 1980 to avoid any possible patrimony-law-based criminal prosecution)? That requirement would, by default, label every undocumented object as suspect. What to do in the absence of evidence is the most significant challenge facing museums in making collecting decisions.

Clearly, gathering any available evidence is the key step. As a general matter, the duty of care required by those who govern museums includes due care at the acquisition stage, as specified in written policy,[30] usually in the museum's collections management policy. The standard of "good faith inquiry with a reasonable amount of diligence and care"[31] required under the duty of care may avoid forfeiture of objects at a later stage. Absent such inquiry, the museum may experience financial loss even if the object had not been purchased but donated, because of the costs expended to curate, conserve, and maintain objects in the collections.[32] In addition to financial loss, any forfeiture is also detrimental to the public image of the museum and may result in loss of public confidence in the institution. Moreover, in the event its title to an object is challenged, a museum may face having to prove in court that it acted reasonably and in good faith by making sufficient inquiry that objects were not stolen at the time of acquisition.[33] Good faith inquiry at the time of acquisition is required for a successful *laches* defense in a civil recovery case for stolen property (*Guggenheim v. Lubell*[34]). To prevail, the defendant must prove prejudice as a result of the claimant's unreasonable delay in bringing the suit. The *laches* doctrine that places a premium on fairness, the conduct of both the holder of the stolen object and the claimant will be examined and balanced. Therefore, with the Arcadian collection

[27] Dealers and auction houses did not normally reveal provenance of an object for sale. In fact, tradition held that such information was rarely sought. The propriety of secrecy was assumed (Bator 84, n.146).

[28] See "Culpable Ignorance?..." *The Art Newspaper Archives* Record Number 14994. The J. Paul Getty Museum revised its policy on acquisition of classical antiquities in 1995 by requiring a publication history for a new acquisition as of the date of that policy (Malaro, Figure IV.10).

[29] For example, the Virginia Museum of Fine Arts (VMFA) was subject to an Egyptian claim demanding return of an object (granite block relief) allegedly recorded as stolen from a temple and acquired by the VMFA in 1963, long before the 1983 patrimony law. Lufkin, Martha. "Egypt Demands Return of Antiquity at Virginia Museum, Threatening Law Suit. Object had been in Collection Since 1963" *The Art Newspaper* (January 9, 2002) (<http://62.253.251.9/access/artnewspaper.html>, accessed January 7, 2005) Record Number 14991. The alleged theft occurred more than forty years ago, raising the possibility for a statute of limitations defense. But, should museums assert such a defense for objects removed from known sites?

[30] Gerstenblith 454.

[31] This standard for the duty of care for nonprofit board members is described in the landmark case, *Stern v. Lucy Webb Hayes National Training School of Deaconesses and Missionaries*, 381 F. Supp. 1003, 1015 (D.D.C. 1974).

[32] Collections are costly to maintain. In a survey published in 1988, the cost of storing objects in accordance with museum-quality methodology showed that the annual operating costs allocable to an object kept in storage – in 1988 dollars – was $30 per square foot. An average object required two square feet of storage space and adjusting for inflation by 2000, the cost per item was $89 per annum. Weil, S *Making Museum Matter* (Washington DC: Smithsonian Press) 2002 citing Hartman *Museum News* (May–June 1988).

[33] The CPIA also makes the importation of certain cultural property illegal as of 1983. This includes any cultural property stolen from museums and other cultural sites of member nations of the UNESCO Convention. 9 U.S.C. Sec. 2607. Any such object is subject to seizure by U.S. Customs.

[34] *Solomon R. Guggenheim Foundation v. Lubell*, 77 N.Y.2d311, 567 NYS2d 623, 569 N.E.2d 426 (N.Y. Ct. App. 1991).

generally, Museum A needs to do a reasonable amount of research in good faith to ensure that the duty of care has been satisfied and to preserve the defense of *laches*.[35] In that regard, if any object in the collection was at one time stolen, there is a chance that it may be listed in one of the stolen art databases. Checking with such databases would be a minimum first step.[36]

In keeping with legal standards, the 2004 AAMD Guidelines were established "to assist members in revising their acquisition policies."[37] The Guidelines state that member museums should require sellers and donors to provide "all available information and documentation" (Section II A. (2) & (3)). Research on provenance, authenticity, quality, and condition of the object is noted; the following specific areas are recommended:

- ownership history,
- the countries in which the work has been located and when,[38]
- exhibition history,
- publication history,
- whether any claims to ownership of the work have been made,
- whether the work appears in relevant databases of stolen works, and
- circumstances under which it is offered to the museum.

Finally, member museums are advised "to make a concerted effort to obtain accurate written documentation with respect to the history of the work of art, including import and export documents."[39] These provisions formalize the inquiry and research process for acquisitions. By doing so, they have set a standard by which art museum practices may be measured in the future. Note that the AAMD Guidelines do not recommend contacting the country of origin for further information about an undocumented object. The Smithsonian Policy dating from 1972 recommends contacting source countries for "substantial proposed acquisitions of foreign provenance where acceptance is in question."[40] Neither does AAMD suggest dealing with only reputable dealers, as does the J. Paul Getty Museum's acquisition policy as of 1995.[41] One commentator suggests *Schultz* "dispelled the myth of 'reputable dealer'."[42]

If, after "rigorous research" and the "concerted effort," the museum is not able to determine securely whether the acquisition complies with applicable law, under the AAMD Guidelines, Museum A is free to use its "professional judgment" whether or not to acquire the object, recognizing that the public may be best served through acquisition of the object by a public-serving institution that may conserve, exhibit, and interpret the work. Therefore, the AAMD Guidelines consider an object innocent until proven guilty and cite the benefits associated with this approach. The AAMD Guidelines offer the following possible benefits of acquisition as examples:

- the possibility of making the work publicly accessible,
- providing material contribution to knowledge, and
- facilitating reconstruction of its provenance, thereby allowing possible claimants to come forward.

In addition, the AAMD further instructs that a museum should take into account:

- whether the work has been outside its probable country for sufficient time that its acquisition would not provide a *direct* and *material* incentive to looting or illegal excavation. The length of time recommended is ten years, although individual museums are advised to determine their own policies on this point (Section II E.) (emphasis added).

Under the AAMD Guidelines, Museum A is left with a dilemma. Although acquisition of the undocumented portion of Bill's collection would lead to public access, and

[35] For recommended steps for a due diligence inquiry for buyers or victims of a theft, see Pinkerton, Linda F. "Due Diligence for Acquisition of Cultural Property in the New Millennium," *IFAR Journal* (2000) Vol. 3, Nos. 3 and 4, pp 50–2.

[36] The Art Loss Register (ALR) is a preeminent international stolen art database that lists approximately 100,000 items reported as stolen or missing. The ALR collects information from law enforcement, insurance companies, and individuals. The charge is approximately $75 per item searched for nonsubscribers, which includes a number of museums. (<http://www.artloss.com/Default.asp>, accessed January 25, 2005). However, ALR cannot list objects that are undocumented, such as those surreptitiously excavated, so its effectiveness for archeological material may be limited. Museums should also check the U.S. Department of State's Web site for objects controlled pursuant to CPIA. The International Property Protection Homepage of the U.S. Department of State is illustrated with thumbnail photographs of the type of objects subject to temporary import restrictions. (<http://exchanges.state.gov/culprop/>, accessed January 23, 2005).

[37] The existing guidelines of the AAMD *Professional Practices in Art Museums (2001)* provided only that:"The Director must not knowingly acquire or allow to be recommended for acquisition any objects that has been stolen, removed in contravention of treaties and international conventions to which United States is a signatory, or illegally imported into the United States." In short, this provision instructed Directors not to violate U.S. law.

[38] The AAMD, in 2002, issued a position paper, *Art Museums and the International Exchange of Cultural Artifacts* (<http://aamd.org/pdfs/Cultural%20Property.pdf>, accessed January 23, 2005). It listed recommended questions to ensure the importation of art is conducted in a lawful and responsible manner, including, "Is there evidence that the work is being legally exported?"

[39] If imported into the United States as a part of the acquisition, the AAMD Guidelines direct that the museum should always obtain import documentation. If the import occurred earlier, then a concerted effort will suffice. *AAMD Guidelines* (Sec. II.A (2)).

[40] *Smithsonian Acquisition Policy* Sec. 3(b) (May 1973).

[41] *J. Paul Getty Museum Acquisition Policy for Classical Antiquities* November 13, 1987, revised November 10, 1995 states "[a]ll transactions will be with vendors of substance and established reputations in order that such transactions shall be covered by enforceable warranties" (Malaro, Figure IV.10).

[42] The revelations about Mr. Schultz's illegal practices were surprising to many because he had enjoyed a reputation in the art trade as a prominent and respected dealer. Mr. Schultz served for years as the President of the National Association of Dealers in Ancient, Oriental and Primitive Art, a U.S. organization that represented the interests of dealers in the cultural property policy debates on the national level. Elia, Ricardo J. "Move in the Right Direction" *The Art Newspaper* (January 9, 2003) (Record Number 17371).

conservation, and enable further provenance research, there is no evidence of when any of these objects left Arcadia and thus there is no way to judge whether any object meets the ten-year out-of-source-country recommendation. Critics may question the assumed rationale for this ten-year limit, namely that if the object was looted more than ten years ago, the acquisition by a museum is less likely to provide "direct, material" incentive for looting in the source country. One may argue that if a major museum in the United States collects an undocumented object, exhibits, and publishes it, the market value of similar objects will increase and the incentive to loot and smuggle similar objects will also increase no matter whether the museum's object was removed from the source country nine or fifteen years ago. AAMD chose to draw a line in the sand – ten years or more outside of a source country for objects of incomplete provenance meets its "direct and material" incentive for looting test.

By comparison, the Smithsonian and Harvard policies both require some documentation showing legal export and excavation before acquisition is authorized. In the absence of any information, the Harvard's policy directs the curators in cases of doubt to "consult widely." As noted previously, the Smithsonian Policy states that "substantial" acquisitions of foreign provenance without proper documentation may be considered only after consultation with the source country.[43] J. Paul Getty Museum's policy on collecting classical antiquities provides that works acquired by the museum as of 1995 must be published as of that date. No unpublished classical antiquities may be accepted.[44] The American Association of Museums ("AAM") directs member museums to conduct collecting activities to "discourage illicit trade" in cultural materials without specifying whether undocumented objects may be acquired.[45] The International Council of Museums ("ICOM") Code of Ethics is more explicit: The governing body or responsible officer of a museum is charged with the obligation to satisfy themselves that the object has not been acquired or exported from its country of origin in violation of that country's laws or subject to a recent unscientific excavation.[46] The ICOM therefore requires evidence to exculpate an object before acquisition. The absence of evidence would prevent the museum from accepting the object into its collections.[47]

[43] *Harvard University Policy* (Sec. 4); *Smithsonian Institution Acquisition Policy* (Section 2(b)).

[44] *J. Paul Getty Museum Policy on Acquisition of Classical Antiquities* (1995 rev.).

[45] *AAM Code of Ethics* 1994.

[46] *ICOM Code of Professional Ethics II 3.2.*

[47] As noted by O'Keefe, Patrick J. "Museum Acquisition Policies and the UNESCO Convention" *Museum International* (1998), Vol. 50, No. 1 20, 21, simply to write a policy is not enough; it must be implemented. He relates a story of how he had to search for the acquisition statement of a major museum because it had been filed away in the archives and forgotten. Indeed, there has been no study of how these existing policies have been implemented. For example, compare the Harvard University Policy of 1972 with the Annual Report (1997–8) of the Harvard University Art Museums by then director James Cuno, "Building Collections and Housing Them: Acquisition, Renzo Piano, and a Master Plan for the Art Museums."

The absence of information about when Bill's objects left the country is somewhat problematic if Museum A follows the new AAMD Guidelines in its decision-making. However, it may be argued that because Collector Bill was active in the art market for the past 65 years, chances are that most of his undocumented objects were removed from Arcadia more than ten years ago. Moreover, the ten-year limitation is simply a recommendation and Museum A is encouraged under the Guidelines to make its own policy on this point.

Objects (described as significant) Documented through the 1973 Exhibition Catalog. Objects that are documented by a catalog publication that pre-dates Arcadia's patrimony law are legally less troublesome. The catalog evidences that the patrimony law is not a basis to assert legal title to objects documented to have been in the United States in 1973. The objects may still have been illegally exported under the 1950 export law, but violation of a foreign export law is not a violation of U.S. law. Legally, the objects maybe acquired. As an ethical issue, illegally exported property from Arcadia is discussed subsequently. In addition, for any such object that may have been stolen in the conventional sense, it could be argued that the 1973 publication triggered the running of the statute of limitations barring civil recovery by the theft victim.

Museum A should be aware that the use of prior museum publication as documentation of provenance has been criticized. As noted earlier, the J. Paul Getty Museum's Policy requires the Getty to acquire only collections documented (published) prior to 1995.[48] This step was hailed, because it precluded future collecting by the Getty to be linked to current or future looting activity. Shortly after this policy was passed, the Getty acquired a large collection of more than 300 objects of Greek, Roman, and Etruscan origin from a private collector. Reportedly, provenience for ninety percent of these objects was unknown. The documentation relied upon by the Getty was Getty's own catalog from a loaned exhibition that it held a few years earlier. Critics accused the Getty of manufacturing documentation to satisfy its own requirements for provenance and thereby tacitly condoning the flow of illegal antiquities.[49]

Objects That May Be Identified as Being in Bill's Collection Only after 1980* and *No Documentation Exists That the Objects Were Removed from Arcadia prior to 1980 (effective date of Arcadia's patrimony law). This category of objects may fall under the *Schultz* doctrine and Museum A may be well advised not to take possession because mere possession may be a criminal violation of NSPA. In this category, the nature of the object may play a role in determining the risk of legal liability. For example, if the object is unique and traceable back to Arcadia post 1980, then clearly the risk of criminal violation is substantial. What if the object was export-ware

[48] *J. Paul Getty Museum Policy on Acquisition of Classical Antiquities* (1995) (Sec. 2.).

[49] Kaufman. *The Art Newspaper Archives* Record Number 2386.

that may have been circulating in the international market for years prior to Bill's purchase? One might argue that the risk of criminal liability is less for objects that are not unique and if similar objects are known to be widely available in international markets for many years. Should museums skirt criminal law or take a more principled stance and decline all such material whether or not criminal liability is likely to attach? Note that this category of objects may also have been subject to an illegal export if they were removed from Arcadia after 1950, as discussed later.

Objects That May Be Traced to Official Excavation Sites in Arcadia. This category of objects is also suspect. The AAMD Guidelines recommend that if the object is "known to have been a part of an official archeological site" and removed without permission of authorities, it should not be acquired (Section D). In fact, the U.S. law of ordinary theft may apply. If the object was "known," it must have been documented and, thus, tracing its ownership is possible. It may be noted that identifying objects as a part of any particular official excavation may be difficult if like objects may also be found elsewhere. The burden to prove that the object could not have come from anywhere else may be formidable.[50] In effect, AAMD is instructing members to avoid potential legal problems arising from theft in the chain of title.

However, AAMD also goes further here. The Guidelines state that museums should not acquire such materials regardless of any applicable statute of limitations provided that the objects were removed from Arcadia post 1970, the date of the UNESCO Convention. In this instance, it asks museums to forego a potential statute of limitations defense for any such object, thereby setting a standard higher than the law may require. This is also true for any object that Museum A may wish to acquire but determines "to have been stolen from a museum, or a religious, or secular public monument or similar institution" as of 1970, the date of the UNESCO Convention. It should be noted that any object with the same history stolen after 1983 and imported into the United States would be a violation of the CPIA and be subject to seizure and return to the source country.[51] In any event, AAMD promotes waiving of potential affirmative defense to justify an acquisition in these two circumstances in which theft from a museum or an official excavation site as of 1970 is at issue.[52]

Any Object Acquired by Bill as of 1950 and That Cannot Be Documented As Being Outside of Arcadia prior to 1950 (the effective date of Arcadia's export law). Illegally exported objects may also have been subject to other legal violations, such as theft. It is also possible that an object, otherwise legally owned, may have been removed from its country of origin in violation of only an export law. This category is therefore broad and may include objects discussed previously under other categories.

As noted earlier, illegal export from a source country is not a violation of U.S. law absent a CPIA-imposed temporary import restriction. In this case, the facts provided indicate that there was no such restriction in place. The AAMD Guidelines do not directly address the issue of "illegal export."[53] This is noteworthy because this issue has been debated broadly and restrictions on illegally exported materials were adopted by many museums years ago. The AAM passed a resolution in 1971 that recommends member museums of all types (including art museums) abstain from acquiring illegally exported antiquities from countries that have "adopted the farsighted policy of making duplicate material available through legal channels, or has installed a procedure for granting export licenses to material which has been approved by a board of review."[54] The internal policies of Harvard University (1972) and the Smithsonian Institution (1973) include restriction on acquiring illegally exported objects as of the early 1970s. These policies were based on the UNESCO Convention's Article 7(a), that required member nations to restrict collecting activities of museums within their borders in illegally exported materials from other member nations. The CPIA that implemented UNESCO specifically declined to pass U.S. law to control the acquisition practices of U.S. museums, noting that U.S. museums voluntarily adopted such provisions by that date.[55] UNESCO Convention's Section 5(a) urged adoption of "ethical principles" set forth in the convention by those concerned (curators, collectors, and antique dealers). Thus, the UNESCO Convention provided moral backing for refusing to collect illegally exported cultural property even if the government itself did not pursue this objective in the implementing legislation.[56]

The AAMD Guidelines bypass Article 7(a) and limit acquisition of objects to what the CPIA prohibits, namely acquisition of "objects stolen from a museum, or a religious, or secular public monument or similar institution." Thus, AAMD's implementation of UNESCO's Article 7 does not require anything significantly more than what the implementing U.S. law directs. Under these standards, any object that falls within this category maybe acquired by Museum A because mere illegal export will not be a deterrent.

[50] See *Peru v. Johnson* at 812 ("plaintiff must overcome legal and factual burdens that are heavy indeed").

[51] The CPIA offers time limitations for seizure depending upon how long the object was held by a U.S. museum and published by it. See 19 U.S.C. Sec. 2611.

[52] Waiving of affirmative defenses by museums is also evident in the guidelines established by the American Association of Museum for Nazi erabased claims for restitution, *AAM Guidelines Concerning the Unlawful Appropriation of Objects During the Nazi Era* issued by AAM November 1999 and amended April 2001. (<http://www.aam-us.org/museumresources/ethics/nazi˙guidelines.cfm0> accessed Feb. 7, 2005).

[53] In fact, the Guidelines do not direct museums to adhere to foreign laws generally, but only to foreign laws (presumable patrimony laws) that may impact legal status of the object under U.S. law.

[54] "Report of the AAM Special Policy Committee" *Museum News*, May 1971, at 22–3.

[55] See note 2 earlier.

[56] O'Keefe. Patrick J. "Museum Acquisition Policies and the UNESCO Convention" *Museum International* (January 1998) Vol. 50, No. 1, pp. 20, 21.

The AAMD's position on illegal export may be justified on several grounds. It may be argued that any attempt to enforce export laws of other countries would require museums to implement laws that may be themselves unjustified and impractical, would require museums to invest in elaborate investigative resources, and possibly would stunt the growth of the collections. It may be noted that post-*Schultz*, elaborate investigations of foreign law are already required. It may also be argued that the effectiveness of such a self-imposed bar would be questionable when restricted only to museums rather than the United States as a whole. Moreover because any such restriction would be voluntary, many museum directors may fear that self-denial would result in objects ending up in rival museums here or abroad. Finally, it may be argued that export laws of other countries are enforced in the United States on a selective basis using legal channels available through the CPIA-mandated process. That process is intended to protect endangered cultural property but only after source countries prove that such help is needed. In other words, the CPIA process is a more effective and targeted solution than a blanket approach applicable only to museum acquisitions.[57] Many also believe that overly restrictive export controls used to embargo property have the opposite effect than intended, namely, fueling the black market.[58]

Paul Bator, a noted authority writing in 1982, argued nevertheless for the adoption by museums of policies preventing acquisition of illegally exported cultural objects. He based his conclusions on several factors. He felt that museums have special obligations flowing from their status of "public-serving" institutions and therefore they should maintain "an especially scrupulous standard of civic virtue, and avoid being tainted by the illegal."[59] He also believed that acquisition of smuggled objects implicates museum in a deeply subversive activity, which is inappropriate for museums that must be the first to commit to the ideal of preservation. Not that every illegally exported object can be traced to looting, but rather he argued that "the satisfaction of the market of illegally exported objects has created a business that depends on and encourages a practice which is frequently destructive" and rewards people who are willing to engage in it.[60] When a museum acquires a smuggled object, it cannot be sure that it did not help reward destruction.

From a practical perspective, if a museum restricts illegally exported artifacts, it will also restrict material subject to potential other claims, including those based on patrimony laws. Generally, export laws exist wherever patrimony laws are in effect and many predate them. Screening for illegal export casts a broader net and may make other, more detailed inquiries unnecessary. But, by such screening, museums would further limit acquisitions. Under the AAMD Guidelines, no consideration of illegal export is indicated for members.

[57] Bator at 82.
[58] Bator at 41–3.
[59] Bator at 83.
[60] Bator at 83.

Any Remaining Objects Documented As Acquired by Bill prior to 1950. Because this group of objects acquired by Bill predate any legal restrictions and are not covered by the AAMD Guidelines, they may be freely acquired provided that standard due care inquiries to uncover any reported thefts were made. In addition, because these objects were outside of Arcadia prior to 1970, the AAMD guidelines on "moral claims" would not apply. Because most acquisition policies of other groups and museums passed in the 1970s were prospective, no policy would direct otherwise.

Post Acquisition AAMD Guidelines

The AAMD strongly urges members to disclose and disseminate information after the object is acquired to make it readily available to an international audience. Transparency in collecting is advisable from a legal standpoint because disclosure may provide notice to claimants for purposes of triggering statutes of limitations. The AAMD further recommends that in the event the museum uncovers information that establishes another party's claim and even if that claim is not enforceable under U.S. law, the museum should seek "equitable resolution." This provision is limited to objects acquired after June 10, 2004. The options provided for such resolutions are not limiting because they include sale, transfer, loan, exchange, or retention of the object. It may be noted that the Guidelines are not subject to sanctions. Members are urged (not required) to accept and be guided by them.

CONCLUSION

This case study exercise demonstrates the complexities that museum professionals face with acquisitions of archeological materials or ancient art privately collected during the past century. The legal and ethical waters are increasingly difficult to navigate requiring elaborate investigative resources. Recognizing this, the AAMD has taken a step to assist its membership in revising their existing acquisition policies by issuing new Guidelines that are commendable in several respects. The Guidelines call for rigorous provenance research for acquisitions and urge full and prompt public disclosure following an acquisition. Compared with the "no questions asked, no information given" practices of the art trade, museums have come a long way. It may be argued that much of this progress may be attributed to developments in the law, citing the *U.S. v. Schultz* case as the latest in a trend to curtail suspect transactions in the art trade. However motivated, the AAMD has set standards for rigorous provenance research and public disclosure of acquisition records by which the future actions of art museum directors may be measured.

It is expected that the Guidelines will be criticized for not going far enough by failing to restrict the acquisition of illegally exported works and condoning acquisition of works with incomplete provenance. By failing to self-regulate more rigorously in this area, the AAMD may be criticized for sidestepping an opportunity to curtail illicit activity in the art market, and thereby help preserve the world's cultural heritage. Indeed, many provisions of the Guidelines reflect a persistent concern that legitimate trade in art not be unduly hampered. The art museum community complains that even in cases in which the objects are fully documented both as to ownership history and provenience, museums are not exempt from moral claims based on misdeeds of the past – some occurring hundreds of years ago.[61] A proposal that museums should cease all collecting in ancient art for decades also has been proposed as a solution.[62]

[61] One commentator notes that "outlandish claims should and will be resisted," and that the *Schultz* case "encourages nations to make unilateral demands and to try to 'pillage back' from the museums of the world," with the result that sharing of cultural heritage between countries through lending and borrowing will be "curtailed by growing demands of cultural nationalism." Hawkins, *The Art Newspaper Archives* Record Number 17370.

[62] Coggins, Clemency C "Essays: A Proposal for Museum Acquisition Policies in the Future" 1 *International Journal of Cultural Property* (1998) pp 434–237.

In response to increasing demands that many feel threaten museum collections, directors of American and European museums signed the "Declaration on the Importance and Value of the Universal Museums" in 2002, reasserting the community's objection to illegal trafficking, but affirming the museums' role as agents in disseminating cultures of ancient civilizations.[63] Because the policy debate continues to be increasingly polarized, it should also be recognized that museums have more at stake, namely, public trust that is essential for any nonprofit, publicly supported organization.[64] A thoughtful dialogue among all interested parties and founded on the principle that all sides hold legitimate values is overdue.

[63] "The Declaration on the Importance and Value of Universal Museums" printed in Bailey, M. "We Serve All Cultures, Say Big Global Museums" *The Art Newspaper* (January 2003) No. 32, pp. 1, 6.

[64] See Cuno, James ed. *Whose Muse? Art Museums and the Public Trust* (Princeton: Princeton University Press 2004) 12–13, noting that press reports of illegally antiquities in museums threatens the public trust.

CHAPTER FIFTY-TWO

Mäori Taonga – Mäori Identity

Arapata Hakiwai

Mäori taonga or treasures are held in many New Zealand museums and are well represented in overseas museum collections. They form important collections in many countries, including the United Kingdom, America, France, Germany, Australia, and Russia. Many Mäori people are not aware that there are Mäori collections held in these overseas museums, much less the large number of Mäori taonga held in museums in New Zealand. In fact, many Mäori have been alienated from their ancestral treasures for a long time. What is certain is that Mäori taonga form an important foundation for Mäori cultural identity. Mäori taonga are well sought after in auctions both in New Zealand and overseas. They have been the object of fascination and intrigue since the time of the early explorers to New Zealand such as Abel Janszoon Tasman (1642) and Captain Cook (1769–1777) and the interest continues today, as seen by images of Mäori treasures that have been used to promote the sale of oceanic and tribal art through auction houses both in New Zealand and overseas.

SIGNIFICANCE OF MÄORI TAONGA

What is the cultural significance of Mäori taonga to Mäori people? Taonga can represent and depict ancestors, events, stories and narratives of culture and history. For Mäori, taonga are reminders of their past and, by association, their present and future. Irrespective of the passing of time, Mäori taonga continue to be powerful symbols and identity markers of Mäori cultural heritage in today's contemporary world. As Barbara Girshemblatt-Gimblett notes, "For taonga the issue is not a second life as an exhibit. What is at stake is the restoration of living links to taonga that never died."[1]

Mäori *taonga tuku iho*, or treasures handed down from our ancestors, form an important dimension of Mäori identity, as well as being an integral part of New Zealand's cultural heritage. However, in this fast changing world, Mäori cultural heritage has become even more important in terms of cultural maintenance, reclamation, restoration, and ongoing cultural development. With strong Mäori language initiatives in New Zealand such as the Kohanga Reo, early childhood language nests, and the Kura kaupapa Mäori schools, combined with a vibrant Mäori performing and visual arts programme around the country, Mäori taonga become even more important in terms of identification to one's identity, history, and social well-being.

Taonga have a whakapapa or genealogical relationship connected to them and form special relationships to their tribal descendants and kin. Carvings depict ancestors and histories and narratives of our knowledge and belief systems. Cloaks, likewise, carry significance with respect to who made them, who they were made for, the occasion on which they were worn, the type of cloak, and repeats the relationships and histories attached to them. Portraits and photographs of ancestors, meeting houses, carvings, and the landscape continue to hold meaning and significance for their tribal descendants because of who they represent, their achievements, and their ongoing connection to descendants today.

Sadly, many Mäori are unaware of the extent of Mäori taonga held in museums both nationally and internationally. Many Mäori have been dispossessed and alienated from their tribal heirlooms and treasures for a long time. In fact, museums have not had the best of reputations for connecting indigenous people with their art and heritage base. Given this context, it is no wonder that Mäori are extremely interested in knowing when Mäori taonga or treasures come up for sale in auction houses.

To see how the spirit can be uplifted when one discovers through the reconnection process an important cultural identity marker is a joy to witness. A recent example at Te Papa was seen with the discovery and reconnection of a significant treasure to its family of origin. To see and experience this occasion was a humbling and rewarding experience.

MUSEUM OF NEW ZEALAND TE PAPA TONGAREWA (TE PAPA)

Te Papa has extensive experience working with auctions and the art market in New Zealand and overseas. The Museum of New Zealand is aware at any one time what taonga are coming up for auction in most parts of the world. Te Papa is different from many other museums in New Zealand. Te Papa is committed to developing as a bicultural organisation based on the partnership implicit in the Treaty of Waitangi. This partnership is reflected in the organisational structure of the museum, where the strategic leadership is shared, with a CEO and kaihautü, or Mäori equivalent. Te Papa's Bicultural Framework recognises key policies, including Mana Taonga, the Bicultural Policy, Iwi Relationship Strategy, Mätauranga Mäori Strategy, and the Iwi Exhibition Strategy. These policies affirm the special relationship that exists between Mäori and taonga.

Mana Taonga is one of Te Papa's key policies that is central to laying a foundation for Mäori participation and

[1] See Girshemblatt-Gimblett (1998:165).

involvement at Te Papa. The concept of Mana Taonga was developed through consultation with Mäori tribes and provides iwi (tribe) and our wider communities the right to define how taonga should be cared for and managed in accordance with their own tikanga or custom. Broadly speaking, the concept recognizes the spiritual and cultural connections of taonga with the people. Mana Taonga enables any Mäori iwi or other culture to stand on the marae[2] and exercise their own tikanga or customs by right of the taonga or collections held within the museum.

The policy of Mana Taonga helps to shape and inform the way Te Papa carries out its business, whether exhibitions, research, events, publications, or the auction process. At the heart of this policy are relationships. Te Papa actively works with our communities of interest and Mäori tribes at all levels. Maintaining strong relationships with iwi has meant working with the art market and negotiating through the different value systems and processes in ways that can help and assist our communities. Te Papa's Chief Executive, Dr. Seddon Bennington, recently said, "Mana Taonga is not just a way of thinking about the relationship for Mäori between objects and their makers. It is also bringing to our consciousness the role and attitude we need to develop in our engagement with other communities."[3]

WORKING TOGETHER, UNDERSTANDING ONE ANOTHER

An example of how museums can work together more to better understand one another can be seen through the restoration project of the carved Mäori meeting house *Ruatepupuke* in the Field Museum of Natural History, Chicago, Illinois, United States. This project was a collaborative initiative among the Field Museum, Te Waka Toi (now Toi Aotearoa – Creative New Zealand) and the Mäori community of Tokomaru Bay in 1991–3. The Field Museum was particularly keen and excited about the relationship established among their museum and the tribe closely connected with the meeting house, Te Whänau-a-Ruataupare, and Te Whänau a Te Aotawarirangi, of Tokomaru Bay, on the East Coast of the North Island of New Zealand.

The Field Museum openly acknowledged that it was "rich in collections, but poor in relations." As a result of the partnership established through the carved meeting house restoration project, the Field Museum wanted to know how to reconnect and engage with the peoples and cultures from whom the treasures in their care originated. The Field Museum established the Center for Cross-Cultural Understanding and invited me to this meeting. My advice was very simple. Engage with the peoples and cultures *kanohi ki te kanohi* or face to face. Reconnect with them and see what happens. I mention this example because the reconnection of taonga with iwi Mäori in museums in this country and overseas is absolutely imperative if we are to talk to one another, much less understand each other. Let me now talk about issues museums face with regard to the buying and selling of Mäori taonga.

ISSUES

Museums are actively involved in the auction and art market but their reasons for being so are perhaps different from those of the general public. For museums, the art market is one way of acquiring and returning taonga back home, be it largely through the mediated experience of a museum. To return something intrinsically linked to any people's sense of well-being and identity is worth all its weight in gold. To see people cry, talk to, and reconnect with their ancestral treasures brings a powerful sense of affirmation and reward.

The curators at Te Papa know the art market and conduct its business according to well-defined principles, policies, and guidelines. Many museums have collection development policies that articulate why they collect, what they collect, and how they collect it. Te Papa is no different, in that we have strategies and collection development plans across disciplines, including the Natural Environment, Art and Visual Culture, History and Pacific Cultures, and Mäori art and History or Mätauranga Mäori. The museum's role and responsibility in acquiring taonga through the auction process has come under fire in recent times, questioning the reasons why museums should collect, on whose behalf, and the processes they undertake. What is certain is that many museums consider auctions as one way where Mäori taonga can be returned.

There is, however, tension between the different value systems of the art market and Mäori towards the buying and selling of Mäori taonga. Whenever Te Papa is informed that a taonga with history or provenance comes up for sale, and in which we may be interested, we consult the relevant tribe, subtribe or family, to let them know that their taonga is coming up for sale. We inform Mäori tribes that their taonga is coming up for sale as part of Te Papa's responsibility and obligation. Often, our role is negotiating between the different interest groups and communities to find a positive solution.

Some tribes seek information regarding to what they can do, even if this means buying back their taonga in auctions. Te Papa is often contacted by tribes throughout New Zealand for guidance and instruction because these tribes have confidence in and respect for Te Papa. We are also aware that some Mäori tribes have registered themselves as collectors within the requirements of the Antiquities Act 1975 as a way in which they can acquire back their material culture.

Representing and advocating for the interests of Mäori – iwi (tribes), hapü (sub-tribes), and whänau (families) can be challenging. The research work and processes that Te Papa

[2] A marae and meeting house was intentionally built for Te Papa when it opened in February 1998. The adoption of such a strong Mäori cultural institution was a strong expression and commitment to biculturalism and Mäori values, beliefs, and knowledge.

[3] See "Te Ara," *Journal of Museums Aotearoa* (May 2004), Volume 29, Issue I, p. 11.

carry out with regard to taonga coming up for sale are comprehensive and rigorous. We carry out our own internal checks to corroborate and validate the information provided in auction catalogues, as well as working closely with the appropriate iwi, hapü, and whänau, to ascertain their wishes. In our role as negotiator and facilitator, we often assist iwi with regard to their options. In some cases, this has resulted in tensions between the reality of the art market and the expectation by Mäori that their taonga should return home, via the National Museum. Clearly, there are different understandings and notions of value for both the seller and buyer.

The role and responsibility of museums to actively assist indigenous peoples to connect and reconnect with their material cultural are great. Certainly, museums have a pivotal role in this process because they possess extensive collections of material culture and have proven experience and expertise in this area. Being able to connect and reconnect indigenous peoples to their cultural heritage is an important priority for museums in today's contemporary society. In fact, enlightened museum practice is, in itself, demanding that museums rethink and reframe themselves about what museums are and what museums should be.

Museums Australia adopted a strong cultural policy document in 1993 called *Previous Possessions, New Obligations*, which addresses secret and sacred material; human remains; the display, access, and return of collection items; the right of self-determination; and issues such as employment and training. The policy states that Aboriginal and Torres Strait Islander peoples should be involved in policy decisions affecting their cultural heritage at all levels. Te Papa's experience strongly reinforces this position, noting that there are clear responsibilities and obligations that the National Museum should have for the indigenous people of Aotearoa, New Zealand.

Examples of best museum practice can be seen in registration and accreditation schemes for museums worldwide, as well as a number of reports commissioned by countries and states on the relationship between museums and indigenous peoples. Clearly, museums have a responsibility and obligation to connect and reconnect the taonga and collections housed in their museums back to indigenous peoples. New Zealand has a museums standards scheme for best museum practice called *The New Zealand Museums Standards Scheme He Kaupapa Whaimana a Ngä Whare Taonga o Aoteraoa.* This continuous improvement scheme recognises the importance of museums in relation to communities of interest and recognises the responsibility to honour the Treaty of Waitangi, New Zealand's founding document. No longer is it acceptable for museums not to engage their communities of interest. As noted by the well-known museum commentator Elaine Gurian, "the exclusive right of museum personnel to decide what shall be included or excluded in their public exhibitions will, and in some cases already has, ended. The display of any objects without consultation with the native group and, by extension, any group importantly affected, will become obsolete. In fact, the involvement of indigenous peoples in the business of museums goes much deeper than mere presentation." (1996:3–4).

An important issue concerns the Antiquities Act 1975. This legislation has a number of long-standing problems that have, and continue to, impact on the art market. Some of these include the outdated and inconsistent definitions of antiquities and artefacts, the low penalties for noncompliance, particularly illegal export, and the decision-making processes for export applications being inconsistent over time, to name a few. Presently we have the passage of the Protected Objects Amendment Bill, which will significantly address many of these issues. This Bill will come into force on 1 July 2005.

PROVENANCE AND INFORMATION

Another issue concerns provenance and information. The Antiquities Act 1975 has created a growing trend by auction houses to deliberately withhold information. Te Papa has noticed a trend to fabricate provenance information because, often, more information can lead to increased taonga sale prices. Contrary to this, Te Papa has also noticed that some auction houses have deliberately withheld information because of the fear of political contestation that can ensue with Mäori people. There have been recent examples of this in which auction sales have been disrupted because of protest and outrage about the selling of precious tribal taonga. Te Papa tries very hard within a relatively short time frame to verify, corroborate, and validate taonga with known provenances and histories attached to them. Although not an easy exercise, Te Papa's experience and expertise in this area is very good. We also know that there have been unethical practises in the fabrication of taonga histories and provenances over the years to help inflate the prices of taonga.

Te Papa's involvement in the art market is judicious and well considered. Te Papa is very cautious when it comes to Mäori taonga coming up for sale on the art market. Te Papa's research of taonga on the national and international art market goes back many years. We know that there are questionable practices that auctions and the art market employ that contribute towards the hyping and inflation of taonga prices. The presence of Te Papa staff at auction sales on occasion has also been used to promote the value of taonga. Many museums have effectively become mediators and facilitators in the process of selling and buying of Mäori taonga, either through the implementation of the Antiquities Act or through advice and instruction. The reasons why museums acquire taonga are, in many cases, quite different from reasons why personal collectors and auction houses buy and sell taonga. Restoring the living links of taonga that never died is a high priority for museums. Recognising the importance of Mäori taonga coming up for sale in auctions and the art market is likewise an important consideration.

REFERENCES

Dekker, Diana (2004) "Treasured Possessions." An article written in *The Dominion Post Newspaper*, Wellington, Saturday August 14, E3.

Hakiwai, Arapata (1995) "Ruatepupuke: Working Together, Understanding One Another." Presented at the Museums Association of Aotearoa New Zealand and Museum Educators Association Annual Conference 1994. Published by the *New Zealand Museums Journal* Vol. 25 Number 1 pp. 42–44.

Hakiwai, Arapata (1997) "Museums – On Whose Terms? Working 'Inside Out.'" Paper presented to the International Symposium "Representing Cultures in Museums" held at the National Museum of Ethnology, Osaka, and the Setagaya Art Museum, Tokyo, October 20–26, 1997.

Hakiwai, A., Terrell, J. (1994) "Ruatepupuke: A Maori Meeting House." Presented under the Field Museum: "Exploring the Earth and Its People," *Field Museum*, Chicago, Illinois.

Kirshenblatt-Gimblett, Barbara (1998) "Destination Museum," taken from *Destination Culture: Tourism, Museums, and Heritage*, Berkeley and Los Angeles: University of California Press.

Mead, S. M. "Te Māori: A Journey of Rediscovery for the Māori people of New Zealand" in *TRIPTYCH*, magazine of the Asian Art Museum, M.H. de Young Memorial Museum, California Palace of the Legion of Honour, June-July 1985, pp. 11–18.

Mead, Hirini Moko (1990) "The Nature of Taonga" in *Taonga Māori Conference*, published by the Cultural Conservation Advisory Council, Department of Internal Affairs, Wellington, pp. 164–9.

Nesus, Cath (2004) "Making the Connection – Biculturalism at Work" in Te Ara *Journal of Museums Aotearoa*, Volume 29, Issue 1, pp. 12–15.

Paterson, Robert K. (1999) "Protecting Taonga: The Cultural Heritage of the New Zealand Māori" in *International Journal of Cultural Property*, Vol. 8, No.1, pp. 108–32.

Tapsell, Paul (1997) "The Flight of Pareraututu: An Investigation of Taonga from a Tribal Perspective," in *The Journal of the Polynesian Society*, December, Vol. 106, No. 4, pp. 323–74.

Tapsell, Paul (1998) "Taonga: A Tribal Response to Museums," Ph.D. thesis, School of Museum Ethnography, University of Oxford.

CHAPTER FIFTY-THREE

Unfolding Intangible Cultural Heritage Rights in Tangible Museum Collections: Developing Standards of Stewardship

Gerald R. Singer

Some of the world's most important cultural property resides in museum repositories of collections of anthropological and archaeological objects and in their archives of study materials – field notes, diaries, maps, research correspondence and reports, unpublished manuscripts, drawings, electronic databases of the collections, illustrations, paintings, photographs, films, audio recordings, language studies, catalogues – considered organic to the collections themselves. Museum repositories document the intangible cultural heritage of indigenous peoples – their ceremonies, music, songs, stories, language, symbols, beliefs, customs, crafts, skills, and ideas – but traditionally have not included participation by the indigenous people whose culture is represented by the collections.

Museum cultural collections have been an arena of contention. Museums assembled and continue to assemble and preserve these repositories as the cultural heritage of mankind, whereas many indigenous peoples have often considered the collections to be the product of conquest and subjugation, resulting in a loss of tangible objects and artifacts of their unique creation that are interdependent with their rituals and traditions, and, in the creation of archives, a loss of privacy for secret or closed rituals and traditions. Use of the collections and archives for research, education, and exhibition has also traditionally proceeded without consultation with the indigenous people represented. Those traditions are changing.

Cultural rights are reported to be the least developed rights within the human rights spectrum.[1] An attempt to provide a practical and more specific definition of cultural rights was made in the Preliminary Draft Declaration of Cultural Rights produced in Friberg, 1995. The rights listed included "participation in cultural life" and the right to "participate in cultural policies either as an individual person or in a community with others." The Universal Declaration on Cultural Diversity adopted by UNESCO in September 1991 declares: "Cultural rights are an integral part of human rights, which are universal, indivisible, and interdependent" and lists, among other cultural rights, that "... all persons have the right to participate in the cultural life of their choice and conduct their own cultural practices, subject to respect for human rights and fundamental freedoms." Such documents serve to establish international norms and a basis for rights legislation within member states of the international community.

Some in the legal community are skeptical that a right of indigenous people "to participate in cultural life" is hopelessly vague. To this, one commentator responded:

> And with regard to the idea that cultural rights are vague – I don't think cultural rights are more vague than any other right. The right to participate in cultural life – is that any more vague than the right to life? Or the right to due process? The right to judicial protection? They are all vague. They have been defined, and we know what the normative content of the right to life is, or the right to due process, because they have been developed in specific factual situations through a judicial process. That's how we know what the normative content is. As more and more cases are being brought in the cultural context, then we know exactly what the right to culture means.[2]

The museum community has anticipated the right to participate with its ethical codes. For example, ICOM's code of professional ethics provides:

> Museums should ensure that the information they present in displays and exhibitions ... gives appropriate consideration to represented groups or beliefs. ... Human remains and materials of sacred significance must be displayed in a manner consistent with professional standards and, where known, taking into account the interests and beliefs of the community, ethnic or religious groups from whom the objects originated. ... Requests for removal from public display of human remains and material of sacred significance ... must be addressed expeditiously with respect and sensitivity.[3]

The right to participate in cultural life has also been adopted into law. For example, within the United States, the 1990 law titled "the Native American Graves Protection and Repatriation Act" provides significantly for participation by Native Americans and Hawaiians. The law requires that institutions receiving federal funds such as museums and universities must consult with Native American tribes and Hawaiian organizations to (1) prepare inventories of their collections comprising human remains as well as "associated funerary objects" (artifacts in their possession that are reasonably believed to have been buried with the remains, or made exclusively for burial purposes, or containing human remains); and to (2) prepare summary descriptions of their holdings of other funerary artifacts, as well as "sacred objects" (specific ceremonial objects needed by traditional Native American religious leaders for the practice of traditional Native American

[1] Halina Niec, "Culture Rights: At the End of the World Decade for Cultural Development."

The author's views are personal and not associated with the American Museum of Natural History.

[2] Tara Melish, edited remarks given at the Cultural Rights Workshop of 9/23/04, Carnegie Council on Ethics and International Affairs.

[3] International Council of Museums.

religions by their present day adherents), and "objects of cultural patrimony" (property that has "ongoing historical, traditional, or cultural importance to the Native American group or culture" and of such "central importance" to the tribe that it was communally owned and could not be "alienated, appropriated, or conveyed by an individual").

Because of this law, many museums adopted policies providing for further participation by Native Americans and Hawaiians in aspects of collection management. For example, one museum's policy declares that "relationships between the Museum and Native American peoples will be governed by respect of the human rights of Native Americans" and that the Museum recognizes the need to pursue historic and scientific research "in a respectful, non-intrusive manner that takes into account the values of the Native American nations and peoples." The Museum policy further pledges "to resolve questions of the disposition and treatment of human remains and cultural items consensually through cooperative and timely discussions between the Museum and all interested Native American groups" and declares that the Museum "recognizes the need to interpret cultural items with accuracy, sensitivity, and respect for their relationship to the cultures of Native peoples" and "to engage in dialogues with Native Americans concerning their beliefs and viewpoints.

The right of indigenous peoples to participate in cultural life is still evolving and, as anticipated, that development is taking place through approaches to specific issues presented to museums. Examples include

. . . in conservation:

- "Can I conserve this using standard museum materials and practices?" One museum's archive included drawings of Navaho dry paintings traditionally destroyed after the healing ceremony. The museum staff questioned whether the drawings should be conserved or allowed to deteriorate and sought advice from the tribe before deciding to proceed with conservation. A number of museums now regularly consult with tribes on the use of standard museum materials and practices.
- "Can female conservation staff handle this object?" One museum decided to turn down a request by indigenous peoples to prohibit handling of an object by female staff that by their traditions was forbidden.

. . . in public display:

- "Should we grant this loan request for display of an object to a museum in a foreign country?" Some museums require assurance of tribal consultation. Some museums have entered into agreements with tribes that require their consent to lend an object and tribal approval of the exhibition text.
- "Should we continue to display this object of a ceremonial mask that is questioned as sacred?" Upon request, many museums have removed religious objects, such as ceremonial masks, from display.
- "Should we remove from public display a painting by a European artist that depicts a religious ceremony of indigenous peoples?" The museum decided to remove it.

. . . in public programming:

- "Should we agree to a protocol that prohibits educational personnel and docents from providing lectures and tours that tell of a tribal group's oral histories and stories?" One museum agreed to this protocol.

. . . in acquisitions:

- "Should we accept a gift of an important research collection with the donor's stipulations that it be retained, knowing that some objects may be subject to repatriation?" A museum decided to advise the donor of the museum's obligations to contact the Native American tribe and to offer to accept the collection with the restrictions, but subject to repatriation obligations.

. . . in research access:

- "Should we grant permission for this researcher to photograph burial remains?" One museum granted permission to photograph for research purposes, but on condition the photograph would not be published. The researcher did not honor the request. Of all of these examples of requests for participation, the most problematic are those restricting research.
- "Should we remove images of some collection objects on our research database that may be considered intrusive to the indigenous peoples?" Museums have removed images of the objects and are cautious of sending the image to bona fide researchers.
- "Should we transfer to the cultural office of indigenous peoples the title, custody, and control of the prints and negatives of selected photographic images in the archive that depict their religious ceremonies?" The museum declined but provided a duplicate set of prints.
- "Should the museum accept the tribe's request for immediate closure of all published or unpublished field data relating to the tribe, including notes, drawings and photographs, particularly those dealing with religious matters, to anyone who had not received the tribe's written permission?" Although it is believed that none of the museums granted the request for closure, a number of them marked the collections and archival material as "sensitive" and adopted a policy of encouraging or requiring scholars to contact tribal authorities before access would be granted.

. . . in overall collection management:

- "Should we accept this proposal of a binding contract to jointly curate the collection?" Some museums have; others have been reluctant to do so.

In the examples just provided, museums have developed, on an ad hoc basis, procedural approaches that provide for varying levels of participation. Some require consent from the cultural office of the indigenous peoples. Some consult with the cultural office of the indigenous peoples but retain the decision making to the museum, informed by policy and ethics of the field. Others have made their decisions without specific consultation and retain decision making to the museum.

A final example illustrating the cultural right to participation: In the Fall of 2000, a delegation from the Confederated Tribes of the Grand Ronde came to the American Museum of Natural History and submitted a claim for repatriation of the Willamette meteorite as a "sacred object" of one of its tribes, the Clackamas.

To the Museum and its scientists, the meteorite represented a rare and important scientific specimen that was preserved as part of a small record of authentic extraterrestrial objects, an important specimen for research in the fields of earth and planetary sciences and astrophysics, and an extraordinary scientific object for public display and education. The Museum had held the meteorite for these purposes for most of a century. From its unusually complicated microscopic structure, scientists have found evidence of collisions from the early history of our solar system.

To the Clackamas of the Grand Ronde, the meteorite was a sacred object. According to the traditions of the Clackamas, the meteorite they call "Tomanowos" is a revered spiritual being that has healed and empowered the people of the valley since the beginning of time. The Clackamas believe that Tomanowos came to the valley as a representative of the Sky People and that a union occurred between the sky, earth, and water when it rested in the ground and collected rainwater in its basins. The rainwater served as a powerful purifying, cleansing, and healing source for the Clackamas and their neighbors, and tribal hunters, seeking power, dipped their arrowheads in the water collected in the Meteorite's crevices. These traditions and the spiritual link with Tomanowos were preserved through the ceremonies and songs of the descendants of the Clackamas. The repatriation claim was the Grand Ronde's effort to re-unite the traditions with the meteorite.

The Grande Ronde and the Museum reached common ground and a resolution that involved, among other things, that the meteorite would be conveyed to the Grand Ronde if the Museum permanently removed it from public display. The meteorite would stay on exhibit at the Museum with a narrative label next to the scientific narrative that provides the history of "Tomanowos" and the Clackamas relationship to it. The settlement also provided for annual, private, ceremonial access to the meteorite.

CHAPTER FIFTY-FOUR

Indigenous Cultural and Intellectual Property Rights: A Digital Library Context

Robert Sullivan

INTRODUCTION

Recently, a watershed moment occurred in the world of intellectual and cultural property rights in Aotearoa, New Zealand, when the "Toi Iho" trademark[1] was launched at the Auckland City Art Gallery. Elders and leaders of the art world and of the tangata whenua – the indigenous local tribe – gathered to celebrate the physical reality of an idea/passion/signifier that had been discussed in various guises by Maori for decades.

The Toi Iho trademark asserts authenticity in the creative arts and provides a cultural context for works that have a Maori lineage or whakapapa. The Toi Iho trademark signifies an ethos of ownership, respect, and active engagement with the Maori people from which the culture sprang.

Within this context, I begin a discussion about the digitization of the creative works of our ancestors. Works cauled in the times of the gods – when Tane separated his parents, the heavens and the earth,[2] when Ruaumoko,[3] the foetal earthquake-god, kicked the belly of the earth mother to create the ravines and mountains of Aotearoa/New Zealand, and when Maui[4] hauled his great fish – the North Island – out of the domain of Tangaroa, the ocean. This created wisdom has been handed down by the ancestors since Kupe[5] first discovered Aotearoa near the end of the first millennium.

[1] Toi Iho, a registered trademark of authenticity and quality for Maori arts and crafts, <http://www.toiiho.com/> (last accessed May 8, 2002).

[2] National Library of New Zealand, <http://www.natlib.govt.nz/flash.html> (last accessed May 8, 2002). This site opens with a summary of the story.

[3] Weka, Hana. Ruamoko, <http://maori.com/kmst1.htm> (last accessed May 8, 2002).

[4] Orbell, Margaret. *The Illustrated Encyclopedia of Maori Myth and Legend.* (Christchurch: Canterbury University Press, 1995), 114–117.

[5] *Ibid.* 92–94.

This chapter originally appeared as an article at <http://www.dlib.org> *D-Lib Magazine*, May 2002, Vol. 8, No. 5, ISSN 1082-9873.

DIGITIZING CULTURAL MATERIALS

Anything can be digitized: any story, legend, map, chart, blueprint, or equation. Any storyteller recorded in video or sound format can be transformed into a digital rendition for access on local or global networks.

When digitizing cultural materials, the important questions are: How do we send a message that strengthens the holistic context of each cultural item and collection? How do we ensure that both indigenous and nonindigenous peoples receive the message? How do we digitize material taking into account its metaphysical as well as its digital life?

In August 2001, I was fortunate to participate in the Hilo, Hawaii, meeting on "Digital Collectives in Indigenous Cultures and Communities."[7] This collaboration of indigenous, technical, financial, and library experts created a vision that needs to be embraced and driven by indigenous communities themselves: "Building a Global Indigenous Library" (a suggested project in the Hilo meeting report).

Various technical digital library models were articulated at the meeting. It was agreed that the challenge in building a successful indigenous digital library model is winning the trust of the people the library aims to serve. Trust is won through the governance and administration of the digital library, and the way that flow-on economic benefits are distributed to the people providing the content. For trust to exist, there must be a mutual ethic of reciprocity.

Many communities want training and employment opportunities. Building a global digital library requires first people and infrastructure, and then content. Various technical protocols and standards must be met to ensure that the resource is accessible – and accessible in the manner intended. Dealing with these technical issues alone provides an enormous employment opportunity. Consequently, there is potential for material returns from sharing the cultures of indigenous communities for the benefit of the world.

A necessary component of Digital Library infrastructure is the equipment to deliver and receive information. Many communities have narrow-width access to the Internet – if they have telecommunications or computers at all. How to resource communities so that they can access the World Wide Web is an issue for everyone – an issue with even more resonance for indigenous groups.

DL infrastructure also includes administrative structures. In the D-Lib Magazine, "Special Issue on Digital Technology and Indigenous Communities,"[8] Professor Loriene Roy articulates a model of governance that could be transferred to the Indigenous Digital Library (IDL). Suffice it to say, governance is an important issue that will impact the IDL's effectiveness in working with communities to gather information.

[7] Digital Collectives in Indigenous Cultures and Communities Meeting, Hilo, Hawaii, August 10–12, 2001, <http://si.umich.edu/pep/dc/meeting/meeting.htm> (last accessed May 8, 2002).

[8] Special Issue on Digital Technology and Indigenous Communities, *D-Lib Magazine*, March 2002, <http://www.dlib.org/dlib/march02/03contents.html> (last accessed May 8, 2002).

Indigenous cultural and intellectual property (ICIP) management must be articulated from the start of any IDL project. Barambah and Kukoyi[9] advocate the development of cultural protocols that overcome legislative deficiencies and difficulties.

A key legislative deficiency affecting IDL projects, in particular, is the temporary and individualistic protection that copyright offers to creators of ICIP. Copyright expires after a defined term. Copyright is assigned to individuals. Therefore, the collective nature and enduring guardianship – care, development, and preservation – with which indigenous communities imbue their cultural and intellectual property, cannot be addressed by copyright alone. The New Zealand initiative of the Toi Iho trademark ameliorates this situation for the Maori artistic community. A similar protocol initiative, to set up systems and procedures to ensure that local indigenous customs are maintained in regard to their information, would ensure the integrity of IDLs.

The New Zealand initiative also enables cross-cultural partnerships. The toi iho TM Maori Made has two companion trademarks: toi iho TM Mainly Maori, and toi iho TM Mauri Co-Production. The first two trademarks cannot be used by businesses, only by individual artists. However, the toi iho TM Maori Co-Production can include use by business entities. The trademark can also be used to authenticate exhibitions and may provide an interesting application for digital repositories.

The protocols articulated by indigenous communities serve many purposes. They satisfy communities that their information will be contextualized in a manner that acknowledges and maintains everything the communities hold to be significant. Protocols perform an educating function for the library and information community. Thus, they potentially reduce infringement in other information spheres.

The Australian Aboriginal article by Barambah et al. raises issues of relevance to New Zealand Maori:

> The issues involved include: Who can speak for what? Who has the authority for what? Whose custom? Whose heritage? Whose culture? And whose identity? All these questions are extremely important.[10]

These issues are also transferable to the global indigenous sphere.

AUTHENTICATING MATERIAL ALREADY HELD BY INSTITUTIONS OF MEMORY

In the Maori context, and indeed the Polynesian context, much information has already been collected and systematically catalogued in institutions of memory such as the Alexander Turnbull Library (<http://www.natlib.govt.nz/en/collections/turnbull/index.html>). Most of this information has been gathered using nineteenth century methods, some involving payments, which thus has encouraged false information to be given and published.[11] If a digital collection were to be created using such material, out of legal copyright, the digitizing institution would have the responsibility of placing the material in its appropriate context, by liaising with the communities where the information originated.

One such case involves the Department for Courts of New Zealand, which holds copies of the Maori Land Court Minute Books of evidence,[12] given to establish legal title to most of the Maori land in New Zealand. "Maori are compelled by statute to deal with the Maori Land Court if they want to transact business over their land" (p. 11). The historical purpose of the Court was to prepare the land for purchase by settlers. Some of the evidence is contentious, and covers historical battles and family feuds.

The Department for Courts is completing a project involving the digitization of all the minute books, covering 12.2 million pages (and growing five percent annually). Prior to the project, a series of consultative meetings were held throughout the country. From these meetings, a number of principles emerged:

1. The information may not be changed or altered.
2. Sacred, genealogical information should only be accessed by individuals after they have consulted with the relevant tribes.
3. Institutions of social memory must be informed that genealogical information contained in copies of the Land Court records that they hold is restricted information.
4. It must be ensured that sacred information "... is not used in a manner contrary to Maori cultural values, or for commercial purposes."
5. Maori assert ownership of the record.

The principal recommendation of the report is that a group be established, with representation from interested tribes, to formulate policies on access to the record – in both documentary and digital formats.

AUTHENTICATING CONTEMPORARY MATERIAL

The process for digitizing contemporary cultural information from indigenous communities is less complex than for older materials, and has been amply covered by the "Digital Collectives" collaboration report.[13] Some of the guiding principles

[9] Barambah, Maroochy and Ade Kukoyi. "Protocols for the use of indigenous cultural material." In Anne Fitzgerald (ed.) *Going Digital 2000: Legal Issues for E-commerce, Software and the Internet.* (NSW, Australia: Prospect Media, 2000).

[10] *Ibid.*, 33.

[11] Walker, Ranginui. "Intellectual property" in *Nga pepa o Ranginui.* (Auckland: Penguin, 1996).

[12] Department for Courts, Information Management Team. "Maori Land Court Information Management Team Report: access to and archiving of Maori Land Court records after imaging." 28 July 1999. For a guide to the Maori Land Court, see <http://www.courts.govt.nz/maorilandcourt/> and <http://www.auckland.ac.nz/lbr/maori/mlcmb.htm> (last accessed May 8, 2002).

[13] Holland, Maurita and Digital Collectives in Indigenous Cultures and Communities. We come from around the world and share similar visions! (Ann Arbor: School of Information, University of Michigan, 2002).

from the report pertaining to ICIP invite digitizing groups to:

1. Affirm indigenous communities as equal partners in future collaborations.
2. Uphold cultural intellectual and property rights of communities.
3. Ensure cultural integrity.
4. Interpret, analyze, and synthesize information for general audiences.
5. Require that "Digital libraries should be developed and controlled by indigenous peoples and self-determined" (p. 6).
6. Understand the "importance of community-based guides [to digitization] that express [sic] tribal values" (p. 8).

Two other informational documents pertaining to ICIP are: "The Mataatua Declaration on Cultural and Intellectual Property Rights of Indigenous Peoples,"[14] ratified by more than 150 indigenous representatives from sixty United Nations member states,[15] and the Draft Declaration on the Rights of Indigenous Peoples. The former document asserts cultural ownership of indigenous knowledge – this includes development, promotion, and protection – and that content creators must be first beneficiaries. Articles 12 and 29 of the 1993 Draft Declaration on the Rights of Indigenous Peoples[16] (UN Commission on Human Rights) also highlights the need for "full ownership, control and protection" of ICIP.

The first international indigenous librarians' forum Proceedings[17] endorses both the Mataatua Declaration and the UN Draft Declaration.

CONCLUSION

A cornerstone of an IDL is that the indigenous communities themselves control the rights management of their cultural intellectual property. Local cultural protocols need to be documented and followed prior to the creation of digital content, and communities must be consulted with regard to the digitization of content already gathered by institutions of social memory. As noted in the Hilo meeting report, indigenous leaders should gather to plan and confirm the path ahead.

FURTHER READING

Cultural and Intellectual Property Rights: Economics, Politics and Colonization. Vol. 2. (Auckland: Moko Productions/IRI, 1997).

[14] "Appendix E," The Mataatua Declaration on Cultural and Intellectual Property Rights of Indigenous Peoples <http://www.tpk.govt.nz/publications/docs/tangata/app_e.htm> (last accessed May 8, 2002).

[15] Biodiversity and Maori (Wellington: Te Puni Kokiri, 1994), 17.

[16] Draft Declaration on the Rights of Indigenous Peoples, <http://www.hookele.com/netwarriors/dec-En.html> (last accessed May 8, 2002).

[17] Sullivan, Robert (ed.). Proceedings (Auckland: International Indigenous Librarians Forum, 2001).

CHAPTER FIFTY-FIVE

The Role of Museums Today: Tourism and Cultural Heritage

Yani Herreman

This chapter looks at the contemporary role of museums in relation to tourism and cultural heritage. The first section provides a general overview of the changes that museums have undergone in recent years that makes them so attractive to tourism. The second section then takes a closer look at the relationship among museums, sustainable development, and cultural tourism. Section III considers ways of enhancing the role of museums in the protection of cultural heritage. Finally, the paper ends with a number of recommendations and conclusions.

MUSEUMS TODAY

Among other major cultural movements typical of the 1960s, the decade marked the beginning of one of the main cultural trends of the twentieth century: the museum boom. Never before have so many museums been built, restored, or enlarged all over the world. Even in the midst of the social and economic changes of the last twenty years, museums have flourished as never before.

Museums have developed and thrived, modifying many of their functions and enriching their scope. This has led them to new positions within a changing, globalised and highly competitive consumer society, where high tech, networking, and tourism are only some of the present constituents. This chapter explains what some of the museum's new roles are, and discusses their relationships to tourism, sustainability, and heritage protection.

One of the most important and permanent changes in the development of the contemporary museum has been to become more audience-conscious and to be more in step with modern social processes. However, it has only been in the past twenty years, and even more abruptly in the last ten, that what appeared to be an outdated, dusty and elitist institution has completely changed by adopting a contemporary outlook on modern life.

According to authors Jacqueline Eidelman and Michel Van Praet,[1] two major issues arose at the beginning of the 1970s as a result of the aforementioned change: "a newly acquired importance for what has been called services for the public" and the widening of the term "museum."

Education, for example, has always been a major aspect of museum work, but it has become more interactive with the help of high-tech resources. The research and collecting oriented tasks, as well as the object-centred institution itself, have moved towards a more modern "service provider" concept that is better suited to today's pluralistic society. In this sense, museums' programs are offered as an entertainment possibility for society. Authors dedicated to marketing, such as Neil Kotler,[2] advocate this trend and have written about the need to implement marketing programs for museums and their activities in order to "position" them correctly in a world full of entertainment.

Other reasons for the museums' recent changes arise from social circumstances. During the 1980s, the era of leisure and consumer society, so characteristic of the end of the twentieth century and the beginning of the twenty-first century, began to unfold. In addition, society has become increasingly multicultural in the so-called developed countries during the last twenty years, while indigenous cultures have demanded equal standing in society in the rest of the world.

Today, society is affected and changed by multiculturalism. It demands new approaches from museums, which have started to integrate innovative and relevant approaches. In a sense, museums not only exhibit and house intellectual and artistic products, but also objects and concepts that reflect society as it exists outside their walls. UNESCO's recent "Declaration on Intangible Cultural Heritage" has strengthened this approach (<http://unescodoc.unesco>). Issues that used to be studied mainly by anthropologists and sociologists are now being retaken by city planners, architects and museum professionals.

Unesco's definition states that:

1. The "intangible cultural heritage" means the practices, representations, expressions, knowledge, skills – as well as the instruments, objects, artefacts and cultural spaces associated therewith – that communities, groups, and, in some cases, individuals recognize as part of their cultural heritage. This intangible cultural heritage, transmitted from generation to generation, is constantly recreated by communities and groups in response to their environment, their interaction with nature and their history, and provides them with a sense of identity and continuity, thus promoting respect for cultural diversity and human creativity. For the purposes of this Convention, consideration will be given solely to such intangible cultural heritage as is compatible with existing international

Researcher, Center for Postgraduate Studies and Research (CIEP). Facultad de Arquitectura. Universidad Nacional Autónoma de México.

[1] Eidelman/Van Praet; 2000; 3. [2] Kotler/Kotler; 2000; 123.

human rights instruments, with the requirement of mutual respect among communities, groups, and individuals, and with sustainable development.

2. The "intangible cultural heritage," as defined in paragraph 1 in this list, is manifested *inter alia* in the following domains:
   (a) oral traditions and expressions, including language as a vehicle of the intangible cultural heritage;
   (b) the performing arts;
   (c) social practices, rituals, and festive events;
   (d) knowledge and practices concerning nature and the universe;
   (e) traditional craftsmanship.
3. "Safeguarding" means measures aimed at ensuring the viability of the intangible cultural heritage, including the identification, documentation, research, preservation, protection, promotion, enhancement, transmission, particularly through formal and nonformal education, in addition to the revitalization of the various aspects of such heritage (UNESCO. Intangible Cultural Heritage Convention. annex III-pag.6).

An early example of this approach in the museum field is the Museo Nacional de Culturas Populares (National Museum of Popular Culture) in Mexico City, opened in 1982, where everyday urban and rural culture is presented in exhibitions such as "Circuses and Vaudeville," "The Radio," "Grinding Coffee" and "Traditional Bread," the Museo de la Nación in Lima (Peru) has a special wing in which children can learn about peasant childhood by seeing and touching tools, games, and toys. More recently, in Birmingham, United Kingdom, a most interesting experiment was launched in the form of a museum/cultural centre where all kinds of art forms are presented by local artists. "The Public" is presently located in an economically depressed part of the city, in an old and abandoned building. Jobless neighbours and newly arrived immigrants are invited to interact in this "common" space through different types of artistic expressions. They have now succeeded in being partially sponsored by the local government to start a new museum that aims to enhance social cohesion through the creation and enjoyment of different cultural expressions.

Mr. Jay Haviser, Former Director of the Kura Hulanda Museum in Curaçao, declares that:

> "Museums be mirror of ourselves, reflecting the vitality of our diversity and richness of our individual cultures and cultural mixing. I believe that in the near future museums will focus more on theatre and the performing arts, such as living oral history, in conjunction with the more traditional artifact exhibit."

The growing number of activities developed within and in relation to museums has expanded the definition of what constitutes a museum. In its contemporary form, it has had to cope with a number of contradictory and ethical issues. This institution has become a factor in socio-economic development and, simultaneously, has enhanced mutual awareness and respect for the other; it has continued being an educational resource and has become a plural interdisciplinary cultural centre. Finally, it is a major tourist attraction and, therefore, plays a central role in culture-oriented national projects that see them as a resource to attain a desired sustainable development

MUSEUMS AND TOURISM

It is well known that tourism means big business. The World Tourism Organisation has published on its Web site that 2004 closed with more than 70 million international arrivals. That means that it has grown more than ten percent in the year (OMT/Sala de Prensa/Comunicados de Prensa). The tourist industry is currently the second largest employer in the United States and the country's largest export industry (WIREMAN; 97; 16), with more than twelve percent growth in 2004 after three years of losses (OMT/Sala de Prensa/Comunicados de Prensa).

In Mexico, the tourist industry is one of the country's largest sources of income – second only to the oil industry – and generates almost US$9 billion in revenues per year. Even after the last two years, when social problems such as the Iraq war and terrorist fear affected many tourist destinations, Mexico received 6.9 percent more foreign visitors, who spent 10.4 percent more than in 2002 (finanzas.com). There has also been a significant increase in the number of tourists visiting Bolivia in the last four years. With 350,000 tourists per year and annual revenues of US$170 million, tourism now ranks as the country's most profitable industry, overtaking the export of zinc and soybeans. In Honduras, tourism is now the third biggest source of hard currency, generating revenues of US$120 million per year. In Cuba, the annual number of tourists has increased from 350,000 to two million in the last ten years. In Barbados and Curacao, finally, tourism is the most important economic activity, according to personal interviews, carried out by the author, with museum directors in those countries last year.

Clearly, tourism became a major economic factor at the end of the twentieth century and still is very much so at the beginning of the twenty-first century. As is well known, future projections foresee enormous growth. Tourism is now recognised as an economic powerhouse, associated with transnational economical interests.

Cultural tourism is different from mass tourism and has been recognized only recently as a very important and profitable sector. The European Association for Tourism and Leisure Education defines it as "the movement of persons to cultural attractions away from their normal place of residence with the intention to gather new information and experiences to satisfy their cultural needs" (<www.gestioncultural.orgportalgc@gestioncultural.org>). For many, cultural tourism is regarded as beneficial for local communities, whereas others see it as Spanish researcher Santana Talavera conceives it, as "a form of alternative tourism that embodies the completion and or success of commercialized forms of culture."

He adds, however, that "it may also enhance local creativity and adaptability to new social circumstances" (Horizontes antropológicos. Turismo cultural). UNESCO, on the other hand, fosters the idea of cultural tourism as a tool for strengthening understanding and tolerance among peoples through knowledge and cultural dialogue.

Cultural tourism includes ethnic and historical tourism and sites or places were intangible cultural heritage may be witnessed. It focuses on local lifestyles and brings tourists closer to local people and their heritage through visits to museums, archaeological and historical sites, and religious buildings.

Cultural tourism has been strongly developed in Europe in the last years. Countries such as Spain have launched ambitious tourism projects that include refurbishing whole urban areas, such as the old town in Barcelona. On the basis of estimates, Europe's cultural tourism has recently jumped from thirty-five to seventy percent of the total volume of international tourism, according to Myriam Jensen. This means that if approximately 698 million international tourists spent in the region of US$467 billion, then the worldwide share of cultural tourism amounts to more than 482 million tourists, who spend more than US$362 billion annually.

Until now, because of tourism's economical impact, heritage protection, sustainability, and social factors have not been a priority. Social studies such as sociology, anthropology, cultural economics, and museology have not become fully involved. Fortunately, cultural tourism is beginning to be recognized as an extremely important activity that implies a complex, worldwide network of travel movements and human behaviour with particular characteristics. A growing group of researchers has been formed and training centres specialised in heritage management and or cultural tourism have been created. The University of Barcelona and the University of Wisconsin are two good examples and on most culture-oriented Web sites one may find sufficient information on these issues. El Portal Iberoamericano de Gestión Cultural and the Portal de Cultura Iberoamericana (Escena cultural. 2002) informed about more than thirty seminars, meetings, and symposia in these fields.

Unfortunately, this type of research has merely begun in Latin America, where the richness and variety of cultural sites and landscapes is extraordinary. In Latin America, UNESCO's World Heritage Centre had classified more than sixty registered archaeological and historical monuments as World Heritage Sites, in comparison to a total of five in Canada and the United States two years ago.

One of the first meetings held in this field was a forum in Barquisimeto, Venezuela in 1995 under the auspices of ICOM's Venezuelan National Committee. In the following ten years, a huge change has taken place. With the support of the Dutch government, ICOM organised a Seminar on Museums, Heritage and Cultural Tourism in Peru and Bolivia in 2001. In addition to its own proceedings, the Seminar also produced the first version of a Charter on Museums and Cultural Tourism and, through its "Working Group on Museums and Tourism," ICOM is conducting interdisciplinary research on the issue in order to advise and establish guidelines. Nevertheless, cultural tourism and heritage management are still deficient.

As for museums . . . it is now recognised that they are tourist attractions. This is now an unquestionable fact in the context of the worldwide tourist industry but very few countries have developed research projects on museums and tourism. The role of museums within the wider range of tourist products, their economic input, their urban impact, and economic spill-over effect, and their relation to development and sustainability have yet to be studied. One of the recent researches carried out by Bonet, of the Universidad de Cataluña, resulted in the following figures: In 1997, during a survey carried out in twenty of Europe's main cities, more than fifty percent of 8,000 of their visitors visited museums and thirty percent, an exhibition. Why?

Because museums have become major cultural centres and trigger multiple and diverse cultural activities that people enjoy and benefit from. Art and Cultural Festivals such as Mexico City's City Historic Center, Havana's and Sau Paulo Visual Arts Bienali, and Bolivia's Chiquitos Latin American Barroque Festival are some of these ambitious and successful programs.

According to the European Commission and because of their ever-growing presence, museums, as part of cultural tourism, are now being positioned strategically to solve one of tourism's main problems: "density management." They are promoted as an option to lower other sites' tourist density. This holds true for Latin America.

Promotion of cultural tourism implies benefits and threats and the lack of a more systematic approach in research projects of production and consumption of products and services in the area of cultural tourism constitutes not only a drawback but a serious risk that should not be underestimated. We must insist over and over that cultural (and natural) heritage must be preserved and the only way to find sustainability is through permanent research programs on tourism's impact on cultural landscapes. To quote Jafar Jafari of the University of Wisconsin, '"preservation and production acts ensemble can result in representative and sustainable tourism products" (Jafari; 2001; 4).

In order to gain a clearer view of the position occupied by museums within the cultural tourism sector, I have included some figures on museum attendance in America. I ask the reader to please bear in mind the lack of a credible system of statistical and economic analysis that includes serious research into museum attendance. The following are numbers given, unofficially, to the author by specialized professionals in the museum field in each stated country, and correspond to the year 2001.

Canada boasts 2,500 museums, galleries, historical houses, and other cultural sites that are visited approximately fifty million visitors per year. As pointed out by John MacAvity, Director of the Canadian Museums Association, these figures are most impressive when it is taken into account that the population of Canada is thirty million. He believes that the majority of these visitors are Canadian.

- The United States has 8,000 museums listed in the Official Museum Directory and perhaps as many as 10,000 museum sites. More than 600 museums have been built in the last thirty years (Newhouse; 2000; 1). Edward Abel, Director of the American Association of Museums, in his kind answer to my query, proudly stated that "America's museums enjoy over 865 million visits a year – more than the total attendance of amateur and professional sports events, performing arts and the movies."
- Mexico, which occupies the eighth place in the world in the tourism chart, has 348 museums, according to Mexico's National Institute for Statistics (INEGI). In 1997, the total number of visitors was 22,039,831, of whom 20,085,238 were Mexican and 1,954,593 were tourists. In addition, the National Institute of Anthropology has noted that twenty-five museums at archaeological sites were opened to the public in recent years, significantly increasing the total number of visitors, especially tourists. In 2000, these sites – including their museums – received 4,434,573 visitors, of whom 2,187,089 were foreign tourists. Together with the figures for Mexico's other museums, the total number of visitors was more than 10 million. These other visitors went to the Institute of Fine Arts, government-funded museums, and private museums. The total number is probably higher than the 22 million quoted by INEGI.
- Cuba boasts 294 museums that were visited by 7,709,000 visitors, of which 1,233,043 were foreign tourists and 6,475,957 were Cuban in 2000. Important to point out are the outstanding results of the Office of the City Historian, which has implemented imaginative strategies.
- Curaçao has twenty-five museums with a variety of themes. The Kura Hulanda Museum is the largest and most important on the island. According to Jay Haviser, Director of the museum, it receives about 60,000 visitors per year, of which sixty percent are tourists.
- Barbados received 126,976 visitors in its museums and heritage sites in 2000. A National Art Gallery is now being planned.
- Peru boasts 206 museums, according to the National Institute for Culture. These museums receive visitors according to their location and their proximity to archaeological sites. Tourism increases constantly if we see that in 1998, 819,530 entries were registered; the following year, 943,917; and, for 2000, more than one million. Sites like Machu-Pichu and the new museum that houses the Señor de Sipán collections are main attractions.

When they are well planned and managed, big travelling exhibitions can be good business. Peggy Wireman (Wireman; 1997; 27) gives an example involving a highly developed country and a developing one. It is well known that many people take their children to Washington, DC, to see the National Air and Space Museum, the National Gallery of Art, and the dinosaurs in the National Museum of Natural History, but who would have thought that 131,000 people would go to San Antonio to see "Mexico: Splendors of Thirty Centuries"? According to Wireman, they did. She adds that the total number of visitors, including local visitors, came to 265,000. Visitors to the exhibitions ended up spending US$80 million on an exhibition that cost US$2.5 million.

MUSEUMS AND CULTURAL HERITAGE PROTECTION

One of Latin America's biggest problems, shared by all developing countries, is illicit traffic in cultural property. Although significant steps have been taken towards its combat, like ICOM's recently published Red List, great ignorance still prevails and government officials do not pay required attention to the problem. Illicit traffic in cultural tangible and intangible and natural heritage by tourists is still common practice and is quite significant, even though it is carried out on a small scale in comparison to the organized networks dedicated to this activity, that are now associated with drug traffic.

A significant part of the problem is located in developed countries, where dealers find a market for their merchandise. The problem has been known for many years and involves all kinds of people in different professions. In 1976, Hughes De Varine, a museologist and former ICOM Secretary General, referred to:

> "Directors of big or very rich museums that want to justify their pretensions through the acquisition of more and more prestigious collections and by record prices. They create a contest looking more after their publicity rather than after their professional or scientific reputation. Collectors without scruples, speculators, tax and public relations specialists that use museums as their investment guide, as a showcase of wealth or for their own prestige.
>
> Heads of state or high-ranking officials that do not hesitate to squander their national cultural and natural heritage or that of other countries.
>
> International experts, airline stewardesses, businessmen, diplomats and tourists." (De Varine; 73; 76)

The situation remains very much the same. Central European countries, such as Switzerland, are known to host, willingly or unwillingly, structured illicit traffic organisations.

At this point, it is important to take note of the work carried out by some nongovernmental organizations (NGOs), such as ICOM, ICOMOS and World Trade Organization (WTO), in relation to the conservation of tangible and intangible cultural heritage and or the ethics of tourism. ICOM's Code of Ethics has become a turning point in the professional behaviour of museum specialists that has also set an example for other NGOs. For instance, the World Federation of Friends of Museums has also developed a code of ethics based on ICOM's Code.

ICOM, as the most important international museum organisation, has launched an extremely valuable resource that aims to curb illicit traffic, looting, and theft in Latin

America. The Red List is a guide made by specialists from various Latin American countries and other researchers from Spain, United States, and Switzerland. It helps identify valuable cultural objects, considered part of the country's heritage. (ICOM: 2002).This publication makes an appeal to museums, auction houses, art dealers, and collectors not to acquire these objects. On the other hand, it becomes a legal argument for the protection of a country's heritage.

In addition to the dissemination of important documents such as the aforementioned Code of Ethics and Red List, it is also vital to devote attention to legislation and international agreements in the field of cultural heritage. In this regard, mention may be made of various international agreements and the extraordinary efforts undertaken by ICOM and UNESCO to attain them, such as the 1970 UNESCO Convention on *Preventing the Illicit Traffic in Cultural Property.* In addition, several regional meetings have been organised on the issue, and a whole edition in the *One Hundred Missing Objects* series was dedicated to Latin America.

Heritage conservation is a responsibility that should be shared by the host country and its visitors, by local people and the government, by the individual and the community.

We have repeated throughout this chapter that tourism, including its cultural field, plays a twofold action with regard to cultural tangible and intangible heritage. It is, without doubt, a valuable resource for human exchange of knowledge and respect, but it is also a threat.

Objects as part of heritage have become relics and tourism is a new form of pilgrimage. According to Donald Horne,

> "[p]atterns of tourism behavior having enormous technical, social and economic repercussions have thus been created. How is it that someone can be so deeply moved that he or she will travel hundreds or thousands of kilometers to see, for instance, an object or an historic site?"

Tangible and intangible cultural heritage and identity, represented in objects, are features that remain the main attraction of museums. This is what gives them their uniqueness and authenticity and makes them as popular as ever, also for tourism. In parallel, the question immediately arises of how to balance the traditional tasks of museums, such as conservation, with newer ones, such as the implementation of a broader approach to education, leisure, and enjoyment, which has already been discussed in this chapter.

Contemporary social science has demonstrated the dangers of unplanned tourism and has determined that vernacular heritage, including the elusive intangible one, must be taken into account in all cultural-related projects. Local entities and multiculturalism should be reaffirmed when seeking national, regional, or local economic and social development. Tourism projects that have ignored such important issues have been unsuccessful in the long run. But as tourism specialist and anthropologist Dr. Jafar Jafari of the University of Wisconsin affirms, "One can use tools and concepts to study and understand tourism, as a phenomenon and as an industry." If correct research and planning are carried out, both economic development and social welfare may be achieved.

The philosophy behind the idea that museums may play a unique role as resources between the local culture and the tourist is based on two assessments:

Sustainability in the field of cultural property is of fundamental importance, and it concerns the preservation of the conditions in which it is possible to renovate or continue the use, consumption, enjoyment, and transmission of cultural objects without exhausting or harming them.

Sustainability of cultural tourism can work in two directions. First, with respect to the natural and cultural environment and, second, with respect to its own viability, and in both cases, suffocation through saturation or destruction of the surrounding conditions needs to be avoided.

The museum may be in the tourism production and consumption of products and services in the area of cultural tourism processes a cultural mediator promoting knowledge, understanding, respect and sense of protection of local heritage, among a group of "one time" visitors, a sort of contemporary cultural nomad.

The new challenge is to balance the desired development that tourism brings and the protection of local heritage; to contribute to attract foreign visitors and simultaneously make them aware of the value of preserving local heritage; to promote a sense of proud ownership in local communities and make them aware of their responsibility of preserving their heritage through correct management and conservation programs.

Museums have multiple assets that enable them to carry out this new trend. Regional and community museums and, later, ecomuseums have been pioneers on this trail. New proposals have been arising lately, like the "Economuseum" that pursues a more direct economic benefit for the local community through special commercial programs based on museum activities. Regional and local museums have also integrated new approaches such as oral history and local indigenous guides, as in the Arts and Crafts Museum in the city of Tlaxcala, in Mexico.

Furthermore, if we agree with UNESCO's definition of protection and safeguarding stated in its Convention on Intangible Cultural Heritage as "the measures aimed at ensuring the viability of the intangible cultural heritage, including the identification, documentation, research, preservation, protection, promotion, enhancement, transmission, particularly through formal and nonformal education, as well as the revitalization of the various aspects of such heritage" (UNESCO. Intangible Cultural Heritage Convention. annex III-pag.6), then we may readily understand the museum's position in contemporary tourism and culture.

Museums have a principal role to play, not only among tourists but also in local communities. Searching for conservationist governmental policies and community awareness of cultural landscapes' value is yet another challenge for us, museum professionals. Present day museums are institutions deeply involved with society that offer their unique resources, as transdiciplinary spaces, to deliver full programs on identification, documentation, research, preservation, protection, promotion, enhancement, transmission, and, particularly, through formal and nonformal education.

Unfortunately, Latin American government officials still seem to disregard the museum's active role in the fields of education, communication, economics, and tourism. The need to seek and devise policies and action plans to regulate cultural heritage tourism turns the correct use of museums in the most contemporary sense, in which they are free to develop their own systems of preservation, interpretation, education, and dissemination, into an urgent issue. Systematic research into this particular issue would result in guidelines for the creation of appropriate cultural and tourist policies that optimise the resources of the museum as a cultural mediator and educator.

Worth underlining are the Señor de Sipán experience, in Peru, and the community museums in the state of Oaxaca, in Mexico. The principle behind these projects was to integrate the community as a way to restore and reconstruct its history and culture.

In the Sipán case, following anthropological methods, head archaeologist Walter Alva worked with the local community, right from the beginning of the excavating process. As work developed, local indigenous inhabitants were taught and trained in different museum fields such as documentation, education, communication, and conservation. Today, with the building finished, the community is still very much involved in its conservation and management.

As for the community museums in Mexico, they have succeeded in establishing a beneficial relationship between national and international public and the communities in which they are located and contribute to the development of local and regional identities. Again, an anthropological approach was used by Mexican anthropologist Cuahutemoc Camarena and his team.

Aware of the importance of monitoring and counselling museum development and the work of museum professionals in tourism, ICOM has undertaken the task of promoting research and advisory programmes on the role of the contemporary museum in this field and its link with other international agencies. In 2001, with the support of the Dutch government, ICOM organised a Seminar on Museums, Heritage and Cultural Tourism in Peru and Bolivia. In addition to its own proceedings, the Seminar also produced the first version of a Charter on Museums and Cultural Tourism. The next step will be to collaborate on the Charter with ICOMOS and the World Tourism Organisation. It is worth emphasising the importance of these kinds of documents, which promote the conservation of heritage and provide for its use as a sustainable resource.

Museums are the ideal resource for research that integrates and interprets tangible and intangible cultural and natural heritage and communicates it through exhibitions to local and foreign audiences. To quote ICOM's proposal for a Charter of Principles for Museums and Cultural Tourism,

> "Museums encourage the active participation of the communities and serve as educator and cultural mediator to an increasing number of visitors belonging to all levels of the community, locality or social group. They play a predominant role in the efforts to stop degradation of cultural and natural resources, according to principles, standards and objectives of national and international measures for the protection and appreciation of cultural heritage."

CONCLUSIONS AND RECOMMENDATIONS

In summary, it can be said that museums:

- are important for today's society;
- will continue to increase in number;
- are developing new functions and activities, but remain faithful to their core aims and commitments as a social institutions;
- are both landmarks and tourist attractions;
- can generate resources for a city or a region, if they are well planned and managed;
- are inextricably linked to cultural tourism;
- form an essential part, together with other heritage and cultural organisations, of sustainable economic development;
- help to strengthen the social fabric;
- can contribute to the development and implementation of policies, strategies, and programmes that promote sustainable development and contribute to the social, ecological, and economic vitality of a community;
- are resources for the interpretation of archaeological and historical sites;
- act as cultural mediators between foreign and local cultures;
- function as education centres for the local community with regard to local and foreign culture; and
- function as research centres for traditional skills and arts such as folk art, music, dance, and other examples of intangible cultural heritage.

In order for museums to realise their full potential, the following measures are suggested:

- promoting interdisciplinary research projects that involve museums and tourism;
- promoting the participation of museum specialists in major economic, urban, and tourist projects;
- appointing ICOM as a permanent consultant on museums and tourism issues;
- promoting professional training on the role of museums and other heritage sites as tourism or educational/communication resources, taking into account their own limitations and the need for special conservation; and

- fostering planning and implementation of sustainability policies in tourist projects that involve museums and other heritage sites.

CLOSING RECOMMENDATIONS

Cultural policies cannot be limited to promoting tourism in the prevailing manner, that is to say, on the basis of profit making. On the contrary, correct cultural property incorporates the criterion of conservation, along with education and, no less importantly, respect for the cultural environment. Museums must never forget this.

This is the current state of affairs with regard to museums, particularly in Latin America. Inasmuch as some of them appear to overdo the entrepreneurial aspect of their activities, they generally remain loyal to their ethical mandate, as described in ICOM's Code of Ethics for Museums, according to which a museum is:

"a non-profit making, permanent institution in the service of society and of its development, and open to the public, which acquires, conserves, researches, communicates and exhibits, for purposes of study, education and enjoyment, material evidence of people and their environment."

QUESTIONS FOR DISCUSSION

1. Read and discuss the main statements of ICOM's proposal for a Charter on Museums and Tourism.

2. Read and discuss the main statements of ICOM's Charter on Heritage and Tourism.

3. Do museums in your city or region associate with tourism activities? If so, discuss how and suggest innovative programs. Don't forget ICOM's definition of museums, its Code of Ethics, and its proposal of a Charter for Museums and Tourism while carrying out this discussion.

4. In which way does cultural tourism affect local indigenous tangible and intangible cultural heritage? Discuss benefits and disadvantages and related possible management strategies or laws. The same applies to natural heritage.

5. Discuss the role of local communities in management of tangible and intangible cultural heritage and the museum's responsibility.

BIBLIOGRAPHY

Annals of Tourism Research

Ballé, C. 1998. *Le musée: définitions nationales et internationales.* Colloque: Publics et projets culturels: un enjeu des musées en Europe. Paris. Musée National du Moyen Age.

Banducci, Alvaro e Barreto Margarida. 2001. *Museo e identidad local: uma visao antropologica.* Campinas, Papirus. Brasil.

Barreto, Margarida. *Turismo e legado cultural.* Campinas, Papirus. Brasil. 2000.

Bonet i Agustí, Luis. 2003. Turismo Cultural : Una reflexión desde la ciencia económica. En Portal Iberoamericao de Gestión Cultural. <www.gestioncultural.org>.

Eidelman, Jacqueline and Michel Van Praet. 2000. *La museologie des sciences et ses publics.* Paris: PUF.

Elderfield, John. 1998 '*Imagining the Future of the Museum of Modern Art.*' Studies in Modern Art, No. 7. New York: MOMA.

Connaissances des Arts. 2000. *Guggenheim, Bilbao.* Edición Española. Paris, France. [UNCLEAR]

Herreman, Yani. 1998. *Museums and Tourism: Culture and Consumption. Tourism (1).* in Museum International. (UNESCO, Paris) No. 199 (Vol.50. No.3).

Herreman, Yani. 2004. *Reflexiones acerca del patrimonio cultural.* In Noticias del ICOM, Paris. No. 2. (Vol. 57).

Herreman, Yani. 2000. *Cultural Tourism, Heritage and Museums in Latin America: A Humanistic Approach* in Museums, Heritage and Cultural Tourism. Paris: International Council of Museums: ICOM.

Horn, Donald. 1984. *The Great Museum: the Re-presentation of History.* Pluto Press. London

ICOM. Red List/Lista Roja. Bienes Culturales latinoamericanos en peligro. 2002. París.

Jafari, Jafar 2001. *Cultural Tourism Product. The Packaging of its Landscape* in proceedings of Cultural Tourism and Management of World Sites.

Jansen-Verbeke, Myriam. 2000. *The market values of museums in cultural tourism.* In Museums, Heritage and Cultural Tourism. Paris: International Council of Museums: ICOM.

Machuca, Jesús Antonio. 2000. *Prospects for Cultural Tourism from the Perspective of Globalisation.* In Museums, Heritage and Cultural Tourism. Paris: International Council of Museums: ICOM.

Minghetti, Valeria, Moretti Andrea and Miccelli Stefan. 2000. 'Re-engineering the Museum's Role in the Tourism Chain: The Challenge of New Technologies.' Conference on the Impact of Technology] on Cultural Tourism, June 27–29. Turkey: Istanbul.

Proceedings of the International Meeting on Patrimony, Museums and Tourism. 1995 Venezuela: Barquisimeto. pp. 78–85.

Pecquet, Claude and O'Byrne, Patrick. 1979. *La programmation, un outil au service du conservateur, du maître d'ouvrage et du maître d'uvre.* Museum. Vol XXXI no. 2. Revue trimestrelle publié par l'UNESCO. Paris: France.

Quentin, Christine. 1994. 'Musées et Tourisme.' Paris: Ministère de la Culture, Direction des Musées de France. Paris: France.

Report on meeting on *Culture, Tourism, Development: Crucial Issues for the XIst Century.* 1996. UNESCO. Paris.

Salazar, Alberto. 1999. Interview. Coordinación Nacional de Museos. Instituto Nacional de Antropología e Historia. Mexico City: Mexico.

Shelton, Anthony. 1999. 'Hermeneútica y la democratización de los espacios museográficos.' ICME Meeting on Ethnography Museums in Multicultural Societies. Mexico City: Mexico.

Stivalet, Isabel. Interview. Coordinación Nacional de Museos. Instituto Nacional de Antropología e Historia. Mexico City: Mexico.

Wireman, Peggy. 1997. Partnership for Prosperity. American Association of Museums. Washington: USA.

World Tourism Organisation. 2001. *World Code of Ethics.*

World Tourism organisation. 2004. Tourist Market Trends: Americas/Africa/Europe.

World Tourism Organisation. National and Regional Tourism Planning:Methodology and case studies. 2003.

3. CODES OF ETHICS OR POLICY GUIDELINES

3.1. ICOM's Code of Ethics.
3.2. ICOM's proposal for a Charter of Principles for Museums and Cultural Tourism.
3.3. ICOMOS'Charter on Cultural Tourism and Heritage.
3.4. WTO Code of Ethics.
3.5. Our Creative Diversity. Report of the World Commission on Culture and Development. UNESCO.
3.6. UNESCO: Culture, Tourism and Development: Crucial issues for the 21st century.

4. RECOMMENDED WEB SITES

<www.gestioncultural.org>
<www.escenacultural.com>
<www.world-tourism.org/english/>
<turismocultural@teleline.es>
<jafari@uwstout.edu>

PART NINE

Caring and Sharing

Innovative Solutions and Partnerships for Natural and Cultural Heritage Conservation

CHAPTER FIFTY-SIX

Finding Solutions for Lost Cities: Indigenous Populations and Biological and Cultural Diversity

Alvaro Soto

ENVIRONMENT AND HUMAN CULTURE

One of the problems we face when tackling environmental issues is that the concept of "environment" is primarily based on sources originating from the world of biology. When the term "ecosystem" was first coined, it referred to a holistic system in which every life form was closely interrelated. Human beings, however, seemed to be left out of the equation; the main focus was, and continues to be, on the conservation of "nature." No one seemed to realise that people, their history, and the traces they leave behind in the form of buildings and monuments are an integral part of the natural world, and that they also depend on nature for their survival.

Similarly, anthropologists and archaeologists who focus on cultures, the history of those cultures, and the remains of their structures and monuments have placed little emphasis on the environment in which people lived. As a result, the "environmental issue" has been overlooked to the extent that traditional anthropologists, with the exception of certain authors like Lesley White, have written very little about the close relationship between the environment and the way its inhabitants live. It is almost as if cultures developed as a kind of "fashion statement" by different human groups, rather than as a response to their surroundings.

WHO ARE THESE INDIGENOUS PEOPLE?

The literature commonly refers to indigenous cultures, both past and present, as if the term applied only to the native populations that existed in Latin America when the first Europeans arrived. In practice, however, indigenous has a much broader definition: All cultures are indigenous in the sense that they all originated in natural habitats, with communities developing their own particular strategies to adapt to and survive in their particular surroundings. Communities that were unable to do this, or whose surroundings changed too fast, simply did not survive.

Every "culture," both past and present, is thus the result of the interaction of a particular community with its particular environment. Because there are many different types of environments, there are many different cultures.

Therefore, individuals that belong (or belonged) to a particular culture have (or had) specific knowledge about their surroundings and knew how to exploit them in order to survive. In other words, they have (or had) the knowledge necessary to make use of the biotic and nonbiotic elements that make up the natural environment with which they interact. Obviously, such knowledge differs from one culture to another. In the process of interacting with nature, communities develop a whole range of technologies, economic systems, beliefs, mythologies, legal systems, customs, and so on, and this contributed to the cultural diversity that exists on the planet. Each human group has developed its own "indigenous" strategies that form part of their particular cultural heritage. The inhabitants of developed countries have established patent laws to protect much of their knowledge. The main issue must be to decide how to develop international laws and policies that will protect the rights and knowledge belonging to other cultures.

Particularly during the process of change or so-called "development," some cultures on the planet have gradually removed themselves from close contact with their original natural environment. Once captivated by technology, they came to believe that the natural world around them was an inexhaustible source of economic resources. Because of this, their economic systems were developed for production on a massive scale, which, in turn, implied extensive use of the natural elements of their environment. Those cultures that call themselves "civilizations" that occupy what is known today as the "developed world" have found that their way of life cannot be sustained without causing serious environmental damage. This damage threatens the very survival of those civilizations: they consequently will have to fall back on the traditional knowledge and the skills of other populations to make their continued existence more viable.

As a result, in the modern world, there are two factors that affect the survival of the planet:

- high rates of consumption in developed countries that outstrip the supply capacity of the environment; and
- a limited global supply of renewable and nonrenewable resources.

Faced with this state of affairs, we need to realize that other cultures on the planet have developed survival strategies that may provide valuable lessons for tomorrow's world.

ROOM FOR HOW MANY?

The carrying capacity of a given environment, or the number of individuals that can be supported by a specific ecosystem, is not a fixed, universal figure. It depends on the way in which the ecosystem is used and, therefore, on the cultural form of the interaction between a community and its environment. There are two strategies to increase the number of inhabitants that can be supported by a specific ecosystem. The first is to develop technologies that enable the population to get more out of the environment without destroying it. The second is to alter the cultural patterns of interaction with the environment to increase its carrying capacity. It is in the use of the second strategy that knowledge acquired from other cultures can determine the outcome. This knowledge includes not only technological expertise and an understanding of natural resources, but also an understanding of cultural aspects, some of which may be described as ethical.

The Second Strategy and the Case of the Sierra Nevada de Santa Marta in Colombia

The Sierra Nevada de Santa Marta is located in the north of Colombia, on the Caribbean coast. As well as being the world's highest coastal mountain range on which the thermal zone passes through every tropical condition, from tropical rain forest to permanent snow, it conceals within in its rainforests the remains of a civilization that lived there from the middle of the first millennium until it was destroyed by the European conquistadors.

In the 1970s, initially through the Colombian Institute of Anthropology, I began to investigate the archaeological remains of this extraordinary Latin American culture on the basis of information drawn from sixteenth century Spanish chronicles. A study of the ruins revealed that these people had managed to maintain a high population density without destroying the fragile natural environment with which they interacted in order to sustain and develop their culture.

OVERALL RESEARCH STRATEGY

The overall research strategy was designed on the basis of three specific anthropological, ecological, and archeological programs, considered essential to provide and integral interpretation of the Sierra.

The first of these programs was aimed at obtaining knowledge on the present indigenous cultures of the Sierra Nevada de Santa Marta, i.e., the Kogui (northern slope), the Ijka (southeastern slope), and Samka (southwestern slope) groups, and on the settler and peasant communities that have been gradually coming to inhabit the sierra since the 40s, progressively displacing the indigenous groups to the heights of the Sierra.

The program was intended to provide an understanding of the intrinsic dynamics of the indigenous communities and of their cultural heritage through the study of the strategies applied by these groups to profit from their natural environment and to establish their means of subsistence. Another important purpose thereof was to define strong measures to defend the existence of these groups against the harassment of settlers and entrepreneurs who, with interests foreign to and far different from those of the indigenous communities, were causing a generalized loss, not only of their ancestral lands but also of their values and traditions.

As a means to consolidate the ecological program, the Project of the Sierra was linked, from the start, to the activities of INDERENA (The National Institute for the Development of Natural Renewable Resources and the Environment), given that, in 1973, this Institute was implementing the initial stages of the ECODESARROLLO Project for the ecological development of the Massif.

This project, financed by United Nations Environment Program (UNEP) was aimed at determining the actions the State could take to efficiently protect the ecosystems of the Sierra against this degradation.

In view of this need together with the INDERENA we undertook the study of the interrelations of the cultural patterns of indians and settlers and the use of the environment.

In the framework of the ECOANDES Project, we provided technical and human resources and logistic support for some vertical transactions between the semi-barren coastline level and the perennial snow region, through the wide range of Sierra forest isohyets.

The large amount of information obtained from pollen samples for hypothesis development and cultural development models, periods, phases, and data interpretation led us to also support a palinology study of the Amsterdam and Utrech universities.

This cooperation resulted in many specialized research papers (Van der Hammen, 1973, 1977, 1983; Herrera de Turbay, 1980, 1985) which are now a major part of the set of research studies on the Sierra Nevada de Santa Marta.

In addition to vegetation surveys, soil profiles, physicochemical tests, and temperature, humidity and rainfall readings, climatological, hydro-biological, and geological data were carefully compiled to identify and make an inventory of the different ecosystems and bioclimatic zones of the Sierra.

The basic criterion on which the research processes were always based – especially where archeological excavations or earthworks were involved – was the importance of preserving the ecosystems and the valuable species of the area. During wall and road reconsolidating works care was always taken to preserve the top soil to the greatest possible extent. It can thus be said that Ciudad Perdida and other Upper Buritaca archeological sites were restored "beneath" the forest.

It was often difficult to make the project workers understand the need to avoid the introduction of exotic species into the work fronts. For instance, during the investigations conducted at Buritaca 200, emphasis was made on the importance of preserving the site's genetic banks even at the expense of having to endure shortages of commodities and agricultural products which could have been potentially grown there to solve the frequent costs problems of having to fly supplies in from Santa Marta by helicopter.

We wanted to preserve and maintain natural resources while the archeological work was underway. The forests in this part of the Sierra are representative of the wide biologic diversity and of the endemisms contained in damp sub-tropical and mountain rainfall forests still characteristic of the zone we worked in. To have acted otherwise, would have meant depriving science of the possibility of studying these ecosystems, unique in our planet and probably affecting the nearby fog forest, with the subsequent damage to the dynamics of the natural watershed mechanisms in that vast region.

The Sierra Nevada must be understood, in itself, as a functional unit with different topsoils varying in type according to altitude, forming individual but closely related sub-units. Large scale human disturbance of any of those ecosystems brings about the disruption of all. Increasing deforestation practices have influenced the gradual recession of the glaciers at the top of the Sierra, with the ensuing loss of hydric potential. This is a phenomenon already affecting the city of Santa Marta, the north coast towns and villages, the western region, the Guajira and the Valledupar area.

The purpose of the third and final program was that of analyzing the impact of the Tayrona civilization on the Sierra's environment. It centered on the historic reconstruction of the Tayrona settlement patterns and socio-cultural characteristics based on the exploration and surveying of the west and north slopes of the Sierra.

The surveys conducted indicated that the references of the Sixteenth and Seventeenth Century chroniclers were well-founded. The numerous villages explored, the magnitude of some of their remnants with clearly defined urban characteristics and the road infrastructure intercommunicating villages, towns and cities are proof of the accuracy of their descriptions which were in no way exaggerated.

"Because if there were to be a paradise in this land of indians, this seems to be it . . . It is crowned by tall peaks that must rise at least eight leagues from the bottom, less at some points, with ragged ridges throughout, with golden sweet water rivers flowing though its ravines. . . . with slopes and deep gorges occupied by large indian villages on all sides of the mountain, offering a pleasant sight" (Sim¢n, 1892, V.IV. pp. 190–1.)

The spatial distribution of the different settlements follows population trends that indicate a direct relationship with ecological and geographical variables, making it possible to infer the ancient settlers' approach and criteria upon establishing at the Sierra Nevada.

TREASURE HUNTERS

The first references to the existence of the Upper Buritaca (B-200) archeological site came in 1975, when I received news at the Colombian Institute of Anthropology, of a monumentally large settlement in imminent risk of destruction caused by treasure hunters.

During the 70s, treasure hunting had become a means of earning a living in Colombia and, in the case of the Sierra Nevada de Santa Marta, regularly, during the rainy season, true hordes of archeological site looters caused major damages to our historic and cultural heritage.

These archeological looting phenomena must be considered within the context of the socio-economic problems affecting that part of our country during the early 70s, prior to the time when marijuana began to be grown there in 1975, bringing a drastic change to that region's economy.

Groups of "guaqueros," unemployed individuals who had come to the north coast from different parts of the country in search of seasonal jobs, set off through the intricate peaks and plateaus of the Sierra hunting for treasures with which they thought they could palliate their economic hardship. The destruction was systematic and continuous. Even a treasure hunters union, with 10,000 affiliates came to be established, approved by the Ministry of Labor by Resolution N§03105 of December 14, 1972, in contradiction with the laws that protect the cultural heritage of Colombia.

The unlawful destruction of these Tayrona culture places was such that many of the sites reported by Alden Mason, Gerardo and Alicia Reichel-Dolmatoff, Bischof, Murdy, and Wynn, have been totally lost to history.

When the Anthropological Station of the Sierra Nevada de Santa Marta was set up, the Archeological Project was implemented at the source of the Buritaca river and, for many years, it was possible to maintain control over a vast region of the invaluable forests of the basin, also significant for being the site of numerous satellite villages probably dependent on Buritaca 200.

As for those that had been Treasure Hunters in the past, many of them found in the archaeological project a less dangerous and more stable job. Through education and re-training that we provided, they acquired and excellent awareness of the Sierra Nevada issues. Today, more than 20 years latter, the "guaqueros" have conformed a legal association of guides which have become experts on conducting visitors to the archaeological remains of the Tayrona, through the trails of the Sierra. Now, they are the principal economic beneficiaries of the historical ruins that they themselves helped to rescue.

During the course of my explorations in the vast region of the Sierra Nevada, which at the time were centered around the upper Buritaca and Nulicuandecue rivers, I found the remains of more than 200 urban settlements, ranging from small villages to one of the largest cities uncovered in the Americas, Buritaca 200, also known as La Ciudad Perdida (the Lost City).

These towns and villages were linked to one another by an impressive network of paths that allowed the exchange of products between the different climatic areas and provided these early settlers with the key to the efficient use of their habitat.

Figure 56.1. Paths of La Ciudad Perdida. © Alvaro Soto.

The study of their agricultural techniques, pest control methods, and the design of their dwellings, which were suited to the climate and made use of locally available resources – the reconstruction of a past way of life – permits us not only to continue to discover a very important part of Colombia's cultural heritage, but also to directly take advantage of this technical expertise for the rational use of the resources of the Sierra Nevada and of other areas and countries.

The Proposal for the Creation of the Environmental, Historical and Cultural Reserve of the Sierra Nevada de Santa Marta

The proposal aims to create special development areas for education and eco-tourism in the archaeological sites located between the valleys of the Nulicuandecue and upper Buritaca rivers, as well as in the major archaeological sites in Tayrona National Park, concentrating particularly on the La Ciudad Perdida and Pueblito.

The project aims to develop an area of approximately 50,000 hectares that, in addition to the La Ciudad Perdida and Pueblito, will include five other archaeological cities set amidst perfectly conserved rainforest. The management of this area and its transformation into the Environmental, Historical and Cultural Reserve of the Sierra Nevada de Santa Marta will lead to the creation of a program similar to those in other regions of major archaeological interest, such as those in Mexico and the Galapagos Islands. The area will be accessible to significant numbers of highly controlled visitors and will be organized in a way that will allow the further exploration,

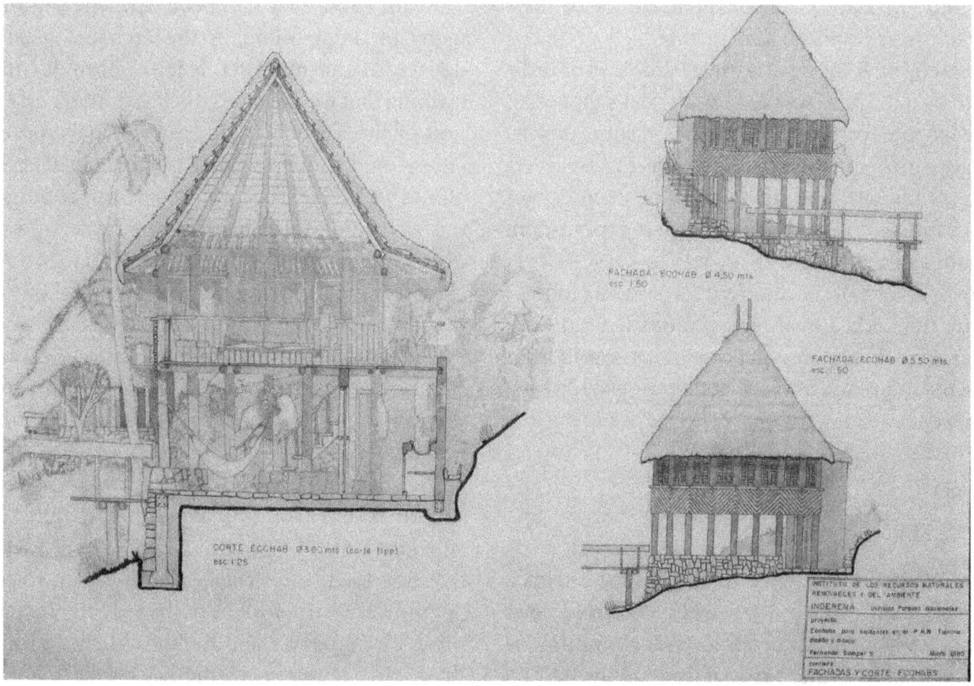

Figure 56.2. Eco hab. © Alvaro Soto.

Figure 56.3. Huts on Hillside Eco hab. © Alvaro Soto (drawing).

study, and conservation of the archaeological monuments and ecosystems.

Based on current figures for La Ciudad Perdida of 2,000 visitors a month, it is fair to say that these numbers will increase if the area in question is properly developed to create a reserve. The reserve could then become an important source of employment in the region and, ultimately, an alternative economy the benefits of which would spread to Santa Marta and the rest of the Atlantic Coast.

If the area is properly managed from the ecological and archaeological point of view, the vast geographic region surrounding La Ciudad Perdida, Pueblito, and other pre-Hispanic cities that we explored in the 1970s could achieve the same economic importance as other Latin American sites of cultural and environmental interest.

THE RATIONALE OF THE PROPOSAL

The current socio-economic situation in the Sierra Nevada de Santa Marta is such that many problems afflicting the nation as a whole come together there. For example, peasant farmers with no economic alternatives in the region find the cultivation of illegal crops highly appealing. This, in turn, leads to the arrival of guerrilla bands and paramilitaries. The indigenous population finds itself increasingly defenseless as the influx of "colonos," or settlers, attracted by the big money to be made from the illegal crops, encroaches on their land.

The arrival of these settlers to the Sierra Nevada has created a permanent state of violence that has led to the massive destruction of archaeological sites as well as natural resources, especially those of the rainforests, which include a wide variety of plant and animal life and the water sources supplying the towns of Santa Marta, Ciénaga, and other parts of Magdalena province, Riohacha, La Guajira, Valledupar, and El Cesar.

The high social cost of the arrival of the settlers in terms of loss of life and the state of chaos in which the inhabitants of the Sierra Nevada live, in addition to the high economic cost in terms of the country's loss of biodiversity and water sources and the irreversible damage to its ecosystems, means that there is an urgent need for viable and legal alternative employment opportunities, which, in turn, will ensure the ecological and protection of the Sierra Nevada and its historical and cultural patrimony.

The establishment of the aforementioned reserve could become a major factor in the transformation of the current state of affairs in the Sierra Nevada, not only because of the local employment opportunities that would be created directly and indirectly, but also because it would give the inhabitants an extra incentive to conserve the environment because conservation activities would be the source of their jobs.

In the framework of the project, the aforementioned archaeological sites, which are currently somewhat neglected, would be restored, their historical significance would be further explored, and the reserve as a whole would be protected as a genuine ecological sanctuary.

The people currently living in the Sierra Nevada are the descendents of the people who built the cities that are the subject of the present proposal. These communities will be the first to benefit from the development of the reserve and the various projects this will involve.

Figure 56.4. Eco hab based on ancient methods. © Alvaro Soto.

WHO IS BEHIND THE PROPOSAL?

Heading the proposal is Neotrópico, legally incorporated in Bogotá, Colombia, on January 26, 1987 as a nonprofit corporation dedicated to conducting research and providing education on subjects related to anthropology, history, culture, geography, economic systems, and the environment in Colombia and other parts of the world. Neotrópico's current activities include projects in the Sierra Nevada de Santa Marta, on Colombia's Pacific coast, and on South America as a whole.

Neotrópico has the knowledge and experience to carry out the proposed project, as well as suitably experienced personnel, many of whom were involved in the first archaeological explorations either as scientists, manual workers, or supervisors, in the framework of the ten-year exploration and restoration of La Ciudad Perdida and other archaeological sites.

STRUCTURE OF THE PROJECT

In order to carry out the project, a long-term agreement covering a period of at least fifteen years must be reached among the Neotrópico corporation, the indigenous communities of the Sierra Nevada de Santa Marta, private industry, and the relevant government agencies. Such an agreement will allow Neotrópico to create a consortium responsible for the effective management and environmental protection of the reserve, to proceed with maintenance work and continue the work begun by the archaeologists, and to protect the area of the proposed Environmental, Historical and Cultural Reserve of the Sierra Nevada de Santa Marta on the upper Buritaca and Nulicuandecue rivers and the Pueblito archaeological site in Tayrona Park, while being able to rely on sufficient financial resources. These resources can be raised mainly through:

a. the private sector
b. national government
c. the indigenous communities

INDIGENOUS COMMUNITIES

No project affecting archaeological sites or land inhabited by indigenous communities should develop without the agreement of the indigenous local population, whose members should also be the main beneficiaries of such projects. The archaeological sites were built by the ancestors of the current inhabitants of the Sierra Nevada and therefore belong to them.

(Unfortunately, this policy has yet to be applied to those archaeological sites that are currently being exploited in other countries, like Machu Picchu or those of the Mayas in Mexico and Guatemala; the Quechuas and the Mayas should be the main beneficiaries of the revenues produced by the tourism generated by their monuments.)

National Government

To initiate the project, permission is needed from the Colombian national government in the form of a concession or an agreement.

Private Sector

Agreements between Neotrópico and the private sector must be reached for the funding needed to cover the project's operating costs during its first year and for partnership arrangements in subsequent years.

These contributions would be regarded as capital investment to be recovered from future income generated by admission charges paid by visitors to the reserve. The indigenous communities and private-sector companies – invited by common agreement between Neotrópico and the indigenous communities to take part in the project – may also earn a significant amount of income from various aspects of the tourist infrastructure such as accommodation, recreation, and other services, in addition to the provision of air and overland transport. Specialized guides will continue to work through the Sierra Nevada de Santa Marta Guides Association.

As a result of the implementation of this proposal, it would be possible to go ahead with other tourist infrastructure projects with a low environmental impact such as the construction of a small railway to take visitors to the proposed reserve through the tropical rainforest along the Buritaca river and additional heliports near the archaeological sites where work would continue under the terms of the project.

BIBLIOGRAPHY

Herrera, Luisa Fernanda. 1980. Buritaca 200. Estudio de polen Arqueologico. Boletin del Museo del Oro, Banco de la República. Mayo-Agosto.

Herrera, Luisa Fernanda. 1985. Agricultura aborigen, y cambios de vegetación en la Sierra Nevada de Santa Marta. Fundación de investigaciones arqueológicas nacionales del Banco de la República. Bogota.

Reichel-Dolmatoff, Gerardo. 1954. Investigaciones arqueólogicas en la Sierra Nevada de Santa Marta. Partes 1 y 2 en Revista Colombiana de Antropologi'a, Vol. II. pp. 145–206, Bogota.

Simón, Pedro. 1625 (1953). Noticias historiales de las conquistas de tierra firme en las Indias occidentales. Ed. Kelly, Bogota.

Soto-Holguin, Alvaro. 1988. *La Ciudad Perdida de los Tayrona, História de su hallazgo y Descubrimiento.* Bogotá: Editorial Gente Nueva.

Van Der Hammen Thomas and Pedro Ruiz. 1984. La Sierra Nevada de Santa Marta (Colombia) – Transecto Buritaca-La Cumbre – J. Cramer in der Gebrüder Borntraeger Verlasgbushhandlung. Berlin – Stuttgart.

White, Lesley. 1969. *The Science of Culture.* Farrar Straus & Giroux.

CHAPTER FIFTY-SEVEN

Cultural Heritage Preservation: A National Trust Perspective

Trevor A. Carmichael

Culture may be defined as the way of life of a people. Although cultural heritage may be reflected in various national and subnational institutions, it also transcends such institutions and is reflected in the essence of how people conduct their lives.

Recognising the tangible–intangible dichotomy, UNESCO acknowledges that tangible heritage includes the landscape of a country, the bodies of water that are its exclusive property, its architectural structures, artefacts, and monuments, and the preservation of the people as nationals of that country. On the other hand, intangible culture embraces all forms of traditional, popular, or folk culture represented by the collective works of a particular society. Inasmuch as the transmission of these works is either oral or by gesture, modification takes place over a period of time through a process of collective re-creation. The intangible, therefore, encompasses oral traditions, music, dance, customs, languages, rituals, festivities, traditional medicine and pharmacopoeia, and culinary arts.

In seeking to explore cultural heritage preservation in relation to law and legislation, one is drawn towards an examination of law and interest-group activity as symbolic elements, as preservation efforts gain their impetus from the structure and function of interest-group action. In the context of the Caribbean, the relationship between the two may be examined by means of a survey of the adequacy of relevant laws and by examining the role of national trusts and conservation societies as advocates of cultural preservation. This chapter adopts such an analysis for the English-speaking Commonwealth Caribbean.

BAHAMAS NATIONAL TRUST: A LEADER

The Bahamas National Trust is a Caribbean leader in its capacity as a vigorous and effective actor in the field of cultural heritage preservation. It has achieved this by skilfully balancing the domestic and international factors of growth and development. The Trust has its origins in a 1959 Act of Parliament, which granted it the ability to make its own by-laws without government approval. From the outset, the Trust adopted a structure that recognises the value of both local and international input. Accordingly, the Board of the Trust elects nine members from the Trust's own membership, six from the Bahamian government, and six from various U.S. institutions, including the American Museum of Natural History, the New York Zoological Society (now Wildlife Conservation International), the Smithsonian Institution, the National Audubon Society, the United States National Parks Service, and the University of Miami's Rosential School of Marine and Atmospheric Sciences.

A significant consequence of this dual structure is that it has provided a wide range of sources of funding for the Trust. With an annual budget of about US$1 million, it has been able to generate income through memberships, special functions, sales, and entrance fees. However, more than fifty percent of its annual income comes from the Trust's own Heritage Fund, the first endowment fund of its kind in the Commonwealth Caribbean – a feature that was facilitated by the Trust's early institutional connections in the United States. The Trust has therefore been able to employ a small cadre of staff of about twenty-four persons, but, more importantly, it has been able to recruit hundreds of volunteers, some of whom were recruited as a result of the international nexus that has been developed.

This international focus is also exemplified by the successful preservation of the Exuma Cays Land and Sea Park. In the mid-1980s, the Trust designated the Exuma Cays as a "no take" replenishment area, thereby establishing the first marine fishery reserve in the Commonwealth Caribbean. Although this step did not receive immediate popular support, the basic philosophy of the Trust, namely, that protecting the habitat would facilitate protection of the resource, was eventually understood and appreciated. Scientists outside the Bahamas were fascinated by this novel action, which introduced the term "marine fishery reserve" as well as the policy of promoting such reserves as a critical tool in sustaining fisheries resources.

The Exuma Cays project, which was mentioned in international publications and discussed at scientific conferences, catapulted the Trust into the international limelight. It also proved to be the catalyst for other preservation efforts outside the Bahamas, such as the collaborative work of the Florida Keys National Marine Sanctuary and the Everglades and Dry Tortugas National Parks, which later established marine replenishment areas in the Dry Tortugas area of the Florida Keys.

This internationalisation has, in turn, resulted in the Trust receiving financial support from the Florida Nature Conservancy and endorsements from officials of the U.S. National Park System. The success of the project was not without local response; the commercial fishermen gave strong and vocal support, and the Trust continued to receive requests to create more national parks. The Trust has also been at the vanguard of preservation projects in eleven other parks and protected areas and oversees 325,000 acres.

BARBADOS NATIONAL TRUST: CONSISTENT STEWARDSHIP

The Barbados National Trust, like its Bahamian counterpart, was established by an Act of Parliament. However, the Barbadian Act of 1961 does not lay down the structure and functions of the Trust in detail, but describes the framework within which the Trust should operate and makes provisions for the further promulgation of a constitution and by-laws.

The Trust, which is registered as a corporation, has also been registered as a charity. In keeping with the many objectives set out in its original mandate, the Trust has been at the forefront of the compilation of a photographic and written record of places of natural beauty and other animal and plant life, the acquisition of properties for the benefit of residents of Barbados and its visitors, and the opening to the public of the island's many sites of historical and architectural interest.

As a result of its activities, the Barbados National Trust has become the owner of a significant amount of property.

- Welchman Hall Gully has a wide range of tropical flora and fauna and is representative of the peculiarly Barbadian gully system, which runs underground and criss-crosses almost the entire island.
- The Andromeda Botanical Gardens, bequeathed to the Trust by the late Mrs. Iris Banochie, contains thousands of plants from virtually every corner of the earth, including many species of hybrids, and forms the largest collection of botanical specimens in the Caribbean.
- Bridgetown Synagogue has been restored by the local Jewish community and is now vested in the National Trust, having earned an American Express President's Award. The synagogue, which is located about 200 yards from the main shopping street in Bridgetown, was founded soon after the establishment of the British settlement in 1627, during the exodus of Jews from Recife to Amsterdam. On learning that Oliver Cromwell had opened British territories to Jews, they applied for permission to settle in Barbados. The Bridgetown Synagogue is one of the two oldest synagogues in the western hemisphere, the other of similar age being in Curaçao.
- The Morgan Lewis Sugar Mill still has its original machinery and ground sugar cane until 1947. Since 1996, it has been listed on UNESCO's List of 100 Endangered Historical Sites and is actually grinding sugar cane once again, having received an American Express President's Award.
- The Sir Frank Hudson Sugar Museum, which complements the Morgan Lewis Sugar Mill, is housed in an old factory boiling house and contains an impressive display of old sugar machinery and artefacts.
- The Trust has also developed the Tyrol Cot Heritage Village, which is built around a property constructed in 1854 by William Farnum, one of Barbados' most prominent builders. The property is the former residence of Sir Grantley Adams, the only prime minister of the short-lived West Indies Federation. The village is a beautiful testimony to the life of Sir Grantley and Lady Adams, who both played an important part in the social development of Barbados between 1930 and 1960. The National Trust has restored the house and garden in the style of the 1930s and has added an arts and crafts village and a collection of chattel houses, emulating Barbados's most well-known cultural icon, the chattel house, as well as a rum shop, a blacksmith's workshop, a standpipe, a replica of a slave hut, and the Chattel House Museum.
- The Trust also owns four signal stations located in different parts of the island, with commanding views of the coastline. These stations were used as defensive positions during the Caribbean stage of the eighteenth and nineteenth century European wars and have also been employed for meteorological purposes. The stations have now been tastefully restored, and the Gun Hill Station, in particular, is so beautifully appointed that it has become a major revenue earner over the years.

The Trust has also made a significant contribution to the preservation of properties in general. In 1982, for example, the Trust participated, together with the Caribbean Conservation Association and the Barbados Museum and with funding from the Canadian government, in the compilation of a list of protected buildings that are identified in legislation affecting town and country planning. This list has been an important tool in the fight to preserve the history and architecture of Barbados. Although a lack of funding has made it impossible to extend the list as desired, the process has nevertheless proved to be an important factor in the encouragement of preservation and the hindering of demolition.

The Trust regularly reviews applications for the demolition, restoration, or alteration of listed buildings, in collaboration with the Town and Country Planning Department. It is often consulted to ensure that its views are taken into account in the area of development.

Like the Bahamas National Trust, the Barbados National Trust has forged links with a variety of international agencies and has received a significant amount of financial assistance over the years through the Mission Administered Funds of the Canadian International Development Association.

The Trust has also forged links with many non-Barbadians through its participation in the Open House Programme. Under this programme, some of the most historically and architecturally significant homes on the island are opened up to the public, one a week for four months of the year. An even greater involvement of locals and visitors is achieved through the National Trust hikes, which started with only eight people in 1982 but are now attended by 300 people every Sunday. At no other event is it possible to find such a wide sample of Barbadians and visitors coming together for the common purpose of enjoyment and education.

BRITISH VIRGIN ISLANDS NATIONAL PARKS TRUST: OPEN-AIR BEAUTY

This Trust was established in July 1961 by the government of the British Virgin Islands to preserve the natural beauty and historical features of the islands. Its Board of Directors is appointed by the government, which provides the Trust with an annual subvention through the Ministry of Natural Resources and Labour. The Trust is a professional organisation with a staff of more than twenty-five and responsibilities that have developed from managing the Sage Mountain National Park in 1964 to managing eighteen national parks in 2002.

The parks system, which is divided into eastern and western regions, is managed by programme coordinators and park wardens. Management responsibilities include the preservation of all the flora and fauna within the parks, and the maintenance and upgrading of facilities such as trails and sites. Scientific research is also part of the Trust's overall mandate. Each park has its own management plan, and the Trust also has a systems plan that helps it in the selection of areas that are designated for protection or conservation.

The Trust has also been instrumental in the return of flamingos to the island of Anegada. The project involved the introduction of eighteen flamingos, and now there are forty flamingos living on the island. The Trust is also involved in the rehabilitation of endangered Anegada iguana population and has made significant efforts to protect the fragile coral reefs by means of a mooring reef protection programme, which was established in 1991.

It is clear from the previous discussion that the focus of the Trust's activities in the British Virgin Islands has been mainly on natural beauty, flora, and fauna, and less on buildings.

CAYMAN ISLANDS NATIONAL TRUST: AN ETHOS OF EDUCATION

The Cayman Islands National Trust was established in 1987 under the National Trust for the Cayman Island Law of 1987, which was subsequently revised as the National Trust Law in 1997. The Trust was formed on the basis of a mission statement seeking to preserve natural environments and places of historic significance for present and future generations of the Cayman Islands. As a result of the Trust's attempts to implement this statement, education has become an integral part of its work, such that educational programmes are fashioned according to the policies of environmental and historical preservation. The Trust has therefore become involved in the new national curriculums for science and social studies established by the Department of Education.

In the area of its environmental programmes, the Trust has been very successful in assisting Cayman Islands in the maintenance of their obligations under important international conventions that foster environmental management and cultural integrity. In their individual and collective ways, the 1992 Convention on Biological Diversity, the 1971 Ramsar Convention on Wetlands, and the 1990 Protocol Concerning Specially Protected Areas and Wildlife (SPAW Protocol) aim to ensure a system of protected areas that, in turn, will also protect the islands' native biodiversity. The National Trust has raised more than US$1 million from private donors for voluntary land purchases at prevailing market rates in an effort to protect areas of the three islands. It has also managed the protected areas.

The assessment and monitoring of native biodiversity have also been important features of the Trust's activities. The Trust manages the Cayman Islands Herbarium and runs an insectarium that contains historic and recent collections. The Islands' biodiversity is maintained by the Trust's extensive forest diversity survey and mapping project and its preservation of important endangered species, such as the Grand Cayman Blue Iguana, the Cayman Brac Parrot, Little Cayman's Red-Footed Boobies, the bats of the Cayman Islands, and endangered plants. The Trust also manages to guarantee public involvement by maintaining the Mastic Trail, the Governor Gore Bird Sanctuary, Heritage Beach, a self-guided trail through the Brac Parrot Reserve, and the Visitor's Centre at the Booby Pond Nature Reserve.

The national curriculum has incorporated much of the aforementioned because the Trust has provided specially produced resources for teachers in the fields of social studies and the sciences. The resources in question are the so-called National Symbols and Mangroves education packages.

The Trust's environmental work is complemented by a vibrant historical preservation programme that includes a commemorative plaque programme, the creation of an inventory of historic buildings and sites, historical preservation awards, and a programme for the acquisition of historic sites. Once again, education receives a lot of attention, and public participation and education have been encouraged through an Historical Education Programme that comprises many activities, including the creation and publication of two self-guided walking tours in George Town and West Bay; the ongoing development of an historical resource library with written publications aimed at schoolchildren and other interested parties; and guided tours to historic properties belonging to the National Trust.

The sustainability of the Trust has been secured through the high level of public participation that has been achieved through the involvement of government, locals, visitors, and the educational establishment.

ST. LUCIA NATIONAL TRUST: A PUBLIC CONNECTION

The St. Lucia National Trust was established for the specific purpose of preserving buildings, objects of historical and architectural interest, and areas of natural beauty. Its work is administered by a Council that includes seven members elected by the Trust's general membership, two representatives from the St. Lucia Archaeological and Historical Society, and two members nominated by the minister responsible for the St. Lucia National Trust. There are a number of committees that are responsible for various aspects of the Trust's work, including the finance, membership, research, and publications committees, in addition to an administrative staff.

The Trust is engaged in the management of parks, nature reserves, and historic and architectural sites. It maintains its focus on public outreach and education with organised tours to the Maria Islands Nature Reserve, the Fregate Islands Nature Reserve, the Pigeon Island National Landmark, the Morne Fortuné, and the Eastern Nature Trail. The Trust takes preservation of cultural heritage to memorable heights by advertising its services as a special kind of wedding planner.

The Trust has developed a special connection with a public that is familiar with the unique beauty and significance of St. Lucia's two Piton mountain triangles and consistently displays a deep awareness of its national culture.

TURKS AND CAICOS NATIONAL TRUST: ONGOING EDUCATION

The Turks and Caicos National Trust sees its role as managing the lands belonging to the Trust and increasing public awareness and education. The Trust owns three important areas of national significance – on Providenciales, North Caicos, and Grand Turk – and has long-term leases on many other sites of environmental and historical significance. It maintains a comprehensive public education profile and has conducted an extensive campaign on the Rock Iguana with a grant from the RARE Centre for Tropical Conservation. It is also operating a preservation programme for the West Indian Whistling Duck on all the islands.

In furthering its educational objectives, the Trust has maintained an international focus with its links to the Royal Society for the Protection of Birds, the Caribbean Ornithology Society and the United Kingdom Territories Conservation Forum. The Trust's educational focus extends to its publications, in particular *Echo Echoes*, a children's environmental publication. This booklet is frequently used by teachers as a resource for lessons on topics such as mangroves, coral reefs, and national parks. The Trust has also recently published the first comprehensive book on the birds of the Turks and Caicos Islands.

CONCLUSION

It might be appropriate to conclude on a note that, on the one hand, appears to be contradictory, but which, on the other hand, is also complementary – a note of fusion. Today, fusion rules in a world that constantly flirts with the meaning of globalisation. Fusion in cuisine and lifestyles has now moved to the realm of musicals, where only a short while ago Sir Andrew Lloyd Webber spoke of his new "Bollywood-inspired" musical "Bombay Dreams," and its Indian composer, A. R. Ralman, noted that "the future of shows in the West lies in Indian music." However, genuine fusion cannot be true to itself and is without merit if the primary product is not safe and sustainable. It is this author's respectful submission that the Caribbean National Trusts are performing this role with competence, grace, and style.

CHAPTER FIFTY-EIGHT

Costa Rica's Biodiversity Law: Searching for an Integral Approach to Cultural and Biological Diversity

Vivienne Solís Rivera[1] and
Patricia Madrigal Cordero[2]

The aim of this chapter is to share the process of drawing up, approving, and enforcing Costa Rica's Biodiversity Law. We think that this is a valuable process in that it discusses the implementation of the Convention on Biological Diversity (the "CBD") at the national level, and has forced us to face the learning process involved in promoting a legal initiative that attempts to regulate existing economic interests. This chapter does not deal in depth with the CBD, nor does it defend its precepts as given truth. We think that each country should seek its own legal means to regulate biodiversity according to its specific social, economic, and political context.

BACKGROUND

Costa Rica's Biodiversity Law, approved on April 23, 1998, is the result of a long process to create a legal framework in response to the ethical and social mandate for a more just and equitable distribution of benefits deriving from the commercial use of components of biological diversity, and according to the principles of the CBD.

It is important to note that when the first Draft Biodiversity Law was presented in June of 1996, six contracts with transnational companies had already been signed in Costa Rica to carry out biodiversity prospecting, and a regulatory legal framework for carrying out such activities was absent.

Laws exist that regulate each individual natural resource, such as the Law for Wildlife Conservation (1992), the Forest Law (1996), the Constitutional Law for the National Parks Service (1972), and the Organic Law on the Environment (1995). But a legal gap existed between the regulation of genetic and biochemical resources, and in access to and the fair distribution of their benefits. The CBD was ratified in 1994.

The administrative framework for the consideration of the theme of the use of biodiversity was restricted to the presence of an Advisory Council to the Minister of the Environment and Energy, known as COABIO, made up of specialists in distinct aspects of biodiversity. And the presence of the National Biodiversity Institute (INBio), a civil nonprofit association that is counterpart to private enterprise interested in the search, for commercial ends, for new sources of chemical compounds, genes, proteins, micro-organisms, and other products of current or potential economic value found in biodiversity.

THE LAW'S HISTORY

The promoter of the initiative was Luis Martínez Ramírez, ex-congressman and former president of the Environmental Commission of the Legislative Assembly, who officially requested the technical support of the World Conservation Union's Regional Office for Mesoamerica (IUCN-ORMA), located in Costa Rica, in drawing up the Draft Biodiversity Law.

This legal initiative's aim was to comply with the mandate of the CBD, which challenged its signatories to legislate on the themes covered by the CBD.

ORMA responded positively to the request and charged the Wildlife Thematic Area with responsibility for the project.[3] Prior to drawing up the draft law, its philosophical framework was defined jointly with the Environmental Commission of the Legislative Assembly. This definition established the following guiding principles:

- equal access to and distribution of the benefits in the use of biodiversity components;
- respect for human rights, principally those of groups who are marginalized because of cultural or economic conditions;
- sustainable use of biodiversity components respecting development options for future generations;
- that democracy guarantees a greater participation by all citizens in decision making, within an environment of peace, and in development options.

With this conceptual base, a consultation process was initiated with groups selected according to certain characteristics: indigenous peoples, closeness to protected areas, small farmer groups, legal experts, scientists, civil servants, and private

[1] Coope Sol i Dar R. L., is a self-managed cooperative made up of professionals from different disciplines, whose mission is: Propose innovative alternatives to achieving cultural and biological wealth, contributing to improving the quality of life for the population, with justice and equality, by working with participatory processes for making decisions individually and collectively at the local, national, and international levels.

[2] Our work assists in establishing common grounds between conservation and development, primarily for local communities through providing technical support to diverse national and Central American projects and institutions to enable progressing toward sustainable development models that can create a synergy among the regional, national, and local levels.

[3] At that time, Vivienne Solís Rivera was the co-ordinator and Patricia Madrigal Cordero was the legal advisor of the Wildlife Thematic Area of the World Conservation Union's Regional Office for Mesoamerica.

enterprise. The objective of this consultation was to learn what the basic content of the draft law should be.

With this input, the preparation of the draft law was started, with it being defined as a general law that would attempt to regulate all those aspects of the CBD in an integral manner, and considering the possibility of, in the future, developing distinct regulations for more specific themes such as biosecurity, biotechnology, access, and intellectual property.

On becoming officially public on June 18, 1996, the draft law was the subject of diverse debates and generated reactions in favour and against its content, making patent the different opinions that exist on the type of regulations and mechanisms that would be covered by a law of this type for the protection of biodiversity resources.

The presentation of the draft law was public and extensive. Three thousand copies of the draft were distributed, including 300 to individuals and institutions, for their comment. It was also made available on the Internet in order to generate discussion groups.

A substitute Draft Law was drawn up with the comments, observations, and suggestions sent to the Environmental Commission in December 1996. However, the discussion process was bogged down because of the polarisation of the different positions.

The proposal for a reconciliation forum by Jorge Mora, Rector of the National University, was accepted by the Environmental Commission. The latter delegated the task of drawing up the draft law to a Special Mixed Sub-commission, made up of representatives of the National Indigenous Forum, the Costa Rican Federation for Environmental Conservation, the National Small Farmers' Board, the University of Costa Rica and the National University, the Union of Chambers for Private Business, INBio, COABIO, and the National Liberation and Christian Socialist Unity parties.

The objective of this subcommission was to draft a consensual project within a period of five months. Debate arose, among other things, about the role of the state as guardian of biodiversity, the concepts of public and private ownership, the administrative organisation, biosecurity and access to genetic and biochemical components, the protection of associated knowledge, and the intellectual rights of the community.

The subcommission submitted the consensual text in November 1997, and five months later, on the April 23, 1998, during the last days of the Figueres-Olsen administration, the Draft Biodiversity Law was approved by a conditional majority vote in the Legislative Assembly to be subsequently signed and become Law of the Republic No. 7788, on May 6, 1998.

CONTENTS OF THE BIODIVERSITY LAW 7788

The Concepts

Since the conception of discussion on the biodiversity law, the relationship between biological and cultural biodiversity has remained clearly established. This relationship is reflected in the concept of biodiversity itself, which includes associated knowledge, recognizing different forms of knowledge, and the right to cultural objection to access to genetic resources.

Article 1 – Objective

The objective of the present law is the conservation of biodiversity and the sustainable use of resources, in addition to the just distribution of benefits and derivatives.

Article 2 – Sovereignty

The State has complete and exclusive sovereignty over the components of biodiversity.

Article 3 – Scope of Application

This law will be applied to components of biodiversity that are under the sovereignty of the State, as well as to the processes and the activities made under its jurisdiction or control, independently of those whose effects are pronounced inside or outside the subject zones of national jurisdiction. This law will specifically regulate the use, the handling, the knowledge and the right distribution of the befits and costs derived from the use of the components of biodiversity.

Article 6 – Public Dominion

The biochemical and genetic properties of wild or domesticated components of biodiversity are of public dominion. The State will authorize the exploration, investigation, bioprospecting, and use of components of biodiversity that constitute public properties, as well as the use of all the genetic and biochemical resources, by the norms of access established in chapter V of this law.

Article 7 – Definitions

The variability of living organisms from any source, existing within terrestrial, aerial, marine, or aquatic ecosystems or in other ecological complexes. It includes the diversity within each species, as well as between species and the ecosystems of which they are part.

For the purpose of this law, the term biodiversity is understood to include those intangible components being: individual or collective knowledge, innovation, and traditional practice, of real or *potential* value associated with biochemical and genetic resources, *protected or not* by intellectual property systems or *sui generis* registry systems.

Generally speaking, "The State recognizes the existence and validity of all forms of knowledge and innovation and the necessity to protect them by means of... [appropriate] legal mechanisms..." (Art 77), which include "... patents, trade secrets, plant breeders' rights, *sui generis community intellectual rights*, copyrights and farmers' rights" (Art. 78).

Knowledge is understood to be traditional, popular, and scientific knowledge.

Knowledge:
A dynamic product generated by society over time and by different mechanisms, and includes that which is produced by traditional means or generated by scientific practice.

Previous informed consent has been established as a necessary requirement for access to genetic resources.

Previous Informed Consent (PIC):
Procedure by which the state, private owners, or local and indigenous communities, having been previously supplied with all requested information, agree to permit access to biological resources or to the intangible component associated with them, under mutually agreed conditions.

Permission of access:
Authorization granted by the Costa Rican State for bioprospecting, acquisition, or commercialization of genetic materials or biochemical abstracts of components of biodiversity, as well as its associated knowledge of people or institutions, nationals, or foreigners, requested by means of a procedure created in this legislation, according to permits, contracts, agreements, or concessions.

Article 10 of the law sets forth as other objectives the "promotion of education and public awareness" and the improvement of administration.

THE ADMINISTRATIVE STRUCTURE

Different proposals for the administrative organisation for the conservation of biological diversity were analysed during the discussion process that accompanied the drawing up of the Draft Biodiversity Law. This section is presented with the idea of recovering the conceptual evolution of the discussion held on this aspect, in recognition of the fact that it will be a highly debated theme for national development within each country.

The First Draft Law

The first draft presented in June 1996 aimed at the establishment of a National System for Biodiversity Planning made up of four sectors: the state, small farmers, scientific/academic groups, and indigenous groups. These sectors named a representative to create the National Biodiversity Commission (CONABI).

This Commission was attached to the Presidency and coordinated by one of the vice presidents, and included the establishment of a National Technical Secretariat that would carry out its measures. It had advisory councils on biosecurity, biotechnology, sustainable use, intellectual property, and indigenous matters. Its judgements were binding. It also made use of a national biodiversity network for the recovery and systematisation of information, the education and training of human resources, and dissemination.

It had diverse functions oriented towards programming for policy definition, providing advice to the executive power, and holding executive functions with regards to the granting of permits.

This system was established on the premise that each sector, made up of different types of institutions and organisations, would organise itself internally and name a representative who would serve as the link between the sector concerned and the national position.

For example, in the case of the public sector, made up of different ministries: Environment and Energy; Health; Agriculture and Livestock; Overseas Trade; conferring the co-ordination to a ministry presented problems of capacity and institutional scope. By being attached to the Presidency, the possibility was contemplated of the vice president co-ordinating governmental action through the policy definition.

A series of comments and proposals for changes to the law started to arrive at the office of the proposing congressperson after the presentation of the Draft Law. Thus, in December 1996, a Substitutive Draft Law, enriched with the contributions from different national institutions, was presented.

The Substitute Project

The administrative organisation was subject to the following basic changes: that the Biodiversity Conservation System would be made up of the National System for Biodiversity Management, and by the National System of Conservation Areas (SINAC).

This proposal was aimed at giving SINAC, which was functioning *de facto*, a stronger legal basis, and considering that the protected areas were a fundamentally important instrument for *in situ* biodiversity conservation.

The National System for Biodiversity Management presented its integration on behalf of a national commission and a technical secretariat, and a proposal for the regionalisation and de-concentration on the part of the regional and local councils.

The CONABI was attached to the Ministry of Environment and Energy, considering its arguments for being the guiding body with regards to biodiversity.

Two more sectors were incorporated: the productive sector, in recognition of its importance as a user of biodiversity components; and nongovernmental organisations, in recognition of their role representing civil society.

Functions were maintained with the same orientation, but in the case of the executive functions for the granting of permits, the necessity of strengthening the capacity of Conservation Areas in the granting of concessions, permits, licenses, or contracts for biodiversity prospecting, use and commercialisation of biodiversity components.

It was foreseen that SINAC should function as a decentralised management system, providing for a five-year period for the gradual transfer of operative functions from the

Technical Secretariat on Biodiversity to the Conservation Areas.

No changes were made either to the Advisory Councils or the National Biodiversity Network.

The Second and Last Substitute Text

July 1997 saw the naming of a Special Mixed Sub-Commission in an attempt to arrive at a Draft Consensual Law, in which stakeholders from different sectors would participate. In November 1997, the Draft Law was submitted and, with slight modifications, it passed on April 23, 1998.

This text maintained the Ministry of Environment and Energy as co-ordinator of the National Commission for Biodiversity Management and the National System of Conservation areas as before, the functions of which are maintained much as they were in the first version and include programming, advisory, and implementation functions.

The main difference is that it is not a system made up of different sectors, but of institutional representatives.

The National Commission for Biodiversity Management is made up of eleven representatives of diverse ministries. This Commission, known as CONAGEBIO, has an Office for Technical Support, made up of the Executive Director and personnel named according to the regulation, and takes care of the processing, co-ordination, and granting of permits. It may name *ad hoc* Expert Committees.

Consultation on the part of the Executive Power is voluntary and not binding.

ACCESS TO GENETIC AND BIOCHEMICAL COMPONENTS AND THE PROTECTION OF ASSOCIATED KNOWLEDGE (ARTICLES 62 AND 76 BIODIVERSITY LAW)

CONAGEBIO is responsible for proposing access policies for biodiversity's genetic *ex situ* and *in situ* and biochemical components, and for acting as obligatory consulting body in procedures for requests for the protection of intellectual rights on biodiversity.

One of the exclusions established in Article 4 of the Law is that of not applying dispositions to the exchange of biochemical and genetic resources or to knowledge resulting from non-profit practices, uses, and customs among indigenous peoples and local communities.

Basic Requirements for Access

The basic requirements for access are:

(1) Previous informed consent of representatives of the place where access is to take place, these being the regional councils of the Conservation Areas, farm owners, or indigenous authorities, when this lies within their territory.
(2) Authorisation of this previous informed consent on the part of the Commission's Technical Office.
(3) Terms of technology transfer and the fair distribution of benefits, when these exist, agreed to in the permits, agreements, and concessions, as well as the type of protection of associated knowledge called for by the representatives of the place where access takes place.
(4) Definition of the means by which such activities will contribute toward the conservation of species and ecosystems.
(5) Designation of a legal representative, resident in the country, in the case of an individual or corporate body resident overseas.

Right to Cultural Objection

Recognises the right of local communities and indigenous peoples to oppose access to their resources and associated knowledge for cultural, spiritual, social, economic, or other reasons.

Any research programme or biodiversity prospecting on genetic or biochemical material from biodiversity to be carried out on Costa Rican territory requires an access permit.

For duly registered *ex situ* collections, this law's regulation establishes the procedure for the authorisation of the respective permit.

Such permits are granted to a researcher or research centre, are personal and not transferable, are limited to the material containing the authorised genetic or biochemical components, and can only be used in the area or territory that is clearly indicated in the permit.

Access permits for research or biodiversity prospecting do not give rights or actions, or delegate them, and only allow for the carrying out of such activities on previously established biodiversity components. These clearly stipulate: the certification of origin, the possibility of or prohibition to extract or export samples or, failing which, the duplication or deposit of materials; periodic reports, monitoring, and control, publicity and ownership of rights, in addition to any other condition which, given the applicable scientific and technical rules, is necessary according to the Commission's Technical Office.

These requirements are established in a different manner for research for noncommercial ends and for those that are commercial; but in the case of the former it must be established beyond any shadow of a doubt that no economic interests exist.

Each request should be addressed to the Technical Office and comply with the following requirements:

(1) Complete name and identification of the interested party. If it is not the interested party making the application, full details about their representative should be indicated as well as the authorisation under which he/she is operating.
(2) Complete name and identification of the responsible professional or researcher.

(3) Exact location of the place and the objects to be subject to research, with an indication of the owner, or the administrator or holder of the real estate.
(4) Descriptive chronogram of the scope of the research and possible environmental impacts.
(5) Objectives and end sought.
(6) Manifestation that the previous declaration has been made under oath.
(7) Place for notifications to be made with the perimeter of the location of the Commission's Technical Office.

The request should be accompanied by the PIC, authorised by the appropriate body, according to Article 65.

Voluntary Registration of Individuals or Corporate Bodies Involved in Biodiversity Prospecting

Individuals or corporate bodies who wish to carry out biodiversity prospecting should first register with the Commission's Registry. This act does not provide rights to carry out activities specific to biodiversity prospecting.

Authorisation for Agreements and Contracts

The Commission's Technical Commission will authorise agreements and contracts signed between individuals, nationals or from overseas, or between them and institutions registered for this purpose, if access to the use of genetic and biochemical components of Costa Rican biodiversity is involved. Their processing and approval are subject to stipulations in Articles 69, 70, and 71.

Public universities and other duly registered centres can draw up periodical framework agreements with the Commission for the processing of access permits and operational reports. In these cases, the legal representatives of the universities or institutions that benefit from this provision will hold criminal and civil liability for the uses to which the access is put.

Concession

When the Technical Office authorises the permanent use of genetic material or biochemical extracts for commercial ends, the interested party is required to obtain a concession for their extraction; and for which the General Norms established by the Commission are applied.

General Rules for Access

In addition to the requirements specifically indicated in the respective articles, in the Technical Office's respective resolution, according to the Commission's General Norms, the interested party will be obliged to deposit up to ten percent of the research budget and up to fifty percent of the royalties charged, in favour of the National System of Conservation Areas, indigenous territory, or private owner of the components to be accessed. An additional amount will be determined and which interested parties will have to pay in each case to cover processing costs, as well as any other benefit or technological transfer that is part of the PIC.

INTELLECTUAL PROPERTY

(Articles 62–67 of the Biodiversity Law)

Recognition of the Forms of Innovation

The state recognises the existence and validity of forms of knowledge and innovation and the need to protect them through appropriate legal means for each specific case.

Forms of and Limits to Protection

The state will grant the protection indicated in the previous article through patents, commercial secrets, rights of the plant improver, unique community intellectual rights, copyright, farmers' rights, and other forms. With the exception of:

(1) Deoxyribonucleic acid sequences per se;
(2) Plants and animals;
(3) Micro-organisms that have not been genetically modified;
(4) Essential biological procedures for the production of plants and animals;
(5) Natural processes and cycles themselves;
(6) Inventions that are essentially derived from knowledge associated with publicly owned traditional or cultural biological practices;
(7) Inventions which, on being commercially exploited in a monopolistic manner, could affect agricultural processes or products considered basic for food and health of the country's inhabitants.

Binding Previous Consultation

Both the National Seed Office and the Registries of Intellectual and Industrial Property are bound to consult with the Commission's Technical Office on innovations that involve biodiversity components prior to granting protection to intellectual or industrial property. They will always be accompanied by the certificate of origin issued by the Commission's Technical Office and the PIC.

Opposition raised by the Technical Office will prevent registration of the patent of protection of the innovation.

Licences

Individuals benefiting from protection of intellectual or industrial property relating to biodiversity will cede, in favour of the state, an obligatory legal license that will allow the use of such rights in cases of declared national emergency for the benefit of the collective, with the sole aim of addressing the emergency, with no need to pay privileges or indemnities.

Sui Generis Community Intellectual Rights

The state recognises and expressly protects, under the common denomination of *sui generis* community intellectual rights, knowledge, practices, and innovations of indigenous peoples and local communities, related to the use of biodiversity components and associated knowledge. This right exists and is legally recognised by the simple existence of the cultural practice or knowledge related to genetic and biochemical resources; it requires no previous declaration, express recognition, or official registration; and it thus may include practices that might acquire such a category in the future.

The recognition implies that none of the forms of protection of the intellectual and industrial rights regulated in this section, special laws, and international law will affect such historical practices.

Participatory Process to Determine the Nature and Scope of Unique Community Intellectual Rights

Within the eighteen months following the entry into effect of this law, the Commission, through its Technical Office, together with the Indigenous Board and the Small Farmers' Board, must define a participatory process with indigenous and small farmer communities, so as to determine the nature, scope, and requirements of these rights for their definitive regulation. The Commission and involved organisations will lay out the form, methodology, and basic elements of the participatory process.

Determination and Registration of *Sui Generis* Community Intellectual Rights

Procedures will be followed to take an inventory of specific unique community intellectual rights for which communities request protection, and the possibility will remain open in the future for the registration or recognition of others with the same characteristics.

The recognition of these rights in the Registry of the Commission's Technical Office is voluntary and free of charge; it should be carried out formally or at the request of the interested parties, without being subject to any type of formality.

The existence of such recognition in the Registry will oblige the Commission's Technical Office to provide a negative reply to any consultation relating to the recognition of intellectual or industrial rights over the same component or knowledge. Such refusal, so long as it is duly well-founded, can be issued for the same reason even when the *sui generis* right is not officially registered.

Use of *Sui Generis* Community Intellectual Rights

The form in which *sui generis* community intellectual rights will be exercised and who will exercise such entitlements will be determined through the participatory process. The recipients of their benefits will be likewise identified.

The most controversial issues and how they were resolved include:

Critcism	Reconciliation
• Too many obstacles to access	• It is clarified that it is a question of access to genetic and biochemical resources and that biological resources are not included. Access conditions are simplified.
• University autonomy is violated with regard to scientific research	• That stipulated in law does not affect university autonomy as far as teaching and research in the field of biodiversity is concerned, except when research has commercial ends
• Issue of protected areas not included	• A chapter was included for the legal establishment of the National System of Conservation Areas (SINAC)
• Indigenous and small farmer groups are not organised, the state cannot lose the co-ordination	• Participation of the Indigenous Board and the Small Farmers' Board is included within the National Commission for Biodiversity Management (CONAGEBIO) directed by the Ministry of the Environment and Energy
• Human genetic material is included within the law	• Access to human biochemical and genetic material is excluded from the law

CURRENT SITUATION AND FOLLOW-UP

Three months after the approval of the law, the Ministry of the Environment and Energy presented to the constitutional chamber a proceeding for unconstitutionality against articles 14 and 22 of the Biodiversity Law. These articles create CONAGEBIO and SINAC. The action is justified on the basis of the recovery of state jurisdiction over the definition of environmental and natural resource policies, and its exclusive jurisdiction and responsibility in the use of public funds. The National Incidence Network, together with other sectors, is analysing the possible consequences of this action and is attempting to ensure that this becomes an insurmountable problem for the enforcement of the Law.

To date, the Constitutional Chamber has not issued a finding on the motion for unconstitutionality. Nevertheless, the Biodiversity Law is applicable, except for the articles that have been appealed. CONAGEBIO has been created and its Executive Secretary has been established. The genetic resource access procedures, after a long consultation process, were approved.[4]

With the aim of ensuring the regulation and enforcement of the Biodiversity Law and strengthening the participation of civil society in debates relating to trade and environment, the National Small Farmers' Board, the National Indigenous Board, the Costa Rican Federation for Environmental Conservation and the National University's CAMBIOS programme make up the network, and the following objectives were proposed:

- Ensure the direct participation of farmers, indigenous populations, academia, and the environmental movement in the regulation of the law.
- Strengthen civil society through CONAGEBIO, the body that was created to draw up national policy in the conservation, sustainable use, and restoration of biodiversity. CONAGEBIO is the body that will propose policies relating to access to the genetic and biochemical components of biodiversity and will act as the obligatory consultative body as far as procedures relating to requests for protection of intellectual rights over biodiversity are concerned.
- Strengthen civil society participation through its effective incorporation into the Regional Councils of the Conservation Areas, created within the framework of the National System of Conservation Areas.
- Support the participatory process with communities so as to achieve the means, scope, and requirements for the regulation of *sui generis* community intellectual rights (rights of local communities to collectively benefit from their knowledge, practices, and innovations relating to the conservation and sustainable use of biodiversity).
- Support education in biodiversity conservation and sustainable use.
- Strengthen international relations with organisations that work in this area so as to share experiences and support proposals that benefit local communities.

The *Sui Generis* Community Rights Consultation Process in Indigenous Lands and Local Communities[5]

The Biodiversity Law established an eighteen-month timeframe after it went into effect to perform a participatory process to determine the nature, scope, and requirements for *sui generis* community intellectual rights. It was not until 2002 when, based on Article 83, the National Indigenous Council and the National Small Farmers' Board began a participatory information, training, and consultation process with the indigenous and small farmer communities that will produce the ideas and principles about the nature, scope, and requirements of community intellectual rights. This process brought forth holding twenty-four territorial consultation workshops and five regional workshops in the indigenous sector. This process is a pioneer in the region and Latin America and defined some initial results, among them: The communities consulted stated that the issue is clad in so much importance that they would like a longer-term process to be able to develop the issues more broadly. They are interested in gaining in-depth knowledge of the progress of discussion in other communities through the results of diverse regional workshops. There is a first draft proposal to set forth norms for the scope of *sui generis* community rights in the indigenous lands and local communities.

Work with the National Biodiversity Commission (CONAGEBIO)

During 2002, the draft of the norms for access to genetic resources was reviewed, mentioning that it should be developed as a complement to the Biodiversity Law. Three consultation workshops were organized with the universities to receive input and contributions to the draft. Likewise, the proposal was reviewed as a function of other norms or regulations that have some level of competence in relation to the issue of genetic resources, such as the Seed Law, the Phyto-Sanitary Protection Law, and the Wildlife Law. The regulation on access to genetic resources was approved by CONAGEBIO and published as an executive decree at the end of 2003.

LESSONS LEARNED

- The regulation of activities that are underway and unregulated is a process that faces strong opposition and considerable political and economic pressure.
- There are no systematised experiences or practices that help analyse how this issue has been developed in the South; this makes for a path that is both empirical and innovative.
- Information available to the population in general on biodiversity and its economic, ethical, and social interests has been very limited, and only an academic/scientific elite is informed.
- There is no adequate or continuous participation by the region in meetings on issues prioritised by developing countries with regard to follow up to the Biodiversity Convention.
- The transcendental points should appear in the Law and not in its regulations.
- The state does not yet want to share decision making with other civil society sectors, and especially the small farmer and indigenous sectors.

But the best lesson we have learned in the legislative advisory processes we have undertaken in Central America is that the law drafting process opens a space for learning and strengthening capacities, which allows for a real change in management, and not necessarily in the law itself.

[4] Executive Decree N°31514 – MINAE, the Ministry of the Environment and Energy, December 15, 2003, La Gaceta Official Publication, N°241 dated December 15, 2003.

[5] Information provided by Donald Rojas (of the Indigenous Council), Carlos Hernández (of the Small Farmer Council), and Marta Lilliana Jiménez, Former Executive Director of CONAGEBIO.

FINAL REFLECTIONS

The relationship that exists between biological and cultural diversity is clear. This relationship has been emphasized since the Global Biodiversity Strategy. The Costa Rican biodiversity law evidences (from the concept of biodiversity) the establishment of *sui generis* rights through a law or policy that should be approached as a "process," a space for awareness and reflection to define a position as a country.

The process of consulting the Indigenous and Small Farmers' Boards in regard to community intellectual rights has brought up more questions than answers. Can a system be established that really protects traditional knowledge? Or would it open the door to that knowledge being usurped instead? Bringing up a participatory process based on consultation is the only viable procedure for establishing a community intellectual rights system that can respond to this commotion. However, this process came upon one of its main obstacles in the form of the marginalization process in relation to the indigenous and small farmer sectors in terms of education, access to resources, and the land. The structural processes that these two sectors face should be dealt with little by little, parallel to the definition and establishment of a community intellectual rights system.

The Biodiversity Law's focus on recognizing genetic and bio-chemical resources as "public dominion" property in Article 5 is accepted by most government agencies. Costa Rica is a state that has received and broadened its jurisdiction in environmental matters, primarily since the 1990s, but one that has watched human and financial resources that are needed to deal with this jurisdiction decrease, posing serious problems in human and financial capacity to deal with the responsibility.

Civil society and the private sector little by little have been assuming some responsibilities that were previously considered to belong to the state. It would seem that in order to fulfill the environmental responsibilities, an effort is needed by all social sectors, in response to an environmental and social responsibility coming more from moral conviction than from a legal or political mandate.

Although the Biodiversity Law has linked biological and cultural diversity, there is a long road to travel so that culture and the environment are seen as part of the same reality. Many of the problems in dealing with the protection of traditional knowledge – the nature and scope of rights, the identification of beneficiaries, and the regulation of the public domain have been left to further development. Finally, as described in the chapter by Sara Castillo Vargas, "Costa Rica's Legal Framework for the Sponsorship and Protection of Its Cultural Heritage," conserving the cultural and architectural heritage in Costa Rica pertains to other administrative offices and is not seen by the environmental movement as part of its tasks.

REFERENCES AND BIBLIOGRAPHY

Solís Rivera, V., 1997 *Una ley de biodiversidad que responde a un compromiso con la vida* (A Biodiversity Law Responsible for a Commitment to Life), in Ramírez, Luis, "El desafío de la biodiversidad" (The Biodiversity Challenge). The Legislative Assembly, San Jose.

Ramírez, L., 1997, *El desafío de la biodiversidad* (The Biodiversity Challenge). The Legislative Assembly, San Jose.

Madrigal, P., 2000, *OGM's y Derechos de Propiedad Intelectual* (Genetically Modified Organisms and Intellectual Property Rights), Seminar on the current situation and outlook for genetically modified organisms and their relation to intellectual property rights.

Federación Costarricense para la Conservación del Ambiente FECON, Press Release, April 15, 2004, "Movimiento ecologista exige moratoria" (Ecology Movement Demands Moratorium).

Salazar, R., Valverde, M., 1999. *Biotecnología, bioseguridad y legislación: el caso de Costa Rica* (Biotechnology, Biosafety and Legislation, the Case of Costa Rica). Revista de Ciencias Ambientales, No. 16, June, Heredia, Costa Rica.

CHAPTER FIFTY-NINE

Partnership Paradigms Combining Microbial Discovery with Preservation of Tropical Biodiversity and Sustainable Development

Barbara T. Hoffman

Over the past fifteen years, the international community has paid increasing attention to the alarming rate of the loss of global biodiversity. Biodiversity is a compound of the words "biology" and "diversity." Biodiversity is commonly used to describe the number and variety of living organisms on the planet including genes, species and ecosystems that are the result of 3 billion years of evolution. Biodiversity can be divided into genetic diversity and species diversity. Only 1.4 million of the 5 to 30 million species have been catalogued.

Species extinction is a natural part of the evolutionary process. Due to human activities, primarily deforestation, however, species and ecosystems are threatened with destruction at an alarming rate. The losses are taking place primarily in tropical rain forests where 50%–90% of identified species live. The most recent predictions indicate losses of some 4,000 species a year. In other words, 25% of the world's biodiversity is lost to extinction each year due to tropical deforestation alone, at which rate it has been estimated that up to 10% of the world's species will be extinct in 25 years.

Historically, over 25% of all U.S. prescription drugs have been developed or derived from natural compounds, many of which are found in the extreme and interesting ecological niches in tropical rain forests. As changes in technology driving discovery efforts have made bioprospecting strategies viable, the notion of biodiversity and the prospect of unlocking the magic of nature for the benefit of both developed and less developed countries has promoted partnerships among government, non-governmental organizations (NGOs), and the pharmaceutical and biotechnology industries that may serve as paradigms for partnerships in other areas of cultural heritage policy.

INBio – MERCK AGREEMENT

The INBio – Merck agreement is one of the most widely recognized and discussed bioprospecting efforts in the world.[1] Before the adoption of the CBD, and before Costa Rica enacted its Biological Diversity Law, the arrangement had already been concluded between the U.S. pharmaceutical company Merck & Co., Inc. and the *Instituto Nacional de Biodiversidad* (INBio). INBio was created in 1989 as an NGO in response to a national concern for the accelerating loss of Costa Rican biological diversity and operates under the premise that a tropical country will succeed in conservation efforts, only if biodiversity contributes to the country's sustainable economic development.

INBio's purpose is to collaborate with private industry in order to create mechanisms to help maintain the conservation areas of Costa Rica by making them economically viable, providing extracts of plants collected from rainforests in Costa Rica's national parks.[2]

Under the Merck agreement, a certain number of plant, insect, and micro-organism samples from the catalogue are made available to Merck. These samples are initially extracted and processed by INBio and their properties are explored at Merck facilities in Spain and the U.S.[3] In exchange for the right to screen this catalogue for biological activities, Merck paid some $1.1 million up front, as well as an unspecified percentage of future royalties. Under this contract, Merck scientists evaluated plant, insect, and animal samples from protected Costa Rican government reserves to determine if they might have pharmaceutical or agricultural applications. Ten percent of the initial fee and 50% of the royalties were then funneled back into conservation and biodiversity protection through an arrangement with the Costa Rican government. Considered a success by all parties involved, the agreement has been renewed twice, most recently in 1997 until 2000.

David Greeley, Merck's Senior Director of Public Affairs and Policy for Latin America, in an executive report provided to the editor, stated that even after Merck's research with InBIO ended, Merck, through its subsidiary in Costa Rica, continued to collaborate with InBIO to highlight some of the aspects of the multi-year collaboration. In 2000 and then again in 2002, Merck provided InBIO with two grants, the main features of which included the development and construction of a permanent exhibit on Biodiversity Prospecting within the INBioparque; funding for the development and construction of a permanent exhibit on the INBio-Merck Collaboration Case Study within the Bioprospecting module of INBioparque; and funding for follow-up training for INBioparque guides during the first year of operation of the park.[4]

Kerry ten Kate and Sarah A. Laird describe research agreements between INBio and a number of other companies. To

[1] Legal and Economic Aspects of Bioprospecting. In: Blakeney (ed.), *Intellectual Property Aspects of Ethnobiology*, p. 63; Columbia University School of International and Public Affairs, Access to Genetic Resources: An Evaluation of the Development and Implementation of Recent Regulation and Access Agreements; Environmental Policy Studies Working Paper No. 4, New York 1999, p. 14.

[2] *Columbia University School of International and Public Affairs* (fn. 362), p. 19.

[3] *Columbia University School of International and Public Affairs* (fn. 362), p. 9.

[4] Editor's files.

date, bioprospecting agreements have contributed more than $2.5 million U.S. to MINAE, Costa Rican conservation areas, Public universities, and other groups at INBio, particularly its Inventory Program.[5]

INTERNATIONAL COOPERATIVE BIODIVERSITY GROUPS (ICBG) PROGRAM

The U.S. government, for its part, has developed similar partnerships with developing countries to promote pharmaceutical prospecting and biodiversity conservation alike. The National Institute of Health (NIH), the National Science Foundation, and the USAID established the five-year International Cooperative Biodiversity Groups (ICBG) program in 1993. The program funded partnerships between academics, companies, government agencies, and local peoples and local institutions in source countries to engage in bioprospecting efforts throughout Latin America and Africa. Its funding accounts for FY95 $2.35 million with capacity in 20 different institutions and training over 130 individuals. The ICBG program stresses three primary goals:

(1) drug discovery,
(2) conservation of the environment and genetic resources of the source country, and
(3) development of sustainable economic activities for the people of the source country.

By adding economic value to biodiversity, therefore, this program aims to enhance the motivations surrounding environmental conservation to the economic, political and health care realms. In late February 1997, representatives from each group convened at NIH for the first evaluation of the program by an outside review panel.

Each of the five projects has developed its own intellectual right structure. For instance, in the ICBG–Peru project discussed below the U.S. side entered into a contract with the indigenous tribe, the Aguaruna, offering a "know-how" license to compensate them for assisting in American bioprospecting efforts. A know-how license covers the intangible resources such as in-depth knowledge that leads to the collection of certain plants. In exchange for annual payments, milestone payments and royalties, the Aguaruna are giving the U.S. interests involved the right to use plant samples with their knowledge for a certain period of time.

ICBG–PERU

The stated purpose of the successfully completed ICBG–Peru[6] project was to identify new pharmaceuticals based originally on ethnobotanical prescreening, while concomitantly conserving biodiversity in northern Peru by enhancing economic growth among the collaborating Aguaruna people. The focus of the research has been both on globally important diseases and syndromes and maladies of serious concern in Peru.

ICBG–Peru originated as a partnership consisting of three universities, a corporate partner, and an indigenous organization. The Principal Investigator is Dr. Walter H. Lewis, Washington University, St. Louis, Missouri.

The legal basis for the ICBG–Peru project is a set of interconnected agreements, including: (1) the basic Biological Collecting Agreement, which outlines who is involved in the program, where and under what circumstances collecting can occur, and what annual collecting fees will be provided to the collaborating Aguaruna organizations by the corporate partner; (2) a License Option and a License Option Amendment Agreement between Washington University and G.D. Searle & Company, detailing a basis for their interactions and establishing royalty rates for pharmaceutical products and how these rates are to be shared; (3) a later negotiated Know-how License Agreement that prescribes an annual license fee to be paid by the corporate partner to the collaborating Aguaruna groups while their knowledge is being used in extraction and screening programs, and also establishes certain milestone payments to be paid by the corporate partner; and (4) two subsidiary agreements outlining the nature of the collaborative relationship between Washington University and the two other academic institutions involved. Annual collection and know-how license fees paid by the corporate partner are to be deposited into a fund that will make grants to assist the Aguarunas with education and that will ensure the development of new conservation and sustainable development projects within the Aguaruna communities. Royalties will be divided equally among the three universities and the Aguaruna peoples, with fully 75% of any royalty income returning to Peru.[7]

Each agreement recognizes that the traditional knowledge of the indigenous people is their cultural legacy and that the people have a right for such knowledge to be protected *from* the public domain. They state that such knowledge is being provided voluntarily and is being retained in confidence. Should such information prove valuable, then the original IPR of the indigenous people over such knowledge would be preserved through the filing of appropriate patents, and by the inventors assigning shared ownership of the patents to the indigenous federations. The agreements also recognize the ownership and patrimony of the Peruvian state over certain tangible resources (whole plants) collected by the researchers in Peru for scientific purposes and for making extracts, fractions, and isolating compounds of potential commercial use as new pharmaceuticals. The agreements assure that collecting activities do not endanger natural populations of the plant

[5] Kerry ten Kate and Sarah A. Laird, The Commercial Use of Biodiversity: Access to Genetic Resources and Benefit-Sharing (1999).

[6] For a complete discussion of ICBG–Peru, see W. H. Lewis, Ethics and Practice in Ethnobiology http:law.wustl.edu/centeris/confpapers/.

[7] See Joshua P. Rosenthal, Drug Discovery, Economic Development and Conservation: The International Cooperative Biodiversity Groups, 37 Pharmaceutical Biology 5 (Supplement 1999). Also Walter H. Lewis *et al.*, Peruvian Medicinal Plant Sources for New Pharmaceuticals (International Cooperative Biodiversity Group Peru) and W. H. Lewis, Ethics, ibid.

species or their habitats and that a program of restoration to help conserve medicinal and other plants would be initiated.

The Prior Informed Consent procedure was divided into two phases. In the first phase, research collectors mainly talked with leaders of the stakeholders to acquaint them with the project, obtain their consent to talk with members of the indigenous communities, and to attend the Aguaruna Congress (IPAAMAMU). The meetings also tried to map out the broad conditions for agreements being reached between the universities and the corporate partner and the stakeholders. These conditions included:

- A flat collection payment for plant samples collected annually over four years;
- A license fee paid as long as Searle continued to make use in assays of plant extracts accompanied by traditional medicinal intellectual property;
- Milestone payments during the development of new products;
- A shared royalty payment based on net sales of products;
- Favorable terms of supply and distribution of products in Peru; and
- Intellectual property rights, such as sharing in patent ownership.

Dr. Lewis, in his Conclusions and Recommendations, observed that:

> The ICBG-Peru project incorporated the goals of the CBD by accessing genetic material and traditional knowledge with the PIC of the people involved. It recognized the rights of the indigenous people to their traditional knowledge and compensated them fairly. It also recognized the sovereign rights of the government of Peru, provided them with benefits, particularly by involving source country institutions and transferring back knowledge and technology to the country. The project has also attempted to fulfill the mandate of conservation and sustainable harvesting.
>
> The ICBG-Peru project succeeded in its mandate to protect the traditional knowledge of indigenous people as it was uncompromisingly fair on three principles: communication, confidentiality, and compensation.[8]

NOVOZYMES

Novozmyes' approach to microbial discovery does not involve the use of traditional knowledge. It has also been discussed as a model for partnerships in combining microbial discovery with the preservation of tropical biodiversity. Flying under the banner of "unlocking the magic of nature," Novozymes has developed certain guiding principles:

- No microbial strains or natural material obtained without prior informed consent from the country of origin will be included in screening;
- All materials screened are covered by contracts and/or material transfer agreements;
- Conditions should be on mutually agreed terms and should include benefit sharing, intellectual property rights, and technology transfer where appropriate;
- Contracts should be cleared by the proper authority in the country of origin; and
- The country of origin should do the collections and will be named in relevant publications and patent applications.

Novozymes has identified three methods for establishing win/win collaborations:

- Include both monetary and nonmonetary compensations (via technology transfer and capacity building);
- Include compensations to country of origin for the mere option to screen accessed strains *and* benefits if later commercialized; and
- Prioritize scientist to scientist collaboration.

Novozymes has also identified five pitfalls of the CBD:

(1) mismatch of expectations;
(2) middle-men take the benefit;
(3) difficulties obtaining prior informed consent;
(4) obstacles for scientist to scientist collaboration; and
(5) academia not fully implementing CBD.

Conclusions and recommendations:

- Access to biological resources should be provided by prior informed consent under mutually agreed terms, preferably through scientist to scientist collaboration, leaving copy strain in country of origin; and
- Code of conduct should be worked out for obtaining prior informed consent and approved templates for mutually agreed terms should be made.

Novozymes' code of conduct for access benefit sharing outlines two phases, the screening phase and the commercial phase.

In the screening phase:

- Industry gets option to evaluate new strains;
- Country of origin receives capacity building and technology transfer.

In the commercial phase:

- Country of origin receives monetary benefits (up front lump sums or royalties), based on the contribution made and on actual sales.[9]

[8] In Editor's files. A presentation by Dr. Lene Lange, Professor of Science and Director, Microbial Discovery, Novozymes Presentation to the World Federation Culture Collections, November 2004, Japan. An excellent article on ICBG initiatives is "Intellectual Property, Genetic Resources and Traditional Knowledge Protection: Thinking Globally Acting Locally" by Charles R. McManis (*Symposium: Traditional Knowledge, Intellectual Property, and Indigenous Culture*, 2003 Yeshiva University Cardozo Journal of International and Comparative Law, Summer 2003, 11 Cardozo J. Int'l & Comp. L. 547). The editor would strongly recommend the entire volume to anyone unlearned in the subject.

[9] *Le Figaro*, Samedi 29 – Dimanche 20, Janvier 2005.

Contractual arrangements have traditionally been used as a means to arrive at a consensus in transactions involving the access to genetic resources and benefit sharing therefrom. Contractual arrangements catapulted into importance following the Merck-INBio agreement, and have since, as illustrated by the example of ICBG and Novozymes, continually been utilized as mechanisms that can be used to resolve the contentious positions adopted by the developed nations on one hand and the biodiversity-rich nations on the other hand. Various committees, including the expert panels of the CBD and the World Intellectual Property Organization (WIPO), have released several reports that comment on the importance of such contractual arrangements. These reports also contain model clauses that the parties to the agreement could use, so that the interests of the provider of biodiversity and/or traditional knowledge, the recipient of the same, and the local community involved are all protected.

CHAPTER SIXTY

Costa Rica's Legal Framework for the Sponsorship and Protection of Its Cultural Heritage

Sara Castillo Vargas

In 2001, for the first time in Costa Rica's history, two people were sentenced to prison for destruction and vandalism of cultural property. The Casona de Santa Rosa case concerned an old hacienda in the northern part of the country, where Costa Ricans fought and won a battle against William Walker and his army. Walker was trying to gain control of Central America in order to use its inhabitants as substitute slaves in the southern United States, following the abolition of slavery. The destruction of the Casona de Santa Rosa by vandals is regarded by Costa Ricans as a national tragedy.

Costa Rica is a small country with four million inhabitants and more than 500 years of post-Columbus history, 221 of which were under the rule of Spain and the rest, as a democratic republic. The dazzling beauty of Costa Rica and the splendour of its forests and coastlines overshadow the relatively small and humble heritage of its cities. A history characterised by civil organisation, civilian governments, and an emphasis on education has left Costa Rica with a patrimony consisting mainly of schools, churches, and vernacular architecture. The emphasis placed on the country's ecological resources has not encouraged Costa Ricans to accord much value to the country's architectural structures and cultural heritage.

INCENTIVES FOR PRESERVATION

As of 1995, Costa Rica has a new law for the protection of its architectural heritage. One of the innovations of Law No. 7555 for the Protection of Cultural Architectonic Heritage is the section on incentives for persons and private organisations that preserve and/or sponsor Costa Rica's heritage. The incentives are intended to encourage landowners, citizens, and communities to regain control and ownership of their cultural heritage, after many years of failed attempts by the state to centralise its control and ownership. The previous law, Law No. 5397 of 8 November 1973, promoted the purchase of property by the state, which was extremely expensive. The state did not have the resources to purchase the property in question, and, during this long and fruitless process, landowners preferred to demolish the buildings instead. As a result, Costa Rica lost many important buildings, which were demolished by their owners or simply abandoned.

The new law introduces several different kinds of incentives:

- Income tax deductions apply to donations and investments made by landowners and ordinary citizens for the preservation of Costa Rica's patrimony and/or the improvement of buildings that have already been classified as historic architectural structures.
- Land transfer tax deductions eliminate the high tax that is imposed on the sale or donation of property classified as being of historical interest.
- Another incentive is an exemption from property tax on luxurious buildings already classified as being of historical interest. This exemption also does away with the payment of stamp duty on paperwork approving construction in locations of historical interest.
- Public institutions are allowed to make investments and donations for the preservation and purchase of properties of architectural and historical value.
- The new law lays down that money collected through fines for violations of the law and bequests made to the state for the purpose of preserving Costa Rica's heritage must be added to the budget of the Ministry of Culture and used for preservation works.
- It is the Ministry of Culture's legal duty to negotiate lines of credit for private and public entities at state banks for the purpose of financing the restoration of property that is of architectural and historical interest.
- Finally, the new law imposes a fifteen percent tax on basic international rates that will be charged by means of a special series of stamps featuring pictures of Costa Rican monuments. The money that is collected in this manner must be used to implement the new law for the preservation of Costa Rica's patrimony.

It is very satisfying to see these measures in legal form. However, because of the fact that the law only entered into force quite recently, and because of a lack of political power to enforce the law, none of these measures has been implemented in a meaningful way.

It was not until very recently that the body responsible for government budget control began to insist that government departments set aside funds for the preservation of buildings of historical value under their administration.

CULTURAL HERITAGE RESEARCH AND CONSERVATION CENTRE

The Cultural Heritage Research and Conservation Centre, the government organ responsible for monitoring the implementation of Law No. 7555, plays a significant role. Using the powers provided by the new law, it files criminal cases against people who have violated the law by damaging or destroying protected buildings. With the assistance of the Prosecutor's Office for the Environment, people are being sentenced to prison or to community service, which often involves work in the field of preservation, for actions that are detrimental to Costa Rica's patrimony.

Even more recent is the effort to include zoning and conservation parameters in the new urban planning proposal for the Great Metropolitan Area, which is currently being drafted.

The authorities, in contrast, have not been so faithful to their duties, and the present administration has not yet signed the bill that reinforces Law No. 7555 by laying down more specific provisions on case procedure and law enforcement.

It is not known how long it will take for the new urban planning proposal to be approved and implemented because it requires strong political will and involves restrictions on developers and others who are used to doing what is in accordance with their interests.

After many years of tense and conflictual relations with representatives of the Roman Catholic Church, a highly satisfactory level of understanding and sensibility has been achieved on their part in matters related to the preservation of their structures. This is very important because some of the most significant examples of Costa Rica's patrimony are churches owned by the Roman Catholic Church.

On the whole, it is fair to say that the officers of the Cultural Heritage Research and Conservation Centre are devoted professionals who do a lot with very little. It cannot be said, however, that the government of Costa Rica has a coherent policy on cultural heritage protection.

STATE–PRIVATE FORMS OF SPONSORSHIP: THE CASE OF ICOMOS

ICOMOS-Costa Rica was formed in 1983 as an asociación – a nongovernmental and nonprofit organisation with professional and cultural goals. It is a branch of the International Council on Monuments and Sites (ICOMOS), a UNESCO "A" type organisation for the preservation of the world's monuments and sites. According to Costa Rican legislation in this area, organisations of this kind enjoy certain benefits because they are regarded as assisting the government and the community in the achievement of certain social objectives. In addition, such organisations must comply with a set of rules concerning their internal organisation and use of resources. Their funding comes from members' dues, donations, grants, payments for services, and other forms of legal fundraising.

At the outset, ICOMOS-Costa Rica had no other funding than the goodwill and fees of the ten or fifteen members who established it. Money for basic expenses such as communications and stationary was provided by the members, who have always been willing to put up extra money for specific projects.

In May 1989, President Oscar Arias of Costa Rica signed a decree by which banana producers donated one colón for each box of bananas they exported to help preserve the country's cultural heritage. The money was collected by the National Banana Association and given to ICOMOS-Costa Rica. This was an historic act on the part of the government and the banana producers for the conservation of Costa Rica's architectural patrimony. Instead of simply applying another tax, the government approved the direct transfer of funds from the banana producers to civil-society organisations. As a result of the aforementioned decree, 43,840,000 colón were collected, which is a significant amount for a resourceless organisation like ICOMOS.

Unfortunately, only eleven months later, in March 1990, the decree was abolished and the money collecting stopped. However, the amount already collected served as initial investment capital for the organisation, which, by means of profitable investments and a policy of budgetary austerity, managed to double this amount by 1996.

These resources provided ICOMOS with new strength and allowed the organisation to initiate new projects, for example, the creation of a master plan for the historic centre of Limón. The significance of this city, located in the Caribbean region, is that it possesses one of the country's richest multi-ethnic heritages. Here, native Costa Ricans and immigrants of European, African, and Asian origin met and mingled, and this is reflected in the architecture and urban structure of the city.

In 1996, using the same resources, ICOMOS purchased a property of great patrimonial value in the historic centre of San José in which to establish its headquarters. The restoration of the building has already been started. This will allow ICOMOS to turn the property into a true centre for the propagation of Costa Rica's cultural heritage.

On the basis of the profits it earns from the original donations of the banana producers, ICOMOS prepares an annual plan of activities that include education, public information, restoration, and the legal defence of Costa Rica's patrimony.

In recent years, ICOMOS members have worked together with schoolchildren and youth organisations, the Costa Rican Tourism Board, and state universities through preservation workshops, research, and restoration projects. ICOMOS has also contributed to the restoration of the National Theatre, the finest piece of European-style architecture in San José, the excavation of two pre-Columbian sites, and many other preservation activities.

In 1994, the government of Costa Rica classified ICOMOS as a public-interest organisation. This status offers tax benefits relating to the purchase and import of goods. Until now, ICOMOS has not made use of this advantage, but it is believed that it will lead to significant savings in the implementation of the organisation's future projects.

ICOMOS has started to sell professional services to its members. An example of this is the contract signed by ICOMOS with the Costa Rican Art Museum regarding the restoration of the building in which it is located. This is a very promising project, because it serves two purposes: It contributes to ICOMOS resources and helps to preserve Costa Rica's architectural heritage.

Attempts to compensate for a reduction in the interest earned on the original donations have led to efforts to find other sources of funding. For example, a private company donated its services during the restoration of the headquarters of ICOMOS, which agreed to recognise the company publicly for donating its services.

In spite of the efforts described so far, the efforts and resources of ICOMOS are but a drop in the ocean in a country that does not have a strong culture of preservation.

CONCLUSION

Costa Rica has taken a few basic steps towards the establishment of a real protection system by enacting adequate legislation, providing direct and indirect funding for restoration activities, and taking a number of cases to court. These steps are significant but, regrettably, not sufficient. In spite of the good intentions of the legislature, Costa Ricans have not learned to value their country's patrimony. The efforts devoted to architectural preservation do not equal the efforts devoted to environmental preservation. In Costa Rica's main cities, landowners are demolishing historic buildings to build parking lots, turning the hearts of these cities into an ugly collection of pavements without identity or soul that are full of vehicles during the daytime and desolate at night.

We must keep up our efforts on behalf of Costa Rica, so that its cities do not become empty spaces the identity, history, and soul of which can be erased by the winds of globalisation and economic pressure.

CHAPTER SIXTY-ONE

Financial Regulations and Tax Incentives with the Aim to Stimulate the Protection and Preservation of Cultural Heritage in Spain

María Rosa Suárez-Inclán Ducassi

Within the present legal framework for the protection, conservation, and management of cultural heritage in Spain,[1] special attention has been paid, in the last two decades, to the implementation of financial regulations by the establishment of stimulating measures and tax incentives. Several of the most recent legal measures in this field have not only served to recognise the increasing importance of the private sector (the so-called *Third Sector* or *Third Way*) in the promotion and safeguard of cultural heritage but also to foster its development.

This tendency is also in accordance with the guidelines of the *European Green Book*, which recognises the need to encourage the social responsibility of business entrepreneurs.

Given both the increasing strength of cultural industries and the limits of the government's action in the field of culture, the economic contribution and the effort of private entities and individuals have become more and more necessary. Public authorities may well exert an influence as well as some important functions of management and control, but the capacity of creating culture belongs to private groups and individuals, and therefore remains in the civil sphere.

This chapter refers to the most important fiscal measures to encourage the protection and preservation of the cultural heritage, which are the special tax regime for foundations and nonprofit associations of public utility and the tax incentives for patronage.

Besides some partial provisions adopted since 1986, the first specific legislation represented by private participation in activities of public interest was the Law 30/1994 24 November on Foundations and Tax Incentives for Private Contributions in Activities of General Interest.[2] Experience with the law over several years showed that despite the limited extent of the incentives, there was a spectacular development of the private sector in this field. This evidence led to the promulgation of a new Law 49/2002 of December 23rd on the Tax Regime of Non-profit Entities and Tax Incentives for Patronage, which was complemented by the Law 50/2002 of December 26th on Foundations. The first of these new legal instruments has introduced a great flexibility on the requirements to benefit from the tax incentives, which can be obtained on free optional basis by simply communicating this purpose to the relevant authorities and without depending on a specific administrative permission. It has also provided a legal security on the development of the role of the private entities. This law is aiming not only to the establishment of a legal framework on tax incentives for the nonprofit entities, but also for patronage activities carried out by private persons and private institutions.

The new tax system for a nonprofit entity is based on two aspects: (1) The concept of this kind of entities, which are defined in the law as foundations, nongovernmental

[1] (Note: The term "Law" or "Act" is used interchangeably in this text to refer to Acts of Parliament.)

[2] The following are some of the key measures:

(1) Relating to *constructors and firms involved in public works, in addition to restorers, owners and holders*, the Law establishes preferential access to official credit for funding, public works, conservation, upkeep and rehabilitation, in addition to archaeological prospectuses and excavations carried out in areas declared to be of cultural interest. In order to do this, the Public Administrations may establish, by means of agreements with public and private entities, the conditions of using credit benefits.

(2) As regards *public works built and development by private persons by virtue of State dispensation without financial contribution from the State*, one percent of the overall budget shall be applied to funding conservation. It can also be applied to enrichment works for the Spanish Historical Heritage, preference being given to the works themselves or their immediate surroundings. An exception is made in the case of public works with and overall budget under 600,000 Euro, which may concern the State Security or the security of public services. The Ministry of Education and Culture drafts a yearly Plan for Conservation and Enrichment debited to the said funds. In order to execute the projects and programs, cooperation from the Administration must be requested.

(3) *Debt payment in different taxes*: Succession and Gift Tax, Property Tax, Personal Income Tax, and Corporate Income Tax may be paid *by handing over assets belonging to the Spanish Historical Heritage* that are registered at the General Registry of Assets of Cultural Interest or included in the General Inventory. In such case, the Board of Classification, Appraisal and Export of Assets belonging to the Spanish Historical Heritage shall appraise the said assets for this purpose.

(4) *Exemptions and other benefits: Assets belonging to the Spanish Historical Heritage registered in the aforementioned Registry and Inventory.* These assets are exempt from Property Tax. They may be subject to appraisal for tax purposes up to their market value, being exempted from increased capital tax, unless they are part of the holder's floating assets. Likewise, the following are exempt from Local Real State Tax:
- Monuments and gardens each declared to be assets belonging to the Spanish Historical Heritage
- Those classified as "specially protected" by the urban development plan for archaeological areas
- When included in classified Historical Sites, those at least fifty years old that receive complete urban protection

There is an exemption from other local taxes on property or its use and conveyance when owners or holders of real property rights have undertaken conservation, improvement, or rehabilitation works on Real State declared to be of cultural interest.

These exemptions shall be applied in the terms established by respective municipal regulations.

organizations, associations of public utility, and sport federations. (2) the special systems established by this law for both corporate income tax and local tax, from which these entities can benefit.

As required in the previous Law of 1994, seventy percent of the total income, gains, and revenues obtained as a result of their economic activities[3] must be devoted to activities of general interest within the next four years, though the necessary expenses for their obtainment can be deducted.[4] The rest, if not applied to the aforementioned activities, must be devoted to increase the property of the entity or its financial savings. For this purpose, the nonprofit entities are now allowed to freely acquire capital assets or share holdings in mercantile companies.

With respect to corporate income tax, the nonexempt economic activities cannot exceed forty percent of the total income of the entity, which represents a considerable increase in this field.

Another requirement for an entity wishing to benefit from the special regime established by this law is that the members of its board of directors cannot receive any kind of salary, though they may obtain economic compensation for their role as director if they develop other activities not directly related to its directive function. This provision helps in practice to guarantee transparency and the real philanthropic role of these entities.

With respect to corporate income tax, the law has introduced the following substantial incentives, which have contributed to the creation of a considerable number of new nonprofit entities and to increase their activities on a much more professional basis:

(1) Tax exemptions for income and gains obtained from the following sources: movable and immovable properties, the sale or purchase of any kind of goods and rights, exempt economic activities, and those specifically assigned by the law to nonprofit entities.
(2) A list of exempt economic activities: thus, it is no longer necessary to apply for specific tax exemptions for income derived from any activity of this kind, as it was necessary before. This innovation has introduced a very positive reduction in bureaucratic aspects and has also provided a framework of legal security for the activities undertaken by these entities.
(3) The application of corporate income tax to the nonexempt activities as described earlier.
(4) The local tax system is well defined so as to determine which activities and entities are exempt by law (*ex lege*), without depending on the power of decision of the local authorities. The new law has also introduced a considerable number of exemptions that were not contemplated in the law of 1994, such as, for instance, that referring to the Urban Land Gain Tax.

For more detailed information on the special tax system of nonprofit entities and their regulation, see the systematic resume included in footnote.[5]

[3] The benefits obtained for the sale of immovable properties where the entity develops its own activity are not considered as income for this purpose, provided that they are reinvested in other immovable properties subject to the same condition.

[4] Expenses derived from external services, staff, and functioning, in addition to financial and tax expenses applied to obtain the above income, gains and revenues are deductible. Only the expenses made for the accomplishment of the specific statutory role cannot be deducted.

[5] Among other entities, *both foundations and associations declared of public utility* may benefit from the special measures provided for in Act 49/2002 of 23 December on the Tax Regime of Nonprofit Entities and Tax Incentives for Patronage.

These entities must meet the following *requirements*:

(1) They must pursue general interest purposes (such as cultural, scientific, promotion of volunteer work, or other aims of general interest);
(2) They must allocate to pursue their specific purposes at least seventy percent of the income and revenues derived from: (a) economic activities; (b) transfers of properties and rights of ownership (income from onerous transfers of immovable properties where they conduct their activity is not included, provided that such income is reinvested in properties and rights of like nature); (c) income obtained by any other means, after deducting the expenses incurred to obtain such income and excluding from this calculation the expenses incurred for compliance with statutory aims or the purpose of the nonprofit entity. Calculation of income will not include contributions or donations received in the form of a capital asset. Nonprofit entities must allocate the remainder of income and revenue to increasing capital assets or reserves.
(3) They must not carry out economic activities unrelated to their purpose or statutory aim. This requirement will be understood to be fulfilled if annual net income from this type of nonexempt activities does not exceed forty percent of the total annual income of the entity and does not violate the laws for the defense of free competition. The leasing of immovable property belonging to the entity does not constitute an economic activity for this purpose.
(4) The founders, associates, patrons, statutory representatives, members of the governing board and their spouses or relatives to the fourth degree inclusive must not be the principal beneficiaries of the foundation's activities or benefit from special conditions. Nevertheless, this rule will not apply to foundations the purpose of which is the conservation and restoration of properties belonging to national historic heritage that comply with the requirements of this specific regulation, in particular with respect to the obligations of public visiting and exhibitions of said properties.
(5) The positions of patrons, statutory representative, and member of the governing board must not be remunerated, notwithstanding the right to be reimbursed for duly justified expenses incurred in the performance of their functions, as long as they do not exceed the limit for per diem allowances exempt from taxation. Patrons, statutory representatives, and board members may receive remuneration for giving services to the entity, including those given within the framework of an employment relationship, other than those involved in the performance of the functions corresponding to them as patrons or members of the governing board, but such persons may not participate in the economic results of the entity, either directly or indirectly through a third party person or entity.
(6) In the case of dissolution, the assets of the foundation must be transferred in their entirety to foundations and associations qualifying as beneficiaries of patronage or other public entities pursuing general interest purposes, and this circumstance must be expressly provided for in the founding business or in the statutes of the dissolved entity.
(7) They are legally registered in the corresponding Registry.
(8) They comply with their accounting obligations, prepare a detailed financial report in accordance with applicable regulations, and file it in due time with the public body in charge of the corresponding registry.

With respect to tax incentives for patronage, the most important measures introduced by the new law are the following:

(1) There is a list of those entities that may benefit from this special system.
(2) Tax incentives for the gift of rights, such as the usufruct over goods, rights, and securities without compensation.

These entities will be granted the following *tax benefits*:
1. *Corporate Income Tax*

1.1 Exempt Income
1. Income derived from the following will be exempt:
   (a) Gifts and donations received to support the purpose of the entity, including contributions and donations in the form of capital assets and financial assistance received through the business – nonprofit entity agreements regulated in article 25 of this Act;
   (b) Membership fees paid by associates, collaborators, or benefactors;
   (c) Public grants, except those used to finance nonexempt economic activities.
2. Income derived from the movable and immovable property of the entity.
3. Income from acquisitions or transfers, whatever their modality, of properties or rights.
4. Income obtained from exempt economic activities in the cases foreseen in the Act.
5. Income obtained from other exempt income sources included in the aforementioned items.

1.2 Exempt Economic Activities
Income derived from economic activities carried out in compliance with the specific purpose of the foundation will be exempt, as is the case of the following:
1. Economic activities related to properties declared of cultural interest in accordance with the National Historic Heritage Act and respective regulations of the Autonomous Communities, in addition to museums, libraries, archives, and documentation centers, provided that they meet the requirements established in said Act, in particular, with respect to the obligations of visiting and public exhibition of these properties.
2. Economic activities consisting of the organizations of exhibits, lectures, symposia, courses, or seminars.
3. Economic activities related to the preparation, editing, publication, and sale of books, magazines, and brochures, in addition to audiovisual and multimedia materials.
4. Economic activities that are merely ancillary or complementary to the exempt economic activities or the activities aimed to comply with statutory aims or purpose of the nonprofit entity. Economic activities will not be considered as ancillary or complementary if their net income exceeds twenty percent of the total income of the entity.
5. Economic activities of minor importance. Economic activities will be considered as minor if their net income does not exceed 20,000 euros.

1.3 Determination of Taxable Base and Tax Rate
1. Nonprofit entities will only be subject to corporate income tax on income derived from nonexempt economic activities.
2. The following will not be considered as tax-deductible expenses: (a) expenses attributable solely to exempt income; (b) amounts allocated to amortize assets not related to taxable economic activities; (c) amounts corresponding to the application of results and, in particular, surpluses from nonexempt economic activities.
3. The positive taxable base corresponding to income derived from nonexempt economic activities will be taxed at a rate of ten percent.

1.4 Income not Subject to Withholding
Exempt income provided for in this Act will not be subject to withholdings or payments on account.

1.5 Obligation to File
Entities that opt for this tax regime are obliged to file a Corporate Income Tax return for their total income, both exempt and nonexempt.

(3) This way, the gifts, donations, and contributions made in favour of nonprofit entities will enable a deduction in the personal net taxable income of twenty-five percent of their amount. In the same cases, the deduction from corporate income tax will be of thirty-five percent in the net taxable income (this represents a great advantage because in the previous law this deduction was made in the taxable base). The amount of this deduction cannot exceed ten percent of the total taxable income in the tax period, but the amount in excess can be deducted in the subsequent ten years. These percentages of deduction may be respectively increased up to a limit of thirty percent and forty percent when the patronage is exerted to favour the priority activities included in a list established by the General Budgetary Act within the scope of general interest purposes.

Finally, the law regulates the benefits applicable to other patronage activities distinct from gifts, donations, and

1.6 Conditions Required for Application of This Special Tax Regime
Application of this special tax regime is subject to compliance with the conditions and requirements described previously. Failure to comply will result in the obligation to pay all amounts that would have been paid if the entity had not benefited from this special tax regime and late payment interests, without prejudice to any fines that may be applicable.

2. *Local Taxes*
1. Properties in the ownership of entities that have opted for this special regime will be exempt from payment of Real Estate Tax (except those related to economic activities not exempt from Corporate Income Tax) and the Transfer Tax on properties acquired by onerous transactions.
2. These entities will also be exempt from the Urban Land Gains Tax.

The application of both exemptions will be subject to communication to the municipal government concerned that the entity has opted for this special regime and compliance with all applicable conditions and requirements. These exemptions are established without prejudice to those provided for in Act 39/1988 of 28 December regulating local taxes.

Nonprofit foundations and associations that opt for this special tax regime are also *qualifying recipients for patronage*, given that the gifts, donations, and contributions they receive enjoy the tax incentives provided for in this Act.

With regard to *charitable building entities* established under article 5 of Act of 15 July 1954, *they may opt for the special tax regime* foreseen for nonprofit foundations and associations, provided that: (a) they comply with the requirements established in the specific Act regulating these entities; (b) those specifically indicated in Act 49/2002 of 23 December regulating the Tax Regime of Nonprofit Entities, and (c) they are duly registered in the corresponding registry of the state or autonomous administration. However, *the status of qualifying recipients for patronage will not be applicable to them* and, therefore, they will not be eligible for the tax incentives for patronage provided for in this Act.

With regard to *religious entities*, refer to the information given at the end of section III and footnotes 2 and 3.

The General State Budget Act may amend, in accordance with the provisions of article 134, paragraph 7 of the Spanish Constitution: (a) The tax rate of nonprofit entities; (b) The percentage of deduction and limits for their application provided for in this Act.

With respect to *Value Added Tax, Real State Tax*, and *Local tax applied to economical activities*, nonprofit entities are exempt from them for the activities carried out in compliance with their purposes that do not imply a financial gain of a nonexempt nature.

contributions. The main new measures introduced by this law are the following:

(1) The expenses derived from business–nonprofit entity agreements on general interest is activities will be deductible from both personal and corporate income tax. The limits fixed by the previous law of 1994 have been suppressed.
(2) The limits for the deduction of the expenses made by an enterprise on activities of general interest have also been suppressed.
(3) A well-defined legal framework for programs of support to the priority activities of general interest is established by law, which will specify the maximum of their contents as well as their duration and basic rules.

The law introduces some additional provisions that have also contributed to stimulate the conservation of cultural heritage. The more notable refer to special benefits in the payment of personal income tax for owners who receive public grants for this purpose. They also include the expenses made in the surroundings of historic cities or in properties inscribed in the World Heritage List of the UNESCO.

The General State Budget Act may amend the tax rate and the percentage of deductions provided for in this law.

Note: For more detailed information on tax incentives for patronage, see the list included in footnote.[6]

In view of the foregoing, it is undeniable that there is a link between fiscal policy and patronage. In this sense, patronage may be understood as an instrument of public intervention in the field of culture. But it should also be said that patronage and the official cultural policies of the European countries, as is the case of Spain, do not necessarily share the same objec-

[6] The tax incentives provided for in Act 49/2002 of 23 December on the Tax Regime of Nonprofit Entities and Tax Incentives for Patronage are applicable to gifts, donations, and contributions made *in favor of*:

(1) Registered foundations and nonprofit associations recognized to benefit the public that opt for the special tax regime provided for them and that fulfill the requirements set out in the Law; (2) the State, autonomous communities, and local entities, and official autonomous institutions linked to them; (3) universities; and (4) other public institutions determined by the Act.

The tax regime allows deductions for *outright and irrevocable gifts, donations, and contributions of the following nature*: (a) monetary gifts, gifts of properties or rights; (b) membership fees; (c) establishment of a right of usufruct over properties, rights, or securities, without compensation; (d) gifts or donations of properties belonging to national historic heritage that are registered in the General Registry of Properties of Cultural Interest or included in the General Inventory; (e) gifts or donations of cultural properties of guaranteed quality to entities whose purposes include the pursuit of museum activities and the promotion and dissemination of historic art heritage.

In the case of revocation, the donor will be liable for payment of the amounts of the deductions made as well as possible late payment interests.

The tax base for deductions made for the aforementioned gifts, donations, and contributions will be the following: (a) for monetary gifts, their amount; (b) for gifts or donations of properties or rights, their book value, or, otherwise, their value as determined by the rules for Property Tax; (c) for the establishment of a right of usufruct over immovable properties, two percent of their cadastral value; (d) for the establishment of a right of usufruct over securities, the annual amount of the dividends or interests perceived by the beneficiary; (e) for the establishment of a right of usufruct over properties or rights, the annual amount resulting from applying the legal interest rate for money; (f) for gifts or donations of works of art of guaranteed quality and properties that belong to national historic heritage, the assessment made by the Classification, Valuation and Exportation Board. In the case of properties not belonging to national historic heritage, the Board will assess whether they are of sufficient quality. The maximum limit for the assessed value of these properties will be their usual market value at the time of transfer.

With regard to the *deduction from personal income tax*, taxpayers are entitled to deduct twenty-five perecnt of the value of donations from their net taxable income. This value will be computed according to the limit provided in Personal Income Tax Act 40/1998 of 9 December and other tax regulations. Nonresident taxpayers operating in Spain through a permanent establishment may apply the same deduction. Nonresident taxpayers operating in Spain not through a permanent establishment can apply the income tax deduction to taxable events occurring within one year of the date of the gift, donation, or contribution and the amount of the deduction may not exceed ten percent of the taxable base of all returns submitted in this period.

With regard to the *deduction from corporate income tax*, the deduction will be thirty-five percent, after applying all other tax deductions and credits corresponding to this tax, and the amounts not deducted in the first year can be deducted in the returns of the tax periods concluding in the subsequent ten calendar years. The amount of this deduction cannot exceed ten percent of total taxable income in the tax period. The amounts in excess of this limit can be deducted in the tax periods concluding in the subsequent ten calendar years.

The General State Budget Act may establish a list of *priority patronage activities* within the scope of the general interest purposes cited in this Act, as well as the qualifying entities for patronage. With respect to these activities and entities, the General State Budget Act may increase up to a limit of five percent the percentages and limits of the deductions established in this Act.

Exemption of incomes and capital gains derived from gifts, donations, and contributions. Capital gains and revenues resulting from gifts, donations, and contributions will be exempt from personal income tax, corporate income tax, and nonresident income tax. Gains derived from transfers of urban land or the establishment or transfer of rights of enjoyment restricting the ownership rights to real property, when carried out for the same purposes, will be exempt from the Urban Land Gains Tax.

The beneficiary entity must issue a *certificate* of the gifts, donations and contributions received and file it with the tax administration.

The Act also covers the *Tax regime for other forms of patronage: (a) Business – nonprofit entity agreements on general interest activities*, by which these entities, in exchange for financial support to achieve their specific aims, agree in writing to publicize by any means the involvement of the company in their activities. The amounts paid or the expenses incurred will be considered deductible expenses and the tax regime applicable to these amounts will be incompatible with the other tax incentives provided for under this law. *(b) Expenses on general interest activities* will be considered as deductible expenses in the determination of taxable income for corporate income tax, nonresident income tax of taxpayers operating in Spain, or the net taxable income of the economic activity of taxpayers subject to direct evaluation regime of personal income tax, provided that they are included in the expenses made for the general interest purpose specified in the Act. This deduction will be incompatible with the other tax incentives provided for under this Act. *(c) Support programs for events of exceptional public interest* which may be established by the Act, as appropriate. This Act will regulate their duration and the creation of a consortium or the designation of an administrative body in charge of implementing the program and certifying the suitability of the expenses and investments made with respect to the established aims and plans, the basic lines of action and the tax benefits that will be applicable. These entities may deduct from their net taxable income fifteen percent of the expenses and investments corresponding to, among others, the rehabilitation of buildings and other constructions that contribute to enhancement of the physical area concerned. These works must comply with the requirements established in architectural and urban planning regulations that may be established in this regard by both the municipalities affected by the respective program and the designated consortium or administrative body. When advertising support refers specifically to dissemination of the event, the deduction will be for the total amount of the investment; otherwise, the tax base for deduction will be twenty-five percent of the investment. This deduction, when added to the other corporate income tax deductions, cannot exceed thirty-five percent of net taxable income after

tives in practice. In fact, a great portion of the activities carried out in the sphere of patronage are even in contradiction with the basic political guidelines of the official sector.

In any case, tax incentives are not the most important methods to stimulate patronage. Often, the primary goal is the promotion of image through a marketing campaign, which allows the introduction of trademarks and products in social sectors initially attracted by the appeal of both cultural events and private cultural agents.

In this sense, Raimon Bergós, a legal expert, considers that "In practice, sponsorship with marketing purposes and philanthropic patronage can benefit from the same kind of deductions, which is really contradictory."[7] But he adds that the law encourages small companies to make gifts and donations to foundations because the deduction they can obtain represents an advantage of five percent in comparison to the deduction obtained if the same activities were carried out directly by them. That is why the percentage for the taxable corporate income of the small companies is fixed at thirty percent and at thirty-five percent for the big companies.

As stated by Bergós, the new legal instruments are very positive, in general terms, from the point of view of the foundations. But there is also a certain degree of disappointment in this sector because the gifts and donations made to philanthropic entities may generate the same tax deductions as the activities of "general interest" carried directly out by those hypothetical donors.

Notwithstanding, it should also be recognised that, thanks to patronage, many cultural activities, such as publications, exhibits, and conferences, in addition to research centres and training programs, may exist. Patronage has also encouraged the creation of many new nonprofit entities and contributed to implement the activities of the existing ones.

The general and most authoritative opinions seem to be reflected in the comments made by Ignacio Camuñas, from the Spanish Centre of Foundations. In his opinion, "The fact that the extraordinary work carried out by the non-profit entities has been officially recognised in legal terms has meant a positive step. Their tax regime has been notably improved. But, still, the tax incentives introduced by the new law do not represent a sufficiently stimulating measure." Teresa Sanjurjo, the director of the Confederation of Spanish Federations, which includes 475 foundations – 150 of them devoted to cultural aspects – thinks that, "The new legal provisions have meant a great improvement in general terms, but tax incentives for patronage could have been contemplated in a more generous way."

QUESTIONS FOR DISCUSSION

1. Several European countries – like the United Kingdom, France, Italy, Germany, and Spain – have developed legal, financial measures and tax incentives to stimulate the participation of private entities in the safeguarding of cultural

subtracting deductions and credits to avoid double taxation. Nondeducted amounts may be deducted in the returns of the subsequent ten calendar years. Calculation of the time period may be deferred until the first year within the period of prescription in which profits are obtained by newly created entities or losses from previous years are offset by the provision of new resources. Taxpayers are entitled to the deductions provided for in this Act for donations and contributions to the consortium. The priority patronage regime will be applicable to programs and activities related to the event, provided that they are approved by the consortium or competent administrative body and are undertaken by the entities foreseen in the Law and the aforementioned consortium, with an increase of five percent in the percentages and limits of the established deductions. Transfers subject to the Transfer Tax and Stamp Duty will benefit from a ninety-five percent tax credit on the tax due when the properties and rights acquired are used directly and exclusively by the taxpayer for the purpose of investments eligible for deduction, including, among others, the rehabilitation of the buildings and constructions indicated earlier. Companies or entities implementing the aims of the respective program will receive a ninety-five percent tax credit on all local taxes and duties that may be chargeable on operations related exclusively to implementation of this program.

Additional Provision 1 of this Act introduces some *amendments to Personal Income Tax Act 40/1998 of 9 December and other tax regulations*, of which the most notable are the following:

- "*Public grants by the competent administrations to owners of properties belonging to national historic heritage* registered in the General Registry of Properties of Cultural Interest referred to in National Historic Heritage Act 16/1985 of 25 June, for the sole purpose of their conservation or rehabilitation, may be allocated in fourths to the year they are obtained and the following three years, provided that they comply with the requirements established in this Act, in particular with respect to the obligations of public visiting and exhibition of said properties."
- Taxpayers will be entitled to a fifteen percent deduction on the tax due for the amount of the investments or expenses made for: (a) *Acquisition of properties belonging to national historic heritage outside of Spain for their introduction in Spain*, provided that the properties remain within Spain and part of the possession of the holder for at least three years. The tax base for this deduction will be the valuation made by the Classification, Valuation and Exportation Board or by the corresponding bodies of the Autonomous Communities. (b) *Conservation, repair, restoration, dissemination, and exhibition of properties owned by the holder that are classified as properties of cultural interest according to the National Historic Heritage Act*, provided that they comply with the requirements of this Act, in particular with respect to the obligations of public visiting and exhibition of said properties. (c) *Rehabilitation of buildings, maintenance and repair of roofs and facades, as well as improvements in infrastructures of property owned by the holder* located in a protected area of Spanish cities or in architectural, archeological, natural, or landscape ensembles or properties locatedin Spain declared World Heritage by the UNESCO."

Additional Provision 2 also introduces *amendments to Corporate Income Tax 43/1995 of 27 December*, including:

- Companies subject to corporate income tax will be entitled to a fifteen percent deduction from net taxable income for the amount of the investments or expenses carried out in for the protection and dissemination of national historic heritage and cities, ensembles and properties declared World Heritage, *in the same circumstances as those specified earlier for private individuals.*
- *Nonprofit entities, to which the tax regime established by Act 49/2002 of 23 December is not applicable*, will be subject to corporate income tax at a rate of twenty-five percent.
- *Nonprofit entities to which the tax regime established by Act 49/2002 of 23 December is applicable* will benefit from the tax exemptions provided for in this Act and pay only ten percent of income derived from nonexempt economic activities *(Note: The special tax regime enjoyed by these entities and the requirements they must fulfill are described in section X of this paper).*

Additional Provision 3 includes another *amendment to Royal Legislative Decree 1/1993 of 24 September approving the Transfer Tax and Stamp Duty Act.* By virtue of this amendment, the aforementioned nonprofit entities that opt for the special tax regime provided in Act 49/2002 of 23 December will be exempt from this tax.

[7] This is, in fact, the system in the United States.

heritage. Both in social comparative terms and from the point of view of tax payers, which are the advantages and disadvantages of these different systems?

2. Which are, in each case, and also in comparative terms, the advantages and disadvantages looking at the promotion of nonprofit entities?

3. Because there is a difference between sponsorship and philanthropic patronage, which is, in comparative terms, the incidence of each of these two possibilities in the development of private participation on the protection and preservation of cultural heritage?

Does sponsorship based on business–nonprofit entity agreements on general interest activities represent a threat for foundations and other nonprofit entities? Is the importance of these institutions sufficiently recognised by public authorities? See Bibliography.

BIBLIOGRAPHY

Comentarios a la Ley 49/2002, de Régimen Fiscal de las Entidades sin Fines Lucrativos y de los Incentivos Fiscales al Mecenazgo. *Fiscalidad de fundaciones, otras entidades sin ánimo de lucro y del mecenazgo.*
Colección: Monografías
Autor: Carlos Herrero Mallol – Marzo 2003
Publica: Editorial Aranzadi
Páginas: 232
ISBN: 84-9767-111-2
Precio con IVA 28 Euros
Reference: <http://www.aranzadi.es/online/catalogo/monografias/ficha_monogra_ley49. html>

FUNDACIONES
Boletín Oficial del Estado
Edición 2.004. 848 paginas
Precio C/IVA: 29 Euros.
Reference: <http://www.actualidadjuridica.com/FUNDACIONES- BOE-.html>

Fiscalidad de fundaciones, asociaciones y del mecenazgo
Miguel Gil del Campo <http://www.actualidadjuridica.com/FISCALIDADFUNDACIONES-CISS-.html>

Informe sobre la Ley de Mecenazgo. De la Fundación Luis Vives <http://www.solucionesong.org/informate3.asp?id_indice=140&id_ area=12&consulta=si>

Ley 49/2002, de 23 de diciembre, del Régimen Fiscal de las Entidades sin Fines Lucrativos y de los Incentivos Fiscales al Mecenazgo (BOE de 24 de diciembre). <http://www.todalaley.com/mostrarLey923p1tn.htm>

Information provided by the Ministry of Culture:

Beneficios fiscales
<http://www.mcu.es/patrimonio/jsp/plantilla.jsp?id=119>
Mecenazgo
<http://www.mcu.es/patrimonio/jsp/plantilla.jsp?id=8>
Bienes prioritarios de mecenazgo:
a – Bienes singulares declarados Patrimonio de la Humanidad
<http://www.mcu.es/patrimonio/jsp/plantilla.jsp?id=120&contenido=/patrimonio/mec/bien/grupo1.html>
b – Edificios eclesiásticos incluidos en el Plan Nacional de Catedrales
<http://www.mcu.es/patrimonio/jsp/plantilla.jsp?id=120&contenido=/patrimonio/mec/bien/grupo2.html>
c – Otros bienes culturales <http://www.mcu.es/patrimonio/jsp/plantilla.jsp?id=120&contenido=/patrimonio/mec/bien/grupo3.html>
Tipos de mecenazgo en patrimonio

CHAPTER SIXTY-TWO

ARPAI: The Successful Intervention of Private Citizens in the Protection of Italy's Artistic and Archaeological Heritage

Alida Tua

Editor's note: ARPAI was established in 1989 in Venice as an Italian not-for-profit organisation dealing with the preservation of artistic monuments in Italy. Since its inception, the organisation has participated in the restoration or preservation of more than fifty museums, churches, and historical sites.

The twentieth century witnessed a new awareness of the need to preserve culture through the recovery of the world's artistic heritage. The Charter of Athens of 1931 and the Charter of Venice of 1964 are two seminal documents that affirmed the need to protect the world's monuments. In October 2000, the International Conference on Preservation resulted in the signing of the Charter of Krakow, which included such concepts as: (1) the entire population – not only the members of a certain stratum – has a right to the benefits of cultural heritage; (2) cultural assets represent the collective memory through which a people finds its identity; (3) a careful selection based on historical or artistic value should determine which cultural assets are preserved, rather than the indiscriminate preservation of all cultural assets; (4) cultural assets as they exist today should be considered authentic, despite all the damage and modifications inflicted upon them over time.

The Association for the Restoration of Italian Artistic Patrimony (ARPAI) is committed to the principle that to respect, preserve, and maintain works of art and monuments is to protect the cultural identity that enables growth and prosperity. ARPAI's interventions are not imposed from above, but are based on working with the community to ascertain priorities, cultivate awareness of cultural heritage, and garner local support for restoration and preservation. The future should be built on the foundations of the past.

Progress is created from the peaceful dialectics of cultural diversity. That is why it is necessary to respect the diversity of other peoples together when preserving one's own cultural identity. We must fight against the negative impact of globalisation that threatens to replace local cultures and traditions with mass culture.

ARPAI not only strives to attain its primary objective, restoration, but also to heighten the awareness of high-ranking bureaucrats and government officials regarding cultural heritage preservation issues. For example, ARPAI lobbied Italy's Ministries of Cultural Heritage and Finance to change certain tax laws that disadvantage individuals and companies that sponsor restoration activities and to reduce their value-added tax rates. ARPAI's efforts paid off when the government enacted a law at the end of 2000 that provides generous tax deductions for cultural projects. Under this law, individuals and corporations are entitled to tax deductions for contributions to recognised private and public institutions that carry out cultural projects, up to a statutory maximum per year.

ARPAI is also committed to refining and stimulating the cultural sensibility of its members by promoting biannual cultural meetings in different Italian regions and by drawing attention to less well-known artistic sites as well as the most representative works of Italy's vast heritage. These efforts also stimulate domestic tourism.

Finally, given the great importance of developing the tourism sector, investment in culture helps to create jobs for local populations and to educate the members of ARPAI.

It is now recognised that the active management of cultural heritage may become the driving force of a new economy. An example of this is provided by the Guggenheim Museum of Bilbao, which has re-launched the economy of the town. In this context, the words of Ibon Areso Mendiguren, the vice-mayor and town planning counsellor of Bilbao, are particularly interesting: "I'm convinced that in the future important economic cities will not exist without being important cultural cities as well."

Since its inception, ARPAI has placed an emphasis on education in conservation and preservation techniques. The preservation of Italy's artistic and historical heritage not only requires money and the surmounting of bureaucratic obstacles, but also cultural education, a scientific approach to the definition of the issues and state-of-the-art intervention methods executed by skilled workers and technicians.

In ARPAI's 2002 review of its activities, Maurizio Diana, the association's scientific coordinator, stressed the importance of technological advances in the preservation and discovery of cultural artefacts:

> Knowledge, analysis, preservation and enhancement are all part of our unique approach: they are intertwined and should not be regarded as separate and autonomous sectors if the objective is the enjoyment of our artistic heritage, not only today but by future generations as well. Knowledge cannot be accumulated without information stemming from the analysis of the materials used in the oeuvre d'art or monument and preservation is always linked to scientific diagnostic and control methods. As for enhancement, it is necessary to remember that it cannot exist without preservation. This means that the final aspect of our approach must be subject to the pressing needs of preservation principles.

Despite the substantial developments in restoration techniques, it remains true that each restoration intervention entails a certain loss, even of the most infinitesimal kind, that leads us to say that, whatever happens, the object in question is no longer the same. It is for this reason that technology surveys play an important role with regard to knowledge and preservation.

However, it is important to stress the need for a synergic approach to what we would like to call "cross-functional" cooperation between scientists and historians, aimed at exploiting information, improving knowledge of works of art and diminishing the frequency of restoration interventions, thereby saving money and improving the preservation of works of art.

Indeed, ARPAI-funded restoration projects have always been characterised by the highest scientific standards, thanks in part to the use of state-of-the-art technologies and non-destructive analysis methods that allow us to study a work without touching it."[1]

Restoration implies saving or enhancing the defence mechanisms that prolong the life of works threatened by time, neglect, or violence. It is not only a question of supplying the means, but also of streamlining the bureaucracy and working with the government authorities to identify the most skilled workers to carry out the intervention.

As Gian Antonio Golin, ARPAI's executive director, has aptly expressed it:

"Although the road is long, it may be traversed by practical steps; every saved work represents a chapter of the history of our civilisation, it is an oasis in the desert of indifference and neglect."[2]

Finally, ARPAI's chairman, Count Paolo Marzotto, observed as follows in his introduction to ARPAI's 2002 review of its activities:

This priceless but fragile heritage has suffered from the ravages of time and carelessness, but it is now widely believed that its recovery is no longer the sole responsibility of the public administration. It is certainly crucial to implement preservation programs involving citizens, both at the individual level and through ad hoc associations.

By acting directly for the restoration and preservation of Italy's artistic heritage and discovering forgotten and even neglected works, our association finds allies in individuals and other associations that share the common goal of giving back to the public a heritage that risks disappearing.

ARPAI stimulates the private and public spheres to act in symbiosis.[3]

[1] ARPAI I Restauri. 2002. Vicenza. p. 5.

[2] *Ibid.*, p. 4.

[3] *Ibid.*, p. 1.

PART TEN

Creating Value

Considering Arbitration or Mediation to Resolve Art and Cultural Property Disputes

The International Bar Association's Committees on Art, Cultural Institutions and Heritage Law and the Committee on Arbitration and Alternative Dispute Resolution have sponsored two sessions on the resolution of art and cultural property disputes, in Cancun in 2001 and Auckland in 2004. Given the interest in and the importance of the subject, we have devoted Part X to a continuation of our exploration of alternatives to litigation in the resolution of art and cultural heritage disputes. Such disputes may be crossborder or within one country. Disputes may be between private individuals, private individuals and states, state to state, state and indigenous populations, and industry and indigenous populations. Art-related disputes may involve museums and auction houses, vis-a-vis claims by individuals and/or states. Claims may be convention based and treaty related or nonconvention based, particularly in view of the nonretroactivity provisions in three of the conventions at issue. In addition, disputes may involve property of a special character, such as art looted during the Holocaust or art looted as a result of war.

As Wend Wendland has noted, there is no one-size-fits-all solution. Several contributors have talked about litigation alternatives in the area of art looted during the Holocaust. One such example of the consultative approach is the American Association of Museums' (AAM) Guidelines Concerning the Unlawful Appropriation of Objects during the Nazi Era. Among these Guidelines, those dealing with claims of ownership specify that "AAM acknowledges that in order to achieve an equitable and appropriate resolution of claims, museums may elect to waive certain available defenses." The Guidelines also state that "when appropriate and reasonably practical, museums should seek methods other than litigation (such as mediation) to resolve claims that an object was unlawfully appropriated during the Nazi era without subsequent restitution."

The New York State Department of Banking Holocaust Claims Processing Office, created in 1997, is helping survivors around the world recover family property and assets. The office has successfully prosecuted a total of eleven art claims, US$60 million in bank claims and almost $9 million in insurance claims. In many instances, the solutions and settlements with respect to the art claims have replicated those in our role-playing mediation clinics dealing with Holocaust art.[1] Similar models have been set up in England and several other European countries.

One of the significant obstacles to the use of arbitration and mediation for nonconvention or contractual disputes is the difficulty of obtaining the consent of the parties. When recently asked by the author about his views on proposals for an arbitration tribunal to consider such claims, E. Randol Schoenberg, counsel for the Bloch-Bauer heirs in their attempt to retrieve the Klimt paintings from Austria, offered the following comments.

> In the Altmann case we have a 140-page expert opinion from the Chairman of the Institute for Civil Law at the Univ. of Vienna, Prof. Rudolf Welser which concludes that under Austrian law the Klimt paintings should be returned to Mrs. Altmann. The government just refuses to follow its own law and every attempt to litigate is met with procedural defenses (whether in the US or in Austria). This is the tactic of the defense in all these cases. In *Bennigson v. Alsdorf* (Picasso case), which is going to the Cal Supreme Court next year, the defendant, Mrs. Alsdorf, had the painting sent out of the state on the day after we filed suit and has been fighting jurisdiction for the past two years. In my experience the defendants have lots of money, and they have the paintings, and so they tend to want to fight until the bitter end. In *Searle v. Goodman* (Degas case) this meant that Searle spent $2 million fighting and only gave in at the end in a settlement where he got to have a charitable deduction for 50% of the value, which turned out to be less than what he had paid for the painting – almost a total loss. But that has not deterred Mrs. Alsdorf from following his footsteps.
>
> So you asked whether an international arbitration court for art claims would be a good idea. yes. it would be a great idea. Which is why it will never happen. The defendants would rather waste their money litigating procedural battles in the hope that they can wear down the plaintiffs and settle the matter without handing over their looted art.

Sir Ian Barker, in his chapter, "Thoughts of an Alternative Dispute Resolution Practitioner on an International ADR Regime for Repatriation of Cultural Property and Works of Art," discusses other concerns related to the ADR structure for cultural property disputes.

[1] I have participated as both mediator and arbitrator with the ADR Committee of the ABCNY conducting training sessions using a model Holocaust art-related dispute between an original owner's heirs and a good-faith purchaser, who purchased from a gallery located in a civil law country. In dividing into six groups with a mediator and six groups with an arbitrator, the mediations were often most likely to lead to successful results and innovative solutions, which are paralleled by several settlements in the real world. The arbitrations were not at all consistent or predictable in their outcomes.

This author is a proponent for the exploration of mediation for the resolution of art and cultural heritage disputes. The ability to create value through the mediation process is particularly suitable to Holocaust era disputes as well as disputes between first nations or indigenous peoples and drug and pharmaceutical companies, and/or large-scale infrastructure construction companies and power providers. Mediation in this area has been used successfully in many hydroelectric projects, with particularly good results in, for example, Quebec, Canada. Mediation as a tool is further explored by Wend Wendland in his chapter.

Innovative solutions to the resolution of disputes involving sacred and ritual objects in museum collections have been generated by the mediation process and there is the opportunity for creative sharing initiatives for objects taken during colonial times. The Code of Ethics of ICOM proposes mediation of disputes and there is much to be said for setting up mediation panels to assist ICOM members in resolving desputes relating to claims for repatriation by source nations or indigenous groups. One has only to compare the model of Bonnischen with Gerald Singer's Meteorite to see the benefits of a non-litigation model.

Folarin Shyllon, in his article in Part II, recommends arbitration and mediation for repatriation claims of source nations. The experience of the Intergovernmental Committee of UNESCO should be studied to learn how it can be made more effective. Brooks Daly discusses the particular attributes of arbitration in the context of the Permanent Court of Arbitration and its ability to successfully resolve disputes between State Parties and individuals and states.

Whatever the readers' conclusions, the development of a consciousness that dialogue and discussion, followed by alternatives to litigation to resolve disputes, is a basic premise on which this book is based.

POLICY QUESTIONS

1. Should a permanent arbitral institution for the resolution of cultural property disputes be set up?

2. What should be the areas of subject matter jurisdiction?

a. Private vs. State
b. State vs. State
c. Private vs. Private
d. Private vs. Non-governmental/Governmental

3. What rules should apply?

4. Do we need new rules of evidence?

5. Should a separate tribunal be set up for Holocaust claims in Europe?

6. If an arbitral system is set up, who should administer it? (The Permanent Court of Arbitration (PCA), Institute for the Unification of Private Law (UNIDROIT), UNESCO, WIPO?)

7. Does it make sense to have multiple tribunals with different subject matter jurisdiction?

8. Who should the panelists be? Museum directors, diplomats, lawyers, trained, arbitrators, or mediators, cultural resources managers.

9. What is the relationship of the various conventions and Codes of Ethics to any arbitration or alternative dispute resolution processes?

CHAPTER SIXTY-THREE

Arbitration of International Cultural Property Disputes: The Experience and Initiatives of the Permanent Court of Arbitration

Brooks W. Daly

PCA GENERALLY

The Permanent Court of Arbitration (PCA) is an international organization founded in 1899 as a mechanism for the peaceful settlement of disputes between States. In recent years, the PCA's 101 Member States[1] have increased their recourse to arbitration for the resolution of international disputes, and have endorsed the expansion of PCA services to cover the resolution of disputes between states and private parties, states and international organizations, and international organizations and private parties. This chapter summarizes the recent work of the PCA relevant to cultural property disputes and describes the potential contributions the PCA may be able to make to the development of a specialized mechanism for the resolution of cultural property disputes.

PCA CULTURAL PROPERTY AND ILS GENERALLY

In May 2003, the PCA organized its Fifth International Law Seminar, choosing as its topic: "The Resolution of Cultural Property Disputes."

The PCA International Law Seminar Program is based on identifying areas in which alternative means of dispute settlement could make a contribution, and then bringing together lawmakers, academic experts, and practitioners in these fields to discuss how to facilitate dispute settlement. The Seminars have addressed such topics as mass claims settlement systems; investments and the protection of the environment; the enforcement of regulatory measures in air, space, and telecommunications law; international water disputes; and international labor disputes, culminating in its most recent Seminar on cultural property disputes.

At each of these Seminars, the view was expressed that arbitration and/or conciliation, in the hands of highly qualified experts, would be useful additions to the existing means of adjudication. Moreover, the PCA could provide an effective platform for such mechanisms. The recommendations of these Seminars have been realized in a variety of forms, some of which are mentioned later.

Each of the Seminars addressed an issue that was of immediate relevance, but perhaps none more so that the question of the resolution of cultural property disputes. Only weeks before the Seminar, the looting of Iraq's cultural treasures occurred and this was the subject of the keynote address by Dr. Lyndel Prott.[2] Another matter of urgency highlighted at the Seminar is the life span of the survivors of the Second World War and, more specifically, the Holocaust, and the need to provide means not only of locating, identifying, and establishing provenance of looted cultural property, but also neutral mechanisms for settling claims to ownership.

The Seminar invited speakers representing a broad range of public and private interests and specializations, so as to provide a balanced examination of dispute resolution mechanisms, which would be acceptable to all potential parties. The program focused on new developments in provenance research, highlighting the creation of online databases; responses by various institutions and governments to World War II looted art; legal issues associated with restitution, such as the notion of good faith and the weight of evidence; and dispute settlement mechanisms relating to cultural property.[3]

Speakers and participants at the Seminar put forward a variety of suggestions for the creation of specialized arbitral tribunals, procedures, and substantive rules, noting that the PCA, an intergovernmental organization with a membership of more than 100 States, offers arbitration and conciliation rules for disputes not only between States, but also between States and non-States (private parties). This unique combination of broad international commitment to peaceful dispute settlement providing a neutral forum for any combination of states and non-states could offer a means in the future for new forms of dispute settlement in this field. The PCA has taken note of these suggestions and intends to take concrete steps in this direction.

ERITREA–ETHIOPIA CLAIMS COMMISSION

Significant interest in the use of arbitration to resolve cultural property disputes has been generated in recent years, but practical examples of its application in this context remain rare. It is therefore worth setting forth the details of a claim related to

[1] PCA Member States are signatories of either the 1899 Hague Convention for the Pacific Settlement of International Disputes or 1907 Hague Convention for the Pacific Settlement of International Disputes.

Special Counsel, Permanent Court of Arbitration, the Hague. The author thanks Ms. Belinda Macmahon, Mr. Dane Ratliff, and Ms. Judy Freedberg for their contributions to this chapter.

[2] Lyndel V. Prott, *Keynote Address: The Prospects for Recovery of Cultural Heritage Looted from Iraq*, in RESOLUTION OF CULTURAL PROPERTY DISPUTES (International Bureau of the Permanent Court of Arbitration ed., Kluwer Law International 2004), at 23.

[3] Seminar papers were published in RESOLUTION OF CULTURAL PROPERTY DISPUTES (International Bureau of the Permanent Court of Arbitration ed., Kluwer Law International 2004).

cultural property recently submitted in a PCA administered arbitration.

Background to the Establishment of the Claims Commission

The Eritrea–Ethiopia Claims Commission[4] is one of two arbitral tribunals established by the Peace Agreement signed in Algiers on December 12, 2000 between the Governments of the State of Eritrea and the Federal Democratic Republic of Ethiopia.[5] The Peace Agreement ended the armed conflict over the two countries' common border that had begun in May 1998. The Claims Commission's role is to resolve questions of State responsibility for violations of international law that occurred during the 1998–2000 conflict. The second arbitral tribunal, the Eritrea Ethiopia Boundary Commission, was given the task of determining a common boundary for the Parties. The two Commissions are independent tribunals with their seat in The Hague, and the PCA acts as Registry for both.[6]

Jurisdiction and Remedies

The Claims Commission is directed under Article 5(1) of the Peace Agreement to:

"decide through binding arbitration all claims for loss, damage or injury by one Government against the other, and by nationals (including both natural and juridical persons) of one party against the Government of the other party or entities owned or controlled by the other party that are (a) related to the conflict that was the subject of the Framework Agreement, the Modalities for its Implementation and the Cessation of Hostilities Agreement,[7] and (b) result from violations of international humanitarian law, including the 1949 Geneva Conventions, or other violations of international law."

A fundamental objective of the Peace Agreement is to address the negative socio-economic impact of the conflict on the civilian populations of both countries. The remedy available for claims for loss, damage, and injury before the Claims Commission is monetary compensation. The Peace Agreement empowers the Commission to issue awards requiring a party to pay compensation to the other party for valid claims, and to pay interest and costs. The Claims Commission may provide other types of remedies in appropriate cases, if the particular remedy can be shown to be in accordance with international practice, and if the Commission determines that a particular remedy would be reasonable and appropriate in the circumstances.[8]

Claims Commission's Work to Date

The Claims Commission decided to bifurcate its work by dealing first with issues of liability and only subsequently with the determination of damages. Three of four scheduled hearings on liability issues between the Parties have now been held: (1) claims for alleged unlawful treatment of prisoners of war, in December 2002 ("POW claims"); (2) claims arising out of the conduct of military operations on the Central Front of the armed conflict, in November 2003 ("Central Front claims"); and (3) claims regarding allegations of mistreatment of civilians and their property in areas not directly affected by the armed conflict, in March 2004 ("Civilians' claims"). The Parties' remaining claims, arising out of the conduct of military operations in the Eastern and Western Front zones, certain diplomatic claims and on the economic impact of certain government actions during the conflict, in addition to claims alleging unlawful resort to the use of force, are scheduled for hearing on liability in 2005. The Claims Commission will then have to move on to the next phase of assessing damages where liability is found.

The Claims Commission has delivered two sets of interim awards arising from the first two hearings: POW Partial Awards in July 2003[9] and Central Front Partial Awards in April 2004.[10] In its Partial Award for Eritrea's Central Front claims, the Commission determined, *inter alia*, Eritrea's claim concerning the alleged deliberate destruction by the Ethiopian military of the Stela of Matara, "an object of great historical and cultural significance to both Eritrea and Ethiopia."[11]

[4] A five member arbitral tribunal was constituted and its members are Prof. Hans van Houtte (President), Judge George Aldrich, Mr. John Crook, Dean James Paul, and Ms. Lucy Reed.

[5] Available at <http://www.pca-cpa.org/ENGLISH/RPC/EEBC/E-E%20Agreement.html> [hereafter, the "Peace Agreement"].

[6] Each tribunal operates in accordance with a modified version of PCA procedural rules. *See* Peace Agreement, *id.*, art. 4(11): "The [Boundary] Commission shall adopt its own rules of procedure based upon the 1992 Permanent Court of Arbitration Optional Rules for Arbitrating Disputes Between Two States" and art. 5(7): "The [Claims] Commission shall adopt its own rules of procedure based upon the 1992 Permanent Court of Arbitration Optional Rules for Arbitrating Disputes Between Two States."

[7] A high-level delegation of the Organization for African Unity ("OAU") presented proposals for a Framework Agreement for a Peaceful Settlement of the Dispute between Eritrea and Ethiopia on November 8, 1998, involving the support of the United Nations, for the consideration of the two governments. The OAU Framework Agreement for a Peaceful Settlement of the Disputes between Eritrea and Ethiopia and the OAU Modalities for the Implementation of the Framework Agreement were endorsed by the 35th Session of the Assembly of Heads of State and Government held in Algiers, Algeria from July 12 to 14, 1999. On June 18, 2000, Eritrea and Ethiopia signed the OAU Agreement on Cessation of Hostilities between the Government of the State of Eritrea and the Government of the Federal Democratic Republic of Ethiopia.

[8] *See* Decision No. 3, Aug. 2001, available at <http://www.pca-cpa.org/ENGLISH/RPC/EECC/Decisions%201-5.htm>.

[9] Partial Award, Prisoners of War, Eritrea's Claim 17 Between the State of Eritrea and The Federal Democratic Republic of Ethiopia (July 1, 2003); Partial Award, Prisoners of War, Ethiopia's Claim 4 Between The Federal Democratic Republic of Ethiopia and The State of Eritrea (July 1, 2003), both available at <http://www.pca-cpa.org/ENGLISH/RPC/#Partial%20Awards>.

[10] Partial Award, Central Front, Eritrea's Claims 2, 4, 6, 7, 8 & 22 Between the State of Eritrea and The Federal Democratic Republic of Ethiopia (April 28, 2004); Partial Award, Central Front, Ethiopia's Claim 2 Between The Federal Democratic Republic of Ethiopia and The State of Eritrea (April 28, 2004), both available at <http://www.pca-cpa.org/ENGLISH/RPC/#Partial%20Awards>.

[11] Partial Award, Central Front, Eritrea's Claims 2, 4, 6, 7, 8 & 22, *supra* note 12, at para. 107.

Applicable Law

Article 5(13) of the Peace Agreement provides that "in considering claims, the Commission shall apply relevant rules of international law." Article 19 of the Claims Commission's Rules of Procedure[12] directs the Claims Commission to look to:

1. International Conventions, whether general or particular, establishing rules expressly recognized by the parties;
2. International custom, as evidence of a general practice accepted as law;
3. The general principles of law recognized by civilized nations;
4. Judicial and arbitral decisions and the teachings of the most highly qualified publicists of the various nations, as subsidiary means for the determination of rules of law.

It is not disputed that the 1998–2000 conflict between Eritrea and Ethiopia was an international armed conflict subject to the international law of armed conflict (international humanitarian law). Ethiopia signed the four Geneva Conventions[13] in 1949 and ratified them in 1969. Consequently, they were in force in Ethiopia in 1993 when Eritrea became an independent State.

Eritrea acceded to the four Geneva Conventions on August 14, 2000, i.e., during the conflict. The Claims Commission has held (in both sets of Partial Awards delivered to date) that the law applicable to those claims prior to August 14, 2000 is customary international humanitarian law. The Commission has also held that the Geneva Conventions have largely become expressions of customary international humanitarian law and, consequently, that the law applicable to all the claims submitted to the Commission is customary international humanitarian law as exemplified by the relevant parts of those Conventions.

In its Central Front Awards, because the subject claims arose from military combat and from belligerent occupation of territory, the Claims Commission made the same holdings with respect to the customary status of the Hague Convention (IV) Respecting the Laws and Customs of War on Land of 1907 and its annexed Regulations ("Hague Regulations").[14] The Commission further held that during the armed conflict between the Parties, most of the provisions of the 1977 Protocol Additional to the Geneva Conventions of 1949 and Relating to the Protection of Victims of International Armed Conflicts ("Protocol I")[15] were expressions of customary international humanitarian law.

The Stela of Matara

Eritrea's Claim

One of Eritrea's Central Front claims against Ethiopia concerned the alleged deliberate destruction by the Ethiopian military of the Stela of Matara, which it asserted to be probably the most famous and historically significant archeological site in Eritrea.[16] The Stela is an obelisk dating from the middle of the first millennium B.C. It stood 4.68 meters high and extended one meter below ground. It displayed a pre-Christian symbol of the sun over a crescent and an inscription in the ancient language of Ge'ez (the ancestor of the modern Ethiopian and Eritrean languages), which (translated), read: "King Agheze dedicates this monument to his forefathers who have defeated the mighty people of Awe'alefene and Wetsebelan."

Eritrea alleged that in May 2000, during the Ethiopian occupation of Senafe, Ethiopian soldiers deliberately destroyed the Stela. Eritrea claimed that inspection by archeological experts near the Stela after the event revealed it to be scattered in pieces. Because of the dispersion of the pieces of the Stela, some almost ten meters away, these experts surmised that explosives were deliberately placed at the base of the Stela. Because of possible lost pieces, it is, according to Eritrea, questionable whether the Stela will ever stand again.

The State of Eritrea seeks monetary compensation for this loss and damage, and in addition requested that the Government of Ethiopia be obligated to apologize for the damage.

Commission's Findings

A hearing on liability for this claim, along with the other Central Front claims by both Eritrea and Ethiopia, was held at the Peace Palace in November 2003. In its Partial Award on Eritrea's Central Front claims, delivered on April 28, 2004, the Claims Commission made the following findings with respect to the Stela of Matara:[17]

"3. The Stela of Matara

107. The stela is an obelisk that is perhaps about 2,500 years old. It is an object of great historical and cultural significance to both Eritrea and Ethiopia. It is located near the small village of Matara a few kilometers south of Senafe Town and off the main highway from Zalambessa to Senafe and Asmara. The stela stood alone on a plain 4.68 meters above ground, with another meter under ground. There were no houses or other structures near the stela.

[12] Available at <http://www.pca-cpa.org/ENGLISH/RPC/EECC/Rules%20of%20Procedure.PDF>.

[13] Geneva Convention for the Amelioration of the Condition of the Wounded and Sick in Armed Forces in the Field, Aug. 12, 1949, 6 U.S.T. p. 3114, 75 U.N.T.S. p. 31; Geneva Convention for the Amelioration of the Condition of the Wounded, Sick and Shipwrecked Members of Armed Forces at Sea, Aug. 12, 1949, 6 U.S.T. p. 3217, 75 U.N.T.S. p. 85; Geneva Convention Relative to the Treatment of Prisoners of War, Aug. 12, 1949, 6 U.S.T. p. 3316, 75 U.N.T.S. p. 135; Geneva Convention Relative to the Protection of Civilian Persons in Time of War, Aug. 12, 1949, 6 U.S.T. p. 3516, 75 U.N.T.S. p. 287 [hereafter Geneva Convention IV].

[14] Hague Convention (IV) Respecting the Laws and Customs of War on Land and Annexed Regulations, Oct. 18, 1907, 36 Stat. p. 2277, 1 Bevans p. 631 [hereafter Hague Regulations].

[15] Protocol Additional to the Geneva Conventions of Aug. 12, 1949, and Relating to the Protection of Victims of International Armed Conflicts, June 8, 1977, 1125 U.N.T.S. p. 3 [hereafter Protocol I].

[16] *Cf* the Obelisk of Axum, removed from Ethiopia by Mussolini's army in the 1930s and erected in Rome. Ethiopia has campaigned for its return for decades. It has recently been dismantled from its Rome site, but has not yet been returned to Ethiopia.

[17] *See* Partial Award, Eritrea's Claims 2, 4, 6, 7, 8 & 22, *supra* note 12.

108. The evidence indicates that the area where the stela is located was controlled by Ethiopian armed forces at least from May 28, 2000, and that those forces established a camp on high ground quite near the stela (perhaps as close as 100 meters). Witnesses who lived not far from the stela and regularly walked by it during the day stated that it was standing on the evening of May 30 and was lying on the ground on the morning of May 31. Some also described hearing an explosion during the night.
109. Eritrea presented an expert witness, highly experienced in the analysis and restoration of stone artifacts and structures, Mr. Laurent Bouillet, who inspected the stela in September 2002. Mr. Bouillet testified that a military type of explosive had been used to bring down the stela, pointing to the nature and areas of fragmentation of the stone and the white traces of explosive as proof of that conclusion. Eritrea's other expert witness, Mr. Arkin, also looked briefly at the stela a few weeks later than Mr. Bouillet, and testified that he saw no evidence of explosive damage. The Commission is satisfied that Mr. Bouillet's expertise is more directly related to the effects of explosives on stone than is Mr. Arkin's, and it is persuaded that the stela was damaged and toppled by an explosive charge of the type Mr. Bouillet described.
110. Ethiopia denied any knowledge about the damage inflicted on the stela. It submitted a statement by Brigadier General Berhane Negash, in which the only thing he said relevant to the damage to the stela of Matara was the following: 'During this campaign, intense fighting occurred in the vicinity of the Eritrean locality of Matara. The only targets that were destroyed by Ethiopian forces in this locality were the barracks used by the Eritrean soldiers.'
111. In effect, Ethiopia asserts that it is unclear what caused the stela to fall, that Eritrea has the burden of proof, and that it has not met that burden.
112. The Commission believes that Eritrea has proved that the stela was felled on the night of May 30–31, 2000, that it was felled by an explosive of a military type fastened at its base, and that an encampment of Ethiopian soldiers was quite near the stela when this occurred. In these circumstances, the Commission concludes that Ethiopia, as the Occupying Power in the Matara area of Senafe Sub-Zoba, is responsible for the damage, even though there is no evidence that the decision to explode the stela was anything other than a decision by one or several soldiers.
113. The Commission holds that the felling of the stela was a violation of customary international humanitarian law. While the 1954 Hague Convention on the Protection of Cultural Property was not applicable, as neither Eritrea nor Ethiopia was a Party to it, deliberate destruction of historic monuments was prohibited by Article 56 of the Hague Regulations, which prohibition is part of customary law. Moreover, as civilian property in occupied territory, the stela's destruction was also prohibited by Article 53 of Geneva Convention IV and by Article 52 of Protocol I. The Commission notes that the applicability of Article 53 of Protocol I may be uncertain, given the negotiating history of that provision, which suggests that it was intended to cover only a few of the most famous monuments, such as the Acropolis in Athens and St. Peter's Basilica in Rome. However, given the clear applicability of the principles reflected in Article 56 of the Hague Regulations, the Commission need not attempt to weigh the comparative cultural significance of the stela.
114. Consequently, Ethiopia is liable for the unlawful damage inflicted upon the Stela of Matara in May 2000. Eritrea's request that Ethiopia also be obligated to apologize for that damage is dismissed. As the Commission stated in its Decision No. 3, in principle, the appropriate remedy for valid claims should be monetary compensation, except where other remedies can be shown to be in accordance with international practice and the Commission determines that another remedy would be reasonable and appropriate. No such showing was made here."[18]

The Eritrea Ethiopia Claims Commission is therefore an example of an arbitral tribunal resolving a dispute relating to cultural property. Although the Hague Regulations have long been recognized as representing customary international law, it is still noteworthy to see the principles relating to the protection of cultural property being applied as customary international law and hence binding on nonsignatories of the relevant Convention. Of course, it is the vast scope of the dispute between Eritrea and Ethiopia that resulted in the creation of the Claims Commission, rather than a special recognition of cultural property as an appropriate subject matter for international arbitration; on its own, a dispute over one artifact may have languished without an appropriate forum, as in the case of the Obelisk of Axum.[19] Also, the work of the Claims Commission is not complete; although a decision on liability has been reached, the complex issue of quantification of damages remains.

ARBITRATION UNDER EXISTING INTERNATIONAL INSTRUMENTS RELATING TO THE PROTECTION OF CULTURAL PROPERTY: THE EXAMPLE OF UNCLOS ANNEX VII ARBITRATION AT THE PCA

Available Arbitration Options under Existing Mechanisms

Contributors to the PCA's Cultural Property volume revealed numerous inadequacies in the dispute resolution mechanisms in existing international instruments. One problem focused upon was the reliance on national courts, often applying national law, to resolve claims and the potential disparities that result from the application of differing substantive and procedural laws to similar disputes. Adaptation of arbitral procedures to certain existing international agreements would therefore appear to be a potential solution to some of these problems, if not in completely resolving the divergences in substantive laws, then at least in facilitating access to a forum that may be perceived as more neutral by potential claimants as compared to the courts of a respondent government.

The arbitration option in Article 8(2) of the UNIDROIT Convention gives no advice on how to design arbitration procedures and has therefore had little practical effect.[20] The organization of arbitral proceedings to be conducted under this provision is left completely up to the agreement of the parties. In view of the natural tension that arises between

[18] *See* Hague Regulations, *supra* note 12, art. 56; Geneva Convention IV, *supra* note 11, art. 53; Protocol I, *supra* note 13, arts. 52 and 53, all reproduced in the Annex to this paper.
[19] *See supra* note 17.
[20] Article 8(1) of the 1995 UNIDROIT Convention provides that "parties may agree to submit the dispute to any court or other competent authority or to arbitration"; UNIDROIT Convention on Stolen or Illegally Exported Cultural Objects, June 24, 1995, 34 I.L.M. 1322.

Parties to an existing dispute, and the resultant difficulty in negotiating agreement on arbitral procedure, it is no surprise that recourse to national courts remains the obvious path for Parties making claims under this convention. The 1954 Hague Convention and the 1970 UNESCO Convention[21] make no mention of arbitration.

One instrument, however, that provides a viable arbitration option is the United Nations Convention on the Law of the Sea (UNCLOS). UNCLOS itself provides for the protection and preservation of archaeological objects found at sea.

Article 303 of UNCLOS reads:

"1. States have the duty to protect objects of an archaeological and historical nature found at sea and shall cooperate for this purpose.
2. In order to control traffic in such objects, the coastal State may, in applying article 33 [contiguous zone], presume that their removal from the seabed in the zone referred to in that article without its approval would result in an infringement within its territory or territorial sea of the laws and regulations referred to in that article.
3. Nothing in this article affects the rights of identifiable owners, the law of salvage or other rules of admiralty, or laws and practices with respect to cultural exchanges.
4. This article is without prejudice to other international agreements and rules of international law regarding the protection of objects of an archaeological and historical nature."

Article 303 of UNCLOS places a duty on States to protect cultural property found at sea. If a dispute between States party to UNCLOS were to arise regarding the interpretation of Article 303, a State could invoke Article 287 of Part XV of UNCLOS, allowing for arbitration by an *ad hoc* tribunal in accordance with Annex VII of UNCLOS. Likewise, the UNESCO Convention on the Protection of Underwater Cultural Heritage[22] ("CPUCH"), which outlaws the plunder of underwater archaeological sites, allows for disputes regarding the Convention's interpretation to be referred to Part XV of UNCLOS.[23]

In practice, the PCA has been involved in the establishment of four arbitral tribunals constituted in accordance with Annex VII of UNCLOS. Although these cases were not concerned with the protection of cultural property, the procedure followed in the conduct of these proceedings should constitute a useful precedent in for conduct of any future arbitration relating to cultural property under either UNCLOS or CPUCH.

[21] UNESCO Convention on the Means of Prohibiting and Preventing the Illicit Import, Export and Transfer of Ownership in Cultural Property, Nov. 14, 1970, 823 U.N.T.S. 231.

[22] Article 25, UNESCO Convention on the Protection of Underwater Cultural Heritage, 41 I.L.M. 40 (2001).

[23] Article 303(3) of UNCLOS has been criticized for undermining the objective of protecting cultural property found at sea, by letting salvage and admiralty laws prevail over the objectives of UNCLOS in protecting and preserving cultural property. However, the same commentator goes on to suggest that Article 303(4) of UNCLOS provides for a more specific treaty to be developed, which could afford further protection to such property, and that CPUCH does serve to fill in some of the gaps left open by UNCLOS. *See* Roberto Garabello & Tullio Scovazzi, The Protection of the Underwater Cultural Heritage – Before and After the 2001 UNESCO Convention 8 (2003).

UNCLOS ANNEX VII Arbitration in Practice

Introduction and Background

The first of the arbitrations under Annex VII of UNCLOS was the Ireland–United Kingdom "MOX Plant Case." On October 21, 2001, Ireland instituted proceedings against the United Kingdom pursuant to Article 287 and Article 1 of Annex VII UNCLOS, and concurrently requested provisional measures from the International Tribunal for the Law of the Sea ("ITLOS") pending constitution of the Annex VII tribunal. A five-member arbitral tribunal was constituted and its members are: Judge Thomas Mensah (President), Prof. Gerhard Hafner, Prof. James Crawford, Maître Yves Fortier, and Sir Arthur Watts. The case concerns discharges into the Irish sea from a Mixed Oxide Fuel (MOX) plant located at Sellafield nuclear facility in the United Kingdom, and related movements of radioactive material through the Irish Sea. Many of the issues on the merits raised by Ireland concern protection and preservation of the marine environment, as well as movements of such fuels and navigation rights and duties.

Hearings in the case took place from June 10, 2003 until June 21, 2003, after which the tribunal issued an order suspending proceedings on jurisdiction and merits, and ruling on a request by Ireland for provisional measures. On November 14, 2003, the tribunal issued another order further suspending proceedings on jurisdiction and merits until the European Court of Justice has given judgment in a related case concerning European Community law issues, or until the tribunal otherwise determines.

Development of Procedural Rules Pursuant to UNCLOS Annex VII

Article 5 of UNCLOS Annex VII provides that "Unless the Parties to the dispute otherwise agree, the arbitral tribunal shall determine its own procedure, assuring to each Party a full opportunity to be heard and to present its case." Thus, for every Annex VII tribunal constituted, either the Parties or the tribunal will have to develop rules of procedure. There are several difficulties associated with developing such rules of procedure, not the least of which is a dearth of precedent because confidentiality requirements may prevent any rules of procedure developed in an Annex VII case from ever being made public.

The parties in the MOX Plant case agreed upon rules of procedure between them, on which the tribunal and the PCA commented, before their adoption. The MOX Plant Rules of Procedure ("ROP") were made public by agreement of the Parties, and have been available as a model for the rules of procedure developed in other Annex VII cases.[24] Annex VII

[24] The PCA currently has three other Annex VII cases pending: (1) Guyana–Suriname: On February 24, 2004, Guyana gave written notification and a statement of claim to Suriname submitting a dispute concerning the delimitation of its maritime boundary with Suriname to an arbitral tribunal to be constituted under Annex VII of UNCLOS. In accordance with Annex VII, an arbitral tribunal composed of the following members was constituted: H. E. Mr. Dolliver Nelson (President), Professor Thomas

provides only a general framework for an arbitral tribunal or parties to the arbitration to develop rules of procedure, and attempts to ensure that any rules of procedure the parties or tribunal adopt, function in accordance with UNCLOS.[25] The only detailed procedures Annex VII provides for are the appointment procedures in Article 3 and procedures for interpretation in Article 12. The remaining procedures provide, *inter alia* and in a general manner: for institution of proceedings, that the parties must cooperate with the tribunal and allow it to call witnesses and gather evidence, that the award will be final and binding, for sharing of costs, for majority decisions, for the form of the award while allowing dissenting or separate opinions, and for application to entities other than State Parties.

The ROP built upon the skeleton arbitral procedure of Annex VII. For example, Article 1(2) of the MOX ROP allows the tribunal, after consulting with the Parties, to decide any question not expressly governed by the ROP or the Convention. Challenge procedures were added in Article 6 ROP. An elaboration on the replacement procedures in Article 3 of Annex VII was added, dealing with replacement as a result of challenge, and allowing for repetition of hearings at the discretion of the arbitral tribunal. The ROP also provide for place of arbitration hearings (Article 9), although this will, in practice, likely not matter for filling in the rules of procedure on the basis of local law or enforcement because the award of an Annex VII tribunal is denationalized.[26] Further, the ROP set out a procedural timetable (Article 10), allowing the Parties to amend or supplement their claims at the discretion of the arbitral tribunal. There are detailed provisions on evidence and confidentiality thereof in Article 12 ROP. Although the Parties ultimately agreed that the public interest in the case was great enough to warrant making the hearings and pleadings public, certain information was considered too sensitive to be made public. Article 13 ROP provides in detail for the hearing of witnesses. The remaining provisions deal with matters such as allocation and sharing of costs, deposits, and publication of the award.

Later Annex VII tribunals at the PCA have closely followed the MOX ROP, but making modifications to the confidentiality provisions and adding provisions regarding interim awards, correction of awards, and making specific provision in one case for the arbitral tribunal to appoint its own expert on hydrography.

Limitations of UNCLOS Annex VII Arbitration

As a model for cultural property disputes in general, the UNCLOS Annex VII procedure has some limitations. One is that it foresees the constitution of a five-member arbitral tribunal, which may not be appropriate for smaller disputes. Another is that compulsory arbitration procedures under Part XV of UNCLOS are only open to States.

PCA WORKING GROUPS

In recent years, the PCA has constituted a number of working groups and charged them with devising means to facilitate the use of arbitration in particular types of international disputes. The two areas dealt with by PCA working groups that have the greatest relevance to cultural property disputes are mass claims arbitration and arbitration of environmental disputes. This section describes the work of those working groups and then describes a number of issues that a new PCA or IBA working group on cultural property disputes could consider.

Mass Claims Steering Committee/Checklist

As part of the PCA's ongoing interest in the field of international mass claims resolution, in 2000, it appointed a steering committee of experts to conduct a comparative study of ten modern mass claims processes, ranging from the Iran–United States Claims Tribunal to the Eritrea–Ethiopia Claims Commission.[27] The Steering Committee is composed of individuals who were active in two or more of the mass claims processes operational in 2000, either as an arbitrator, an administrator or as counsel. The study, which is being prepared, takes the form of a "checklist" of matters that designers of future international mass claims processes might wish to consider, by describing how the ten claims processes of the study dealt with numerous issues, including: establishing the claims process; the legal nature of the claims process; starting the claims

Franck, Professor Hans Smit, Prof. Dr. Allan Philip, and Dr. Kamal Hossain. The PCA is acting as registry in this case. By agreement of the two governments, both the written and oral proceedings in this arbitration are to be confidential. It is, however, expected that the award of the tribunal will be made public. (2) Barbados–Trinidad and Tobago: Barbados submitted a dispute concerning the delimitation of the exclusive economic zone and continental shelf between it and Trinidad and Tobago to an arbitral tribunal constituted under Annex VII. In accordance with Annex VII, an arbitral tribunal composed of the following members was constituted: Judge Stephen Schwebel (President), Mr. Ian Brownlie CBE QC, Professor Vaughan Lowe, Professor Francisco Orrego Vicuña, and Sir Arthur Watts KCMG QC. By agreement of the two governments, both the written and oral proceedings in this arbitration are to be confidential. It is, however, expected that the award of the tribunal will be made public. (3) Malaysia–Singapore: No information about Malaysia–Singapore is currently available.

[25] Article 4 of UNCLOS Annex VII provides "An arbitral tribunal constituted under article 3 of this Annex shall function in accordance with this Annex and the other provisions of this Convention."

[26] On denationalized awards, see Thilo Rensman, *Anational Arbitral Awards – Legal Phenomenon or Academic Phantom?* in J.O.I.A. 15, 37–66 (1998).

[27] It is expected that the study will include material on the Iran–U.S. Claims Tribunal, the United Nations Compensation Commission, the Commission for Real Property Claims of Displaced Persons and Refugees, the Claims Resolution Tribunal for Dormant Accounts in Switzerland, the second Claims Resolution Tribunal for Dormant Accounts in Switzerland, and the Housing and Property Claims Commission (Kosovo), processes administered by the International Organization for Migration (Holocaust Victim Assets Program and German Forced Labor Compensation Program), the Eritrea–Ethiopia Claims Commission, one of the subprograms of the International Commission on Holocaust Era Insurance Claims, and an "illustrative case" by the American Arbitration Association (a confidential mass claims settlement).

process; procedures; administration, facilities, and computer support; financing the claims process; and transparency. The annotated checklist will be published as a book in 2005.

Group of Experts and Drafting Committee on Environmental Disputes – Development of Specialized Procedural Rules

From Concept, to Drafting, to Adoption

At a conference of the PCA's Members of the Court[28] in 1993, participants considered a number of initiatives relating to the role the PCA could play in the United Nations Decade on International Law.[29] Among these initiatives, under the general heading of "Broadening the Scope and Improving the Effectiveness of Mechanisms for Dispute Settlement Offered by the Permanent Court of Arbitration," was the appointment of future Members of the Court who would be "specialists in areas of international law where disputes between States are more frequent, e.g., delimitation of maritime boundaries or the protection of the environment."[30] In a resolution of the PCA Administrative Council (the assembled PCA Member States acting as a governing body) at the same conference, the proposal to convene a "Group of Experts" tasked with drafting "appropriate rules of procedure" was welcomed.[31] The explicit reference to the environment at that conference was influenced by the 1992 UN Conference on Environment and Development, and its call in Principle 26 of the Rio Declaration[32] for States to settle their international environmental disputes peacefully, in accordance with Article 33 of the UN Charter.

The Group of Experts commissioned papers and held meetings in 1996 and 1998 aimed at identifying gaps in the international environmental dispute resolution architecture of the time, and making recommendations regarding how the PCA could fill such gaps.[33]

By early 1999, the Group of Experts had completed its work and one of its recommendations was the drafting of a new set of specialized rules tailored to environmental dispute resolution. The Secretary-General approved this recommendation and established a Drafting Committee, which, in September of 2000, presented its first draft of the PCA Optional Rules for Arbitration of Disputes Relating to the Environment and/or Natural Resources (the "Environmental Rules," or the "Rules") to the Administrative Council.[34] The Environmental Rules were adopted nine months thereafter, following drafting sessions in Administrative Council meetings. One year later, a set of complementary Rules for Conciliation of Environmental Disputes was adopted.

Unique Provisions of the Environmental Rules

Modifications to the UNCITRAL Arbitration Rules. All PCA procedural rules adopted since 1976 are based on the United Nations Convention on International Trade Law Arbitration Rules ("UNCITRAL Rules"),[35] with modifications meant to suit the targeted area of application.[36] The UNCITRAL Rules were chosen as a template in view of their wide acceptance and perceived neutrality from the standpoint of both States and private parties.[37]

Examples of Special Provisions of the Environmental Rules as Compared with the UNCITRAL Rules

SCOPE OF APPLICATION. Whereas the UNCITRAL Rules were drafted with international commercial arbitration in mind[38] and the scope of application therein refers to disputes arising from a "contract," the PCA Environmental Rules were drafted in the hope that disputes would be submitted to arbitration under (environmental) treaties or international agreements, and private contracts, thus expanding the scope of the Environmental Rules. It was also the intention of the drafters that the use of the Rules not be limited to States, and the variety of public and private instruments in which the arbitration clause could reside, including "reference upon consent of the parties by a court" listed in Article 1(1) of the Environmental Rules, is meant to indicate that. The "waiver of any right of sovereign immunity" in Article 1(2) of the Rules further underlines the multiplicity of actors of mixed origin (States and non-States in any combination) who were contemplated as potential users of the Rules. Finally, a provision was added setting out that the International Bureau of the PCA shall take charge of the archives of the proceedings, and may provide secretariat and registry services.

CONFIDENTIALITY. The Drafting Committee determined a need for confidentiality clauses stronger than those found in

[28] Pursuant to the PCA's founding conventions, each Member State may designate up to four potential arbitrators as Members of the Court. Parties to PCA administered dispute resolution may, but are not required to, select arbitrators from this list.

[29] *See* Permanent Court of Arbitration: First Conference of the Members of the Court, 10 and 11 September 1993, VII, 1–7 (T.M.C. Asser Institute ed., 1993).

[30] *Id.* at 5.

[31] *Id.* at 16.

[32] Rio Declaration on Environment and Development, 31 I.L.M. 874 (1992).

[33] See Philippe Sands & Ruth MacKenzie, *Annex I: Guidelines for Negotiating and Drafting Dispute Settlement Clauses for International Environmental Agreements, in* International Investments and Protection of the Environment: The Role of Dispute Resolution Mechanisms 307 (PCA Int'l. Bureau ed., Kluwer Law International 2001) [hereafter International Investments and Protection of the Environment].

[34] See Dane P. Ratliff, *The PCA Optional Rules for Arbitration of Disputes Relating to the Environment and/or Natural Resources,* 14 Leiden J. Int'l L. 887–96, at 888 (2001).

[35] The UNCITRAL Arbitration Rules are available at <http://www.uncitral.org>.

[36] In addition to the Environmental Rules, the PCA has Optional Rules based on the UNCITRAL Arbitration Rules for arbitrating disputes between two States; between two Parties, only one of which is a State; involving international organizations; and, between international organizations and private Parties. PCA Optional Rules are available at <http://www.pca-cpa.org>.

[37] PCA Optional Rules for Arbitration and Optional Rules for Conciliation of Disputes Relating to Natural Resources and/or the Environment, 41 I.L.M. 202 (2002).

[38] For a discussion of the drafting of the provision on "Scope" in the UNCITRAL Arbitration Rules *see* Jacomijn J. van Hof, Commentary on the UNCITRAL Arbitration Rules 13, 14 (1991).

existing mechanisms, given the generally sensitive nature of environmental matters. Although some Member States noted that the arbitral process relating to environmental matters should be fully transparent and in the public domain, the majority felt that including strong confidentiality provisions would actually encourage the resolution of environmental disputes where they might otherwise go unresolved because the consent to arbitrate might not be given if certain information were to be made public. The confidentiality procedures in Article 15(4–6) of the Environmental Rules were designed with the protection of information impacting national security, intellectual property, trade secrets, and other proprietary information in mind. Article 15(4) of the Environmental Rules takes confidentiality requirements of existing agreements, especially those obliging parties to share information, into consideration, and provides that experts appointed by the tribunal be held to confidentiality requirements. Article 15(5) allows the tribunal to determine whether information is of such a nature that the absence of special measures of protection would cause harm to a party invoking confidentiality, and to set conditions for its handling. Determination of whether information is of such a nature that it needs to be "classified" does not necessarily entail discovery of the information by the tribunal. Article 15(6) allows for a confidentiality advisor to be appointed as an expert to report on confidential issues, without disclosing them to the party "from whom the confidential information does not originate, or to the tribunal." Article 25(4) follows the UNCITRAL Rules in requiring hearings to be held *in camera* unless the parties otherwise agree.

INTERIM MEASURES OF PROTECTION. The tribunal may order provisional measures of protection and security under Article 26(1) of the Rules that it deems necessary to "preserve the rights of any party or to prevent serious harm to the environment falling within the subject matter of the dispute." Some Member States were initially concerned that a tribunal enabled to order measures to prevent environmental harm in general might overextend its jurisdiction to affect third parties not involved in the arbitration. The drafters attempted to address this concern by limiting provisional measures to the "subject matter of the dispute" and to the preservation of "the rights of any party" to the dispute.[39] Before ordering provisional measures, the tribunal must have "obtained the views of all parties." It is unclear whether this should act as a bar to the granting of measures should one Party not provide a view. Some Member States expressed this concern, but the drafter's apparent conclusion was that the tribunal's general power to conduct the arbitration "in such a manner as it considers appropriate, provided that the parties are treated with equality and that at any stage of the proceedings each party is given a full opportunity of presenting its case"[40] would allow the tribunal to proceed with the granting of such measures after giving the Parties a deadline for the submission of views.

SPECIALIZED LISTS. At the time of the drafting of the Rules, one of the main criticisms leveled at courts deciding environmental matters was that judges generally did not have the requisite expertise in environmental issues to effectively deal with such cases. In response to this criticism, the Drafting Committee and PCA Member States decided that lists of Member State-appointed experts in environmental law and science should be made, in order to aid Parties in constituting tribunals with expertise in the subject matter of environmental disputes. Article 8(3) of the Environmental Rules thus provides that the Secretary-General shall assist the Parties by making "available a list of persons considered to have expertise in the subject matter of the dispute at hand for which [the] Rules have been designed."[41] Article 27(5) provides that the PCA Secretary-General "will provide an indicative list of persons considered to have expertise in the scientific or technical matters in respect of which these Rules might be relied upon." The Secretary-General has not limited the use of these lists to disputes under the Environmental Rules, having also provided them as a resource for UN development projects where environmental or environmental law expertise may be required.[42]

Areas of Application of the Environmental Rules

Since their adoption, the Environmental Rules have been referred to in a number of agreements related to the environment, including greenhouse gas emissions trading contracts between private parties, investment agreements between States under the Kyoto Protocol,[43] and treaties on civil

[39] The full text of Article 26(1) is as follows: "Unless the parties otherwise agree the arbitral tribunal may, at the request of any party and having obtained the views of all the parties, take any interim measures including provisional orders with respect to the subject matter of the dispute it deems necessary to preserve the rights of any party or to prevent serious harm to the environment falling within the subject matter of the dispute."

[40] PCA Optional Rules for Arbitration of Disputes Relating to Natural Resources and/or the Environment, Art. 15(1), 41 I.L.M. 202 (202).

[41] The Secretary-General may also appoint persons considered to have the necessary expertise to the list mentioned in Article 8(3) of the Rules. The lists are available at <http://www.pca-cpa.org/ENGLISH/EDR>.

[42] The PCA has an informal agreement with the American Bar Association and the United Nations Development Program International Legal Resource Center (ABA/UNDP ILRC) to make available these lists on request for their (environmental) capacity-building projects. See <http://www.abanet.org/intlaw/ilrc> for more information on the ABA/UNDP ILRC.

[43] Kyoto Protocol to the United Nations Framework Convention on Climate Change, Dec. 10, 1997 and May 22, 1992, reprinted in 37 I.L.M. 22 and 31 I.L.M. 849, respectively. On the Kyoto Protocol see generally Ott, H., and Oberthür, S., The Kyoto Protocol: International Climate Policy for the 21st Century (1999). The Kyoto Protocol includes provisions allowing developed countries to meet their greenhouse gas emissions reduction targets set out in an annex to the protocol, by using so-called "flexible mechanisms." Articles 6 and 12 of the Protocol outline how two of these that allow the participation of private actors to generate and trade emissions reductions, operate. These are the "Clean Development Mechanism" (CDM) and "Joint Implementation" (JI) mechanisms, respectively. Simply put, the CDM allows a developed country to invest in projects in a developing country that allow the developing country to develop cleanly, and thereby emit fewer greenhouse gases than would occur in the absence of the project. The project-resultant emissions reductions can be used by the developed country to meet its targets under the Kyoto Protocol, and/or surplus emissions reductions sold on the open market. JI is similar, except that two developed countries undertake activities jointly that lead

liability.[44] The Environmental Rules have also been used as a model for *ad hoc* arbitral tribunals drafting their own rules of procedure in cases submitted to arbitration pursuant to Annex VII to the UNCLOS, such as in the rules drafted for the previously discussed Ireland–UK MOX Plant Case. Almost half of the PCA's recent caseload has an environmental or natural resource component. Certainly, the adoption of the Environmental Rules has raised the PCA's profile in environmental dispute resolution in general, and encouraged parties to submit environmental disputes to arbitration.[45] Taken together, the unique provisions of the Environmental Rules satisfy a number of the goals of those who have called for an international environmental court,[46] although there remains no multilateral agreement accepting broad arbitral jurisdiction for the resolution of international environmental disputes.

Establishment of an IBA Working Group on Cultural Property Disputes

A number of issues may be ripe for consideration by a specialized working group of the IBA or PCA, which would include members from both IBA's Committee on Art, Cultural Institutions and Heritage Law and the Committee on Arbitration and Alternative Dispute Resolution. The working group would first have to decide what additions to the existing dispute resolution framework would be most useful and whether they are practically obtainable. The goals of the working group could range from general guidelines for parties seeking to submit a cultural property dispute to arbitration or mediation, to the establishment of a standing tribunal to hear such disputes. The following are a number of topics that the working group should consider:

1. Guidelines or Checklist

As previously discussed, one PCA working group is preparing an annotated checklist to be used in the constitution of mass claims tribunals. Organization of expert advice in a similar form could also prove useful to Parties seeking to arbitrate or mediate a cultural property dispute in the future, not only as a guide for designing procedures, but also to make potential claimants aware of the existing dispute resolution mechanisms available. Such guidelines could go over both institutional and ad hoc arbitration options as well as other ADR options and would not have to be tied to a particular institution or type of dispute resolution. Although some of the complexities of these disputes may argue for an institutional solution, *ad hoc* procedures may also be designed to include institutional support, as in example of the Eritrea–Ethiopia Claims Commission.

2. Procedural Rules

The working group should consider whether a full set of procedural rules is necessary, or if more detailed arbitration clauses used in combination with existing rules would suffice. Existing procedural rules allow Parties great freedom in areas such as the choice of applicable law or rules of law, confidentiality provisions, and use of experts. Certain concerns could therefore be addressed by clauses specially tailored clauses for cultural property disputes.

It should also be decided whether clauses or rules will be developed for general use, or for use with specific existing mechanisms. For example, rules developed for use in disputes under the UNIDROIT Convention might increase the chances that such disputes could be brought to arbitration rather than national courts. Also, weaknesses in the UNCLOS Annex VII provisions, such as default to a five member tribunal, could be remedied and facilitate the conduct of efficient proceedings under that convention and the CPUCH.

More complex provisions involving increased participation in evidence gathering by a tribunal or tribunal secretariat or burden shifting and reduced evidentiary standards seem more appropriate for a full set of procedural rules. Because some standards may not be appropriate for each case, tribunal flexibility must be built in to a more complex procedural regime than what might normally be seen in an arbitration clause.

3. Panels

The working group should decide whether the establishment of panels of arbitrators and experts with expertise in the area of cultural property would be worthwhile. Such panels may be considered useful even if procedural rules are not adopted

to emissions reductions. Articles 6 (3) and 12 (9) of the Protocol afford non-State actors a role in JI and CDM projects respectively. Decision 18/CP.7 in UN Doc.FCCC/CP/2001/13/Add.2, 21 January 2001, sets out the requirements for involvement of non-State actors under Article 17 of the Protocol dealing with international emissions trading. Generally on the role of non-State actors in the Kyoto Protocol see Campbell, L. B., *The Role of the Private Sector and Other Non-state Actors in the Implementation of the Kyoto Protocol*, in Inter-linkages: The Kyoto Protocol and the International Trade and Investment Regimes, W. B. Chambers (ed.), 17–41 (2001). Emissions trading under the Protocol is already underway, but a significant increase is expected to take place once the Protocol enters into force, probably sometime in 2005. Numerous government contracts for CDM projects, as well as private Emissions Reduction Purchase Agreements, contain references to the PCA Environmental Rules (examples include contracts of the World Bank Prototype Carbon Fund, the International Finance Corporation, and the International Emissions Trading Association Model Agreement). Because of uncertainty in the market, and unpredictability, it is expected that disputes regarding performance of contract in terms of emissions reduction delivery, verification, validation, monitoring, etc., will arise.

44 Article 14 of the Protocol on Civil Liability to the Watercourses and TEIA Conventions contains a reference to the Environmental Rules allowing private claimants in one State to arbitrate claims that are found to be the result of an accident caused by an operator of an industrial facility (who is liable for damage caused by any such accident under the Protocol) in another State along a transboundary watercourse. The consent of the operator is, however, required to arbitrate. During the negotiations, some States argued for compulsory arbitration, but others considered such a provision to be at odds with public policy requirements. UNECE Convention on the Transboundary Effects on Industrial Accidents, Mar. 17, 1992, 31 I.L.M. 1330, 1334 (1992); Convention on the Protection and Use of Transboundary Watercourses and International Lakes, Mar. 17, 1992, 31 I.L.M. 1312, 1314–15 (1992); Convention on Civil Liability for Damage Resulting from Activities Dangerous to the Environment, June 21, 1993, 32 I.L.M. 1228, 1232 (1993).

45 Recently, the Executive-Director of the United Nations Environment Program (UNEP) recognized the PCA's unique role in peaceful resolution of environmental disputes. See letter from the Executive-Director of UNEP to the PCA Secretary-General, Feb. 18, February 2004 (on file with the PCA International Bureau).

46 See Ellen Hey, *Reflections on an International Environmental Court, in* International Investments and Protection of the Environment, *supra* note 29, at 287–95.

because they may be referred to in a number of contexts, as the Environmental Panels have been. In addition, the participation of PCA Member States may increase their acceptance of the view that this type of dispute should be submitted to an international forum.

4. **Implementation of the Washington Principles**
The working group should explore whether the PCA would provide an appropriate platform for the implementation of any of the Washington Principles, such as the establishment of a central registry for confiscated art.[47]

5. **Liaise with the European Commission**
The working group should establish contact with the European Commission regarding European Parliament Resolution No. 0408/2003 of 17 December 2003 calling for, *inter alia*, exploration of possible dispute resolution mechanisms to help owners of Nazi-era looted art, in order to see what efforts may considered most useful to the Commission.

CONCLUSION

The resolution of claims related to looted art presents unique challenges that justify a specially designed mechanism functioning on an international level, free from the inconsistent approaches of national jurisdictions. Until now, the incentives and resources have not been present to create such a system, but recent developments such as the work of the European Parliament and Commission, may indicate a change. Based on its experience with mass claims and other types of international disputes, in addition to its special nature as an intergovernmental organization, the PCA may be well positioned to act as a platform for those seeking to develop such a mechanism. Based on the success of prior PCA working groups, a working group established to explore methods for more efficient resolution of cultural property disputes and liaising with other interested parties would likely produce a useful contribution to the existing dispute resolution framework.

Annex

Hague Regulations

(Hague Convention (IV) Respecting the Laws and Customs of War on Land and Annexed Regulations, Oct. 18, 1907)

"Art. 56 (Section III: Military authority over the territory of the hostile state):

The property of municipalities, that of institutions dedicated to religion, charity and education, the arts and sciences, even when State property, shall be treated as private property.

All seizure of, destruction or wilful damage done to institutions of this character, historic monuments, works of art and science, is forbidden, and should be made the subject of legal proceedings."

Geneva Convention IV

(Convention relative to the Protection of Civilian Persons in Time of War, Aug. 12, 1949)

"Art. 53 (Section III: Occupied Territories):

Any destruction by the Occupying Power of real or personal property belonging individually or collectively to private persons, or to the State, or to other public authorities, or to social or cooperative organizations, is prohibited, except where such destruction is rendered absolutely necessary by military operations."

[47] Principle 6, Washington Conference Principles on Nazi-Confiscated Art.

Protocol I

(Protocol Additional to the Geneva Conventions of Aug. 12, 1949, and Relating to the Protection of Victims of International Armed Conflicts, June 8, 1977)

"Art. 52 (Part IV: Civilian population; Section I – General protection against effects of hostilities; Chapter 3 – Civilian objects):

General protection of civilian objects
1. Civilian objects shall not be the object of attack or of reprisals. Civilian objects are all objects which are not military objectives as defined in paragraph 2.
2. Attacks shall be limited strictly to military objectives. In so far as objects are concerned, military objectives are limited to those objects which by their nature, location, purpose or use make an effective contribution to military action and whose total or partial destruction, capture or neutralization, in the circumstances ruling at the time, offers a definite military advantage.
3. In case of doubt whether an object which is normally dedicated to civilian purposes, such as a place of worship, a house or other dwelling or a school, is being used to make an effective contribution to military action, it shall be presumed not to be so used.

Art. 53:

Protection of cultural objects and of places of worship
Without prejudice to the provisions of the Hague Convention for the Protection of Cultural Property in the Event of Armed Conflict of 14 May 1954, and of other relevant international instruments, it is prohibited:

(a) to commit any acts of hostility directed against the historic monuments, works of art or places of worship which constitute the cultural or spiritual heritage of peoples;
(b) to use such objects in support of the military effort;
(c) to make such objects the object of reprisals."

CHAPTER SIXTY-FOUR

Mediation as an Option for Resolving Disputes between Indigenous/Traditional Communities and Industry Concerning Traditional Knowledge

J. Christian Wichard[1] and
Wend B. Wendland[2]

INTRODUCTION

Disputes between indigenous/traditional communities and industry are particularly sensitive. They involve parties that could hardly be more diverse in terms of economic power and cultural and linguistic background; often relate to cultural, moral, ethical, or religious concerns; may involve community calls for the application of indigenous and customary laws and practices to non-indigenous parties; are likely to engage public authorities as well as nongovernmental organizations (NGOs); may call for culturally appropriate remedies less familiar to more formal legal forums; and often receive a high degree of public attention. In addition, parties to such disputes are frequently in different jurisdictions and the interests involved may well span national boundaries, leading to uncertainty in determining the applicable law and difficulties with enforcement.

The purpose of this chapter is to explore the viability of alternative dispute resolution (ADR), especially mediation, as a means for resolving disputes between industry and indigenous and traditional communities in so far as intellectual property (IP) and the protection of traditional knowledge, genetic resources, and traditional cultural expressions are concerned, with a view to making potential parties aware of mediation as an option for resolving such disputes. Although such communities as well as industry may each have ample experience with informal means of dispute resolution, mediation has hardly been used so far for resolving disputes between parties from both groups.

The chapter does not promote the establishment of a comprehensive mediation-based institutional framework that would apply to all types of disputes between indigenous/traditional communities and industry, nor does it seek to pre-empt the outcome of ongoing international, regional, and national discussions on the possible establishment of enforceable measures for the protection of traditional knowledge and cultural expressions (see chapter "Intellectual Property and the Protection of Traditional Knowledge and Cultural Expressions" in this volume). This chapter suggests rather a more evolutionary approach. A first step could consist in raising potential parties' awareness of mediation as a means for resolving their dispute and assisting them in making the necessary arrangements for using it. If necessary, the experience gained through individual mediations may eventually lead to a more institutional approach.

We analyze the interests typically involved in such disputes, describe the characteristics and benefits of mediation, and identify a number of issues that would seem to require special attention in the context of disputes between parties from indigenous/traditional communities and industry. In a separate section, we examine how far mediation can be included in institutional arrangements. Annex A provides four examples of cases involving IP and traditional know-how, traditional cultural expressions, and genetic resources in which ADR was used or contemplated.

INTERESTS TYPICALLY INVOLVED IN DISPUTES BETWEEN INDIGENOUS/TRADITIONAL COMMUNITIES AND INDUSTRY

The term indigenous and traditional communities embraces an enormous diversity of peoples, communities, and cultures found in almost every country of the world. Although it therefore is hard to generalize, this section attempts to identify some of the interests that appear to be often present in disputes between indigenous/traditional communities and industry. An overview of the interests of potential parties and how they can be addressed in mediation is provided in Annex B.

Indigenous and Traditional Communities

The interests of such communities are often not formally recognized under the statutory or common laws of the countries in which they are based, where the activity that gives rise to the dispute is occurring, or where the company undertaking the activity is based.

These interests, deriving often from indigenous and customary laws and protocols, may be voiced in nonlegal terms, and refer to cultural, religious, moral, or ethical considerations that cannot always be addressed in formal court proceedings. In addition, such communities, although formally represented by an individual, might often be seeking to vindicate communal interests not recognized by current legal systems. The remedies that such communities seek may also not easily be addressed by regular courts. The remedies that courts have at their disposal, such as injunctions and monetary damages, are, in some cases, inadequate or inappropriate

[1] Deputy Director and Head, Legal Development Section, Arbitration and Mediation Center, World Intellectual Property Organization (WIPO) in Geneva, Switzerland. The views expressed in this article are not necessarily those of WIPO or any of its Member States.

[2] Head, Traditional Creativity and Cultural Expressions Section, Global Intellectual Property Issues Division, World Intellectual Property Organization (WIPO) in Geneva, Switzerland. The views expressed in this article are not necessarily those of WIPO or any of its Member States.

when dealing with the kinds of cultural and spiritual harm at issue. The claims of communities might also draw upon rights derived from a wide variety of related and, in some cases, overlapping legal areas, such as cultural heritage preservation, human rights, indigenous peoples' rights, and the conservation of the environment and biological diversity.

Being Heard

At a minimum, indigenous and traditional communities will have an interest in being recognized as "stakeholders" whose interests need to be taken into account. Because such groups typically find themselves in a weaker bargaining position, they might seek the assistance of individuals or groups outside their own group to help them formulate and express their interests. Particularly where industry is unresponsive and legal relief is unavailable, indigenous and traditional communities might rely on a high degree of publicity in order to increase the visibility of their interests and to build up their bargaining position.

Positive and Defensive Objectives

In general terms, indigenous and traditional communities call for legal and practical recognition of the principle that they must give their "free, prior and informed consent" before their know-how and cultural expressions are used in any way by industry and other third parties.

Communities also articulate a range of more finely calibrated IP-related needs and strategies. Some wish to be able to claim IP rights in order to be able to control and benefit from the commercialization of their tradition-based creations and innovations. Exclusive IP rights can also be used to ensure that where industry exploits an asset in which an indigenous community claims traditional, moral, or religious rights (such as a plant that is considered part of its biological heritage, or a design or piece of music that identifies and forms part of its cultural heritage) the community receives acknowledgment for its creation and preservation of the asset in question, appropriate customary and indigenous protocols are respected and there is benefit sharing between the community and industry. On the other hand, some others may wish to claim IP rights in order to prevent activities undertaken by industry that are considered culturally inappropriate and offensive, even though they might not be illegal in the sense that they violate statutory or common law in the relevant country. Because both of these sets of needs involve claiming IP rights, albeit with different objectives, they may be referred to as needs for "positive protection."

In other cases, however, communities may wish to prevent altogether the acquisition of IP rights over their traditional know-how and cultural expressions. This may be described as a need for "defensive protection." In many cases, a single community may wish both positive and defensive protection.

Procedural Interests

Indigenous and traditional communities typically consider themselves in a weaker bargaining position than industry members, with their superior economic power and legal or technical expertise. They will therefore participate in negotiations or procedures only if these proceedings are neutral and under their control, allow for third party assistance, and are affordable. Strict neutrality is necessary to alleviate concerns that proceedings are manipulated to their disadvantage. In order to reinforce their position, such groups might need the assistance and advice of third parties, such as NGOs or public authorities, to help them formulate and express their interests. Because of their economic position, indigenous and traditional communities will typically not be able to participate in expensive proceedings or travel to distant locations.

Industry

Industry typically tends to perceive and express its position in terms of the existing legal framework. In disputes with indigenous and traditional communities, however, industry might need to take account of religious or moral interests that lie outside the purely legal sphere.

Preserving Reputation

Disputes with indigenous and traditional communities may have particularly adverse consequences for a company's reputation because such disputes are charged with moral, ethical, or religious considerations, involve other players, such as public authorities and NGOs, and receive a high degree of public attention. Industry will therefore typically have an interest in controlling the effect of the dispute on its reputation as much as possible, which can more easily be achieved when a dispute remains confidential. In some circumstances, however, industry might even seek publicity itself, for example in order to improve or restore its public reputation by promoting its willingness to negotiate or to make a generous offer as a sign of goodwill.

Access

Where a dispute relates to an asset in which an indigenous or traditional community claims traditional rights, industry will often be interested in gaining or retaining access. This interest will be particularly strong if the entity in question has made considerable investments in the expectation of using the asset, or has already started to use it.

Legal Certainty

If industry engages in negotiations or dispute resolution procedures, it will often require that such procedures, and their results, provide legal certainty. Legal certainty in the procedure requires that the parties as well as the interests involved are clearly defined, which may be difficult if indigenous/traditional interests are not organized; it also implies that parties retain some form of control over the procedure and the outcome. The outcome itself should provide a comprehensive resolution of the dispute (which requires that all stakeholders and interests have been identified), be binding and enforceable, and, ideally, also regulate future behavior.

Procedural Interests

Disputes distract from core business operations and the costs of a protracted dispute are typically high, both in terms of management time and financial resources. Disputes, in particular if they are likely to be widely covered by the media, place significant burdens on business and operational personnel and have an adverse impact on financing, marketing activities, and business expansion plans. Industry will therefore typically be interested in resolving any disputes as quickly as possible. Because of the involvement of third parties and the potentially damaging effect of adverse publicity for its reputation, industry will also have a strong interest in preserving strict neutrality of any dispute resolution process.

CHARACTERISTICS OF MEDIATION

Introduction

Both sides have several options to deal with a dispute once it has arisen. A party might simply refuse to negotiate with the other side, thus risking that the dispute becomes public and gets out of control. Alternatively, parties might resort to formal court proceedings, which are, however, not likely to lead to a comprehensive resolution of the dispute because many important interests at stake might not (yet) be recognized under the applicable statutory law. ADR provides additional options, ranging from formal structured procedures, such as arbitration, to informal and unstructured negotiations. Mediation is an informal and flexible ADR procedure that involves a neutral intermediary, the mediator, who facilitates negotiations between the parties by helping them to identify the issues in dispute, understand the interests involved, develop a working relationship, and explore options for settling the dispute. The following paragraphs highlight the characteristics of mediation and its potential for resolving disputes between indigenous and traditional communities and industry.[3]

Mediation Is a Nonbinding Process That Is Controlled by the Parties

Mediation is nonbinding because the mediator does not have the power to impose a settlement on the parties, and either party can abandon the process at any time after the first meeting and before signing a settlement agreement. Mediation is largely in the hands of the parties, who therefore risk hardly anything by participating in it. This feature can make mediation attractive to both indigenous and traditional communities as well as industry because both groups typically fear that procedures might become subject to undue influence. Indigenous and traditional communities might fear industry's superior economic power and legal expertise, industry, the influence of pressure groups and the media.

Mediation Provides a Neutral Forum

The assistance of neutral and experienced mediators can be particularly helpful if parties differ widely in terms of cultural or educational background, or economic power. Parties are also less likely to be subject to "undue influence" from either side in the presence of an impartial and independent mediator. In the case of WIPO mediation, the neutrality of the process is safeguarded by an institution that is likely to be trusted and respected by both sides.

Mediation Is an Interest-based Process

In mediation, parties can address their real interests and needs and go beyond their factual and legal positions. Parties can take account of interests that, as in disputes involving indigenous and traditional communities, may not find expression in statutory provisions, but are based on religious, moral, or ethical considerations. Mediation allows parties to develop solutions that would be unavailable in court litigation. Instead of being limited to "all-or-nothing" solutions involving injunctions or monetary damages, parties can develop solutions that regulate future behavior and provide for comprehensive package deals that include nonmonetary benefits, such as technology transfer agreements, training programs, or infrastructure development. If the mediation is successful, it will result in a settlement that is enforceable as a contractual agreement, thus providing legal certainty in a tangible outcome to a dispute that might have been argued largely in moral or ethical terms.

Mediation Is a Confidential Process

Mediations are confidential unless the parties provide otherwise. The WIPO Mediation Rules,[4] for example, prohibit the disclosure of the existence as well as the outcome of a mediation, and prevent any admissions, proposals, or offers for settlement made during the mediation from being used in subsequent court or arbitration proceedings. Although effects of public proceedings are more likely to get out of control, mediation's confidentiality allows parties to focus on the critical issues without fear of adverse publicity.

[3] Further information about mediation is available on the Web site of the WIPO Arbitration and Mediation Center at <http://arbiter.wipo.int/mediation/index.html>, in the *Guide to WIPO Mediation*, WIPO Publication No. 449 (E), and in the Module on the WIPO Arbitration and Mediation Center in the UNCTAD Course on Dispute Settlement in International Trade, Investment, and Intellectual Property (UNCTAD), available at <http://arbiter.wipo.int/center/publications/index.html>.

[4] The WIPO Mediation Rules are available at <http://arbiter.wipo.int/mediation/rules/index.html>.

Mediation Is a Flexible Process

Mediations are not constrained by strict formal rules on pleadings, evidence, or relief. The parties can tailor the process to fit the dispute at hand. If necessary, the mediator or an administering institution, such as the WIPO Arbitration and Mediation Center, can assist parties in structuring the procedure in the most appropriate and cost-effective manner. Its flexibility makes mediation particularly suitable for disputes between highly diverse parties like indigenous and traditional communities and industry.

Given its flexibility, mediation can be conducted in various ways:

- *Facilitative mediation.* The mediator endeavors to facilitate communication between the parties and helps each side understand the other's perspectives, positions, and interests with a view to settling the dispute.
- *Evaluative mediation.* The mediator takes a more active role by providing a nonbinding evaluation of the dispute, which the parties may then accept or reject as the settlement of the dispute. Evaluative mediation is sometimes referred to as "early neutral evaluation" and treated as a separate ADR category.
- *Mini-Trial.* Mini-trials are often considered as a distinct ADR procedure. Like mediation, they are nonbinding procedures. In contrast to facilitative or evaluative mediation, however, mini-trials take the form of a mock trial, in which the parties make submissions to a panel comprised not only of the neutral party but also of senior representatives of the disputing parties. The panel renders a decision based on the parties' submissions. Any such decision is, however, not binding on the parties.

Although mediations usually involve only one mediator, there is no limitation on the number of mediators acting in a given case, except that the costs are likely to increase with the number of mediators involved. Various circumstances may suggest the participation of more mediators: if, for example, a case involves a number of complex issues, the appointment of two mediators each with different subject matter expertise may be warranted; when it is difficult to find an experienced mediator with sufficient technical or cultural expertise, parties may engage the services of both an experienced mediation specialist and a technical or cultural expert. The appointment of several mediators might also be necessary if the parties cannot agree on a common mediator; in such a case, each party could appoint one mediator. The appointment procedures are further explored subsequently.

PROCEDURAL ISSUES

Introduction

Mediation is a consensual process that can only be used with the agreement of both parties. In disputes between indigenous and traditional communities and industry, both sides will often not have had any prior contacts with each other. In many instances, mediation can therefore not be based on a prior agreement. This means that the parties will have to agree on the means to resolve their dispute as well as on the details of the procedure after the dispute has arisen. Experience shows that this is very difficult. It will be even more difficult when the parties come from widely different backgrounds, the dispute is charged with religious, moral, or ethical concerns, and it has already become public. This might explain why mediation is still not a common means of resolving disputes between indigenous/traditional communities and industry.

For parties involved in a dispute, it will be easier to submit to a set of institutional mediation rules that regulate all issues that typically need to be addressed in a mediation proceeding, such as the WIPO Mediation Rules (the "Rules"), than having to determine all relevant details *ad hoc* by themselves. The agreement submitting the dispute to WIPO mediation can be fairly short because all relevant issues are covered in the Rules. To facilitate the submission of disputes, the WIPO Arbitration and Mediation Center has developed model contract clauses and submission agreements.[5] Parties are free to modify the Rules in accordance with their needs and preferences, and the WIPO Arbitration and Mediation Center can assist them in fine-tuning the procedure. The following paragraphs attempt to identify a number of issues that would typically seem to be relevant in disputes between indigenous and traditional communities and industry.

Parties

A mediation can only work if the parties are clearly identified, are in a position to express their interests, and can commit to any settlement that may ultimately be reached. Mediation will only result in a comprehensive settlement if all stakeholders are involved in the proceeding. Partial solutions will rarely produce reliable outcomes.

In disputes involving disperse indigenous/traditional communities, it may sometimes be difficult to identify the persons or entities that are involved in a dispute, and those individuals that are entitled to represent their interests and commit the communities to any settlement that will eventually be reached. Although communities may be well organized for their own purposes, it should be borne in mind that indigenous and customary ways of internal consultation and decision-making may seem cumbersome for outsiders.

Indigenous and traditional communities might need assistance in organizing and expressing their interests. Providing such assistance in the mediation itself is a delicate task for the administering institution as well as the mediator because both must avoid any appearance of partiality. One of the first tasks of the mediator will, however, consist of identifying the issues in dispute, the scope of the dispute, the parties involved, and the persons authorized, or at least recognized, as representatives. This exercise will be crucial for the success

[5] The Model submission agreements and contract clauses are available on the Center's Web site, <http://arbiter.wipo.int/mediation/contract-clauses/index.html>.

of the mediation. In addition, both sides should be free to retain the assistance of persons they trust, which, in the case of indigenous and traditional communities, may well include NGOs.

The need for comprehensive participation and competent representation should, however, be balanced against efficiency concerns: If too many parties participate, and if too many representatives are involved, the mediation will not only be extremely difficult to manage, but is also likely to become charged with unrelated concerns.

Neutrals

The success of a mediation depends to a large extent on the expertise and skill of the mediator. This is particularly true for conflicts between indigenous and traditional communities and industry. The mediator will have to bridge widely different cultural, linguistic, and economic backgrounds and is likely to be faced with an acrimonious dispute charged with ethical, moral, or religious considerations. In such a situation, building trust in the mediator and between the parties will be essential, a task that requires an experienced mediator.

In addition, the dispute may often involve both intricate technical issues (e.g., when a pharmaceutical substance or method is concerned) and concerns of a cultural or anthropological nature. Ideally, candidates should have expertise in all relevant areas. However, in some situations, it might be difficult to find a mediator with the relevant expert knowledge who is equally trusted by both sides. A mediator with sufficient technical expertise might be unacceptable for the indigenous and traditional communities, whereas industry might consider a mediator as biased who has expert knowledge in the relevant cultural or religious issues. It should be noted, however, that, because a mediator does not have the power to impose a binding decision on the parties, solid procedural experience in mediation would seem more important than specialist technical or anthropological knowledge, which could, if necessary, be gained from external experts.

Where parties cannot agree, the administering institution could be given the authority to appoint a mediator, possibly from a short list of candidates previously provided to the parties and on the basis of any comments received from them. Alternatively, each side could be given the right to select a mediator of its choice, if necessary on the basis of recommendations made by the administering institution. Both mediators would have to cooperate in the mediation, possibly with the help of external experts. In very complex cases, a third mediator could be appointed either by agreement of the two other mediators or directly by the institution after consulting the parties. However, the costs of the mediation will inevitably increase with the number of mediators involved.

Neutrality

Any procedure for resolving disputes between indigenous and traditional communities and industry must be as neutral and impartial as possible. Mediations are built on trust. Trust is, however, not likely to develop if parties fear that the process might become subject to unfair pressure. The possibility to end one's participation can function as a safety valve. Strict neutrality of the procedural framework will, however, be an absolute precondition for both parties' submission to mediation in the first place.

If the mediation is administered by an institution that no party considers as being too closely affiliated with the other side, this might further the acceptability of the process. The role of the institution would be to oversee the integrity and independence of the process as a whole and to provide procedural advice and support. Among other things, the institution would assist parties in identifying qualified neutral mediators, and perform conflict checks prior to a mediator's appointment to ensure the mediator's impartiality and independence from either party.

Confidentiality

In disputes between indigenous and traditional communities and industry, the latter would typically seem to have a greater interest in preserving confidentiality whereas indigenous and traditional communities may well be interested in publicity to enhance their bargaining position. Once a dispute has become public, however, no side will be able to negotiate freely. In order to avoid liability, industry might not be willing or even able to make concessions, agree to conditions for access, commit to benefit-sharing arrangements or provide other benefits such as transfer of know-how or training. Preserving confidentiality might therefore enable indigenous and traditional communities to explore the other party's willingness to understand and to take account of their interests. It would seem, therefore, that both groups have at least an initial interest in preserving confidentiality. Confidentiality should extend to the existence of the mediation proceedings as well as to their outcome and to any statement or offer made during the proceedings. The WIPO Mediation Rules contain, in Articles 14 to 17, a number of confidentiality safeguards. In addition, both parties would normally sign appropriate confidentiality undertakings prior to the mediation in order to allow the process to develop unencumbered by fear of leaks.

Venue, Fees and Cost, and the "Balance of Convenience"

Strict neutrality would require that any meeting be held in a neutral venue, that each party carries its own cost, and that all fees are borne by the parties in equal shares. In view of the typically weaker economic position of indigenous and traditional communities, the balance of convenience might tip in their favor and require some adjustments to this principle.

The venue of any mediation meeting should be determined by party agreement. If the parties decide to hold their meeting in Geneva, the WIPO Arbitration and Mediation Center can provide meeting rooms free of charge. When the meeting takes place in another location, the Center can assist the parties in organizing appropriate meeting rooms. For indigenous and traditional communities, it will, however, typically be more difficult and burdensome to travel to distant, albeit neutral, venues than it is for industry. Parties may therefore agree to hold any meeting in, or close to, the country where the community in question is located. Alternatively, parties are free to dispense completely with face-to-face meetings and rely on video and telephone conferences. It should be noted, however, that, particularly in disputes between parties who are as diverse as industry and indigenous and traditional communities, face-to-face meetings are often the only means to develop the trust and confidence necessary for a fruitful cooperation in the mediation.

As far as cost is concerned, it may sometimes be difficult for indigenous and traditional communities to fully cover their share of the institution's fees as well as the mediator's fees, which can be significant, particularly when more than one mediator is involved. Alternatively, the industry party could agree to cover all of the fees of the mediation. If this were the case, a neutral institution safeguarding the strict neutrality of the proceedings would seem even more important in order to avoid the procedure from being regarded as potentially biased in favor of industry.

INSTITUTIONAL MEDIATION

The role of an administering mediation institution has already been addressed in the preceding paragraphs. The WIPO Arbitration and Mediation Center, for example, assists parties in reaching agreement on the elements of the mediation procedure, can help them find a suitable mediator (or suitable mediators), provides administrative assistance throughout the procedure, and generally safeguards the neutrality of the proceedings. For parties already involved in a dispute, it will be easier to submit this dispute to such a trusted neutral institution rather than having to develop all the procedural rules themselves. Given the special characteristics of disputes between indigenous and traditional communities and industry, it is likely that more specific determinations will have to be made. If requested, the WIPO Arbitration and Mediation Center could tailor its proceedings and services to the specific needs of the parties. Eventually, learning from the experience of administering mediations involving indigenous and traditional communities and industry, the Center might be in a position to develop and offer specific mediation procedures for such types of disputes.

The successful resolution of individual disputes may then raise potential parties' awareness of the benefits of mediation and encourage them to include mediation clauses in contractual agreements they may conclude with each other, thus regulating the dispute resolution mechanism before a conflict arises. As stated earlier, the WIPO Arbitration and Mediation Center provides model mediation contract clauses and can assist parties in developing tailor-made clauses.

Submission to mediation can be facilitated if one party has, prior to the dispute, unilaterally pledged to resolve certain types of (future) disputes through mediation. In this case, the other party could simply accept this offer by initiating the mediation. Industry would seem to be better placed to make such a pledge given that is often their activity that triggers the dispute. If mediation becomes an accepted means for resolving such disputes, pledges may become part of individual companies' standard practices, or, in the case of industry groups which, like the pharmaceutical industry, are likely to become involved in such conflicts or have relevant prior experience, may be incorporated in industrywide best practices.

CONCLUSIONS

The adaptability of ADR mechanisms and rules means that a flexible, culturally sensitive procedure can yield a result that provides legal certainty, predictability, and mutual confidence, because the outcome, a contract, will typically be legally binding. This is even the case were enforceable rights in traditional knowledge and cultural expressions to be established in law because consideration of ADR does not pre-empt or detract from this possibility (it could even serve as a means for developing and implementing such legal solutions). The procedure provides for mutual interests to be identified and promoted, so that dispute settlement can be a positive outcome for the two parties, and, indeed, may form the basis for a continuing relationship as a sustainable form of equitable benefit sharing. By contrast, it may be difficult or procedurally burdensome in formal legal proceedings to establish the standing, legal identity or personality, and legal or equitable interests that form the basis of a successful legal action, especially when recognition of legal personality or other interests is, in part, structured by customary law considerations. Although such determinations may be still be manageable under the national laws of the country in which a traditional community is based, their legal and practical difficulties are likely to be magnified in the context of a dispute with an international dimension. ADR would also provide a flexible and adaptable means of recognizing and giving effect to customary law considerations, particularly if procedural rules were established to facilitate this and to deal with other distinctive elements of disputes involving traditional holders of traditional knowledge and cultural expressions. For industry, it can be a means to preserve, or even enhance, a company's reputation while, at the same time, achieving a tangible outcome.

The benefits of the successful resolution of a number of disputes between indigenous and traditional communities and industry may well reach beyond individual disputes. When potential parties become aware of, and develop trust in, mediation as a means for resolving their disputes, mediation may become an accepted procedural model. On a substantive level, the outcomes reached in individual mediations may provide model solutions, or "best practices" that can then be used or adapted in similar disputes.

ANNEX A

I. Lego, a Danish toy company, launched a new range of toys, many of which were given names using Maori and Polynesian words and names (for example, "tohunga," meaning "spiritual healer"). Lego did not seek to trademark the names of the new toys in New Zealand or elsewhere. Maori considered the use of the Maori language by Lego to be inappropriate and offensive. Following approaches from Maori groups claiming expropriation of their cultural heritage, Lego, although initially claiming that it had not done anything illegal, later acknowledged that it had acted inappropriately.

Representatives of Maori groups and Lego met to discuss the development of an international self-regulating code of conduct for toy manufacturing companies. The possibility of Maori authorizing Lego to produce a range of toys using Maori designs, symbols, and words was also discussed. Discussions did not proceed and a code of conduct was not developed.

II. The Maca plant has been cultivated and used in Peruvian highlands for many hundreds of years. Today it can be found in most Peruvian pharmacies advertised as a food supplement and for its medicinal properties. It is also widely available, especially in the United States, as an herbal product, usually related to increased libido (MacaMagic^{TM}, Royal Maca^{TM}, Imperial Gold Maca^{TM} etc.). Consumption of Maca is frequently by means of a blend of the roots with water or fruit juice and some form of alcohol.

Pure World Botanicals (PW) recently launched Macapure^{TM}, a sex-enhancing standardized extract of Maca. PW claims that it has discovered 'several previously unknown compounds in the plant'. MacaPure^{TM} is standardized to these novel compounds and thus "represents a significant botanical breakthrough." PW has apparently already obtained one patent on Maca in the United States and filed one further patent application on Maca there. The patents relate to an extracted composition of Maca and the process of its extraction. A certain amount of ethno-botanical literature is quoted in both patent applications.

A Peruvian indigenous NGO, called ANDES, claims, *inter alia*, that the nature of the extract and the process are considered standard approaches in botanical extraction by those skilled in the art. The PW patent does not meet the standard of novelty or nonobviousness, it is claimed. ANDES does not have the funds to challenge the patent in question, it has stated.

III. A popular hit song of 1993 by the group Enigma, "Return to Innocence," included a direct sampling of a performance of a traditional song by two Aboriginal singers. No acknowledgment was made for the use of their voices. The traditional song was not regarded as a copyright work, and whether the performance itself was protected was uncertain.

After lawyers intervened on behalf of the two singers, a settlement was reached between the singers, Enigma, and its record label. Under the mediated settlement, the singers' contribution was acknowledged and they received some money. In addition, the record label established a Foundation to encourage similar aboriginal musicians and performers to compose and record music. As a result, contemporary but culturally distinct music from those communities has flourished.

IV. Aveda Corporation launched a range of skin care products under the name "Indigenous," which it also trademarked. According to the company, the Aveda Indigenous line was originally introduced to connect the modern consumer to the timeless wisdom and values of indigenous peoples. Aveda's intent was to raise awareness about the beauty of their sustainable lifestyles, and to generate funding for key indigenous programs through sales of these products.

Following intense lobbying and discussions with indigenous groups, Aveda later announced the discontinuation of its Indigenous product line and its intention to abandon the Indigenous trademark. The decision was reached following a meeting among representatives of several indigenous nations of the Americas and Australasia and representatives of Aveda.

"We are discontinuing the Indigenous product line to demonstrate our ongoing support and respect for indigenous peoples in their efforts to protect their traditional knowledge and resources," explained Dominique Conseil, president of Aveda. "Aveda will discontinue marketing any products under the 'Indigenous' trademark and, to emphasize its respect, will begin the formalities necessary to abandon any rights it may have in this trademark," Conseil added.

According to Conseil, Aveda remains committed to its indigenous partnerships and will continue to seek the guidance and knowledge of these wisdom-keepers. "Aveda will continue its ongoing partnerships with indigenous communities in the sustainable sourcing of plant and flower ingredients," explains Conseil. "Aveda also intends to develop new frameworks for enhanced partnerships, based on sustainable business and conservation models, and, even more importantly, self determination. We hope to achieve a solid sense of interdependence in the greater 'web of life.'"

ANNEX B

Interests in Mediations Between Indigenous and Traditional Communities and Industry

Indigenous and traditional communities	Industry	Mediation
Recognition of (traditional, religious, moral) interests ("being heard")	Preserving (or enhancing) reputation	Taking account of "intangible" interests
Control ("informed consent"), consideration ("benefit sharing")	Legal certainty regarding (conditions of) access	Developing contractually binding solutions
Neutrality of proceedings, control, third party assistance, affordability	Neutrality of proceedings, control, efficiency	Neutrality safeguarded by mediator and institution, process flexible and under the parties' control. Although mediation tends to be faster than court litigation, affordability depends on the duration of the process and the number of mediators involved

CHAPTER SIXTY-FIVE

Thoughts of an Alternative Dispute Resolution Practitioner on an International ADR Regime for Repatriation of Cultural Property and Works of Art

Ian Barker

The following thoughts are offered by one with no specialized knowledge of art law and of the problems associated with the misuse of cultural property and works of art. The basis for comment comes from a background as barrister, judge, arbitrator, and mediator. I see problems apparent from even a superficial consideration. I do not speak as one with any expert knowledge or credentials in the field of art law and leave that task to others. I am aware of the various International Conventions (notably the 1970 UNESCO and 1995 UNIDROIT), which provide a strong foundation for an international regime for repatriation but which suffer from difficulties of inter-state enforceability. Accordingly, my comment is that of an interested observer.

The *Ortiz* case demonstrates the difficulty attending any attempt to create a compulsory regime to deal with disputes about stolen works of art and cultural property, the aim of which is restoration to original owners. Dealers and collectors are unlikely to consent to any consensual process such as arbitration or mediation in other than particular disputes. They would probably prefer to rely on their rights under the general law of possession and ownership of chattels. Consequently, any compulsory scheme for ADR of these disputes would have to be tightly drawn in all jurisdictions so as to encompass unwilling participants. Possibly the rules of a trade association or auction houses or a representative museum organisation could require consent to arbitration of disputes as a condition of membership. Also, standard contracts with vendors and purchasers cold mandate arbitration.

The conflict of laws problems are exacerbated by the *nemo dat* principle of the common law whereby, save in a few exceptions, a purchaser cannot obtain title to a chattel from a person who has no title him/herself. This principle is enshrined in the Sale of Goods Act, which was one of those examples of statutory codification of the common law, adopted by most British colonies, and which is still found, more or less without amendment, in many of those former colonies, now independent countries. The civil law, on the contrary, addresses the plight of the *bona fide* purchaser for value over that of the original owner. A purchaser can obtain legal title from a thief or receiver, when buying in good faith.

The scale of the need for some international solution to the problem of stolen art is exemplified, starkly and overwhelmingly, by the Holocaust looting of works of art. The Resolution of the European Parliament of 17 December 2003 is a significant step forward in achieving a workable and binding system to resolve disputes about property looted by the Nazis. Items of cultural and spiritual value to indigenous peoples have also been purloined over the centuries – often by citizens of the colonizing power. Many of the developing nations that have been so plundered are very poor and may lack infrastructure conducive to protecting effectively items of cultural heritage.

From the viewpoint of one with domestic and international arbitration experience of more than seven years, as well as some twenty years as a Judge, I have been asked to offer some thoughts on a possible international treaty creating a binding arbitration regime for disputes of this nature, imposing obligations on member states. I note, for example, that the 1970 UNESCO Treaty Article 13(d) has no enforcement provisions. I understand that further Conventions on underwater archeological heritage and intangible cultural heritage, likewise, have no enforcement provisions.

BENEFITS OF ARBITRATION

The greatest advantage of international arbitration lies in the enforceability of arbitral awards. More than 120 countries have now acceded to the "New York Convention." In simple terms, this Convention provides that an award of an Arbitral Tribunal in one country can be enforced in any other of the Convention countries, merely by registering the award in a Court in that country. This ease of enforcement accounts for the upsurge in international arbitration over recent years.

Judgments of national Courts encounter severe problems in being enforced in the Courts of other jurisdictions. There is reciprocal enforcement of judgment legislation applicable to many parts of the British Commonwealth. That relic of the colonial past (former colonies in this part of the world adopted legislation passed in Britain in the 1930s) is seen as inefficient and costly – not as cost-effective or as reliable as enforcing an arbitration award under the New York Convention. Although there can be questions about the prompt enforcement of international arbitral awards in some countries, which are signatories to the New York Convention, but which have Judges unfamiliar with arbitration, there are very few exceptions to the almost automatic enforcement of awards found in what is now Article 36 of the UNCITRAL Model Arbitration Law.

The second principal advantage of arbitration is confidentiality. One can imagine that many claimants of looted property may not wish to have their sad and harrowing family histories ventilated publicly nor that some museums or other cultural institutions would necessarily wish to have the provenance of some exhibits openly dissected. Mediation also has the advantage of confidentiality.

Arbitration has advantages over litigation in national Courts, although arbitration cannot necessarily be seen as cheaper. Lawyers cost the same, whether they appear in Court or in an arbitration. However, arbitrations can usually be less formal than Courts and arbitrators tend to tailor the procedure according to the needs of the particular dispute, while not infringing the principles of natural justice. The prevalence of international commercial arbitration – whether *ad hoc* or administered by a respected international body – shows an acceptance by the commercial community of crossing national boundaries and of operating under a variety of legal systems. Most of the ICC, LCIA, World Intellectual Property Organisation (WIPO), and similar-style arbitrations arise from the dispute resolution clause in a contract between the parties. If an international art/cultural heritage arbitration regime were to be established, then appropriate resolution clauses could be inserted in the standard sale and purchase agreements of dealers and museums.

DIFFICULTIES WITH TREATIES

Those with greater international law experience than I are better able to speak of the difficulties involved with implementing an international treaty or convention. Obvious comments spring to mind:

(a) Treaties take a long time to reach their final form. There are always numerous international conferences of a gestational nature. Compromises appear in the final version.
(b) Once the wording of the treaty has been fixed, there usually is a stated number of signatory states that have to accede to the treaty before the treaty comes into effect.
(c) Some treaties (e.g., those relating to the Kyoto Protocol and the International Criminal Court) are not supported by some major countries. Although many smaller countries may accede to a treaty, it may not be particularly effective unless the major powers adopt it wholeheartedly, particularly "market nations." Accessions to the treaty may come with reservations that may block or defeat some claimants.
(d) Most common law jurisdictions do not acknowledge a treaty as part of the domestic law unless it is followed up with a specific Act of the local legislature incorporating the provisions of the treaty into domestic law. This is what is happening in New Zealand, as noted earlier. This domestic law may or may not see local add-ons or deletions to the original text imposed during the legislative process (as has happened to the UNCITRAL model arbitration law).

Even assuming that it would be possible to achieve a treaty in force throughout most of the world, establishing a system of registration of works of art and cultural heritage and a regime of international arbitration, the following problems are seen to emerge.

CONSTITUTION OF THE ARBITRAL TRIBUNAL

There are models provided by the rules of international arbitral institutions (such as ICC, LCIA, and WIPO). Normally, three arbitrators, one appointed by each party and one as independent chair from another country, are approved by the arbitral organization. Party-appointed arbitrators in an emotional situation such as art and cultural disputes might not be ideal, but might have to be accepted if the proposal were to command wide acceptance. There could be questions raised about their partiality or lack of independence, as there sometimes are, even in commercial arbitrations. It may be better to have the administering organisation choose all the arbitrators, possibly one from the country to which each participant belongs with an independent chairperson from a third country. See the discussion on International Centre for Settlement of Investment Disputes (ICSID) later in this chapter.

WHO SHOULD BE THE ARBITRATORS?

In some of the material I have read, it is suggested that lawyers or retired Judges are not suitable to arbitrate art disputes because a considerable knowledge of art history, art dealing and auctions, gallery and museum practice, and so on is required. Such a blanket statement is not correct. Matters for decision in the arbitration would include the provenance of the work of art or artifact in question, how it got to where it now is, and whether there exists a valid moral and/or legal claim for its return and, possibly, the assessment of compensation. The Chair of the arbitral tribunal should be a lawyer or retired Judge because legal issues would be pivotal in most disputes and procedural and case management skills, important. Art dealers, art historians, museum curators, and such subject matter specialists could be members of the arbitral tribunal. There also could be a power for the tribunal to appoint its own experts.

Without wishing to appear "lawyercentric," it must be noted that successful counsel, judges, and international arbitrators are used to dealing with complicated factual situations, requiring the necessity for them to "bone-up" on highly technical subject matters. Judges and lawyers frequently have to "come up to speed" in matters with a level of complexity every bit as daunting as issues in the art world; e.g., the composition of pharmaceutical patents, the design of bridges, and other arcane subjects. Many international arbitral panels include technical persons as co-arbitrators and a legal Chair. For example, in construction arbitrations, there is usually on the tribunal an engineer type person with appropriate knowledge and experience in the issues raised in the particular dispute.

WHO WOULD BE THE PARTIES?

Under most systems of criminal law, certainly in common law jurisdictions, in additional to the offence of theft, there is an offence known as either receiving or handling – i.e., obtaining goods knowing them to have been dishonestly obtained, although the exact method by which the goods had been obtained need not be known by the receiver. The equivalent in the law of tort is the tort of conversion. The receiver/converter has no good title to give a purchaser, even a *bona fide* one for value. Over time, it is possible that some collectors or museums could have acquired, in good faith, originally stolen works. Maybe the acquisition took place in a civil law jurisdiction, which might give title to the *bona fide* purchaser under the *lex situs* but this title would not necessarily be recognised in a common law country to which the work had been transported. The circumstances of acquisition would need to be investigated – particularly where compensation is sought. The standard criminal defendant's response, "I bought it from a man in a pub" or "it fell off the back of a truck" – although more elegantly phrased to suit sophisticated art world conditions – would have to be critically and skeptically assessed.

I am able only to speak of the statute law of my own country, but I believe that in most countries that follow the common law and standard British statute law exported in colonial times, it is possible for *bona fide* purchasers to obtain good title to dishonestly obtained goods from a mercantile agent or a factor in possession of the goods with the consent of the owner. The British "market overt" principle might also apply to some transactions and give a purchaser good title, although this exception to the *nemo dat* rule is now abolished. Otherwise, the *nemo dat* rule prevails.

The parties to any dispute over cultural property could include (a) the ultimate and current holder of the work; and (b) those claiming it was stolen from his/her forebears or a representative of the country from which it had been removed. There could be other interested parties entitled to be heard, such as persons in the chain of legal owners, especially where ownership has been acquired under a civil law *lex situs*. Claims for compensation for innocent purchasers might have to be considered, if it were thought that a legal title ought to be defeated by strong moral claims. All of these people would be entitled to be heard as parties to any arbitral process, which could add to the cost, time, and complexity of the process. Arguments and difficulties concerning the legitimacy of claims to title, problems of proof, limitation statutes, and *locus standi* of claimants are eminently foreseeable. Moreover, any system would not be retrospective in its operation. The International Bar Association's Rules of Evidence in Commercial Arbitrations could provide a useful precedent when the arbitration was ready for hearing. Moreover, there could be the difficulty, exemplified in *Ortiz*, of upholding a penal statute of another country that declared all artifacts of that country to be national inalienable property.

CHOICE OF LAW

I have been looking at matters from a common law perspective. What the common law says as to rules of ownership may have been altered by statute in common law jurisdictions. As noted earlier, civil law countries take a different approach. So what law should govern the arbitration? Is it the law of the place where the work of art is currently located? Is it the law of the place where the current "owner" acquired the item? Is it the law of the place where the work of art originally existed? If that law has been altered by a revolutionary or confiscatory regime, then should the law be that obtaining before the change? What was the law applicable in the place when a *bona fide* purchaser acquired the work of art in good faith from a person in unlawful possession?

These problems may not be insoluble, but they certainly require a good deal of thought to overcome. If compensation is to be paid to anyone who may have purchased the work *bona fide*, who should pay any compensation? It should not have to be the heirs of the victims of theft.

OTHER PROBLEMS

Where would this tribunal have its base? Would it be financed by the United Nations? What country should provide the bureaucracy? Should parties have to pay for the ADR process? Should costs be awarded for and against parties depending on the success of their claim or defence? Should a system of discovery (not particularly favoured in civil law jurisdictions) apply? Discovery could be very important in establishing title and/or proving the history of the work of art. What arrangements would there be for archives or customs records to be opened and for general cooperation by states that have signed up to the treaty, especially when the work of art or cultural heritage item may only have been within their borders for a short time? Should the tribunal act as *amiable compositeur* or *ex aequo et bono*?

ARBITRATION OR SOMETHING ELSE?

Arbitration is probably the only option for an international tribunal that will have to deal with conflict of law problems and function under its own rules. Power could be given to the tribunal to act *ex aequo et bono* or as an *amiable compositeur*. Litigation in national courts can be difficult in some jurisdictions for all sorts of reasons; e.g., systemic delays, unskilled judges. The enforceability problem of judgments of national courts is a major drawback to litigation.

Conciliation (which is a form of mediation) could be useful in emotionally fraught situations. Its processes are more user-friendly and less adversarial than those of arbitration. However, any form of mediation depends on the goodwill and consent of all disputants. Moreover, any agreement reached at mediation or conciliation could be enforceable as a contract only in the jurisdiction where the agreement was made, unless there were some international enforceability mechanism that could turn an agreement reached at conciliation into an arbitration or mediation award, enforceable internationally under the New York Convention, i.e., a "med/arb" solution, in ADR parlance.

Any arbitration regime would have to make provision for interim measures and for diminishing the possibility of interference by national Courts. Although rights of appeal *per se* could be written out by statute, Article 34 of the UNCITRAL Model Law demands a minimum standard of natural justice that would have to apply to give redress to national Courts unless there was some other mechanism in the Convention for redressing egregious jurisdictional errors or a denial of natural justice by the arbitral tribunal. As noted subsequently, the equivalent of Article 34 in the ICSID jurisdiction – annulment – is said to slow the process.

PRECEDENTS

International Centre for the Settlement of Investment Disputes

An international precedent that could give some guidance is the arbitration system established by the Washington Convention; i.e., the Convention on the Settlement of Investment Disputes between States and Nationals and other States. This treaty created the ICSID. It established a self-contained jurisdictional system, dependent on the international law of treaties, so that an ICSID arbitration is delocalized or denationalized. The system is unique in that resort to national Courts is limited. Court-ordered ancillary relief is generally not available. ICSID awards are subject to attack only by an annulment procedure: absent annulment, ICSID awards are enforceable in signatory States as if final judgments of the Courts of those States. I am advised by those more familiar than I with ICSID disputes, that the ready enforceability of ICSID awards is hampered by the potential for delay under the annulment procedure.

ICSID is administered by a Council with a representative from each contracting State with a Secretariat in Washington DC. Each contracting State may designate four persons to both a panel of conciliators and a panel of arbitrators. Persons so designated shall be "*of high moral character and recognized competence in the fields of law, commerce, industry or finance who may be relied upon to exercise independent judgment. Competence in the field of law shall be of particular importance in the case of persons on the panel of arbitrators.*"

Jurisdiction of the ICSID extends to any legal dispute arising directly out of an investment between a contracting State, or any constituent subdivision or agency of a contracting State designated to the Centre by the State, and a national of another contracting State that the parties to the dispute consent in writing to submit to the Centre. Once the parties have given their consent, no party may withdraw its consent unilaterally. Such a consent is deemed to be a consent to arbitration to the exclusion of any other remedy, but a contracting State may require the exhaustion of local administrative or judicial remedies as a condition of its consent to arbitration. Once having given a consent to submit to arbitration, no contracting State shall give diplomatic protection or bring an international claim in respect of a dispute that one of its nationals and another contracting State shall have submitted to arbitration.

Conciliation is also provided under the ICSID Convention as an option to arbitration. It is the duty of the Conciliation Commission, normally three conciliators, to clarify the issues in dispute between the parties and to endeavor to bring about an agreement between them upon mutually acceptable terms. To that end, the Commission may recommend terms of settlement to the parties. The parties are obliged to cooperate in good faith with the Commission to enable it to carry out its function and shall give the most serious consideration to its recommendations. In the event of an agreement, the Commission draws up a report, noting the issues in dispute and recording the agreement. If there appears no likelihood of agreement, the Commission shall close its proceedings and draw up a report noting the failure to reach agreement. Conciliation is, generally speaking, conducted on a "without prejudice" basis.

In an ICSID arbitration, the arbitral panel is three, but a sole arbitrator can be appointed by consent of the parties. The majority of the arbitrators shall be nationals of States other than those to which the parties belong. The parties may agree on the appropriate law or whether the tribunal can decide a dispute *ex aequo et bono*. In the absence of agreement, the parties shall apply, for the dispute, the law of the contracting State party, including its rules on conflict of laws and such rules of international law as may be applicable.

Any award issued by an arbitral tribunal shall be binding on the parties and not subject to any appeal or other remedy except those provided in the Convention. Every contracting State to the Convention shall recognize an award rendered pursuant to the Convention as binding and shall enforce the pecuniary obligations imposed by that award, as if a final judgment of the Court in that State.

Maybe there are some areas in the ICSID Convention and Rules (of which I have given a very broad summary) that may be of precedent value for any proposed Convention for dealing with art and cultural heritage disputes. One of them could be that the process is not confined to State versus State disputes. Individuals (usually corporations) from State A can sue State B.

Domain Name Disputes

An example of an international dispute resolution process that does not depend on any national system of law is the ICANN Policy for the resolution of domain name disputes. Accredited dispute resolution providers, notably WIPO (Geneva) and the National Arbitration Form (Minneapolis), administer disputes concerning domain names. Claims are brought by those asserting rights under a trademark, whether a registered or a common law mark, against persons who reflect the mark in a domain name. The domain name will be ordered to be transferred to the complainant if: (a) the domain name is identical or confusingly similar to a mark in which the complaintant has rights, and (b) the domain name user has no legitimate rights or interest in the name, and (c) the domain name has been registered and continues to be used in bad faith. Thousands of domain name disputes have been resolved under this process, purely on the papers, by independent panelists throughout the world.

I am not suggesting that art disputes can be resolved as simply as domain name disputes. The precedent value in the domain name disputes' procedure is that it is the ICANN Policy alone that provides the legal basis for determining these disputes. All persons registering a top-level domain name must agree to submit to the process under the Policy. Any national law, although sometimes important as a trademark law precedent, is subservient to the Policy.

It may be possible to establish a "policy" for art/cultural property disputes which, like the ICANN policy, incorporates a general agreement as to the appropriate legal framework under which any proposed arbitration system might operate. In other words, just as the contract between a domain name registrant and his/her registrar must contain an agreement that the registrant will accept the Policy to resolve any disputes over the domain name registration, then standard forms of contract for purchasers of art/cultural items such as auction houses and museums could have a standard clause bringing both parties into the new arbitral system.

The ICSID procedure shows that there has to be some international administering body for such a scheme. Because WIPO concentrates on intellectual property and has a section dealing with cultural property, it might be the appropriate body to administer art/cultural heritage disputes. The WIPO Arbitration and Mediation Center has extensive experience dealing not only with domain name disputes, but also arbitration and mediation. WIPO is a UN agency, a fact that would assist in its acceptance by many countries.

UNIDROIT CONVENTION

Any compulsory ADR system would have to build on the 1995 UNIDROIT Convention. A helpful summary of the advantages of that Convention is found in New Zealand's "national interest" analysis of the advantages and disadvantages of New Zealand's accession to the Convention. The analysis was presented to the House of Representatives, and annexed to the Report of a Parliamentary Select Committee examining both the 1970 and 1995 Conventions, as part of New Zealand's process of discernment in deciding whether to accede to those Conventions.

"The advantages to New Zealand of accession to the UNIDROIT Convention include:

- The UNIDROIT Convention provides that possession of the cultural object by a good faith purchaser would not extinguish a claim for recovery of a stolen cultural object. This is consistent with New Zealand domestic law. It would benefit New Zealand by allowing the recovery of stolen or illegally exported objects overseas where this would not otherwise be available in countries whose law favours good faith purchaser.
- The UNIDROIT Convention harmonises the domestic laws of State Parties in respect of recovery of cultural objects, making it easier for New Zealanders to seek the return of stolen or illegally exported cultural objects in foreign courts.
- Improvements in private law rights for the recovery of stolen cultural objects means that individuals will not have to rely on the New Zealand Government to seek the return of their objects on their behalf. This has two benefits – it provides a choice of action for private citizens, and it lessens the burden on the New Zealand Government.
- The rights contained in the UNIDROIT Convention are additional to existing mechanisms for the return of cultural objects, such as State-to-State channels under the UNESCO Convention, or negotiating separate bilateral arrangements or agreement regarding specific object (New Zealand does not participate in any such arrangements). If the UNIDROIT Convention mechanisms are not appropriate in a particular case, State Parties and individuals remain free to use other means to seek return of the object at issue.
- The UNIDROIT Convention does not require objects to be registered or designated as cultural property by the State. Accordingly, objects of which the State had no prior knowledge, such as those illegally removed from archaeological sites, or stolen from private collections, can be covered by the convention.

The disadvantages of New Zealand's accession primarily relate to the UNIDROIT Convention's shortcomings.

- The UNIDROIT Convention has relatively few ratifications (23) compared to the UNESCO Convention (103). This is not unusual taking into account the length of time the Convention has been in force. It reduces the efficacy of the UNIDROIT Convention's protections because New Zealand can only invoke the Convention against other State Parties.
- Accession to the UNIDROIT Convention means that the New Zealand Government may not be involved in the management of the repatriation of objects where private court actions are pursued in the country of an object's destination.
- Because the Convention's application is prospective, it would not apply to objects stolen or illegally exported prior to entry into force of convention for New Zealand.

In summary, New Zealand would benefit from accession to the UNIDROIT Convention in tandem with the UNESCO Convention, as this would offer New Zealand a variety of options for pursuing the return of cultural objects to suit the circumstances of the case. The UNIDROIT Convention is intended to complement the UNESCO Convention – both adopt the same definition of cultural objects, both are prospective in application, and the problem of the illicit trade of cultural objects is addressed through the framework of principles established by the UNESCO Convention and the specific legal actions of the UNIDROIT Convention."

APPENDIX

A Guide to Art and Cultural Heritage Resources

LEGAL DOCUMENTS

International Conventions

- Hague Convention Concerning the Laws and Customs of War on Law, October 8, 1907, 36 Stat. 2277, 15 U.N.T.S. 9.
<http://www.icrc.org/ihl.nsf/0/1d1726425f6955aec125641e0038bfd6?OpenDocument>
- Convention for the Protection of Cultural Property in the Event of Armed Conflict, May 14, 1954, 249 U.N.T.S. 240.
<http://www.unesco.org/culture/laws/hague/html_eng/page1.shtml>
- The Second Protocol of the Hague Convention for the Protection of Cultural Property in the Event of Armed Conflicts, 26 March 1999, 38 I.L.M. 769.
<http://www.unesco.org/culture/laws/hague/html_eng/protocol2.shtml>
- Convention on the Means of Prohibiting and Preventing the Illicit Import, Export and Transfer of Ownership of Cultural Property, November 14, 1970, 823 U.N.T.S. 231.
<http://www.unesco.org/culture/laws/1970/html_eng/page1.shtml>
- Convention Concerning the Protection of the World Cultural and Natural Heritage, November 23, 1972, 27 U.S.T. 37, 1037 U.N.T.S. 151.
<http://whc.unesco.org/world_he.htm>
- Convention on Biological Diversity, June 5, 1992, 31 I.L.M. 818.
<http://www.biodiv.org/doc/legal/cbd-en.pdf>
- UNIDROIT Convention on Stolen or Illegally Exported Cultural Objects, June 24, 1995, 34 I.L.M. 1322.
<http://www.unidroit.org/english/conventions/ccult.htm>
- Convention on the Protection of the Underwater Cultural Heritage, November 6, 2001, 41 I.L.M. 40.
<http://www.unesco.org/culture/laws/underwater/html_eng/convention.shtml>
- Convention for the Safeguarding of the Intangible Cultural Heritage, October 17, 2003.
<http://unesdoc.unesco.org/images/0013/001325/132540e.pdf>

Regional Legal Documents

European Union

- European Union Directive on the Return of Cultural Objects, Council Directive 93/7/EEC.
<http://europa.eu.int/scadplus/leg/en/lvb/l11017b.htm>
- Council Regulation (EEC) No. 3911/92 of 9 December 1992 on the export of cultural goods.
<http://exchanges.state.gov/culprop/eu3911.html>

Africa

- Model Legislation for the Recognition and Protection of Rights of Local Communities, Farmers, Breeders and for the Regulation of Access to Biological Resources (Organization of African Unity Model Law, now African Union, 2000)

Americas

- Convention on the Protection of the Archeological, Historical and Artistic Heritage of the American Nations, June 16, 1976 ("Convention of San Salvador") directed at the registration, protection and surveillance of the assets that constitute the cultural heritage of the American nations, specifically in order to prevent unlawful exportation of cultural assets.
<http://www.oas.org.juridico/english/treaties/c16.html>.

South Pacific

- The Pacific Regional Framework, comprising the Model Law and a comprehensive explanatory memorandum, has been developed through close collaboration between SPC, PIFS, UNESCO, Pacific Island member countries and territories, and the Council of Pacific Arts. It is reflective of international developments taking place within UNESCO and WIPO.
<http://www.wipo.int/documents/en/meetings/2002/igc/pdf/grtkf_ic_4_inf2a4_attach.pdf>

Selected National Legal Documents

Brazil

- Decreto-Ley n° 25 sobre Protección del patrimonio histórico y artístico nacional (30.XI.1937).
<http://www.iphan.gov.br/legislac/decretolei25.htm>
- Ley 3924 sobre Monumentos prehistóricos y arqueológicos (26.VI.1961).
<http://www.iphan.gov.br/legislac/lei3924.htm>

Canada

- Canada Cultural Property Export and Import Act, R.S.C. 1985, c C-51, §37: Foreign Cultural Property <http://www.pch.gc.ca/pc-ch/mindep/acts/culture.htm>

Costa Rica

- Ley 7788, de Defensa del Diversidad Biologico (X.5.1983)

Switzerland

- Swiss Federal Act on the International Transfer of Cultural Property (Cultural Property Transfer Act, CPTA), June 20, 2003 <http://www.kultur-schweiz.admin.ch/arkgt/files/kgtg2_e.pdf>

United Kingdom

- United Kingdom Dealing in Cultural Objects (Offences) Act 2003, 2003 Ch. 27. <http://www.hmso.gov.uk/acts/acts2003/20030027.htm>

United States

- Convention on Cultural Property Implementation Act, January 12, 1983, 19 U.S.C. §301–315 <http://exchanges.state.gov/culprop/97-446.html>
- U.S. Senate Report No. 97-564 <http://exchanges.state.gov/culprop/97-564.html>
- 19 U.S.C.§2600, Chapter 14, Convention on Cultural Property <http://exchanges.state.gov/culprop/2600.html>
- Executive Order 12555 of March 10, 1986 <http://exchanges.state.gov/culprop/12555.html>
- Regulation of Importation of Pre-Columbian Monumental or Architectural Sculpture or Murals <http://exchanges.state.gov/culprop/92-587.html>
- National Historic Preservation Ac of 1966, 16 U.S.C. 470 et. seq. §101–402 <http://www2.cr.nps.gov/laws/NHPA1966.htm>
- National Stolen Property Act, 18 U.S.C. §2314–2315 <http://exchanges.state.gov/culprop/18-2314.html>
- Archeological Resources Protection Act of 1979 <http://exchanges.state.gov/culprop/96-95.html>
- Native American Graves Protection and Repatriation Act, 1990, P.L. 101-601 <http://exchanges.state.gov/culprop/101-601.html>
- Abandoned Shipwreck Act of 1987, 43 U.S.C. 2101 et. seq., P.L. 100-298 (April 28, 1988) <http://exchanges.state.gov/culprop/100-298.html>

CODES OF ETHICS AND POSITION PAPERS

- International Council of Museums (ICOM) Code of Ethics for Museums <http://icom.museum/ethics.html#begin>
- International Council on Monuments and Sites (ICOMOS) Ethical Commitment Statement <http://www.international.icomos.org/ethical_e.htm>
- UNESCO International Code of Ethics for Dealers in Cultural Property <http://portal.unesco.org/culture/en/ev.php-URL_ID=13095&URL_DO=DO_TOPIC&URL_SECTION=201.html>
- American Association of Museums (AAM) Code of Ethics for Museums <http://www.aam-us.org/museumresources/ethics/coe.cfm>
- College Art Association (CAA) Code of Ethics for Art Historians and Guidelines for the Professional Practice of Art History <http://www.collegeart.org/caa/ethics/art_hist_ethics.html>
- Archaeological Institute of America Code of Ethics <http://www.archaeological.org/pdfs/AIA_Code_of_EthicsA5S.pdf>
- Association of Art Museum Directors (AAMD) Code of Ethics <http://www.aamd.org/about/#Code>
- Art Museums and the Identification and Restitution of Works Stolen by the Nazis <http://www.aamd.org/pdfs/Nazi%20Looted%20Art.pdf>
- AAM Guidelines Concerning the Unlawful Appropriation of Objects During the Nazi Era <http://www.aam-us.org/museumresources/ethics/nazi_guidelines.cfm>
- Report of the AAMD Task Force on the Acquisition of Archaeological Materials and Ancient Art <http://www.aamd.org/papers/documents/June10FinalTaskForceReport_001.pdf>
- T. Hill and T. Nicks, "The Task Force on Museums and First Peoples" (1992) 10:2, 10:3, Muse.

BIBLIOGRAPHY

Books

- Konstantin Akinsha et al, *Beautiful Loot: the Soviet Plunder of Europe's Art Treasures* (New York: Random House, 1995).
- Richard T. Arndt, *The First Resort of Kings. American Cultural Diplomacyin the Twentieth Century* (Washington, D.C.: Potomac Books, 2005).
- Paul Bator, *The International Trade in Art* (Chicago: University of Chicago Press, 1983).
- Martine Briat, Judith A. Freedberg, eds., *Legal Aspects of International Trade in Art – Les aspects juridiques du commerce international de l'art* (Paris; New York: ICC Pub.; The Hague; Boston: Kluwer Law International, 1996).
- Michael F. Brown, *Who Owns Native Culture?* (Harvard University Press, 2003).
- Ed. Guido Camarda & Tullio Scovazzi, *The Protection of the Underwater Cultural Heritage: Legal Aspects* (Giuffre Editore).

- Kevin Chamberlain, *War and Cultural Heritage* (Great Britain: Institute of Art and Law, 2004).
- Roberta Garabello & Tullio Scovazzi, ed., *Protection of the Underwater Cultural Heritage: before and after the 2001 UNESCO Convention* (Brill Academic Publishers, January 2003).
- Ghose, Saroj, ed. *Handbook of Standards: Documenting African Collections*, (ICOM; Paris, 1996).
- Jeannette Greenfield, *The Return of Cultural Treasures* (Cambridge; New York: Cambridge University Press, 1996).
- International Bureau of the Permanent Court of Arbitration/Peace Palace Papers, ed., *Resolution of Cultural Property Disputes*, (Hague, London New York: Kluwer Law International, 2004).
- Silke von Lewinski, ed., *Indigenous Heritage and Intellectual Property*, (Hague, London. New York: Kluwer Law International, 2004).
- John Henry Merryman, *Thinking About the Elgin Marbles: Critical Essays on Cultural Property, Art and Law* (The Hague, Boston: Kluwer Law International, 2000).
- Patrick J. O'Keefe, *Trade in Antiquities: Reducing Destruction and Theft* (Paris: UNESCO pub; London: Archetype, 1997).
- Karl E. Meyer, *The Plundered Past*, (New York: Simon & Shuster Adult Publishing Group, 1973).
- The Protection of Movable Cultural Property I: Compendium of Legislative Texts (Paris: UNESCO, 1984–).
- Lyndel V. Prott, *Commentary on the Unidroit Convention on Stolen and Illegally Exported Cultural Objects 1995* (Leicester: Institute of Art and Law, 1997).
- Joseph L. Sax, *Playing Darts With a Rembrandt* (University of Michigan Press, 1999).
- Tullio Scovazzi, ed., *La Protezione del Patrimonio Culturale sotto Marino nel Mare Meditteraneo*, (Guiffre Editore, Milan, 2004) (articles in Italian and English).
- Nancy H. Yeide, Konstantin Akinsha, and Amy L. Walsh, *The AAM Guide to Provenance Research* (Washington, D.C.: American Association of Museum, 2001).

Internet Bibliographies

- *Selected Bibliography on Art Theft*, ((c) Getty Museum) <http://www.museum-security.org/bibliogr.html>
- *Selected Titles on European Art Loss and Restitution* (The Art Institute of Chicago) <http://www.artic.edu/aic/libraries/provenance.html>
- Legal Protection of Cultural Property: A Selective Resource Guide (By Louise Tang) <http://www.llrx.com/features/culturalproperty.htm>

Journals and Periodicals

- *Archeology* (The Archeological Institute of America)
- *Art, Antiquity and Law* (Institute of Art and Law, UK)
- *IFAR Journal* (International Foundation for Art Research)
- *International Journal of Cultural Property* (International Cultural Property Society, Cambridge University Press)
- *Spoils of War* (International Newsletter published by the German Coordination Office of the Federal States for the Return of Cultural Treasures)
- *Arts Journal: The Daily Digest of Art, Culture & Ideas* <http://www.artsjournal.com/>
- *ARTNews* <http://www.artnewsonline.com/>
- *The Art Newspaper* <http://www.theartnewspaper.com/index.asp>
- Joseph Wong, ed., *University of British Columbia Law Review* (U.B.C. Law Review Society, 1995).

EFFORTS TO PROTECT CULTURAL PROPERTY

International

- Art Loss Register <http://www.artloss.com/Default.asp>
- European Heritage Network (HEREIN) <http://www.european-heritage.net/>
- International Council of Museums (ICOM) <http://icom.museum/>
- International Council on Monuments and Sites (ICOMOS) <http://www.icomos.org/>
- InterPol <http://www.interpol.int/Public/WorkOfArt/Default.asp>
- Object ID <http://www.object-id.com/>
- Red List ICOM <http://icom.museum/redlist/>
- World Heritage Center <http://whc.unesco.org/pg.cfm>
- World Customs Organization (WCO) <http://www.wcoomd.org/ie/index.html>
- UNESCO <http://portal.unesco.org/culture/fr/ev.php-URL_ID=22554&URL_DO=DO_TOPIC&URL_SECTION=201.html>

United States

- FBI Art Theft Program <http://www.fbi.gov/hq/cid/arttheft/arttheft.htm>
- United States Central Bureau of InterPol Cultural Property Program <http://www.usdoj.gov/usncb/cultprop/cultureabout.htm>
- The President's Cultural Property Advisory Committee <http://exchanges.state.gov/culprop/committee.html>

RESTITUTION OF WORLD WAR II ERA STOLEN ART

Books

- Hector Feliciano, *The Lost Museum: The Nazi Conspiracy to Steal the World's Greatest Works of Art* (New York: Basic Books, 1997).
- Wojciech W. Kowalski, *Art Treasures and War: a Study on the Restitution of Looted Cultural Property, Pursuant to Public International Law* (London: Institute of Art and Law, 1998).
- Michael J. Kurtz, *Nazi Contraband: American Policy on the Return of European Cultural Treasures, 1945–1955* (New York: Garland, 1985).
- Lynn H. Nicholas, *The Rape of Europa: the Fate of Europe's Treasures in the Third Reich and the Second World War* (New York: Knopf, 1994).
- *OSS Art Looting Investigation Unit Reports, 1945–46* (Washington, D.C., National Archives and Records Administration, 2000) (microfilm).
- Jonathan Petropoulos, *Art as Politics in the Third Reich* (Chapel Hill: University of North Carolina Press, 1996).
- Jonathan Petropoulos, *The Faustian Bargain: The Art World in Nazi Germany* (New York: Oxford University Press, 2000).
- Elizabeth Simpson, ed., *The Spoils of War: World War II and its Aftermath: The Loss, Reappearance and Recovery of Cultural Property* (New York: H.N. Abrams in association with the Bard Graduate Center for Studies in the Decorative Arts, 1997).

Internet Resources

- *Looted Art: A Teacher's Guide to the Holocaust* (Florida Center for Instructional Technology, College of Education, University of South Florida)
  <http://www.fcit.usf.edu/holocaust/resource/biblio/ARTBIBLT.HTM>
- *Holocaust-Era Assets* (US National Archives and Records Administration)
  <http://www.archives.gov/research_room/holocaust_era_assets/bibliographies/bibliographies.html>
- Spoliation of Jewish Property / Spoliation des biens juifs: Bibliography Compiled by the UNESCO.ICOM Information Centre
  <http://icom.museum/biblio_spoliation.html>
- *Focus on Looted Art* (Collection of Art Newspaper articles related to Nazi looted art (1997–2001)).
  <http://www.theartnewspaper.com/looted/lootedart.asp>

International Agencies

- Conference on Jewish Material Claims against Germany
  <http://www.claimscon.org/>
- Central Registry of Information on Looted Cultural Property 1933–1945
  <http://www.lootedart.com/>
- International List of Current Activities Regarding Holocaust-Era Assets, Including Historical Commissions, and Forced and Slave Labor
  <http://www.ushmm.org/assets/>
- Commission for Looted Art in Europe (Resolution 1205 of the Council of Europe)
  <http://www.lootedartcommission.com/lootedart_councilofeurope.htm>
- Vilnius International Forum on Holocaust Era Looted Cultural Assets
  <http://www.vilniusforum.lt/>
- The World Jewish Congress Commission for Art Recovery (WJCCAR)

United States

- Washington Conference on Holocaust-Era Assets
  <http://www.state.gov/r/pa/ho/hear/>
- Holocaust Era Assets (National Archives and Records Administration)
  <http://www.archives.gov/research_room/holocaust_era_assets/index.html>
- American Association of Museums Nazi-Era Provenance Internet Portal
  <http://www.nepip.org/>
- New York State Holocaust Claims Processing Office – Art Claims
  <http://www.claims.state.ny.us/art.htm>
- Plunder and Restitution: Findings and Recommendations of the Presidential Advisory Commission on Holocaust Assets in the US and Staff Report December 2000
  <http://www.holocaustassets.gov/PlunderRestitution.html/html/Home_Contents.html>
- Presidential Commission on Holocaust Assets in the US
  <http://www.pcha.gov/>
- Project for the Documentation of Wartime Cultural Losses (the Documentation Project)
  <http://docproj.loyola.edu/>

United Kingdom

- Art and Antiques Stolen Property Database (A.C.I.S.)
  <http://www.met.police.uk/artandantiques/ACIS_database.htm>
- National Museum Directors' Conference: spoliation of Works of Art during the Holocaust and World War II Period: Progress Report on UK Museums' Provenance Research for the Period 1933–1945
  <http://www.nationalmuseums.org.uk/spoliation/spoliation.html>

Other Countries

- Provenance Research Project (National Gallery of Victoria, Australia)
  <http://www.ngv.vic.gov.au/provenance/>
- Landesmuseum Joanneum (Austria)
  <http://www.museum-joanneum.at/restitution/>
- Restitution Art (Czech Republic)
  <http://www.restitution-art.cz/english/main.html>
- Catalogue des MRN (Musées Nationaux Récupération)
  <http://www.culture.gouv.fr/documentation/mnr/pres.htm>
- Schloss Collection Non-restituted Works Looted (Ministère des affaires étrangères, France)
  <http://www.france.diplomatie.fr/archives/dossiers/schloss/index_ang.html>
- Lost Art Internet Database (Germany)
  <http://www.lostart.de/index.php3?lang=english>
- Art Treasures Removed from Italy During the War Period, 1940–1945 (Interministerial Commission for Art Works, Italy)
- Origins Unknown (The Netherlands)
  <http://www.herkomstgezocht.nl/eng/index.html>
- Wartime Losses Polish Painting: Oil Paintings, Pastels, Watercolours Lost between 1939–1945 within Post-1945 Borders of Poland
  <http://www.polamcon.org/lostart/index.html>

A SELECTIVE LIST OF NON-PROFIT ORGANIZATIONS IN CULTURAL AND NATURAL HERITAGE CONSERVATION

- Association for the Restoration of the Italian Artistic Patrimony (ARPAI): <www.arpai.org>
  See Part IX of this Book.
- Global Heritage Fund: <www.globalheritagefund.org>
  The Global Heritage Fund (GHF) was founded to address a critical need in world heritage conservation to preserve and protect endangered cultural heritage sites in developing counties. The Fund works only in developing countries and regions where the need for protection is most urgent, where expertise and management skills exist, but conservation is inadequately supported, and where GHF involvement and funding at critical stages bridge the gap between success and failure. GHF encompasses the entire lifecycle of planning, conservation, advocacy, and economic development necessary for long-term success. It also teaches how humans have lived their lives and made sense of the world – from the microcosm of family to the macrocosm of society. GHF believes sustainable conservation creates parks and preserves for enjoyment, knowledge, and research – a legacy for future generations.
- The Nature Conservancy: <www.nature.org>
  The Nature Conservancy is a leading international organization dedicated to preserving the diversity of life on Earth. The mission of The Nature Conservancy is to preserve the plants, animals, and natural communities that represent the diversity of life on Earth by protecting the lands and waters they need to survive. The Nature Conservancy works closely with partners, corporations, indigenous people, and traditional communities all over the world to achieve tangible results using a nonconfrontational, collaborative approach and exercising integrity beyond reproach and operating openly and transparently, and accountable to all those who have a stake in preserving our precious natural resources.
- The Tairona Trust: <www.taironatrust.org>
  The Tairona Trust is a registered charity in the United Kingdom that provides support for the Kogi under the direction of the Mamas. It has provided help for land purchase and administration and is currently exploring strategies to assist in the defense of their culture.
- World Monuments Fund: <www.wmf.org>
  The World Monuments Fund (WMF) is dedicated to the preservation of historic art and architecture worldwide through fieldwork, advocacy, grantmaking, education, and training. It works with local communities and partners to stem the loss of more than 430 irreplaceable sites in eighty-three countries. Cutting across geographic, cultural, and national boundaries, WMF projects have ranged from the renowned stone carvings of Easter Island to the historic synagogue in Krakow, Poland, to Cambodia's jungle temples, to the adobe churches of New Mexico, to the frescoed ceilings of Venetian churches.

UNIDROIT CONVENTION ON STOLEN PROPERTY, JUNE 24, 1995

THE *STATE PARTIES* TO THIS CONVENTION:

ASSEMBLED in Rome at the invitation of the Government of the Italian Republic from 7 to 24 June 1995 for a Diplomatic Conference for the adoption of the draft Unidroit Convention on the International Return of Stolen or Illegally Exported Cultural Objects,

CONVINCED of the fundamental importance of the protection of cultural heritage and of cultural exchanges for promoting understanding between peoples, and the dissemination of culture for the well-being of humanity and the progress of civilisation,

DEEPLY CONCERNED by the illicit trade in cultural objects and the irreparable damage frequently caused by it, both to these objects themselves and to the cultural heritage of national, tribal, indigenous or other communities, and also to the heritage of all peoples, and in particular by the pillage of archaeological sites and the resulting loss of irreplaceable archaeological, historical and scientific information,

DETERMINED to contribute effectively to the fight against illicit trade in cultural objects by taking the important step of establishing common, minimal legal rules for the restitution and return of cultural objects between Contracting States, with the objective of improving the preservation and protection of the cultural heritage in the interest of all,

EMPHASISING that this Convention is intended to facilitate the restitution and return of cultural objects, and that the provision of any remedies, such as compensation, needed to effect restitution and return in some States, does not imply that such remedies should be adopted in other States,

AFFIRMING that the adoption of the provisions of this Convention for the future in no way confers any approval or legitimacy upon illegal transactions of whatever kind which may have taken place before the entry into force of the Convention,

CONSCIOUS that this Convention will not by itself provide a solution to the problems raised by illicit trade, but that it initiates a process that will enhance international cultural co-operation and maintain a proper role for legal trading and inter-State agreements for cultural exchanges,

ACKNOWLEDGING that implementation of this Convention should be accompanied by other effective measures for protecting cultural objects, such as the development and use of registers, and the physical protection of archaeological sites and technical co-operation,

RECOGNISING the work of various bodies to protect cultural property, particularly the 1970 UNESCO Convention on illicit traffic and the development of codes of conduct in the private sector,

HAVE AGREED as follows:

Chapter I – Scope of Application and Definition

Article 1. This Convention applies to claims of an international character for:

a. the restitution of stolen cultural objects;
b. the return of cultural objects removed from the territory of a Contracting State contrary to its law regulating the export of cultural objects for the purpose of protecting its cultural heritage (hereafter "illegally exported cultural objects").

Article 2. For the purposes of this Convention, cultural objects are those which, on religious or secular grounds, are of importance for archaeology, prehistory, history, literature, art or science and belong to one of the categories listed in the Annex to this Convention.

Chapter II – Restitution of Stolen Cultural Objects

Article 3

(1) The possessor of a cultural object which has been stolen shall return it.
(2) For the purposes of this Convention, a cultural object which has been unlawfully excavated or lawfully excavated but unlawfully retained shall be considered stolen, when consistent with the law of the State where the excavation took place.
(3) Any claim for restitution shall be brought within a period of three years from the time when the claimant knew the location of the cultural object and the identity of its possessor, and in any case within a period of 50 years from the time of the theft.
(4) However, a claim for restitution of a cultural object forming an integral part of an identified monument or archaeological site, or belonging to a public collection, shall not be subject to time limitations other than a period of three years from the time when the claimant knew the location of the cultural object and the identity of its possessor.
(5) Notwithstanding the provisions of the preceding paragraph, any Contracting State may declare that a claim is subject to a time limitation of 75 years or such longer period as is provided in its law. A claim made in another Contracting State for restitution of a cultural object displaced from a monument, archaeological site or public collection in a Contracting State making such a declaration shall also be subject to that time limitation.
(6) A declaration referred to in the preceding paragraph shall be made at the time of signature, ratification, acceptance, approval or accession.
(7) For the purposes of this Convention, a "public collection," consists of a group of inventoried or otherwise identified cultural objects owned by:
   a. a Contracting State
   b. a regional or local authority of a Contracting State;
   c. a religious institution in a Contracting State; or
   d. an institution that is established for an essentially cultural, educational or scientific purpose in a Contracting State and is recognised in that State as serving the public interest.
(8) In addition, a claim for restitution of a sacred or communally important cultural object belonging to and used by a tribal or indigenous community in a Contracting State as part of that community's traditional or ritual use, shall be subject to the time limitation applicable to public collections.

Article 4

(1) The possessor of a stolen cultural object required to return it shall be entitled, at the time of its restitution, to payment of fair and reasonable compensation provided that the possessor neither knew nor ought reasonably to have known that the object was stolen and can prove that it exercised due diligence when acquiring the object.
(2) Without prejudice to the right of the possessor to compensation referred to in the preceding paragraph, reasonable efforts shall be made to have the person who transferred the cultural object to the possessor, or any prior transferor,

pay the compensation where to do so would be consistent with the law of the State in which the claim is brought.

(3) Payment of compensation to the possessor by the claimant, when this is required, shall be without prejudice to the right of the claimant to recover it from any other person.

(4) In determining whether the possessor exercised due diligence, regard shall be had to all the circumstances of the acquisition, including the character of the parties, the price paid, whether the possessor consulted any reasonably accessible register of stolen cultural objects, and any other relevant information and documentation which it could reasonably have obtained, and whether the possessor consulted accessible agencies or took any other step that a reasonable person would have taken in the circumstances.

(5) The possessor shall not be in a more favourable position than the person from whom it acquired the cultural object by inheritance or otherwise gratuitously.

Chapter III – Return of Illegally Exported Cultural Objects

Article 5

(1) A Contracting State may request the court or other competent authority of another Contracting State to order the return of a cultural object illegally exported from the territory of the requesting State.

(2) A cultural object which has been temporarily exported from the territory of the requesting State, for purposes such as exhibition, research or restoration under a permit issued according to its law regulating its export for the purpose of protecting its cultural heritage and not returned in accordance with the terms of that permit shall be deemed to have been illegally exported.

(3) The court or other competent authority of the State addressed shall order the return of an illegally exported cultural object if the requesting State establishes that the removal of the object from its territory significantly impairs one or more of the following interests:

a. the physical preservation of the object or of its context;
b. the integrity of a complex object;
c. the preservation of information of, for example, a scientific or historical character;
d. the traditional or ritual use of the object by a tribal or indigenous community, or establishes that the object is of significant cultural importance for the requesting State.

(4) Any request made under paragraph I of this article shall contain or be accompanied by such information of a factual or legal nature as may assist the court or other competent authority of the State addressed in determining whether the requirements of paragraphs 1 to 3 have been met.

(5) Any request for return shall be brought within a period of three years from the time when the requesting State knew the location of the cultural object and the identity of its possessor, and any case within a period of 50 years from the date of the export or from the date on which the object should have been returned under a permit referred to in paragraph 2 of this article.

Article 6

(1) The possessor of a cultural object who acquired the object after it was illegally exported shall be entitled, at the time of its return, to payment by the requesting State of fair and reasonable compensation, provided that the possessor neither knew nor ought reasonably to have known at the time of acquisition that the object had been illegally exported.

(2) In determining whether the possessor knew or ought reasonably to have known that cultural object had been illegally exported, regard shall be had to the circumstances of the acquisition, including the absence of an export certificate required under the law of the requesting State.

(3) Instead of compensation, and in agreement with the requesting State, the possessor required to return the cultural object to that State may decide:

a. to retain ownership of the object; or
b. to transfer ownership against payment or gratuitously to a person of its choice residing in the requesting State who provides the necessary Guarantees.

(4) The cost of returning the cultural object in accordance with this article shall be borne by the requesting State, without prejudice to the right of that State to recover costs from any other person.

(5) The possessor shall not be in a more favourable position than the person from whom it acquired the cultural object by inheritance or otherwise gratuitously.

Article 7

(1) The provisions of this Chapter shall not apply where:

a. the export of a cultural object is no longer illegal at the time at which the return is requested; or
b. the object was exported during the lifetime of the person who created it or within a period of 50 years following the death of that person.

(2) Notwithstanding the provisions of sub-paragraph (b) of the preceding paragraph, the provisions of this Chapter shall apply where a cultural object was made by a member or members of a tribal or indigenous community for traditional or ritual use by that community and the object will be returned to that community.

Chapter IV – General Provisions

Article 8

(1) A claim under Chapter II and a request under Chapter III may be brought before the courts or other competent authorities of the Contracting State where the cultural

object is located, in addition to the courts or other competent authorities otherwise having jurisdiction under the rules in force in Contracting States.

(2) The parties may agree to submit the dispute to any court or to other competent authority or arbitration.

(3) Resort may be had to the provisional, including protective, measures available under the law of the Contracting State where the object is located even when the claim for restitution or request for return of the object is brought before the courts or other competent authorities of another Contracting State.

Article 9

(1) Nothing in this Convention shall prevent a Contracting State from applying any rules more favourable to the restitution or the return of stolen or illegally exported cultural objects than provided for by this Convention.

(2) This article shall not be interpreted as creating an obligation to recognise or enforce a decision of a court or other competent authority of another Contracting State that departs from the provisions of this Convention.

Article 10

(1) The provisions of Chapter II shall apply only in respect of a cultural object that is stolen after this Convention enters into force in respect of the State where the claim is brought, provided that:

a. the object was stolen from the territory of a Contracting State after the entry into force of this Convention for that State; or

b. the object is located in a Contracting State after the entry into force of the Convention for that State.

(2) The provisions of Chapter III shall apply only in respect of a cultural object that is illegally exported after this Convention enters into force for the requesting State as well as the State where the request is brought.

(3) This Convention does not in any way legitimise any illegal transaction of whatever nature which has taken place before the entry into force of this Convention or which is excluded under paragraphs (1) or (2) of this article, nor limit any right of a State or other person to make a claim under remedies available outside the framework of this Convention for the restitution or return of a cultural object stolen or illegally exported before the entry into force of this Convention.

Chapter V – Final Provisions

Article 11

(1) This Convention is open for signature at the concluding meeting of the Diplomatic Conference for the adoption of the draft Unidroit Convention on the International Return of Stolen or Illegally Exported Cultural Objects and will remain open for signature by all States at Rome until 30 June 1996.

(2) This Convention is subject to ratification, acceptance or approval by States which have signed it.

(3) This Convention is open for accession by all States which are not signatory States as from the date it is open for signature.

(4) Ratification, acceptance, approval or accession is subject to the deposit of a formal instrument to that effect with the depositary.

Article 12

(1) This Convention shall enter into force on the first day of the sixth month following the date of deposit of the fifth instrument of ratification, acceptance, approval, or accession.

(2) For each State that ratifies, accepts, approves or accedes to this Convention after the deposit of the fifth instrument of ratification, acceptance, approval or accession, this Convention shall enter into force in respect of that State on the first day of the sixth month following the date of deposit of its instrument of ratification, acceptance, approval or accession.

Article 13

(1) This Convention does not affect any international instrument by which any Contracting State is legally bound and which contains provisions on matters governed by this Convention, unless a contrary declaration is made by the States bound by such instrument.

(2) Any Contracting State may enter into agreements with one or more Contracting States, with a view to improving the application of this Convention in their mutual relations. The States which have concluded such an agreement shall transmit a copy to the depositary.

(3) In their relations with each other, Contracting States which are Members of organizations of economic integration or regional bodies may declare that they will apply the internal rules of these organizations or bodies and will not therefore apply as between these States the provisions of this Convention the scope of application of which coincides with that of those rules.

Article 14

(1) If a Contracting State has two or more territorial units, whether or not possessing different systems of law applicable in relation to the matters dealt with in this Convention, it may, at the time of signature or of the deposit of its instrument of ratification, acceptance, approval or accession, declare that this Convention is to extend to all its territorial units or only to one or more of them, and may substitute for its declaration another declaration at any time.

(2) These declarations are to be notified to the depositary and are to state expressly the territorial units to which the Convention extends.
(3) If, by virtue of a declaration under this article, this Convention extends to one or more but not all of the territorial units of a Contracting State, the reference to:
   a. the territory of a Contracting State in Article 1 shall be construed as referring to the territory of a territorial unit of that State;
   b. a court or other competent authority of the Contracting State or of the State addressed shall be construed as referring to the court or other competent authority of a territorial unit of that State;
   c. the Contracting State where the cultural object is located in Article 8 (1) shall be construed as referring to the territorial unit of that State where the object is located;
   d. the law of the Contracting State where the object is located in Article 8 (3) shall be construed as referring to the law of the territorial unit of that State where the object is located; and
   e. a Contracting State in Article 9 shall be construed as referring to a territorial unit of that State.
(4) If a Contracting State makes no declaration under paragraph 1 of this article, this Convention is to extend to all territorial units of that State.

Article 15

(1) Declarations made under this Convention at the time of signature are subject confirmation upon ratification, acceptance or approval.
(2) Declarations and confirmations of declarations are to be in writing and to be formally notified to the depositary.
(3) A declaration shall take effect simultaneously with the entry into force of this Convention in respect of the State concerned. However, a declaration of which the depositary receives formal notification after such entry into force shall take effect on the first day of the sixth month following the date of its deposit with the depositary.
(4) Any State which makes a declaration. under this Convention may withdraw it at any time by a formal notification in writing addressed to the depositary. Such withdrawal shall take effect on the first day of the sixth month following the date of the deposit of the notification.

Article 16

(1) Each Contracting State shall at the time of signature, ratification, acceptance, approval, or accession, declare that claims for the restitution, or requests for the return, of cultural objects brought by a State under Article 8 may be submitted to it under one or more of the following procedures:
   a. directly to the courts or other competent authorities of the declaring State;
   b. through an authority or authorities designated by that State to receive such claims or requests and to forward them to the courts or other competent authorities of that State;
   c. through diplomatic or consular channels.
(2) Each Contracting State may also designate the courts or other authorities competent to order the restitution or return of cultural objects under the provisions of Chapters II and III.
(3) Declarations made under paragraphs 1 and 2 of this article may be modified at any time by a new declaration.
(4) The provisions of paragraphs I to 3 of this article do not affect bilateral or multilateral agreements on judicial assistance in respect of civil and commercial matters that may exisit between Contracting States.

Article 17. Each Contracting State shall, no later than six months following the date of deposit of its instrument of ratification, acceptance, approval or accession, provide the depositary with written information in one of the official languages of the Convention concerning the legislation regulating the export of its cultural objects. This information shall be updated from time to time as appropriate.

Article 18. No reservations are permitted except those expressly authorised in this Convention.

Article 19

(1) This Convention may be denounced by any State Party, at any time after the date on which it enters into force for that State, by the deposit of an instrument to that effect with the depositary.
(2) A denunciation shall take effect on the first day of the sixth month following the deposit of the instrument of denunciation with the depositary. Where a longer period for the denunciation to take effect is specified in the instrument of denunciation it shall take effect upon the expiration of such longer period after its deposit with the depositary.
(3) Notwithstanding such a denunciation, this Convention shall nevertheless apply to a claim for restitution or a request for return of a cultural object submitted prior to the date on which the denunciation takes effect.

Article 20. The President of the International Institute for the Unification of Private Law (Unidroit) may at regular intervals, or at any time at the request of five Contracting States, convene a special committee in order to review the practical operation of this Convention.

Article 21

(1) This Convention shall be deposited with the Government of the Italian Republic.

(2) The Government of the Italian Republic shall:
  a. inform all States which have signed or acceded to this Convention and the President of the International Institute for the Unification of Private Law (Unidroit) of:
    i. each new signature or deposit of an instrument of ratification, acceptance approval or accession, together with the date thereof;
    ii. each declaration made in accordance with this Convention;
    iii. the withdrawal of any declaration;
    iv. the date of entry into force of this Convention;
    v. the agreements referred to in Article 13;
    vi. the deposit of an instrument of denunciation of this Convention together with the date of its deposit and the date on which it takes effect;
  b. transmit certified true copies of this Convention to all signatory States, to all States acceding to the Convention and to the President of the International Institute for the Unification of Private Law (Unidroit).
  c. perform such other functions customary for depositaries.

IN WITNESS WHEREOF the undersigned plenipotentiaries, being duly authorised, have signed this Convention.

DONE at Rome, this twenty-fourth day of June, one thousand nine hundred and ninety-five, in a single original, in the English and French languages, both texts being equally authentic.

Annex

a. Rare collections and specimens of fauna, flora, minerals and anatomy, and objects of palaeontological interest;
b. property relating to history, including the history of science and technology and military and social history, to the life of national leaders, thinkers, scientists and artists and to events of national importance;
c. products of archaeological excavations (Including regular and clandestine) or of archaeological discoveries;
d. elements of artistic or historical monuments or archaeological sites which have been dismembered;
e. antiquities more than one hundred years old, such as inscriptions, coins and engraved seals;
f. objects of ethnological interest;
g. property of artistic interest, such as:
  i. pictures, paintings and drawings produced entirely by hand on any support and in any material (excluding industrial designs and manufactured articles decorated by hand);
  ii. original works of statuary art and sculpture in any material;
  iii. original engravings, prints and lithographs;
  iv. original artistic assemblages and montages in any material;
h. rare manuscripts and incunabula, old books, documents and publications of special interest (historical, artistic, scientific, literary, etc.) singly or in collections;
i. postage stamps, revenue and similar stamps, singly or in collections;
j. archives, including sound, photographic and cinematographic archives; articles of furniture more than one hundred years old and old musical instruments.

PUBLIC SUMMARY REQUEST OF THE PEOPLE'S REPUBLIC OF CHINA TO THE GOVERNMENT OF THE UNITED STATES OF AMERICA UNDER ARTICLE 9 OF THE 1970 UNESCO CONVENTION[1]

Pillage of archaeological sites and smuggling of cultural artifacts in China has become rampant in recent years despite the law enforcement efforts of the Chinese government. Artifact smuggling is a major threat to the protection of Chinese and world cultural heritage. To address this problem, the State Administration of Cultural Heritage, on behalf of the Government of the People's Republic of China, is making a request to the Government of the United States for assistance under Article 9 of the 1970 UNESCO Convention.

Cultural History and Archaeology of China

...

Pillage and Looting

Since the mid-19th c., through invasion and other means, foreign powers have looted Chinese archaeological artifacts. From the beginning of the 20th c., adventurers came into China to pillage sites and illicitly remove countless artifacts. Since its inception in 1949, the People's Republic of China has devoted many resources to the protection of its cultural heritage. However, in the last 10 years looting has again become a serious problem.

The world-wide popularity and high prices for Chinese archaeological artifacts have encouraged illegal excavation and smuggling of cultural property. Although Chinese customs and other functional departments have intensified their efforts to crack down on smuggling and illicit excavation, pillage and smuggling continues to be a real problem.

In 1997, for example, Tianjin Customs traced a container of over 4,000 archaeological artifacts which were destined for abroad. Later that year, Tianjin customs identified two shipments destined for South Korea of over 513 pieces including stone horse statues, stone tortoises and Buddhist statuary. In June, a shipment traced to Beijing and destined for the United States contained over 2,200 pieces of smuggled items including ancient porcelain, Buddhist stone statues, and Tibetan sutras. Other examples abound. Although many shipments have been intercepted, others are successfully smuggled abroad for sale on the international market.

[1] Provided by the U.S. government at <http://exchanges.state.gov/culprop/cn04sum.html>.

This huge demand for Chinese cultural artifacts has caused serious damage to ancient tombs and ancient sites. Gangs of criminals have been identified with their own networks of pillage, transportation, smuggling and sales abroad. The Chinese government has devoted many resources to stopping the pillage and smuggling, but many ancient sites, tombs, stone statuary, and temples are scattered throughout the undeveloped countryside where protection is difficult.

The looting and destruction of so many artifacts from archaeological sites and monuments has caused great damage to Chinese cultural heritage. One notable example are the Tombs of the Marquis of the Jin State in Shanxi Provence. The inscribed artifacts excavated from this site are crucial to the study of the history of the Jin State. However, since the tombs have been pillaged and their artifacts smuggled abroad, the continuity of historical record has been broken. Elsewhere, many stone Buddhist statues dating to the Northern Wei and Song Dynasty were looted. These were important to the study of development of style and chronology of Buddhist statuary, now seriously compromised. These and other examples of looting illustrate the damage to scholarship and knowledge caused by illicit excavation and removal of artifacts.

Efforts of the Chinese Government to Protect Cultural Heritage

The Government of China attaches great importance to the protection of cultural heritage and has instituted a system of laws to protect archaeological sites and archaeological objects. In 1950, just a year after the founding of the People's Republic of China, the government promulgated the Provisional Methods on the Prohibition of Export of Rare Cultural Relics and Books and the Provisional Methods Governing Survey and Excavation of Ancient Cultural Sites and Tombs. In addition, Article 22 of the Constitution of the People's Republic of China stipulates "places of historic interest and scenic beauty, rare cultural relics and other important historical and cultural heritage are protected by the State." Articles on the protection of artifacts are included in the Criminal Law of the People's Republic of China. The Cultural Relics Protection Law of the People's Republic of China was passed in 1982 and amended in 1991. [A new Cultural Relics Protection Law was passed in 2002.] Rules and regulations issued by the Ministry of Culture and State Administration of Cultural Heritage guide the implementation of these laws.

The State Bureau for Museums and Archaeological Data was set up in 1949 and renamed the State Administration for Cultural Heritage (SACH) in 1988. This institution is responsible for the protection of cultural relics throughout the country, planning for the development, rules and regulations, management of sites and museum, approval of archaeological excavation projects, salvage archaeology, and study and formulation of new regulations governing the circulation of archaeological artifacts.

The Ministry of Public Security, General Administration of Customs, and the State Administration for Industry and Commerce also take part in the protection and administration of cultural heritage. Special administrations on protection of cultural relics are set up in the provinces, autonomous regions, municipalities, counties and cities. Institutes for Archaeological Research and Cultural Artifacts, museums, and institutes for the protection of ancient buildings have been set up by the central government in all regions. These institutions are responsible for survey, excavation, study, conservation, and collection of archaeological remains.

Offices for the protection of cultural relics are set up in each county. These are the grass-roots organs to conserve and administer local archaeological sites and artifacts. Some villages and towns have set up teams to care for sites and cultural artifacts in their areas of jurisdiction.

Museums have existed in China for one hundred years. The first to be established was the Nantong Museum in 1905. By 1982, China had established over 1,900 museums. These museums received over 100 million visitors in the year 2000. The collections include almost 10 million pieces of cultural heritage. Most museums are run by the government and their main financial support is government funding. More recently, however, private museums have opened in a number of cities.

National cultural inventory of archaeological collections was begun in 1989 to enhance the protection of the collections. Inspection, registration, and establishment of an archive is almost complete. Collections are classified into rare and general cultural artifacts. The rare cultural artifacts are further classified into three grades for which there are different protection and conservation standards.

Export of cultural artifacts is regulated by law. It states in the cultural artifacts protection law that, except for those approved by the State Council for the purpose of exhibition overseas, cultural relics with important historical, artistic and scientific value are prohibited from being exported overseas. SACH has set up State appraisal stations for exporting cultural artifacts in seventeen cities nationwide. The government has arranged for many college graduates in archaeology to work in the Customs office each year. The regional SACH offices also cooperate with Customs to organize training for Customs staff.

Private collections and the trade in cultural artifact is also regulated by law. Citizens of China may register their private collections with SACH. Citizens may sell their private collections to institutions with collections of cultural artifacts or to cultural artifact dealers as regulated by SACH. Businesses which buy and sell cultural artifacts do so must be approved by SACH or the administrations of provincial, autonomous region, or municipal government and are subject to registration in the Administration of Industry and Commerce. Rare cultural artifacts are subject to the most stringent controls.

In recent years, more regulation of the market has been put into effect through the government Notice on Enhancing the Administration of the Cultural Artifacts Market and the Notice on Rectifying and Regulating the Market Order in the

Cultural Artifacts Market (2000). SACH has helped cultural artifact dealers meet the legitimate domestic and overseas demand while cooperating with Customs and police entities to eradicate the black market in illegal transactions, and to punish the criminals engaged in illicit trade and smuggling.

The Chinese government has also cooperated with the international community to protect cultural heritage through ratification of the 1970 Convention on the Means of Prohibiting and Preventing the Illicit Import, Export and Transfer of Ownership of Cultural Property (1989), UNIDROIT (1995), and the 1954 Hague Convention (1999). The government of China participated in the formulation of the UNESCO Convention on the Protection of Underwater Cultural Heritage and plans to adopt it soon. In order to enhance the implementation of these conventions, in recent years SACH has conducted a nationwide public awareness campaign that included experts from INTERPOL, World Customs Organization, International Council on Museums, Art Loss Register and others.

Through INTERPOL or with the cooperation of authorities in other governments, the Chinese government has been able to identify and return many artifacts looted from archaeological sites or stolen from museums. For example, in 1998 the Chinese government received over 3,000 artifacts from the authorities in the UK.

The Chinese government has been very active in promoting cultural heritage protection through public education. In 1989, for example, the Ministry of Culture and SACH issued the Promotion Outline for the Program of Everyone Cherishing the Cultural Heritage of the Motherland.

Museums, memorial halls, and cultural heritage protection institutions are open to the public and provide many programs on cultural heritage protection. Each year over 6,000 artifacts are on exhibit for over 100 million visitors. In addition, newspapers and journals report recent finds and comment on the important historical, scientific and artistic value of Chinese cultural heritage. Major newspapers have special sections devoted to Cultural Relics Protection Law and articles on cultural heritage protection.

US Market for Chinese Cultural Artifacts

Although the Chinese government has instituted a series of laws and regulations governing the export of Chinese cultural artifacts, the great number of artifacts, their wide distribution within China, and their attractiveness and high prices on the international market has resulted in rampant pillage and smuggling. Driven by high prices, many looted and smuggled artifacts appear for sale in the US market. This has been demonstrated by the appearance of Chinese excavated material in galleries and auctions and in the interception of shipping containers filled with archaeological artifacts bound for US ports.

Some examples include: November 1997, Seattle Customs discovered large amounts of illicitly exported cultural artifacts in containers shipped from Hong Kong. These were returned to Hong Kong. In June 1998, a stone sculpture from Tomb of Yongtai was identified in an auction catalog in California and returned to China. In 1998 and 1999, shipments were identified in New Jersey and San Diego.

Because of the increase in smuggling and illicit export to the US, the Chinese government believes a bilateral agreement imposing US import restrictions on certain categories of archaeological artifacts from China would prove a useful deterrent.

Significance of Chinese Cultural Heritage to the International Community

Cultural artifacts are a reflection of social systems, modes of production, social life, spiritual culture and beliefs of their respective historical periods. They do, therefore, have great historical, artistic, and scientific value for China and for the international community. China boasts rich sources of cultural knowledge and potential for reconstructing history in thousands of archaeological sites and monuments. Some of the most important of these related to the origins of man, domestication of rice and millet, origins of writing, paper, and printing, as well as silk and porcelain technology. In addition, China is one of the few cultures in the world with an unbroken cultural record from the prehistory to the present. Chinese history and archaeology is, therefore, a key to understanding the process of development of human society and civilization.

THE WORLD BANK OPERATIONAL MANUAL BANK PROCEDURES: PHYSICAL CULTURAL RESOURCES

Introduction

1. Physical cultural resources[1] are important as sources of valuable scientific and historical information, as assets for economic and social development, and as integral parts of a people's cultural identity and practices.
2. Physical cultural resources are seriously threatened throughout the world, partly as a result of modernization and development. The loss of these resources is irreversible, but fortunately, it is often avoidable.
3. The Bank assists countries to avoid adverse impacts on cultural resources from development projects that it finances, or to mitigate such impacts. This policy applies to all components of such projects, regardless of the source of financing.

[1] For the purposes of this policy, "cultural resources" (also termed "cultural heritage," "cultural patrimony," "cultural assets," or "cultural property") refers exclusively to *physical* cultural resources. This includes movable or immovable objects, sites, structures, groups of structures, natural features and landscapes that have archaeological, paleontological, historical, architectural, religious, aesthetic, or other cultural significance. Cultural resources may be located in urban or rural settings, and may be above ground, underground, or underwater.

Cultural Resources and Environmental Assessment

4. The Bank requires the borrower to address impacts on cultural resources in projects proposed for Bank financing as an integral part of its Environmental Assessment (EA) process.[2] The Bank advises the borrower on the Bank's EA requirements, and reviews the findings and recommendations of the EA to determine whether they provide an adequate basis for processing the project for Bank financing.
5. Given that cultural resources may not be known or visible, it is important that a project's potential impacts on cultural resources are considered at the earliest possible stages of project processing.

Screening

6. During environmental screening, projects that are either located in a known cultural heritage site or that involve excavations, demolition, movement of earth, flooding, or other environmental changes should be classified as EA Category A or B. The procedures of the cultural resources component of EA, as set out in this policy, apply to both Category A and B projects.

Scoping

7. As part of the initial, scoping phase of the EA, the borrower, in consultation with the Bank and project-affected groups, identifies the likely major impacts, if any, of the project on cultural resources. This phase should normally include a preliminary on-site inspection of physical cultural resources.
8. The findings of the scoping phase form the basis for the Terms of Reference (TOR) for the cultural resources component of the EA. The TOR normally specifies that a further on-site investigation of physical cultural resources be included in the baseline data collection phase of the EA.

Cultural Resources Component of the Environmental Assessment

9. The borrower informs the Bank of the relevant requirements of its legislation pertaining to the management of physical cultural resources, including provisions for the management of physical cultural resources encountered during project implementation and operation (hereafter referred to as chance finds).
10. The borrower identifies physical cultural resources likely to be affected by the project, and assesses the project's potential impacts on these resources as an integral component of the EA process, in accordance with the Bank's EA requirements.[3]
11. Where the project is likely to have adverse impacts on physical cultural resources, the borrower consults with project-affected groups to identify appropriate measures for mitigating these impacts as part of the EA process.
12. These measures may range from full site protection to selective mitigation, including salvage and documentation where a portion or all of the cultural resources may be lost.
13. The borrower develops a management plan that includes measures for mitigating any adverse impacts, provisions for the management of chance finds, any necessary measures for strengthening institutional capacity, and a monitoring system to track progress of these activities. The management plan is approved by competent authorities and submitted to the Bank for review and approval.

Consultation

14. As part of the EA process, the borrower consults with competent authorities, project-affected groups and, where appropriate, relevant experts, in documenting the presence and significance of physical cultural resources, assessing potential impacts, and exploring mitigation options.

Disclosure

15. The findings of the cultural resources component of the EA are disclosed as part of, and in the same manner as, the EA report, except where the borrower, in consultation with the Bank, determines that such disclosure would jeopardize the safety or integrity of the cultural resources involved.

Emergency Recovery Projects

16. This policy normally applies to emergency recovery projects processed under OP8.50, *Emergency Recovery Assistance*. However, when compliance with any requirements of this policy would prevent the effective and timely achievement of the objectives of an emergency recovery project, the Bank may exempt the project from such a requirement. The justification for such exemption is recorded in the loan documents.

Sector Investment Loans and Financial Intermediary Loans

17. The cultural resources aspects of EAs for subprojects under sector investment loans (SILs) and financial intermediary loans (FILs) are addressed as part of the EA process.[4]

Capacity Building

18. When the borrower's capacity is inadequate to manage physical cultural resources that are affected by a

[2] See OP4. 01, *Environmental Assessment*.
[3] See OP4. 01, *Environmental Assessment*.

[4] As set out in paragraphs 9 and 11 of OP4.01.

Bank-financed project, the project normally includes components to strengthen that capacity.

19. Given that the borrower's responsibility for cultural resources management extends beyond individual projects, the Bank may consider broader capacity building activities as part of its overall country assistance program.

THE WORLD BANK OPERATIONAL MANUAL BANK PROCEDURES: INDIGENOUS PEOPLES

1. This policy[5] contributes to the Bank's[6] mission of poverty reduction and sustainable development by ensuring that the development process fully respects the dignity, human rights, economies and cultures of Indigenous Peoples. For all projects proposed for Bank financing that affect Indigenous Peoples,[7] the Bank requires the borrower to engage in a process of free, prior and informed consultation.[8] The Bank will provide project financing only where free, prior and informed consultation results in broad community support to the project by the affected Indigenous Peoples.[9] Such Bank-financed projects include measures to: (a) avoid potentially adverse effects on the Indigenous Peoples' communities; or (b) when avoidance is not feasible, minimize, mitigate, or compensate for such effects. Bank-financed projects are also designed to ensure that the Indigenous Peoples receive social and economic benefits that are culturally appropriate and gender and intergenerationally inclusive.
2. The Bank recognizes that the identities and cultures of Indigenous Peoples are inextricably linked to the lands on which they live and the natural resources on which they depend. These distinct circumstances expose Indigenous Peoples to different types of risks and levels of impacts from development projects, including loss of identity, culture, and customary livelihoods, in addition to exposure to disease. Gender and intergenerational issues among Indigenous Peoples also are more complex. As social groups with identities that are often distinct from dominant groups in their national societies, they are frequently among the most marginalized and vulnerable segments of the population. As a result, their economic, social, and legal status often limits their capacity to defend their interests in and rights to lands, territories, and other productive resources, and/or restricts their ability to participate in and benefit from development. At the same time, the Bank recognizes that Indigenous Peoples play a vital role in sustainable development and that their rights are increasingly being addressed under both domestic and international law.
3. *Identification.* Because of the varied and changing contexts in which Indigenous Peoples live and because there is no universally accepted definition of "Indigenous Peoples," this policy does not define the term. Indigenous Peoples may be referred to in different countries by such terms as indigenous ethnic minorities, aboriginals, hill tribes, minority nationalities, scheduled tribes, or tribal groups.
4. For purposes of this policy, the term Indigenous Peoples is used in a generic sense to refer to a distinct, vulnerable, social and cultural group[10] possessing the following characteristics in varying degrees:
   (a) self-identification as members of a distinct indigenous cultural group and recognition of this identity by others;
   (b) collective attachment to geographically distinct habitats or ancestral territories in the project area and to the natural resources in these habitats and territories;[11]
   (c) customary cultural, economic, social, or political institutions that are separate from those of the dominant society and culture; and
   (d) an indigenous language, often different from the official language of the country or region.

   A group that has lost "collective attachment to geographically distinct habitats or ancestral territories in the project area" (paragraph 4 (b)) because of forced severance remains eligible for coverage under this policy.[12]

[5] This policy should be read together with other relevant Bank policies, including *Environmental Assessment* (OP 4.01), *Natural Habitats* (OP 4.04), *Pest Management* (OP 4.09), *Physical Cultural Resources* (OP 4.11, forthcoming), *Involuntary Resettlement* (OP 4.12), *Forests* (OP 4.36), and *Safety of Dams* (P 4.37).

[6] "Bank" includes IBRD and IDA; "loans" includes IBRD loans, IDA credits, IDA grants, IBRD and IDA guarantees, Project Preparation Facility (PPF) advances; and grants made under the Institutional Development Fund (IDF), but does not include development policy loans, credits, or grants. For social aspects of development policy operations, see OP 8.60, Development Policy Lending, paragraph 10. The term borrower includes, wherever the context requires, the recipient of an IDA grant, the guarantor of an IBRD loan, and the project implementing agency, if it is different from the borrower.

[7] This policy applies to all components of the project that affect Indigenous Peoples, regardless of the source of financing.

[8] "Free, prior and informed consultation with the affected Indigenous Peoples' communities" refers to a culturally appropriate and collective decision-making process subsequent to meaningful and good faith consultation and informed participation regarding the preparation and implementation of the project. It does not constitute a veto right for individuals or groups (see paragraph 10).

[9] For details on "broad community support to the project by the affected Indigenous Peoples," see paragraph 11.

[10] The policy does not set an *a priori* minimum numerical threshold because groups of Indigenous Peoples may be very small in number and their size may make them more vulnerable.

[11] "Collective attachment" means that for generations there has been a physical presence in and economic ties to lands and territories traditionally owned, or customarily used or occupied by the group concerned, including areas that hold special significance for it, such as sacred sites. "Collective attachment" also refers to the attachment of transhumant/nomadic groups to the territory they use on a seasonal or cyclical basis.

[12] "Forced severance" refers to loss of collective attachment to geographically distinct habitats or ancestral territories occurring within the concerned group members' lifetime because of conflict, government resettlement programs, dispossession from their lands, natural calamities, or incorporation of such territories into an urban area. For purposes of this policy, "urban area" normally means a city or a large town, and takes into account all of the following characteristics, no single one of which is definitive: (a) the legal designation of the area as urban under domestic law; (b) high population density; and (c) high proportion of nonagricultural economic activities relative to agricultural activities.

Ascertaining whether a particular group is considered as Indigenous Peoples for the purpose of this policy may require a technical judgment (see paragraph 8).

5. *Use of Country Systems.* If the borrower has a system that recognizes and protects the rights of Indigenous Peoples and provides an acceptable basis for achieving the objectives of this policy, the Bank may rely on that system. In deciding whether the borrower's system is acceptable, the Bank assesses the system and identifies all relevant legal, policy, or institutional aspects that need to be strengthened. Aspects thus identified must be strengthened by the borrower prior to the Bank's agreement to rely upon the system to achieve the objectives of this policy.

Project Preparation

6. A project proposed for Bank financing that affects Indigenous Peoples requires:
   (a) screening by the Bank to identify whether Indigenous Peoples are present in, or have collective attachment to, the project area (see paragraph 8);
   (b) a social assessment by the borrower (see paragraph 9 and Annex A);
   (c) a process of free, prior and informed consultation with the affected Indigenous Peoples' communities at each stage of the project, and particularly during project preparation in order to fully identify their views and to ascertain their broad community support to the project (see paragraphs 10 and 11);
   (d) the preparation of an Indigenous Peoples Plan (see paragraph 12 and Annex B) or an Indigenous Peoples Planning Framework (see paragraph 13 and Annex C); and
   (e) disclosure of the Indigenous Peoples Plan or Indigenous Peoples Planning Framework (see paragraph 15).
7. The level of detail necessary to meet the requirements specified in paragraph 5 (b), (c), and (d) is proportional to the complexity of the proposed project and commensurate with the nature and scale of the proposed project's potential effects on the Indigenous Peoples, whether adverse or positive.

Screening

8. Early in project preparation, the Bank undertakes a screening to determine whether Indigenous Peoples (see paragraph 4) are present in, or have collective attachment to, the project area.[13] In conducting this screening, the Bank seeks the technical judgment of qualified social scientists with expertise on the social and cultural groups in the project area. The Bank also consults the Indigenous Peoples concerned and the borrower. The Bank may follow the borrower's framework for identification of Indigenous Peoples during project screening, when that framework is consistent with this policy.

Social Assessment

9. *Analysis.* If, based on the screening, the Bank concludes that Indigenous Peoples are present in, or have collective attachment to, the project area, the borrower undertakes a social assessment to evaluate the project's potential positive and adverse effects on the Indigenous Peoples, and to examine project alternatives where adverse effects may be significant. The breadth, depth, and type of analysis in the social assessment are proportional to the nature and scale of the proposed project's potential effects on the Indigenous Peoples, whether positive or adverse (see Annex A for details). To carry out the social assessment, the borrower engages social scientists whose qualifications, experience, and terms of reference are acceptable to the Bank.
10. *Consultation and Participation.* Where the project affects Indigenous Peoples, the borrower shall engage in free, prior and informed consultation with them. To ensure such consultation, the borrower:
    (a) establishes an appropriate gender and intergenerationally inclusive framework that provides opportunities for consultation at each stage of project preparation and implementation among the borrower, the affected Indigenous Peoples' communities, the Indigenous Peoples Organizations (IPOs) if any, and other local civil society organizations (CSOs) identified by the affected Indigenous Peoples' communities;
    (b) uses consultation methods[14] appropriate to the social and cultural values of the affected Indigenous Peoples' communities and their local conditions and, in designing these methods, gives special attention to the concerns of Indigenous women, youth, and children and their access to development opportunities and benefits; and
    (c) provides the affected Indigenous Peoples' communities with all relevant information about the project (including an assessment of potential adverse effects of the project on the affected Indigenous Peoples' communities) in a culturally appropriate manner at each stage of project preparation and implementation.
11. In deciding whether to proceed with the project, the borrower ascertains, based on the social assessment (see paragraph 9) and the free, prior and informed consultation (see paragraph 10), whether the affected Indigenous Peoples' communities provide their broad support to the

[13] The screening may be carried out independently or as part of a project environmental assessment (see OP 4.01, *Environmental Assessment*, paragraphs 3, 8).

[14] Such consultation methods (including using indigenous languages, allowing time for consensus building, and selecting appropriate venues) facilitate the articulation by Indigenous Peoples of their views and preferences. The "Indigenous Peoples Guidebook" (forthcoming) will provide good practice guidance on this and other matters.

project. Where there is such support, the borrower prepares a detailed report that documents:
(a) the findings of the social assessment;
(b) the process of free, prior and informed consultation with the affected Indigenous Peoples' communities;
(c) additional measures, including project design modification, that may be required to address adverse effects on the Indigenous Peoples and to provide them with culturally appropriate project benefits;
(d) recommendations for free, prior and informed consultation with and participation by Indigenous Peoples' communities during project implementation, monitoring, and evaluation; and
(e) any formal agreements reached with Indigenous Peoples' communities and/or the IPOs.

The Bank subsequently satisfies itself through a review of the process and the outcome of the consultation carried out by the borrower that the affected Indigenous Peoples' communities have provided their broad support to the project. The Bank pays particular attention to the social assessment and to the record and outcome of the free, prior and informed consultation with the affected Indigenous Peoples' communities as a basis for ascertaining whether there is such support. The Bank will not proceed further with project processing if it is unable to ascertain that such support exists.

Indigenous Peoples Plan/Planning Framework

12. *Indigenous Peoples Plan.* On the basis of the social assessment and in consultation with the affected Indigenous Peoples' communities, the borrower prepares an Indigenous Peoples Plan (IPP) that sets out the measures with which the borrower will ensure that: (a) Indigenous Peoples affected by the project receive culturally appropriate social and economic benefits; and (b) when potential adverse effects on Indigenous Peoples are identified, those adverse effects are avoided, minimized, mitigated, or compensated for (see Annex B for details). The IPP is prepared in a flexible and pragmatic manner[15] and its level of detail varies depending on the specific project and the nature of effects to be addressed. The borrower integrates the IPP into the project design. When Indigenous Peoples are the sole or the overwhelming majority of direct project beneficiaries, the elements of an IPP should be included in the overall project design, and a separate IPP is not required. In such cases, the Project Appraisal Document (PAD) includes a brief summary of how the project complies with the policy, in particular the IPP requirements.
13. *Indigenous Peoples Planning Framework.* Some projects involve the preparation and implementation of annual investment programs or multiple subprojects.[16] In such cases, and when the Bank's screening indicates that Indigenous Peoples are likely to be present in, or have collective attachment to, the project area, but their presence or collective attachment cannot be determined until the programs or subprojects are identified, the borrower prepares an Indigenous Peoples Planning Framework (IPPF). The IPPF provides for the screening and review of these programs or subprojects in a manner consistent with this policy (see Annex C for details). The borrower integrates the IPPF into the project design.
14. *Preparation of Program and Subproject IPPs.* Should the screening of an individual program or subproject identified in the IPPF indicate that Indigenous Peoples are present in, or have collective attachment to, the area of the program or subproject, the borrower ensures that, prior to implementing the individual program or subproject, a social assessment is carried out and an IPP is prepared in accordance with the requirements of this policy. The borrower provides each IPP to the Bank for review before the respective program or subproject is considered eligible for Bank financing.[17]

Disclosure

15. The borrower makes the social assessment report and draft IPP/IPPF available to the affected Indigenous Peoples' communities in an appropriate form, manner, and language.[18] Before project appraisal, the borrower sends the social assessment and final IPP/IPPF to the Bank for review.[19] Once the Bank accepts the documents as providing an adequate basis for project appraisal, the Bank makes them available to the public in accordance with the Bank's Disclosure Policy, and the borrower makes them available to the affected Indigenous Peoples' communities in the same manner as the earlier draft documents.

Special Considerations

Lands and Related Natural Resources

16. Indigenous Peoples are closely tied to land, forests, water, wildlife, and other natural resources, and therefore special considerations apply if the project affects such ties. In this situation, when carrying out the social assessment

[15] When non-Indigenous Peoples live in the same area with Indigenous Peoples, the IPP should attempt to avoid creating unnecessary inequities for other poor and marginal social groups.

[16] Such projects include community-driven development projects, social funds, sector investment operations, and financial intermediary loans.

[17] If the Bank considers the IPPF to be adequate for the purpose, however, the Bank may agree with the borrower that prior Bank review of the IPP is not needed. In such case, the Bank reviews the IPP and its implementation as part of supervision (see OP 13.05, *Project Supervision*).

[18] The social assessment and IPP require wide dissemination among the affected Indigenous Peoples' communities using culturally appropriate methods and locations. In the case of an IPPF, the document is disseminated using IPOs at the appropriate national, regional, or local levels to reach Indigenous Peoples who are likely to be affected by the project. Where IPOs do not exist, the document may be disseminated using other CSOs as appropriate (see paragraphs 13 and 14 of this policy).

[19] An exception to the requirement that the IPP (or IPPF) be prepared as a condition of appraisal may be made with the approval of Bank management (see BP 4.10, paragraph —) for projects meeting the requirements of OP 8.50, *Emergency Recovery Assistance.*In such cases, management's approval stipulates a timetable and budget for preparation of the social assessment and IPP (or for preparation of the IPPF).

and preparing the IPP/IPPF, the borrower pays particular attention to:

(a) the customary rights[20] of the Indigenous Peoples, both individual and collective, pertaining to lands or territories they traditionally owned, or customarily used or occupied, and where access to natural resources is vital to the sustainability of their cultures and livelihoods;

(b) the need to protect such lands and resources against illegal intrusion or encroachment;

(c) the cultural and spiritual values that the Indigenous Peoples attribute to such lands and resources; and

(d) their natural resources management practices and the long-term sustainability of such practices.

17. If the project involves: (a) activities that are contingent on establishing legally recognized rights to lands and territories that Indigenous Peoples traditionally owned, or customarily used or occupied (such as land titling projects), or (b) the acquisition of such lands, the IPP sets forth an action plan for the legal recognition of such ownership, occupation, or usage. Normally, the action plan is undertaken prior to project implementation; in some cases, however, the action plan may need to be carried out concurrently with the project itself. Such legal recognition may take the form of:

(a) full legal recognition of existing customary land tenure systems of Indigenous Peoples; or

(b) conversion of customary usage rights to communal and/or individual ownership rights.

If neither option is possible under domestic law, the IPP includes measures for legal recognition of perpetual or long-term, renewable custodial or use rights.

Commercial Development of Natural and Cultural Resources

18. If the project involves the commercial development of natural resources (such as minerals, hydrocarbon resources, forests, water, or hunting/fishing grounds) on lands or territories that Indigenous Peoples traditionally owned, or customarily used or occupied, the borrower ensures that as part of the free, prior and informed consultation process the affected communities are informed of: (a) their rights to such resources under statutory and customary law; (b) the scope and nature of the proposed commercial development and the parties interested or involved in such development; and (c) the potential effects of such development on the Indigenous Peoples' livelihoods, environments and use of such resources. The borrower includes arrangements in the IPP to enable the Indigenous Peoples to share equitably in the benefits[21] to be derived from such commercial development; at a minimum, the IPP arrangements must ensure that the Indigenous Peoples receive, in a culturally appropriate way, benefits, compensation and rights to due process at least equivalent to that to which any landowner with full legal title to the land would be entitled in the case of commercial development on their land.

19. If the project involves the commercial development of Indigenous Peoples' cultural resources and knowledge (for example, pharmacological or artistic), the borrower ensures that, as part of the free, prior and informed consultation process, the affected communities are informed of: (a) their rights to such resources under statutory and customary law; (b) the scope and nature of the proposed commercial development and the parties interested or involved in such development; and (c) the potential effects of such development on Indigenous Peoples' livelihoods, environments and use of such resources. Commercial development of the cultural resources and knowledge of these Indigenous Peoples is conditional upon their prior agreement to such development. The IPP reflects the nature and content of such agreements and includes arrangements to enable Indigenous Peoples to receive benefits in a culturally appropriate way and share equitably in the benefits to be derived from such commercial development.

Physical Relocation of Indigenous Peoples

20. Because physical relocation of Indigenous Peoples is particularly complex and may have significant adverse impacts on their identity, culture and customary livelihoods, the borrower will explore alternative project designs to avoid physical relocation of Indigenous Peoples. In exceptional circumstances, when it is not feasible to avoid it, the borrower will not carry out such relocation without obtaining broad support for it from the affected Indigenous Peoples' communities as part of the free, prior and informed consultation process. In such cases, the borrower prepares a resettlement plan, in accordance with the requirements of OP 4.12, *Involuntary Resettlement*, that is compatible with the Indigenous Peoples' cultural preferences, and includes a land-based resettlement strategy. As part of the resettlement plan, the borrower documents the results of the consultation process. The resettlement plan should allow the affected Indigenous Peoples, where possible, to return to the lands and territories which they traditionally owned, or customarily used or occupied should the reasons for their relocation cease to exist.

21. In many countries, the lands set aside as legally designated parks and protected areas may overlap with lands and territories that Indigenous Peoples traditionally owned, or customarily used or occupied. The Bank recognizes the significance of these rights of ownership, occupation, or usage as well as the need for long-term sustainable management of critical ecosystems. Therefore, involuntary restrictions on the access of Indigenous Peoples to legally

[20] "Customary rights" to lands and resources refers to patterns of long-standing community land and resource usage in accordance with Indigenous Peoples' customary laws, values, customs, and traditions, including seasonal or cyclical use, rather than formal legal title to land and resources issued by the State.

[21] The "Indigenous Peoples Guidebook" (forthcoming) will provide good practice guidance on this matter.

designated parks and protected areas, in particular access to their sacred sites, should be avoided. In exceptional circumstances, where it is not feasible to avoid restricting access, the borrower prepares, with the free, prior and informed consultation of the affected Indigenous Peoples' communities, a process framework in accordance with the provisions of OP 4.12. The process framework provides guidelines for preparation, during project implementation, of an individual parks and protected areas' management plan. The process framework is also designed to ensure that the Indigenous Peoples participate in the design, implementation, monitoring, and evaluation of the management plan, and share equitably in the benefits of the parks and protected areas. The management plan should give priority to collaborative arrangements that enable the Indigenous Peoples, as the custodians of the resources, to continue to use them in an ecologically sustainable manner.

Indigenous Peoples and Development

22. In furtherance of the objectives of this policy, the Bank may, at a member country's request, support the country in its development planning and poverty reduction strategies by providing financial assistance for a variety of initiatives. Such initiatives may be designed to:
    - (a) strengthen local legislation, as needed, to establish legal recognition of the customary or traditional land tenure systems of Indigenous Peoples;
    - (b) make the development process more inclusive of Indigenous Peoples by incorporating their perspectives in the design of development programs and poverty reduction strategies, and providing them with opportunities to benefit more fully from development programs through policy and legal reforms, capacity building, and free, prior and informed consultation and participation;
    - (c) support the development priorities of Indigenous Peoples through programs (such as community-driven development programs and locally managed social funds) developed by governments in cooperation with Indigenous Peoples;
    - (d) address the gender[22] and intergenerational issues that exist among many Indigenous Peoples, including the special needs of indigenous women, youth, and children;
    - (e) prepare participatory profiles of Indigenous Peoples to document their culture, demographic structure, gender, and intergenerational relations and social organization, institutions, production systems, religious beliefs, and resource use patterns;
    - (f) strengthen the capacity of Indigenous Peoples' communities and IPOs to prepare, implement, monitor, and evaluate development programs;
    - (g) strengthen the capacity of government agencies responsible for providing development services to Indigenous Peoples;
    - (h) protect indigenous knowledge, including by strengthening intellectual property rights; and
    - (i) facilitate partnerships among the government, IPOs, CSOs, and the private sector to promote Indigenous Peoples' development programs.

[22] See OP/BP 4.20, *Gender and Development.*

Annex A. Social Assessment

1. The breadth, depth, and type of analysis required for the social assessment are proportional to the nature and scale of the proposed project's potential effects on the Indigenous Peoples.
2. The social assessment includes the following elements, as needed:
    - (a) A review, on a scale appropriate to the project, of the legal and institutional framework applicable to Indigenous Peoples.
    - (b) Gathering of baseline information on the demographic, social, cultural, and political characteristics of the affected Indigenous Peoples' communities, and the land and territories which they traditionally owned, or customarily used or occupied and the natural resources on which they depend.
    - (c) Taking the review and baseline information into account, the identification of key project stakeholders and the elaboration of a culturally appropriate process for consulting with the Indigenous Peoples at each stage of project preparation and implementation (see paragraph 9 of this policy).
    - (d) An assessment, based on free, prior and informed consultation with the affected Indigenous Peoples' communities, of the potential adverse and positive effects of the project. Critical to the determination of potential adverse impacts is an analysis of the relative vulnerability of, and risks to, the affected Indigenous Peoples' communities given their distinct circumstances and close ties to land and natural resources, as well as their lack of access to opportunities relative to other social groups in the communities, regions, or national societies in which they live.
    - (e) The identification and evaluation, based on free, prior and informed consultation with the affected Indigenous Peoples' communities, of measures necessary to avoid adverse effects, or if such measures are not feasible, the identification of measures to minimize, mitigate, or compensate for such effects; and to ensure that the Indigenous Peoples receive culturally appropriate benefits under the project.

Annex B. Indigenous Peoples Plan

1. The Indigenous Peoples Plan (IPP) is prepared in a flexible and pragmatic manner, and its level of detail varies

depending on the specific project and the nature of effects to be addressed.

2. The IPP includes the following elements, as needed:
   (a) A summary of the information referred to in Annex A, paragraph 2, (a) and (b).
   (b) A summary of the social assessment.
   (c) A summary of results of the free, prior and informed consultation with the affected Indigenous Peoples' communities carried out during project preparation (Annex A) leading to broad community support to the project.
   (d) A framework for ensuring free, prior and informed consultation with the affected Indigenous Peoples' communities during project implementation (see paragraph 10 of this policy).
   (e) An action plan of measures to ensure that the Indigenous Peoples receive social and economic benefits that are culturally appropriate, including, if necessary, measures to enhance the capacity of the project implementing agencies.
   (f) When potential adverse effects on Indigenous Peoples are identified, an appropriate action plan of measures to avoid, minimize, mitigate, or compensate for these adverse effects.
   (g) The cost estimates and financing plan for the IPP.
   (h) Accessible procedures appropriate to the project to address grievances by the affected Indigenous Peoples' communities arising from project implementation. When designing the grievance procedures, the borrower takes into account the availability of judicial recourse and customary dispute settlement mechanisms among the Indigenous Peoples.

   Mechanisms and benchmarks appropriate to the project for monitoring, evaluating and reporting on the implementation of the IPP. The monitoring and evaluation mechanisms should include arrangements for the free, prior and informed consultation with the affected Indigenous Peoples' communities.

Annex C. Indigenous Peoples Planning Framework

1. The Indigenous Peoples Planning Framework (IPPF) sets out:
   (a) The type of programs and subprojects likely to be proposed for financing under the project.
   (b) The potential positive and adverse effects of such programs or subprojects on Indigenous Peoples.
   (c) A plan for carrying out the social assessment (see Annex A) for such programs or subprojects.
   (d) A framework for ensuring free, prior and informed consultation with the affected Indigenous Peoples' communities at each stage of project preparation and implementation (see paragraph 10 of this policy).
   (e) Institutional arrangements (including capacity building where necessary) for screening project-supported activities, evaluating their effects on Indigenous Peoples, preparing IPPs, and addressing any grievances.
   (f) Monitoring and reporting arrangements, including mechanisms and benchmarks appropriate to the project.
   (g) Disclosure arrangements for IPPs to be prepared under the IPPF.

ICOM CODE OF ETHICS FOR MUSEUMS

Introduction

This edition of the *ICOM Code of Ethics for Museums* is the culmination of six years' revision. Following a thorough review of the ICOM's *Code* in the light of contemporary museum practice, a revised version, structured on the earlier edition, was issued in 2001. As envisaged at that time, this has now been completely reformatted to give it the look and feel of the museum profession and is based on key principles of professional practice, elaborated to provide general ethical guidance. The *Code* has been the subject of three periods of consultation with the membership. It was approved at the 21st General Assembly of ICOM, Seoul in 2004 with acclamation.

The whole ethos of the document continues to be that of service to society, the community, the public and its various constituencies, and the professionalism of museum practitioners. Although there is a changed emphasis throughout the document resulting from the new structure, the accentuation of key points, and the use of shorter paragraphs, very little is totally new. The new features will be found in paragraph 2.11 and the principles outlined in sections 3, 5, and 6.

The *Code of Ethics for Museums* provides a means of professional self-regulation in a key area of public provision where legislation at a national level is variable and far from consistent. It sets minimum standards of conduct and performance to which museum professional staff throughout the world may reasonably aspire as well as a providing a statement of reasonable public expectation from the museum profession.

ICOM issued its *Ethics of Acquisition* in 1970 and a full *Code of Professional Ethics* in 1986. The present edition – and its interim document of 2001 – owe much to that early work. The major work of revision and restructuring, however, fell on the current members of the Ethics Committee and their contribution in meetings – both actual and electronic – and their determination to meet both target and schedule is gratefully acknowledged. Their names are listed subsequently.

Like its precursors, the present *Code* provides a global minimum standard on which national and specialist groups can build to meet their particular requirements. ICOM encourages the development of national and specialist codes of ethics to meet particular needs and will be pleased to receive copies of them. These should be sent to the Secretary-General of ICOM, Maison de l'UNESCO, 1 rue Miollis, 75732 Paris Cedex 15, France. E-mail: <secretariat@icom.org>

Geoffrey Lewis
Chair, ICOM Ethics Committee

ICOM Ethics Committee for the Period 2001–4

Chair: Geoffrey Lewis (UK)
Members: Gary Edson (USA); Per Kåks (Sweden); Byung-mo Kim (Republic of Korea); Pascal Makambila (Congo) – from 2002; Jean-Yves Marin (France); Bernice Murphy (Australia) – to 2002; Tereza Scheiner (Brazil); Shaje'a Tshiluila (Democratic Republic of Congo); Michel Van-Praët (France).

VI. Preamble

VII.

Status of the Code of Ethics for Museums

This *Code of Ethics for Museums* has been prepared by the International Council of Museums (ICOM). It is the statement of ethics for museums referred to in the ICOM Statutes. This *Code* reflects principles generally accepted by the international museum community. Membership in ICOM and the payment of the annual subscription to ICOM is an affirmation of this *Code of Ethics.*

A Minimum Standard for Museums

This *Code* represents a minimum standard for museums. It is presented as a series of principles supported by guidelines of desirable professional practice. In some countries, certain minimum standards are defined by law or government regulation. In others, guidance on and assessment of minimum professional standards may be available in the form of "Accreditation," "Registration," or similar evaluative schemes. Where such standards are not defined, guidance can be obtained through the ICOM Secretariat, the National Committee of ICOM, or the appropriate International Committee of ICOM. It is also intended that individual nations and the specialised subject organisations connected with museums should use this Code as a basis for developing additional standards.

VIII.

Translations of the *Code of Ethics for Museums*

The ICOM *Code of Ethics for Museums* is published in three versions: English, French, and Spanish. ICOM welcomes the translation of the Code into other languages. However, a translation will be regarded as "official" only if it is endorsed by at least one national committee of a country in which the language is spoken, normally as the first language. Where the language is spoken in more than one country, it is preferable that the national committees of these countries should also be consulted. Attention is drawn to the need for linguistic as well as professional expertise in providing official translations. The language version used for the translation and the names of the national committees involved should be indicated. These conditions do not restrict translations of the Code, or parts of it, for use in educational work or for study purposes.

Sections

1. Museums preserve, interpret, and promote aspects of the natural and cultural inheritance of humanity.
   - Institutional standing
   - Physical resources
   - Financial resources
   - Personnel
2. Museums that maintain collections hold them in trust for the benefit of society and its development.
   - Acquiring collections
   - Removing collections
   - Care of collections
3. Museums hold primary evidence for establishing and furthering knowledge.
   - Primary evidence
   - Museum collecting and research
4. Museums provide opportunities for the appreciation, enjoyment, understanding, and promotion of the natural and cultural heritage.
   - Display and exhibition
   - Other resources
5. Museum resources provide opportunities for other public services and benefits.
   - Identification services
6. Museums work in close collaboration with the communities from which their collections originate as well as those they serve.
   - Origin of collections
   - Respect for communities served
7. Museums operate in a legal manner.
   - Legal framework
8. Museums operate in a professional manner.
   - Professional conduct
   - Conflicts of interest

Glossary

Appraisal The authentication and valuation of an object or specimen. In certain countries, the term is used for an independent assessment of a proposed gift for tax benefit purposes.

Conflict of interest The existence of a personal or private interest that gives rise to a clash of principle in a work situation, thus restricting, or having the appearance of restricting, the objectivity of decision making.

(a) Conservator-Restorer *Museum or independent personnel competent to undertake the technical examination, preservation, conservation and restoration of cultural property. For further information, see ICOM News 39 (1), pp 5–6 (1986)*

Cultural Heritage Any thing or concept considered of aesthetic, historical, scientific, or spiritual significance.

Dealing Buying and selling items for personal or institutional gain.

Due diligence The requirement that every endeavour is made to establish the facts of a case before deciding a course of action, particularly in identifying the source and history of an item offered for acquisition or use before accepting it.

Governing Body The persons or organisations defined in the enabling legislation of the museum as responsible for its continuance, strategic development, and funding.

Income-generating Activities intended to bring financial gain or profit for the benefit of the institution.

Legal title Legal right to ownership of property in the country concerned. In certain countries, this may be a conferred right and insufficient to meet the requirements of a due diligence search.

Minimum Standard A standard to which it is reasonable to expect all museums and museum personnel to aspire. Certain countries have their own statements of minimum standards.

Museum[1] A museum is a non-profit-making permanent institution in the service of society and of its development, open to the public, which acquires, conserves, researches, communicates, and exhibits, for purposes of study, education, and enjoyment, the tangible and intangible evidence of people and their environment.

(a) Museum professional[1] *Museum professionals consist of the personnel (whether paid or unpaid) of museums or institutions as defined in Article 2, paras. 1 and 2, of the Statutes, who have received specialised training, or possess an equivalent practical experience in any field relevant to the management and operations of a museum, and independent persons respecting the ICOM Code of Ethics for Museums and working for museums or institutions as defined in the Statute quoted above, but not persons promoting or dealing with commercial products and equipment required for museums and museum services.*

Natural Heritage Any natural thing, phenomenon, or concept, considered to be of scientific significance or to be a spiritual manifestation.

Non-profit organisation A legally established body, corporate or unincorporated, whose income (including any surplus or profit) is used solely for the benefit of that body and its operation. The term *Not for profit* has the same meaning.

Provenance The full history and ownership of an item from the time of its discovery or creation to the present day, from which authenticity and ownership is determined.

Valid title Indisputable right to ownership of property, supported by full provenance of the item from discovery or production.

[1] It should be noted that the terms"museum" and "museum professional" are interim definitions for use in interpreting the *ICOM Code of Ethics for Museums*. The definitions of "museum"and "professional museum workers" used in the *ICOM Statutes* remain in force until the revision of that document has been completed.

1. Museums Preserve, Interpret, and Promote Aspects of the Natural and Cultural Inheritance of Humanity

Principle: *Museums are responsible for the tangible and intangible natural and cultural heritage. Governing bodies and those concerned with the strategic direction and oversight of museums have a primary responsibility to protect and promote this heritage as well as the human, physical, and financial resources made available for that purpose.*

Institutional Standing

1.1. Enabling Documentation. The governing body should ensure that the museum has a written and published constitution, statute or other public document, in accordance with national laws which clearly states the museum's legal status, mission, permanence, and non-profit nature.

1.2. Statement of the Mission, Objectives, and Policies. The governing body should prepare, publicise and be guided by a statement of the mission, objectives, and policies of the museum and of the role and composition of the governing body.

Physical Resources

1.3. Premises. The governing body should ensure adequate premises with a suitable environment for the museum to fulfil the basic functions defined in its mission.

1.4. Access. The governing body should ensure that the museum and its collections are available to all during reasonable hours and for regular periods. Particular regard should be given to those persons with special needs.

1.5. Health and Safety. The governing body should ensure that institutional standards of health, safety, and accessibility apply to its personnel and visitors.

1.6. Protection Against Disasters. The governing body should develop and maintain policies to protect the public and personnel, the collections and other resources, against natural and man-made disasters.

1.7. Security Requirements. The governing body should ensure appropriate security to protect collections against theft or damage in displays, exhibitions, working or storage areas, and while in transit.

1.8. Insurance & Indemnity. Where commercial insurance is used for collections, the governing body should ensure that the cover is adequate and includes objects in transit or on loan and other items currently the responsibility of the museum. When an indemnity scheme is in use, it is necessary that material not in the ownership of the museum is adequately covered.

Financial Resources

1.9. Funding. The governing body should ensure that there are sufficient funds to carry out and develop the activities of the museum. All funds must be accounted for in a professional manner.

1.10. Income-generating Policy. The governing body should have a written policy regarding sources of income that it may generate through its activities or accept from outside sources. Regardless of funding source, museums should maintain control of the content and integrity of their programmes, exhibitions and activities. Income-generating activities should not compromise the standards of the institution or its public (See 6.6).

Personnel

1.11. Employment Policy. The governing body should ensure that all action concerning personnel is taken in accordance with the policies of the museum as well as the proper and legal procedures.

1.12. Appointment of the Director or Head. The director or head of the museum is a key post and when making an appointment, governing bodies should have regard for the knowledge and skills required to fill the post effectively. These qualities should include adequate intellectual ability and professional knowledge, complemented by a high standard of ethical conduct.

1.13. Access to Governing Bodies. The director or head of a museum should be directly responsible, and have direct access, to the relevant governing bodies.

1.14. Competence of Museum Personnel. The employment of qualified personnel with the expertise required to meet all responsibilities is necessary (See also 2.18; 2.24; 8.12).

1.15. Training of Personnel. Adequate opportunities for the continuing education and professional development of all museum personnel should be arranged to maintain an effective workforce.

1.16. Ethical Conflict. The governing body should never require museum personnel to act in a way that could be considered to conflict with the provisions of this *Code of Ethics*, or any national law or specialist code of ethics.

1.17. Museum Personnel and Volunteers. The governing body should have a written policy on volunteer work which promotes a positive relationship between volunteers and members of the museum profession.

1.18. Volunteers and Ethics. The governing body should ensure that volunteers, when conducting museum and personal activities, are fully conversant with the *ICOM Code of Ethics* and other applicable codes and laws.

2. Museums That Maintain Collections Hold Them in Trust for the Benefit of Society and Its Development

Principle: *Museums have the duty to acquire, preserve, and promote their collections as a contribution to safeguarding the natural, cultural, and scientific heritage. Their collections are a significant public inheritance, have a special position in law and are protected by international legislation. Inherent in this public trust is the notion of stewardship that includes rightful ownership, permanence, documentation, accessibility, and responsible disposal.*

Acquiring Collections

2.1. Collections Policy. The governing body for each museum should adopt and publish a written collections policy that addresses the acquisition, care, and use of collections. The policy should clarify the position of any material that will not be catalogued, conserved, or exhibited (See 2.7; 2.8).

2.2. Valid Title. No object or specimen should be acquired by purchase, gift, loan, bequest, or exchange unless the acquiring museum is satisfied that a valid title is held. Evidence of lawful ownership in a country is not necessarily valid title.

2.3. Provenance and Due Diligence. Every effort must be made before acquisition to ensure that any object or specimen offered for purchase, gift, loan, bequest, or exchange has not been illegally obtained in, or exported from, its country of origin or any intermediate country in which it might have been owned legally (including the museum's own country). Due diligence in this regard should establish the full history of the item from discovery or production.

2.4. Objects and Specimens from Unauthorised or Unscientific Fieldwork. Museums should not acquire objects where there is reasonable cause to believe their recovery involved the unauthorised, unscientific, or intentional destruction or damage of monuments, archaeological or geological sites, or species and natural habitats. In the same way, acquisition should not occur if there has been a failure to disclose the finds to the owner or occupier of the land, or to the proper legal or governmental authorities.

2.5. Culturally Sensitive Material. Collections of human remains and material of sacred significance should be acquired only if they can be housed securely and cared for respectfully. This must be accomplished in a manner consistent with professional standards and the interests and beliefs of members of the community, ethnic or religious groups from which the objects originated, where known (See also 3.7; 4.3).

2.6. Protected Biological or Geological Specimens. Museums should not acquire biological or geological specimens that have been collected, sold, or otherwise transferred in contravention of local, national, regional, or international law or treaty relating to wildlife protection or natural history conservation.

2.7. Living Collections. When the collections include live botanical and zoological specimens, special considerations should be made for the natural and social environment from which they are derived as well as any local, national, regional or international law, or treaty relating to wildlife protection or natural history conservation

2.8. Working Collections. The collections policy may include special considerations for certain types of working collection where the emphasis is on preserving cultural, scientific, or technical process rather than the object, or where objects or specimens are assembled for regular handling and teaching purposes (See also 2.1).

2.9. Acquisition Outside Collections Policy. The acquisition of objects or specimens outside the museum's stated policy should only be made in exceptional circumstances. The governing body should consider the professional opinions available to them, and the views of all interested parties. Consideration will include the significance of the object or specimen including its context in the cultural or natural heritage, and the special interests of other museums collecting such material. However, even in these circumstances, objects without a valid title should not be acquired (See also 3.4).

2.10. Acquisition by Members of the Governing Body and Museum Personnel. Special care is required in considering any item, either for sale, as a donation or as a tax-benefit gift, from members of governing bodies, museum personnel, or the families and close associates of these persons.

2.11. Repositories of Last Resort. Nothing in this *Code of Ethics* should prevent a museum from acting as an authorised repository for unprovenanced, illicitly collected, or recovered specimens and objects from the territory over which it has lawful responsibility.

Removing Collections

2.12. Legal or Other Powers of Disposal. Where the museum has legal powers permitting disposals, or has acquired objects subject to conditions of disposal, the legal or other requirements and procedures must be complied with fully. When the original acquisition was subject to mandatory or other restrictions, these conditions must be observed unless it can be shown clearly that adherence to such restrictions is impossible or substantially detrimental to the institution and, if appropriate, relief obtained through legal procedures.

2.13. Deaccessioning from Museum Collections. The removal of an object or specimen from a museum collection must only be undertaken with a full understanding of the significance of the item, its character (whether renewable or non-renewable), legal standing, and any loss of public trust that might result from such action.

2.14. Responsibility for Deaccessioning. The decision to deaccession should be the responsibility of the governing body acting in conjunction with the director of the museum and the curator of the collection concerned. Special arrangements may apply to working collections (See 2.7; 2.8).

2.15. Disposal of Objects Removed from the Collections. Each museum should have a policy defining authorised methods for permanently removing an object from the collections through donation, transfer, exchange, sale, repatriation, or destruction, and that allows the transfer of unrestricted title to the receiving agency. Complete records must be kept of all deaccessioning decisions, the objects involved, and the disposition of the object. There will be a strong presumption that a deaccessioned item should first be offered to another museum.

2.16. Income from Disposal of Collections. Museum collections are held in public trust and may not be treated as a realisable asset. Money or compensation received from the de-accessioning and disposal of objects and specimens from a museum collection should be used solely for the benefit of the collection and usually for acquisitions to that collection.

2.17. Purchase of Deaccessioned Collections. Museum personnel, the governing body, or their families or close associates, should not be permitted to purchase objects that have been deaccessioned from a collection for which they are responsible.

Care of Collections

2.18. Collection Continuity. The museum should establish and apply policies to ensure that their collections (both permanent and temporary) and associated information, properly recorded, are available for current usage and will be passed on to future generations in as good and safe a condition as practicable, having regard to current knowledge and resources.

2.19. Delegation of Collection Responsibility. Professional responsibilities involving the care of the collections should be assigned to persons with the appropriate knowledge and skill or who are adequately supervised (See also 8.11).

2.20. Documentation of Collections. Museum collections should be documented according to accepted professional standards. This documentation should include a full identification and description of each item, its associations, provenance, condition, treatment and present location. Such data should be kept in a secure environment and be supported with retrieval systems providing access to the information by the museum personnel and other legitimate users.

2.21. Protection Against Disasters. Careful attention should be given to the development of policies to protect the collections during armed conflict and other man-made and natural disasters

2.22. Security of Collection and Associated Data. The museum should exercise control to avoid disclosing sensitive personal or related information and other confidential matters when collection data are made available to the public.

2.23. Preventive Conservation. Preventive conservation is an important element of museum policy and collections care. It is an essential responsibility of members of the museum profession to create and maintain a protective environment for the collections in their care, whether in store, on display, or in transit.

2.24. Collection Conservation and Restoration. The museum should carefully monitor the condition of collections to determine when an object or specimen may require conservation-restoration work and the services of a qualified conservator-restorer. The principal goal should be the stabilisation of the object or specimen. All conservation procedures should be documented and as reversible as possible, and all alterations should be clearly identifiable from the original object or specimen.

2.25. Welfare of Live Animals. A museum that maintains living animals should assume full responsibility for their health and well-being. It should prepare and implement a safety code for the protection of its personnel and visitors, as well as the animals, that has been approved by an expert in the veterinary field. Genetic modification should be clearly identifiable.

2.26. Personal Use of Museum Collections. Museum personnel, the governing body, their families, close associates, or others should not be permitted to expropriate items from the museum collections, even temporarily, for any personal use.

3. Museums Hold Primary Evidence for Establishing and Furthering Knowledge

Principle: *Museums have particular responsibilities to all for the care, accessibility, and interpretation of primary evidence collected and held in their collections.*

Primary Evidence

3.1. Collections as Primary Evidence. The museum collections policy should indicate clearly the significance of collections as primary evidence. The policy should verify that this is not governed by current intellectual trends or museum usage.

3.2. Availability of Collections. Museums have a particular responsibility for making collections and all relevant information available as freely as possible, having regard to restraints arising for reasons of confidentiality and security.

Museum Collecting and Research

3.3. Field Collecting. Museums undertaking field collecting should develop policies consistent with academic standards and applicable national and international laws and treaty obligations. Fieldwork should only be undertaken with respect and consideration for the views of local communities, their environmental resources, and cultural practices in addition to efforts to enhance the cultural and natural heritage.

3.4. Exceptional Collecting of Primary Evidence. In very exceptional cases, an item without provenance may have such an inherently outstanding contribution to knowledge that it would be in the public interest to preserve it. The acceptance of such an item into a museum collection should be the subject of a decision by specialists in the discipline concerned and without national or international prejudice (See also 2.11).

3.5. Research. Research by museum personnel should relate to the museum's mission and objectives and conform to established legal, ethical, and academic practices.

3.6. Destructive Analysis. When destructive analytical techniques are undertaken, a complete record of the material analysed, the outcome of the analysis, and the resulting research, including publications, should become a part of the permanent record of the object.

3.7. Human Remains and Material of Sacred Significance. Research on human remains and materials of sacred significance must be accomplished in a manner consistent with professional standards and taking into account the interests and beliefs of the community, ethnic, or religious groups from whom the objects originated where these are known (See also 2.5; 4.3).

3.8. Retention of Rights to Research Materials. When museum personnel prepare material for presentation or to document field investigation there must be clear agreement with the sponsoring museum regarding all rights to the work.

3.9. Shared Expertise. Members of the museum profession have an obligation to share their knowledge and experience with colleagues, scholars, and students in relevant fields. They should respect and acknowledge those from whom they have learned and should pass on such advancements in techniques and experience that may be of benefit to others.

3.10. Co-operation Between Museums and Other Institutions. Museum personnel should acknowledge and endorse the need for co-operation and consultation between institutions with similar interests and collecting practices. This is particularly so with institutes of higher education and certain public utilities where research may generate important collections for which there is no long-term security.

4. Museums Provide Opportunities for the Appreciation, Enjoyment, Understanding, and Promotion of the Natural and Cultural Heritage

Principle: *Museums have an important duty to develop their educational role and attract wider audiences from the community, locality, or group they serve. Interaction with the constituent community and promotion of their heritage is an integral part of the educational role of the museum.*

Display and Exhibition

4.1. Displays, Exhibitions, and Special Activities. Displays and temporary exhibitions, physical or electronic, should be in accordance with the stated mission, policy, and purpose of the museum. They should not compromise either the quality or the proper care and conservation of the collections.

4.2. Interpretation of Exhibits. Museums should ensure that the information they present in displays and exhibitions is well-founded, accurate, and gives appropriate consideration to represented groups or beliefs.

4.3. Exhibition of Sensitive Materials. Human remains and materials of sacred significance must be displayed in a manner consistent with professional standards and, where known, taking into account the interests and beliefs of members of the community, ethnic, or religious groups from whom the objects originated. They must be presented with great tact and respect for the feelings of human dignity held by all peoples.

4.4. Removal from Public Display. Requests for removal from public display of human remains or material of sacred significance from the originating communities must be addressed expeditiously with respect and sensitivity. Requests for the return of such material should be addressed similarly. Museum policies should clearly define the process for responding to such requests.

4.5. Display of Unprovenanced Material. Museums should avoid displaying or otherwise using material of questionable origin or lacking provenance. They should be aware that such displays or usage can be seen to condone and contribute to the illicit trade in cultural property.

Other Resources

4.6. Publication. Information published by museums, by whatever means, should be well-founded, accurate, and give responsible consideration to the academic disciplines, societies, or beliefs presented. Museum publications should not compromise the standards of the institution.

4.7. Reproductions. Museums should respect the integrity of the original when replicas, reproductions, or copies of items in the collection are made. All such copies should be permanently marked as facsimiles.

5. Museum Resources Provide Opportunities for Other Public Services and Benefits

Principle: *Museums use a wide variety of specialisms, skills, and physical resources which have a far wider application than in the museum. This may lead to shared resources or the provision of services as an extension of the museum's activities. They should be organised in such a way that they do not compromise the museum's stated mission.*

Identification Services

5.1. Identification of Illegally or Illicitly Acquired Objects. Where museums provide an identification service, they should not act in any way that could be regarded as benefiting from such activity, directly, or indirectly. The identification and authentication of objects that are believed or suspected to have been illegally or illicitly acquired, transferred, imported, or exported should not be made public until the appropriate authorities have been notified.

5.2. Authentication and Valuation (Appraisal). Valuations may be made for the purposes of insurance of museum collections. Opinions on the monetary value of other objects should only be given on official request, from other museums, or competent legal, governmental, or other responsible public authorities. However, when the museum may be the beneficiary, appraisal of an object or specimen must be undertaken independently.

6. Museums Work in Close Collaboration with the Communities from which Their Collections Originate as well as Those They Serve

Principle: *Museum collections reflect the cultural and natural heritage of the communities from which they have been derived. As such, they have a character beyond that of ordinary property, which may include strong affinities with national, regional, local, ethnic, religious, or political identity. It is important therefore that museum policy is responsive to this possibility.*

Origin of Collections

6.1. Co-operation. Museums should promote the sharing of knowledge, documentation, and collections with museums and cultural organisations in the countries and communities of origin. The possibility of developing partnerships with museums in countries or areas that have lost a significant part of their heritage should be explored.

6.2. Return of Cultural Property. Museums should be prepared to initiate dialogues for the return of cultural property to a country or people of origin. This should be undertaken in an impartial manner, based on scientific, professional, and humanitarian principles as well as applicable local, national, and international legislation, in preference to action at a governmental or political level.

6.3. Restitution of Cultural Property. When a country or people of origin seek the restitution of an object or specimen that can be demonstrated to have been exported or otherwise transferred in violation of the principles of international and national conventions, and shown to be part of that country's or people's cultural or natural heritage, the museum concerned should, if legally free to do so, take prompt and responsible steps to co-operate in its return.

6.4. Cultural Objects from an Occupied Country. Museums should abstain from purchasing or acquiring cultural objects from an occupied territory and respect fully all laws and conventions that regulate the import, export, and transfer of cultural or natural materials.

Respect for Communities Served

6.5. Contemporary Communities. Where museum activities involve a contemporary community or its heritage, acquisitions should only be made based on informed and mutual consent without exploitation of the owner or informants. Respect for the wishes of the community involved should be paramount.

6.6. Funding of Community Facilities. When seeking funds for activities involving contemporary communities, their interests should not be compromised (See 1.10).

6.7. Use of Collections from Contemporary Communities. Museum usage of collections from contemporary communities requires respect for human dignity and the traditions and cultures that use them. Such collections should be used to promote human well-being, social development, tolerance, and respect by advocating multisocial, multicultural, and multilingual expression (See 4.3).

6.8. Supporting Organisations in the Community. Museums should create a favourable environment for community support (e.g., Friends of Museums and other supporting organisations), recognise its contribution, and promote a harmonious relationship between the community and museum personnel.

7. Museums Operate in a Legal Manner

Principle: *Museums must conform fully to international, regional, national, or local legislation and treaty obligations. In addition, the governing body should comply with any legally binding trusts or conditions relating to any aspect of the museum, its collections, and operations.*

Legal Framework

7.1. National and Local Legislation. Museums should conform to all national and local laws and respect the legislation of other states as they affect their operation.

7.2. International Legislation. Museum policy should acknowledge the following international legislation which is taken as a standard in interpreting the *ICOM Code of Ethics*:

Unesco Convention for the Protection of Cultural Property in the Event of Armed Conflict (The Hague Convention, First Protocol, 1954 and Second Protocol, 1999);

Unesco Convention on the Means of Prohibiting and Preventing the Illicit Import, Export and Transfer of Ownership of Cultural Property (1970);

Convention on International Trade in Endangered Species of Wild Fauna and Flora (1973);

UN Convention on Biological Diversity (1992);

Unidroit Convention on Stolen and Illegally Exported Cultural Objects (1995);

Unesco Convention on the Protection of the Underwater Cultural Heritage (2001);

Unesco Convention for the Safeguarding of the Intangible Cultural Heritage (2003).

8. Museums Operate in a Professional Manner

Principle: *Members of the museum profession should observe accepted standards and laws and uphold the dignity and honour of their profession. They should safeguard the public against illegal or unethical professional conduct. Every opportunity should be used to inform and educate the public about the aims, purposes, and aspirations of the profession to develop a better public understanding of the contributions of museums to society.*

Professional Conduct

8.1. Familiarity with Relevant Legislation. Every member of the museum profession should be conversant with relevant international, national, and local legislation and the conditions of their employment. They should avoid situations that could be construed as improper conduct.

8.2. Professional Responsibility. Members of the museum profession have an obligation to follow the policies and procedures of their employing institution. However, they may properly object to practices that are perceived to be damaging to a museum or the profession and matters of professional ethics.

8.3. Professional Conduct. Loyalty to colleagues and to the employing museum is an important professional responsibility and must be based on allegiance to fundamental ethical principles applicable to the profession as a whole. They should comply with the terms of the *ICOM Code of Ethics* and be aware of any other codes or policies relevant to museum work.

8.4. Academic and Scientific Responsibilities. Members of the museum profession should promote the investigation, preservation, and use of information inherent in the collections. They should, therefore, refrain from any activity or circumstance that might result in the loss of such academic and scientific data.

8.5. The Illicit Market. Members of the museum profession should not support the illicit traffic or market in natural and cultural property, directly or indirectly.

8.6. Confidentiality. Members of the museum profession must protect confidential information obtained during their work. In addition, information about items brought to the museum for identification is confidential and should not be published or passed to any other institution or person without specific authorisation from the owner.

8.7. Museum and Collection Security. Information about the security of the museum or of private collections and locations visited during official duties must be held in strict confidence by museum personnel.

8.8. Exception to the Obligation for Confidentiality. Confidentiality is subject to a legal obligation to assist the police or other proper authorities in investigating possible stolen, illicitly acquired, or illegally transferred property.

8.9. Personal Independence. While members of a profession are entitled to a measure of personal independence, they must realise that no private business or professional interest can be wholly separated from their employing institution.

8.10. Professional Relationships. Members of the museums profession form working relationships with numerous other persons within and outside the museum in which they are employed. They are expected to render their professional services to others efficiently and to a high standard.

8.11. Professional Consultation. It is a professional responsibility to consult other colleagues within or outside the museum when the expertise available is insufficient in the museum to ensure good decision-making.

Conflicts of Interest

8.12. Gifts, Favours, Loans, or Other Personal Benefits. Museum employees must not accept gifts, favours, loans, or other personal benefits that may be offered to them in connection with their duties for the museum. Occasionally professional courtesy may include the giving and receiving of gifts but this should always take place in the name of the institution concerned.

8.13. Outside Employment or Business Interests. Members of the museum profession, although entitled to a measure of personal independence, must realise that no private business or professional interest can be wholly separated from their employing institution. They should not undertake other paid employment or accept outside commissions that are in conflict with, or may be viewed as being in conflict with the interests of the museum.

8.14. Dealing in Natural or Cultural Heritage. Members of the museum profession should not participate directly or indirectly in dealing (buying or selling for profit) in the natural or cultural heritage.

8.15. Interaction with Dealers. Museum professionals should not accept any gift, hospitality, or any form of reward from a dealer, auctioneer, or other person as an inducement to purchase or dispose of museum items, or to take or refrain from taking official action. Furthermore, a museum professional should not recommend a particular dealer, auctioneer, or appraiser to a member of the public.

8.16. Private Collecting. Members of the museum profession should not compete with their institution either in the acquisition of objects or in any personal collecting activity. An agreement between the museum professional and the governing body concerning any private collecting must be formulated and scrupulously followed.

8.17. Use of the Name and Logo of ICOM. Members of ICOM may not use of the words "International Council of Museums," "ICOM," or its logo to promote or endorse any for-profit operation or product.

8.18. Other Conflicts of Interest. Should any other conflict of interest develop between an individual and the museum, the interests of the museum should prevail.

EXISTING OPTIONS FOR THE RESOLUTION OF ART AND CULTURAL PROPERTY DISPUTES

Convention on the Means of Prohibiting and Preventing the Illicit Import, Export and Transfer of Ownership of Cultural Property (Paris 1970)

The General Conference of the United Nations Educational, Scientific and Cultural Organization, meeting in Paris from 12 October to 14 November 1970, at its sixteenth session,

Article 3. The import, export or transfer of ownership of cultural property effected contrary to the provisions adopted under this Convention by the States Parties thereto, shall be illicit.

Article 7. The States Parties to this Convention undertake:

a. To take the necessary measures, consistent with national legislation, to prevent museums and similar institutions within their territories from acquiring cultural property originating in another State Party which has been illegally exported after entry into force of this Convention, in the

States concerned. Whenever possible, to inform a State of origin Party to this Convention of an offer of such cultural property illegally removed from that State after the entry into force of this Convention in both States;

b. i. to prohibit the import of cultural property stolen from a museum or a religious or secular public monument or similar institution in another State Party to this Convention after the entry into force of this Convention for the States concerned, provided that such property is documented as appertaining to the inventory of that institution;

ii. at the request of the State Party of origin, to take appropriate steps to recover and return any such cultural property imported after the entry into force of this Convention in both States concerned, provided, however, that the requesting State shall pay just compensation to an innocent purchaser or to a person who has valid title to that property. Requests for recovery and return shall be made through diplomatic offices. The requesting Party shall furnish, at its expense, the documentation and other evidence necessary to establish its claim for recovery and return. The Parties shall impose no customs duties or other charges upon cultural property returned pursuant to this Article. All expenses incident to the return and delivery of the cultural property shall be borne by the requesting Party.

Intergovernmental Committee for Promoting the Return of Cultural Property to its Countries of Origin or its Restitution in Case of Illicit Appropriation

The Committee held its first session at the UNESCO headquarters in Paris in 1980, and since then has met nine times. The body, composed of 22 UNESCO member States,[17] is primarily a negotiating forum aimed at facilitating bilateral negotiations and agreements for the return or restitution of cultural property, particularly that resulting from colonisation and military occupation to its countries of origin either when all the legal means have failed or where bilateral negotiations have proved unsuccessful.

UNIDROIT Convention on Stolen or Illegally Exported Cultural Objects (Rome, 24 June 1995)

Chapter IV – General Provisions
Article 8

(1) A claim under Chapter II and a request under Chapter III may be brought before the courts or other competent authorities of the Contracting State where the cultural object is located, in addition to the courts or other competent authorities otherwise having jurisdiction under the rules in force in Contracting States.

(2) The parties may agree to submit the dispute to any court or other competent authority or to arbitration.

(3) Resort may be had to the provisional, including protective, measures available under the law of the Contracting State where the object is located even when the claim for restitution or request for return of the object is brought before the courts or other competent authorities of another Contracting State.

Convention on the Protection of the Underwater Cultural Heritage (Paris, 2 November 2001)[23]

Article 1 – Definitions
For the purposes of this Convention:

1. (a) "Underwater cultural heritage" means all traces of human existence having a cultural, historical or archaeological character which have been partially or totally under water, periodically or continuously, for at least 100 years such as:
   (i) sites, structures, buildings, artefacts and human remains, together with their archaeological and natural context;
   (ii) vessels, aircraft, other vehicles or any part thereof, their cargo or other contents, together with their archaeological and natural context; and
   (iii) objects of prehistoric character.
   (b) Pipelines and cables placed on the seabed shall not be considered as underwater cultural heritage.
   (c) Installations other than pipelines and cables, placed on the seabed and still in use, shall not be considered as underwater cultural heritage.
2. (a) "States Parties" means States which have consented to be bound by this Convention and for which this Convention is in force.
   (b) This Convention applies mutatis mutandis to those territories referred to in Article 26, paragraph 2(b), which become Parties to this Convention in accordance with the conditions set out in that paragraph, and to that extent "States Parties" refers to those territories.
3. "UNESCO" means the United Nations Educational, Scientific and Cultural Organization.
4. "Director-General" means the Director-General of UNESCO.
5. "Area" means the seabed and ocean floor and subsoil thereof, beyond the limits of national jurisdiction.
6. "Activities directed at underwater cultural heritage" means activities having underwater cultural heritage as their primary object and which may, directly or indirectly, physically disturb or otherwise damage underwater cultural heritage.
7. "Activities incidentally affecting underwater cultural heritage" means activities which, despite not having underwater cultural heritage as their primary object or one of

[23] It is in this committee that Greece, since 1984, has argued its request for the return of the Parthenon models, to no avail.

their objects, may physically disturb or otherwise damage underwater cultural heritage.

8. "State vessels and aircraft" means warships, and other vessels or aircraft that were owned or operated by a State and used, at the time of sinking, only for government non-commercial purposes, that are identified as such and that meet the definition of underwater cultural heritage.
9. "Rules" means the Rules concerning activities directed at underwater cultural heritage, as referred to in Article 33 of this Convention.

Article 25 – Peaceful Settlement of Disputes

1. Any dispute between two or more States Parties concerning the interpretation or application of this Convention shall be subject to negotiations in good faith or other peaceful means of settlement of their own choice.
2. If those negotiations do not settle the dispute within a reasonable period of time, it may be submitted to UNESCO for mediation, by agreement between the States Parties concerned.
3. If mediation is not undertaken or if there is no settlement by mediation, the provisions relating to the settlement of disputes set out in Part XV of the United Nations Convention on the Law of the Sea apply mutatis mutandis to any dispute between States Parties to this Convention concerning the interpretation or application of this Convention, whether or not they are also Parties to the United Nations Convention on the Law of the Sea.
4. Any procedure chosen by a State Party to this Convention and to the United Nations Convention on the Law of the Sea pursuant to Article 287 of the latter shall apply to the settlement of disputes under this Article, unless that State Party, when ratifying, accepting, approving or acceding to this Convention, or at any time thereafter, chooses another procedure pursuant to Article 287 for the purpose of the settlement of disputes arising out of this Convention.
5. A State Party to this Convention which is not a Party to the United Nations Convention on the Law of the Sea, when ratifying, accepting, approving or acceding to this Convention or at any time thereafter shall be free to choose, by means of a written declaration, one or more of the means set out in Article 287, paragraph 1, of the United Nations Convention on the Law of the Sea for the purpose of settlement of disputes under this Article. Article 287 shall apply to such a declaration, as well as to any dispute to which such State is party, which is not covered by a declaration in force. For the purpose of conciliation and arbitration, in accordance with Annexes V and VII of the United Nations Convention on the Law of the Sea, such State shall be entitled to nominate conciliators and arbitrators to be included in the lists referred to in Annex V, Article 2, and Annex VII, Article 2, for the settlement of disputes arising out of this Convention.

Bi-lateral Agreements

Counsel of Europe Resolution 1205 1999

Spoliation, Recovery and Restitution Commissions Related to the Holocaust in Europe and the United States, Both Governmental and Non-Government

Codes of Conduct, i.e., AAMD, UNESCO Code for Art Dealers

Index

CPSIA information can be obtained
at www.ICGtesting.com
Printed in the USA
BVHW011707300822
645849BV00010B/458

9 780521 122979